THE ENCYCLOPEDIA
OF THE
ARAB-ISRAELI
CONFLICT

A Political, Social, and Military History

THE ENCYCLOPEDIA
OF THE
ARAB-ISRAELI
CONFLICT

A Political, Social, and Military History

VOLUME III: P–Z

Dr. Spencer C. Tucker
Volume Editor

Dr. Priscilla Roberts
Editor, Documents Volume

Dr. Paul G. Pierpaoli Jr.
Associate Editor

Major General David Zabecki, USAR (retired)
Dr. Sherifa Zuhur
Assistant Editors

FOREWORD BY
General Anthony C. Zinni, USMC (retired)

A B C ⬢ C L I O

Santa Barbara, California   Denver, Colorado   Oxford, England

Cataloging-in-Publication Data is on file with the Library of Congress

ISBN 978-1-85109-841-5 (hard copy : alk. paper) — ISBN 978-1-85109-842-2 (ebook)

10 09 08 07 06 05   10 9 8 7 6 5 4 3 2 1

This book is also available on the World Wide Web as an ebook.
Visit abc-clio.com for details.

ABC-CLIO, Inc.
130 Cremona Drive, P.O. Box 1911
Santa Barbara, California 93116–1911

This book is printed on acid-free paper ⊗ .
Manufactured in the United States of America

Contents

List of Entries

List of Maps

General Maps

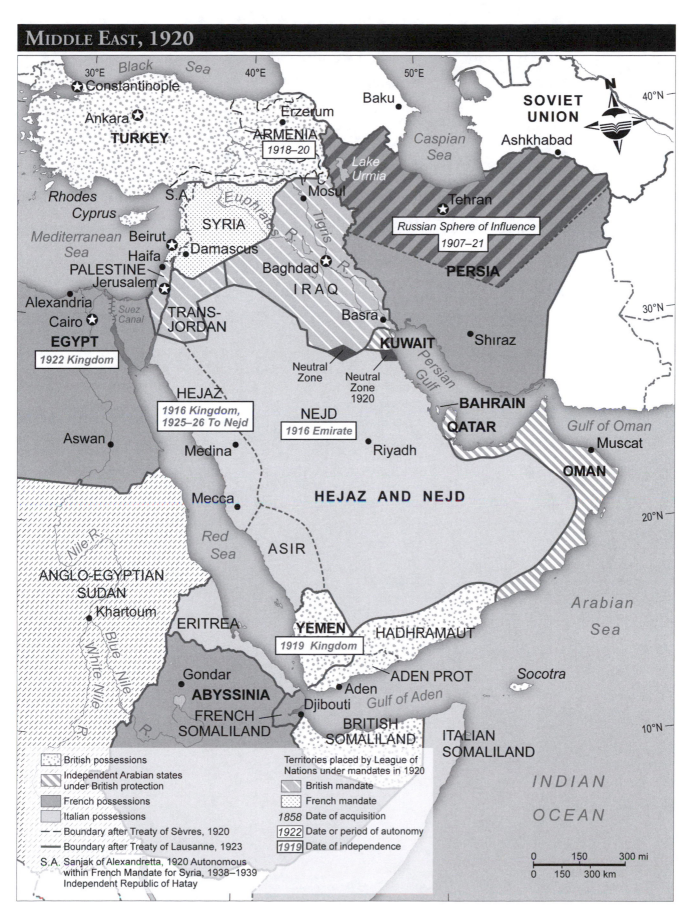

MIDDLE EAST, 1920

Constantinople
Ankara
TURKEY
30°E
40°E
50°E
Black Sea
Erzerum
Baku
SOVIET UNION
40°N
Ashkhabad
ARMENIA
1918–20
Caspian Sea
Lake Urmia
S.A.
Mosul
Tehran
Rhodes
Cyprus
SYRIA
Euphrates R.
Tigris R.
Russian Sphere of Influence 1907–21
Mediterranean Sea
Beirut
Damascus
Baghdad
PERSIA
Haifa
PALESTINE
Jerusalem
I R A Q
Alexandria
30°N
Cairo
TRANS-JORDAN
Basra
Shiraz
Suez Canal
EGYPT
1922 Kingdom
KUWAIT
Neutral Zone
Neutral Zone 1920
Persian Gulf
Aswan
HEJAZ
1916 Kingdom, 1925–26 To Nejd
NEJD
1916 Emirate
BAHRAIN
QATAR
Gulf of Oman
Muscat
Medina
Riyadh
OMAN
Mecca
HEJAZ AND NEJD
20°N
Red Sea
ASIR
ANGLO-EGYPTIAN SUDAN
Khartoum
Nile R.
ERITREA
YEMEN
1919 Kingdom
HADHRAMAUT
Arabian Sea
Gondar
ABYSSINIA
FRENCH SOMALILAND
Djibouti
Aden
ADEN PROT
Socotra
Gulf of Aden
BRITISH SOMALILAND
ITALIAN SOMALILAND
10°N
Blue Nile R.
White Nile R.
INDIAN OCEAN

British possessions
Independent Arabian states under British protection
French possessions
Italian possessions
Boundary after Treaty of Sèvres, 1920
Boundary after Treaty of Lausanne, 1923
S.A. Sanjak of Alexandretta, 1920 Autonomous within French Mandate for Syria, 1938–1939 Independent Republic of Hatay

Territories placed by League of Nations under mandates in 1920
British mandate
French mandate
1858 Date of acquisition
1922 Date or period of autonomy
1919 Date of independence

0   150   300 mi
0 150 300 km

MIDDLE EAST, 1945 – 1990

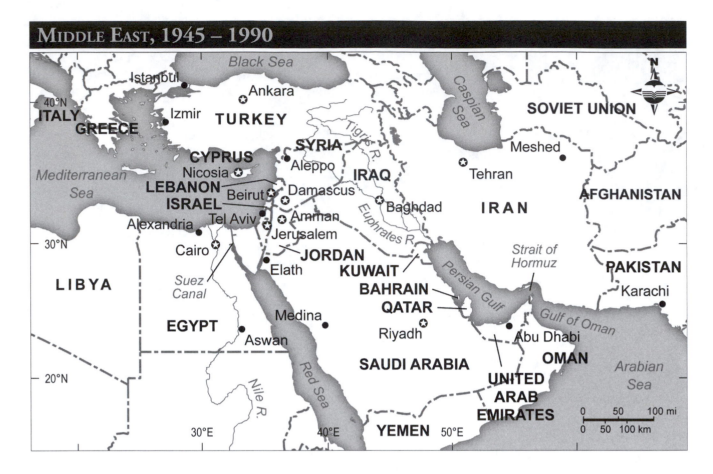

EUROPE, 1945 – 1990

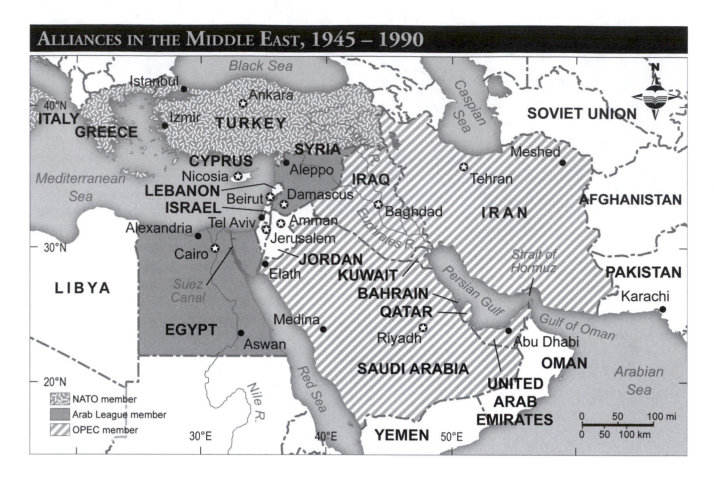

ALLIANCES IN THE MIDDLE EAST, 1945 – 1990

P

Pale of Settlement

The western border region of imperial Russia within which Jews were expected to reside. In the late 19th century, some 40–50 percent of the world's Jews lived in Russia. The 5 million Russian Jews differed from the great majority of the Russian population in terms of religion, language, and social customs, and in consequence the government and many ordinary Russians suspected their loyalty. During the 1880s and 1890s a number of anti-Jewish measures legally restricted the Jews regarding their residence, educational opportunities, political rights, and economic status.

All Jews were expected to live within the Pale. Created by Czarina Catherine II the Great in 1791 as an alternative to the expulsion of the Jews from Russia, it comprised a wide swath of western Russia running north from the Black Sea to the Baltic and comprising present-day Ukraine, Moldavia, Poland, Belarus, Lithuania, and part of western Russia. Within the Pale, Jews were generally compelled to live in towns and cities—although they were forbidden to live in some cities, such as Kiev, Sevastopol, and Yalta—where they could be kept under government surveillance. They were forbidden to move into the smaller villages. Thousands of Jews were forced to relocate into the Pale, including Jews from Moscow and St. Petersburg as late as 1891. Only a limited number of Jews were permitted to live outside the Pale. The government might grant exceptions and issue special licenses to Jews who were university graduates, wealthy merchants, professionals, or skilled artisans to permit them to reside outside the Pale.

The government also sharply restricted Jewish political rights. Jews could not vote for the dumas (representative assemblies) in the cities. The government appointed their representatives. In education, Jews were limited to a fixed percentage of the total student body in any particular school. This figure ranged from 3 percent to

Jewish children in the Warsaw Ghetto in Poland (then belonging to Russia), part of the Russian Pale of Settlement, circa 1896. (Library of Congress)

10 percent, depending on location and the level of institution. In consequence, many Jews were forced to go abroad to obtain an advanced education or were deprived of it altogether.

Jews could also not legally buy or lease land in rural districts. Government approval was required for a Jew to become a lawyer, and Jews were not permitted to be civil servants. Government regulations also sharply limited the number of Jewish stockholders in industrial corporations. And while Jews were required to serve in the Russian Army, they could not be officers in it. Finally, no Christian could legally marry a Jew. As a consequence of these regulations, many Jews became of necessity moneylenders, bankers, or retail merchants. In these capacities they were often hated by the peasants because of the high interest charged for loans.

The legislation was entirely on religious grounds. That is, conversion to Russian Orthodoxy would remove all restrictions. Also, the anti-Jewish laws were not always and everywhere enforced. And with the low salaries paid to local officials, corruption was rampant, and Jews might thereby secure a certain immunity. On the other hand, Russian officials sometimes went to the other extreme and did not give the Jews the protection to which they were entitled. Anti-Jewish riots, known as pogroms, broke out, often with the full approval of the authorities. Jews were systematically subjected to beatings or even death and their property might be plundered or destroyed as the police looked on. Such pogroms occurred throughout Russia, especially during 1881–1883 and 1903–1906. The most notorious of pogroms of this period occurred in April 1903 in the city of Kishinev, Bessarabia, when hundreds of Jews were killed or wounded. Both the anti-Jewish legislation and pogroms led many Jews to immigrate, most of them to the United States but a number to Palestine. Jews within the Pale of Settlement developed a system of volunteer social welfare organizations to look after the least fortunate among them.

The Pale officially ceased to exist in 1917, when two revolutions swept the czarist regime out of power. Yet it had contributed substantially to the alienation of the Jewish community from Russian society at large, and thus it indirectly advanced Zionism. Also, the concentration of most of Soviet Jewry in the western reaches of the subsequent Soviet Union had tragic consequences, as it made it easier for the Nazis to carry out their plan to exterminate the Jews of Europe (the Holocaust) following the Nazi invasion in June 1941.

SPENCER C. TUCKER

See also

Holocaust; Kishinev Pogrom; Pogroms

References

Dubnow, Simon. *History of the Jews in Russia and Poland: From the Earliest Times until the Present Day (1915)*. 10 vols. Philadelphia: Jewish Publication Society of America, 1916–1929.

Gitelman, Zvi Y. *A Century of Ambivalence: The Jews of Russia and the Soviet Union, 1881 to the Present*. New York: Schocken, 1988.

Klier, John Doyle. *Russia Gathers Her Jews: The Origins of the "Jewish Question" in Russia, 1772–1825*. De Kalb: Northern Illinois Press, 1986.

Palestine, British Mandate for
Event Date: 1922–1948

The British Mandate for Palestine refers to a period from 1922 to 1948 when Great Britain, following World War I, assumed control over the territory known as Palestine as a League of Nations mandate. This area had been part of the Ottoman (or Turkish) Empire until the end of 1917. Beginning in the 1920s, Palestine became increasingly subject to violent clashes between Arabs and Jews, as both groups claimed the territory as their homeland. Complicating matters was the fact that both groups believed that Britain had promised Palestine to them.

The region now known as Palestine has, at one time or another, been home to the Canaanites, Philistines, and other tribes but has also been under the authority of the Egyptians, the Jews, the Assyrians, the Persians, the Hellenic Empire, the Roman Empire, the Byzantine or Eastern Roman Empire, the Arab-Islamic Empire, Crusader Europeans, the Turkish or Ottoman Empire, the British, and, since 1948, the Jews again. Jews trace their origin 4,000 years ago to the prophet Abraham. Egyptian documents first mention the Jews in 1220 BC. After suppressing a series of Jewish revolts in the first century AD, the Roman Empire expelled most of the Jews from Palestine. As a result, over the next 1,000 years Jews migrated first to Western Europe, next to Eastern Europe, and then starting in the 1880s gradually back to Palestine.

The Palestinians are descended from the land's original inhabitants who either converted to Islam or retained their Christian faith as well as tribes that were part of or followed the Islamic conquests of the seventh century. Palestine was conquered by the Ayyubids, the Mamluks, the Crusaders, and, later, the Ottomans. Under Ottoman rule, Palestine was divided into districts, which in turn were part of provinces. Until 1841, much of Palestine had been part of the province of Syria governed from Damascus. However, northern Palestine was ruled by Sheikh Zahir al-Omar and later by Ahmad Jazzar Pasha, whose territory extended to Damascus. During 1831–1840 the region was under Egyptian occupation. In 1841, however, some areas were reorganized for purposes of taxation to form a northern district that was part of the province of Beirut, while other areas remained under the sanjak of Damascus. In the late 19th century the Arab population of Palestine numbered about 446,000 people, representing 90 percent of the total population.

The Jewish population of Palestine at the beginning of the 19th century numbered some 25,000 people and at the end of the century 60,000 people, approximately 10 percent of the area's total population. Although the notion of returning to Palestine had been a Jewish dream for centuries, it did not find serious consideration until the late 19th century. A significant increase in anti-Semitism during that time, particularly in Eastern Europe (in Poland and especially in Russia) prompted the beginning of the Zionist movement. Zionism was committed to settling Jews in Palestine and establishing a Jewish homeland there. The Holocaust significantly increased the appeal of Zionism, as many Jews came to believe that their survival could only be assured by the creation of a country of their own.

In the 1880s Jewish groups in Russia were formed to secure Jewish settlement in Palestine, but owing to poor organization and a lack of funds and participants, these early settlements were not very successful. In 1882 a seminal pamphlet titled *Autoemancipation*

British and Arab troops stand guard at a checkpoint in Jerusalem following the Arab Riots in April 1920. (Library of Congress)

by Leo Pinsker, a Polish-Russian Jew, gave Zionism its political-ideological foundations. Pinsker argued that anti-Semitism was too entrenched in European society for Jews to secure equal rights through assimilation, and he thus rejected assimilation as impossible. According to Pinsker, Jews were persecuted because they were foreigners everywhere they lived, and their only hope was to establish an independent Jewish state. Although Pinsker never insisted that this Jewish state be in Palestine, his book persuaded many Russian Jews to accept his arguments about the logic and necessity of a Jewish homeland.

Theodor Herzl, an Austro-Hungarian Jew, is most responsible for uniting the various early European Jewish groups into an international Zionist movement. As with Pinsker, Herzl rejected the impossibility of eliminating anti-Semitism in Europe by legislation and assimilation and called for the establishment of a Jewish state. He did not specify Palestine as the location of this state. Herzl's greatest contribution to the Zionist cause was his organizing in 1887 the First Zionist Congress in Basel, Switzerland, in which more than 200 delegates pledged that the goal of Zionism was to secure a legally recognized Jewish state in Palestine. At the same congress, the World

Zionist Organization (WZO) was created to coordinate the Zionist movement and unite the various East European Jewish groups.

Herzl's efforts paid off in that future congresses attracted more delegates and supporters of the Zionist cause. Gradually, the Zionist movement not only became united but also grew into an international rather than a regional phenomenon. By the time of Herzl's death in 1904, a Jewish state in Palestine still remained an unfulfilled dream, but Herzl's efforts had organized many of Europe's Jews and forged Zionism into a unified and dedicated international political movement.

During World War I, the British government began to take a greater interest in and more favorable position toward Zionism, and so its political prospects improved significantly. During the war, Britain sought Jewish support to secure British war aims, one of which was control of certain Ottoman territories in the Middle East after the end of the war. British leaders recognized that British support for Zionism would bring Jewish support for Britain's Middle Eastern imperial ambitions. Meanwhile, Chaim Weizmann, a leading Zionist in Britain, lobbied the British government to support Zionism and skillfully exploited London's desire to curry favor

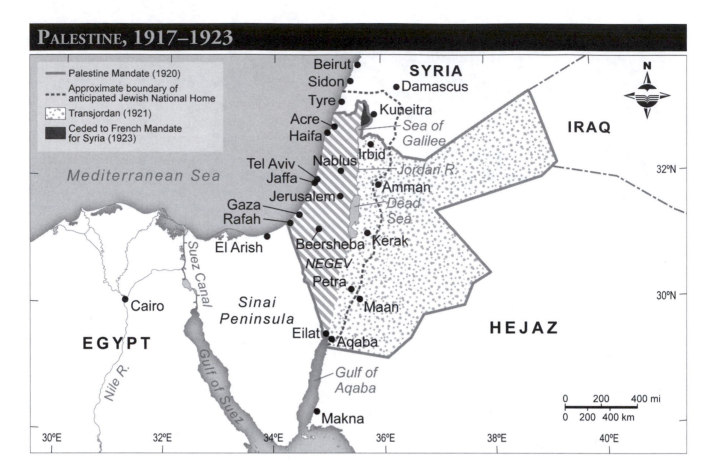

PALESTINE, 1917–1923

Legend:
- Palestine Mandate (1920)
- Approximate boundary of anticipated Jewish National Home
- Transjordan (1921)
- Ceded to French Mandate for Syria (1923)

with Jews. On November 2, 1917, British foreign secretary Arthur Balfour wrote to Lord Walter Rothschild, another prominent Zionist figure in Britain, pledging British support for Zionism. Balfour declared that London viewed "with favor the establishment in Palestine of a National Home for the Jewish people and will use [its] best endeavors to facilitate the achievement of this object." Yet seemingly in contradiction to this pledge, Balfour went on to say, "it being clearly understood that nothing shall be done which may prejudice the civil and religious rights of existing non-Jewish communities in Palestine," namely the Arabs.

At the same time, Britain also sought help from the Arabs, who were agitating for independence from the Ottoman Empire. This it accomplished with pledges of support for independence and self-rule in exchange for Arab support for Britain during World War I. Thus, while promising a homeland for Jews in Palestine, the British also promised independence to the Arabs, including those living in Palestine. While this may have been a shrewd wartime strategy, it would later prove impossible for the British to deliver on both sets of promises and satisfy both Arabs and Jews.

Two years before the Balfour Declaration, British high commissioner in Egypt Sir Henry McMahon exchanged a series of letters with Abdullah, the son of Sharif Hussein of Mecca, and with the sharif himself. Abdullah's July 14, 1915, letter asked for British approval of an Arab caliphate and independence for Arab lands en-

compassing all of present-day Syria, Iraq, Jordan, Palestine, and the entire Arabian Peninsula. McMahon's first response only concerned the caliphate, but then due to crisis on the British front at Gallipoli in the Dardanelles, he wrote to Hussein on October 24, 1915, promising to "recognize and support the independence of the Arabs within the territories included in the limits and boundaries proposed by the Sherif of Mecca." There were some reservations to the territory previously specified by Abdullah (Mersina, Alexandretta, and some lands just west of the Syrian cities; British administrative control of Baghdad and Basra; and British commitments to other tribes of the Arabian Peninsula), but these did not pertain to Palestine. This promise was in exchange for an Arab uprising against the Turks. In these letters, McMahon announced "Great Britain's sympathy with the aspirations of her friends the Arabs and that it will result in a lasting and solid alliance with them."

The British government later maintained that the McMahon correspondence did not apply to Palestine and that the Balfour Declaration did not contradict any earlier pledges made to the Arabs. Indeed, McMahon's letter of October 25, 1915, had not explicitly mentioned Palestine. It also had not mentioned the sanjak of Jerusalem, which was the former Ottoman administrative department that covered much of Palestine. The Arabs held that because these areas were not specifically excluded from the Arab sphere, they should come under Arab control. McMahon and Hussein had agreed that land not purely Arab in makeup was to be excluded from the understanding. The British argued that because Palestine was neither completely Arab nor Muslim, it was not part of the agreement. The Arabs, however, saw things differently. They held that Palestine was overwhelmingly Arab and should therefore be Arab-controlled.

Despite their agreements with Hussein on behalf of the Arabs, in the 1916 Sykes-Picot Agreement the British negotiated with the French to divide present-day Lebanon, Jordan, Iraq, and Syria between them. This clearly contradicted the terms of the McMahon correspondence. Following the end of World War I, the British and the French refused to let the Arabs rule themselves and, per the Sykes-Picot Agreement, assumed control of these Arab territories. They called them mandates, which were given legitimacy by the League of Nations. In each mandate, the European powers pledged to grant Arabs independence when they were deemed ready for self-government.

At the San Remo conference in April 1920, a new entity called Palestine was also placed under British authority, defined for the first time to consist of the present-day countries of Israel and Jordan. The British then divided Palestine and turned the territory east of the Jordan River into the state of Transjordan and announced that the Balfour Declaration did not apply to Jordan. This is why some Jews claim that present-day Jordan is part of Palestine, or the homeland of the Palestinian Arabs.

The Arab elites of Palestine were intensely opposed to the Jewish pursuit of a state in Palestine, which the British government certainly understood by 1918. The Arabs believed that the creation of a Jewish homeland in Palestine would eventually turn them into a marginalized minority among a majority Jewish population. Thus, the 500,000-strong Arab community of Palestine, approximately 85–90 percent of the total population, was unwilling to compromise with either the British or the Jews.

The British Mandate government in Palestine during 1922–1948 failed to keep the peace between the Arabs and the Jews. The escalating violence between Arabs and Jews was the result of the British policy that sought to achieve mutually exclusive goals: implementing the Balfour Declaration while safeguarding the interests and rights of the majority Arab population. Much of the tension arose over the numbers of Jewish immigrants admitted to the country. In response to Arab violence and riots, the British considered suspending Jewish settlements and Jewish land purchases in Palestine, which were often from wealthy absentee Arab landowners but then led to the eviction of Arab peasants. But London relented in the face of strong Jewish opposition.

In 1920 Palestinian Arabs began sporadically attacking Jewish settlements, and in response Jews formed a clandestine defense organization known as Haganah in 1921. To encourage cooperation between Arabs and Jews, the British in 1922 and 1923 attempted to create a legislative council, but Arabs refused to participate. Indeed, they not only suspected British manipulation and Jewish favoritism but also believed that their participation would signal their acceptance of the British Mandate and recognition of the Balfour Declaration.

Violence between Arabs and Jews throughout 1929 led the British to halt all Jewish settlement in Palestine. But in the face of outcries by Jews in Palestine and Zionists in London, the British government quickly reversed its policy. By 1936 the Jewish population of Palestine was approximately 400,000, or 30 percent of the total population. That same year, the British resurrected the idea of a legislative council, but this time both Arabs and Jews rejected the idea. Also in 1936, a full-fledged Arab rebellion began that lasted until 1939. This forced Britain to dispatch 20,000 troops to Palestine. The Arab Revolt led to a temporary collaboration between the British and Jews against Arabs to suppress the rebellion.

In 1937 the British recommended partitioning Palestine into separate Arab and Jewish states, but a year later they rejected partition as not feasible. By the end of the Arab Revolt in 1939, some 5,000 Arabs had been killed and thousands more wounded or arrested. That same year, the British announced that Palestine would become an independent state within 10 years. They also seemingly repudiated the Balfour Declaration by severely limiting future Jewish immigration and also restricting the sale of land to Jews.

By 1939, with the threat of world war looming, Britain sought to secure its Middle East interests by placating the Arabs. For the first time, the Jews found themselves marginalized and ignored by the British. As a result, some Jews began taking up arms against the British administration in Palestine. There was a temporary lull in fighting between Arabs and Jews owing to the German threat in the Middle East, but by the end of 1942 and the looming defeat of the Axis in North Africa, Arabs and Jews resumed fighting. At the same time, Jewish groups stepped up their attacks against the British.

News of the Holocaust gradually became public knowledge in 1942, and Zionists became increasingly impatient in their demands for not just more Jewish settlement in Palestine but also the immediate creation of a Jewish state there. At the same time, some Jewish groups such as Lohamei Herut Israel (also known as Lehi or the Stern Gang) and the Irgun Tsvai Leumi (National Military Organization) were resorting to increasing violence. The Holocaust facilitated the creation of Israel by further legitimizing Zionism and by uniting Jews around the idea that Jews would be essentially defenseless in the face of a government-sponsored genocide. Seemingly only a sovereign state could really protect Jews. The employment of terrorism and guerrilla warfare by armed Zionist groups in Palestine against the British throughout the 1940s became a major factor in Britain's decision to relinquish control of Palestine in 1948.

As for the Arabs, they took the view that because they neither caused nor were responsible for the Holocaust, they should not be forced to sacrifice for it by accepting the creation of a Jewish state in Arab territory. Many Arabs regard the creation of Israel as a product of Western guilt and shame over the Holocaust, with Arabs paying the price and bearing the burden of Western guilt. Thus, albeit for different reasons, both Jews and Arabs regard themselves as victims. Yet it is worth pointing out that the Holocaust almost certainly gave moral and political legitimacy to the Zionist cause. Israeli writer Amos Elon has argued that the genocide of the Jews in the Holocaust has been turned into a legitimizing myth for the existence of the State of Israel.

At the end of World War II, European governments struggled with what to do with more than 250,000 displaced Jews, survivors of the Holocaust. Britain resisted Zionist demands that they be allowed to settle in Palestine, especially while experiencing mounting terrorist violence there perpetuated by Jewish groups. This included the bombing by Irgun of the British military headquarters at the King David Hotel in Jerusalem on July 22, 1946, which killed some 90 people. Between November 1945 and July 1946 Jewish terrorism increased, with some 40 British soldiers and police killed by Irgun and Lehi along with the sabotage of infrastructure. Britain resented Jewish efforts to embarrass London by sending ships of Jewish refugees from Europe to Palestine only to have them intercepted by the Royal Navy. Meanwhile, the terrorist violence only reinforced Britain's uncompromising position.

British unwillingness to allow at least some of these displaced European Jews to settle in Palestine encouraged further attacks by militant Jewish organizations and anti-British sentiment among Jews. A joint attempt by the United States and Britain to resolve the Jewish refugee problem in Europe failed when Britain refused to abide by the Anglo-American Committee of Inquiry recommendation to admit 100,000 Jewish refugees into Palestine. On February 14, 1947, seeking to extricate itself from Palestine, Britain gave the newly created United Nations (UN) the responsibility of solving the Palestinian problem.

On August 31, 1947, the UN Special Commission on Palestine (UNSCOP) recommended the termination of the British Mandate for Palestine and the granting of Palestinian independence. A majority of UNSCOP members agreed to partition Palestine into both Arab and Jewish states, with Jerusalem remaining an international city. Although the Arab population was 1.2 million and the Jewish population just 600,000, the Arab state would have constituted only 43 percent of the land of Palestine. The Jewish state would take up 56 percent. It is worth noting that Jews already owned 6–8 percent of the total land area.

While not getting as much as they had hoped for, Jews supported the partition plan. The Arabs viewed the partition as unjust, granting more productive lands to the Jews and legitimizing the claim of the Jews—the majority of whom had been in Palestine for less than 30 years—as equal in terms of rights to those who had been living there for thousands of years. The newly created Arab League threatened war if the UN approved and implemented the partition plan. Desperate to quit Palestine, the British government announced that it would accept the UN recommendation and declared in September 1947 that the British Mandate for Palestine would terminate on May 14, 1948. By announcing the end of the British Mandate before the UN had approved the UNSCOP proposal and by refusing to enforce whatever decision the UN made, Britain undermined the UN's attempt to solve the Palestine problem.

President Harry S. Truman supported the UNSCOP plan. As a Democrat, he recognized that he needed the Jewish vote to win reelection in 1948, which may have influenced his decision. Truman also resented the more pro-Arab State Department, which worried about both the Arab reaction and the Middle East oil supply if the United States aligned itself with the Jews.

On November 29, 1947, the UN officially approved the partition of Palestine according to the UNSCOP report by a vote of 31 to 13 with 10 abstentions. This assured the establishment of a Jewish state in Palestine. In January 1948 the Arab Liberation Army (ALA) began entering Palestine and initially enjoyed considerable success in isolating rural Jewish settlements from Jews living in the major cities such as Haifa, Jerusalem, and Tel Aviv. But in April 1948 following the arrival of arms shipments from abroad, the Jews took the offensive and seized much territory, including Haifa and Jaffa. Arabs evacuated or were attacked and fled their villages and towns as Jews advanced during the spring 1948 offensive. The cause for this mass exodus remains controversial and disputed. Arabs had believed that the Jews would be swiftly defeated. Survivors also reported that in the chaos and invasions or hurried exits of their homes, they had no idea that they would be forbidden from returning. During this time, both Arabs and Jews resorted to terrorism with little regard for noncombatants. By May 2, 1948, Jews had militarily occupied a state roughly the equivalent of that approved by the UN. Thus, on May 14, 1948, the State of Israel was declared. The next day the Arab armies of Egypt, Lebanon, Jordan, Syria, and Iraq invaded Palestine, thus sparking the Israeli War of Independence (1948–1949).

STEFAN BROOKS

See also
Anti-Semitism; Arab Liberation Army; Arab Revolt of 1936–1939; Balfour Declaration; Haganah; Herzl, Theodor; Holocaust; Irgun Tsvai Leumi; Israel; Israeli War of Independence, Overview; Lohamei Herut Israel; McMahon-Hussein Correspondence; Sykes-Picot Agreement; United Kingdom, Middle East Policy; United Nations, Role of; United Nations Special Commission on Palestine; United States, Middle East Policy; Weizmann, Chaim; World War I, Impact of; World War II, Impact of; Zionism; Zionist Conference

References
Bickerton, Ian J., and Carla L. Klausner. *A Concise History of the Arab-Israeli Conflict.* 4th ed. Upper Saddle River, NJ: Prentice Hall, 2004.

Dowty, Alan. *Israel/Palestine.* Malden, MA: Polity, 2005.

Kamrava, Mehran. *The Modern Middle East.* Berkeley: University of California Press, 2005.

Sachar, Howard M. *A History of Israel: From the Rise of Zionism to Our Time.* 3rd ed. New York: Knopf, 2007.

Shepherd, Naomi. *Ploughing Sand: British Rule in Palestine, 1917–1948.* New Brunswick, NJ: Rutgers University Press, 1999.

Smith, Charles D. *Palestine and the Arab-Israeli Conflict: A History with Documents.* 6th ed. New York: Bedford/St. Martin's, 2006.

Yapp, M. E. *The Making of the Modern Near East 1792–1923.* London: Longman, 1987.

Palestine, Partition of

The idea of partitioning Palestine into Jewish and Arab political entities emerged early in Zionist thought. In his negotiations with the Ottoman government in 1902, Zionist leader Theodor Herzl suggested that a charter be granted for a Zionist entity that would run from Haifa by the Jezreel Valley to Lake Kinneret (the Sea of Galilee) and include all Galilee to the Litani River. Zionist leader and organizer of agricultural settlements in Palestine Arthur Rupin planned to concentrate Jewish settlements in Judea and around Lake Kinneret in an effort to achieve a sufficient population mass to achieve Jewish autonomy in these areas.

Zionists were active during the Paris Peace Conference following World War I, proposing the creation of a large Palestinian state under the assumption that rapid Jewish migration would soon allow them to constitute the majority of its population. This found a sympathetic ear in the British delegation if only because a large Palestine would ipso facto extend British influence in the region. Strong French opposition, however, excluded from the 1920 Palestinian Mandate areas of western Galilee to the Litani River and the Golan Heights to the Yarmuk River. Then, in 1922 the lands east of the Jordan River were placed under the rule of Emir Abdullah.

Following increasing violence in Palestine between Arabs and Jews and especially the Arab riots of 1929, in 1932 Victor Jacobson, World Zionist Organization (WZO) representative to the League of Nations, suggested to the League of Nations the possibility of Palestinian partition. He proposed that the Jewish area include the coastal plain and the relatively thinly populated valleys. With the beginning of the Arab Revolt of 1936–1939, calls for partition became more frequent and widespread and were even mentioned in the press. The British Peel Commission of 1936–1937 supported the partition of Palestine, with the Jews having an area of the country in which they would be the majority of the population. It also reached the rather erroneous conclusion that partition could end Jewish-Arab conflict. Zionists were divided on the issue, but the majority was inclined to accept partition as a means of rescuing Europe's Jews, then under increased persecution in both Germany and Poland. The British government was inclined to accept partition whereby there would be two separate states in Palestine, both of which would be tied to Britain.

Arab leaders adamantly opposed partition, however. The one exception was Abdullah. Faced with the strong opposition by the Arabs and German and Italian support for this, the British government reconsidered its stance. Indeed, the subsequent Woodhead Commission, charged with recommending ways of implementing partition, devised a plan that was disadvantageous to the Jews. The British government White Paper of 1939 and regulations the next year sharply restricting Arab land sales to Jews were strongly detrimental to the Jewish position. British policies were at this point in large part conditioned by London's desire to win Arab support for the war against the Axis. Meanwhile, the Zionist Biltmore Program of 1942 called for Jewish rule over all Palestine and extensive Jewish immigration there.

In late 1943 a British ministerial committee appointed by Prime Minister Winston Churchill proposed a partition plan in which there would be Arab and Jewish states and a British-mandated area that would include Jerusalem. The two states carved from Palestine would be part of a larger federation of states under the protection of Britain, France, and the United States. The Labor government that came to power in July 1945 did not initially favor partition or the granting of independence. Rather, it supported autonomous districts with ultimate authority to remain in British hands. The British government tended to be anti-Zionist, while the U.S. government was pro-Zionist. For a number of reasons, London was forced to follow Washington's position. The Anglo-American Committee of Inquiry of 1946, created under U.S. pressure, recommended creation of a single Arab-Jewish state, under the trusteeship of the United Nations (UN), and the admission of 100,000 Jewish refugees to Palestine. In the summer of 1946, Zionist leaders informed U.S. president Harry S. Truman that they were withdrawing their demands for a Jewish state that would encompass the whole of Palestine and were prepared to accept a Jewish state in part of the country.

Unable itself to resolve the Palestinian issue and under increasing financial pressures, the British government was determined to divest itself of Palestine. In February 1947 British foreign secretary Ernest Bevin announced that Britain was referring the matter to the UN, which in turn appointed the UN Special Commission on Palestine (UNSCOP) to come up with a recommendation. The two alternatives before the committee were the partition of Palestine into two separate sovereign states or one state in which there would be a federated state with an Arab majority and autonomy for a Jewish minority. A majority of the committee members favored partition. The UNSCOP plan called for Jerusalem to be internationalized. The original plan also called for the Jewish state to receive the Negev area for future immigration, but in negotiations with the General Assembly, the Negev was restored to the Arab state. While the Jews were willing to accept the UN plan, the Arabs firmly rejected it. Indeed, approval of the plan by the UN on November 29, 1947, led to the beginning of the Arab-Jewish Communal War. On May 14, 1948, the Jews announced the independence of the State of Israel, and this immediately led to an Arab invasion and the Israeli War of Independence (1948–1949). Israel won that war and at the conclusion of the armistice agreements of early 1949 ended up with three-quarters of the territory of the Palestine Mandate.

SPENCER C. TUCKER

See also

Abdullah I, King of Jordan; Anglo-American Committee of Inquiry; Arab Revolt of 1936–1939; Bevin, Ernest; Biltmore Program; Churchill, Sir Winston; Herzl, Theodor; Peel Commission; Truman, Harry S.; United Kingdom, Middle East Policy; White Paper (1939); Woodhead Report; Zionism

References

Sachar, Howard M. *A History of Israel: From the Rise of Zionism to Our Time*. 3rd ed. New York: Knopf, 2007.

Shepherd, Naomi. *Ploughing Sand: British Rule in Palestine, 1917–1948.* New Brunswick, NJ: Rutgers University Press, 1999.

Palestine, Pre-1918 History of

Palestine is a geographical area of the eastern Mediterranean coast bounded by the Jordan Valley to the east, the Negev Desert to the south, and Lebanon to the north. What constitutes Palestine has varied over time, but because it occupied an important transportation route between larger empires, it was destined for a stormy existence and has been fought over and disputed since ancient times. The current dispute is primarily between Palestinian Arab nationalists and the State of Israel, but on a larger scale it involves Islam, Judaism, Christianity, the United States, Europe, and the predominantly Muslim countries of the Middle East.

The Bible introduces the geographical region as Canaan. The Old Testament book of Numbers first names the area as Eretz Israel (the Land of Israel) in Chapter 34 and there clearly delineates Israel's boundaries that include portions of present-day Jordan. Palestine has been settled, disputed, conquered, and ruled by the Canaanites, Philistines, Samaritans, Nabataeans, Greeks, Romans, Byzantines, Ottomans, British, Jews, Muslims, and Christians.

Even the ownership of Palestine is disputed. As is true of most things in the Middle East, perspective is everything. For example, the Muslim perspective on the inheritance of the land revolves around the story in Genesis, the first book of the Bible, of a man named Abraham who had a special relationship with God. The major character in Genesis is Abraham, and many groups both present and past, such as the Edomites, the Arab peoples, and the Jews, trace their origins to Abraham. The Arabs assert that the story of Genesis accepted by Jews and Christians is fiction, a reconstructed story created by the Jews to establish Jewish ownership of the land. The Arab and Muslim perspective is that God's promise to make of Abraham a great nation and to give Abraham's offspring the land now disputed as Palestine or Israel was actually a promise to Ishmael, Abraham's son by his Egyptian wife Hagar, and to Ishmael's descendants through Ishmael's 12 sons. Muslims assert that the story was rewritten to make the promise to Isaac, Abraham's son by his wife Sarah. Isaac's first son, Esau, was the progenitor of the Edomites, who returned as enemies of Jacob's descendants later in biblical history.

The origin of the name "Palestine" is also subject to dispute, and Israelis and Palestinians have different perspectives on this too. Israeli prime minister Golda Meir asserted that the name was unknown until the British revived it after the demise of the Ottoman Empire at the end of World War I. And the radical American Israeli Rabbi Meir Kahane claimed that the idea of a Palestinian people as an ethnic group was a myth fabricated and perpetuated after 1948 by Arab states that did not and do not want to absorb the inhabitants who assumed residence in biblical Israel before the land was regained by present-day Israel. Kahane primarily based this contention on his assertion that no reference to Palestinian Arabs or a Palestinian people existed prior to the 20th century. Meir ridiculed the name as an Arab mispronunciation, "Falastin," of the name "Palaestina," given the area when it was under Roman rule.

The radical pro-Israel group Masada2000.org has asserted that the name "Palestine" was created by a Roman procurator following the AD 135 defeat of the Jews by the Romans in the Third Jewish Revolt, also known as the Simon Bar Kokhba (Kochba) Revolt. The procurator supposedly asked the name of the greatest enemy of the Jews in their history and, having been told the Philistines, declared that the area would forever be known as Philistia so as to erase the Jews from history. The Palestinians and Arab peoples assert that "Palestine" is the ancient name for the region, and both worldwide Jewry and Israel assert that "Israel" is the ancient name.

Both perspectives are built on partial truths. The name "Philistia" is an anglicized form of the Hebrew word "Plesheth," common in the Bible. The name was based on the Hebrew root *palash* that generally refers to rolling movements or migratory behavior and may have been a reference to the Philistines' multiple invasions of the coastal and southern regions of the area prior to the conquest of Canaan by Hebrews following the Hebrew exodus from Egypt. As early as the fifth century BC, the Greek historian Herodotus used the Greek-language equivalent of the English "Philistine Syria" to designate the eastern coast of the Mediterranean Sea. This designation was used six centuries later when the Bar Kokhba Revolt so angered the Roman emperor Hadrian that he wanted to erase from history the name "Provencia Judaea," the Latin name for the region. Hadrian renamed the area "Provincia Syria Palaestina," the Latin version of the name used by Herodotus. The name was later shortened to "Palaestina," the Latin name from which the English name "Palestine" is derived.

The Romans divided the region into three parts in the fourth century and named them First Palestine, Second Palestine, and Third Palestine. This division remained until the Romans lost control of the region to the Persians in AD 614. Palestine continued as the general name of the region until the end of the Crusader Kingdom in 1291 and thereafter as a colloquial term for the areas east and west of the Jordan River in the province of Damascus until the demise of the Istanbul-based non-Arab Muslim Ottoman Empire (1517–1917) following World War I.

BC History of Palestine

Ancient Canaan was a loose confederation of city-states paying tribute to Egypt's pharaohs until it was conquered by the Hebrews at the end of their 40-year wilderness wandering led by Moses, believed in Jewish tradition to have been 1240–1200 BC, although some scholars assert a date as early as 1500–1460 BC and others as late as 1140–1100 BC. The Edomites also resided in the area south of the Dead Sea during this time. The lands west of the Jordan River were divided among 11 of the 12 tribes of Israel, and the lands east of the Jordan River were divided among the two tribes descended from the 12th tribe of Joseph.

Tel Beth Shean, archaeological remains of the clay-brick–built Canaanite sanctuary dating from 14th–12th centuries BC. The tel is the site of a major Canaanite and Philistine city; King Saul and Jonathan were killed in battle with the Philistines near Beth Shean. (Zev Radovan/Land of the Bible Picture Archive)

There is general agreement that Saul became the first king of united Israel around 1025 BC after periods of oppression from neighboring peoples during the time of the Judges that followed Joshua's incomplete conquest. This left pockets of Canaanites throughout the land. David eventually became king after the death of Saul, and David's reign is generally dated by his 1004–1000 BC conquest of the Jebusite city of Jerusalem. David's son Solomon (Suleiman) became king during 970–962 BC and built the First Temple during 960–950 BC on land chosen by his father.

There was a brief period of unity after Solomon died around 928 BC, but during 930–920 BC the United Kingdom (Israel) split into a Northern Kingdom and a Southern Kingdom. The Northern Kingdom, known also as Israel and later as Samaria after its capital, consisted primarily of the ancestral lands of the descendants of the 10 northern tribes. The Southern Kingdom, known also as Judah, had Jerusalem as its capital and was constituted primarily of the ancestral lands of the descendants of the tribes of Judah and Benjamin.

The Northern Kingdom was destroyed in 722 BC after Assyrian King Sennacherib laid siege to Samaria. Sennacherib resettled the 10 northern tribes into other parts of his empire and forced them to integrate culturally, religiously, and linguistically, thereby reducing the opportunity for the conquered people to organize and support a rebellion. This forced integration, and the ensuing loss of ethnic and religious identity was why these tribes were called "lost." Sennacherib then moved another conquered people into the area vacated by the northern tribes and forced them to integrate into what remained of the culture and religion of the 10 lost tribes. These outsiders became the Samaritans, referred to in the New Testament. One reason they were hated by the Jews of the first century is that these outsiders were not the people of the promise given to Abraham. Although Sennacherib was unsuccessful in his siege of Jerusalem in 701 BC, the Assyrians maintained control of the region until they were conquered by the Babylonians.

A series of three confrontations between Babylonians under Nebuchadnezzar and Judah beginning in 608 BC and ending with the siege and surrender of Jerusalem in 597 BC sent three waves of captives to exile in Babylon. Their departure left only a small remnant of the descendants of Abraham, Isaac, and Jacob in the land to which they claimed Divine promise. Unlike the Assyrians, however, the Babylonians allowed the exiles from Judah to maintain their ethnicity, language, and religion, although they no longer had the First Temple, Solomon's Temple. As these exiles congregated, they

The ruins of a Roman aqueduct leading to Caesarea in northern Israel. (iStockPhoto.com)

became known as the people from Judah, or Jews. Because they could not sacrifice to make themselves right with their God, they began to codify the law contained in the Torah, the first five books of the Bible, believing that if they could not atone for their sins through sacrifice, they might avoid sin by following the minutiae of the Torah law.

This period was known as the Babylonian Captivity. Many of the inhabitants of Judah fled to or were taken as slaves to Egypt, Syria, Mesopotamia, and Persia. The forced movement of the inhabitants of Judah into Babylon and throughout the Middle East is called the First Dispersion, or Diaspora, of the Jews.

Cyrus the Great became king of Persia in 559 BC and conquered Babylon in 539 BC, allowing a group of the Jews led by Sheshbazzar and Zerubbabel to return to resettle on their ancestral land and rebuild Jerusalem. Darius I, also known as Darius the Great, became the king of Persia in 521 BC, and in 520–515 BC he allowed the construction of the Second Temple in Jerusalem under the prophets Haggai and Zechariah. Nehemiah, a cupbearer to Darius's successor Artaxerxes I (ruled 465–424 BC), was allowed to go to the region in 446 BC, 11 years after Ezra returned to restore true temple worship. Nehemiah rebuilt the walls of Jerusalem, and Ezra instituted synagogues similar to those that had developed in Babylonia to study the Torah law during the Captivity. He also publicly reintroduced

the Torah to the people in a General Assembly. The Samaritans built their temple on Mount Gerizim in 428 BC and began to worship the god of the region in a manner not in agreement with the Jewish understanding of the Torah law or of God's nature.

The region remained a province of Persia until 333 BC, when Alexander the Great of Macedonia conquered Persia and brought the region under Greek rule. The control of the region was disputed and alternately ruled by the dynasties of the generals, the Ptolemies in Egypt, and the Seleucids in Syria, who fought for control of Alexander's empire upon his death in 323 BC. During this period, the Nabataeans and other Arab tribes from the Arabian Peninsula began to encroach into the region and eventually occupied the area between Syria and Arabia bounded on the east by the Euphrates River and on the west by the Jordan River, the Dead Sea, and the Red Sea. The Nabataeans occupied Petra in 312 BC and made it their capital, although overall control remained with the Greek dynasties.

Seleucid ruler Antiochus IV, known also as Antiochus Epiphanes (ruled 175–163 BC), attempted to Hellenize the Jews under his governance. When they resisted, he occupied Jerusalem, profaned the Temple with swine's blood in 168 BC, and in 167 BC outlawed Jewish religious practices. The Jews, led by a Hasmonean Jewish priest named Mattathias and then by his son Judas Maccabeus, rebelled during 167–164 BC and in 165 BC regained the Temple.

The cleansing and rededication of the Temple was remembered annually in the Jewish festival of Hanukkah (Chanukah). The Essenes established their religious community at Qumran (Qumrun, Qumron) around 160 BC. Even though the environs of Jerusalem and Judea became semiautonomous following the Maccabean Revolt, the first fully autonomous Jewish state since the Babylonian conquest was not established until the Hasmonean dynasty was founded by Simon Maccabaeus in 142–140 BC.

The Hasmonean Empire expanded to encompass Transjordan, Samaria, Galilee, and Idumea, reaching its zenith under John Hyrcanus (134–104 BC). Hyrcanus forced many of the peoples in these incorporated territories to convert to Judaism, a practice that the Hasmonean king Alexander Jannaeus (103–76 BC) continued in his burgeoning rivalry with the Nabataeans, who had previously allied themselves with the Maccabees against the Seleucids.

In 63 BC Roman consul Pompey the Great invaded Judah, sacked Jerusalem, brought the Hasmoneans under Roman control, and called the area Judea. In 57–55 BC the Roman proconsul of Syria, Aulus Gabinius, divided the Hasmonean Kingdom into Galilee, Samaria, and Judea. The Idumean Herod the Great, appointed the king of the Jews in 74 BC by the Roman Senate, made Jerusalem his capital in 37 BC and began restoring the Second Temple in 20 BC. Herod Antipas, the son of Herod the Great, was made tetrarch ("ruler of the quarter") of Galilee and Perea under the rule of the Roman procurators at about the time of the births of Jesus and John the Baptist (6 BC–0). At the same time, Herod Archelaus (23 BC–AD 18), the brother of Herod Antipas, became ethnarch (a leader of an ethnic group within a designated area) of Judea (4 BC–AD 6).

AD History of Palestine

Jewish antipathy and Zealotian resistance to the Romans swelled after Jerusalem was made part of the Roman province of Judea in AD 6, when Caesar Augustus removed Herod Archelaus as ethnarch and brought Samaria, Judea, and Idumea under direct Roman rule as part of the Province of Iudaea (Judea). Augustus made Caesarea on the Mediterranean coast the capital of the province and placed the province under the control of Quirinius, the legate (governor) of Syria. Pontius Pilate served as the governor (procurator) of the Province of Judea (26–36) at the time of the crucifixion of Jesus (30–33).

Roman emperor Claudius first appointed Herod Agrippa I king of the Jews (ruled 41–44) and then appointed Herod Agrippa II king of the Jews, the seventh and last Herodian king, giving him control of the Temple in 48. Agrippa I ordered James the Great, the leader of the Christians in Jerusalem, killed in 44, but this only served to disperse the Christians and spread their religion.

The Christian leadership endorsed the Apostle Paul's evangelism and inclusion of gentiles in the religion at the Council of Jerusalem around 50. In 59–60 Paul was brought before Herod Agrippa II, who then sent Paul on to Rome when Paul exercised his right as a Roman citizen to have his case heard before Caesar. Both Peter and Paul died around 64–69 during Nero's persecution of the Christians.

Herod Agrippa II fled Jerusalem to Galilee and the safety of the Romans when the First Jewish Revolt (66–73), also known as the Great Revolt and the First Jewish-Roman War, began. The Romans under Vespasian destroyed Jerusalem and the Second Temple in 70 after a 134-day siege. This destruction of the Second Temple during the reign of the Emperor Titus marked the end of a Jewish state and the beginning of the Second Diaspora of the Jews.

It was during the Great Revolt that a small band of Zealots ("the zealous ones") under the command of Eleazar ben Ya'ir fled to the Masada fortress built by Herod the Great on a rock mesa overlooking the Dead Sea in the eastern Judean Desert near Ein Gedi. As the Romans prepared to surmount the redoubt after a lengthy siege, Eleazar exhorted the Zealot defenders and their families to a final act of defiance. The defenders and their families burned their personal belongings and selected by lot 10 defenders to kill the general population. These 10 then killed each other in turn, leaving only the final defender to commit suicide.

The Nabataean Empire was incorporated into the Roman Empire in 102. There were then two Jewish revolts against the Romans: the Second Jewish-Roman War, also known as the Kitos War (115–117), and the Third Jewish-Roman War (132–135), also known as the Bar Kokhba Revolt or the Third Jewish Revolt. Jericho and Bethlehem were destroyed in the Bar Kokhba Revolt. Roman emperor Hadrian retaliated by barring the Jews from Jerusalem, razing the city, building a pagan city named Aelia Capitolina over the ruins, and changing the name of the region to Palaestina from which the contemporary name "Palestine" is derived. Many Jews were killed or sold into slavery. Although many of the Jews who survived fled the region in the Third Diaspora of the Jews, a remnant remained.

Byzantine emperor Constantine, after adopting Christianity in 312, sought to rebuild Jerusalem after it came under Byzantine rule in 324. Although Constantine removed some of the restrictions that had been placed on the Jews following the Bar Kokhba Revolt and even permitted them to mourn annually the destruction of the city and the Temple, he continued to bar Jews from residing in the city. In 326 Constantine's mother Helena, a Christian, made a pilgrimage to the region and initiated construction of the Church of the Holy Sepulcher in Jerusalem and the Church of the Nativity in Bethlehem. In 362 the Byzantine emperor Flavius Claudius Iulianus (361–363), also known as Julian the Apostate, allowed Jews to resettle in Jerusalem.

Jerusalem fell to the Persians in 614 but was retaken by the Byzantines in 629 only to be lost again in 638 to the Arab Muslim caliph Omar Ben Hatav, also known as Omar ibn al-Khattaab. The Arab-Muslims adopted the Greco-Roman name "Palastina," pronouncing it as "Falastin." Control of Palestine (661–750) passed to the Damascus-based Umayyad caliphate—an Islamic government that governed and applied Sharia (Islamic law) to all Muslims—under the leadership of Caliph Abdal-Malik (685–705).

Abdal-Malik, also known as Abdul Malik ibn Marwan, built the Dome of the Rock (Mosque of Omar) in 690. The Dome of the Rock is the oldest holy building in Islam and surrounds the large rock from

Jewish Settlement in Palestine, 1880 – 1914

Mediterranean Sea

35°E

36°E

N

Metula

Yesod Hamaala

Ayeiet Hashaar

Mishmar Hayarden

Ein Zeitim

Rosh Mahanayim

33°N

Safed Rosh Pina

Acre

Sea of Galilee

Migdal

Kfar Hittim

Bnei Yehuda

Haifa

Tiberias Mizpa

Poriya

Nazareth Sejera

Kinneret

Atlit

Sharona

Deganya

Kfar Tavor

Beitanya

Tantura

Bat Shelomo

Biet Gan

Menahemya

Shefeiya

Merhavya

Yavneel

Zikhron Yaakov

Gan Shmuel

Givat Ada

Beisan

Karkur

Heftzibah

Nahliel

Hadera

Jenin

Tulkarm

Nablus

Kfar Mahal

Kfar Sava

Mikve Israel

Ein Hai

Tel Aviv

Petah Tikvah

Jaffa

Ein Ganim

Nahalat Yehuda

Mahane Yehuda

Ben Sheman

32°N

Rishon le Zion

Ramla

Ramallah

Beer Yaakov

Rehovot

Jericho

Nes Ziona

Ekron

Hulda

Motza

Gedera

Kfar Uriya

Jerusalem

Hartuv

Beer-Toviya (Kastinia)

Jordan R.

Gaza

Hebron

Dead Sea

Ruhama

○ Arab towns with few, if any, Jewish inhabitants by 1914

◉ Jewish Settlements established between 1880 and 1914

● Towns with Jewish as well as Arab Populations

0   5   10 mi

0 5 10 km

Beersheba

which Islamic tradition believes the Prophet Muhammad ascended (621) on his horse Al-Buraq to heaven at the end of his Night Journey. This rock is also considered to be the place that Abraham was to sacrifice his son. Jews and Christians assert that the potential sacrifice was Isaac, and Muslims assert that it was Ishmael. The Dome of the Rock was erected near what the Jews believe was the site of the Temple of Solomon and the Second Temple. The only remaining physical remnant, the Western Wall (Wailing Wall), was a retaining wall built at the base of the Temple Mount during Herod the Great's reconstruction of the Second Temple about 19 BC. Muslims today generally dispute any connection between the Western Wall and any previous Jewish religious site.

Abdal-Malik also planned the building on the same site of the al-Aqsa Mosque, which was completed in AD 710 by his son al-Walid (705–715). The al-Aqsa Mosque complex became a center of Islamic learning and worship when law schools were established there.

Palestine came under the control of the Baghdad-based Abbasid caliphate in 750 and remained under its administration until the North African (Egyptian) Fatimid dynasty and caliphate took Palestine by force in the ninth century. The Fatimid caliph al-Hakim (996–1021) persecuted the Christians and Jews residing in Palestine and commanded the destruction of many of the region's churches and synagogues. The Turkic Muslim Saljuqs took control of Jerusalem and a portion of Palestine in 1071, bringing the administration of these areas again under the Abbasid caliphate.

European Crusaders invaded the region in 1099 seeking to regain the Holy Land for Christendom. The Crusaders captured Jaffa and Jerusalem and began referring to the region as Palestine. The Crusader Latin Kingdom of Jerusalem, ruled by Godfrey of Bouillon, was responsible for the deaths of so many Jews and Muslims that a Papal Bull was issued in 1119 directing that the Jews no longer be killed. The Bull reiterated St. Augustine's 427 entreaty that the Jews should be made to wander Earth as evidence that they rejected Jesus, the true God. Crusader control of Palestine ended in 1187 when the (half-Kurdish) Muslim Saladin (Salah al-Din al-Ayyubi) defeated a large Crusader force at the Battle of Hattin, captured Jerusalem, and made Palestine part of the Province of Syria. English king Richard I the Lionheart tried to recapture Palestine and Jerusalem in 1192 during the Third Crusade but was unsuccessful.

Three hundred French and English rabbis were allowed to settle in Jerusalem in 1212, but Jerusalem was despoiled by the Tartars in 1244 and then by the Mongols in 1259–1260. The Mamluks, dynasties of professional soldier-slaves and then rulers of Egypt, ousted the Mongols from Palestine in 1260 and administered the region from Cairo. The Mamluks eradicated the last Crusader states in Palestine, Acre (Akka) and Qaysariyya, in 1291. Although Jews from Spain and other parts of the Mediterranean began to resettle in Palestine during the 1300s, the poor administration of the Mamluks and Palestine's 1351 Black Death epidemic contributed to a decrease in the population of Palestine to just over 200,000 people by 1500.

The Ottoman Turkish Muslims began just over 400 years of rule over Palestine when Sultan Selim I (1457–1520), the ruler of the Ottoman Empire during 1512–1520, defeated the Mamluks in Syria in 1516, captured Jerusalem, and seized Gaza. Mamluk Egypt was incorporated into the Ottoman Empire in 1517. Suleiman I (1494–1566), known also as the Magnificent and the Lawgiver, reconstructed Jerusalem during 1535–1538, and in 1541 he sealed the Golden Gate through which Jewish tradition holds that the Messiah would enter the city. The importance of Palestine as an overland trade crossroads diminished as sea routes were discovered to the east. There is little change to the area, and there were no conflicts during the 18th century and first quarter of the 19th century. In 1705 the Ottomans restricted Jewish immigration after Judah the Pious and 1,000 followers took up residence in Jerusalem. In 1831 a new personal tax on Muslim subjects caused a revolt in Damascus and the murder of the Ottoman governor and other officials.

In 1831 Muhammad Ali Pasha, the khedive (viceroy) of Egypt from 1805 to 1849, ostensibly an administrator for Ottoman sultan Mahmud II (ruled 1808–1839), conquered and occupied Syria under troops led by his son Ibrahim. Muhammad Ali had previously demanded that the sultan place Syria under his governorship in exchange for his military assistance in quelling a Greek revolt against the empire. The Egyptian administration raised taxes and increased the size of the bureaucracy and army. It also encouraged cash crops. In 1839 Mahmud II lost his army and his naval fleet in an attempt to regain Syria. A coalition of European nations together with a popular uprising finally drove out Muhammad Ali's government in 1840. Palestine, like other parts of the Ottoman Empire with the exception of Egypt under Muhammad Ali, suffered from lowered export tariffs, meaning that early industrial development, mainly textiles, could not compete with imports.

Meanwhile, oppression and persecution of the Jews in Eastern Europe in the latter part of the 19th century gave impetus to the Zionist emigration for Palestine and led to the establishment of Petach Tikva, the first agricultural community (i.e., Zionist settlement) in Palestine a year after the first Ottoman parliament (1876–1877). Jews accounted for 24,000 of the 400,000 residents of Palestine in 1880, but that number more than doubled after the initial wave of immigration (the First Aliya) of East European Zionists. These immigrants settled on small farms throughout Palestine and at first employed Arab labor. By 1895 Jews accounted for 47,000 of the 500,000 residents of Palestine and owned 0.5 percent of the land. The Jewish Colonization Association began aiding Zionist settlements in Palestine in 1896.

In 1897 Austrian-Jewish journalist Theodor Herzl convened the First Zionist Congress in Basle, Switzerland, in response to increasing European anti-Semitism following the Dreyfus Affair in France in 1894 and his call for a Jewish state in his influential short book *Der Judenstaat* (*The Jewish State*), published in 1896. The First Zionist Congress created the World Zionist Organization (WZO), elected Herzl as the first WZO president, authorized the WZO to establish branches in all countries with consequential Jewish populations,

Samaritan women carry water from a well near Nablus, circa 1890, an area now part of the West Bank in the Palestinian Autonomous Region. (Library of Congress)

and determined Zionism's goal to be the creation of a legal (guaranteed) Jewish homeland in Palestine (Israel). The WZO was formed to unite the Jewish people politically so that Judaism acting as one organic whole might exert more power in addressing the plight of world Jewry and in creating a homeland in Israel (Palestine) for Jews.

At the First Zionist Congress, the political Zionism of the Jews of Western Europe merged with the settlement activities in Turkish Palestine, promoted and successfully engaged in by the East European Hovevei Tsion. The WZO created companies and institutions designed to accomplish its policies, the most prominent among many being the Jewish Colonial Trust, established in 1899; the Jewish National Fund (Keren Keyemeth), established in 1901; the Anglo-Palestine Bank, the Jewish Colonial Trust's subsidiary, established in 1902; and Keren Hayesod, established in 1920. The Jewish National Fund was created to acquire land in Palestine. Keren Hayesod funded Zionist and Yishuv (Jewish communities in Palestine) activities and created companies such as the Palestine Electric Company, the Palestine Potash Company, and the Anglo-Palestine Bank.

The WZO's actions promoted and facilitated the Second Aliya (1904–1914), which brought primarily secular Jews (including socialists) into Palestine and raised the Jewish population to 6 percent of the Palestinian total. The many farms and factories bought or built by the Baron Edmond de Rothschild Foundation were insufficient to employ this number of people, and so many participants in the Second Aliya eventually left Palestine.

Fearing that the publication in 1904 of Najib Azury's (*The Awakening of the Arab Nation in Turkish Asia*), which publicly warned the Arabs of the Zionist plan for Palestine, would hamper its plans, the 1904 Fourth Zionist Congress determined that there was a need for an alternative Jewish national homeland in Argentina. However, the 1906 Fifth Zionist Congress reaffirmed Palestine as the future Jewish national homeland. The Arabic-language newspaper *Al-Karmil* was founded in 1908 in Haifa with the express purpose of opposing Zionist colonization, but this did not prevent the 1909 establishment of the first Zionist kibbutz (collective) farm. By 1910, Arabic-language newspapers in Beirut and Damascus sounded the alarm over Zionist land acquisitions and the growing Jewish population, and in 1911 the Arab newspaper *Filastin* began calling Arabs living in Palestine "Palestinians." One of the earliest books in Arabic, Najib Nassar's *Zionism: Its History, Objectives and Importance,* was also published in 1911. The Jews accounted for 85,000 (12 percent) of the 700,000 total population of Palestine by 1913, the same year the First Arab Nationalist Congress met in Paris.

During World War I the British government, eager to secure the support of both Arabs and Jews, made promises to the Arabs and the Zionists that Britain never kept in whole for either side. Britain promised independence for Arab lands under Turkish Ottoman rule while at the same time courting world Jewry. By 1915, the Anglo-Jewish politician and diplomat Herbert Samuel (1870–1963), eventually to be the first high commissioner of the British Mandate for Palestine in 1920, secretly proposed that Britain annex Palestine and populate it with 3–4 million European Jews. The Arabs, on the other hand, were opposed to plans that would divest them of their land and property. Many understood the 1916 talks and correspondence between Hussein ibn Ali, sharif of Mecca and later the king of the Hejaz, and Sir Henry McMahon, British high commissioner in Egypt, as ensuring their rights in Palestine as part of a postwar Arab nation.

On May 16, 1916, the British and French secretly concluded the Sykes-Picot Agreement that specified their respective interests in the Arab provinces of the Ottoman Empire, dividing them into postwar areas directly or indirectly administered by the French and British. Later in 1916, uninformed of British participation in the Sykes-Picot Agreement and acting on his correspondence with McMahon, Sharif Hussein declared independence from the Ottoman Empire and began an Arab revolt against its control.

The British government issued the Balfour Declaration on November 2, 1917, expressing official British support for a Jewish homeland in Palestine. In December 1917, Ottoman forces in Jerusalem surrendered to British general Sir Edmund Allenby. Allenby's allied forces then occupied all of Palestine by September 1918. World War I and the Ottoman Empire's rule of Palestine ended in October

1918, paving the way for a British mandate over the area that would endure until 1948.

RICHARD M. EDWARDS

See also

Al-Aqsa Mosque; Balfour Declaration; Church of the Holy Sepulcher; Church of the Nativity; Dome of the Rock; Jerusalem; Kibbutz Movement; Masada; Masada2000.org; Ottoman Empire; Palestine, British Mandate for; Samaritans; Sykes-Picot Agreement; World Zionist Organization; Zionism; Zionist Conference

References

Ahlstrom, Gosta W. *The History of Ancient Palestine.* Minneapolis, MN: Augsburg, 1993.

Avi-Yonah, Michael. *The Jews of Palestine: A Political History of Palestine from the Bar Kokhba War to the Arab Conquest.* New York: Schocken, 1984.

Biale, David. *Cultures of the Jews: A New History.* New York: Schocken, 2002.

Bright, John. *A History of Israel.* 4th ed. Louisville, KY: Westminster John Knox Press, 2000.

Coogan, Michael D. *The Oxford History of the Biblical World.* New York: Oxford University Press, 2001.

Dimont, Max. *Jews, God and History.* New York: Simon and Schuster, 1962.

Farsoum, Samih K., and Naseer H. Aruri. *Palestine and the Palestinians: A Social and Political History.* 2nd ed. Jackson, TN: Westview, 2006.

Pappe, Ilan. *A History of Modern Palestine: One Land, Two Peoples.* Cambridge: Cambridge University Press, 2003.

———. *The Israel/Palestine Question: Rewriting Histories.* Minneapolis, MN: Augsburg, 1999.

Parkes, James. *A History of Palestine from 135 AD to Modern Times.* Elibron Classics Replica Edition. Brighton, MA: Adamant Media Corporation, 2005.

Provan, Iain W., et al. *A Biblical History of Israel.* Louisville, KY: Westminster John Knox Press, 2003.

Russell, Michael. *Palestine or The Holy Land from the Earliest Period to the Present Time.* Kila, MT: Kessinger, 2004.

Thompson, Thomas L. *Early History of the Israelite People: From the Written & Archaeological Sources.* Leiden: Brill Academic, 2000.

Palestine Executive Committee

An elected body of delegates granted semiautonomous rule over Palestine during the British Mandate period. The Palestine Executive Committee (PEC) assumed a variety of forms but was dominated from 1920 until 1934 by Musa Kazim al-Husayni. The PEC was first elected at the Third Palestinian Arab Congress, which met in Haifa in 1920. Al-Husayni headed the congress and was the resounding choice to chair the Executive Committee. The committee, which initially had no legal standing to represent the Palestinian people, repeatedly demanded the creation of a democratic, representative government in Palestine. When the British Mandate government, headed by High Commissioner Herbert Samuel, refused to acknowledge al-Husayni's group, the committee voted to send a delegation to Europe to explain the situation and plead for assistance.

The PEC's delegates, led by al-Husayni, went to Cairo, Rome, London, and Geneva. While their visits generated some publicity, particularly when they obtained an audience with Pope Pius XI, the delegation did not meet with any British officials. The delegates demanded that the British government renounce its pro-Zionist stance, espoused in the 1917 Balfour Declaration, but met with little success. Upon returning to Palestine, they declared a boycott of British government offices, hoping to force an end to legal Jewish immigration and open the possibility of the creation of a Palestinian state.

After the Seventh Palestinian Arab Congress (June 20–27, 1927), the new British governor of Palestine, High Commissioner Herbert Plumer, recognized the PEC as the representative of the Palestinian people. At the Seventh Congress the PEC was reconstituted, and all previous committees were formally dissolved. The newest iteration of the PEC included 48 members, 36 Muslims and 12 Christians. The Muslim representatives were elected by local associations, with 2 delegates per region. The Christian delegates were elected at-large, as no district contained a Christian majority. Al-Husayni remained the chairman of the PEC, holding the position until his death in 1934. Although the PEC claimed to represent all Palestinians, it was plagued by a lack of internal unity and was but one of many organizations claiming a mandate for the Palestinian people.

The PEC's relationship with the British Mandate authorities was tumultuous at best. In 1924 the PEC boycotted the visit of former British foreign secretary and prime minister Arthur Balfour, who presided over the inauguration of Hebrew University. The PEC met with Colonial Secretary Leopold Amery, but its importance was undercut by the National Party, which demanded and received a separate meeting. This division clearly demonstrated the factionalism inherent in Palestinian politics. By 1932 the PEC's importance had declined, and it represented but one faction among many. This minor status remained until 1936, when the Arab Revolt (1936–1939) demonstrated the need for unity in opposition to the British Mandate. The push for unification resulted in the creation of the Arab Supreme Committee and the formal dissolution of the PEC.

PAUL JOSEPH SPRINGER

See also

Arab Revolt of 1936–1939; Balfour, Arthur James; Balfour Declaration; Palestine, British Mandate for; Samuel, Sir Herbert Louis

References

Cohn-Sherbok, Dan, and Dawoud El-Alami. *The Palestine-Israeli Conflict: A Beginner's Guide.* Oxford, UK: Oneworld, 2001.

Kimmerling, Baruch, and Joel S. Migdal. *Palestinians: The Making of a People.* New York: Free Press, 1993.

Tannous, Izzat. *The Palestinians: A Detailed Documented Eyewitness History of Palestine under British Mandate.* New York: I.G.T., 1988.

Palestine Liberation Army

Military organization established by the first Palestinian National Congress in 1964. Proposed by Ahmad Shukeiri, the Palestine Liberation Army (PLA) was created to serve as the conventional military arm of the Palestine Liberation Organization (PLO). The PLO

Members of the Palestine Liberation Army undergo training in the Gaza Strip, April 26, 1966. (Bettmann/Corbis)

was originally a forum for traditional, influential Palestinian notables. Its leadership did not consider guerrilla or commando activities at that time. Instead, they established the PLA as a force of
three brigades, totaling some 20,000–30,000 men, to be hosted and
trained in Egypt, Iraq, and Syria that would fight alongside these
Arab armies under their command.

Although nominally under PLO direction, in practice the PLA
has always been firmly under the control of its host nations, and
PLA units have been incorporated into their military establishments.
Thus, the Ayn Jalut Brigade in Gaza came under Egyptian Army
control, the Hittin Brigade came under Syrian control, and the
Qadisiyya Brigade came under Iraqi control. In Jordan where much
larger numbers of Palestinians resided, Shukeiri had to promise
King Hussein that Palestinians would not arm or organize Palestinians. Later, however, the Yarmuk Brigade formed with defectors
from the Jordanian Army. The presence of Palestinian troops has
proved a convenient circumstance on a number of occasions particularly for Syria, which utilized PLA troops during its armed
actions in Jordan and Lebanon.

The 1967 Six-Day War made it impossible for the Egyptian
government to oppose commando activities. Hence, Gamal Abdel

Nasser met with Fatah leaders and arranged to help arm and train
them. Shukeiri was overthrown as PLO leader and replaced first by
Yahya Hammuda in 1967 and then by Yasser Arafat in 1969. This
period saw a displacement of the PLO leaders who had emphasized
politics and diplomacy for those who wanted more independent
Palestinian military activities. Arafat, who had opposed the creation of the PLA out of concern that it would be dominated by its
host nations, argued that the PLA hurt the recruitment of Palestinian fighters. This lack of unity demonstrated the inherent weakness
of the PLO, which had never maintained even rudimentary control
over its military wing. In 1970 Arafat was named the head of the
PLA at the Seventh Palestinian National Council, but the commander of the PLA, Uthman Haddad, refused to recognize Arafat's
supremacy and remained in power. In a face-saving gesture, Haddad was renamed the PLA's chief of staff, and in this position he
continued his policy of maintaining PLA autonomy from Arafat's
control. Haddad maintained close ties with the Syrian Army and
effectively continued the policy of subordinating the PLA to the
Syrians.

In 1970 both Syria and Jordan deployed PLA troops to Jordan
during the events of Black September. More than 5,000 PLA troops

remained on Jordanian territory until the threat of foreign intervention compelled their withdrawal. Syria also used PLA units in Lebanon. However, some of these refused to fight other Palestinians. The Yarmuk and Hittin Brigades comprised a major part of the Syrian assault on Lebanese sovereignty. In 1976 Egypt deployed the PLA's Ayn Jalut Brigade to fight alongside Fatah forces resisting the Syrian advance, with the result that PLA units were ordered to fight one another. The PLA presence in Lebanon was virtually destroyed in 1982 when Israel invaded the southern portion of the country. However, the PLA quickly recruited new members from Palestinian refugee populations in Syria, Egypt, Iraq, and Jordan. By the mid-1980s, the PLA had grown to a peak strength of approximately 14,000 permanent forces divided into eight brigades.

After the signing of the Declaration of Principles and the Cairo Agreement on May 4, 1994, some of the PLA was redeployed into the autonomous area to serve as the police force of the Palestinian Authority (PA).

The Syrian brigade, in principle autonomous as it is staffed entirely by drafted Palestinian refugees, is in fact controlled by Syria. It organizes pro-Syrian events to demonstrate Syrian solidarity with the Palestinian cause.

PAUL J. SPRINGER, SPENCER C. TUCKER, AND SHERIFA ZUHUR

See also

Arafat, Yasser; Fatah; Palestine Liberation Organization; Palestinian Authority

References

Amos, John W., II. *Arab-Israeli Military/Political Relations: Arab Perceptions and the Politics of Escalation.* New York: Pergamon, 1979.

Brand, Laurie. *Palestinians in the Arab World: Institution Building and the Search for State.* New York: Columbia University Press, 1988.

Khouri, Fred J. *The Arab-Israeli Dilemma.* 3rd ed. Syracuse, NY: Syracuse University Press, 1985.

Norton, Augustus Richard, and Martin H. Greenberg, eds. *The International Relations of the Palestine Liberation Organization.* Carbondale: Southern Illinois University Press, 1989.

Palestine Liberation Front

Militant Palestinian group that was characterized by the United States and some European nations as a terrorist organization. The Palestine Liberation Front (PLF) was first founded in 1959 by Ahmed Jibril with Syrian backing. In 1967 it merged with two other organizations, the Heroes of the Return and the Youth of the Revenge Group, to form the Popular Front for the Liberation of Palestine (PFLP), led by George Habash. In 1968, however, Jibril split off part of the membership to form the Popular Front for the Liberation of Palestine–General Command (PFLP-GC) that supported Syria in doing battle with the Palestine Liberation Organization (PLO) in 1976 during the Lebanese Civil War.

The PFLP-GC action led to the reestablishment of the PLF in April 1977 under Abu Abbas (Muhammad Zaidan) and Talat Yaqub. PLF leaders were angry that the PFLP-GC did not oppose Syrian support for the Phalangists against the PLO in Lebanon. Some fight-

ing occurred thereafter between the PLF and the PFLP-GC, including the bombing of PLF headquarters in August 1977 in which some 200 people died.

In 1983 following the Israeli invasion of Lebanon, the PLF split into three factions. The two principal groups were a pro-Syrian faction led by Yaqub, and a larger pro-Iraq group was led by Abbas. Both kept the same name and claimed to represent the original organization. Yaqub died in November 1988, and only then did his group rejoin that led by Abbas.

Reportedly receiving some Libyan funding, the PLF believed strongly in armed struggle against Israel in the form of terrorist attacks, most of them mounted along Israel's northern border from Lebanon. The most notorious of its terrorist actions was the hijacking of the Italian cruise ship *Achille Lauro* on October 7, 1985. It also mounted an unsuccessful attack on Nizamim Beach near Tel Aviv on May 30, 1990. The attack was to kill both Israelis and tourists in the hopes of torpedoing any move toward peace talks between the PLO and Israel. Abbas came under heavy criticism from within the PLO leadership for this and was forced to resign from the PLO Executive Committee. Following the 1993 Oslo Accords, the PLF accepted the PLO policy of halting terrorist activity against Israel. The PLF campaigned in the 2006 Palestinian elections under the name of Martyr Abu Abbas but failed to win any seats.

SPENCER C. TUCKER

See also

Abbas, Abu; *Achille Lauro* Hijacking; Habash, George; Syria

References

Alexander, Yonah. *Palestinian Secular Terrorism.* Ardsley, NY: Transnational Publishers, 2003.

Bohn, Michael K. *The Achille Lauro Hijacking: Lessons in the Politics and Prejudice of Terrorism.* Dulles, VA: Potomac Books, 2004.

Cassese, Antonio. *Terrorism, Politics and Law: The Achille Lauro Affair.* Princeton, NJ: Princeton University Press, 1989.

Nassar, Jamal R. *The Palestine Liberation Organization: From Armed Struggle to the Declaration of Independence.* New York: Praeger, 1991.

Palestine Liberation Organization

A political and military organization founded in 1964 and dedicated to protecting the human and legal rights of Palestinians and creating an independent state for Palestinian Arabs in Palestine. Since the 1960s, the Munazzamat al-Tahrir Filastiniyyah (Palestine Liberation Organization, PLO) has functioned as the official mouthpiece for the Palestinian people. There are numerous factions and organizations that loosely fall under the PLO's umbrella. In addition to Fatah which is the largest of these groups, the PLO has also encompassed the Popular Front for the Liberation of Palestine (PFLP), the Democratic Front for the Liberation of Palestine (DFLP), the Palestinian People's Party, the Palestine Liberation Front (PLF), the Arab Liberation Front, al-Saiqa (Syrian Baathists), the Palestine Democratic Union, the Palestinian Popular Front Struggle, and the Palestinian Arab Front. Two groups no longer associated with the

General Wagih el Madany, commander of the Palestine Liberation Organization (PLO) Army, and Ahmad Shukeiri, first chairman of the PLO, in Cairo during a meeting of the Arab Defense Council, December 7, 1955. (AFP/Getty Images)

PLO include the Popular Front for the Liberation of Palestine–General Command (PFLP-GC) and the Fatah Uprising. The PLO is comprised of centrist-nationalist groups (such as Fatah), rightist groups, leftist groups (including communists), militant groups, and nonmilitant groups. It has purposely eschewed embracing any one political philosophy so as to be as inclusive as possible in its membership. The PLO has been enormously successful in attracting funding over the years. Indeed, a 1993 survey estimated the PLO's total assets at between $8 billion and $10 billion and its average yearly income at $1.5 billion to $2 billion.

The PLO was founded in 1964 by the Arab League and Egypt. Its first president was Ahmad Shukeiri. The stated purpose of the PLO was the liberation of Palestine, condemnation of Zionist imperialism, and the dissolution of Israel through the use of armed force. Throughout its existence, the PLO has often used violence to express its viewpoints and gain international attention. This has earned it the reputation of being a terrorist organization, although Palestinians and many international observers dispute that characterization. In 1988, PLO chairman Yasser Arafat—who led the organization from 1969 to 2004—renounced violence as a means to achieve Palestinian goals, but a number of PLO groups did not follow this decree and have continued to mount terrorist attacks in Israel and elsewhere.

Although the PLO has been reorganized many times since its inception, its leading governing bodies have been the Palestinian National Council (PNC), the Central Council, and the Executive Committee. The PNC has 300 members and functions as a nominal legislature. The Executive Committee has 15 members elected by the PNC and holds the PLO's real political and executive power. The Palestinian Revolutionary Forces are the PLO's military arm. (The Palestine Liberation Army, or PLA, a military group in Syria during the 1970s, was never part of the PLO.)

The PLO has always had a variety of viewpoints represented, some more radical and prone to violence than others, and Egyptians dominated the organization in its first years. As the 1960s wore on, fedayeen organizations, groups that existed expressly to take up the armed struggle against the Israelis, became more powerful. These groups used guerrilla and paramilitary tactics to resist the encroachment of Israelis on what they considered Palestinian territory.

In 1968 Fatah took control of the PLO's activities after Arafat appeared on the cover of *Time* magazine as the chairman of the Palestinian movement. On February 3, 1969, the PNC in Cairo officially appointed Arafat chairman of the PLO. Over the next four years, Arafat had become the commander in chief of the PLO's military branch, the Palestinian Revolutionary Forces, and the political leader of the organization. He based the PLO in Jordan.

In 1968 and 1969, the PLO functioned as a well-organized unofficial state within Jordan, with its uniformed soldiers acting as a police force and collecting their own taxes. In 1968 King Hussein of Jordan and the PLO signed an agreement by which the PLO agreed that its members would stop patrolling in uniform with guns, stop searching civilian vehicles, and act as Jordanian civilian citizens. The PLO did not comply with this agreement, however, and both attacks on civilians and clashes between Palestinians and Jordanian soldiers increased. By 1970 Hussein decided that the Palestinians threatened national security and ordered his army to evict them. This led to several months of violence, during which Syria aided the Palestinians and the United States aided Jordan. The events of Black September (including an attempt on Hussein's life), several airliner hijackings by the PFLP, and a declaration of martial law in Jordan culminated with the PLO agreeing to a cease-fire on September 24 and promising to leave the country.

Arafat now relocated the PLO to Beirut, Lebanon. There Palestinians moved into existing refugee settlements. The Lebanese government tried to restrict the PLO's movements, which led to tensions, but the Palestinians used their position to launch periodic attacks across the Israeli border. Lebanese Muslims and members of Kamal Jumblatt's progressive coalition supported the Palestinian cause, seeing the Palestinians as allies in their struggle against certain Christian factions who dominated the government and the Lebanese Forces (Maronite militias). The latter disliked the PLO presence and wanted to drive the Palestinians out by force.

During the early 1970s, Arafat and the various groups that comprised the PLO often came into conflict over the proper means of achieving the organization's goals. Although Arafat agreed that a

Palestinians carry posters of President Yasser Arafat during a mock funeral in the Gaza Strip, November 12, 2004. Arafat was buried in a chaotic scene of grief and gunfire at the compound where he spent his final years. (Suhaib Salem/Reuters/Corbis)

certain amount of violence against Israel was necessary to accomplish the PLO's purposes, he believed that diplomacy and compromise were also key to gaining international support. After 1968 the more politically radical groups, such as the PFLP, the DFLP, and other smaller factions, strongly disagreed because it seemed apparent that the Arab countries could not defeat Israel militarily. Such groups gained notoriety for their airplane hijackings in the late 1960s and early 1970s, carried out in Europe and the Middle East. These attacks were intended to further efforts to destroy Israel and create a socialist secular Arab society in its stead. Arafat himself condemned overseas attacks because he believed that they hurt the PLO's international image.

When the radical Black September organization killed several Israeli athletes at the Olympic Games in Munich in 1972, Arafat promptly stated that the PLO was not responsible for the attacks. Arafat closed down the Black September organization in 1973, and

in 1974 he ordered the PLO to restrict its violent attacks to Israel, the Gaza Strip, and the West Bank.

In 1974 the Arab Summit recognized the PLO as the sole representative of the Palestinian people. Arafat then appeared before the United Nations (UN) that same year as the official representative of the Palestinians. Speaking before the UN General Assembly, he condemned Zionism and said that the PLO would continue to operate as freedom fighters but also said that he wanted peace. This was the first time the international community had heard directly from the PLO, and many international observers praised Arafat and came to support the Palestinian cause. The UN granted the PLO observer status on November 22, 1974.

Also in 1974, the leaders of Fatah, in the guise of the PNC, created a Ten-Point Program that set forth the PLO's goals. This program called for a secular state in Israel and Palestine that would welcome both Jews and Arabs and provide all citizens equal rights regardless of religion, race, or gender. It also called for the creation of a Palestinian Authority (PA) on free Palestinian territory. Israel rejected the Ten-Point Program. Meanwhile, the radical guerrilla groups the PFLP and the PFLP-GC, which had earlier split from the PFLP, departed from the PLO in protest of its attempt to negotiate with Israel.

In 1975 the Lebanese Civil War broke out. Israel pursued a strategy of support of the Lebanese Forces, the Maronite militias who opposed the Palestinians. The PLO and Fatah joined forces with the National Front, a more left-wing coalition of Muslims, Druze, and Christians. Syria intervened at first on behalf of Muslim forces but later came to the aid of the Maronites and in the 1980s also supported the Shia militias.

On January 12, 1976, the UN Security Council voted to grant the PLO the right to participate in Security Council debates. The PLO became a full member of the Arab League that same year.

During the late 1970s, PLO members continued to enter Lebanon and maintain positions in Beirut, from which they exchanged attacks with Israel. On July 24, 1981, the PLO and Israel agreed to a cease-fire within Lebanon and on the border between Lebanon and Israel. Arafat interpreted the cease-fire agreement literally and continued to allow the PLO to attack Israel from Jordan and the West Bank. The Israelis violated the cease-fire numerous times, bombing PLO targets in Beirut. That autumn, Israeli prime minister Menachem Begin and Defense Minister Ariel Sharon planned an invasion into Lebanon to occupy southern Lebanon and territory all the way up to Beirut, where they planned to destroy the PLO. Israeli troops invaded, occupied much of southern Lebanon, and rounded up much of the male population of the area. The UN passed one resolution demanding that Israel withdraw its troops, but the United States vetoed another resolution repeating this demand. The United States demanded that the PLO withdraw from Lebanon. Sharon ordered the bombing of West Beirut beginning on June 15. The UN once again demanded that Israel withdraw, but the United States again vetoed the resolution.

On August 12, 1982, the two sides agreed to another cease-fire in which both the PLO and Israel would leave Lebanon. As a result, about 15,000 Palestinian militants left Lebanon by September 1. The Israelis, however, claimed that PLO members were still hiding in Beirut and returned to the city on September 16, killing several hundred Palestinians, none of whom were known to be PLO members. Sharon resigned as defense minister after the Sabra and Shatila massacres, which were carried out by Lebanese Christian militias with Israeli foreknowledge and approval.

Arafat and many surviving PLO members spent most of the 1980s in Tunisia rebuilding the organization, which had been severely damaged by the fighting in Beirut. During this time, Iraq and Saudi Arabia donated substantial sums of money to the organization. But relations between the PLO and Israel remained intractably bad. The Israel Defense Forces (IDF) bombed the PLO headquarters in Tunis in 1985, an attack that killed 73 people.

In December 1987 the First Intifada broke out spontaneously in the West Bank and Gaza, surprising Israelis with its intensity. On November 15, 1988, the PLO officially declared the formation of the State of Palestine. The PLO claimed all of Palestine as defined by the former British Mandate. However, the PLO had decided to seek a two-state solution. That December Arafat spoke before the UN, promising to end terrorism and to recognize Israel in exchange for the Israeli withdrawal from the occupied territories, according to UN Security Council Resolution 242. This was a distinct change from the PLO's previous position of insisting on the destruction of Israel. The PNC symbolically elected Arafat president of the new Palestinian state on April 2, 1989.

Arafat and the Israelis began conducting peace negotiations at the Madrid Conference in 1991. Although the talks were temporarily set back when Arafat and the PLO supported Iraq in the 1991 Persian Gulf War, over the next two years the two parties held a number of secret discussions. These negotiations led to the 1993 Oslo Accords in which Israel agreed to Palestinian self-rule in the Gaza Strip and the West Bank and Arafat officially recognized the existence of the State of Israel. Despite the condemnation of many Palestinian nationalists, the peace process appeared to be progressing apace. Israeli troops withdrew from the Gaza Strip and Jericho in May 1994.

In 1994 the PLO established a Negotiations Affairs Department (NAD) in Gaza to implement the Interim Agreement. Mahmoud Abbas, then secretary-general of the PLO Executive Committee, headed the NAD until April 2003, when the Palestinian Legislative Council chose him as the first prime minister of the PA. He was replaced by Saeb Erakat. The Gaza office of NAD handled Israeli affairs, agreements between Israel and Palestine, colonization, and refugees. It also kept careful track of Israeli expansion into Palestinian territory. The NAD also opened an office in Ramallah to handle the implementation of the Interim Agreement and prepare the Palestinian position for negotiations toward permanent status. The government of the United Kingdom began assisting the NAD with its preparation for permanent status talks in 1998.

In 1996 the PNC agreed to remove from the PLO charter all language calling for armed violence aimed at destroying Israel, and Arafat sent U.S. president Bill Clinton a letter listing language to be removed, although the PLO has dragged its feet on this. The organization claimed that it was waiting for the establishment of the Palestinian state, when it would replace the charter with a constitution.

Arafat was elected leader of the new PA in January 1996. The peace process began unraveling later that year, however, after rightist hard-liner Benjamin Netanyahu was elected prime minister of Israel. Netanyahu distrusted Arafat and condemned the PLO as a terrorist organization responsible for numerous suicide bombings on Israeli citizens. The accord collapsed completely in 2000 after Arafat and Israeli prime minister Ehud Barak failed to come to an agreement at a Camp David meeting facilitated by Clinton. After that, the Second (al-Aqsa) Intifada began when Palestinians, already experiencing the intractability of the Israeli government, saw Ariel Sharon lead security forces onto the Haram al-Sharif. During that period, suicide bombings increased. These attacks were in some instances claimed by Islamic Jihad of Palestine (PIJ), Hamas sympathizers, and other groups. Arafat and the PLO disavowed any support for such attacks. But whether right or wrong, the Israeli media continued to state or suggest that Arafat clandestinely supported the work of the terrorists.

Arafat died on November 11, 2004. There was much dissension over the succession, but Abbas eventually came to represent the PLO's largest faction, Fatah. In December 2004 he called for an end to the violence associated with the Second Intifada that began in September 2000. In January 2005 he was elected president of the PA but has struggled to keep the PLO together and Fatah from losing its political and financial clout. In the January 2006 PA parliamentary elections, Abbas and Fatah were dealt a serious blow when Hamas captured a significant majority of seats. An even greater blow came in June 2007 when Hamas seized control of Gaza.

AMY HACKNEY BLACKWELL

See also

Abbas, Mahmoud; Arafat, Yasser; Black September; Black September Organization; Fatah; Hamas; Jordan; Lebanon; Lebanon, Civil War in; Lebanon, Israeli Invasion of; Madrid Conference; Oslo Accords; Palestinian Authority; Palestinian Elections of 2006; Palestinian National Council; Suicide Bombings; Terrorism

References

Abbas, Mahmoud. *Through Secret Channels: The Road to Oslo; Senior PLO Leader Abu Mazen's Revealing Story of the Negotiations with Israel.* Reading, UK: Garnet, 1997.

Aburish, Said K. *Arafat: From Defender to Dictator.* New York: Bloomsbury, 1998.

Gabriel, Richard. *Operation Peace for Galilee: The Israeli-PLO War in Lebanon.* New York: Farrar, Straus and Giroux, 1985.

Hart, Alan. *Arafat: A Political Biography.* Rev. ed. London: Sidgwick and Jackson, 1994.

Kushner, Arlene. *Disclosed: Inside the Palestinian Authority and the PLO.* Philadelphia: Pavilion, 2004.

Livingstone, Neil C., and David Haley. *Inside the PLO.* New York: William Morrow, 1990.

Rubin, Barry. *Revolution until Victory? The Politics and History of the PLO.* Reprint ed. Cambridge: Harvard University Press, 2003.

Palestine Liberation Organization Phased Plan
Event Date: June 9, 1974

Three-part strategy designed to further the goals of the Palestine Liberation Organization (PLO). Sometimes also known as the 1974 Political Program, the Phased Plan was adopted during the 12th session of the Palestinian National Council. The council convened in Cairo, Egypt, on June 9, 1974. Occurring just nine months after the October 1973 Yom Kippur War, the Phased Plan reflected the new realities of the Arab-Israeli struggle as a result of the war. It also added more urgency to the Palestinian issue.

In many ways, the Yom Kippur War had been a bitter pill for most Arab nations to swallow. Instigated by Egypt and Syria, the

war had witnessed a fast and unexpected strike on the part of the Egyptians into the Sinai Peninsula, while the Syrians launched a simultaneous attack on the Golan Heights. Following initial successes, Arab coalition forces were sent into retreat by Israeli forces, and the war did not result in any land gains for the Arabs. Although Egypt and Syria especially could take some solace that they had caught the Israelis by surprise and had inflicted serious damage to Israeli forces, the fact remained that the situation after the war was largely the status quo antebellum. Now realizing that destroying Israel had become harder than ever, Arab and Palestinian leaders began to plot their next steps in the ongoing Arab-Israeli struggle.

For the Palestinians, these new realities meant a reinvigorated effort to attain their objectives. As such, the Palestinian National Committee adopted the Phased Plan, which consisted of three primary objectives. First, the PLO would create an independent combatant force in any areas that were freed from Israeli control in the future. Second, using both conventional and nonconventional military tactics, the PLO would continue its fight against Israel from its current base of operations (Lebanon). Third, the plan would liberate all Palestinian territory by instigating a general war with Israel that would result in its destruction by Arab nations. The plan also called for the overthrow of the Jordanian monarchy and the creation of a Palestinian state in its stead. PLO chairman Yasser Arafat had argued consistently that the Kingdom of Jordan was illegitimate and that its land was actually part of greater Palestine.

Although the Phased Plan did not incorporate any radically new objectives for the PLO, it did suggest new tactics and served as a call to arms. It remained the operative plan for the next 20 years. Some have argued, in fact, that the Phased Plan remains operational, even after the 1993 Oslo Accords and the peace process that followed. Indeed, in a September 1993 address Arafat made reference to the 1974 Phased Plan.

PAUL G. PIERPAOLI JR.

See also

Arafat, Yasser; Palestine Liberation Organization; Palestinian National Council; Yom Kippur War

References

Laqueur, Walter, and Barry Rubin, eds. *The Israel-Arab Reader: A Documentary History of the Middle East Conflict.* London: Penguin, 2001.

Nassar, Jamal R. *The Palestine Liberation Organization: From Armed Struggle to the Declaration of Independence.* New York: Praeger, 1991.

Palestine National Fund

The Palestine National Fund (PNF) is the main financial body of the Palestine Liberation Organization (PLO) and the Palestinian Authority (PA). In theory, the PNF oversees all PLO and PA funds. Its finances come from two primary sources: voluntary contributions from Arab governments, which have dwindled since the Oslo Accords (1993), and a tax imposed on Palestinian workers employed in Arab nations. The tax is collected by the host nations and forwarded to the PNF, although in recent years some Arab states have withheld the taxed funds from PLO control.

The large budget of the PNF, an estimated $233 million in 1990, has led to accusations of corruption and massive infighting within the PLO. One-third of the PNF budget is spent on the military forces of the PLO. In the aftermath of the Oslo Accords, Israel has transferred taxes collected in the West Bank and Gaza to the PA, which has kept the funds separate from the PNF.

The largest source of taxable income for the PNF comes from middle-class workers outside of Israel. These individuals live a precarious existence, as they have no secure position or legal status within their host nations. Without the diplomatic protections offered to other foreign nationals, these Palestinians could be deported at any time, and thus they cannot afford to complain about being taxed, ostensibly for the PNF, even if the taxed funds do not reach the PNF. By the mid-1980s, the liberation tax of 5–7 percent of income was collected but not sent to Palestine by Kuwait, Libya, Qatar, and the United Arab Republic (UAR). After 1993, most collecting nations began withholding a portion of the liberation tax. Despite the withholding, the liberation tax remains the source of 60 percent of PNF finances. The remainder is provided by direct contributions or as interest on PNF investments.

The financial resources of the PNF are a closely guarded secret. In 1989, most estimates placed the cash reserve of the PNF at $1.5 billion, although some estimates were as high as $14 billion. Experts identified a growing focus on money within the PLO rather than on the revolutionary struggle to create an independent Palestinian state. Throughout the 1990s, the leader of the PLO, Yasser Arafat, took steps to transfer the majority of PLO funds out of the PNF and have the money placed under his direct control. This included massive amounts of foreign assistance from the United States and Europe that totaled more than $1 billion annually after 1993.

The PNF is formally managed by a board of directors, led by a chairman selected by the Palestinian National Council (PNC). The chairman receives a seat in the PNC's Executive Committee, which selects the remainder of the PNF board. However, Arafat's personal control over PLO money allowed him to direct substantial funds to militia forces under his authority. He was also accused of delivering millions of dollars to terrorist organizations. Despite the allegations, he refused to allow any audits or oversight by external authorities, citing an unwillingness to comply with economic occupation by Western powers.

PAUL J. SPRINGER

See also

Arafat, Yasser; Oslo Accords; Palestine Liberation Organization; Palestinian Authority; Palestinian National Council

References

Khouri, Fred J. *The Arab-Israeli Dilemma.* 3rd ed. Syracuse, NY: Syracuse University Press, 1985.

Kimmerling, Baruch, and Joel S. Migdal. *Palestinians: The Making of a People.* New York: Free Press, 1993.

RAND Palestinian State Study Team. *Building a Successful Palestinian State.* Santa Monica, CA: RAND, 2005.

Palestine Partition Plan, United Nations

See United Nations Palestine Partition Plan

Palestinian Authority

The Palestinian Authority (PA) is an interim self-governing entity authorized by the 1993 Oslo Accords and established in 1994 to govern what would be the Palestinian autonomous regions of the West Bank and the Gaza Strip and what Palestinians specified as a future autonomous state. The Oslo Accords were finalized after a series of secret meetings between Israel and the Palestine Liberation Organization (PLO). The accords scheduled incremental Israeli withdrawals from the designated territories as refined in ensuing agreements. Israel, as scheduled, withdrew from Jericho on May 13, 1994; the Gaza Strip on May 18, 1994; Janin on November 13, 1995; Tulkarem and Nablus on December 11, 1995; Qalqiliyya on December 16, 1995; Bethlehem on December 21, 1995; Ramallah on December 27, 1995; and 80 percent of Hebron on January 17, 1997.

The autonomous areas were chosen so that the PA would govern 91 percent of the Palestinian populace. The PA was given control over 85 percent of the Gaza Strip. (The Jewish settlements comprised the other 15 percent.) Prime Minister Ariel Sharon imposed an Israeli withdrawal from these settlements in August 2005 despite some governmental and popular opposition and in the absence of any agreement with the Palestinians. The PA was initially given control over 39.7 percent of the West Bank.

The Oslo Accords specified that the PA would have control over all civilian- and security-related issues in most of the urban areas of the autonomous regions, termed "Area A," but would have control over only civilian affairs in certain rural areas, termed "Area B." By 1997 the urban areas under the control of the PA included most of the major Arab population centers in the West Bank, excepting East Jerusalem. Israel retained control over all travel, civilian affairs, and security in "Area C"; all of the remaining disputed territories; all Israeli settlements and military installations and access to them in all of the autonomous regions; the Jordan Valley; connecting roads between Palestinian communities; and any common borders.

The PA's elected presidency is its highest-ranking political office. The Palestinian Legislative Council (PLC), representing the Gaza Strip and the West Bank, was originally composed of 88 elected members but now has 132. It elects a member from its ranks for the president to declare as prime minister, an office first created by the PLC in March 2003. The prime minister ostensibly reports to the president. Even though the president and prime minister share power, in theory at least the preponderance of power rests with the prime minister. The prime minister, with the approval of the PLC, chooses a cabinet that runs the PA's government agencies. As chief of the national security services, the prime minister also directs the PA's security forces. The president, as the head of state, repre-

New security force recruits, operating under the purview of the Palestinian Authority (PA), train in Gaza City, July 9, 2005. (Ali/epa/Corbis)

sents the PA in negotiations with governmental entities apart from the PA.

The PA is headquartered in Ramallah and seats the PLC in Gaza City. Since the death of President Yasser Arafat in November 2004, the ability of the PA to govern has been challenged by various Palestinian subgroups, and the PA is also constrained by the Israeli government and military. This conflict was made clear following the January 2006 PLC elections, when Hamas won a majority of seats. A Hamas prime minister, Ismail Haniyeh, was then chosen to govern with the previously elected Fatah PA president, Mahmoud Abbas.

The PA regulates businesses within its borders and levies taxes and duties that are collected for it by Israel and then are distributed back to it by Israel. It is responsible for social services, education, and health care within the regions it governs and represents the Palestinians in all negotiations with Israel. The PA is also responsible for publicly denouncing, discouraging, and stopping any Palestinian terrorism against Israel. Attempts to carry out this mandate, however, have placed the PA at odds with groups within its own ranks.

Funding for the PA comes from the duties and taxes levied and distributed as well as in the form of aid from Western nations, Russia, and some Arab states. Most Western aid was cut off, however, after the 2006 election of a Hamas-oriented PLC. This meant that the PA could not in fact provide many of the educational, health care, and other social services under its mandate. Most of the PA budget is dedicated to paying its employees, who also went unpaid for months, especially its police and security agencies. The lack of sufficient indigenous sources of income and resources coupled with a history of corruption and patronage together with the freezing

of donor funds left the PA with insufficient funds to meet its basic responsibilities. These gaps have been filled in part by groups such as Hamas, which although cut off from most sources of external funding and prevented by the Israelis from operating their normal charitable associations, still obtain in-country contributions and provide volunteer services, as from physicians or instructors who donate their time.

The Oslo Accords limit the PA to an official uniformed security force (police force) totaling 30,000 personnel. Although the PA officially claims a force under that number, external sources estimate the true size at 40,000–80,000 men. The force is also restricted to armored cars and a limited number of automatic weapons, but external estimates judge its capabilities to be much more powerful.

The unemployment rate and number of people living below the regional poverty level was substantial in the Palestinian autonomous regions before the creation of the PA. However, continued violence and curfews, the Israeli Security Fence, and strict Israeli border control have cost jobs within the region and prevented others from the region from entering Israel where they were historically employed as guest workers. In fact, the Israeli government intends to cut off employment of workers from the PA areas by 2008.

The Oslo Accords envisioned the withdrawal of Israel from the proposed autonomous regions and the transfer of administrative responsibilities to the PA during a five-year interim to be followed by a second phase that would begin in 1999 and would develop a permanent solution to the problem. However, despite repeated final status agreements signed at the 2000 Camp David Summit and the 2001 Taba Summit and the 2003 Geneva Draft Permanent Status Agreement, an official peace agreement between Israel and the PA remains elusive.

The issues that remain are the same issues that existed before the PA, including the status of Jerusalem, the Palestinian right of return, recognition of the right of Israel to exist, security issues, economic issues, and borders. Actual negotiations over the status of Jerusalem were postponed, and in fact this issue has not yet been settled. The PA also remains committed to the creation of a Palestinian state with its capital in Jerusalem. The Oslo period was at first accompanied by more Israeli travel to Arab countries and the grassroots formations of Cousin's Clubs, or discussion groups for Palestinians and Israelis, and generally advanced the propeace faction within Israel and among the Palestinians. The sporadic violence and then suicide bombings from 1996 troubled many, but the spirit of Oslo did not truly break down until the Second (al-Aqsa) Intifada.

Following the signing of the Oslo Accords, Arafat immediately returned to the region from his exile in Tunisia and in 1994 appointed a 19-member interim PA until elections could be held. The elections were delayed for 18 months beyond the intended date. As with most events in the Middle East, the reasons for the delay depend upon one's perspective. The Israelis asserted that Arafat caused the delay so that he had time to regain control over the area, allowing him to control the election and select those who might run in it. The interim PA asserted that the delay was prompted by the need to develop an administrative system from scratch, the logistics of setting up an election, and Israeli intransigence in dealing with Arafat.

The elections for the presidency and the 88-member PLC occurred on January 20, 1996. Arafat was elected president of the PA, and his Fatah party was represented by 55 of the 88 PLC members in March 1996.

Additional areas of the West Bank were placed under PA control in 1997 as Israel continued its phased withdrawals. Israel agreed to additional withdrawals as part of the October 23, 1998, Wye River Agreement, but the continued failure of the PA to enforce the agreed-upon security provisions of the agreement caused the Israelis to halt their withdrawals. The agreement allowed the PA to open the Gaza International Airport in Rafah, although Israel maintained control over its security so that the facility could not be used to launch terrorist attacks or import weapons. The airport opened in November 1998 but was closed and then completely razed by Israel in December 2001 following the outbreak of the Second Intifada.

The signing of the Oslo Accords and the creation of the PA effectively ended the violence of the First Intifada (1987–1993). The Second Intifada began in September of 2000 after Israeli politician Sharon brought troops onto the Haram al-Sharif (Temple Mount). The intifada ended most of the discussions concerning the implementation of the Oslo Accords, for as the violence increased and suicide bombings became more prevalent, Israel responded by attacking PA infrastructure and facilities and reoccupying territory previously ceded to the PA. Israel also added to the tension by doubling the number of Jewish settlements in the West Bank between 1991 and 2001. Whether it was a valid reason or not, the violence of the intifada was used as the reason for the PA's delay of its scheduled 2001 PA presidential and legislative elections.

The PLC created the position of prime minister in March 2003 and named Abbas to the position, which he held from March to October 2003. Although considered a moderate, he was a longtime PLO associate of Arafat. Arafat saw the addition of a PA prime minister as weakening his position as PA president, and tension between the two seemed to escalate. By this point, both Israel and the United States had cut off all contact with Arafat and dealt only with Abbas, further isolating the PA president. A short lull in the cycle of Palestinian violence and Israeli reprisals soon ended, and Abbas resigned. Abbas's appointed successor, Ahmad Quray (Qurei), also battled with Arafat over the administration of the PA and the control of the PA security forces, but Arafat remained firmly in control of both the PLO and the PA.

Although he never formally assumed the title, Rawhi Fattuh, then PLC Speaker of the house, became the interim PA president following Arafat's death on November 11, 2004. Fattuh assumed the duties of the office until Abbas, who had been elected PLO chairman after Arafat's death, was elected president of the PA on January 9, 2005, with 62.3 percent of the vote.

Although Abbas's attempts to reengage the U.S. Road Map to Peace proposal were challenged by most of the militant Palestinian groups, he and Israeli prime minister Sharon agreed in an early 2005 summit to suspend hostilities. This agreement effectively ended the Second Intifada and led to the March 2005 reestablishment of PA control of Jericho and a few northern West Bank towns over which Israel had reassumed control during the conflict.

While continuing to encourage new settlements in the West Bank and against the extremely vocal opposition of the Israeli settlers, Sharon began a unilateral withdrawal of all Israeli military and civilians from the Gaza Strip in August 2005. The withdrawal and razing of the settlements completed on September 12, 2005, ceded control of all of Gaza to the PA. While the PA gained control of the territory and benefited from the appearance of having successfully negotiated a withdrawal on quite favorable terms to the PA, the jobs lost when Israeli farms and industries no longer provided employment drove more than 75 percent of the population of the Gaza Strip below the poverty line.

A pledge of $50 million and continued support of a free Palestinian state from the United States in May 2005 coupled with the Israeli withdrawal from Gaza led Abbas to set PLC elections for January 25, 2006. However, when Hamas did well in local elections (December 15, 2005), Abbas sought to no avail to postpone the PLC election.

Violence continued within Gaza and against Israel after the withdrawal. Abbas's power as PA president dissipated rapidly when Sharon experienced a debilitating stroke on January 4, 2006, that ended his premiership. The elections that Abbas had called but could not cancel led to a Hamas majority in the expanded 132-seat PLC. Although Abbas remained as PA president, his party's hold on the PA was weakened. Hamas selected Ismail Haniyeh as the new PA prime minister, and he formed a new PA government while Abbas remained as PA president. Israel's opposition to Hamas due to its previously stated refusal to recognize the right of Israel to exist caused the European Union (EU) and the United States to withhold their financial support that together totaled approximately $1 billion in 2005 alone. Some nations, including Canada, also terminated aid. Other nations did not terminate aid, but it remained frozen.

This aid withdrawal and the worsening unemployment situation exacerbated the PA's economic crisis and stoked tensions between Fatah and Hamas. The security and military situation drastically worsened after funds and political encouragement were received by some elements in Fatah who aimed to displace Hamas. Hamas operatives dug a tunnel from inside Gaza to an IDF border outpost inside Israeli territory and captured an Israeli soldier in June 2006, taking him back into Gaza. Israel responded by invading Gaza and arresting PA leaders, primarily members of Hamas.

The already-weak PA economic and security conditions worsened as the political friction between Fatah and Hamas grew and the potential for civil war seemed palpable. Abbas called for early parliamentary elections, which many Palestinians rejected as a gambit to undo the previous Hamas electoral victory. Instead, a truce was negotiated in Mecca between Fatah and Hamas representatives in February 2007.

On March 17, 2007, Abbas managed to put together a Palestinian unity government that included both Hamas and Fatah. In it, Hamas leader Ismail Haniyeh became prime minister. Despite the agreement, in May violence between Hamas and Fatah escalated. Then on June 14 in an unexpected move, Hamas fighters seized control of Gaza. In retaliation, Abbas dissolved the Hamas-led unity government and declared a state of emergency. On June 18, having been assured of EU support, Abbas dissolved the National Security Council and swore in an emergency Palestinian government. Concurrently, the United States ended its 15-month embargo on the PA and resumed aid to it in an effort to strengthen Abbas's government, which was now limited only to the West Bank. On June 19 Abbas cut off all ties and dialogue with Hamas, pending the return of Gaza. In a further move to strengthen the perceived moderate Abbas, on July 1 Israel restored financial ties to the PA. The situation remained stalemated, with Gaza under increasing economic and diplomatic isolation.

RICHARD EDWARDS

See also

Abbas, Mahmoud; Arafat, Yasser; Cairo Accord; Fatah; Geneva Accord; Hamas; Hebron Protocol; Intifada, First; Intifada, Second; Israeli Security Fence; Jerusalem; Oslo Accords; Palestine Liberation Organization; Ramallah; Right of Return, Palestinian; Settlements, Israeli; Sharon, Ariel; Wye River Agreement

References

Abbas, Mahmoud. *Through Secret Channels: The Road to Oslo; Senior PLO Leader Abu Mazen's Revealing Story of the Negotiations with Israel.* Reading, UK: Garnet, 1997.
Gelvin, James L. *The Israel-Palestine Conflict: One Hundred Years of War.* New York: Cambridge University Press, 2005.
Hall, John G. *Palestinian Authority: Creation of the Modern Middle East.* Langhorne, PA: Chelsea House, 2002.
Makovsky, David. *Making Peace with the PLO: The Rabin Government's Road to the Oslo Accord.* Boulder, CO: Westview, 1996.
Pappe, Ilan. *A History of Modern Palestine: One Land, Two Peoples.* Cambridge: Cambridge University Press, 2003.
Parsons, Nigel Craig. *The Politics of the Palestinian Authority: From Oslo to Al-Aqsa.* London: Routledge, 2003.

Palestinian Christians

A term that refers to Palestinian Arabs who are by birth Christians. Palestinian Christians comprise approximately 10 percent of the worldwide Palestinian population. Even as Christianity continues to grow and thrive into the 21st century, Christianity in the Holy Land (Israel and Palestine) faces a continued reduction of its population primarily from emigration.

Christian emigration from the Holy Land has reduced the Christian population to just 1.6 percent of the Palestinian population in the West Bank, Jerusalem, and the Gaza Strip. The Palestinian Christian population that accounted for 10 percent of the total population in the Holy Land prior to 1947 now accounts for about 2.3 percent of the entire Arab and Jewish population there. The majority of Palestinian Christians (51 percent) belong to the Palestinian Orthodox Church (Greek Orthodox) and the Roman Catholic Church (32 percent). However, the spectrum of Christianity in the Holy Land includes Maronites, Melkites, Jacobites, Greek Orthodox, Syrian Catholics, Copts, and a broad range of Protestants. The major Christian Holy Sites are spread between Israel (Jerusalem, Nazareth, and the Sea of Galilee) and the West Bank (Bethlehem, Hebron, and the Jordan River). Israel allows the appropriate religious authorities to administer their respective holy places.

Western Christianity became interested in and more committed to the Palestinian Christian community in the Holy Land in the 19th century. This came about when the Ottomans under Abdulmecid I (1835–1861) implemented changes in the law that granted more rights to all Ottoman subjects, even infidels, and equality in civil matters. They already possessed the right to practice their religious faith under the Ottoman practice of delegating authority over religious minorities to their respective leaders in return for political loyalty, known as the millet system. Ironically, the economic changes and the same edicts that granted Christians more equality under the law also heightened sectarianism in the Ottoman Empire. Western Christian groups hoped to convert Muslims, but as Muslims are strictly forbidden from conversion, their main target was the Eastern Christian communities. Western Christian groups created missionary-sponsored schools that promoted an educated Palestinian class. Along with development funds, health care, and social services and its economic advantages gained through commerce, the Palestinian Christian community prospered economically. The great out-migration of Palestinian Christians since 1947, the loss of property, and negative aspects of life under Israeli control mean that many churches survive only through the support of partner denominations and churches and missionary organizations.

Father Athanas, priest of the Maronite Arab village of Gush Halav, talks with villagers, May 1950. (Fritz Cohen/Israeli Government Press Office)

As a percent of the population of Jerusalem, the Palestinian Christian presence remained stable through the first half of the 20th century. Palestinian Christians comprised 18.5 percent of Jerusalem's population in 1910, 23.4 percent in 1922, 21.3 percent in 1931, 19 percent in 1946, 4.8 percent in 1967, 3.2 percent in 1983, 2.3 percent in 1995 after the First Intifada, and 2.2 percent in 2000 before the beginning of the Second (al-Aqsa) Intifada. The total Palestinian Christian population of the West Bank, Jerusalem, and the Gaza Strip fell to an estimated 1.6 percent by 2005. Although these numbers demonstrate the dramatic reduction of the Palestinian Christian population in Jerusalem, the drop was dramatic in the western areas of Jerusalem, which were taken over by the Israelis in 1948, as well as other areas of East Jerusalem and the affiliated villages. The first census conducted by the British Mandate government in 1922 fixed West Jerusalem's Palestinian Christian population at approximately 51 percent of the total. The total Palestinian Christian population of Jerusalem and the British Mandate for Palestine remained basically proportional through the post–World War I aliyas until after the end of World War II. There was

then a precipitous decline in the Palestinian Christian population following the Israeli War of Independence (1948–1949). Palestinian emigration at that time was a matter of refugee flight from the country, emigration to join relatives in the West, and church-sponsored programs.

The fact that large numbers of Palestinians fled or were expelled from Jerusalem and the newly created Israel in 1948–1949 is well documented. The number of refugees is disputed, however. Estimates range from the Israeli figure of 400,000 to the Arab estimate of 950,000 and an official United Nations (UN) figure of 710,000.

Zionists had debated the status of the non-Jewish population in Palestine since Jewish settlement there first began. Although some Zionists believed in sharing power with the non-Jewish population once the Jewish state was founded, most argued for a voluntary transfer encouraged through economic incentives and sanctions. Other Zionists advocated involuntary transfer (i.e., expulsion). It was this latter solution that was used to reduce the Palestinian Christian population in West Jerusalem by 50 percent during 1948–1949. The proportion of Christian refugees who were either expelled or fled Jerusalem was twice that of the Muslim refugees who left Jerusalem. On the other hand, 34 percent of the land seized by Israel without remuneration came from the Palestinian Christian community and churches, while 66 percent came from the Muslim community, even though the population sizes were roughly equal.

The drop in the total Christian population in the Holy Land was less precipitous. The decline in the total to roughly 2.3 percent following the 1967 Six-Day War, the First Intifada, and the 1993 Oslo Accords was obviously more precipitous. Israel was not the only Middle East country seeing the emigration of its Christian population, however. Every one of the Muslim countries in the Middle East experienced declining Christian populations during the same period. In fact, even though the percentage decline in the Christian population in the Holy Land was drastic during this period, Israel actually experienced a real increase in the Palestinian Christian population: 34,000 in 1948 and 125,000–130,000 in 2005. None of the 20 Muslim countries of the Middle East experienced a real increase in their Christian populations during this period.

Israel has long maintained differing policies regarding Arab Christians and Muslims. Such policies and attempts to win over the Palestinian Christian leadership did not diminish the Palestinian Christian participation in the nationalist movement and the Palestine Liberation Organization (PLO). Some Israelis assert that the Christian population decline was a consequence of the rise of Muslim fundamentalism in the region. Israelis also make much of the fact that the constitution of the Palestinian Authority (PA) draws on Islam as a source of law and imply that it discriminates against Christians, who are subject to their own religious courts in matters of personal status.

Palestinian Christians also admit fears about the rising influence of Muslim fundamentalism. They tended within the PLO to be more numerous among the progressive committees than within

Fatah. Hamas, however, took up the protection of Christians in Ramallah when youths in the area threatened some Christians after a beer industry was established there.

It is true that in certain areas of the West Bank and Gaza, Christian women (as well as Muslim women) who do not wear hijab, the Islamic head covering, have been subjected to harassment and may still encounter it although the political leadership tried to discourage such behavior. Tensions about intermarriage occasionally erupt as well. Palestinian Christian women are allowed to marry Muslim men, but Muslim women are not allowed, under Islamic law, to marry non-Muslims. Most importantly, families still exert control over a daughter's choice of a spouse, preferring to keep such choices within religious sects or families. Israelis have made much of honor killings that occasionally are committed by Palestinian Christians as well as Muslims. Another source of tension comes from Christian evangelical activities, such as those by the Mormons, the Seventh-day Adventists, and Jehovah's Witnesses that are based in the West and smaller, lesser-known initiatives. Israel and the PA both limit such Christian evangelism.

The PA and many Palestinian Christians assert that the population decline is due to the harshness of the Israeli occupation that forestalls economic development and the creation of jobs, lessens educational opportunities, and restricts tourism to the historic Christian sites. The PA points to a survey of Palestinian Christians in Bethlehem that contends that 73.3 percent of the respondents feel respected and protected by the PA, with 78 percent of the respondents attributing the emigration to Israeli border policies and the Israeli Security Fence that effectively stops all commerce and tourism. These policies also prevent Palestinian Christians from traveling to and from Israel to work there.

There are correlative reports of anti-Christian acts perpetrated in Israel by both private Israeli citizens and the Israeli government. The Arab Human Rights Association (AHRA) asserts that Israel denies permits to properly maintain the churches and monasteries, denies open access to holy sites, and promotes and allows the intimidation of both Christian and Muslim clerics. The AHRA also asserts that Israel ignores the complaints of Palestinian Christians and enacts and enforces policies that restrict their religious, economic, and civil liberties. Israel denies these allegations and responds that the Israeli government has itself paid in recent years for repairs on some of the Christian holy sites. The Israeli government also asserts that it is Palestinian-perpetrated violence, particularly suicide bombings, that has damaged the tourism industry and caused commerce and access to be restricted. Polls indicate that Palestinian Christians contemplating emigration are primarily concerned with the violence and political conditions (47 percent) and economic conditions (40 percent).

Most Palestinian Christians who remain in Israel work in white-collar professions such as education, civil service, church and church-related ministries, and commerce. A smaller percentage own their own businesses, work in various trades, and farm. Few are unskilled laborers. The occupational profile is different in the West Bank and the Gaza Strip, where the percentage of white-collar professionals is much smaller, as it is in general within the entire population of the territories. One business that has been decimated by the Second (al-Aqsa) Intifada was tourism and its related industries, such as film production and merchandising. Many Palestinian Christians were employed in tourism, and an extremely high number of those from this industry remain unemployed or underemployed. Palestinian Christians are still among the most important intellectual and academic leaders of the Palestinian movement, and they resist any efforts to divide the community.

RICHARD EDWARDS AND SHERIFA ZUHUR

See also

Arab-Jewish Communal War; Intifada, First; Intifada, Second; Israel; Israeli War of Independence, Overview; Jerusalem; Jerusalem, Old City of; Oslo Accords; Palestinian Authority

References

Bailey, Betty Jane, and J. Martin Bailey. *Who Are the Christians in the Middle East?* Grand Rapids, MI: Eerdmans, 2003.
Lutz, Charles P., and Robert O. Smith. *Christians and a Land Called Holy: How We Can Foster Justice, Peace, and Hope.* Minneapolis, MN: Fortress, 2006.
O'Mahony, Anthony. *Palestinian Christians: Religion, Politics and Society in the Holy Land.* London: Melisende, 1999.
Raheb, Mitri. *I Am a Palestinian Christian.* Minneapolis, MN: Augsburg Fortress, 1995.

Palestinian Elections of 2006
Event Date: January 25, 2006

Legislative elections held on January 25, 2006, to determine the makeup of the Palestinian Authority (PA) and resulting in the unexpected victory of the Islamic Resistance Movement (Hamas). While a wide array of factors rendered the Palestinian Legislative Council (PLC) elections highly significant, the most important were its political ramifications for the Palestine question and for the future of the region as a whole. Equally important, perhaps, were the democratic implications engendered by the new electoral system agreed upon among the various Palestinian political parties and organizations that allowed for wider representation.

The 2006 elections were the result of a new Palestinian electoral law, ratified by the first PLC after an agreement had been reached between the various political Palestinian parties. Originally, the Interim Agreement on the West Bank and the Gaza Strip (known as the Taba Agreement or Oslo II) signed between Israel and the PLO on September 24, 1995, in Taba, Egypt, structured the PA and the PLC and identified their mandates and authority.

The old electoral law had divided the West Bank, the Gaza Strip, and East Jerusalem into 16 voting districts. The number of representatives for each district ranged from 1 to 16, depending on the population of each district. The district-based system had enabled

Hamas supporters in the West Bank city of Ramallah celebrating their victory in the Palestinian legislative elections of January 25, 2006. (Pedro Ugarte/AFP/Getty Images)

Fatah to control 66 of the 88 seats, or 75 percent, in the first legislative elections, held on January 20, 1996. This was in spite of the fact that Fatah's popular support was under 55 percent. The original law excluded smaller parties that were unable to compete at the district level. This weakened the system of checks and balances, as Fatah controlled both the legislative and executive branches of the PA.

Furthermore, the original electoral system included a Christian quota that many, including leading Palestinian Arab Christians, perceived to be a step toward sectarianism. Palestinian Christians had been an integral part of the Palestinian national movement and in most Palestinian political parties. Those framing the new electoral system believed that the Christians should be represented politically based on their respective parties, not their religious convictions.

Palestinian political factions meeting in Cairo on the eve of the 2006 elections agreed to change the electoral system. The new law, ratified by the first PLC, divided the 132 PLC seats, which replaced the previous 88, between a majority system (66 district seats) and a proportional representation system (66 seats from party lists). Not only did the new law help end Fatah's hegemony, but it also allowed smaller political parties to be proportionally represented in half of the seats, thus producing a more diverse legislative body. In addition, the new electoral system allowed for more representa-tion of women in the PLC, in contrast to the old district-based system in which women were highly disadvantaged.

Beginning at 7:00 a.m. on January 25, 2006, more than 1 million Palestinians, representing almost 77 percent of the 1.3 million registered voters, cast their ballots in one of the 2,721 polling stations distributed among the 1,008 polling centers scattered throughout the West Bank and the Gaza Strip. They would choose 132 representatives from among more than 400 candidates representing 11 lists and districts. The elections were monitored primarily by more than 850 international observers from the European Union (EU), Canada, the United States, Australia, Russia, Jordan, Turkey, and Egypt. Additionally, 25,713 monitors representing the different participating parties joined 20,000 Central Election Committee–Palestine (CEC) employees responsible for voter registration, voting, and ballot counting. With the exception of few minor and isolated incidents, the international observers expressed satisfaction and admiration for what was characterized as a highly transparent and democratic experience.

On January 27, 2006, the CEC announced the outcome of the elections. Hamas had won 74 seats, or 65 percent, of which 30 seats were gained from Hamas's national list. Fatah secured only 45 seats, or 34 percent, of which 27 seats were gained from Fatah's national list. The Popular Front for the Liberation of Palestine (PFLP) won

3 seats, Badeel secured 2 seats, Independent Palestine won 2 seats, Third Way won 2 seats, and independents affiliated with Hamas took 4 seats. The new PLC also included 17 woman, 6 from Hamas, 8 from Fatah, and 1 each from the PFLP, Independent Palestine, and Third Way lists. Additionally, the new PLC's composition included 84 representatives from the West Bank and East Jerusalem and 48 representatives from the Gaza Strip.

The most important outcome of the election was the landslide electoral victory for Hamas. Its electoral success in securing almost two-thirds of the PLC seats came as a surprise to much of the international community and was a stunning rebuff for the ruling Fatah movement, which had dominated Palestinian politics since the late 1960s. The results could be attributed not only to the new electoral law but also to widespread dissatisfaction among Palestinians over the failure of the peace process, continued difficult economic conditions, and widespread corruption in Fatah.

While the Fatah leadership had been engaged in political negotiations with Israel since 1993 in an attempt to reach a resolution to the Palestinian-Israeli conflict, Hamas rejected negotiations as well as agreements already concluded between the two sides. Thus, the elections saw the Palestinian-Israeli conflict enter a new stage.

Additionally, the electoral success of the Islamist movement in free elections in Palestine was encouraging to other Islamist movements, notably in Egypt and Jordan. Were they to come to power in these states, it might well jeopardize existing political agreements signed between the governments of both Egypt and Jordan with Israel.

LAURA J. EL-KHOURY

See also

Fatah; Hamas; Palestinian Authority; Popular Front for the Liberation of Palestine

References

Abu-Amr, Ziad. "The Palestinian Legislative Council: A Critical Assessment." *Journal of Palestine Studies* 26 (Summer 1997): 90–97.

Amr, Hady. "Israel and Palestine: Two State, Bantustans, or Binationalism?" *Middle East Report* 201 (October–December 1996): 19–22.

Khalidi, Ahmad S. "The Palestinians' First Excursion into Democracy." *Journal of Palestine Studies* 25 (Summer 1996): 20–28.

Shikaki, Khalil. "The Palestinian Elections: An Assessment." *Journal of Palestine Studies* 25 (Spring 1996): 17–22.

Palestinian General Security Services

Organization that encompassed 10 Palestinian security organizations, including a Special Security Force and a Presidential Guard (Amn al-Riiasah) that reported directly to President Yasser Arafat. In 2004 Arafat attempted to consolidate all of these forces under his nephew Moussa Arafat and faced a rebellion from within Fatah and the al-Aqsa Martyrs Brigades. They were modified under President Mahmoud Abbas. With the Hamas-Fatah dissension that followed the 2006 elections, various security forces represent each faction.

The Palestinian General Security Services (PGSS) was formally created as a part of the 1994 Gaza-Jericho Agreement (Cairo Accord), although the foundation for the PGSS was established in the 1993 Oslo Peace Accords. The PGSS incorporated military and intelligence operations that were overseen by a director general, but due to the leadership style of President Arafat, they were also under his personal management. The origins of the PGSS can thus be traced back to the incorporation of the Palestine Liberation Organization (PLO) and its military wing, the Palestine Liberation Army (PLA) in 1964. The elements of the PGSS were extremely diverse, particularly in terms of training and equipment. Each was nominally responsible for a separate sector of security functions, but in reality some amount of overlap existed between the separate arms of the PGSS, which operated out of two independent headquarters, one in Gaza and one in the West Bank. In addition, a great deal of distrust between the branches coupled with accusations of corruption and factionalism within the Palestinian Authority (PA) hindered the effectiveness of the PGSS in its attempts to promote the autonomy of an independent Palestinian state. The PGSS had 10 services, and some were ostensibly independent of the others and reported only to the PGSS command. These covered the functions of intelligence, interior security, and national security.

The intelligence services of the PGSS included the Mukhabarat al-Amma (General Intelligence), the Istikhbarat al-Askariyya (Military Intelligence), and, subordinate to it, the Military Police, which was not an official entity of the PGSS. The Mukhabarat al-Amma was the official Palestinian intelligence agency and was responsible for both domestic and foreign intelligence operations in the regions under control of the PA. The Mukhabarat al-Amma employed more than 3,000 agents in both espionage and counterespionage operations. The Istikhbarat al-Askariyya, although officially considered the military intelligence service, served primarily to investigate, arrest, and interrogate Palestinians opposed to the PA. The Istikhbarat al-Askariyya was also tasked with investigating the other security agencies in the PGSS. However, the Special Security Force established by Arafat also gathered information on other Palestinian security services and Palestinian opposition groups in other countries. The Military Police maintained the Palestinian penal system, including civilian prisons; performed riot control; and provided security for important members of the PA.

The Interior Branch included five separate agencies: al-Shurta Madaniyya (Civil Police), al-Difa al-Madani (Civil Defense), al-Shurta Mahafzat (Governorate Security), al-Amn al-Wiqai (Preventive Security Force), and al-Amn al-Riasah (Presidential Security Force). Al-Shurta Madaniyya, nicknamed the "Blue Police," employed approximately 10,000 officers (6,000 in the West Bank and 4,000 in Gaza) in a traditional community policing capacity. The force was lightly armed, and most members received only cursory police training (all of the Palestinian security organizations were envisioned under Oslo as a police force) with the exception of its rapid deployment unit of nearly 1,000 officers, who respond to riots or supplement military operations. Most of al-Shurta Madaniyya's force was dedicated to criminal investigations, arrests, and traffic control. Al-Difa al-Madani provides emergency services, including fire and rescue services. Governorate Security comprises a group of small security forces protecting regional governors and administrations. Five governorates were recognized by 2001, and 16 were recognized by 2007. Al-Amn al-Wiqai is the Interior Branch's intelligence force and includes more than 5,000 officers in the West Bank and Gaza. Its primary function is to prevent or counteract Israeli military action, although it often cooperates with the Mukhabarat al-Amma on specific cases. Al-Amn al-Riasah is the most highly trained of the PGSS forces and includes more than 3,000 officers, many drawn from Arafat's Force 17, a private security detail created to protect him during his exile.

The National Security Branch of the PGSS was tasked with the duties of traditional national military forces, protecting the borders of areas under the direct control of the PA. Al-Amn al-Watani (National Security Forces) is the closest force to an army possessed by the PA and includes former elements of the PLA as well as recent recruits from the Palestinian population. Al-Amn al-Watani patrols border regions, occasionally partnered with elements of the Israel Defense Forces (IDF), and is also often used for crime prevention, although its leadership has been continually plagued by accusations of incompetence and corruption. It is by far the largest of the security forces, with a strength of 14,000 men by 2005. The Shurta Bahariya (Coast Guard) patrols the Gaza coast with five small motorboats crewed by a force of 1,000 men. Its primary responsibility is to reduce smuggling from Egypt, particularly in weapons and narcotics. Since the Hamas electoral victory, this force was replaced with a Marine Police in August 2007. The Shurta al-Jawiya (Air Guard), which flew and maintained PA helicopters, serves primarily as a rapid-transport service for top PA officials traveling between Gaza and the West Bank. Most of its small membership was initially drawn from Force 14, the PLO's aerial unit that served in a similar capacity.

Control of the PGSS has been a continual point of contention since its inception. Most of the individual security services remained personally loyal to Arafat and his top lieutenants. Because Arafat selected and often replaced the commanders of each service, he maintained intense rivalries between the services. Furthermore, his Fatah Party often directly paid the salaries of PGSS members, particularly at times when funding for the PA remained precarious. The overlapping missions of the various services increased the intense internecine struggles. Occasionally, rival elements of the PGSS openly clashed in Gaza and the West Bank.

When Arafat's health began to decline, he agreed to relinquish some of his personal control over the PGSS, at least on paper. On September 11, 2003, Arafat announced that the PGSS would be supervised by a National Security Council. The council includes members of the PA cabinet, the commanders of al-Amin al-Watani forces in Gaza and the West Bank, and the chiefs of al-Difa al-Madani, the Mukhabarat al-Amma, the Istikhbarat al-Askariyya, and al-Amn al-Riasah. While this nominally broadened the PA's control over the PGSS and eliminated some of Arafat's personal authority, he retained the firm loyalty of the service chiefs and remained the titular head of the council. Arafat's transfer of the services to his nephew was one of various sparks igniting battles between the al-Aqsa Martyrs Brigades of various cities and towns and the PGSS. After Arafat's death in late 2004, PA president Abbas restructured the council, greatly reducing its membership and increasing civilian control.

The general perception of the PGSS in the PA was that it had failed to provide stability or secure the borders. In addition to internal divisions, the PGSS has been beset by Israeli attacks on Palestinian security installations. Such attacks have often been in retaliation for terrorist attacks in Israel, which the PGSS has failed to prevent or even measurably reduce. The PGSS also lacks sufficient equipment and training, further reducing its potential effectiveness. Only in terms of manpower is the PGSS sufficient. In Gaza, the current security ratio is 1 officer per 50 residents, making it one of the most-policed societies in the world. Despite the large numbers, the election of a Hamas-led government in 2006 was accompanied by the announcement that Hamas's militias would be integrated into the PGSS. Hamas ceded the presidential authority to Abbas, but the forces of the Interior Ministry came under the leadership of Said Siam. Abbas and the Fatah faction then battled Hamas, with Abbas demanding that Hamas destroy its Executive Force, then about 6,000 members strong. Hamas seized control of the Gaza Strip in June 2007. Its forces also remain in the West Bank, where it chose not to battle the PA forces under an emergency government declared by Abbas in 2007. Hamas now possesses an undetermined number of forces in addition to its Izz al-Din al-Qassam Brigades.

Paul J. Springer

See also

Abbas, Mahmoud; Arafat, Yasser; Fatah; Gaza Strip; Hamas; National Security Forces, Palestinian; Oslo Accords; Palestine Liberation Army; Palestine Liberation Organization; Palestinian Authority; Presidential Security, Palestinian; West Bank

References

Farsoum, Samih K., and Naseer H. Aruri. *Palestine and the Palestinians: A Social and Political History.* 2nd ed. Jackson, TN: Westview, 2006.

Giacaman, George, and Dag Jorund Lonning, eds. *After Oslo: New Realities, Old Problems.* Chicago: Pluto, 1998.

Hunter, Robert E., and Seth G. Jones. *Building a Successful Palestinian State: Security.* Santa Monica, CA: RAND, 2006.

RAND Palestinian State Study Team. *Building a Successful Palestinian State.* Santa Monica, CA: RAND, 2005.

Palestinian Islamic Jihad

See Islamic Jihad, Palestinian

Palestinian Legislative Council

Legislative arm of the Palestinian Authority (PA), the governing body of the Palestinians. An elected assembly that is organized along parliamentary lines, the unicameral Palestinian Legislative Council (PLC) was established in 1995 by the Israeli-Palestinian Interim Agreement (Oslo II Agreement) and was the result of the Oslo Accords of 1993. The PA began the process of Palestinian self-government in the occupied territories, namely in the West Bank and the Gaza Strip.

The first elections to the PLC were held in January 1996. Fatah, the largest and most powerful Palestinian political entity, dominated the elections. Fatah and its affiliated Liberation Movement of Palestine captured 55 of the 88 total seats in the PLC. Hamas, Fatah's chief rival, boycotted the elections. At the same time, Palestinians voted for the first president of the PA. That post was won handily by Yasser Arafat, chairman of the Palestine Liberation Organization (PLO) and the leader of the Fatah faction.

Reacting to complaints that the 1996 elections were not truly representative of all the Palestinian people and that some districts and parties (such as Hamas) were overrepresented, the PLC enacted a change in the election law in June 2005. This resulted in a considerable increase in the size of the legislative body. Instead of 88 seats, the PLC would have 132 seats representing 16 districts. The legislation that amended the election laws was rife with controversy, particularly because Hamas had announced that it would run candidates in the 2006 PLC elections.

The PLC's election law of 2005 now meant that half of the seats would be elected by proportional representation, while the other half would be chosen on the basis of a plurality vote mechanism in which the division of seats is determined by multidistrict counts with winner usually taking all (often referred to as a majority system). In the January 2006 PLC elections, Hamas garnered a majority of seats, replacing Fatah in that spot. Hamas captured 74 seats to Fatah's 45. The rise of a Hamas majority in the PLC presented a major challenge to Mahmoud Abbas, Fatah leader and president of the PA. It also brought with it condemnation from the West, and many nations—including the United States—rescinded funding for the Palestinians to protest the election of Hamas.

Despite the predictable complaints about Hamas's victory, by all measures the 2006 PLC elections were fair and well run. International observers described the election procedures as "extremely professional" as well as "free, transparent, and without violence." The PLC has proven to be a much-needed arm of the PA. It helps to act as a check against an overzealous executive and is able to engage in informed debate comprising a multitude of positions before legislation is passed. After Arafat created the position of prime minister in 2003 (to which he appointed Abbas), the PLC now works somewhat like a parliamentary system in which the prime minister is elected by the legislative body. Nevertheless, the office of president still wields considerable clout, and the president has the power to call for new elections in certain situations.

PAUL G. PIERPAOLI JR.

See also

Abbas, Mahmoud; Arafat, Yasser; Fatah; Hamas; Oslo Accords; Palestinian Authority; Palestinian Elections of 2006

References

Abu-Amr, Ziad. "The Palestinian Legislative Council: A Critical Assessment." *Journal of Palestine Studies* 26 (Summer 1997): 90–97.

Amr, Hady. "Israel and Palestine: Two State, Bantustans, or Binationalism?" *Middle East Report* 201 (October–December, 1996): 19–22.

Khalidi, Ahmad S. "The Palestinians' First Excursion into Democracy." *Journal of Palestine Studies* 25 (Summer 1996): 20–28.

Shikaki, Khalil. "The Palestinian Elections: An Assessment." *Journal of Palestine Studies* 25 (Spring 1996): 17–22.

Palestinian National Charter
Event Date: May 28, 1964

The Palestinian National Charter, also referred to as the Palestinian National Covenant, was formally adopted on May 28, 1964. This agreement was considered the charter of the Palestine Liberation Organization (PLO), then headed by Ahmad Shukeiri. The charter, which called for an independent Palestinian state, is one of the pillars of disagreement between Palestinians and Israelis.

Following World War II the United Nations (UN), seeking to make amends for the Nazi-inspired Holocaust, called for the division of Palestine into two states. Israel was to be a homeland for Jews, and Palestine was to be a homeland for the remaining Arabs in the region. The Arabs vehemently rejected this decision and refused to recognize the Jewish state when it declared independence in May 1948. The Palestinians challenged Israel's right to exist and, through a series of wars, sought to reclaim that territory.

The PLO was formed in 1964 and quickly became instrumental in helping to provoke conflict with Israel. Shukeiri in fact gave a speech to the UN detailing what the PLO would do to Israel if the PLO struck first. However, the Arab defeat during the 1967 Six-Day War led to differing opinions as to how this could be accomplished. Shukeiri resigned from the PLO in December 1967, and Yasser Arafat gained considerable influence within the organization and became its chairman.

During July 10–17, 1968, the Fourth Palestine National Assembly met in Cairo to revise the Palestinian National Charter to provide a clearer cause and more concrete aims, as the 1964 version had focused more on the aims of the PLO. The assembly drastically changed the charter to focus more on Palestinian national identity and the liberation of their homeland. For the first time, this produced a clear and consistent demand for an independent Palestinian state rather than a conquest of Palestine by Arab nations. In addition, it used more belligerent language, stating that the partition of Palestine and the creation of a Jewish state were "entirely illegal." It also spoke of the "Zionist invasion" and detailed its aim to eliminate Zionism worldwide. The charter was soon followed by a detailed program for a secular democratic state. This program also called for the exile from Palestine of all Jews arriving in Palestine after 1917 and their descendants.

In 1993 Israeli prime minister Yitzhak Rabin called for changes to the Palestinian National Charter in accordance with the Oslo Accords. In a letter to Rabin on September 9, 1993, Arafat committed to changing the charter to confirm that those articles denying Israel's right to exist and those contrary to such commitments were declared null and void. These changes were formally ratified by the Palestinian National Council on April 24, 1996.

PAUL G. PIERPAOLI JR.

See also

Arafat, Yasser; Oslo Accords; Palestine Liberation Organization; Rabin, Yitzhak

References

Becker, Jillian. *The PLO: The Rise and Fall of the Palestine Liberation Organization.* New York: St. Martin's, 1985.

Nassar, Jamal R. *The Palestine Liberation Organization: From Armed Struggle to the Declaration of Independence.* New York: Praeger, 1991.

Palestinian National Council

Quasi parliament and legislative body of the Palestine Liberation Organization (PLO). The Palestinian National Council (PNC) was made up of representatives from various Palestinian organizations, such as professional associations, trade unions, and women's organizations from both the occupied territories and the Palestinian Diaspora. Two-thirds of the membership constituted a quorum, and votes were by simple majority. The PNC set policy, approved the budget of the PLO, and received the report of the Palestinian National Fund. Until fairly recently, identities of the individual representatives were kept secret for fear of Israeli reprisals.

The first PNC met in Jerusalem in May 1964. Its 422 representatives came from Palestinian communities in the West Bank, the Gaza Strip, Jordan, Lebanon, Syria, Kuwait, Iraq, Egypt, Qatar, Libya, and Algeria. The PNC representatives adopted the Palestinian National Charter and established the PLO as the representative body of the Palestinian people. They also elected Ahmad Shukeiri as the first chairman of the PNC Executive Committee. The Executive Committee acts as the leadership of the PNC when the latter is not in session. Because the PNC did not meet regularly, the Executive Committee occupied the top position in the governmental hierarchy.

The PNC was to meet annually, although this was not always the case. Subsequent PNC meetings were held in Cairo (1965), Gaza (1966), Cairo (1968–1977), Damascus (1979–1981), Algiers (1983), Amman (1984), and Gaza (1996 and 1998). The number of representatives to the PNC fluctuated. There were 422 at its first meeting in 1964, and in 1993 there were 452. The representatives normally served two- or three-year terms. Because of the PNC's political and military influence, more than half of the members were from Fatah. In 2004 the PNC had 669 members: 88 from the Palestinian Legislative Council (PLC), 98 from the Palestinian population in the West Bank and the Gaza Strip, and 483 from the Palestinian Diaspora. It was chaired by Salim Zanum (Abu Adib).

In January 1996 Palestinian elections were held in the West Bank and Gaza, supervised by some 1,500 international observers. The elections saw 676 candidates vying for a PLC of 88 seats and 2 running for president. The elections were limited to the West Bank and Gaza, however. Members of the Palestinian Diaspora were not allowed to vote. The PLC was the first elected Palestinian Council and in effect replaced the PNC. The council only represented Palestinians in the West Bank and Gaza, however. It also has no real policymaking power. Like the PNC, the PLC was dominated by Fatah members. With Hamas boycotting the voting, Fatah secured 55 seats and, with those affiliated with it, constituted 71 of the 88 members. Unlike the PNC, the PLC was not a forum to debate and establish policy. Until his death in November 2004, President Yasser Arafat kept that power firmly in his own hands.

Among memorable PNC meetings were the February 1969 meeting in Cairo in which Arafat was named the chairman of the PLO. In 1974 the PNC stated that it would establish a national authority in any territory that Israel would vacate. On November 15, 1988, during the meeting in Algiers, the PNC declared the independence of the Arab State of Palestine.

In the April 24, 1996, meeting in Gaza following the Oslo Accords of 1993, the PNC voted 504 to 54, with 14 abstentions, to void those parts of the covenant that denied Israel's right to exist, although no formal change to or redrafting of the covenant occurred.

SPENCER C. TUCKER

See also

Arafat, Yasser; Fatah; Oslo Accords; Palestine Liberation Organization

References

Laqueur, Walter, and Barry Rubin, eds. *The Israel-Arab Reader: A Documentary History of the Middle East Conflict.* London: Penguin, 2001.

Nassar, Jamal R. *The Palestine Liberation Organization: From Armed Struggle to the Declaration of Independence.* New York: Praeger, 1991.

Palestinian Refugee Camps

Refugee encampments for Palestinians who fled or were forced to leave their towns and villages by Israeli military forces during the 1948–1949 Israeli War of Independence. The United Nations (UN) defines a Palestinian refugee as a person whose primary residence was Palestine for a minimum of two years prior to events leading up to the establishment of the State of Israel in May 1948. Originally, these Palestinian refugees numbered 750,000 (out of a total population of 1.5 million Palestinians). After 1948, the Israelis barred their return to their original homes and instead encouraged their permanent settlement in Arab countries. They were immediately forbidden from returning to their lands or homes under several military and civil laws. Then in 1950 the Israeli government adopted the Law of Return, which allowed any person of Jewish descent to immigrate and obtain citizenship in Israel and facilitated the absorption of European Jewish refugees into Israel. Some of these refugees were resettled in formerly Palestinian villages, towns, or new settle-

Balata refugee camp, West Bank, 1989. (M. Nasr/UN Relief and Works Agency)

ments built on these lands. These policies effectively prevented most Palestinians from returning to their homes. That same year, the Knesset (Israeli parliament) passed the Absentee Property Law, which established December 29, 1947, as the cutoff date for the refugees' permissible return to Palestine. Thus, Palestinians who left their homes after that date because of the hostilities lost all claims to their property and citizenship. However, on December 11, 1948, the UN adopted General Assembly Resolution 194, which recognized the Palestinians' right of return to their homes provided they lived in peace with their neighbors. They were also to be compensated for their lost properties upon their return. Nevertheless, Israel's laws effectively negated the UN resolution.

Refugee camps were originally built on municipal lands and were intended to be temporary. They appeared in Syria, Lebanon, Jordan, the Gaza Strip, the West Bank, and Egypt. In time, however, they became permanent locations because the ongoing Arab-Israeli and Palestinian-Israeli conflicts remained unresolved. The UN Relief Works Association for Palestine Refugees in the Near East (UNRWA) was not established until December 1949, and it took about two years until its relief activities were functioning effectively. In the meantime, Palestinian charitable associations brought food, cloth-

ing, and tenting to these areas. Most of the refugees initially subsisted on food rations consisting of 1,600 calories per day.

According to the 1966 Casablanca Protocol of the League of Arab States, host countries were expected to grant refugees unrestricted residency rights and the freedom to travel and seek employment. These governments were also expected to maintain the Palestinian national identity until their repatriation. The UN High Commission on Refugees (UNHCR), created in 1951, does not include the Palestinians under its mandate. Instead, they were relegated to a purely humanitarian organization, the UNRWA, which was created specifically to provide relief services for them.

Many Palestinians initially sought refuge in Jordan because the Jordanians controlled eastern Palestine, naming it the West Bank, and extended citizenship rights to its citizens. About 264,000 refugees still inhabit 10 camps in the vicinity of Amman, Jordan, and other cities. The Jordanian camps were eventually supervised by teachers of UNRWA schools who came from the ranks of the refugees and played a pivotal role in enhancing their national identity. The Jordanian refugee camps were also briefly involved in the 1970 Jordanian civil conflict that resulted in the expulsion of Palestine Liberation Organization (PLO) fighters from that country.

PALESTINIAN REFUGEES BY JUN 30, 1989

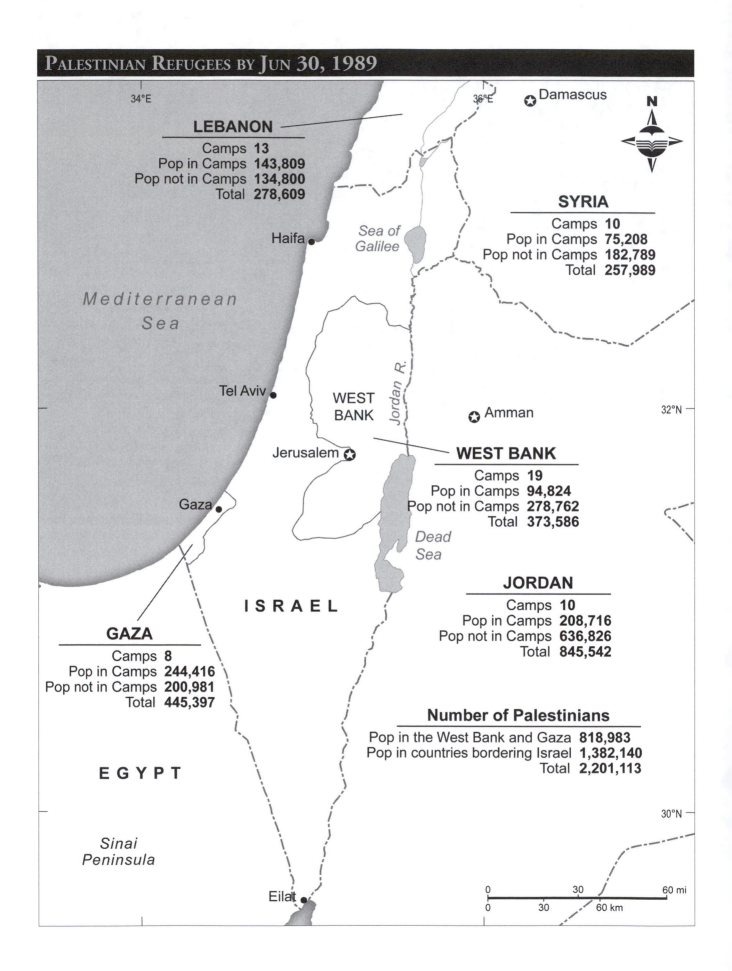

LEBANON

Camps **13**
Pop in Camps **143,809**
Pop not in Camps **134,800**
Total **278,609**

SYRIA

Camps **10**
Pop in Camps **75,208**
Pop not in Camps **182,789**
Total **257,989**

Damascus

Sea of Galilee

Haifa

Mediterranean Sea

Tel Aviv

WEST BANK

Jordan R.

Amman

Jerusalem

WEST BANK

Camps **19**
Pop in Camps **94,824**
Pop not in Camps **278,762**
Total **373,586**

Gaza

Dead Sea

JORDAN

Camps **10**
Pop in Camps **208,716**
Pop not in Camps **636,826**
Total **845,542**

I S R A E L

GAZA

Camps **8**
Pop in Camps **244,416**
Pop not in Camps **200,981**
Total **445,397**

Number of Palestinians

Pop in the West Bank and Gaza **818,983**
Pop in countries bordering Israel **1,382,140**
Total **2,201,113**

E G Y P T

Sinai Peninsula

Eilat

34°E   36°E   32°N   30°N

0   30   60 mi
0   30   60 km

Palestinian Registered Refugees (1965–2005)

Year	Registered Refugees
1955	912,425
1965	1,300,117
1975	1,652,436
1985	2,119,862
1995	3,246,044
2005	4,255,120

In Syria, about 370,000 refugees remain on UNRWA's rolls. Most of the camps are in Damascus, which alone account for 67 percent of the refugees. Al-Yarmuk (Yarmouk) Camp is the largest and is considered a suburb of Damascus. The UNRWA recognizes 10 such camps throughout the country, providing them with educational and health services. Most of the camps are constituted as homogenous neighborhoods reflecting the refugees' original towns and villages. This alone worked to strengthen their national identity since 1948 and helped defeat U.S. plans to resettle them in the country. In 1956, Syria's Law 260 granted the refugees equal rights with Syrian citizens in the areas of employment, commerce, and military service. They were also allowed to join trade unions, reside outside the camps, and reenter the country without a visa. But they were restricted to the ownership of just one residence and were prohibited from owning land in order to discourage their permanent settlement in Syria.

Palestinian refugees faced particularly difficult conditions in the camps in Lebanon prior to 1970 and during the Lebanese Civil War. The camps bore the brunt of Israeli military actions because of the Palestinian Resistance Movement's raids and strikes staged from Lebanon. Yet even before the PLO's arrival in the Lebanese camps in 1970, the refugees were subject to police harassment and surveillance. Largely of peasant origins, the Palestinian camps were located in southern Lebanon, in Beirut's southern slum areas, and in the Bekáa Valley at Anjar as well as in some other areas. Today, Lebanon has recognized 12 camps, although 16 others emerged as a result of various wars. There were some 110,000 refugees in Lebanon in 1948, and today that number has grown to more than 350,000.

Some of their camps, such as Ayn al-Hilwah in the southern city of Sidon, claim as many as 60,000 residents. The Lebanese Civil War in combination with the Israeli invasions of 1978 and 1982 resulted in the loss of at least 50,000 Palestinian lives. The situation in the Lebanese camps deteriorated badly after the 1982 Israeli invasion of Lebanon, culminating in the massacres at the Sabra and Shatila camps at the hands of local militias with the tacit collusion of the Israeli Army. Following the PLO's withdrawal from Lebanon in 1982, the refugees there were embroiled in the so-called War of the Camps against the Amal militia. The 1989 Taif Agreement resulted in a stipulation that banned the settlement of any non-Lebanese groups in the country. The Palestinians had been restricted from many types of employment, property ownership, and political rights in Lebanon during the entire period of their stay. Following the Taif Agreement these restrictions were reinstated, legally barring Palestinians from 75 professions, which resulted in an unemployment rate of 70 percent within the camps. In 2001, more legislation further restricted the refugees from owning property.

Nineteen refugee camps are located in the Palestinian territories. Around 26.5 percent of the West Bank's population is comprised of refugees, while 65 percent of the Gaza Strip's population is made up of refugees. The largest of these, the Jabalya camp in Gaza, often suffers from incursions by the Israeli military. A single camp located within the Jerusalem area, Shufat, has been affected by the encirclement of expanding Israeli settlements such as Pisgat Zeev. A sprawling refugee camp along the Iraqi-Jordanian border, al-Ruwayshid, is the latest Palestinian displacement camp. Movement outside this refugee camp remains severely restricted.

In addition to the fact that a Palestinian right of return has not been addressed in the various stages of peace negotiations, Palestinian refugees have suffered and continue to suffer from extraordinarily poor conditions in the refugee camps. Education is substandard, medical care is often nonexistent, unemployment rates are tragically high in all but a few camps, and living conditions are far from optimal. In the West Bank and Gaza, these conditions led to stronger support from camp residents for militant slogans and recruitment. Refugees in Jordan were offered full citizenship, but many others remain in a state of citizenship limbo of sorts. The Jordanians made no effort to form a Palestinian state in the West Bank when they controlled it, nor did Egypt create a nation for the Palestinians when it controlled the Gaza Strip. In fact, the Egyptian government denied citizenship to Palestinians and generally forbade them from leaving the Gaza Strip.

GHADA HASHEM TALHAMI

See also

Expellees and Refugees, Palestinian; Gaza Strip; Lebanon, Israeli Invasion of; Palestine Liberation Organization; Right of Return, Palestinian; Sabra and Shatila Massacre; United Nations General Assembly Resolution 194; West Bank

References

Aruri, Naseer, ed. *Palestinian Refugees: The Right of Return.* London: Pluto, 2001.
Morris, Benny. *The Birth of the Palestinian Refugee Problem Revisited.* 2nd ed. Cambridge: Cambridge University Press, 2004.
Sayigh, Rosemary. *Too Many Enemies: The Palestinian Experience in Lebanon.* London: Zed, 1994.
Talhami, Ghada Hashem. *Palestinian Refugees: Pawns to Political Actors.* Happauge, NY: Nova Science Publishers, 2003.
Viorst, Milton. *Reaching for the Olive Branch: UNRWA and Peace in the Middle East.* Washington, DC: Middle East Institute, 1989.

Palestinian Special Security Force

Part of the Palestinian General Security Service (PGSS), the Palestinian Special Security Force (SSF), also known as al-Amn al-Khass, is one of the 10 domestic Palestinian security forces formed following the May 1994 Cairo Agreement. That agreement had turned over the majority of territory in the Gaza Strip as well as land in and around Jericho to the Palestinian Authority (PA). Created in January 1995, the SSF was officially tasked with the conduct of intelligence operations against foreign opposition groups, especially those operating in Arab nations. However, it has dedicated most of its efforts to the oversight of Palestinian intelligence agencies, activities or corruption among PA leadership, and the activities of domestic opposition groups operating within the PA.

The PGSS officially serves as the PA's senior-most intelligence and security authority, responsible for the coordination of efforts among its 10 police, military, and civilian intelligence agencies. However, the SSF bypasses the PGSS reporting protocol and answers directly to the Palestinian president. For nearly a decade, the SSF's function as a domestic intelligence-gathering agency contributed greatly to President Yasser Arafat's ability to retain control until his death in November 2004. General Abu Yusuf al-Wahadi served as the first and only known leader of the SSF.

Following the signing of the 1994 Cairo Agreement and the formation of the PGSS, multiple organizations embarked on often overlapping domestic intelligence collection, analysis, and reporting missions. These conflicting roles and responsibilities led to continual conflict throughout the PGSS intelligence and security force structure. The SSF, as a highly autonomous organization within the PGSS with direct access to the Palestinian prime minister, served as Arafat's independent source of intelligence monitoring internal conflict within the PGSS.

Throughout the 1990s, PGSS leadership continued to fracture between former Palestine Liberation Army (PLA) veterans and those with historical ties to the First Intifada. Arafat sought out and engaged outsiders with connections to neither the PLA nor the intifada to lead critical intelligence agencies within PGSS. General al-Wahadi was one such outsider brought to the Palestinian territories from abroad to lead the SSF. His lack of affiliation with either of the parties and his deep loyalty to Arafat made him a critical and trusted component of Arafat's human intelligence capabilities.

The SSF played another vital role for Arafat, as it monitored the equilibrium of power among general staff members. Arafat used the SSF to ensure that no senior member of his staff accumulated sufficient influence or power to pose a threat to the stability of the PA. The intelligence provided by the SSF in this role proved invaluable in neutralizing emerging threats to the PA's stability.

Although the headcount is not known for certain, it is generally believed that SSF membership does not exceed more than 100 personnel. Most estimates suggest significantly fewer, perhaps as few as a dozen core members. Their utility as a mechanism to monitor, report, and enforce allegiance to the prime minister suggests that they exert disproportionate influence on Palestinian politics. Because the SSF was never a formally recognized organization within the PGSS, the size, disposition, and staffing levels within this organization are generally unknown.

C. Scott Blanchette

See also
Arafat, Yasser; General Intelligence Agency, Palestinian; Palestine Liberation Organization; Palestinian Authority; Palestinian General Security Services

References
Hunter, Robert E., and Seth G. Jones. *Building a Successful Palestinian State: Security.* Santa Monica, CA: RAND, 2006.
RAND Palestinian State Study Team. *Building a Successful Palestinian State.* Santa Monica, CA: RAND, 2005.
Usher, Graham. "The Politics of Internal Security: The PA's New Intelligence Services." *Journal of Palestine Studies* 25(2) (Winter 1996): 21–34.

Palmach

Jewish fighting force numbering at its height a few thousand soldiers. It was created jointly by the British and the Jewish Haganah on May 15, 1941. Haganah (Hebrew for "defense"), the Jewish underground self-defense and military organization formed in 1920, was the precursor of the Israel Defense Forces (IDF). Haganah leadership realized the need for a permanently mobilized military organization to defend Jewish settlements that from time to time came under harassment from Arab bands. More important to the British was that if Axis forces were ever to enter the British Mandate for Palestine, the Palmach (Palmakh) would fight them as well.

The new, elite Palmach, which is the Hebrew abbreviation of Plugot Mahats, or "strike force," was originally commanded by Yitzhak Sadeh. Composed of 9 assault teams, it was trained and equipped by the British and dispersed throughout Palestine, including one in Jerusalem. A third of its members were young women. The Palmach eventually grew to 12 assault teams that initiated scouting and sabotage missions as well as preemptive strikes into Syria and Lebanon. Yigal Allon, Moshe Dayan, Yitzhak Rabin, Chaim Bar-Lev, Uzi Narkiss, and Ezer Weizman were some of its more notable members.

The Palmach was officially disbanded when the British defeated the German forces at El Alamein in the summer of 1942 and the threat to the British position from Syria and Lebanon had abated after the Allied invasion of Syria. The Haganah converted the Palmach after its supposed dissolution into an underground commando force and initially assigned it to the protection of the Yishuv (Jewish settlements) in Palestine in August 1942. Yitzhak Tabenkin, head of the kibbutzim union, conceived of a plan that assigned Palmach platoons to various kibbutzim. These would provide the Palmachniks (Palmach members) with food, shelter, and other needs as they arose. In return, the Palmach protected the kibbutz to which they were assigned, worked in the agricultural enterprises of the kibbutz, and participated in Zionist education. This combination of training, protection, education, and work was called Akhshara Meguyeset, or Drafted/Recruited Training. Each Palmachnik was to train 8 days a month, stand guard 14 days a month, and rest 7 days a month. However, Palmachniks were always on call in case of an attack.

Two members of the Jewish Palmach (Strike Force) firing through a hole in a wall while training in Jerusalem for city fighting, March 1948. (Bettmann/Corbis)

The role of the Palmach was not limited to the protection of the Yishuv. By 1943 the Palmach had organized itself into six regular companies and a like number of special units. The Ha-Makhlaka Ha-Germanit, or German Department, operated against the Nazi infrastructure in the Middle East and the Balkans. The Ha-Makhlaka Ha-Aravit, or Arab Department (known also as the Arab Platoon because members often dressed in Arabic attire), operated against Arab militias. After the formation of Israel, they formed the basis of the border police and IDF infiltration units. The Pal-Yam was the sea force of the Palmach and focused on facilitating the illegal entry of Jewish refugees from Europe in violation of the British White Paper of 1939 that limited Jewish immigration to Palestine. The Palmach's Sabotage Units eventually formed the nucleus of the IDF Engineering Corps. The Palmach Air Force consisted of British-trained Jewish pilots who had no planes until 1948, when they commenced observation and scouting operations. Additionally, Zionist youth movement participants aged 18–20 were formed into Nahal (Hebrew acronym for *noar halutzi lohem,* meaning "fighting pioneer youth") or nucleus groups. They were trained by Palmachniks and eventually formed the basis of the Nahal settlements, created as strategic strongholds in case of war.

Palmachniks received basic training in physical fitness, small arms, topography, squad operations, and Krav Maga (Hebrew for "contact combat"), a martial art developed in Czechoslovakia in the 1930s. Most Palmachniks also received additional training in one or more of the following combat specialties: sabotage and explosives, reconnaissance, sniping, light and medium machine gunnery, and mortars. Group and platoon training also included live-fire drills using artillery, machine guns, and mortars. Palmach officer training emphasized the development of independent and innovative field commanders who took initiative and led by example.

When it was clear following World War II that the British were unwilling to create a Jewish state or allow the immigration of large numbers of Jewish refugees into Palestine, the Palmach attacked British infrastructure such as bridges, railways, radar stations, and police stations during 1945 and 1946. These attacks stopped when the British arrested en masse many of the Palmach and Haganah leadership on June 19, 1946, a date known in Israeli history as the Black Sabbath.

Palmach units assumed responsibility for protecting the Jewish settlements from Arab militias when the Israeli War of Independence (1948–1949) erupted following the partition of Palestine and the formation of the State of Israel. These Palmach units persevered until the Haganah relieved them. The Palmach was then formed into two units of the newly created IDF, the Negev Brigade and Yiftah Brigade. These units stopped the Egyptian Army in the Negev and then seized the Gaza Strip and Sharm al-Sheikh.

Many Palmachniks entered Israeli politics, including Rabin, Dayan, Bar-Lev, Mordechai Gur, Mati Peled, Yair Tsaban, Shulamit Aloni, Rehavam Zeevi, and Rafael Eitan. Indeed, Palmachniks dominated the IDF command structure for many years and helped shape its distinctive ethos.

RICHARD M. EDWARDS

See also

Bar-Lev, Chaim; Dayan, Moshe; Eitan, Rafael; Gur, Mordechai; Haganah; Israel Defense Forces; Kibbutz Movement; Narkiss, Uzi; Rabin, Yitzhak; Sadeh, Yitzhak; Weizman, Ezer

References

Bar-On, Mordechai, ed. *A Never-ending Conflict: A Guide to Israeli Military History.* Westport, CT: Praeger, 2004.

Goldstein, Yaacov N., and Dan Shomron. *From Fighters to Soldiers: How the Israeli Defense Forces Began.* Brighton, UK: Sussex Academic, 1998.

Van Creveld, Martin. *The Sword and the Olive: A Critical History of the Israeli Defense Force.* New York: PublicAffairs, 2002.

Pan-Arab Congress
Event Date: September 8, 1937

Conference of some 400 Arab leaders that convened on September 8, 1937, in Bludan, Syria. The Pan-Arab Conference took place in the middle of the Great Palestinian Rebellion in Palestine (1936–1939), sometimes called the Arab Revolt. More specifically, the congress met during the second major phase of the rebellion (July

1937–October 1938). The rebellion, which was aimed primarily at British interests in Palestine, also saw widespread violence against Jews, whose numbers in Palestine had been steadily increasing. By 1936, Palestinian Arabs had grown weary and annoyed with British policies that had allowed more and more Jewish immigrants into Palestine. Many Arabs had also grown fearful that Jewish purchases of Arab land were relegating the Palestinian Arabs to a decidedly second-rate status and threatening their economic well-being.

The Arab Revolt was led by two primary groups. The first was the politically conscious Arab elite, dominated by the two rival clans of the Husseini family, led by the mufti of Jerusalem Haj Amin al-Husseini, and their rivals, the Nashashibi family (represented by Fakhri al-Nashashibi). The second (and the true center of the leadership) resided among local committees that had emerged in Jerusalem, Nablus, Jaffa, Tulkarm, and elsewhere.

The primary triggering mechanism of the hastily convened Pan-Arab Congress, however, was the 1937 Peel Commission, sponsored by the British government. As a response to the violence of the uprising, the British government had charged the Peel Commission with making recommendations that would ease Arab-Jewish tensions and bring an end to the rebellion.

Issued in July 1937, the Peel Commission Report concluded that the Arab Revolt was the result of the Palestinians' drive for independence and their enmity toward the concept of a Jewish state in Palestine. To bring an end to the violence, the Peel Commission recommended the partitioning of Palestine into Jewish and Palestinian states (the latter to be part of Transjordan) and common areas controlled by the mandate (Jerusalem, for example).

The Palestinian Arabs—and most other Arabs—were incensed with the Peel Commission's conclusion that partition was necessary. Instead of mitigating Palestinian anger, the report served only to fan the flames of resentment. Violence reached new heights in the late summer and early autumn of 1937, and by September as many as 10,000 well-armed Palestinian guerrillas were prowling the countryside. They were joined by at least several hundred Arab fighters, sponsored by the Arab Higher Commission, from other states.

It was amid this incredibly tense political and military atmosphere that the Pan-Arab Conference convened. It resulted in unanimous support for the Palestinians' right to a homeland and took considerable pains to condemn the Peel Commission and the suggestion of a bifurcated Palestine. It also called for scrapping the 1917 Balfour Declaration, the immediate suspension of all Jewish immigration to Palestine, an end to the British Mandate, and the creation with all due haste of a Palestinian state. For Jews already living in Palestine, the Pan-Arab Congress agreed to give them guaranteed minority status. In addition, the congress agreed to create a permanent executive committee to help Palestinians economically and to engage in public relations activities. Finally, delegates voted to expand the Arab economic boycott to include British as well as Jewish goods.

The 1937 Pan-Arab Congress not only gave voice to Palestinian grievances but also unified the effort to help them attain a homeland. Also, Syria quickly emerged as the linchpin of the rebellion in Palestine. It hosted key leaders of the insurgency and funneled money to the Palestinian cause. The Arab Revolt continued for almost two additional years, with many more deaths and casualties.

PAUL G. PIERPAOLI JR.

See also

Arab Revolt of 1936–1939; Balfour Declaration; Husseini, Haj Amin al-; Nashashibi, Fakhri al-; Palestine, British Mandate for; Peel Commission; Syria

References

Gelvin, James L. *The Israel-Palestine Conflict: One Hundred Years of War.* New York: Cambridge University Press, 2005.

Morris, Benny. *Righteous Victims: A History of the Zionist-Arab Conflict, 1881–2001.* New York: Vintage Books, 2001.

Porath, Yehoshua. *The Palestinian National Movement, 1929–1939: From Riot to Rebellion.* London: Cass, 1974.

Swedenburg, Ted. *Memories of Revolt: The 1936–1939 Rebellion and the Palestinian National Past.* Minneapolis: University of Minnesota Press, 1995.

Pan-Arabism

A philosophical and political movement based on Arab nationalism that calls for the solidarity of Arab peoples and, sometimes more specifically, a union of Arab nations in the Middle East. Beginning with intellectual debate about the major unifying factor in the region—language, history, and ethnicity versus the role of Islam—Pan-Arabism next considered the appropriate response of Arab nations against increased Western imperial expansion. Pan-Arabism ultimately became a political doctrine, the application of which had far-reaching consequences for power relations in the Middle East and beyond.

In the second half of the 19th century, a variety of Middle Eastern intellectuals began to theorize about the future of the Islamic world in relation to the increasingly powerful imperial nations of Europe. One influential movement was that of Pan-Islamism. Led by Jamal ad-Din al-Afghani, early Pan-Islamists were fiercely anti-imperialist and framed their desires for parity with the West along religious lines. Al-Afghani did not believe that the West was superior to the Muslim East. Rather, he believed that over time Middle Eastern governments and religion had become corrupt and had lost touch with the true message of Islam.

For al-Afghani, there were two major Islamic tenets that needed to be revised for the Muslim world to become as powerful as the West: unity and action. Unity of the Muslim world was crucial in the eyes of al-Afghani. He looked back to the early Muslim kingdoms and the success of early Islam as something that could be achieved anew in the Middle East. Muslims need only unify behind a progressive Islam, which would encourage its followers throughout the world to forget their ethnic and national differences and see themselves as part of one supernation of believers. In doing so,

Egyptian president Gamal Abdel Nasser (*left*) and Syrian president Shukri al-Quwatli clasp hands to symbolize the merger of the two countries into the United Arab Republic (UAR) on al-Quwatli's arrival in Cairo with members of his cabinet, March 2, 1958. (Bettmann/Corbis)

Muslims would actively unite against European expansionism and economic exploitation.

One of al-Afghani's most influential students was Muhammad Abduh, a well-respected theologian who ultimately became the mufti of Egypt in 1899. Abduh formulated one of the most influential modern interpretations of Islam in a book entitled *Risalah al-Tawhid* (A Treatise on the Oneness of God), published in 1897. It asserted not only that Islam and modernity were compatible but also that modernity complemented Islam rather than restricted it. Abduh founded the Salafiyya movement, which called for the reintroduction into Sunni Islam of a legal principle of Islamic law (*ijtihad*) allowing for more reinterpretation. As Pan-Islamists, both al-Afghani (who was not an Arab) and Abduh were concerned about Islamic affairs more than Arab affairs.

Abd al-Rahman al-Kawakibi (1849–1903), a journalist from Aleppo, was of Kurdish descent. He spent the last three years of his life in Cairo and published two key books in which he voiced his disgust toward the corruption of the Ottoman Empire, which ruled large segments of the Arab world. He blamed the decline of Muslim rule on the fact that non-Arabs had taken control of the Middle East. He looked at Islam as the greatest achievement of the Arabs, and because God had chosen to reveal Islamic teachings to an Arab prophet in Arabic, the Arabs were an ideal people for leadership. He wanted to see the restoration of an Arab caliphate, which, he

believed, would hasten a revival in the region as well as in the religion. Al-Kawakibi's ideology gave some Arabs a framework for opposing the Ottomans, which eventually took on nationalist tones.

Arab nationalism also evolved from Syrian nationalism and a movement of revival for the Arabic language called the *nahda,* or renaissance. Many of these Arab nationalists were Christians, including Jurji Zaydan, who wrote histories and novels; Ibrahim al-Yaziji, who established a secret society in 1875 that focused on Arab pride and rejected the Ottoman claim to the caliphate; and Najib Azury, who founded the Ligue de la Patrie Arabe (League of the Arab Fatherland) in 1903 in Cairo and wrote *The Awakening of the Arab Nation* in 1905. By 1913 other secret nationalist societies had formed and survived rounds of suppression from the Ottoman government.

As the Ottoman Empire collapsed at the end of World War I and Britain and France secured control over much of the Middle East, other Arab intellectuals challenged European expansionism. It is in the ideas of those thinkers that the foundations of Pan-Arabism were laid.

One of the first Pan-Arabists to gain serious recognition was a Syrian Arab named Sati al-Husri, who had made a name for himself during the Ottoman era as a Westernized bureaucrat committed to educational reform. After the collapse of Ottoman rule in 1918, al-Husri became a leading voice for the Pan-Arabist cause in the interwar years, heading up the ministry of education in King Faisal I's Iraqi government. While helping the Iraqis build an educational infrastructure in the 1920s and 1930s, al-Husri wrote a series of pamphlets—*Arabism First, On Arab Nationalism,* and *What Is Nationalism?*—in which he called for the creation of a single, independent Arab state. He believed that the Arab people constituted one nation and that language was the primary marker of that fact. Because the Arabic language came before Islam, both Muslim and Christian Arabs should be united under this nation. Al-Husri hoped that the common language, shared culture, and shared history would inspire Arabs to unite against the Western forces and found a modern nation-state.

Another pair of influential thinkers who picked up on al-Husri's ideas were the Syrian intellectuals Michel Aflaq and Salah al-Din al-Bitar. As students in Paris in the 1930s, they were attracted to socialist ideology, particularly its anti-imperialism and messages of social justice. Calling their movement Baath (Arabic for "resurrection"), they expressed a Pan-Arabist agenda in the context of social restructuring to build a powerful and independent Arab society. Members of the Baath movement believed that the Arabs could regain their confidence only with unity. That unity would hearken back to Arab greatness under the conquering caliphs of early Islam and would put the Arab world on par with the West. In that way, Aflaq and al-Bitar were influenced by al-Kawakibi. Indeed, the Baath movement, although inclusive of Muslims and Christians, idealized Islam as a cultural system and a symbol of what the Arab world was capable of producing: a great religion that had spread across the globe. In that way, the Baath movement did not alienate

Muslims but instead attracted them. Yet its inclusive rhetoric also appealed to non-Muslim Arabs who wished to see their nation resurrected as well. The ideology of the Baath movement was coupled with two other powerful political developments in the Arab world: the dispossession of the Palestinians from their homelands and the emergence of Nasserism in Egypt during the rule of President Gamal Abdel Nasser.

Like al-Husri, many Pan-Arab thinkers called on Egypt to take the lead to promote the Arabist cause, and such ideas took hold during the 1930s and 1940s. At that time, Western imperialism seemed to the Arab world to be most destructive to the Arabs in Palestine, who were on the eve of losing their homeland to the Zionist settlers from Europe (who wanted to create a Jewish state in the region). In 1945, seizing on the hope that strength could be achieved in a postwar world, the Arab League was formed in Cairo, the city with the most active movement for Pan-Arabism. The league was a coalition of Egypt, Syria, Lebanon, Iraq, and Transjordan (later Jordan). The leaders of these states pledged to support each other in building economic, political, and cultural strength and cooperation.

In May 1948 during the Israeli War of Independence, the member nations of the Arab League invaded Palestine to halt the formation of the State of Israel, but they were defeated by the Israelis in December. The defeat of this "Liberation Army" was a turning point for the Pan-Arabist movement. The loss of Palestine to the Israelis was made more bitter by the humiliating crisis of the Palestinian refugees, who were trapped in dismal refugee camps while the Arab countries looked on, unable or unwilling to assimilate those people into their own societies yet also unable to liberate them from the Israelis and implement Palestinian national sovereignty in the Holy Land. For Arabs throughout the world, the rhetoric of uniting in an effort to restore the Palestinians to their homeland and defeat the Israeli state became a powerful tool of political unification.

Nasser ultimately became the most well-known spokesperson for Pan-Arabism. During his period in power (1952–1970), he promoted Pan-Arabism to rally the Arab world behind Egypt's policies in standing up to the West, in the Suez War, and in opposing what he regarded as British and U.S. plans to divide the region. He convinced Jordan and Syria not to join the British-sponsored Baghdad Pact of 1954, and in 1956 he successfully faced off against the Western powers and nationalized the Suez Canal. Nasser used his oratorical skills, following the failure of the British, French, and Israelis in the Suez Crisis to defeat him, to define the cause that the Arab nation was one nation. Later, he defined Egypt's style of Pan-Arabism as a progressive and populist cause, in contrast to that of traditional monarchies such as Saudi Arabia. As a propaganda war mounted between these two nations and others, Nasser utilized the Voice of Cairo, a powerful radio network that broadcasted throughout the Arab world and beyond to spread the doctrines of Pan-Arabism and Arab socialism.

In late 1957 the Baath Party in Syria turned to Nasser and asked him to join a union of the two countries, since they were at that time under threat by a rival faction. In February 1958 the United Arab Republic (UAR), the political unification of Syria and Egypt, was founded. Baath leaders believed that the union would assure their control over Syria, while the Egyptians saw the move as the first step to a larger Pan-Arabist state led by Egyptians. Yemen soon joined the union. The unification of Baath ideology and the potent leadership of Nasser was a dream combination for millions of Arabs, who ardently believed that the UAR was the beginning of a new Arab superstate that could challenge Western hegemony.

It was not to be. It soon became clear that there was resentment among the Syrian bourgeoisie, who could justifiably claim that the relationship between Egypt and Syria was not an equal one. Some of the Egyptian bureaucrats and officials who went to Syria were highly unpopular there. The unification also demonstrated that resistance to the programs of land reform and industrialization in Syria were politically destabilizing. The UAR was not a well-thought-out formation but rather a hasty attempt by the Syrian opposition to capitalize on Nasser's power in a way that he could not refuse. In September 1961 Syrian military units staged an insurrection against the Egyptian commanders, and the UAR came to an end. Nasser accepted this defeat, but his subsequent statements dwelt on the issues of class struggle that led to the union's failure and thus contributed to the discourse on Arab socialism at that time.

The failure of the UAR was followed by a lengthy Egyptian military involvement in Yemen and then in 1967 by the humiliating defeat of Egypt, Syria, and Jordan by the Israelis in the Six-Day War. The war brought great territorial losses for the Arab side and dramatic increases in the number of Palestinian refugees. For the Arab world, it appeared that Arab unity was now more necessary than ever. Yet the governments of the Arab nations were further divided by the 1967 defeat. Moreover, with the 1967 defeat it was clear to Palestinians that their cause could not be left in the hands of the Arab states. Although the Palestinian cause remained a symbol for Arab unity, real action for change was moved away from the Arab League and was concentrated in the Palestine Liberation Organization (PLO) and other Palestinian movements.

In the 1970s and 1980s, Arab leaders employed the rhetoric of Arab nationalism and Pan-Arabism to rally their populations behind a number of issues, particularly the struggle against Israel. Saddam Hussein of Iraq, in particular, used the Arab cause as a rationale for his policies. But in 1990 an event occurred that spelled the beginning of the end of Pan-Arabism. After Iraq invaded Kuwait in August 1990, the Western powers, led by the United States working through the United Nations (UN), convinced a number of other Arab nations to join their alliance against Iraq. Egypt and Syria committed troops to the Persian Gulf War in exchange for debt cancellation and other economic rewards, while Saudi Arabia agreed to host coalition forces. With the punishing defeat of Iraq in February 1991, wrought in part because Arab states were willing to fight other Arab states, Pan-Arabism seemed all but dead.

Today, although there are still dreams of Arab unity, millions of people in the Arab world search for other alternatives to their political, social, and economic problems. Many turned instead to Islamist or Muslim fundamentalist movements.

NANCY STOCKDALE

See also

Arab League; Baathism; Egypt; Expellees and Refugees, Palestinian; Nasser, Gamal Abdel; Palestine Liberation Organization; Persian Gulf War; Six-Day War; Syria; United Arab Republic; Zionism

References

Hourani, Albert. *Arabic Thought in the Liberal Age, 1798–1939.* New York: Cambridge University Press, 1983.
Khalidi, Rashid, et al., eds. *The Origins of Arab Nationalism.* New York: Columbia University Press, 1993.
Tibi, Bassam. *Arab Nationalism: Between Islam and the Nation-State.* New York: St. Martin's, 1997.

Passfield White Paper

See White Paper (1930)

Patria, Destruction of
Event Date: November 25, 1940

French ship blown up at Haifa on November 25, 1940. Early in November 1940 three ships carrying Jewish immigrants sailed for Palestine from the Romanian port of Tulcea. In effect, the German government saw an opportunity to create difficulties for the British and abetted the departure of the refugees and the ships. On November 1, the *Pacific* arrived at Haifa with some 1,100 illegal Jewish immigrants from Germany and Austria. A few days later, the *Milos* arrived with another 700 immigrants from Czechoslovakia.

The year 1940 was a difficult one for the British. Germany had defeated France, and Britain was the only major military opponent remaining against the Germans and Italians. There were fears in London that the Axis powers would soon conquer Egypt and take the Suez Canal. In these circumstances and despite the documented persecution of Jews by Germany, London was anxious to placate the Arabs regarding Jewish immigration into Palestine. The German government saw in these circumstances an opportunity to embarrass the British.

Warned in advance of the arrival of the ships, British authorities secured the aging *Patria,* a 12,000-ton French transport. They then transferred the immigrants to it, supposedly for reasons of quarantine. The British then announced that the immigrants would not be admitted to Palestine and would instead be shipped on to Mauritius in the Indian Ocean for the duration of the war, after which a decision would be rendered as to where the immigrants would be sent.

On November 24, 1940, the *Atlantic,* the third ship carrying illegal immigrants, arrived at Haifa. The British then prepared to transfer its passengers to the *Patria* as well, refusing all appeals to the contrary from Jewish representatives. The Zionists did all they could to persuade the British to change their minds. A general strike had no impact.

Finally, on November 21 a mine was smuggled aboard the ship by members of the Jewish self-defense organization, Haganah. The plan was to blow a small hole in the ship's hull, forcing the British to disembark the passengers. Unfortunately, when the mine went off at 9:00 a.m. on November 25 as passengers from the *Atlantic* were being transferred to it, the *Patria* sank almost immediately. Some 267 people died, including 50 crew members and British soldiers and policeman. Later the members of Haganah claimed that the *Patria* was in such poor condition at the time that it would have sunk at sea anyway, with far greater loss of life.

Following this incident and ensuing widespread outrage, British authorities decided to make an exception and allow the 1,560 survivors of the *Patria* to enter Palestine, although the number of refugees was to be deducted from subsequent Jewish immigration quotas. The immigrants not yet transferred from the *Atlantic* were not included in the special consideration and were indeed deported to Mauritius on December 9, 1940. After the war, they were given the option to return to Palestine, and more than 80 percent chose to do so.

SPENCER C. TUCKER

See also

Holocaust; Palestine, British Mandate for

References

Chazan, Meir. "The *Patria* Affair: Moderates vs. Activists in Mapai in the 1940s." *Journal of Israeli History* 22(2) (2003): 61–95.
Israeli, R., and M. N. Penkower. *Decision on Palestine Deferred: America, Britain and Wartime Diplomacy, 1939–1945.* New York: Routledge, 2002.
Ofer, S. "The Rescue of European Jewry and Illegal Immigration to Palestine in 1940: Prospects and Reality; Berthold Storfer and the Mossad le'Aliyah Bet." *Modern Judaism* 4(2) (1984): 159–181.
Shepherd, Naomi. *Ploughing Sand: British Rule in Palestine, 1917–1948.* New Brunswick, NJ: Rutgers University Press, 1999.

Patriot Missile System

Defensive antiaircraft and antiballistic missile system. The U.S. Patriot missile system was untested in combat until the 1990–1991 Persian Gulf War, when it was used to shoot down Iraqi Al Hussein short-range theater ballistic missiles (a locally built version of the Soviet Scud missile) launched at Israel and Saudi Arabia. The Patriot was developed at the Redstone Arsenal in Huntsville, Alabama, in the late 1970s as an antiaircraft weapon and was modified in the 1980s as an antitheater ballistic missile weapon. U.S. Patriot units based in Germany were deployed to Israel during the 2003 Iraq War. During the 2006 Israel-Hezbollah War, three Israel Defense Forces (IDF) Patriot batteries were deployed around Haifa in August 2006

American Patriot antiballistic missile battery, positioned to counter a possible Iraqi missile attack, located in northern Tel Aviv, Israel, March 13, 2003. (Moshe Milner/Israeli Government Press Office)

and tasked with intercepting various types of missiles launched at the area from Lebanon by Hezbollah.

The Patriot is a long-range, high-altitude, all-weather missile defense system designed to defeat aircraft, theater ballistic missiles, and cruise missiles. The Patriot's multifunction phased array radar and track-by-missile guidance systems can simultaneously detect and engage multiple targets, despite electronic countermeasure. The Patriot missile is a single-stage, solid-fuel, 7.4-foot, 2,200-pound projectile operating at mach 3 speed with an effective range of 43 miles.

The missile is armed with a proximity-fused 200-pound high-explosive warhead designed to disable or destroy an inbound target by detonating and dispersing fragmentation in a fanlike pattern immediately ahead of the threat. The Patriot is deployed as a Patriot Fire Unit, having 32 missiles loaded (4 each) in 8 M-901 storage and transportation canister launchers. Each launcher is arrayed atop an M-860 semitrailer launch platform. The Patriot Fire Unit also includes a 5-ton, M-818 tractor truck variant mounted with an

MSQ-104 engagement control station, which houses the fire control, radar, and computer engagement systems.

The Patriot is a three-phase intercept system that uses its engagement control radar to detect an inbound target. The engagement control computer plots an intercept trajectory and programs the intercept data into the missile's guidance system, elevates and trains the launcher, and then fires the missile. The missile's onboard radar then guides the missile to the optimal intercept point.

The Patriot missile was first launched in combat on January 18, 1991, when it mistakenly fired at a computer glitch misinterpreted as a Scud fired at Saudi Arabia. The Patriot engaged more than 40 theater ballistic missiles during the Persian Gulf War, but its intercept rate was well below the 97 percent claimed by U.S. officials at the time. The U.S. Army eventually claimed a 70 percent effective intercept rate for the Saudi Arabian theater of operations and a 40 percent effective intercept rate in Israel. The IDF estimated the effective intercept rate at 10 percent or less. This substantially lower estimate may have been a function of the IDF's definition of success and effectiveness that counted any ground warhead detonation as a failure regardless of whether the incoming missile had been hit, disabled, or deflected.

Since the Patriot missile systems in both theaters of operation were manned by U.S. Army crews, there was much speculation concerning the higher reported effective intercept rate in Saudi Arabia. One reason may have been that the Saudi government simply lied because all Saudi press reports on Scud strikes were censored. The Israeli targets were heavily populated areas where any debris or detonation could be reported by the uncensored Israeli press. The Saudi targets, on the other hand, were primarily desert military installations far from Saudi population centers.

Regardless of the reasoning used to explain the theater effective intercept rate differential, the success rate for the Patriot was not what had been anticipated, especially in Israel. One reason may simply have been that Iraqi modifications to the Soviet-built Scud made to increase the range and speed of the Al Hussein variant structurally weakened the missile. Many of the Al Husseins broke up as they reentered Earth's atmosphere, and those multiple pieces stretched the target so that the Patriot engagement control radar and onboard missile radar could not differentiate between general debris and the warhead.

The Patriot was originally designed to intercept and destroy or disable aircraft, but when it was modified to defend against theater ballistic missiles, the targeting protocols were not sufficiently modified to compensate for the faster speed of the missile or the detonation point at the target's center of mass. Thus, the Patriot tended to spray its fragmentation at the tail of the Al Hussein, leaving the warhead in the nose intact.

A software error that was subsequently corrected caused a third of a second drift in the system's internal clock that translated into a 600-meter error in the targeting trajectory. The more time the system remained in use before a shutdown reset the clock, the greater the error. On February 25, 1991, that error caused a Patriot to miss the inbound Scud that hit the billets of the U.S. Army's 14th Quartermaster Detachment in Dharan, Saudi Arabia, killing 28 American soldiers.

The Patriot continues to be used by the United States, the Netherlands, Germany, Japan, Israel, Saudi Arabia, Kuwait, Taiwan, and Greece. The IDF continues joint development with the United States of the Arrow 2 antimissile system that was also deployed by Israel in the 2006 Israel-Lebanon War.

RICHARD EDWARDS

See also

Hezbollah; Iraq; Iraq War; Iraq, Armed Forces; Israel; Israel Defense Forces; Lebanon; Lebanon, Israeli Operations against; Persian Gulf War; Saudi Arabia; Saudi Arabia, Armed Forces

References

Atkinson, Rick. *Crusade: The Untold Story of the Persian Gulf War.* New York: Mariner Books, 1994.

Clancy, Tom, and Chuck Horner. *Every Man a Tiger: The Gulf War Air Campaign.* Rev. ed. New York: Berkley Publishing, 2005.

Dinackus, Thomas D. *Order of Battle: Allied Ground Forces of Operation Desert Storm.* Central Point, OR: Hellgate Press/PSI Research, 1999.

Hildreth, Steven A. *Evaluation of U.S. Army Assessment of Patriot Antitactical Missile Effectiveness in the War against Iraq.* Washington, DC: Congressional Research Service, 1992.

Patterson, John Henry

Born: November 10, 1867
Died: June 18, 1947

British Army officer, author, and supporter of Zionism. John Henry Patterson was born in Forgney, Ballymahon, County Westmeath (now Longford), Ireland, on November 10, 1867. He joined the British Army at age 17, eventually rising to the rank of lieutenant colonel. He saw service in Africa and India and fought in the South African (Boer) War (1899–1902). Patterson was stationed in Egypt at the beginning of World War I and worked with Zionist Joseph Trumpeldor to establish and recruit members for the Zion Mule Corps, a Jewish volunteer auxiliary formation. Patterson also became fast friends with another Zionist in Egypt, Vladimir Jabotinsky. Trumpeldor and Jabotinsky hoped that the establishment of a Jewish military unit fighting with the British would help their goal of a Jewish state in Palestine. Patterson commanded the Zion Mule Corps on the Gallipoli Peninsula in 1915 with Trumpeldor as his second-in-command.

After the British Empire troops were evacuated from Gallipoli and the Zion Mule Corps disbanded, Patterson assumed command of an Irish battalion and then the 1st Jordan Regiment (38th Royal Fusiliers or Jewish Legion). A devout Protestant, he saw to it that the men in his command were able to observe the Sabbath whenever it proved possible. Patterson's subsequent book about his wartime experiences earned him the admiration of Jews but very much displeased the War Office.

Returning to Britain after the war, Patterson became an articulate spokesman for the Zionist cause and especially for Revisionist Zionists, no doubt sacrificing his military career as a result. During World War II he lobbied ardently both in Britain and the United States for the formation of a Jewish army to fight on the Allied side. He also sharply criticized British policy in Palestine. Patterson died in Bel-Air, California, on June 18, 1947. A well-known writer, his first and best-known book is *The Man-Eaters of Tsavo* (1907), the true story of how he had been engaged in 1898 to hunt man-eating tigers that were killing workers building a railroad bridge in Kenya. The book became the basis for three films.

SPENCER C. TUCKER

See also

Jabotinsky, Vladimir Yevgenyevich; Jewish Legion; Revisionist Zionism; Trumpeldor, Joseph; Zion Mule Corps; Zionism

References

Patterson, John Henry. *With the Judeans in the Palestine Campaign.* New York: Macmillan, 1922.

———. *With the Zionists in Gallipoli.* New York: George H. Doran, 1916.

Streeter, Patrick. *Mad for Zion: A Biography of Colonel J. H. Patterson.* Harlow, Essex, UK: Matching Press, 2004.

PEACE FOR GALILEE, Operation

See Lebanon, Israeli Invasion of

Peace Movements

While most news coverage of the Middle East has focused on issues pertaining to war and conflict, significant efforts for peace have been undertaken by state officials, groups, and individuals in the region from before the establishment of the State of Israel in 1948. These efforts have tended to take two paths. One way is that of dialogue, encounter, and reform, which seeks to modify relationships and human behavior through learning about the Other. A second way is that of nonviolent protest or peace and human rights activism designed to alter existing patterns of relationships and remove the causes of war (seen to be in part the result of injustice and inequality). Although the term "peace" is not always included in the name or description of some of these groups, the aim of such initiatives is to create a region free of war and based on relationships of trust and coexistence if not necessarily close friendship.

Peace groups have been particularly prevalent in Israel and Palestine, not only because the region is the center of the Arab-Israeli conflict but because of the more democratic government there and the strong Israeli and Palestinian civil societies. Throughout the region the term "peace" is contentious, as it is often considered a sign of surrender or submission. Consequently, when the term is used, it is often modified, as seen in Israeli calls for peace with security and Palestinian calls for peace with justice. Because of the politics of the region and the controversy surrounding the term

Israeli peace activists are interviewed while demonstrating against the Israel Defense Forces (IDF) shelling of Beit Hanoun, November 2006. (Rachel Avnery)

"peace" (what peace signifies in political terms), it is often more instructive to look at initiatives for nonviolent social change that promote dialogue, diversity, democracy, and human rights and thereby create the conditions for peace. This is especially important because groups suspected of peace activities are viewed as suspect or traitorous by other groups within society.

A number of official Middle East peace initiatives have occurred over the decades, from the well-known 1978 Camp David Accords between President Anwar Sadat of Egypt and Prime Minister Menachem Begin of Israel to the quieter dealings of Jordan's King Hussein prior to the 1994 signing of the Israel-Jordan Peace Treaty. Saudi Arabia proposed the eight-point plan for peace in 1981 as well as the more recent 2002 proposal that was accepted by the Arab League. Dialogue groups and problem-solving workshops led primarily by U.S. academics pairing semiofficial Palestinians and Israelis (and sometimes other national groupings) have been a regular occurrence since the 1970s, bringing individuals together for several days of communications training, dialogue, and brainstorming with the help of third parties. Such activities do not generate official documents or agreements but instead lead to rela-

tionships across national divides and can lead to policy initiatives suggested by workshop attendees in their home communities. Several of the parties involved in the Oslo negotiations, which led to the 1993 Oslo Accords, were graduates of such workshops. More recent civil society initiatives such as the December 2003 Geneva Accord and the People's Voice Campaign also resulted from personal relationships developed between Israelis and Palestinians in high positions but not in official government capacities.

Numerous institutions have promoted nonviolent social change and coexistence over the years. The Israeli Givat Haviva Institute has been promoting peace, mutual understanding, and partnership in the region since 1949. Founded by the Kibbutz Artzi movement, Givat Haviva has expanded its programs over the years to include educational, athletic, and dialogue activities. The Israeli Palestinian Center for Research and Information (IPCRI) was founded in 1988 as a joint think tank promoting practical policy alternatives to the conflict. Palestinian nongovernment organizations (NGOs)—including Wi'am, a Palestinian conflict resolution center drawing on the principle of *sulha,* a traditional form of reconciliation, and the Palestinian Center for Rapprochement between Peoples—work on issues of conflict resolution, human rights, and democracy within Palestinian society.

On the individual level, Israeli journalist and activist Uri Avnery has been advocating pluralism, peace, and democracy for all living in the region since before the outbreak of the 1948–1949 Israeli War of Independence through his activities as a journalist, member of the Knesset (Israeli parliament), and founder of the Israeli peace group Gush Shalom. In all of these venues, Avnery has pushed for a two-state solution to the Palestinian-Israeli conflict and has sought and maintained dialogue with many Palestinians. Palestinian nonviolent activist Mubarak Awad, who had been called the "Palestinian Gandhi," was deported from Israel in 1988 because his nonviolent efforts to achieve a just and lasting peace were seen as threatening to the status quo.

Peace groups in Israel and the Palestinian territories have undergone a series of changes as the local, regional, and international scene has shifted. Many early initiatives bringing Israelis and Arabs together, such as Matzpen, were socialist in scope, aspiring to supranationalist aims based in equality and solidarity regardless of ethnic or religious origin. An intentional community of Arabs and Jews living together, Neve Shalom-Wahat al-Salam, was founded in the early 1970s and developed the first Jewish-Palestinian bilingual education program as well as an encounter program, the School for Peace, to promote dialogue and understanding between Israeli and Arab youths. Such programs are extremely rare in Israel, however, where many Israelis have never exchanged visits with Arabs and the separated residential communities and schools have remarkably little personal knowledge of each other.

The peace movement in Israel really began in the late 1970s and early 1980s in response to the Camp David Accords and the 1982 Israeli invasion of Lebanon. Groups such as Peace Now had their origins in this time period and were able to draw crowds of 100,000 to protests in Tel Aviv. After the outbreak of the largely nonviolent First Intifada in 1987 additional groups emerged, such as Rabbis for Human Rights and Women in Black. After the signing of the Oslo Accords in 1993, there was a proliferation of new Israeli-Palestinian joint initiatives and peace groups, largely because of the atmosphere of hope, an official sanctioning of peace activity by Israeli and Palestinian officials, and funding priorities of donor agencies. Many of these organizations, however, were put together hastily without much relationship building among the members and were criticized for replicating asymmetrical power relationships, evident through language of communication (often Hebrew or English rather than Arabic) and location of decision-making authority (often with Israeli

Palestinian and Israeli children taking part in a Darbuka drum workshop at the Hebrew University Campus on July 17, 2002, in Jerusalem, Israel. Wellspring for Democratic Education organized this summer camp for 160 children (80 Palestinians and 80 Israelis). (Quique Kierszenbaum/Getty Images)

directors). With the collapse of the Oslo process and the outbreak of the Second (al-Aqsa) Intifada in September 2000, many of these groups disappeared, although groups with a lasting history of cooperation and joint activity and research, such as the Alternative Information Center that has offices both in the Palestinian town of Beit Sahour and in West Jerusalem, were able to continue.

A new generation of peace groups—often explicitly rejecting the word "peace" because of the failure of the Oslo Accords and focusing on issues of human rights, justice, and equal partnership as the necessary prerequisites for peace—emerged shortly after the beginning of the Second Intifada. These groups, such as Ta'ayush (Arab-Jewish Partnership in Life), Machsom Watch (Checkpoint Watch), and al-Mubadara (Palestinian National Initiative), tend to focus on issues internal to Israeli and Palestinian societies—such as racism within Israel and the need for political reform within the Palestinian Authority (PA)—rather than dialogue and encounter per se. Such groups seek partners for campaigns and the pursuit of common goals but do not pursue dialogue and encounter as ends unto themselves. Cross-border relationships, according to these groups, are built out of a sense of common struggle for peace, with justice conducted in the sociopolitical arena.

At the same time, an increasing focus on nonviolence as a strategy for social change has gained prominence within both Palestinian and Israeli society. In April 2005, Panorama Center and Holy Land Trust organized a conference on nonviolence that drew 120 Palestinians from all districts in the West Bank to discuss nonviolent strategies for resistance and to develop mechanisms for communication and sharing accumulated experience. In December 2005 an International Nonviolence Conference was held in Bethlehem, and in February 2006 another one was held in Bil'in with a special focus on the joint nonviolent struggle against the separation barrier.

Military service evasion in Israel, which has a tradition dating back to the 1970s, has expanded from the refusal to serve in the occupied Palestinian territories or in Lebanon (the original aims of Yesh Gvul when it began in 1982) to the refusal of some to serve in the military at all on grounds of politics and conscience. Several letters have been written to Israeli officials from high school seniors and Israeli soldiers, including the 2002 Combatants Letter and a 2003 letter signed by a group of pilots and members of an elite commando unit voicing concern as to the immoral nature of the occupation in terms of violating Palestinian civilians' rights and corrupting the moral fabric of Israel.

While most of these groups, such as the Courage to Refuse, focus on refusal to serve beyond the 1967 borders, New Profile, an Israeli organization committed to combating the militarization of all aspects of Israeli society through an emphasis on building a civil society, supports conscientious objectors, including those who refuse to serve in the military at all, even within 1967 borders. They have recently put together an exhibit that documents the effects of militarism on Israeli education, advertising, and popular culture using materials found in the course of everyday life.

Numerous challenges face civil society groups promoting peace, democracy, and human rights in the Middle East because of the authoritarian nature of many Arab regimes. Since the early 1990s, civil society efforts have been increasingly visible. Most of these groups struggle first and foremost to create the conditions conducive to an active civil society—freedom of speech, freedom of assembly, and freedom of the press—within their own countries. Such an environment is necessary before openly propeace movements can be created, such as can be seen in Israel and the Palestinian territories. In Syria, for example, the brief period of mild political opening known as the Damascus Spring just after Bashar al-Assad's accession to power was organized around small civil society groups meeting in private homes discussing political affairs and calling for reform.

The Ibn Khaldun Center for Development Studies, based in Egypt and closed by the government, which arrested, tried, and sentenced to prison its director Saad Eddin Ibrahim and other employees, studied the major protracted conflicts in the Middle East–North Africa region and has brought together conflict parties when possible and has focused on issues of peacemaking and ethnopolitics at its annual conferences. Nonetheless, the main focus of Ibn Khaldun was its effort to promote democratization in Egypt.

NGOs in Jordan such as the Amman Center for Peace and Development, Palestinian organizations such as Miftah and Panorama, and Israeli organizations such as the Yakar Center and Physicians for Human Rights have promoted peace through their work for democracy, development, human rights, and dialogue. Many of these and other organizations have been involved in the Search for Common Ground's Middle East program, founded in 1991.

Arab and Israeli journalists have worked with Search for Common Ground on promoting peace and nonviolent, cooperative solutions through the media as well as through dialogue efforts and cooperative projects. Articles promoting peace and coexistence are translated and circulated in Arabic, Hebrew, and English to news outlets and individual subscribers around the Middle East and elsewhere.

Despite these challenges, several Arab peace groups have been successful in maintaining and creating new programs locally and regionally. One such group is the Lebanon Conflict Resolution Network (LCRN), which was established in 1996 with the aim of developing and disseminating the skills and principles of conflict resolution, negotiation, and collaborative problem solving. The network has provided training, conducted interventions, and organized study groups for NGOs, political parties, and other organizations in countries throughout the Middle East, including Lebanon, Syria, Iraq, Jordan, Morocco, Tunis, Algeria, Yemen, Bahrain, and Qatar. A more recently established group, the Middle East Citizen's Assembly (MECA), began in 2001 and convened in 2005 and 2006 to create a network of those working on promoting peace, freedom, democracy, and human rights in order to build cross-border alliances and lay the groundwork for overcoming social and political divides. MECA includes representatives from Turkey, Iran, Morocco, Jordan, Palestine, Iraq, Yemen, Saudi Arabia, Tunisia, and Israel.

MAIA CARTER HALLWARD

See also

Camp David Accords; Geneva Accord; Intifada, Second; Oslo Accords

References

Gidron, Benjamin, Stanley Katz and Yeheskel Hasenfeld, eds. *Mobilizing for Peace: Conflict Resolution in Northern Ireland, Israel/Palestine, and South Africa.* London: Oxford University Press, 2002.

Hall-Cathala, David. *The Peace Movement in Israel, 1967–1987.* New York: St. Martin's, 1990.

Hallward, Maia Carter. "Building Space for Peace: Challenging the Boundaries of Israel/Palestine." PhD dissertation, American University, Washington, DC, 2006.

Lonning, Dag Jorund. *Bridge over Troubled Water: Inter-Ethnic Dialogue in Israel-Palestine.* Bergen, Norway: Norse Publications, 1995.

Peel Commission
Start Date: August 1936
End Date: July 7, 1937

Commission to study the British-held mandate in Palestine. In August 1936 the British government appointed a Royal Commission of Inquiry headed by Lord Robert Peel to examine the effectiveness of the mandate system and to make proposals concerning future British policy in Palestine. Peel was the former secretary of state for British-held India. Members of the Royal Commission arrived in Jerusalem on November 11, 1936. While all of the committee's members were experienced in foreign affairs, none had any particular connection to either the Arab cause or the Jewish cause.

The Peel Commission, as it came to be called, was established at a time of increasing violence in Palestine. Indeed, serious clashes between Arabs and Jews broke out in 1936 and were to last three years. The commission was charged with determining the cause of the unrest and judging the merit of grievances on both sides. Chaim Weizmann gave a memorable speech on behalf of the Zionist cause. However, the mufti of Jerusalem, Haj Amin al-Husseini, refused to testify in front of the commission. Instead, he demanded full cessation of Jewish immigration into Palestine. Although the Arabs continued to boycott the commission officially, there was a sense of urgency to respond to Weizmann's speech. The former mayor of Jerusalem, Raghib Bey al-Nashashibi, was thus sent to explain the Arab perspective through unofficial channels.

The commission returned to Britain on January 18, 1937, and published its report on July 7, 1937. The Peel Commission attributed the underlying cause of the Arab Revolt of 1936–1939 to the Arabs' desire for independence and their hatred and fear of the establishment of a Jewish homeland in Palestine. Therefore, the commission recommended freezing Jewish immigration to Palestine

at 12,000 people per year for five years. It also urged that a plan be developed for formal partition of the territory.

With regard to partition, the commission recommended that the mandate be eventually abolished except for a corridor surrounding Jerusalem and stretching to the Mediterranean coast just south of Jaffa and that the land under its authority be apportioned between an Arab and an Israeli state. The Jewish side was to receive a territorially smaller portion in the midwest and the north, from Mount Carmel to south of Be'er Tuvia, as well as the Jezreel Valley and the Galilee, while the Arab state was to receive territory in the south and mideast, which included Judea, Samaria, and the Negev Desert.

The Peel Commission recommended that until the establishment of the two states, Jews should be prohibited from purchasing land in the area allocated to the Arab state. To overcome demarcation problems, the commissioners proposed that land exchanges be carried out concurrently with the transfer of population from one area to the other. Demarcation of the precise borders of the two states would be entrusted to a specialized partition committee.

These recommendations marked the beginning of the end of British rule in Palestine. The British government accepted the recommendations of the Peel Commission regarding the partition of Palestine, and Parliament announced its endorsement of the commission's findings. Among Jews, bitter disagreements erupted between supporters and opponents of the partition proposal, while the Arabs rejected it outright. Ultimately, the plan was shelved. A new commission, the Woodhead Commission, was subsequently established to determine borders for the proposed states.

MOSHE TERDIMAN

See also

Arab Nationalism; Balfour Declaration; Husseini, Haj Amin al-; Jerusalem; Nashashibi, Raghib; Palestine, British Mandate for; United Kingdom, Middle East Policy; Weizmann, Chaim; Zionism

References

Ayaad, Abdelaziz A. *Arab Nationalism and the Palestinians, 1850–1939.* Jerusalem: Passia, 1999.

Cohen, Aharon. *Israel and the Arab World.* New York: Funk and Wagnalls, 1970.

Palestine Royal Commission Report Presented by the Secretary of State for the Colonies to Parliament by Command of His Majesty, July 1937. London: His Majesty's Stationery Office, 1937.

Swedenburg, Ted. *Memories of Revolt: The 1936–1939 Rebellion and the Palestinian National Past.* Minneapolis: University of Minnesota Press, 1995.

Peled, Elad
Born: 1927

Israeli military officer. Elad Peled was born in 1927 and as a youth in Palestine joined the permanently organized Jewish military organization of the Palmach. He fought in the Israeli War of Independence in 1948 and was wounded during the defense of Safed.

PEEL COMMISSION PARTITION PLAN, JUL 1937

33°E · 34°E · 35°E · 36°E

N

Damascus

LEBANON

Metulla

SYRIA

33°N

Acre

Haifa · Tiberias · Sea of Galilee

Deraa

Afula

Beit Shean

Mediterranean Sea

Nablus

Jerash

Tel Aviv-Jaffa · Petah Tikva

Amman

32°N

Ramla · Lod

Rehovot · Jericho

Jerusalem

Bethlehem

Gaza · Hebron

Dead Sea

TRANS-

Al Arish

JORDAN

31°N

N e g e v

EGYPT

Petra

Maan

30°N

—·— Frontier of the Palestine Mandate

Proposed Jewish state, 1937

Proposed Arab state, 1937;
Transjordan was already barred
to Jewish settlement

Proposed area to remain under
British control

0   20   40 mi
0   20   40 km

Aqaba

thus able to break into the city relatively easily. However, serious fighting followed until the entire city was taken during the next six hours.

By the end of the Six-Day War, Peled also controlled an infantry brigade and a parachute brigade, which he used to help secure Israeli positions in the Golan Heights. These troops took the southern area of the Golan Heights in the area of Tawfiq and the Yarmuk Valley.

Following his retirement from the army, Peled served in the Ministry of Education. He then entered local politics and became deputy mayor of Jerusalem.

RALPH MARTIN BAKER

See also
Golan Heights; Jenin; Six-Day War

References
Hammel, Eric. *Six Days in June: How Israel Won the 1967 Arab-Israeli War.* New York: Scribner, 1992.
Oren, Michael B. *Six Days of War: June 1967 and the Making of the Modern Middle East.* Novato, CA: Presidio, 2003.

Peres, Shimon
Born: August 16, 1923

Israeli politician, leader of the Labor Party, and prime minister (1984–1986 and 1995–1996). Born Shimon Perski on August 16, 1923, in Wieniawa, Poland (now Vishniev, Belarus), Peres immigrated with his family to the British Mandate for Palestine in 1934. He grew up in Tel Aviv and was educated at the Geula School in Tel Aviv and at the agricultural school of Ben Hemen. He spent several years in Kibbutz Geva and was one of the founders of Kibbutz Alumot. He was elected secretary of the Labor-Zionist youth movement in 1943 and then returned to Alumot as a farmer and shepherd.

In 1947 Peres joined the Jewish self-defense organization Haganah, and while working in manpower and arms management he came under the political mentorship of David Ben-Gurion who, as Israel's first prime minister, put the 24-year-old Peres in charge of the Israeli Navy following the Israeli War of Independence (1948–1949). In 1952 Peres was appointed deputy director-general of the Israeli Ministry of Defense and was head of the procurement delegation in the United States, where he studied at the New York School for Social Research and at Harvard. During 1953–1959 he served as the general director for procurement for the Ministry of Defense, developing a close relationship with the French government that led to the acquisition of the advanced Dassault Mirage III French jet aircraft, the establishment of Israel's avionics industries, the acquisition of a nuclear reactor, and planning for the 1956 Sinai Campaign.

Peres increased indigenous weapons production while serving as deputy defense minister during 1959–1965, and he also started Israel's nuclear research program and further developed foreign military alliances. Peres was first elected to the Knesset (Israeli

Israeli Army general Elad Peled, November 1965. (Fritz Cohen/Israeli Government Press Office)

Continuing in the Israeli Defense Army after the war, Peled graduated from the French École de Guerre and was assigned command of the Golani Brigade. Promoted to major general in 1967 just prior to the start of the Six-Day War, he had command of a reserve division based around Galilee. Known as the Peled Division, this force originally consisted of two armored brigades. Colonel Uri Ram led one brigade, and Colonel Moshe Bar-Kochva led the other. Peled's division included three types of tanks—the British A-41 Centurion, the French AMX-13, and the Israeli-modified U.S. M-4 Super Sherman—as well as an additional battalion of half-tracks.

During the Six-Day War, Peled's division operated in the West Bank under the Israeli Northern Command. Peled was one of the group of senior army generals who persuaded the Israeli political leadership to accept the feasibility of the planned attack.

In the initial stages of the Six-Day War, Peled's units engaged Jordanian forces in the Dotan Valley area in an effort to protect the Ramat David airfield. Bar-Kochva's armored brigade led the attack and succeeded in pushing the Jordanian armored units back and capturing Kabatiya and Jenin. This assault was assisted by close aerial support. Peled's forces then advanced on Nablus, where the Israeli troops were initially mistaken for Syrian forces and were

Shimon Peres, Israeli politician, leader of the Labor Party, and prime minister (1984–1986 and 1995–1996). (Ya'acov Sa'ar/Israeli Government Press Office)

parliament) in 1959 and remains a member. In 1965 he helped Ben-Gurion found the failed political party called Rafi (Israel's Worker's List) and then in 1967 helped merge the Mapai Labour Party (Ben-Gurion's former party), Rafi, and the more leftist Ahdut Ha'avodah workers' party into what would become the Labor Party, with Peres as its deputy secretary-general.

In 1969 Peres became the minister of immigrant absorption. He then served as the minister of transport and communications (1970–1974), minister of information (1974), and defense minister (1974–1977). In the latter position he improved the strength and readiness of the Israel Defense Forces (IDF), helped negotiate the second interim peace agreement with Egypt, authored the Good Fence concept that sought to improve relationships with residents of southern Lebanon, and was instrumental in planning the Entebbe rescue mission (1976).

Peres became acting prime minister upon the resignation in 1977 of Labor prime minister Yitzhak Rabin and in the same year led Labor to its first defeat in a general election in 30 years. Peres lost the premiership to Menachem Begin but was elected as the Labor Party chairman that same year and served in that capacity

until 1992. Peres was again chairman of the Labor Party during 1995–1997 and has held that post since 2003.

Peres again lost to Begin and the Likud Party in 1981 but joined with Begin's Likud successor, Yitzhak Shamir, to form a national unity government after an indecisive general election in July 1984. Peres served as Israeli prime minister for the first half of a 50-month term, and Shamir served as deputy prime minister and foreign minister, with the positions rotating for the second 25 months. During Peres's prime ministership, Israel withdrew its forces from Lebanon in 1985, established a security zone in southern Lebanon, and dramatically reduced the inflation rate.

Following another indecisive election in 1988, Likud and Labor formed a new coalition government in which Shamir remained prime minister and enlisted Peres to serve as deputy prime minister and minister of finance. When this coalition government failed in 1990, Shamir formed a new government that included members of some ultraconservative parties and excluded Labor.

Rabin assumed the leadership of Labor from Peres in February 1992 following Rabin's victory in the first primary in Israeli history and went on to be elected Israel's prime minister in July 1992, making Peres his minister of foreign affairs. Following the understanding established at the Madrid Peace Conference in September 1991, Peres and Rabin negotiated in September 1993 the Declaration of Principles with the Palestine Liberation Organization (PLO) that led to the 1993 Israel-PLO peace accords, which began Israel's withdrawal from the West Bank and the Gaza Strip and for which Peres, Rabin, and Arafat were awarded the 1994 Nobel Peace Prize. A peace treaty with Jordan followed in October 1994, and Peres sought to establish relations with additional Arab countries in North Africa and the Persian Gulf that he hoped would lead to a so-called New Middle East.

In November 1995 Peres assumed the premiership following the assassination of Rabin and concurrently held the post of minister of defense. Peres lost the general elections in May 1996 to the Likud Party's Benjamin Netanyahu largely because of a wave of suicide bombings that killed 32 Israeli citizens and that Peres seemed powerless to prevent.

In 1996 Peres founded the Peres Center for Peace, promoting socioeconomic development, cooperation, and mutual understanding through Arab-Israeli projects in economy, culture, education, health care, agriculture, and media. He served on the Knesset Foreign Affairs and Defense Committee (1996–1999) and as minister of regional cooperation (July 1999–March 2001). He was minister of foreign affairs and deputy prime minister in Prime Minister Ariel Sharon's national unity government (March 2001–October 2002), leaving office only in advance of the 2003 elections. Peres led the party into a coalition with Likud following Sharon's announcement of disengagement from Gaza. Peres served as vice premier from January 2005. Although he was the leader of the party, at the end of November 2005 he announced that he was leaving Labor to support Sharon and the new Kadima Party. In March 2006 Peres was elected to the Knesset as a member of Kadima. He was then minister for the development of the Negev, Galilee, and the regional economy and second vice prime minister.

On July 1, 2007, Moshe Katsav resigned as president of Israel, and on July 13 Peres was elected by the Knesset to succeed him as the ninth president of Israel. Peres resigned his position as a member of the Knesset the same day, having served in that body since November 1959 (except for three months in early 2006), the longest such tenure in Israeli political history. He was sworn in to the largely honorific position of president on July 15, 2007.

Peres is a prolific author. Among his books are *The Next Step* (1965), *David's Sling* (1970), *And Now Tomorrow* (1978), *From These Men: Seven Founders of the State of Israel* (1979), *Entebbe Diary* (1991), *The New Middle East* (1993), *Battling for Peace: A Memoir* (1995), *For the Future of Israel* (1998), and *A History of Israel and the Holy Land* (2003).

RICHARD EDWARDS

See also

Begin, Menachem; Ben-Gurion, David; Entebbe Hostage Rescue; Gaza Strip; Labor Party; Lebanon; Likud Party; Netanyahu, Benjamin; Shamir, Yitzhak; Sharon, Ariel; Sinai Campaign

References

Corbin, Jane. *The Norway Channel.* New York: Atlantic Monthly, 1994.
Freedman, Robert Owen, ed. *Israel under Rabin.* Boulder, CO: Westview, 1995.
Golan, Matti. *The Road to Peace: A Biography of Shimon Peres.* New York: Warner, 1989.
Laqueur, Walter, and Barry Rubin, eds. *The Israel-Arab Reader: A Documentary History of the Middle East Conflict.* London: Penguin, 2001.
Makovsky, David. *Making Peace with the PLO: The Rabin Government's Road to the Oslo Accord.* Boulder, CO: Westview, 1996.
Peleg, Ilan, ed. *Middle East Peace Process: Interdisciplinary Perspectives.* Albany, NY: SUNY Press, 1998.
Perry, Mark. *A Fire in Zion: The Israeli-Palestinian Search for Peace.* New York: Morrow, 1994.
Quandt, William B. *The Peace Process: American Diplomacy and the Arab-Israeli Conflict since 1967.* Washington, DC: Brookings Institution, 1993.
Said, Edward W. *Peace and Its Discontents: Essays on Palestine in the Middle East Process.* New York: Vintage, 1995.
Savir, Uri. *The Process: 1,100 Days That Changed the Middle East.* New York: Random House, 1998.
Tessler, Mark. *A History of the Israeli-Palestinian Conflict.* Bloomington: Indiana University Press, 1994.

Persian Gulf War
Start Date: August 2, 1990
End Date: February 27, 1991

A conflict between Iraq and an international coalition of 34 nations mandated by the United Nations (UN) and led by the United States. The Persian Gulf War was sparked by Iraq's August 2, 1990, invasion and subsequent occupation of Kuwait, which was met with immediate economic sanctions by the UN against Iraq. The war

commenced on January 17, 1991, with a heavy aerial attack against key Iraqi assets, including its air force, antiaircraft facilities, and command, control, and communications centers. The ground war began on February 24. Declaring a cease-fire on February 27, President George H. W. Bush announced the liberation of Kuwait, and the war thus ended.

Relations between Iraq and Kuwait had been strained for some time. Despite improvement during the Iran-Iraq War (1980–1988), when Kuwait assisted Iraq with loans and diplomatic support, relations worsened when Iraqi president Saddam Hussein, who had launched a costly reconstruction program, demanded that Kuwait forgive its share of Iraq's war debt and help with other payments. Also at issue was oil. As Hussein tried to increase the price of the commodity by slackening production within the Organization of Petroleum Exporting Countries (OPEC), Kuwait undercut his plans by increasing its own production. Kuwait's alleged slant-drilling into Iraqi oil fields also rankled Hussein. Meanwhile, Washington miscalculated Hussein's intentions and sent mixed signals as to its possible action.

Iraqi forces invaded Kuwait shortly after midnight on August 2, 1990. About 150,000 Iraqi soldiers with almost 2,000 tanks easily overwhelmed the unprepared and inexperienced Kuwaiti forces, which numbered only about 20,000 men. By dawn, Iraq had assumed control of Kuwait City, the capital, and was soon in complete control of the small country.

The Iraqis initially posed as liberators, hoping to appeal to Kuwaiti democrats who opposed the ruling Sabah monarchy. When this claim attracted neither Kuwaiti nor international support, it was dropped. In place of the Sabahs, most of whom fled during the invasion, Iraq installed a puppet government.

The UN Security Council and the Arab League immediately condemned the Iraqi invasion and imposed an economic embargo that prohibited nearly all trade with Iraq. Iraq responded to the sanctions by formally annexing Kuwait on August 8, prompting the exiled Sabah family to call for a stronger international response to evict Iraqi forces from their homeland. In response, the UN passed a total of 12 resolutions condemning the invasion.

After consulting with U.S. secretary of defense Dick Cheney, King Fahd of Saudi Arabia invited American troops onto Saudi soil. The Americans and their West European allies were now concerned about the Iraqi threat to the Saudi oil fields. Other Arab countries, including Egypt, Syria, and the smaller states along the Persian Gulf, also joined the growing coalition, fearing that even if Iraq's conquests stopped at Kuwait, Iraq could still intimidate the rest of the region.

Beginning a week after the Iraqi takeover of Kuwait and continuing for several months, a large international force gathered in Saudi Arabia. The United States sent more than 500,000 troops, and more than 200,000 additional troops came from Saudi Arabia, the United Kingdom, France, Kuwait, Egypt, Syria, Senegal, Niger, Morocco, Bangladesh, Pakistan, the United Arab Emirates, Qatar, Oman, and Bahrain. Other countries including Canada, Italy,

M-60A1 main battle tanks of the 1st Tank Battalion, U.S. 1st Marine Division, advance toward Kuwait City during the third day of the ground offensive phase of Operation DESERT STORM, February 26, 1991. (U.S. Department of Defense)

Australia, Belgium, Denmark, Greece, Norway, Portugal, Spain, Czechoslovakia, New Zealand, the Netherlands, Poland, and South Korea contributed ships, air forces, and medical units. Still other countries made other contributions. Turkey allowed air bases on its territory to be used by coalition planes, and Japan and Germany lent financial support.

On November 29, with coalition forces massing in Saudi Arabia and Iraq making no signs of retreat, the UN Security Council passed a resolution authorizing the use of "all necessary means" to force Iraq from Kuwait if Iraq remained in the country after January 15, 1991. The Iraqis flatly rejected the ultimatum. Soon after the vote, the United States agreed to a direct meeting between Secretary of State James Baker and Iraq's foreign minister, Tariq Aziz. The two sides met on January 9, 1991. Neither side offered to compromise. The United States underscored the ultimatum, and the Iraqis refused to comply with it, even threatening to attack Israel.

When the UN deadline of January 15 passed without an Iraqi withdrawal, the coalition forces had reached a strength of 700,000 troops. President Bush, in consultation with the other key leaders of the coalition, waited two days after the UN deadline before ordering the coalition to commence operations against Iraq. In the early morning hours of January 17, 1991, coalition forces began a massive U.S.-led air attack on Iraqi targets.

The air assault, which had been named Operation DESERT STORM, had three goals: to neutralize Iraqi air assets, to disrupt command and control, and to weaken ground forces in and around Kuwait. After five and a half weeks of intense bombing and more than 10,000 sorties by coalition planes, Iraq's forces were severely damaged.

In an attempt to pry the coalition apart, Iraq fired Scud missiles at both Saudi Arabia and Israel, which especially disrupted Israeli civilian life. Iraq could thus portray its Arab adversaries as fighting on the side of Israel. The strategy failed to split the coalition, in part because the Israeli government did not retaliate.

The ground war, code-named Operation DESERT SABRE, began at 8:00 p.m. on February 24 with a massive ground offensive. This was launched northward from northeastern Saudi Arabia into Kuwait and southern Iraq. The main U.S. armored thrust drove deep, some 120 miles into Iraq, and struck the Iraqi armored reserves from the rear. This maneuver surrounded Kuwait, encircling the Iraqi forces there and allowing coalition forces (mainly Arab) to move up the coast and take Kuwait City. Some Iraqi units resisted, but the coalition offensive advanced more quickly than anticipated. Thousands of Iraqi troops surrendered. Others deserted. Iraq then focused its efforts on withdrawing its elite units and sabotaging Kuwaiti infrastructure and industry. Many oil wells were set on fire, creating huge oil lakes, thick black smoke, and other environmental damage. The coalition forces destroyed most of Iraq's elite Republican Guard units when they tried to make a stand south of Basra in southeastern Iraq.

On February 27, with the collapse of Iraqi resistance and the recapture of Kuwait, the coalition's stated goals had been achieved. President Bush declared a cease-fire, to go into effect on February 28. The land war had lasted precisely 100 hours. The cease-fire came shortly before coalition forces would have surrounded Iraqi forces. On March 2, the UN Security Council issued a resolution laying down the conditions for the cease-fire, which were accepted by Iraq in a meeting of military commanders on March 3. They agreed to pay reparations to Kuwait, reveal the location and extent of Iraqi stockpiles of chemical and biological weapons, and eliminate weapons of mass destruction (WMDs).

President Bush's decision to terminate the ground war so soon was criticized because it allowed the escape of a large amount of military equipment and personnel later used to suppress the postwar rebellion of Shiite and Kurdish citizens. Bush asserted that the war had accomplished its mandate. More extensive aims, such as overthrowing the Iraqi government or destroying Iraqi forces, did not have the support of all coalition members. Most Arab members, for example, believed that the war was fought to restore one Arab country, not to destroy another.

In terms of casualty counts, the outcome of the Persian Gulf War was very one-sided. The number of Iraqi combat casualties is very much in dispute, and estimates range from 10,000 to 100,000 Iraqis killed. Western military experts now seem to agree that Iraq sustained between 20,000 and 35,000 casualties. Coalition losses were extremely light by comparison: 240 killed in action, 148 of whom were Americans. The number of coalition wounded totaled around 900, of whom 467 were Americans.

In military terms, the campaign was clearly successful. Politically, however, the outcome of the war was more clouded. The end of the fighting left Hussein still in power with a large part of his combat capability intact. The war had failed to resolve a number of key issues. The UN sanctions against Iraq did not end with the war. On April 2, 1991, the Security Council laid out strict demands for ending the sanctions. Iraq would have to accept liability for damages, destroy its chemical and biological weapons and ballistic missiles, forgo any nuclear weapons programs, and accept international inspections to ensure that these conditions were met. If Iraq complied with these and other resolutions, the UN would discuss removing the sanctions. Iraq resisted, claiming that its withdrawal from Kuwait was sufficient compliance.

The UN continued to maintain most of the economic embargo on Iraq after the war, and several coalition nations enforced other sanctions, such as the no-fly zones over Iraq. In 1995 the UN amended the sanctions to allow Iraq to sell limited amounts of oil

Kuwaiti oil wells set afire by withdrawing Iraqi troops during Operation DESERT STORM in 1991. (U.S. Department of Defense)

for food and medicine if it also designated some of the revenue to pay for damages caused by the war. Iraq initially rejected this plan but then accepted it in 1996.

JAMES H. WILLBANKS

See also

Bush, George Herbert Walker; Hussein, Saddam; Iran-Iraq War; Iraq; Iraq, Armed Forces; Israel; Kuwait; Kuwait, Armed Forces; Organization of Petroleum Exporting Countries; Saudi Arabia, Armed Forces; United Nations, Role of

References

Atkinson, Rick. *Crusade: The Untold Story of the Persian Gulf War.* New York: Mariner Books, 1994.

De la Billiere, Sir Peter. *Storm Command: A Personal Account of the Gulf War.* New York: HarperCollins, 1992.

Finlan, Alastair. *The Gulf War, 1991.* Oxford, UK: Osprey, 2004.

Gordon, Michael R., and Bernard E. Trainor. *The Generals' War.* Boston: Little, Brown, 1995.

Khaled bin Sultan. *Desert Warrior: A Personal View of the Gulf War by the Joint Forces Commander.* New York: Perennial, 1996.

Pollack, Kenneth M. *Arabs at War: Military Effectiveness, 1948–1991.* Lincoln: University of Nebraska Press, 2002.

Schwarzkopf, Norman H. *It Doesn't Take a Hero.* New York: Bantam, 1992.

Perski, Shimon

See Peres, Shimon

Pineau, Christian

Born: October 14, 1904
Died: April 5, 1995

French Resistance fighter, socialist National Assemby deputy, and cabinet minister, including minister of foreign affairs (1956–1958). Born in Chaumont (Haut-Marne) on October 14, 1904, Christian Pineau attended the École alsacienne in Paris and earned degrees in law and political science from the École libre des sciences politiques. He then held banking positions while also becoming active in the trade union movement as secretary of the Economic Council of the Conféderation générale du travail (General Confederation of Labor, CGT) during 1936–1940. He also established a journal, *Banque et bourse* (Bank and Exchange).

On the defeat of France by the Germans in June 1940, Pineau joined the Resistance. In November 1940 he began publishing a newspaper, *Libération.* He also established his own resistance net, known as Phalanx. Arrested by the Germans in Lyon in May 1943, he was deported to Buchenwald. Released in April 1945, he was recognized for his Resistance work by being awarded the Legion of Honor and Medal of the Resistance with rosette. He served in the provisional government of General Charles de Gaulle as minister of supply in 1945.

Christian Pineau, former foreign minister of France, arriving at Lod Airport in Israel with his wife, met by Defense Minister Shimon Peres and French ambassador to Israel Pierre Gilbert, January 29, 1959. (David Gurfinkel/Israeli Government Press Office)

Pineau was a member of both constituent assemblies in 1945 and 1946 and was elected to the National Assembly of the Fourth Republic in 1946, serving as a socialist deputy from the Department of the Sarthe until 1958. Active in the reestablishment of credit and banking institutions, he held a number of cabinet posts, including minister of public works and transport (1947–1948), minister of finance (1948), and minister of public works, transport, and tourism (1948–1950). He was designated premier in 1955 but failed to win a confirmation vote in the National Assembly.

Increasingly involved in foreign affairs, Pineau was a staunch supporter of the European Defense Community, especially as a means of guaranteeing that Germany rearmed within a European context, and he backed the movement toward European economic integration. From February 1956 until November 1958 he was minister of foreign affairs in the government of Premier Guy Mollet. In that post Pineau sought to promote closer ties between Western and Eastern Europe, strongly supported the European Common Market, and favored independence for Morocco and Tunisia.

The chief foreign policy issue of Pineau's tenure was the 1956 Suez Crisis. That July, Egyptian president Gamal Abdel Nasser nationalized the Suez Canal. Nasser was a vocal supporter of the National Liberation Front that was fighting France to secure Algerian independence, and Pineau, Mollet, and many others in France believed falsely that Egyptian arms and money were the chief support of the Algerian revolt. The French government thus seized on Nasser's action of nationalizing the canal as an opportunity to cooperate with the British government of Prime Minister Anthony Eden in securing control of the canal and toppling Nasser from power. Pineau did disagree with Mollet, however, over the latter's characterization of Nasser as a new Adolf Hitler.

Pineau conducted a number of talks with British and Israeli leaders, resulting in a secret agreement, dubbed the "Treaty of Sèvres," of October 23, 1956, that provided for an Israeli invasion of the Sinai followed by French and British military operations against Egypt. Subsequent heavy U.S. pressure forced the British to withdraw, and Mollet was unwilling to continue on without Britain. Pineau, who from the beginning had been less enthusiastic than Mollet about the military intervention, urged the premier to persevere in cooperation with the Israelis. Mollet refused, and the French and the Israelis then also withdrew.

In the crisis of May 1958 caused by the Algerian War, de Gaulle returned to power as the last premier of the Fourth Republic, but Pineau opposed the general's plans to establish a Fifth Republic. Pineau retired from public office that same year but remained active in socialist politics until the early 1970s. In retirement, he wrote a number of books, including one on the Suez Crisis. Pineau died in Paris on April 5, 1995.

SPENCER C. TUCKER

See also
Eden, Robert Anthony; Eisenhower, Dwight David; France, Middle East Policy; Mollet, Guy; Suez Crisis

References
Beaufre, André. *The Suez Expedition, 1956.* Translated by Richard Barry. New York: Praeger, 1969.
Pineau, Christian. *1956: Suez.* Paris: Robert Laffont, 1976.
Simmons, Harvey G. *French Socialists in Search of a Role, 1956–1967.* Ithaca, NY: Cornell University Press, 1970.
Thomas, Hugh. *Suez.* New York: Harper and Row, 1967.

Pistols

At the beginning of the Arab-Israeli wars in 1948, the pistols employed by both sides in the fighting were of World War II vintage. The majority were American and British. From the mid-1950s, Israel employed U.S. and West European small arms. By the 1980s Israel was also producing its own firearms. At the same time, most Arab states adopted weapons, including pistols, of East European and Soviet manufacture.

Initially both sides used whatever weapons were available, and they were of a wide variety. Israel began the Israeli War of Independence (1948–1949) short of all types of firearms, and pistols were no exception. Among them were Mauser Model 1896/1912 semiautomatic pistols that had been used in World War I. German World War II pistols, such as the Walther P-38 semiautomatic firing the 9×19-mm Parabellum round, were also in use on both sides. Among other prominent pistol types were the British-manufactured Webley .38-caliber and .453-caliber revolvers and the semiautomatic U.S. Colt M-M-1911A1, firing the .45-caliber ACP round.

When the Israel Defense Forces (IDF) came into being, standardization of arms became a primary goal for purposes of both maintenance and ammunition supply. The IDF selected as its official sidearm the Italian Beretta M-1951 semiautomatic. Firing the 9-mm Parabellum round, it had an eight-round magazine. The Beretta was the standard service pistol not only in Israel but also in Egypt by the mid-1960s. The Egyptians produced the pistol under license, and there it was known as the Helwan. Egypt also adopted the Soviet Tokarev TT-33 semiautomatic. Introduced in 1936 and firing a 7.62-mm round, this pistol had an eight-round magazine. The Hungarians manufactured the TT-33 for Egypt, where it was known as the Tokagypt. The Tokarev was commonly carried by tank crews. Syrian tank crews were similarly armed. The Egyptian police were also armed with the Tokagypt, even after it was withdrawn from military service.

The Makarov was another Eastern bloc pistol that came into general use in the Arab countries in the late 1950s. Introduced in 1951, it was essentially a Soviet version of the semiautomatic Walther PP of 1929. The Makarov fired a 9×17-mm round that lacked the hitting power of the 9×19-mm Parabellum round. Although the Makarov was not produced by any of the Arab states in the region, many of these pistols were shipped to them by the Soviets as a normal part of military aid packages.

Although most of the Arab states used predominantly Soviet firearms, there were exceptions. Iran initially had close ties to the

United States, and the Iranian military used the U.S. Colt M-1911A1. After the overthrow of Mohammad Reza Shah Pahlavi in 1979 and a severing of U.S. ties, there was a general influx of Soviet weaponry. Many of the smaller Gulf states, such as Bahrain, Kuwait, and Oman, adopted various Italian, German, and French pistols. Morocco adopted both the Italian Beretta and the French MAS-1950 9-mm semiautomatic pistol with a nine-round magazine. Saudi Arabia purchased a variety of pistols for its defense personnel and did not establish a standardized sidearm.

Arab militias and the Palestine Liberation Organization (PLO) carried a wide variety of weapons. Snub-nosed revolvers, including the U.S. Smith and Wesson .38-caliber Model 38 Bodyguard, were popular because they could be easily concealed.

In the mid-1980s the Israelis produced their own pistol, the Jericho 941 designed by Israel Military Industries (IMI). The descriptor "941" comes from initial chambering of this gun. The gun was produced with two interchangeable barrels and magazine sets, one for a 9-mm Parabellum and another for a more powerful .41-caliber cartridge. The .41-caliber weapon, however, was not a financial success and was discontinued in favor of models chambered for .40-caliber and .45-caliber ammunition.

The Jericho also came to be called the Baby Eagle, following development by IMI of the Desert Eagle that fires either a .357-magnum or a .44-magnum round. This weapon is not in use by the military but is designed for the civilian market. The latest IMI pistol is the semiautomatic Barak SP-21 Lightning, introduced in 2002. It was originally intended solely as a replacement for all then-existing IDF pistols, but IMI has since marketed the SP-21 abroad. It became available in Europe early in 2003 and in the United States by late 2003. The Barak SP-21 is chambered for 9-mm Parabellum, .40-caliber Smith & Wesson, and .45-caliber ACP ammunition. It has a magazine capacity of 10–15 rounds, depending on the caliber.

RALPH MARTIN BAKER AND SPENCER C. TUCKER

See also
Rifles

References

Arnold, David. *Classic Handguns of the 20th Century.* Iola, WI: Krause, 2004.

Hogg, Ian V. *Pistols of the World.* Iola, WI: Krause, 2004.

———. *Small Arms: Pistols and Rifles.* London: Military Book Club, 2003.

Mullin, Timothy. *The 100 Greatest Combat Pistols: Hands-On Tests and Evaluations of Handguns from Around the World.* Boulder, CO: Paladin, 1994.

Pius XII, Pope
Born: March 2, 1876
Died: October 9, 1958

Roman Catholic prelate and pope. Pope Pius XII was born Eugenio Maria Giuseppe Pacelli on March 2, 1876, in Rome, Italy, to a family of Vatican legal officials. He was ordained in 1899, entered the Vat-

Pope Pius XII. (Library of Congress)

ican's Foreign Affairs Office in 1901, and became a protégé of Pietro Cardinal Gaspari, whom Pacelli would succeed in 1930 as cardinal secretary of state. In 1904 Pacelli received his doctorate in canon and civil law from the St. Apollinaris Institute. His diplomatic career took him throughout Europe and America, notably to Munich during World War I as papal nuncio, which also brought promotion to archbishop. He negotiated the unsuccessful papal peace effort of 1917 and then later immersed himself in prisoner-of-war issues. He was in Munich during the unrest there in 1919 and then in 1920 went to Berlin as nuncio. He remained in Berlin until late 1929 and then returned to Rome as Vatican secretary of state.

Pacelli negotiated the Concordat between the Church and German dictator Adolf Hitler's Nazi regime, initialed in July 1933 and signed two months later. Pacelli's diplomatic background led him to favor bilateral agreements between the Vatican and other states. Such arrangements favored the signatories, usually to the detriment of local or national church leaders who now had to defer to the Vatican, which now enjoyed legal recognition as the voice of the Church, rather than to the local primate.

The concordat assured the Catholic Church of full religious freedom. Its bishops were promised free communication with Rome and the right to publish pastoral letters, and its religious orders were allowed to continue work of a pastoral character. The church also received assurances regarding the continuation of its schools.

In return, Rome ordered bishops to take an oath of loyalty to the state and agreed to the dismantling of the Christian labor union movement and the dissolution of the Catholic Center Party. Clergy were also prohibited from participating in political activities. The concordat was of great benefit to Hitler, for it helped to allay German Catholic concerns about the National Socialists. The concordat, coupled with Pacelli's years in Germany and his subsequent public silence concerning Nazi atrocities, led to the sobriquet "the German pope."

Pacelli was elected pope in 1939 and took the name Pius XII. The beginning of his papacy coincided with the start of World War II, which led to savage criticism of the pope after the war. The furor was a reaction to the public silence of the Church with respect to Nazi atrocities, most notably the Holocaust. A recent work by English author John Cornwell on this controversy takes the title *Hitler's Pope,* representing the latest fusillade in a barrage begun in 1959 by Swiss playwright Rolf Hochhuth, whose play *The Deputy: A Christian Tragedy* accused Pius XII of being Hitler's accessory in genocide. The terms of this debate are stark. They allege that the pope knew of the genocide against the Jews and chose to remain silent about it. His strongest criticism of the Holocaust came in his 1942 Christmas speech in which he noted the "hundreds of thousands who, without any fault of their own, sometimes only by reason of their nationality or race, are marked down for death or gradual extinction." Cornwell dismisses this statement as worse than paltry, calling it shocking and evasive because it leaves out the words "Jew" and "Nazi" and scales the deaths of millions down to hundreds of thousands. Pius's silence, says Cornwell, reflected his indifference to the Jews, making him Hitler's pawn.

Pius's defenders, however, cite pragmatic grounds for the pope's reticence. They note that Church protests would lead to Nazi reprisals, creating more death and suffering, not less, and that Hitler's regime was indifferent to public opinion, which, in a war, was all that the Church could mobilize. Other defenders note that for the Church and Pacelli the enemy was on the political Left rather than on the Right. In the 1930s communism was rampant in the Soviet Union and seemed to be gaining ground in other parts of the world, and its official and unrelenting atheism clearly marked the Church's major theater of war.

After the war, relations between the Vatican and Israel remained distant. Indeed, Pius XII did not recognize the new State of Israel, although his private writings and utterances seem to indicate that he was at least sympathetic to a Zionist vision. Israeli-Vatican relations would not substantively improve until the papacy of John Paul II (1978–2005). Pope Pius XII died in Rome on October 9, 1958.

MICHAEL B. BARRETT

See also

Germany, Federal Republic of, Middle East Policy; Holocaust; John Paul II, Pope

References

Cornwell, John. *Hitler's Pope: The Secret History of Pius XII.* New York: Viking, 1999.
Goldhagen, Daniel Jonah. *A Moral Reckoning.* New York: Knopf, 2002.
Sanchez, Jose M. *Pius XII and the Holocaust.* Washington DC: Catholic University of America Press, 2002.

Pogroms

Rioting and violence directed against Jews. The term "pogrom" is derived from the Russian word meaning "to wreak havoc." The term dates from the 19th century and is used to describe the organized persecution, even massacre, of a minority group. Most commonly, however, the term "pogrom" is used in reference to the persecution of Jews.

Attacks by Europeans against Jews date back as least as far as the Crusades. In 1348 a large number of Jews were massacred, mostly in Germany, in hysteria surrounding the plague known as the Black Death. Reportedly, 12,000 Jews perished in the city of Mainz alone. Many Jews then fled Germany to Poland.

Other Jews were murdered in a Cossack uprising in Ukraine during 1648–1654, but reportedly the first action against Jews in Russia in which the term "pogrom" was used took place during rioting in Odessa in 1821. This occurred in reaction to the murder of the patriarch of the Greek Orthodox Church in Constantinople. Fourteen Jews died. Other sources identify the first pogrom as having occurred in Odessa in 1859. The term came into common use after a series of violent actions against Jews following the 1881 assassination of Russian czar Alexander II. These events triggered the First Aliya to Palestine (1882–1904). Pogroms continued through the 1880s, and a second wave occurred during 1903–1906. One of the worst of pogroms was at Kishinev, Bessarabia, in April 1903.

Pogroms remained concentrated in southern Russia, although they spread to other areas of the empire, such as Warsaw and Novgorod. The Russian government was clearly involved in some of this anti-Jewish activity. The government also restricted the area of Russia in which Jews might reside—the Pale of Settlement—and promulgated laws that sharply restricted educational opportunities for Jews and closed numerous occupations to them. Thus, while Jews were required to serve in the Russian Army, they were prohibited from being officers.

The pogroms led to the organization of Jewish self-defense groups in Russia. They also fostered widespread immigration of Jews from Russia, chiefly to the Americas and to Palestine. An estimated 2 million Jews left Russia in the three decades before World War I. The pogroms had another profound effect. They greatly propelled the Zionist movement, the desire of Jews to create a sovereign Jewish national state in Palestine in which all Jews would be welcome and might peaceably reside and that would guarantee protection of their basic human rights.

Pogroms again occurred in Russia coinciding with chaos surrounding the Russian revolutions of 1917 and the civil war that raged for several years thereafter. This saw the most dramatic loss of Jewish life. At least 60,000 Jews died, hundreds of thousands more were

Bodies of Jews massacred in a pogrom at Proskurov (present-day Khmelnytskyi, Ukraine), February 15, 1919. Perhaps 1,500 Jews died in the pogrom in a single day. (Getty Images)

wounded, and many Jewish communities were either partially or totally destroyed.

Widespread persecution of Jews began in Germany after the Nazis came to power there in 1933. The ensuing Nuremberg Laws turned Jews into a class of untouchables within Germany, and many who could do so fled abroad. Anti-Semitism and pogroms also occurred in Poland in the 1930s.

These actions, horrific as they were, paled in comparison with what occurred during World War II. Following their invasion of the Soviet Union in June 1941, the Nazis unleashed their so-called Final Solution to the Jewish question. Now known as the Holocaust, this was nothing less than a systematic effort to kill all Jews within Nazi reach. An estimated 6 million Jews died, many of them with the complicity of non-Germans. Pogroms did not end with World War II, however, for there was persecution of Jews thereafter, especially in Poland and in the Soviet Union.

SPENCER C. TUCKER

See also

Anti-Semitism; Holocaust; Kishinev Pogrom; Pale of Settlement; Zionism

References

Judge, Edward H. *Easter in Kishinev: Anatomy of a Pogrom.* New York: New York University Press, 1995.

Perry, Marvin, and Frederick Schweitzer. *Anti-Semitism: Myths and Hate from Antiquity to the Present.* New York: Palgrave Macmillan, 2005.

Pollard, Jonathan
Born: August 7, 1954

American spy for Israel and one of the most notorious spies in American history. Born in Galveston, Texas, into an affluent family on August 7, 1954, Jonathan Pollard graduated from Stanford University. He then attended the Fletcher School of Law and Diplomacy in Boston for two years but did not graduate. In 1977 he applied for a position at the Central Intelligence Agency (CIA) but apparently failed a polygraph test. Two years later, however, he secured a position with U.S. Naval Intelligence as a research specialist, working in the Field Operational Intelligence Office in Suitland, Maryland. Unmasked as a spy and arrested in November 1985, he confessed and entered into a plea bargain by which he would agree to be interviewed, submit to polygraph examination, and provide damage assessment information. In return the government extended a plea bargain to Pollard's wife, Anne, and promised Pollard that he would be charged with only one count of conspiracy to deliver national intelligence information to a foreign government, which carried a maximum sentence of life in prison. In 1986 Pollard was sentenced to life in prison. Before sentencing, U.S. secretary of defense Caspar Weinberger delivered a lengthy classified memorandum to the sentencing judge, the contents of which were not made available to Pollard's attorneys. Pollard began his sentence in 1987. Anne Pollard was sentenced to five years in prison but was released after three and a half years for health reasons.

In the years since Pollard's sentencing, many books and articles have appeared on the case, a number of them claiming that Pollard is either innocent or that his sentence was unjust, either because Israel is a U.S. ally or because Pollard had entered into a plea bargain agreement (which, however, did not detail sentencing). Because Pollard was never actually brought to trial and because of the nature of his crimes, a great many questions about the case remain. Certainly, Pollard's behavior was bizarre and should have alerted his superiors much earlier in his espionage career.

Extraordinarily costly to the United States in terms of sensitive information lost, by his own admission Pollard gathered and transferred to Israeli intelligence an astonishing 1 million pages of classified material occupying about 360 cubic feet. Although the exact information passed to the Israelis by Pollard remains classified, investigative reporters have charged that it included information on the U.S. global electronic surveillance network, the names of American agents in the Soviet Union (information that some say Israel may have traded to the Soviet Union in return for a continued flow of Jewish immigrants to Israel), and U.S. Navy techniques for tracking Soviet submarines.

The notion that Pollard spied for Israel because of his Jewish heritage is preposterous, because Pollard first approached four other nations about selling the information to them. Although the Israeli government refused Pollard asylum in 1985, it also initially denied that he had spied for Israel. Nonetheless, the Israeli government continues to make efforts to secure Pollard's release. Not until 1998 did Israeli prime minister Benjamin Netanyahu admit that Pollard had spied for the Jewish state. That same year the Israeli government declared Pollard to be an Israeli citizen. Thus far, all appeals for Pollard's release have gone unanswered. The U.S. courts have also repeatedly rejected Pollard's appeals for a new trial on the grounds of ineffective assistance by counsel.

SPENCER C. TUCKER

See also
Mossad; Netanyahu, Benjamin; Weinberger, Caspar

References
Goldenberg, Elliot, and Alan M. Dershowitz. *The Hunting Horse: The Truth behind the Jonathan Pollard Spy Case.* Amherst, NY: Prometheus, 2000.
Olive, Ronald J. *Capturing Jonathan Pollard: How One of the Most Notorious Spies in American History Was Brought to Justice.* Annapolis, MD: Naval Institute Press, 2006.

Popular Front for the Liberation of Palestine

Marxist-Leninist organization founded in 1967 that seeks to create a socialist state for Palestinians. The Popular Front for the Liberation of Palestine (PFLP) has always been opposed to the existence of Israel and has committed numerous terrorist attacks since 1968, focusing on Israeli and moderate Arab targets. Founded by George Habash on December 11, 1967, just after the Six-Day War, the PFLP arose from the merger of the Arab Nationalist Movement, which Habash had founded in 1953, with the Palestine Liberation Front and Youth for Revenge. Habash created the PFLP to represent the Palestinian working class and stated that its goal was the creation of a democratic socialist Palestinian state and the elimination of Israel. Habash saw the elimination of Israel as a necessary step in purging the Middle East from Western capitalist influences. He also claimed after the 1967 Arab defeat that it would be necessary to combat the Arab regimes before that could be accomplished. Although Habash was himself a Palestinian Christian, he wanted the PFLP to be an entirely secular organization based on Marxist principles and socialism and positioned on the vanguard of a world socialist revolution.

Palestinian students with posters of Popular Front for the Liberation of Palestine (PFLP) leader Ahmed Sadat during a protest in the West Bank town of Halhoul near Hebron, March 15, 2006. (Nayef Hashlamoun/Reuters/Corbis)

The PFLP quickly spread into other Arab countries and acquired financial backing from Syria and Jordan. The group joined the Palestine Liberation Organization (PLO) in 1968 and immediately generated two splinter factions, the terrorist organization Popular Front for the Liberation of Palestine–General Command (PFLP-GC) and the orthodox Marxist Democratic Front for the Liberation of Palestine.

Most members of the PFLP were trained as guerrillas. The group soon became known for its terrorist activities, especially its airliner hijackings, many of which targeted the Israeli airline El Al. Most of the early attacks were coordinated by Wadi' Haddad, known as "The Master." On July 23, 1968, the PFLP commandeered an El Al airplane on its way from Rome to Tel Aviv and landed it in Algeria, mistakenly believing that Major General Ariel Sharon, later to become an Israeli prime minister, was on board. The group held the passengers and crew captive until August 31.

Other hijackings and attacks followed. On December 26, 1968, PFLP guerrillas shot at an El Al jet about to leave Athens for Paris, killing 1 passenger. On February 18, 1969, its members attacked another El Al jet in Zurich, killing the copilot. Two days later they bombed a supermarket in Jerusalem. That August, the PFLP hijacked a TWA flight flying from Rome to Tel Aviv and forced it to land in Damascus. One of the leaders of this attack was Leila Khaled, who had joined the Arab Nationalist Movement in 1958 at the age of 14. She was arrested in Damascus but was quickly released. On September 9, 1969, 6 Palestinians threw grenades at Iraqi embassies in Bonn and The Hague and at the El Al office in Brussels. The PFLP also attacked a bus at the Munich airport on February 10, 1970. On February 21, 1970, the group detonated a barometric pressure device on Swissair Flight 330, flying from Zurich to Tel Aviv. The bomb damaged the plane sufficiently that the pilots were unable to return to the Zurich airport. The jet crashed and killed all on board, including 38 passengers and 9 crew members.

On September 6, 1970, the PFLP launched its most ambitious hijacking scheme yet. Group members simultaneously hijacked jets in Brussels, Frankfurt, and Zurich and forced them to fly to Cairo or Zarqa, Jordan. The group hijacked a fourth plane three days later. They blew up the three aircraft in Zarqa on September 12. The PFLP announced that the hijackings were intended to teach the Americans a lesson and to punish them for supporting Israel. On September 16, 1970, King Hussein of Jordan formed a military government and began attacking Palestinian guerrillas in Jordan. He ultimately expelled the PLO from the country. This crisis, which became known as Black September, reinforced Habash's claim that Arab regimes were inhibiting the Palestinian guerrilla movement.

Khaled, who had undergone six months of cosmetic surgery to disguise her appearance, and her colleague Patrick Arguello attempted to hijack a fourth aircraft departing from Amsterdam on September 6. They failed in this task. Arguello was shot, and Khaled was overpowered and then imprisoned in London. This arrest provoked the PLFP to seize five more civilian airplanes in an effort to persuade British authorities to release Khaled. She was released after 28 days in exchange for 56 Western hostages.

In 1973 Habash agreed that the PFLP would cease terrorist activities abroad, on the advice of the Palestinian National Council. Thereafter he restricted his terrorist activity to Israel, Jordan, and Lebanon. On May 30, 1972, the PFLP attacked Lod Airport in Israel, killing 24 people. Two months later on July 9, 1972, Israelis killed PFLP member and creative writer Ghassan Kanafani. Throughout the 1970s the group attacked numerous Israeli targets. The PFLP withdrew from the PLO in 1974, complaining that the PLO was no longer interested in destroying Israel completely and seemed instead to be willing to compromise.

When the First Intifada began on December 8, 1987, elements of the PFLP organized terrorist attacks in the Gaza Strip and the West Bank. In 1990 the Jordanian branch of the PFLP was converted into an actual political party, the Jordanian Popular Democratic Party. Habash stepped down as leader on April 27, 2000, and was replaced by Abu Ali Mustafa, who was killed by Israeli commandos on August 27, 2001. The PFLP retaliated on October 17, 2001, by killing Rehavam Zeevi, the Israeli minister of tourism. Ahmed Sadat became general secretary of the organization on October 3, 2001. The armed militia of this group continued its terrorist activity in the early 2000s, using car bombs and other small-scale bombing techniques and sometimes simply shooting targets. Sadat was subsequently arrested by the Palestinian Authority (PA) and held in Jericho. The PFLP opposed the 1993 Oslo Accords, partially because of its resentment of Fatah control over the PLO and subsequently the PA. The group has maintained its Marxist-Leninist beliefs, and this has always contributed to its smaller size and led to its decline as Islamism became much more influential.

AMY HACKNEY BLACKWELL

See also

Arab Socialism; Habash, George; Intifada, First; Palestine Liberation Organization; Terrorism

References

Hourani, Albert. *A History of the Arab Peoples*. Cambridge: Harvard University Press, 1991.

Popular Front for the Liberation of Palestine. *A Radical Voice from Palestine: Recent Documents from the Popular Front for the Liberation of Palestine*. Oakland, CA: Abraham Guillen, 2002.

Smith, Charles D. *Palestine and the Arab-Israeli Conflict: A History with Documents*. 6th ed. New York: Bedford/St. Martin's, 2006.

Popular Front for the Liberation of Palestine–General Command

Militant Palestinian organization that carried out military-style operations and terrorist attacks against Israeli targets and Arab political opponents. Founded in October 1968 as a splinter group of the Popular Front for the Liberation of Palestine (PFLP) and the Arab Nationalist Movement, the Popular Front for the Liberation

A masked member of the Popular Front for the Liberation of Palestine–General Command stands guard at the entrance to a military base belonging to the pro-Syrian organization, which was attacked by Israeli jets, in Naameh, 20 km south of Beirut, December 28, 2005. (AFP/Getty Images)

of Palestine–General Command (PFLP-GC), led by Ahmad Jibril, a former Palestinian officer in the Syrian Army, dedicated itself to conducting armed revolutionary action. It did so as a result of ideological debates about political strategies and directions among the more militant groups of that period. Based in Syria and Lebanon, the PFLP-GC is an organization of negligible size (a few hundred fighters) and limited influence within the Palestinian nationalist movement.

The roots of the organization can be traced to the experiences of dispossession shared by many Palestinians. The group's founder, Ahmad Jibril (1928–), was born in Jaffa in present-day Israel. Following his family's relocation to Syria in late 1947, he yearned for a return to Palestine. Together with like-minded Palestinians serving in the Syrian Army during the 1950s and early 1960s, he conducted covert cross-border raids into Israel. In 1965 he and other army veterans formed the Palestine Liberation Front (PLF). Jibril's militancy grew out of the Arab defeat in the 1967 Six-Day War, following which in October 1967 the PLF joined the Palestinian wing of the Arab Nationalist Movement to found the PFLP led by George Habash. However, within a year Jibril withdrew from the collaboration, reportedly over disputes involving control and command. He then formed the PFLP-GC.

The new organization quickly established itself as one commit-ted to mounting spectacular operations with skill and tenacity. In February 1970 the group killed 47 people in its first major terrorist attack, bringing down a Swissair passenger plane bound for Israel. Just four years later, a team of 3 PFLP-GC fighters killed another 18 people in a raid to seize hostages in the northern Israeli town of Qiryat Shmona. Major attacks also targeted the Palestine Liberation Organization (PLO) as the myriad Palestinian groups became embroiled in the Lebanese Civil War and feuded over leadership of the nationalist movement. And even as the PFLP-GC was increasingly marginalized by its affiliation with both Syrian and Libyan interests, the group's actions still served to inspire and support the popular Palestinian drive to end the Israeli occupation.

In late November 1987, only days before the outbreak of the First Intifada (1987–1993), an innovative operation saw the PFLP-GC use hang gliders to ferry guerrillas into northern Israel and attack army positions, underscoring the group's desire to defy the political realities on the ground.

With ongoing backing from Syria and bases in Lebanon, the PFLP-GC continues to retain a role in the Palestinian nationalist movement. However, its future has been tenuous since the death of Jibril's son, Muhammad Jihad, whose assassination on May 20, 2002, in Beirut robbed the group of its commander of armed operations and the heir apparent to overall leadership.

Jonas Kauffeldt

See also

Habash, George; Intifada, First; Israel; Lebanon; Palestine Liberation Organization; Popular Front for the Liberation of Palestine; Syria; Terrorism

References

O'Neill, Bard E. *Armed Struggle in Palestine: A Political-Military Analysis.* Boulder, CO: Westview, 1978.

Sayigh, Yezid. *Armed Struggle and the Search for State: The Palestine National Movement, 1949–1993.* New York: Oxford University Press, 2000.

Shemesh, Moshe. *The Palestinian Entity, 1959–1974: Arab Politics and the PLO.* 2nd ed. London: Frank Cass, 1996.

Port Said

The second-largest port city in Egypt after Alexandria, Port Said is the northern terminus of the Suez Canal. Port Said lies near the Mediterranean Sea to the north, Sinai to the east, Manzalah Lake to the west, and the Ismailiyya governorate to the south.

Port Said was established as a working camp in 1859 when construction began on the Suez Canal. The port is named after Khedive Said, who granted permission for the digging to begin.

Port Said prospered from the movement of ships through the canal, and by the end of the 19th century it had become an important shipping city. All the major maritime powers had established consulates there. A transit point for ships traveling to and from Europe and the Far East, the city became a major refueling station

Mosque at Port Said, Egypt. (PhotoDisc, Inc.)

but was also a shipping point for Egyptian exports such as cotton and rice.

During the 1956 Suez Crisis, Port Said was heavily damaged when British and French paratroopers carried out a vertical envelopment of the city and it was shelled by French and British destroyers. It sustained other damage during the 1967 Six-Day War. During the Yom Kippur War of 1973, Israeli bombing destroyed the center of the city. In 1976 Port Said was declared a duty-free zone. Since the 1979 Camp David Accords, the city has prospered. At present, there are approximately 400,000 residents. Port Said's economic base rests on fishing, chemicals, processed food, and cigarette manufacture. It is also a popular summer resort for Egyptians and a duty-free zone that links Asia, Africa, and Europe.

CHARLES FRANCIS HOWLETT

See also
Egypt; Six-Day War; Suez Canal; Suez Crisis; Yom Kippur War

References
Dupuy, Trevor N. *Elusive Victory: The Arab-Israeli Wars, 1947–1974.* Garden City, NY: Military Book Club, 2002.
Love, Kennett. *Suez: The Twice-Fought War.* New York: McGraw-Hill, 1969.
Ovendale, R. *The Origins of the Arab-Israeli Wars.* London: Longman, 1999.

Presidential Security, Palestinian

The security agency tasked with the personal protection of the president of the Palestinian Authority (PA). Al-Amn al-Riyasa (Palestinian Presidential Security, PPS) is largely composed of former elements of Force 17, the Palestinian security unit that protected Yasser Arafat during his exile from Israel. The force includes more than 3,000 highly trained individuals, split into two divisions. The Presidential Guard protects current PA president Mahmoud Abbas. The intelligence unit investigates domestic opposition to the president, including threats to his safety. Under Arafat, the intelligence division largely served to silence critics of his rule, while the Presidential Guard supplied many of his most trusted advisers.

The unit is one of 12 independent security organizations, all coordinated by the Palestinian General Security Services (PGSS). The PGSS was formally established by the 1993 Oslo Accords and subsequent Israeli-Palestinian peace initiatives. The PGSS was largely composed of existing security services, most of them under the personal control of Arafat. The PGSS, with its responsibility for Arafat's safety, was comprised of fanatically loyal officers who remained extremely well rewarded for their service. While nominally under the Interior Branch of the PGSS, presidential security forces have

Presidential security personnel in training in Ramallah prior to their deployment in the West Bank, June 2007. (Atef Safadi/epa/Corbis)

earned a reputation for operating independent of the formal security hierarchy. With the election of a Hamas-led government in January 2006, an international economic boycott of that government has prevented thousands of Palestinian civil servants from receiving their pay, provoking a crisis within the PGSS at large and the PPS in particular.

PAUL J. SPRINGER

See also

Abbas, Mahmoud; Arafat, Yasser; Oslo Accords; Palestinian General Security Services

References

Giacaman, George, and Dag Jorund Lonning, eds. *After Oslo: New Realities, Old Problems.* Chicago: Pluto, 1998.

Hunter, Robert E., and Seth G. Jones. *Building a Successful Palestinian State: Security.* Santa Monica, CA: RAND, 2006.

Preventive Security Organization, Palestinian

A branch of the Palestinian police force, established under the May 1994 Cairo Accord and further defined by the September 1995 Oslo II Agreement. The Palestinian police are responsible for security and law enforcement for Palestinians and other non-Israelis in areas of the West Bank and the Gaza Strip controlled by the Palestinian Authority (PA). The police are charged with the usual duties of a police force, including maintenance of internal order, protecting the public and public property, and preventing crime. The Oslo Agreement assigned to them the additional duties of combating terrorism and preventing incitements to violence.

The Palestinian Preventive Security Organization or Force (PSO) (al-Amn al-Wiqai) is a plainclothes unit, comprising some 5,000 armed members. Prior to the September 2000 outbreak of the Second (al-Aqsa) Intifada, the PSO proved itself to be reasonably effective, but its agents earned a reputation for human rights abuses, including abduction of civilians, harsh interrogations, and routine use of torture. The U.S. Central Intelligence Agency (CIA) maintained a close relationship with the PSO during the 1990s and provided extensive training to its agents. The PSO also worked closely with Israeli security and intelligence agencies in counterterrorism and crime prevention operations.

The PSO leadership has included powerful figures who were well connected politically within Palestine Liberation Organization (PLO) chairman Yasser Arafat's Fatah organization, including West Bank chief Colonel Jibril Rajub and Gaza Strip chief Colonel Muhammad Dahlan. Both were deeply involved in Fatah's rampant corruption. Given the PA's control over the lucrative import and export of goods and services, it is alleged that both Rajub and Dahlan made fortunes through graft and bribery.

As the Second Intifada unfolded, the PSO faced mounting criticism from hard-line Palestinian elements for its previous collaboration with Israel. To retain credibility with the Palestinian public, the PSO leadership transformed the organization and entered into clandestine cooperation with Palestinian terrorist organizations. In Gaza, its headquarters became a center for the manufacture and stockpiling of ammunition, explosives, and weapons and a safe haven for terrorists.

Dahlan and his deputy, Rashid Abu Shabak, facilitated the October 2000 creation of the Popular Resistance Committees (PRC), unifying the efforts of Palestinian armed groups such as the al-Aqsa Martyrs Brigades, Hamas, and the Islamic Jihad of Palestine. The PRC's ideology rested on nonrecognition of Israel's right to exist and support for violent jihad against Israel. The PSO leadership provided financial, logistical, and weapons support to terrorists, personally directing and sponsoring terror attacks. In October 2003, PSO chief Abu Shabak was involved in a deadly Gaza Strip convoy attack in which three American civilian contractor security guards were killed.

With the PSO then a part of the problem of violence, Israel changed its approach toward the organization, destroyed its headquarters, and marked its key leadership for arrest or assassination. Pressed by internal tensions and wary of their growing power, Arafat sacked both Dahlan and Rajub in June 2002 and instituted some limited reforms, whose principal effect was the tightening of his own control over the conduct of terror operations against Israel.

Arafat's death in November 2004 spurred the disintegration of Fatah's power and influence within the PA. Furthermore, Hamas's January 2006 electoral victory left PA president Mahmoud Abbas struggling to maintain control over the PSO. Estimates hold that about 40 percent of members of the Palestinian security forces voted for Hamas, which has now taken over the PSO's functions in Gaza.

CLARE M. LOPEZ

See also
Abbas, Mahmoud; Al-Aqsa Martyrs Brigades; Arafat, Yasser; Cairo Accord; Dahlan, Muhammad Yusuf; Fatah; Gaza Strip; Hamas; Intifada, Second; Islamic Jihad, Palestinian; Jihad; Oslo Accords; Palestinian Authority; Terrorism; West Bank

References
Cordesman, Anthony. *Palestinian Forces: Palestinian Authority and Militant Forces*. Washington, DC: Center for Strategic and International Studies, 2006.
Luft, Gal. "The Palestinian Security Services: Between Police and Army." *Middle East Review of International Affairs* 3(2) (June 1999): 1–3.
Parsons, Nigel Craig. *The Politics of the Palestinian Authority: From Oslo to Al-Aqsa*. London: Routledge, 2003.

Project Babylon

Iraqi attempt to develop a supergun capable of launching a small satellite into Earth's orbit or firing a weapon of mass destruction (WMD) against Israel. The director of Project Babylon was Dr. Gerald V. Bull, a Canadian aerophysical engineer who believed that specially designed guns could launch small payloads into orbit at a fraction of the cost of missile launches. In the early 1960s Bull was the director of the joint Canadian and American High Altitude Research Project (HARP). Based on the island of Barbados, he and his team managed to fire projectiles from a 7-inch gun to as high as 60 miles. By 1966 the HARP team working in Arizona fired a 185-pound projectile to an altitude of 108 miles using two welded-together tubes from 16-inch naval guns to form a barrel 30 meters long.

Despite the HARP team's impressive progress, funding for the project was cancelled in 1967. Frustrated at what he regarded as Canadian and American small-minded bureaucracy, Bull turned his impressive engineering talents to the design of conventional field artillery. In the 1970s he introduced the GC-45 howitzer. One of the most revolutionary artillery designs ever produced, the GC-45 was capable of accurately firing a 155-mm projectile to ranges of some 42,700 yards, almost double the maximum range of the American M-109 howitzer that was the standard of most Western armies of the time.

Reportedly with Central Intelligence Agency (CIA) funding, Bull sold a version of the gun, designated the G-5, to South Africa, which was then involved in a war with Angola. The G-5 vastly outranged and quickly defeated almost all of the Cuban artillery in Angola. By 1980, however, a change in the U.S. presidential administration and increasing world opposition to South Africa's apartheid regime eroded Bull's political protection. He was convicted of illegal arms sales and imprisoned in the United States for six months.

Upon his release, Bull established a company in Brussels and began to work with Iran, Chile, Taiwan, the People's Republic of China (PRC), and other countries. In the early 1980s he sold 200 of his GC-45 howitzers to Iraq. Designated the GHN-45 in Iraqi service, the guns quickly gave Iraq a significant tactical advantage in its war with Iran, which was armed primarily with aging American-built guns. Bull also helped modify the warheads of Iraq's Scud missiles to extend their range. Despite his previous conviction for illegal arms sales to South Africa, his work for Iraq had the covert support of many Western governments that viewed Iraq as a far lesser evil than Iran. When Iraqi dictator Saddam Hussein assumed an increasingly aggressive posture in the region following the Iran-Iraq War, that support evaporated.

Still trying to revive his old dream of launching satellites from large guns, Bull argued to Hussein that Iraq would never become a major power unless it could launch its own satellites, a capability already possessed by Israel. A supergun would be a relatively inexpensive and fast way for Iraq to achieve this. Such a gun also could be used to launch an antisatellite weapon designed to explode in the proximity of its target, either destroying it or at least neutralizing it. Hussein also might have believed that such a gun could be used to fire chemical or nuclear projectiles against Israel, although it is questionable whether Bull himself was thinking along those lines.

Bull started working on Project Babylon in March 1988. The initial prototype, dubbed Baby Babylon, was completed in May 1989 at Jabal Hamrayn, about 100 miles north of Baghdad. The barrel was 45 meters long with a 350-mm bore. The entire gun weighed close

United Nations (UN) weapons inspectors stand at the base of Iraq's supergun, November 1991. (Corel)

to 110 tons. Not designed to be mobile, it was emplaced on a hill-side at a fixed elevation of 45 degrees. That, of course, was too low an elevation to achieve the altitude necessary for an orbital shot, but it was the optimal elevation for maximum horizontal range, which has been estimated at some 450 miles.

Bull contracted with the Iraqis to build two full-size Babylon guns. With a bore of 1,000 mm, the barrel would be assembled from 26 sections, each 6 meters in length, for a total barrel length of 156 meters. The completed barrel would weigh 1,655 tons and the entire gun 2,100 tons. With a specially designed propellant charge that weighed almost 10 tons, the gun was designed to fire a 1,320-pound projectile to a range of some 600 miles or fire a 4,400-pound rocket-assisted projectile with a 440-pound payload into orbit. The launch cost would be less than $300 per pound.

Neither of the Babylon guns was ever completed. Bull was assassinated in Brussels on March 22, 1990. Although it is widely assumed that he was killed by operatives of Mossad, the Israeli agency responsible for intelligence and special operations outside Israel, the Israeli government has neither confirmed nor denied involvement. If Mossad did do it, it is far more likely that the reason was the work Bull was doing on extending the Iraqi Scuds rather than Project Babylon. As the Babylon guns were incapable of being elevated or traversed, the Israelis did not see them as a significant military threat. Their immobility also made them very vulnerable to air attack.

Project Babylon effectively died with Bull. In November 1990 British customs agents seized the final eight sections of the Babylon barrel that had been manufactured in the United Kingdom. At the end of the Persian Gulf War of 1991 the Iraqis admitted the existence of Project Babylon. United Nations (UN) teams destroyed the 350-mm Baby Babylon, the existing components of the 1,000-mm Babylon, and a quantity of supergun propellant. Some of the 1,000-mm barrel sections are on display at the Royal Armouries at Fort Nelson Museum in Portsmouth, England.

DAVID T. ZABECKI

See also

Artillery; Bull, Gerald Vincent; Mossad

References

Adams, James. *Bull's Eye: The Assassination and Life of Supergun Inventor Gerald Bull.* New York: Times Books, 1992.

Lowther, William. *Arms and the Man: Dr. Gerald Bull, Iraq, and the Supergun.* Novato, CA: Presidio, 1991.

Promised Land

Biblical reference to the land of Judea (Palestine) and Jerusalem, which God promised to Abraham and his descendants. Jews argue that the biblical books of Genesis, Ezekiel, and Isaiah foretold a literal return to Jerusalem and Israel. Until the late 19th century, many Christians, however, believed that Jerusalem, or Zion, was a metaphorical reference to heaven. The notion that Zion was only a metaphor for paradise supported the Arab perspective that centuries of residence on the Palestinian land justified Arab territorial claims over Jewish claims to the land.

During the 18 centuries of the Diaspora, Jews had always found hope in their notion of Zion. Jewish nationalism reemerged as a powerful political force in the late 19th century, particularly in Russia, as racist sentiments led to pogroms. In reaction, some Russian Jews began to turn to Zion.

As prejudices against Jews became more overt and widespread in Europe, as evidenced by events such as the Dreyfus Affair beginning in 1894, European Jews began to believe that only a separate, political entity could protect them from anti-Semitism. In 1896 Theodor Herzl published *Der Judenstaat* (*The Jewish State*) in which he called for a Jewish nation-state. This opened the floodgates, as it were, for Zionism among Jews the world over. Following World War II, the political idea that Jews required a state of their own, which the Holocaust seemed to confirm, merged with the religious belief that the Jews were fated to restore their nation.

The rise of nationalism and racism in 19th-century Europe also influenced Arab nationalism, which arose partly as a response to heightened tensions between Turks and Arabs. The British abetted Arab nationalism during World War I as a means of undermining the Ottoman Empire. Westerners then became torn between the Arab and Jewish perspectives during the first decades of the 20th century as more Christians came to reside in Palestine. Coupled with the rise of premillennialism that relied on a literal interpretation of the Bible among British and American evangelicals, more Christians became openly supportive of the Jewish position, leading to eventual American and British support for the establishment of the State of Israel.

LISA ROY VOX

See also
Anti-Semitism; Arab Nationalism; Genesis, Book of; Herzl, Theodor; Jerusalem; Zionism; Zionist Conference

References
Lustick, Ian S. *For the Land and the Lord: Jewish Fundamentalism in Israel.* New York: Council on Foreign Relations, 1988.

Vogel, Lester I. *To See a Promised Land: Americans and the Holy Land in the Nineteenth Century.* University Park: Pennsylvania State University Press, 1993.

Wilken, Robert L. "Early Christian Chiliasm, Jewish Messianism, and the Idea of the Holy Land." *Harvard Theological Review* 79(1–3) (January–July 1986): 298–307.

Q

Qabbani, Nizar
Born: March 21, 1923
Died: April 30, 1998

Syrian diplomat, poet, and publisher. Born in Damascus, Syria, on March 21, 1923, into a distinguished Syrian family, Nizar Qabbani (Kabbani) was educated at a time when strong conventions were observed both in subject matter and the form of Arabic poetry. His work broke with both sets of conventions. His father, a factory owner, supported the Syrian resistance to French rule and was several times arrested by the French, events that sharply affected Qabbani's own outlook.

Qabbani studied at the National Scientific College School in Damascus and then went on to the University of Damascus, where he graduated in 1945 with a law degree. He wrote his first collection of poems while still a college student when he was only 19 years old. Following his legal studies and with the establishment of an independent Syria at the end of World War II, he embarked on a diplomatic career. Although his publication of the poem "Bread, Hashish and a Moon" caused some Syrian parliament members to demand that he be fired from his job and put on trial, he continued his diplomatic career. From 1945 to 1966 he held diplomatic assignments in Cairo, Ankara, London, Beijing, Beirut, and Madrid.

Resigning from the diplomatic service in 1966, Qabbani established his own publishing house in Beirut. The death of his second wife, Balqis, in the bombing of the Iraqi embassy in Beirut in December 1981 during the Lebanese Civil War had a profound effect on Qabbani. He traveled to Europe and eventually moved to London.

Qabbani's first book made outspoken references to women's bodies, an Islamic taboo, and he challenged the traditions that constrained Arab women. When he was just a child, the suicide of his older sister Wisal, who took her own life when prohibited from marrying the man she loved, affected him deeply. He referred to Wisal as "the martyr for love," saying that she was "buried in the depths of my heart, not in the cemetery." Thus, in addition to writing volumes of overtly romantic poetry, which broke from the conservative conventions of traditional Arab literature, he often wrote about the oppression of women in Arab society, even addressing the issue of abortion and noting that the relationship of men and women in Arab society was not a healthy one.

Qabbani's work was thoroughly imbued with Arab nationalism and criticism of the ineffective leadership and hypocrisies of the Arab world. He idolized Gamal Abdel Nasser for standing up to the British, but Qabbani's poetry about the Arab defeat in the 1967 Six-Day War blamed the defeat on the Arab armies and the lack of freedom in the Arab world. As a result, his work was banned in Egypt. Many people obtained copies illegally, however, memorizing Qabbani's controversial words ("In a flash / You changed me from a poet who writes poems of love and longing / To a poet who writes with a knife"). Yet he mourned Nasser at his death with the poem "We Murdered the Prophet." Much of Qabbani's work assailed other Arab leaders, and in his 1990 poem "Abu Jahl" he reviled the Arab journalists whom he believed prostituted their profession to Gulf sponsors. Yet he supported Saddam Hussein of Iraq. Qabbani opposed censorship, including that which the Muslims wanted to impose on Salman Rushdie. Qabbani's opposition to authoritarian governments notwithstanding, he was revered as a national hero in Syria.

A frequent contributor to the Arabic-language newspaper *Al-Hayat,* Qabbani authored more than 35 collections of poetry and prose during his life. Among his early works were *Qalat liya al-samra'* (The Brunette Told Me), published in 1942, and *Tufulat nahd*

Syrian diplomat, poet, and publisher Nizar Qabbani. (AP/Wide World Photos)

(Childhood of a Breast), published in 1948. Several of his poems were used as the lyrics for songs by Arab singers Umm Kulthum, Abdel Halim Hafiz, Fayruz, and Najat al-Saghira and more recently by Majida al-Rumi and Kadhim al-Sahir. Qabbani died of a heart attack in London on April 30, 1998. He is often hailed as one of the great modern poets of the Arab world.

SPENCER C. TUCKER AND SHERIFA ZUHUR

See also

Literature of the Arab-Israeli Wars; Nasser, Gamal Abdel; Syria

References

Jayyusi, Lena, et al. *On Entering the Sea: The Erotic and Other Poetry of Nizar Qabbani.* Northampton, MA: Interlink, 1996.
Kabbani, Nizar. *Arabian Love Poems.* Boulder, CO: Lynne Rienner, 1998.

Qaddafi, Muammar
Born: June 1942

Libyan military officer and head of state (1970–present). Born the youngest child of a nomadic Bedouin family in the al-Nanja community in Fezzan in June 1942, Muammar Qaddafi attended the Sebha preparatory school from 1956 to 1961. He subsequently graduated from the University of Libya in 1963, the same year he entered the Military Academy at Benghazi, where he became part of a cabal of young military officers whose plans included the overthrow of Libya's pro-Western monarchy.

Qaddafi and the secret corps of militant, Pan-Arabist officers seized power in Libya on September 1, 1969, following a bloodless coup that overthrew King Idris. After a brief internal power struggle that consolidated his rule, Qaddafi renamed the country the Libyan Arab Republic and officially ruled as president of the Revolutionary Command Council from 1970 to 1977. He then switched his title to president of the People's General Congress during 1977–1979. In 1979 he renounced all official titles but remained the unrivaled head of Libya.

Domestically, Qaddafi's reign was based upon Islamic socialism. Loosely following the model of his hero, Egyptian president Gamal Abdel Nasser, Qaddafi promoted a middle path that was neither communist nor Western. He sought the privatization of major corporations, the creation of a social welfare system, and the establishment of state-sponsored education and health care systems. He also outlawed alcohol and gambling. His political, economic, and Islamic ideas are included within his Green Book. Qaddafi's regime encompassed a dark side, however, including the sometimes violent suppression of Libyan dissidents and the sanctioning of state-sponsored assassinations.

In foreign policy, Qaddafi promoted the ideals of Pan-Africanism, Pan-Arabism and anti-imperialism. He was a major proponent of the Organization for African Unity (OAU) and supported various anticolonial liberation struggles in sub-Saharan Africa, including those in Mozambique and Angola. He also supported Zimbabwe's Robert Mugabe and was a staunch ally of Nelson Mandela and the African National Congress (ANC) in South Africa, stances that annoyed the United States, which had maintained a certain loyalty to European interests in Africa and viewed the South African apartheid regime as a bulwark against communism.

Qaddafi's Middle East policies further alienated him from the West. He viewed himself as heir to Nasser's notion of Pan-Arabism, which sought to unify all Arab states into one Arab nation. In 1972 Qaddafi proposed a union of Libya, Egypt, and Syria, and in 1974 he signed a tentative alliance agreement with Tunisia, although neither scheme worked out. At the same time, he became a strong supporter of the Palestine Liberation Organization (PLO) and is rumored to have been a chief financier of the radical Islamic Black September organization, which most notoriously engineered the killing of Israeli athletes at the 1972 Munich Olympics. He was also linked to other non-Arab movements such as the Irish Republican Army (IRA) and terrorist attacks, including the December 1988 bombing of a Pan Am 747 airline jet over Lockerbie, Scotland. As with many other Arab nationalists, Qaddafi generally held a visceral hatred for the State of Israel, which he viewed as a tool of Western imperial domination. He made frequent threats of engaging Israel militarily and expressed public hope that the nation could be wiped

Libyan leader Muammar Qaddafi at a news conference on the island of Majorca during a meeting with Spanish prime minister Felipe González, December 18, 1984. (Bettmann/Corbis)

off the map. He also urged several African states to withdraw support for Israel as a precondition for receiving foreign aid.

Qaddafi's ties to Islamic terrorism drove a deep wedge in Libyan-U.S. relations. By the early 1980s, he had marginally allied himself with and received significant weapons supplies from the Soviet Union. Meanwhile, tensions between Libya and the United States reached fever pitch during the presidency of Ronald Reagan. In 1986 Reagan authorized the U.S. bombing of Tripoli in retaliation for the bombing of a West Berlin discotheque, which had been tied directly to Qaddafi. The bombing raid, designed to kill Qaddafi, instead killed his infant adopted daughter and scores of civilians.

The end of the Cold War witnessed an easing of tensions in U.S.-Libyan relations as Qaddafi took a more conciliatory stance toward the West. He publicly apologized for the Lockerbie bombing and offered compensation to victims' families. He also openly condemned the September 11, 2001, terrorist attacks in the United States and has taken a more moderate line in the Palestinian-Israeli conflict. In February 2004, Libya renounced its weapons of mass destruction (WMDs) program, and that June the United States and

Libya resumed formal diplomatic relations, after which most economic sanctions against Libya were lifted.

JEREMY KUZMAROV

See also

Black September Organization; Camp David Accords; Libya; Munich Olympic Games; Nasser, Gamal Abdel; Palestine Liberation Organization

References

Davis, Brian L. *Qaddafi, Terrorism and the Origins of the U.S. Attack on Libya.* New York: Praeger, 1990.
Lemarchand, Rene. *The Green and the Black: Qadhafi Policies in Africa.* Bloomington: Indiana University Press, 1988.
Sicker, Martin. *The Making of a Pariah State.* New York: Westport, 1987.
Vanderwalle, Dirk, ed. *Qadhafi Libya, 1969–1994.* New York: St. Martin's, 1995.

Qassam, Izz al-Din al-
Born: 1882
Died: November 20, 1935

Arab nationalist and militant credited with helping to instigate the Great Palestinian Rebellion (or Arab Revolt) of 1936–1939. Born in Jaballah, Syria, in 1882, Izz al-Din al-Qassam was sent at age 14 to Cairo to study at al-Azhar University. He returned to Syria in 1903, then returned to Alexandria, Egypt, to try to create an armed force to fight the Italians in Libya. He also studied Sharia (Islamic law). In 1922 he moved to Haifa in the British Mandate for Palestine. He led a masjid and taught militant and charismatic religious leaders who believed in the necessity of armed struggle, and he was also a representative of the Naqshabandi Sufi order and was elected the head of the Young Men's Muslim Association in 1928. He was then made a registrar for the Islamic court in the Haifa area. Al-Qassam attracted many followers, particularly from among the lower classes, and believed in both Arab and Muslim solidarity.

Al-Qassam argued for the immediate departure from Palestine of both the British and the Jews. When Mufti Haj Amin al-Husseini rejected al-Qassam's plan to transfer funds dedicated to mosque repairs in order to purchase weapons, al-Qassam proceeded to organize a military effort on his own in response to the British firing on a crowd of Palestinian demonstrators. Leading a group against the British at Ya'bud outside the town of Jenin, he was killed on November 20, 1935. He is regarded by Palestinian militants as a hero and martyr. His followers, the Qassamiyun, or Izz al-Din al-Qassam Brigades, fought in the 1936–1939 Arab Revolt. The Hamas military divisions and the Qassam rocket, which is employed by both Hamas and Hezbollah, are named for him.

SPENCER C. TUCKER

See also

Arab Revolt of 1936–1939; Hamas; Hezbollah; Husseini, Haj Amin al-; Nabhani, Taqi al-Din al-; Qassam Rocket

References

Nafi, Basheer M. "Shaykh 'Izz Al-Din Al-Qassam: A Reformist and a Rebel Leader." *Journal of Islamic Studies* 8(2) (1997): 185–215.

Schleifer, Abdullah. "Izz al-Din al-Qassam: Preacher and Mujahid."
Pp. 164–178 in *Struggle and Survival in the Modern Middle East,*
edited by Edmund Burke III. Berkeley: University of California Press,
1993.

Sherman, A. J. *Mandate Days: British Lives in Palestine, 1918–1948.*
Baltimore: Johns Hopkins University Press, 2001.

Wasserstein, Bernard. *The British in Palestine: The Mandatory
Government and Arab-Jewish Conflict.* London: Blackwell, 1991.

Qassam Rocket

Locally fabricated weapon used to launch terror attacks against Israel. The Qassam rocket was developed to surmount the security barrier between Israel and the Gaza Strip. Almost all Qassam attacks have been launched from Gaza, either into Israel proper or against the Israeli settlements in Gaza prior to the Israeli pullout in 2005. Most of the attacks have been conducted by Hamas, but Palestinian Islamic Jihad and the al-Aqsa Martyrs Brigades have also launched Qassams.

The rockets are named after Sheikh Izz al-Din al-Qassam, a militant cleric who in the 1920s and 1930s advocated rebellion and formed a military force of Palestinians who fought the British. The rockets are generally crudely made and wildly inaccurate and have a relatively short range. They can, however, be set in place and fired within a matter of minutes, making them ideal hit-and-run harassment weapons.

The first Qassam rocket was launched against Israel in October 2001, but the rocket never made it out of Gaza. The first Qassam rocket to strike Israeli territory was launched on February 10, 2002. The first Israeli city hit by a Qassam rocket was Sderot on March 5, 2002. The first Israelis killed by Qassam fire were two children, ages

Remains of Qassam rockets fired from the Gaza Strip into Israel, April 21, 2007. (Mark Neyman/Israeli Government Press Office)

two and four, in Sderot on September 29, 2004. By mid-2006, more than 1,000 Qassams had been launched, only 1 from the West Bank.

Propelled by a crude mixture of potassium nitrate and sugar, the Qassam rocket has evolved since its introduction. The Qassam-1 rocket was less than 3 feet long and 60 mm in diameter. It weighed about 12 pounds and had a warhead of just more than 1 pound. Its range was only 3,000 yards. The Qassam-2, which appeared in 2002, is 6 feet long and 150 mm in diameter. It weighs some 80 pounds and has a warhead of up to 15 pounds. It has maximum range of slightly more than 10,000 yards. The Qassam-3, which appeared at the start of 2005, is 6.5 feet long and 200 mm in diameter. It weighs almost 200 pounds and has a 45-pound warhead. Its maximum range varies between 11,000 and 22,000 yards. New variants of the Qassam continue to appear. In July 2006, militants fired a Qassam rocket with two engines.

DAVID T. ZABECKI

See also

Al-Aqsa Martyrs Brigades; Gaza Strip Disengagement; Hamas; Islamic Jihad, Palestinian

Reference

Karon, Tony. "The Homemade Rocket That Could Change the Mideast." *Time Magazine,* February 10, 2002.

Qassem, Abdul Karim
Born: November 21, 1914
Died: February 8, 1963

Iraqi general and leader of a 1958 coup that overthrew the British-imposed monarch King Faisal II, sweeping away the last vestiges of colonial rule in Iraq. Abdul Karim Qassem (Kassem), son of a Sunni Arab and a Shia Kurdish mother, was born in a poor section of Baghdad on November 21, 1914. His father raised corn along the Tigris River, and as a young boy Qassem experienced poverty, which influenced his later efforts at social reform. He attended school in Baghdad, and at age 17, following a brief period teaching elementary school (1931–1932), he enrolled in the Iraqi Military College. Two years later, in 1934, he graduated as a second lieutenant. In 1935 he took part in suppressing unrest in the middle Euphrates region of Iraq.

In December 1941 Qassem graduated with honors from the al-Arkan (General Staff) College and became a staff officer. In 1942 while stationed in Basra near the Persian Gulf, he struck up a friendship with Abd al-Salam Arif. The two men shared a desire to overthrow the Iraqi monarchy. In 1945 Qassem commanded a battalion against rebellious Kurdish tribesmen in northern Iraq, a campaign that earned him the highest Iraqi military decoration.

In 1948 during the Israeli War of Independence (1948–1949), Qassem commanded a battalion of the Iraqi 1st Brigade in Palestine. Following the Arab defeat, he attended a senior officers' school in Britain for six months. Upon his return to Iraq, he was promoted to colonel and a year later attained the rank of brigadier general. During the Suez Crisis of 1956, he commanded Iraqi troops in Jor-

Abdul Karim Qassem, Iraqi general and leader of a 1958 coup that overthrew the British-imposed monarch King Faisal II. (Central Press/Hulton Archive/Getty Images)

dan, where his schooling and his combat experience earned him respect and prominence.

In 1956 Qassem helped organize and then headed the central organization of the Free Officers, a clandestine association working to overthrow the Iraqi monarchy. He worked closely with Arif waiting for the right moment to stage a coup. That time came in 1958 when a revolt broke out in Jordan followed by a crisis in Lebanon, and the Iraqi monarchy ordered troops into Jordan.

Arif's battalion entered Baghdad on July 13 en route to Jordan, but on the next day his troops occupied the central radio studio and proclaimed the overthrow of the king. The following day, the king, the crown prince, some other members of the royal family, and Prime Minister Nuri al-Said Pasha were assassinated. Qassem arrived in Baghdad with his troops after the assassinations. Some historians attribute the apparent delay in his arrival to a calculated decision to allow Arif to take the initial risk. Regardless, Qassem became prime minister and minister of defense, with Arif as deputy prime minister and interior minister.

Disputes soon arose between Qassem and Arif over the direction of the revolutionary government. Arif was more popular with the crowds than Qassem, and this also led to tension. Arif favored the unionist wing of the Baathists who first argued for unity with Egypt and later Syria, while Qassem was attempting to balance the Baath Party with its several factions against the Arab nationalists

and the communists. These tensions eventually resulted in a showdown with Arif and his imprisonment on charges of conspiracy.

Qassem allowed the Communist Party to operate, and he embarked on serious land reform to address rural poverty. The new government launched a series of attacks on opponents that prompted a public outcry. Two incidents in particular inspired revulsion. The first occurred in March 1959 when Qassem's communist allies, after crushing a revolt by army units in Mosul, went on a rampage, killing anticommunist supporters of the rebellion. The second incident occurred later that summer when Kurdish communists were involved in massacres, particularly of Turcomen in Kirkuk.

Meanwhile, Qassem launched several important domestic and foreign policy reforms. First, he addressed the maldistribution of land by limiting the size of holdings. Second, he expanded women's rights in the areas of marriage, divorce, and inheritance. Third, in a highly successful move, he reduced the influence of oil companies by confiscating large amounts of land held by the foreign-owned Iraq Petroleum Company. This step prepared the way for full nationalization in 1973.

In foreign affairs Qassem followed a policy of nonalignment, but his actions, including substantial arms purchases from communist-bloc nations, tilted Iraq toward the Soviet Union. Relations with Egypt deteriorated, encouraging unionists to contemplate Qassem's overthrow. In October 1959 the Iraqi branch of the Arab Baath Socialist Party concluded that Qassem's policies, particularly his antagonism toward Egypt and alliance with the communists, necessitated his removal. The Baathists plotted to kill Qassem in the streets of Baghdad, and on October 7 they attacked but only succeeded in wounding him. Several of the conspirators fled Iraq, including the young Saddam Hussein.

Following this attempt on his life, Qassem permitted the free organization of political parties but only if they did not threaten national unity. In practice, this meant that no independent party could exist, a fact confirmed in late 1960 when Qassem suppressed all parties. His increasingly narrow support became restricted to segments of the military, and he lived an increasingly isolated existence, barricaded in the office of the Ministry of Defense.

Qassem's growing unpopularity was exacerbated by two military failures. One was the inability to quell a Kurdish rebellion in northern Iraq. The second was his bungled attempt to absorb Kuwait in 1961, when he announced that the small Persian Gulf nation was in reality a renegade Iraqi province. When British and later Arab League troops moved to protect Kuwait, Qassem was forced to back down. Another blow came in the form of an economic slump. All these factors led to growing disaffection in the army, Qassem's last bastion of support. On February 8, 1963, a military coup led by Arif Baathists toppled Qassem. Following a bloody street battle, he was captured and executed. Qassem achieved much in societal reform, health, education, housing for the poor, and agriculture, but perhaps his greatest accomplishment was the establishment of a truly independent Iraq.

NEIL HAMILTON AND SPENCER C. TUCKER

See also

Faisal II, King of Iraq; Iraq; Iraq, Armed Forces; Israeli War of
Independence, Overview; Nasser, Gamal Abdel; Suez Crisis; United
Arab Republic

References

Batatu, Hanna. *The Old Social Classes and the Revolutionary Movements
of Iraq: A Study of Iraq's Old Landed and Commercial Classes and of Its
Communists, Ba'thists and Free Officers.* Princeton, NJ: Princeton
University Press, 1978.

Dann, Uriel. *Iraq under Qassem: A Political History, 1958–1963.* New
York: Praeger, 1969.

Khadduri, Majid. *Republican Iraq: A Study in Iraqi Politics during the
Revolution of 1958.* Oxford: Oxford University Press, 1969.

Makiya, Kanaan [Khalil, Samir al-]. *Republic of Fear: The Politics of
Modern Iraq.* Berkeley: University of California Press, 1998.

Marr, Phebe. *The Modern History of Iraq.* 2nd ed. Boulder, CO: Westview,
2003.

Qawuqji, Fawzi al-

Born: 1890
Died: December 1976

Arab nationalist and insurgency commander. Born in Tripoli in
present-day Libya in 1890, Fawzi al-Qawuqji (Kaukji) pursued a
military career and served as a junior officer in the Ottoman Army
during World War I. In the wake of the defeat, he joined the struggle to assert Arab interests in the face of European occupation and
Zionist inroads in Palestine.

Al-Qawuqji greatly resented the British and French occupation
of Arab lands after World War I and became a regional leader of
the Great Syrian Revolt (1925–1927), which sought unsuccessfully
to end French rule there. After the resistance faded, he fled via Iraq
to the Hejaz in western Arabia with the other fighters and Sultan
al-Atrash.

Defeat and exile did not deter al-Qawuqji, who emerged as a key
figure in the Arab drive for self-determination. For a time he served
as a military adviser to Ibn Saud, future king of Saudi Arabia. In
1932 al-Qawuqji made his way to Iraq, where he joined the Iraqi
Army and became an instructor at the military college in Baghdad.
Over the next few years, his image as a fervent Arab nationalist and
a legendary military figure seemingly made him the ideal man to
lead the next regional uprising. In 1936 he was encouraged to take
command of contingents of armed volunteers in the struggle against
British rule in Palestine and the stream of Jewish immigrants into
the mandate.

Despite numbering only in the hundreds of men, al-Qawuqji's
forces quickly elevated the quality of Arab resistance, as they included both veteran fighters and professional soldiers. However,
facing thousands of British troops and an Arab decision to suspend
the fighting, his men eventually had to retreat back across the Jordan River in October 1936.

During al-Qawuqji's brief stay in Palestine, he also embroiled
himself in local politics and generated a mutual enmity for Haj Amin

Fawzi al-Qawuqji, military officer, Arab nationalist, and commander of
Arab units opposing British rule in Palestine, shown here as an Iraqi
Army officer in September 1936. (Austrian Archives/Corbis)

---

al-Husseini, the mufti of Jerusalem. The bitter rivalry between the
two men, in a sense symbolic of Arab divisions over the fate of Palestine, would intensify during the decade following the 1939 defeat of
the Arab Revolt in the mandate. As fellow nationalists, al-Qawuqji
and al-Husseini reluctantly collaborated, first during the failed
Iraqi uprising against the British in 1941 and later as joint exiles
in Nazi Germany, but throughout those years the friction between
them grew.

Tensions hardly lessened with al-Qawuqji's appointment in
1947 to be field commander of the Arab Liberation Army (ALA), a
motley fighting force sponsored by the Arab League and intended
for deployment to Palestine. Organized and trained in southern
Syria, the ALA gradually slipped into the mandate during the early
months of 1948, and by April shortly after al-Qawuqji arrived to
assume direct command, the ALA of some 7,500 men was poised
to begin major operations.

The ALA, heavily influenced by Syrian interests (Syrians made
up about a third of the force), was as much sent to block the ambitions of Jordan and those of al-Husseini as to fight Jewish military
forces. During the weeks before the neighboring Arab states directly
joined the conflict, al-Qawuqji failed to achieve any significant suc-

cesses on the field of battle, and it is even asserted that he intentionally withheld men and supplies from assisting the Palestinian forces loyal to al-Husseini. The ALA commander later rejected such criticisms. He instead blamed the Arab League for poor logistical support and attributed the overall defeat of Arab forces to the lack of a unified command.

Al-Qawuqji's participation in the Israeli War of Independence ended by November 1948. His remaining ALA forces, unable to further resist a superior enemy, retreated permanently from Palestine. The defeat disillusioned al-Qawuqji greatly, as he soon retired from military service and withdrew entirely from public life. He published his memoirs in 1975 and died in Beirut, Lebanon, in December 1976.

JONAS KAUFFELDT

See also

Arab League; Arab Liberation Army; Husseini, Haj Amin al-; Israeli War of Independence, Overview; Zionism

References

Morris, Benny. *Righteous Victims: A History of the Zionist-Arab Conflict, 1881–2001.* New York: Vintage Books, 2001.

Pollack, Kenneth M. *Arabs at War: Military Effectiveness, 1948–1991.* Lincoln: University of Nebraska Press, 2002.

Porath, Yehoshua. *The Palestinian Arab National Movement: From Riots to Rebellion.* London: Frank Cass, 1977.

Provence, Michael. *The Great Syrian Revolt.* Austin: University of Texas Press, 2005.

Rogan, Eugene L., and Avi Shlaim, eds. *The War for Palestine: Rewriting the History of 1948.* Cambridge: Cambridge University Press, 2001.

Qibya Massacre
Event Date: October 14, 1953

Israel assault on the West Bank village of Qibya on October 14, 1953, that resulted in the deaths of some 60 Palestinians and the nearly wholesale destruction of the town. At the time, the West Bank was under Jordanian administration. Code-named Operation SHOSHANA by the Israel Defense Forces (IDF), the Qibya attack was launched soon after nightfall and carried out by a unit of Israeli paratroopers, a specialized force of counterinsurgency troops known as Unit 101 that was commanded by Major Ariel Sharon, who much later became the Israeli prime minister.

The Israeli government asserted that the Qibya raid was in retaliation for a steady stream of Palestinian attacks and incursions via Jordan and the West Bank that had killed scores of Israeli citizens since late 1949. In 1953 the pace and severity of the Palestinian raids had increased dramatically, so much so that 32 Israelis had died from January to September alone. The immediate triggering event was the October 12, 1953, murders of a Jewish woman and her two young children in the village of Yehud, Israel. Determined to exact revenge on the Palestinians, Israeli defense minister Pinhas Lavon, in consultation with Prime Minister David Ben-Gurion, made plans

for a quick and heavy retaliation. Qibya was chosen because of its close proximity to the Israeli border and the fact that several Palestinian attacks had seemed to come from there.

The assault on Qibya commenced with an Israeli artillery strike as IDF ground forces moved into position. Roads leading to and from the village were mined to prevent the Jordanians from sending in reinforcements and to cause maximum damage to fighters trying to flee the town. IDF forces maintain that they conducted a house-to-house search to warn civilians to leave the area. Palestinians dispute that this occurred. After the village had been secured militarily, IDF troops blew up a number of homes that had not already been leveled by the artillery barrage. Many Palestinians thus died because they either never received the warnings from the IDF or could not leave their homes as they were being fired on. At dusk the following morning, 60 Palestinians lay dead, and an undetermined number were injured. The dead included a high percentage of women and children. Forty-five houses, the village mosque, the school, and water facilities lay in ruins. The Israelis then withdrew across the border in the early hours of the morning.

A high degree of uncertainty and conflicting stories exist as to what precisely happened in Qibya that night. The IDF claimed that it had given fair warning to the villagers before the fight began, but it is also likely that the initial artillery strike killed several villagers, who at that point would have had no warning at all. Sharon himself said that he believed all the homes demolished by explosives had been empty, but other reports claim that those who died in their homes had been forced at gunpoint to remain in them and had not been given the chance to escape before they were blown up.

Initially, the Israeli government tried to downplay the raid. Indeed, when news of the raid first came to light, Ben-Gurion's government denied having had anything to do with it. Ben-Gurion claimed it had been carried out by civilians. This denial did not wash, however, and as word of the massacre circulated, the Israeli government came under harsh criticism from many Israelis. On the international front, the Qibya Massacre was a public relations catastrophe for the Israelis. Virtually every Western nation including the United States denounced the attack, and the United Nations (UN) Security Council passed a resolution that November condemning the raid. Clearly, the Qibya Massacre only served to enrage Palestinian guerrillas all the more.

PAUL G. PIERPAOLI JR.

See also

Ben-Gurion, David; Israel; Israel Defense Forces; Sharon, Ariel; West Bank

References

Laqueur, Walter, and Barry Rubin, eds. *The Israel-Arab Reader: A Documentary History of the Middle East Conflict.* London: Penguin, 2001.

Morris, Benny. *Israel's Border Wars, 1949–1956: Arab Infiltration, Israeli Retaliation, and the Countdown to the Suez War.* Oxford, UK: Clarendon, 1993.

Pappe, Ilan. *The Making of the Arab-Israeli Conflict, 1949–1951.* London: Tauris, 1994.

Qumran and the Dead Sea Scrolls

Qumran (Qumrun, Qumron) was a second-century BC to second-century AD Essene settlement, a persecuted messianic and apocalyptic Jewish sect located 13 miles east of Jerusalem in the desert and just east of 11 cliff-side caves in which the Dead Sea Scrolls were discovered between 1947 and 1956.

The first settlement was established on the site during the eighth to seventh centuries BC and was resettled in the second century BC when the Essenes, then numbering about 4,000 throughout Judea and Syria, began to separate from Judaism and the then-Hebrew Hasmonean rulers of Judea. The persecution of the Essenes began after the Maccabees wrested control of the area from Seleucid Empire ruler Antiochus IV (ruled 175–163 BC). The Jews led by a Hasmonean Jewish priest named Mattathias and then his son Judas Maccabeus rebelled (167–164 BC), and on the 25th day of Kislev in 165 BC they retook the Temple that Antiochus had desecrated with swine's blood.

The cleansing and rededication of the Temple is remembered annually in the Jewish festival of Hanukkah. The Essenes began expanding their community at Qumran around 160 BC in response to Jonathan Maccabeus's rise to power as the founder of the Hebrew Hasmonean dynasty in Judea (161–143 BC). Jonathan attempted to solidify his power base by naming himself the high priest (153 BC) in violation of Jewish law and the traditional prohibition against any Hebrew king being both king and priest. The persecution of the Essenes began after they opposed this commandeering of the high priesthood. From this time forward, the Essenes considered any high priest and all of the priests in Jerusalem to be ungodly and illegitimate. The persecution of the Essenes increased when Jonathan's youngest brother Simon Maccabeus (ruled 143–135 BC) assumed the throne and, against the continued opposition of the Essenes, the high priesthood.

Much of what physically remains of the Qumran settlement was constructed during the reigns of the Hasmonean kings John Hyrcanus I (134–104 BC) and his son Alexander Jannaeus (103–76 BC). An earthquake in 31 BC and a fire during the reign of Herod the Great (37–4 BC) caused the site to be abandoned for a short period. Rebuilt, it remained inhabited until the First Jewish Revolt (AD 66–73), when the Romans under General Vespasian destroyed it in the summer of AD 68. Roman soldiers were garrisoned there until about AD 73.

The 1947 discovery by Bedouin of the Dead Sea Scrolls in a cave west of Qumran led to an organized search of the area in 1949. This exploration was carried out under the joint auspices of the Depart-

The excavation of the ancient Jewish settlement at Qumran, near the Qumran Caves north of the Dead Sea, 1982. (Herman Chanania/Israeli Government Press Office)

Professor James Bieberkraut of Hebrew University works on the restoration of one of the Dead Sea Scrolls, February 1955. (Israeli Government Press Office)

compose a portion of the Dead Sea Scrolls, and the writings of Philo Judaeus (20 BC–AD 40), Pliny the Elder (AD 23–79), and the Jewish historian Flavius Josephus (AD 37–100).

The Essenes lived in small communities throughout Judea and Syria, but Qumran is the best-known and perhaps the largest of their settlements. The Essenes were ascetics who lived communally and subsisted on farming, as participation in any form of trade or commerce was forbidden for fear that it might taint the community. They held their property in community, met the needs of each member, and ate together, especially at times of great messianic feasts. They ritually bathed and wore white as part of their active prayer and worship lives. The Essenes forbade animal sacrifice, swearing, oath taking (except for entry into the sect), and the making of weapons.

The Essenes were Sabbath and Torah observant, meaning that they strictly followed the Hebrew Bible (Tanakh) laws concerning the Sabbath and studied the Torah, the first five books of the Hebrew Scriptures, as well as other books of the Tanakh, which the Christians later adopted as their Old Testament. The Essenes had an organized religious leadership that oversaw the community and instructed its members. The Essenes asserted that the community's past and present spiritual leaders, known as correct expositors or teachers of righteousness, rightly divined the scriptures and that the Essenes were the repositories of that true understanding.

Essene beliefs and practices were messianic and apocalyptic. They anticipated a final expositor and prophet known as the Teacher of Righteousness who may or may not have appeared and may or may not have been killed by the Jerusalem priestly establishment. They also anticipated a concluding war between themselves—the true followers of God, the sons of light—and the sons of darkness, generally regarded to have been the priestly and aristocratic Sadducean establishment in Jerusalem. They believed themselves to be the true priesthood and the true Israel. The Essenes were baptistic, believing that baptism symbolized repentance and entry into the presence of the Elect of God. Some modern scholars have advanced the theory that John the Baptist was an Essene. Entry into full membership in the community followed a two- to three-year probationary period finalized by an oath committing oneself to the complete obedience to the community standards, practices, and beliefs. A member who broke the oath faced expulsion.

The Dead Sea Scrolls are a collection of an estimated 800–870 separate scrolls plus roughly 15,000 small and brittle scroll fragments torn and broken from the more than 500 additional manuscripts. The Bedouin who discovered the original 7 scrolls sold them to two antiquities dealers in Bethlehem who in turn sold 4 of the scrolls to Athanasius Samuel, the Syrian Orthodox Metropolitan at St. Mark's Monastery. The other 3 scrolls were sold to Hebrew University archaeologist E. L. Sukenik, the father of Yigal Yadin, the second chief of staff of the Israel Defense Forces (IDF). The initial sales prompted the Bedouin to search for more scrolls, and some thought that more money could be generated by selling the manuscripts in pieces. In 1955 Yadin earned his doctorate in archaeology,

ment of Antiquities of Jordan (the site was in Jordan at that time), the Dominican École Biblique et Archéologique of Jerusalem, and the Palestine Archaeological Museum, now the Rockefeller Museum. This search located 10 additional caves, some of them lined with shelves as if they were used as libraries and others filled with debris that led to speculation that those scrolls and fragments may have been dumped there during the First Jewish Revolt. The primary archaeological excavation of Qumran began under the French archaeologist Roland de Vaux in 1951 and lasted until 1956. The work unearthed a large cistern that fed the extensive Jewish ritual baths as well as a possible scriptorium (an area dedicated to copying and studying sacred writings), a large room that could have been used for assemblies or communal dining. Also uncovered were a watchtower, storage and living facilities, and a nearby cemetery with more than 1,000 graves.

There is no mention of the Essenes in the Bible or any rabbinical literature of the period. What is known of the lifestyle, religious practices, and beliefs has been deduced from the organization of the community, the community manuals and commentaries that studying the Dead Sea Scrolls, at Hebrew University. He happened to be lecturing in New York in 1955 when he noticed an advertisement by Metropolitan Samuel seeking to sell the 4 scrolls in his possession. Yadin convinced the Israeli government to buy the scrolls for $250,000.

Based on the theory that the Essenes began developing their community at Qumran in 200 BC and the fact that it was destroyed in AD 68, it is believed that the majority of the Dead Sea Scrolls were compiled, copied, or written in that period. However, many of the manuscripts, the manuscript of Isaiah in particular, date much closer to the original date of traditional authorship. This means that at least some of the biblical material in the corpus is much older than Qumran's Essene community.

Approximately 30 percent of the material is from the Hebrew Bible, including at least 19 copies of the book of Isaiah, 25 copies of Deuteronomy, and 30 copies of the Psalms. The only book of the Hebrew Bible not found is the book of Esther. A fragment of what is believed to be the book of Nehemiah has also been found. This corpus is the oldest Old Testament manuscript collection known to exist and is remarkable for the lack of variation in the multiple copies. In a similar vein, a comparison of these copies to those generated by the Masoretes during the 7th to 11th centuries AD demonstrates that there were very few copying errors over this 900–1,300-year span.

Additional material concerning biblical figures was also found. There were heretofore unknown prophecies ascribed to Ezekiel, Jeremiah, and Daniel; the last words of Joseph, Judah, Levi, Naphtali, and Amram (the father of Moses) were recorded; unknown psalms attributed to David and Joshua were found; and there were unknown stories concerning biblical figures such as Enoch, Abraham, and Noah. Abraham's story includes an explanation of why God asked Abraham to sacrifice Isaac. This story and its date are problematic for Islam, however. Islamic apologists generally assert that unknown Jews at an unknown time altered the book of Genesis to elevate Isaac to the position of the first son and Isaac's descendants, the Jews, to being the Chosen People of God with a divine right to the land now occupied by Israel. This find and the copy of Genesis are problematic in that they assert the Chosen People status of the Jews at least 800 years before Muhammad and long before most Islamic scholars assert that the change was first made.

About 25 percent of the corpus consists of noncanonical traditional religious texts from the Intertestamental Period, the approximately 400 years between Malachi, the last book of the Old Testament canon, and Matthew, the first book of the New Testament canon. These texts include the Apocryphal books of Enoch, Jubilees, and the Testament of Levi.

Approximately 30 percent of the corpus is composed of what appears to be Essene-based Bible commentaries and material related to the practice and faith of the Essene community, such as the Community Rule, also known as the Discipline Scroll or Manual of Discipline, and the War Scroll, also known by the name War of the Sons of Light against the Sons of Darkness. The last 15 percent of the corpus is yet to be identified.

There is no New Testament literature included in the corpus. There are some factions that argue that Jesus was actually the Teacher of Righteousness, that the Teacher of Righteousness was actually a foreshadowing of Jesus, or that the Teacher of Righteousness was the forerunner of Muhammad. Still others claim that the Essene community was more indigenously Palestinian than Jewish.

Most of the Dead Sea Scrolls were written in one of three Hebrew variations: proto-Hebrew, believed to date from the 10th to 8th centuries BC; biblical or classical Hebrew, common in the 7th through 6th centuries BC; and Dead Sea Scroll Hebrew that dates from the 3rd century BC to the 1st century AD. There is also material written in Aramaic, the language of Judea at the time of Jesus, and Koine Greek. There is little punctuation in the manuscripts, and in some cases there are no spaces between the words.

Most of the scrolls were written on brownish animal skins that may be *gevil,* an ancient Hebrew writing surface. Some of the corpus was written on papyrus, and one, the Copper Scroll, has text incised on thin sheets of copper. The Copper Scroll is also unique in that it contains a list of 64 underground sites throughout Israel that contain gold, silver, aromatics, manuscripts, and perhaps even treasures from the Temple in Jerusalem.

Each manuscript and scroll was numbered based on the cave from which it was retrieved. Although the major intact texts were published by the late 1950s, much of the corpus remained unpublished and unavailable for study even for academics. However, in September 1991 after scholars at Cincinnati's Hebrew Union College created a computer-generated text from fragments published in concordance, the two repositories of the unpublished material—the Huntington Library, Art Collections, and Botanical Gardens of San Marino, California, and the Israel Antiquities Authority—made photographs of the material available.

Most of the scrolls and fragments are now housed in the Shrine of the Book and the Rockefeller Museum in Jerusalem and the Museum of the Department of Antiquities in Amman, Jordan.

RICHARD EDWARDS

See also

Archaeological Sites and Projects; Genesis, Book of; Palestine, Pre-1918 History of

References

Davies, Philip R., George J. Brooke, and Philip R. Callaway. *The Complete World of the Dead Sea Scrolls.* New York: Thames and Hudson, 2002.

Golb, Norman. *Who Wrote the Dead Sea Scrolls? The Search for the Secret of Qumran.* New York: Touchstone, 1996.

Hirschfield, Yizhar. *Qumran in Context: Reassessing the Archaeological Evidence.* Peabody, MA: Hendrickson, 2004.

Magness, Jodi. *The Archaeology of Qumran and the Dead Sea Scrolls.* Grand Rapids, MI: Eerdmans, 2003.

VanderKam, James, and Peter Flint. *The Meaning of the Dead Sea Scrolls: Their Significance for Understanding the Bible, Judaism, Jesus, and Christianity.* San Francisco: HarperSanFrancisco, 2004.

Vermes, Geza. *The Dead Sea Scrolls in English.* 4th ed. London: Penguin, 1995.

Whitelam, Keith W. *The Invention of Ancient Israel: The Silencing of Palestinian History.* New York: Routledge, 1996.

Qur'an

See Koran

Qurei, Ahmed Ali Mohammed
Born: March 29, 1937

Palestinian Arab leader and prime minister of the Palestinian Authority (PA) during 2003–2006. Born in Abu Dis, an area of Jerusalem, into a well-to-do Arab family on March 26, 1937, Ahmed Qurei joined the Fatah wing of the Palestine Liberation Organization (PLO) in 1968 and became a close associate of PLO leader Yasser Arafat. Known by his nickname of Abu Alaa, Qurei had expertise in banking. He managed the PLO's foreign investment branch and also its economic branch, including its extensive business enterprises in Lebanon.

Following the Israeli invasion of Lebanon in 1982 and the expulsion of the PLO the next year, Qurei went to Tunis with the rest of the PLO leadership and rose to greater prominence in the mid-1980s. He was elected a member of the Fatah Central Committee in August 1989. He was a key participant in the talks leading to the Oslo Peace Accords of 1993, especially concentrating on economic issues. Also in 1993, he established the Palestinian Economic Council for Development and Reconstruction and presented an economic development plan to the World Bank aid conference.

In January 1996 Qurei was elected speaker of the 88-member Palestinian Legislative Council. He held this post until 2003. In July 2000 he played a prominent role in negotiating at Camp David, Maryland, with the Israelis, headed by Prime Minister Ehud Barak.

Following a power struggle with Arafat, Mahmoud Abbas resigned as Palestinian Authority (PA) prime minister on September 7, 2003. Arafat appointed Qurei to replace him. However, Qurei tried to resign in 2004, a move blocked by Arafat. Following the resounding defeat of Fatah in the 2006 Palestinian elections, Qurei submitted his resignation on January 26 but remained in office as a caretaker until February 19, 2006, when he was succeeded by Ismail Hamiya. Seen as a moderate, Qurei supports Jerusalem as the capital of a Palestinian state and asserts the Palestinian Arab right of return.

SPENCER C. TUCKER

Ahmed Qurei, Palestinian Arab leader and prime minister of the Palestinian Authority (PA) during 2003–2006. (European Community)

See also
Arafat, Yasser; Barak, Ehud; Oslo Accords; Right of Return, Palestinian

References
Livingstone, Neil C., and David Haley. *Inside the PLO*. New York: William Morrow, 1990.
Parsons, Nigel Craig. *The Politics of the Palestinian Authority: From Oslo to Al-Aqsa*. London: Routledge, 2003.

Quwatli, Shukri al-
Born: 1891
Died: June 30, 1967

Syrian political leader and president of Syria (1943–1949 and 1953–1958). Shukri al-Quwatli was born in 1891 in Damascus, Syria, which was then part of the Ottoman Empire. His family owned land and engaged in trade. Al-Quwatli attended secondary school in Damascus and college in Turkey, where he earned a degree in political science and associated with Arab nationalists. Returning to Syria, he joined Fatah, a secret Syrian nationalist organization opposing Turkish rule.

Ottoman authorities arrested al-Quwatli in 1916 for his association with Fatah. Fearful that under torture he would reveal information about comrades in Fatah, he attempted suicide by slashing his wrists but was saved from death at the last minute by colleague and friend Dr. Ahmad Qadri. This event made al-Quwatli a nationalist hero.

Following the end of World War I and the collapse of the Ottoman Empire, al-Quwatli became a civil servant and helped to organize the Arab Independence Party, a radical group seeking Syrian nationhood. In 1920, however, Syria passed under French control as a League of Nations mandate. When the Syrians resisted this arrangement, French troops expelled the Syrian monarch, King Faisal I.

Forced into exile himself, al-Quwatli lived for a time in Egypt and then in Geneva. In exile, he worked with Syrian, Lebanese, and Palestinian nationalists to establish the Syrian-Palestinian Congress. In 1922 France separated Lebanon from Syria and centralized its control. The French also built roads and schools, established the University of Damascus, and reformed agriculture. Yet their high-handed policies angered the nationalists and produced the Great Syrian Revolt of 1925–1927. Having returned to Syria in 1924, al-Quwatli participated in these events.

Exiled again in 1927, al-Quwatli raised money for the Arab nationalist movement. He returned to Syria under an amnesty in 1932 and developed his landholdings into the Syrian Conserves Company, which produced fruit and vegetables for export. At the same time, he continued to raise money for the nationalist cause. He joined the National Bloc, which rejected armed conflict in favor of popular protests and negotiated concessions to secure greater Syrian autonomy. He was uncomfortable with this moderate approach but used his influence to ensure that the Nationalist Bloc did not agree to unfavorable terms.

Shukri al-Quwatli, president of Syria during 1943–1949 and 1953–1958. (UPI/Bettmann/Corbis)

When the French resisted meaningful concessions, in 1936 al-Quwatli helped organize a 50-day general strike. This led to negotiations and a French agreement to allow Syrian independence. In elections to establish a transitional government, he was returned to the legislature and served as minister of defense and finance. In 1938, however, he resigned to protest the Syrian government's acquiescence to changes in the independence treaty that were more favorable to France. As it turned out, the French government did not ratify the treaty.

During World War II on March 20, 1941, al-Quwatli demanded Syria's immediate independence. Food shortages and unemployment plagued Syria, and nationalist riots had become widespread. On September 27, 1941, France formally recognized Syrian independence. However, troops remained present, and elections were delayed. Finally, in August 1943 al-Quwatli was chosen president by Syria's new legislature, and following further riots in 1945 and al-Quwatli's insistence that French troops remain in their barracks, France withdrew in April 1946, beginning Syria's complete independence.

As leader of Syria, al-Quwatli embraced Pan-Arabism and led

Syria into the League of Arab States in 1945. He also attempted agricultural reforms, but his administration suffered from continued economic difficulties brought by the devaluation of the French franc, by misspending, and, in 1948, by Israel's defeat of the Syrian forces during the Israeli War of Independence (1948–1949).

On March 30, 1949, although al-Quwatli had in 1948 secured reelection, he was ousted in a bloodless coup and charged with corruption. Held in a hospital for a month, he was then released to go into exile, first in Switzerland and later in Egypt. This coup began a series of similar upheavals. Two additional coups occurred in 1949, and a new constitution was adopted in 1950. The following year, the Nationalist Party (successor to the Nationalist Bloc), which was dominated by the business leaders in Damascus, sought al-Quwatli's return, but another coup led to a military dictatorship, and he did not return to Syria until 1954.

Al-Quwatli regained the presidency in 1955, but in the power shift to the military the position of president had been greatly weakened. He supported Egypt in the Suez Crisis of 1956. He also supported the merger of Egypt and Syria into the United Arab Republic (UAR), resigning the Syrian presidency in 1958 so that Egyptian leader Gamal Abdel Nasser could serve as president of the UAR. Al-Quwatli quarreled with Nasser in 1959, however, and was again forced into exile, ending his political career. Al-Quwatli died in Beirut, Lebanon, on June 30, 1967, but was subsequently given a state funeral in Damascus by the successor Baath Party leadership.

NEIL HAMILTON AND SPENCER C. TUCKER

See also

France, Middle East Policy; Franco-Syrian Treaty; Nasser, Gamal Abdel; Syria; United Arab Republic

References

Devlin, John F. *Syria: Modern State in an Ancient Land.* Boulder, CO: Westview, 1983.

Hitti, Philip Kuri. *History of Syria, including Lebanon and Palestine.* 2 vols. Piscataway, NJ: Gorgias, 2002.

Khoury, Philip. *Syria and the French Mandate: The Politics of Arab Nationalism, 1920–1945.* Princeton, NJ: Princeton University Press, 1987.

Seale, Patrick. *The Struggle for Syria: A Study of Post-War Arab Politics, 1945–1958.* New Haven, CT: Yale University Press, 1987.

Tibawi, Abdul L. *A Modern History of Syria including Lebanon and Palestine.* London: Macmillan, 1969.

R

Rabat Summit

Start Date: October 26, 1974
End Date: October 29, 1974

Meeting of 20 Arab heads of state as well as leaders of the Palestine Liberation Organization (PLO) in Rabat, Morocco, in October 1974. Convened as the seventh summit of the Arab League, the conference produced a series of resolutions on October 28 and 29, the most notable of which conferred upon the PLO de facto Arab recognition as the sole and legitimate representative of the Palestinian people. The same meeting also welcomed Somalia to the Arab League. The summit met exactly one year after the 1973 Yom Kippur War and was an attempt to solidify the Arab position vis-à-vis Israel and the West as well as an effort to deal with the Palestinian question in a coherent and uniform fashion. It was in this period that the idea of a Palestinian state in the West Bank and the Gaza Strip began to take shape, although neither the Arab states nor the Palestinians were in full agreement at this time. The summit also dealt with a variety of other issues, including the Palestinian situation in the wake of the 1973 Yom Kippur War. Some conference participants were concerned that areas such as the West Bank might be returned to Jordanian control. In fact, Palestinians in the West Bank had taken part in a series of demonstrations, strikes, and sit-ins that rejected both Israeli occupation and any restoration of Jordanian rule. Prior to the conference, PLO officials had met clandestinely with officials from President Richard M. Nixon's administration in hopes of securing U.S. recognition of the PLO. Such recognition was not forthcoming.

Arafat believed that it was important for the PLO to push for formal recognition from as many Arab countries as possible. Thus, as plans for the Rabat Summit progressed, Palestinian leaders made their case clearly: they would walk out of the meeting if the Arab League refused to grant the PLO formal recognition as the solitary representative of the Palestinian people. Once the meeting began, Arafat demanded that any land earmarked for Palestinian settlement (such as the West Bank) be turned over to the PLO. This included land won in war or sacrificed for peace. The Jordanians balked at this because Jordan was home to such a large number of Palestinians whose interests could lie either with Jordan, where they had the right to citizenship, or with the West Bank.

After some hard-fought wrangling, the conferees hammered out a compromise. It stated that the Palestinians had a right to their own homeland but that its territory was not to be limited to the West Bank exclusively. Even more important for the short term, the summit issued a resolution, which passed unanimously, acknowledging the PLO as the sole legitimate Palestinian representative body. Arafat had won his point. Finally, the summit resolutions promised cooperation between the PLO and Arab nations but warned against meddling in the PLO's internal affairs, just as the Arab League advised against member interference in all of its member states.

The Rabat Summit formalized the PLO's legitimacy in the Arab world and also codified Arab acceptance of the PLO's claims to the West Bank. Not surprisingly, King Hussein of Jordan, having experienced such tensions with the PLO leadership, recoiled at the summit's conclusions and at first refused to endorse the resolutions. Indeed, some sources allege that he signed on to them only after he had been promised some $300 million per year in subsidies from the Persian Gulf and other oil-producing Arab states. Other sources emphasize Hussein's desire to implement fully the summit's intentions. In terms of the Arab-Israeli conflict, the Rabat Summit sent an unambiguous signal to Israel that the Arab world was united in its advocacy of a Palestinian state. In succeeding years Hussein gave

Chairman of the Palestine Liberation Organization (PLO) Yasser Arafat flashes the victory sign on October 30, 1974, in Rabat during an Arab Summit meeting after Arab leaders recognized the PLO as the sole legitimate representative of the Palestinian people. (Bennati/AFP/Getty Images)

the more than 900,000 Palestinians in the East Bank the opportunity to choose either a Jordanian or Palestinian identity. The Rabat resolutions also meant that Jordan's House of Representatives, at that point made up only of West Bank politicians, would have to be reorganized. Jordan continued its responsibilities in the West Bank, however, including paying the salaries of civil servants and teachers there.

PAUL G. PIERPAOLI JR.

See also

Arab League; Arafat, Yasser; Hussein, King of Jordan; Jordan; Palestine Liberation Organization; West Bank; Yom Kippur War

References

Al-Shuaibi, Issa. "The Development of Palestinian Entity-Consciousness." *Journal of Palestinian Studies* 9(3) (1979): 50–70.

Nassar, Jamal R. *The Palestine Liberation Organization: From Armed Struggle to the Declaration of Independence.* New York: Praeger, 1991.

Norton, Augustus Richard, and Martin Harry Greenberg, eds. *The International Relations of the Palestine Liberation Organization.* Carbondale: Southern Illinois University Press, 1989.

Rabinovich, Abraham. *The Yom Kippur War: The Epic Encounter That Transformed the Middle East.* New York: Schocken, 2005.

Rabin, Yitzhak
Born: March 1, 1922
Died: November 4, 1995

Israeli army general, diplomat, leader of the Labor Party, and prime minister of Israel (1974–1977 and 1992–1995). Born in Jerusalem on March 1, 1922, Yitzhak Rabin moved with his family to Tel Aviv the following year. He attended the Kadoori Agricultural High School, graduating in 1940. He then went to work at the Kibbutz Ramat Yochanan, where he joined the Palmach, an elite fighting unit of Haganah, the Jewish self-defense organization that ultimately became the Israel Defense Forces (IDF).

In 1944 Rabin was second-in-command of a Palmach battalion and fought against the British Mandate authorities. He was arrested by the British in June 1946 and spent six months in prison. He became chief operations officer of the Palmach in 1947.

Rabin spent the next 20 years fighting for Israel as a member of the IDF. During the 1948–1949 Israeli War of Independence he commanded the Harel Brigade and fought for Jerusalem. He participated in the armistice talks and served as a deputy to Yigal Allon.

Yitzhak Rabin, Israeli Army general, diplomat, leader of the Labor Party, and prime minister of Israel (1974–1977 and 1992–1995). (Ya'acov Sa'ar/Israeli Government Press Office)

During 1956–1959 Rabin headed the Northern Command. During 1959–1961 he was chief of operations, and during 1961–1964 he was deputy chief of staff of the IDF. On January 1, 1964, he became IDF chief of staff and held this position during the Six-Day War in 1967. Following the Israeli capture of the Old City of Jerusalem in the war, he was one of the first to visit the city, delivering what became a famous speech on the top of Mount Scopus at the Hebrew University.

On January 1, 1968, Rabin retired from the army and shortly thereafter was named Israeli ambassador to the United States. He held this position until the spring of 1973, when he returned to Israel and joined the Labor Party. He was elected to the Knesset (Israeli parliament) in December 1973. Prime Minister Golda Meir appointed Rabin to her cabinet as minister of labor in April 1974. Meir retired as prime minister in May 1974, and Rabin took her place on June 2.

As prime minister, Rabin concentrated on improving the economy, solving social problems, and strengthening the IDF. He also sought to improve relations with the United States, which played a key role in mediating disengagement agreements with Israel, Egypt,

and Syria in 1974. Egypt and Israel signed an interim agreement in 1975. That same year Israel and the United States signed their first Memorandum of Understanding. The best-known event of Rabin's first term as prime minister was the July 3–4, 1976, rescue of hostages of Air France Flight 139 held at Entebbe, Uganda.

In March 1977 Rabin was forced to resign as prime minister following the revelation that his wife Leah held bank accounts in the United States, which was at that time against Israeli law. Menachem Begin replaced him, and Rabin was praised for his integrity and honesty in resigning.

Between 1977 and 1984 Rabin served in the Knesset as a member of the Labor Party and sat on the Foreign Affairs and Defense Committee. He published his memoirs, *Service Notebook,* in 1979. He served as minister of defense in the national unity governments between 1984 and 1990. In 1985 he proposed that IDF forces withdraw from Lebanon and establish a security zone to protect the settlements along the northern border of Israel.

In February 1992 Rabin was elected chairman of the Labor Party in its first nationwide primary. He led the party to victory in the June elections. He became prime minister for the second time that July. In an effort to achieve peace in the Middle East, he signed a joint Declaration of Principles with Palestine Liberation Organization (PLO) chairman Yasser Arafat, shaking hands with him on September 13, 1993, during the Oslo Peace Accords. This agreement created the Palestinian Authority (PA) and gave it some control over the West Bank and the Gaza Strip. Rabin, Arafat, and Shimon Peres shared the 1994 Nobel Peace Prize for their efforts to achieve peace. In 1995 Rabin continued his negotiations, signing an agreement with Arafat expanding Palestinian autonomy in the West Bank.

A number of ultraconservative Israelis believed that Rabin had betrayed the nation by negotiating with the Palestinians and giving away land they considered rightfully theirs. On November 4, 1995, right-wing extremist Yigal Amir shot Rabin after a peace rally in Kings of Israel Square, afterward renamed Yitzhak Rabin Square. Rabin died of his wounds soon afterward in Ichilov Hospital in Tel Aviv. November 4 has since become a national memorial day for Israelis. Numerous squares, streets, and public foundations have been named for Rabin, who is revered by many for his efforts on behalf of peace.

AMY HACKNEY BLACKWELL

See also

Arafat, Yasser; Begin, Menachem; Haganah; Israel Defense Forces; Jerusalem, Old City of; Labor Party; Meir, Golda; Oslo Accords; Palestinian Authority; Palmach; Zionism

References

Freedman, Robert Owen, ed. *Israel under Rabin.* Boulder, CO: Westview, 1995.

Kurzman, Dan. *Soldier of Peace: The Life of Yitzak Rabin, 1922–1995.* New York: HarperCollins, 1998.

Makovsky, David. *Making Peace with the PLO: The Rabin Government's Road to the Oslo Accord.* Boulder, CO: Westview, 1996.

Rabin, Yitzhak. *The Rabin Memoirs.* 1st English-language ed. Boston: Little, Brown, 1979.

Slater, Robert. *Rabin of Israel.* Rev. ed. New York: St. Martin's, 1993.

Tessler, Mark. *A History of the Israeli-Palestinian Conflict.* Bloomington: Indiana University Press, 1994.

Rafah Tunnels

Rafah, a city of about 150,000 people, lies at the far southern end of the Gaza Strip, adjacent to the Egyptian border and only about three miles from what was once the Gaza International Airport. It was the scene of fighting in both the 1956 Sinai Campaign and the 1967 Six-Day War. Under the terms of the 1993 Oslo Accords, Israel controlled a narrow strip of land between the Gaza and Egyptian borders, running in an almost straight line from the southernmost corner of the strip near the town of Kerem Shalom in Israel north-northwest to the Mediterranean coast. The road running along this narrow buffer zone is called the Philadelphi Road.

Following the Israel-Egypt Peace Treaty in 1979, Rafah became a key center for smuggling between Egypt and Palestinian-held territory. Tunnels dug from Rafah under the Philadelphi Road and to the Egyptian side became a major conduit for contraband cigarettes, pirated cassette tapes and videos, and drugs. With the start of the Second (al-Aqsa) Intifada in September 2000, the Rafah Tunnels became the major entry point for weapons, ammunition, and explosives into Gaza, all in violation of the Oslo Accords. The tunnels were also used to exfiltrate terrorists and suicide bombers to attack Israel within its borders. Emerging on the Egyptian side, the terrorists headed south into the Sinai and then cut back to the east, entering Israel through the porous border between the Sinai and the trackless southern Negev Desert.

Over the years, the Rafah Tunnels have become complex and sophisticated. To camouflage the entrances in Rafah, almost all are built on private property or within homes. In some cases, the homes belong to the tunnel's owners, members of the various militant groups or criminal gangs. In other cases, private citizens with no other connections to the tunnel operations are paid quite well for the use of their property. Both the criminal and the militant groups use small children to move material back and forth through the tunnels.

The packed clay subsoil in the area is relatively easy to dig yet firm enough to support tunnels. The tunnel builders could dig down 90 feet and more before starting the horizontal section, which can run anywhere between 500 and 2,000 feet. The construction of a single tunnel could take more than three months. The tunnels were reinforced with wooden supports, and most had some sort of ventilation system. Some were outfitted with lighting and phone lines, and some even had trolleys running their horizontal lengths.

For security purposes tunnel construction work was carried out in hours of darkness. Dirt and sand were removed from the excavation sites in flour sacks and dispersed in remote locations. Once the tunnel was operational, its entrance in a private home was concealed under furniture, under showers or bathtubs, or behind specially constructed double walls.

To counter the smuggling operations through the tunnels, the Israel Defense Forces (IDF) constructed a 12-feet-deep underground barrier along the Philadelphi Road. This only forced the tunnelers to go deeper, which also made their operations more difficult for the Israelis to detect with listening devices. The IDF also built an above-ground wall along the road to shield its soldiers from snipers in Gaza while conducting countertunnel operations.

The Egyptian government has operated against the tunnels on their side of the border, but the Israelis complained that the Egyptians were not sufficiently aggressive or effective. Nonetheless, in 2002 and 2003 the Egyptians intercepted more than two tons of explosives headed into Gaza. Prodded by the U.S. Coordinating and Monitoring Mission (USCMM), the Palestinian Preventive Security Organization (PSO) in Gaza under Muhammad Dahlan conducted raids in Rafah during August 23–24, 2003, that seized five tunnels. Israeli intelligence, however, dismissed the action as a show raid, claiming that all the tunnels were old and inactive. Israeli intelligence also told USCMM officials that at least two of the tunnels were owned by officers in other Palestinian security organizations who had been forewarned about the PSO raid.

Thus far, the only way that has shown any results at all in reducing the tunnel operations has been for the IDF to enter Rafah itself, find the tunnel entrances, and physically destroy the tunnels. Most all such incursions meet stiff opposition and usually result in casualties on both sides. Experience has shown that once a tunnel is found, filling in its entrance with dirt, or even cement, will rarely keep it closed for very long. Most tunnels have multiple openings. The only way to neutralize the tunnel completely is with large explosive charges, which almost always results in the complete destruction of the private home where the tunnel originates. The incursions and the destruction of private homes in Rafah create even more resentment among the Palestinians as well as far wider public relations problems for the Israelis. Since the start of the Second Intifada, the IDF located and destroyed more than 90 tunnels in Rafah.

DAVID T. ZABECKI

See also

Dahlan, Muhammad Yusuf; Gaza Strip; Hamas; Intifada, Second; Oslo Accords; United States Coordinating and Monitoring Mission

References

Guyatt, Nicholas. *Absence of Peace: Understanding the Israeli-Palestinian Conflict.* New York: St. Martin's, 1998.

Tessler, Mark. *A History of the Israeli-Palestinian Conflict.* Bloomington: Indiana University Press, 1994.

Ramadan War

See Yom Kippur War

Ramallah

West Bank Palestinian city located about 9 miles north of Jerusalem and perhaps 35 miles inland from the Mediterranean. It is today

A general view from the Kalandia checkpoint in the West Bank of the Israeli separation barrier surrounding Ramallah, May 22, 2006. (Uriel Sinai/Getty Images)

the headquarters of the Palestinian Authority (PA). Located among mountains about 3,000 feet above sea level, Ramallah is in a watershed area. The climate is moderate, and there is adequate rainfall.

Originally a Canaanite settlement dating from perhaps 3500 BC, modern Ramallah was founded in the 1500s by Yemenite Christian Arabs. Originally an agricultural village, it was declared a city in 1908. The city owed its importance to its location. It is a major crossroads astride the main north-south road from Lebanon to Egypt and an east-west road from Jaffa (Yafo) to Jericho. Today Ramallah has a population of some 57,000 people. With nearby al-Bireh, it forms a single constituency for PA elections.

One of the first Palestinian newspapers, *The Mirror,* was published in Ramallah beginning in 1919, and the city was also the site of a large radio tower erected by the British that was capable of broadcasting to all Palestine. During the Arab-Jewish Communal War of 1947–1948, many Arab refugees crowded into the city, more than doubling its population. The Jordanian Arab Legion took over control of the Ramallah–al-Bireh area during the Israeli War of Independence (1948–1949), preventing Israeli forces from captur-

ing the cities and also serving to prevent an exodus of civilians from the area. A number of refugee camps were also established around the city. Al-Jalazon, Kalandia, al-Amari, and Kadura today house some 30,000 refugees. Following the war, Jordan annexed the entire West Bank of the Jordan River. Ramallah was relatively peaceful during the years of Jordanian control (1948–1967), but that changed as a consequence of the Six-Day War in June 1967. Following Jordan's entry into the war, Israel captured Ramallah on June 7 and assumed control over the entire West Bank. The city now came under Israeli military rule.

Resistance to Israeli control was subdued but grew in the 1980s, culminating in the First Intifada (1987–1993). With the violence and clashes between intifada fighters and Israel Defense Forces (IDF), businesses were open only sporadically, and schools were closed by order of the IDF. Many students lost an entire year of education during 1988–1989. Arrests by the authorities were also commonplace, and public services were sharply curtailed. The intifada ended in 1993 as a result of the Oslo Accords. In December 1995 the IDF departed from the city center, and the new Palestinian Authority (PA) took full civilian control and security responsibilities.

The years from 1995 to 2000 saw general peace and considerable prosperity in the city. A number of Ramallah residents who had previously immigrated to the United States now returned and opened businesses. Unemployment among the general population remained high, however. IDF forces remained on the outskirts of the city, and residents had no access to nearby Jerusalem without work permits, which were difficult to secure.

Confidence in the Palestinian-Israeli peace process gradually ebbed, and when the Second (al-Aqsa) Intifada began in September 2000, Ramallah became a flashpoint. On October 12, 2000, Ramallah was targeted by Israeli attack helicopters when two Israeli army reservists were captured by a mob and killed. A number of the suicide bombers who struck in Jerusalem came from the city or from its surrounding refugee camps. In 2002 the IDF, which had already destroyed most of the PA buildings in the city by air strikes, reoccupied Ramallah in Operation DEFENSIVE SHIELD. During that period, Ramallah residents were living in a state of siege.

Conditions in Ramallah steadily deteriorated, and there were confirmed instances of looting by Israeli soldiers. Most of the expatriates who had returned departed once again. Making matters worse, large sections of the Israeli West Bank barrier erected near the city increased the difficulties for anyone traveling from one point to another. Ramallah was plagued in 2004–2005 with inter-Palestinian violence and rivalries. However, it remains an important commercial center, and as home to Bir Zayt University and to the various political parties, it has a lively atmosphere.

Ramallah is known for the Muqataa, a series of governmental buildings dating to the British Mandate for Palestine and located on high ground. They also served as the governmental headquarters of the PA, sometimes referred to as "Arafat's Compound" for PLO chairman Yasser Arafat. In 2002, IDF troops isolated Arafat in his compound by bulldozing buildings nearby, cutting him off from the rest of Ramallah. This act engendered bitter denouncements in much of the Arab world. Ramallah is also the burial site of Arafat. He is buried in a tomb on the Muqataa near his former headquarters.

SPENCER C. TUCKER

See also

Al-Bireh; Arab-Jewish Communal War; Arafat, Yasser; Intifada, First; Intifada, Second; Palestinian Authority; West Bank

References

Hass, Amira. *Reporting from Ramallah: An Israeli Journalist in an Occupied Land.* Cambridge, MA: MIT Press, 2003.

Shaheen, Azeez. *Ramallah: Its History and Genealogies.* Birzeit, Palestine: Birzeit University Press, 1982.

Shehadeh, Raja. *When the Birds Stopped Singing: Life in Ramallah under Siege.* South Royaltown, VT: Sheerforth, 2003.

Ramla

City located in central Israel with a population of approximately 65,000 people. Ramla is the largest Israeli city between Tel Aviv and Jerusalem. It is approximately 10 miles from the Mediterranean Sea and includes Israel's major airport at Lod, Ben-Gurion International Airport. The city dominates the central plain of Israel and straddles the main road from the capital to Jerusalem.

Ramla was the original capital of Arab Palestine. The city was one of the first objectives seized by Arab armies during the Israeli War of Independence (1948–1949). Ramla was captured and held by the Arab Legion, which also occupied Lod's major rail junction. This position effectively isolated Tel Aviv from Jerusalem. Arab Legion units heavily fortified Ramla and Lod, holding the area through the first truce of the war.

When fighting resumed on July 8, 1948, Israeli forces mounted a major assault on Ramla. Operation DANNY (July 9–12, 1948) captured the twin settlements and reopened the vital Tel Aviv–Jerusalem Road. Under the orders of Prime Minister David Ben-Gurion, Israeli forces attempted to consolidate their hold on the region by expelling thousands of Arabs from the area. Fewer than 500 Arab inhabitants, mostly Christians, were allowed to remain. The homes of the exiled Arabs were turned over to newly arriving immigrants, instantly transforming the demographics of the town. Eighty percent of the current population of Ramla is Jewish, 16 percent is Arab Muslim, and the remainder is Arab Christian.

PAUL J. SPRINGER

See also

Israel; Israeli War of Independence, Overview; Jerusalem

References

Herzog, Chaim. *The Arab-Israeli Wars: War and Peace in the Middle East from the War of Independence to Lebanon.* Westminster, MD: Random House, 1984.

Lustick, Ian. *From War to War: Israel vs. the Arabs, 1948–1967.* New York: Garland, 1994.

Rantisi, Abd al-Aziz
Born: October 23, 1947
Died: April 17, 2004

Palestinian political leader and head of operations for Hamas in the Gaza Strip. Abd al-Aziz Rantisi was born on October 23, 1947, in Yabna (Jibna), a town near Ashdod (Isdud) and Jaffa, Palestine. His family fled their home for Khan Yunis in the Gaza Strip in 1948 during the Israeli War of Independence (1948–1949). Following Israel's independence in May 1948, Egypt administered the Gaza Strip until its occupation by Israel in the aftermath of the Six-Day War in 1967.

Rantisi excelled in school, and upon graduating from secondary school in 1965 he was admitted to Alexandria University in Egypt to study medicine. He graduated with a bachelor's degree in medicine in 1972 and returned to Gaza for two years before resuming his studies in Egypt and obtaining a master's degree in pediatrics in 1976. It was during his nine years in Egypt that he became exposed to the ideals of Islamic fundamentalism espoused by the Muslim Brotherhood, an organization with a long history and affiliates throughout the Muslim world. These same ideals lay at the heart of Hamas, which is, in contrast, also a nationalist organization.

Upon returning to Gaza in 1976, Rantisi worked as a resident physician at the government-run Nasser Hospital in the city of Khan Yunis until 1986. He also busied himself with posts in several organizations dedicated to public works, including service as a board member of the Islamic Complex, as a member of the Arab Medical Society in Gaza, and as a member of the Palestinian Red Crescent (the Islamic counterpart to the Red Cross). In 1978 he was promoted to the post of chief pediatrician in the Khan Yunis hospital and joined the faculty of science at the Islamic University of Gaza in its inaugural year.

Rantisi's political convictions first landed him in trouble in 1983, when he was arrested for refusing to pay taxes to Israel. However, his political involvement with the organization that came to be known as Hamas first became widely known in 1987. The triggering event was the killing of four Palestinians after an Israel Defense Forces (IDF) truck ran into a group of residents of the Jabalya refugee camp in the Gaza Strip on December 8, 1987. Rantisi has claimed that he and six other associates—Sheikh Ahmed Yassin foremost among them—on the following day helped to channel the seething discontent of Palestinians into the civilian uprising that spread like wildfire across the occupied territories. This was the origin of what came to be known as the First Intifada. Hamas emerged after its outbreak.

Rantisi was arrested twice in 1988. The first time he was held for 21 days, and the second time he was held for a year and a half. His release in September 1990 was short-lived, for he was arrested again in December 1990 and held in detention for a year. On December 15, 1992, he was expelled to Marj Al-Zuhur, in southern Lebanon, along with 415 other Hamas and Islamic Jihad activists. The expellees

Hamas leader Abd al-Aziz Rantisi and the Hamas flag, Gaza, June 14, 2003. (Reuters/Corbis)

were not permitted by the Lebanese government to leave the area where they were dropped off by Israeli air transport, and with no rights or supplies, they attracted international attention.

Rantisi then became a leading spokesperson for the expelled Palestinians. Allowed to return to the Gaza Strip in September 1993 with other expellees, he was frequently imprisoned by the Palestinian Authority (PA) for his open criticism of it and Palestine Liberation Organization (PLO) chairman Yasser Arafat.

Following the signing of the Declaration of Principles on Interim Self-Government Arrangements (1993), which Hamas opposed, the organization staged several knife attacks on soldiers and settlers in the occupied territories. However, following the massacre of 29 Palestinians by Israeli settler Baruch Goldstein in the Cave of the Patriarchs (Hebron Mosque Massacre) on February 25, 1994, Hamas and other organizations and unaffiliated individuals embarked on a campaign of suicide bombings. Although peaking in the years 2001 and 2002, Hamas continued these bombings with occasional breaks.

Upon the return of Sheikh Ahmed Yassin to Gaza in 1997, Rantisi worked with him to reconstitute Hamas's Gaza leadership. In mid-1999, following Rantisi's release from a PA prison, Rantisi became Yassin's right-hand man and the public spokesperson for Hamas in the Gaza Strip, in part because of his fluent command of English.

Despite Hamas's attempts to portray its political leadership as separate from its military wing (known as the Izz al-Din al-Qassam Brigades), Israel recognized no such separation and targeted the political department of Hamas for assassination. Rantisi narrowly avoided such a fate on June 10, 2003, when a helicopter rocket attack on his car missed its mark.

Within Hamas, Rantisi was always considered a hard-liner who never missed an opportunity to use his rhetorical skills to further inflame any situation. He vehemently denied the Holocaust engineered by Nazi Germany, and he was uncompromising in his call for an Islamic Palestine—in contrast to the Palestine Liberation Organization (PLO), which is secular and includes many Christian Palestinians—and refused to recognize Israel's right to exist. Following the March 2004 assassination by Israeli forces of Sheikh Yassin, Rantisi took the opportunity of Yassin's funeral to seize the leadership of Hamas in the Gaza Strip, having himself proclaimed Yassin's appointed heir during the accompanying protest rally. Rantisi was recognized as Hamas's Gaza leader by Khaled Mashal, whom Rantisi recognized in return as the leader of Hamas in the West Bank. (Mashal was operating in exile in Damascus, Syria.) Not surprisingly, Rantisi, who had already been targeted for assassination by Israel once, was again targeted, and on April 17, 2004, only hours after Hamas had claimed responsibility for the assassination of an Israeli soldier, an Israeli helicopter gunship fired a missile at his car, killing Rantisi, his 27-year-old son, and a bodyguard.

SPENCER C. TUCKER

See also

Arafat, Yasser; Hamas; Hebron Mosque Massacre; Holocaust; Intifada, First; Islamic Jihad, Palestinian; Muslim Brotherhood; Palestine Liberation Organization; Palestinian Authority; Terrorism; Yassin, Ahmed Ismail

References

Mishal, Shaul, and Avraham Sela. *The Palestinian Hamas: Vision, Violence, and Coexistence.* New York: Columbia University Press, 2000.

Nusse, Andrea. *Muslim Palestine: The Ideology of Hamas.* London: Routledge, 1999.

Reeve, Simon. *The New Jackals.* Boston: Northeastern University Press, 1999.

Souryal, Sam. *Islam, Islamic Law, and the Turn to Violence.* Huntsville, TX: Office of International Criminal Justice, Sam Houston State University, 2004.

Reagan, Ronald Wilson
Born: February 11, 1911
Died: June 5, 2004

U.S. politician and president of the United States (1981–1989). Born on February 11, 1911, in Tampico, Illinois, Ronald Reagan graduated from Eureka College, worked as a sports announcer, and in 1937 won a Hollywood contract with Warner Brothers, eventually appearing in 53 movies. As president of the Screen Actors Guild during the late 1940s and early 1950s, the once-liberal Reagan purged alleged communists and veered strongly to the political Right. His politics grew increasingly conservative in the late 1950s and early 1960s.

In 1966 the genial Reagan won the first of two terms as the Republican governor of California. During his campaign he supported U.S. intervention in Vietnam and condemned student antiwar protestors. He soon became one of the leading figures of the increasingly powerful Republican Right, supporting high defense budgets, a strong anticommunist international posture, and deep cuts in taxes and domestic expenditures. These positions he affirmed while seeking the Republican presidential nomination in 1976 and 1980.

In November 1980 when Reagan defeated Democratic incumbent Jimmy Carter for the presidency, the United States was suffering from spiraling inflation and high unemployment. In Iran, radical Muslims had overthrown Mohammad Reza Shah Pahlavi in 1979, sending oil prices soaring. For more than a year radical Iranian students held U.S. diplomatic personnel hostage in Tehran. An almost simultaneous Soviet-backed coup in Afghanistan intensified a sense of American impotence, as did communist insurgencies in Central America and Africa. Reagan opposed compromise with communism. Believing firmly that a U.S. victory in the Cold

Ronald Reagan, president of the United States (1981–1989). (U.S. Department of Defense)

War was attainable, the ever-optimistic Reagan used blatantly triumphalist, anti-Soviet rhetoric, famously terming the Soviet Union "The Evil Empire."

Reagan purposefully engaged the Soviet Union in an arms race whereby he and his advisers hoped that American technological and economic superiority would strain the Soviet economy. The Reagan administration hiked the defense budget from $171 billion to $376 billion between 1981 and 1986 in the hope of helping the United States to combat communism around the world. In 1983 Reagan announced that the United States would begin research on an expensive new ballistic missile defense system. The Strategic Defense Initiative (SDI), popularly known as "Star Wars," was a largely theoretical plan to intercept and destroy incoming nuclear missiles.

Breaking with Carter's foreign policies, Reagan also deliberately de-emphasized human rights, consciously supporting dictatorships provided they were pro-American while assailing human rights abuses within the Soviet sphere. Covert operations intensified as the United States offered support to anticommunist forces around the world, providing economic aid to the dissident Polish Solidarity trade union movement and military and economic assistance to antigovernment rebels in Angola, mujahideen guerrillas in Afghanistan and the anti-Sandinista Contras in Nicaragua. Aid to the Contras included covert support. When Congress responded by passing the 1984 Boland Amendment forbidding funding for

Nicaraguan covert actions, the Reagan administration embroiled itself in an ill-fated secret enterprise to sell arms to Iran—thereby evading its own embargo but, officials suggested, enhancing the political standing of Iranian moderate elements—and using the proceeds to aid the Nicaraguan Contras. Revelations of these illegal activities embarrassed Reagan during his second term.

Notwithstanding his bellicose rhetoric, in practice Reagan was surprisingly pragmatic and cautious. In potentially difficult guerrilla settings, his administration favored covert operations, preferably undertaken by surrogates such as the Afghan mujahideen or the Nicaraguan Contras, over outright military intervention. Wars were kept short and easily winnable, as in the small Caribbean island of Grenada in 1983 when American troops liberated the island from Marxist rule. When almost simultaneously radical pro-Syrian Druze Muslims bombed the Beirut barracks of an American peacekeeping force in Lebanon, killing 241 American soldiers, the United States quickly withdrew. In 1986 suspected Libyan involvement in terrorist incidents provoked only retaliatory American surgical air strikes on Tripoli.

The Reagan administration's Middle East policies were characteristic of its approach toward other regions of the world. Anticommunism—laced with anti-Soviet rhetoric—was buffered by pragmatism and caution. U.S. officials took a hard line against regional terrorist organizations including Lebanon's Hezbollah, which was routinely taking Americans hostage and assaulting civilian targets. This became particularly acute after the June 1982 Israeli invasion of Lebanon. When radical Palestinians began a major terror campaign in the Gaza Strip and on the West Bank, Reagan administration officials sharply denounced the activity and made veiled hints of retaliation. In 1982 when the United Nations (UN) called for a limited peacekeeping force in Lebanon, Reagan sent U.S. marines. Their job was not an easy one, given that Israel completely occupied Beirut and was attempting to flush out Palestine Liberation Organization (PLO) members. In September 1982, the massacre of Palestinian civilians in Lebanon's Sabra and Shatila refugee camps by Maronite Christian militias shocked and embarrassed the Reagan administration. As a result, Reagan helped form a new multinational peacekeeping force. Intensive diplomatic efforts by the United States to broker a peace deal between Israel and Lebanon ultimately bore fruit, although the October 1983 bombing of the U.S. marine barracks in Beirut put an effective end to the American military presence there. In an attempt to keep American ties with Saudi Arabia on track, in 1981 Reagan pushed through the controversial sale of American-made Airborne Warning and Control System (AWACS) planes to the kingdom. Israel fiercely denounced the move.

Reagan had become president only months after the outbreak of the Iran-Iraq War (1980–1988). At first, the United States attempted to stay neutral. As time went on, the administration attempted to help both sides. However, Reagan administration officials began tilting toward Iraq as the war dragged on. A clear consensus had emerged that Iraqi dictator Saddam Hussein was the lesser of two evils. Indeed, the United States had more to fear from a triumphant Iran, which might foment fundamentalist revolutions in neighboring Arab states, than it did from a secular, albeit autocratic, Iraq. By 1982, when an Iranian victory looked likely, the Reagan administration launched Operation STAUNCH, an effort to prevent arms from making their way to Iran. The United States also began to provide financial and intelligence assistance to Hussein. At the same time, however, Reagan administration officials were secretly selling arms to Iran to fund its covert aid to the Nicaraguan Contras. It is also believed that the administration shipped so-called dual-purpose materials (such as biological and chemical agents) to Iraq, which was supposed to use them for civilian purposes. It is highly likely that they were used in Iraq's secret programs to manufacture chemical and biological weapons. The longer-term implications of these policies are now manifest. The United States has since been compelled to wage two separate wars against Iraq, the first one in 1991 and the second one in 2003, which is far from resolved.

Despite campaign pledges to the contrary, Reagan did not shun Mainland China or restore U.S. relations with Taiwan. Sino-American trade increased, and Reagan made a 1984 state visit to Beijing. By 1984, international and domestic politics suggested that the president moderate his anti-Soviet line. In September 1984, Reagan proposed combining all major ongoing nuclear weapons talks into one package, and Soviet leaders soon agreed.

Reagan's mellowing coincided with the culmination of long-standing Soviet economic problems as military spending rose, diverting funds from domestic programs. Most East European countries resented Soviet domination. The Solidarity Movement in Poland proved remarkably persistent, undercutting Soviet control. Assertive Soviet policies in Africa and Latin America carried a high price tag too, while the decade-long Afghan intervention had embroiled Soviet troops in a costly and unwinnable guerrilla war.

In 1985 the young and energetic Mikhail Gorbachev became the general secretary of the Communist Party of the Soviet Union (CPSU). He immediately sought to address Russia's problems and reform the communist economic and social systems. American and European leaders were initially wary of Gorbachev's overtures, although he quickly won great popularity. After British prime minister Margaret Thatcher urged Reagan—her ideological soul mate—to work with Gorbachev, the president did just that. Domestic economic factors may have also impelled Reagan toward rapprochement. Deep tax cuts meant that heavy government budget deficits financed the 1980s' defense buildup, and in November 1987 an unexpected Wall Street stock market crash suggested that American economic fundamentals might be undesirably weak. Reagan had several summit meetings with Gorbachev, and in 1987 the superpowers signed the Intermediate Nuclear Forces (INF) Treaty, eliminating all medium-range missiles in Europe. This marked the beginning of a series of arms reduction agreements, continued under Reagan's successor George H. W. Bush, and of measures whereby the Soviet Union withdrew from its East European empire and, by 1991, allowed it to collapse.

Reagan left office in 1989. After a decade-long battle with Alzheimer's disease, he died of pneumonia at his home in Los Angeles, California, on June 5, 2004.

PRISCILLA ROBERTS

See also

Carter, James Earl, Jr.; Iran; Iran-Iraq War; Iraq; Lebanon; Lebanon, Civil War in; Lebanon, Israeli Invasion of; Qaddafi, Muammar; Reza Pahlavi, Mohammad, Shah of Iran; Shultz, George Pratt; Weinberger, Caspar

References

Cannon, Lou. *President Reagan: The Role of a Lifetime.* New York: Simon and Schuster, 1991.

Fischer, Beth A. *The Reagan Reversal: Foreign Policy and the End of the Cold War.* Columbia: University of Missouri Press, 1997.

FitzGerald, Frances. *Way Out There in the Blue: Reagan, Star Wars, and the End of the Cold War.* New York: Simon and Schuster, 2000.

Matlock, Jack F., Jr. *Reagan and Gorbachev: How the Cold War Ended.* New York: Random House, 2004.

Mervin, David. *Ronald Reagan and the American Presidency.* New York: Longman, 1990.

Pemberton, William E. *Exit with Honor: The Life and Presidency of Ronald Reagan.* Armonk, NY: M. E. Sharpe, 1997.

Smith, Geoffrey. *Reagan and Thatcher.* New York: Norton, 1991.

Strober, Deborah Hart, and Gerald S. Strober. *The Reagan Presidency: An Oral History of the Era.* Washington, DC: Brassey's, 2003.

Reagan Plan
Event Date: September 1, 1982

Middle Eastern peace initiative put forth by President Ronald W. Reagan on September 1, 1982. The so-called Reagan Plan (or Reagan Peace Plan) came on the immediate heels of the August 12, 1982, cease-fire agreement between the Palestine Liberation Organization (PLO) and Israel, both of which had been heavily involved in the Lebanese Civil War (1975–1990). One of the terms of this agreement was that the PLO would abandon its operational base in Lebanon, resulting in the exodus of some 15,000 Palestinian fighters by September 1, 1982. PLO chairman Yasser Arafat relocated the PLO's headquarters to Tunisia shortly thereafter. The war in Lebanon had been a protracted and tragic affair for all involved and had left the country a virtual wasteland. Thus, in order to breathe new life into the moribund Middle East peace process and to begin the process of rebuilding in the region, the Reagan administration unveiled its plan to coincide with the September 1 deadline.

The Reagan Plan had six primary points. First, the Palestinians would achieve autonomy in the Gaza Strip and the West Bank after elections that would constitute a Palestinian governing entity. Full autonomy would be achieved after a five-year transitional period. Second, Israel would bar the construction of any more settlements in disputed or occupied territories. Third, the United States would not support a fully independent Palestinian state in the West Bank or the Gaza Strip. The United States would also not tolerate Israeli control over these areas. Fourth, the United States supported a negotiated settlement over the disputed areas and believed that an autonomous Palestinian entity under Jordanian jurisdiction offered the best potential for an enduring peace. Fifth, Israel would withdraw from Gaza and the West Bank entirely in exchange for peace. Sixth, Jerusalem would remain intact and not be divided, subject to future negotiations.

The Reagan Plan had been drawn up in great secrecy and was not divulged to either the Israelis or Arab nations until its formal announcement on September 1. Implicit in the announcement was the fact that the United States would continue to refuse any contacts with the PLO until it officially recognized Israel and accepted United Nations (UN) Resolutions 242 and 338. Another condition not initially made public was that the United States would not press for the dismantlement of any Israeli settlements until after the five-year transitional period had ended.

Israel's Likud government, led by Menachem Begin, flatly rejected the plan. Indeed, Begin allegedly said that reading the plan was the "saddest day" of his life. The Labor Party, however, believed that the Reagan Plan might provide a solid base from which negotiations would follow. In several aspects, the plan echoed the party's own plan for peace. The PLO also rejected the plan, albeit for different reasons. Arafat's biggest problem with the plan was that it provided no mechanism for full Palestinian sovereignty and self-determination. The PLO also refused to accept the plan because it had not been previously consulted, and the Americans refused to meet with its leadership. On the other hand, the PLO had to have been heartened somewhat by the Americans' call for a freeze on new Israeli settlements and their opposition to Israeli claims of sovereignty over the West Bank and the Gaza Strip.

The Jordanians rejected the Reagan Plan too and by so doing essentially rendered the entire initiative moot because it depended on Jordanian control over an autonomous Palestinian Authority (PA). Some have argued that the plan was destined to fail because it addressed only part of the larger Palestinian problem. Indeed, it did not mention the plight and status of as many as 2.5 million Palestinian refugees, did not earmark any additional land to the Palestinians besides Gaza and the West Bank, and did not speak to UN-mandated specifications for restitution to those Palestinians who lost their property since 1948.

Occurring as it did during the height of the renewed Cold War between Moscow and Washington, the Reagan Plan became quickly embroiled in superpower politics. Upon learning of King Hussein of Jordan's rejection of the peace plan, Tass, the Kremlin's official government news agency, stated that the plan "has nothing to do with a genuine peace settlement, but aims at splitting up the Arabs, perpetuating Israeli occupation of Arab lands, and building up . . . the United States military presence in the region."

PAUL G. PIERPAOLI JR.

See also

Arafat, Yasser; Begin, Menachem; Gaza Strip; Hussein, King of Jordan; Lebanon, Civil War in; Palestine Liberation Organization; Reagan, Ronald Wilson; Settlements, Israeli; United Nations Security Council

Resolution 242; United Nations Security Council Resolution 338; West Bank

References

Gabriel, Richard. *Operation Peace for Galilee: The Israeli-PLO War in Lebanon.* New York: Farrar, Straus and Giroux, 1985.

Hart, Alan. *Arafat: A Political Biography.* Rev. ed. London: Sidgwick and Jackson, 1994.

Laham, Nicholas. *Crossing the Rubicon: Ronald Reagan and U.S. Policy in the Middle East.* Aldershot, Hampshire, UK: Ashgate, 2004.

Rubin, Barry. *Revolution until Victory? The Politics and History of the PLO.* Reprint ed. Cambridge: Harvard University Press, 2003.

Red Cross

See International Red Cross

Red Sea

The Red Sea is a large body of water separating the continents of Africa and Asia. The most northern of all tropical seas, it dominates the physical and geopolitical landscape of the Middle East. Egypt, Sudan, Eritrea, and Ethiopia lie on its western borders; Saudi Arabia and Yemen lie on its eastern borders; and Egypt, Israel, and Jordan are at its northern apex.

In the north the Red Sea is separated by the Sinai Peninsula into two channels. The first is the Gulf of Suez to the west. It is about 180 miles long and some 20 miles wide on average. To the east is the Gulf of Aqaba. It has a length of roughly 100 miles and an average width of about 15 miles.

The Red Sea is some 1,450 miles in length from its northern edge, where the city of Suez is located, to its southern boundary at the Straits of Bab al-Mandab, where it connects via the Gulf of Aden to the Indian Ocean. The Red Sea is never more than 200 miles in width.

Why the Red Sea was so named remains obscure. It may be from a misinterpretation of the Hebrew word for "Reed Sea" or from the occasional abundance of blooms of red algae that cause so-called red tides.

The Red Sea is connected to the Mediterranean Sea to the north via the Suez Canal, which opened to ship traffic in 1869. The Red Sea varies in depth from more than 8,000 feet in the central trench, where there are numerous metal-rich deposits, to less than 2,000 feet. There are extensive shallow-water shelves around its periphery that are well developed in the Gulf of Suez. The tidal flow ranges from about 2 feet close to the mouth of the Gulf of Suez to some 3 feet near the Gulf of Aden. The central region is virtually tideless. The predominance of an arid climate and torridly hot temperatures in the region means that evaporation is high, resulting in the highest salinity concentrations of all the nonlandlocked seas.

There are several important cities along the Red Sea's coastal plain, such as Jiddah (in Saudi Arabia) and Port Sudan (in Sudan). Along the Sinai coast lie the cities of Eilat, Israel; Aqaba, Jordan; and

The Red Sea, shown in a satellite image from September 29, 2004. (NASA)

Sharm al-Sheikh, Egypt. All have capitalized on the rich geological and ecological resources of the region to develop economically important tourism industries. Much of this is based on the abundance of near-coastal coral reefs in shallow waters, which provide many opportunities for ecotourism and other marine activities.

The Red Sea is not merely a key geographic feature and important economic resource. It is also a significant piece of the geopolitical equation in the Middle East. Indeed, the Suez Canal is critical to the regional power balance, as was shown in the 1956 Suez Crisis. The closing off of the Gulf of Aqaba and the Strait of Tiran to Israeli shipping from 1949 to 1956 represented a significant hardship for the Israelis. The strait was again briefly closed in 1967 prior to the Six-Day War. While the area was blockaded, Israeli ships bound for the East had to circumnavigate the African continent, adding many days and considerable expense to such voyages. During the Iran-Iraq War (1980–1988), the Gulf of Aqaba was crucial to the Iraqis as a resupply route via Jordan. In the run-up to the Persian Gulf War of 1991, the Gulf again took on critical importance as coalition forces interdicted goods bound for Iraq.

Antoinette Mannion

See also

Aqaba, Gulf of; Climate of the Middle East; Eilat, Israel; Sharm al-Sheikh; Strait of Tiran Crisis; Straits of Tiran; Suez Canal; Suez Crisis

References

Ghisotti, Andrea. *The Red Sea.* Florence, Italy: Casa Editrice Bonechi, 1995.

Mallory, Kenneth. *The Red Sea.* New York: Franklin Watts, 1991.

Reform Judaism and Zionism

A branch of Judaism that originated in Germany in the early 1800s and that is now the dominant movement in North American Judaism. Although its doctrines have changed over time, Reform Judaism has a history of liberalism and progressivism. Although its emphasis on Judaism as a religion rather than a nationality initially put it at odds with Zionism and the creation of a Jewish homeland, changing world events have done much to reconcile these two ideological strains of Judaism.

Reform Judaism has its roots in the Jewish Enlightenment (Haskalah) of the late 18th and early 19th centuries. During this period, German Jewish intellectuals used the expanded rights and freedoms granted to Jews during the 18th-century European Enlightenment as a basis for a new form of Judaism. Reform Jews argued that Judaism was a religion, not a nationality. This meant that Jews should work to integrate themselves into the larger civic structure of the nation. To this end, certain aspects of Jewish religious observation were changed to streamline them with non-Jewish practices. For instance, previously banned musical accompaniment was incorporated into religious observations, and services were conducted in German rather than Hebrew. Other practices that set Jews apart from their non-Jewish neighbors, such as circumcision and the following of dietary restrictions, were also abolished. In addition to their ideological basis, these changes had a practical purpose. They helped stem the flow of conversions to Christianity by Jews who found their religion overly rigid, difficult to understand, and a source of alienation.

Reform Judaism spread to other European states, including Britain, the Netherlands, Denmark, Hungary, and Austria. It was brought to the United States by a wave of almost 150,000 Jewish immigrants from German-speaking countries between 1840 and 1870. Although the American Reform movement had many important intellectual and religious leaders, the most important was undoubtedly Isaac Mayer Wise. A Bohemian rabbi who immigrated to the United States in 1846, Wise wrote the first prayer book edited for American Jews in 1857. He also established many important institutions in American Reform Judaism, including the Union of American Hebrew Congregations in 1873, the Hebrew Union College in 1875, and the Central Conference of American Rabbis (CCAR) in 1889. Although Reform Judaism met with opposition from the Orthodox Jewish community as it had in Europe, it quickly became the dominant form of Judaism in the United States. The 1885 Declaration of Principles (also known as the Pittsburgh Platform) was the first official statement made by American Reform rabbis.

By the 1930s, however, Reform Judaism had begun to reincorporate elements of traditional Jewish observation that it had previously eschewed. The changing landscape of Reform Judaism was addressed in a series of platform statements issued by the CCAR in 1937, 1976, 1997, and 1999. Reform Judaism remains more liberal than Orthodox Judaism. For instance, it welcomes gay and lesbian Jews and allows members to trace their Jewish lineage through either the mother or the father rather than just the mother.

This gradual evolution of doctrine in Reform Judaism may be best exemplified by the movement's attitude toward Zionism and Israel. Many of the first leaders of the Reform movement believed that pushing for the creation of a Jewish homeland in Israel undermined the concept of Judaism as a religious rather than national identity. They maintained that Jews should not think of themselves as exiled from Israel but instead should embrace the place of their birth as their homeland. It was feared that working for the creation of a Jewish state would only further alienate the Jewish population. A desire to create a Jewish homeland would promote dual loyalties and might even be seen by non-Jewish authorities as treasonous. However, after the 1917 Balfour Declaration, which pledged Britain's support for the creation of a Jewish homeland in the Middle East, Reform Judaism began to warm to the Zionist cause.

The 1948 creation of the State of Israel significantly helped to infuse Zionism into the Reform movement. In 1997, in accordance with the centennial of the World Zionist Organization (WZO), the CCAR issued "Reform Judaism and Zionism: A Centenary Platform" (also known as the Miami Platform) in which it formally declared its support of Israel and Zionism. Today, a small number of Reform Jews maintain anti-Zionist positions.

PAUL G. PIERPAOLI JR.

See also

Ashkenazic Judaism; Wise, Isaac Mayer; World Zionist Organization; Zionism

References

Greenstein, Howard R. *Turning Point: Zionism and Reform Judaism.* Otterup, Denmark: Scholars Press, 1981.

Kaplan, Dana Evan. *American Reform Judaism: An Introduction.* Piscataway, NJ: Rutgers University Press, 2003.

Meyer, Michael A. *Response to Modernity: A History of the Reform Movement in Judaism.* Detroit: Wayne State University Press, 1995.

Refugees

See Expellees and Refugees, Palestinian; Palestinian Refugee Camps

Religious Sites in the Middle East, Christian

Jerusalem is the principal holy city for Christianity. It contains the traditional tomb of Jesus and the route Jesus traveled to his crucifixion after his condemnation by the Roman procurator Pontius Pilate. It is also the place of Jesus's crucifixion (Golgotha). The Church of the Holy Sepulcher, in the northwest quarter of the Old City of Jerusalem, sits atop what most of Christendom believes to

Room, alleged to be the site of Jesus's Last Supper, located on the second floor of a building on Mount Zion, near the Dormition Church in Jerusalem. The traditional name for this upper chamber is the Cenacle. (Corel)

be the site of both Jesus's tomb and his crucifixion. The original church was built by Constantine the Great, the first Roman emperor (AD 306–337) to profess his Christianity. It was destroyed, however, in 1009. A new structure went up in the mid-12th century that underwent major renovations during the 19th century and major restorations in the mid-20th century.

The Via Dolorosa (Italian for "Street of Sorrows") is a street in the Old City of Jerusalem that is the supposed path trod by Jesus to Golgotha. It is divided by the Roman Catholic Church into the 14 Stations of the Cross, which pilgrims follow to remember Jesus's steps to his death. The final 5 stations, the last being the laying of Jesus's body in the tomb, are within the walls of the Church of the Holy Sepulcher.

There remains a dispute over the correct site of both Jesus's crucifixion and burial. Some Protestants, most notably British general Charles George Gordon in the late 19th century, asserted that both the tomb (the Garden Tomb) and Calvary (Golgotha, the place of the Skull) are in East Jerusalem, just north of the walls of the Old City. The uncertainty arises because the inhabitants of Jerusalem fled to Pella in AD 66 during the Jewish uprising and subsequent destruction of the Second Temple by the Roman general Titus in AD 70. There was no tradition of the correct location until Con-

stantine ordered its determination in AD 325, which was carried out subjectively at best.

Other significant Christian sites in Jerusalem include the Garden of Gethsemane (near the base of the Mount of Olives) where Jesus was betrayed and the Tomb of the Virgin Mary close by. Farther up on the Mount of Olives is the traditional place where Christians believe Christ made his final ascent to heaven. A mosque currently sits on the site, which is venerated by Muslims.

The Church of the Nativity in Bethlehem (the House of Bread) is the second major holy site for Christendom in the Middle East. It was built by Saint Helena (AD 248–328), the mother of Constantine the Great, on the site identified by Saint Justin the Martyr who lived in the second century. The Church of the Nativity is administered by the Greek, Roman, and Armenian churches.

Bethlehem, Jesus's traditional birthplace, has been under control of the Palestinian Authority (PA) since 1995. Palestinian militants fleeing the Israel Defense Forces' (IDF) Operation DEFENSIVE SHIELD seized the church on April 2, 2002, and set fire to a portion of the building. They were deported to Cyprus and European Union (EU) countries following a negotiated settlement 38 days later.

Nazareth, the town where Jesus grew up, is located some 15 miles west of the southern end of the Sea of Galilee. The shore of the Sea

Important Religious Sites in the Middle East

City	Location	Important in	
Bethlehem	West Bank	Christianity	birthplace of Jesus and site of the Church of the Nativity
Hebron	West Bank	Islam Judaism	site of the Tomb of the Patriarchs and Matriarchs
Jerusalem	Israel	Christianity Islam Judaism	site of Jesus's crucifixion and burial site of the al-Aqsa Mosque site of the Solomonic Temple and Second Temple
Mashad	Iran	Islam	burial place of Imam Reza
Mecca	Saudi Arabia	Islam	birthplace of Muhammad and site of the Kaaba
Medina	Saudi Arabia	Islam	burial place of Muhammad and original seat of the Muslim empire
Qom	Iran	Islam	site of Shia Islamic scholarship
Tiberias	Israel	Judaism	site of Jewish history and scholarship
Tzfat	Israel	Judaism	site of the writing of much of the Talmud

of Galilee itself is the site of much of Christ's early ministry, especially Capernaum, the original home of Simon Bar Jonah (later known as Saint Peter), and the Mount of Beatitudes near Tabgha, the traditional site of the Sermon on the Mount.

A less-accepted and less-venerated Christian holy site is what is believed to be the Church of John the Baptist. It was erected by the Roman emperor Anastasius (AD 491–518) to mark the spot on the bank of the Jordan River where Jesus is thought to have left his outer garments before being baptized by John the Baptist. There are, however, several places along the Jordan that claim to be the site of the baptism.

Israel allows unrestricted access to all religious shrines and holy sites. Nevertheless, entry checkpoints into Israel from the West Bank and Gaza limit access to the religious sites in Israel and Jerusalem in particular. The Israeli Security Fence, however, does restrict access to and from Bethlehem, Hebron, and the Jordan River. Israel does allow the appropriate religious authorities to administer their respective holy places. In Jerusalem, for example, the Church of the Holy Sepulcher is administered by the Greek Orthodox, Roman Catholic, Armenian Orthodox, and Coptic churches. Each controls a separate section of the church.

RICHARD EDWARDS AND DAVID T. ZABECKI

See also
Bethlehem; Jerusalem

References
Bahat, Dan. *The Illustrated Atlas of Jerusalem.* New York: Simon and Schuster, 1990.
Crown-Tamir, Hela. *How to Walk in the Footsteps of Jesus and the Prophets: A Scripture Reference Guide for Biblical Sites in Israel and Jordan.* Jerusalem: Gefen, 2000.
Mansour, Atallah. *Narrow Gate Churches: The Christian Presence in the Holy Land under Muslim and Jewish Rule.* Carol Stream, IL: Hope Publishing House, 2004.
Poole, Karen, ed. *Jerusalem & the Holy Land.* New York: Dorling Kindersley, 2007.

Religious Sites in the Middle East, Jewish

Jerusalem is the principal holy city for Judaism and was made the ancient capital of the United Kingdom of Israel by King David in the 10th century BC. It remained the capital of the Southern Kingdom of Judah in the Divided Kingdom. Jerusalem is the current capital of the State of Israel, although it is unrecognized as such by the majority of the world community. With the exception of the Israel Defense Forces (IDF), it is the location of the primary offices of all the branches of the Israeli government and the Israeli parliament (Knesset).

Jerusalem is the site of King Solomon's Temple (the First Temple) and the Second Temple erected during the rule of the Persian Darius (522–486 BC). The Second Temple was completely rebuilt starting around 19 BC under the reign of Herod the Great. The temple was destroyed by the Roman general Titus in the Jewish revolt that ended at Masada in AD 70. The only surviving remnant of the Second Temple is the Western Wall, which was actually a retailing wall at the base of the Temple Mount erected during Herod's reconstruction.

The Western Wall is also known as the Wailing Wall, so called by Europeans who saw pious Jews bemoaning the destruction of the Temple and praying for its restoration, and is a place of Jewish prayer and pilgrimage. The wall is central to the plans for a new temple by such groups as the Temple Mount Faithful Movement. Even though the cornerstone for this new temple was laid in July 2001, the building of a Third Temple on the site of the first two is highly problematic.

Currently, the Temple Mount is occupied by the al-Aqsa Mosque, Islam's third-holiest site. Both access to the Noble Sanctuary and the potential encroachment on the precinct by the proposed new temple have led to many clashes between Jews and Muslims since the Israelis captured the Old City of Jerusalem in the 1967 Six-Day War. The latest such disturbance began with a visit by Prime Min-

View of the Western Wall at the Dome of the Rock. (PhotoDisc, Inc.)

ister Ariel Sharon on September 28, 2000, to the al-Aqsa precinct. This event triggered the Second (al-Aqsa) Intifada.

The Tomb of David, located on Mount Zion just outside the walls of the Old City, is the traditional burial place of ancient Israel's greatest king. Until the Israeli capture of the Old City in 1967, the Tomb of David was the major site for Jewish prayers because Jews were not allowed access to the Western Wall. Also outside the current-day walls of the Old City and just to the south of the Temple Mount lie the excavated ruins of the City of David, the original city of Jerusalem conquered by King David about 1004 BC.

The Kidron Valley also lies outside the current-day Old City walls in East Jerusalem, between the Mount of Olives to the east and the high ground of the Temple Mount and Mount Zion to the west. The Kidron is known in the Bible as the Valley of Jehoshaphat, meaning "the valley where God will judge." It is the site of many significant Jewish tombs, including the Tomb of Bene Hezir, the Tomb of Zechariah, and the Pillar of Absalom.

The Tomb (Cave) of the Patriarchs and Matriarchs in Hebron (ancient Judea and now the southern part of the West Bank) is the second-holiest site in Judaism. It is the purported burial place of the great patriarchs and matriarchs buried as couples—Abraham and Sarah, Isaac and Rebecca, Jacob and Leah, and Adam and Eve —and is sacred to Muslims as well. Hebron was the capital of Judah, the Southern Kingdom, and the first capital of the United Kingdom,

before Jerusalem. Hebron came under Israeli control in the Six-Day War. The Jewish settlements built in Hebron since then remain a flashpoint in Israeli-Palestinian relations, despite the 1997 Hebron Protocol. Both a mosque (Sanctuary of Abraham) and a synagogue are built on top of the tomb. Jacob's second wife is buried in the Tomb of Rachel on the Jerusalem-Hebron Road near the Iron Gate of Israel's security fence at Bethlehem's northern entrance. Both tombs are holy to Jews and Muslims, who claim a common ancestry through Abraham.

Tzfat, or Safed, is sacred to Jews as the site of the writing of much of the Jerusalem (Palestinian) Talmud (AD 400–550) and for the development of Jewish kabbalistic mysticism (15th and 16th centuries). Tiberias is considered sacred as the last meeting place of the Sanhedrin (AD 426), as an ancient center of Jewish learning, and for the tombs of the ancient Jewish scholars.

RICHARD EDWARDS AND DAVID T. ZABECKI

See also

Al-Aqsa Mosque; Bethlehem; Hebron Protocol; Intifada, Second; Jerusalem; Religious Sites in the Middle East, Christian; Religious Sites in the Middle East, Muslim; Sharon, Ariel; Six-Day War; Western Wall

References

Bahat, Dan. *The Illustrated Atlas of Jerusalem.* New York: Simon and Schuster, 1990.

Crown-Tamir, Hela. *How to Walk in the Footsteps of Jesus and the Prophets: A Scripture Reference Guide for Biblical Sites in Israel and Jordan.* Jerusalem: Gefen, 2000.

Hoffman, Lawrence A. *Israel: A Spiritual Travel Guide; A Companion for the Modern Jewish Pilgrim.* 2nd ed. Woodstock, VT: Jewish Lights, 2005.

Mansour, Atallah. *Narrow Gate Churches: The Christian Presence in the Holy Land under Muslim and Jewish Rule.* Carol Stream, IL: Hope Publishing House, 2004.

Poole, Karen, ed. *Jerusalem & the Holy Land.* New York: Dorling Kindersley, 2007.

Religious Sites in the Middle East, Muslim

The Middle East is home to all of the holiest shrines of Islam. The three holiest Islamic sites are Mecca, Medina, and the al-Aqsa Mosque in Jerusalem. Other venerated sites are located in Damascus, Cairo, Najaf, Karbala, Qum, Mashhad, and Fez, to mention only a few. Also important in Palestine are Khalil (Hebron), Jericho, and numerous other mosques and tombs of holy persons. The holy sites in Israel and Palestine remain a focal point of the Palestinian-Israeli conflict because there is no freedom of worship for Muslims at these religious sites and also because of certain groups that propose to destroy them in order to rebuild the Temple. Israel restricts access to all religious sites for Palestinians, allowing entry only to those who are permitted to reside or travel in that specific area. Thus, Muslims who wish to visit the al-Aqsa Mosque must first obtain permission to visit Israel, which is restricted by many Muslim nations, and they will then most likely be denied entry to the country by Israel. Even Muslims from European nations or Turkey who can obtain entry must then satisfy soldiers at entry checkpoints. More recently, Israel's security fence restricted access to and from the West Bank and Gaza. An Islamic waqf, a trust or endowment that is required to be administered by Muslims, has been instead controlled by Israel. It is delegated to representatives approved by Israel, and since Oslo there has been an agreement that Palestinian security personnel will guard entry to the al-Aqsa complex in East Jerusalem. This is a site holy to both Islam and Judaism and has been a source of conflict since long before Israel gained control of it after the 1967 Six-Day War. The principal reason that Israeli prime minister Ehud Barak and Palestine Liberation Organization (PLO) chairman Yasser Arafat were unable to reach an agreement at the Camp David talks in July 2000 was the failure to reconcile Jewish and Muslim claims to the Bayt Maqdis, or al-Aqsa complex, known to Israelis as the Temple Mount.

Mecca, in Saudi Arabia, was the birthplace of the Prophet Muhammad and is Islam's holiest site. Muslim religious obligations include the pilgrimage (hajj) to Mecca, held annually during the Dhul-Hijjah (month of hajj), the last month of the Islamic calendar. Devout Muslims are expected to make at least one hajj if they can afford to do so.

Mecca's Great Mosque (Masjid al-Haram) is constructed around the Kaaba (meaning "cube"), the holiest place in Islam. Muslims believe that the Kaaba, a windowless granite and masonry cube covered with a black silk cloth, was built by Adam and then rebuilt by Ibrahim (Abraham). It is believed that he placed in its southeastern corner a gift, known as the Black Stone, from the angel Gabriel. The Zamzam, a dome-covered sacred well created by Allah, is located 115 feet from the Kaaba and provides water for the pilgrims.

Muhammad was welcomed in Medina after finding few adherents in Mecca. Medina was the nucleus of the new Muslim community until the rise of the Umayyad caliphs, when the capital was moved to Damascus in AD 661. It is home to the Mosque of the Prophet. This mosque contains the tombs of Muhammad and his daughter Fatimah. It also houses the tomb of Omar, the second caliph. The caliphs were the political successors to Muhammad. However, prayer was conducted in the direction of Jerusalem for many years, and this only later was changed to Mecca after the reconquest of that city.

The third-holiest Islamic site is the Bayt al-Maqdis, later known as the Haram al-Sharif (Noble Sanctuary) at the end of the Old City of Jerusalem (al-Quds). The al-Aqsa Mosque (Masjid al-Aqsa, meaning the "farthest mosque") is both a building and a complex of buildings. The site is dominated and bounded by two major structures, the al-Aqsa Mosque building on the east and the Dome of the Rock on the west. The Dome of the Rock, or the Mosque of Omar, is a *mashhad,* or a shrine for pilgrims. It is not a mosque used for public worship. The Dome of the Rock surrounds and covers a large rock (the Noble Rock). From this rock, Islamic tradition believes that Muhammad, at the end of his Night Journey from Mecca to Jerusalem in AD 621, ascended in the company of Gabriel through the heavens to Allah. Before returning to Earth, Muhammad met at the rock with the prophets, including Moses, and negotiated the number of the obligatory Islamic prayers. According to a prophetic tradition (hadith), the site is so sacred that Muslims believe that 1 prayer there is equivalent to 500 normal prayers. Some Jewish traditions assert that the rock was the platform upon which Abraham intended to fulfill God's divine command to sacrifice Isaac.

The Tomb (Cave) of the Patriarchs and Matriarchs in Hebron (ancient Judea and now the West Bank) is the burial place of Ibrahim and his family. He was the father of Ishmael, the ancestor from whom all Arab peoples believe they descended. The Orthodox Jewish settlements in Hebron that went up after the 1967 Six-Day War remain a flashpoint in the Palestinian-Israeli conflict despite the 1997 Hebron Protocol. The Sanctuary of Ibrahim, a mosque, and a synagogue are built atop of the tomb. Muslims consider the cave too sacred to enter. The Oak of Ibrahim (Oak of Mamre), sitting just over a mile west of Hebron, is believed to be the place where three angels told Ibrahim that his wife Sarah would bear his son Isaac. Also at Hebron is the tomb of Fatima, the daughter of Imam Husayn.

Although the prophet Moses died on Mount Nebo in present-day Jordan, his tomb, Maqam al-Nabi Musa near Jericho, is also venerated in Islam.

Throughout Israel and especially in the Negev, there are the tombs of Muslim saints. Those in the Negev are venerated by the Bedouin,

Evening prayer at the Mosque of the Prophet in Medina, Saudi Arabia. During the annual hajj, nearly 2 million pilgrims visit here. (Kazuyoshi Nomachi/Corbis)

who also believe that they may be cured by visiting these tombs. Oil or fabric scraps may be left to acquire the charismatic blessing of the saint. Just outside of the city of Herzliya is the tomb of 'Alin ibn 'Alim, known as the Mashhad Sayyidna Ali.

There are also sites holy to the Druze such as the grave of the prophet Jethro at Nabi Shu'ayb. Rather than a gravestone, a huge Christ's Thorn jujube tree was the focus and prayer site for pilgrims, and it is called the Sidrat Nabi Shu'ayb. There are numerous Islamic sites, historic mosques, and centers of Islamic scholarship outside of Palestine, but that does not detract from its importance. Religiously, Muslims consider all of Palestine a waqf.

For the Shia Muslims, the four most important sites are the holy cities of Najaf and Karbala in present-day Iraq and also two places in the cities of Mashhad and Qum in Iran. Mashhad is the burial place and shrine of the ninth-century Imam Reza (AD 766–818), the eighth Shia imam to follow the Prophet Muhammad. For the Twelver Shia Muslims, this imam was one of the infallible successors to Muhammad, descended through his son-in-law Ali. Qum, also in Iran, is a center for Shia Islamic studies and is a counterpart to the city of Najaf, known as Najaf the Noble, to Muslims in Iraq. Ayatollah Ruhollah Khomeini taught in both cities. Qum is also home to the gold-plated dome shrine to Fatima the Pure, the sister of Imam Reza. Karbala is a city important to the Shia because Imam Husayn and his forces were murdered here, and these deaths are honored annually in the mournful holiday of Ashura.

RICHARD EDWARDS AND SHERIFA ZUHUR

See also
Al-Aqsa Mosque; Arafat, Yasser; Barak, Ehud; Camp David Accords; Dome of the Rock; Haram al-Sharif; Hebron; Hebron Protocol; Israeli Security Fence; Jericho; Jerusalem; Khomeini, Ruhollah; Palestinian Authority; Six-Day War

References
Bahat, Dan. *The Illustrated Atlas of Jerusalem.* New York: Simon and Schuster, 1990.
Canaan, Taufik. *Mohammedan Saints and Sanctuaries in Palestine.* London: Luzac, 1927.

Crown-Tamir, Hela. *How to Walk in the Footsteps of Jesus and the Prophets: A Scripture Reference Guide for Biblical Sites in Israel and Jordan.* Jerusalem: Gefen, 2000.

Mansour, Atallah. *Narrow Gate Churches: The Christian Presence in the Holy Land under Muslim and Jewish Rule.* Carol Stream, IL: Hope Publishing House, 2004.

Nasr, Seyyed Hossein, and Ali Kazuyoshi Nomachi. *Mecca the Blessed, Medina the Radiant: The Holiest Cities of Islam.* New York: Aperture, 1997.

Poole, Karen, ed. *Jerusalem & the Holy Land.* New York: Dorling Kindersley, 2007.

Taragan, Hana. "The Tomb of Sayyidna 'Ali in Ar[sdotu]uf: The Story of a Holy Place." *Journal of the Royal Asiatic Society* 14 (2004): 83–102.

Reshef-Class Guided-Missile Boat

Israeli missile boat. The Reshef-class guided-missile boat is the follow-on design to the earlier Saar-class missile boats. Repeatedly upgraded, they continue to serve in the Israeli Navy.

Hoping to counter the Osa- and Komar-class missile boats supplied by the Soviet Union to Egypt and Syria in the 1960s, Israel funded the development of an antiship missile, which became the Gabriel, and hired the German firm Lürssen to design a fast ship to carry it. Fearing reprisal from the Arab world, West Germany prohibited their construction in West Germany, so Israel arranged to build 12 Saars in Cherbourg, France. The last of these neared completion when the 1967 Six-Day War began. Although French president Charles de Gaulle's arms embargo prevented their transfer to Israel, Israeli agents nonetheless managed to smuggle the Saars out of Cherbourg and into Israel.

The French embargo, however, convinced Israeli officials that they had to construct future warships in Israel. Fortunately, the growing sophistication of the Israeli arms industry made this possible, and plans were begun to build a new class of boats, the Reshefs, in the early 1970s.

Only two Reshef-class vessels were completed in time for the 1973 Yom Kippur War, however. Designed as a squadron leader, the Reshef-class guided-missile boats each displaced 446 tons, almost twice that of the Saar-class boats. Each was equipped with advanced electronics and could carry eight Gabriel antiship missiles. In the 1973 war the Reshefs proved themselves in battle alongside Israel's 12 Saars, sinking several Egyptian and Syrian warships without any loss on the Israeli side.

Israel continued production of the Reshef class after the war, and by 1980 10 had joined the Israeli fleet. During the 1980s, Israel added 8 U.S.-made Harpoon missiles to the Reshefs by removing 2 Gabriel missiles. The long-range Harpoon created a need for ships to carry helicopters to locate enemy ships and guide missiles to targets over the horizon. To meet this need, Israel Shipyards produced

The Israeli Navy's Sa'ar 4–class missile boat *Reshef* launching a ship-to-ship missile, 1989. (Israeli Government Press Office)

a stretched version of the Reshef, the Saar 4.5 or Hetz, the additional 12 feet of which allowed it to accommodate a helicopter platform. During the 1990s Israel modernized the class, improving electronics and air and missile defense systems and adding 32 Barak point defense missiles to the Hetz class (renamed the Nirit class after this refit). Reshef- and Hetz/Nirit-class warships continue to serve in the Israeli Navy. In addition, Israel has sold them to South Africa, Mexico, Chile, and other nations.

STEPHEN K. STEIN

See also

Arms Sales, International; Israel Defense Forces; Missiles, Cruise; Warships, Surface

References

Rabinovich, Abraham. *The Boats of Cherbourg: The Secret Israeli Operation That Revolutionized Naval Warfare.* New York: Seaver, 1988.

Tzalel, Moshe. *From Ice-Breaker to Missile Boat: The Evolution of Israel's Naval Strategy.* Westport, CT: Greenwood, 2000.

Restoration Movement

A Christian religious movement that originated in the early 19th century in the United States and advocated Zionism as part of its dogma. Indeed, the various U.S. Protestant groups in this period were among the first advocates of Zionism, and that Christian religious dogma came to cast a long shadow over the foreign policy of the United States.

The Restoration Movement was one of many reformations that emerged during the Second Great Awakening and revolved around the idea that sectarian Christian churches had become too enshrined in dogmatic arguments and too separated from the fundamental biblical teachings of the New Testament. Adherents to the Restoration Movement, also called the Stone-Campbell Restoration Movement, believed that all Christians should abandon their divisive denominations and forge a new relationship with God by simplifying their religious practices.

Two of the earliest founders of the Restoration Movement were Barton W. Stone and Alexander Campbell. Both urged followers to abandon their churches in favor of a more simple form of worship. Each emphasized the need for baptism by total immersion as a means of cleansing sins. After being reborn, believers celebrated their faith through a weekly communion ceremony, or the Lord's Supper. At the ceremony, each adherent ate bread, which symbolized Jesus Christ's body, and drank grape juice, which symbolized his blood that was shed during the crucifixion. Stone and Campbell's followers, centered in Kentucky, Indiana, and Ohio, came together into a single movement in 1832.

Many of the religious movements of the early 19th century strongly supported Zionism. They argued that when Jews reoccupied the Holy Land it would signal the Second Coming of Christ, which would institute a new reign of heaven on Earth. To hasten the Messiah's return, members of the Restoration Movement actively supported the creation of a Zionist state in Palestine.

Despite the movement's foundation as a solution to sectarian disagreements, the Restoration Movement was not immune to its own internal divisions. After seven decades of unity, the Stone-Campbell group split in 1906. Two major groups emerged from the schism, the Church of Christ and the Christian Church, the latter often called the Disciples of Christ. Further splits have occurred in the past century, with splinter groups peeling off from each of the core divisions of 1906. The lack of unity within the churches of the Restoration Movement is in direct contradiction of the original tenets of the Restorationists, but it is unlikely that the disparate congregations will choose to reunify in light of doctrinal and procedural differences within each group.

PAUL J. SPRINGER

See also

Zionism

References

Allen, C. Leonard, and Richard T. Hughes. *Discovering Our Roots: The Ancestry of Churches of Christ.* Abilene, TX: Abilene Christian University Press, 1988.

Hughes, Richard T. *Reviving the Ancient Faith: The Story of Churches of Christ in America.* Grand Rapids, MI: Eerdmans, 1996.

Jorgenson, Dale A. *Theological and Aesthetic Roots in the Stone-Campbell Movement.* Kirksville, MO: Thomas Jefferson University Press, 1989.

North, James B. *Union in Truth: An Interpretive History of the Restoration Movement.* Cincinnati, OH: Standard Publishing, 1994.

Oren, Michael B. *Power, Faith, and Fantasy: America in the Middle East, 1776 to the Present.* New York: Norton, 2007.

Revisionist Zionism

A form of Zionism that gained hold after 1925. Revisionist Zionism argued that the British Mandate for Palestine should be revised to create a sovereign Jewish state encompassing both sides of the Jordan River. Revisionist Zionists also held that Zionism should shift its emphasis from social and economic development in Palestine to the immediate creation of a Jewish state aligned with the United Kingdom.

Vladimir Jabotinsky founded Revisionist Zionism in 1925 as a variant of Theodor Herzl's Political Zionism. Jabotinsky was the Russian-born Jewish Zionist who helped found the Jewish Legion that fought for the British in World War I. Israel's present-day Likud and Kadima parties and many prominent Israeli politicians are inheritors of the Revisionist legacy.

Revisionist Zionism is part of the pantheon of Zionist movements that developed at the end of the 19th century in response to increased Jewish persecution in Europe. Zionism sought to resolve this growing problem by seeking to create a legal (guaranteed) Jewish homeland in Palestine. These Zionist movements spanned the spectrum from the purely secular to the purely religious.

Revisionist Zionism was one of the major influences in Jewish Palestine following World War I. Jabotinsky's experience in World War I led him to believe that swift and strong retaliatory action could forestall Arab attacks on the Yishuv (Jewish community in

Vladimir Jabotinsky (*center*) and Menachem Begin (*right*) in Pinsk, Poland, December 1933. (Israeli Government Press Office)

Palestine). Jabotinsky was one of the founders of the United Jewish Appeal (Keren Hayesod), the main Zionist fund-raising organization, and in 1921 was elected to the Executive Council of the World Zionist Organization (WZO) that was chaired by Chaim Weizmann. Jabotinsky disagreed with the measured goals advocated by Weizmann. Thus, in 1923 Jabotinsky resigned and then in 1925 formed the Revisionist Zionist Alliance, also known as the Alliance of Revisionists-Zionists. Jabotinsky's Revisionist Zionism sought to change the WZO's moderate plan and the timetable of the other Zionist movements to a more aggressive plan with speedier implementation. Revisionism advocated shifting the emphasis of Zionism away from social and economic development in Palestine to the immediate creation of a Jewish state in Palestine. Jabotinsky advocated massive European immigration into Palestine, rapidly producing a Jewish voting and fighting majority; the immediate creation of a Jewish state in Palestine; and the creation of a Jewish self-defense organization.

The Revisionists advocated two additional revisions. Jabotinsky rejected what he perceived to be the fanciful hope of David Ben-Gurion's Labor Zionism that a Jewish state would eventually arise from an established Jewish working and middle class flourishing in Palestine and asserted that more direct and immediate action was needed. Revisionism also sought to revise, reexamine, or realign the

relationship of Zionism to the British mandatory government in Palestine and to the United Kingdom itself. Weizmann and Ben-Gurion emphasized and promoted the independent settlement of Palestine with the approval of the dominant world communities. Revisionism originally advocated a more direct alliance with the British.

Revisionists under Jabotinsky's leadership sought to develop a symbiotic relationship with the United Kingdom and through that relationship alter the British Mandate for Palestine to be more favorable to Zionism. Jabotinsky tried to bring this change about through worldwide and internal social and political pressure on the British government by using petitions, demonstrations, and other forms of public appeal and protest. He also sought to reason with the British, arguing that it was in the United Kingdom's best interest to have a loyal friend in the region, something the British had learned in World War I. Jabotinsky also argued that British aid and cooperation would be reciprocated by a strong Zionist state with European, particularly British, roots. He even asserted that such a Zionist state would be a loyal autonomous extension of the United Kingdom, allowing it to project power into the region with minimal military commitment.

Jabotinsky used the latter reasoning to argue for the revision of the 1922 decision by the League of Nations to divide the mandate into two geographical units, one east of the Jordan River and one west of the Jordan River that remained under the direct administration of the British. The Emirate of Transjordan had been created as a semiautonomous political division of the British Mandate for Palestine east of the Jordan River, encompassing an area roughly equivalent to the 1942–1965 Kingdom of Jordan. The creation of Transjordan was an attempt to appease the Arab nations in light of the 1917 Balfour Declaration that expressed official British support for a Jewish homeland in Palestine. Jabotinsky argued that this appeasement would create neither a loyal nor a strong British advocate and partner in the region and that he and other Zionists had demonstrated their loyalty to the United Kingdom when they had fought with the British in World War I. Jabotinsky pressed the British to convert all of the mandate east and west of the Jordan River into a dependable sovereign Jewish state with a proven pro-British propensity. Such a friend would be achieved in part by a British-sponsored, -promoted, and -funded mass Jewish immigration from Europe into the mandate, and this would make European Jewry the majority in Palestine. Jabotinsky also advocated the formation and sponsorship of two Jewish Legion groups to be stationed in Palestine and military training of Jewish youths for self-defense and potential mobilization if needed.

The British rejected his ideas and even barred his return to Palestine following the Sixteenth World Zionist Congress in 1929, but these ideas were implemented in the Yishuv. Revisionist settlers brought their Betar youth movement into the Yishuv and created their own self-defense force, the Irgun Tsvai Leumi (National Military Organization), based on theories of Middle East warfare advocated by Jabotinsky.

Irgun was a right-wing paramilitary Zionist underground movement in Palestine during 1931–1948 known for immediate and harsh retaliation for attacks on the Jewish community in Palestine and its advocacy of military action against the British. The Irgun movement itself was classified by the British as a terrorist organization, and many of its operations were declared terrorist by the Jewish Agency for Palestine, Haganah, and the Histadrut (Israeli trade union). Haganah, organized after the Arab riots of 1920–1921, was the main Jewish self-defense and military organization during 1920–1948 in Palestine. Jabotinsky, one of the founders of Haganah, led the organization against Arab riots in Jerusalem during Passover in 1920. His swift response was deemed criminal by the British mandatory government, and he was sentenced to 15 years' hard labor but was soon granted amnesty and released. The Irgun was created in 1931 as an alternative to what the Revisionists perceived was Haganah's overly restrained responses to Arab attacks on the Yishuv. The Revisionists sought in similar fashion to confront and at times counter with force what they perceived as the British mandatory government's pro-Arab bias.

Jabotinsky founded the Betar youth movement, also known as Beitar, in Riga, Latvia, in 1923. He asserted five major goals for Betar: teach Jewish youths to defend themselves, prepare the youths of the Yishuv to protect their homes against Arab attacks, prepare the

youths of the Yishuv to fight for a Jewish state in Palestine, prepare the youths of the Yishuv to lead the Jewish state in Palestine, and encourage Jewish youths from outside Palestine to immigrate to Palestine.

Menachem Begin exemplified the ideals of Jabotinsky and Betar. Begin joined Betar when he was 16 years old and in 1932 led the Organization Department of Betar Poland before graduating from the University of Warsaw in 1935. Begin assumed the leadership of Betar Czechoslovakia in 1936, and in 1938 Betar Poland's 100,000 members engaged in self-defense, weapons, agricultural, and communications training and transported immigrants to Palestine whom the British deemed illegal. Begin advocated the establishment of a Jewish national homeland in Palestine by conquest and pushed Betar and Jabotinsky to adopt this position at the 1938 Betar convention. Begin openly criticized the Jewish Agency for Palestine and worldwide Zionism as being too timid in their approach to a Jewish state and forcefully advocated the Revisionist Zionists' belief that a Jewish homeland must be created in Palestine and if need be by military action. Begin joined the Irgun in 1942 and commanded the organization from 1943 to 1948. The Irgun stopped its attacks on the British during 1941–1943 as World War II worsened and supported the Allies against Germany and Germany's Arab allies in the Middle East. It was under Begin's leadership that the Irgun declared war on the British in February 1944 and resumed attacks on Arab villages and British interests. Some Betar graduates also joined the more radical Stern Gang, also known as Lehi (Jewish Freedom Fighters).

Ever the Anglophile, Jabotinsky disagreed with the attacks on the British and asserted that the real enemy was the Arabs and that the British could still be enticed to side with the Yishuv. The Irgun and Lehi, on the other hand, felt it necessary to war against both the British and the Arabs. Jabotinsky and the Irgun-Lehi branch of Revisionist Zionism also disagreed on the status of the Arabs in Palestine and their status in the future Jewish state. An essential element of almost all of the Zionist strategies was the creation of a Jewish majority that would vote for a Jewish state. Almost all Zionists sought to produce this Jewish majority through aliya. Many argued, however, that aliya should be augmented by a correlative strategy, the outmigration of the Arab population. Most Zionists argued for a voluntary transfer encouraged through economic incentives and sanctions. Still others advocated involuntary transfer (i.e., expulsion). It was this latter technique that was used during 1948–1949 to reduce the Palestinian Christian population in West Jerusalem by 50 percent following the Israeli War of Independence (1948–1949).

The argument for transfer was simply that reductions in the Arab population hastened the creation of the Jewish majority and created a more stable and secure state by decreasing the danger of having pockets of Arabs living within the Jewish state. The Revisionists generally supported involuntary transfer. The Irgun-Lehi branch of Revisionism adamantly opposed any power sharing with Arabs in Palestine and advocated their involuntary expulsion. Jabotinsky never made a clear statement concerning transfer.

Although Revisionism advocated shifting the emphasis of Zionism away from social and economic development in Palestine, Revisionism did not ignore those needs. Revisionism created a labor union, the National Labor Federation, and health services to compete with the community services offered by Labor Zionism's Histadrut (General Federation of Laborers in the Land of Israel).

Labor Zionism was strongest in the rural Jewish communities of Palestine, in the kibbutzim and moshavim, and with the working class. Revisionism had few followers in the areas dominated by Labor Zionism. General Zionism dominated the Yishuv middle class. Revision was strongest in Poland and Eastern Europe. This strength was primarily due to the pervasiveness of Betar in the Jewish communities there that were formed from the remnants of World War II Holocaust survivors.

As the 1920s and 1930s passed with what the Revisionists saw as little progress toward the creation of a Jewish state and as attacks on the Yishuv grew in the face of what some Revisionists asserted was a profound British pro-Arabism, the Revisionists became more strident in their demands for action. The Revisionists' more aggressive approach was rejected by the WZO in 1935, and the Revisionists resigned from the WZO. The Revisionists returned to the WZO in 1946 and asserted that the position of the WZO had come into line with Revisionism with the 1942 Biltmore Program's rejection of the binational solution to Palestine in favor of the immediate creation of a Jewish state in Palestine.

Revisionist Zionism diverged into three distinct branches at the end of the 1930s: the centrists, the Irgun and Lehi, and the national messianists. All three branches advocated the creation of a Jewish state spanning the Jordan River with boundaries similar to those of Israel after the conquest of the land of Canaan under Joshua. The centrists favored the voluntary transfer of the Arab population, a British parliamentary form of government, and a more cooperative approach seeking the long hoped-for alliance with the United Kingdom. Irgun and Lehi opposed any power sharing, favored Arab expulsion, and saw the British as much the enemy as the Arabs. Irgun and Lehi did favor a parliamentary form of government such as that in the United Kingdom. The national messianists opposed any power sharing, favored Arab expulsion, and opposed any agreements or alliances with any foreign powers. The national messianists leaned more toward an authoritarian, theocratic (divinely directed) regime, choosing the leader as God had chosen David and Saul.

Betar members and former members played important roles in the fight against the British during the time of the mandate and in the creation of Israel and all branches of the Israeli military. Betar and Revisionist Zionism also produced two more Israeli prime ministers besides Begin—Yitzhak Shamir and Ehud Olmert—as well as Israel's former defense minister Moshe Arens. Betar remains active in support of worldwide Jewry and continues to encourage aliya to Israel through its young adult and university campus programs in North America.

RICHARD EDWARDS

See also

Balfour Declaration; Begin, Menachem; Ben-Gurion, David; Haganah; Herzl, Theodor; Irgun Tsvai Leumi; Jabotinsky, Vladimir Yevgenyevich; Labor Zionism; Lohamei Herut Israel; Palestine, British Mandate for; Reform Judaism and Zionism; Weizmann, Chaim; World Zionist Organization; Zionism; Zionist Conference

References

Baume, Judith Taylor. *The "Bergson Boys" and the Origins of Contemporary Zionist Militancy*. Translated by Dena Ordan. Syracuse, NY: Syracuse University Press, 2005.

Brenner, Lenni. *The Iron Wall: Zionist Revisionism from Jabotinsky to Shamir*. London: Zed, 1984.

Brenner, Michael. *Zionism: A Brief History*. Translated by Shelley Frisch. Princeton, NJ: Markus Wiener, 2003.

Kaplan, Eran. *The Jewish Radical Right: Revisionist Zionism and Its Ideological Legacy*. Madison: University of Wisconsin Press, 2005.

Morris. Benny. *Righteous Victims: A History of the Zionist-Arab Conflict, 1881–2001*. New York: Vintage, 2001.

Sachar, Howard M. *A History of Israel: From the Rise of Zionism to Our Time*. 3rd ed. New York: Knopf, 2007.

Shavit, Yaacov. *Jabotinsky and the Revisionist Movement, 1925–1948*. New York: Routledge, 1988.

Reza Pahlavi, Mohammad, Shah of Iran
Born: October 26, 1919
Died: July 27, 1980

Ruler of Iran from 1941 to 1979. Mohammad Reza Pahlavi, who was also known by the deferential title Aryamehr, which means "Light of the Aryans," was the second monarch of the Pahlavi dynasty and the last shah of Iran. He was born in Tehran on October 26, 1919, the son of Shah Reza Pahlavi, who ruled Iran from 1925 to 1941. His father was a military leader, Reza Khan, who had overthrown the Qajar dynasty and established the Pahlavi dynasty.

During the last decades of the Qajar dynasty, the British and Russians established spheres of influence in Iran. At the beginning of the 20th century, the Qajar shah had granted a concession to the British government, which resulted in British domination of the lucrative Iranian oil industry. Reza Pahlavi sought to decrease British and Russian influence in Iran by seeking closer ties with Germany and Italy. The shah's policy had the opposite effect, resulting in the occupation of Iran by British and Soviet forces in 1941 during World War II. Meanwhile, Mohammad Reza Pahlavi completed his education at a Swiss boarding school in 1935 and, upon returning to Iran, attended a military academy in Tehran, graduating in 1938. Two brief marriages had ended in divorce by 1948. Concerned that Reza Pahlavi was planning to ally his nation with Nazi Germany, the British forced him to abdicate in favor of Mohammad Reza Pahlavi on September 16, 1941, shortly before the latter's 22nd birthday.

Unlike his father, Mohammad Reza Pahlavi was willing to cooperate with the Allied war effort. The British and Americans used Iran as a conduit to ferry supplies to the Soviet Union during the war.

Mohammad Reza Pahlavi, shah of Iran (1941–1979), at his desk in Tehran, November 1960. (Bettmann/Corbis)

For many Iranians, the new shah's legitimacy was in question because he was viewed as a puppet of the Western powers.

After World War II Iran was plagued by economic problems, including a large and impoverished peasantry, little foreign capital and investment, and high unemployment. Although tremendous wealth was being generated by Iranian oil production, most of the profits were going to the British-owned Anglo-Iranian Oil Company (AIOC).

In 1951 the Iranian parliament nationalized the AIOC, and Dr. Mohammad Mosaddeq, a nationalist who was a member of the Qajar family, became prime minister of Iran. It had been Mosaddeq who advocated for the nationalization of AIOC. The British imposed a naval blockade on Iran and refused to allow Iran to export any of its oil. On April 4, 1953, President Dwight D. Eisenhower's administration approved $1 million in funding for the overthrow of Mosaddeq, who was being supported by radical Islamic clerics and the Tudeh Party, which was nationalist and prosocialist. The plan called for the shah to dismiss Mosaddeq. Although this initially failed and the shah was forced to flee Iran, within a few days a military coup, with support from the Central Intelligence Agency (CIA), restored the shah to this throne. Mosaddeq was placed under house arrest and then tried and imprisoned.

After being restored to power, the shah imposed an authoritarian regime funded by an increased profit-sharing plan negotiated with the foreign oil companies. By the early 1960s, the Iranian treasury was awash in money. The shah's secret police, Sazeman-e Ettelaat va Amniyat-e Keshvar (SAVAK, National Information and Security Organization), crushed all politically and religiously based resistance in Iran. SAVAK was notorious for its brutal persecutions and torturing of prisoners. During the White Revolution of 1963, the shah nationalized large estates and distributed the land to 4 million landless peasants. And influenced by his third wife, Farah Diba, whom he married in 1959, the shah also granted women the right to vote. The move was fiercely unpopular among traditional Muslims and conservative clerics. In 1975, citing security reasons, the shah effectively banned the multiparty system in Iran and ruled with even greater authority through his Rastakhiz (Resurrection) Party. These moves toward increased autocracy angered not only Islamic fundamentalists but also growing numbers of the middle class and intelligentsia. In 1976 the shah replaced the Islamic calendar, which begins in 622 when the Prophet Muhammad ibn Abdullah led his followers to Medina, with the Persian calendar that began more than 25 centuries earlier.

In foreign affairs, the shah was decidedly pro-Western. Under President Richard Nixon's administration, which came to view the shah's Iran as the central citadel in the Middle East, sales of U.S. arms and weaponry to Iran increased dramatically. Not surprisingly, the shah's pro-Western orientation did not sit well with Iran's

Islamic clerics and other traditionalists. In particular, the shah was considered far more friendly to Israel than to his Arab neighbors.

The shah managed to straddle the fence during the 1967 Six-Day War and 1973 Yom Kippur War by maintaining reasonably cordial relations with the Persian Gulf nations. He also enjoyed generally good relations with Jordan and Egypt. Relations with Iraq remained strained until the 1975 Algiers Accord brought a thaw. With revenues from the petroleum industry, the shah had built the largest military force in the Persian Gulf by the late 1970s.

By the end of the 1970s, however, the shah's strong-arm tactics, brutal suppression of dissidents, and increasing secularization had begun to take their toll. Following a year of intense political protests against the monarchy from both Islamic traditionalists and the middle class, a revolution occurred on January 16, 1979, and the shah and his family were forced to flee Iran. In February 1979 on his return from exile in France, the Ayatollah Ruhollah Khomeini was hailed by millions of Iranians. He and his supporters began to consolidate their political control of the country by eliminating opposing factions and clerics and establishing an Islamic government.

Mohammad Reza Pahlavi first went into exile in Egypt. Although President Jimmy Carter allowed the shah to seek treatment for lymphatic cancer in New York City, he was compelled to leave the United States after his treatment. He lived for a few months in Panama before returning to Cairo, Egypt, where he died on July 27, 1980. The shah's oldest son, Reza Pahlavi II, who lives in the United States, is heir to the Pahlavi dynasty.

MICHAEL R. HALL

See also

Iran; Iran, Armed Forces; Khomeini, Ruhollah

References

Barth, Linda, et al. *Mohammed Reza Pahlavi.* New York: Chelsea House, 2002.

Farmanfarmaian, Manucher, and Roxane Farmanfarmaian. *Blood and Oil: A Prince's Memoir of Iran, from the Shah to the Ayatollah.* New York: Random House, 2005.

Gasiorowski, Mark. *U.S. Foreign Policy and the Shah: Building a Client State in Iran.* Ithaca, NY: Cornell University Press, 1991.

Ghani, Cyprus. *Iran and the Rise of the Reza Shah: From Qajar Collapse to Pahlavi Power.* London: Tauris, 2001.

Rice, Condoleezza
Born: November 14, 1954

U.S. national security adviser (2001–2005) and secretary of state from 2005. Condoleezza Rice was born on November 14, 1954, in Birmingham, Alabama, to a prominent African American family. She graduated from the University of Denver at age 19 in 1973, then earned a master's degree from Notre Dame University in 1975. After working in the State Department during Jimmy Carter's presidency, Rice returned to the University of Denver and received a doctorate in international studies in 1981. She joined the faculty at Stanford

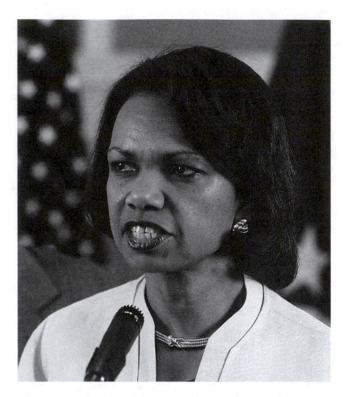

U.S. secretary of state Condoleezza Rice addresses the media following a meeting at the U.S. embassy in Baghdad, Iraq, April 2006. (U.S. Department of Defense)

University as a professor of political science and fellow at the Hoover Institute.

In 1989 Rice joined the administration of President George H. W. Bush, where she worked closely with Secretary of State James Baker. She was the director of Soviet and East European affairs on the National Security Council (NSC) and a special assistant to the president on national security affairs. She impressed Bush, who subsequently recommended her to his son George W. Bush when the Texas governor began to prepare for his 2000 presidential campaign. From 1993 to 2000, Rice was the provost of Stanford University.

Rice served as a foreign policy adviser to the younger Bush in the 2000 presidential campaign and, on assuming the presidency, Bush appointed her in January 2001 as the nation's first female and second African American national security adviser. Following the September 11, 2001, terrorist attacks on the United States, Rice emerged as a central figure in crafting the U.S. military and diplomatic response and in advocating war with Iraq. She played a central role in the successful implementation of Operation ENDURING FREEDOM in Afghanistan in late 2001.

In 2002 Rice helped develop the U.S. national security strategy commonly referred to as the Bush Doctrine that emphasized the use of preemptive military strikes to prevent the use of weapons of mass destruction (WMDs) and acts of terrorism. She was also instrumental in the administration's hard-line policy toward the Iraqi regime of Saddam Hussein, including the effort to isolate Iraq and formulate an international coalition against it. Rice was one of the main proponents of the 2003 U.S.-led invasion of Iraq, Operation IRAQI FREEDOM.

During the 2004 presidential campaign, Rice became the first national security adviser to openly campaign on behalf of a candidate. She faced criticism by Democrats for her hard-line security policies and for her advocacy against affirmative action policies. After the election, on the resignation of Colin Powell, Rice was appointed secretary of state.

Once in office in 2005, Rice worked to repair relations with U.S. allies such as France and Germany, the governments of which opposed the U.S.-led invasion of Iraq. She also endeavored to increase international support for the continuing U.S. efforts in Iraq. Rice's closeness with Bush provided her with greater access and therefore more influence than Powell. One result of this was that in the second Bush administration, Secretary of Defense Donald Rumsfeld had less influence in broad security policy, while Rice increased the role of the State Department in formulating such policy.

In 2005 Rice led the U.S. effort to develop a multilateral approach toward Iran in light of that country's refusal to suspend its nuclear program. In June 2006 the permanent members of the United Nations (UN) developed a plan to offer incentives in exchange for the cessation of Iran's nuclear program. Rice supported European Union (EU) high commissioner for foreign policy Javier Solana's efforts to negotiate with Iran after Tehran refused to meet an August 2006 deadline to suspend its nuclear enrichment.

Rice was a staunch supporter of Israel. She endeavored to gain support for the Road Map to Peace, which endorsed the creation of a Palestinian state in exchange for democratic reforms and the renunciation of terrorism by the Palestinians. During the second half of 2003, the U.S. Coordinating and Monitoring Mission (USCMM) in Israel attempted to advance the Road Map to Peace initiative. The chief of the mission, Ambassador John Wolf, reported directly to Rice.

Rice led the negotiations in 2005 for the Israeli withdrawal from the Gaza Strip and the subsequent agreement on border crossings. When fighting broke out in July 2006 between Israel and Hezbollah guerrillas in Lebanon, she supported Israel's use of force and refused to call for a cease-fire, arguing that the fighting was part of the birth of a new Lebanon. This turned many Lebanese against the United States. She subsequently worked to delay a UN-brokered cease-fire through UN Security Council Resolution 1701. Belatedly in the opinion of many observers, Rice worked to put together talks in Annapolis, Maryland, in late November 2007 between Arab and Israeli government representatives with the stated goal of achieving an Arab-Israeli peace agreement before President Bush leaves office.

TOM LANSFORD

See also
Bush, George Herbert Walker; Bush, George Walker; Hezbollah; Hussein, Saddam; Iran; Iraq; Iraq War; Israel; Lebanon, Israeli Operations against; Nuclear Weapons; Terrorism; United States Coordinating and Monitoring Mission; Wolf, John Stern

References
Felix, Antonia. *Condi: The Condoleezza Rice Story*. New York: Newmarket, 2002.
Lusane, Clarence. *Colin Powell and Condoleezza Rice: Foreign Policy, Race, and the New American Century*. Westport, CT: Praeger, 2006.
Morris, Dick, and Eileen McGann. *Condi vs. Hillary: The Next Great Presidential Race*. New York: Regan Books, 2005.

Rifles

The rifle is a shoulder-fired weapon that is the soldier's primary firearm. Although the soldier may be attached to a crew-served weapon such as a machine gun, artillery piece, mortar, or tank, the rifle remains his or her basic weapon for self-defense, position defense, or general security duties. The infantry soldier's survival and success on the battlefield depend on his skill with his rifle.

The Arab-Israeli conflicts were typical of all modern wars, with the vast majority of the combatants carrying rifles into combat. As in most other modern armies, however, officers and section leaders frequently carried pistols or submachine guns instead of rifles. The infantry squad is usually equipped with a light machine gun or a heavy-barrel automatic rifle, but the rifle remains the primary infantry tool.

The Arab-Israeli wars were a testing ground for various new armament technologies, as infantry weapons evolved from bolt-action rifles to the current generation of magazine-fed, semiautomatic, and automatic assault rifles. When Israel declared statehood in May 1948, Palestine and much of the immediate region had been a mandate of the United Kingdom. The British equipped and trained the standing military and police forces there, and British small arms therefore predominated in the region. The Transjordan Arab Legion and the Egyptian Army in particular were relatively well equipped with British armaments.

By the end of World War II, the standard issue British rifle was the bolt-action Lee Enfield Rifle Number 4 Mark I. It was an evolutionary development of the 1895 Lee Medford rifle first produced by the Royal Small Arms Factory located near London at Enfield Lock. In 1906 the Short Magazine Lee Enfield Mk I, universally known as the SMLE, was approved for standard issue to British infantry units.

A carbine is a more compact version of a standard rifle, usually with a shorter barrel and sometimes chambered for a smaller caliber. Carbines were first developed for cavalry and mounted troops and later were issued as substitutes for pistols. The British, however, considered a carbine version of the SMLE for cavalry use to be an unnecessary duplication of effort.

The most common version of the SMLE during World War I was the Mk III. In 1939 it was replaced with the Enfield Rifle No. 4 Mk I, which weighed 10.3 pounds, had a rate of fire of 20–30 rounds per

Young women from settlements in northern Israel practice firing the Uzi submachine gun, April 1980. (Moshe Milner/Israeli Government Press Office)

minute, and had a maximum effective range of 900 meters. The Rifle No. 4 Mk I remained in British service until replaced in 1957 by the Belgian-designed Fabrique Nationale FAL (Fusil Automatic Legiere).

The Enfield was rugged and easily maintained and was one of the most widely produced weapons of the 20th century. It had a 10-round magazine external to the rifle and one of the best bolt-action operating systems ever designed. Many small arms experts believe that the Enfield's bolt-action system was equal to or better than the German-made Mauser system, which was and still is considered the world standard.

The Enfield fired the uniquely British .303-caliber round, which was common to all British small arms of the period including the Bren gun squad automatic weapon and the Vickers and Lewis machine guns. The British submachine gun, the Sten, was chambered for the 9×19-mm parabellum round. Introduced in 1941, it weighed 7 pounds, had a cyclic rate of fire of 500 rounds per minute, and had a maximum effective range of only 50 meters.

As the Jewish state became a reality, so did its need for weapons. Israel's preindependence underground army, Haganah, had approximately 10,000 rifles, pistols, and submachine guns, far short of the number needed to arm a regular army that had to face the combined standing armies of Egypt, Syria, Transjordan, and Iraq. Complicat-

ing Israel's situation, most of the world embargoed arms shipments to the new nation.

In 1948 Israeli agents negotiated an agreement with Czechoslovakia, one of the leading arms manufacturers in Eastern Europe. Ironically, the Israelis bought weapons that the Czechs had produced under German occupation for the Third Reich. The Israelis acquired substantial numbers of the Mauser K-98k, the standard shoulder arm of the World War II Wehrmacht.

The original version of the Mauser, the Gewehr-98, was first adopted by the German Army in 1898 and was its standard rifle through World War I. In 1935 the Wehrmacht adopted an updated carbine version, the K-98, and the even shorter-barreled K-98k. The first "K" in the designation stood for *Karabiner* ("carbine"), and the second "k" stood for *kurz* (short). The bolt-action K-98k was chambered for a 7.92×57-mm round and weighed 9 pounds. It had a maximum rate of fire of 20 rounds per minute and a maximum effective range of 700 meters. The K-98k was the standard issue weapon of the Israel Defense Forces (IDF) until the 1956 Sinai Campaign and continued in service with IDF reserve and rear-echelon units until 1967.

The Czechs also supplied Israel with German-designed light and heavy machine guns. The Israelis purchased various other weapons wherever they could on the international market. They also raided British and Arab weapons depots at every opportunity.

By 1955 the Israelis decided that they could not remain dependent on other nations for their armaments. They purchased a license to manufacture the Belgian FN FAL rifle, initially introduced in 1951. The Israeli-made FAL, called the Romat, fired a standard NATO 7.62×51-mm round and weighed 9.8 pounds. It had a cyclic rate of fire of 650 rounds per minute and a maximum effective range of 600 meters. By the time of the 1967 Six-Day War, the FAL was standard issue in the IDF but was not a popular weapon. It had a tendency to jam in the fine sand of the Middle East, and Israeli soldiers complained about having to clean the weapon constantly in combat. The FAL's weight also limited the amount of ammunition a soldier could carry in combat, and its 43-inch length was impractical for the crews of tanks and other armored vehicles.

During the late 1940s, Israeli ordnance officer Uzi Gal designed an innovative submachine gun that bears his name. The Uzi was adopted by the IDF in 1955 and quickly became a universally recognized symbol of the State of Israel. Weighing only 7.7 pounds, it was chambered for the 9×19-mm Parabellum round. It had a cyclic rate of fire of 600 rounds per minute but a maximum effective range of only 200 meters. Subsequent variants have been chambered for the .45-caliber ACP round.

The Uzi was immensely popular with IDF soldiers, who all too frequently discarded their issue rifles if they had a chance to acquire an Uzi. The basic version was only 18.5 inches long and was especially well suited for armored vehicle crews and special operating forces. In December 2003 the IDF announced that it was completely retiring the Uzi, but it would continue to manufacture the weapon for both domestic law enforcement and security service work as well as for export. More than 90 countries have bought the Uzi.

After the Six-Day War, the IDF started to phase out the FAL in favor of the Uzi and the Soviet-produced AK-47 (Automvat Kalashnikov), captured in large numbers from the Arabs. In the late 1960s Israel produced its own infantry rifle. The Galil, adopted by the IDF in 1974, was chambered for the NATO 7.62×51-mm round, weighed 8.6 pounds, had a cyclic rate of fire of 650 rounds per minute and a maximum effective range of 450 meters. A later sniper version, designated the Galat'z, had a longer and heavier barrel, weighed 13.6 pounds, and had a maximum effective range of 600 meters without optical sights.

In the 1960s NATO adopted a second smaller but higher-velocity standard rifle round, driven largely by the American experience in Vietnam, which demonstrated that most encounters were at shorter

An Israeli soldier points his M16 assault rifle at a Palestinian at the Kalandia checkpoint between Ramallah and Jerusalem, December 8, 2001. (Reuters/Corbis)

ranges and required higher rates of fire. The first American infantry weapon chambered for the 5.56×45-mm round was the M-16 rifle, initially adopted in 1960 and widely issued to American troops from 1966 on. The initial version weighed only 6.4 pounds, had a cyclic rate of fire of 750 rounds per minute, and had an official maximum effective range of 500 meters. Most American combat infantrymen, however, knew that the M-16's maximum effective range was far shorter.

The initial version of the M-16 had serious design flaws, and the propellant used in the cartridges was especially corrosive, causing frequent jams. Once these flaws were corrected, the M-16 developed into an adequate but hardly outstanding infantry weapon. Nonetheless, the Israelis in the late 1960s and early 1970s started buying M-16s in large numbers at very favorable prices. The vastly improved M-16A2 had a heavier barrel, which increased accuracy, but also had a heavier weight at 8.6 pounds. A modification to the selector switch eliminated the full automatic fire mode of the earlier models in favor of a three-round burst option.

The IDF also bought large numbers of the carbine version of the M-16. First introduced in the mid-1960s as the XM-177, it was finally standardized in American service in 1994 as the M-4 carbine. With a weight of 5.5 pounds and a length of 29.8 inches, the M-4 has the same cyclic rate of fire as the M-16 but a maximum effective range of only 300 meters.

The IDF also bought from the United States the M-203 grenade launcher, which attaches underneath the barrel of the M-16 rifle or M-4 carbine, thereby adding an additional 3 pounds to the overall weight of the combined system. The M-203 has a 12-inch barrel and fires a 40-mm grenade out to a maximum effective range of 150 meters. A well-trained grenadier can fire five to seven grenades per minute.

Although a later version of the Galil was chambered for 5.56×45 mm, the rifle was expensive to manufacture. By the 1973 Yom Kippur War, the Galil was still being carried by IDF artillery and air force units, but the M-16 had become the standard Israeli shoulder weapon. Because Israel depended on massive resupply of arms and ammunition from the United States during the 1973 war, the commonality of small arms was a significant advantage.

The M-16 remains the standard Israeli rifle at the start of the 21st century, but Israeli small arms designers have been experimenting with new technology to replace the aging American-designed rifles. Developed in 1991 and fielded to IDF units in 2000, the Tavor TAR-21 assault rifle is chambered for the NATO standard 5.56×45-mm round. Weighing only 6.2 pounds, it has a cyclic rate of fire of up to 900 rounds per minute and a maximum range of 500 meters.

As with the Israelis, the Arab armies immediately after World War II were armed with various versions of the British Enfield rifle and other British automatic weapons and submachine guns. As the political balance changed in the Middle East and the Arabs increasingly aligned with the Soviet Union, the Soviets became the principal arms supplier in the region, especially after the 1956 Suez War.

Starting in the late 1950s, the Soviets completely reequipped and trained the armies of Egypt, Jordan, Syria, Iraq, and Yemen.

The ubiquitous Soviet-designed AK-47 is arguably the world's finest assault rifle. First designed in 1944 by Mikhail Kalashinkov while he was recovering from war wounds, the weapon was derived from the hard lessons of combat that the Soviets learned at the hands of the Germans. The AK-47 combined characteristics of both the rifle and the submachine gun, most significantly the high rate of fire of the latter. The result became known in the West as an assault rifle.

The weapon was type classified in 1947 and adopted for general issue by the Soviet Army in 1949. Chambered for the 7.62×39-mm round (which is not compatible with the NATO 7.62×51-mm round), the basic version of the AK-47 weighs 8.4 pounds and has a cyclic rate of fire of 600 rounds per minute and a maximum effective range of 300 meters. All of the AK-series weapons are known for their rugged reliability, ease of maintenance, and moderate accuracy. They almost never jam.

The AK-47 was quickly adopted and manufactured under license by many other countries, including China, Iraq, Egypt, and most of the Warsaw Pact nations. More than 55 armies worldwide have issued the AK-47 to their troops. More than 11 major AK-47 variants exist, including models with fixed stocks of wood or polymers and the more popular folding-stock models for paratroopers. More than 100 million copies of all versions have been manufactured over the years. The AK-47's very shape has become an iconic symbol of liberation movements and wars of resistance. After the fall of Saddam Hussein in 2003, the units of the new Iraqi Army being trained by the Americans still insisted on carrying the AK-47 rather than the M-16.

Introduced in 1974, the AK-74 variant of the AK-47 is chambered for the 5.45×39-mm round. Weighing 7.3 pounds, it has a cyclic rate of fire of 650 rounds per minute and a maximum effective range of 500 meters. Other Soviet small arms carried by the various Arab armies included the RPD (Ruchnoy Pulemet Degtyarov) light machine gun, chambered for the same ammunition as the AK-47, and the RPG-7 rocket-propelled grenade (Ruchnoy Protivotankovy Granatomyot).

Immediately following World War II, the Soviets also introduced a conventional semiautomatic infantry carbine. The SKS (Samozariyadnyi Karabin Simonova) is chambered for the same round as the AK-47, weighs 8.5 pounds, and has a maximum rate of fire of 35 rounds per minute and a maximum effective range of 400 meters. It has a fixed-blade bayonet attached to the barrel that folds down and back underneath the barrel when not in use. The utility and popularity of the AK-47 made the SKS almost instantly obsolete, but vast numbers were produced in China and the Soviet satellite countries and given in large numbers to Soviet clients in the Middle East.

The Arab armies used the AK-47 and other Soviet small arms in the 1967 Six-Day War, the 1973 Yom Kippur War, and most Arab-

Israeli conflicts since. They remain the standard-issue small arms in most Arab and African nations, with the SKS still being used by various insurgent movements.

JAY A. MENZOFF AND DAVID T. ZABECKI

See also

Arms Sales, International; Machine Guns

References

Bishop, Chris, and Ian Drury, eds. *Combat Guns: An Illustrated History of Twentieth Century Firearms.* Secaucus, NJ: Chartwell, 1987.

Isby, David. *Russia's War in Afghanistan.* London: Osprey, 1986.

Laffin, John. *The Israeli Army in the Middle East Wars, 1948–1973.* London: Osprey, 1982.

Poyer, Joe. *The AK-47 and AK-74 Kalashnikov Rifles and Their Variants.* Tustin, CA: North Cape Publications, 2006.

Smith, W. H. B., and Edward C. Ezell. *Small Arms of the World.* New York: Barnes and Noble, 1992.

Right of Return, Palestinian

An internationally recognized principle that holds that an ethnic, religious, or national group has the right to settle in—or become a citizen of—the country that it considers to be its homeland, regardless of national changes that may have occurred in that state. Usually, the right of return involves ethnically dispersed peoples. In the Middle East, it applies to Palestinians who were driven from their homes and homeland during the various Arab-Israeli wars since 1948. The Palestinians' right of return to lands now controlled by Israel has been a perennial sticking point in Arab-Israeli relations, and it continues to present a major impediment to a lasting peace in the region.

At present, there are an estimated 4 million Palestinian refugees residing in refugee settlements throughout the Middle East in addition to a much larger number dispersed throughout the world. Most refugees live in the Gaza Strip, West Bank, Lebanon, Syria, Egypt, Iraq, and Jordan. The vast majority of these refugees were displaced from their ancestral homeland (lands now controlled by Israel) during the 1948–1949 Israeli War of Independence and the 1967 Six-Day War. This number also includes the children and even grandchildren of those first displaced in 1948 and 1967. Palestinians believe that these refugees and their offspring have an unalienable right to return to their homes. In fact, many of them retain legal documents, deeds, and even keys to homes and businesses that they owned prior to the Diaspora.

Indeed, the Palestinians' belief that they have an absolute right to return to areas now controlled by Israel is far from unfounded. United Nations (UN) Resolution 194 (specifically Article 11) passed by the General Assembly on December 11, 1948, calls for the return of all refugees from the conflict "at the earliest practicable date." The UN made no distinction between Israeli and Palestinian refugees. Quite naturally, the Palestinians have used this resolution as the linchpin of their right of return. Over the years, the UN has also specified that the right of return applies to both Palestinians and their direct descendants. This stands in contrast to its normal policies regarding refugees, which usually hold that only those actually displaced have a right of return and that the right does not extend to descendants. To bolster their claims further, Palestinians also point to the UN's Universal Declaration of Human Rights, which was adopted on December 10, 1948, just one day prior to UN Resolution 194. That document holds that an individual has the right to "leave any country, including his own, and to return to his country."

But while the Palestinian right of return seems justified based upon the various UN dictates, the issue is far more complicated to put into practice, especially after so many years have passed since the Palestinian Diaspora. From the Israeli perspective, the issue raises several critical concerns. First, Israel maintains that as a sovereign nation, it must be the sole arbiter of Israeli immigration policy. Arguing that every nation has the right to set its own policies in this regard, the Israelis insist that to surrender to the right of return would involve surrendering a piece of their sovereignty. Second, and more important perhaps, the Israeli government claims that allowing as many as 4 million Palestinians to return to Israel would threaten the very survival of the nation and seriously alter the ethnic and national identity of the state. It has repeatedly been argued that relatively few of the 4 million would want to return. However, Israel refused to discuss this issue even with its inclusion in the Oslo Accords, and otherwise liberal negotiators argued that it was Palestinians who were unreasonable to advance such a position. Many of the property rights that predate the founding of Israel have actually been argued in court and settled in favor of Palestinians, but the government has refused to honor these rulings.

Besides Israeli concerns, there are other potential roadblocks in the right of return. One is certainly determining the Palestinians who became refugees in 1948 and 1967. Another is determining the exact circumstances of their departure. Be that as it may, there are fairly accurate figures for Palestinian refugees that have been kept by the UN over the years. In 1951, for example, the UN determined that there were approximately 860,000 Palestinians who lost their homes, livelihoods, or both as a result of the Arab-Israeli conflict that began in 1948. After Israel annexed the West Bank and the Gaza Strip in 1967, there were an additional 300,000 Palestinians who left their homeland. Most went to neighboring Jordan.

Most Israelis see the right of return as a fundamental issue that is not to be implemented, for to agree to do so would be a tacit admission that their very existence as a people and a nation might be at risk. Indeed, they equate the concept with Israel's destruction. But the likelihood that anything like 4 million Palestinians would stream into Israel if the right of return were granted is highly unlikely. A recent survey of Palestinians living in Jordan, Lebanon, the Gaza Strip, and West Bank indicated that only about 10 percent would actually attempt to return to their homes if allowed. The vast majority preferred to stay where they were or wait for the creation of a bona fide Palestinian nation. Thus, the number of likely Palestinian refugees returning to Israel would be far less than 4 million, perhaps only 1 million to 1.5 million or even fewer. This blunts Israeli assertions that the right of return would drastically alter or destroy their nation. Still, even with this knowledge, many Israelis (even some of whom support a limited right of return) argue that an influx of even several hundred thousand Palestinians would be enormously expensive and would create major challenges in terms of infrastructure, housing, education, health care, etc.

In the final analysis, the right of return continues to stand as a contentious and outstanding issue that would benefit from serious efforts at negotiation. Most Arabs assert that no peace can be brokered without allowing Palestinians the right of return. The 1993 Oslo Accords were negotiated chiefly because both sides consented to take up the issue in future talks. And the 2000 Camp David discussions between Palestine Liberation Organization (PLO) chairman Yasser Arafat and Israeli prime minister Ehud Barak in part broke down because Barak would not consent to a right of return.

PAUL G. PIERPAOLI JR.

See also

Arafat, Yasser; Barak, Ehud; Gaza Strip; Israel; Israeli War of Independence, Overview; Oslo Accords; Palestine Liberation Organization; Six-Day War; United Nations, Role of; United Nations General Assembly Resolution 194; West Bank

References

Aruri, Naseer Hasan, ed. *Palestinian Refugees: The Right of Return.* London: Pluto, 2001.

Bowker, Robert. *Palestinian Refugees: Mythology, Identity, and the Search for Peace.* Boulder, CO: Lynne Rienner, 2003.

Ginat, Joseph, Edward J. Perkins, and Hassan bin Talal, eds. *Palestinian Refugees: Traditional Positions and New Solutions.* Norman: University of Oklahoma Press, 2002.

United Nations. *The Right of Return of the Palestinian People.* New York: United Nations, 1979.

Road Map to Peace
See United States Coordinating and Monitoring Mission

Rogers, William Pierce
Born: June 23, 1913
Died: January 2, 2001

U.S. secretary of state (1969–1973). William Rogers was born on June 23, 1913, in Norfolk, Virginia. Brought up in modest circumstances, Rogers graduated from Colgate University in Hamilton,

U.S. secretary of state William Rogers addresses the press on his arrival at Lod Airport in Israel on May 6, 1971. Israeli foreign minister Abba Eban is seated behind Rogers. (Israeli Government Press Office)

New York, in 1934, and Cornell Law School in 1937. Following service as an assistant district attorney in New York state, in 1947 Rogers became chief counsel to the U.S. Senate Investigations Subcommittee of the Executive Expenditures Committee. There he first met Congressman Richard Nixon with whom he worked on the Alger Hiss case. Nixon and Rogers became friends, partly due to their shared experience of achieving legal success from unpretentious family backgrounds.

An energetic and respected lawyer with excellent Republican political connections, Rogers became deputy U.S. attorney general in 1953 and attorney general in 1958. Following Nixon's defeat in the 1962 California gubernatorial election, Rogers helped him establish a New York legal practice.

In 1969 Nixon, having been elected president in November 1968 and seeking to retain personal control of foreign policy, named Rogers his secretary of state. In so doing, Nixon cited his appointee's negotiating skills. Throughout his tenure Rogers remained marginalized by Henry Kissinger, Nixon's dominating, driven, and intellectually brilliant national security adviser under whose direction the National Security Council almost immediately wrested from the State Department the crucial power to set the agenda for U.S. foreign policy discussions. Nixon and Kissinger often kept Rogers ignorant of and excluded from major foreign policy initiatives, including arms control talks, secret negotiations to end the Vietnam War, and the opening to China, which Rogers first learned of through newspaper accounts of Kissinger's 1971 trip to Beijing. Rogers did, however, handle crises in Korea and dealings with the Southeast Asian Treaty Organization (SEATO).

Until 1973 Rogers also played the major role in Nixon's Middle East policy, which Nixon and Kissinger initially relegated to Rogers while they themselves concentrated on big-power diplomacy. Seeking to resolve outstanding issues from the 1967 Six-Day War, in 1969 Rogers and Joseph Sisco, assistant secretary of state for Near Eastern and South Asian affairs, developed a peace plan (the Rogers Plan) envisaging Israeli withdrawal from occupied territories in return for evenhanded Soviet and U.S. policies toward both Arabs and Israel in the Middle East and a brokered peace settlement guaranteed by the Soviet Union and the United States, to be implemented by them in collaboration with Britain, France, and the United Nations (UN). Rogers unveiled this proposal on December 9, 1969, without prior detailed consultation with Israel, whose government rejected the Rogers Plan on December 22. Egypt followed suit, while in 1970 70 U.S. Senators and 280 congressional representatives rejected the Rogers Plan as insufficiently favorable to Israel. Kissinger apparently undermined the Rogers Plan by privately informing Soviet ambassador Anatoly Dobrynin that the White House had no interest in it. U.S. Middle Eastern policy thereafter remained largely static until the October 1973 Yom Kippur War, when Kissinger took over the major role in policy formulation and implementation.

In 1972 Nixon rejected Rogers's advice to fire those presidential aides responsible for the burglary of the Democratic National Committee headquarters in the Watergate Hotel. After winning reelection, in September 1973 Nixon replaced Rogers with Kissinger. Rogers resumed the practice of law in New York City, taking little further interest in foreign affairs. He died on January 2, 2001, in Bethesda, Maryland.

PRISCILLA MARY ROBERTS

See also
Kissinger, Henry Alfred; Nixon, Richard Milhous; Rogers Plan

References
Ambrose, Stephen E. *Nixon.* 3 vols. New York: Simon and Schuster, 1986–1991.
Isaacson, Walter. *Kissinger: A Biography.* New York: Simon and Schuster, 1992.

Rogers Plan
Event Date: December 9, 1969

Comprehensive U.S. peace initiative for the Middle East proposed in 1969 in the aftermath of the 1967 Six-Day War and named for U.S. secretary of state William Rogers. The Rogers Plan was unveiled on December 9, 1969.

Peace efforts in the ongoing Arab-Israeli conflict had been under way since the end of the Six-Day War. On November 22, 1967, some five months after the cessation of hostilities, the United Nations (UN) Security Council passed Resolution 242 calling for the withdrawal of Israeli troops from occupied territories. The following day, the Security Council appointed Swedish diplomat Gunnar Jarring as special envoy to the Middle East with the task of negotiating with all parties concerned in the Middle East dispute. Over the next 18 months, Jarring was unsuccessful in his attempts to hammer out a lasting peace arrangement. In the meantime, the War of Attrition continued to threaten the region with another full-scale war.

With the advent of the Richard Nixon administration in January 1969, the United States began pushing hard for an end to the War of Attrition and, more importantly, a comprehensive peace settlement between Israel and its Arab neighbors. Indeed, Nixon's focus on détente with the Soviet Union played a sizable role in this renewed American commitment to Middle East peace. Because the Soviet Union did not have diplomatic relations with Israel at the time, U.S. policymakers sought to take a tougher line against the Israelis in an effort to curry favor with the Kremlin.

By 1969, the Soviets had presented their own peace plan calling for a bilateral arrangement between Egypt and Israel. In March, William Rogers met with Israeli ambassador to the United States Yitzhak Rabin and called for an Israeli withdrawal from occupied territories gained in the Six-Day War. Tel Aviv rejected the request, claiming that such a move offered no guarantee of security from future Arab attacks. Rogers then presented the proposal to the Soviets and Arabs, who refused to deal bilaterally with the Israelis and asked instead for a UN-sponsored proposal.

Hostilities meanwhile continued, with sporadic fighting occurring between Israeli and Egyptian forces. In September 1969, Israeli prime minister Golda Meir visited Washington and consulted personally with Nixon and Rogers. Rabin was also a party to most of the discussions, in which the Israelis informed the Americans that peace proposals without security arrangements were not acceptable. Throughout the fall, Nixon had continued to confer with both Meir and Rabin.

At the same time, the U.S. Department of State was readying a comprehensive peace proposal to be presented to all sides. On December 9, 1969, Rogers took the initiative and unveiled the so-called Rogers Plan in the course of a prescheduled speech. The proposal called for cooperation among the United States, the Soviet Union, the United Kingdom, and France in helping the Jarring Mission arrive at an agreement acceptable to all parties. It also envisaged a central role for the UN as per the spirit of Resolution 242. For the first time in U.S.-Israeli relations, such a proposal had not been revealed to the Israelis beforehand. Indeed, both Meir and Rabin were caught off guard by the announcement.

More specifically, the Rogers Plan requested the withdrawal of Israeli forces from Egyptian territory to the heretofore internationally recognized border. Egypt, for its part, would have to commit specifically to a binding peace settlement. The status of Jerusalem would be determined in accordance with consultations among Israel, Jordan, and the international community. The plan also addressed the issue of Palestinian refugees rendered homeless by the 1948 and 1967 wars. Lastly, the Rogers Plan reiterated the U.S. commitment to peace and cooperation with all parties concerned in the region.

Immediately after the Rogers speech, Rabin was called home for consultations. On December 22, 1969, Israel formally rejected the Rogers Plan following a contentious cabinet debate. The Israelis refused to consider a proposal that did not address the question of its long-term security. In 1970, 70 U.S. Senators and 280 U.S. Representatives also rejected the Rogers Plan on the grounds that it ran counter to the interests of Israel. For his part, Egyptian president Gamal Abdel Nasser had also rejected the proposal.

The War of Attrition continued until full-scale war again erupted in the October 1973 Yom Kippur War. In the interim, the failure of both the Jarring Mission and the Rogers Plan strained U.S.-Israeli relations considerably. It was not only the content of the plan that had angered the Israelis. They were also resentful that Rogers had announced it with no prior consultation with Tel Aviv.

PATIT PABAN MISHRA AND PAUL G. PIERPAOLI JR.

See also

Attrition, War of; Expellees and Refugees, Palestinian; Jarring, Gunnar; Jarring Mission; Jerusalem; Meir, Golda; Nasser, Gamal Abdel; Rabin, Yitzhak; Rogers, William Pierce; Six-Day War; United Nations Security Council Resolution 242; Yom Kippur War

References

Bailey, Sydney D. *Four Arab-Israeli Wars and the Peace Process.* New York: St. Martin's, 1982.

Dupuy, Trevor N. *Elusive Victory: The Arab-Israeli Wars, 1947–1974.* Garden City, NY: Military Book Club, 2002.

Herzog, Chaim. *The Arab-Israeli Wars: War and Peace in the Middle East from the War of Independence to Lebanon.* Westminster, MD: Random House, 1984.

Roosevelt, Franklin Delano
Born: January 30, 1882
Died: April 12, 1945

U.S. politician, assistant secretary of the U.S. Navy (1913–1920), governor of New York (1929–1933), and president of the United States (1933–1945). Born at his family's Hyde Park estate in Dutchess County, Hyde Park, New York, on January 30, 1882, Franklin Roosevelt studied at the Groton School, Harvard College, and Columbia Law School. He then entered Democratic politics, consciously modeling his career on that of his distant cousin President Theodore Roosevelt. In 1905 Franklin married Theodore's niece Eleanor. After serving two terms as a New York state senator, in 1913 Franklin Roosevelt became assistant secretary of the navy in the administration of President Woodrow Wilson. During World War I Roosevelt was vehemently pro-Allied and interventionist, lobbying strenuously for major increases in defense spending. In 1920 he ran unsuccessfully as the Democratic vice presidential candidate on a pro–League of Nations ticket.

In 1921 Roosevelt contracted polio, which left him permanently disabled but did not prevent his return to politics. Elected governor of New York in 1928, four years later he ran successfully for the presidency. He did so in the midst of the Great Depression, a dark time for the nation in which unemployment hovered at 25 percent and banks were folding with frightening rapidity. In his first term, he concentrated primarily on domestic affairs, launching a major reform program, the New Deal, to tackle the Great Depression and its effects. Even so, by the mid-1930s Roosevelt displayed far greater determination than most Americans to check the growing influence and territorial designs of fascist dictatorships in both Europe and Asia.

While the economy began a very slight and gradual upturn by the mid-1930s, unemployment remained high, and business investments were still well below the levels seen prior to the October 1929 stock market crash. Under pressure by Republicans and conservatives in his own party who decried high government spending and many New Deal programs, Roosevelt felt obliged to cut public spending beginning in 1936. The result was a sharp downturn in the economy, sometimes referred to as the recession in the depression. Despite the Roosevelt administration's best efforts, the U.S. economy did not see marked improvement until preparations for war were undertaken beginning in 1940.

Appreciable popular resistance to American intervention notwithstanding, when World War II began in September 1939, Roosevelt unequivocally and immediately placed the United States in the Allied camp. Two years of fierce debate over U.S. foreign policy

Franklin D. Roosevelt, president of the United States (1933–1945). (Library of Congress)

continuation of Western imperialism after the war, sentiments that greatly irritated Churchill, who believed profoundly in the British Empire. Roosevelt was also dedicated to ending French colonial rule.

The British and U.S. decision to defer the invasion of Europe via the English Channel until the spring of 1944 effectively ensured that after the war Soviet military forces would control most of Eastern Europe and the Balkans. At the February 1945 Yalta conference, the three leaders signed the Declaration on Liberated Europe supposedly promising free elections on democratic principles to all areas taken over by the Allies, but only the goodwill of the occupying powers, who could interpret them as they pleased, guaranteed these pledges. At Yalta, the Big Three also agreed to divide Germany into three temporary, separate occupation zones to be administered by their occupying military forces. Roosevelt's acquiescence in the Yalta provisions exposed him to fierce posthumous attacks from conservatives, but given the military situation on the ground, the United States and Britain had few effective means of preventing Soviet domination of the area. By the time of Roosevelt's death in April 1945, Soviet-American relations were deteriorating, as the brutality with which Stalin intended to impose effective Soviet domination upon much of Eastern and Central Europe became increasingly apparent to often shocked Allied observers.

Like many men of his age and era, Roosevelt had conflicted feelings toward Jews. While he sometimes in private made decidedly anti-Semitic remarks, he also cultivated several close Jewish political allies, including Wall Street financier Bernard Baruch and mobilization czar Henry Morgenthau, and Felix Frankfurter. Roosevelt appointed Frankfurter to the U.S. Supreme Court and named Morgenthau secretary of the treasury. The Roosevelt–New Deal political coalition counted Jews among its most ardent supporters. Nevertheless, some have criticized the Roosevelt administration's slow and small response to Nazi Germany's horrific treatment of Jews beginning in the mid-1930s. Roosevelt sharply condemned German dictator Adolf Hitler's treatment of German Jews. After 1937 when persecution of German Jews became far more pronounced, Roosevelt rebuffed requests that Jewish refugees be allowed to resettle in the United States, fearing that acquiescence to this would provoke his political adversaries, some of whom were openly anti-Semitic. In the end, on the eve of World War II only a token number of Jews had been allowed to enter the United States from Europe.

By 1942 Roosevelt had become aware of the horrific Holocaust unfolding against Jews in Germany and Eastern Europe. His prescription for this was the complete destruction of Nazi Germany. Still, however, he stuck by the restrictive immigration laws that kept many Jews from seeking refuge in the United States. Only in 1944 did Roosevelt decide to increase the number of Jews entering the country, and only then at the considerable urging of Morgenthau. Unfortunately, the action was too little too late, as several million Jews had already been exterminated. Near the end of his life and as the war was winding down, Roosevelt made it clear that he would

ensued during which Roosevelt moved his country ever closer to outright war with Germany while providing massive quantities of aid to Great Britain, France, and, from summer 1940, Free French forces, the Soviet Union (after June 1941), and China.

The United States entered the war as a result of the concurrent crisis in the Pacific, where Roosevelt sought to use economic weapons to force the Japanese to withdraw from China and Indochina. The Japanese refused and on December 7, 1941, mounted a preemptive attack on Pearl Harbor.

From then until 1945, the United States, Great Britain, and the Soviet Union were the senior coalition partners in the Grand Alliance against the Axis powers: Germany, Italy, and Japan. As president, Roosevelt set the parameters of American and Allied strategy. He consciously chose to place winning the war in Europe ahead of the Pacific theater and authorized the development of atomic weapons. He also presided over the forging of close, permanent ties among the U.S. military establishment, science, and industry, links that later hardened into the postwar military-industrial complex.

During the war Roosevelt met repeatedly with Soviet leader Joseph Stalin and British prime minister Winston S. Churchill to reach agreement on Allied strategy and to plan for the postwar world. Roosevelt frequently expressed strong opposition to the not support the creation of a Jewish state in Palestine. He also opposed increased Jewish immigration to Palestine, then still under a British mandate. Indeed, Roosevelt appeared to favor the status quo in the Middle East and pointedly told Saudi Arabia's King Ibn Saud in the winter of 1945 that he was against the creation of a Jewish state.

In the larger context, Roosevelt himself erroneously assumed that the postwar understanding among Britain, the Soviet Union, and the United States would endure beyond victory, envisaging a peace based on the delegation to each great power of a regional sphere of influence. During the war Roosevelt endorsed postwar American membership in the United Nations (UN) and newly created international economic institutions, effectively setting the United States on the path of continued internationalism, moves for which he cannily obtained bipartisan political support.

Under Roosevelt, the United States became the world's greatest economic and military power, a position it retained throughout the 20th century, and moved decisively away from its pre-1940 quasi isolationism. In poor health in his final year, he did not survive to view the results of his labors. Roosevelt died of a stroke at Warm Springs, Georgia, on April 12, 1945.

PRISCILLA ROBERTS

See also

Churchill, Sir Winston; Stalin, Joseph; United States, Middle East Policy

References

Beschloss, Michael. *The Conquerors: Roosevelt, Truman, and the Destruction of Hitler's Germany, 1941–1945.* New York: Simon and Schuster, 2002.

Dallek, Robert. *Franklin D. Roosevelt and American Foreign Policy, 1932–1945.* New York: Oxford University Press, 1995.

Hoopes, Townsend, and Douglas Brinkley. *FDR and the Creation of the U.N.* New Haven, CT: Yale University Press, 1997.

Kimball, Warren F. *The Juggler: Franklin Roosevelt as Wartime Statesman.* Princeton, NJ: Princeton University Press, 1991.

Sainsbury, Keith. *Churchill and Roosevelt at War: The War They Fought and the Peace They Hoped to Make.* New York: New York University Press, 1994.

Rothschild, Edmond de

Born: August 19, 1845
Died: November 2, 1934

Prominent Jewish banker. Edmond de Rothschild was born in Paris on August 19, 1845. He was educated by private tutors and at the Lycée Condorcet and served in the French Army, but did not see combat, during the Franco-Prussian War (1870–1871). A well-known art collector and patron of scientific research, in the early 1880s he took up the cause of refugee Jews from Russia.

Insisting on strict financial accountability, Rothschild helped establish Jewish agricultural colonies in Palestine. He proceeded cautiously, trying to avoid antagonizing the Ottoman authorities, and provided his settlements with engineers, agronomists, and other experts along with strong-willed administrators. By 1900, resentment over his tight supervision coupled with the rise of more militant organizations dominated by Zionists limited his influence.

During World War I, Rothschild shifted his position on a Jewish homeland. He abandoned the caution that he had believed was necessary while Palestine was under Turkish control. With the collapse of the Ottoman Empire likely, he aligned himself with the Zionists and encouraged the British government to issue the 1917 Balfour Declaration supporting a Jewish homeland in Palestine.

Rothschild visited Palestine five times until 1925, when his health began to deteriorate. He died in Paris on November 2, 1934. In 1954, the Israeli government moved his remains and those of his wife to graves in the state he had helped to establish.

NEIL M. HEYMAN

See also

Balfour Declaration; Kibbutz Movement; Zionism

References

Aaronsohn, Ran. *Rothschild and Early Jewish Colonization in Palestine.* Lanham, MD: Rowman and Littlefield, 2000.

Schama, Simon. *Two Rothschilds and the Land of Israel.* London: Collins, 1978.

Wilson, Derek. *Rothschild: A Story of Wealth and Power.* London: Andre Deutsch, 1988.

Rubashow, Shneur Zalman

See Shazar, Shneur Zalman

S

Sabra and Shatila Massacre
Start Date: September 16, 1982
End Date: September 18, 1982

Mass Phalangist killing of inhabitants of the Sabra and Shatila refugee camps located in Beirut, Lebanon, during September 16–18, 1982. The incident occurred as part of the Lebanese Civil War (1975–1990) and following the Israeli invasion of Lebanon in 1982. Estimates of the number of individuals killed ranged from 700 to 1,800 to more than 3,500. Included among the dead were many women, children, and elderly, some of whom were raped or castrated and killed in the most brutal ways possible. In addition, bulldozers were used to destroy dwelling places in the camps, and a number of camp residents were hauled off in trucks, never to be seen again. Hospitals in each camp were attacked, and in one case a crowd of 500 persons escaped from the hospital but were driven back into the camp by Israelis. The massacre created a firestorm of international outrage and resulted in significant political and military repercussions in Israel. At the time, Israel Defense Forces (IDF) occupied the area that included Sabra and Shatila. The IDF was in direct contact with the militia that committed the massacre, surrounded the camps, and gave the Phalangist forces access into the camps. The IDF subsequently prevented civilians and residents from exiting the camps and escaping what went on there. The IDF was thus responsible, along with the Phalangist forces, for actions that took place in the camps. Most IDF personnel would later claim that they were not aware of the actions within the camps because they were patrolling the perimeter areas only. Worse still, it was later confirmed that the Lebanese Christian Phalangist militia had been invited to Sabra and Shatila by top-level Israeli military officials to flush out Palestine Liberation Organization (PLO) fighters who were supposedly using the refugee camps as safe havens. Israeli journalists and others later presented evidence revealing that this plan was concocted not to flush out fighters but to kill camp residents, destroy the buildings there, and terrorize Palestinians who remained in Beirut into leaving. Israeli defense minister Ariel Sharon claimed there were as many as 2,000 fighters in the camps who had not been part of the September 1 evacuation from Beirut.

The mission involving the Phalangists had been approved by Sharon and was carried out by IDF chief of staff General Rafael Eitan. Those who believe that the operation was planned in advance argue that the Phalangists deliberately waited until after the September 1 evacuation of the Palestinians and then used the assassination of Lebanon's Maronite Christian president Bashir Jumayyil (Gemayel) as the pretext for their actions. The Israeli forces later argued that the Phalangists seemed determined to exact revenge for the assassination on the Palestinians—any Palestinians. The deliberate methods used, including carving the sign of the cross on victims, dismemberment, rape, torture, the killing of children, and the destruction of buildings point instead to much more than the actual claim made at the time, pursuit of what Israelis called terrorists, PLO fighters who were in fact not in evidence. The idea that this was a revenge spree for the death of Jumayyil was also problematic, as it was quickly known that the Syrians and not the PLO were behind the murder of Jumayyil because of his alliance with Israel. Furthermore, the Phalangists were accompanied by southern Lebanese under Saad Haddad's command, pointing additionally to Israeli foreknowledge or coordination.

Israeli soldiers, who had already sealed off the Sabra and Shatila camps, admitted the Phalangists and Haddad's fighters into them on September 16, 1982. The Phalangist and South Lebanon Army (SLA) personnel then began an indiscriminate 62-hour killing spree

Bodies of Palestinians killed the day before in the Sabra refugee camp outside Beirut, Lebanon, lie in the middle of a road as civil defense workers prepare to remove them, September 18, 1982. (AFP/Getty Images)

that involved the murder of many innocent Palestinians. All the while, IDF forces were providing illumination flares for nighttime operations and were observed monitoring activities from rooftop observation posts. Some Phalangists would later claim that they had made specific reports to Israelis about the killings, including those of civilians. The bloodletting continued unabated, as IDF troops barred exits from the camps. It is hard to comprehend that Israeli commanders were not aware of the activities inside Sabra and Shatila. Additional Phalangist and SLA troops came into the camps. The medical staff, mostly Europeans, were forced out of the Gaza Hospital at Sabra after the Palestinians and a Syrian medic were killed. Israelis took custody of the Europeans and later released them. Not until the morning of September 18 did the militia units leave the camps.

A little more than an hour after the Phalangists left the refugee camps, foreign journalists caught their first glimpses of the carnage. What they saw was deeply disturbing. Inside the camps were many hundreds of dead bodies, some of which had been mutilated. Included among the dead were women, children, and the elderly. Journalists saw evidence of the discarded Israeli illumination flares as well. By noon local time on September 18, the first reports of the massacre had hit the news wires. At least a quarter of the victims were Lebanese, and the remainder were Palestinian. The Red Cross tallied 350 dead, the Israelis claimed 700–800 dead, several foreign

journalists claimed 2,000 dead, and an Israeli journalist claimed 3,000–3,500 dead, a figure that most Palestinians cite as fact. Whatever the number, the Sabra and Shatila Massacre was horrific, and the event elicited sharp international condemnations and strong reactions in Israel. In December 1982 the United Nations (UN) General Assembly denounced the killings, calling them an act of genocide.

Amid street protests condemning the killings and genuine outrage in Israel, the Israeli government established a commission of inquiry to investigate the incident on September 28, 1982. Israeli Supreme Court justice Yitzhak Kahan headed the inquiry. On February 8, 1983, after a detailed investigation, the Kahan Commission issued its report on the massacre at Sabra and Shatila. The report concluded that while the Phalangists themselves were directly accountable for the killings, Israeli forces were indirectly responsible. Defense Minister Sharon was deemed personally responsible for the incident because of his complacency and his failure to anticipate the obvious: that the Phalangists were driven by revenge and therefore should not have been allowed into the camps. The report recommended that Sharon be removed as minister of defense, and he resigned shortly thereafter. Chief of Staff Eitan was also held partially accountable, and he too was forced to resign his post. In addition, the director of Israeli military intelligence, Yehoshua Saguy, was required to resign.

The Kahan Commission was and still is a controversial inquiry. Many people, both inside Israel and beyond, claim that it was motivated mainly by political expediency. Some hold that it was an outright distortion of the true facts and dimensions of the massacre. Indeed, Noam Chomsky termed the Kahan Commission a "shameful whitewash," while Israeli journalist Shimon Lehrer claims that its conclusions were "untenable." The Israeli writer Benny Morris alleges that the IDF provided bulldozers to bury as many dead as possible so as to lessen the grim impact of the event. Elie Hubayka (Hobeika), the Phalangist commander whom most consider responsible, was killed in a bomb blast in 2002, allegedly to prevent his testimony to the International Court in The Hague, where Palestinians had hoped to charge Sharon. The probable reason that no charges were made against the Lebanese perpetrators (with the exception of those in the SLA) is that the Taif Agreement was forged on the understanding that war crimes, massacres, kidnappings, and assassinations as well as battle casualties could not be prosecuted, as that would render the cessation of violence impossible.

PAUL G. PIERPAOLI JR. AND SHERIFA ZUHUR

See also

Eitan, Rafael; Lebanon; Lebanon, Armed Forces; Lebanon, Civil War in; Lebanon, Israeli Invasion of; Palestine Liberation Organization; Sharon, Ariel

References

Al-Hout, Bayan Nuwayhed. *Sabra and Shatila: September 1982.* London: Pluto, 2004.

Black, Ian, and Benny Morris. *Israel's Secret Wars: A History of Israel's Intelligence Services.* New York: Grove, 1994.

Brynen, Rex. *Sanctuary and Survival: The PLO in Lebanon.* Boulder, CO: Westview, 1990.

Chomsky, Noam. *Fateful Triangle: The United States, Israel, and the Palestinians.* Cambridge, MA: South End Press, 2002.

Kapeliouk, Amnon. *Sabra et Chatila: Enquete sur un massacre.* Paris: Seuil, 1982.

Morris, Claud. *Eyewitness Lebanon: Eyewitness Evidence of 91 International Correspondents.* London and New York: Morris International, 1983.

Sadat, Anwar
Born: December 25, 1918
Died: October 6, 1981

Egyptian nationalist leader, vice president (1966–1970), and president of Egypt (1970–1981). Born on December 25, 1918, in Mit Abu al-Kum, near Tala in the Minufiyya province of Egypt, Muhammad Anwar Sadat was 1 of 13 children of an Egyptian father, who was an army clerk, and a Sudanese mother. Sadat attended the Royal Egyptian Military Academy, from which he graduated in 1938 as a second lieutenant. Early on he supported the Misr al-Fatat (an Islamist youth party) and the Muslim Brotherhood. His first posting was in the Sudan, where he met fellow nationalist and future Egyptian president Gamal Abdel Nasser. Stemming from their mutual disdain of the continuing British influence over the Egypt-

Anwar Sadat, president of Egypt (1970–1981). (U.S. Department of Defense)

ian government, Sadat joined with Nasser in forming the secret organization that would eventually be called the Free Officers Movement, comprised of young Egyptian military officers dedicated to ousting the British and replacing the government of King Farouk.

In May 1941 Sadat took part in a plot led by the ex-chief of staff General Aziz al-Masri to join forces with Iraqi military leader Colonel Rashid Ali al-Gaylani and make common cause with the Axis powers and expel the British from Egypt. British authorities foiled the plot, and Sadat was among those jailed in 1942. He escaped from prison in 1944 but was arrested again in 1946 and tried in the planning of the assassination of Amin Uthman. Sadat was released in 1948 and regained his commission in 1950.

Nasser, Sadat, and a group of younger officers shared a mutual disdain of the continuing British influence in Egyptian affairs. Nasser took the lead in forming the secret organization called the Free Officers Movement, dedicated to ousting the British, and replacing the government of King Farouk. Sadat joined the organization in 1950 and helped Nasser plan the July 23, 1952, Free Officers' bloodless revolution against King Farouk. Farouk was forced to abdicate and departed Egypt on July 26. When Egypt was declared a republic in June 1953, Major General Mohammad Naguib became its president, with Nasser as vice president. In October 1954 after an attempt on Nasser's life, Naguib was removed from office while Nasser consolidated his power. In February 1955 Nasser became prime minister, and seven months later he became president. Sadat,

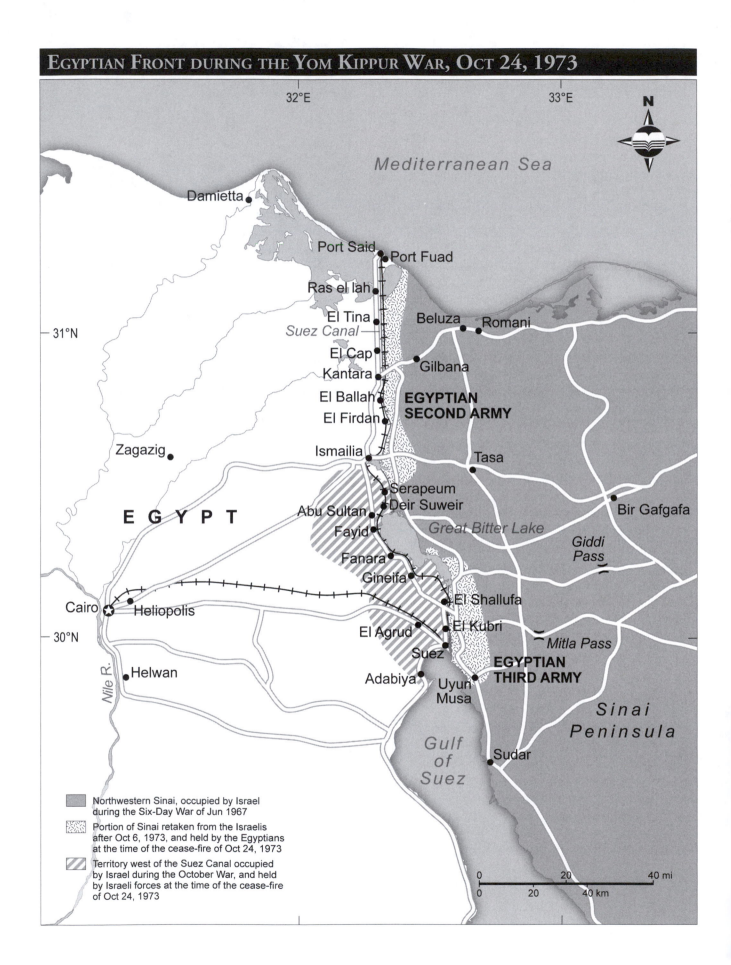

EGYPTIAN FRONT DURING THE YOM KIPPUR WAR, OCT 24, 1973

Mediterranean Sea

Damietta

Port Said
Port Fuad

Ras el Iah

El Tina
Suez Canal
Beluza
Romani

El Cap
Gilbana

Kantara

El Ballah
EGYPTIAN
SECOND ARMY

El Firdan

Zagazig

Ismailia
Tasa

Serapeum

Deir Suweir
Bir Gafgafa

Abu Sultan
Great Bitter Lake

E G Y P T
Fayid
Giddi
Pass

Fanara

Gineifa

El Shallufa

Cairo
Heliopolis
El Kubri

El Agrud
Mitla Pass

Suez
EGYPTIAN
THIRD ARMY

Helwan
Adabiya
Uyun
Musa
Sinai
Peninsula

Sudar

Gulf
of
Suez

Northwestern Sinai, occupied by Israel
during the Six-Day War of Jun 1967

Portion of Sinai retaken from the Israelis
after Oct 6, 1973, and held by the Egyptians
at the time of the cease-fire of Oct 24, 1973

Territory west of the Suez Canal occupied
by Israel during the October War, and held
by Israeli forces at the time of the cease-fire
of Oct 24, 1973

0   20   40 mi
0   20   40 km

31°N

30°N

32°E

33°E

Nile R.

meanwhile, served loyally under Nasser, a trusted member of his government. Sadat edited the newspaper *al-Jumhuriyya* from 1953 to 1956 and chaired the United Arab Republic (UAR) national assembly during 1960–1961.

In 1969 Colonel Sadat became vice president of Egypt because Nasser wished to squelch the ambitions of Ali Sabri and his leftist supporters. Apparently Nasser had planned to replace Sadat as vice president, but Sadat became temporary president upon Nasser's death in September 1970 and then was elected president by the National Assembly on October 7. This decision was later confirmed in a popular vote. In November Sadat was elected president of the Arab Socialist Union.

This was not a seamless transition by any means. A number of prominent individuals in Egypt's government and armed forces as well as many of the country's intellectuals and youths opposed Sadat. They wanted power for themselves, but they also favored an orientation closer to Nasser's own policies or even further to the Left and the maintenance of Egypt's alliance with the Soviet Union. In May 1971 the government uncovered a plot to overthrow Sadat, and this led to the arrest, trial, and imprisonment of the four ringleaders. Sadat then appointed a trusted associate, Mamdouh Salim, to be the new minister of the interior.

In domestic affairs, despite professing his adherence to Nasser's policies, Sadat soon began to move away from Nasser's positions. The new regime was not much more politically liberal than its predecessor, however, so Sadat's dissenters had virtually no avenue to dispute the changes in direction. Egyptians were given more freedom in traveling to the West as relations improved with these countries. Censorship continued in journalism and print media, and this was extended even to verbal discussion of various political subjects by the end of Sadat's rule. However, as a means of defeating the leftist opponents of Sadat, journalists with pro-Islamist and anti-Nasserist views were now allowed to publish. The National Assembly and the Arab Socialist Union had virtually no autonomy from the executive. Indeed, Sadat legislated reforms while the National Assembly was in recess in 1979. In 1976 Sadat ran unopposed for a second six-year term as president and was confirmed. Many Egyptians took note of and were critical of Sadat's opulent lifestyle, which was in sharp contrast to his predecessor's modest ways.

The Egyptian economy had been adversely affected by Nasser's government takeover of the large industries and corporations. Sadat now began a new economic policy intended to encourage joint investments by foreigners and Egyptians and attempted to privatize some industries. The courts restored a number of individual properties that had been confiscated by the previous regime. The Sadat government encouraged expansion of the private sector, although tax and other regulation structures inhibited this. The government also sought foreign investment not only from the oil-rich states but also from the United States and other Western nations. As such, several large American oil companies received offshore drilling concessions.

Unfortunately for the government, this liberalization was slow to bring tangible economic benefits to the Egyptian people. Following several decades of socialism and expropriation of properties, foreign governments were wary of investing in Egypt, and it would take some time to overcome this. The bloated Egyptian bureaucracy also had much to lose to the reforms, and many leading Egyptians disapproved of the reforms and the increasing gap in wages that they would introduce. Certain Egyptian entrepreneurs also took immediate advantage of the situation to enrich themselves, much to the embarrassment of the government. The population growth slowed in cities but actually increased in rural areas and in the new desert cities that Sadat established, which were overall an economic failure. In addition, the vaunted Aswan High Dam that was supposed to solve so many of Egypt's economic problems proved a mixed blessing. It did provide much more electricity, but the dam also had a negative impact on the agricultural sector, preventing the annual silting that had enriched the soil, and also adversely impacted the fisheries industry in the eastern Mediterranean. All of this together with an increasing trade imbalance meant that the Sadat government was continually forced to seek new foreign loans and the refinancing of existing loans, while the national debt continued to spiral upward.

In foreign affairs, Sadat improved ties with the Arab Gulf states. This relationship had several intended and unintended effects, including growing legitimacy for and support given to Islamist groups in Egypt and aid granted to the Egyptian government. Many wealthy Gulf Arabs preferred to vacation in Egypt, where socially conservative mores were corruptible by riches. This trend came under criticism from the Islamist groups, however. The Camp David Accords largely ended this relationship when Egypt was ousted from the Arab League.

Sadat sought in the early years of his rule to develop a common policy toward Israel. Libyan strongman Muammar Qaddafi earnestly sought an Egyptian-Syrian-Libyan federation, which was signed in Damascus in August 1971. This arrangement was nothing like the former UAR and did not lead to any actual sharing of government. Warm relations with Libya did not last long, however, and in April 1974 Cairo announced that it had discovered a plot to overthrow the Egyptian government and pointed to Qaddafi as the mastermind behind it.

When Sadat became president, Egypt's once robust relationship with the Soviet Union was already showing signs of serious strain. In fact, Nasser had been moving away from the Soviet Union at the time of his death. Part of the reason for this had been the failure of the Soviet Union, then preoccupied by supporting India during the latter's war with Pakistan, to sell advanced weapons systems to Egypt. On July 18, 1972, a frustrated Sadat ordered the expulsion of all Soviet military advisers and experts from Egypt and placed all of their bases in the country under Egyptian control.

Meanwhile, Sadat did all he could to prepare Egypt for war, especially by increasing military training. He privately expressed the view to United Nations (UN) envoy Gunnar Jarring that he was willing to recognize the State of Israel and even to sign a peace treaty with the Jewish state but that the precondition for this was the return of all territory conquered by Israel to Egypt and the Palestinians. Sadat feared that the recent situation of no war and no peace might go on indefinitely and that the world would ultimately come to accept this as a permanent situation, giving Israel de facto control over the annexed territories. Sadat believed that the only way to change this was for him to initiate a new war, which in turn would produce an international crisis that would force the world to deal with the situation once and for all.

Over a protracted period, Egyptian forces engaged the Israelis in low-level skirmishing across the Suez Canal. Then, on October 6, 1973 (Yom Kippur, the Jewish Day of Atonement), Sadat launched a massive cross-canal attack that caught the Israeli government and military completely by surprise, partly because of its timing. He had carefully coordinated his plans with Syria in order to oblige the Israelis to fight a two-front war. In the Yom Kippur War, Syrian forces simultaneously struck Israel in the north along the Golan Heights. The war ended with Israeli forces poised to achieve total victory. On the Golan Heights front, Israeli forces held during desperate fighting and then counterattacked deep into Syria. Against Egypt they had rallied from early setbacks, crossed the canal, and were in position to drive on Cairo. However, the Egyptians had achieved a psychological victory with the initial Egyptian crossing of the canal. This and the relatively satisfactory cease-fire brokered by the United States and the Soviet Union earned Sadat great respect among his people and in the Arab world.

Painfully aware that only the United States could elicit any substantive concessions from Israel, Sadat completely severed relations with the Soviet Union in March 1976 and began working with the Americans toward a peace settlement with the Israelis. In a courageous move, on November 19, 1977, Sadat traveled to Jerusalem on a two-day visit, the first Arab leader to make an official trip to the Jewish state. He met with Prime Minister Menachem Begin and even addressed the Israeli Knesset. In September 1978 Sadat signed the Camp David Accords. This agreement and the peace treaty of March 1979 produced a comprehensive peace agreement with Israel. The accords were highly unpopular in the Arab world and became less popular in Egypt within a short period of time.

Although the Camp David Accords and the peace treaty of March 1979 were, in the long run, beneficial for Egypt, which with its larger army had borne the brunt of much of the previous three wars, many in the Arab world saw them as a great betrayal and Sadat as a traitor. In September 1981 his government cracked down on extremist Muslim organizations and also on many other non-Islamist and liberal opponents of the president, in the process arresting more than 1,600 people. Sadat's strong-arm tactics angered many in the Arab community and only exacerbated his problems, which included economic stagnation and charges that he had quashed dissident voices through force.

On October 6, 1981, Sadat was assassinated in Cairo while re-viewing a military parade commemorating the Yom Kippur War. His assassins were radical Islamist army officers who belonged to the Islamic Jihad organization, which hoped to overthrow the government and had bitterly denounced Sadat's un-Islamic rule and failure to implement Islamic law, his peace overtures with Israel, and his suppression of dissidents. Sadat was succeeded in office by Hosni Mubarak.

DALLACE W. UNGER, JR., SPENCER C. TUCKER, AND SHERIFA ZUHUR

See also

Begin, Menachem; Camp David Accords; Carter, James Earl, Jr.; Egypt; Farouk I, King of Egypt; Nasser, Gamal Abdel; Yom Kippur War

References

Beattie, Kirk J. *Egypt during the Sadat Years.* New York: Palgrave, 2000.

Finklestone, Joseph. *Anwar Sadat: Visionary Who Dared.* Portland, OR: Frank Cass, 1996.

Hirst, David, and Irene Beeson. *Sadat.* London: Faber and Faber, 1981.

Sadat, Anwar. *In Search of Identity: An Autobiography.* New York: Harper and Row, 1978.

Sadeh, Yitzhak
Born: August 10, 1890
Died: August 21, 1952

Israeli soldier and founder of the Palmach. Yitzhak Sadeh was born in Lublin, Poland, on August 10, 1890. Having completed his basic education, he joined the Imperial Russian Army. He saw considerable action in World War I and was one of the first officers to be commissioned in the Red Army following the November 1917 Bolshevik seizure of power. In 1918 he was a major in command of a battalion. During the ensuing civil war he developed his skills in mobile warfare and small unit tactics.

In 1920 Sadeh immigrated to Palestine and joined Haganah, the Jewish underground self-defense organization. In 1929 he took part in the defense of Haifa. In 1936 as a response to Arab threats, he formed the Nodedet (Patrol). By 1937, this force had become known as the Fosh and operated as a mobile force to protect Jewish settlements throughout Palestine.

In 1938 Sadeh worked closely with British Army captain and militant Zionist Orde Wingate to set up the Special Night Squads, which consisted of both British and Jewish troops. In 1941 Haganah leadership ordered Sadeh to form the Palmach (Phugot Machaz, or Strike Companies), a permanently mobilized Jewish military force. The Palmach was essentially an armed youth movement, but Sadeh quickly trained its recruits into a highly effective military force. He also aided in bringing numbers of illegal Jewish immigrants into Israel.

At the start of the 1948–1949 Israeli War of Independence, Sadeh helped defend territory under attack by the Syrians. The Palmach was absorbed into the newly established Israel Defense Forces (IDF). Later in 1948, he took command of the 8th Brigade in the IDF. The 8th Brigade was, on paper at least, an armored brigade and included the battalion of jeep commandos raised by Major Moshe

Israeli Army major general Yitzhak Sadeh, founder of the Palmach, March 1949. (Israeli Government Press Office)

Dayan. These forces captured the Lod airport and took part in operation KHOREV, reaching El Arish in the Sinai.

Following the end of the war, Sadeh left the military as a major general and pursued a literary career under the pen name of Y. Noded. While in the Palmach, he had been given the nickname "The Old Man" because so many of the recruits were only in their teens. Nevertheless, his charisma and outgoing personality made him a vital figure in establishing the ethos of the Israeli military. Sadeh died in Tel Aviv on August 21, 1952.

RALPH MARTIN BAKER

See also

Dayan, Moshe; Haganah; Israel Defense Forces; Israeli War of
    Independence, Israeli-Jordanian Front; Israeli War of Independence,
    Israeli-Syrian Front; Israeli War of Independence, Overview; Palmach;
    Wingate, Orde Charles

References

Goldstein, Yaacov N., and Dan Shomron. *From Fighters to Soldiers: How the Israeli Defense Forces Began.* Brighton, UK: Sussex Academic, 1998.
Kurzman, Dan. *Genesis 1948: The First Arab-Israeli War.* New York: Da Capo, 1992.

Said, Abu al-

See Khalid, Hasan

Said, Edward
Born: November 1, 1935
Died: September 23, 2003

Edward Said was a literary theorist, writer, critic, pianist, and pro-Palestinian activist. The son of Wadie Said of Jerusalem and Hilda Musa of Nazareth, Said was born on November 1, 1935, in Jerusalem, then part of the British Mandate for Palestine. He spent his early years living in Cairo and Jerusalem and visiting Lebanon every year. When he was 12 years old and attending St. George's School in Jerusalem, his immediate family left for Egypt. Then, his remaining relatives and neighbors in West Jerusalem were forced out. At age 16 he attended the Mount Hermon School in Massachusetts before going to college. He received his bachelor's degree at Princeton University in 1957 and his master's degree from Harvard University in 1960. During these years, his family and many friends would be forced to leave Egypt as a consequence of arrests and sequestrations under Gamal Abdel Nasser's Arab socialist policies. Said's parents urged him to avoid politics, and they sent his four younger sisters to college in the United States as well.

In 1963 Said joined the faculty at Columbia University as a professor of English and Comparative Literature Studies. A year later he earned his PhD from Harvard. Said spoke Arabic, English, and French fluently, and he was proficient in Latin, Spanish, Italian, and German. He remained on the Columbia faculty for several decades, ultimately becoming the Old Dominion Foundation Professor of Humanities in 1977. He also taught at Harvard, Johns Hopkins, and Yale universities.

Said's early work focused on the novelist Joseph Conrad. Perhaps Said's greatest intellectual contribution was his critique of orientalism that in turn spawned postcolonialist theory in political, literary, and historical forms. In his important book *Orientalism* (1978), he examined the prejudices and presumptions of the major European scholars of the Middle East. He argued that the European interest in the Middle East was rooted in a political agenda of domination and served as the justification for imperialist, colonial policies in the region. Said believed that these scholars and other writers had created a false, romantic, and exotic sense of the region, thus rendering it an Other and an enemy. He claimed that these counterproductive stereotypes still held sway in Western culture and worked to shape the study of and policy toward the Middle Eastern, African, and Asian worlds. In essence, he broke new ground in both cultural studies and literary theory. He also profoundly shook the academic establishment, opening the door to new Middle Eastern scholars and interpretations.

Said is also identified with postmodernism and discursive theory, which was perhaps best illustrated by the work of French philosopher Michel Foucault. The deconstructionist theory as propounded by the French literary theorist Jacques Derrida can also be found in Said's work. Said's critics claimed, however, that he had merely helped to create another type of academic dogma in place of

Literary theorist, writer, critic, pianist, and pro-Palestinian activist Edward Said. (UPI-Bettmann/Corbis)

Said wrote against the cultural boycott of Israeli Jews. His love of music and friendship with conductor-musician Daniel Barenboim led to the founding of a unique workshop in Europe for young Palestinian, Arab, and Israeli musicians to work together with figures such as Barenboim and cellist Yo-Yo Ma. Said died on September 23, 2003, in New York City after a decade-long struggle with leukemia.

DANIEL KUTHY AND SHERIFA ZUHUR

See also
Arafat, Yasser; Expellees and Refugees, Palestinian; Jerusalem; Nasser, Gamal Abdel; Palestine Liberation Organization; Persian Gulf War

References
Hussein, Abdirahman. *Edward Said: Criticism and Society.* London: Verso, 2004.
Said, Edward. *Culture and Imperialism.* New York: Knopf, 1999.
———. *The End of the Peace Process: Oslo and After.* New York: Vintage Books, 2001.
———. *Orientalism.* New York: Pantheon, 1978.
———. *The Politics of Depression: The Struggle for Palestinian Self-determination, 1969–1994.* New York: Pantheon, 1994.
———. *The Question of Palestine.* New York: Vintage Books, 1992.

Said, Nuri al-
Born: 1888
Died: July 15, 1958

Prominent pro-British Iraqi politician who served as prime minister 14 times between 1930 and 1958. Born in Baghdad in 1888, Nuri al-Said was the son of a minor Ottoman government official. Trained at the Staff College in Constantinople as an officer in the Ottoman Army, Nuri al-Said was converted to the Arab nationalist cause and fought with T. E. Lawrence in the Arab Revolt (1916–1918) as an adviser to Emir Faisal of Hejaz, who would later reign briefly as the king of Syria before becoming King Faisal I of Iraq. In 1918 Nuri al-Said commanded the Arab troops who took Damascus for Faisal and accompanied Faisal to the Paris Peace Conference following World War I.

Nuri al-Said secured his first cabinet position, as director-general of the police in Iraq, in 1922. He used this post to staff the police with his own followers, a tactic he would repeat again and again. In 1924 he became deputy commander of the Iraqi Army, and in 1930 he became prime minister for the first time, signing the Anglo-Iraqi Treaty. The treaty provided for Iraqi independence in 1932 but was unpopular because it also provided for a 25-year alliance between Britain and Iraq that included the leasing of bases to Britain. Nuri al-Said held numerous cabinet positions and served many times as prime minister.

Although he was dismissed from office in 1932, Nuri al-Said, a trusted ally of the British, was never far from the seat of power. In early 1941 he denounced Prime Minister Rashid Ali al-Gaylani's anti-British, pro-German policies, which were strongly influenced by Haj Amin al-Husseini, the mufti of Jerusalem. At the end of January

orientalism. In another important work, *Culture and Imperialism* (1993), Said shows the breadth of imperial vision and how it deals with resistance. He also opened the door in the 1980s to the hiring of other Arab academics, who with the exception of language specialists or Israeli Arabs had been mostly excluded from academic institutions.

As a Palestinian activist, Said initially supported the creation of a single, independent Palestinian state. He later lobbied for the establishment of a single Jewish-Arab state. He was an independent member of the Palestinian National Council (PNC), the Palestinian parliament in exile, during 1977–1991. However, he left the organization because of Palestine Liberation Organization (PLO) chairman Yasser Arafat's decision to support Iraq in the Persian Gulf War (1991). After that, Said became an outspoken opponent of Arafat. For different reasons, he denounced the 1993 Oslo Accords as counterproductive to Palestinian interests. In 1995, an infuriated Arafat banned sales of Said's books to Palestinians. In 2000, however, Said softened his position vis-à-vis Arafat when the PLO leader turned down Israeli peace offers at the Camp David Summit in 2000.

Nuri al-Said, Iraqi prime minister on 14 different occasions between 1930 and 1958, shown here in 1957. (Time Life Pictures/Getty Images)

1941, al-Gaylani fled into exile, only to return to power in April. It was then Nuri al-Said's turn to flee, to Jordan. When al-Gaylani attempted to restrict British troop movements in Iraq, British forces, supported by Jordan's Arab Legion, deposed al-Gaylani and installed Nuri al-Said as the new prime minister. This time Nuri al-Said held office until June 1944.

Nuri al-Said was prime minister for the 9th through 14th times during the periods November 1946–March 1947, January–December 1949, September 1950–July 1952, August 1954–June 1957, and March–May 1958. In February 1954 Nuri al-Said signed the Baghdad Pact with Iran, Turkey, Pakistan, and the United Kingdom as a buffer against Soviet encroachments in the region.

Nuri al-Said's pro-Western position brought him into conflict with Egyptian leader Gamal Abdel Nasser, who opposed Western influence in the region. Nasser launched a media campaign that challenged the legitimacy of the Iraqi monarchy and called on the Iraqi military to overthrow it. In response to the Egyptian-Syrian union known as the United Arab Republic, on February 12, 1958, the Hashemite monarchies of Jordan and Iraq declared an Iraqi-Jordanian union known as the Arab Federation. In May 1958 Nuri al-Said resigned to become the first prime minister of the short-lived Arab Federation.

Nuri al-Said's pro-Western policies and his increasingly heavy-handed methods, from crushing a miners' strike in November 1946 to putting down demonstrations against the Baghdad Pact, made him very unpopular in Iraq. On July 14, 1958, a military coup led by Abdul Karim Qassem ended the Arab Federation, the Iraqi monarchy, and Nuri al-Said's life. King Faisal II and other members of the royal family were executed. Nuri al-Said, disguised as a veiled woman, escaped capture for one day but was caught on July 15 and promptly put to death. His body was buried but then dug up and reportedly tied to the back of a car and paraded through the streets of Baghdad until nothing remained but a portion of one leg.

MICHAEL R. HALL

See also
Arab Revolt of 1916–1918; Baghdad Pact; Faisal I, King of Iraq; Faisal II, King of Iraq; Glubb, Sir John Bagot; Husseini, Haj Amin al-; Iraq; Lawrence, Thomas Edward

References
Birdwood, Lord. *Nuri as-Said*. London: Cassell, 1959.
Dodge, Toby. *Inventing Iraq: The Failure of Nation-Building and a History Denied*. New York: Columbia University Press, 2003.
Gallman, Waldemar J. *Iraq under General Nuri: My Recollection of Nuri Al-Said, 1954–1958*. Baltimore: Johns Hopkins University Press, 1964.

Samaritans

Religious minority group of ancient origin whose modern members live in both the State of Israel and in the occupied West Bank. The Samaritans are Palestinian Arabs who practice one of the world's oldest religions, and they are also the smallest minority group in current-day Palestine and Israel. According to their own tradition, they are the sole practitioners in pure form of the ancient Israelite religion as it was observed even before the building of the First Temple at Jerusalem in the 10th century BC. Modern Samaritans speak Palestinian Arabic and Modern Hebrew because that is now the language of Israel but pray in Ancient Hebrew, and their religious texts are written in Old Hebrew script. Jewish religious authorities have not considered the Samaritans to be Jews since at least the time of the building of the Second Temple around 515 BC, and the relationship between the two religions remains strained to this day.

Mentioned multiple times in both the Old and New Testaments and in the writings of Josephus, the Samaritans at the dawn of the Common Era were a generally despised minority group. The key points of the New Testament parable of the Good Samaritan (Luke 10:25–37) are nondiscrimination and interracial harmony. That message has become largely lost to modern audiences, who no longer have any idea who the Samaritans were or what their status was in the broader society at the time of Jesus Christ.

The Samaritans derive their name from the land of Samaria, one of the two principal regions of the present-day West Bank. The split between Samaritanism and Judaism has its roots in the rivalry between the ancient Israelite kingdoms of Israel in the north (present-day Samaria) and Judah in the south (present-day Judea). According to the Samaritans, their final split with Judaism resulted from the capture of Jerusalem in 586 BC, when the First Temple was destroyed and the religious leaders and elite of Judah were deported to Babylon.

When the Jews were allowed to return to Jerusalem in 539 BC, their religion had changed so much that the schism between Samaritanism and Judaism was unbridgeable.

There are several significant differences between the modern Jewish and Samaritan religions. The only sacred writings the Samaritans recognize are the five books of the Torah, and the Samaritan version has several minor variations from the Jewish version. The Samaritans do not recognize the books that make up the Prophets or the Writings, the other two major sections that with the Torah comprise the Jewish Bible (Tanakh). The Samaritan religious holidays are only those cited in the Torah, and the Samaritans do not observe Hanukkah or Purim. Unlike the Jews, who abandoned the high priesthood after the fall of the Second Temple in AD 70, Samaritan religious leadership remains invested in a hereditary priesthood that claims descent from the line of Aaron, the first high priest of Israel.

The Samaritans completely rejected the primacy of the Temples at Jerusalem. For them, the one true Temple to God existed on Mount Gerizim, near the West Bank city of Nablus. Archeological evidence indicates that a Samaritan temple was built there as early as 330 BC. It was destroyed by the Jewish Hasmonean king John Hyrcanus (Yohanan Girhan) about 128 BC. The Samaritans rebuilt their temple at Gerizim after the Romans crushed the Bar Kokhba Revolt, about AD 135. It was destroyed again during the wave of repressions carried out under the Byzantine emperor Zeno in the late fifth century.

In 529 the Samaritans revolted in an attempt to establish their own independent state. They were crushed by the forces of Emperor Justinian I. Tens of thousands of Samaritans died or were forced into slavery, and their religion was outlawed throughout the Byzantine Empire. The Samaritans suffered further repressions under first the Mamluks and then the Ottomans. Many Samaritans were forced to convert to Islam, and their synagogues were destroyed or turned into Mosques.

In the fourth and fifth centuries, some 1.2 million Samaritans lived in the region that stretched from southern Syria to northern Egypt. Samaritan communities existed as far abroad as Sicily and Thessalonica. By 1919, however, an issue of *National Geographic* magazine reported that only 150 Samaritans remained. By 1948 the community had grown to 250, and in 2003 their numbers stood at almost 700 people. The current population is almost equally divided between the area around Mount Gerizim and the Israeli city of Holon, just south of Tel Aviv. Until recently there was a Samaritan community in Nablus, but the upheavals of the First Intifada (1987–1993) forced them to consolidate on the slopes of Mount Gerizim.

Samaritans do not accept converts and almost never marry outside their own faith. The current population consists of only four clans, and in recent years they have shown signs of genetic disease resulting from the relatively small gene pool. Depending on where they live, the Samaritans carry either Israeli or Palestinian Authority (PA) passports. Despite their historical roots and close ties to

Judaism, the Samaritans have avoided taking sides in the Israeli-Palestinian conflict, fearing reprisals from both sides.

DAVID T. ZABECKI

See also

Ashkenazic Judaism; Palestine, Pre-1918 History of; Sephardic Judaism; West Bank; Western Wall

References

Anderson, Robert T., and Terry Giles. *The Keepers: An Introduction to the History and Culture of the Samaritans.* Peabody, MA: Hendrickson, 2002.

———. *Tradition Kept: The Literature of the Samaritans.* Peabody, MA: Hendrickson, 2005.

Samu Raid, West Bank
Event Date: November 13, 1966

Retaliatory raid by Israel Defense Forces (IDF) on the Palestinian village of Samu in the West Bank, not far from the city of Hebron, on November 13, 1966. At the time, the West Bank was under Jordanian control. In the months leading up to the Samu Raid, Israel had come under attack by a number of Palestinian guerrillas who had been staging increasingly destructive assaults, many of which had involved civilians. However, the majority of these attacks had been emanating from neighboring Syria. Those responsible for them were members of Fatah, the military faction of the Palestine Liberation Organization (PLO). Nevertheless, when a mine exploded near the Israeli-Jordanian border, resulting in the deaths of three Israeli policemen (a fourth police officer was seriously injured), the Israeli government decided to respond with a major incursion and assault into the West Bank.

The IDF assembled a large strike force of about 400 men reinforced by 10 tanks and 40 trucks for transport. Aircraft of the Israeli Air Force provided cover for the ground operation. Dubbed Operation SHREDDER, the raid began in the early hours of November 13, 1966. As the force crossed into the Jordanian-held West Bank, it initially encountered little resistance. Moving toward the settlement of Rujm al-Madfa, IDF forces leveled the police station there. Still encountering light resistance, the assault force continued toward Samu, the next major village. Here the town's inhabitants fled in panic as the IDF soldiers targeted homes, blowing them up or bulldozing them with their tanks.

By now, the Jordanians had managed to mobilize a small counterforce (an armored column, smaller in number than the Israelis) and began advancing toward Samu. As the Jordanians approached, the Israelis partly surrounded them in a near-perfect ambush. The ensuing short battle resulted in the deaths of 15 Jordanian soldiers and the wounding of 54 others. The Israelis suffered 1 dead and 10 wounded. Meanwhile, Jordanian fighters were scrambled to provide air cover, but arrived too late. In a momentary dogfight, the Israelis shot down a Jordanian fighter before the Jordanian planes withdrew. Casualties went beyond military personnel, however, and

The Palestinian village of Samu on the West Bank after an Israeli Army raid in November 1966. (Time & Life Pictures/Getty Images)

when the raid and brief battle had ended, 3 Arab civilians were among the dead, and an additional 96 civilians were wounded.

The Samu Raid did not go well from the Israeli perspective. The Israelis suffered casualties, lost equipment, and engendered the wrath of the international community. In the Middle East, the operation fanned the flames of Arab resentment against Israel during a time in which Arab-Israeli tensions were already running high. Indeed, just six months after the Samu Raid, the June 1967 Six-Day War broke out. And more than one Arab government would name the raid as a contributing factor to the conflict. In the United States, President Lyndon B. Johnson's administration was far from pleased with the Israeli action, arguing that it was too large, was not commensurate with the provocation, and ignored the fact that Syria had been supporting the lion's share of attacks against Israel. U.S. policymakers were also in a quandary because Jordan was one of the few Arab nations in the Middle East that had continued to remain a fairly reliable friend and ally of the United States.

The United Nations (UN) Security Council, in Resolution 228, formally censured Israel for its attack on the West Bank. In Jordan, the attacks brought widespread unrest and riots in Jordan's cities. A number of Jordanians were outraged by the government's seeming ineffectiveness in preventing or blunting the attack, and still others were incensed that nothing had been done to safeguard Palestinian civilians residing in the West Bank.

PAUL G. PIERPAOLI JR.

See also

Israel; Israel Defense Forces; Jordan; Jordan, Armed Forces; Six-Day War; West Bank

References

Broyles, Matthew. *The Six-Day War.* New York: Rosen, 2004.

James, R. S., and Rebecca Stettof. *The West Bank and Gaza Strip.* New York: Chelsea House, 1988.

Parker, Richard B., ed. *The Six-Day War: A Retrospective.* Gainesville: University Press of Florida, 1996.

Samuel, Sir Herbert Louis
Born: November 6, 1870
Died: February 5, 1963

British diplomat and Zionist. Born on November 6, 1870, in Toxteth, England, the son of a successful banker, Herbert Louis Samuel was an observant Orthodox Jew. He received his education at University College School in Hampstead, London, and at Balliol College,

British diplomat and Zionist Sir Herbert Samuel in 1920. (Library of Congress)

Oxford University. Interested in politics, Samuel won election to Parliament on the Liberal Party ticket in 1895. He failed to win reelection in 1900 but won another seat in a by-election in 1902. In 1905 he became undersecretary of state for the Home Office. In 1910 Prime Minister Herbert H. Asquith appointed Samuel postmaster general, and he held that position until 1916. During January–December 1916 he was home secretary. Samuel was the first practicing Jew to become a member of the cabinet.

The entry of the Ottoman Empire into World War I on the side of the Central Powers led Samuel to suggest in a conversation with Foreign Secretary Sir Edward Grey that the British government work to establish a protectorate over Palestine that would permit increased Jewish immigration there and "serve as a center for a new culture" as well as promote British interests in the Middle East. In January 1915 he sent a formal memorandum on the same subject to Prime Minister Asquith. Although nothing came of the proposal at the time, it was the basis for the 1917 Balfour Declaration, which Samuel strongly supported. Following the Liberal Party split in 1916, he sided with Asquith against David Lloyd George and was thus excluded from the cabinet when Lloyd George became prime minister. Samuel failed to win reelection to Parliament in the general election of 1918.

In late 1919 the Foreign Office asked Samuel to travel to Palestine, report on the situation there, and make recommendations regarding policies to be followed, pending formal recognition of its assignment as a British Mandate. Lloyd George then offered Samuel the position of the first high commissioner of Palestine following its acquisition as a mandate the next year, this despite protests that the appointment would be offensive to the Arabs.

Arriving in Palestine in June 1920, Samuel held the post of high commissioner for five years until 1925. He was, in effect, the first Jew to govern Palestine in 2,000 years. During his first several years, he was preoccupied with setting up the administrative and legal machinery of the mandate. He did his best to follow policies that would not alienate either the Jews or the Arabs. Toward that end he appointed as mufti of Jerusalem Haj Amin al-Husseini, who turned out to be a thorn in the side of the British administration. Following the Arab riots of May 1921, Samuel sought to appease the Arabs by somewhat slowing the pace of Jewish immigration into Palestine, angering the Zionists. Nonetheless, between 1918 and 1925 the Jewish population of Palestine grew from 55,000 to 108,000 people.

Samuel left Palestine in July 1925 and returned to Britain. That same year, Prime Minister Stanley Baldwin appointed him to head a commission to examine the coal mining industry. The Samuel Commission report, published in March 1926, recommended reorganization but not nationalization. It also recommended an end to the government subsidy, which meant in effect a reduction in worker wages. Dissatisfaction on the part of the miners with the report was one of the factors leading to the great General Strike of May 1926.

Again elected to Parliament in 1929, in 1931 Samuel became the head of the Liberal Party, the first practicing Jew to head a major British political party. He served as home secretary during 1931–1932 in the government of Prime Minister Ramsay MacDonald. Samuel remained the leader of the Liberals until he lost his seat in elections in 1935. Created Viscount Samuel in 1937, he led the Liberal Party in the House of Lords during 1944–1955.

Samuel retained his interest in Palestine and was regarded as the leading Anglo-Jewish statesman of his generation. In 1936 he became chairman of the board of directors of the Palestine Electric Corporation. In 1939 he urged that the British government not implement provisions of the White Paper regarding Palestine announced that year, and during World War II he urged the British government to adopt a pro-Zionist policy. Samuel died on February 5, 1963. Although many Zionists were disappointed with his tenure as high commissioner in Palestine, all acknowledge the importance of his work in setting up the administrative framework of the mandate that contributed greatly to the establishment of the State of Israel. His son, Edwin Herbert Samuel, 2nd Viscount Sterling, served in the Jewish Legion during World War II.

SPENCER C. TUCKER

See also

Balfour Declaration; Husseini, Haj Amin al-; Lloyd George, David; Palestine, British Mandate for; White Paper (1939); Zionism

References

Bowle, John. *Viscount Samuel: A Biography.* London: Victor Gollancz, 1957.

Samuel, Edwin, 2nd Viscount Samuel. *A Lifetime in Jerusalem: The Memoirs of Lord Samuel.* London: Valentine Mitchell, 1970.

Samuel, Herbert, 1st Viscount Samuel. *Grooves of Change: A Book of Memoirs.* Indianapolis: Bobbs-Merrill, 1946.

Wasserstein, Bernard. *Herbert Samuel: A Political Life.* Oxford: Oxford University Press, 1992.

San Remo Conference

Start Date: April 19, 1920
End Date: April 26, 1920

International summit held in San Remo, Italy, during April 19–26 to discuss unresolved issues arising from World War I (1914–1918) and the Paris Peace Conference of 1919. The most pressing issue at San Remo was the official disposition of Middle Eastern territories formerly belonging to the Ottoman Empire, which had dissolved as a result of the war. In attendance at the San Remo Conference were the prime ministers of France, Great Britain, and Italy and top-level representatives from Greece, Belgium, and Japan.

In regard to the disposition of lands in the Middle East, the San Remo Conference simply codified and elaborated upon the secret Sykes-Picot Agreement of 1916 in which the French and British agreed to create spheres of control in the Middle East. Although other issues were discussed at the meeting including the particulars of the 1919 Treaty of Versailles and the creation of a peace treaty with the Turks, the main item on the agenda was the establishment of mandates. In this case, mandates would be administered via the League of Nations, although the mandate powers (France and Great Britain) would administer their mandate governments with almost complete autonomy.

The mandates were organized into three categories depending on the location and sociopolitical development of the nations involved. The mandates in the first category included Iraq and Palestine (to be administered by the British) and Syria and Lebanon, which fell under French aegis. Unlike the other mandates in this category, the people of Palestine would not be treated as citizens of a nation-state because of the varied ethnic and religion makeup of the region.

Nor surprisingly, many Arabs viewed the British Mandate for Palestine with considerable trepidation particularly given the 1917 Balfour Declaration, which seemed to suggest that the British favored the creation of a Jewish homeland in Palestine. Furthermore, many Arabs believed that Arabs living in Palestine had been singled out by denying them political autonomy. Indeed, as early as December 1920, Arab leaders were already planning for the formation of an autonomous Palestinian state within the borders of the British Mandate.

PAUL G. PIERPAOLI JR.

See also

Balfour Declaration; League of Nations Covenant, Article 22; Palestine, British Mandate for; Sykes-Picot Agreement; World War I, Impact of

References

Méouchy, Nadine, and Peter Sluglett, eds. *The British and French Mandates in Comparative Perspective,* Vol. 93. Leiden, UK: Brill Academic, 2004.

Sherman, A. J. *Mandate Days: British Lives in Palestine, 1918–1948.* Baltimore: Johns Hopkins University Press, 2001.

Saud, Abd al-Aziz ibn Abd al-Rahman ibn Faisal ibn Turki, al-

See Ibn Saud, King of Saudi Arabia

Saud, Abdullah ibn Abd al-Aziz, al-

See Abdullah, King of Saudi Arabia

Saudi Arabia

Middle Eastern nation located on the Arabian Peninsula. The Kingdom of Saudi Arabia, founded in 1932, covers 756,981 square miles, nearly three times the area of the U.S. state of Texas. Saudi Arabia borders on Jordan, Iraq, and Kuwait to the north; the Persian Gulf, Qatar, and United Arab Emirates to the east; Oman and Yemen to the south; and the Red Sea to the west.

Saudi Arabia has been dominated by its ruling family, the House of Saud, for all of its modern history. King Abd al-Aziz al-Saud, known as Ibn Saud, the founding monarch, ruled until his death in 1953. All succeeding kings have been his sons, of which he had 48. The House of Saud has historical ties to the descendents of Muhammad abd al-Wahhab, the founder of Wahhabism (a sect of Islam), and as a result Saudi Arabian law and society are based on the Hanbali school of Islamic law and Wahhabi interpretations. Indeed, the Koran serves as the basic constitution for Saudi Arabia.

The role of Ibn Saud in Saudi Arabia cannot be overstated. The state grew inexorably as a result of his domination of the Arabian Peninsula in the early 20th century as the Ottoman Empire declined. After the end of World War I, he consolidated his position and became king in 1925. The realm was renamed the Kingdom of Saudi Arabia seven years later. The fortunes of the kingdom were transformed with the discovery of petroleum in the 1930s. The nation's vast oil reserves would bring with them trillions of dollars of revenue and turn the kingdom into one of the world's wealthiest nations. After the 1960s, at which point the influence of foreign oil companies was on the wane, Saudi Arabia's oil assets gave the kingdom a great deal of geopolitical clout as well.

Initially, American oil companies (Chevron in particular) played the leading role in oil exploration and formed a partnership with the Saudi monarchy, paying royalties for the right to extract and ship Saudi oil. The importance of oil during World War II enhanced the Saudi-American relationship, and in 1944 the Arab-American Oil Corporation (ARAMCO) was formed. President Franklin Roosevelt

MIDDLE EAST, 1920

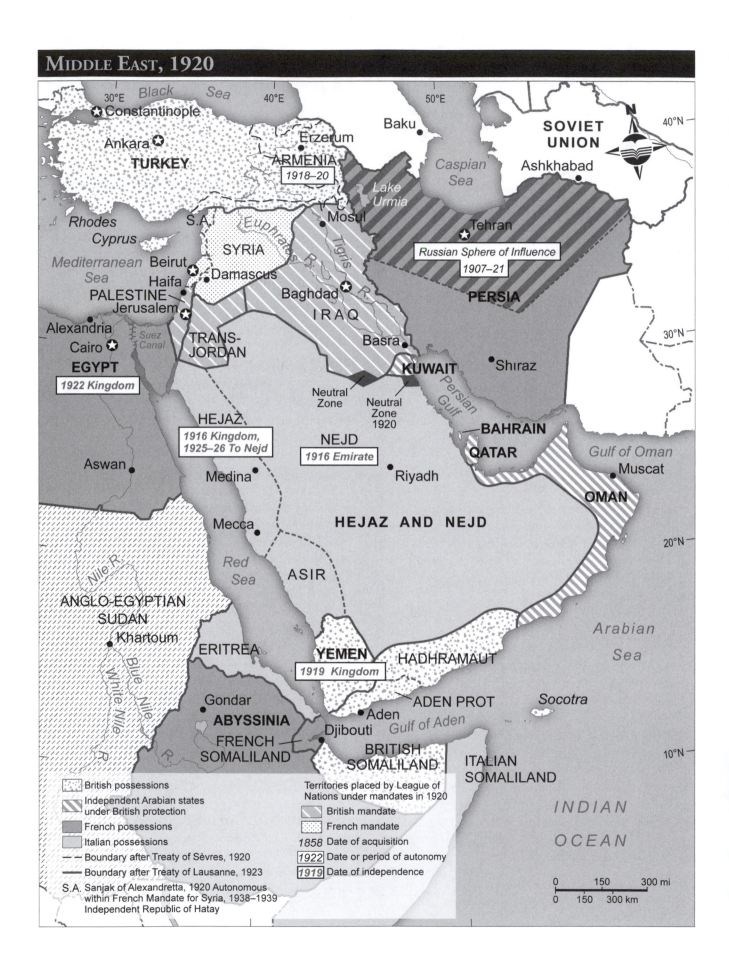

Black Sea

30°E ✪ Constantinople
Ankara ✪
TURKEY
Erzerum
40°E
Baku •
50°E
SOVIET UNION
40°N
Ashkhabad •

ARMENIA
1918–20

Caspian Sea

Rhodes
Cyprus
S.A.
Mosul •
Lake Urmia
✪ Tehran
Russian Sphere of Influence 1907–21

Mediterranean Sea
Beirut ✪
SYRIA
Damascus •
Baghdad ✪
IRAQ
PERSIA

Haifa •
PALESTINE
Jerusalem ✪
Basra •
Shiraz •
30°N

Alexandria •
Suez Canal
TRANS-JORDAN
KUWAIT
Cairo ✪
EGYPT
1922 Kingdom
Neutral Zone
Neutral Zone 1920
Persian Gulf

HEJAZ
1916 Kingdom, 1925–26 To Nejd
BAHRAIN
QATAR
Gulf of Oman
Muscat •

Aswan •
NEJD
1916 Emirate
Riyadh •
OMAN

Medina •
HEJAZ AND NEJD

Mecca •
Red Sea
ASIR
20°N

ANGLO-EGYPTIAN SUDAN
Arabian Sea

Khartoum •
ERITREA
YEMEN
1919 Kingdom
HADHRAMAUT

Gondar •
ABYSSINIA
FRENCH SOMALILAND
Djibouti •
ADEN PROT
Aden •
Gulf of Aden
Socotra

Blue Nile
White Nile
Nile R.
BRITISH SOMALILAND
ITALIAN SOMALILAND

10°N

INDIAN OCEAN

Legend

- ⣿ British possessions
- ⫽ Independent Arabian states under British protection
- ▨ French possessions
- ▨ Italian possessions
- – – – Boundary after Treaty of Sèvres, 1920
- —— Boundary after Treaty of Lausanne, 1923

S.A. Sanjak of Alexandretta, 1920 Autonomous within French Mandate for Syria, 1938–1939 Independent Republic of Hatay

Territories placed by League of Nations under mandates in 1920
- ⫽ British mandate
- ⣿ French mandate
- *1858* Date of acquisition
- *1922* Date or period of autonomy
- *1919* Date of independence

0   150   300 mi
0   150   300 km

helped to cement the growing relationship when he met with Ibn Saud on February 14, 1945, aboard the heavy cruiser USS *Quincy*. The Saudi monarchy maintained close economic and strategic ties to the United States throughout the remainder of the century.

Nevertheless, the Israeli issue greatly complicated U.S.-Saudi relations. The Saudis firmly objected to the 1948 formation of Israel, opposed the displacement of Palestinian Arabs, and played a minor military role in the Israeli War of Independence (1948–1949). Opposition to Israel became a central theme of Saudi foreign policy, and as with other Arab nations, the Saudis refused to recognize Israel for the remainder of the 20th century. However, strong American ties led Saudi diplomacy to depart significantly from that of the other leading Arab states. Because of the growing strategic importance of the Middle East and its oil reserves to Cold War geopolitics, both the United States and the Soviet Union sought increased influence in the region. The Soviets endorsed the rise of secular, socialist, Arab nationalist regimes in Egypt, Iraq, and Syria, and Soviet military assistance was crucial to these nations in their ongoing struggle with Israel. The United States countered these Soviet moves by tightening its links to the royal regimes in Iran and Saudi Arabia, which included vast arms sales.

In 1962 civil war broke out in Yemen when a nationalist faction supported by Egyptian president Gamal Abdel Nasser sought to overthrow the royal government there. Despite previous rivalries with the ruling house of Yemen, the Saudis gave financial support and military assistance to the Yemeni monarchy. Egypt and Saudi Arabia thus confronted each other directly in the conflict. The devoutly Muslim House of Saud opposed the rise of secular, socialist Arab nationalism and refused to tolerate the spread of Nasser's Pan-Arabism in the region. In addition, the respective affiliations of Egypt and Saudi Arabia with the Soviet Union and the United States turned the Yemeni Civil War into a regional theater of Cold War confrontation.

The resounding victory of Israel in the June 1967 Six-Day War led to a warming of relations between Saudi Arabia and the various Arab nationalist states, especially Egypt. As U.S. support for Israel increased, the Saudis sought to influence American policy in favor of the Arabs. This conflict ultimately laid the foundation for the 1973 oil embargo. Saudi oil was largely controlled by American-owned oil companies until the early 1970s. At that point, the House of Saud negotiated the gradual takeover of ARAMCO by Saudi interests. By 1973, the transfer of control had begun. When Egypt and Syria attacked Israel in October 1973 prompting the Yom Kippur War, Saudi Arabia's King Faisal obtained U.S. president Richard M. Nixon's assurances of American nonintervention.

The Israelis suffered severe reversals in the opening stages of the conflict, however, prompting Nixon to send U.S. military aid to Israel on October 19. The next day, working through the Organization of Petroleum Exporting Countries (OPEC), the Saudi government implemented an oil embargo directed mainly at the United States. The embargo hobbled the already weak U.S. economy, created inflationary pressures, and decimated the U.S. automobile and

The Kingdom Center Tower in Riyadh, capital of Saudi Arabia. (iStockPhoto.com)

steel industries. American fuel prices rose 40 percent during the five months of the crisis. The net result was a major economic recession coupled with high inflation (sometimes referred to as stagflation). Even after the embargo ended, oil prices remained high for the remainder of the decade.

Saudi Arabia emerged from the crisis as the clear leader of OPEC and with renewed respect in the Arab world. Massive increases in oil revenues (from $5 billion per year in 1972 to $119 billion per year in 1981) transformed Saudi Arabia into an affluent, cosmopolitan, urbanized society with generous government subsidies and programs for its citizens and no taxation. However, the House of Saud maintained strict control over Saudi society, culture, and law. Saudi Arabia remained an absolute monarchy until 1992, when the royal family promulgated the nation's Basic Law following the 1991 Persian Gulf War.

The U.S.-Saudi relationship eventually recovered and remained close. Indeed, Saudi Arabia often used its influence in OPEC to keep oil prices artificially low from the mid-1980s to the late 1990s. However, the Saudis continued to oppose the State of Israel. Saudi relations with Egypt declined precipitously after the signing of the Camp David Accords between Israel and Egypt in 1978. The Saudis objected to any individual peace deals with Israel that did not settle the entire Arab-Israeli conflict and address the plight of the Palestinian Arabs and the refugees of the 1948–1949 war. In 1981, King Fahd proposed a peace plan based on a Palestinian state in the West Bank and the Gaza Strip, removal of Israeli settlements in those areas, and a plan to address the needs of Palestinian refugees. Indeed, Saudi Arabia became a primary source of economic aid for the Palestine Liberation Organization (PLO) after the Camp David Accords. While the PLO's support for Saddam Hussein during the Persian Gulf War of 1991 effectively curtailed Saudi financial support for Fatah, the regime in Riyadh did not change its position on a comprehensive peace and in 2002 proposed another comprehensive plan to which the Israeli government did not respond.

During the Persian Gulf War the Saudis took the unusual step of allowing some 500,000 troops to use its territory as the main staging area for a strike against Iraq, which had invaded and annexed Kuwait in August 1990. The decision caused a negative reaction among the ultraconservatives and morals police in Saudi Arabia, and consequently the king had to rein them in. The conservatives argued that the foreigners were defiling Islamic traditions and law. But the troop deployment was seen in Riyadh as a necessary evil of sorts, as Iraqi dictator Hussein could not be trusted to end his land grab in Kuwait.

After the September 11, 2001, terrorist attacks on the United States, which involved 15 Saudi Arabian nationals or citizens, U.S.-Saudi relations took a nosedive. The Saudis disapproved of the 2003 Iraq War and refused to allow their territory as a base of operations for the invasion. In August 2003 just five months after the war began, all remaining U.S. troops were withdrawn from the kingdom. During 2003–2005 a series of attacks by Al Qaeda on the Arabian Peninsula killed Saudis and Westerners. These included the bombing in May and November 2003 of two housing compounds for foreign workers in Saudi Arabia that resulted in many deaths (including Americans) and an attack on the American consulate in Jiddah. Despite these developments, the Saudis have repeatedly dedicated themselves to fighting the so-called war on terror, and the Saudi government has continued to work with the Americans in the areas of counterterrorism and counterintelligence.

ROBERT S. KIELY

See also

Arab Nationalism; Arab Oil Embargo; Fahd, King of Saudi Arabia; Faisal, King of Saudi Arabia; Faisal II, King of Iraq; Ibn Saud, King of Saudi Arabia; Nasser, Gamal Abdel; Organization of Petroleum Exporting Countries; Pan-Arabism; Wahhabism; Yom Kippur War

References

Hourani, Albert. *A History of the Arab Peoples.* Cambridge: Harvard University Press, 1991.
Lacey, Robert. *The Kingdom.* London: Hutchinson, 1981.
Wynbrandt, James. *A Brief History of Saudi Arabia.* New York: Checkmark, 2004.
Zuhur, Sherifa. *Saudi Arabia: Islamic Threat, Political Reform and the Global War on Terror.* Carlisle Barracks, PA: Strategic Studies Institute, 2005.

Saudi Arabia, Armed Forces

Saudi Arabia's military forces are currently divided into five major branches: the Saudi Arabian National Guard (SANG), the Royal Saudi Land Forces (RSLF), the Royal Saudi Air Force (RSAF), the Royal Saudi Naval Force (RSNF), and the Saudi Coast Guard. Operational control of these forces rests with the minister of defense and aviation in Riyadh. The head of the SANG is the first deputy prime minister and answers directly to the king.

SANG evolved from Ikhwan (the Brotherhood), or the White Army as it was sometimes called from the traditional Arab garb rather than uniforms worn by its members. King Ibn Saud, the first king of Saudi Arabia, organized and led the White Army in the early decades of the 20th century to subdue tribal resistance and unify the tribes of the Arabian Peninsula into what is now the Kingdom of Saudi Arabia. From this origin, SANG has a long-honored tradition of bravery and loyalty to the nation and its ruling family.

Existing parallel to but separate from the regular Saudi military forces, SANG is a full-time standing, land-based, defensive force of approximately 75,000 regulars and 25,000 militia. It is headquartered in the capital city of Riyadh and has two regional headquarters at Dammam in the east and Jeddah in the west.

SANG is a mechanized infantry and light infantry force that relies on rapid mobility and firepower to defeat its adversaries. Armed with eight-wheeled light armored vehicles and towed artillery, SANG complements the heavier armor of the RSLF and is fully capable of conducting integrated operations. However, it primarily acts as a very effective internal security force that can provide rear-area security for the army and help defend Riyadh.

The RSLF is headquartered in Riyadh and has field commands organized into eight zones under military zone commanders. The RSLF consists of armored, mechanized, and airborne forces with associated support elements. The RSLF has about 75,000 troops and an inventory of 1,000 tanks, 3,000 other armored vehicles, and 500 major artillery pieces. These forces are normally dispersed over much of the kingdom and focus on territorial defense.

The RSAF employs a mix of Sikorsky UH-60 Blackhawk utility and support helicopters, Boeing-Vertol CH-47 Chinook transport helicopters, and Bell AH-64 Apache attack helicopters. The RSLF has its own air defense resources. As of 2002, these forces included 17 antiaircraft artillery batteries, organized and equipped to protect its maneuver forces in combat. These forces are armed with Crotale, Shahine, Mistral, Stinger, and Redeye surface-to-air missiles (SAMs). In addition, they employ a number of different antiaircraft gun systems, including the Vulcan, Bofors, and Oerlikon guns.

Prior to 1984, the Royal Saudi Air Defense Force fell under the command of the land forces commander (army), but that year the kingdom established a separate professional service dedicated to the relatively high-technology air defense mission. This separate force controls Saudi Arabia's heavy SAMs and fixed air defenses. It

A Royal Saudi Air Force F-15 Eagle fighter aircraft approaches a KC-135 Stratotanker for refueling during Operation DESERT SHIELD. (H. H. Deffner/U.S. Department of Defense)

is a relatively static force of about 16,000 men designed for point defense that cannot easily support the army in mobile operations.

Saudi Arabia has given the modernization and expansion of the RSAF a higher priority than that of the land forces, navy, and air defense force. This is primarily because the RSAF is the only service that can cover Saudi Arabia's 2.3 million square km of territory. The RSAF is headquartered at Riyadh and has a total strength of about 20,000 men. Its operational command is structured around its air command and operations center and base operations. The main air command and operations center is near Riyadh, and there are ancillary sector operating centers at Tabuk, Khamis Mushayt, Riyadh, Dhahran, and Al-Kharj that control fighter aircraft, SAMs, and air defense artillery.

The RSAF has operational command facilities at a number of air bases located throughout the kingdom. According to one source, the RSAF's combat forces are organized into six wings with a total of 15 combat squadrons and more than 400 fixed-wing combat and training aircraft. The RSAF flies a mix of aircraft to include various models of the F-15, F5, and Tornado.

The RSNF is headquartered in Riyadh and has east and west fleets for its Gulf and Red Sea coasts. It has a total strength of 13,500 to 15,500 men. In 2002 the combat strength of the RSNF included 4 frigates, 4 missile corvettes, and 9 guided missile ships. It also included 3 torpedo boats, 20 inshore fast craft, 17 coastal patrol craft, 7 mine warfare ships, and a number of support and auxiliary craft. The RSNF also includes the Royal Saudi Marine Division. This 3,000-man force is organized into one regiment with two battalions.

The Saudi Coast Guard is part of the Frontier Force, has a separate command chain, and maintains its primary base at Aziziah. The Coast Guard contains up to 4,500 men who man a variety of coastal patrol craft. Its primary mission is antismuggling, but it does have an internal security mission as well.

Saudi Arabia emerged as a significant regional military force during the 1991 Persian Gulf War. Two Arab task forces were organized under the command of Prince Khalid Bin Sultan al Saud. By the time the land phase of the war began in February 1991, the Saudi ground forces in theater totaled nearly 50,000 men, some 270 main battle tanks, 930 other armored fighting vehicles, 115 artillery weapons, and more than 400 antitank weapons. The RSAF flew a total of 6,852 sorties between January 17 and February 28, 1991, second only to the United States in total air activity. In the four-day ground war that began on February 24, Saudi troops, including the National Guard, helped defeat the Iraqis and drive them out of Kuwait. Saudi forces did not participate in the Iraq War that began in 2003, however.

James H. Willbanks

See also
Persian Gulf War; Saudi Arabia

References
Cordesman, Anthony H. *Saudi Arabia: Guarding the Desert Kingdom.* Boulder, CO: Westview, 1997.
———. *Saudi Arabia Enters the Twenty-First Century: The Military and International Security Dimensions.* New York: Praeger, 2003.
Khaled bin Sultan. *Desert Warrior: A Personal View of the Gulf War by the Joint Forces Commander.* New York: Perennial, 1996.
Pollack, Kenneth M. *Arabs at War: Military Effectiveness, 1948–1991.* Lincoln: University of Nebraska Press, 2002.

Saudi King as Custodian of the Two Holy Mosques

A title given to the king of Saudi Arabia as the temporal protector of al-Masjid al-Haram (the Sacred Mosque) in Mecca and the Masjid al-Nabawi (the Prophet's Mosque) in Medina, both of which are located in Saudi Arabia. These two cities and the sacred spaces in them are the first and second most holy places to Muslims. Muslims are obliged, if possible, to make the pilgrimage to Mecca at least once in their lifetime if possible. When Muslims pray in the five obligatory daily prayers, or in additional supernumerary prayers, they face in the direction of Mecca (*qiblah*). At the very outset of Islam, the *qiblah* was in the direction of Jerusalem, the third-holiest site to Muslims. Because Medina is not far from Mecca, many Muslims also extend their pilgrimage to include a visit to that city, as the Prophet Muhammad lived and died there. Pilgrims visit the Prophet's Mosque and other sites in Medina.

The title "Custodian of the Two Holy Mosques" goes back centuries. However, the political locus of the Islamic empires shifted early on from the Arabian Peninsula, first to Damascus, then to Baghdad, and then to multiple other points. Still, the annual pilgrimage went on, and governance and administration were necessary to accommodate it. Later, the sharif family, or descendents of the Prophet's clan, were named guardians of the holy city of Mecca, and in particular they maintained the Kaaba, the structure at the center of the pilgrimage. At the same time the House of Saud began to gain more control over the Arabian Peninsula. In 1925 King Abd al-Aziz al-Saud (Ibn Saud) decisively defeated Hashemite sharif Hussein ibn Ali and took control of Mecca and the Sacred Mosque. The following year, Ibn Saud was crowned king of the Hejaz (present-day western Saudi Arabia), which included both Mecca and Medina.

From that time forward, the royal House of Saud has exercised temporal control over these holy sites. In 1982 Saudi King Fahd bin Abdul Aziz (King Fahd) formally adopted the honorific title "Custodian of the Two Holy Mosques."

Some Muslims including Osama bin Laden take a dim view of Saudi control of the holy cities of Mecca and Medina. The Islamic Republic of Iran also opposes the Saudi royal family, mainly because they are Wahhabi, and in the past the Wahhabis attacked the Shia and their holy places. The Iranians also oppose the Saudi royal family because they are, in principle, against monarchies, which they claim are un-Islamic. It is true that the Saudis by virtue of their governance of the holy cities have a strong influence on Islamic institutions and education in the region, something they actively promote. On the practical side, King Fahd spent hundreds of millions of dollars expanding and improving the holy sites in Mecca and Medina, including the installation of air conditioning in the Sacred Mosque and its environs.

Paul G. Pierpaoli Jr. and Sherifa Zuhur

See also
Fahd, King of Saudi Arabia; Ibn Saud, King of Saudi Arabia; Mecca; Medina; Saudi Arabia; Wahhabism

References
Al-Rasheed, Madawi. *A History of Saudi Arabia.* New York: Cambridge University Press, 2002.
Peters, F. E. *Mecca: A Literary History of the Muslim Holy Land.* Princeton, NJ: Princeton University Press, 1994.
Waines, David. *An Introduction to Islam.* Cambridge: Cambridge University Press, 1995.
Wintle, Justin. *The Timeline of Islam.* New York: Barnes and Noble, 2004.

Sayeret Matkal

Sayeret Matkal, also known as the General Staff Reconnaissance Unit, is the elite special forces unit of the Israel Defense Forces (IDF). Originally formed in 1957 as Unit 269, its organizing army intelligence officer was Avraham Arnan, and its first leader was Lieutenant Meir Har-Zion. The original members of Sayeret Matkal were drawn from the Paratroopers Brigade, Unit 101, and Aman, the intelligence branch of the IDF, to which it reports.

Sayeret Matkal was initially patterned after the British Special Air Service (SAS) and even adopted its motto: "Who Dares Wins." Sayeret Matkal's primary tasks are counterterrorism, deep reconnaissance, and intelligence collection. Bedouin taught the unit members desert tracking, and training emphasized knowledge of Arab attire, cultures, and language variations.

Sayeret Matkal conducts two selection camps (*gibush*) annually. Initially, new recruits were secretly selected from the personal acquaintances and families of its members. From the 1980s it has accepted volunteers. The 20-month training regime stresses small arms proficiency, hand-to-hand combat, martial arts, orienteering, camouflage, disguise, reconnaissance, evasion, survival, adaptation, unit cohesiveness, flexibility, creativity, and the patient execution of well-ordered plans. The top graduates join Unit 269, which specializes in counterterrorism activities outside of Israel. Unit 269 frequently deploys with the Israeli Navy's Flotilla 13.

Notable former members of Sayeret Matkal include Ehud Barak, Benjamin Netanyahu, and Jonathan (Yoni) Netanyahu. Among its many operations are THUNDERBOLT, the 1976 raid on Entebbe; Operation ISOTOPE, the 1972 capture of a Sabena flight hijacked by the Black September organization; Operation SPRING OF YOUTH, the 1973 killing of Black September leaders in Beirut, Lebanon; the 1974 Ma'alot Massacre school hostage rescue; the Savoy Hotel hostage rescue in Tel Aviv in 1975; the 1989 kidnapping of Sheikh Abdul-Karim Obeid in Lebanon; and numerous behind-the-lines operations in all of Israel's wars since 1957.

Sayeret Matkal is also known for war-fighting innovations such as deep-penetration helicopter infiltration and weapons innovations such as the folding stock that increased the Uzi submachine gun's accuracy without a commensurate increase in size and weight. Because of the clandestine nature of their mission, members of Sayeret Matkal are the only IDF soldiers not allowed to wear their unit insignia in public.

RICHARD M. EDWARDS

See also

Barak, Ehud; Entebbe Hostage Rescue; Netanyahu, Benjamin; Netanyahu, Jonathan

References

Katz, Samuel M. *The Hunt for the Engineer: The Inside Story of How Israel's Counter-terrorist Forces Tracked and Killed the Hamas Master Bomber.* New York: Lyons, 2002.
———. *The Illustrated Guide to the World's Top Counter-Terrorist Forces.* Hong Kong: Concord, 2001.
———. *Israeli Special Forces.* Osceola, WI: Motorbooks International, 1993.

Sea of Galilee

See Lake Kinneret

Second Aliya

See Aliya, Second

Sephardic Judaism

One of the two principal branches of Judaism whose origins can be traced to the Iberian Peninsula, North Africa, and the eastern Mediterranean. During the Middle Ages, Judaism diverged into two cultures that differed in laws, customs, liturgy, and language. While Ashkenazic Judaism evolved and flourished in Central and Eastern Europe, the environs of the Holy Roman Empire, Sephardic Judaism evolved and flourished in the Moorish Iberian Peninsula, primarily Spain, and North Africa.

Sephardic customs and halakic (Jewish law) rulings are based on the Palestinian Talmud and ritual traditions. Ashkenazic customs and halakic rulings, meanwhile, are based on the Babylonian Talmudic and ritual traditions. This division of Sephardic and Ashkenazic Judaism can be seen in the structure of the chief rabbinate of Israel that represents all of Judaism in Israel and is the final arbiter of halakic and kashruth (Jewish food laws). The chief rabbinate has two chief rabbis, one Sephardic and one Ashkenazic. The Jewish community in Rome predated the destruction of the Solomonic Temple and the Diaspora and along with Yemenite, Ethiopian, and Oriental Jewry, is neither Sephardic nor Ashkenazic.

Sephardic Judaism derives its name from the Hebrew *Sefarad* (Spain). Spain's Ferdinand and Isabella expelled the Jews from Spain in 1492 along with the last of the Moors. These Sephardim were dispersed throughout the Mediterranean region and the Ottoman Empire. Many, however, also settled in Southwest Asia, France, Italy, the Spanish Americas (present-day Southwest United States, Mexico, Central America, and South America), Brazil, the Netherlands (including the former Dutch possessions of Aruba, Suriname, and Curacao), Hungary, Denmark, Germany, Austria, and England. Benjamin Disraeli, a Sephardic Jew who converted to Anglicanism, served two terms as the British prime minister in the late 19th century. The majority of the Jews of this Sephardic Diaspora settled in Morocco and North Africa, however.

The first Jewish congregation in North America, Shearith Israel (New York, 1684), was founded by Sephardim. But by 1751 Ashkenazim dominated the American Jewish community. Sephardic Jews, who represented 97 percent of world Jewry in the 11th century, comprised only 8 percent in 1931 before the decimation of Ashkenazic Jews in the Nazi Holocaust. The Sephardim now comprise approximately 15 percent of world Jewry.

In addition to their differences in Talmudic traditions, Sephardic and Ashkenazic Jews differ in their indigenous languages and in some legal and ritual practices. Ladino, a hybrid of Judeo/Hebrew-Castilian/Spanish, is the traditional vernacular of Sephardic Jewry. Yiddish (Judeo/Hebrew-German) is the traditional vernacular language of Ashkenazic Jews. Just as the Gileadites and the Ephramites of biblical times varied in their pronunciation of "Shibboleth," Sephardim and Ashkenazim vary in their pronunciation of one Hebrew consonant and some vowels.

Sephardim and Ashkenazim also vary in some halakic and kashruth (kosher) practices. Sephardim eat rice, corn, peanuts, legumes, peanuts, and millet during the observance of Passover (*Pesach*). Ashkenazim abstain from these foods. Sephardim and Ashkenazim also vary in some other halakic and kashruth practices. Sephardim are generally stricter than Ashkenazim in their understanding of which meats are kosher. There are also differences in the permissibility of specific slaughter practices.

Although they have much in common, Sephardic and Ashkenazic Torah and worship practices also differ. The terms "Sephardic" and "Ashkenazic" are often used to refer to liturgical traditions (*nusackh*). Those traditions vary in the content of the prayers, the order of the prayers, the text of the prayers, the melodies of the prayers, and the prayer book (*Siddur*). Sephardic brides and grooms do not refrain from meeting for one week prior to their wedding, while Ashkenazic brides and grooms do. Sephardic Torahs stand during a Torah service, and Ashkenazic Torahs lie flat. The Sephardic understanding of Jewish law is based on the writings of Rabbi Joseph Caro, and the Ashkenazic understanding of Jewish law is based on the writings of Rabbi Moses Isserles.

Sephardim and Ashkenazim have generally lived together peacefully where both have settled, with the possible exception of the Sephardic migration to France following the French withdrawal from Morocco in 1956 and Algeria in 1962. Sephardim and Ashkenazim rarely intermarry. Sephardim have maintained their religious and variant ethnic heritages by settling or grouping themselves according to their countries or culture of origin. Thus, among the myriad of cultures from which and into which the Sephardim have settled, they have formed Castilian, Aragonian, Catalonian, Portuguese, Cordovan, Romaniotes, Mallorcan, Sicilian, Sevillian, Moroccan, Algerian, and numerous other culturally and geographically rooted congregations.

Even though the Ashkenazim, Sephardim, and Mizrahi Jews have lived peacefully with one another and fought together to preserve the State of Israel since 1948, present-day Israel continues to be dominated by Ashkenazic Jews of European descent. This peaceful and fruitful coalition is endangered by a rising Mizrahi post-Zionist backlash that asserts that Mizrahi or Arab Jews are discriminated against by Israel's Ashkenazic Jewish political establishment. These Mizrahim contend that the Zionist immigration policies that promoted Ashkenazic Jewish immigration from the late 19th through the 20th centuries reduced Mizrahi Jews to second-class citizenship. This, they argue, has created social, political, and economic discrimination that separates Sephardic and Mizrahi Israelis from Ashkenazic Israelis.

RICHARD EDWARDS

See also

Ashkenazic Judaism

References

Assis, Yom Tov. *The Jews of Spain: From Settlement to Expulsion.*
    Jerusalem: Hebrew University of Jerusalem, 1988.
Bartlett, John R. *Jews in the Hellenistic World: Josephus, Aristeas, the
    Sibylline Oracles, Eupolemus.* Cambridge: Cambridge University Press,
    1985.
Raphael, Chaim. *The Sephardi Story: A Celebration of Jewish History.*
    London: Valentine Mitchell, 1991.

Settlements, Israeli

Although the term "settlement" is used broadly within Israel to describe residential communities and neighborhoods that were settled by Jewish pioneers, the phrase "Israeli (Jewish) settlements" is more specifically used to describe residential communities built in the areas occupied by Israel after the June 1967 Six-Day War. These areas include the Golan Heights, the Sinai Peninsula, the Gaza Strip, and the West Bank. Settlements are one of the "final status"

A young Jewish settler plants the Israeli flag on Artis Hill next to the settlement of Bet El in Samaria in the West Bank, 1995. (Avi Ohayan/Israeli Government Press Office)

issues that remain unresolved in the Israeli-Palestinian conflict. Because of the size of the settlements, some of which, such as Ma'ale Adumim, are cities of 45,000 or more residents, some argue that they are irreversible facts on the ground that pose a roadblock to a two-state solution. The settlements are illegal according to international law because they are in occupied territory under a military administration. Yet Israel does not recognize the applicability of the Fourth Geneva Convention, claiming that the land is disputed and that settlements are built on state land.

There are approximately 250,000 Jewish settlers living in the West Bank, a number that rises to more than 400,000 if one includes the settlements of East Jerusalem, which is also occupied territory according to international law but has been formally annexed by Israel. Settlers are Israeli citizens with all the rights, responsibilities, and services entailed, including infrastructure services (roads, water, electricity), military and police protection, and military service. Settlers are governed by Israeli civil law, whereas the Palestinians among whom they live are governed by a combination of Israeli military law, Ottoman law, British Mandate law, and a mixture of Palestinian and Jordanian laws.

Some Israeli settlers live in the West Bank, Gaza (until 2005), and the Golan Heights for economic reasons. Housing in the settlements is highly subsidized by the government, and the communities are advertised as suburbs of Tel Aviv and Jerusalem because of the road network that has been constructed for the use of settlers (much of which is prohibited to Palestinians). Others move to settlements on ideological grounds and believe that they are redeeming the land by settling on it in accordance with Jewish scripture. Most of these religious settlements are found in areas of biblical significance. One example is Kiryat Arba, which is near the Cave of Machpelah in Hebron where Abraham, Isaac, Rachel, and Rebecca are believed buried.

While there are more than 120 official settlements consisting of permanent dwellings, schools, shops, and even some universities in the West Bank (excluding East Jerusalem), there are also about 100 outposts. These are usually small communities that have been erected without official government sanction and involve a few individuals or families living in mobile home units. Although these outposts are deemed illegal under Israeli law and the government has committed to evacuate them at various times, construction of new housing units, permanent buildings, and infrastructure projects continues apace.

Jewish settlements (deemed such because Arab and Druze Israelis are not generally permitted to live in these communities) are often found on hilltops, strategically placed along the main aquifers in the West Bank, and ringing the city of Jerusalem. Israeli policy regarding the settlements has evolved since 1967. The construction of settlements has been pursued for a variety of reasons, including defense, religious beliefs, and political leverage in the Arab-Israeli conflict.

The Alon Plan, which was prepared shortly after the 1967 Six-Day War, proposed Jewish settlement in strategic areas such as the Jordan Valley, East Jerusalem, and the Judean desert. After the 1977 Likud Party victory, settlement activity turned toward areas in the central West Bank, where the majority of the Palestinian population was located. At times Gush Emunim (Bloc of the Faithful) established new settlements. Gush Emunim is a religious group ideologically committed to the building of settlements throughout the West Bank, which they call Judea and Samaria. The government recognized them only after several years of struggle.

Although elected government officials have been involved in articulating settlement policy over the years, much of the work has been designed and carried out by officials in a wide range of ministries, the civil administration, and the settler councils in the West Bank. The Settlement Division of the World Zionist Organization (WZO), whose full budget comes from the Israeli treasury, has worked with the Israeli government in establishing settlements. However, according to one recent government report, this group often acts without official authorization from elected officials.

Both of the major Israeli parties—Labor and Likud—have supported and encouraged the building of settlements, although Labor has traditionally advocated the use of settlements as a bargaining chip with the Palestinians. The Likud Party, meanwhile, has been committed to settlement expansion for ideological reasons as well. Neither party, however, envisions dismantling major settlement blocs, such as Ariel, Gush Etzion, or Ma'ale Adumim, and instead advocates a land swap with the Palestinians.

Many Israeli peace groups, such as Peace Now, object to Israel's settlement policy, arguing that it prevents the emergence of a viable Palestinian state and therefore challenges Israel's existence as a Jewish state. They also argue that the presence of settlers and Israeli military personnel deep in the West Bank reduces Israeli security by instigating Palestinian anger and by diluting defense forces. Several groups have argued that the route of the Israeli Security Fence has been designed to incorporate not only current settlements but also future settlement growth and therefore results in a poor line of defense, as it is twice the length of the 1949 Green Line.

Officially sanctioned settlements have been dismantled by the Israeli government in two historical cases: the withdrawal from the Sinai Peninsula after the signing of the 1979 Camp David Accords with Egypt, and the unilateral Gaza disengagement in September 2005. In April 2006, Israeli prime minister Ehud Olmert formed a new government with the vision of a convergence or consolidation plan that called for the withdrawal of some 60,000 Israeli settlers from smaller settlements in the eastern portion of the West Bank. The plan also called for the consolidation of settlers into major settlement blocs. This plan was shelved, however, after the war with Hezbollah in the summer of 2006.

Israeli settlements have been identified as an ongoing obstacle to peace in the 1993 Oslo Accords, the 2002 Road Map to Peace, and other peace initiatives. Even the U.S. government has raised the settlement issue as a major impediment to peace. Be that as it may, throughout the Oslo Peace Process (1993–2000) the number of Israeli settlers in the West Bank almost doubled, and settlement growth has continued. Indeed, permits for the construction of more than 952 new settlement housing units have been issued as of mid-2006, while the Israelis issued permits for 1,184 housing units in 2005.

MAIA CARTER HALLWARD

See also

Gaza Strip; Golan Heights; Israeli Security Fence; Jerusalem; Jerusalem, Old City of; Six-Day War; West Bank

References

Efrat, Elisha. *The West Bank and Gaza Strip: A Geography of Occupation and Disengagement.* New York: Routledge, 2006.
Gorenberg, Gershom. *The Accidental Empire: Israel and the Birth of the Settlements, 1967–1977.* New York: Times Books, 2006.
Lein, Yehezkel. *Land Grab: Israel's Settlement Policy in the West Bank.* Jerusalem: B'Tselem, 2002.

Settlers' Council

See Yesha Council

Shaath, Nabil
Born: 1938

Palestinian politician and, during 2003–2005, the first foreign minister of the Palestinian Authority (PA). Born in 1938 in Safed, Galilee, in the British Mandate for Palestine, Nabil Shaath was the son of a Palestinian Arab father and a Lebanese mother. He immigrated with his family to Egypt after the creation of the State of Israel in 1948 and the beginning of the Israeli War of Independence. After studying in Alexandria, he traveled to the United States in 1959 to obtain a degree at the University of Pennsylvania.

Shaath returned to Cairo in 1965 and became an Egyptian citizen. In 1969 he moved to Beirut, Lebanon, to teach business administration at the American University of Beirut. Since 1975 he has headed a consulting, engineering, and management company known as TEAM International, located in several Arab countries. He was also active in the Fatah organization and a close associate of Palestine Liberation Organization (PLO) chairman Yasser Arafat.

Regarded as a moderate, Shaath played an important role in establishing PLO contacts abroad. He took part in the 1991 Madrid peace talks, serving as the liaison between the PLO leadership in Tunis and the official Palestinian delegation. He was also involved,

Nabil Shaath, minister of foreign affairs for the Palestinian Authority (PA), during a visit to European Community headquarters in Brussels, December 2004. (European Community)

to a lesser degree, in the secret talks that led to the Declaration of Principles and is credited with having drafted the Palestinian proposition for it. Shaath headed the negotiations that ended in the Gaza-Jericho Autonomy Agreement (Cairo Accord) and took part in the talks at Camp David in 2000 and at Taba in 2001.

In 1994 Shaath joined the PA as minister of planning and international cooperation. In January 1996 he won election as a Fatah representative to the Palestinian Legislative Council. He retained his ministry post despite a strongly critical internal audit resulting from European Union (EU) pressure.

In April 2003 Shaath became the first foreign minister of the PA in the new cabinet headed by Mahmoud Abbas (Abu Mazen). He held this post until February 2005. Shaath was also acting prime minister of the PA for nine days in December 2005 when Ahmed Qurei briefly stepped aside. Shaath caused something of a stir when he told BBC television in 2005 that President George W. Bush had said to him that he had a mission from God in his Middle East policies, a statement that both Bush and Abbas subsequently denied.

SPENCER C. TUCKER

See also
Abbas, Mahmoud; Arafat, Yasser; Bush, George Walker; Fatah; Madrid Conference; Oslo Accords; Palestinian Authority; Qurei, Ahmed Ali Mohammed

References
Hall, John G. *Palestinian Authority: Creation of the Modern Middle East.* Langhorne, PA: Chelsea House, 2002.
Parsons, Nigel Craig. *The Politics of the Palestinian Authority: From Oslo to Al-Aqsa.* London: Routledge, 2003.

Shaba Farms

Small strip of disputed territory located at the juncture of southeastern Lebanon, southeastern Syria, and northeastern Israel. This narrow strip of fertile land runs from southwest to northeast and is about 1.6 miles wide and 8.7 miles long. It lies to the south and southwest of the Lebanese village of Shaba (Chebaa) on the slopes of Mount Hermon and north of the Druze village of Majdal al-Shams in the Golan Heights.

Dispute over ownership of the territory reaches back to the period of the French mandate following World War I, when France controlled Syria and Lebanon. In a French-British agreement of 1935, the Lebanese-Syrian border was defined so that the western side of Mount Hermon was Lebanese and the eastern slopes were Syrian, but no formal boundary was set.

Beginning in the 1950s and extending to 1964, a series of disputes occurred between Syria and Lebanon over their joint border, leading the two governments to establish a commission to resolve these issues. In 1964 the commission recommended to the two governments that the Shaba Farms be made part of Lebanon. Neither the Syrian nor Lebanese governments took any formal action at that time, however. Indeed, the Syrian government imposed its authority there, and by 1967 the Shaba Farms area was firmly under its control.

Israel captured the Shaba Farms area from Syria in the Six-Day War of 1967 and denied the Lebanese landowners the right to farm it. Israel officially annexed the area in 1981. Hezbollah claims that the Israeli annexation of the Shaba Farms is illegal because it is Lebanese land and that Israel should have withdrawn from it in 2000. This is one of the territorial justifications for its terrorist attacks on Israel. The controversy began in 2000 when the United Nations (UN) certified that Israel had withdrawn from all Lebanese territory following its invasion of that country in 1982. The government of Lebanon then officially protested to the UN that the Shaba Farms was its territory and that it remained under Israeli control. However, UN secretary-general Kofi Annan held that Israel had indeed complied with UN Security Council Resolutions 425 and 426 to withdraw from all Lebanese territory and that maps available to the UN all placed the Shaba Farms within Syria. Most independent experts claim the same. Nonetheless, Syrian president Bashar al-Assad has said repeatedly that the Shaba Farms area belongs to Lebanon.

SPENCER C. TUCKER

See also

Assad, Bashar al-; Hezbollah; Lebanon; Lebanon, Israeli Invasion of

References

Evron, Yair. *War and Intervention in Lebanon: The Israeli-Syrian Deterrence Dialogue.* Baltimore: Johns Hopkins University Press, 1987.

Hajjar, Sami G. *Hezbollah: Terrorism, National Liberation, or Menace?* Carlisle Barracks, PA: Strategic Studies Institute, U.S. Army War College. 2002.

Kaufman, Asher. *The Shebaa Farms: A Case Study of Border Dynamics in the Middle East.* Jerusalem: Hebrew University of Jerusalem and Gitelson Peace Publications, 2002.

Shafi, Haidar Abdel
Born: 1919
Died: September 25, 2007

Leading Palestinian secular nationalist leader, physician, and founder of the Palestinian Red Crescent Society in Gaza. Born in Gaza in 1919, the son of Sheikh Muheiddin Abdul Shafi, head of the Higher Islamic Council (Waaf), Haidar Abdel Shafi attended primary school in Gaza and secondary school at the Arab College in Jerusalem, graduating in 1936. He studied medicine at the American University in Beirut and there joined the Arab Nationalist Movement. Upon graduation in 1943, he went to work at the Municipal Hospital in Jaffa. In 1944 he joined the British Army in Jordan. Resigning his commission at the end of the war, he entered private medical practice in Gaza and cofounded a branch of the Palestine Medical Society in 1945. Always fiercely independent politically, in 1948 he urged acceptance of the United Nations (UN) partition plan that would have established two separate states in Palestine.

During the Israeli War of Independence (1948–1949), Shafi helped provide medical assistance to the estimated 200,000 Palestinian refugees who flooded into Gaza. In 1951 he studied surgery at Miami Valley Hospital in Dayton, Ohio. Returning to Gaza in 1954, he worked as a surgeon, and during 1957–1967 he was director of health services in the Gaza Strip.

Following the opening of the Palestinian National Congress in Jerusalem in May 1964 and establishment of the Palestine Liberation Organization (PLO), Shafi became a member of its 16-man Executive Committee. By 1966 he was the leading PLO figure in the Gaza Strip but in the 1960s came under attack in the Arab press for urging negotiations with Israel to achieve a peaceful resolution of the Arab-Israeli conflict.

Following the 1967 Six-Day War, Israeli authorities charged Shafi with encouraging protests against their rule and expelled him from Gaza to a village in the Sinai Desert for three months. In September 1970 they deported him to Lebanon for two months. From 1972 he was the founder and director of the Palestinian Red Crescent Society in the Gaza Strip, providing free medical care and a forum for cultural activities.

Shafi was a sharp critic of the Camp David Accords of September 1978, which he saw as a sellout of the Palestinians by Egypt so that it might recover the Sinai. In the early 1990s he became the chief Palestinian negotiator in talks in Washington, D.C., with the Israeli government but resigned in 1993 over the settlements issue. He continued to be a sharp critic of continued construction of Jewish settlements in the West Bank and the Gaza Strip, which he regarded as contrary to the peace process and a violation of international law. Indeed, he called on Palestinians to fight, if necessary, to prevent their construction. However, he opposed suicide bombings. At the same time, he called for a two-state solution for Palestine but with the restoration of the 1967 borders. Elected to the Palestinian Legislative Council in 1996, he resigned two years later, frustrated by what he called its ineffectiveness and lack of movement toward democratic institutions. He remained a sharp critic of Yasser Arafat's rule and the concentration of power in Arafat's hands. Critical of Palestinian disunity, in April 1998 Shafi initiated unity talks for all factions in Gaza, to include Fatah, Hamas, the Islamic Jihad, and others. He was also one of the founders of the Palestinian National Initiative, begun in June 2002, that advocated national unity, democracy, and honest government.

Shafi died in Gaza of colon cancer on September 25, 2007. His death resulted in the rare occurrence of tributes from leaders of both Hamas and Fatah.

SPENCER C. TUCKER

See also

Arafat, Yasser; Camp David Accords; Fatah; Gaza Strip; Hamas; Palestine Liberation Organization; United Nations Palestine Partition Plan

References

Ashrawi, Hanan. *This Side of Peace.* New York: Simon and Schuster, 1995.

Wallach, John, and Janet Wallach. *Still Small Voices.* New York: Harcourt Brace Jovanovitch, 1989.

Shakur, Yusuf bin Raghib
Born: 1928

Syrian major general and commander of Syrian armed forces against Israel in the Yom Kippur War of October 1973. Yusuf bin Raghib Shakur was born in 1928 near Homs, Syria. Upon graduation from secondary school he attended the Military Academy in Homs. He then took an advanced course in artillery at Châlons-sur-Marne, France, in 1949 and also pursued higher military studies in the Soviet Union.

A gifted linguist, Shakur was fluent in Arabic, French, English, Spanish, Russian, and Armenian. These language skills brought him diplomatic assignments, and he served as Syrian consul general to Venezuela and Brazil during 1961–1964.

Following his return to Syria, Shakur became the director of security forces. He was promoted to colonel and then to brigadier general before the Six-Day War with Israel in 1967, in which he saw action. He was promoted to major general in 1970, not only for his military accomplishments but also for his loyalty to Hafez al-Assad, who assumed power in Syria that year. In April 1972 following the appointment of Mustafa Tlas as minister of defense, Shakur was moved into his former post as chief of staff of the Syrian armed forces.

In his new position Shakur was closely involved in planning for war with Israel in 1973. The idea for a joint Egyptian-Syrian invasion of Israel originated with Egyptian president Anwar Sadat, and Shakur participated in a final review of the plans with his Egyptian counterparts in Alexandria during the summer of 1973. Among the chief concerns were how to deceive the United States and Israel into believing that the massing of Syrian forces along Israel's northern and southern borders was simply in connection with routine autumn maneuvers.

The beginning of the Yom Kippur War on October 6, 1967, caught Israel completely off guard. Shakur committed substantial resources to exploit the initial success achieved in the Golan Heights, the primary territory that Syria hoped to recover from Israel in the war. Although Syrian forces fought hard and well, Shakur's commanders often failed to exercise initiative in what was a developing situation. Hoping for a knock-out punch, he committed too much of his available armor too soon in unfavorable territory and thus lacked the resources to meet the inevitable Israeli counterattack.

Shakur and the remainder of the Syrian high command were also not aware that their Egyptian allies had different goals for the war. The strategy of a simultaneous invasion from north and south had been designed to split the Israel Defense Forces (IDF), but Egypt had limited goals. Sadat merely hoped to provoke new peace negotiations. Syria, however, sought an all-out military victory. This divergence in strategies enabled the Israelis to concentrate their attention on the Syrian forces in the Golan Heights and prevent a Syrian breakthrough there.

On October 8 the Israelis halted the Syrian drive in the Golan Heights and began counterattacking. Under this Israeli pressure Shakur authorized a Syrian withdrawal, which was initially accomplished in good order. A subsequent all-out Israeli push, however, reached almost to Damascus and was halted only by the injection of Iraqi and Jordanian armor units and the cease-fire accepted by Syria on October 22.

Al-Assad made Shakur one of the scapegoats for the Syrian military failure. In the reshuffling that followed the war, Shakur was forced into retirement in August 1974.

Spencer C. Tucker

See also

Assad, Hafez al-; Sadat, Anwar; Syria; Syria, Armed Forces; Yom Kippur War

References

Herzog, Chaim. *The War of Atonement: October, 1973.* Boston: Little, Brown, 1975.

Pollack, Kenneth M. *Arabs at War: Military Effectiveness, 1948–1991.* Lincoln: University of Nebraska Press, 2002.

Rubin, Barry, and Thomas A. Keaney, eds. *Armed Forces in the Middle East: Politics and Strategy.* Portland, OR: Frank Cass, 2002.

Seale, Patrick. *Assad of Syria: The Struggle for the Middle East.* Berkeley: University of California Press, 1988.

Shallah, Ramadan Abdullah
Born: January 1, 1958

Leader of Palestinian Islamic Jihad. Born in Sajaya in the Gaza Strip on January 1, 1958, Ramadan Abdullah Shallah studied at Zagaziq University in Egypt, where he became friends with Fathi Shiqaqi, the founder of Islamic Jihad of Palestine. Returning to Gaza, Shallah worked for a time at Al-Azhar University. He established Islamic Jihad in the West Bank.

Shallah returned to Egypt in 1984 and then went on to the United States, where he studied political science and economics. He then settled in Britain, where he earned a doctorate in banking and economics from the University of Durham. He also helped coordinate activities of Islamic Jihad in Europe. In 1991 he moved to the United States, becoming director of the World and Islam Studies Enterprise in Tampa, Florida; publishing a journal, *Qira'at Siyasiya* (Political Readings); and teaching as an adjunct professor at the University of Florida. Following the assassination of Shiqaqi by the Mossad, the Israeli intelligence service, Shallah was selected in October 1995 to succeed him as head of Islamic Jihad. Shallah resides in Damascus, Syria.

Spencer C. Tucker

See also

Islamic Jihad, Palestinian; Mossad; Shiqaqi, Fathi

References

Abu-Amr, Ziad. *Islamic Fundamentalism in the West Bank and Gaza: Muslim Brotherhood and Islamic Jihad.* Bloomington: Indiana University Press, 1994.

Hatina, Meir. *Islam and Salvation in Palestine: The Islamic Jihad Movement.* Syracuse, NY: Syracuse University Press, 2001.

Shamir, Yitzhak
Born: October 15, 1915

Israeli politician and prime minister (1983–1984, 1986–1992). Yitzhak Shamir was born Yitzhak Jaziernicki on October 15, 1915, in Ruzinoy, Poland (now in Belarus). While a young man, he joined the Polish Betar Zionist youth movement. His law studies in Warsaw ended when he immigrated to the British Mandate for Palestine (Eretz Israel) in 1935, where he ultimately enrolled in Jerusalem's Hebrew University.

That same year, 1935, Jaziernicki formally changed his name to Shamir. He then joined the Irgun Tsvai Leumi (National Military Organization), a right-wing paramilitary Zionist underground movement in Palestine. Irgun was known for its immediate and harsh retaliation for Arab attacks on the Jewish community in Palestine and its advocacy of military action against the British mandatory government.

When the Irgun split into right-wing and left-wing factions in 1940, Shamir affiliated himself with the more militant Lohamei Herut Israel (Israel Freedom Fighters), a group that was classified by the British as a terrorist organization and later became known as the Stern Gang (after its founder, Avraham Stern). Shamir was arrested by the British in 1941 and escaped from their custody in 1943 following the death of Stern in 1942. Shamir now became one of those who led the organization and who re-formed it and renamed it Lehi. It was under Shamir's leadership that in 1944 Lehi assassinated Walter Edward Guinness, Lord Moyne, heir to the Guinness fortune and the British minister resident in the Middle East.

Shamir served as Lehi's principal director of operations until he again was arrested by the British in 1946 and exiled to a British prison camp in Eritrea. Shamir escaped from there in 1947 to the neighboring French colony of Djibouti and, although granted political asylum by France, returned to Israel in 1948 to command Lehi until it was disbanded in 1949. Shamir directed the 1948 assassination of Count Folke Bernadotte, the United Nations (UN) representative in the Middle East, whom Shamir and his collaborators saw as an anti-Zionist and in league with the British.

Shamir served as a Mossad (Israeli intelligence service) operative from 1955 to 1965 and then engaged in business until he joined Menachem Begin's Herut movement (which became the Likud Party) in 1973. Shamir was elected to the Knesset (Israeli parliament) in 1973 and two years later became Herut's chairman. In the Knesset,

Yitzhak Shamir, Israeli politician and prime minister (1983–1984 and 1986–1992), June 21, 1977. (Israeli Government Press Office)

Shamir served on the Foreign Affairs and Defense Committee as well as on the State Comptroller's Committee. The Likud Party's victory in the national elections for the ninth Knesset in May 1977 saw Begin become Israel's first non-Labor prime minister and Shamir become the Speaker of the Knesset. Begin immediately challenged King Hussein of Jordan, President Hafez al-Assad of Syria, and President Anwar Sadat of Egypt to meet to negotiate a peace treaty. Sadat subsequently agreed to the Camp David Accords and the Israel-Egypt Peace Treaty that extended full Egyptian diplomatic recognition to Israel in exchange for the return of the Sinai Peninsula, which Israel had seized in the Six-Day War in 1967. Shamir presided over the ratification of the treaty in the Knesset.

Following the resignation of Moshe Dayan, Shamir served as Israel's foreign minister during 1980–1983. In that capacity he oversaw the posttreaty normalization process with Egypt, reestablished diplomatic contacts with African countries severed during the Yom Kippur War in 1973, and negotiated a postoperation peace agreement for Galilee with Lebanon. This treaty was later revoked by the Lebanese under Syrian pressure soon after Begin's resignation as prime minister in October 1983. Shamir succeeded Begin both as leader of the Likud and as prime minister.

Shamir's failure to decrease the inflation that racked Israel's economy led to an indecisive national election in July 1984 and the formation of a government of national unity that allied Likud with the Labor Party headed by Shimon Peres. Peres served as prime minister with Shamir as vice premier until October 1986, when Shamir and Peres rotated positions and Shamir again became prime minister. While serving in these capacities, Shamir and Defense Minister Moshe Arens collaborated with U.S. president Ronald Reagan and Defense Secretary Caspar Weinberger to advance U.S.-Israeli strategic cooperation and free trade.

Following another indecisive election in 1988, Likud and Labor formed a new coalition government that retained Shamir as prime minister but did not have the rotation arrangement of its predecessor agreement. When this coalition government failed in 1990, Shamir formed a new government that included members of some ultraconservative parties and excluded Labor.

In 1991 Shamir's government ordered the rescue of thousands of Ethiopian Jews in Operation SOLOMON. At Washington's urging, Shamir did not retaliate in 1991 for unprovoked Iraqi Scud missile attacks during the Persian Gulf War that were designed to bring Israel into the conflict and break up the allied coalition. In September 1991 Shamir's government participated in the Madrid Peace Conference, which led to the 1993 peace accords between Israel and the Palestine Liberation Organization (PLO) that began Israel's withdrawal from the West Bank and the Gaza Strip.

Shamir's premiership ended in 1992 with the defeat of Likud in general elections. He resigned from the leadership of Likud in March 1993, although he retained his seat in the Knesset until 1996. Since that time, he has largely withdrawn from public scrutiny. In recent years he has reportedly been in failing health.

RICHARD EDWARDS

See also
Begin, Menachem; Camp David Accords; Irgun Tsvai Leumi; Israel-Egypt Peace Treaty; Likud Party; Lohamei Herut Israel; Madrid Conference; Mossad; Peres, Shimon; Persian Gulf War; Reagan, Ronald Wilson; Weinberger, Caspar

References
Brinkley, Joel. *The Stubborn Strength of Yitzhak Shamir.* New York: New York Times, 1988.
Enderlin, Charles. *Shamir.* Paris: O. Orban, 1991.
Shamir, Yitzhak. *Summing Up: An Autobiography.* London: Orion, 1994.

Shammout, Ismail
Born: 1930
Died: July 3, 2006

Prominent Palestinian artist and director of arts and national culture for the Palestine Liberation Organization (PLO). Born in al-Lydd in the British Mandate for Palestine in 1930, Ismail Shammout studied as a boy with the well-known Palestinian artist Daoud Zalatimo. At age 16 Shammout convinced his father that he could make a living with his art but was forced to flee his birthplace with his family in July 1948 during the Israeli War of Independence (1948–1949). He settled in the refugee camp of Khan Younis in the Gaza Strip.

Continuing to pursue his art career, in 1950 Shammout enrolled in the College of Fine Arts in Cairo and in 1953 held his first art exhibition in Gaza. Many of his paintings depicted the flight of his people from Palestine in 1948. A year later he had a major exhibition of his paintings in Cairo with the participation of another Palestinian artist, Tamam Arif al-Akhal, who became his wife in 1959. Egyptian president Gamal Abdel Nasser opened the exhibit. That same year Shammout moved to Rome, where he studied at the Academy of Fine Arts. In 1956 he settled in Beirut.

Shammout was widely regarded as the greatest Palestinian artist and art teacher of his day. His brightly colored works with their folkloric inspiration were popular among Palestinians for their depiction of the suffering of the Palestinian people. In 1965 Shammout joined the PLO as its director of arts and national culture. In 1969 he was elected first secretary-general of the Union of Palestinian Artists. Two years later he was chosen the first secretary-general of the Union of Arab Artists.

In 1983 following the Israeli invasion of Lebanon, Shammout moved from Beirut to Kuwait. After the 1991 Persian Gulf War he moved again, this time to Köln (Cologne), Germany. In 1994 he settled in Amman, Jordan, where he died on July 3, 2006.

SPENCER C. TUCKER

See also
Israeli War of Independence, Overview; Nasser, Gamal Abdel; Palestine Liberation Organization

References
Ankori, Gannit. *Palestinian Art.* Chicago: University of Chicago Press, 2006.

Nassar, Jamal R. *The Palestine Liberation Organization: From Armed Struggle to the Declaration of Independence.* New York: Praeger, 1991.

Zuhur, Sherifa, ed. *Colors of Enchantment: Theater, Music, Dance, and Visual Arts of the Middle East.* Cairo: American University in Cairo Press, 2001.

Sham'un, Kamil

See Chamoun, Camille

Shara, Farouk al-
Born: January 17, 1938

Syrian foreign minister (1984–2006) and then vice president (2006–). Farouk al-Shara was born in Dara, Syria, on January 17, 1938. He received a bachelor's degree in English literature at Damascus University in Syria in 1963 and later studied international law at the University of London. He pursued a career in business and in 1968 was regional manager of Syria Air in London. In 1972 he became the commercial director of the airline. An active member of the Baath Party, he left his position with Syria Air in 1976 to become Syrian ambassador to Italy. In 1980 he became deputy foreign minister, and in March 1984 he became foreign minister, a post he held until 2006. He also served on the Baath Party central committee.

As foreign minister and a key figure of the Hafez al-Assad regime, al-Shara maintained a high profile on the international scene. Among the events in which he has been involved are the 1991 Persian Gulf War, when he warned Israel not to respond to Iraqi missile attacks, and the Middle East peace conference held in Madrid in October 1991, where he headed the Syrian delegation. He was sporadically involved in peace negotiations with Israeli delegates, which were overshadowed by the Palestinian-Israeli peace initiatives after September 1993. Negotiations between Israel and Syria remained deadlocked on the future of the Golan Heights.

Following the death of al-Assad in 2000, his son Bashar al-Assad succeeded him as Syrian president. Although he reshuffled the cabinet and replaced many of his father's longtime associates, he retained al-Shara. In October 2005, however, al-Shara came under international criticism and was accused of lying when he denied any Syrian involvement in the assassination of former Lebanese prime minister Rafik Hariri. The matter did lead to the death, allegedly by suicide, of Syrian interior minister Ghazi Kanan.

In February 2006, however, al-Shara left his post as foreign minister when he was appointed vice president of Syria. Many international observers saw this as a demotion, for the vice president has traditionally had little power and chiefly carries out ceremonial

Farouk al-Shara, Syrian foreign minister (1984–2006) and vice president (2006–). (European Community)

functions. But in his new post he traveled extensively abroad, and there were hints that he might have a far more active role in policy formation. According to the Syrian constitution, in the event that al-Assad should die in office or resign, al-Shara would become the president of Syria.

SPENCER C. TUCKER

See also

Assad, Bashar al-; Assad, Hafez al-; Baathism; Golan Heights; Hariri, Rafik; Madrid Conference; Syria

References

Lesch, David W. *The New Lion of Damascus: Bashar Al-Assad and Modern Syria.* New Haven, CT: Yale University Press, 2005.

Pipes, Daniel. *Greater Syria: The History of an Ambition.* New York: Oxford University Press, 1990.

Seale, Patrick. *Assad of Syria: The Struggle for the Middle East.* Berkeley: University of California Press, 1988.

Sharett, Moshe

Born: October 15, 1894
Died: July 7, 1965

Israeli politician, first foreign minister (1948–1956), and second prime minister (1953–1955). Moshe Sharett was born Moshe Shertok in Kherson, Ukraine, in the Russian Empire on October 15, 1894. He attended traditional Hebrew schooling until 1908, when his family moved to Palestine, then part of the Ottoman Empire. His family settled in the Arab village of Ein Sinia, where he learned Arabic and Arab customs. In 1910 his family moved to Jaffa (Yofa) and helped to establish Ahuzat Bayit, the early nucleus of Tel Aviv. Sharett graduated as part of the first class of Herzliya Gymnasium, the first Hebrew high school in Palestine.

Sharett went on to study law in Constantinople until the beginning of World War I, when he joined the Turkish Army and served as an interpreter. Following the war, he worked in land acquisition for the Palestine Jewish Community's Representative Council and joined the Ahdut Ha'avodah (Unity of Labor) Party. Later, he joined the Mapai (Labor Party). During 1922–1924 he studied at the London School of Economics. Around that time he became involved in Zionist activities and joined the Po'ale Zion (Workers of Zion). Returning to Palestine, in 1925 he became a deputy editor of the Histadrut (General Federation of Labor) daily newspaper, *Davar.*

In 1931 Sharett became secretary of the Political Department of the Jewish Agency. In 1933 he became head of the department when his predecessor was murdered. In that position, Sharett was specifically responsible for public relations with the British mandatory authorities in Palestine and the ambassador of Zionism. He was one of the witnesses advocating an independent Jewish state before the Peel Commission in 1936. At the Jewish Agency, he became associated with David Ben-Gurion.

In 1944 Sharett helped establish the British Army's Jewish Brigade, which fought in World War II and secretly assisted Jewish

Moshe Sharett, Israeli politician, first foreign minister (1948–1956), and second prime minister (1953–1955), shown here in 1952. (Israeli Government Press Office)

immigration to Palestine. In 1946 he represented the Jewish Agency in Palestine before the Anglo-American Committee of Inquiry. In 1947 the British government arrested Sharett and other leaders of the Jewish Agency and held them for four months at a Latrun detention camp. Golda Meir replaced Sharett as head of the Political Department and worked for his release as well as the release of the other detainees. Upon his release, Sharett actively lobbied the United Nations (UN) to accept partition. Sharett, known for his oratorical skills, was the chief advocate of a Jewish state before the UN.

In 1948 Sharett was one of the signatories of the Israeli Declaration of Independence. It was at this time that he changed his name from Shertok to the Hebrew Sharett. He also became the new nation's first foreign minister, working to establish the Israeli Foreign Service and developing the new state's diplomatic relationships. His work in this area proved invaluable during the Israeli War of Independence (1948–1949). He played a leading role in concluding the armistice agreements that ended the war.

With the beginning of the Cold War, Sharett followed a policy of nonidentification in which Israel would not take sides in order to retain diplomatic relations with both sides. He is also credited with recognizing the impact of decolonization and working to develop ties with the emerging states of Africa, Asia, and Latin America.

In 1953 Sharett was elected Israeli prime minister on the retirement of Ben-Gurion, at the same time retaining the post of foreign minister. As prime minister, Sharett was known for his efforts to avoid the confrontational approach toward the Arab states of his predecessor. He was also able to maintain Israeli economic growth and to manage the large influx of new immigrants.

Ben-Gurion returned to the prime ministership in November 1955. Sharett remained at the foreign ministry until his resignation in June 1956 over disagreements with Ben-Gurion and the imminent Suez Crisis. Sharett continued his writing career and managed the Mapai's publishing house of Am Oved (Working Nation). He was also chairman of Beit Berl College and in 1960 was elected chairman of the World Zionist Organization (WZO) and the Jewish Agency. In that position he devoted his energies to relations between Israel and the Jewish community worldwide. Sharett died in Jerusalem on July 7, 1965.

SPENCER C. TUCKER

See also

Anglo-American Committee of Inquiry; Ben-Gurion, David; Histadrut; Israel; Jewish Agency for Israel; Jewish Brigade; Palestine, British Mandate for; Peel Commission; World Zionist Organization; Zionism

References

Sachar, Howard M. *A History of Israel: From the Rise of Zionism to Our Time.* 3rd ed. New York: Knopf, 2007.

Sheffer, Gabriel. *Moshe Sharett: Biography of a Political Moderate.* New York: Oxford University Press, 1996.

Shepherd, Naomi. *Ploughing Sand: British Rule in Palestine, 1917–1948.* New Brunswick, NJ: Rutgers University Press, 1999.

Sharm al-Sheikh

Egyptian coastal city on the Red Sea, now a major resort and tourist destination, located on the southern tip of the Sinai Peninsula. After the Israeli War of Independence (1948–1949) ended, the Egyptian government closed the Strait of Tiran to Israeli shipping. Because of the negative impact that the closure caused to the Israeli economy, the Israel Defense Forces (IDF) had long planned for a military operation that would seize Sharm al-Sheikh and reopen the straits. When the 1956 Suez Crisis began, the IDF's plan to cross the Sinai included an assault against the city. As the main attack smashed toward the Suez Canal in October 1956, the IDF's 9th Infantry Brigade attacked southward from Eilat toward Sharm al-Sheikh, beginning on October 29.

Traversing difficult terrain and overcoming stiff Egyptian resistance along the west coast of the Gulf of Aqaba, the brigade reached

Israeli Army personnel show United Nations Emergency Forces (UNEF) personnel around Sharm al-Sheikh in preparation for the Israeli withdrawal from the Sinai, March 8, 1957. (Israeli Government Press Office)

the outskirts of the city on November 4. Meanwhile, the 202nd Parachute Brigade had been dropped on al-Tur, 40 miles west of Sharm al-Sheikh, in support of the 9th Brigade. The combined force began its attack on November 4. After the Egyptians repulsed a night attack, the Israelis broke through early in the morning of November 5. By 9:00 a.m., Sharm al-Sheikh was in IDF hands, and an internationally negotiated truce began the next day.

Sharm al-Sheikh remained under Israeli control until March 11, 1957, when the Israelis were promised that the straits would remain open—under international law—to all shipping. In order to monitor the Strait of Tiran, United Nations Emergency Forces (UNEF) were then stationed in Sharm al-Sheikh.

The city remained under United Nations (UN) supervision until May 1967, when Egyptian president Gamal Abdel Nasser ordered all UNEF forces out of the Sinai, to include Sharm al-Sheikh. When the Six-Day War began in June 1967, the IDF had planned for a combined naval-airborne attack to seize the city once more. With the stunning success of the overall Israeli war plan, IDF chief of staff Yitzhak Rabin moved up the attack against Sharm al-Sheikh, afraid that an early cease-fire might prevent the IDF from taking that city. Meanwhile, the Egyptian garrison at Sharm al-Sheikh had been ordered to retreat without a fight.

The Israelis cancelled a planned paratroop assault against al-Tur and dropped their airborne troops directly into the city on June 7, 1967. With support from naval forces, the IDF captured the city virtually without a fight, as most of the defenders had already been withdrawn. Israel immediately declared the Strait of Tiran open to international shipping.

During the 15 years of Israeli occupation of the Sinai Peninsula, the city was renamed Mifratz Shlomo. In 1982, three years after the initial Israel-Egypt Peace Treaty was signed, Israel returned Sharm al-Sheikh to the Egyptians.

Known today for its vibrant tourism, upscale hotels and resorts, fishing, and deep-sea diving, Sharm al-Sheikh was the site of several diplomatic conferences. On September 4, 1999, the city hosted a joint peace conference that produced the Sharm al-Sheikh Memorandum, which implemented parts of the interim agreements reached via the Oslo II agreement of September 1995 to include the Israeli transfer of portions of the West Bank to the Palestinian Authority (PA). Another summit held at Sharm al-Sheikh on October 17, 2000, failed to stem the violence of the Second (al-Aqsa) Intifada. New terrorist cells threatened Sinai tourism with a series of bombings during 2004–2006, the first of which targeted Israeli tourists at Taba.

THOMAS VEVE

See also

Geography of the Middle East; Israel-Egypt Peace Treaty; Nasser, Gamal Abdel; Red Sea; Sinai Campaign; Six-Day War; Straits of Tiran; Suez Crisis

References

Herzog, Chaim. *The Arab-Israeli Wars: War and Peace in the Middle East from the War of Independence to Lebanon.* Westminster, MD: Random House, 1984.

Oren, Michael B. *Six Days of War: June 1967 and the Making of the Modern Middle East.* Novato, CA: Presidio, 2003.

Sharon, Ariel
Born: February 27, 1928

Israeli Army general, politician, and prime minister (2001–2006). Ariel Sharon was born Ariel Scheinermann (also known by the diminutive Arik) on February 27, 1928, in Kfar Malal, Palestine, to Russian immigrants. In 1942 at age 14 he joined the Gadna, the paramilitary youth organization of the Haganah, the Jewish defense force that protected kibbutzim (collective-farming settlements) from Arab attacks.

Sharon commanded an infantry company in the Alexandroni Brigade during the Israeli War of Independence (1948–1949) and was severely wounded by Jordanian forces in an effort to relieve the besieged Jewish population of Jerusalem during the Second Battle of Latrun. Following the war he founded and commanded a special commando unit (Unit 101) that specialized in reconnaissance, intelligence gathering, and retaliatory raids designed to punish and deter Palestinian and Arab protagonists while enhancing Israeli morale.

Sharon was criticized for targeting both Arab soldiers and non-combatants and condemned for the killing of 69 civilians, half of whom were women and children, during a raid on the West Bank village of Qibya in the fall of 1953. In an effort to end the criticism, in 1954 Unit 101 was folded into the 202nd Paratrooper Brigade. However, it continued to attack military and civilian targets, including the Kalkiliya police station raid in October 1956.

During the 1956 Suez Crisis, Sharon commanded the 202nd Brigade in the Israeli invasion of the Sinai Peninsula, capturing the strategically important Mitla Pass at the onset. Later he received heavy criticism for taking the pass rather than merely holding the ground east of it. Taking the pass claimed 38 Israeli dead. This incident hindered Sharon's military advancement during the next several years.

After studying at the British Staff College in Camberley, England, in 1957, Sharon commanded an infantry brigade and then the Israeli Army Infantry School. In 1962 he earned his bachelor of law degree from the Hebrew University of Jerusalem. He was appointed chief of staff of the Northern Command in 1964 and then in 1966 headed the Israel Defense Forces (IDF) Training Department.

Sharon was promoted to major general just before the 1967 Six-Day War, when forces under his command again took the Mitla Pass. He assumed leadership of the Southern Command in 1969. He retired from the IDF in June 1972 only to be recalled to command the armored division that crossed the Suez Canal into Egypt at the end of the 1973 Yom Kippur War. His direction of that crossing and the subsequent encirclement of Egyptian forces is widely considered one of the masterpieces of tactical command in modern mobile warfare.

Sharon helped found the Likud Party in September 1973 and

Ariel Sharon, Israeli Army general, politician, and prime minister (2001–2006), speaking during a press conference at his office in Jerusalem, May 2001. (Ya'cov Sa'ar/Israeli Government Press Office)

was elected to the Knesset in December 1973. He resigned in 1975 to serve as security adviser to Prime Minister Yitzhak Rabin until 1977 and then became minister of agriculture in Likud prime minster Menachem Begin's first government (1977–1981). In this position Sharon actively promoted the construction of Jewish settlements in the occupied Arab territories. In June 1981 he became Begin's minister of defense, and in this position he designed and prosecuted Israel's 1982 invasion of Lebanon, known as Operation PEACE FOR GALILEE because the ostensible intent was to force the Palestine Liberation Organization (PLO) Katyusha rockets out of the range of Israel's northern border and to destroy the terrorist infrastructure there. Sharon and Begin deliberately expanded the invasion to include a drive against Beirut. Although the PLO was driven from Lebanon, the invasion intensified the Lebanese Civil War, allowing Syria to become entrenched in the politics of that country. The Israeli presence in force lasted three years (a limited Israeli force remained until 2000) and resulted in such a high number of Palestinian civilian deaths that worldwide public opinion turned against Israel. Following the September 1982 massacre of Palestinians at the Sabra and Shatila refugee camps by Israel's Lebanese Christian Phalangist allies, Sharon was found to be indirectly responsible for failing to provide adequate protection for the refugees and thus resigned as Begin's minister of defense. This event overshadowed Sharon's diplomatic rapprochement with a number

of African nations and his role in developing the first strategic cooperation agreement with the United States (1981), Operation MOSES (1984), and a free trade agreement with the United States (1985).

Sharon served in various Israeli governments as a minister without portfolio (1983–1984), minister of industry and trade (1984–1990), and minister of construction and housing and chairman of the ministerial committee on immigration and absorption (1990–1992). The latter post allowed him to double the number of Jewish settlements throughout the West Bank and the Gaza Strip during his tenure in office. He hoped that these settlements would not only provide a strategic buffer for Israel proper but would also reduce the possibility of the return of these territories (Judea and Samaria) to Palestinian Arabs.

Sharon then served on the Knesset's Foreign Affairs and Defense Committee (1992–1996) and as minister of national infrastructure (1996–1998) under Likud prime minister Benjamin Netanyahu. As foreign minister (1998–1999), Sharon led Israel's permanent status negotiations with the Palestinian Authority (PA) and sought to promote long-term solutions to the region's water disputes and inadequacies.

Sharon assumed the leadership of the Likud Party after Ehud Barak's victory in the general elections of May 1999 led to the resignation of Prime Minister Netanyahu. The failure of Barak's land for peace initiative at the Camp David Summit in 2000 coupled with the collapse of his governing coalition and the eruption of Palestinian violence led to Barak's defeat by Sharon in the general election of February 2001, even though much of the civil violence was precipitated by Sharon's visit to the Temple Mount on September 28, 2000. The ensuing violence was known as the Second (al-Aqsa) Intifada (2000–2004).

Palestinians charged that as prime minister, Sharon pursued a policy of confrontation and nonnegotiation. On July 2004, he also angered the French government when he called for French Jews to emigrate for Israel following an upswing in anti-Semitic incidents in France. With 600,000 Jews, France had the largest Jewish population after the United States and Israel.

In 2004 Sharon began a bold policy of disengagement, or unilateral withdrawal, from the Gaza Strip, a policy opposed by his own Likud Party but supported by the Labor Party, the U.S. government, and many European nations. In January 2005 Labor Party leader Shimon Peres accepted the position of vice premier in Sharon's unity government that included members of Likud, Labor, Meimad, and United Torah Judaism. Sharon completed the withdrawal from Gaza of all Israeli settlers on August 30, 2005, and the destruction of all Israeli settlements and the complete withdrawal of the Israeli military on September 11, 2005.

Sharon narrowly defeated a challenge to his leadership of Likud by Netanyahu on September 27, 2005, and then on November 21, 2005, resigned his Likud position, dissolved parliament, formed a new center-right party known as Kadima (Forward), and set new elections for March 2006. On December 18, 2005, Sharon was hospitalized for what was thought to be a minor ischemic stroke and shortly thereafter was released anticipating surgery to repair a newly discovered hole in the atrial septum of his heart. He suffered a massive cerebral hemorrhage at his Negev ranch (Havat Hashikmim) on January 4, 2006, before the surgery could be accomplished. He underwent several brain surgeries at Jerusalem's Hadassah Hospital, but he remains in a persistent vegetative state with little potential for the recovery of cognitive function. On April 11, 2006, the Israeli cabinet declared Sharon incapacitated and ended his prime ministership three days later, naming Ehud Olmert as interim prime minister, a position made official after Kadima won the most Knesset seats in the national election. Perhaps the most controversial of Sharon's projects as prime minister was a security wall designed to separate and secure Israel proper from territory to be ceded to the Palestinians.

RICHARD EDWARDS

See also

Arafat, Yasser; Barak, Ehud; Begin, Menachem; Gaza Strip; Intifada, Second; Katyusha Rocket; Lebanon, Israeli Invasion of; Likud Party; Mitla Pass; Netanyahu, Benjamin; Palestine Liberation Organization; Palestinian Authority; Peres, Shimon; Rabin, Yitzhak; Suez Crisis; Yom Kippur War

References

Finkelstein, Norman H. *Ariel Sharon.* Minneapolis, MN: First Avenue Editions, 2005.

Gelvin, James L. *The Israel-Palestine Conflict: One Hundred Years of War.* New York: Cambridge University Press, 2005.
Kimmerling, Baruch. *Politicide: Ariel Sharon's War against the Palestinians.* London: Verso, 2003.
Miller, Anita, Jordan Miller, and Sigalit Zetouni. *Sharon: Israel's Warrior-Politician.* Chicago: Academy Chicago Publishers, 2002.
Sharon, Ariel, and David Chanoff. *Warrior: An Autobiography.* 2nd ed. New York: Simon and Schuster, 2001.

Shas

Israeli religious party founded in 1984 and dedicated to promoting the interests of the Orthodox Sephardic community. Focused on defending and strengthening the role of Judaism in the daily lives of Israelis, the Shas party platform is guided by a council of religious scholars known as Moetzet Hachmei Hatorah (Council of the Wise of Torah). The spiritual leader of the party is Ovadia Yosef, an Iraqi-born Jew who is the former Sephardic chief rabbi of Israel.

Shas has enjoyed considerable electoral success over the two decades of its existence. In 1984 in its first foray into Israeli politics, Shas won four seats in the Knesset (Israeli parliament), and just four years later it was the third-largest party in parliament. During the subsequent decade, Shas continued to increase its popularity, especially through its national network of social service institutions working to alleviate the struggles facing the lower classes. However, in 1999 the party's political leadership was severely damaged by charges of fraud and corruption, and Arye Deri, the party leader, was even jailed for his role in the affair. From its peak of 17 seats in the Knesset in 1999, support for Shas plummeted in the next election in January 2003, leaving the party with only 11 seats.

Shas remains a significant factor in Israeli politics. Party members have served in the governing coalitions of both Likud and Labor, and Shas continues to represent the interests of a devoted and entrenched Sephardic population within the country.

JONAS KAUFFELDT

See also

Knesset; Labor Party; Likud Party; Sephardic Judaism

References

Peretz, Don. *The Government and Politics of Israel.* Boulder, CO: Westview, 1979.
Sharkansky, Ira. *Rituals in Conflict: Religion, Politics and Public Policy in Israel.* Boulder, CO: Lynne Rienner, 1996.

Shaw Commission
Start Date: August 1929
End Date: March 31, 1930

Commission sent by the British government to Palestine to investigate Arab violence against Jews in Palestine that occurred in August 1929. The riots had resulted following a confrontation in Jerusalem at the location of the Western (Wailing) Wall, the most sacred of Jewish sites, and the al-Aqsa Mosque precinct, Islam's

A crowd of Arab demonstrators protests the arrival of the Shaw Commission in Jaffa in 1929. The sign in the background reads "Down with the Balfour Declaration." (Corbis)

third-holiest site. The proximity of these two sacred religious sites provided a volatile setting. The Western Wall had been the scene of confrontation between Jews and Arabs on every Jewish holy day when Jews sought to go there to pray.

On August 16, 1929, a right-wing Jewish youth group secured permission from the British authorities for a march to the Western Wall to commemorate the fast of the Ninth of Ab. Learning of this, the Muslim leadership in Jerusalem hastily organized a counter-demonstration near the wall, replete with inflammatory speeches. Some minor clashes then occurred between the two groups. During the next week, Muslim agitators traveled throughout Palestine and urged Arab peasants to come to Jerusalem in order to protect the al-Aqsa Mosque against Jewish attacks.

During the night of August 23 and the next day, crowds of Arabs moved into Jerusalem near the al-Aqsa Mosque and at noon on August 24 attacked the orthodox Jewish quarter. Jews also came under Arab attack elsewhere in Palestine, such as Hebron and Safed. British authorities were obliged to call in additional troops from Egypt, and it was not until August 28 that order was restored. By that date, 133 Jews had been killed and 399 wounded. The Arab

side lost 87 killed and 91 wounded. The riots proved to be a turning point in the history of the mandate, for hopes that both Arab and Jew might live together in the same state now dimmed considerably.

The Colonial Office in Prime Minister Ramsay MacDonald's Labour government then dispatched a commission headed by Sir Walter Shaw to report back on the causes of the riots and to make recommendations to prevent a reoccurrence. Shaw, a retired chief justice of the Turkish Straits Settlements, headed the commission, which conducted formal hearings in Palestine over a five-week period and issued its report on March 31, 1930.

The Shaw Commission Report blamed the Arabs for the rioting but also found fault with the British authorities and police for failing to provide adequate protection. The report concluded that widespread Arab dissatisfaction over the intentions of Jews in Palestine, including Arab concern for their economic future, was the chief factor behind the rioting. The report noted that the British government had promised to provide but had never issued a statement that spelled out its obligations to the non-Jewish population of Palestine. Pending that, the commission urged that the British government tighten Jewish immigration into Palestine and restrict

Jewish land purchases so that Jews could not evict Arab tenants. London should also ensure that the Jewish Agency be made to understand that it had no role in the government of Palestine.

Zionists received the Shaw Commission Report with shock and anger. Worse was to come. In May, the British government sent Sir John Hope Simpson, a retired Indian civil servant and authority on agricultural economies, to Palestine. He spent three months there and on October 20, 1930, issued a massive report that held that the land available to Arabs was less than had been thought previously, and that Arabs were being driven off the land by Jewish land purchases. He blamed Arab poverty on Jewish land purchases and concluded that steps should be immediately taken to restrict Jewish immigration into Palestine. The report's conclusions were embodied in a White Paper issued by the British government the same day that called for restrictions on Jewish purchases of land and suspending Jewish immigration into Palestine as long as there was extensive poverty in Palestine. It also called on Zionist leaders to rethink their national home policy. Greeted by a storm of protest, the White Paper was quickly withdrawn.

SPENCER C. TUCKER

See also

Haram al-Sharif; Palestine, British Mandate for; Zionism

References

Sachar, Howard M. *A History of Israel: From the Rise of Zionism to Our Time.* 3rd ed. New York: Knopf, 2007.

Sanders, Ronald. *The High Walls of Jerusalem: A History of the Balfour Declaration and the Birth of the British Mandate for Palestine.* New York: Holt, Rinehart and Winston, 1983.

Zalman Shazar, Israeli writer, scholar, politician, and president of Israel (1963–1973), shown here in May 1963. (Israeli Government Press Office)

Shazar, Shneur Zalman
Born: 1889
Died: October 5, 1974

Israeli writer, scholar, politician, and president of Israel (1963–1973). Born Shneur Zalman Rubashow to a Habid Hasidic Jewish family in Mir, Russia, in 1889, Shazar (which was a mix of letters from his original name) was raised in nearby Stolbtsy, where he received a formal Jewish education. In his teens he rejected Hasidism for Zionism. In 1905 he joined the Zionist labor Poalei Zion movement. He also helped organize Jewish self-defense units during the 1905 Russian Revolution. In 1907 Shazar was arrested by Russian authorities along with other members of the staff of the Poalei Zion newspaper and spent two months in jail. Upon his release he entered the Academy for Jewish Studies in St. Petersburg, where he studied for four years under such professors as Simon Dubnow. At the same time Shazar worked on the editorial staff of a Yiddish newspaper.

In 1911 Shazar visited Palestine and worked for a time in Kibbutz Merhavya. Returning to Russia, he reported for military service but was given an exemption and went to Germany to study history and philosophy at the universities in Freiburg and Stras-

bourg. He was especially interested in the study of the Jews of Eastern Europe.

At the beginning of World War I Shazar, as an enemy alien, was restricted to Berlin, where he continued to study and to pursue his Zionist activities and cultural work among German Jews. He was one of the founders of both the Zion Labor Movement and the Hehalutz (Pioneers of Zion) movement. In 1919 he completed his studies at the University of Berlin. That same year he was named to the study commission of Poalei Zion sent to Palestine and edited its report. In 1921 he was a delegate to the Twelfth Zionist Congress in Karlovy Vary. At the Thirteenth Zionist Congress in 1923 at Karlovy Vary, he was named a member of the Zionist Actions Committee. In 1922 he became a lecturer in Jewish history at the Hebrew Pedagogium in Vienna, which trained Jewish teachers.

Shazar immigrated to Palestine in 1924, settling permanently there and continuing his Zionist activities. Appointed to the Executive Committee of Histadrut, the General Federation of Labor, he then joined the staff of its daily newspaper, *Davar,* and soon was its editor. Later he headed the Histadrut publishing house Am Oved. He was the author of numerous articles, poems, essays, biographies, and monographs in both Yiddish and Hebrew. His most important scholarly work was in the study of the Shabbatian movement. Politically, he took an active role in the founding of Mapai, the Palestine Jewish labor party, and he often traveled abroad for it and for Histadrut.

In 1947 Shazar was part of the Jewish Agency delegation to the United Nations (UN) concerning the future of the British Mandate for Palestine, and in April 1948 in Israel he drafted the declaration passed by the Zionist General Council calling for an independent Jewish state immediately upon the termination of the British Mandate. In 1949 he was elected to the first Knesset (Israeli parliament), and he became Israel's first minister of education and culture that same year, serving until 1951. He put forward the plan for free and compulsory education passed by the Knesset in 1949. In 1951 he resigned from the cabinet to become Israeli ambassador to Moscow. When that post failed to materialize, in 1952 he was named a member of the Jewish Agency Executive, and from 1956 to 1960 he was acting chairman of its Jerusalem Executive. In recognition of his myriad achievements, in May 1963 the Knesset elected him to the largely ceremonial post of president of Israel. Reelected in 1968, he retired at the end of his second term in May 1973. Shazar died on October 5, 1974.

SPENCER C. TUCKER

See also

Dubnow, Simon Meyervich; Hehalutz Movement; Histadrut; Jewish Agency for Israel; Labor Zionism

References

Bernstein, Deborah S. *Constructing Boundaries: Jewish and Arab Workers in Mandatory Palestine.* Albany, NY: SUNY Press, 2000.

Gilbert, Martin. *Israel: A History.* New York: William Morrow, 1998.

Sachar, Howard M. *A History of Israel: From the Rise of Zionism to Our Time.* 3rd ed. New York: Knopf, 2007.

Shazly, Saad el-
Born: April 1, 1922

Egyptian military officer and diplomat, largely responsible for the planning and successful execution of the Egyptian Suez Canal offensive in the Yom Kippur War of 1973. Born in Cairo on April 1, 1922, Saad el-Shazly began his military career by attending the Egyptian Military Academy between 1939 and 1943. His first combat assignment was as a platoon commander in the Israeli War of Independence (1948–1949). His performance in combat earned him a nomination to the Junior Officer's Command Course and Military Staff College, from which he graduated in 1952 with a master's degree in military science. A year later el-Shazly was selected to attend the U.S. Army Infantry School at Fort Benning, Georgia. Upon his return to Egypt he was assigned to Egypt's Parachute School, which he commanded from 1954 to 1956.

El-Shazly faced combat for the second time as a paratroop company commander in the 1956 Sinai Campaign. In 1958 he attended the Command Leadership Course in the Soviet Union and was later appointed chief of staff of a Paratroop Brigade. Between 1960 and 1961 he commanded the Egyptian United Nations (UN) contingent in the Congo. He then became Egypt's military attaché to the United Kingdom for the next two years. In 1965 he went to Yemen as part of the Egyptian forces intervening in the Yemeni Civil War.

By 1967 el-Shazly had been promoted to the rank of major general. As a special task force commander in the June 1967 Six-Day War, he was tasked with cutting off the Israeli city of Eilat in an attempt to deny Israeli forces access to the Gulf of Aqaba. Israeli forces preempted this move, however, effectively cutting off his force. El-Shazly successfully avoided decisive engagements and eventually led his troops out of Israeli encirclement to safety.

After the end of the Six-Day War, el-Shazly was seen as the most qualified Egyptian officer to lead and train Egyptian Special Forces. His two-year tenure brought significant improvements to the training program, including the establishment of al-Saiqa (commandos) and the Mizidat (paratroops).

In September 1970 Anwar Sadat assumed the Egyptian presidency and immediately initiated a political and military restructuring. As a result, el-Shazly, now a lieutenant general, became chief of the General Staff of the Egyptian armed forces on May 16, 1971. Later that year he was named assistant secretary-general for military affairs for the Arab League.

After the losses in the Six-Day War, Sadat was looking to strike back at Israel and recapture at least a portion of the Sinai Peninsula in an attempt to force the Israelis to negotiate. As such, el-Shazly and his staff developed an attack plan that focused on crossing the Suez Canal and establishing strong defensive positions that would lure the Israel Defense Forces (IDF) into a killing zone. Unlike his predecessors, el-Shazly managed to synchronize air, ground, and naval forces. The plan worked, and the Egyptians were able to cross the canal. They then used their Soviet-supplied defensive firepower, in the form of antiaircraft missiles to drive off Israeli aircraft and antitank missiles to destroy counterattacking Israeli armor.

With this success, Sadat then sought to expand the offensive in an attempt to regain the whole of the Sinai. El-Shazly strongly opposed any additional advances beyond the coverage of the Egyptian surface-to-air missile (SAM) batteries. Sadat disregarded his advice. Upon the successful Israeli counteroffensive, el-Shazly pleaded with Sadat to withdraw Egyptian troops that were in danger of encirclement and later orchestrated an ineffective counterattack. On October 20, 1973, after continued pleas and requests to shift troops to address possible encirclement, Sadat removed el-Shazly from his post in the field. El-Shazly was officially fired in December 1973.

As a result of his open protests, el-Shazly was appointed Egypt's ambassador to the United Kingdom in 1974. A year later, he was appointed Egypt's ambassador to Portugal. El-Shazly openly criticized the Arab-Israeli peace process and predicted failure for the 1978 Camp David Summit. He argued that the only solution to the Arab-Israeli conflict was a military one and criticized Sadat for being weak, even calling for the Egyptian leader's overthrow.

El-Shazly was forced into permanent exile in Libya. He eventually settled in Algeria, where he founded the Egyptian National Front
opposition party in March 1980. While in exile he was tried in
absentia and court-martialed for allegedly disclosing classified information in his memoirs, published in 1976. He was sentenced to 3
years in prison. After 14 years of exile he returned to Egypt in 1992
and was immediately imprisoned. Although Egypt's High Court
reversed the earlier sentencing, el-Shazly ended up serving out his
sentence in full.

VADIM SIMHAKOV

See also

Egypt; Egypt, Armed Forces; Sadat, Anwar; Sinai Campaign; Six-Day
War; Suez Crisis; Yom Kippur War

References

Aboul-Enein, Youssef. "Egyptian General Saad-Eddine El-Shazly:
Controversial Operational Winker and Architect of the 1973 Yom-
Kippur War." *Infantry* (January–February 2005): 20–24.
An-Nahar Arab Report Research Staff. "General Saaduddin Shazli."
Pp. 176–178 in *The October War: Documents, Personalities, Analyses
and Maps,* edited by Riad N. el-Rayyes and Dunia Nahas. Beirut,
Lebanon: An-Nahar Press Services S.A.R.L., 1973.
El Shazly, Saad. *The Arab Military Option.* San Francisco: American
Mideast Research, 1986.
———. *The Crossing of the Suez.* San Francisco: American Mideast
Research, 1980.

Shertok, Moshe

See Sharett, Moshe

Shia Islam

Smaller of the two predominant branches of Islam. Adherents to
Shia Islam account for 12–15 percent of all Muslims worldwide. The
Sunni sects or schools of Islam account for 67 percent. Shiism is
divided into several major subgroups: the Ithna Ashariyya, called
Twelvers by Westerners and Jafariyya by adherents, for their school
of Islamic law; the Ismailiyya (Seveners); and the Zaydiyya (Fivers),
named according to the prominent figures in the chain of religious
leaders (imams) that each recognizes as constituting the proper line
of leadership succession from the Prophet Muhammad. Shiism is
the dominant branch of Islam in Iran (90 percent of the population), Iraq, Lebanon, Bahrain, Azerbaijan, and Yemen. Shiism also
has adherents in Syria, East Africa, India, Pakistan, Afghanistan,
Turkey, Qatar, Kuwait, the United Arab Emirates, and the Eastern
Province of Saudi Arabia. Shiism accounts for a small percentage of
the Islamic population in South Asia and Europe, although Shiism's
presence in the latter, particularly Great Britain, is increasing.

The Shiites were originally referred to as the Shiat Ali (Party of
Ali). Upon the Prophet's death, they preferred the succession of Ali
ibn Abu Talib, the son-in-law of Muhammad by marriage to Muhammad's only surviving daughter Fatima. Some suggest that in

**Religious Makeup of Selected Middle Eastern and
North African Countries**

Country	Sunni Muslims	Shiite Muslims	Other Religions
Algeria	95%	4%	1%
Bahrain	30%	70%	0%
Egypt	93%	1%	6%
Iran	10%	89%	1%
Iraq	34%	63%	3%
Jordan	92%	2%	6%
Kuwait	65%	35%	0%
Lebanon	24%	36%	40%
Libya	96%	1%	3%
Morocco	97%	2%	1%
Oman	89%	10%	1%
Qatar	85%	0%	5%
Saudi Arabia	90%	10%	0%
Syria	77%	13%	10%
Tunisia	96%	2%	2%
United Arab Emirates	82%	14%	4%
Yemen	57%	42%	1%

the mixture of southern and northern Arab Muslim tribes, it was
the southerners, Aws and Khazraj of Medina, who most strongly
supported hereditary rights in leadership. Ali accepted Abu Bakr
as caliph (khalifa), or political leader of the Muslims, but his supporters agitated again when Uthman became the third caliph.
Uthman was so disliked for nepotism and the enrichment of his
Umayyad relatives that a revolt occurred in which he was killed.
Ali's followers recognized him as the fourth caliph in AD 656. However, the Umayyads claimed the caliphate for Muawiya, and this led
to two civil wars in Islam and Ali's assassination in 661. Following
Ali's death, his son Hasan was forced to abdicate, and his other son
Husayn fought the Umayyads and was killed at Karbala. With the
accession of the Umayyads, its preachers regularly cursed Ali in
their Friday sermons.

While all Muslims revere the Prophet and his family, Sunni
Muslims also recognize the Prophet's early companions at Medina
for their political role and strength as transmitters of hadith, the
short texts relating Muhammad's words, actions, or preferences. In
contrast, the Shiites extend the notion of the Prophet's family, the
Ahl al-Bayt (People of the House), from the Prophet, his daughter
Fatima, and Ali on to Ali's sons Hasan and Husayn and the succession of imams who followed them.

Shiites believe that Ali was the first imam. The imam is the sole
legitimate successor of the Prophet. Each imam designates his own
successor. In Shia Islam, each imam is held to have special knowledge of the truth of the Koran, Muhammad's *sunnah* (traditions
or practices), and Islam. The aimah, or chain of imams, are believed
to be infallible, sinless, and personally guided by Allah (God) and
are also believed to possess the divine authority over Islam and
humanity granted to Ali by Muhammad.

Shiites and Sunnis hold to the same views of Allah, who has
omnipotence over all beings, and yet Allah is also believed to be, as

The Imam Ali Mosque in Najaf, Iraq, was originally built in 977 over the tomb of Ali ibn Abu Talib, son-in-law of the Prophet Muhammad and Islam's fourth caliph. It has been reconstructed twice since, in 1086 and in 1500. (Corel)

expressed in his other names, Merciful and Beneficent, closer to man than his own "jugular vein," and one who cares deeply about his creation. In both, there is also a dynamic between faith and the acceptance of divine will with the responsibility of the human believer. Indeed, apart from the differences in the Shia view of leadership, the two sects are very similar in many aspects. They diverge, however, in their legal systems.

The Shia recognize all the same religious duties as the Sunnis, which are described in the study of Islam in the West as the five pillars with two additional duties. However, the Ismailiyya sect and its subsects also stress the inner truths, or esoteric knowledge of Islamic principles. The Shia stress the unicity or oneness (tawhid) of Allah, a strict monotheism, and the avoidance of any trace of polytheism. They support social justice (adalah), which means equity within society, and aid to the oppressed and the needy. As with Sunni Muslims, the Shia adhere to the principle of the hisba, or commanding the good and forbidding the reprehensible. This refers to all that is licit or recommended in Islamic law as opposed to sins that are forbidden. Entrance into Paradise is based on doing more

good than evil or upon martyrdom. All Muslims, Shia as well as Sunni, respect the prophets, including Abraham, Moses, Jesus, and Muhammad, whom they believe revealed to humans the true religion of Allah.

The concept of the aimah (imamate)—that specific leaders are appointed by Allah and then by other imams (nass or designation) —grew in strength thanks to the sixth imam, Jafar al-Sadiq (d. 765). His followers developed the Twelver legal and theological tradition. The last of these Twelve imams, Muhammad al-Mahdi, did not make himself known at the death of the 11th imam, al-Hasan al-Askari. Al-Mahdi is believed to be hiding on Earth, neither alive nor dead but in a state of occultation, and will return at the Day of Judgment and the Resurrection (Qiyamah) when Allah will decide the fate of all humanity, Muslim and non-Muslim alike.

The Twelvers believe that al-Mahdi was the son of al-Hasan, born in 869. The Shia believe that al-Mahdi was in hiding from the caliph and that between the years 874 and 941 he communicated by letters with his people. During this period, called the Lesser Occultation, the community recognized four regents for Muhammad al-Mahdi. In his last letter, he wrote that he would no longer communicate with humanity. Thus, the period from 941 to the present is known as the Greater Occultation.

In Islam, every human is held accountable for his or her deeds. The deeds of each individual are judged by Allah and weighed on a scale. If the good outweighs the evil, then the individual gains entrance into Paradise. If the evil outweighs the good, the individual spends eternity in Hell. The Shia further believe that the prophets, imams, and martyrs can intercede with Allah for a soul on the Day of Judgment and may seek this intercession (shafaa), if possible, through prayer, religious rituals, or appeals to the Fourteen Infallibles: the Prophet Muhammad, his daughter Fatima, and the Twelve imams. They also seek redemption through ritual of repentance performed on the Day of Ashura, the commemoration of Imam Husayn's death.

Shiism's Twelvers, the largest Shia group, proclaim the necessity of obligatory religious duties or acts of outward worship. The first is the shahada or testimony that there is no God but God and that Muhammad is his prophet and Ali his imam. The next is prayer (salat), recited five or more times a day. The third is fasting (sawm) during the daylight hours for all of the month of Ramadan, the ninth month of the Islamic calendar. The fourth religious practice is the pilgrimage (hajj), a journey to the holy city of Mecca that should be made at least once during a person's life if he or she is physically and financially able to undertake it. The fifth religious practice is the paying of zakat, a voluntary tax that is used to support the poor, spread Islam, or sometimes other purposes such as aid to travelers and the funding of jihad. The assessment of zakat should be 2.5 percent of one's income and assets in any given year. (All Muslims also give gifts of money during and at the end of Ramadan and the Id al-Adha, but these are not technically zakat.) Another form of tithing, the khums, is a 20 percent tax on all annual profits from any source levied on all adult males and is used to support the mosque and the

Ayatollah Ali Khamenei leading Friday prayers on the campus of Tehran University during the first Friday of the holy month of Ramadan in Tehran, Iran, on September 14, 2007. Khamenei was named supreme leader of Iran and is the highest religious authority in the predominantly Shiite nation. (Document Iran/Corbis)

clerics. Jihad is also a commanded duty in Shiism and refers to the struggle of the faithful to please Allah as well as to defend Islam by waging war. The idea of the *walaya* is important in Shiism (but also in Sufi Islam), as is the *tabarra*. These mean a special reverence for all members, past and descended, of the Household of the Prophet Muhammad, the Ahl al-Bayt, and the guardianship of the imamate and the disassociation from all enemies of the Ahl al-Bayt.

In addition to the Shia groups mentioned above, there are others. The Druze are an offshoot of the Ismailiyya sect, and the Alawites found in Syria and Turkey are a distinct sect. The Shaykhiyya of Basra and Bahrain are a subsect of the Ithna-Ashariyya, or Twelver Shia, influenced by Akhabari thought. Sunni Muslims and some Shia, however, consider the Alawi sect deviant because of some of its syncretic practices. Nonetheless, it was declared a licit school of Islam in a fatwa issued by Imam Musa al-Sadr in order to legitimate the rule of President Hafez al-Assad, an Alawi, in Syria. Although all branches of Islam believe in a divine savior, Mahdi, who will come at the Day of Judgment, the Twelver branch of Shiism holds that the Twelfth Imam, or Hidden Imam since he is in occultation, is the Mahdi and call him the Imam Mahdi.

Mahmoud Ahmadinejad, elected president of Iran in 2005, and his cabinet have pledged to work to make the conditions right for the return of the Imam Mahdi, a return that Shia Muslims believe will lead Islam to world domination. In Iran, many believe that the Imam Mahdi will reappear from a well at the mosque in Jamkaran just outside of the holy city of Qum, Iran. The site is frequently visited by Shiite pilgrims who drop messages into the well hoping that the Hidden Imam will hear them and grant their requests. Along with the Imam Mahdi's return at the Day of Judgment, there are various beliefs about other millenarian events and wars that will occur before this period.

Since the disappearance of the Twelfth Imam, the Shia ulama (clerics) have served as his deputies, interpreting the law and leading the Shiite faithful under the authority of the Hidden Imam. In Twelver Shiism it is believed that four persons acted as the deputies or special vice-regents (*wakala al-khassa*) of the Hidden Imam during the Lesser Occultation. These persons were called the *bab* (gate) or *naib* (deputy) for the imam. From 941 there have been no overt claims of a *bab* except for Sayyid Ali Muhammad, known as The Bab, who established Babism in the 19th century, and the Shaykhi Shia, who put forth the idea of the perfect Shia who lives in each age. Generally in this period, the idea is that there is a *wakala al-amma*, or a general idea of vice-regency delegated to the Shia clerics. When Ayatollah Ruhollah Khomeini and his government established the system of rule of the cleric (*vilayat-e faqih*) in Iran, he was referred to as the naib al-Imam, or deputy of the Hidden Imam. The idea of rule of the cleric, developed from the increasingly activist opinions of one branch of Shiism—the *usulis* (*usuliyya*)—opposed the akhbaris, a different intellectual tradition. Khomeini's official title became Supreme Faqih (Jurist), and he served with the Council of Guardians as its supreme religio-political authority. However, his successor, Ali Husayni Khamenei, was not the most senior of the possible clerics to follow Khomeini and was granted the title of ayatollah more as a political appointment.

Ismaili Shiites, also known as Ismailiyya, or the Seveners, are followers of the living Aga Khan and constitute the second-largest branch of Shia Islam. Ismailis believe that the imamate is a position that continues unbroken since the caliphate of Ali, although the living imams since the Seventh Imam serve as regents awaiting the return of the Hidden Imam. Ismailis acknowledge only six of the Twelve Imams and assert that the real Seventh Imam was Ismail Ibn Jafar. Other Muslims assert that Ismail's son Muhammad was the Seventh Imam and that he is presently occulted awaiting the end of time to reveal himself as the last Imam. The Ismaili movement spread through missionary activity as a secret organization beginning in the later ninth century. It split in a factional dispute about leadership in 899. Ismaili Shiites are found primarily in South Asia, Syria, Saudi Arabia, Yemen, China, Tajikistan, Afghanistan, and East Africa but have in recent years immigrated to Europe and North America.

Ismailis mandate the same religious practices as the Twelvers, but their emphasis is on an inner or deeper interpretation of each that can make them distinct. As with the Twelvers, the Ismailis evince love and devotion (*walayah*) for Allah, the prophets, the Ahl al-Bayt, the imam, and the Ismaili dai (the preacher) and also believe in personal purity and cleanliness (*taharah*). The third pillar is prayer, and the fourth is almsgiving, or purifying religious dues. The fifth is the fast, and the sixth is the pilgrimage. The seventh pillar is jihad.

Zaydis, also known as Zaydiyya or the Fivers, are in theology and the view of the law closer to a Sunni school of the law. Zaydism is strongest in India, Pakistan, and Yemen. Zaydis derive their name from Zayd ibn Ali ibn Abi Talib, the son of Husayn ibn Ali ibn Abi Talib (626–ca. 680), the grandson of the Prophet Muhammad. Most Zaydis regard Husayn as the third rightful imam. After Ali, Hasan, and Husayn, the Zaydis assert that the succession of the imamate was determined by engaging in armed rebellion against evil caliphs. Although Zayd's rebellion against the corrupt Umayyad caliph Hisham ibn Abd al-Malik (691–743) in 740 was unsuccessful, the attempt was sufficient to make Zayd the fourth Zaydi imam.

Zaydism does not support the infallibility of the imams and asserts that no imam after Husayn receives any divine guidance. Zaydis reject the Hidden Imam and the idea that the imamate must be passed from father to son, although they do believe that the living imam must be a descendant of Ali. Zaydi Islamic law (*fiqh*) is most like the Sunni Hanafi school.

While there was never a concept of Sunni Islam as a sect, the non-Alid Muslims accepted the institution of the caliphate even though the caliph was not a spiritual descendent of the Prophet. Still, the caliph received an oath of allegiance from his people and had to be pious and promote and protect Islam. Alids (supporters of Ali), later the Shia, accepted their temporal rulers but did not regard them as being spiritually legitimate in the manner of the imams. For purposes of survival, they could deny their Shia beliefs if need be in the practice known as *taqqiya* (dissimulation). Non-Shia Muslims accepted the authority of the first three caliphs—Abu Bakr, Umar, and Uthman—and often cited hadith that are traced to the companions (*sahaba*) of the Prophet as well as the Prophet Muhammad himself. The hadith explain the practice or beliefs of the Prophet and constitute his Way, or *sunnah*. Shia Muslims often cite hadith as having passed through the Ahl al-Bayt or relating back to the imams. Minor differences pertain to the times for prayer and the commencement of holidays.

Shia Islamic education is centered in Najaf and Karbala in Iraq and in Qum and Mashhad in Iran, with additional centers of learning elsewhere. Shia clerics from Lebanon typically studied in Iraq or in Iran. The most prominent Shia theorist in Iran following the Islamic Revolution was probably Abd al-Karim Sorush, who is famous for his idea of the expansion and contraction of Islamic law (*qabz va bast-e shariat*). The most senior cleric in Iraq today is the Shia Grand Ayatollah Sistani. The clerical establishment in Iraq is referred to as the hawza, and its duty is to train the future clerics of Shiism.

Alongside the hadiths traceable to the Prophet Muhammad, Sunni Islam most highly regards the testimony of the companions as it passed through the ages, while Shia Islam also highly regards the teachings of the Twelve Imams and their representatives. The testimony of the companions is sometimes at variance with Shia traditions in interpretations (*tafsir*) of the Koran, Islamic history, and the practices (*sunnah*) of Muhammad.

Sunnis and Shiites have different approaches to jurisprudence, or the making of Islamic law, and therefore also in the issuance of fatawa to broader religious questions of Muslims. The different Sunni schools of law use as sources (*usul al-fiqh*) the Koran, the hadith, analogy (*qiyas*), and *ijma,* or the consensus of the community at Medina or of the jurists. In earlier periods, these legal schools also used *ray* (opinion of the jurist) or *ijtihad,* a particular technique of intellectual problem solving. In the 10th century, the Sunni jurists decided to stop using *ijtihad* so as to avoid the introduction of too many innovations into Sharia. However, the Shia legal school of the Twelvers retained this principle. Consequently, Shia cleric-jurists who train in this technique and qualify receive the title of mujtahid, or one who can enact *ijtihad.*

There are various ranks of clerics in Shia Islam in addition to the mujtahid, such as the elevated designations of ayatollah and grand ayatollah that other clerics should agree on. In addition, the Shia may follow his or her own preferred *marja* (source). Above all of these clerics, there may be one agreed-upon *marja-e taqlid* (source of emulation of the age).

These are not the only differences between Sunni and Shia Islam. Other legal and sociocultural or even economic differences exist in such countries as Lebanon and Saudi Arabia, where the Shia have been an underclass. Both Sunni and Shia Islam have produced Sufi movements or brotherhoods. Both have also produced militant versions of Islamism, including parties that aim at Islamic governance. There has been some effort to recognize Shiism in Sunni Islam. Indeed, the al-Azhar University did so and teaches Shiism as a madhhab or legal school of Islam in spite of the fact that the government of Egypt outlawed Shiism. It should also be noted that Shia and Sunni Muslims had coexisted peacefully and frequently intermarried in Iraq. Shia Muslims were often members of the Communist Party or the Baath Party, and the clerics began an Islamic movement in Iraq in part to dissuade youths from joining the secular parties. This resulted in Saddam Hussein's suppression of the Shia Islamist movement. Sadly, the end of Hussein's rule brought Shia-Sunni sectarian conflict to Iraq, fueled in part by Sunni Islamists and nationalists who viewed the new Shia-dominated majority as conspirators with the Americans and who called the Shia apostates or renegades.

RICHARD EDWARDS AND SHERIFA ZUHUR

See also

Imam; Iran; Jihad; Khomeini, Ruhollah; Koran; Mecca; Saudi Arabia; Sunni Islam; Syria

References

Ajami, Fouad. *The Vanished Imam: Musa al-Sadr and the Shia of Lebanon.* Ithaca, NY: Cornell University Press, 1986.

Daftari, Farhad. *The Isma'ilis: Their History and Doctrines.* Cambridge: Cambridge University Press, 1990.

Fuller, Graham E., and Rend Rahim Francke. *The Arab Shi'a: The Forgotten Muslims.* Hampshire, UK: Palgrave Macmillan, 2001.

Gregorian, Vartan. *Islam: A Mosaic, Not a Monolith.* Baltimore: Brookings Institute Press, 2004.

Halm, Heinz. *Shi'a Islam: From Religion to Revolution.* Princeton, NJ: Markus Wiener, 1997.

Momen, Moojan. *An Introduction to Shi'i Islam: The History and Doctrines of Twelver Shi'ism.* New Haven, CT: Yale University Press, 1987.

Nasr, Seyyed Hossein. *Islam: Religion, History, and Civilization.* New York: HarperCollins, 2003.

Sachedina, A. A. *Islamic Messianism: The Idea of the Mahdi in Twelver Shi'ism.* Albany, NY: SUNY Press, 1981.

Sobhani, Ayatollah Jafar, and Reza Shah Kazemi. *Doctrines of Shi'i Islam: A Compendium of Imami Beliefs and Practices.* London: Tauris, 2001.

Shield of David

See Star of David

Shin Bet

The Israeli counterintelligence and internal security service. Shin Bet, also known as the General Security Service, or Shabak, is the sister agency to the Mossad, which handles external security and foreign intelligence, and Aman, the military intelligence branch of the Israel Defense Forces (IDF). Isser Harel, also founder of the Mossad, founded Shin Bet in 1947. Originally known as the General Security Service, it was under the aegis of the IDF but later was transferred to the direct control of the prime minister's office. The motto of Shin Bet was "Shield who shall not be seen."

Originally tasked with counterintelligence, Shin Bet was also given responsibility for monitoring Palestinians who chose to stay and live in Israel after 1948. During the Cold War era, Shin Bet focused much of its energy on the Soviet Union. Shin Bet infiltrated Soviet-backed dissident organizations in Israel during the 1950s and 1960s. In 1961 it also uncovered top Soviet spy Dr. Israel Bar, both a lieutenant colonel in the IDF reserves and a friend of Prime Minister David Ben-Gurion, who had access to a great deal of classified information. Also in 1961, Shin Bet unmasked Kurt Sita, an operative for Czech intelligence who was working as a professor in Israel.

After the 1967 Six-Day War, Shin Bet began to focus more of its attention and resources on monitoring Arabs in the occupied territories. It received considerable leeway when dealing with suspects, and many Israelis feared that Shin Bet would become an instrument of totalitarianism. Internal checks and balances within Shin Bet have prevented this. As the lead organization tasked with combating terrorism, Shin Bet nonetheless has resorted to extrajudicial methods that evoked great criticism in Israel and the Arab world.

The most notorious incident involving Shin Bet is known as the KAV 300 Affair or the Shabak Affair and involved the summary execution of two suspected terrorists who participated in a bus hijacking. The KAV 300 Affair spotlighted Shin Bet and some of its more questionable activities and led to a purging of the organization and more public oversight. Avram Shalom, the head of Shin Bet at the time, was forced to resign, and the Knesset (Israeli parliament) established the so-called Landoy Committee to monitor Shin Bet activities. One of Shin Bet's major responsibilities was the protection of senior Israeli ministers, including the prime minister. Thus, Shin Bet's reputation received a further blow in 1995 when it failed to prevent the assassination of Israeli prime minister Yitzhak Rabin. An internal investigation actually implicated Shin Bet agents in stirring up provocations and anti-Rabin sentiments as part of its domestic counterterrorism operations that may have actually contributed to his assassination. Another housecleaning occurred. Avi Dichter, a tough-minded ex-commando, was eventually placed in charge of Shin Bet in 2003.

Shin Bet is believed to be organized into three operational departments. The Arab Affairs Department handles intelligence gathering on Arab terrorist organizations via informers and through interrogation. The Non-Arab Department was formerly divided between communist and noncommunist sections and was charged with debriefing Soviet refugees and countering Soviet intelligence. Since 1991 its mission has changed to monitoring all non-Arab immigrants in Israel. The Protective Security Department provides uniformed personnel to secure government buildings, scientific research facilities, airports, and ports. It also provides bodyguards for Israeli dignitaries and undercover operatives for El Al Airline flights. Supporting departments include, among others, finance, logistics, personnel, and transportation.

Shin Bet relies mainly on informants and human intelligence (HUMINT) sources for its information. The organization is believed to run extensive networks of Arab informants throughout Israel and abroad. Shin Bet is also tasked with interrogation of suspects and has received a great deal of criticism from the public and the press in Israel for its use of physical coercion and torture to extract information. The organization has also received negative press for infiltrating domestic leftists and rightist Jewish organizations and political parties. Shin Bet has been widely implicated in the assassination program conducted against Arab targets including members of Hamas, the Palestine Liberation Organization (PLO), and Hezbollah. In 2002 Shin Bet agents assassinated Yahya Ayyash, a terrorist known as "the Engineer" and chief bomb maker for Hamas, by placing an explosive device in his cell phone. Shin Bet continues to work directly with the Israeli Air Force to target terrorist leaders and bases and also uses commandos and trained agents to root out terror networks that threaten Israel.

The counterterrorist role is a difficult one and often corrupts those engaged in it. Shin Bet remains perhaps the world's premier counterterrorist organization and is believed to have been of great assistance to the U.S. government in the wake of the September 11, 2001, terrorist attacks.

ROD VOSBURGH

See also

Ben-Gurion, David; Hamas; Mossad; Rabin, Yitzhak

References

Black, Ian. *Israel's Secret Wars: The Untold History of Israeli Intelligence.* London: Viking, 1991.

Katz, Samuel M. *Guards without Frontiers: Israel's War against Terrorism.* London: Arms and Armour, 1990.

———. *Soldier Spies: Israeli Military Intelligence.* New York: Presidio, 1992.

Melman, Yossi. *The Imperfect Spies: The History of Israeli Intelligence.* London: Sedgewick and Jackson, 1989.

Sprinzak, Ehud. *Brother against Brother: Violence and Extremism in Israeli Politics from Altalena to the Rabin Assassination.* New York: Free Press, 1999.

Thomas, Gordon. *Gideon's Spies: The Secret History of the Mossad.* New York: St. Martin's Griffin, 2000.

Shiqaqi, Fathi

Born: 1951
Died: October 26, 1995

Founder of Islamic Jihad of Palestine. Born in the Gaza Strip in 1951 to a Palestinian family that had fled Jaffa during the Israeli War of Independence (1948–1949), Fathi Shiqaqi studied mathematics in Beirut and then medicine at the Zagazig University in Egypt during the 1970s. Graduating with a degree in medicine, he worked as a

doctor in Egypt and joined the Muslim Brotherhood. He practiced medicine for a time in Jerusalem, then returned to Gaza in 1981.

In Gaza in the early 1980s, Shiqaqi and Sheikh Abd al-Aziz Awda founded Islamic Jihad of Palestine, which carried out suicide bombings inside Israel. The U.S. government subsequently designated Islamic Jihad as an international terrorist organization. Reportedly, Shiqaqi was the first to publish a booklet that legitimized suicide martyrdom attacks, which he called sacrifices, as justifiable in jihad (holy war).

Arrested by the Israelis in 1983, he was imprisoned for a year. Again arrested in 1986, he was again imprisoned and then was deported in 1988. He settled in the Palestinian refugee camp at Yarmuk in Damascus. There in January 1994 he played a leading role in creating the National Alliance, a coalition of eight Palestine Liberation Organization (PLO) groups, Islamic Jihad, and Hamas. Early the next year, he sharply disagreed with Sheikh Awda over both the funding and organization of Islamic Jihad.

Shiqaqi rejected the 1993 Oslo Peace Accords and was said to have been behind a number of suicide bombings in Israel in 1995. He was shot to death, allegedly by several agents of Mossad, the Israeli intelligence service, in front of the Diplomat Hotel in Sleima, Malta, on October 26, 1995. Reportedly, he was on his way to Libya to meet with Muammar Qaddafi to secure funding for Islamic Jihad terrorist activities. Shiqaqi's funeral, held in Damascus on November 1, was attended by some 40,000 people. Ramallah Abdullah Shallah succeeded Shiqaqi as head of Islamic Jihad.

SPENCER C. TUCKER

See also

Islamic Jihad, Palestinian; Jihad; Qaddafi, Muammar; Shallah, Ramadan Abdullah

References

Abu-Amr, Ziad. *Islamic Fundamentalism in the West Bank and Gaza: Muslim Brotherhood and Islamic Jihad.* Bloomington: Indiana University Press, 1994.

Hatina, Meir. *Islam and Salvation in Palestine: The Islamic Jihad Movement.* Syracuse, NY: Syracuse University Press, 2001.

Shishakli, Adib al-

Born: 1909
Died: September 27, 1964

Syrian Army general and strongman of Syria (1949–1954). Adib al-Shishakli was born in 1909 in Hamah, Syria, then part of the Ottoman Empire. By the time he joined the military, France ruled Syria under a League of Nations mandate. Al-Shishakli studied at the Syrian military academy in Damascus and was commissioned in the Special Troops organized by France. Al-Shishakli early on joined the Syrian Social Nationalist Party (SSNP), which was headed by Antun Saada and advocated a Greater Syria.

Syria achieved independence as a consequence of World War II, and in 1948 during the Israeli War of Independence (1948–1949)

al-Shishakli served as a deputy commander of the Arab Liberation Army (ALA) sponsored by the Arab League against Jewish forces. However, the ALA had a poor combat record in the war. This was one factor in a coup in March 1949, in which al-Shishakli played a role, that brought Husni al-Zaim to power in Syria.

Al-Zaim distrusted al-Shishakli and soon dismissed him. In August 1949, however, al-Shishakli participated in a coup that toppled al-Zaim and brought Sami al-Hinnawi to power. Al-Hinnawi became chief of staff of the army, and longtime Syrian nationalist Hashim al-Atasi became prime minister. When al-Atasi sought to secure a union with Hashemite Iraq, al-Shishakli strongly objected and in December 1949 was the prime mover behind yet a third coup that toppled al-Hinnawi. Al-Shishakli now took power himself.

At first, al-Shishakli was content running things behind the scenes and allowed the Syrian parliament to continue to function. By 1951, however, his opposition to the pro-Iraqi bent of the People's Party led him to organize another coup that November during which he assumed complete power and ordered the arrest of the prime minister, his cabinet, and a number of other key leaders. Al-Shishakli suppressed most Syrian political parties and appointed his associate, Colonel Fawzi Salu (later promoted to general), as chief of state, premier, and minister of defense, but it was al-Shishakli who now openly controlled affairs.

Throughout those early years of his rule, al-Shishakli pursued several goals. His experience in the fighting with Israel made him acutely aware of the failings of the Syrian military, and he worked hard to build up and improve the armed forces. He sometimes spoke of his wish to transform Syria into the "Prussia of the Arab states." A strong Syrian nationalist, he made the Druze minority a particular target of his campaign against so-called centrifugal tendencies, even shelling their strongholds.

In foreign affairs, al-Shishakli sought improved relations with the West but continued an uncompromising stance toward Israel. He also very much feared the expansion of Egyptian president Gamal Abdel Nasser's Pan-Arabism. Al-Shishakli nonetheless refused to join a Middle East defense organization that became the 1955 Baghdad Pact. Although tempted, he also rejected a U.S. offer of financial assistance in return for Syrian acceptance of Palestinian refugees and an effort to turn them into Syrian citizens.

In August 1952 al-Shishakli banned all political organizations and created a one-party state based on his own Arab Liberation Movement. In June 1953 he assumed more of the trappings of power by becoming premier and then securing the presidency of Syria by means of a popular referendum. This same referendum also provided approval for a new constitution that increased the president's powers.

In January 1954, resistance to his government became more open. Prominent Syrian political leaders had refused to support his Arab Liberation Movement, the Druze community engaged in violent demonstrations, and others followed suit. By February, elements within the army had determined that al-Shishakli had to go. The coup on February 25, 1954, in which the Baath Party also played

an important role began in the mutiny of troops in Aleppo and rapidly spread. Forced to resign, al-Shishakli sought exile first in Lebanon, then in Saudi Arabia, and subsequently in France.

Although reportedly al-Shishakli subsequently negotiated with foreign agents over a possible coup attempt to topple the more pro-Soviet Syrian government and replace it with one headed by himself, nothing came of these efforts. In 1957, moreover, the Syrian government tried al-Shishakli in absentia on charges of conspiracy to overthrow the government. In 1960 al-Shishakli thought it prudent to move to a more distant location, and he settled in Brazil. There on September 27, 1964, a Druze militant assassinated al-Shishakli for attacks on the Druze minority during his presidency.

SPENCER C. TUCKER

See also

Druze; Nasser, Gamal Abdel; Pan-Arabism; Syria

References

Lenczowski, George. *The Middle East in World Affairs*. 4th ed. Ithaca, NY: Cornell University Press, 1980.

Pipes, Daniel. *Greater Syria: The History of an Ambition*. New York: Oxford University Press, 1990.

Roberts, David. *The Ba'th and the Creation of Modern Syria*. New York: St. Martin's, 1987.

Shkolnik, Levi

See Eshkol, Levi

Shomron, Dan
Born: 1937

Israeli Army officer and chief of staff of the Israel Defense Forces (IDF) during 1987–1991. Dan Shomron was born in 1937 at Ashdot Yaacov in the British Mandate for Palestine. He graduated with a BA in geography from Tel Aviv University. Drafted into the IDF in 1956, he continued in its service.

Although as a junior officer he was trained in armored warfare, Colonel Shomron commanded a paratroop unit at the Suez Canal during the Six-Day War (1967) and later as a brigadier general commanded the 401st Armored Brigade defending the Suez Canal at the beginning of the Yom Kippur War (1973). Rallying from the initial Egyptian attacks, Shomron and his unit then crossed the Suez under the command of Major General Ariel Sharon on October 14, 1973.

In 1974 Shomron commanded the IDF's Infantry and Paratroopers Branch and in this capacity had overall operational command of Operation THUNDERBOLT in July 1976. This operation successfully liberated the Israeli passengers and crew of Air France Flight 139 held hostage at the Entebbe Airport in Uganda.

As head of the IDF's Southern Command (1978), Shomron directed the dismantling of Israeli settlements and military bases in the Sinai Peninsula mandated by the 1978 Camp David Accords. He was on study leave in the United States when Israel invaded

Lieutenant General Dan Shomron, chief of staff of the Israel Defense Forces (IDF) during 1987–1991, pictured here in July 1976. (Israeli Government Press Office)

Lebanon in September 1982. In 1983 Major General Shomron was directed to integrate all of the IDF infantry, armor, artillery, and engineer corps into a single field command. He then assumed command of this new organization with the title of chief of the Ground Forces Command, reporting directly to the IDF chief of staff. Promoted to lieutenant general, Shomron succeeded Moshe Levi as the IDF chief of staff on April 19, 1987, and held that position until April 1, 1991.

During the Persian Gulf War (1990–1991) when Iraq launched Scud missiles against Israel in an effort to draw it into the fighting and unhinge the coalition against Iraq, Shomron authorized the deployment of American Patriot missiles and cautioned Israel's Prime Minister Yitzhak Shamir against retaliation against Iraq. As IDF chief of staff, Shomron also began the process of converting the IDF into a smaller and smarter army, reduced the number of its special operations, hinted publicly at an Israeli nuclear capability, and oversaw the Israeli initial response to the First Intifada (1987–1993). Later, he asserted that there was no military solution to the intifada.

Although Shomron had no formal higher education or experience in business, following his retirement as chief of staff in 1991

he became chairman of the Israel Military Industries (later Ta'as Israel Industries). He remained in that position until 1995, when Ta'as was unable to provide the Labor government of Israel with accurate financial records. Shomron remained active in business and in 2004 signed a cooperative agreement with the Israeli defense contractor Bynet Systems for an artificial intelligence video motion detector–based system for securing installations and settlements.

In 1995 Shomron helped found the Third Way political party that later joined Likud. He served as Likud prime minister Benjamin Netanyahu's chief negotiator in finalizing the 1997 Hebron Protocol with the Palestine Liberation Organization (PLO). Shomron criticized any loosening of Israeli gun control laws that would make private firearms more readily available and increase the already high Israeli violent crime rate. He advocated trading territory for peace and asserted that there could be no peace unless Hamas was challenged and a strong Palestinian leadership that was willing to negotiate emerged. He also served on the Committee for the Prevention of Destruction of Antiquities on the Temple Mount, the International Advisory Board of the Begin-Sadat Center for Strategic Studies at Bar-Ilan University, and the presidium of the Israeli Media Watch that monitors, reports, and responds to political and cultural media bias against Israel.

RICHARD EDWARDS

See also

Camp David Accords; Entebbe Hostage Rescue; Intifada, First; Israel Defense Forces; Netanyahu, Benjamin; Persian Gulf War; Shamir, Yitzhak

References

Goldstein, Yaacov N., and Dan Shomron. *From Fighters to Soldiers: How the Israeli Defense Forces Began.* Brighton, UK: Sussex Academic, 1998.
Porat, Yesha Yahu Ben. *Entebbe Rescue.* New York: Delacorte, 1977.
Van Creveld, Martin. *The Sword and the Olive: A Critical History of the Israeli Defense Force.* New York: PublicAffairs, 2002.

Shultz, George Pratt
Born: December 13, 1920

U.S. secretary of labor (1969–1970), secretary of the treasury (1972–1974), and secretary of state (1982–1989). Born in Englewood, New Jersey, on December 13, 1920, George Shultz graduated from Princeton University, majoring in economics, in 1942 and then joined the U.S. Marine Corps, serving in the Pacific theater as an artillery officer and ending World War II as a captain. After demobilization, in 1949 he obtained a doctorate in industrial economics from the Massachusetts Institute of Technology, where he subsequently taught industrial relations, moving to the University of Chicago in 1957.

Under Republican president Richard Nixon, Shultz served successively as secretary of labor (1969–1970), the first director of the Office of Management and Budget (1970–1972), and secretary of the treasury (1972–1974). He resigned in March 1974 to become

George Shultz, U.S. secretary of labor (1969–1970), secretary of the treasury (1972–1974), and secretary of state (1982–1989). (U.S. Department of State)

vice president of Bechtel Corporation, an international construction company, where he remained until 1982.

In June 1982 Shultz became Republican president Ronald Reagan's second and last secretary of state, replacing the forceful but divisive Alexander M. Haig and adopting a low-key, nonconfrontational style. Even so, Shultz's cautious readiness to negotiate arms control agreements with the Soviet Union brought repeated clashes with the more hawkish secretary of defense, Caspar Weinberger, who favored major increases in weapons systems.

Shultz's tenure of office saw the emergence in 1985 of Mikhail Gorbachev as general secretary of the Communist Party of the Soviet Union. Gorbachev was a conciliatory leader who became increasingly committed to reducing his country's international military commitments and improving Soviet-American relations. Shultz, initially somewhat skeptical and inclined to discountenance the more optimistic Reagan's readiness in his 1986 Reykjavik meeting with Gorbachev to consider abolishing all nuclear weapons, nonetheless negotiated the 1987 Intermediate Nuclear Force (INF) Treaty that removed all such weapons from Europe. In 1988 the Soviets also concluded an agreement to withdraw all their forces from Afghanistan, where since 1979 they had been at war with U.S.-backed mujahideen guerrillas.

From the time he took office, one of Shultz's major preoccupations was with initiatives to resolve or at least ease the entrenched disputes dividing Israel and its Arab opponents after Israel's June 1982 invasion of Lebanon. Except in Afghanistan, the warming in Soviet-American relations had relatively little impact on the nearly intractable Middle Eastern situation. Shultz drafted the September 1982 Reagan Plan envisaging partial Israeli withdrawal from occupied territory in return for Arab acceptance and respect for Israeli security interests, proposals that the Israeli government strongly rejected. Throughout his years in office, Shultz repeatedly but unsuccessfully tried to broker similar schemes. In December 1988 he prevailed upon Palestine Liberation Organization (PLO) leader Yasser Arafat to renounce the use of terrorism, a stance enabling the United States to open direct talks with the PLO, but Arafat failed to force his more radical followers to respect this stance, and within a year the U.S.-PLO talks broke down.

Shultz was a determined opponent of international terrorism and of governments such as those of Libya and Iran that sponsored such tactics. After powerful bombs from Imad Mughniya's radical Shiite group destroyed the barracks of the U.S. marine peacekeeping force in Beirut, Lebanon, in October 1983, killing 241 American servicemen, Shultz began to press Reagan to respond forcefully to such attacks on Americans. Shultz supported the use of force as well as military and economic sanctions, not just against individual terrorists but also against states that sponsored terrorism. He applauded Reagan's readiness in 1985 to employ military personnel to capture Palestinian hijackers of the American cruise ship *Achille Lauro* and to mount bombing raids on Libya in April 1986.

Shultz opposed and was therefore deliberately left in ignorance of efforts by national security adviser Robert McFarlane and others based in the Reagan White House to sell arms to the fundamentalist Islamic regime in Iran and surreptitiously use the proceeds to fund the activities of anticommunist Contra guerrillas in Nicaragua. The Iran-Contra Scandal, which broke in 1986, damaged but did not destroy Reagan's presidency, and his final years in office saw further incremental warming in Soviet-American relations that came to full fruition under his successor, George H. W. Bush.

Shultz retired at the end of Reagan's presidency and became a senior fellow at the conservative Hoover Institution in Palo Alto, California. In retirement Shultz has written lengthy memoirs.

PRISCILLA ROBERTS

See also

Arafat, Yasser; Bush, George Herbert Walker; Iran; Lebanon, U.S. Interventions in; Libya; Nixon, Richard Milhous; Palestine Liberation Organization; Reagan, Ronald Wilson; Reagan Plan; Terrorism; Weinberger, Caspar

References

Brands, H. W. *Into the Labyrinth: The United States and the Middle East, 1945–1953.* New York: McGraw Hill, 1994.

FitzGerald, Frances. *Way Out There in the Blue: Reagan, Star Wars, and the End of the Cold War.* New York: Simon and Schuster, 2000.

Laham, Nicholas. *Crossing the Rubicon: Ronald Reagan and US Policy in the Middle East.* Aldershot, UK: Ashgate, 2004.

Martin, David C., and John Walcott. *Best Laid Plans: The Inside Story of America's War against Terrorism.* New York: Harper and Row, 1988.

Matlock, Jack F., Jr. *Reagan and Gorbachev: How the Cold War Ended.* New York: Random House, 2004.

Oberdorfer, Don. *The Turn from the Cold War to a New Era: The United States and the Soviet Union, 1983–1990.* New York: Poseidon, 1991.

Quandt, William B. *The Peace Process: American Diplomacy and the Arab-Israeli Conflict since 1967.* Washington, DC: Brookings Institution, 1993.

Shultz, George P. *Turmoil and Triumph: My Years as Secretary of State.* New York: Scribner, 1993.

Woodward, Bob. *Veil: The Secret Wars of the CIA, 1981–1987.* New York: Simon and Schuster, 1987.

Shultz Plan
Event Date: March 4, 1988

Middle East peace proposal formally enunciated by U.S. secretary of state George P. Shultz on March 4, 1988. The Shultz Plan was part of President Ronald Reagan's response to the First Intifada, which had broken out in the occupied territories the preceding year. Dozens of people had already been killed during the uprising since it first began in December 1987. The plan was also part of an American attempt to become more actively engaged in the ongoing Arab-Israeli peace process. Since 1983, American policymakers had shied away from active engagement in the Middle East. The reasons for this are multifaceted. The abortive U.S. involvement in the Lebanese Civil War, the failure of the 1982 Reagan Plan, and the October 1983 destruction of the U.S. Marine Corps barracks in Beirut in which 241 Americans died all had forced Reagan to reverse course and pull American troops out of the region. These negative experiences had convinced the Americans that peace in the Middle East was a chimera. Also, the renewed Cold War with the Soviets and then negotiations with the Soviets beginning in late 1985 had diverted the Reagan administration's attention from the problems in the Middle East.

By the late 1980s, however, the Americans realized that they could no longer stay out of the Middle East. Yet the Palestinians would not make the Americans' jobs any easier. The U.S. State Department had tried on more than one occasion to engage the Palestine Liberation Organization (PLO), but the organization refused to alter its goal of destroying Israel. And as long as this persisted, the United States refused to enter into negotiations with the PLO. In October 1987, just weeks before the First Intifada began, Shultz asserted in a speech—which was clearly a precursor to the Shultz Plan—that "the Palestinians must be involved in the peace process if it is to mean anything." Yet in the same breath, he also stated that "there isn't a role in the peace process for people whose tactics are violent." Shultz, a consummate diplomat, seemed to be holding out a vision of direct U.S.-PLO talks in return for that group's denunciation of violence.

The Shultz Plan had three primary parts. First, negotiations should begin at once, to be comprised of all pertinent parties that accepted United Nations (UN) Resolutions 242 and 338 and denounced violence. The talks would be sponsored by the five permanent members of the UN Security Council. Second, the Palestinians would be part of the Jordanian delegation that would negotiate for all the Palestinians a three-year period of transitional self-government in the occupied territories (Gaza and the West Bank). Third, the initial multination conferences would be spun off into binational negotiations in which the details of the larger negotiations would be hammered out. The secretary of state's plan was predicated in part on the 1978 Camp David Accords, the 1982 Reagan Plan, and peace ideas prescribed by Israeli foreign minister Shimon Peres and King Hussein of Jordan.

The Shultz Plan initially caused quite a stir. And to make headway in getting it accepted, Shultz embarked on a flurry of shuttle diplomacy in and around the Middle East that lasted from March to June 1988. While the plan was generally accepted by Peres, Israeli prime minister Yitzhak Shamir had grave reservations about it. He was especially suspect of the land for peace formula, which would have given to the Palestinians control over land currently occupied by Israel. He also disagreed with the three-year transitional period that Shultz had proposed, believing that it should be considerably longer. Thus, there was a split within Israel over the plan and an overt rift between the foreign minister and prime minister. The Egyptians and Jordanians ultimately gave the Shultz Plan a lukewarm endorsement but with few large reservations. Syria expressed serious concerns with the plan as did the PLO, which had not yet denounced violence against Israel. When Shultz traveled to the West Bank and Gaza to talk with key Palestinian leaders, none would meet with him, apparently on orders of the PLO.

As the summer of 1988 approached, Shultz had made little headway in getting the key players in the region to sign on to the plan. Israel was proving intransigent, as were the Palestinians. As with the Reagan Plan that preceded it, the Shultz Plan fell short on specifics. It did not offer any breakthroughs on Palestinian self-determination and did not specifically include the PLO. Without the PLO's participation, no peace settlement could be brokered. After June, Shultz continued to press his case for the plan, but the little momentum he had gained initially was gone. While he could say that no party had rejected the plan outright, neither was it met with much zeal.

The Shultz Plan became a dead letter after the November 1988 elections ushered Reagan's vice president, George H. W. Bush, into the Oval Office. Yet Shultz's laudable effort set the stage for important developments in the Middle Eastern peace process. By laying out the exact conditions under which the United States would engage with the PLO, the Shultz Plan forced a lively internal debate among PLO factions and their leaders. The plan, in fact, had given PLO chairman Yasser Arafat the opportunity to seize the initiative and overcome hard-line resistance within the organization. In so doing, he outflanked them by announcing, with much fanfare, the

November 15, 1988, Algiers Declaration. This statement implied PLO acknowledgment of Israel and a vow to cease and desist from engaging in or promoting terrorism. Although it was not enough to satisfy Washington, it was nevertheless a historic step toward a direct U.S.-PLO dialogue. The Shultz Plan also laid the groundwork for the Oslo Accords of 1993.

PAUL G. PIERPAOLI JR.

See also

Algiers Declaration; Arafat, Yasser; Intifada, First; Lebanon, Civil War in; Oslo Accords; Palestine Liberation Organization; Peres, Shimon; Reagan Plan; Shamir, Yitzhak; Shultz, George Pratt

References

Laham, Nicholas. *Crossing the Rubicon: Ronald Reagan and U.S. Policy in the Middle East.* Aldershot, Hampshire, UK: Ashgate, 2004.

Quandt, William B. *The Peace Process: American Diplomacy and the Arab-Israeli Conflict since 1967.* Washington, DC: Brookings Institution, 1993.

Rubin, Barry. *Revolution until Victory? The Politics and History of the PLO.* Reprint ed. Cambridge: Harvard University Press, 2003.

Shultz, George P. *Turmoil and Triumph: My Years as Secretary of State.* New York: Scribner, 1993.

Sidqi, Atif

Born: August 21, 1930
Died: February 25, 2005

Egyptian prime minister (1991–1996), lawyer, and professor. Born in Tanta-Gharbiyya, Egypt, on August 21, 1930, Atif Sidqi graduated from Cairo University Faculty of Law in 1951 and then earned a doctorate in finance and economics from the Sorbonne in 1958. He taught at Cairo University during 1958–1973. From 1980 to 1985 he presided over the Advisory Council for Economic and Financial Affairs in Egypt. He has written several books on economics and taxation.

From 1987 to 1991 Sidqi served as Egyptian minister for international cooperation, and in November 1991 he became Egyptian prime minister. Often eclipsed by President Hosni Mubarak, Sidqi was seen as a moderate and effective administrator of Mubarak's conservative political and economic reform program. In October 1993 Sidqi carried out a government overhaul in which key ministers retained their posts, while most others were merely assigned to a different ministry. Despite his unassuming leadership style, Sidqi was the target of a failed assassination attempt in November 1993 by members of al-Jihad.

On January 2, 1996, shortly after controversial legislative elections, President Mubarak dismissed Sidqi, who then chaired the national specialized councils. Sidqi died on February 25, 2005, from a heart condition.

SPENCER C. TUCKER

See also

Egypt; Mubarak, Hosni

References

Kassem, Maye. *Egyptian Politics: The Dynamics of Authoritarian Rule.* Boulder, CO: Lynne Rienner, 2004.

Solecki, John. *Hosni Mubarak.* New York: Chelsea House, 1991.

Sinai

The Sinai Peninsula is the triangle-shaped peninsula belonging to Egypt that links Africa and Asia. The peninsula is part of West Asia, while the remainder of Egypt is part of North Africa. The Sinai is bordered by the Gulf of Suez and the Suez Canal on the west and the Gulf of Aqaba and the Negev Desert on the east. The Mediterranean Sea is to the north, and the Red Sea is to the south. The Sinai constitutes an area of some 23,166 square miles and is almost entirely desert and high mountains.

During ancient Egyptian times the Sinai was inhabited by the Monitu people, who called it the Country of Turquoise, and both turquoise and copper were mined in the region. Arab tribes have resided there since before Islam. From 1260 the peninsula was controlled by the Egyptian Mamluks. In 1518 the Ottoman Turks defeated the Mamluks and took control of the Sinai and the rest of Egyptian territory. In 1882 the British took control of Egypt, and in 1906 Constantinople agreed, under British pressure, to hand over control of the Sinai to Egypt. British authorities then set the border of the Sinai, which is now the border between Egypt and Israel. The Turks reoccupied the Sinai during World War I, but it was returned to Egyptian control thereafter. The British maintained a governor in the Sinai until 1936, when they withdrew from all areas except for the Suez Canal region.

In response to the 1948 creation of the State of Israel, a huge number of Bedouin were expelled, and others were prevented from reentering. During the Israeli War of Independence (1948–1949) Egyptian troops traversed the Sinai Peninsula, where they were met and halted by Israeli forces. Israeli forces occupied much of the northeastern corner of the Sinai during the war, but British and American pressure forced them to withdraw.

In 1956 Egyptian president Gamal Abdel Nasser instituted a blockade of the Israeli port of Eilat. During the ensuing Suez Crisis, the Israeli, British, and French governments worked out a secret plan whereby Israel would invade the Sinai followed by French and British moves to reestablish control of the canal. Israeli forces drove deep into the Sinai toward the canal, prompting the excuse of British and French military intervention to allegedly protect the canal. The United States forced all three countries to withdraw from Egyptian territory. Subsequently, a United Nations Emergency Force (UNEF) took up position along the Egyptian-Israeli border.

In the spring of 1967 Nasser reinforced Egyptian troops in the Sinai, ordered the UNEF observers to depart, and reimposed a blockade of Eilat. Israel's response was the preemptive air strike of June 5, 1967, that wiped out the Egyptian Air Force and opened what became known as the Six-Day War. This time Israel occupied the entire Sinai.

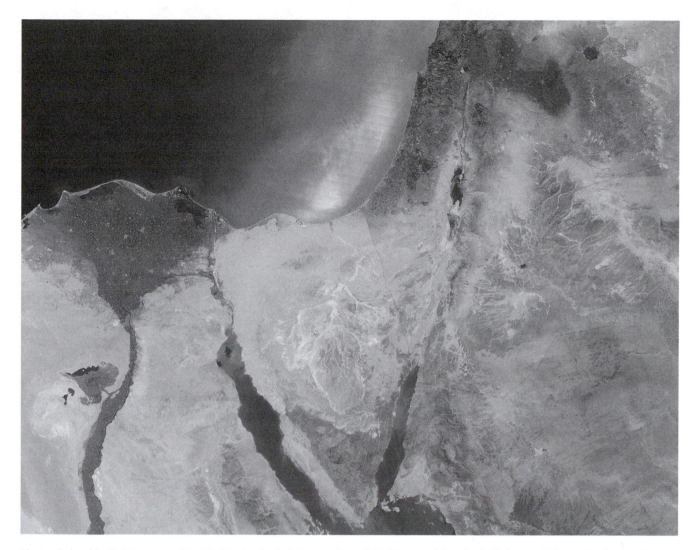

The two forks of the Red Sea surround the Sinai Peninsula; the left branch is the Gulf of Suez, the right is the Gulf of Aqaba. This satellite photograph was taken on June 5, 2006. (NASA)

In the 1973 Yom Kippur War, Egyptian forces crossed the Suez Canal, penetrating the Israeli Bar-Lev Line, and proceeded a short distance into the Sinai. Although the Egyptians were at first successful, the Israelis soon gained the upper hand. They crossed over the canal and isolated an Egyptian army on the east bank when a cease-fire was declared. Under the subsequent Sinai Disengagement Agreements, Israel agreed to withdraw its forces west of the canal and from an additional strip of the western Sinai, allowing the Suez Canal to be reopened under Egyptian control.

In 1979 Israel and Egypt signed a peace agreement in accordance with the Camp David Accords of a year earlier. The peace treaty stipulated that the entire Sinai was to be returned to Egyptian control. Israel completed its withdrawal from the peninsula in 1982. The Israeli pullout required that several Jewish settlements be destroyed.

According to biblical tradition, Jabal Musa (Mount Sinai) is where Moses received the Ten Commandments from God. The monastery of St. Catherine at the foot of the mountain is said to be the world's oldest Greek Orthodox monastery and is a major tourist attraction. There has been little development in the Sinai except for tourism. Conditions are quite difficult for the Bedouin, particularly in the north, and Palestinians. Several Sinai coastal cities are popular tourist destinations for Israelis as well as others and have been the scene of terrorist bombings, as in October 2004 when explosions in Taba killed more than 30 people, a number of them Israelis.

SPENCER C. TUCKER

See also

Aqaba, Gulf of; Bar-Lev Line; Camp David Accords; Egypt; Israeli Air Strikes Beginning the Six-Day War; Sinai Campaign; Six-Day War; Suez Canal; Suez Crisis

References

Beck, John A. *The Land of Milk and Honey: An Introduction to the Geography of Israel.* St. Louis: Concordia, 2006.

Henriques, Robert D. Q. *A Hundred Hours to Suez: An Account of Israel's Campaign in the Sinai Peninsula.* New York: Viking, 1957.

Orni, Ephraim. *Geography of Israel.* Philadelphia: Jewish Publication Society of America, 1977.

Quandt, William B. *Camp David: Peacemaking and Politics.* Washington, DC: Brookings Institution Press, 1986.

Sinai Campaign

Start Date: October 29, 1956
End Date: November 6, 1956

On October 29, 1956, Israeli forces invaded the Egyptian Sinai Peninsula, opening what became known as the Sinai Campaign. The Israeli attack had been prearranged with the governments of Britain and France, which were then to intervene in a claim to protect the Suez Canal from fighting between Egypt and Israel.

On July 26, 1956, Egyptian president Gamal Abdel Nasser nationalized the Suez Canal, heretofore owned and operated by a company controlled largely by the British. This action and Nasser's support for Algerian rebels fighting France as well as his support for raids against Israel led to the opening of secret talks among the French, Israeli, and British governments regarding common action designed to topple Nasser from power and remove any military threat by Egypt to Israel. The Israelis were especially anxious to end the blockade imposed by Egypt on the Straits of Tiran at the southern tip of the Sinai Peninsula. The blockade cut off the Israeli port of Eilat at the head of the Gulf of Aqaba, halting Israeli shipping from that port with East Africa and Asia. The Israelis also wanted to wipe out Palestinian fedayeen guerrillas located on Egyptian territory, especially in the Gaza Strip. Fedayeen attacks on Israel had been a major problem for Israel.

Israel was anxious that the attack be carried out soon. A year earlier, on October 27, 1955, Egypt had arranged for the purchase of a large quantity of Soviet military equipment from Czechoslovakia. This included some 230 tanks and 200 modern jet aircraft, including 120 MiG-15 and MiG-17 fighters and 50 Ilyushin IL-28 bombers. Much of this equipment was superior to anything in the Israeli arsenal. In June 1956, however, the Egyptians had not fully integrated the new weapons into their military establishment. Thus, only about 30 pilots had been fully trained to fly the MiG-15, and only 10 bomber crews were trained in the IL-28. In all, in October 1956 the Egyptian Air Force numbered about 254 aircraft, including 84 British Gloster Meteor and de Havilland Vampire fighters.

Intelligence deception aided the Israelis in gaining surprise at the start of the war. The Egyptians believed that the bulk of Israeli forces were in place facing Jordan and that no major attack on Egypt was imminent. With the nationalization of the canal, the Egyptians had positioned a large part of their military assets in the Nile Delta area to defend against a possible British and French attack there. As a result, Egyptian defenses in the Sinai were undermanned. The Egyptian defensive plan for the Sinai had called for a force of four infantry divisions, one armored division, and several independent infantry battalions, all to be deployed in a defense in-depth. The armored division was to act as a mobile reserve. However, in October 1956 only one-third of the Egyptian Army, about 30,000 men, was stationed in the Sinai, a far smaller force than was required. Egyptian troops there were organized into two divisions and a number of scattered smaller independent units. Nonetheless, two infantry divisions and the sole armored division were positioned in the Ismailia area just across the canal and could presumably easily move into the Sinai if necessary. On the up side, the Egyptians had constructed extensive field fortifications around the Sinai towns of Rafah and Abu Ageila. Former German Army officer Wilhelm Frambecher had overseen their construction and had also drawn up the Egyptian defense plan for the Sinai.

Egyptian minister of defense and commander in chief General Abdel Hakim Amer was supremely confident of victory should any armed clash occur. He had announced on September 3 that the Egyptian Army was "prepared to the smallest detail." Indeed, just a few days before the start of the Israeli invasion, Amer traveled to Jordan and then on to Syria to sign the new tripartite Arab pact. He was in Syria when the fighting began. Israeli intelligence discovered the return route of his aircraft, and an Israeli jet shot it down. Amer was not aboard, having decided to remain in Syria an additional day, but 18 senior officers died in the crash, which was a serious blow to Egyptian military operations.

When fighting began on the afternoon of October 29, 1956, Israel had concentrated 45,000 men in 10 brigades, including one armored and three mechanized brigades with some 200–250 tanks. Israel also had 136 aircraft, 54 of them jet fighters: 16 Dassault Mystère IVAs, 22 Dassault Ouragans, and 16 Gloster Meteors. There were also 42 propeller aircraft—29 P-51D Mustangs and 13 de Havilland Mosquitos—for ground-attack missions. Although the Israeli Air Force was at great disadvantage in terms of number of aircraft as well as their technical quality, these disadvantages were more than offset by far superior pilot training and expertise.

Israel Defense Forces (IDF) chief of staff Lieutenant General Moshe Dayan developed the Israeli strategic plan. It called for the chief initial Israeli attacks to come in the central Sinai against the Abu Ageila complex and Mitla Pass. Four of the Israeli brigades were committed to the central Sinai effort. Three other Israeli brigades would then attack Rafah and the Gaza Strip before turning west and heading toward the canal. Two brigades would be held in reserve, while another would strike south toward Sharm al-Sheikh.

The Sinai offensive began with an Israeli parachute battalion of the 202nd Brigade dropped on the eastern side of the Mitla Pass on the afternoon of October 29. This key terrain feature guarded the approach to the Suez Canal, 30 miles west. The pass was of major strategic importance and was heavily defended by the Egyptians. The paratroopers established a defensive perimeter and then settled in for the night, while the remainder of the brigade, under command of Major Ariel Sharon, raced for Mitla Pass to link up with the paratroopers. Sharon's unit easily brushed aside scant Egyptian resistance and linked up with the airborne unit the next morning. Over the next several days, heavy fighting occurred at the pass as

Sɪɴᴀɪ Cᴀᴍᴘᴀɪɢɴ, 1956

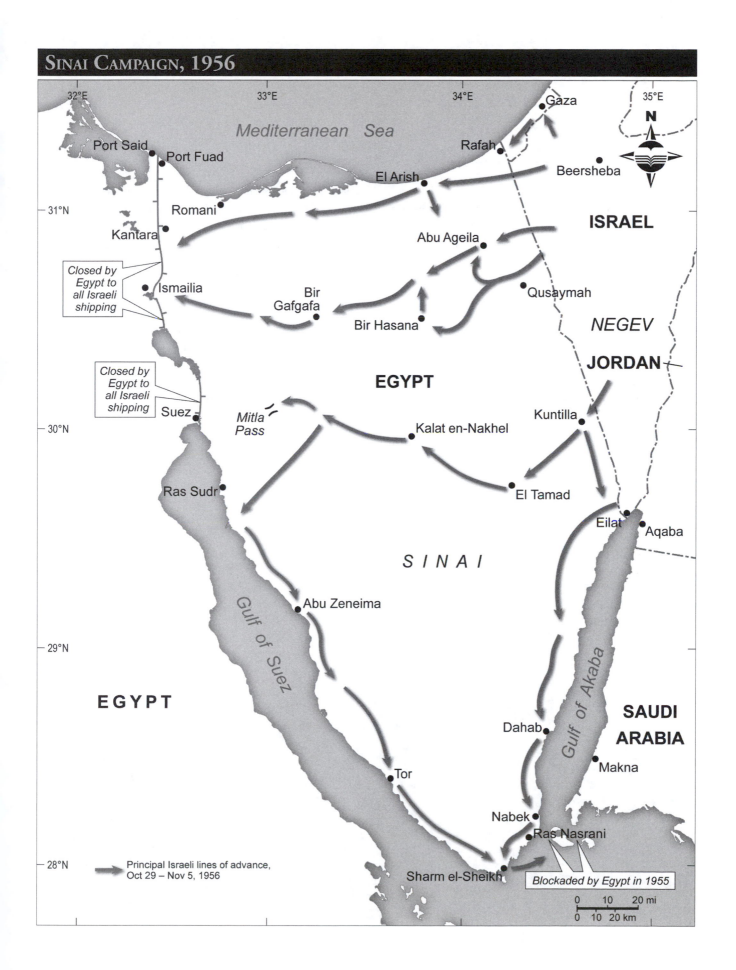

Mediterranean Sea

Gaza

Port Said
Port Fuad
Rafah
Beersheba

El Arish

Romani

ISRAEL

Kantara

Abu Ageila

Closed by Egypt to all Israeli shipping

Ismailia

Bir Gafgafa

Qusaymah

NEGEV

Bir Hasana

EGYPT

JORDAN

Closed by Egypt to all Israeli shipping

Suez

Kalat en-Nakhel

Kuntilla

Mitla Pass

Ras Sudr

El Tamad

Eilat
Aqaba

S I N A I

Abu Zeneima

EGYPT

Gulf of Suez

Gulf of Akaba

SAUDI ARABIA

Dahab

Makna

Tor

Nabek
Ras Nasrani

Sharm el-Sheikh

Blockaded by Egypt in 1955

Principal Israeli lines of advance,
Oct 29 – Nov 5, 1956

0   10   20 mi
0 10 20 km

Estimated Casualties of the 1956 Sinai Campaign

	Egypt	Israel	Israel's Allies (Britain and France)
KIA	1,000	189	26
WIA	4,000	900	129
POW	6,000	0	0
Aircraft Lost	215	15	0

Sharon violated orders by attempting to take the pass rather than merely holding the ground east of it. The fighting there claimed 38 Israeli dead, and Sharon subsequently came in for heavy criticism.

It took perhaps a dozen hours for the Egyptians to figure out Israeli intentions. Nasser and key military leaders all assumed that the thrust against Mitla Pass was the main attack, and they committed major resources, including the 4th Armored Division, against it. Other Israeli forces meanwhile easily broke through Egyptian border defenses in the central and southern Sinai. South of Abu Ageila, the Israeli 4th Infantry Brigade easily overran Egyptian defenses at Qusaymah. The Egyptians there simply broke and ran. Part of the 4th Brigade then continued into the central Sinai, screening Sharon's more southerly advance. The Israelis then moved against Abu Ageila itself and adjacent Umm Qatif. There the Egyptians beat back a number of Israeli attacks between October 29 and November 1.

Despite losing Abu Ageila, the Egyptian garrison at Umm Qatif fought on stubbornly. The Israelis did not take it until Nasser ordered a general retreat from the Sinai. However, Egyptian counterattacks farther north were completely unsuccessful.

Additional Israeli units bypassed Egyptian strong points and poured into the Sinai. The 4th Armored Division had already crossed the Suez Canal and moved into the Sinai to block the Israeli advance. However, the Egyptians had difficulty piecing together what was happening in the Sinai because of their poor communications.

On October 30, meanwhile, the British and French governments issued an ultimatum, nominally to both the Egyptian and Israeli governments but in reality only to Egypt, expressing the need to "separate the combatants" and to protect the security of the Suez Canal. The ultimatum demanded that both sides withdraw their forces 10 miles from the canal. The Egyptian and Israeli governments were given 12 hours to reply. The Israelis immediately accepted the ultimatum, while the Egyptians promptly rejected it. On the evening of October 31, therefore, the British and French began air strikes against the Egyptians.

Nasser concluded that the British and French threat was the more serious. Therefore, the 4th Armored Division, which had been advancing slowly into the Sinai, was ordered to turn around and head back to the canal. The Israelis thus were able to occupy the central Sinai with minimal opposition. At the same time, on No-

Israeli tanks in the Sinai Desert during the 1956 Sinai Campaign. (Israeli Government Press Office)

vember 1 Nasser ordered all Egyptian Army units in the Sinai to begin a withdrawal toward the canal. Egyptian forces thus finally abandoned Umm Qatif and began pulling out of their defenses in the Gaza Strip and Rafah. This Egyptian retreat soon turned into a catastrophic rout as the withdrawing Egyptian columns came under heavy attack from Israeli Air Force aircraft.

In sharp contrast to the superb support rendered to its ground units by the Israeli Air Force, the Egyptian Air Force played virtually no role in the fighting. It mounted several strikes against the Israelis at the Mitla Pass, but the lack of trained pilots as well as poor maintenance meant that most Egyptian jets remained on the ground for much of the war. Indeed, many Egyptian aircraft were moved to southern Egypt simply to avoid their destruction. The Egyptians carried out exactly one bombing raid on Israeli territory, sending six bombers to attack an Israeli air base near Jerusalem. However, five of the Egyptian bombers failed to find Israel and had to return to base. The sixth bomber located Jerusalem but dropped its bomb load in an open field. The raid was a testimony to the abysmal state of Egyptian training.

Besides suffering Israeli air attacks, the retreating Egyptian columns simply moved too slowly to escape the much more mobile Israeli forces. Some Egyptian Army units could fight well from static defenses, as they did at Umm Qatif and the Mitla Pass, although other formations broke and ran at the first sign of an Israeli attack. In mobile warfare, the Egyptians were completely outclassed by the Israelis. Egyptian weaknesses in this became abundantly clear during the retreat to the Suez Canal after November 1. The marksmanship of Egyptian tank crews was especially poor, even though they operated superior tanks. Possibly half of Egypt's new Soviet-built tanks remained immobilized during the war because of maintenance problems in the harsh desert environment. Egyptian advances and counterattacks also moved far too slowly. Had the Egyptian 4th Armored Division moved quickly into the Sinai, the entire Israeli plan of attack might have come undone. Its snail's pace advance contrasted sharply with the rapid attacks of the Israelis. Egyptian counterattacks seemed completely disorganized, and they were unable to operate around the vulnerable flanks of Israeli units.

The Israeli conquest of the Sinai proceeded rapidly after November 1. The Israelis broke into Egyptian defenses at Rafah, meeting sporadic resistance. Gaza was quickly overrun as additional Israeli columns stormed along the north shore of the Sinai toward the canal. Finally, in the south the Israelis captured Sharm al-Sheikh at the very tip of the Sinai Peninsula, ending the Egyptian blockade of the Straits of Tiran. By November 3, major combat operations in the Sinai were virtually at an end, with only mopping up remaining.

Meanwhile, British and French airborne assaults began on November 5. The British captured Port Said, while the French took Port Fuad. Egyptian defenses crumbled quickly under the British and French air and commando attacks. Once again, Egyptian counterattacks failed, despite the bravery of many Egyptian soldiers. The British and French both prepared to move south and seize the rest of the Canal Zone, but international pressure, chiefly from the United States, forced a cease-fire at midnight on November 6.

Estimates vary, but in the brief conflict the Egyptians suffered about 1,000 troops killed in action, 4,000 wounded, and just under 6,000 taken prisoner. The Egyptians also lost at least 215 aircraft and 100 tanks. The usual tally given for Israeli casualties is 189 dead and some 900 wounded. The Israelis lost only 15 aircraft. The British and French counted 26 dead and 129 wounded.

In December 1956 the British and French withdrew their forces from Port Said and Port Fuad, while the Israelis withdrew from the Sinai in March 1957. A specially created United Nations (UN) Emergency Force then took up station in Sharm al-Sheikh and in the Gaza Strip.

The Israelis, at least, had achieved their objectives. They defeated the Egyptian Army, lifted the blockade of the Straits of Tiran, and smashed Palestinian fedayeen operations in Gaza. The British and French failed to accomplish their goals. Curiously, Nasser emerged from the war with his reputation enhanced in the Arab world, even though the Egyptians had fared badly in the actual fighting. Many Arabs saw Nasser as a hero for having stood up to the old colonial powers and to Israel. Egypt's military losses could be excused on the grounds that the British and French had intervened and that Egypt could not have been expected to defeat these forces. Egyptian Army leaders also concluded that it had nothing to learn from the Sinai Campaign, again because they had supposedly lost to the British and the French. The British and French intervention allegedly meant that the Egyptian defenses in the Sinai were not fully manned and that their best units could not engage the Israelis. Although partially true, this line of reasoning ignored serious Egyptian Army shortcomings in tactics, training, leadership, communication, and control revealed during the fighting. The Egyptians paid a heavy price for ignoring the lessons of 1956 when they next fought Israel in 1967. The Israelis, by contrast, learned a great deal from the war and made major efforts to improve their armed forces. Indeed, the Israelis made mobility, maneuver, and air supremacy the keystones of their armed forces doctrine.

PAUL DOERR

See also

Airpower, Role in the Arab-Israeli Wars; Amer, Abdel Hakim; Aqaba, Gulf of; Dayan, Moshe; Eden, Robert Anthony; Egypt; Egypt, Armed Forces; France, Middle East Policy; Gaza Strip; Israel; Israel Defense Forces; Nasser, Gamal Abdel; Sharon, Ariel; Straits of Tiran; Suez Canal; Suez Crisis; United Kingdom, Middle East Policy

References

Bregman, Ahron. *Israel's Wars, 1947–93*. London: Routledge, 2000.

Dayan, Moshe. *Diary of the Sinai Campaign*. Cambridge, MA: Da Capo, 1991.

Dupuy, Trevor N. *Elusive Victory: The Arab-Israeli Wars, 1947–1974*. Garden City, NY: Military Book Club, 2002.

Pollack, Kenneth M. *Arabs at War: Military Effectiveness, 1948–1991*. Lincoln: University of Nebraska Press, 2002.

Sheffy, Yigal. "Unconcern at Dawn, Surprise at Sunset: Egyptian Intelligence Appreciation Before the Sinai Campaign, 1956." *Intelligence and National Security* 5(3) (1990): 7–56.

Troen, Selwyn. *The Suez-Sinai Crisis, 1956: Retrospective and Reappraisal.* Edited by Moshe Shemesh. New York: Columbia University Press, 1990.

Sinai I and Sinai II Agreements
Event Dates: January 19 and September 4, 1974

Comprehensive cease-fire agreements between Israel and Egypt. Sinai I was signed on January 19, 1974, while Sinai II was signed on September 4, 1974. The United States played a critical role in both agreements. After the Yom Kippur War of October 1973, Israel and Egypt began a process of negotiations that would lead to the Israeli withdrawal from most of the territory it had captured from Egypt, not just in 1973 but also in the Six-Day War of June 1967. This was a significant departure from what had happened following previous conflicts. In 1956 the United States pressured Israel as well as Britain and France to give up all territories seized from Egypt in October during the Suez Crisis and Sinai Campaign. In 1967 Israel kept all territories gained. Thus, the Sinai I and Sinai II agreements ushered in a new era in Israeli-Egyptian relations that would ultimately lead to formal diplomatic relations by 1978.

The Sinai agreements followed the October 6 surprise attack by Egyptian forces on the Bar-Lev Line defending the Suez Canal line in Sinai and the Syrian assault on Israeli positions on the Golan Heights. The Egyptians were able to cross the canal and take Israeli strongholds on its east bank. In the north, Syria penetrated into the Golan Heights. Although Israel managed to repel the attacks on both fronts, it was not accomplished in the lightning fashion of 1956 or 1967. By the time the United Nations (UN) had brokered a cease-fire on October 24, Israel was within artillery range of Damascus and had attacked Egypt west of the canal, splitting the two major Egyptian armies from mutual support. The Egyptian Third Army was cut off east of the canal, and Israeli forces were in position to threaten Cairo. Serious talks now began, this time with significant results in the Sinai.

U.S. secretary of state Henry Kissinger played a key role in structuring the Sinai agreements. He hoped to prevent the Middle Eastern conflict from escalating into a wider war or conflict with the Soviets, and he also wanted to enhance the position of the United States in the Middle East. Keeping these strategic goals in mind, he understood that achieving a durable agreement would require a step-by-step approach, breaking each issue into discrete parts for resolution. He was also willing to be an active participant in the negotiations, focusing on specific tactical goals for each step of the way. This involved frequent trips to the Middle East, soon dubbed shuttle diplomacy, as he sometimes functioned as the conduit for proposals and counterproposals between Israel and Egypt.

The Sinai I process began even before the UN cease-fire. Kissinger's first goal was Soviet agreement to a cease-fire. Kissinger met with Soviet premier Leonid Brezhnev in Moscow on October 21, 1973. Brezhnev agreed to a cease-fire. Kissinger's task was then to attain Israeli agreement. Israel reacted positively but wanted continued U.S. arms shipments and a face-to-face meeting between Kissinger and Israeli prime minister Golda Meir.

The preliminary Israeli agreement led to UN Resolution 338, ordering a cease-fire within 12 hours. This allowed sufficient time for Kissinger to fly to Tel Aviv, where he obtained Meir's commitment. The guns fell silent about 7:00 p.m. on October 22, an hour after Kissinger flew back to Washington.

The lull in the fighting did not last, however. Because the Israeli military had cut off a large part of the Egyptian army east of the Suez Canal, the Egyptians tried to escape. That gave Israel the chance to open fire and further denigrate Egyptian forces. UN Resolution 339, passed on October 23, reaffirmed Resolution 338 and called for a return to the lines of the previous day. The fighting ended on October 24. Intense negotiations continued in Washington and New York, leading to UN Resolution 340 on October 25, again reaffirming Resolution 338 and authorizing a UN buffer force in the Sinai. Both sides then agreed to it. Kissinger's step-by-step process had thus far worked to prevent expansion of the conflict and broker a cease-fire.

Maintaining the cease-fire required more work, and Kissinger led the effort. The first discussions in Washington resulted in the Israeli agreement to allow nonmilitary supplies to reach the Third Egyptian Army in exchange for return of Israeli prisoners held by Egypt. On November 5, 1973, Kissinger set off for the Middle East for several weeks of negotiations. He concentrated on talks with Arab leaders in Morocco, Egypt, Saudi Arabia, and Jordan and dispatched others to treat with Tel Aviv. Another trip in December included meetings between Meir and Kissinger as well as meetings in Cairo, Riyadh, and Damascus in preparation for a general conference on Middle East problems in Geneva on December 21.

Kissinger could not obtain Syrian agreement to participate in the Geneva talks, but his approach did lead to a settlement between Israel and Egypt in the Sinai after Geneva and another set of shuttle diplomacy in January 1974. On January 18, 1974, both the Egyptian and Israeli sides agreed to extend the cease-fire indefinitely. Egypt accepted a UN observer force, reduced its demands to maintain armored forces in the Sinai, and agreed to allow Israeli shipping through the Suez Canal and out of the Gulf of Aqaba. Israel received assurances of major U.S. military aid, while Egypt received a promise from the Americans to work toward implementation of UN Resolution 242, passed in November 1967. Hostilities between Israel and Egypt would not resume, and the United States had now become the dominant superpower in the Middle East.

The question now was how much more could be accomplished in Israeli-Egyptian relations. The negotiations that led to Sinai II would answer this decisively. The cast of players in the negotiations changed, as President Gerald Ford replaced Richard Nixon and Yitzhak Rabin replaced Meir. But Anwar Sadat remained in control of Egypt, and Kissinger remained as secretary of state. As with Nixon, Ford gave Kissinger a great deal of leeway in negotiations. Kissinger continued his course of step-by-step diplomacy with personal involvement in almost all of the negotiations. The Egyptians' goal was for Israel to concede to more concessions. These included withdrawal from the key passes in the Sinai, limiting Israel's intelligence gathering abilities, and the return of oil-producing regions to Egypt. Israel, in turn, demanded a path to ultimate peace with its Arab neighbors, especially Egypt, in return for concessions. Kissinger wanted the United States to remain the major superpower in the Middle East with influence on both sides of the conflict.

After preliminary posturing, diplomacy resumed with meetings among Ford and both Sadat and Rabin in June 1975. Kissinger carefully managed shuttle diplomacy that involved the U.S. ambassador to Egypt traveling back and forth between Cairo and Washington, while Kissinger concentrated his efforts with a visit to Tel Aviv in August 1974. By August 31, he had persuaded both sides to agree to what would become the Sinai II Agreement.

Sinai II was formally signed in Geneva on September 4, 1974. Israel agreed to a return of the oil fields and withdrawal from key Sinai passes. The United States committed itself to continue arms supplies and economic aid to Israel, along with support for a UN presence in the Sinai and support for oil supplies to replace those from the Sinai. Egypt agreed to concessions on Israeli trade through the Suez Canal and the Gulf of Aqaba and to limitations on the size of forces kept in the Sinai. Although Israel was not completely satisfied with the wording of Sinai II regarding U.S. guarantees in case of Soviet intervention in the Middle East, Kissinger had essentially ended any effective Soviet role in the region.

Following direct talks between Sadat and Israeli prime minister Menachem Begin at Camp David in 1978, Egypt and Israel finally made peace with each other on September 17, 1978. That peace has been sustained. In the final analysis, it was Sinai I and Sinai II that paved the way.

DANIEL E. SPECTOR

See also

Begin, Menachem; Camp David Accords; Kissinger, Henry Alfred; Meir, Golda; Rabin, Yitzhak; Sadat, Anwar; Sinai Campaign; Six-Day War; Suez Crisis; United Nations Security Council Resolution 242; United Nations Security Council Resolution 338; Yom Kippur War

References
Herzog, Chaim. *The War of Atonement: October, 1973.* Boston: Little, Brown, 1975.
Quandt, William B. *The Peace Process: American Diplomacy and the Arab-Israeli Conflict since 1967.* Washington, DC: Brookings Institution, 1993.
United States Army. *Area Handbook Series: Israel, a Country Study.* Washington, DC: U.S. Government Printing Office, 1978.

Siniura, Fuad
Born: 1943

Prime minister of Lebanon. Fuad Siniura (Siniora) was born in the coastal city of Sidon, Lebanon, in 1943 and is a Sunni Muslim. A fluent English speaker, he received a master's degree in business administration from the American University of Beirut, where he was a lecturer during the 1970s. His career background is in banking and finance. He held an important post within the Central Bank of Lebanon from 1977 to 1982. He became a financial adviser and subsequently a close political ally to Rafik Hariri, Lebanon's two-time prime minister who was assassinated in 2005. Siniura served in both of Hariri's cabinets, as minister of state from 1992 to 1998 and as finance minister from 2002 to 2004. During his time at the Finance Ministry, critics complained about his handling of the state budget and ballooning national debt. Highlights of Siniura's tenure in the Hariri administration included his efforts to secure international economic assistance for Lebanon in 2002 to combat debt caused by the country's 15-year civil war and enormous reconstruction costs. Siniura is probusiness and a proponent of free trade.

With the elections in May and June 2005, an alliance led by Saad Hariri, the son of Rafik Hariri, won control of Lebanon's National Assembly. Lebanese president Émile Lahoud appointed Siniura prime minister on June 30, 2005, to succeed Najib Mikati. A member of Hariri's Future Movement political party, Siniura formed his cabinet on July 19, 2005. It was the first in more than a decade to have a majority of members who opposed Syrian influence in Lebanon. Syria, which had a military presence in the country for 29 years, withdrew its forces from Lebanon in April 2005. The withdrawal left Lebanon free from foreign occupation by the forces of Israel and Syria (along with Palestinian groups) for the first time in 35 years. The cabinet was also the first to include a minister from Hezbollah.

Upon taking office, Siniura promised to implement a reform program begun by Rafik Hariri. In April 2006 Siniura visited Washington, D.C., and met with President George W. Bush and members of his administration.

In response to the devastating conflict between Hezbollah fighters in Lebanon and Israel that began on July 12, 2006, Siniura presented a seven-point plan in Rome on July 27, 2006. It called for an immediate and comprehensive cease-fire and the release of Lebanese and Israeli prisoners and detainees (through the International Committee of the Red Cross), the withdrawal of Israel's army from Lebanon, the deployment of a United Nations (UN) international force in southern Lebanon to conduct humanitarian and relief work and ensure the stability of the region, the extension of Lebanese armed forces throughout its territory, the enforcement of the armistice agreement signed by Lebanon and Israel in 1949, and the international community's commitment to assist Lebanon with relief, reconstruction, and the rebuilding of its national economy.

Siniura's government lost support during the crisis because of the devastation wrought by the Israeli attacks on the country. Many Lebanese criticized Siniura's tearful addresses to the nation, since it was Hezbollah and not the government that had responded with assistance and because it was understood that some coordination has occurred between the government and the Israelis. Also, Siniura's government was powerless to prevent Lebanese pro-Syrian elements from acting. On November 21, 2006, assassins shot to death

Lebanese prime minister Fuad Siniura during a visit to European Community headquarters in Brussels, Belgium, in March 2006. (AP/Wide World Photos)

Minister of Industry Pierre Germayel, the fourth high-level outspoken critic of Syria to be assassinated since the murder of former Prime Minister Hariri. After repeated calls for changes in the government and the cabinet, six ministers resigned from it in November, bringing about a constitutional and governmental crisis. This was followed by huge public demonstrations and picketing against Siniura for many weeks, with some accompanying minor violence. In February 2007 both the Arab League and the Saudi Arabian government presented compromise plans in an effort to resolve affairs.

SPENCER C. TUCKER

See also

Hezbollah; Lebanon; Lebanon, Israeli Operations against

References

Fisk, Robert. *Pity the Nation: The Abduction of Lebanon.* 4th ed. New York: Nation Books, 2002.

Khalf, Samir. *Civil and Uncivil Violence in Lebanon.* New York: Columbia University Press, 2004.

Siniura, Hanna
Born: November 6, 1937

A Palestinian Christian and peace activist known for his campaign for a negotiated peace between Israel and the Palestinians and for

his publishing activities. Hanna Siniura was born on November 6, 1937, in Jerusalem. He studied pharmacy in India and received a bachelor of science degree in 1969 but quickly decided to go into journalism.

In 1974 Siniura was named editor of the Jerusalem daily newspaper *Al-Fajr* after its editor was kidnapped. He became editor-in-chief of the pro–Palestine Liberation Organization (PLO) newspaper in 1983 and served until the paper ceased publication in 1993. *Al-Fajr* was an Arabic-language paper that appealed mostly to Arab readers. Siniura recognized the need to get the Palestinian side of issues to the larger world, so in 1980 he founded *Al-Fajr Weekly,* an English-language newspaper. The newspaper continued to publish until 1993.

Siniura has worked constantly for a peaceful settlement to the conflict between Israelis and Palestinians. He met privately with Israeli citizens in an effort to foster better relations and also traveled throughout the world and established contacts in Europe and the United States. The articulate businessman was able to serve as an unofficial representative of the PLO. In 1986 he met with U.S. secretary of state George P. Shultz as a representative from the occupied territories. As such, Siniura helped lay the groundwork for U.S. recognition of the PLO at the end of Ronald Reagan's presidency. In 2002 it was rumored that Siniura was being considered for appointment as the PLO's representative in Washington. He obtained U.S. citizenship in 2000, one of the requirements for the position.

Siniura continued his political activities on behalf of the Palestinians and peace efforts. Between 1985 and 1987 he served on a joint Palestinian-Jordanian delegation to international conferences. In 1991 he was appointed as an adviser to the Palestinian delegation to the Madrid Peace Conference. He has also served since 1990 as a member of the Palestinian National Council. He ran unsuccessfully for the Palestinian Legislative Council in January 2006 in an election that swept Hamas into power.

Siniura was philosophical about the Hamas victory, as he believed that it would force Hamas to adopt a more moderate stance. He continues his own private efforts to promote peace and since 1994 has published *The Jerusalem Times,* a weekly English-language newspaper. He also serves as the chairman of the European-Palestinian Chamber of Commerce and was chairman of the Palestinian-American Chamber of Commerce until 2003. He has joined with Jewish peace movement leaders to form the Israel/Palestine Center for Research and Information and the Israeli-Palestinian Peace Tours Company.

Tim J. Watts

See also

Hamas; Madrid Conference; Palestine Liberation Organization; Palestinian Christians; Palestinian Elections of 2006; Palestinian Legislative Council; Palestinian National Council; Peace Movements

References

Hallward, Maia Carter. "Building Space for Peace: Challenging the Boundaries of Israel/Palestine." Unpublished PhD dissertation, American University, Washington, DC, 2006.

Lonning, Dag Jorund. *Bridge over Troubled Water: Inter-Ethnic Dialogue in Israel-Palestine.* Bergen, Norway: Norse Publications, 1995.

Parsons, Nigel Craig. *The Politics of the Palestinian Authority: From Oslo to Al-Aqsa.* London: Routledge, 2003.

Six-Day War
Start Date: June 5, 1967
End Date: June 10, 1967

By May 1967, long-simmering tensions between Israel and its Arab neighbors brought the Middle East to the brink of yet another war, known as the Six-Day War. While Israel's Arab neighbors still clamored for its destruction and refused to recognize it as a sovereign state because of the occupation of the West Bank and the Gaza Strip and the dispossession of the Palestinians, military setbacks in 1948 and 1956 had left even the most belligerent Arab leaders reluctant to directly engage Israel in a contest of force. Instead, they allowed the conflict to proceed via low-intensity state-sponsored terrorist attacks against Israel. Yasser Arafat's Palestinian Fatah movement led the way. Operating from Syria's Golan Heights, Fatah and other insurgents staged daily attacks against Israeli farmers living in the north.

Estimated Casualties of the 1967 Six-Day War

	Israel	Arab Nations
KIA	679	21,000
WIA	2,563	45,000
POW	15	6,000
Aircraft Lost	36	452

For years Israel managed the undeclared war on a retaliatory basis, staging its own overt and covert counterstrikes on guerrilla camps and villages in the Golan Heights and in Jordan. An Arab attempt to divert the flow of the Jordan River and seriously reduce Israel's water supply resulted in a series of Israel Defense Forces (IDF) attacks against the diversion sites in Syria in 1965.

On November 13, 1966, the IDF launched a large-scale attack against Es Samu in Jordan, a Palestinian refugee village that the Israelis believed was a base for Syrian terrorists. On April 7, 1967, a major aerial battle over the Golan Heights resulted in the downing of six Syrian MiG-21s. The ongoing cycle of strikes back and forth across the border seemingly had become institutionalized by the late spring of 1967.

With the United States heavily engaged in Vietnam, the leaders of the Soviet Union saw an opportunity to alter the balance of power in the Middle East to favor their own client states, including Egypt and Syria. On May 13, 1967, the Soviets provided the Egyptians an intelligence report falsely indicating that Israeli forces were building up along the Syrian border. The motivation behind the Soviet disinformation campaign also may have been an attempt to create problems for West Germany, then a strong supporter of Israel.

Egyptian president Gamal Abdel Nasser, mindful of the Israeli attack 11 years earlier and fearful of a future attack but also unrealistically hoping to get the best of Israel, announced that Egypt would stand alongside Syria in the present crisis. Israel's protestations that the Soviet report was untrue fell on deaf ears, as there was little reason for the Egyptians to believe the Israelis. Politically, Nasser sought to exploit the situation as much as his Soviet sponsors, and he would not allow the opportunity to pass. Scholars disagree over whether Nasser actually intended to go to war. Most believe that he thought he could bluff his way through the crisis without actual recourse to arms, extricating himself diplomatically.

Nasser met with members of the Arab press and proposed closing the Strait of Tiran to Israeli shipping, a step that would severely disrupt the Israeli economy. Nasser certainly should have known that Israel, which used the straits as its primary access to the Arabian Sea and the Far East, could not allow it to be closed and would be forced to react militarily. Nasser probably assumed that the United States would refuse to support Israel and that the Soviet Union in turn would support Egypt and its allies.

Initially, Nasser's gambit appears to have been as much bluff as substance. If his threat to close the straits forced Israel to withdraw its allegedly mounting forces along the Syrian border, he could emerge as a regional hero without even risking a military

Six-Day War, 1967

N

LEBANON

Damascus ✪
Sassa
Kuneitra

GOLAN
HEIGHTS

SYRIA

Mediterranean
Sea

Nazareth
Jenin
Tulkarm
Nablus
WEST
BANK
Tel Aviv
Damia
Bridge
Amman ✪
Jericho
Jerusalem ✪
Allenby
Bridge
Bethlehem
GAZA
STRIP
Gaza
Hebron
Dead
Sea
Khan Yunis
Port Said
Beersheba
Port Fouad
Ras el-Aish
El Arish
Kantara
Abu Ageila
Ismailia
Lake Timsah
NEGEV

JORDAN

Bir Gafgafa

Bitter
Lakes
Suez
S I N A I

Kuntilla

E G Y P T
Eilat
Aqaba

Abu Zeneima

EGYPT

SAUDI

ARABIA

Tor

Gulf of Suez

Gulf of Aqaba

0   25   50 mi
0   25   50 km

Sharm al-Sheikh
Strait
of Tiran

Suez Canal

Jordan River

Israeli territory, 1949–Jun 4, 1967
Israeli conquests, Jun 5–10, 1967

32°E   33°E   34°E   35°E   36°E   37°E

33°N

32°N

31°N

30°N

29°N

28°N

Egyptian field marshal Abdel Hakim Amer speaking to Egyptian Air Force pilots on May 20, 1967, in Egypt less than a month before Israel's devastating air strikes. (Bettmann/Corbis)

confrontation. If the Israelis did not react, he could close the straits and force Israel to take the next step, in which case he still could play the part of hero and protector of the Arab world. Nasser's options, however, disappeared on May 22 when Egyptian minister of defense Field Marshal Abdel Hakim Amer, acting under the president's orders, directed Egyptian forces to close the Strait of Tiran the next day. Knowing full well that Israel would have to go to war to reopen the straits, Nasser issued orders for the Egyptian military to prepare for war. Any negotiation or compromise over the situation alleged to be developing along the Syrian border was now moot.

Israel, meanwhile, continued to maintain its innocence regarding affairs with Syria but simultaneously signaled its determination to keep open the Strait of Tiran. Hoping to find an international solution to the crisis, Israel sent Foreign Minister Abba Eban to Washington on May 26. President Lyndon B. Johnson, however, had little to offer. On the one hand, Johnson steadfastly refused to assist Israel if it initiated hostilities. On the other hand, the U.S. promise to look for a coalition of international partners to help in keeping the straits open offered only the remotest possibility of success. The United States supported a British proposal for an international maritime force, but only Britain and the Netherlands offered to contribute ships to it. Israel's diplomatic initiatives appeared to be going nowhere.

In Egypt, meanwhile, the military mobilizations swept Nasser and his generals closer to war with Israel. On May 16 Nasser ordered the United Nations Emergency Force (UNEF) to leave the Sinai, and United Nations (UN) secretary-general U Thant complied. Formed at the conclusion of the Suez Crisis in 1956, the UNEF had maintained a relatively demilitarized Sinai for more than 10 years.

Jordan's King Hussein arrived in Cairo on May 30, 1967, to finalize a tripartite alliance among Egypt, Jordan, and Syria. As Nasser declared, "Our basic objective will be the destruction of Israel." The alliance strengthened Egypt's position, but Nasser encountered new obstacles from his Soviet sponsors. The Soviet Union, having first set the chain of events in motion, now urged Nasser to show restraint. The Soviets were responding to a direct hot-line message sent to the Kremlin by President Johnson on May 26. In a discussion similar to that between the Israeli ambassador and the Johnson administration, the Soviets on May 27 insisted to the Egyptians that they not strike first.

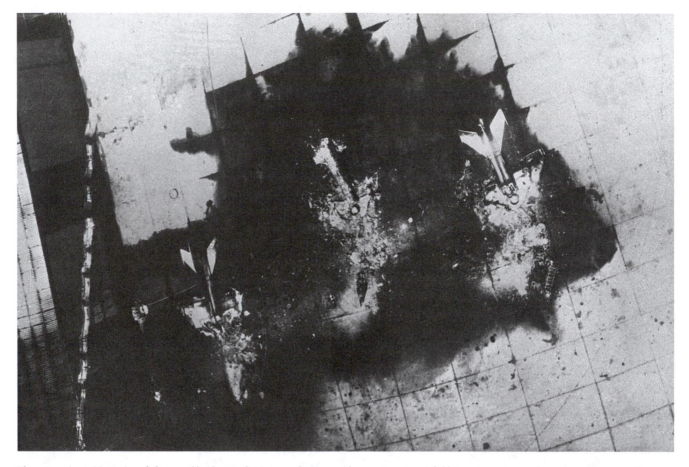

Three Egyptian MiG-21 aircraft destroyed by the Israeli Air Force during a raid on an Egyptian airfield, June 5, 1967. (Israeli Government Press Office)

Nasser countered that a surprise first strike by Israel could neutralize Egypt's numerical superiority. The Soviets remained firm. Despite having Israel surrounded—Syria to the north, Jordan to the east, and Egypt to the south—and outnumbered, Egypt and its allies would have to wait for Israel to initiate hostilities. Meanwhile, other Arab states, including Iraq, Algeria, and Sudan, began mobilizing.

Egypt and Israel both subsequently played a waiting game in which Egypt appeared to have the advantage. Each day brought the Israeli economy closer to the brink of disaster. The mobilization for war alone had a catastrophic impact on Israel's economy, which ground to a near halt as all males between the ages of 16 and 55 entered active service. Israel recognized that the waiting game could defeat the country even more readily than a war. Unlike Israel's economy, that of Egypt remained unaffected by the closing of the Strait of Tiran. Nonetheless, the prospect of war was destabilizing to Egypt, whose economy was in difficult times with peasant complaints, riots, and inconclusive reforms. A war, if it proved disastrous, could mean the end of the regime.

On June 2, 1967, Israel tried the diplomatic route one final time, sending a special envoy to meet again with the Johnson administration. The distant hope of an international flotilla capable of keeping the Strait of Tiran open had by now disappeared altogether, with Japan and Canada reluctant to join and with the United States unwilling to take action unilaterally. Perhaps to reassure its Middle Eastern ally, the United States revealed to the Israeli envoy the results of a U.S. Defense Department analysis, which concluded that Israel could defeat Egypt, Jordan, and Syria within two to three weeks even if it allowed them to strike first. Israel, however, could not continue to wait for its enemies to strike first.

Following a heated exchange with his advisers on June 4, Israeli prime minister Levi Eshkol finally authorized a preemptive strike against Egypt despite the absence of U.S. support for such an action. For weeks Egypt had moved large numbers of armored units into the Sinai Peninsula in preparation for a clash with Israel. Israeli defense minister Moshe Dayan and IDF chief of staff Yitzhak Rabin, however, planned to bypass Egypt's armor and strike instead at its air force. If Israel could neutralize or even seriously degrade Egyptian airpower, Dayan and Rabin were confident that Israel would prevail in the Sinai.

The Egyptian Army had a nominal strength of 150,000 men, but more than 50,000 of its best troops were tied down in the civil war in Yemen. Nasser must have realized the impact of this and, for that reason, probably did not plan to enter into a war. The IDF had a core force of 50,000 highly trained troops plus more than 200,000 mobilized reservists. The Israeli Air Force (IAF) had only about 200 combat aircraft against 420 Egyptian planes, mostly relatively modern Soviet models. The IAF's chief advantage lay in its highly trained and efficient ground crews' ability to turn their aircraft around very quickly after each sortie, allowing each IAF aircraft to launch up to four times per day as opposed to the one or two sorties per day on average for aircraft in the Arab air forces.

At dawn on the morning of June 5, 180 Israeli aircraft launched against targets in Egypt and the Sinai. Coming in low and out of the sun to avoid Egyptian radar and visual detection, the Israeli strike force caught the Egyptians by surprise. Trapped on the ground when the IAF began to bomb and strafe the airfields, Egyptian aircraft were sitting ducks. Within minutes, all of Egypt's airfields were under attack. By noon, Egypt had lost more than 300 aircraft and 100 pilots. The Israelis lost only 19 aircraft.

The loss of Egypt's air force had an immediate and dramatic impact on the balance of power. The Egyptian forces in the Sinai consisted of some 100,000 troops, more than 900 tanks, 1,100 armored personnel carriers, and 1,000 artillery pieces, all organized into seven divisions. The IDF fielded some 70,000 troops and 700 tanks organized into three armored divisions under the IDF's Southern Command. Although Egypt outnumbered the Israelis on the ground, the absence of air support left Egyptian armor extremely vulner-

able to Israeli attacks from above. Egypt suffered tremendous losses. When the IDF armored division under Major General Ariel Sharon broke through at Abu Ageila, Egypt's Marshal Amer ordered a general withdrawal, but the damage was already done. Israel thoroughly routed the Egyptians. By the end of the fighting in the Sinai, Egypt had lost 80 percent of its military equipment and 11,500 troops killed, 20,000 wounded, and 5,500 captured. The IDF had, by contrast, lost only 338 troops killed.

The war might have ended with Egypt losing the Sinai Peninsula and the Gaza Strip were it not for the critical lack of communications between Egypt and Jordan. Shortly after the surprise attack on the Egyptian airfields, Israel notified Jordan's King Hussein that its conflict lay with Egypt and that it had no interest in Jordan so long as Hussein kept his forces out of the fray. Simultaneously, however, Hussein received Egyptian state-run radio broadcasts claiming staggering victories and predicting the end of the Israeli nation. Hussein decided that the Israeli communiqué was a desperate ploy and ordered his forces to attack the Israeli-held West Jerusalem. Only then did Nasser admit to his ally what actually was occurring in the Sinai. By then it was too late for Hussein to withdraw from the conflict.

Israeli prime minister Eshkol ordered the IDF to attack on June 6 to seize all of Jerusalem, including the Old City, and force the

Prime Minister Levi Eshkol and General Shlomo Erell in an Israeli fast patrol boat in the Strait of Tiran, June 20, 1967. (Ilan Bruner/Israeli Government Press Office)

Jordanian military completely out of the West Bank. The Jordanian Army had 55,000 troops and 300 Western-built tanks, organized into 11 brigades. The Jordanian Air Force, however, had only 20 relatively obsolescent British aircraft. IDF's Central Command had only 5 brigades.

Israeli air superiority was decisive once more. Within days Israel successfully pushed the Jordanian forces back across the Jordan River. Israeli paratroopers entered the Old City of Jerusalem on June 7. The defeat was a staggering blow to Jordan, which lost almost 7,000 dead and more than 12,000 wounded. The Israelis lost only about 300 dead. King Hussein called upon Nasser for help, but the Egyptian president, his military machine little more than broken and twisted wreckage, could offer little assistance. Nasser did, however, offer a ruse that if successful might bring the Soviet Union to the rescue.

Since Israel had struck first, Egypt could claim to have honored its earlier agreement with the Soviets. The agreement, however, failed to specify what support, if any, the Soviets would provide. Nasser assured Hussein that the Soviet Union would waste no time becoming involved if it believed that the United States already had done so. Thus emerged what some later dubbed the "Great Lie." In calling upon the Soviets for support, Nasser alleged that the United States had led the initial air strikes against Egypt. King Hussein supported Nasser's claim, and the war appeared on the verge of becoming a major Cold War superpower confrontation.

The Soviets were disappointed that their plans to change the Middle East balance of power had failed. Israel now controlled the Sinai Peninsula, the Gaza Strip, and the West Bank and had sent its forces north to the Golan Heights. Initially giving credence to the Egyptian claim that the Americans had been involved, the Soviet Union planned to defend Syria. Soviet help in retaking the West Bank and Sinai would follow.

When the Johnson administration learned that the Soviets were mobilizing air units for possible commitment to the region, President Johnson ordered the *Independence* carrier group in the Mediterranean to alter course and head for Israel. Then, in one of the most controversial incidents of the war, on June 8 IAF aircraft attacked and nearly sank USS *Liberty,* an American electronic intelligence ship operating just outside of Egypt's territorial waters, 13 nautical miles off El Arish. The Israelis later claimed that they had committed a tragic error amid the fog of war, but much about the incident still remains unclear.

The U.S. message to the Soviet Union was unequivocal. If the Soviets sought to raise the stakes, the United States would match them. Neither superpower relished the prospect of direct confrontation —the Cuban Missile Crisis had taken place a scant five years earlier— but neither wanted to be perceived as weak. For the United States, that meant standing firm against the Soviets publicly while pursuing diplomatic alternatives through the UN. In resorting to the UN, the Johnson administration sought to end the conflict multilaterally before it could escalate.

While the Israeli ambassador to the UN had little trouble justifying Israel's actions against Egypt, the UN demanded an immediate withdrawal from the West Bank and an end to hostilities with Syria in the Golan Heights. Arab delegates demanded an Israeli withdrawal on all fronts of the war.

For Israel, however, the opportunity to seize control of the strategic Golan Heights and thereby deny its use as a terrorist staging area was too important to pass up. Consequently, Eshkol ordered his country's UN ambassador to stall for time and to claim that Israel had no further designs on Arab territory. When President Johnson demanded that the Israeli ambassador convey the American insistence to withdraw from the Golan Heights, Eshkol shrewdly claimed to be unable to understand the message because of problems with the phone lines.

As the situation stabilized on the IDF's southern and central fronts, Dayan was able to turn his attention to the Golan Heights and Syria. The IAF had already destroyed some two-thirds of the Syrian Air Force in a series of air strikes executed on the evening of June 5. The Syrians had 75,000 troops organized into nine brigades. The IDF's Northern Command attacked with four brigades, and by June 9 they had broken through to the Golan Heights' high ground. By the morning of June 10 Israel controlled the Golan Heights, having lost only 141 soldiers killed. The Syrians lost 2,500 dead, 5,000 wounded, and almost all of their tanks and artillery that had been on the Golan Heights.

Having occupied the Sinai, the Gaza Strip, the West Bank, and the Golan Heights, Israel prepared to face the UN. With the fighting over, the United States and the Soviet Union pulled back from the brink. By this point, Soviet intelligence had concluded that the U.S. carrier group in the Mediterranean had been too far removed to have participated in the early morning attacks of June 5, 1967, as Nasser had claimed. It had been the IAF's impressive sortie turnaround rate that had contributed significantly to the initial belief that more than just the 200 Israeli aircraft had been involved in the first day's strikes.

The Soviets' ensuing coolness toward their Middle Eastern allies for having maneuvered them into a direct confrontation with the United States ensured that Soviet support for recovering the lost territories would be a very long time in coming. The Soviet Union did, however, sever diplomatic relations with Israel, and Soviet-sponsored regimes in Eastern Europe quickly followed suit. Although yet another cease-fire officially ended the 1967 conflict, the first formal peace treaty between Israel and an Arab nation remained 12 years in the future.

The defeat was regarded as an utter disaster both in Egypt and the Arab world. In Egypt, Nasser resigned but then was returned to power by popular intervention. He then blamed his military advisers for the debacle. In the Arab world, people were so angry that they entered into a new stage of resistance against their own governments and elites. The defeat also led to a militant period of irregular armed struggle against Israel.

The war between the Arabs and the Israelis meanwhile simply entered another stage, later called the War of Attrition. As the protracted fighting dragged on, the diplomats continued to wrangle. Arab and Soviet demands that Israel return the captured territories did not subside with the signing of the cease-fire. By the end of the year the UN passed Resolution 242, which called upon the Israelis to return the captured territories. The resolution also stipulated that the Arab nations should negotiate and sign peace treaties with Israel. Neither the Israelis nor the Arab states, however, were in much of a mood for compromise.

Israel argued that because of its national security requirements it should not be required to return the territories. By more than doubling the territory under its control, Israel for the first time now had viable geographic buffer zones between it and most of its Arab enemies. Meaningful peace treaties would have to precede any discussion of territorial returns. The Arab states predictably countered that they would not consider peace treaties until after Israel returned the territories. Israel retorted that no nation had ever willingly returned territory that it had captured in a war, and Israel ignored Resolution 242 until the 1993 Oslo Agreements.

The Six-Day War had four long-term effects. First, Egypt and Syria quickly resumed the low-intensity conflict that had preceded the war, often using state-sponsored terrorism to execute attacks too risky for their own militaries. Israel's relations with its immediate neighbors had come full circle.

Second, outraged by UN impotence and Arab reluctance to confront Israel's superior military, armed groups such as Arafat's Fatah along with disorganized refugees called for a revolution. The armed groups and their political counterparts argued about tactics and methodology, with the most radical, violent, and antielitist elements holding sway for approximately the next six years. This was the origin of the high-profile media-focused attacks mounted by various Palestinian groups.

Third, Israel's control of the contested territories greatly complicated the long-term prospects for peace. Right-wing Israelis and ultraorthodox Jews considered a surrender of land that had belonged to biblical Israel (i.e., the West Bank and the Gaza Strip) to be completely out of the question. This, in turn, created a huge problem for Israel in retaining its essential identity as both a Jewish state and a democracy. With some 600,000 more Arabs now under Israeli control and with long-term demographic trends in the region favoring the Arabs, their inclusion in the nation's political process would eventually undercut the state's Jewish character. However, denying the Arabs full political rights would also erode Israel's democratic foundations.

Fourth, Israeli settlements subsequently established in the occupied territories have since become a force of their own and a major fault line in Israeli domestic politics. To this day the settlements cast a long shadow over any prospects of trading land for peace with the Arabs.

During the 40 years following the Six-Day War, the Gaza Strip, the West Bank, and the Golan Heights remained under Israeli control. Israel formally annexed East Jerusalem and the Golan Heights, although no other nations have given formal recognition to these actions. Under the Camp David Accords, Israel returned the Sinai Peninsula to Egypt in 1978. The Israelis finally withdrew from Gaza in 2005 but continued to launch military incursions against terrorist groups as they thought necessary.

While Israel, Egypt, and Jordan are finally officially at peace, Syria's relations with Israel remain strained at best. The West Bank and the Gaza Strip remain breeding grounds for anti-Israeli sentiment and direct action, most notably the First Intifada (1987–1993) and the Second (al-Aqsa) Intifada (2000–2004). As with the Arab world of the 1960s and 1970s, today's Palestinians insist that there can be no peace until Israel returns the occupied territories to Palestinian control. Israel maintains, as it has in the past, that peace and security must precede any cession of territory. And Israel must still come to terms with itself over the issue of the settlements.

BRYAN VIZZINI AND DAVID T. ZABECKI

See also

Aqaba, Gulf of; Arafat, Yasser; Attrition, War of; Dayan, Moshe; Eban, Abba Solomon; Eshkol, Levi; Fatah; Gaza Strip; Golan Heights; Hussein, King of Jordan; Israeli Air Strikes Beginning the Six-Day War; Jerusalem; Johnson, Lyndon Baines; *Liberty* Incident; Nasser, Gamal Abdel; Palestine Liberation Organization; Rabin, Yitzhak; Settlements, Israeli; Sharon, Ariel; Suez Crisis; Terrorism; West Bank

References

Bowen, Jeremy. *Six Days: How the 1967 War Shaped the Middle East.* New York: Thomas Dunne, 2005.

Finkelstein, Norman G. *The Rise and Fall of Palestine: A Personal Account of the Intifada Years.* Minneapolis: University of Minnesota Press, 1996.

Friedman, Thomas. *From Beirut to Jerusalem.* New York: Anchor Books, 1995.

Goldschmidt, Arthur. *Modern Egypt: The Formation of a Nation State.* Boulder, CO: Westview, 2004.

Herzog, Chaim. *The Arab-Israeli Wars: War and Peace in the Middle East from the War of Independence to Lebanon.* Westminster, MD: Random House, 1984.

Morris, Benny. *Righteous Victims: A History of the Zionist-Arab Conflict, 1881–2001.* New York: Vintage Books, 2001.

Netanyahu, Benjamin. *A Durable Peace: Israel and Its Place among the Nations.* New York: Warner, 2000.

Ochsenwald, William, and Sydney Nettleson Fisher. *The Middle East: A History.* Boston: McGraw-Hill, 2004.

Oren, Michael B. *Six Days of War: June 1967 and the Making of the Modern Middle East.* Novato, CA: Presidio, 2003.

Smilansky, Yizhar

Born: September 21, 1916
Died: August 21, 2006

Israeli author and politician. Yizhar Smilansky was born on September 21, 1916, in Rehovat, then part of Ottoman-controlled Palestine. His parents had been Russian immigrants and were among the Zionist intelligentsia who had begun to arrive in Palestine near the turn of the century. Smilansky usually wrote under the name S. Yizhar.

Israeli writer and politician Yizhar Smilansky, September 1951. (Israeli Government Press Office)

Smilansky became well known—and quite controversial—for his sharp critiques of the Israeli military and for his peace overtures. In the 1930s he taught at the Ben Shemen Youth Village. In 1938 he published his first work, a novella entitled *Ephraim Returns to Alfalfa*. During the 1948–1949 Israeli War of Independence he served as an intelligence officer. When the war ended in 1949 he was elected to the Knesset (Israeli parliament) representing the Mapai Labor Party. He served in the Knesset until 1966 while continuing to write. Following his political career, he attended Harvard University for a time and earned a PhD in literature from the Hebrew University of Jerusalem, where he also taught.

Smilansky was a supporter of the Zionist cause. Modest and unassuming in the political realm, his greatest cause as a Knesset member was land preservation. Yet his writing revealed a mind deeply conflicted and sometimes disturbed by modern Israeli politics. He was a critic of Israeli government policies and of Israeli society in general, positions that made many of his literary works controversial. Some of his first works involved the 1948–1949 war and the many acts of cruelty that Israeli soldiers and civilians inflicted on innocent Arab Palestinians. In one such story about the war, a Jewish character reminds the reader that the Jews were a people accustomed to perpetual exile. How then, he asks, can they now be sending another people into exile? Smilansky's work transcends the Israeli condition, however. In its broadest context, many of his books and stories deal with the vagaries and cruelty of modern warfare and are designed to penetrate the consciences of those involved in it.

Some critics consider Smilansky to have been a great stylist in the tradition of James Joyce, while others have dismissed his writing style as overwrought. Much of his work melds fiction, biography, autobiography, geography, and climate to paint the portrait of complete and grittily real scenes. There can be little doubt, however, that Smilansky's work is polarizing. Some in Israel have viewed his writing as bordering on traitorous. Others, however, have lauded it for its great sensibility and flowing prose. Between 1961 and 1992 Smilansky all but ceased writing long, expository works and concentrated on short essays and children's literature. In 1992 he published a long semiautobiographical novel set in pre-Israeli Palestine that was very well received. In 1998 he famously called for a "peace revolt" in Israel. Smilansky died in Gedera, Israel, on August 21, 2006.

Paul G. Pierpaoli Jr.

See also
Literature of the Arab-Israeli Wars

References
Abkel-Malek, Kamal, and David C. Jacobson, eds. *Israeli and Palestinian Identities in History and Literature.* New York: Palgrave Macmillan, 1999.
Ramras-Rauch, Gila. *The Arab in Israeli Literature.* Bloomington: Indiana University Press, 1989.

Smuts, Jan Christian
Born: May 24, 1870
Died: September 11, 1950

South African politician, prime minister, British field marshal, and staunch friend of the Zionist cause. Born to Afrikaner parents on a farm near Riebeck West, Cape Colony, on May 24, 1870, Jan Christian Smuts won highest honors at Christ's College, Cambridge. He then practiced law in Cape Town. During the South African War (Boer War) of 1899–1902 he fought against the British, leading Boer commandos as a general. Following the war, Smuts, who was a close ally of Louis Botha, helped draft the constitution of the Union of South Africa and sought accommodation with the British.

When World War I began, Smuts was defense minister under Prime Minister Botha and headed the southern offensive that took control of German Southwest Africa (the future Namibia) from the Germans. Made a British Army general, Smuts then commanded British operations in East Africa. Before the end of the war he had joined the British Imperial War Cabinet as minister of air and helped to organize the Royal Air Force, the world's first independent air force. A deeply religious Christian, Smuts found in the Bible inspi-

Jan Smuts, South African prime minister, British field marshal, and Zionist. (Library of Congress)

Nazi sympathizers, although he refused to suppress his fascist opponents completely.

Longtime friend British prime minister Winston Churchill frequently consulted Smuts on strategic matters. Smuts was a strong advocate of holding on to Egypt no matter what the cost. Thus, South African forces, following their participation in the East Africa campaign, deployed to Egypt in late 1941. The next year they helped to take the island of Madagascar. In 1941 Smuts was made an honorary British field marshal.

Smuts was also a staunch advocate of the formation of the United Nations (UN). He wrote its preamble and helped draft its charter. In April 1945 he attended the San Francisco conference and was thus one of the UN's official founders. His internationalist outlook undoubtedly cost him political support at home, and in 1946 he retired following his defeat in the general elections. Smuts died at his home near Pretoria on September 11, 1950.

SPENCER C. TUCKER

See also

Balfour Declaration; Churchill, Sir Winston; United Kingdom, Middle East Policy

References

Hancock, W. K. *Smuts*. 2 vols. Cambridge: Cambridge University Press, 1962, 1968.

Ingham, Kenneth. *Jan Christian Smuts: The Conscience of a South African*. New York: St. Martin's, 1986.

Kraus, René. *Old Master: The Life of Jan Christian Smuts*. New York: Dutton, 1944.

Society of Muslim Brothers

See Muslim Brotherhood

Sokolow, Nahum
Born: January 10, 1859
Died: May 17, 1936

One of the most prolific writers to work in Hebrew in the modern era and a major leader of the Zionist movement that worked to promote Jewish settlements in Palestine. Nahum Sokolow was born on January 10, 1859, in Wyszogrod in Russian Poland. He came from a rabbinic family and was destined to become a rabbi. He was an excellent student and displayed a command of traditional Jewish learning, and most unusually for a Russian Jew of his generation, he also studied science, the arts, and world literature. He was fluent in German, French, English, Italian, Polish, and Spanish as well as Hebrew and Yiddish.

Sokolow contributed articles to various Hebrew publications, especially the weekly Hebrew newspaper *Ha-Zefirah*. He moved to Warsaw in 1880 and became a regular columnist in *Ha-Zefirah*. In 1886 he took over as managing editor and turned the newspaper into a daily. Thanks to his facile writing, *Ha-Zefirah* changed from

ration for his support of a Jewish claim to Palestine, and he participated in the drafting of the 1917 Balfour Declaration by the British government that called for the establishment of a Jewish homeland in Palestine. Smuts represented South Africa during the 1919 Paris Peace Conference, where he supported the League of Nations and helped develop the mandate system.

On the death of Botha, Smuts became prime minister of South Africa in August 1919. He remained in that post until the Nationalists attained power in 1924. In 1929 after publication of the Passfield White Paper, Smuts wrote an angry letter to the British government in which he accused it of reneging on the Balfour Declaration. Smuts continued to advocate free and unrestricted Jewish immigration to Palestine.

In 1933 Smuts formed a coalition with Nationalist Party leader James Barry Hertzog and served as deputy prime minister. On the outbreak of war with Germany, Hertzog favored South African neutrality. Smuts, who advocated war with Germany, narrowly defeated Hertzog in Parliament and became prime minister again in September 1939. Smuts was also minister of defense, and from June 1940 he commanded South African armed forces during World War II. Despite his unprecedented power, during the conflict Smuts overcame significant opposition to his policies from

Nahum Sokolow, prolific Jewish author and Zionist leader. (Library of Congress)

a plodding informative newspaper to a popular and lively source of literature, opinions, news about the gentile world, and scientific advances.

Sokolow also directed his efforts into other projects. He wrote and edited journals in Polish and Yiddish for Jews who spoke those languages, while his poems, essays, and stories were published in other journals. He even published the first Hebrew literary annual, *HeAsif*, between 1885 and 1894.

Sokolow also wrote a number of books on Jewish topics. Early works included a Jewish geography and an anthology on anti-Semitism. In 1901 he published *L'Maranan V'Rabbanan* (To Our Masters and Teachers). The book was an appeal to religious Jews who usually opposed Zionism to understand why the movement did not conflict with their beliefs. It proved to be an effective argument and persuaded many traditionalist Jews not to oppose Zionism. With his roots in both aspects of Jewish society, Sokolow was able to appeal to both traditionalist and secular Jewish readers. When Theodor Herzl's book *Old-New Land* was published in 1902, Sokolow translated it into Hebrew with the title *Tel Aviv* (Hill of Spring). The title inspired Zionists to name their main settlement in Palestine Tel Aviv.

Sokolow's conversion to Zionism occurred in 1897 when he attended the First Zionist Congress in Basle. He had previously been neutral on emigration for Palestine, but he was inspired by the political agenda of Zionism. In 1907 he became secretary-general of the World Zionist Organization (WZO). He broke with David Wolffsohn, the WZO's president, in 1909 because Sokolow supported agricultural settlements in Palestine. Sokolow was selected in 1911 as a member of the Zionist Executive and spent most of his time trying to win support for Zionism from around the world. He gained many followers in the United States and Great Britain in particular. During World War I he helped lay the groundwork for the 1917 Balfour Declaration and received formal pro-Zionist pledges from France and the Vatican.

At the Paris Peace Conference of 1919, Sokolow headed the Jewish delegation. His speeches argued for the Zionist cause but also for the rights of Jews in the newly formed countries of Eastern Europe. At the League of Nations he headed the recognized delegation of Jews throughout the world, and he was elected at the 1920 Zionist Congress to head the WZO along with Ezer Weizmann. Sokolow traveled the world extensively, raising support for the Zionist movement among Jews and non-Jews. He met with world leaders including Winston Churchill, Benito Mussolini, and Pope Pius XI. Sokolow succeeded Weizmann as president of the WZO in 1931 and followed most of his predecessor's policies. Sokolow hoped that the Jewish Agency's political and economic policies would promote good relations between Jews and Arabs. When Weizmann was re-elected in 1935, Sokolow returned to fund-raising. Sokolow died in London on May 17, 1936. As a mark of respect, his body was interred in Jerusalem on Mount Herzl.

Tim J. Watts

See also

Balfour Declaration; Herzl, Theodor; Jewish Agency for Israel; World Zionist Organization; Zionism

References

Bauer, Ela. *Between Poles and Jews: The Development of Nahum Sokolow's Political Thought.* Jerusalem: Hebrew University Magnes Press, 2005.

Kling, Simcha. *Nachum Sokolow: Servant of His People.* New York: Herzl, 1960.

Sokolow, Florian, and Joseph Leftwich. *Nahum Sokolow: Life and Legend.* London: Jewish Chronicle Publications, 1975.

Somoa Raid
Event Date: November 13, 1966

Israeli raid on the Jordanian town of Somoa, designed to end cross-border Palestinian raids against Israel. At 5:30 a.m. on November 13, 1966, a large force of Israeli armored vehicles crossed the border into Jordan, heading for the small West Bank town of Somoa. A mechanized infantry brigade, consisting of 40 half-tracks and 400 infantrymen, was supported by 10 tanks and air cover, making it the single-largest strike force organized by Israel since the 1956 Sinai Campaign.

The events of that November morning were prompted by Israel's growing frustration with cross-border raids carried out by Palestinian guerrillas. Only a day earlier, an attack, reportedly the 70th since January 1965, resulted in the deaths of three Israeli border policemen when their patrol vehicle struck a land mine planted by Palestinian infiltrators. Determined to eliminate the staging areas from which such raids originated, Israeli commanders opted to retaliate more forcefully than before by launching a bold daylight strike deep into the West Bank. Advancing nearly four miles to Somoa, the armored force encountered no resistance en route. Once in town, the soldiers set about demolishing houses and municipal buildings in an effort to punish the local residents for supporting or condoning Palestinian attacks. Intent on driving a wedge between the civilian population and the guerrillas, the Israelis hoped to expose the weakness of the local resistance and convince the local people to support King Hussein and seek the protection of the Jordanian Army.

But the political outcome of the military operation served only to complicate the existing regional tensions and further aggravate the animosity between Israel and its Arab neighbors. Rather than a bloodless punitive raid into the West Bank, the Israeli incursion deteriorated into a fierce firefight that saw numerous casualties among the civilian population (3 killed and 17 wounded). By the end of the day dozens of buildings in Somoa lay in ruins, and a company of soldiers from the Royal Jordanian Hittin Infantry Brigade was severely bloodied after being caught in an Israeli ambush. The 100-man Jordanian contingent suffered more than 50 percent casualties (15 dead and 37 wounded) and lost 15 vehicles, while the Israelis sustained only 1 fatality and 10 wounded in the entire operation.

Israeli hopes of turning the local people against the Palestinian guerrillas were entirely dashed. Instead of blaming the Palestinian fighters for bringing about the forceful Israeli attack, the people turned their resentment against the Jordanian government for its failure to provide adequate protection along the border. The raid fueled a deepening rift between the Palestinian population and the Jordanian monarchy, and as pressure mounted on King Hussein to solidify his commitment to the defense of Arab lands, Jordan soon entered into a defense pact with Egypt. In short, the Somoa raid convinced the Jordanian leadership that its only option was to align itself fully with Egypt and Syria in any future conflict.

The Israeli incursion into Jordanian territory also served to further isolate the State of Israel as the United Nations (UN), including all five permanent members of the Security Council, voted to censure Israel for the attack.

JONAS KAUFFELDT

See also

Hussein, King of Jordan; Israel; Jordan

References

Hammel, Eric. *Six Days in June: How Israel Won the 1967 Arab-Israeli War*. New York: Scribner, 1992.
Mutawi, Samir A. *Jordan in the 1967 War*. Cambridge: Cambridge University Press, 1987.
Oren, Michael B. *Six Days of War: June 1967 and the Making of the Modern Middle East*. Novato, CA: Presidio, 2003.

South Lebanon Army

An Israeli trained and funded Lebanese Christian militia that grew out of the Lebanese Civil War (1975–1976) and helped control and administer the Israeli security zone in southern Lebanon from 1982 to 2000. The South Lebanon Army (SLA), also known as the Free Lebanon Army, numbered 5,000–10,000 fighters at its peak strength in the early 1980s.

Conflict between the Palestine Liberation Organization (PLO) and the broader Palestinian Resistance Movement and some elements in Lebanon began to grow as the Palestinian resistance increased attacks on northern Israel. The Lebanese Civil War began on April 13, 1975, when Phalangist (Christian militia) forces ambushed a bus carrying Palestinians back from a political rally. Syria entered the war in May 1976 on the side of the Lebanese National Movement, an alliance of Druze, Muslims, and some Christians after the Lebanese Army began to disintegrate in March 1976. Lebanese Army major Saad Haddad, whose battalion had been allowed to withdraw after being besieged by the PLO in southern Lebanon, joined 400 Christian soldiers who occupied the southern Lebanon border town of Qlaya since leaving the Lebanese Army in 1968 in response to the growing power of the PLO. This new group became known as the Free Lebanon Army (FLA), and its members were still drawing Lebanese government salaries until 1979.

Although a cease-fire in November 1976 brought some calm to Lebanon, the many internal Lebanese issues that had actually sparked the civil war remained unsolved. Israel increased its support of the FLA, while the Palestinians continued their incursions into northern Israel. Israel responded to these attacks by invading southern Lebanon in March 1978 and creating a security zone defended by Israeli forces as well as the approximately 2,000-member SLA. This invasion resulted in a huge loss of life on the Lebanese side, turning many in the area more firmly against Israel and the SLA. The Israel Defense Forces (IDF) withdrew in June 1978. On April 18, 1979, Haddad declared the security zone, roughly 62 miles long and 6–12 miles wide with a population of 100,000 people (60 percent Shiite Muslim and 35 percent Christian), to be Independent Free Lebanon, also known as the Government of Free Lebanon. The government of Lebanon did not recognize his claim. The FLA was renamed the South Lebanon Army in May 1980.

During 1980–1982 the ferocious and complex civil war in which Christians fought Christians and Muslims fought Muslims as well as each other continued. Seeing the chaos and weakness of the Lebanese government, Israeli leaders claimed that they feared the growing influence and power of Syria and the PLO in Lebanon. Following PLO attacks on Israeli diplomats in London and Paris, Israeli forces invaded Lebanon on June 6, 1982. The Israeli invasion, known as Operation PEACE FOR GALILEE, sought to secure an area that would push the PLO's Katyusha rockets out of the range of Israel's northern border. The Israelis also hoped to destroy the terrorist infrastructure that had developed in Lebanon.

After effecting the ouster of the PLO, the IDF hoped to push all remaining Palestinian civilians out of Beirut if possible. The IDF surrounded Beirut and then moved into West Beirut following the assassination of Lebanon's president-elect Bashir Gemayal on September 14, 1982. On September 17, 700–3,500 Palestinian civilians, including women and children, were massacred in the Sabra and Shatila refugee camps by Lebanese Christian Phalangists who were authorized to enter the camps and were monitored there by the IDF. The Phalangist force responsible for the massacre included 150 SLA fighters. While the latter denied their participation in the attacks, survivor testimony noted their southern accents and uniforms.

From 1982 to 2000 the SLA was supplied and supported by Israel, while the SLA administered the security zone and fought the Islamic Resistance movement comprised mostly of Lebanese Shiites, Hezbollah, Amal, Islamic Amal, and some Palestinians. Although the PLO was effectively driven from Lebanon by Operation PEACE FOR GALILEE, the Israeli presence in force lasted until 2000 and resulted in such a high number of Palestinian civilian deaths that worldwide public opinion turned against Israel. A treaty ending the engagement was signed on May 17, 1983, only to be revoked by the Lebanese under Syrian pressure soon after Menachem Begin resigned as prime minister of Israel.

SLA head Haddad died of cancer in January 1984 and was replaced by Antoine Lahad. Israel partially withdrew from Lebanon in 1985 but continued to operate in the security zone and supply and support the SLA. In 1985 the SLA occupied Jezzin and its environs, 12 miles north of the security zone, and also opened a detention center in al-Khiam. The SLA was later accused by Amnesty International of using the al-Khiam facility for torture. Israel contended that al-Khiam was exclusively controlled by the SLA. However, many Lebanese who survived their stay in Israeli-run prison camps from 1982 or who were kidnapped into detention without charges attested to the same types of torture.

Israel redeployed infantry and armor into the security zone in May 1991 in support of its 1,000 soldiers garrisoned there and the approximately 2,500-member SLA. The IDF also deployed soldiers to Jezzin in July 1991. The 1991 SLA-IDF positions remained the status quo until 1999. Ehud Barak was elected prime minister of Israel in May 1999, and in June 1999 he initiated the withdrawal of the IDF and the SLA from the Jezzin area. Hezbollah reentered Jezzin in June 1999. Israel announced its complete withdrawal from southern Lebanon in April 2000 and completed that withdrawal on May 24, 2000. The SLA was too small to hold the security zone against the much larger Hezbollah force without the direct support of Israeli armor and infantry. Barak's rapid withdrawal was blamed in part for the collapse of the SLA.

Once the Israeli withdrawal had been completed, the Lebanese government began hunting down SLA members so that they could be brought to trial for various war crimes. Lahad petitioned the

Lebanese government for mercy, but the petition was denied. Approximately 4,000 SLA fighters and their families sought refuge in Israel. Some SLA members sought asylum in Europe, with Germany accepting the largest number. More than 3,000 former SLA members were in the custody of the Lebanese government by June 2000, and 2,700 of those were tried by military courts before the year ended. Approximately one-third of those tried were sentenced to less than a month imprisonment, and one-third were sentenced to one year of imprisonment. The 21 SLA members sentenced to death eventually had their sentences reduced, and 2 SLA members convicted of torture at al-Khiam continue to serve life sentences.

Even though some of the SLA members who fled to Europe and Israel were allowed to return, others were barred from reentry for various spans of time. Those who stayed in Israel were given full citizenship and financial packages equivalent to those given new immigrants to Israel. The Israeli Knesset Finance Committee agreed on April 6, 2006, to pay the families of each SLA veteran 40,000 Israeli shekels in seven annual installments.

RICHARD EDWARDS

See also

Barak, Ehud; Hezbollah; Katyusha Rocket; Lebanon; Lebanon, Armed Forces; Lebanon, Civil War in; Lebanon, Israeli Invasion of; Palestine Liberation Organization; Sabra and Shatila Massacre; Syria

References

Bechara, Souha. *Resistance: My Life for Lebanon.* Translated by Gabe Levine. Brooklyn, NY: Soft Skull, 2003.
Bregman, Ahron. *Israel's Wars: A History since 1947.* 2nd ed. New York: Routledge, 2002.
Fisk, Robert. *Pity the Nation: The Abduction of Lebanon.* 4th ed. New York: Nation Books, 2002.
Scluiff, Ze'ev, and Ehud Ya'ari. *Israel's Lebanon War.* Translated by Ina Friedman. New York: Touchstone, 2002.

Soviet Jews, Immigration to Israel

For many years, the issue of Russian Jewish immigration to Israel was fraught with controversy and stymied by the vagaries of the Soviet system. The limited nature of Jewish emigration from the Soviet Union prior to 1990 was governed by both domestic policies and Cold War politics.

From 1948 until the death of Soviet dictator Joseph Stalin in 1953, Soviet authorities initiated a campaign intent on the complete liquidation of Jewish culture. Stalinist policies did not allow for the emigration of Jews from the Soviet Union and revolved around systematic arrests, imprisonments, and internal exile. From 1948 to 1953, only 8,163 Soviet Jews were permitted to immigrate to Israel. Soviet leader Nikita Khrushchev's de-Stalinization policies briefly allowed a greater number of Jews to emigrate. However, Khrushchev's later campaign against all religions led to a policy of forced assimilation into Soviet culture as opposed to emigration. Many Soviet Jews nevertheless applied for exit visas, but the Soviet government made emigration increasingly difficult and costly by often charging an exorbitant emigration tax. During the 1970s, in

Immigration to Israel (1950–2005)

Year	Immigrants
1950	170,563
1955	37,528
1960	24,692
1965	31,115
1970	36,750
1975	20,028
1980	20,428
1985	10,642
1990	199,516
1995	76,361
2000	60,192
2005	22,818

the spirit of détente and to gain favored-nation trade status with the United States, Soviet premier Leonid Brezhnev eased emigration policy, resulting in the exodus of 137,000 Jews to Israel from the Soviet Union between 1970 and 1980.

Soviet premier Mikhail Gorbachev's glasnost and perestroika reform initiatives, begun in the mid-1980s, ultimately led to the reversal of the long-standing Soviet policy of severely limiting the emigration of the Soviet Union's large Jewish population. The end of the Cold War, of course, also affected these policies. The result was a period of significant immigration to Israel from the Soviet Union between 1990 and 1993.

Although the long history of Russian/Soviet persecution of Jews was often portrayed as the main motivating factor in the desire of Soviet Jews to emigrate, severe economic dislocations consonant with the end of the Cold War created an additional impetus to take advantage of the new emigration policy. Because of the restrictive nature of U.S. immigration policies, many Soviet Jews interested in emigrating to the United States were redirected to Israel. The influx of more than 400,000 Soviet Jews to Israel between 1990 and 1993 not only produced severe demographic challenges for Israel but also placed additional strains on Arab-Israeli relations and Israeli-Soviet relations.

In an attempt to absorb the unprecedented number of immigrants arriving in Israel after 1990, the Israeli government initiated a series of reforms that included a complete overhaul of Israel's assimilation policies. In contrast to prior waves of immigrants who used so-called absorption centers, a system of direct absorption was put in place for the Soviet immigrants. Under this new system, immigrants arriving in Israel received an initial stipend, health insurance, and mortgage benefits from the Israeli government. Although the policy initially offered much-needed practical assistance to the immigrants, it ultimately resulted in high levels of unemployment, a massive housing shortage, and an effort by the Israeli government to secure loans from the United States and France.

As a result of the housing shortage, Soviet immigrants began migrating to settlements in the occupied Palestinian territories. This controversial policy fulfilled Israeli prime minister Yitzhak Shamir's prophecy first postulated in his January 14, 1990, address known as the "Greater Israel Speech." Shamir had stated that constructing settlements in the occupied territories was the only way to fully incorporate the new immigrants into Israel. Furthermore, Shamir believed that the rapid demographic changes in the West Bank would overwhelm the Palestinian populace, resulting in a consolidated Israel. Between June 1990 and January 1992, the Shamir government invested $1.3 billion to construct more than 18,000 homes in the occupied territories. After June 1992, Prime Minister Yitzhak Rabin greatly modified Shamir's plan of constructing an additional 106,000 housing units in the occupied territories. Rabin's plan called for the construction of just 9,000 residences. Not surprisingly, Israel's settlement policies caused serious friction between the Israelis and Palestinians and their Arab supporters.

The influx of settlers into the occupied territories was not the only issue that strained Arab-Israeli relations, however. The Soviet immigrants were generally better educated than the Palestinian Arab minority in Israel, and this permanently altered the socio-economic makeup of Israeli society. Palestinians feared that the disparities between the Arab minority and the Jewish majority would grow ever more pronounced. Future Arab university graduates

New immigrants from Soviet Russia and former "Prisoners of Zion" stage a hunger strike in solidarity with Russian Jews standing trial in Leningrad, December 12, 1970. (Moshe Milner/Israeli Government Press Office)

would now have to compete with the highly educated immigrants, and Arabs would face greater job competition. Indeed, some of the less well-educated Jewish immigrants began taking lower-paying jobs once relegated to Arab laborers.

The immigration of Soviet Jews had other ramifications as well. Relations among the Soviet Union, United States, Israel, and the Arab states were thrown into further disarray. Maintaining their policy of condemning Israeli colonization in the occupied territories, Arab states placed considerable pressure on the Soviet Union to halt the emigration of Soviet Jews to Israel. While the Soviet Union continued to issue exit visas to those who wished to emigrate, in response to Shamir's "Greater Israel Speech" the Soviet Union refused to seal an agreement offering direct flights between Moscow and Tel Aviv, which in effect limited the ability of some emigrants to leave.

Israeli initiatives to secure $400 million in loan guarantees from the United States to pay for the immigrant absorption packages led to an impasse in Israeli-U.S. relations. The U.S. government, attempting to alter Israeli settlement policy in the West Bank, threatened to rescind funds if Soviet Jews were settled in the West Bank, including East Jerusalem. Thus, the immigration of some 400,000 Soviet Jews to Israel between 1990 and 1993 resulted in a long-term demographic shift in Israel while simultaneously intensifying the Arab-Israeli conflict.

JONATHAN H. L'HOMMEDIEU

See also

Immigration to Palestine/Israel; Rabin, Yitzhak; Settlements, Israeli; Shamir, Yitzhak; Soviet Union and Russia, Middle East Policy; United States, Middle East Policy

References

Al Haj, Majid. *Immigration and Ethnic Formation in a Deeply Divided Society: The Case of the 1990's Immigrants from the Former Soviet Union to Israel.* Boston: Brill Academic, 2004.

Freedman, Robert O. *Emigration and the Dynamic of Resettlement.* Durham, NC: Duke University Press, 1989.

Gurevitz, Baruch. *Open Gates: The Story behind the Mass Immigration to Israel from the Soviet Union and Its Successor States.* Jerusalem: Jewish Agency for Israel, 1996.

Lazin, Fred. *The Struggle for Soviet Jewry in American Politics: Israel versus the American Jewish Establishment.* Lanham, MD: Lexington Books, 2005.

Soviet Union and Russia, Middle East Policy

Geography and oil made the Middle East a crucial arena of Cold War competition. The foreign policy of the Soviet Union in the region sought to reduce British, French, and American influence and gain dominance for itself. The Soviets supported Arab states for geopolitical reasons, such as access to the Mediterranean Sea, the Suez Canal, and the Indian Ocean, and for ideological reasons because the Arabs shared Soviet opposition to Western imperialism and colonialism. The Soviets backed the Arab side during the various Arab-Israeli wars for political as well as ideological reasons and sought to keep the region polarized to preserve Egyptian and Syrian dependence on the Soviet Union. Soviet efforts to dominate the Middle East failed due to vigorous American counteraction and ended when the Soviet Union collapsed in 1991.

Since 1991 Russia, a nation hobbled by financial crises and political turmoil, has taken a far more pragmatic and reactive stand in the Middle East. This does not mean, however, that the Soviet successor state had abdicated its strategic or economic interests and commitments in the region. Since the late 1990s, in fact, the Kremlin had showed a renewed interest in the region. But this has not been driven by the old Soviet ideologies. Rather, it is based upon economic imperatives as well as traditional Russian conceptions of security and international power.

The primary vehicle of Soviet influence was military aid, sometimes transferred using East Europeans as deniable proxies. Soviet arms were available in large quantities, at low prices, and on favorable credit terms. The Soviet Union was the chief military patron of Egypt (1955–1973), Syria (after 1958), Iraq (after 1958), Libya (after 1974), Algeria (after 1962), Somalia (1962–1977), Ethiopia (after 1977), North and South Yemen (after 1967), and Afghanistan (after 1973). During the Iran-Iraq War (1980–1988), the Soviets supplied both Iraq and Iran via intermediaries. The Soviets provided advisers to their clients, obtained air and naval basing rights in the region, and deployed combat forces in Egypt (1970–1972) and Afghanistan (1979–1989).

The Soviets had negligible influence in the Middle East before World War II. After that war decisively weakened Britain and France, the Soviets hoped to gain influence in the region but had limited means at their disposal. They decided to support the Zionist movement in order to weaken British power and create tensions between the United States and Britain but also in part because of the common suffering of the war that had claimed up to 27 million Soviet citizens and 6 million Jews. In 1947 Soviet diplomats supported the partition of Palestine, which led to the creation of Israel in 1948. To strengthen Israel, the Soviets transferred Jews from Soviet-occupied territories to Poland, fully expecting them to emigrate. The Soviets instructed Poland, Czechoslovakia, Romania, and Hungary to permit Jewish emigration. From 1948 to 1951, more than 302,000 Jews emigrated from Eastern Europe to Israel. Israel's Jewish population was only 806,000 in 1948, so this was a vital demographic boost.

At Soviet direction, Czechoslovakia provided $22 million in arms to Israel in 1948, including 50,000 rifles, 6,000 machine guns, 90 million rounds of ammunition, and Supermarine Spitfire and Avia S-199 fighter aircraft. Czech arms played a crucial role in securing air superiority over Israel and halting Arab ground advances in the Israeli War of Independence (1948–1949).

The Soviets may have initially contemplated a strategic alliance with Israel. However, relations deteriorated with the onset of the

Haganah members train with a Czech-made light machine gun in Tel Aviv, February 1948. (Zoltan Kluger/Israeli Government Press Office)

Cold War when Soviet dictator Joseph Stalin launched an anti-Semitic, anti-Western propaganda campaign. In late 1952 Soviet security services manufactured an alleged conspiracy of Jewish doctors to poison Soviet leaders, and in this atmosphere the Soviet Union broke relations with Israel. Official anti-Semitism eased with the death of Stalin in March 1953. Diplomatic relations with Israel were restored, but Israel had shifted permanently into the Western camp.

In 1955 the United Kingdom signed the Baghdad Pact, a defense alliance with Iraq, Turkey, Pakistan, and Iran. The alliance's ostensible purpose was to contain Soviet advances to the south, yet ironically the Baghdad Pact prompted Egypt, Syria, and Yemen to seek closer relations with the Soviet Union. In the 1950s the United States, Britain, and France sought to maintain an Arab-Israeli arms balance and would not sell advanced weapons to Egypt. Egyptian president Gamal Abdel Nasser approached the Soviets, who agreed in September 1955 to supply arms via Czechoslovakia. The Egyptian-Soviet arms deal included 230 tanks, 200 armored personnel carriers, 100 self-propelled guns, 500 artillery pieces, several hundred MiG-

15 jet fighters, 50 Il-28 jet bombers, transport aircraft, and assorted naval vessels. This development greatly alarmed Israel as well as Britain and France, which had their own difficulties with Nasser.

Anglo-French tensions with Egypt came to a head in 1956. The United States withdrew funding from the proposed Aswan High Dam project, forcing Egypt to nationalize the Suez Canal. The British, French, and Israelis invaded Egypt in October in order to regain control of the canal and overthrow Nasser. At that time the Soviets were busy crushing the Hungarian Uprising and in any case had little military capability to intervene on Egypt's behalf. However, the Soviets sent diplomatic notes with veiled threats of force against Britain and France unless they withdrew from Egypt and proposed a joint U.S.-Soviet military intervention to halt the fighting. Washington rebuffed Soviet threats, rejected the proposal for joint action, and employed political and economic pressure to force Britain and France to abandon their occupation. After the Suez Crisis, the Soviets portrayed themselves as Egypt's friend and protector even though their bluster had risked nothing and achieved little. During the brief war, British, French, and Israeli forces destroyed large quantities of Soviet-supplied equipment at little cost to themselves. The Soviets attributed this discreditable performance to poorly trained Egyptian operators.

The British and French defeat at Suez facilitated increased Soviet influence in the Middle East. The Soviets agreed to replenish Egypt's lost equipment and supplied more modern MiG-17 and MiG-19 fighters. In 1963 Egypt received first-line T-54/55 tanks, MiG-21 supersonic fighters, Tu-16 bombers, and SA-2 surface-to-air missiles (SAMs). The Soviets provided similar modern equipment to the progressive regimes in Syria and Iraq, the latter of whose pro-British government was overthrown in 1958. Some 1,300 Soviet and East European advisers trained Egyptian forces to use the new equipment. The number of Soviet tanks and combat aircraft given to the Arabs vastly exceeded Western supplies to Israel, not least because the United States refused to supply significant quantities of modern equipment to Israel before 1967.

Soviet strategy in the Middle East from 1965 to 1973 was subordinate to Soviet strategy toward Indochina. In response to the escalating war in Vietnam after 1965, the Soviets supplied many tens of thousands of tons of weapons and equipment to Hanoi. The overland supply route from the Soviet Union across China to North Vietnam was not secure due to Sino-Soviet antagonism and the turmoil created by China's Great Proletarian Cultural Revolution. Nor could supplies travel via Vladivostok given the limited capacity of the Trans-Siberian Railroad and the need to increase Soviet forces in the Far East to confront China. Thus, the Soviets shipped supplies to North Vietnam primarily via the Black Sea port of Odessa. The sea route from Odessa to Haiphong via the Cape of Good Hope was more than twice as long as the route via the Suez Canal. Closing the Suez Canal would thus more than halve the quantity of supplies the Soviets could deliver. From 1965 to 1967 the Soviets sought to prevent Egyptian-Israeli conflict, which would likely close the Suez Canal. After the 1967 Six-Day War closed the canal, the Soviets urgently sought to reopen it both by demanding Israeli withdrawal from the Canal Zone and by arming Egypt in order to open the canal by force.

The argument that the Soviets instigated the Six-Day War or encouraged Arab aggression in 1967 defies logic. The Soviets needed to keep the Suez Canal open. Furthermore, Egyptian and Syrian forces had not yet received all the weapons or training that the Soviets intended to provide. About a third of Egypt's army (55,000 troops, including the best units) was deployed in Yemen and was unavailable to fight Israel. When tensions rose in May 1967, the Soviets warned Egypt that Israel planned to attack Syria. Possibly, the Soviets hoped that a display of Egyptian resolve would deter Israel from striking Syria, but if so this backfired. Nasser's decision to close the Strait of Tiran, to order United Nations (UN) peacekeepers to leave the Sinai, and to mobilize Egyptian forces simply induced Israel to crush Egypt. On May 26, 1967, the Soviets pressured Egypt and Syria to moderate their rhetoric and prevent armed conflict with Israel by whatever means necessary, but this came too late to prevent Israeli action.

Soviet premier Nikita Khrushchev sickles a bushel of wheat on a new 20,000-acre model farm, located about 30 miles south of Alexandria, Egypt, May 22, 1964. (Bettmann/Corbis)

Soviet behavior during the Six-Day War was restrained. The Soviets expressed resolute support for the Arabs but did not resupply them or risk confrontation with the United States. The Soviets only threatened overt involvement on June 10 when they feared that Israel would take Damascus and overthrow the Syrian government. They broke relations with Israel and alerted their airborne divisions for deployment, but intervention proved unnecessary when Israel accepted a cease-fire.

After the Six-Day War, the Soviets replaced Egypt's and Syria's lost equipment and dispatched huge quantities of arms to Sudan, Iraq, and Yemen. The Soviets sent 13,000 military advisers to Egypt in late 1967—rising to 20,000 in 1970—with advisers attached to every Egyptian unit down to battalion level. The Soviets demanded an overhaul of the Egyptian high command, and thousands of Egyptian officers visited the Soviet Union for training. Diplomatically, the Soviets continued to insist that Israel withdraw from the Canal Zone without preconditions. Washington responded that a comprehensive solution to the Arab-Israeli conflict must precede Israeli withdrawal from occupied territories. The Soviets and the East Europeans began to train, fund, and equip terrorist organizations such as the Palestine Liberation Organization (PLO) and the Popular Front for the Liberation of Palestine (PFLP) in order to harass Israel, Western Europe, and the United States.

In April 1969 Egypt launched the War of Attrition, which sought to avoid major ground combat while causing continual Israeli casualties. Israel countered with air strikes that destroyed Egypt's air defenses in the Canal Zone. When this did not force Egypt to desist, Israel began deep-penetration raids throughout Egypt. Egypt then convinced the Soviets to take control of Egypt's air defenses. More than 12,000 Soviet operators manned air defenses that included 85 SA-2 and SA-3 missile sites, radar-guided artillery pieces, and more than 100 MiG-21 fighters with Soviet pilots. Although initially restricted to defense of the Nile River Valley, in July 1970 the Soviets began moving SAM batteries closer to the Suez Canal, creating the prospect that Egyptian forces could cross the canal under this umbrella. The United States equipped Israeli aircraft with advanced electronic countermeasures and air-to-surface missiles to defeat the SAM threat.

The effort to put a SAM umbrella over the Suez Canal coincided with a crisis in Jordan. In September 1970 King Hussein violently suppressed increasingly uncontrollable Palestinian guerrilla groups. In response, the Soviets sponsored a Syrian invasion of Jordan. Soviet advisers planned the operation and accompanied Syrian tanks until they crossed the border. The Soviets hoped that either Israel would intervene, which would discredit Hussein, or that the Americans would intervene, which would discredit the United States in the Arab world. However, the Jordanian Air Force smashed Syria's tank columns, making outside intervention unnecessary.

After Nasser's death in September 1970, Egypt's new president, Anwar Sadat, sought to improve relations with Israel and the United States. When the Soviets tried to influence the Egyptian succession struggle in favor of pro-Soviet vice president Ali Sabri, Sadat dismissed and arrested Sabri. More than 100 pro-Soviet officials were purged from the Egyptian government in the Corrective Revolution of May 1971. To prevent a complete break in relations, the Soviets demanded—and obtained—a Soviet-Egyptian Treaty of Friendship. The treaty restricted the Soviet role in Egypt to providing military aid and training, and Egypt agreed not to join any anti-Soviet alliance.

Having lost influence in Egypt, the Soviets tried to strengthen their relations with other Arab states through arms deliveries to Syria, Iraq, Somalia, North and South Yemen, and Sudan. This effort succeeded except in Sudan, where the government followed Sadat's lead in purging local communists. Desperate Sudanese communists launched a coup attempt but were crushed. Soviet military advisers were then expelled.

Sadat understood that the Soviets preferred to perpetuate Arab-Israeli antagonism in order to keep Egypt isolated and dependent on the Soviet Union. He also knew that only the Americans could deliver a political settlement with Israel and the return of the Sinai to Egyptian control. Sadat hoped that Washington could broker a political solution, but American efforts to do so in 1971 and 1972 foundered on Israeli intransigence. Sadat signaled his independence and desire for improved relations with the United States—for example, he expelled Soviet military advisers in July 1972—but could not completely burn his bridges with the Soviets because he needed Soviet arms. Sadat's strategy was to prepare for a limited war in the expectation that victory would enable Washington to force Israel to accept a peace agreement and withdraw from the Sinai. Sadat informed the Soviets in February 1973 that he intended to attack Israel, and he demanded their support. The Soviets had little choice but to agree since failure to support Egypt would destroy Soviet influence in the Middle East. Furthermore, reopening the Suez Canal would facilitate arming Hanoi for a future attack on South Vietnam.

From late June 1967 until early 1973, the Soviets gave Egypt sufficient weaponry to defend itself but not advanced offensive weapons. The Egyptians were especially displeased that the Soviets did not provide their latest MiG-23 and MiG-25 fighters to counter Israeli F-4 Phantoms. Before the October 1973 Yom Kippur War, the Soviets provided first-line T-62 tanks and large numbers of anti-aircraft and antitank missiles, which would enable Egypt to take and hold a bridgehead on the east bank of the Suez against Israeli air and armored counterattacks. Syria and Iraq also received significant quantities of Soviet weapons before the war.

The main Soviet objective before and during the Yom Kippur War was to ensure that the region remained polarized. This required either stampeding Israel into a preemptive attack on Egypt that would make Sadat's goal of a limited victory over Israel impossible or prodding Washington into a premature display of full support for Israel that would ruin Washington's credibility as an honest broker. Moscow tried to provoke Israeli preemption by circulating warnings in the communist press that an attack was imminent and by evacuating Soviet civilians from Egypt and Syria. These gambits failed, not least because the United States sternly warned Israel not to preempt.

Once the war began, the Soviets sought a cease-fire at the point of maximum Arab gain—when Egypt had taken the east bank of the canal and Syria had taken the Golan Heights—but this effort failed. Israel quickly counterattacked the Syrians, and Moscow asked Egypt to advance in order to divert Israeli attention. The Soviets also began resupplying Syria and Egypt by air and sea and alerted their airborne divisions for deployment to Damascus. Israel, however, stopped short of Damascus and shifted its forces south to inflict a catastrophic defeat on the Egyptians, who had advanced into the Sinai beyond their air-defense umbrella. Israeli forces then crossed the Suez Canal and threatened to destroy Egyptian forces trapped on the east bank. The UN Security Council called for a cease-fire on October 22, 1973, but Israel disregarded this and continued encircling the Egyptians. The Soviets proposed sending joint U.S.-Soviet military contingents to enforce the cease-fire and threatened to act unilaterally if the United States refused. To emphasize their determination, the Soviets made further preparations to deploy airborne forces, and Soviet troops in Egypt fired two Scud ballistic missiles into Israel. At this point there was a real prospect of renewed fighting and the commitment to nuclear weapons. Washington raised its military alert level, informed Moscow of its willingness to cooperate in maintaining a cease-fire (although not with U.S. troops), asked Sadat to withdraw his request for superpower military intervention (which he did), and demanded that Israel cease operations (which, under extreme duress, it eventually did).

The Yom Kippur War yielded only one positive result for Moscow: the opening of the Suez Canal. Otherwise, the outcome was profoundly negative. Washington reestablished ties with Egypt and excluded Moscow from any substantive role in the Egyptian-Israeli peace process. Moscow's only recourse was to strengthen ties with Syria and to forge a relationship with Libya, which bought $20 billion in Soviet arms from 1974 to 1985.

In 1969 Mohamed Siad Barre seized power in Somalia and proclaimed it a socialist state. Somalia bought Soviet arms and gave the Soviets access to ports on the Indian Ocean and the Gulf of Aden. In 1975 the Ethiopian military seized power and embraced socialism. Two years later Haile Mengistu, the new Ethiopian leader, obtained substantial Soviet military aid. Siad Barre wished to control Ethiopia's ethnically Somalian province of Ogaden and feared that Soviet support for Mengistu would prevent this. Siad Barre rejected Soviet efforts to mediate the Ogaden dispute and appealed to the Americans for military aid. The United States agreed in principle to provide defensive arms, and Siad Barre, assuming that he had secured an alternate arms supplier, invaded Ethiopia in July 1977. In August the United States reversed itself and declined to provide arms to Somalia. Siad Barre begged the Soviets to restore military support but was denied. The Soviets poured $1 billion in military aid into Ethiopia, including 600 tanks, thousands of advisers, and 15,000 Cuban combat troops. These forces drove the Somalians out of Ethiopia by March 1978. Somalia renounced its Treaty of Friendship and Cooperation with the Soviets, expelled Soviet personnel from Somalia, and became a U.S. client state.

After defeating Somalia, Ethiopia focused on suppressing its nationwide internal rebellion. Despite prodigious Soviet military aid worth more than $4 billion from 1978 to 1984, the Ethiopians never managed to crush the rebels. After 1985, Soviet leader Mikhail Gorbachev dramatically reduced Soviet aid to Ethiopia, gradually withdrew Soviet advisers, and urged the Ethiopians to negotiate a settlement of their internal disputes.

In 1974 Iran began a determined effort to shift Afghanistan into its orbit. With Iranian assistance, Afghan president Mohammed Daoud lessened his dependence on Moscow and attempted to suppress Afghan communists. To arrest this trend, in April 1978 Moscow approved a coup that killed Daoud and installed Noor Mohammed Taraki. Afterward, the Soviet political and military presence in Afghanistan rapidly escalated.

In June 1978 a pro-Soviet coup in South Yemen reversed that country's drift toward the West, thus securing the important port of Aden for Soviet use. Energetic Soviet-sponsored action in Ethiopia, South Yemen, and Afghanistan in 1978 raised serious questions in the United States regarding the Soviet commitment to détente. Collectively, pro-Soviet regimes in these countries together with Syria and Iraq gave the Soviets tremendous potential leverage against the pro-American regimes in Saudi Arabia and Iran.

American efforts to guide Iran from autocracy to constitutional monarchy in the late 1970s completely failed, and Mohammad Reza Shah Pahlavi abdicated in early 1979. The shah's trip to the United States for medical care in October 1979 gave Ayatollah Ruhollah Khomeini a pretext to seize the U.S. embassy in Tehran. This allowed him to destroy his domestic opponents who sought improved relations with the United States. Major U.S. forces began gathering in the region, and the Soviets, perceiving a geopolitical opportunity, warned the Americans not to intervene militarily in Iran. The crisis in Iran coincided with an anticommunist revolt in Afghanistan that the Afghan government was unable to quell. After Hafizullah Amin assassinated Taraki and became president of Afghanistan in September 1979, the Soviets decided on military action there. In December 1979 80,000 Soviet troops invaded Afghanistan—and executed Amin—in order to suppress the revolt and deter a U.S. invasion of Iran, which the Soviets mistakenly believed was imminent.

The Soviet Army originally intended to garrison key points and allow the Afghan Army to fight the resistance but was soon drawn into combat itself. Soviet equipment and tactics designed for conventional opponents proved poorly suited to fighting guerrillas in rugged Afghan terrain. The indiscriminate use of firepower aroused the intense hatred of the Afghan people and created millions of refugees. With American, British, and Saudi support, Pakistan provided a sanctuary in which resistance fighters could train and launch attacks into Afghanistan. Equipping the resistance fighters with Stinger antiaircraft missiles in 1986 deprived the Soviets of the crucial advantage of low-altitude air support. Soviet general secretary Mikhail Gorbachev decided to abandon the debilitating occupation and withdrew Soviet troops in 1989. The Soviet-Afghan War cost 15,000 Soviet dead and 470,000 sick and wounded over a 10-year period. Afterward, Afghanistan sank into civil war. From a larger perspective, the Soviet war in Afghanistan galvanized American leadership of a global anti-Soviet crusade. The Afghan debacle was in fact a major factor in the collapse of the Soviet Union.

Before 1979 Iraq was a long-standing Soviet client, receiving 90 percent of its arms from Soviet sources, while Iran was a U.S.-armed client. The fall of the shah of Iran caused Iraq to improve relations with Saudi Arabia, Jordan, and the United States, while Iran strengthened its relations with Syria, Libya, and the Soviets. After Iraq invaded Iran in September 1980, the Soviets tried to manipulate the conflict to bring a pro-Soviet regime to power in Iran. The Soviets believed that Iran's war with Iraq, Iran's need for Soviet arms to fight that war, the presence of Soviet troops in Afghanistan, and American forces in the Persian Gulf would create irresistible pressure on Tehran to turn to Moscow to solve its problems and escape hostile encirclement.

Soviet strategy required time to come to fruition. Moreover,

Soviet surface-to-air missiles (SAMs) during a military review in Kassasin, Egypt, October 1978. (Time & Life Pictures/Getty Images)

prolonged conflict would weaken Iran and, because Iran could not obtain Western arms, increase its dependence on the Soviet Union. Thus, the Soviets armed both sides to protract the fighting. Some regard Iraq as an American puppet during the Iran-Iraq War. In fact, the Soviet bloc and its clients provided the vast majority of Iraq's tanks, armored personnel carriers, artillery, small arms, and combat aircraft. At the same time, Soviet clients—Syria, Libya, North Korea, Cuba, and Vietnam—supplied Iran with arms that played a critical role in blunting the initial Iraqi offensive and allowing Iran to counterattack. The Soviets backed Iranian communist resistance groups that three times attempted to overthrow the Khomeini regime, but each time the coups were brutally suppressed. Ultimately, Soviet strategy did not succeed. Only after the end of the Iran-Iraq War, the death of Khomeini, and the Soviet withdrawal from Afghanistan were the Iranians willing to accept a close relationship with Moscow (which persists to this day).

Syrian alignment with Iran in the 1980s created fear of a Syrian attack that Iraq, fully engaged against Iran, could not withstand. The Soviets did not intend to authorize such Syrian action, but Israel, with U.S. backing, moved to pin down the Syrians in any case. After Iran expelled Iraq from Iranian soil in May 1982 and began driving into Iraq, Israel launched a powerful incursion into Lebanon, mauling Syrian forces there. The deployment of the Multi-national Force in Lebanon further fixed Syrian attention in the West and eased pressure on the Iraqi rear. The minimum Soviet goal during the Syrian-Israeli confrontation was to ensure that Israel did not destroy Syria, although the Soviets took no direct steps to support Syria or counter Israel in Lebanon itself. After the destruction of Syrian air defenses in 1982, the Soviets rebuilt it with the more modern SA-5 SAMs and provided additional modern weapons such as Su-24 and MiG-29 aircraft and T-72 tanks. Soviet military presence in Syria peaked at 13,000 Soviet and East European advisers in 1984 and declined after 1985.

The Soviets were on the defensive worldwide from 1985 to 1991. This was driven by serious internal economic dislocations, the disastrous Soviet intervention and occupation of Afghanistan, and Soviet leader Mikhail Gorbachev's efforts to reform Soviet society and government (glasnost and perestroika). In the Middle East, the Soviets' willingness to provide unstinting military largesse to their clients declined, and the Soviets sought to extract themselves from the Afghan quagmire. Diplomatically, the Soviets improved relations with Egypt, Israel, Saudi Arabia, and the Gulf States in the late 1980s and joined the UN consensus in condemning Iraq's invasion of Kuwait in August 1990.

Indeed, Soviet cooperation completely changed the character of the U.S. confrontation with Iraq during 1990–1991 that culminated in the 1991 Persian Gulf War. The Kremlin declined to aid—or even shield—its regional client as it had done during the Cold War. The Persian Gulf War would have in fact been unimaginable at the height of the U.S.-Soviet Cold War rivalry. The movement of major American forces from Germany to Saudi Arabia most certainly would not have been possible during the Cold War. The Soviets attempted to persuade Iraqi strongman Saddam Hussein to withdraw unscathed from Kuwait, but he obstinately refused a diplomatic solution. Thus, the Soviets did not block the use of force in January and February 1991. The Soviet collapse in December 1991 ended four decades of bipolar superpower competition in the Middle East and ushered in a less peaceful and unpredictable era in the region.

With the familiar bipolarity of the Cold War now gone, nations in the Middle East are far less likely to heed Great Power admonitions to exercise restraint. The lack of restraining forces on Middle Eastern states has literally sent some of them into centrifugal chaos. Both religious and political radicalism have been on the rise, and few regional governments have been able to contain them entirely. This turn of events has been key to the rise of terrorism—both regionally and worldwide—and sectarian violence. Nowhere is this more apparent than in war-torn Iraq, where Shiites, Sunnis, and Kurds battle it out to win supremacy in a nation that Anglo-American forces have been unable to pacify or control. In addition, perceived American hegemony in the Middle East since the fall of the Soviet Union has begun to look far more menacing without the countervailing power of the Soviet Union.

Under Russian presidents Boris Yeltsin and Vladimir Putin, Russian policy in the Middle East has largely eschewed the ideologically oriented prescriptions of the communist era. Russian policies now tend to be grounded in pragmatism. And while both administrations in theory supported democracy in the region, they were (and are) more concerned with political and economic stability in the region. Another change from the Soviet era is the role of private enterprise in the direction and creation of foreign policies. In the pre-1991 era, the state controlled Soviet industry. In addition to promoting economic autarky, the government largely dictated the policies and direction of industry. Thus, there was no process of push-pull in foreign policymaking. The state dictated industrial policies that were consonant with its foreign policies and vice versa. In the post-1991 era of emerging free market capitalism, however, Russian industrial concerns in the Middle East have begun to play a more central role in overall Russian policy in the region. To spur and protect Russian private investments in the Middle East, the Kremlin has had to cleave to policies that are economically and politically advantageous to Russian industry.

Much to the annoyance and occasional chagrin of the West, the Russians have cultivated relations with Middle East nations that are both friendly to and antipathetic to the West. Indeed, Russian diplomats have played a masterful juggling act by maintaining relations with Syria and Iran while at the same time keeping relations with Washington and London on a relatively even keel. To show-

case this ecumenical approach, in 2005 Putin visited Israel, Egypt, and the Palestinian Authority (PA). In January 2005 Syrian president Bashar al-Assad traveled to Moscow on an official state visit. Clearly, the Kremlin is hedging its bets by attempting to stay on firm footing with a number of diverse regimes in the Middle East.

Some of the Kremlin's caution in the region is derived from its long-standing struggle with Chechnya, the renegade Russian Republic territory that is peopled largely by Sunni Muslims. From 1994 to 1996 Yeltsin fought a bloody—and unsuccessful—war with Chechnya, which desired to be completely independent. In 1999 military conflict between Russia and Chechnya inaugurated the Second Chechen War, which is still technically being fought. Hoping to quell Chechen rebels and court Chechen moderates, Putin has tried to cultivate positive relations with Islamic states to demonstrate Moscow's presumption of being an honest broker.

Russia has been supportive of the Israeli-Palestinian peace process since 1993 and has courted positive relations with Tel Aviv. Because of the large number of Israeli Jews from Russia (some 30 percent of Israel's population is now of Russian origin), there has been a natural affinity between the two nations. Russian businesses have also benefited from economic ties with Israel. Relations between Moscow and Tel Aviv have not been without tension, however, as the Kremlin's support of Iran and Syria has at times caused much dismay among Israeli policymakers.

Since the 1990s, the Kremlin has engaged in major economic and technology deals with Iran, as Russian-Iranian ties owe much to the two nations' proximity and shared geopolitical interests. Indeed, Iran concluded a major arms agreement and became Russia's third-largest arms client (after China and India) in the 1990s. Iran purchased advanced weapons, including Kilo-class submarines, T-72 tanks, S-300 SAMs, and Su-24 and MiG-29 aircraft. Iran also acquired the rights to produce Russian weapons. Iranian officers attended Russian military schools, and Russian advisers trained Iranian forces in the use of Russian weapons. In 1995 under American pressure, Russia agreed not to conclude any new arms deals with Iran, but Putin abrogated this agreement in 2000. A particular U.S. concern has been the transfer of nuclear and missile technology. Russia sold Iran important missile components and manufacturing technologies in the 1990s and trained Iranian scientists in ballistics, aeronautic design, booster design, and missile guidance. Iranian Shahab ballistic missiles were derived from Soviet SS-4 and SS-5 designs. In 1995 Russia obtained a contract to build a nuclear power plant at Bushehr and despite U.S. protests remained determined to finish the project. Russia subsequently agreed to provide fuel for Bushehr and to build additional reactors in Iran.

The Russians notably abstained from voting when the International Atomic Energy Agency (IAEA) found Iran in noncompliance with Nuclear Non-Proliferation Treaty safeguards on uranium enrichment and reprocessing in September 2005 and opposed referring the issue to the UN Security Council. Russia has consistently opposed the imposition of sanctions on Iran and sought to protract negotiations for as long as possible. Moreover, in late 2006 Russia began delivering advanced Tor-M1 air defense missiles to Iran that would seriously complicate any military action to destroy Iran's nuclear facilities.

In recent years Russian ties to Syria have been strengthened, and in 2005 President Putin seemed to support the position of Hezbollah in Lebanon, which is heavily funded by the Syrians and Iranians (who in turn have received weapons systems and armaments from Russia). Moscow's links with Iran, Syria, and Hezbollah have strained relations with Washington over the last several years, and Moscow's repeated dilution of U.S. efforts to enact UN sanctions against Iran for its nuclear program has only added to the tension.

In March 2003 as the Anglo-American invasion of Iraq commenced, Putin issued an unequivocal if not prescient statement labeling the endeavor a grave political miscalculation. Unlike the 1991 war against Iraq, the Russians refused to endorse in any way the 2003 invasion. While Putin stopped short of warning Washington and London of any Russian countermeasures, he made it clear that the move was not in the best interests of Moscow or the Middle East. The ongoing war in Iraq therefore continues to strain Russia's relations with the West. On the other hand, after the September 11, 2001, terror attacks on the United States, Putin offered full Russian cooperation in the war on terror, which he shrewdly linked to his war against Chechen rebels.

During the Israeli-Hezbollah Lebanon War in the summer of 2006, the Putin government did not openly oppose the Israeli incursion into southern Lebanon. Nevertheless, Hezbollah had obtained Russian-made Spandrel, Kornet, and Vampir antitank missiles from Syria and Iran. These missiles played a major role in blunting Israel's armored offensive. Once more, the Kremlin was attempting to hedge its bets by staying out of any direct conflict in the region. But behind the scenes, it played an important role while attempting to appear neutral. There can be little doubt that Moscow had known from the very beginning that the armaments it sold to the Syrians and Iranians were going to end up in the hands of groups such as Hezbollah.

Very recently, some right-wingers in the United States have begun to assert that Russia is seeking to revive the Soviet Union's hegemonic policies in the Middle East. This seems unlikely. Moscow's continuing war in Chechnya, its ever-decreasing military power, and its shaky economic underpinnings will more than likely guarantee the continuation of the cautious, pragmatic approach in the region for some time to come.

JAMES D. PERRY AND PAUL G. PIERPAOLI JR.

See also

Attrition, War of; Baghdad Pact; Egyptian-Soviet Arms Deal; Hezbollah; Iran; Iran-Iraq War; Iraq; Iraq War; Israel; Lebanon, Israeli Operations against; Persian Gulf War; Suez Canal; Suez Crisis; Six-Day War; Syria; Yom Kippur War

References

Hiro, Dilip. *The Longest War: The Iran-Iraq Military Conflict.* London: Routledge, 1991.

Israelyan, Victor. *Inside the Kremlin during the Yom Kippur War.* University Park: Pennsylvania State University Press, 1995.
Oren, Michael B. *Six Days of War: June 1967 and the Making of the Modern Middle East.* Novato, CA: Presidio, 2003.
Pollack, Kenneth M. *Arabs at War: Military Effectiveness, 1948–1991.* Lincoln: University of Nebraska Press, 2002.
Rumer, Eugene. *Dangerous Drift: Russia's Middle East Policy.* Washington, DC: Washington Institute for Near East Policy, 2000.
Thornton, Richard. *The Carter Years.* New York: Paragon House, 1991.
———. *The Nixon-Kissinger Years.* New York: Paragon House, 1989.

Special Night Squads

Military formations in the British Mandate for Palestine consisting of both British soldiers and members of Haganah, the secret Jewish self-defense organization. The Special Night Squads were organized as a consequence of the Arab Revolt (1936–1939) when Arab militants and terrorists attacked Jews and their property in Palestine. The Special Night Squads were established in 1938 by British captain Orde Charles Wingate, who was attached to British military intelligence in Galilee. Despite his Arabist training and the pro-Arab sentiment of the British administration in Palestine, Wingate learned Hebrew and became a fanatical Zionist.

Wingate secured official permission to organize the Special Night Squads, which were designed to protect Jewish settlements against Arab attack. Active in the Lower Galilee and in the Jezreel Valley, the squads operated at night and set ambushes for Arab raiders conducting attacks on the Jewish settlements. The Special Night Squads also attacked known Arab terrorist bases and helped protect the Iraq-Haifa oil pipeline. A special squad also patrolled the Palestine Electric Corporation high-voltage cable located in the Sharon Plain. Although the squads were highly successful in both offensive and defensive operations, they were also much criticized for their ruthless, brutal methods, including the torture of prisoners.

Wingate both commanded the squads and participated in a number of their raids until his politically inspired transfer from Palestine at the end of 1938. His passport was stamped with the words that he was not to be allowed to reenter Palestine. The British administration then greatly limited the effectiveness of the squads, and they were completely disbanded in late 1939. Among the members of the Special Night Squads were future Israeli leaders Moshe Dayan and Yigal Allon. Many regard the Special Night Squads as Britain's first special forces, the predecessor of the Special Air Service (SAS) formed in October 1941.

SPENCER C. TUCKER

See also

Allon, Yigal; Arab Revolt of 1936–1939; Dayan, Moshe; Haganah; Palestine, British Mandate for; Wingate, Orde Charles

References

Kaniuk, Yoram. *Commander of the Exodus.* New York: Grove, 2001.
Katz, Sam. *Israeli Units since 1948.* London: Osprey, 1988.

Spector, Yiftah
Born: 1940

Israeli Air Force (IAF) brigadier general. Yiftah Spector was born in Palestine in 1940. His mother was a secretary for various Haganah commanders, and his father was one of the 23 Men in the Boat, a group of commandos during World War II sent to destroy oil installations in Vichy French–controlled Lebanon. That entire force disappeared without a trace.

Over a span of almost 40 years Spector became the second–highest-scoring Israeli ace and one of the highest-scoring jet aces of all time. He is credited with 15 kills. During his military career, Spector flew more than 8,500 sorties, including 334 combat missions. He flew a General Dynamics F-16 in the Osiraq Raid, an Israeli strike on the Iraqi nuclear reactor on June 7, 1981. Although he was the senior-ranking pilot on the mission, he was not its commander. In order to participate in the mission, he volunteered to fly as a wingman.

Spector was also the first Israeli pilot to reach and fire on USS *Liberty* on June 8, 1967, during the Six-Day War. Spector's aircraft was not armed with bombs, but he raked the ship with 30-mm armor-piercing rounds. Both the Israeli and American governments later conducted multiple investigations and officially concluded that the attack was the result of a tragic mistake in identification. Speaking about the incident publicly for the first time on October 10, 2003, Spector told the *Jerusalem Post* that he could tell that it was a military ship and that it was not Israeli. He insisted that the ship was not flying a flag, and he photographed it just to make sure. Assuming that the ship was Egyptian and would open fire on him at any minute, he fired first. He expressed deep regret for the mistake. Despite the official investigations and Spector's later apology, the *Liberty* incident remains highly controversial.

Spector was the senior figure in the 2003 Pilots' Revolt. Although a retired brigadier general, he still worked for the IAF training instructor pilots. Along with 26 other active, reserve, and retired pilots, he signed an open letter to IAF commander Major General Dan Halutz that was published on September 24. In the letter the pilots stated their opposition on moral and legal grounds to many of the attack missions the IAF was carrying out in the occupied Palestinian territories in response to the Second (al-Aqsa) Intifada. The fact that the letter was signed by a retired general officer and a national hero with impeccable military credentials sent shock waves through the Israel Defense Forces (IDF) and the nation as a whole. On October 3, 2003, Halutz personally stripped Spector of his wings.

DAVID T. ZABECKI

See also

Intifada, Second; Israel Defense Forces; *Liberty* Incident; Osiraq Raid; Six-Day War; Yesh Gvul

References

Claire, Rodger W. *Raid on the Sun: Inside Israel's Secret Campaign That Denied Saddam the Bomb.* New York: Broadway, 2004.

Weizman, Ezer. *On Eagles' Wings: The Personal Story of the Leading Command of the Israeli Air Force.* New York: Macmillan, 1977.

St. James Palace Conference
See London Round Table Conference

Stalin, Joseph
Born: December 21, 1879
Died: March 5, 1953

Communist revolutionary and dictator of the Soviet Union (1929–1953). Much of Joseph Stalin's early life remains obscure, in part because he took pains to rewrite it. He was born in the town of Gori in Georgia in the Caucasus on December 21, 1879, as Josef Dzhugashvili. In 1894 he entered a theological seminary on a scholarship. He was either expelled or quit the seminary, where, he claimed, he was introduced to Marxism. In 1901 he joined the Russian Social Democratic Labor Party, where his activities to secure funds included robberies and counterfeiting operations. Exiled to Siberia in 1903, he escaped a year later. One of his aliases, the one by which he became best known, was that of Stalin ("Steel"), given to him by his fellow revolutionaries for his strength and ruthlessness. During the March 1917 Revolution he returned to Petrograd and became editor of the party newspaper, *Pravda* ("Truth").

Stalin was active in the Russian Civil War (1918–1921) and the Russo-Polish War (1920–1921), and from 1920 to 1923 he was com-

Joseph Stalin, Bolshevik revolutionary and absolute ruler of the Soviet Union from 1929 until his death in 1953. (Library of Congress)

missar of nationalities. In 1923 he assumed the post of secretary-general of the Communist Party, a position he used as a springboard to power. His political rise has been ascribed to his skill at in-fighting and playing one faction against another as well as his absolute ruthlessness. But he also put in long hours and deserves considerable credit for his achievement.

By the late 1920s Stalin had triumphed over his rivals to wield absolute power in the Soviet Union. He created the Soviet bureaucratic system and refined both the secret police and slave labor camps. He abandoned Vladimir Lenin's New Economic Policy that permitted a degree of capitalism in Russia and initiated a series of five-year plans to modernize the economy, concentrating on heavy industry. Stalin's economic policies also included the forced collectivization of agriculture that claimed an estimated 10–15 million lives. He was directly responsible for the Great Purge trials of the 1930s that consumed virtually all of the top party leadership. Also falling victim to the Great Purge were military leaders, including 60 percent of Red Army officers above the rank of major.

During World War II Stalin grew in stature as a military commander and strategist. Learning the art of war and absorbing specialist military information, he made all of the important strategic decisions for the Red Army as well as making many decisions on the tactical level. He also carried out his own foreign policy during the war.

The Soviet Union suffered grievously during the war, with perhaps 27 million people dead and widespread physical destruction. Stalin put the population to work rebuilding, although his people paid for this in retention of the 48-hour workweek and living standards well below those of 1940. In a new Five-Year Plan he continued his emphasis on building heavy industry, although some attention was paid to pressing housing needs.

To unite the Soviet people under his leadership, Stalin proclaimed the belief of a communist world threatened by encircling enemies. Everything was done to maintain the intense nationalistic sentiments aroused by the long struggle against the Germans in World War II. Andrei Zhdanov, political boss of Leningrad, became the guiding spirit of this ideology, known as the Zhdanovshchina. It championed Russian nationalism and attacked Western influence, glorified communism, and above all trumpeted the accomplishments and inspiration of the "Great Leader," Stalin, attributing to him all Soviet successes.

In foreign affairs, Stalin seized opportunities that presented themselves in Eastern Europe and the Balkans. Knowing exactly what he wanted, he met with Western leaders in Moscow and at the Tehran, Yalta, and Potsdam conferences. Following World War II, he insisted on East European governments that were friendly to the Soviet Union, this in order to provide security for a badly wounded Soviet empire. Although there were fears in the West that Stalin's plans included the communization of Western Europe, the dictator's immediate motivation was simply that of securing Soviet border areas. Because of the Red Army presence on the ground, there was little that Western leaders could do to prevent this short of war

with the Soviet Union. Stalin's regime emerged from the war with all of Eastern Europe, and much of Central Europe, under its control.

Once Stalin rejected a closer relationship with the West, the Cold War began in earnest. He refused to allow the East European Soviet satellites to participate in the European Recovery Program (Marshall Plan), and following an impasse over German reunification on Soviet terms, in the summer of 1948 Soviet troops cut off Western land access to the city of Berlin. Stalin's tactics and saber rattling resulted in the 1949 formation of the North Atlantic Treaty Organization (NATO) and prompted the movement toward West European unity.

Stalin pushed hard to develop an atomic bomb, a process greatly accelerated by Soviet espionage. Following the explosion of the Soviet Union's first nuclear device in late 1949, he adopted a less militant foreign policy in favor of one that was comparatively defensive in nature. Agitation against colonialism was increasingly used to weaken the Western hold on global military bases, while Soviet foreign policy also sought to sow discord between the United States and its allies.

Early in 1950 Stalin gave his blessing to plans by North Korean leader Kim Il Sung to invade South Korea and reunify the peninsula under communist rule. Stalin evidently believed Kim's contention that the United States would either do nothing or would not react in time to save South Korea. Later, when the war went badly for Kim and North Korea, Stalin sanctioned military intervention by the People's Republic of China (PRC), promising to provide the PRC with Soviet air support.

Stalin's Middle Eastern policies, particularly those regarding Israel, were deceptive. On the surface he gave the impression that he favored a strong, unified State of Israel. However, his motives were not so altruistic. Indeed, there is every indication that he hoped to lure Israel into the Soviet orbit while at the same time ridding the Soviet Union of its Jewish population. Representatives at the United Nations (UN) were astonished to hear Soviet ambassador Andrei Gromyko declare Soviet endorsement for a Jewish state under the UN partition plan. Because the Soviet Union had a veto in the Security Council and was thus in position to block decisions there, its support was crucial.

Millions of Jews lived in Russia and Eastern Europe. Stalin's position seemed to signal hope for Jews there and in Palestine. The Soviet Union was, in fact, the second state to recognize Israel, after the United States. At the same time, Stalin instigated anti-Jewish campaigns in Russia. Soviet and East European Jews immigrated by the thousands to Israel, perhaps laying bare Stalin's true goals in recognizing Israel.

At the same time Stalin also supplied Soviet arms to Israel, despite a UN embargo. Deliveries took place via Czechoslovakia and were crucial in the defense of Jerusalem when five Arab armies attacked in 1948. Many Russians also volunteered to work in Israel or to be part of the Jewish defense forces.

Stalin tried to leverage his influence in Israel to push for socialism or communism. But when these efforts failed, he turned to the

Arab countries instead. He supported them politically at first and then militarily as well.

Stalin's reversal on Israel found expression in active anti-Semitism within the Soviet Union. The last act in the Stalinist drama was the so-called Doctors' Plot. Fed by Stalin's continuing paranoia, nine doctors, six of them Jewish, were accused of employing their medical skills to assassinate prominent individuals, among them Stalin's heir apparent Andrei Zhdanov. Many in the Soviet Union believed that this heralded a return to the purges of the 1930s. But it may only have been a maneuver to strike out against the growing ascendancy of a leadership group headed by Georgy Malenkov and Lavrenty Beria or perhaps an effort to imbue the bureaucracy with renewed revolutionary zeal. Certainly it was in part prompted by anti-Semitism. Whatever the reasons, Stalin's death in Moscow on March 5, 1953, following a paralytic stroke came as a relief to many in highly vulnerable Soviet leadership positions.

THOMAS J. WEILER

See also

Anti-Semitism; Soviet Union and Russia, Middle East Policy

References

Deutscher, Isaac. *Stalin: A Political Biography*. New York: Oxford University Press, 1969.

McNeal, Robert. *Stalin: Man and Ruler*. New York: New York University Press, 1988.

Rayfield, Donald. *Stalin and His Hangmen: The Tyrant and Those Who Killed for Him*. New York: Random House, 2004.

Tucker, Robert C. *Stalin as Revolutionary, 1879–1929*. New York: Norton, 1973.

———. *Stalin in Power: The Revolution from Above, 1928–1941*. New York: Norton, 1990.

Star of David

Symbol most commonly associated with Judaism and Jewish identity. The Star of David (Magen David), also known as the Shield of David, is alleged to represent the shield of biblical King David or at least a symbol on that shield or a royal seal. Some have attributed profound theological significance to the Star of David, but there is no religious or scriptural basis for that claim. Indeed, the symbol of two intertwined equilateral triangles (one pointed up and the other down), or hexagram, was a common one in the Middle East and North Africa and was long associated with good luck.

In medieval Europe, it became the practice to place Stars of David on synagogues to identify them as Jewish places of worship, much as crosses appeared on Christian churches. But it was the menorah rather than the Star of David that was the primary Jewish symbol. The Star of David achieved its close identification with Judaism only in the 19th century. Although the step was at first controversial, in 1897 the World Zionist Organization (WZO) adopted the Star of David as its official symbol. Then in 1948 the Star of David appeared on the flag of the new State of Israel. The Magen David Adom (Red Star of David) is the Israeli equivalent of the Red

The Israeli flag on the side of a building in Tel Aviv. The Magen David, or Star of David, has become the most recognizable symbol of Judaism and Jewish identity. (James Margolis/iStockphoto.com)

Cross or Red Crescent. The Israeli organization of that name is a member of the International Committee of the Red Cross.

SPENCER C. TUCKER

See also

World Zionist Organization

Reference

Frankle, Ellen, and Betsey Platkin Teutsch. *The Encyclopedia of Jewish Symbols*. Northvale, NJ: Jason Avonson, 1992.

Stern, Avraham
Born: December 23, 1907
Died: February 12, 1942

Fervent Zionist and founder and leader of the Lehi (Lohamei Herut Israel) terrorist group, also known as the Stern Gang. Avraham Stern was born in Suwałki, Poland, on December 23, 1907. He studied at the Hebrew High School there but immigrated to Palestine in

Avraham Stern, leader of the Lehi underground terrorist organization operation known as the Stern Gang, who was murdered by the British in Palestine in February 1942. (Israeli Government Press Office)

1925 before graduating and continued his high school studies in Jerusalem. He then studied philosophy and classical languages at Jerusalem's Hebrew University. Fluent in Latin and Greek, he won a scholarship to study in Florence, Italy. There he was impressed by dictator Benito Mussolini as well as Italian fascism.

A natty dresser and a womanizer, Stern on his return to Palestine sought a calling to which he could dedicate his talents, as academic work no longer held his attention. Considered a gifted albeit eccentric poet, his attempts to make a living from writing failed. Instead, he turned to politics.

By the late 1920s Stern embraced Revisionist Zionism, a movement founded by Vladimir Jabotinsky. Revisionist Zionists agreed with mainline Zionists on the goal of establishing a Jewish state in Palestine, but its approach was more militant and envisioned an armed struggle to achieve the end. Palestine was then ruled by Britain under a League of Nations mandate, and tensions between Jews and Arabs owing to increased Jewish migration into Palestine and Jewish land purchases there spilled over into violence. Stern became an active member of the Haganah Jewish self-defense organization that helped to protect Jews against Arab attack. Stern par-

ticipated in the defense of Jewish homes and shops in Jerusalem during the Arab Riots of 1929 in which some 133 Jews were killed and 400 injured in Jerusalem, Hebron, and Safed.

Although the British finally quelled the riots, sporadic violence continued throughout the next decade. Indeed, the official response from the British government seemed to favor the Arabs in that London sought means to curb Jewish immigration and land purchases in Palestine. Stern was convinced of the need to organize a more active defense of Jewish interests. In 1931 he helped found the radical group known as the Irgun Tsvai Leumi (IZL, National Military Organization). It advocated counterterrorist tactics against the Arabs and the military liberation of Palestine. Subsequently, Stern directed a training program that emphasized the use of small arms and explosives. He quickly rose through the ranks and became the Irgun's top field commander.

Despite Stern's success, in 1937 he formed a splinter group of Irgun commonly referred to as the IZL. By that time he was drifting away from Jabotinsky and turned to Abba Achimeir, whose Brith Habiryonim faction was even more radical than the Revisionists. Achimeir and Stern agreed to take a more aggressive approach regarding their enemies. Designed with such tactics in mind, the IZL prepared for a campaign of terror. Stern's watchwords were "study, train, and think," but his emphasis was on the use of force.

Formation of the IZL coincided with another Arab uprising known as the Arab Revolt, which began in 1936, as Haj Amin al-Husseini, grand mufti of Jerusalem, led a successful general strike. For the next three years, unrest was commonplace throughout the country. British authorities seemed unable or unwilling to end the violence and continued to offer peace plans and then retract them. Stern organized a bombing campaign and instructed his IZL squads to "kill, be killed, but do not surrender." By 1938, civil government had largely broken down in Palestine. Martial law brought a semblance of peace, but new British policies helped push Stern into a different strategy.

Recognizing the strong possibility of a world war, London opted to protect Britain's significant Middle Eastern holdings by placating Arab opinion. On May 17, 1939, an official British White Paper declared that only 75,000 more Jews would enter Palestine. After that, local Arabs would decide immigration policy. To Zionists in Palestine, the White Paper was a dangerous blow against their future. Furthermore, few Western countries were willing to accept Jewish refugees.

For Stern, Britain's decision was a declaration of war. He called for action but was overruled by Jabotinsky. To avoid controversy, Stern returned to Poland. There, he hoped to expand IZL operations and recruit fighters. Although he established a daily newspaper, *Die Tat* (Action), the German invasion of September 1, 1939, interrupted Stern's mission. Escaping back to Palestine, Stern made a complete break with Jabotinsky and the IZL, which argued the need for cooperation with the British, who had gone to war against Germany on September 3. Stern, asserting that World War II was a conflict "between *Gog* and *Magog*," called instead for a campaign against Great Britain. A year later, Stern formed his last underground unit, Lohamei Herut Israel (Fighters for Israel's Freedom, also known as Lehi for its Hebrew acronym). Recruited chiefly from the IZL, Lehi numbered about 200 men and women. Although a small organization, its members were dedicated and extremely dangerous. Lehi lived up to Stern's dark poetry, for assassination, bombing, and robbery were all Lehi tactics.

British authorities labeled Lehi the Stern Gang, and during 1940–1941 Stern led a clandestine existence that required numerous safe houses, codes, and a quick wit. His alias, Yair, was picked to honor Eliezar ben Yair, the Zealot leader who had defied the Roman armies from the fortress of Masada centuries before. In a controversial action, Stern sent agents to contact Nazi Germany. Arguing that "the enemy of my enemy is my friend," he attempted to forge an alliance between Lehi and the Abwehr, Germany's military intelligence service. Although nothing ever came of that tentative outreach, word of Stern's activities caused most Jews to sever all ties with Lehi.

In January 1942 following a bomb explosion in Tel Aviv that killed three policeman, British authorities offered a reward of £1,000 for Stern's arrest. Cut off from support and now hunted, he went into hiding. He escaped several dragnets but was finally discovered in Tel Aviv. On February 12, 1942, six British policemen broke into his safe house and shot him on the spot. In 1978 an Israeli postage stamp was issued in Stern's honor, and he is also memorialized in the town of Kochav Yair (Yair's Star), after his nickname.

SPENCER C. TUCKER

See also

Arab Revolt of 1936–1939; Gog and Magog; Haganah; Husseini, Haj Amin al-; Irgun Tsvai Leumi; Jabotinsky, Vladimir Yevgenyevich; Palestine, British Mandate for; White Paper (1939); Zionism

References

Bell, J. Bowyer. *Terror out of Zion: Irgun Zvai Leumi, Lehi and the Palestine Underground, 1929–1949.* New York: St. Martin's, 1979.

Bethell, Nicholas. *The Palestine Triangle: The Struggle for the Holy Land, 1935–48.* New York: Putnam, 1979.

Brenner, Lenni. *The Iron Wall: Zionist Revisionism from Jabotinsky to Shamir.* London: Zed, 1984.

Stern Gang

See Lohamei Herut Israel

Strait of Tiran Crisis

Start Date: 1956
End Date: 1967

The Strait of Tiran is a strategically important three-mile-long narrow body of water between the Sinai Peninsula and the island of Tiran that connects the Red Sea to the Gulf of Aqaba. It is the westernmost passage of the Straits of Tiran. Egyptian closure of the waterway helped precipitate the opening of hostilities during both the 1956 Suez Crisis and the 1967 Six-Day War. The eastern shore of the Straits of Tiran is part of Saudi Arabia, while the western shore is at the southern tip of the Sinai Peninsula, overlooked by the Egyptian city of Sharm al-Sheikh. All shipping to and from the Israeli port of Eilat and the Jordanian port of Aqaba must pass through these narrow straits.

In the aftermath of the Israeli War of Independence (1948–1949), Egypt closed the Strait of Tiran from 1949 to 1956. This action was in violation of both the 1949 armistice agreement and international law. As such, the Israel Defense Forces (IDF) General Staff planned for a preemptive war that would begin with an attack to reopen the strait.

The Israelis found common cause with the British and French when Egyptian president Gamal Abdel Nasser nationalized the Suez Canal on July 26, 1956. The Israeli government secretly conspired with the British and French governments whereby the IDF would attack across the Sinai, providing the British and French an excuse to intervene with their forces allegedly to protect the canal. Cooperating with its allies, the IDF hoped to be able to reopen the Strait of Tiran to Israeli shipping but also to destroy Egyptian military forces in the Sinai and halt fedayeen terrorist attacks originating from the Gaza Strip.

The IDF's Sinai Campaign, launched on October 29, 1956, proved a huge success. During the final phase of the campaign, the IDF's 9th Infantry Brigade captured Sharm al-Sheikh and reopened the Strait of Tiran on the night of November 2–3.

Now in complete control of the Sinai, the Israelis were not content with a mere armistice. They refused to evacuate the Sinai until they secured international promises that would guarantee unfettered Israeli access to the Strait of Tiran. After 17 nations had agreed that Israel was entitled to the right of passage through the waterway, on March 1, 1957, Israel began to withdraw its forces. All IDF personnel had departed the Sinai by March 11.

Recognizing Egypt's blockade of the strait as a violation of international passage, United Nations (UN) Resolution II of February 2, 1957, called for a UN Emergency Force (UNEF) to be placed in the Sinai upon Israel's withdrawal. An element of the UNEF was garrisoned at Sharm al-Sheikh to ensure that the waterway remained open to all international shipping. The United States further pledged to the Israelis that it would consider any blockade of the Strait of Tiran to be an act of war against Israel and thus subject to an Israeli military response. Further protections were afforded Israel in April 1958 when the UN Conference on the Law of the Sea adopted the Convention on the Territorial Sea and Contiguous Zone, which forbade any future blockade of the strait.

As Israeli-Egyptian tensions heated up again in 1967, President Nasser demanded that the UNEF be withdrawn from the Sinai. In a mistaken decision, UN secretary-general U Thant complied with the request without seeking the counsel of the General Assembly. On May 23, 1967, Nasser announced that Egypt had again closed the Strait of Tiran to Israeli shipping. The following day, Nasser an-

An Israeli gunboat passing through the Strait of Tiran during the Six-Day War, June 8, 1967. (Ya'acov Agor/Israeli Government Press Office)

nounced that the waterway had been mined. Both moves were in blatant violation of international law.

The Israeli government first sought a diplomatic solution to the crisis by asking both the United States and the UN to reopen the Strait of Tiran, as had been promised in 1957. With no sign of international action against Egypt, however, Israel launched the Six-Day War on June 5, 1967. The IDF General Staff planned Operation LIGHTS to seize Sharm al-Sheikh and open the waterway. Although originally planned as a night offensive, with paratroops landing at A-Tur to support a naval assault, the IDF conducted a morning attack on June 7, when it was determined that most of the Egyptian forces had already withdrawn. After a brief fight, the Israelis declared the strait reopened. Israel remained in control of the Strait of Tiran until 1982, when they evacuated Sharm al-Sheikh under the provisions of the 1978 Camp David Accords and the 1979 Israel-Egypt Peace Treaty. The eastern part of the Sinai, including the strait, is currently demilitarized and remains under the supervision of the Multinational Force and Observers (MFO).

THOMAS D. VEVE

See also

Aqaba, Gulf of; Camp David Accords; Eilat, Israel; Geography of the Middle East; Israel-Egypt Peace Treaty; Nasser, Gamal Abdel; Red Sea; Sharm al-Sheikh; Sinai Campaign; Six-Day War; Straits of Tiran; Suez Canal; Suez Crisis; U Thant

References

Halderman, John W., ed. *The Middle East Crisis: Test of International Law.* Dobbs Ferry, NY: Oceana, 1969.

Herzog, Chaim. *The Arab-Israeli Wars: War and Peace in the Middle East from the War of Independence to Lebanon.* Westminster, MD: Random House, 1984.

Oren, Michael B. *Six Days of War: June 1967 and the Making of the Modern Middle East.* Novato, CA: Presidio, 2003.

Smith, Charles D. *Palestine and the Arab-Israeli Conflict: A History with Documents.* 6th ed. New York: Bedford/St. Martin's, 2006.

Straits of Tiran

Narrow passages of water located between the Sinai Peninsula to the west and the Arabian Peninsula to the east. The westernmost of these waterways, the roughly 3-mile-wide stretch between the Sinai Peninsula and the island of Tiran, is known as the Strait of Tiran and is the most important of the passages in terms to the Arab-Israeli conflict. Just 4.3 miles northeast of the Egyptian city of Sharm al-Sheikh, the Strait of Tiran connects the Gulf of Aqaba with the Red Sea. This area has been the focus of ongoing tensions between Egypt and Israel over the Israeli right of access to the Strait of Tiran and to the Red Sea. Indeed, this very issue precipitated the 1967 Six-Day War. Israel was guaranteed the right of access to the strait as codified in the Convention on the Territorial Sea and Contiguous Zones, adopted by the United Nations (UN) Conference on the Law of the Sea in 1957. Following the adoption of the convention, Israel held that any blockade of the Strait of Tiran would justify military action to maintain its access to the critical port of Eilat.

Following a decade of relative peace between Egypt and Israel, political and military brinksmanship between the two nations led to Egyptian president Gamal Abdel Nasser ordering Egyptian forces to institute a blockade of the Strait of Tiran on May 23, 1967. This move effectively cut off Israel's only supply route with Asia as well as halted Israel's flow of oil from Iran, its major supplier. Acting in accordance with international law, Israel considered the closure of the strait to be an act of war but for the moment held back from an immediate attack on Egypt.

Further alarmed by an agreement placing the Egyptian and Jordanian military command under Egyptian control, by Egypt's mutual defense treaty with Syria, and by the militarization of the Sinai by Egyptian forces, Israel launched a preemptive military strike on June 5, 1967. This attack destroyed Egypt's air force, much of it on the ground, while ground forces quickly brought the Sinai Peninsula under Israeli control. When Syria and Jordan joined the war on Egypt's side, Israel quickly defeated their forces as well, capturing the Golan Heights from Syria and East Jerusalem and the West Bank from Jordan. The Strait of Tiran has remained open to Israeli shipping since the end of the Six-Day War.

THOMAS D. VEVE AND KEITH A. LEITICH

See also

Aqaba, Gulf of; Egypt; Eilat, Israel; Israel; Jordan; Nasser, Gamal Abdel; Sharm al-Sheikh; Sinai; Syria

References

Barker, A. J. *Arab-Israeli Wars.* New York: Hippocrene, 1980.
Halderman, John W., ed. *The Middle East Crisis: Test of International Law.* Dobbs Ferry, NY: Oceana, 1969.
Herzog, Chaim. *The Arab-Israeli Wars: War and Peace in the Middle East from the War of Independence to Lebanon.* Westminster, MD: Random House, 1984.
Khouri, Fred. *The Arab-Israeli Dilemma.* 3rd ed. Syracuse, NY: Syracuse University Press, 1985.
Smith, Charles D. *Palestine and the Arab-Israeli Conflict: A History with Documents.* 6th ed. New York: Bedford/St. Martin's, 2006.

Submarines

Submarines played only a small role in the 20th-century Arab-Israeli conflicts. The conflicts were of such short duration and involved such a small area of operations that submarines could make little impact other than conducting covert intelligence collection or, in the case of Israel, delivering special forces units. Because all the Middle Eastern conflicts—the Israeli War of Independence (1948–1949), the Suez Crisis (1956), the Six-Day War (1967), and the Yom Kippur War (1973)—involved nations sharing contiguous borders, naval operations were less important than land and air forces. However, the advent of submarine-launched cruise missiles

may lead to submarines having a greater role in any future conflicts that may erupt. Israel, Egypt, Libya, and Iran all have submarine fleets, albeit of varying size, quality, and capability. Iran and Israel have received or are developing land-attack cruise missiles for their submarines.

The nature of their fleets' operating areas and the limited size of their defense budgets have precluded the countries involved in the Arab-Israeli wars from operating nuclear-powered submarines. Instead, they have had to opt for the cheaper and much shorter-ranged conventional diesel-electric models. In fact, prior to the late 1990s they were limited to operating secondhand obsolescent submarines. Since that time, they have acquired increasingly modern top-of-the-line conventionally powered submarines.

Israel acquired its first submarines from Great Britain in 1958: two World War II–era Type S diesel boats. Capable of 9 knots submerged and equipped with six 21-inch torpedo tubes and various deck guns and machine guns, the Type S boats were already obsolete. Israel later acquired three 1940s-era Type-T submarines. At 1,700 metric tons submerged and with a submerged speed of 15 knots, the Type Ts were larger and faster than their predecessors but carried a similar armament. Originally designed to attack enemy surface vessels in the Atlantic, the Type S and Type T submarines in Israeli service operated mostly in the Mediterranean Sea, the Red Sea, and the Persian Gulf, where their primary mission was to land covert operations forces. The *Tanin*, an Israeli Type S submarine, saw brief action during the 1967 Six-Day War when it landed a team of commandos at the Egyptian port of Alexandria and subsequently attacked an Egyptian sloop. The Type T submarines served during the War of Attrition that lasted from 1967 through 1973, successfully conducting several special operations forces raids.

Israel upgraded its submarine fleet in 1976 with the introduction of the Gal-class boats, which were specially designed to operate in the region. Smaller and faster than the World War II–era boats, they displaced 660 metric tons and had a top submerged speed of 17 knots. The three Gal-class subs supported extensive covert operations, especially during the Israeli 1982 invasion of Lebanon and against Palestinian targets there and in North Africa. Israel began to replace the Gals in 1997, when it bought three 1925-ton German-built Dolphin-class submarines. Capable of 20 knots submerged, the Dolphins carry both torpedoes and possibly the 900-mile-range Popeye Turbo cruise missile. Estimates of the Dolphin's number of launch tubes range from 6 to 10. Israel has never confirmed or denied that it has nuclear weapons, but the general assumption is that Israel does have them. Although there are no firm indicators that any of Israel's presumed nuclear weapons are capable of being launched from a submarine, most of Israel's enemies in the region suspect that this is the case.

While Israel acquired Western submarines, the Arab countries primarily relied on Soviet designs to equip their fleets. Egypt acquired its first submarines, four Soviet-built Romeo-class boats, in 1957. Egypt secured eight in all (four in 1957, three in 1958, and one in 1962). Two of these were returned to the Soviet Union in 1966,

A new Israeli Dolphin-class submarine arrives at Haifa, July 1999. (Reuters/Corbis)

and two more were returned during 1971–1972; all four were exchanged for Whiskey-class boats. The 1,700-ton Romeos are based on the German Type XXI design of World War II, have a top speed of 14 knots submerged, and are equipped with eight 21-inch torpedo tubes (six in front, two astern). Although of a later design than the Romeos, the slightly smaller (at 1,080 tons) submerged Whiskey-class units offered no performance improvements over the Romeos. The Whiskey-class subs had a lower submerged top speed at 13.5 knots and fewer torpedo tubes (four forward, two aft) but did have a longer underwater duration (30 hours versus 24 at a speed of 3 knots).

Egypt's Romeos and Whiskeys played almost no role in the country's many conflicts with Israel. Their employment was limited to coastal defense and minelaying (in the Gulf of Aqaba). Finally, Egypt purchased four British-built Oberon-class submarines in 1989 and had their combat systems, electronics, and sonars updated. The Oberons are among the quietest submarines in the world and have a submerged displacement of 2,000 tons and a top underwater speed of 17 knots. Their eight 21-inch torpedo tubes can be used to fire torpedoes or Harpoon cruise missiles.

Syria acquired three Romeo-class submarines from the Soviet Union during 1985–1986. An older Whiskey-class sub was also transferred to Syria in 1986 but to serve as a battery-charging hulk to support the Romeo boats.

Farther west, Libya used its oil wealth to purchase six of the more modern Foxtrot-class submarines from the Soviet Union during 1978–1980. With a submerged displacement of 2,045 tons, the Foxtrot class was the largest of the Soviet submarine designs exported before the Kilo class was introduced in the late 1980s. The Foxtrot's 15-knot maximum submerged speed was not particularly impressive. However, it could remain submerged on batteries for up to four days and was the quietest Soviet submarine of its day, making it difficult to detect in the coastal waters off North Africa. However, Libya's submarines have suffered from poor maintenance and crew training and are believed to have never ventured far from the Libyan coast.

After Iran's fundamentalist revolution in 1979, it pursued an aggressive program of modern weapons acquisition and clearly stated its national policy of eliminating the State of Israel. Consequently, both the United States and Germany withheld deliveries of submarines previously contracted for by the Iranian Navy. This drove Iran to purchase three Soviet-built Kilo-class submarines in the early 1990s. The Kilo-class displaces more than 3,900 tons submerged and has a top underwater speed of 17 knots. The Kilos are armed with six 21-inch torpedo tubes and one surface-to-air missile (SAM) launcher.

The Iranian and Israeli submarines represent the best of the submarine designs in service among Middle Eastern nations. Once considered obsolete by many American defense analysts, modern diesel submarines are now recognized as a serious threat in constricted waters, such as those of the Middle East's potential conflict zones. Moreover, modern diesels are quieter when operating on their batteries than are nuclear submarines and can remain submerged on their batteries for up to 15 days with snorkeling. Nonetheless, prior to the introduction of submarine-launched land-attack missiles in 1991, submarines traditionally have had their greatest impact in wars that last long enough for attacks on an enemy's fleet and shipping to have a strategic impact on the fighting ashore. This has now changed. More importantly, Iran's Kilo-class submarines provide Tehran with the capacity to seriously disrupt if not decimate oil shipments coming out of the Persian Gulf.

BRYAN VIZZINI AND CARL OTIS SCHUSTER

See also

Arms Sales, International; Attrition, War of; Iran, Armed Forces; Iraq, Armed Forces; Israel Defense Forces; Mines and Mine Warfare, Sea; Warships, Surface

References

Eldar, Maik. *Dakar and the Story of the Israeli Submarines.* Tel Aviv: Modan: Aryeh Nir, 1997.

Erell, Shlomo. *Hed artsi* [Submarine Diplomacy]. Tel Aviv: Yehudah, 2000.

Katzman, Kenneth. *Iran: U.S. Policy and Options.* Washington, DC: Library of Congress, 2000.

Moore, John. *Jane's Fighting Ships, 1977–78.* London: Jane's, 1977.

Revelle, Daniel J., and Lora Lumpe. "Third World Submarines." *Scientific American* (August 1994): 16–21.

Sharpe, Richard. *Jane's Fighting Ships, 1991–1992.* Surrey, UK: Jane's, 1991.

Südfeld, Simon Maximilian

See Nordau, Max

Suez Canal

Canal that links the Mediterranean Sea and the Red Sea and is one of the world's most important shipping lanes. Just more than 100 miles in length, the Suez Canal, which opened in 1869, has been a source of great controversy since its construction in the mid-19th century. Although the canal had been built by Egyptian labor, control of the canal and its revenues remained in French and British hands until 1956, when it was nationalized by Egyptian president Gamal Abdel Nasser.

From its inception, the Suez Canal has been the source of diplomatic struggles. Although a canal had cut through the Sinai Peninsula in ancient times, it was filled in during the Abbasid era in the eighth century. However, as the centuries passed, engineers and local rulers speculated about the possibility of creating a new canal that would connect the Red Sea and the Mediterranean Sea. In the 18th century, European trade in India led to an increased desire to find a faster route between the subcontinent and Europe. A canal through the Sinai Peninsula would serve to eliminate the long journey to India around Africa's Cape of Good Hope.

However, despite years of speculation, it was not until 1854 that the modern Suez Canal project began. The brainchild of French entrepreneur Ferdinand de Lesseps, planning commenced when the khedive (viceroy) of Egypt, Said Pasha, granted de Lesseps a concession for the canal's construction. Over the next several years, de Lesseps and his Compagnie Universelle du Canal Maritime de Suez (Universal Maritime Company of the Suez) sold shares to numerous European investors in an effort to raise the funds necessary to build the canal.

In 1856 Said Pasha granted the French company the right to operate the canal for 99 years. This concession became a source of immense consternation among Egyptians, and anger was further inflamed by de Lesseps's shady business practices. When he was unable to sell all of the necessary shares to European investors, de Lesseps announced that Said Pasha had purchased those remaining. In reality, the Egyptian leader had not done so and did not have the money to do so. To protect his honor and that of his country, Said Pasha borrowed vast amounts of money from European banks to purchase the shares, using Egypt's cotton crops and other natural resources as collateral. This was the beginning of a long legacy of debt that would cripple the Egyptian economy. Meanwhile, profits to European financiers soared.

Construction on the monumental canal began in 1859 and took a decade to complete. In the first years of building, Egyptian corvée (indentured) labor was used to dig the canal by hand at great expense to the life and liberty of the Egyptian population. The corvée practice was perceived as a further insult among the Egyptians. In the final years of construction, dredging machines and other mechanized equipment from Europe were employed, and in November 1869 to great fanfare the canal finally opened. In consequence, ships could now pass between the Mediterranean Sea and the Red Sea, greatly cutting the time and expense of a journey between Europe and Asia.

In 1875 Ismail Pasha, now khedive of Egypt, offered for sale his nation's shares in the canal to pay back loans made to Egypt by European lenders. By now two-thirds of the tonnage transiting the canal was British. The British government could not be indifferent to its control. Thus, British prime minister Benjamin Disraeli, without waiting for parliamentary consent, boldly and quickly purchased the shares for Great Britain (176,602 of the total of 400,000 shares) at a cost of £4 million. The British government was now the largest shareholder in the company. Egypt was also completely cut out of the canal's profits, a condition that would last until 1949 when the Suez Canal Company granted Egypt 7 percent of the canal's profits.

For nearly a century, Egyptians watched helplessly as foreign governments and investors made huge profits from the canal built on their soil and with their labor. Meanwhile, Britain occupied Egypt in 1881 ostensibly to restore order following antiforeign riots there and in so doing it reduced the sovereignty of the Egyptian monar-

The U.S. aircraft carrier *Dwight D. Eisenhower* transiting the Suez Canal en route to the Mediterranean Sea to support Operation DESERT SHIELD, August 22, 1990. (Frank A. Marquart/U.S. Department of Defense)

chy to puppet status. The Egyptian population and politicians harbored great resentment, and this resentment eventually found a voice in the policies of Egyptian nationalist leader Nasser.

A leader of the 1952 Free Officer Coup against King Farouk I, Nasser became the undisputed leader of Egypt by 1954 and was elected president (as the only candidate) in 1956. A man of modest background who spoke of social justice, Nasser was a leading light in the international Non-Aligned Movement and a founder of modern Arab nationalism.

In 1955 Nasser had announced plans to build a new high dam at Aswan and had secured funding from the World Bank, with the United States and Great Britain as the primary lenders. However, when Egypt purchased weapons from Soviet-allied Czechoslovakia and recognized the People's Republic of China (PRC), the United States, followed by Britain, pulled out of the loan program. In response, Nasser determined that the only way his country could raise the money necessary for the dam's completion was by seizing control of the Suez Canal. Thus, on July 26, 1956, Nasser's troops took control of the Canal Zone.

Britain and France, the two primary shareholders in the Suez Canal Company, not only feared the loss of their profits but also worried that the Egyptians would restrict their supplies of oil. At the same time, Israel was in crisis because Nasser had coupled the Suez seizure with a blockade of Israeli shipping through the Strait of Tiran. These three nations then clandestinely plotted to band together, depose Nasser, and reassert control over the canal.

The event known as the Suez Crisis began on October 29, 1956, when Israel sent forces into Egypt's Sinai Peninsula. Meanwhile, as per the secret plan they had hatched with the Israelis, the British and French sent both Egypt and Israel an ultimatum regarding the canal. When Egypt rejected their demands, prepositioned British and French forces attacked Egypt, even landing troops.

Angry at having been caught by surprise by the British and French action, U.S. president Dwight Eisenhower brought heavy diplomatic and financial pressure on Britain to withdraw. When the British announced that they would do so, France and Israel were forced to follow suit. The Soviet Union also applied pressure, but it was the U.S. move that was decisive. Nasser found himself an instant hero not only in Egypt and the larger Arab world but also in countries fighting against imperial oppression. After nearly 100 years, Egypt finally controlled the Suez Canal.

From 1956 until 1975 the Suez Canal was closed to Israeli shipping while Israel and Egypt continued to skirmish across their border. In 1967 the canal closed during the June Six-Day War, with ships scuttled in the waterway and with Israel's occupation of the Sinai. The canal remained closed to all traffic until June 1975. During this long period, the Suez Canal Zone was the site of many engagements between Egypt and Israel. However, the Suez Canal reopened to ships in 1975. When peace was achieved between Egypt and Israel in 1979, Israeli troops withdrew from the Sinai, and Egypt once again took full control of the waterway. Today, all ships are able to pass through the Suez Canal, one of the most important shipping lanes of the world.

NANCY STOCKDALE

See also

Egypt; Egypt, Armed Forces; Nasser, Gamal Abdel; Sinai Campaign; Six-Day War; Suez Crisis

References

Gorst, Anthony, and Lewis Johnman. *The Suez Crisis*. London: Routledge, 1997.

Karabell, Zachary. *Parting the Desert: The Creation of the Suez Canal*. New York: Knopf, 2003.

Schonfield, Hugh Joseph. *The Suez Canal in Peace and War, 1869–1969*. Coral Gables, FL: University of Miami Press, 1969.

Varble, Derek. *The Suez Crisis, 1956*. London: Osprey, 2003.

Winckler, Onn, and Elie Podeh, eds. *Rethinking Nasserism: Revolution and Historical Memory in Modern Egypt*. Gainesville: University of Florida Press, 2004.

Suez Crisis
Start Date: July 26, 1956
End Date: March 6, 1957

The Suez Crisis was one of the major events of both the Cold War and the Arab-Israeli wars. It ended Britain's pretensions to be a world superpower and fatally weakened Britain's hold on what remained of its empire. It also placed a dangerous strain on U.S.-Soviet relations, strengthened the position of Egyptian leader Gamal Abdel Nasser throughout the Middle East, and distracted world attention from the concurrent Soviet military intervention in the Hungarian Revolution.

The Suez Crisis had its origins in the development plans of Gamal Abdel Nasser. In 1952 a reformist and anti-British coup d'état in Egypt, led by young army officers, toppled the government of King Farouk I. During the months that followed, Nasser emerged as the strongman and ultimately became president of Egypt. Nasser hoped to enhance his prestige and improve the quality of life for his nation's burgeoning population by carrying out long-discussed plans to construct a high dam on the upper Nile River south of Aswan to provide electric power. To finance the project, Nasser sought assistance

Representatives of 22 nations assemble for the Suez Conference in London, August 1956. (Hulton-Deutsch Collection/Corbis)

from the Western powers. But Nasser had also been endeavoring to build up and modernize the Egyptian military. Toward that end he had sought to acquire modern weapons from the United States and other Western nations. When the U.S. government refused to supply the advanced arms, which it believed might be used against the State of Israel, in 1955 Nasser turned to the communist bloc. In September 1955, with Soviet encouragement, he reached a barter arrangement with Czechoslovakia for substantial quantities of weapons, including jet aircraft and tanks, in return for Egyptian cotton.

This arms deal impacted on the Aswan High Dam construction project for which Nasser had sought Western financing. In December 1955 Washington declared its willingness to lend $56 million for financing the dam, while Britain pledged $14 million and the World Bank $200 million. The condition to the aid was that Egypt provide matching funds and that it not accept Soviet assistance.

Nasser was unhappy with the attached strings. With Nasser expecting a Soviet offer of assistance, the controlled Egyptian press launched an all-out propaganda offensive against the West, especially the United States. But when no Soviet offer was forthcoming, Nasser finally accepted the Western aid package on July 17, 1956. Much to his chagrin, two days later U.S. secretary of state John Foster Dulles announced that it had been withdrawn. Britain immediately followed suit. The official U.S. reasons were that Egypt had failed to reach agreement with the Sudan over the dam (most of the vast lake created by the dam would be in Sudanese territory), and the Egyptian part of the financing for the project had become uncertain. The real reasons were objections from some U.S. congressmen, especially Southerners fearful of competition from Egyptian cotton and Dulles's determination to teach Nasser and other neutralists a lesson. Dulles was angry over Nasser's flirtation with the communist bloc to include the arms purchases and was especially upset over Egypt's recent recognition of the People's Republic of China (PRC).

Nasser's response to this humiliating rebuff came a week later on July 26 when he nationalized the Suez Canal. He had contemplated such a move for some time, but the U.S. decision prompted its timing. In 1955 the canal produced net revenues of nearly $100 million, of which Egypt received only $2 million. Seizure of the canal would not only provide additional funding for the Aswan High Dam project, but it would make Nasser a hero in the eyes of many Arab nationalists.

The British government regarded the sea-level Suez Canal, which connected the eastern Mediterranean with the Red Sea across Egyptian territory, as its lifeline to Middle Eastern oil and the Far East. Indeed, fully 60 percent of all oil consumed in Western Europe passed through the canal. The canal, built by a private company headed by Frenchman Ferdinand de Lesseps, had opened to much fanfare in 1869. It quickly altered the trade routes of the world, and two-thirds of the tonnage passing through the canal was British. Khedive Ismail Pasha, who owned 44 percent of the company shares, found himself in dire financial straits, and in 1875 the British government stepped in and purchased his shares. In 1878 Britain acquired the island of Cyprus north of Egypt from the Ottoman Empire, further strengthening its position in the eastern Mediterranean north of Egypt. The British also increased their role in Egyptian financial affairs, and in 1882 they intervened militarily in Egypt, promising to depart once order had been restored. Britain remained in Egypt and in effect controlled its affairs through World War II.

In 1954 Nasser, determined to end British influence in Egypt, succeeded in renegotiating the 1936 treaty with the British to force the withdrawal of British troops from the Suez Canal Zone. The last British forces departed the Canal Zone on June 13, only six weeks before Nasser nationalized the canal.

The British government took the lead in opposing Nasser. London believed that Nasser's growing popularity in the Arab world was encouraging Arab nationalism and threatening to undermine British influence throughout the Middle East. British prime minister Anthony Eden developed a deep and abiding hatred of the Egyptian leader. For Eden, ousting Nasser from power became nothing short of an obsession. In the immediate aftermath of Nasser's nationalization of the canal, the British government called up 200,000 military reservists and dispatched military resources to the eastern Mediterranean.

The French government also had good reason to seek Nasser's removal. Paris sought to protect its own long-standing interests in the Middle East, but more to the point, the French were now engaged in fighting the National Liberation Front (NLF) in Algeria. The Algerian War, which began in November 1954, had greatly

expanded and had become an imbroglio for the government, now led by Socialist premier Guy Mollet. Nasser was a strong and vocal supporter of the NLF, and there were many in the French government and military who believed that overthrowing him would greatly enhance French chances of winning the Algerian War. This position found considerable support when on October 18, 1956, the French intercepted the Egyptian ship *Athos* and found it loaded with arms and documents proving Egyptian support for the NLF.

Israel formed the third leg in the triad of powers arrayed against Nasser. Egypt had instituted a blockade of Israeli ships at the Gulf of Aqaba, Israel's outlet to the Indian Ocean. Also, Egypt had never recognized the Jewish state and indeed remained at war with it following the Israeli War of Independence (1948–1949). In 1955 Israel mounted a half dozen cross-border raids, while Egypt carried out its own raids into Israeli territory by fedayeen (guerrilla fighters).

Over the months that followed Egyptian nationalization of the Suez Canal, the community of interest among British, French, and Israeli leaders developed into secret planning for a joint military operation to topple Nasser. The U.S. government was not consulted and indeed opposed the use of force. The British and French governments either did not understand the American attitude or, if they did, believed that Washington would give approval after the fact to policies undertaken by its major allies, which the latter believed to be absolutely necessary.

The British government first tried diplomacy. Two conferences in London attended by the representatives of 24 nations using the

British troops advance through Port Said, Egypt, as oil installations burn during the Anglo-French invasion of the Suez Canal area, November 10, 1956. (Bettmann/Corbis)

Yugoslav troops with the United Nations Emergency Forces (UNEF) on patrol in El Arish, Egypt, 1957. After Egypt nationalized the Suez Canal in 1956, the UNEF was established to oversee the withdrawal of foreign forces from the area. (Corel)

canal failed to produce agreement on a course of action, and Egypt refused to participate. A proposal by Secretary of State Dulles for a canal users' club of nations failed, as did an appeal to the United Nations (UN) Security Council. On October 1 Dulles announced that the United States was disassociating itself from British and French actions in the Middle East and asserted that the United States intended to play a more independent role.

Meanwhile, secret talks were going forward, first between the British and French for joint military action against Egypt. Military representatives of the two governments met in London on August 10 and hammered out the details of a joint military plan known as MUSKETEER that would involve occupation of both Alexandria and Port Said. The French then brought the Israeli government in on the plan, and General Maurice Challe, deputy chief of staff of the French Air Force, undertook a secret trip to the Middle East to meet with Israeli government and military leaders. The Israelis were at first skeptical about British and French support. They also had no intention of moving as far as the canal itself. The Israelis stated that their plan was merely to send light detachments to link up with British and French forces. They also insisted that British and French military intervention occur simultaneously with their own attack.

General André Beaufre, the designated French military commander for the operation, then came up with a new plan. Under it, the Israelis would initiate hostilities against Egypt in order to provide the pretext for military intervention by French and British forces to protect the canal. This action would technically be in accord with the terms of the 1954 treaty between Egypt and Britain that had given Britain the right to send forces to occupy the Suez Canal Zone in the event of an attack against Egypt by a third power.

On October 23 Mollet and French foreign minister Christian Pineau met in the Paris suburbs at Sèvres with Israeli prime minister David Ben-Gurion, Defense Minister Shimon Peres, and chief of the Israeli General Staff Lieutenant General Moshe Dayan. The French agreed to provide additional air cover for Israel. French ships supposedly searching for Egyptian arms shipments to the Algerian rebels would move to the Israeli coast immediately, and French Mystère aircraft flown by French pilots would be repositioned in Israel. That afternoon British foreign secretary Selwyn Lloyd and Foreign Office undersecretary of state Patrick Dean joined the discussions. The British, while staunchly prointervention, were deeply concerned about their position in the Arab world and were not anxious to be seen in collusion with the Israelis. Thus, an Israeli strike toward the canal through the Sinai would enable the British to have it both ways: they could join the French in demanding of Nasser the right to protect the canal. When he refused, as he certainly would, they could join the French in destroying the Egyptian

Air Force, eliminating the one possible threat to Israeli success on the ground. All parties agreed to this new plan, dubbed the "Treaty of Sèvres" and signed by Dean, Pineau, and Ben-Gurion.

On October 23, meanwhile, unrest began in Hungary. The next day Soviet tanks entered Budapest to put down what had become the Hungarian Revolution. French and British planners were delighted at this international distraction that seemed to provide them a degree of freedom of action.

On the afternoon of October 29 Israeli forces began Operation KADESH, the invasion of the Sinai Peninsula. Sixteen C-47 transports took off from Israeli fields, each with a paratroop platoon. The objective of the 395-man paratroop battalion was the key Mitla Pass, 156 miles from the Israeli border and only 45 miles from the canal. Meanwhile the remainder of Colonel Ariel Sharon's 202nd Parachute Brigade would race for the pass in French-provided trucks, linking up with the paratroopers within 36 hours. This operation was designed to trigger a major Egyptian response and threaten the canal in order to trigger the planned British-French response.

The announced objective of Operation KADESH was the eradication of the fedayeen bases, but it was begun so as to appear to the Egyptians as if it was the beginning of an all-out war. Dayan's detailed plan called for nothing less than a week-long lightning advance that would end with Israeli forces securing the entire Sinai and a total victory over Egypt. The destruction of Nasser's prestige in the Arab world and final Egyptian recognition of the impossibility of an Arab military victory over Israel were the goals rather than destruction of the Egyptian Army or acquisition of its new Soviet equipment.

A day later, October 30, the British and French governments issued an ultimatum, nominally to both the Egyptian and Israeli governments but in reality only to Egypt, expressing the need to separate the combatants and demanding the right to provide for the security of the Suez Canal. The ultimatum called on both sides to withdraw their forces 10 miles from the canal and gave them 12 hours to reply. The Israelis, of course, immediately accepted the ultimatum, while the Egyptians just as promptly rejected it.

At dusk on October 31, British and French aircraft struck Egyptian airfields and military installations from bases on Cyprus and Malta and from aircraft carriers. The aircraft attacked four Egyptian bases that day and nine the next. On November 1, meanwhile, a British and French naval task force sailed from Malta to join with other ships at Cyprus. In all, the allied landing force numbered some 80,000 men: 50,000 British and 30,000 French. There were 100 British and 30 French warships, including 7 aircraft carriers (5 British) and the French battleship *Jean Bart*, hundreds of landing craft, and some 80 merchant ships carrying 20,000 vehicles and stores. Yet when Eden reported to the House of Commons on events, he encountered a surprisingly strong negative reaction from the opposition Labour Party.

Also, following the initial British and French military action, the Egyptians immediately sank a number of ships in the canal to make it unusable. The Israelis, meanwhile, swept across the Sinai in only four days against ineffective Egyptian forces. Finally, on November 5, British and French paratroopers carried out a vertical envelopment of Port Said, Egypt, at the Mediterranean terminus of the canal, while at the same time French and British destroyers carried out a shore bombardment against those targets likely to impede a landing. Early on November 6, British troops began coming ashore at Port Said and the French at Port Fuad. A single day of fighting saw the ports in allied hands. French and British forces then began a virtually unopposed advance southward along the canal.

President Dwight D. Eisenhower had already entered the picture. On October 31 he described the British attack as "taken in error." He was personally furious at Eden over events and is supposed to have asked when he first telephoned the British leader, "Anthony, have you gone out of your mind?" The United States applied immediate and heavy financial threats, both on a bilateral basis and through the International Monetary Fund, to bring the British government to heel. Eisenhower also refused any further dealings with Eden personally.

The Soviets, preoccupied by Hungary, took some five days to come to the conclusion that the United States was actually opposing the British and French action. On November 5, Moscow threatened to send "volunteers" to Egypt. This proved a further embarrassment for the British government, but it was U.S. pressure that was decisive. Nonetheless, the world beheld the strange spectacle of the United States cooperating with the Soviet Union to condemn Britain and France in the UN Security Council and call for an end to the use of force. Although Britain and France vetoed the Security Council resolution, the matter was referred to the General Assembly, which demanded a cease-fire and withdrawal.

Israel and Egypt agreed to a cease-fire on November 4. At midnight on November 6, the day of the U.S. presidential election, the British and French governments also accepted a cease-fire, the French only with the greatest reluctance. By the time the cease-fire went into effect, the French and British controlled about half of the canal's length. French and British losses in the operation were 33 dead and 129 wounded. Egyptian losses are unknown.

A 4,000-man UN Emergency Force (UNEF) authorized on November 4 and made up of contingents from the Scandinavian countries, Brazil, Colombia, India, and Indonesia then arrived in Egypt to take up positions to keep Israeli and Egyptian forces separated. At the end of November the British and French governments both agreed to withdraw their forces from Egypt by December 22, and on December 1 Eisenhower announced that he had instructed U.S. oil companies to resume shipping supplies to both Britain and France. Under pressure from both the United States and the UN, Israel withdrew its forces from the Sinai, to include the Gaza Strip, during February 5–March 6, 1957. A UN observer force of 3,500 men then took up station in Gaza, at Sharm al-Sheikh, and along the Sinai border. Although Israel had been assured that Egyptian forces would not return to Gaza, they were there within 48 hours of the Israeli withdrawal.

Nasser and Arab self-confidence were the chief beneficiaries of the crisis. The abysmal performance of Egyptian military forces in the crisis was forgotten in Nasser's ultimate triumph. Nasser found his prestige dramatically increased throughout the Arab world. Israel also benefited. The presence of the UN force guaranteed an end to the fedayeen raids, and Israel had also broken the Egyptian blockade of the Gulf of Aqaba, although its ships could still not transit the Suez Canal. The crisis also enhanced Soviet prestige in the Middle East, and the UN emerged with enhanced prestige, helping to boost world confidence in that organization.

The Suez Crisis ended Eden's political career. Ill and under tremendous criticism in Parliament from the Labour Party, he resigned from office in January 1957. Events also placed a serious, albeit temporary, strain on U.S.-British relations. More importantly, they revealed the serious limitations in British military strength. Indeed, observers are unanimous in declaring 1956 a seminal date in British imperial history that marked the effective end of Britain's tenure as a great power. The events had less impact in France. Mollet left office in May 1957 but not as a result of the Suez intervention. The crisis was costly to both Britain and France in economic terms, for Saudi Arabia had halted oil shipments to both countries.

Finally, the Suez Crisis could not have come at a worse time for the West because the event diverted world attention from the concurrent brutal Soviet military intervention in Hungary. Eisenhower believed, rightly or wrongly, that without the Suez diversion there would have been far stronger Western reaction to the Soviet invasion of its satellite.

SPENCER C. TUCKER

See also

Aqaba, Gulf of; Aswan High Dam Project; Baghdad Pact; Ben-Gurion, David; Border War; Dulles, John Foster; Eden, Robert Anthony; Egypt; Eisenhower, Dwight David; France, Middle East Policy; Gaza Strip; Hussein, King of Jordan; Israel; Lloyd, John Selwyn; Mollet, Guy; Nasser, Gamal Abdel; Sharon, Ariel; Sinai Campaign; Straits of Tiran; Suez Canal; United Kingdom, Middle East Policy

References

Beaufre, André. *The Suez Expedition, 1956.* Translated by Richard Barry. New York: Praeger, 1969.

Cooper, Chester L. *The Lion's Last Roar: Suez, 1956.* New York: Harper and Row, 1978.

Eden, Anthony. *The Suez Crisis of 1956.* Boston: Beacon Press, 1968.

Freiberger, Steven Z. *Dawn over Suez: The Rise of American Power in the Middle East, 1953–1957.* Chicago: Ivan R. Dee, 1992.

Gorst, Anthony, and Lewis Johnman. *The Suez Crisis.* London: Routledge, 1997.

Hahn, Peter. *The United States, Great Britain, and Egypt, 1945–1956: Strategy and Diplomacy in the Early Cold War.* Chapel Hill: University of North Carolina Press, 1991.

Kelly, Saul, and Anthony Gorst, eds. *Whitehall and the Suez Crisis.* London: Routledge, 2000.

Kingseed, Cole C. *Eisenhower and the Suez Crisis of 1956.* Baton Rouge: Louisiana State University Press, 1995.

Kyle, Keith. *Suez: Britain's End of Empire in the Middle East.* London: Weidenfeld and Nicolson, 1991.

Louis, William R., and Roger Owen, eds. *Suez, 1956: The Crisis and Its Consequences.* New York: Oxford University Press, 1989.

Lucas, W. Scott. *Divided We Stand: Britain, the United States and the Suez Crisis.* Rev. ed. London: Spectre, 1996.

Varble, Derek. *The Suez Crisis, 1956.* London: Osprey, 2003.

Suicide Bombings

Bombing in which an explosive is delivered and detonated or caused by a person or persons who expect to die in the explosion along with the intended target or targets. In recent years the number of suicide bombings or attacks has risen exponentially, and not just in the Middle East. The United States was struck by aircraft piloted by suicide hijackers on September 11, 2001, resulting in the deaths of almost 3,000 people.

Suicide bombers employ several different techniques. Japanese pilots in World War II were known for crashing their airplanes straight into targets, causing tremendous devastation. These pilots were known as kamikaze ("divine wind"), the name given to a typhoon that destroyed a Mongol invasion fleet off Japan in the 13th century. Kamikazes exacted a heavy toll on Allied warships at the end of World War II, especially off Okinawa. Other attackers use bombs secured in cars or trucks.

Individual suicide bombers strap explosives and shrapnel to their bodies and wear vests or belts specially designed for the purpose. They then drive or walk to their targets. Because military targets are heavily defended, typically the targets are crowded shopping areas, restaurants, or buses, or suicide bombers may approach softer targets directly linked to the military or police, such as a line of recruits in the street as during the Iraq War. Detonating the explosives will kill or injure people in the vicinity as well as destroy property, such as a religious shrine. An explosion in an enclosed area is more destructive than one in the open, and suicide bombers pick their targets accordingly. Forensic investigators at the site of a suicide bombing can usually identify very quickly the bomber and the general type of device he or she used. A suicide vest decapitates the bomber, while a belt cuts the bomber in two.

The explosives themselves are easily constructed. They include gunpowder, a battery, acetone, mercury, cable, a light switch detonator, and a custom-made belt or vest to hold the explosives. Explosives may also be carried in a briefcase or other bag. The bomber sets them off by flipping a switch or pressing a button. Muslim extremists typically leave a written or video will and pronounce the Fatiha, or opening verse of the Koran, and the words "Allahu akbar," or "Allah is great," as they detonate their bombs.

Suicide bombings have been common in the Middle East since the late 1970s, when they were employed in Syria by the Islamic resistance against the Baathist government. In November 1982 an Islamic resistance suicide bomber destroyed a building in Tyre, Lebanon, and killed 76 Israelis. The Organization of Islamic Jihad and other militant Islamist groups including Hezbollah as well as numerous Christians carried out another 50 suicide attacks between 1982 and 1999, when the Israelis withdrew from Lebanon. A massive bombing in October 1983 forced American and French troops

A Palestinian boy wearing an explosive belt surrenders at the entrance checkpoint to the Palestinian West Bank city of Nablus on March 24, 2004. Israeli troops arrested the 14-year-old Palestinian would-be suicide bomber before he could detonate his explosive belt. (FLASH 90/Reuters/Corbis)

from Lebanon. The belief that such attacks bring martyrdom has encouraged suicide bombings all over the world, including in Afghanistan, Chechnya, Croatia, Tajikistan, Pakistan, Yemen, Panama, Argentina, and Algeria, but such attacks were also employed prior to this period by the Tamil Tigers in Sri Lanka. In 1995 a suicide bomber dressed as a priest attempted to assassinate Pope John Paul II in Manila.

Palestinians began suicide bombings in the early 1990s. The inspiration for the attacks was the so-called War of the Knives, a battle between Palestinians and Jews praying at the Western Wall that took place on October 8, 1990. Eighteen Palestinians were killed in the melee, and the radical Hamas organization called for a jihad, or holy war. Omar abu Sirhan took this call literally. He walked to a neighborhood in Jerusalem and killed three people with a butcher knife. He claimed that he had seen the Prophet Muhammad in a dream and that the Prophet had ordered him to take revenge for the slain Palestinians. Abu Sirhan had fully believed that he would die during his killing spree.

Hamas declared abu Sirhan a hero and quickly transformed his act into the inspiration for a generation of suicide killers. Hamas and Islamic Jihad, another radical Islamic organization, informed their faithful that martyrdom actions or suicide attacks were a righteous act because jihad was individually required of Muslims under the circumstances of Israeli occupation.

The first Palestinian suicide bombing occurred in April 1993 in the West Bank. There were 198 known suicide bombing attacks in Israel and Palestine between 1993 and July 2002. The bombers died in 136 of those attacks. These attacks usually occurred within Israel's pre-1967 borders. Attacks increased after the beginning of the Second (al-Aqsa) Intifada in September 2000. Although suicide bombings comprised only a small percentage of actual attacks launched by Palestinians against Israelis, they accounted for perhaps half the Israelis killed between 2000 and 2002.

Although some 70 percent of the suicide attackers in Lebanon in the 1980s were Christians, Palestinian suicide bombers have been Muslims. However, a Greek Orthodox religious figure, Archimandrite Theosios Hanna, supported fidayeen shahids (fighter martyrs) in several speeches. It is obvious from the Tamil, Japanese, or anarchist violence that the motivation is primarily nationalist, and in fact Islam strictly forbids suicide and engaging recklessly in jihad so as to obtain martyrdom. There are set rules regarding who may participate in jihad, and these exclude young people, those with

The remains of the South Tower at the World Trade Center in New York City, September 14, 2001. The use of hijacked commercial airliners in a suicide attack was unheard of before September 11, 2001. (U.S. Navy)

dependents, and also traditionally women. The main religious justification is that jihad is really a defense of Islam and is required of believers under Israeli authority who need not wait for jihad to be formally declared as under normal circumstances. To Muslims, there is a difference between an individual and a collectively incumbent religious duty. Religious authorities who decry the linkage of Islam with suicide and the killing of innocent people try to convince their audiences that the greater jihad, the striving to be a good Muslim in every possible aspect of life, can substitute for jihad as armed struggle or that if armed struggle is necessary, it should not involve attacks of this type. Not all religious authorities take this position, of course, and unfortunately the televised footage or videos of suicide bombers serves as a recruiting tool for others.

For many young Muslims, the temptation of martyrdom with its promise of rewards in paradise is irresistible. They are taught that martyrdom cleanses them of sins and that they will have special power to intercede on behalf of their relatives and close friends on the Day of Judgment. The families of suicide bombers are often extremely proud of their loved ones and praise them publicly as heroes. These families acquire higher status in the Muslim communities. Some Palestinians were at one time receiving financial support from Iraqi leader Saddam Hussein, and in this way the bombers were able to provide for their dependents. Successful suicide bombers believe that they will be remembered as popular heroes.

A major motivation of many Muslim suicide bombers is revenge on Israelis, who have killed numerous Palestinians, often including relatives and friends of the bombers. Suicide bombers have left statements explaining their actions in which they list specific victims of Israeli attacks, particularly women, children, and the elderly. Suicide attackers convince themselves that they are not killing innocent victims. They often use the argument that all Israelis serve in the military, at least as reserves, and therefore are combatants and not really civilians. Some Hamas members made such arguments in the past, but the organization itself observed a truce on such attacks from 2004 to 2007.

A large proportion of Palestinians support armed resistance to the Israeli presence, and many support the work of suicide attackers. Numerous other Palestinians do not support this position and consider attacks on civilians reprehensible, but they have not been nearly as prominent as those who praise suicide bombers, in much the same way as the fedayeen were praised in the past.

Cynics point out that using suicide bombers is an inexpensive method for the radical Palestinians to wage war against Israel, an extreme form of asymmetric warfare. The ingredients for the explosives do not cost much, and many bombers even collect and recycle the shrapnel from past explosions so they can kill Israelis with the same shrapnel that killed Palestinians. Palestinians argue that it is impossible to put a price on human capital, so they are not only losing their own youths but are also paying a very high public relations cost if the world believes that Palestinians are only capable of such violence.

The fiqh al-jihad, or rules of jihad, specify that women and parents of dependent children or the children of the elderly should not volunteer for jihad, but in the five-year period when such attacks were most prevalent in Israel, bombers came from both genders, all ages, and all levels of education and income, although the majority are young unmarried men who grew up in refugee camps in an atmosphere of hatred against Israel. Those who were recruited to such actions were chosen for their psychological predispositions, not to suicide but suggestibility, and were prevented, if possible, from contacting those close to them.

Those attackers who authorities said were traceable to Hamas and Islamic Jihad were persons with no major family responsibilities and who were over the age of 18. In some cases recruiters sought individuals who could speak Hebrew well.

Understandably, suicide bombings are enormously upsetting to potential civilian victims. Suicide bombers turn up when they are least expected as their victims go about their daily business, so victims and bystanders are taken completely by surprise. The victims are often civilians, and children often make up a sizable percentage of those killed. Because the bomber has no concern for his or her own life, it is difficult to prevent such attacks. In Israel, many businesses have hired security guards who are specially trained to spot potential bombers. As with all acts of terror, the fact that such bombings spread fear among the Israeli population is as valuable to the radicals' cause as actually killing Israelis.

AMY H. BLACKWELL AND SHERIFA ZUHUR

See also

Hamas; Hezbollah; Intifada, Second; Islamic Jihad, Palestinian; Jihad

References

Aboul-Enein, Youssef H., and Sherifa Zuhur. *Islamic Rulings on Warfare.* Carlisle Barracks, PA: Strategic Studies Institute, 2004.

Friedman, Lauri S. *What Motivates Suicide Bombers?* Farmington Hills, MI: Greenhaven, 2004.

Khosrokhavar, Farhad. *Suicide Bombers: Allah's New Martyrs.* Translated by David Macey. London: Pluto, 2005.

Rosenthal, Franz. "On Suicide in Islam." *Journal of the American Oriental Society* 66 (1946): 239–259.

Skaine, Rosemarie. *Female Suicide Bombers.* Jefferson, NC: McFarland, 2006.

SUMMER RAINS, Operation
Start Date: June 27, 2006
End Date: November 26, 2006

Large-scale, Israeli-launched incursion into the Gaza Strip that began on June 27, 2006, in response to attacks allegedly by Hamas that killed two Israeli soldiers and captured Israel Defense Forces (IDF) corporal Gilad Shalit. The stated Israeli intention of Operation SUMMER RAINS was to secure the release of the captive soldier and to stop the firing of Qassam rockets from the Gaza Strip into Israeli territory. Many Palestinians, however, believe that the Israeli operation was launched in an attempt to topple the Hamas-led government of the Palestinian Authority (PA). Israel carried out strikes against militant Palestinian groups, destroyed infrastructure that the groups used to support their actions, and applied political pressure on the Hamas-led government.

Operation SUMMER RAINS began on June 27 with the Israeli bombing of three bridges and a power plant as Israeli ground troops moved into the Gaza Strip. Also, Israeli fighter jets flew over the summer residence of Syrian president Bashar al-Assad as a warning against his continued support of Hamas and Hezbollah. The following day, Israeli troops entered the Gaza Strip with the aim of securing and destroying Qassam rocket sites. Israeli warships also shelled suspected rocket sites from offshore. Israeli air strikes mainly targeted Hamas training camps and arms caches. Israeli aircraft also dropped thousands of leaflets warning Palestinian civilians to leave their homes in areas of northern Gaza from which it claimed Qassam rockets were being fired.

During the operation, Israeli forces arrested a number of members of the Hamas leadership as well as members of the Palestinian Legislative Council. Unsurprisingly, this led to charges by many

Palestinians, and especially those in Hamas, that Israel was trying to oust the Hamas government that had been democratically elected in January 2006. The operation also destroyed the only power plant in the Gaza Strip, leaving most of the territory without electricity during the brutally hot days of summer. Most Palestinians were also left with no running potable water and no facilities for sanitation and waste processing. This made it difficult for businesses, hospitals, and basic services to function. In addition to the economic consequences of the operation, a building humanitarian crisis in Gaza caught the attention of various international organizations, including the United Nations (UN). Indeed, UN officials decried the toll that the conflict was taking on civilians and urged both sides to resolve their differences peacefully.

By most counts, the majority of Palestinians killed in the Israeli operations in Gaza were militants. However, many civilians also died in the attacks. There was never any conclusive settlement to the crisis, and Gilad Shalit was not returned to Israel. Operation SUMMER RAINS was slowed through a truce agreement between Israel and militant Palestinian organizations on November 26, 2006, although rockets continued to fly from Gaza to Israel through December. Precise casualty figures are difficult to determine, but it is safe to conclude that the majority of casualties occurred among Palestinians.

DANIEL KUTHY

See also

Gaza Strip; Hamas; Palestinian Authority; Qassam Rocket

References

Efrat, Elisha. *The West Bank and Gaza Strip: A Geography of Occupation and Disengagement.* New York: Routledge, 2006.

Gelvin, James L. *The Israel-Palestine Conflict: One Hundred Years of War.* New York: Cambridge University Press, 2005.

Hroub, Khaled. *Hamas: A Beginner's Guide.* Ann Arbor, MI: Pluto, 2006.

Sunni Islam

Largest of the two predominant branches of Islam. Approximately 67 percent of Muslims worldwide are adherents of Sunni Islam. The word "Sunni" is rarely used by Muslims themselves. It derives from a medieval phrase, *Ahl al-Sunna wa al-Jama'a,* meaning those who live according to the Prophet's model and who congregate. In the early period, this term did not refer to all Muslims but rather to those who were engaged in Islamic scholarship and learning. The sunna, or way, of the Prophet Muhammad refers to his practice of Islam during his 23 years of life following the initial revelation of Allah's words to him. It is mostly in the West that Muslims are differentiated as Sunnis or Shia. If asked, a Muslim may instead identify himself by a school of Islamic law or jurisprudence, such as the Hanafi school, which was the official legal doctrine of the Ottoman Empire. If a contemporary Muslim is identified as a sunni, in some countries this indicates his stronger religiosity or that he is an Islamist (frequently called a fundamentalist in the West).

In contrast with the more institutionalized clerics, courts and systems of Sunni Muslim learning, Sufi Islam is a mystical movement

Lebanese Sunni Muslims pray at al-Mansour Mosque during Friday prayers in the port city of Tripoli, October 12, 2001. (Jamal Saidi/Reuters/Corbis)

within Islam that recognizes personal guides (*shaykh* or *pir*) and is organized into brotherhoods (*tariqat*). There are Shia as well as Sunni Sufi orders.

Sunni Muslims do not adhere to the doctrine of the *a'imah,* or imams, as do several sects of Shia Muslims. In the past, they generally judged the validity of the caliph (the temporal political and military leader) or the caliphate (Islamic government) itself by his or its adherence to the faith and the order and harmony that he or it maintained. In contrast with the Shia, Sunni Muslims believe that Abu Bakr, Omar, and Uthman—the first three Rashidun caliphs following Muhammad—were legitimate successors of Muhammad and that they are of equal standing with the fourth caliph, Ali, Muhammad's son-in-law. Ali became the fourth caliph in AD 656 after the murder of Caliph Uthman and was himself assassinated in 661.

It was not a requirement that the political and religious leadership in Sunni Islam trace its lineage through Ali, although the requirements of a caliph as defined by the scholar Abu al-Hasan Ali Ibn Muhammad Ibn Habib al-Mawardi (972–1058) indicated that

he must be of the Prophet Muhammad's Quraysh tribe. Any link to the Ahl al-Bayt, the immediate family members of the Prophet, was highly regarded. Sunnis ascribe no particular religious importance to the position of imam and emphasize the historic role of the caliphate in governing Islam. For example, according to most Sunni schools of law, an offensive (and collective) jihad can only be declared by the caliph, the successor to the Prophet Muhammad and the lawful temporal and spiritual authority for the entire Islamic community. This was highly problematic, as the caliphs lost their real authority in 1055, regaining it only partially until the Mongol sack of Baghdad in 1258. When the Ottoman sultans later declared themselves to be caliphs in order to wage jihad, their religious claim was questioned by other Muslims. By this period, Muslims understood the caliphate as an ideal structure but one that could be replaced by other forms of authority.

In the absence of the caliphate, Muslim politics had continued under the precept that other rulers, sultans, or emirs would rule to the best of their ability in accordance with the Sharia, or Islamic law, and "order the good and forbid the evil," a key principle in Islam. Clerics or *ulama* (those who possess *ilm,* religious knowledge) were to be consulted by the ruler, issue *fatawa,* and help to guide the believers.

Disputes have occurred over the duly Islamic nature of rulers or their governance and have given rise to purist, separatist, or millenarian movements. For example, an early Muslim group, the Khwaraij (Kharijites), called for a return to the piety of the Prophet and refused to acknowledge certain caliphs. A Kharijite actually killed Ali ibn Abu Talib. However, among the capital sins in Islam are sedition and regicide. In the late 19th century, the Mahdist movement in the Sudan fought against the British in the belief that their leader was the Mahdi and that his appearance heralded the Day of Judgment.

To justify Islamic rule the Ottomans, who were Sunni Muslims, later governed under a particular theory called the circle of equity in which mutual responsibilities were to provide equity and justice. In the 20th century both Sunni and Shia politicized Islamic movements have argued for a more intensely Islamic government. The Muslim Brotherhood, Hamas, Hezbollah, the Gamaat Islamiya, and Al Qaeda have all taken this position. These groups draw on very important arguments about governance and the state that have developed in Islamic history. The Muslim Brotherhood rejected jihad as armed struggle and seeks to change society through education. Hezbollah and Hamas argue for both armed struggle and education. Gamaat Islamiya and Al Qaeda focused on armed struggle until the truce between Gamaat Islamiya and the Egyptian government in 1999.

In general, Sunnis believe that the individual interpretation of Islamic law by scholars may vary. Their legal schools employ a principle of lawmaking known as *ijma,* or consensus, that is not employed by the Shia legal schools. However, there are differences in where legal scholars locate that consensus. There is no central authority in Sunni Islam, so Muslims may seek advice from various clerics or authorities, and advice columns in newspapers and on the Internet all provide differing opinions to them.

Muslims believe that the Koran is the literal word of God pronounced in Arabic by the angel Gabriel to Muhammad over a period of 23 years. Any desecration of the Koran is therefore a desecration of the very words of Allah. Although the Koran is the final statement of Allah to humanity, where it does not offer explicit advice on a matter a Muslim may appeal to a jurist to look to the Prophet's *sunnah* as recorded in the *ahadith,* or collected materials concerning the tradition, behavior, practices, and sayings of the Prophet. They may also use *qiyas,* or a type of analogy, in determining the licitness of any action, or behavior, or the principle of *ijima,* a kind of consensus.

The hadith are sometimes related by the companions (*sahabh*) of Muhammad or by his wives. An important companion was Abu Bakr, also known as "The Most Truthful" (*al-Siddiq*), the first caliph. The next companions in level of importance are the next two caliphs, Omar and Uthman. Shiites reject the top ranking of the testimony of these companions, asserting the primacy of Ali. Although these three are important companions, Sunnis consider anyone who knew or even saw Muhammad, accepted his teachings, and died as a Muslim to be a companion. Early Sunni scholars identified these companions and listed them in various reference texts. This identification was essential because their testimonies and their reputation for veracity affirm and determine the content of the hadith and, therefore, the sunna.

There are many collections of these original oral traditions, but they are graded according to their soundness with six respected collections, two of which—that of Muslim and al-Bukhari—are considered most reliable. However, many Muslims repeat and believe in hadith that are not necessarily the most sound, and since the reform movement of the 19th century, some Muslims believe that the hadith brought many unwanted innovations or, conversely, too much imitation of tradition (*taqlid*) into Islam. Shia Islamic law generally uses hadith that pertain to Muhammad as told to members of Ali's family. These variations lead to some differences in Sunni Islamic law and Shia Islamic law.

Muslims must practice their faith through demonstrated religious rituals and obligations. Many sources speak of five religious practices or duties, often referred to as the Five Pillars. The first pillar is called bearing witness (*shahadah*) and is the recitation of the creed or confession of faith, called the Testimony of Faith: "There is no God, but Allah; and Muhammad is His prophet." Shiites generally add "and Ali ibn Abi Talib is the friend of God" to the *shahadah.* The *shahadah* is also uttered as part of the Muslim call (*adhan*) to prayer and is part of the Tashahud segment of the prayers recited at least five times daily. The second pillar is prayer (*salat*) performed at least five times a day (dawn, noon, midafternoon, sunset, and evening). Muslims purify themselves before prayer by washing their hands, face, mouth, nose, ears, and feet. During prayer, all Muslims face Mecca. The third pillar is fasting (*sawm*) during the daylight hours for all of the month of Ramadan, the ninth month of the Islamic lunar calendar. This fasting means that no food or beverages are consumed and that there is no smoking or sexual intercourse. Those who are sick are excused from fasting.

The fourth pillar is almsgiving, effectively a tax (*zakat*) levied on one's assets at the end of the year. It is used for the community's poor, the promotion of Islam, and the maintenance of the mosque and other religious institutions. The fifth pillar is the required pilgrimage (hajj) once in a lifetime to the holy city of Mecca re-creating Muhammad's pilgrimage there in 632.

The responsibility for performing these duties falls on the individual, but stricter Muslims hold that it is the duty of the state to command the good and enforce their performance. There are other strictures. For example, Muslims must not drink alcohol, not simply as a forbidden substance but because it clouds alertness and judgment and makes it impossible to pray. Pork is forbidden, as are games of chance. Many Muslim women believe that covering their heads is a required individual duty, but others do not. Modest behavior is, however, required of both men and women.

Many Westerners know little about Muslims with the exception of the Five Pillars. Yet ethical behavior is very important to Islamic belief, including the protection of the weak and aid to the poor and socially disadvantaged. Islam seeks to promote an ethical life lived within a community. It is more difficult in many ways to be a good Muslim while fulfilling one's obligations to family and community than to live as a hermit, and the Prophet Muhammad is said to have promoted marriage and discouraged celibacy or an extreme ascetic lifestyle. Many of the rules regarding relations between men and women, which non-Muslims find very strict and hard to understand, are indeed intended to provide a moral and ethical grounding for the community.

Muslims are concerned with iman, or faith, and many religiophilosophical principles guide them. The most basic aspect of Islam is belief in Allah and the Oneness (tawhid) of Allah. This monotheism is expressed in many ways. Muslims believe in the prophets and believe that they brought important messages to mankind, but Muhammad is considered the Seal of Prophecy or the last prophet. Nonetheless, Jesus, Moses, Abraham, and others are revered. However, Muslims believe that the Jews did not heed the word of God and that the Jews changed the revelation of Moses to support their assertion that they, and not the descendants of Ishmael, are the chosen people of Allah. The Christians, Sunnis argue, distorted the revelation of Jesus because the doctrine of the Trinity violates the idea of the Oneness of Allah.

Muslims recognize the scriptures as revelations of Allah. Allah was the creator, but he did not simply create the world and humankind and leave man to fend for himself. Rather, Allah provided revelations for the guidance of men. The Koran is the transcending revelation of Allah that cannot be contradicted by any other revelations of Allah. Still, Muslims recognize other revelations, which include the Jewish and Christian holy scriptures as well as the Zoroastrian texts.

Muslims believe in the angels (malaika) who are the servants of Allah. Angels were not given the free will that Allah granted to humans. Their duties include recording all human deeds, ensouling the fetus at 120 days of gestation (although some Islamic scholars believe ensoulment occurs on the 40th day), watching over and caring for creation, the gathering of souls at death, and much more.

All Muslims also believe in the Day of Judgment and in the Resurrection (qiyama) when Allah will return to judge all of humanity, Muslim and non-Muslim, including the dead. After the Resurrection, every human is held accountable for his or her deeds. The deeds of each individual are judged by Allah and weighed on a scale. If the good outweighs the evil, then the individual gains entrance into Paradise. If the evil outweighs the good, the individual spends eternity in Hell.

In the pre-Islamic era, referred to as the jahilliya or time of barbarity, people believed entirely in preordination. Islam rejects this passivity because people possess free will and can thus choose to do good or evil and are held accountable for their decisions. At the same time, it is difficult to retain faith in the face of tragedy, poverty, or disaster. The Muslim belief in the omnipotence of God, his transcendence and simultaneous immanence, is meant to solace the believer.

The application of reason, in the form of Hellenic philosophical arguments to law and theology in order to derive the correct rules and meaning of the Koran and the Sunnah, gave rise to multiple Sunni traditions, or schools of law and theology. These schools share the basic theology described above and assert the primacy of the Koranic revelation, but there are notable differences.

Sunni Islamic law (Sharia) is based on the Koran and the Sunnah as nuanced by the particular hadith collection accepted. Different scholars using different assumptions, reasoning, hermeneutics (guiding interpretive principles), and source materials arrived at different applications of Islamic law organized into schools known as madhahib. Muslims assert that Sharia never changes but that the understanding and application (fiqh) do. For example, the Koran and derived Sharia never envisioned the use of the telegraph. Thus, the application of the Sharia to the use of the telegraph was a matter of interpretation. In addition to the usual sources of law, jurists took into account maslaha, public benefit or the common good, in considering new technology.

There are four major schools of law in Sunni Islam, yet there have been other schools that have died out and smaller schools that continue to exist. The various schools predominate in different regions. These dominant Sunni schools of law are Hanbali, Hanafi, Maliki, and Shafi, and all use the Koran as their primary source.

Hanbali is the strictest tradition and has fewer than 10 percent of Sunnis as adherents. It was founded by Ahmad ibn-Hanbal and is the dominant tradition on the Arabian Peninsula, although it has adherents in Iraq and Syria as well. The clear statements of the Koran and the Sunnah as transmitted through its accepted hadith override any opinion from any source.

Hanafi is the largest school. It was founded by Abu Hanifa and encompasses 30 percent of Sunnis. Its adherents are mainly in Turkey, Central Asia, the Balkans, Iraq, Afghanistan, Pakistan, India, Bangladesh, lower Egypt, Russia, and parts of China. Both the Mongol Empire and the Ottoman Empire promoted the Hanafi tradition. When the Ottoman Sultan Selim the Grim (1512–1520) captured Palestine, he imposed Hanafi law on the region. The official judicial traditions and systems in contemporary Syria, Jordan, and Palestine are derived from the Hanafi tradition.

Maliki has approximately 15 percent of Sunnis as adherents. It was founded by Malik ibn Anas and has adherents in North Africa and West Africa, particularly upper Egypt, Algeria, Tunisia, Morocco, Mauritania, and Libya as well as the Sudan, Kuwait, Dubai, and Abu Dhabi. The Maliki school derives its fiqh through consensus more than any of the other traditions. The Malikite system of lawmaking is built on the Koran and the hadith, supplemented by the consensus of the People (ijma), analogy (qiyas), and the agreed practice of the people of Medina. In addition, Malik considered the statements of the Prophet's companions, the public good (*masalih mursala*), customary law (*urf*), common practice (*adat*), and several other legal principles.

Shafi was founded by Muhammad ibn Idris al-Shafi and has adherents in the southern Arabian Peninsula, Syria, Indonesia, Malaysia, the Philippines, Sudan, Ethiopia, Somali, North Yemen, and lower Egypt. The Shafi school utilizes the *usul al-fiqh* (roots of lawmaking) in a way that places *ijma* ahead of analogy, the Koran, the Sunnah of the Prophet, and consensus.

Historically, there were many Sunni schools and trends in theology. Among the important or well-known trends were the Mutazilah, whose doctrine was abandoned, and the Ash'ariyyah, Maturidiyyah, and Salafism (which has at least two versions).

The Mutazilah school was established in Iraq by Wasil bin 'Ata (699–749). Abbasid caliph Al-Mamun (813–827) made Mutazila theology the state religion and persecuted all dissenters. At the time, Muslims had debated the uncreatedness versus the created (manmade) nature of the Koran. Mutazilites did not accept the doctrine of the uncreated Koran, but with their downfall Muslims accepted precisely that doctrine. They took an intermediate position on the question of sin, asserting that Muslims who commit grave sins and die without repentance are neither believers nor nonbelievers. The Mutazilites rejected anthropomorphic interpretations of God. For instance, the phrase "hand of God" might refer symbolically to God's power.

The Ashariyya school was founded by Abu al-Hasan al-Ashari (873–935) and became the dominant Sunni theology in that era. It emphasizes divine revelation and stresses the understanding of that revelation through the application of human reasoning.

The Maturidiyyah was founded by Abu Mansur al-Maturidi (d. 944). Maturidis believe that the existence of Allah as understood in Islam can be derived through reason alone and that such is true of major concepts of good and evil, legal and illegal. Salafism, a reform movement in Islam, actually developed in two different contexts in 18th-century Arabia and in 19th-century Egypt and the Ottoman Empire. The 19th-century to early-20th-century reformers Jamal al-Din al-Afghani, Muhammad Abduh, Qasim Amin, and Rashid Rida initiated a discussion about the decline of the Muslim world and the reforms it should carry out to overcome the negative influence of Western colonialism and imperialism. While al-Afghani looked for an Islamic ruler who would stand up to the West and believed that Pan-Islam could solve the problem, Muhammad Abduh, an Egyptian jurist, recommended reform of Islamic education and methodology in which blind imitation of the past would cease. He thought that Sunni Muslims should consider a return to *ijtihad* (a Shia methodology of lawmaking) to meet contemporary requirements, and he wanted Western sciences introduced into the educational curriculum. Qasim Amin argued for an end to enforced marriages, female seclusion, and lack of education, while Rashid Rida pursued a somewhat stricter idea of a cleansed Islamic way of life.

Earlier, a strictly monotheistic sect of Islam was developed under Muhammad abd al-Wahhab in Arabia and referred to as Wahhabism by that leader's enemies. Its adherents were known both as Ikhwan (Brethren) and Salafis because they wanted to cleanse Islamic practice and society of its un-Islamic accretions and innovations (*bid'a*) that had arisen through cultural synthesis. The Wahhabis adhered to the Hanbali school of law, although some Salafis speak of rejecting all legal tradition and utilizing only the Koran and the sunnah. The Salafis were anti-Ottoman, anti-Shia, and anti-Sufi and opposed such practices as Sufi ceremonies and visiting tombs. These Salafis called for jihad in its active form with which they, in alliance with the Saud family, drove out first the Ottomans and then in a later historical period the al-Rashids and the Hashemites.

Osama bin Laden is a neo-Salafi. He believes that the Saudi Arabian royal family does not strictly uphold Wahhabi or Salafi values and should be militantly opposed for its alliance with the West. Other Salafis have been part of the resistance in post-2003 Iraq to U.S. occupation and the new Iraqi government.

Some Salafis consider the Shias to be renegades or apostates, apostasy being a capital crime in Islam. Shiites feared and hated the Wahhabis because of their raids on their areas, but this is not true of all Sunnis and Shia who, in general, lived peacefully alongside each other in prewar Iraq. Some charge that the United States and Israel as well as certain Arab countries are heightening fears in the region of a Shia crescent of influence running from Iran to the Shia of Iraq and the Gulf States and then to the Shia of Lebanon. Such discourse could create more problems between Muslims in the region. Therefore, clerics in Saudi Arabia, Egypt, and elsewhere are trying to quiet sectarian discord or at least represent the Shia as a legitimate madhhab or legal school of Islam.

RICHARD EDWARDS AND SHERIFA ZUHUR

See also

Al Qaeda; Hezbollah; Jihad; Koran; Mecca; Medina; Shia Islam

References

Ahmed, Akbar S. *Islam Today: A Short Introduction to the Muslim World.* Rev. ed. London: Tauris, 1999.

Armstrong, Karen. *Islam: A Short History.* New York: Modern Library, 2002.

Esposito, John L. *The Oxford History of Islam.* New York: Oxford University Press, 2000.

———. *What Everyone Needs to Know about Islam.* New York: Oxford University Press, 2002.

Fuller, Graham E., and Rend Rahim Francke. *The Arab Shi'a: The Forgotten Muslims.* Hampshire, UK: Palgrave Macmillan, 2001.

Gregorian, Vartan. *Islam: A Mosaic, Not a Monolith.* Baltimore: Brookings Institute Press, 2004.

Sachiko, Muratam, and William C. Chittick. *The Vision of Islam.* New York: Paragon House, 1994.

Salamah, Ahmad Abdullah. *Shia & Sunni Perspective on Islam: An Objective Comparison of the Shia and Sunni Doctrines Based on the Holy Quran and Hadith.* Jedda, Saudi Arabia: Abul-Qasim Publication House, 1991.

Surface-to-Air Missiles

See Missiles, Surface-to-Air

Sykes-Picot Agreement
Event Date: May 16, 1916

Agreement reached between the British, French, and Russian governments regarding claims of territory belonging to the Ottoman Empire. In the spring of 1915 British high commissioner in Egypt Sir Henry McMahon promised Sharif Hussein ibn Ali of Mecca British support for an Arab state under Hussein in return for Arab military support against the Ottoman Empire. Confident of British support, in June 1915 Hussein proclaimed the Arab Revolt. The French government was alarmed over this, and on October 24 McMahon informed Hussein of limitations on a postwar Arab state. Britain was to have direct control of the Baghdad-Basra region so that the area west of Hama, Homa, Aleppo, and Damascus could not be under Arab control. Any Arab state east of the Hama-Damascus area would have to seek British advice. McMahon also warned Hussein that Britain could make no promises that would injure French interests.

Aware of the British agreement with Hussein, Paris pressed London for recognition of its own claims in the Ottoman Empire. Englishman Sir Mark Sykes and Frenchman François Georges Picot were appointed by their respective governments to conduct the negotiations, and because discussions of the future of Asiatic Turkey necessarily affected the Russians, the two proceeded to Petrograd in the early spring of 1916 and there presented their draft agreement. They secured Russian support in the formal Sazonov-Paléologue Agreement of April 26, 1916, named for Russian foreign minister Sergei D. Sazonov and French ambassador to Russia Georges Maurice Paléologue. It is most often known as the Sykes-Picot Agreement, however. The agreement was officially concluded on May 16, 1916.

The Sykes-Picot Agreement provided extensive territorial concessions to all three powers at the expense of the Ottoman Empire. Russia was to receive the provinces of Erzerum, Trebizond, Van, and Bitlis (known as Turkish Armenia) as well as northern Kurdistan from Mush, Sairt, Ibn Omar, and Amadiya to the border with Persia (Iran). France would secure the coastal strip of Syria, the vilayet of Adana, and territory extending in the south from Ayntab and Mardin to the future Russian border to a northern line drawn from Ala Dagh through Kaysariya Ak-Dagh, Jidiz-Dagh, and Zara to Egin-Kharput (the area known as Cilicia). Britain would secure southern Mesopotamia with Baghdad as well as the ports of Haifa and Acre in Palestine. The zone between the British and French territories would be formed into one or more Arab states, but this was to be divided into British and French spheres of influence. The French sphere would include the Syrian hinterland and the Mosul province of Mesopotamia, while the British would have influence over the territory from Palestine to the Persian border. The agreement also provided that Alexandetta would become a free port, while Palestine would be internationalized.

The parties involved agreed to maintain strict secrecy regarding the plan. Despite this, the Italian government learned of its existence by early 1917 and forced the French and British governments to agree in the St. Jean de Maurienne Agreement of April 17, 1917, that Italy would receive a large tract of purely Turkish land in southern Anatolia and a sphere of influence north of Smyrna. This was the final agreement among the Allies regarding the future partition of the Ottoman Empire. It was contingent on the approval of the Russian government, which was not forthcoming because of revolutionary upheaval there. Hussein did not learn of the Sykes-Picot Agreement until December 1917 when the information was published by the Bolshevik government of Russia and relayed to Hussein by the Turks, who vainly hoped thereby to reverse his pro-British stance.

The Sykes-Picot Agreement proved a source of bitter conflict between France and England at the 1919 Paris Peace Conference. French premier Georges Clemenceau expected to receive British support for French claims to Lebanon, Cilicia, and Syria. He based this belief on a December 2, 1918, meeting in London with British prime minister David Lloyd George where, in a verbal understanding without witnesses, Clemenceau agreed to modify the Sykes-Picot Agreement. Recognizing the British role in victory in the Middle East, Clemenceau agreed that the oil-producing area of Mosul, assigned to France in the Sykes-Picot Agreement, would be transferred to the British sphere. Palestine, which had been slated for some form of international status, would also be assigned to the British. In return, Clemenceau believed that Lloyd George had promised British support for French claims to Syria and Cilicia.

At the Paris Peace Conference, however, Lloyd George jettisoned the Sykes-Picot Agreement. Appealing to U.S. president Woodrow Wilson's principles of national self-determination, Lloyd George argued that the Arab Revolt entitled the peoples of Lebanon and Syria to self-rule. Lloyd George wanted Hussein's son Emir Faisal, who was under British influence, to rule Lebanon and Syria. But Lloyd George also insisted that Britain retain control of Iraq and Palestine. Clemenceau protested. The standoff was resolved on April 24, 1920, at the San Remo Conference, whereby the British and French governments reached agreement on mandates in the Middle East. Britain would receive Palestine and Iraq, while France secured Lebanon and Syria. Self-determination was thus rejected.

Spencer C. Tucker

See also
Faisal I, King of Iraq; Hussein ibn Ali, Sharif of Mecca

References

Andrew, Christopher, and A. F. Kanya-Forstner. *The Climax of French Imperial Expansion, 1914–1924.* Stanford: Stanford University Press, 1981.

Kent, Marian, ed. *The Great Powers and the End of the Ottoman Empire.* London: Routledge, 1996.

Lenczowski, George. *The Middle East in World Affairs.* 4th ed. Ithaca, NY: Cornell University Press, 1980.

Nevakivi, Jukka. *Britain, France and the Arab Middle East, 1914–1920.* London: Athlone, 1969.

Tanenbaum, Jan Karl. *France and the Arab Middle East, 1914–1920.* Philadelphia: American Philosophical Society, 1978.

Tauber, Eliezer. *The Arab Movements in World War I.* London: Frank Cass, 1993.

Syria

Arab nation in the Middle East covering 71,498 square miles, just slightly larger than the U.S. state of North Dakota. The Syrian Arab Republic borders on Jordan and Israel to the south, Lebanon and the Mediterranean Sea to the west, Turkey to the north, and Iraq to the east. For much of its history Syria was dominated by larger powers. Syria was part of the Ottoman Empire until the end of World War I, and the country's economy and educational system had left its populace in relative destitution. In 1920 France received a League of Nations mandate over both Syria and neighboring Lebanon.

French rule resulted in repeated uprisings, particularly among the Druze. After a tortuous series of negotiations and anti-French violence in the late 1920s, Syria was granted considerable autonomy in 1936. Following the defeat of France by Germany in June 1940, Syria was controlled by the Vichy French government headed by Marshal Henri Philippe Pétain. It appointed General Henri Dentz as high commissioner to Syria with a cabinet headed by Khalid al-Azm. Pétain ordered Dentz to allow German and Italian aircraft landing rights in Syria on their way to support Radhid Ali's regime in Iraq.

This situation was intolerable to the Allies. British, Australian, and Free French forces as well as the Transjordan Arab Legion crossed from Palestine into Lebanon and Syria in June 1941. By mid-July they were fully in control of both Syria and Lebanon. Syria was then turned over to the Free French authorities. Although the French recognized Syrian independence, they continued to occupy the country, declared martial law, imposed strict press censorship, and arrested political subversives.

In July 1943 under pressure from its allies, the Free French government-in-exile announced new elections. A nationalist government came to power that August, electing as president Syrian nationalist Shukri al-Quwatli. France granted Syria independence on January 1, 1944, but the country remained under Allied occupation for the remainder of the war. In February 1945 Syria declared war on the Axis powers and then the next month became a member of the United Nations (UN).

In early May 1945 anti-French demonstrations erupted throughout Syria, whereupon French forces bombarded Damascus, killing 400 people before the British intervened. A UN resolution in February 1946 called on France to evacuate the country, and by mid-April all French and British forces were off Syrian soil. Evacuation Day, April 17, is still celebrated as a Syrian national holiday.

The Umayyad Mosque, framed by Roman ruins at Damascus, Syria. (Flemming Pless/iStockphoto.com)

On March 22, 1945, Syria cofounded the Arab League, which advocated Pan-Arab nationalism but without the consolidation of states and the resultant problems that such a movement would have witnessed. The Arab League was also aimed at blocking the creation of a Jewish state in Palestine, which the Syrians strongly opposed.

Syria played a relatively small role in the failed Israeli War of Independence (1948–1949) that arose from the creation of the Jewish state in May 1948. At the beginning of the fighting, Syria had only some 4,500 troops to commit, almost all of whom were dispatched to the Syrian-Palestinian border. Just six days into the fighting, Syrian troops had been repelled, with heavy casualties. News of the Syrian defeat spread rapidly and many Syrians blamed al-Quwatli for the setback. Al-Quwatli reacted by firing his defense minister and chief of staff. As time progressed, however, Syrian troops enjoyed some success and managed to occupy a small strip of Palestinian territory along the border. They also occupied a small piece of land in northeastern Palestine. After these initial successes, the small Syrian military contingent remained rather inactive for the rest of 1948. For al-Quwatli, whose popularity was quickly eroding, the chief issue of the 1948–1949 war was whether Syria would fight alongside other Arab nations in a show of Pan-Arabism or whether it would fight to retain its Syrian identity. In so doing, he diluted the Syrian effort against the Israelis and engendered opponents in other Arab states.

The Israeli victory in the war and disagreements over Syria's potential union with Iraq torpedoed al-Quwatli's government. There were three separate coups in 1949, the last one headed by Lieutenant Colonel Adib al-Shishakli, who governed with a heavy hand until 1954. In 1952 after a series of lengthy talks, al-Shishakli agreed in principle with a U.S. offer that would have brought $400 million of aid to Syria in exchange for Syria's settling of as many as 500,000 displaced Palestinians. The plan was doomed from the start, however, as many Syrians—especially those on the political Left—decried the plan as an attempt to deny Palestinians their right of return to Palestine, which by now had UN backing.

Al-Shishakli was ousted in 1954, and late that year elections were held to determine the makeup of the new government, which would now be civilian. In the end, a three-party coalition (People's Party, National Party, and Baath Party) emerged with National Party chief Sabri al-Asali as its head. The coalition was a shaky one, and political instability plagued the new government. In the succeeding years the Baathists, who combined Arab nationalism with socialist economic policies, became the most powerful political force in Syria, and Syria gradually entered into economic and military agreements with the Soviet Union.

In February 1958 Syria and Egypt joined to form the United Arab Republic (UAR), with Syrian political parties supposed to refrain from all political activity. Complete Egyptian domination of the UAR forced yet another coup against the Syrian government in September 1961. Carried out by military officers, the coup promptly pulled Syria out of the UAR and established the Syrian Arab Republic. In December 1961 elections for a national assembly were held, and the body chose two conservative People's Party members to lead the new regime. However, another coup in late 1962 again toppled the government.

In 1963 a joint Baath-military government came to power. The new government nationalized most industrial and large commercial concerns and engaged in land reforms that redistributed land to the peasants. Meanwhile, Syria continued to cultivate relations with the Soviet bloc. A schism in the Baath Party resulted in more instability, and in 1966 the radical wing of the party staged a coup and installed Yussuf Zayan as prime minister. Nur al-Din al-Atasi became president. This new regime tightened Syria's ties with both the Soviets and Egyptians.

Syria fought Israel yet again in the June 1967 Six-Day War, with disastrous consequences. This time, its defeat included the loss of the Golan Heights to the Israelis. The outcome of the war eviscerated the ruling government, and when Syrian forces had to pull back after attempting to aid the Palestinians in Jordan during Black September (1970), the scene had been set for yet another change of government. On November 13, 1970, General Hafez al-Assad, the minister of defense, seized power in a bloodless coup. Al-Assad referred to it as the Corrective Resolution, which essentially ousted from power civilian Baathists in favor of the military Baathists. An ardent Baathi nationalist, al-Assad sought to strengthen ties to other Arab states, de-emphasize Syrian reliance on the Soviet Union, and defeat Israel.

In early 1971 al-Assad was elected president and immediately began to consolidate his power. He would rule the country until his death in 2000. During the early years of his presidency, he modernized the Syrian Army and engaged in modest economic reforms, while the Baath Party gained even more strength. Befitting his Baathist philosophy, the state played a central role in economic planning and implementation. Al-Assad's tactics could be brutal, and there was little room for dissent or democracy in Syria.

Syria joined with Egypt against Israel in the October 1973 Yom Kippur War. At the beginning of the fighting, Syria launched a massive ground attack that included 1,500 tanks (900 in the initial attack and 600 in reserve) and 144 batteries of artillery in an attempt to retake the Golan Heights. After some initial success and although their forces this time fought quite well, the Syrian attackers were finally driven back beyond their original positions. Syria did not take the Golan Heights, although it did regain control over a small portion of it as a result of U.S.-led negotiations after the war.

In the late 1970s and 1980s Sunni Muslim fundamentalists began challenging the government's authoritarian rule, as the Sunni majority greatly resented the way they were treated by Alawites who had settled in the larger cities. The Islamic parties opposed the Baath Party's secular outlook. From 1976 to 1982, urban areas all across Syria became hotbeds of political unrest. Al-Assad's brother brutally crushed a February 1982 uprising by the Muslim Brotherhood in Hama, and troops killed as many as 30,000 people.

Al-Assad also sent his army into Lebanon in 1976, ostensibly as a peacekeeping force during the civil war there. The troops stayed on, however, with al-Assad siding at certain points with the progressive Christian, Druze, and Muslim forces and then later with certain Christian militias. By the mid-1980s Syrian forces in Lebanon played a dominating military and political role there. In 1990 the conflict was declared to have ended, although Syrian troops were not withdrawn from Lebanon until 2005. As a result of the long Syrian presence in Lebanon, many thousands of Syrians moved into Lebanon after the civil war to seek work. Syrian produce was cheaper than that grown in Lebanon, and smuggling continued from Lebanon into Syria. In 1994 the Lebanese government granted citizenship to 250,000 Syrians, a move that was, for obvious reasons, controversial among the Lebanese people.

At the same time, the 1980s saw the al-Assad regime taking harder-line Arab positions and moving closer to the Soviets. Al-Assad's get-tough approach in regional politics included funding and encouragement of terrorism both in the Middle East and internationally. Al-Assad, who was always in the end a pragmatist, sought to ameliorate relations with the West as the Soviet Union began to implode in 1990. When Iraq invaded Kuwait in August 1990, al-Assad was the first Arab leader to denounce the attack. His government also provided 20,000 troops to the international coalition that defeated Iraqi forces in the 1991 Persian Gulf War. Al-Assad's frontline position in the war reflected both his desire to strengthen relations with the West and his strong dislike of Iraqi dictator Saddam Hussein. For although Hussein was a Baathist—at least in name—he was also a direct threat to al-Assad, who saw himself as the pivotal leader in the region.

In 1991 al-Assad's government entered into peace negotiations with Israel, although the process broke down with no firm agreement in January 2000. Al-Assad died unexpectedly in June 2000 after 30 years in power. He was succeeded by his son, Bashar al-Assad, who had been carefully groomed as the heir apparent after the death of his brother Basil in 1993. Allegedly a free market proponent, the younger al-Assad attempted some economic reforms, but the process has been fraught with setbacks and obstacles. In 1998, 65 percent of all Syrian revenues came from petroleum products. The younger al-Assad also promised both political and democratic reform, but neither has come to fruition.

After the September 11, 2001, terror attacks against the United States, Syria pledged its cooperation in the so-called war on terror. But with the beginning of the 2003 Iraq War, which al-Assad refused to support, U.S.-Syrian relations sharply deteriorated. Syria's continued support, or at least hosting of militant Palestinian groups and terrorist organizations such as Hezbollah, let alone the insurgents fighting U.S. and coalition troops in Iraq, all further strained relations with the United States. And although Syrian troops were out of Lebanon by 2005, there is considerable evidence to suggest that the Syrians continue to involve themselves in the internal politics of that nation. Indeed, most observers agree that Syrian operatives were responsible for the assassination of former Lebanese prime minister Rafik Hariri in February 2005 as well as other assassinations of leading Lebanese figures into late 2007.

PAUL G. PIERPAOLI JR.

See also

Assad, Bashar al-; Assad, Hafez al-; Arab League; Arab Nationalism; Arab Socialism; Baathism; Black September; Golan Heights; Hezbollah; Iraq War; Israeli War of Independence, Israeli-Syrian Front; Israeli War of Independence, Overview; Lebanon; Lebanon, Civil War in; Persian Gulf War; Six-Day War; Syria, Armed Forces; United Arab Republic; Yom Kippur War

References

Lesch, David W. *The New Lion of Damascus: Bashar Al-Assad and Modern Syria.* New Haven, CT: Yale University Press, 2005.

Maoz, Moshe, and Avner Yaniv, eds. *Syria under Assad: Domestic Constraints and Regional Risks.* London: Croom Helm, 1987.

Pipes, Daniel. *Greater Syria: The History of an Ambition.* New York: Oxford University Press, 1990.

Roberts, David. *The Ba'th and the Creation of Modern Syria.* New York: St. Martin's, 1987.

Seale, Patrick. *Assad of Syria: The Struggle for the Middle East.* Berkeley: University of California Press, 1988.

Syria, Armed Forces

Syria has been inhabited continuously for thousands of years and has been the site of dozens of conquests by invading forces. Dam-ascus, the capital of Syria, is one of the oldest surviving cities in the world. It became a Muslim city in AD 636 and was the heart of the Islamic world until the Abbasid Caliphate was established in Baghdad in the eighth century. By 1517 Syria had been incorporated into the Ottoman Empire, where it remained until World War I. After World War I when the Ottoman Empire was partitioned, Syria became a French protectorate. Syria did not achieve full independence until April 1946.

The modern Syrian Army was first formed as a mandate volunteer force in 1920. Designated the Troupes Speciales du Levant (Levantine Special Forces) in 1925, all of the unit's officers were originally French. During World War II this force was under Vichy French control until the British occupied Syria. When the force passed to the control of the Free French, it was redesignated the Troupes du Levant (Levantine Forces). When the French finally departed in 1946, the Levantine Force became the Syrian Army, which by 1948 had grown to 12,000 troops.

In May 1948 the British Mandate for Palestine came to an end. The Jews there declared the independence of the State of Israel, and the forces of Egypt, Iraq, Lebanon, Syria, and Transjordan (later renamed Jordan) immediately invaded Israel.

Syrian involvement in the Israeli War of Independence (1948–1949) began with an advance of infantry and armored vehicles into the Galilee region. The newly established Israel Defense Forces (IDF) had few means to repel armored forces, which it faced on three fronts. The IDF also began the war with no combat aircraft. The Syrian Air Force in 1948 had 50 aircraft, although only 10 were of relatively modern World War II design. French influence on the Syrian military was still significant in 1948. Most Syrian tanks were French models, including the Renault R-35 and R-37. The Syrians also had a small number of French artillery pieces.

The first Syrian advances into Israel targeted the village of Zemach (Samakh), situated at the southern edge of the Sea of Galilee. Despite deploying tanks, armored cars, and artillery against a defensive force armed only with rifles, machine guns, and two small anti-tank guns, the Syrian Army took three days to capture the village. After the fall of Zemach, the Syrians pushed toward the Degania Kibbutzim. At Degania A, 70 Israelis armed with rifles and Molotov cocktails repelled a Syrian infantry company reinforced by tanks and artillery. After a similar defeat at Degania B, the Syrians withdrew, abandoning all their previous gains and providing a one-month respite to the exhausted Israeli defenders.

On June 10, 1948, Syrian forces successfully forced the Jordan River and attacked Mishmar Hayarden, a kibbutz north of the Sea of Galilee. The Israelis launched a series of fierce counterattacks but could not drive the Syrian Army back from Mishmar Hayarden. From that point on, however, the Syrians were content to consolidate their defensive positions and hold what Israeli territory they had.

The Syrian Army occasionally supported the Arab Liberation Army (ALA), a multinational force commanded by Syria's Fawzi al-Qawuqji. When the IDF launched an offensive to destroy the ALA in October 1948, however, Syria refused to support ALA units or to

SYRIAN FRONT AT THE YOM KIPPUR WAR CEASE-FIRE, OCT 24, 1973

Legend:
- ▪▪▪▪ Border between Israel and Syria, 1949–1967
- Israeli territory from the ceasefire after the Six-Day War of Jun 1967, until the Syrian attack on Oct 6, 1973
- Syrian territory held by Israel at the cease-fire of Oct 24, 1973

N

Mediterranean Sea

LEBANON

• Bar Elias

• Sidon

Damascus ☆

• Rasheiya
Hasbaya •
Marjayoun •
Litani R.

• Katana
▲ *Mount Hermon*
Mazraat
Beit Jann
• Kiswe

Sassa •
Kanakir •

SYRIA

Tyre •

Jubbata •

Kiryat Shmona •
Khan Erenbe •
Jeba •

Bint Jubail •

Golan
• Kuneitra
Kafr Shams •

Heights
El Harra •
Es Sanamein •

— 33°N
Khushniye •
Jasim •

Safed •
Rafid •

Rosh Pina
Butmiye •

Sea of Galilee
Ramat Magshimim •
Sheikh Miskin •

Tiberias •
Sham al Golan •

Yarmuk R.

• Nazareth

Jordan R.

• Afula
• Deraa

ISRAEL
Irbid •

• Beit Shean

JORDAN

0   10   20 mi
0   10   20 km

36°E

Syrian armor on review in Damascus, December 12, 1955. (Bettmann/Corbis)

allow them to withdraw into Syrian territory. On July 20, 1949, Syria and Israel agreed to a cease-fire. Syria withdrew from the Mishmar Hayarden area, which became a demilitarized zone.

Dissatisfaction with the outcome of the Israeli War of Independence ran deep in the Syrian military. Although Syrian president Shukri al-Quwatli envisioned a greater Arab nation, encompassing both Syria and Palestine, he also believed in a republican form of government. He was removed from power during a series of military coups that erupted in 1949. In December Colonel Adib al-Shishakli seized power. In 1951 he orchestrated his own election as president and dissolved the Syrian parliament. Another coup removed him from power in 1954, and he was replaced by an Arab nationalist coalition. In September 1961 another military coup occurred. Following more turmoil, Syrian Army officers created the National Council of the Revolutionary Command (NCRC), dominated by the Baath Party. The NCRC assumed power on March 8, 1963, and remained in place until 1970, although internal coups changed the face of the NCRC on a regular basis.

Meanwhile, two decades of sporadic raids across the Israeli-Syrian border exploded into an aerial battle over the Golan Heights on April 7, 1967. Israeli aircraft shot down six Syrian Mikoyan-Gurevich MiG-21 fighters, after which IDF warplanes flew over Damascus in a triumphant show of force.

Although the United Arab Republic had dissolved, Egypt and Syria continued to maintain close military ties. On May 30, 1967, Jordan joined the alliance. All three nations began mobilizing their military forces, deploying them to the Israeli border. In response to

the overwhelming intelligence indicators, the IDF launched a preemptive strike against Egyptian airfields on June 5, 1967, triggering the Six-Day War. After destroying virtually the entire Egyptian Air Force on the ground, Israeli warplanes launched attacks against Jordanian, Syrian, and Iraqi airfields with much the same results.

With two-thirds of the Syrian Air Force destroyed and the remainder dispersed to distant airfields, Syrian military options against Israel were limited. After an abortive attack on the Tel Dan water plant, Syrian units began shelling Israeli towns from fortified positions atop the Golan Heights. The IDF retaliated with air strikes, attempting to silence Syrian artillery and disorganize or destroy the armored units.

On June 9, Israeli forces broke the Syrian defensive lines atop the Golan Heights plateau. The Syrian Army retreated in disarray, abandoning much of its heavy equipment. When the cease-fire took effect on June 11, IDF troops held the Golan Heights. During the Six-Day War, Israel lost only 141 soldiers on the Syrian front. The war cost Syria 2,500 killed as well as almost all of its equipment that had been deployed on the Golan Heights.

The Israeli occupation of the Golan Heights was a critical factor in the next outbreak of hostilities between the two nations. On October 6, 1973, Egyptian and Syrian forces launched a coordinated surprise attack against Israel. During the Yom Kippur War, Syria's primary objective was to retake the Golan Heights. Syria also sought to reclaim some measure of the respect it had lost in the humiliating 1967 defeat. During the first two days of fighting Syrian forces made significant advances, regaining much of the lost territory.

Syrian tanks outnumbered those of Israel by as much as 10 to 1 in some sectors of the battlefield.

For the IDF, the primary front of the war was the Golan Heights, the loss of which would represent the single most serious threat to the security of Israel. Combat against Egypt in the Sinai became the secondary theater, as the IDF rushed reserves to the northern front.

Early Syrian advances pushed the IDF back to the outskirts of Nafah. But as the Syrian units advanced, they left the protective umbrella of their antiaircraft defensive network, increasing their own vulnerability to Israeli air attack. By October 8 the initiative and momentum shifted to the Israelis, who began to push the Syrian forces from the Golan Heights and back into Syria. On October 14, Israeli forces began shelling the outskirts of Damascus. Israeli progress was halted by a surprise Iraqi and Jordanian attack into the IDF's flank, but even the combined Arab armies were insufficient to push the IDF out of Syria.

On October 22 the United Nations (UN) imposed a cease-fire on Egypt and Israel. Syria acceded to the cease-fire on October 23. U.S. secretary of state Henry Kissinger engaged in a series of diplomatic meetings in Syria and Israel, eventually brokering a long-term armistice agreement signed on May 31, 1974. Israel agreed to withdraw its forces to the post–Six-Day War border, which left Israel in control of the Golan Heights. Both sides also agreed to the establishment of a demilitarized zone policed by UN troops.

In 1976 Syria sent 40,000 troops into neighboring Lebanon to intervene in the Lebanese Civil War. This led to a 30-year Syrian presence in Lebanon, as Syria sought to impose internal stability while also pursuing its own interests. In 1982 Israel invaded southern Lebanon in an attempt to preempt terrorist attacks across the border, primarily those launched by the Palestine Liberation Organization (PLO). During the first week of Operation PEACE FOR GALILEE, the Syrian Air Force lost 86 aircraft to the Israeli Air Force (IAF) in the skies over Lebanon. Although the Syrian-Israeli border remained relatively quiet thereafter, the two nations effectively fought a proxy war in Lebanon, as Syria funded and trained Lebanese and Palestinian fighters.

During the 1991 Persian Gulf War, Syria participated on the side of the UN coalition, led by the United States. This was an abrupt departure from previous Syrian policy, especially considering that Syria had been allied with Iraq in three wars against Israel. Following the Persian Gulf War, Syrian president Hafez al-Assad, in power since 1970, conducted discreet face-to-face negotiations with the Israeli government. The talks failed to produce a peace settlement, but the Israeli-Syrian border remained relatively peaceful and secure. When al-Assad died on June 10, 2000, he was succeeded by his son, Bashar al-Assad, who has attempted to continue his father's lower-profile policy toward Israel.

Prior to the 1991 Persian Gulf War, Syria imported most of its military technology from the Soviet Union. As a reward for its participation in that war, Syria received financial assistance from several Arab states in the Persian Gulf, including Kuwait and Saudi Arabia. Much of that funding was earmarked for military spending, in part to offset the costs of participation in the war. With the collapse of the Soviet Union, however, and the unwillingness of most Western governments to sell arms to Syria, that nation has experienced difficulty in procuring quality military hardware. Domestic manufacturing of conventional weapons in Syria remains limited primarily to small arms.

Syria currently fields one of the largest military forces in the world and the second-largest Arab force, behind only Egypt. The Syrian military is organized into the Syrian Arab Army, the Syrian Arab Navy, the Syrian Arab Air Force, the Syrian Arab Air Defense Forces, and the Police and Security Force. All Syrian men serve a compulsory two years in the Syrian military, beginning at age 18. The officer corps is highly politicized, with membership in the Baath Party being a virtual prerequisite for advancement to flag rank. Annually, Syria spends approximately $1 billion on its military, representing almost 6 percent of its gross domestic product (GDP).

The Syrian Army consists of about 200,000 regular troops and 280,000 conscripts organized into seven armored and three mechanized divisions, a Special Forces division, and a Republican Guard division. Its 4,700 main battle tanks included 1,700 Soviet T-72s and 2,000 T-54/55s and T-62s. Many of the T54/55s are emplaced in hull-down static positions in the heavily fortified defensive zone between Damascus and the Golan Heights. Almost all of Syria's armored infantry fighting vehicles and armored personnel carriers are older Soviet BRDMs and BMP-1s. Syria also has significant numbers of field artillery pieces, including the 122-mm 2S-1 and 152-mm 2S-3.

The Syrian Air Force, established in 1948, has some 100,000 regular troops and another 37,000 reservists. Its 1,100 combat aircraft includes Mikoyan-Gurevich MiG-21s, MiG-23s, MiG-25s, MiG-29s, and Sukhoi Su-24s. It also has some 90 attack helicopters, including Mil Mi-24s. The 65,000-strong Air Defense Command fields some 25 air defense brigades, each with six surface-to-air missile (SAM) batteries, as well as about 4,000 antiaircraft guns ranging from 23 mm to 100 mm.

The Syrian Navy was established only in 1950. The relatively small force of 4,000 operates some 40 vessels, including two older Soviet diesel submarines and 22 missile attack craft. Syria has one of the most advanced unconventional weapons programs of all the Arab nations. Most intelligence assessments agree that Syria has developed, stockpiled, and weaponized a significant amount of chemical agents, including the nerve agents GB (Sarin) and VX and the blister agent HD (mustard). Syria's biological warfare agents include anthrax, cholera, and botulism. Syria has a number of delivery options for its chemical weapons, including an arsenal of SAMs. In its pursuit of missile technology, Syria has been aided by shipments of weapons and technological assistance from North Korea, which in the 1990s supplied variants of the Scud-C missile, with a range of 300 miles, and the Scud-D, with a range of 430 miles.

PAUL J. SPRINGER AND DAVID T. ZABECKI

See also

Arab Liberation Army; Assad, Bashar al-; Assad, Hafez al-; Baathism; Biological Weapons and Warfare; Chemical Weapons and Warfare; Israeli War of Independence, Israeli-Syrian Front; Israeli War of Independence, Overview; Kissinger, Henry Alfred; Lebanon, Civil War in; Lebanon, Israeli Invasion of; Persian Gulf War; Quwatli, Shukri al-; Six-Day War; Syria; United Arab Republic; Yom Kippur War

References

Draper, Thomas. *Israel and the Middle East.* New York: H. W. Wilson, 1983.

Herzog, Chaim. *The Arab-Israeli Wars: War and Peace in the Middle East from the War of Independence to Lebanon.* Westminster, MD: Random House, 1984.

Lustick, Ian. *From War to War: Israel vs. the Arabs, 1948–1967.* New York: Garland, 1994.

Pollack, Kenneth M. *Arabs at War: Military Effectiveness, 1948–1991.* Lincoln: University of Nebraska Press, 2002.

Rabil, Robert G. *Embattled Neighbors: Syria, Israel, and Lebanon.* Boulder, CO: Lynne Rienner, 2003.

Rubin, Barry, and Thomas A. Keaney, eds. *Armed Forces in the Middle East: Politics and Strategy.* Portland, OR: Frank Cass, 2002.

Solomon, Brian. *Chemical and Biological Warfare.* New York: H. W. Wilson, 1999.

Torr, James D. *Weapons of Mass Destruction: Opposing Viewpoints.* San Diego: Greenhaven, 2005.

T

Tal, Israel
Born: 1924

Israeli general and armor expert. Israel Tal (Talik) was born in 1924 on a Jewish kibbutz in Palestine. He joined the British Army, served with the Jewish Brigade, and saw action in the Western Desert during World War II. Mustered out of the service as a sergeant, he returned to Palestine and joined the Jewish covert military organization Haganah. In the 1956 Sinai Campaign he served as a brigade commander.

Tal took command of the Israel Defense Forces (IDF) Armored Corps in 1964 and immediately went to work to instill a new professionalism and discipline in that unit. The improved ability of the corps was important in the June 1967 Six-Day War, during which Tal commanded the armored Ugdah Division, the northernmost unit of the Israeli advance into the Sinai.

Tal's division launched the Sinai attack on June 5, 1967, at the northern end of the main Egyptian defensive line, anchored at El Arish. Breaking through at Rafa and Khan Yunis within 12 hours, Tal's success allowed Avraham Yoffe's division to attack between Tal and Ariel Sharon's forces deep into the Sinai. Tal ordered a separate armored task force to race ahead for the Suez Canal. The force arrived at the canal on June 7, making Tal the first to reach the waterway. Tal's main force advanced on two axes toward Suez, including along the coastal road, while Yoffe and Sharon headed toward the Mitla Pass in hopes of trapping the Egyptian Army in the Sinai. Fending off desperate Egyptian counterattacks at Bir Gifgafa, Tal reached the canal across from Ismailia, and the IDF completed its conquest of the Sinai within four days.

In the aftermath of the Six-Day War and the War of Attrition (1968–1970), the IDF decided that the heavily fortified Bar-Lev Line

Israel Tal, Israel Defense Forces (IDF) general and commander of its Armored Corps, April 21, 1966. (Moshe Milner/Israeli Government Press Office)

was the best means for maintaining Israel's hold on the Sinai. Tal, now the IDF vice chief of staff, strongly opposed the line's strong point system, which he saw as an easy target for the Egyptian Army.

Having relied on purchased tanks for many years, in the 1970s the IDF decided to avoid the political winds of overseas tank acquisitions. Thus, the IDF asked Tal to head the design committee for the Merkava (Chariot) main battle tank.

After Tal's retirement from the IDF, he served as assistant minister of defense from 1975 to 2000. He published a book, *National Security: The Israeli Experience* (2000), in which he recognized that the ability of the IDF to defend Israel rested on its ability to launch quick offensive strikes. Tal urged Israel to avoid defensive warfare and attrition while maintaining air superiority and the option of preemptive strikes to meet the future challenge of likely missile attacks.

THOMAS D. VEVE

See also

Bar-Lev Line; Haganah; Israel Defense Forces; Merkava Tank; Sinai Campaign; Six-Day War; Suez Canal

References

Bloom, Jeremy. *Six Days: How the 1967 War Shaped the Middle East.* New York: St. Martin's, 2003.

Herzog, Chaim. *The Arab-Israeli Wars: War and Peace in the Middle East from the War of Independence to Lebanon.* Westminster, MD: Random House, 1984.

Oren, Michael B. *Six Days of War: June 1967 and the Making of the Modern Middle East.* Novato, CA: Presidio, 2003.

Tal, Israel. *National Security: The Israeli Experience.* Translated by Martin Kett. Westport, CT: Praeger, 2000.

Talmud

An extensive set of interpretations of the writings (or scriptures) of the Torah dealing with the law, customs, ethics, and history of the Jewish people. The Torah is the first of three parts of the written Hebrew Bible. The Torah is also essentially the same as the first five books of the Christian Old Testament—Genesis, Exodus, Leviticus, Numbers, and Deuteronomy—often referred to as the Five Books of Moses or the Pentateuch. The Talmud began as an oral commentary on the Torah and was designed to offer insights into the writings of the Torah as well as how to interpret and apply the laws mandated in the Torah. The Talmud also treats issues relating to Jewish history, ethics, and traditions.

Jews of the orthodox tradition believe that God handed down the Oral Torah directly to Moses, who then taught it to others. In this fashion, it was handed down from generation to generation. However, the oral teaching of the Talmud lasted only until the second century AD. At that time, much of it was written down in the form of the Mishna (repetition), which is a compilation of all the laws contained in the Torah.

In the succeeding few centuries, more commentaries were written by rabbis and Jewish scholars both in Babylon and Jerusalem.

These newer writings came to be known as the Gemara (completion), a set of commentaries on the various teachings of the Mishna. Taken together, the Mishna and Gemara make up the Talmud. By the fifth century, most of the writings had been completed.

There are two different Talmuds. The so-called Jerusalem Talmud consists of the Gemara writings and interpretations compiled by scholars, mostly in the Galilee town of Safed. The Babylonian Talmud was compiled by rabbis and scholars in Babylonia. The latter Talmud is the most expansive, and it is the one that many Jews mean when they reference the Talmud.

The Talmud has not remained a static set of writings or interpretations, however. Over the centuries, Rabbis and scholars had added to it and have provided new interpretations of the old laws and scriptures. Currently, a new commentary is being prepared for the Mishna, Gemara, and older commentaries.

Reading the Talmud and comprehending its meaning is not always an easy task. Thus, it is no surprise that reading and interpreting it has often been left to rabbinic scholars and rabbis, although many observant Jews make it a habit of reading a little bit of it daily. The writing is often not linear and can have large gaps in reasoning as well as interpretation. References to passages in the Torah are sometimes little more than a few words, making familiarity with the Torah essential for full comprehension. The writings also may provide more than one interpretation of a law or custom without explicitly stating which interpretation is the preferred one. It takes a well-trained eye and a learned scholar to navigate around such complexities.

The Mishna is organized into six sedarim (orders), and each order has one or more sections known as masekhtot (tractates). The first seder is called Zera'im (Seeds) and contains 11 tractates. Zera'im covers agricultural laws, tithing, blessings, and prayers. The second seder is Mo'ed (Festival), containing 12 tractates. This section deals primarily with laws relating to the Sabbath and the observance of festivals or holidays. The third seder is Nashim (Women), with 7 tractates, and covers subjects relating to marriage, divorce, and certain oaths. The fourth seder is Nezikin (Damages) and includes 10 tractates. Nezikin covers criminal and civil laws and the functions of courts. The fifth seder, comprising 11 tractates, is Kodashim (Things Holy) and speaks to dietary laws, sacrificial ceremonies, and the laws guiding the temple. Toharot (Purity), the sixth seder with 12 tractates, interprets things that are both pure and impure. Taken as a corpus of writings, the Mishna covers religious, social, and judicial laws and interpretations that are meant to guide observant Jews' lives on a daily basis, the oral law as handed down to Moses.

In the 300 years or so after the Mishna had been written down, rabbinic scholars in both Babylonia and Safed began debating and discussing the Mishna. Many of the Gemara writings are in the form of legal syntheses based on the Mishna or Torah and appear in the form of a Socratic, or dialectical, exchange between fictional or anonymous characters. One voice asks the question (makshan), and another voice replies (tartzan).

Because the work proceeded independently in Palestine and Babylon, the Gemara is divided in like fashion. The first is called the Palestinian Talmud (ca. fourth century AD), while the second is known as the Babylonian Talmud (ca. fifth century AD). The Babylonian Talmud is usually the one referred to when the general term "Talmud" is invoked and includes the Mishna as the entire body of work. Over the centuries, rabbinic scholars have placed considerably greater emphasis on the Babylonian Talmud. Part of this preference may stem from the fact that the Babylonian Talmud is far easier to read and interpret than the Palestinian version. The Babylonian Talmud, however, is more than four times the size of the Palestinian Talmud.

The first complete edition of the Babylonian Talmud was printed in the mid-16th century in Italy. In modern times, Orthodox Jews eschew any attempt to apply historical syntheses or interpretations to the Talmud and do not attempt to second-guess the writers and interpreters of the Talmud. Some modern scholars claim that because it is not possible to cobble together all of the various versions and interpretations of the Talmud, it is unwise to try to reinterpret the law. Others claim that it is indeed possible to reconstruct the corpus of writings and apply historical segmentation to them.

Not all Jews have embraced the Talmud as an absolute and authoritative text. Reform Judaism tends to view the Talmud as a guide to moral conduct and inspiration but does not ascribe to it the sacrosanct nature that Orthodox Jews lend to it. Jews of the Conservative tradition have made the Talmud a central part of their system of belief but tend to see it more as a historical guide rather than an inviolable set of laws.

PAUL G. PIERPAOLI JR.

See also

Ashkenazic Judaism; Hasidic Judaism; Mizrahic Judaism; Sephardic Judaism

References

Biale, David. *Cultures of the Jews: A New History.* New York: Schocken, 2002.

Dimont, Max. *Jews, God and History.* New York: Simon and Schuster, 1962.

Robinson, George. *Essential Judaism: A Complete Guide to Beliefs, Customs, and Rituals.* New York: Pocket Books/Simon and Schuster, 2001.

Seltzer, Robert. *Jewish People, Jewish Thought.* New York: Macmillan, 1980.

Tammuz I Reactor

Iraqi nuclear reactor destroyed by Israeli aircraft in 1981 while in the final stages of construction. The Tammuz I reactor was also known as the Osiraq reactor. Beginning in the late 1950s, the Iraqi government headed by Saddam Hussein had sought to acquire

Journalists are shown the destroyed Tammuz Iraqi nuclear reactor bombed by Israel during an air raid in 1981 and hit again during the 1991 Persian Gulf War, September 9, 2002. The site is at al-Toweitheh, some 18 miles southeast of Baghdad. (AFP/Getty Images)

nuclear technology. Iraq claimed that this effort was for peaceful purposes, but many governments, most notably Israel, surmised that the ultimate Iraqi goal was the production of nuclear weapons. Iraq's first foray into the nuclear field came in 1959 when it entered into an agreement with the Soviet Union to build a small 5-megawatt research reactor near Baghdad. The project was completed in 1968, but its small size and close supervision by Soviet technicians frustrated Iraq's goal of acquiring a facility capable of producing weapons-grade plutonium byproducts.

In light of this, Iraq began to look to other sources, notably France and Italy, for more sophisticated nuclear technology. After the 1973–1974 Organization of Petroleum Exporting Countries (OPEC) oil embargo, Iraq's huge energy reserves gave it a powerful bargaining chip as it negotiated an agreement with France for nuclear technology. In 1978 a French-led consortium signed a formal agreement to construct a nuclear plant with the Iraqi government. The terms of the agreement stipulated that Iraq would provide France with oil at discounted prices and agree to large purchases of French military hardware in exchange for construction of a nuclear complex centered on a 70-megawatt nuclear reactor.

The fuel for the proposed reactor was to be 93 percent enriched (weapons-grade) uranium. The project was originally named Osiraq, an Iraqi derivation of the name of a similar reactor in France. However, the name was soon changed to Tammuz to commemorate the time of the year in which the ruling Iraqi Baath Party came to power.

Italian firms would provide expertise in the extraction of weapons-grade plutonium from the reactor's spent fuel. As the reactor complex neared completion in 1980, the Israeli government embarked on a public information campaign designed to alert the world to the dangers of allowing Iraq to acquire nuclear technology. There were also indications by then that Israel had conducted several covert intelligence and sabotage missions against scientists and equipment associated with the program.

In September 1980 Iraq invaded neighboring Iran, triggering the eight-year-long Iran-Iraq War. One of the first Iranian Air Force targets was the Tammuz I reactor. A September 30, 1980, raid by Iranian bombers failed to inflict serious damage on the facility but did precipitate an evacuation of several hundred French and Italian workers and brought construction on the site to a standstill. By the spring of 1981, however, many of the technicians had returned, and work was proceeding with a target date for completion of the complex later that year.

Israeli aircraft struck the Tammuz I reactor site on June 7, 1981. The mission, more than a year in planning and rehearsals, involved eight McDonnell-Douglas F-15 Eagle fighter-bombers with six General Dynamics F-15 Fighting Falcon fighters flying top cover. The strike package flew the 700-mile approach at low altitudes. Battle damage assessment indicated that the reactor building was struck and completely destroyed by 14 bombs.

Iraqi attempts to rebuild Tammuz I in the 1980s were slowed by a diversion of resources to the war with Iran and a breakdown in negotiations with France for the reconstruction of the reactor. The

Tammuz site was again heavily bombed by coalition aircraft in 1991 during the Persian Gulf War, after which there were no significant efforts to rebuild.

ROBERT M. BROWN

See also

Iran-Iraq War; Iraq; Nuclear Weapons; Osiraq Raid; Persian Gulf War; Spector, Yiftah

References

Claire, Rodger W. *Raid on the Sun: Inside Israel's Secret Campaign That Denied Saddam the Bomb.* New York: Broadway, 2004.

Nakdimon, Shelomoh. *First Strike: The Exclusive Story of How Israel Foiled Iraq's Attempt to Get the Bomb.* New York: Summit Books, 1987.

Perlmutter, Amos, Michael Handel, and Uri Bar-Joseph. *Two Minutes over Baghdad.* 2nd ed. London: Frank Cass, 2003.

Tank Warfare

Although the tank only made its first halting appearance on the battlefield in September 1916 during World War I, it quickly became the dominant weapon system in modern ground combat. Combining both of the key elements of combat power—fire and maneuverability—the tank was also the product of the major paradigm shift from muscle (both human and animal) power to machine power that occurred in warfare between 1914 and 1918.

Despite its impressive armor and armament, the tank is not invulnerable, nor can it single-handedly accomplish every task on the battlefield. Tanks can be defeated by physical barriers, land mines, aircraft, artillery, other tanks, and a wide range of infantry weapons. For these reasons, tanks are most effective when they are committed as part of a combined-arms team. Accompanying friendly infantry and engineers reduce barriers and neutralize enemy infantry fire. Friendly aircraft augment the fires of the tanks, suppress enemy antitank fire, and attack enemy tanks. Friendly artillery suppresses enemy antitank and antiaircraft fire and supports the accompanying infantry.

The key problem in coordinating all of these elements of the combined arms team is the varying speeds at which they maneuver, especially when under fire. Tanks and aircraft obviously move much faster than conventional infantry or towed artillery. The requirement to keep up with the tanks gave rise to modern mechanized infantry and self-propelled artillery. Nonetheless, in the years since the end of World War I, armored warfare theorists have gone through several cycles of advocating that tanks and airpower could do it all, with infantry and artillery relegated to mopping up operations. With each new technological advancement in armor or airpower, it seemed to work for a while. But infantry and artillery weapons technology then caught up, and the cycle began all over again. This pattern can be seen very clearly in the history of the Arab-Israeli wars. Tank warfare, therefore, is far more complex than simple tank-against-tank fighting.

Tanks are far more terrain-dependent than infantry, just as airpower is far more weather-dependent than artillery. Tanks are

Israeli tanks cross a pontoon bridge built by the Israel Defense Forces (IDF) over the Suez Canal, October 21, 1973. (Ron Ilan/Israeli Government Press Office)

more effective in open, flat terrain where their ability to maneuver is not restricted by roads, vegetation, or extreme elevations. The deserts of the Middle East are classic tank warfare terrain, and virtually all of the major tank battles since World War II have occurred in that part of the world.

The various categories of tank kills are a function of the damage done to the tank combined with the tactical situation. A mobility kill occurs when the tank's power train or running gear has been damaged to the point that the tank cannot move. The tank may still be able to fire its weapons, but its inability to maneuver severely degrades its combat value. A firepower kill occurs when the tank's main gun or its fire control optics and electronics have been severely damaged. A total kill occurs when the tank can neither move nor fire. This usually means that the tank has been totally destroyed, but it can also mean that the crew has been killed, even though the physical damage to the tank itself may be relatively light. The crew, obviously, is the most vulnerable element of any tank. It is also the most easily replaced as long as highly trained crew members are available.

Whether fired by artillery, aircraft, another tank, or infantry weapons, the warheads of all antitank rounds are classified as either chemical energy or kinetic energy. Most main battle tanks are capable of firing both types of rounds through their main guns. The most common and effective chemical energy projectile, the high-explosive

antitank (HEAT) round, has a shaped charge warhead that relies on the Munroe Effect to burn a hole through the tank's armor in the form of an expanding cone. What actually kills the tank crew members is the fragmented armor of their own tank. HEAT rounds can also set off fuel and ammunition fires. Nonexploding kinetic energy rounds are very heavy and dense and are fired at an extremely high velocity. The most common is some form of sabot round in which an outer casing falls away as soon as the round leaves the muzzle. On impact the sabot literally punches its way through the target's armor. The result inside the tank is no less catastrophic than that caused by a HEAT round.

Because kinetic energy rounds require a flat, line-of-sight trajectory and an extremely high velocity, they must be fired from a gun, as opposed to a howitzer, and from a very heavy platform. Thus, only tanks and antitank artillery can fire sabot rounds. A tank's most vulnerable area to a sabot round is at the slip ring, where the turret joins the main hull. Smaller nonsabot kinetic energy rounds are fired from rotary or fixed-wing aircraft armed with special antitank Gatling guns that deliver a high volume of fire to defeat the target's armor, usually from above where the armor is the weakest. Although common in World War II, purpose-built antitank artillery fell into disuse in the years following 1945. By the 1960s, the Soviet Union, West Germany, and Sweden were among the few remaining countries still building antitank artillery. Most armies came to

An Israeli tank employing a smoke screen to protect against antitank missiles during operations on August 1, 2006, on the Israeli side of the Israeli-Lebanese border. (Getty Images)

regard the tank itself as the premier but certainly not the only anti-tank weapon.

Chemical energy rounds do not require a heavy launching platform and are thus ideal for infantry antitank weapons, which include rocket launchers, recoilless rifles, and antitank guided missiles (ATGMs). When wire-guided ATGMs first appeared in the early 1970s, they were quickly fitted onto helicopters. They were soon replaced by a new generation of ATGMs with fire-and-forget guidance systems. Field artillery HEAT rounds include projectiles that are guided onto the target by a forward observer using a laser designator and projectiles that produce air bursts over tank for-mations, releasing numbers of HEAT submunitions that attack the tank's top surfaces.

The best way to defeat a HEAT warhead is to cause it to detonate prematurely, which will prevent the Munroe Effect from forming properly on the outer skin of the tank's armor. Something as sim-ple as a mesh outer screen mounted on the side of a tank with a few inches of standoff distance will cause that premature detonation. Reactive explosive armor, also called appliqué armor, mounted on the tank's integral armor is also relatively effective against HEAT rounds but is not at all effective against sabot rounds. Each element of reactive armor contains a small explosive charge that detonates when it is hit, causing the impacting HEAT round to detonate pre-

maturely, spoiling the Munroe Effect. Finally, the sloped surfaces of the tank's armor can cause the HEAT round to deflect, which will also spoil the Munroe Effect. Sloped armor surfaces can also deflect sabot rounds in certain instances.

Tanks can be defeated by a blast from conventional high explo-sives if the charge is large enough and close enough. Antitank mines frequently produce mobility kills by blowing off the tread or dam-aging the road wheels and sometimes produce total kills. High-explosive projectiles delivered by artillery or air require a direct or very close hit, which usually exceeds the circular probable error of all but the most advanced precision munitions. Field artillery can also be used to place antitank minefields deep in the enemy's rear by firing special cargo-carrying rounds that disperse the mines upon detonating in the air. The mines are relatively small, usually just large enough to produce a mobility kill, but the advantage is that the enemy tank is immobilized far from the line of contact.

The Israeli War of Independence (1948–1949) was primarily an infantry war, with tanks performing a supporting role. The Israel Defense Forces (IDF) had 15 tanks, 280 half-tracks, and some 20 other armored vehicles that carried guns. The Arabs had 45 tanks and some 620 other armored vehicles, of which 180 carried guns.

The 1956 Sinai Campaign was the first true armored war between the Israelis and the Arab states. The IDF deployed about 200 tanks in the Sinai and lost 40. The Egyptians deployed about 150 and lost 30. Although Israeli losses were greater, the actions of the 7th Armored Brigade at the Dyka Pass and Abu Ageila convinced IDF chief of staff Moshe Dayan that rapidly striking armored forces were the best way to defeat the rigid and linear Arab command systems.

Following the Sinai Campaign, Israel methodically built up its Armored Corps under the leadership of General Israel Tal, who later headed the design team that created the Merkava tank. The Armored Corps became an elite organization on the same level as the air force and paratroopers. But IDF leaders soon realized that they did not have the resources to maintain a state-of-the-art air force and an elite corps of paratroopers and develop a well-balanced mechanized ground force. As a result, the tank branch of the mechanized force acquired modern British Centurion and American Patton tanks, while the mechanized infantry branch still rode in ancient World War II–era open M-3 half-tracks that had limited mobility and increasing maintenance problems. Tal believed that the balanced tank-mechanized infantry team, then the standard in the North Atlantic Treaty Organization (NATO), was a requirement of the European terrain and not all that important in the classic tank country of the Middle East.

The IDF's experiences in the 1967 Six-Day War seemed to confirm the relatively low value of infantry. Both sides deployed a combined total of 2,500 tanks during that short war, with the Israelis losing upwards of 200 and the Arabs losing almost 1,000. During the armored exploitation to the Suez Canal, the World War II–era half-tracks could not keep up with the modern tanks, and the Israeli Air Force's (IAF) air supremacy seemed to make field and air defense artillery all but useless, especially in highly fluid situations.

IDF leaders came to see the tank–fighter-bomber combination as the key to battlefield success in all situations, the same mistake the Germans made in World War II. Between the 1967 Six-Day War and the 1973 Yom Kippur War, the IDF Armored Corps grew from 9 armored and 2 mechanized brigades to 16 armored and 4 mechanized brigades. In the early 1970s, the IDF even turned down an opportunity to purchase American TOW missiles because the Israelis were convinced that the best way to kill a tank was with another tank.

When he became chief of the Armored Corps in 1969, Major General Avraham Adan tried to upgrade the mechanized infantry branch by improving recruiting standards and purchasing American-made M-113 armored personnel carriers (APCs) to replace the decrepit M-3 half-tracks. Tal, who was still a senior IDF commander, opposed spending scarce resources on the M-113s. He believed that the proper role of mechanized infantry was to fight mounted. Since the M-113 was designed to carry troops to the battle who then fought dismounted, it was not the proper armored infantry fighting vehicle (AIFV) that Tal believed the IDF needed. The tank–fighter-bomber combination continued as the IDF's primary tactical focus.

Egypt, meanwhile, had very carefully analyzed its defeat in 1967 and totally rebuilt its force with Soviet equipment and doctrine that relied on large numbers of surface-to-air missiles (SAMs) and the new ATGMs, especially the Soviet Sagger. When the Egyptians

attacked across the Suez Canal on October 6, 1973, they advanced only about 2.5 miles and established defensive positions well within their massive SAM umbrella. When the Israelis launched immediate counterattacks to relieve their cutoff outposts on the Bar-Lev Line, the IAF ran into the most withering air defenses they had ever encountered, and the almost pure IDF tank forces ran into a solid wall of ATGM fire. With the fighter-bombers separated from the tanks and with the tanks having no infantry or field artillery support, the Israeli tankers and pilots both paid a high price.

On the Golan Heights, meanwhile, the Soviet-equipped Syrians launched a massive attack that moved forward on a rigid schedule characteristic of Soviet doctrine, which presented the Israelis with massed targets. The Syrians had better tanks—and many more of them—equipped with the latest night sights, which the IDF tanks did not have. Although the IDF units on the Golan Heights were also almost tank-pure during the initial stages of the war and the IAF ran into the same problems with Syrian SAMs, the Israelis had the advantage of fighting from well-prepared hull-down positions. As much as possible, the IDF tanks did not maneuver during engagements, only moving between engagements to rearm, refuel, and reposition.

After their initial attack failed, the Syrians made a desperate plea to the Egyptians to increase the pressure in the Sinai. Thus, on October 14 the Egyptians attacked eastward from their defensive positions and eventually came out from under the cover of their fixed SAM sites on the other side of the canal. By that time, the Arabs had completely lost the element of surprise. The IDF was mobilized and deployed and ready to carry the fight to its enemies. More than 6,200 tanks on both sides were committed to the Yom Kippur War. The Israelis lost close to 800 main battle tanks and 400 other armored vehicles. The Arab armies lost more than 2,500 main battle tanks and more than 850 other armored vehicles.

The Yom Kippur War was a watershed in the development of modern armored warfare doctrine. An intense study of the IDF experience started the U.S. military on the road that led to the M-1 Abrams tank and the doctrine of AirLand Battle. The Israelis too learned from their mistakes in 1973 and rebalanced their force, placing a greater emphasis on fire support and mechanized infantry and acquiring thousands of the M-113 APC and its variants. Convinced that they had to achieve self-sufficiency in the production of tanks, the Israelis began development of the Merkava series.

During the long and protracted fighting in southern Lebanon between 1982 and 2000, the IDF lost approximately 150 main battle tanks, mostly M-48s and M-60s, and between 5 and 10 Merkavas. Arab losses amounted to more than 350 main battle tanks and the same number of other armored vehicles. As of 2002, the IDF had 3,930 main battle tanks (including 1,280 Merkavas) and some 6,300 APCs and other armored vehicles. Syria had 4,700 tanks and 5,600 APCs and other armored vehicles. Lebanon had 327 tanks and 1,450 APCs and other armored vehicles. Jordan had 1,058 tanks and 1,150 APCs and other armored vehicles. And Egypt had 3,860 tanks and 4,200 APCs and other armored vehicles.

The 2006 Lebanon War produced some of the same rude surprises for the IDF as they experienced in the Yom Kippur War 33 years earlier. Israel started its campaign against Hezbollah almost entirely from the air, apparently trying to replicate what they saw as the successful U.S. air campaign in Kosovo in 1999. When the air campaign failed and the IDF moved into southern Lebanon, it encountered deeply entrenched Hezbollah fighters well supplied with state-of-the-art Russian-made ATGMs, including the Sagger AT-3A, the Metis-M, and the Kornet. Israel claims that of more than 400 IDF tanks operating in southern Lebanon, Hezbollah fighters only managed to hit a few dozen, of which only 20 were penetrated. Thirty IDF tank crewmen were killed. Arab sources claim that the Israelis lost more than 120 tanks. The 2006 Lebanon War may have shown that the highly vaunted Merkava has been overrated.

DAVID T. ZABECKI

See also

Antitank Weapons; Dayan, Moshe; Hezbollah; Israel Defense Forces; Israeli War of Independence, Overview; Lebanon, Israeli Invasion of; Lebanon, U.S. Interventions in; Sinai Campaign; Six-Day War; Tanks; Yom Kippur War

References

Herzog, Chaim. *The Arab-Israeli Wars: War and Peace in the Middle East from the War of Independence to Lebanon.* Westminster, MD: Random House, 1984.

House, Jonathan M. *Toward Combined Arms Warfare: A Survey of 20th Century Tactics, Doctrine, and Organization.* Fort Leavenworth, KS: U.S. Army Command and General Staff College, 1984.

Kahalani, Avigdor. *The Heights of Courage: A Tank Leader's War on the Golan.* Westport, CT: Praeger, 1992.

Ripley, Tim. *Tank Warfare.* Drexel Hill, PA: Casemate, 2003.

Tanks

The first tanks employed in the Arab-Israeli wars were leftover pieces of equipment from World War II. Although the Transjordan Arab Legion was the best-equipped fighting force in the Middle East at the time, it only possessed armored cars. All sides in the Israeli War of Independence (1948–1949) used a wide variety of armored cars, many of which were locally fabricated. The first real Israeli armored vehicles were U.S. M-3 half-tracks, which Haganah agents had managed to procure in Europe.

When Syrian forces invaded Palestine on May 14, 1948, they were supported by a battalion of R-35 light tanks. Entering French service in 1935, the Renault R-35 was designed to replace the FT-17 light tank of World War I. The R-35 had a crew of two, a road speed of 12.4 mph, and a maximum range of 84 miles and weighed just under 12 tons. Its main gun was 37 mm, and its maximum armor protection was 37 mm.

Egyptian forces in 1948 had several different models of British tanks that were left over from the fighting in North Africa. These included Matildas, Valentines, and Crusaders. The Matilda was an infantry support tank, which under the British doctrine of the time did not require much more speed than that of a man walking, a con-

Medium Tanks in Selected Middle Eastern and North African Countries (1972, 1982)

Country	1972	1982
Algeria	590	630
Egypt	1,900	2,100
Iran	860	1,110
Iraq	860	2,200
Israel	1,700	3,600
Kuwait	80	240
Lebanon	40	0
Libya	221	2,900
Qatar	0	24
Saudi Arabia	25	450
Syria	1,140	3,990

cept that would prove extremely faulty in World War II. The Mk II variant of the Matilda entered service in 1940. It had a crew of four, a road speed of 14 mph, and a range of 48 miles and weighed just short of 30 tons. Its main gun was 40 mm, and its maximum armor thickness was 78 mm.

The Valentine entered service in 1940 and remained in production until 1944. It had a crew of three, a road speed of 15 mph, and a range of 87 miles and weighed 19.5 tons. Its main gun was 75 mm, and its maximum armor thickness was 65 mm. At 6,855 units, it was Britain's most mass-produced tank, with more than one-third going to the Soviet Union under Lend-Lease.

The Crusader entered service in 1941. A so-called cruiser tank, it was the mainstay of the British armored divisions in North Africa. It was fast but undergunned. The Crusader had a crew of three, a road speed of 27 mph, and a range of 180 miles and weighed 22 tons. Its main gun was only 57 mm, and its maximum armor thickness was 49 mm.

Before the end of the Israeli War of Independence, Egyptian forces had acquired a handful of American-built M-4 Sherman tanks in Palestine. The Sherman was also the first real Israeli tank, ultimately serving in the Israel Defense Forces (IDF) up through the Yom Kippur War in 1973. By scavenging scrap yards in Italy, Haganah agents in 1948 managed to procure 35 junked Shermans. The hulks were shipped to Israel, where their demilitarized main armament was removed and replaced by a number of different guns. Before the end of the war, 14 of the retrofitted Shermans were in service.

Throughout the 1950s, the Israelis continued to procure Shermans from any source available, and it became the standard tank in the IDF's armored units. Over the years the Sherman underwent many modifications, and more variants of it were produced than any other tank. The Sherman chassis served as the basis for self-propelled artillery, combat engineer vehicles, tank recovery vehicles, and antiradar missile launchers. Prior to being modified by the IDF, the two most common American variants of the Sherman acquired by the Israelis were the M-4A1 and the M-4A3. The M-4A1 entered U.S. service in 1942 and was armed with a 75-mm main gun. The far more capable M-4A3 entered service in 1944. It had a crew of five, a road speed of 24 mph, and a range of 96 miles and

Israel Defense Forces (IDF) tank crews pass in review at the conclusion of a training course, July 1957. The U.S.-made M-4 Sherman tanks are upgraded World War II–vintage tanks. (Israeli Government Press Office)

weighed 33 tons. Its main gun was 76 mm, and its maximum armor was 51 mm.

The most significant of the Israeli modifications to the Sherman included the French-supplied M-1 Super Sherman, with a 76.2-mm main gun; the M-50 Super Sherman, fitted with a French-made 75-mm high-velocity CN 75–50 gun; the M-51 Isherman, with a new turret and a modified French-made 105-mm CN 105 F1 gun; and the M-60 (HVMS), with a 60-mm hypervelocity medium support gun that fired a kinetic energy round. Israel sold most of its M-60 Shermans to Chile in the 1980s. The Egyptians too had modified versions of the Sherman, including an M-4A4 fitted with a diesel engine and the FL-10 turret and 75-mm high-velocity main gun of the French AMX-13 light tank. The IDF captured a number of Egyptian Shermans during the 1956 Sinai Campaign and put them into Israeli service during the 1967 Six-Day War and the 1973 Yom Kippur War.

Egypt, Lebanon, and Israel all acquired limited numbers of the French AMX-13 light tank during the 1950s. Really more a self-propelled tank destroyer than a true tank, the AMX-13 entered French service in 1953. It had a crew of three, a road speed of 36 mph, and a range of 240 miles and weighed 18 tons. Initially the main gun was 75 mm, but some versions had a 105-mm gun. The AMX-13's maximum armor thickness was 25 mm.

By the mid-1950s many of the Arab armies, especially Egypt, were beginning to acquire Soviet-built arsenals, including the PT-76, the IS-3, and the T-34/85, the best tank of World War II. During the Sinai Campaign the Egyptians used the T-34, and the Iraqi Army used the T-34 into the early 1990s. The T-34/76, with a 76-mm main gun, entered service in 1940. The improved T-34/85 entered service in early 1944. It had a crew of five, a road speed of 35 mph, and a range of 196 miles and weighed 32 tons. Its main gun was 85 mm, and its maximum armor was 90 mm.

Egypt also received a small number of Joseph Stalin 3 (IS-3) heavy tanks. Entering service in 1944, the IS-3 had a crew of four, a road speed of 23 mph, and a range of 144 miles and weighed 51 tons. Its main gun was 122 mm, and its maximum armor was 160 mm. The IS-3 probably did not operate in combat in the Middle East.

The PT-76 light amphibious tank entered Soviet service in 1952 and was used by the Egyptians in the Six-Day War and the Yom Kippur War. It had a crew of three, a road speed of 26 mph, and a range of 156 miles and weighed 15 tons. Its main gun was 76 mm, and its maximum armor was only 14 mm.

In the 1950s Iran, Iraq, Egypt, and Syria all acquired the T-54 and T-55 Soviet main battle tanks (MBTs). First built in 1945, the T-54 was replaced by the improved T-55 beginning in 1958. All T-54s in service were upgraded to T-55 standards. The most-produced

Egyptian marines operate a Soviet-made T-54 main battle tank during a multinational joint service exercise in Egypt, August 1985. (Mark Beberwyck/U.S. Department of Defense)

tank series in the world, the Soviets manufactured the T-55 until 1981. China continued to manufacture the T-55 for export, designated the Type-69, through the end of the century. The T-55 had a crew of four, a road speed of 30 mph, and a range of 300 miles and weighed 40 tons. Its main gun was 100 mm, and its maximum armor was 203 mm. Various upgrades for the T-55 included Kontakt-5 explosive reactive armor.

During the Six-Day War and the Yom Kippur War, Israel captured more than 1,000 T-55s from Egypt and Syria and retrofitted many of them for IDF service. Designated the Trion-4 and Trion-5, they remained in service with IDF reserve units into the early 1990s. The Trion-4 had a 100-mm main gun, and Trion-5 was fitted with a 105-mm North Atlantic Treaty Organization (NATO) standard M-68 main gun. Egypt also attempted a radical upgrade of the T-55, with a laser range finder and an automatic fire-suppression system. Designated the Ramses II, very few ever entered actual service, however.

Produced between 1964 and 1985, the Soviet T-62 was the most advanced tank on the battlefields of the Yom Kippur War. Still in service with many countries, it has a crew of four, a road speed of 30 mph, and a range of 270 miles and weighs 46 tons. Its main gun is a smoothbore 115 mm, and its maximum armor is 275 mm. Em-

ployed by both Syria and Egypt, the T-62's state of the art night sights were far superior to anything on IDF tanks in 1973. Nonetheless, Israel managed to capture many T-62s and put about 100 of them into service as the Trion-6. Iran also bought the T-62.

The most advanced Soviet-designed tank in the Middle East today is the T-72. Introduced in the early 1970s, it was the most common tank in the Soviet Army at the time of the collapse of the Soviet Union. Iran, Iraq, and Syria all bought the T-72, which has a crew of three, a road speed of 45 mph, a range of 270 miles, and weighs 45 tons. Its main gun is a smoothbore 125 mm, and its maximum armor is 250 mm. The T-72M, which is in the current Syrian arsenal, is equipped with a laser range finder that ensures a high hit probability at ranges of less than 2,000 yards. During the 1991 Persian Gulf War, Iraqi T-72s performed very poorly against the U.S. M-1 Abrams.

During the 1956 Sinai Campaign, the Israelis captured a number of British-built Centurion tanks from Egypt. In 1966 Israel entered into a deal with the British to help finance the development of their new Chieftain tank. In return, Britain allowed Israel to buy hundreds of older Centurions with an option to purchase the Chieftains. Under heavy Arab pressure, Britain withdrew from the deal in 1969 but not before Israel had acquired a substantial number of Centurions. Retrofitted and designated the Sho't tank in IDF service, Israel committed 293 to combat during the Six-Day War and more than 1,000 of the upgraded Sho't Kal tanks during the Yom Kippur War. Israel also captured 30 Centurions from Jordan during the Six-Day War. The Centurion had a crew of four, a road speed of 30 mph, and a range of 300 miles and weighed 51 tons. Its main gun was 105 mm, and it was protected by 152-mm armor.

The U.S.-built M-47 and M-48 Patton tanks were used by both sides in the Six-Day War. The M-47, which had a five-man crew, entered production in 1951. It was exported to Iran and Jordan. The following year the improved M-48 was introduced. The early versions had a gasoline engine, which easily caught fire whenever the tank took a hit. The M-48A3 version, introduced in 1959, had a diesel engine. The M-48 had a crew of four, a road speed of 40 mph, and a range of 250 miles and weighed 48 tons. Its main gun was 90 mm, and its maximum armor was 180 mm. Jordan also bought the M-48.

Israel tried unsuccessfully to buy M-47s from the United States during the 1950s. In the early 1960s West Germany agreed to sell Israel 150 M-48A2s, but under pressure from the Arab countries only 40 were delivered. But then in 1965, the United States decided to cover the shortfall in the West German order and also to sell Israel an additional 100 M-48s. By the start of the Six Day-War, the IDF

had some 250 M-48s in service, which it designated the Magach-3. A later M-48 upgrade, the Magach-5, had a 105-mm main gun. Israeli M-48s in the Sinai routinely defeated Egyptian T-34s and T-54s, while in the West Bank the IDF defeated Jordanian M-48s using their World War II–era Shermans. The IDF captured about 100 M-48s from Jordan. M-48s were also used by the Lebanese Army and by Christian Lebanese Forces militia during the Lebanese Civil War.

In 1971 the United States sold Israel 150 M-60 tanks, the last of the Patton line. The M-60 entered U.S. service in 1960. It had a crew of four, a road speed of 40 mph, and a range of 270 miles and weighed 60 tons. Its main gun was 105 mm, and its maximum armor thickness was 225 mm. The M-60 was designated the Magach-6 in IDF service. The Magach-6B upgrade had explosive reactive armor. The Magach-7 upgrade had new fire controls, a thermal sleeve, and smoke dischargers. During the Yom Kippur War, a number of M-60s served in both the Sinai and the Golan Heights. In the late 1970s the United States supplied Israel with another 150 M-48A5s, and in the early 1980s with an additional 300 M-60A3s. The IDF deployed both models to Lebanon during Operation PEACE FOR GALILEE.

In 2005 Israel Military Industries upgraded 170 M-60A3s for the Turkish Army. Designated the Sabra, it has a radically redesigned

An Egyptian Army U.S.-manufactured M60A1 main battle tank participating in a live-fire exercise in Egypt, November 1993. (Jeffrey T. Brady/U.S. Department of Defense)

turret and the same 120-mm smoothbore main gun as the Israeli Merkava III tank. The Sabra Mk II has explosive reactive armor.

The most advanced American tanks in the Middle East in 2006 do not belong to the IDF. Following the Yom Kippur War, Egypt embarked on a peace process with Israel that eventually led to the Israeli withdrawal from the Sinai. Simultaneously, Egypt began converting its armored fleet from Soviet tanks to the most modern American tanks. Prior to the 1991 Persian Gulf War, Egypt started acquiring M-60A3s from the United States. Egypt has some 1,700 M-60 tanks in its current arsenal.

In 1984 Egypt and the United States entered an agreement to coproduce the M-1 Abrams tank in Egypt. The M-1, which had a 105-mm main gun, entered U.S. Army service in 1980. The M-1A1, with a 120-mm smoothbore main gun, followed in 1985. It has a crew of four, a road speed of 45 mph, and a range of 280 miles and weighs 63 tons. The Abrams is constructed of Chobham Composite Armor, which uses depleted uranium. Its exact details remain classified, but its maximum Rolled Homogeneous Armor Equivalent (RHAe) has been estimated at 900 mm against kinetic energy projectiles (i.e., sabot) and 1,620 mm against chemical energy rounds (i.e., high-explosive antitank). Egypt has approximately 750 M-1 tanks.

After decades of operating with retrofitted hand-me-downs, the Israeli leadership finally concluded that the nation had to become self-sufficient in tank production. The years of constantly improving and upgrading the designs of other countries gave Israel the technological base to proceed. Introduced in 1979, Israel's Merkava I tank has a crew of four, a road speed of 30 mph, and a range of 240 miles and weighs 63 tons. Its main gun is 105 mm. The precise details of the laminated steel and nickel composite modular armor on all the Merkavas remain classified. The Merkava has an innovative suspension system specifically designed to cope with the rough and boulder-strewn ground of the Golan Heights. The Merkava is the only MBT in the world that was designed to carry a squad of eight infantry soldiers, or three litter casualties, internally under complete armor protection. The Merkava is also unique in the placement of its engine in the front rather than the rear as with all other MBTs. The Merkava I served with the IDF in southern Lebanon during Operation PEACE FOR GALILEE.

The Merkava II was introduced in 1983 and incorporated many upgrades specifically for urban warfare, including an internal 60-mm mortar system. It weighs slightly more than the Merkava I but has a road speed of 33 mph and a range of 500 km. The Merkava III, introduced in 1990, has an improved 1,200-horsepower engine and a 120-mm smoothbore main gun. The Merkava IV, introduced in 2002, weighs 65 tons. It has a 1,500-horsepower engine and the most advanced fire-control computers and electronics. All onboard ammunition is stored in blast-proof containers. Its top road speed is 36 mph. Prior to the 2006 War in Lebanon, many observers considered the Merkava IV to be the most advanced MBT in the world. The IDF's experience in southern Lebanon, however, shows that the Merkava may not have lived up to its high expectations.

DAVID T. ZABECKI

See also

Antitank Weapons; Arab Legion; Israeli War of Independence, Overview; Lebanon, Israeli Invasion of; Sinai Campaign; Six-Day War; Tank Warfare; Valley of Tears, Battle of the; Yom Kippur War

References

Foss, Christopher F., ed. *The Encyclopedia of Tanks and Armored Fighting Vehicles.* San Diego: Thunder Bay, 2002.

Herzog, Chaim. *The Arab-Israeli Wars: War and Peace in the Middle East from the War of Independence to Lebanon.* Westminster, MD: Random House, 1984.

Katz, Samuel M. *Merkava MBT Mks I, II, & III: Chariot of Steel.* Oxford, UK: Osprey, 1997.

Tucker, Spencer C. *Tanks: An Illustrated History of Their Impact.* Santa Barbara, CA: ABC-CLIO, 2004.

Tel Aviv–Jaffa

The second-largest city in Israel, located along the Mediterranean Sea and made up of both Tel Aviv and Jaffa (Yafo). After the creation of the State of Israel, the ancient city of Jaffa was incorporated into Tel Aviv in 1950. Jaffa's first inhabitants appeared in the Neolithic Age (ca. 5000 BC) and by 2000 BC it was an established Canaanite town. The town changed hands nearly 30 times during its history. Among the early rulers were Egyptian king Thutmose II in 1468 BC and Jewish king David four and a half centuries later. The city prospered under Persian rule and then came under the rule of the Ptolemies, Herod, and the Umayyads. As one of the key port cities near Jerusalem, it changed hands several times during the Crusades but then languished for centuries afterward. Napoleon Bonaparte besieged and took the city in 1799, although the Ottoman Turks ruled Jaffa for much of the 19th century.

European funding led to a road from Jaffa to Jerusalem followed by a French-made railroad track connecting the two cities. Also during this time the city came to enjoy a diverse influx of Jews from around the world, some with Zionist dreams, and it was forced to broaden its limits toward the end of the century. Prior to the creation of Tel Aviv, Jaffa was the home of the Palestine bureau of the World Zionist Organization (WZO), the central committees of different labor movements, and headquarters for various sports and educational groups.

Tel Aviv was founded by Jewish pioneers in 1909 as a European city on the edge of the Orient. It was to be the first all-Jewish city of the modern era. It had a 2006 population of 370,000, while the greater metropolitan area incorporates more than 2.7 million people. The city spreads nine miles along the coastline and two to four miles inland. It shares borders with Bat Yam and Holon to the south, Ramat Gan and Givataym to the east, and Herzliya and Ramat Hasharon to the northeast.

Tel Aviv grew rapidly during the era of British control in Palestine immediately following World War I. By 1921 it was declared a town, and in 1934 it separated from Jaffa and formally became a city of its own. Following World War II there was another influx of Jews to the city, and by 1948 it had become the largest city in Palestine.

View of Tel Aviv, Israel's second largest city. (Corel)

With the 1948 creation of the State of Israel and the subsequent Israeli War of Independence (1948–1949), Jewish immigrants to Israel were led off their arriving boat, handed a gun, and sent off to the front. For an eight-month period during this war amid an Arab blockade of Jerusalem, Tel Aviv served as the temporary capital of Israel. The post–World War II United Nations (UN) partition plan stipulated that Jaffa was supposed to stay within the Arab world, but the city was captured by Jewish troops just prior to the creation of the State of Israel and was thus incorporated into Tel Aviv in 1950.

The Tel Aviv Stock Exchange was established in the city in 1953, and this along with earlier developments of financial institutions meant that Tel Aviv became Israel's financial center. Today, the city is the center for 51 percent of all banking jobs in the country, thereby asserting its clear supremacy over Jerusalem and Haifa. Tel Aviv has been able to consolidate its position as a preferred location for high-tech industry, given this sector's dependence on all the services in which the city excels: financial services, expert manpower, and research and development institutions. The planned extension of the Atidim Science-Based Industrial Park, which will provide space for new enterprises, will help to extend Tel Aviv's role in this sector. The Diamond Exchange, founded in 1921, is also located here, and the city remains a crucial player in the global diamond market.

In addition, more than half of Israel's industrial plants are found in the Tel Aviv metropolitan area, including textiles, diamond polishing, food processing, and furniture production. All the major bus and truck companies have their headquarters here, and it is a transport hub for the country via the airport and railway systems. The city is also a center of higher education, boasting the Tel Aviv University, founded in 1953, and the Bar-Ilan University, founded in 1955. There are also several rabbinical and theological institutions.

Despite being Israel's business capital, there are several underlying problems in Tel Aviv–Jaffa. For instance, the city has a high crime rate, and drug use is also high. Russian organized crime has reportedly moved into the city, bringing drug trafficking and money laundering. The city has an estimated 10,000 prostitutes, more than 70 percent of whom are from the former Soviet Union. The city was the target of Iraq's Scud missiles during the 1991 Persian Gulf War, and numerous terrorist attacks during the last 15 years have made its citizens cautious about going out to its numerous cafés. Indeed, during suicide bomber attacks in 1994, 1996, 2001, 2002, 2003, and 2006, nearly 130 people died in the city.

PAUL G. PIERPAOLI JR.

See also

Haifa; Jerusalem; World Zionist Organization

References

Schlor, Joachim. *Tel Aviv: From Dream to City*. London: Reaktion, 1999.
Sofer, Arnon. *Changes in the Geography of the Middle East*. Tel Aviv: Am Oved, 1992.

Temple Mount

See Haram al-Sharif

Terrorism

The use of violence by nongovernmental organizations to pursue political goals that they believe cannot be accomplished by legal methods within the normal political process. This limits the discussion to terror that is the product of extragovernmental groups while still recognizing that governments do use their power to terrorize opponents for political objectives. Governments also fund terrorism by nonstate actors. Terrorism has been a key ingredient in the Arab-Israeli conflict. Indeed, Arab-Jewish conflict predates the 1948 founding of Israel by several decades. Both sides have used terrorism as a means of accomplishing their objectives, and this will likely continue for the foreseeable future.

Following World War I, Britain governed Palestine as a League of Nations mandate to prepare the territory for eventual independence. The nearly 30 years between the beginning of the mandate and the creation of the State of Israel witnessed violent actions by both Arabs and Jews aimed at each other and the British. On the Arab side, these began as demonstrations against British rule, especially as the Palestinian Arabs accused the British of favoring the growing Jewish population, and as sporadic violence against Jews. Throughout the 1920s these clashes became increasingly violent and by 1936 had culminated in the Arab Revolt (1936–1939).

Violence and conflict evolved more slowly on the Jewish side, as the Jewish population initially had looked to the British for protection. The 1921 British decision to divide the mandate into Palestine and Transjordan led to the rise of the Revisionist Zionist movement, which sponsored violent actions against the British, Palestinian Arabs, and other Jews. Mainstream Zionists also had clandestine groups that used violence to pursue their goals. The roots of terrorism in the Arab-Israeli conflict formed from these early experiences.

Before Israeli independence in 1948, the Irgun Tsvai Leumi (National Military Organization) and the Lohamei Herut Israel (Lehi, or Stern Gang) were the major Jewish terrorist groups in Palestine. After 1948 Jewish terrorism diminished but saw a revival with the creation of the Kach Party by Rabbi Meir Kahane in 1979. All three had roots in the Revisionist Zionist movement created by Vladimir Jabotinsky in April 1925, which rejected the split of the mandate and called for a Jewish state in all the territory controlled by ancient Israel.

In 1931 Abraham Tehoni founded the Irgun as a nonsocialist Zionist movement that advocated active resistance to British rule and retaliation against Arab attacks on Jewish targets. For several years Irgun conducted scattered attacks on Arab targets in Palestine. In 1936 Irgun allied with the Revisionist Movement and during the 1936–1939 Arab Revolt conducted reprisal raids against Palestinian Arabs. About 250 Arab deaths resulted. The 1939 British White

Rescue workers search the ruins of the British central government offices in Jerusalem's King David Hotel, blown up by the Jewish terrorist organization Irgun, July 22, 1946. (Hugo Mendelson/Israeli Government Press Office)

Paper limiting Jewish immigration briefly caused Irgun to focus on ending British rule. However, World War II led to a truce with the British and the enlistment of many Irgun members into the British Army's Jewish Brigade.

Menachem Begin took control of Irgun in early 1944 as the war was winding down and ordered a resumption of terrorist attacks against the British. The most spectacular of these was the July 22, 1946, bombing of British military headquarters in the King David Hotel in Jerusalem that killed 91 people. Irgun also attacked other targets, including an officers' club in Jerusalem. Irgun launched raids against Arab targets, of course, including the April 9, 1948, massacre of 254 villagers at Deir Yassin near Jerusalem. Irgun formally disbanded on September 1, 1948, with its military forces becoming part of the Israel Defense Forces (IDF).

Avraham Stern, a member of the Irgun who disagreed with the 1940 decision to cooperate with the British, formed the militant Lehi, or Stern Gang, to continue the fight against the British. The British killed Stern in February 1942, but the group continued under the leadership of Yitzhak Shamir. The assassination of key figures

Prominent Terrorist Organizations in the Middle East

Name	Founded	Still Active?	Membership
Irgun	1931	no	Jewish
Lehi	1940	no	Jewish
Palestine Liberation Front (PLF)	1959	yes	Arab
Popular Front for the Liberation of Palestine (PFLP)	1967	yes	Arab
Black September	1970	no	Arab
Fatah	1974	yes	Arab
Hezbollah	1982	yes	Arab
Hamas	1987	yes	Arab
Al Qaeda	1988	yes	Arab
Kahane Chai	1994	yes	Jewish
Al-Aqsa Martyrs Brigades	2000	yes	Arab
al-Zarqawi Network	2003	yes	Arab

was Lehi's trademark. These included assassination attempts outside Palestine, notably the assassination of Lord Moyne in Cairo in November 1944. Count Folke Bernadotte, who was attempting to broker a United Nations (UN) end to the Israeli War of Independence (1948–1949), fell victim to a Lehi assassin's bullet on September 17, 1948. Other attacks included the use of letter bombs and the mining of bridges, railroads, and oil facilities.

Both sides employed terrorism or the threat of it during the Arab-Jewish Communal War (1947–1948) and the Israeli War of Independence (1948–1949). Many Palestinian Arabs fled their homes during the fighting as a consequence. This created a large Palestinian refugee population, chiefly in Jordan.

After 1948 Jewish terrorism decreased but did not disappear. Notable is the Kach Movement, founded by Rabbi Kahane after his immigration to Israel in 1969. After his assassination in 1990, the movement continued with both political and terrorist wings intact. The group's political efforts did not succeed, but Kach did organize militia training camps in the United States, purchased weapons, and carried out a number of attacks in Israel. A November 1992 attack killed an Arab shop owner in East Jerusalem and wounded several others. In February 1994 a Kach partisan killed 29 Arabs in a Hebron mosque and wounded another 100. Kach members have made numerous attacks on Arabs, particularly in the West Bank. The movement continued to raise funds and carry out attacks, including plots against Arab targets in the United States, in alliance with the Jewish Defense League, also founded by Kahane.

Arab terrorism is more complicated than Jewish terrorism for a number of reasons. Jewish terrorism, while not monolithic, relied on a homogeneous religious base. Arab terrorist groups often have to manage the sectarian differences between Christians and Muslims as well as Sunnis and Shiites. Moreover, various Arab nations sponsor different terrorist groups to further what are often competing interests. With some exceptions, Jewish terrorism was focused on Palestine. After the creation of Israel, which has a strong internal security system, Arab groups had to resort to targets outside Israel. As a result, the list of active Arab terrorist movements is considerably longer than that of Jewish terrorist organizations.

Before independence, Arab terrorism was largely managed by

Palestinian Arabs and instigated by Haj Amin al-Husseini, appointed mufti of Jerusalem in 1921. In 1920 he incited the Abu Musa riots in Palestine and continued to foment other rebellions for many years. In August 1929 he directed armed attacks on Jews in Jerusalem, Hebron, Tel Aviv, Haifa, and Jaffa and on agricultural outposts, killing 133 Jews and wounding almost 400. The Arab toll was 87 dead and nearly 100 wounded. Inspired by the anti-Semitism of Nazi Germany, the mufti orchestrated the Arab Revolt of 1936–1939, aimed at mainly Jewish targets. This began with the killing of 2 Jews on a bus followed by a Jewish retaliation that took 2 Arab lives.

During the Arab Revolt violence quickly escalated, with numerous attacks on Jewish civilians and property. Much of this was directed by Fawzi al-Qawuqji, a Syrian Arab who had been an officer in the Ottoman Army and then worked with French intelligence in Damascus. A general Arab strike was also ordered to support the revolt and paralyze the country. The British put down the uprising by October 1936. By then, 197 Arabs along with 80 Jews and 28 British had been killed.

Encouraged by Germany and Italy, al-Husseini renewed the revolt in 1937, resulting in more casualties, including many Palestinians. This time the terrorists targeted British troops, and casualties exceeded those of 1936. The revolt did ultimately fail, and the mufti fled to French-held Lebanon. He then went to Germany, where he helped Nazi officials coordinate movements with Palestinian activities in Palestine.

Arab terrorism in the postwar years and during the Israeli War of Independence (1948–1949) merged with guerrilla activities and conventional war, with the mufti directing some activities and al-Qawuqji leading a Palestinian army to cooperate with regular forces from neighboring Arab nations to crush Israel. As often happens in conflicts, the distinct lines between terrorism, guerrilla actions, and conventional war blurred over time. The end result was a victory for Israel. There would be more conventional wars, but Arab terrorism would emerge as a major factor that continues with suicide bombings and other attacks on Israeli targets today.

Several Arab terrorist groups developed and evolved after Israeli independence. The Palestinians at first relied on support from the Arab nations bordering on Israel. The year 1964 saw the founding

Members of the Israeli security services sift through debris for clues as to the type of explosives used by a terrorist who planted a bomb on a Jerusalem bus, December 12, 1983. (Ya'acov Sa'ar/Israeli Government Press Office)

of the Palestine Liberation Organization (PLO) as an umbrella movement to coordinate efforts to set up an independent Palestinian state. After the Arab defeat in the June 1967 Six-Day War, the Fatah group, led by Yasser Arafat, came to dominate the PLO. Arafat became the PLO chairman in 1969, a position he held until his death in 2004.

Under Arafat the PLO was engaged in terrorist activities, although he often denied such involvement. Under the PLO umbrella were several movements often in conflict and supported by Arab and other Muslim nations competing with each other. For example, Libya and Syria sponsored the Popular Front for the Liberation of Palestine–General Command (PFLP-GC), while Iraq backed the Palestine Liberation Front (PLF). PLO control of the groups under its umbrella has varied significantly. Some are closely controlled, while others operate with a great deal of independence. Some terrorist organizations not directly related to the PLO sometimes cooperate with PLO groups.

The PLO terrorist groups include Fatah, Force 17, the PLF, the Popular Struggle Front, the Popular Front for the Liberation of Palestine (PFLP), the PFLP-GC, the Democratic Front for the Liberation of Palestine (DFLP), the al-Aqsa Martyrs Brigades, the Popular Resistance Committees, and Black September. The number of groups

and the varying control exercised by the PLO demonstrate the complexity of Arab terrorism. These groups have conducted—or have attempted to conduct—actions against Israeli interests all over the world.

Some terrorist attacks over the last three decades by Arab groups have included the hijacking of a Greek airliner in Beirut in July 1970 by the Popular Struggle Front, the Black September massacre of Israeli athletes at the Munich Olympics in September 1972, the May 1974 attack on a school in Ma'alot by the DFLP that resulted in 161 Israeli casualties, and the 1985 hijacking of the cruise ship *Achille Lauro* and murder of an American Jewish passenger by the Popular Struggle Front.

Major non-PLO terrorist groups are the Abu Nidal Organization, Hamas, Islamic Jihad of Palestine, and Hezbollah. The Abu Nidal Organization formed in 1974 after Sabri al-Banna (aka Abu Nidal) broke with the PLO. The group conducted numerous attention-getting attacks in 20 countries, including attacks on the Rome and Vienna airports in 1985 and the hijacking of an American airliner in Pakistan in 1986.

Hamas is a radical Islamic organization that competes with the PLO for the loyalty of Palestinians. Modeled on Egypt's Muslim Brotherhood, it has a military wing established by Ahmed Yassin in

1982 to combat both the PLO and Israel. It has launched dozens of

1982 to combat both the PLO and Israel. It has launched dozens of attacks on Israel and in both the Gaza Strip and the West Bank. The fact that the political wing of Hamas gained a majority in the Palestinian Authority (PA) parliament in January 2006 increased its importance as a major player in the Arab-Israeli conflict. Indeed, in March 2007 the leader of Hamas, Ismail Haniyeh, became PA prime minister. Then in June 2007, in a surprise move, Hamas seized control of the entire Gaza Strip.

The Palestinian Islamic Jihad began in 1979, inspired by the success of Ayatollah Ruhollah Khomeini in Iran, but is not Shia in religious orientation. Its activities focus on bombings and kidnappings in Israel.

Also inspired by Khomeini and aided by both Iran and Syria, Hezbollah operates from bases in southern Lebanon. It has conducted numerous attacks on Israeli targets by rocket and artillery fire, assault of Israeli military positions, and kidnappings. As with Hamas, it has a political wing that wields power in the Lebanese government. Hezbollah precipitated a month-long war with Israel in July and August 2006 after kidnapping two Israeli soldiers.

Terrorist groups receive support from numerous sources. Some Middle Eastern governments have sponsored various movements. Sympathizers on both sides of the Arab-Israeli conflict contribute money, arms, training, and expertise. There is also ad hoc cooperation among international terrorist groups. An example of the latter is the Japanese Red Army, a group plotting a communist revolution in Japan. The Japanese Red Army found friendly organizational and training grounds in Lebanon's Bekáa Valley during 1970–1971. The PFLP-GC lent its support, and the first attack of the Japanese Red Army was carried out at the Lod Airport in Israel in May 1972, causing 104 casualties including 26 dead. With support from the same Palestinian terrorist group, the Japanese Red Army hijacked an airliner over Europe in July 1973. Germany's Red Army Faction also participated in the Entebbe hijacking.

DANIEL E. SPECTOR

See also

Al-Aqsa Martyrs Brigades; Arab Revolt of 1936–1939; Black September Organization; Democratic Front for the Liberation of Palestine; Fatah; Hamas; Hezbollah; Husseini, Haj Amin al-; Irgun Tsvai Leumi; Islamic Jihad, Palestinian; Lohamei Herut Israel; Palestine Liberation Front; Palestine Liberation Organization; Popular Front for the Liberation of Palestine–General Command; Zionism

References

Laqueur, Walter, and Alexander, Yonah, eds. *The Terrorism Reader: The Essential Source Book on Political Violence Both Past and Present.* New York: Signet, 1987.

Sachar, Howard M. *A History of Israel: From the Rise of Zionism to Our Time.* 3rd ed. New York: Knopf, 2007.

Satloff, Robert B., ed. *War on Terror: The Middle East Dimension.* Washington, DC: Washington Institute for Near East Policy, 2002.

Third Aliya

See Aliya, Third

Tiberias

Israeli city located in the Galilee region on the western shore of the Sea of Galilee (Lake Kinneret), a freshwater lake approximately 14 miles long and 8 miles wide at its widest. Tiberias is named after the Roman emperor Tiberius. It is a major tourist destination and the most popular city for vacationing Israelis in the northern half of Israel and has a current population of about 35,000 people.

Besides the pleasant scenery and lakeside locale, Tiberias boasts 17 natural mineral hot springs in which people have bathed since antiquity. Numerous spas afford vacationers ample opportunities to take in the mineral springs. Not far away is the Jordan River, which many Christians consider holy because of the baptism of Jesus by John the Baptist in its waters, which heralded the commencement of the ministry of Jesus Christ.

Tiberias is brimming with historical significance, for antiquity as well as for Jews and Christians. Around AD 20, the town of Tiberias was constructed atop the ruins of Rakkat by Herod Antipas, Herod the Great's son. In the book of Joshua, Tiberias was part of the region given to Naphtali, and during the era of the Second Temple, the Sanhedrin (Jewish High Court) was located there. Around AD 200, it is believed that much of the Talmud (Mishna) was written down in the vicinity of Tiberias, making the town a center of Jewish spirituality and scholarship.

The city saw many calamities over the next 1,300 years, including earthquakes, invasions, and wars. The area fell under both Arab and Byzantine rule for many years and was fought over during the Crusades, as was the case with much of Palestine. In the mid-16th century, Tiberias became a preferred destination for Jews escaping the Spanish Inquisition. The town suffered more devastation by earthquake and fire and then became a haven for Hassidic Jews fleeing persecution. In the 1700s and 1800s while the Ottoman Empire still ruled the region, many rabbis and Jewish scholars moved to Tiberias, reestablishing its role as a center of Judaism.

For Christians, Tiberias and the Sea of Galilee hold dramatic significance. Much of Jesus's ministry was centered in this region. In the Gospel of Matthew, Jesus walked on the water and calmed the stormy sea on the Sea of Galilee. Only a few miles outside Tiberias, Jesus performed the miracle involving the feeding of a throng of followers by multiplying loaves of bread and fishes. Also close by is the so-called Mount of the Beatitudes, from which Jesus preached his Sermon on the Mount. Not far from Tiberias down the coast lies the ancient city of Capernaum (Kfar Nahum), the home of two of Jesus's disciples and where Jesus based his ministry for three years.

Several kibbutzim are located in the vicinity of Tiberias, including Kibbutz Ginosar, Degania Aleph (Israel's oldest kibbutz), and Degania Bet. During the 1948–1949 Israeli War of Independence, advancing Arab forces moving south were repelled from Tiberias by fighters associated with Degania Aleph. To commemorate this defensive stand, a French-manufactured Syrian tank was left just outside the kibbutz's main entrance.

PAUL G. PIERPAOLI JR.

See also
Galilee; Jordan River; Kibbutz Movement; Lake Kinneret

References
Beck, John A. *The Land of Milk and Honey: An Introduction to the Geography of Israel.* St. Louis: Concordia, 2006.
Horsley, Richard A. *Archaeology, History, and Society in Galilee.* New York: Continuum International, 1996.
Orni, Ephraim. *Geography of Israel.* Philadelphia: Jewish Publication Society of America, 1977.

Tiran Straits

See Strait of Tiran Crisis; Straits of Tiran

Tlass, Mustafa
Born: May 11, 1932

Syrian general and longtime minister of defense of Syria (1972–2004). Born into a Sunni Muslim family in al-Rastan, Syria, on May 11, 1932, Mustafa Tlass completed his elementary and secondary studies in nearby Homs, graduating in 1951. At age 15 he joined the Baath Socialist Party. Tlass wanted to study literature and philosophy, but his family did not have the financial means. Thus, in 1951 he enrolled in the military academy, where education was free. He graduated in 1954 and was commissioned an army second lieutenant that same year.

At the military academy, Tlass formed a lifelong friendship with Hafez al-Assad. Routine military assignments followed. Inevitably, however, the military careers of Tlass and many of his contemporaries were affected by international politics. In 1958 Syria and Egypt unified in the United Arab Republic (UAR) under the presidency of Egyptian Gamal Abdel Nasser. Both Tlass and al-Assad were assigned to Egypt, and Tlass was in an armored unit there. They remained in Egypt until the UAR dissolved in 1961. Nasser had al-Assad arrested and briefly held, and al-Assad chose Tlass to escort his wife and daughter back to Syria.

A military coup had caused Syria's withdrawal from the UAR and brought about the creation of the Syrian Arab Republic. Although Tlass remained in the army, he belonged to a different group of officers than those responsible for the coup, and so he continued to seek greater social change in Syria. Having joined the Liberal Officers Movement in Homs, he was arrested with his colleagues in 1962 and imprisoned until a revolution of March 1963 brought other military revolutionaries, including al-Assad, to power.

Following the 1963 revolution, Tlass was assigned as a battalion commander in the 5th Armored Brigade and was brought into the more political leadership of the Military Committee. His career continued along these dual tracks of military command and political leadership in the Baath Party. When the more radical branch of the Baath Party to which Tlass belonged took power during the Third of October Movement in 1966, Tlass led forces from Homs to defeat those officers who were loyal to the former government.

Mustafa Tlass, Syrian general and longtime minister of defense (1972–2004). (AFP/Getty Images)

During the Six-Day War in June 1967, Tlass commanded the Army General Command Reserve Forces, but his troops did not see action because the cease-fire occurred before the reserves were brought up. In 1970 following the debacle of the attempted Syrian intervention in Jordan on behalf of the Palestinian militants, the military and civilian elements of the Baath Party definitively split. Both Tlass and al-Assad held political office in the Syrian legislature but found themselves increasingly isolated in a body dominated by civilians under the leadership of Salah al-Jadid. Al-Jadid's followers had a more socialist orientation and wished to focus the government's energy on internal change. Al-Assad and Tlass, on the other hand, were more representative of the nationalist orientation of the army, more preoccupied with strategic questions, and more interested in opposition to Israel. For some time, al-Assad had been removing Jadist officers from the army and had secured Tlass's appointment as first deputy of the minister of defense and chief of staff of the army in 1968.

When al-Assad finally carried out his takeover of the government in his Corrective Movement of 1970, he charged Tlass with ensuring that there would be no resistance from the army. From this point forward, Tlass remained al-Assad's most important ally.

Tlass was especially valuable as one of the few Sunnis in what was essentially an Alawite government. Al-Assad promoted Tlass to a specially created rank, *imad,* giving him precedence over all other Syrian generals. Then in 1972, Tlass was rewarded with the post of minister of defense.

In his new position, he was one of the officials who drew up the invasion plans for the Yom Kippur War of 1973. Along with Chief of Staff Yusuf bin Raghib Shakur and other commanders, Tlass met with opposite numbers among the Egyptian high command, then accompanied Egyptian chief of staff Hosni Mubarak to a resort west of Damascus where they briefed al-Assad and Egyptian president Anwar Sadat during August 26–27, 1973. During the war, Tlass remained by al-Assad's side.

The fighting, which started out well, did not end up that way for Syria. It failed to defeat Israel or even to recover the Golan Heights. Much of the blame for this lay in the divergence of goals with the Egyptians, and Syria's failure did not affect Tlass, who continued to accumulate honors and positions. After the war he made a number of trips to Moscow to secure additional Soviet arms and equipment and used these to greatly expand the size of the Syrian military.

Although Tlass was not involved in al-Assad's decision to intervene in Lebanon in 1976, he did take part in the strategic planning for it. In 1984 when al-Assad's brother Rifaat attempted a takeover of power, Tlass remained loyal to the president.

During the 1980s Tlass started a publishing house, Tlass Books, that has been widely criticized for publishing anti-Semitic tracts, including *The Protocols of the Elders of Zion* and one written by Tlass himself and titled *The Matzoh of Zion.* In this book Tlass claimed that the blood libel myth—that Jews employ the blood of murdered non-Jews in religious rituals such as the baking of Matza bread—was in fact truth. In 1991 when Syria was a member of the U.S.-led coalition against Iraq, Tlass, who frequently made outrageous statements on a wide variety of topics, expressed his overwhelming joy when Iraq launched Scud missiles against Israel.

Following the death of Hafez al-Assad and replacement by his son Bashar al-Assad, Tlass and others were seen as opponents of liberal reforms (which the younger al-Assad initially favored) and supporters of hard-line policies toward Israel and as having profited from rampant corruption. In the subsequent shake-up of the military and civilian power structure, Tlass retired as defense minister in May 2004. Lieutenant General Hassan al-Turkmani replaced him.

SPENCER C. TUCKER

See also

Assad, Bashar al-; Assad, Hafez al-; Black September; Mubarak, Hosni; Nasser, Gamal Abdel; Sadat, Anwar; Shakur, Yusuf bin Raghib; Syria; United Arab Republic; Yom Kippur War

References

George, Alan. *Syria: Neither Bread Nor Freedom.* London: Zed, 2003.
Patterson, Charles. *Hafiz Al-Asad of Syria.* Englewood Cliffs, NJ: Prentice Hall, 1991.
Seale, Patrick. *Assad of Syria: The Struggle for the Middle East.* Berkeley: University of California Press, 1988.

Tnuat Hamoshavim

Tnuat Hamoshavim is the general movement in Palestine, and later Israel, to organize and settle collective farming villages, called moshavim. Whereas in a kibbutz all property is considered communal, in a moshav collective farming is blended with private tracts of land. Moshav settlements purchase or lease land, normally from the Israel Lands Authority or the Jewish National Fund. By obtaining a substantial tract, the moshav is able to obtain favorable lending rates for the entire community. The tract is then subdivided into individual family farms. Most moshavim incorporate approximately 60 individual farms. The moshav members pool their resources to purchase heavy machinery for collective use, thereby utilizing group purchasing power and sales practices to maximize productivity among the members.

The first moshavim were founded in 1921 at Nahalal, initially by 20 families drawn from the Second and Third Aliyas. Within a year they were joined by an additional 55 families, most of them members of Hapoel Hatzair. The land was supplied by the Jewish National Fund with support from the Foundation Fund. The land was located in the Jezreel Valley, a malaria-infested swampland that had never been the site of significant agricultural production. The area was extremely isolated, and the pioneering group suffered from a shortage of strong laborers; thus settlers relied upon hired labor to supplement their own abilities. It took more than three years to drain the swamps and begin breaking the soil at Nahalal, but by 1925 the fundamental characteristics of the moshav had emerged.

As soon as practicable, the temporary workers were released, increasing the self-reliance of the settlers. Each family received 25 acres for initial planting. While the farmland developed, members of the moshav sustained their families through outside employment. However, this was perceived as a temporary measure. Once the moshav became self-sustaining, outside employment was strongly discouraged, as was the use of hired laborers. No individual land transfers were permitted, nor could a farm be divided as an inheritance. These provisions ensured the continuity of the moshav and firmly bound the members into the collective success or failure of the experiment.

By 1930 the moshavim movement had proven economically viable. Many Zionist organizations considered moshavim less revolutionary than kibbutzim and thus more likely to thrive. However, moshavim never proved as numerous or populous as the kibbutzim, despite a massive expansion in popularity. In 1931 the moshavim contained 1,000 members. By 1937 this number had swelled to 12,000. During the 1930s the number of separate moshavim also dramatically grew. In 1933 there were 13 settlements in operation, and 25 more were organized but not yet functional. A mere four years later, 35 moshavim existed, with 16 more in the planning stages.

Government in the first moshav and in subsequent settlements took the form of a general assembly. All adults in the community were members and met once per year to decide general policies and elect executive officers to oversee the moshav. These officers, later formed into an executive committee, controlled education, health, security, and social functions within the moshav. Furthermore, the executive committee oversaw the economic development of the moshav, distributing supplies, handling marketing, offering credit, and coordinating the use of collective property such as machinery or storehouse space. In 1930 the Committee of the Moshavim held its first conference at Nahalal. A 21-member council was named, led by a 5-member executive secretariat and dedicated to creating policies to govern the moshavim movement as a whole.

The constant emphasis within each moshav is upon self-sustaining production, with any additional produce sold on the open market. The most successful moshavim have maintained a great diversity of products rather than concentrating on a single agricultural sector. While this reduces the vulnerability of the settlement to uncontrollable environmental factors, it also reduces the overall productivity of each family plot. In addition to economic autonomy, moshavim also seek to provide for all of the social needs of their members. As such, the houses of individual members are not scattered widely, which would promote the most efficient farm management, but rather are clustered in a ring at the center of the development with each family tract radiating outward like the spokes of a wheel. Collective buildings are in the center, as are the households of moshavim professionals who provide vital services to the community but do not farm. This arrangement breaks with the original ideological vision of the moshav as a pure agricultural settlement, but it also allows increased self-reliance within the collective.

The first generation of moshavim settlers considered the experiment an unmitigated success, but as succeeding generations have matured, the voluntary nature of moshav membership has caused controversy. Some moshavim do not have sufficient land to allow all family members to remain within the collective. Others have had trouble retaining membership. Those moshavim that adopted centralized control methods have proven more economically efficient but less attractive to new members. Independent farms, so vital to the system as a whole, have proven too susceptible to individual disasters, such as the death of a parent, permanent disability, or lingering illnesses preventing cultivation. Voluntary assistance from other moshav members has proven insufficient to solve the problems of nonproductive farms, but members are hesitant to create welfare taxation systems. More recently, some moshavim members have been forced to seek supplemental outside employment in times of economic scarcity.

Many moshavim have had difficulty recruiting professionals to join their community without offering comparable benefits to those enjoyed by urban professionals. The number of professionals within the moshavim has generally risen, reaching 40 percent of adult members in well-established moshavim. These professionals are not integrating into the system, however, and demand a higher standard of living than their agricultural compatriots.

Some moshavim do not allow cooperative nonagricultural enterprises, preventing members from obtaining supplemental incomes that can serve as a safety net during times of poor agricultural yield. This sole emphasis upon agriculture, coupled with the lack of active recruitment of new members, has put the moshavim at a competitive disadvantage with the kibbutzim in the recruitment of trained workers, particularly the prized HeHalutzim immigrants. Nevertheless, moshavim have remained productive and stable communities. More than 300 moshavim exist in Israel, with a total population of between 100,000 and 150,000.

Paul J. Springer

See also
Hapoel Hatzair; Hehalutz Movement; Jewish National Fund; Kibbutz Movement

References
Bregman, Ahron. *A History of Israel*. New York: Palgrave Macmillan, 2003.
Laqueur, Walter. *A History of Zionism: From the French Revolution to the Establishment of the State of Israel*. Reprint ed. New York: Schocken, 2003.
Patai, Raphael. *The Jewish Mind*. New York: Scribner, 1977.
Reinharz, Jehuda, and Anita Shapira, eds. *Essential Papers on Zionism*. New York: New York University Press, 1996.
Weintraub, D., M. Lissak, and Y. Azmon. *Moshava, Kibbutz, and Moshav: Patterns of Jewish Rural Settlement and Development in Palestine*. Ithaca, NY: Cornell University Press, 1969.

Tomb of the Patriarchs

The second-holiest site for Judaism and one of the holiest sites for Islam. The Tomb (Cave) of the Patriarchs and Matriarchs in Hebron (Hevron), the capital city of the United Kingdom of Israel (1021–922 BC) before King David made Jerusalem his capital, lies in the heart of ancient Judea in the southwestern part of the West Bank.

Herod the Great (37–4 BC) had a large rectangular structure built over the tombs, and during Byzantine times a roof was added along with a basilica. In AD 614 the Persians conquered the area and destroyed the basilica. In 637 the Muslims took charge and converted the whole structure into a mosque. In 1100 the Crusaders captured the area. The structure again became a church, and Muslims were barred from its precincts. In 1188 the area fell to Saladin, who converted the building back to a mosque but allowed Christians access. In 1267 Mamluk sultan Baybars closed access to the tomb to non-Muslims. It was opened to all faiths when Hebron and the tomb came under the control of Israel in the June 1967 Six-Day War.

The Jewish settlements adjacent to the Tomb of the Patriarchs that began to spring up following the 1967 war remained a flash point for the Israeli-Palestinian conflict until the 1997 Hebron Protocol, but the Second (al-Aqsa) Intifada has rendered the Hebron Protocol meaningless. The settlements are still there.

Both a mosque—the Sanctuary of Ibrahim (al-Haram al-Ibrahimi)—and a synagogue are built atop the Tomb of the Patriarchs. Although each faith has exclusive control of its respective worship sites, both Jewish and Muslim services are held within the

The Tomb of the Patriarchs, Hebron. (Peter Spiro/iStockPhoto.com)

tomb. The tomb, known in Judaism as the Cave of Machpelah (Me'arat ha-Makhpela), is revered in Judaism as the resting place of the great patriarchs and matriarchs buried in two caves as couples, including Abraham and Sarah, Isaac and Rebecca, Jacob and Leah, and Adam and Eve. Jacob's second wife is buried in the Tomb of Rachel along the Jerusalem-Hebron Road near the Iron Gate of Israel's security fence at Bethlehem's northern entrance. Both tombs are holy to Jews and Muslims, who claim a common ancestry through Abraham (Ibrahim).

Every year in the fall, tens of thousands of Jews go to Hebron for the reading of Chayei Sarah. This is the portion of the Torah (Genesis 23) that retells of Abraham's purchase of the Cave of Machpelah. The reading reminds the Jews in attendance of their ancestral claim to the land.

The Tomb of the Patriarchs is revered in Islam as the burial place of Ibrahim and his family. Ibrahim was the father of Ishmael, the ancestor from whom all Arab peoples believe they are descended. Ishmael's mother was Hagar (Hajar), the Egyptian handmaiden of Ibrahim's wife Sarah. Islamic tradition asserts that Ibrahim loved Ishmael and Hagar, but Sarah grew so jealous of the mother and child that she asked Ibrahim to banish them. Allah instructed Ibrahim to take Ishmael and Hagar away and, under the guidance of

Allah, abandoned them in the land of Mecca. This abandonment taught Hagar to trust Allah and is commemorated as part of the obligatory hajj, the Islamic pilgrimage to Mecca. Ishmael returned to Canaan for Ibrahim's funeral and together with his half brother Isaac, the son of Abraham by Sarah and the progenitor of the ancestral line of his second son Jacob (Israel) through whom Jews trace their origins, buried their father in the Tomb of the Patriarchs.

RICHARD EDWARDS

See also

Genesis, Book of; Hebron Protocol; Religious Sites in the Middle East, Jewish; Religious Sites in the Middle East, Muslim; West Bank

References

Crone, Patricia, and Michael Cook. *Hagarism: The Making of the Islamic World.* Cambridge: Cambridge University Press, 1980.

Crown-Tamir, Hela. *How to Walk in the Footsteps of Jesus and the Prophets: A Scripture Reference Guide for Biblical Sites in Israel and Jordan.* Jerusalem: Gefen, 2000.

Feiler, Bruce. *Abraham: A Journey to the Heart of Three Faiths.* New York: HarperCollins, 2002.

Hoffman, Lawrence A. *Israel, A Spiritual Travel Guide: A Companion for the Modern Jewish Pilgrim.* 2nd ed. Woodstock, VT: Jewish Lights, 2005.

Mansour, Atallah. *Narrow Gate Churches: The Christian Presence in the Holy Land under Muslim and Jewish Rule.* Carol Stream, IL: Hope Publishing House, 2004.

Peters, F. E. *The Children of Abraham: Judaism, Christianity, Islam; A New Edition.* Princeton Classic Editions. Princeton, NJ: Princeton University Press, 2006.

Poole, Karen, ed. *Jerusalem & the Holy Land.* New York: Dorling Kindersley, 2007.

Tripartite Declaration
Event Date: May 25, 1950

The Tripartite Declaration was a joint declaration issued by the governments of the United Kingdom, France, and the United States on May 25, 1950, to control arms shipments to the Middle East, to solidify current territorial borders, and to ensure a measure of stability in the region. The declaration, formally known as the Tripartite Declaration Regarding the Armistice Borders, was issued after a meeting in London of the foreign ministers of Britain, France, and the United States. The conference undertook a review of security and stability in the Middle East. Concerned about access to oil in the Middle East as well as the containing threat of Soviet encroachment, the three governments agreed to regulate arms sales and preserve the territorial status quo in the region. They hoped that by neutralizing the simmering Arab-Israeli conflict, they would be able to create a regional buffer against potential Soviet expansionism.

The declaration recognized the need for the Arab states and Israel to maintain their armed forces at certain levels for internal security and legitimate self-defense. But it also stipulated that all future arms purchases in the Middle East would be carefully scrutinized. The governments of the United Kingdom, France, and the United States agreed that all future requests for arms and military equipment would be considered within the context of several principles.

First, the signatories mutually recognized their opposition to the development of an arms race between Israel and neighboring Arab states. Second, the three governments agreed that they would seek to gain assurances from any state supplying arms to Middle Eastern nations that the states requesting arms would not undertake hostile or aggressive actions against another state. Third, the signatories declared their opposition to the use of force or the threat of the use of force between states in the region. Finally, it was mutually agreed that should any government attempt to violate established frontiers or the 1949 armistice borders in the region, the signatories would take action to prevent such violations, within or outside of the United Nations (UN).

A broader aim of the Tripartite Declaration was to create a lasting status quo in the Middle East. The declaration can also be seen as one of the earliest attempts at arms control and limiting arms proliferation in the Middle East. Unfortunately, the declaration was

Foreign Ministers Robert Schuman of France, Dean Acheson of the United States, and Ernest Bevin of Britain meeting press photographers at Lancaster House in London following the conclusion of the Tripartite Declaration on the Middle East, May 27, 1950. (Getty Images)

largely ineffective at stopping the proliferation of arms in the region. The clause requiring that governments sell arms only with the assurance of the purchasing state that it would not use them for acts of aggression against other states proved entirely unenforceable. In addition, the Tripartite Declaration had no effect at all on arms purchases arranged between nonsignatories and Middle Eastern nations. Indeed, there was nothing to stop the Soviet Union or other nations in the communist bloc from supplying weaponry to the Middle East. In fact, within a few years of the Tripartite Declaration, Egypt turned to the Soviets for significant military support after the advent of the Gamal Abdel Nasser regime there. Iraq would follow suit after 1958, and Syria would begin purchasing large amounts of armaments from the Soviets beginning in the early 1960s. By that time the declaration was essentially null and void, as the Middle East became yet another region caught up in the superpower Cold War rivalry.

KEITH A. LEITICH

See also

Egypt; France, Middle East Policy; Iraq; Israel; Nasser, Gamal Abdel; Soviet Union and Russia, Middle East Policy; Syria; United Kingdom, Middle East Policy; United States, Middle East Policy

References

Podeh, Elie. "The Desire to Belong Syndrome: Israel and Middle-Eastern Defense, 1948–1954." *Israel Studies* 4(2) (Fall 1999): 121–144.
Reich, Bernard. *Arab-Israeli Conflict and Conciliation: A Documentary History*. Westport, CT: Greenwood, 1995.
Shlaim, Avi. "Israel between East and West, 1948–1956." *International Journal of Middle East Studies* 36 (July 2004): 657–673.

Truman, Harry S.
Born: May 8, 1884
Died: December 26, 1972

U.S. senator (1935–1944), vice president (January–April 1945), and president (1945–1953). Born in Lamar, Missouri, on May 8, 1884, Harry S. Truman worked as a construction timekeeper, bank teller, and farmer before seeing combat in World War I as an artillery captain in France. He then opened a clothing store in Kansas City, but it soon failed, leaving him with large debts. He won election as a county judge in 1922 with the backing of nearby Kansas City's political Pendergast Machine, and his record of efficiency and fair-mindedness earned him considerable respect. A Democrat, in 1934 he gained election to the U.S. Senate, where colleagues appreciated his hard work, modesty, and amiability. Reelected in 1940, he earned national prominence during World War II as chair of a Senate committee investigating corporate waste, bureaucratic incompetence, contractor fraud, and labor abuse in defense industries.

Truman was the surprise choice to be the vice presidential candidate on President Franklin D. Roosevelt's successful 1944 reelection ticket. Truman had no international experience when he assumed the presidency upon Roosevelt's sudden death in April 1945. Truman closely guarded his authority and took actions that

Harry Truman, president of the United States (1945–1953). (Library of Congress)

were decisive and at times impulsive. This was especially true in foreign affairs, where he immediately faced the challenge of emerging discord with the Soviet Union. Only days into his presidency, he sharply rebuked Soviet foreign minister Vyacheslav I. Molotov, sternly lecturing him about trying to dominate Poland. This contretemps was a harbinger of Truman's hard-line policy toward the Soviet Union.

In July and August 1945 Truman and Soviet leader Joseph Stalin met at the Potsdam Conference but did not reach agreement on any major issues. While there, Truman received word that the test explosion of an atomic bomb had succeeded, although he only made an ambiguous reference about this to Stalin. Truman subsequently ordered atomic attacks on two Japanese cities in August. His justification was to save American lives, but he may have also used Hiroshima and Nagasaki to intimidate the Soviets and prevent them from occupying portions of northeastern Asia. Although the Soviets did enter the war in the Pacific just before Japan surrendered, Truman rejected Stalin's request to participate in the occupation of Japan.

Meanwhile, Truman struggled to end the civil war in China between the Guomindang (Nationalists) and the communists under the leadership of Mao Zedong. Late in 1945 Truman sent General George C. Marshall to negotiate a cease-fire and a political settlement, which never took hold. Marshall returned home in early 1947, became secretary of state, and advised Truman to disengage from

China. By then, Truman had decided to initiate what eventually became the strategy of containment against the Soviet Union.

Truman's containment policy had implications not only for Europe and Asia but also for the Middle East. In 1946 he applied pressure via the United Nations (UN) to force the Soviets to withdraw from Iran. Clearly, the president worried about Soviet influence in the region and knew that the Middle East must remain aligned with the Western powers because of its vast oil reserves. The president's Truman Doctrine speech in March 1947 called for U.S. aid to any nation resisting communist domination. Congress then approved Truman's request for $400 million for Greece (to suppress a communist insurgency) and Turkey (to check Soviet advances). A proposal in June 1947 to help Europe avert economic collapse and keep communism at bay led to the Marshall Plan, an ambitious and successful endeavor that helped reconstruct war-torn economies.

Truman broke with his predecessor's policies on the establishment of a Jewish state in Palestine. Unlike Roosevelt, Truman had been on record since 1940 as a supporter of a Jewish homeland in the Middle East. By 1947 the British were under pressure to leave Palestine as pro-Zionist attacks against their assets in the area increased. That same year the UN, acting on a British proposal that Truman favored, passed a resolution calling for the division of Palestine into two states. In the spring of 1948 British troops began to leave Palestine as neighboring Arab nations began massing troops along the border, poised to prevent the permanent establishment of a Jewish state following Britain's departure.

On May 14, 1948, the State of Israel declared its independence. Truman was under considerable pressure not to recognize Israel. Most of his advisers, including Secretary of State Marshall, believed that doing so would jeopardize U.S. interests and invite the enmity of Arab nations. Nevertheless, Truman recognized the State of Israel just 11 minutes after it had announced its statehood.

Fighting had already broken out between Arabs and Jews in Palestine in reaction to the UN partition, which the Arab world flatly rejected. The creation of Israel sparked the outbreak of a full-scale war that pitted the Israelis against Syria, Jordan, Egypt, Iraq, and Lebanon. Jewish forces consisting of Haganah and the Irgun Tsvai Leumi (National Military Organization) managed to blunt the offensives into Israel, but the Truman administration did not intervene in the conflict. Instead, it pushed aggressively for a cease-fire through the UN. In March 1949 negotiations resulted in the declaration of a cease-fire and the drawing of temporary borders to separate the Jews from the Arabs.

Truman's decision has received much scrutiny. Some have argued that his decision was the product of crass political motives and the influence of Jewish lobbying groups that were heavily Democratic. Others have said that Truman was bought by influential lobbyists. None of these allegations pass history's litmus test, however. What moved Truman principally was humanitarian concern for hundreds of thousands of refugees. He also believed that the Balfour Declaration was valid. In the end, while Truman's decision genuinely seemed to be the product of pragmatic and humanitar-

ian motives, it nevertheless paved the way for a new approach to U.S. policymaking in the Middle East.

Stalin's reaction to Truman's pursuit of containment greatly intensified the Cold War, beginning early in 1948 with the communist coup in Czechoslovakia. The Soviets then blockaded West Berlin to force U.S. and British abandonment of the city, but Truman ordered an airlift of food and supplies that compelled Stalin to restore access one year later. Countering the Soviet threat led to the 1949 creation of the North Atlantic Treaty Organization (NATO) and a U.S. commitment of military defense for Western Europe. Truman sent U.S. troops and huge amounts of military assistance across the Atlantic, but he refused to execute a similar policy in China. This led to charges that he had allowed disloyal American diplomats to undermine the Nationalists and lose China after the communists triumphed in October 1949. Soviet explosion of an atomic bomb that September only increased popular anxiety in the United States. As fears of internal subversion grew, Truman appeared to be soft on communism when Senator Joseph R. McCarthy, an obscure Wisconsin Republican, charged that 205 communists worked in the U.S. State Department.

Early in 1950 Truman approved development of a hydrogen bomb, but he initially refused to approve National Security Council Paper 68 (NSC-68) that called for massive rearmament. When North Korea attacked South Korea in June, Truman, after brief hesitation, committed U.S. troops there because he believed that Stalin had ordered the invasion and that inaction would encourage more expansionist acts. Truman then ordered military protection for Chiang Kai-shek's regime on Taiwan and greater support for the anticommunist efforts of the British in Malaya and the French in Indochina. Even before UN forces commander General Douglas MacArthur halted the initial invasion, Truman approved the plans for a follow-up offensive into North Korea that eventually provoked Chinese intervention. Truman's courageous decision to recall MacArthur in April 1951 for trying to widen the war was highly unpopular but won acclaim from most military observers and European allies.

Armistice talks began in July 1951 but deadlocked in May 1952 after Truman refused to force the repatriation of communist prisoners of war. Unable to end the Korean War, he initiated steps to deter communist expansion on the other side of the world by implementing NSC-68, strengthening NATO militarily, and approving the initial steps that would lead to the rearming of West Germany. Truman left office in January 1953 and returned to Independence, Missouri, to write his memoirs and build his presidential library. He died on December 26, 1972, in Kansas City, Missouri.

JAMES I. MATRAY

See also

Balfour Declaration; Haganah; Irgun Tsvai Leumi; Israeli War of Independence, Overview; Stalin, Joseph; United Kingdom, Middle East Policy; United States, Middle East Policy

References

Cohen, Michael Joseph. *Truman and Israel*. Berkeley: University of California Press, 1990.

Donovan, Robert J. *Conflict and Crisis: The Presidency of Harry S. Truman, 1945–1948.* New York: Norton, 1977.
———. *Tumultuous Years: The Presidency of Harry S. Truman, 1949–1953.* New York: Norton, 1982.
Hamby, Alonzo L. *Man of the People: A Life of Harry S. Truman.* New York: Oxford University Press, 1995.
McCullough, David. *Truman.* New York: Simon and Schuster, 1992.

Trumpeldor, Joseph
Born: 1880
Died: February 29, 1920

Influential Zionist leader. Joseph Trumpeldor was born in Pyatigorsk, in the north Caucasus in Russia, in 1880. In his youth he observed and was influenced by a commune established by followers of Russian writer Leo Tolstoy. Refused admission to high school because of the Russian government's imposed Jewish quota, Trumpeldor studied dentistry.

In 1902 he was drafted into the Russian Army. During the Russo-Japanese War of 1904–1905 he fought at Port Arthur, besieged by the Japanese. He was wounded and had his left arm amputated but refused to be demobilized upon his release from the hospital. He was awarded all four degrees of the Cross of St. George for bravery and became the most highly decorated Jewish soldier of the war.

In a Japanese prison camp, Trumpeldor helped establish educational courses for Russian soldiers and also organized a Zionist group for those Jews who planned to immigrate to Palestine. In 1906 following his repatriation to Russia, Trumpeldor was commissioned a lieutenant, one of the first Jewish officers in the czarist army.

After graduating from a high school for adults, Trumpeldor studied first agriculture and then law at the University of St. Petersburg. Intensely interested in establishing a Jewish community in Palestine, he immigrated there in 1912, but his attempt to establish a commune at Migdal failed. He then worked as an agricultural laborer in Kibbutz Degania and assisted in the organization of the defenses of Jewish settlements in lower Galilee. He attended the Eleventh Zionist Conference in Vienna in 1913 and then traveled to Russia to recruit new members for communal settlements in Palestine.

Trumpeldor returned to Palestine, but at the beginning of World War I Ottoman authorities deported him to Egypt when he refused to accept Ottoman citizenship. In Alexandria he met with Vladimir Jabotinsky, and the two men began a campaign to establish a Jewish military unit to fight on the British side. Trumpeldor and Jabotinsky were convinced that the Allies would win the war and that Britain would dominate the Middle East. They believed that if Jews actively aided the Allied war effort, it would advance the possibility of the creation of a Jewish state in Palestine. In 1915 the two men formed the Zion Mule Corps, the first Jewish military organization of the war. The corps distinguished itself in the Gallipoli Campaign of 1915. Trumpeldor, as a captain, was the unit's deputy commander and was wounded in the shoulder during the fighting.

With the disbandment of the Zion Mule Corps at the end of the Gallipoli Campaign, Trumpeldor joined Jabotinsky in London. There the two men continued efforts to create a Jewish fighting unit. With the Russian Revolution of March 1917, Trumpeldor traveled to Russia with the goal of establishing a Jewish military unit of 100,000 men that would fight its way to Palestine via the Caucasus. While awaiting approval of this project from the government, he helped found the Zionist Socialist Party. He also founded the General Organization of Jewish Soldiers in Russia and commanded a large number of men in the defense of Petrograd against forces loyal to the czar. With Jewish communities endangered as a consequence of the upheaval in Russia, Trumpeldor helped organize self-defense units until these were suppressed by the Bolsheviks.

Trumpeldor also became a key figure in the emerging Hehalutz organization to train Jewish youths for immigration to Palestine, where they would work primarily in agriculture. Leaving Russia in August 1919, he returned to Palestine that autumn. There he offered to Lieutenant General Edmund H. H. Allenby to bring 10,000 Russian Jewish soldiers to Palestine, but his offer was refused. Trumpeldor then busied himself with efforts to unite the Zionist Socialist movement in Palestine.

In January 1920 following Arab attacks on Jewish settlements in northern Galilee, Trumpeldor was called upon to organize their defense. Taking command at Tel Hai, he was killed in combat there, along with five others, on February 29, 1920. His last words were reported as, "Never mind; it is good to die for our country." His passion for the establishment of a Jewish state and the circumstances of his death combined to make Trumpeldor a powerful symbol both for Zionism and for Jewish armed self-defense. To commemorate his colleague, Jabotinsky named the Revisionist Zionist youth movement Betar (a Hebrew acronym for B'rit Trumpeldor, the League of Joseph Trumpeldor) for him.

SPENCER C. TUCKER

See also
Hehalutz Movement; Jabotinsky, Vladimir Yevgenyevich; Jewish Legion; Zionism

References
Jabotinsky, Vladimir. *The Story of the Jewish Legion.* New York: Bernard Akerman, 1945.
Sachar, Howard M. *A History of Israel: From the Rise of Zionism to Our Time.* 3rd ed. New York: Knopf, 2007.
Sanders, Ronald. *The High Walls of Jerusalem: A History of the Balfour Declaration and the Birth of the British Mandate for Palestine.* New York: Holt, Rinehart and Winston, 1983.
Shepherd, Naomi. *Ploughing Sand: British Rule in Palestine, 1917–1948.* New Brunswick, NJ: Rutgers University Press, 1999.

Tschlenow, Yehiel
Born: 1863
Died: 1918

Russian physician and head of Russian Zionists. Born in Kremenchug, Russia, in 1863, Yehiel Tschlenow grew up in Moscow, where he was educated, became a physician, and practiced medicine. As a youth he was active in Hoveve Zion (Lovers of Zion). Later he joined the World Zionist Organization (WZO), and at the Second Zionist Congress he was elected to the Greater Actions Committee. He also headed the Moscow Zionist District and was director of the Jewish National Fund. He supported the Hoveve Zion position of increased settlement in Palestine and efforts to revive Hebrew literature and culture.

At the Sixth Zionist Congress of 1903 when Theodor Herzl presented the British government's East Africa Scheme, Tschlenow led the walkout of delegates opposed to it. He continued to insist that Palestine was the only possible Jewish homeland, but understanding the importance of Zionist unity, he refused to break with Herzl. Tschlenow declined to accept the presidency of the WZO following Herzl's death, preferring instead to remain the head of Russian Zionists.

Tschlenow strongly supported Hebrew, rather than German, as the language of instruction for Jews in Palestine. In the so-called Language War, he raised funds to make Hebrew the language of instruction for all Jewish schools in Palestine.

Named vice president of the WZO Executive in 1913, Tschlenow temporarily moved to Berlin, its headquarters, but he was forced to return to Russia on the outbreak of World War I. He then traveled to Copenhagen for WZO Executive meetings there and strongly supported WZO neutrality in the war rather than siding with either the Entente or Central Powers. He also helped draft the statement of Zionist demands issued as the Copenhagen Manifesto at the end of the war.

Tschlenow traveled to London, where he met with Chaim Weizmann and other British Zionist leaders. Returning to Russia, Tschlenow helped organize relief efforts for civilians fleeing the fighting on the eastern front. Following the March 1917 Revolution that toppled the czar, Tschlenow chaired the All-Russian Zionist Conference in Petrograd, where he continued to argue for neutrality rather than expose the Yishuv (Jewish community of Palestine) to reprisal by Turkish authorities. Heeding the call by Weizmann to go to London for consultations, Tschlenow died there in 1918.

SPENCER C. TUCKER

See also
Copenhagen Bureau; East Africa Scheme; Hoveve Zion; Weizmann, Chaim; World Zionist Organization; World Zionist Organization Executive

References
Brenner, Michael. *Zionism: A Brief History*. Translated by Shelley Frisch. Princeton, NJ: Markus Wiener, 2003.
Laqueur, Walter. *A History of Zionism: From the French Revolution to the Establishment of the State of Israel*. Reprint ed. New York: Schocken, 2003.

Tsomet

Secular right-wing Israeli political party founded in 1983 by former Israel Defense Forces (IDF) chief of staff Lieutenant General Rafael (Raful) Eitan. Eitan formed the party shortly after he had been compelled to resign his military post because of failures associated with the 1982 invasion of Lebanon. Tsomet (Tzomet), meaning "crossroads," urged a distinct separation between the state and religion, conservative socioeconomic policies, and a hard line on national security and military issues. The party had a strong agricultural base in terms of both philosophy and support, as Eitan had come from an agricultural background. Many of its initial supporters were his neighbors in Tel Adashim, a small agricultural community and cooperative. From 1996 to 1998 he served as Israel's minister of agriculture and environment in the cabinet of Prime Minister Benjamin Netanyahu.

Tsomet was perhaps best known for its vociferous opposition to the 1993 Oslo Accords and the larger land for peace process between the Israeli government and the Palestinians. Indeed, Eitan and Tsomet were essentially against any Israeli concessions to the Palestinians or the Palestine Liberation Organization (PLO). The party is still very nominally viable, although its political influence all but ended in 1999 when it failed to pick up any seats in the Knesset (Israeli parliament). Also in 1999, Eitan retired from public life.

In the 1984 elections Tsomet, which ran along with Tehiya, a like-minded rightist party, picked up one Knesset seat, which Eitan himself assumed. After separating itself from Tehiya, Tsomet gained two Knesset seats in the 1988 elections. Its biggest political gain came in 1992 when the party secured eight Knesset seats. It soon became apparent, however, that none of the Tsomet Knesset members except Eitan had any experience or clout in national politics. Soon, jokes about Tsomet being comprised of "Raful and the seven dwarfs" began to circulate around the country.

By 1996 several key Tsomet members had left the party, allegedly because of philosophical differences. But Eitan's iron-fisted rule over the party undoubtedly had something to do with the exodus as well. With its political star already having been eclipsed, Tsomet ran in the 1996 elections on a joint ballot with the Likud and Gesher parties. Three Tsomet candidates won seats in the election, and Eitan would serve as agriculture and environment minister from 1996 to 1998. From 1998 to 1999 he served as deputy prime minister. These high-level posts were basically political payback by Likud and were designed to mollify Eitan's ambitions for the premiership.

In 1999 Tsomet stood alone for the Knesset elections and failed to gain even a single seat. Dispirited, Eitan retired from politics that same year. Four years later, Tsomet again ran candidates for the Knesset but was again unsuccessful. In 2004 Eitan died in a freak accident in which a large wave washed him out to sea while he was overseeing a port renewal project at Ashod, on the Mediterranean coast. With Eitan gone and with back-to-back failures in Knesset elections, Tsomet has all but ceased to be a player in Israeli politics.

PAUL G. PIERPAOLI JR.

See also
Eitan, Rafael; Israel; Likud Party; Netanyahu, Benjamin; Oslo Accords

References
Eitan, Rafael. *A Soldier's Story: The Life and Times of an Israeli War Hero*. New York: S.P.I. Books, 1992.

Israeli president Chaim Herzog (*center*) meets with Tsomet Party leader Rafael Eitan (*to the right of Herzog*) and the members of his Knesset faction, June 29, 1992. (Ziv Koren/Israeli Government Press Office)

Karsh, Efraim, ed. *From Rabin to Netanyahu: Israel's Troubled Agenda*. London: Frank Cass, 1997.

Sharkansky, Ira. *Ambiguity, Coping and Governance: Israeli Experiences in Politics, Religion, and Policymaking*. Westport, CT: Praeger, 1999.

Tunisia

North African nation. The Republic of Tunisia, an overwhelmingly Sunni Muslim nation, covers 63,170 square miles, about twice the size of the U.S. state of South Carolina. Tunisia borders Algeria to the west, Libya to the south, and the Mediterranean Sea to the east and north. Tunisia had a 2006 population of approximately 10 million people.

Until the late 19th century, Tunisia was dominated by various larger powers as well as Arab and Berber dynasties. In 1881 the French signed an agreement with the bey, the local Tunisian ruler, establishing a French protectorate there. Prior to that, Tunisia had been part of the Ottoman Empire. Tunisian society and culture were greatly affected by the long period of French colonial rule, which did not officially end until 1956.

Following World War II, a strong nationalist movement in Tunisia engaged in a protracted struggle against French colonial rule. When the State of Israel was founded in May 1948, the Jewish population of Tunisia numbered approximately 85,000 persons. Of these, nearly 15 percent emigrated during the following four years. On March 20, 1956, following arduous, delicate, and behind-the-scenes negotiations, an independence protocol was signed by French foreign minister Christian Paul Francis Pineau and Tunisian prime minister Tahar ben Amara. Some 6,500 Jews left Tunisia during the year following its independence from France, leaving the country with a population of 58,000 Jewish citizens.

On July 25, 1957, the Tunisian Constituent Assembly ousted the bey, Muhammad VIII al-Amin, who was sympathetic to France and had long been unpopular. It also declared the formation of the Tunisian republic and elected Habib Bourguiba as president. Bourguiba, who would rule until 1987, was decidedly pro-Western in his outlook and foreign policy. He maintained cordial communications with Israeli officials, although this was not made public until years later. In discussions of common interests and subsequent public statements, he made known his opinion that Arab states should accept the existence of Israel and pertinent United Nations (UN) resolutions as a condition for solving the Palestinian problem.

Bourguiba's efforts to transform Tunisia into a modern democratic state had the backing of the majority of young Westernized

Tunisian intellectuals. His main political support came from the well-organized Neo-Destour Party, which he had founded in 1934 and which constituted the country's chief political force. The Bourguiba administration was very tolerant of its Jewish citizens, always distinguishing between the unpopular policies of the State of Israel and the Jewish population living in the country. Bourguiba was not without political rivals, however. Early in his presidency he was strongly challenged by Salah ben Youssef, who leaned toward Egypt and Pan-Arabism and championed the continuation of Tunisia's ancient Islamic traditions.

But Tunisia has always aligned itself squarely with the West and has been considered a strong American ally. During the June 1967 Six-Day War, for example, Bourguiba refused to sever relations with the United States over its support of Israel, despite considerable pressure to do so from other Arab states. Tunisia also faced hostility from Egyptian leader Gamal Abdel Nasser with whom Bourguiba often found himself at odds, even going so far as to briefly sever diplomatic relations in October 1966. During the Six-Day War, there were many anti-Jewish demonstrations and attacks on Jewish citizens, property, and synagogues throughout Tunisia. Bourguiba severely rebuked such events.

In spite of Bourguiba's support of Western-style democracy, his regime exerted strong centralized authority. The economy was closely controlled by Tunis, and as fears of Islamic fundamentalism increased, especially after the late 1970s, the government increasingly relied on censorship, illegal detentions, and other decidedly undemocratic schemes to smother radical movements.

As the country increasingly lost influence among its Arab neighbors, Tunisia's stance on Israel hardened and has often been marked by contradictory and paradoxical policies. For instance, Tunisia supported the October 1973 Egyptian-Syrian attack on Israel that sparked the Yom Kippur War and sent close to 1,000 combatants to fight, despite historically urging a diplomatic solution to Arab-Israeli conflicts. Although Tunisia distanced itself from the Middle East's continued problems throughout the rest of the decade, from 1979 to 1989 Tunis served as the headquarters of the Arab League when the organization suspended Egypt's membership and abandoned Cairo following President Anwar Sadat's peace agreement with Israel.

In 1982 Tunisia reluctantly allowed the Palestine Liberation Organization (PLO) to move the majority of its operations from Beirut to Tunis after Israel's invasion of Lebanon. On October 1, 1985, Israel killed 68 Palestinians and injured many more in the bombing of a Palestinian compound in a Tunis suburb. The bombing was Israel's response to the murder of 3 of its citizens in Cyprus for which the PLO claimed responsibility. On April 16, 1988, Israeli commandos killed the PLO's second-in-command, Khalil al-Wazir (Abu Jihad), at his home in Tunis.

Bourguiba's heavy-handed rule and frail health combined to bring about his ouster on November 7, 1987. General Zine al-Abidine Ben Ali carried out a bloodless coup and succeeded him as president. Under Ben Ali's tenure, Tunisia has taken a moderate, nonaligned stance in its foreign relations.

Following the PLO's acceptance of Israel's right to exist in December 1988, the organization left Tunis and returned to the Middle East, much to the relief of Tunisia. Domestically, it has sought to defuse rising pressures for a more open political system while at the same time dealing with increased Islamic fundamentalist activities and growing anti-Western sentiments.

In April 1996 Tunisia followed the lead of Morocco and opened a liaison office in Tel Aviv to strengthen cultural ties to Israel, especially with respect to Jewish tourism. While the rise of Israel's conservative Likud Party strained emerging Tunisian-Israeli relations over the next several years, on February 6, 2000, Tunisia's secretary of state met with the Israeli foreign minister in Tel Aviv, marking the first ever visit of such high-ranking officials.

The 21st century has witnessed another cooling of relations between Israel and Tunisia. At the 2002 Arab Summit in Beirut, President Ben Ali supported the peace plan that called for an independent Palestinian state with Jerusalem as its capital and the return of all occupied territories. In 2004 he won a fourth five-year term.

MARK SANDERS

See also

Nasser, Gamal Abdel; Palestine Liberation Organization; Pan-Arabism; Six-Day War; Wazir, Khalil al-; Yom Kippur War

References

Geyer, Georgie Anne. *Tunisia: The Story of a Country That Works.* London: Stacey International, 2002.

Laskier, Michael M. *Israel and the Maghreb: From Statehood to Oslo.* Tallahassee: Florida State University Press, 2004.

Perkins, Kenneth. *A History of Modern Tunisia.* New York: Cambridge University Press, 2004.

Turkey, Middle East Policy

The Ottoman Empire aligned itself with Germany and Austria-Hungary at the beginning of World War I. The decision by Turkey's leaders to plunge the nation into war had profound consequences for the entire Middle East. The war brought the Arab Revolt, and under the terms of the Treaty of Sèvres (August 1920) and subsequent Treaty of Lausanne (July 1923), Turkey was shorn of its Arab lands. France received mandates over Syria and Lebanon, while Britain secured mandates over Iraq and Palestine.

Kemal Ataturk's Republic of Turkey, proclaimed in October 1923, limited the influence of Islam in this overwhelmingly Muslim state. The new Turkey, while much more homogeneous than before, was now only a medium-sized state consisting chiefly of Anatolia. The foreign policy of the republic centered on preserving the status quo. This was certainly true during World War II, when Turkey resisted pressure from both the Axis powers and the Allies to join the war. Not until February 1945 did Turkey declare war on Germany, and this was to assure membership in the United Nations (UN).

Following the war, the Soviet Union applied tremendous pressure on Turkey to secure Kars and Ardahan. These two northeastern Turkish provinces had long been in contention between the two nations. Moscow also demanded a share of control over the defense of the Bosporus and Dardanelles. This Soviet pressure on Turkey and the simultaneous communist threat to Greece led to the 1947 Truman Doctrine and to Turkish membership in the North Atlantic Treaty Organization (NATO) in 1952. During the Cold War, Turkey was firmly in the Western camp.

Generally speaking, aside from its interest in the Kurdish problem (Turkey has a large Kurd minority and is opposed to the creation of a Kurdish state beyond Turkey's borders), Turkey maintained a policy of noninvolvement in Middle Eastern affairs for fear of being dragged into one of the region's internecine conflicts, particularly the Arab-Israeli conflict.

Turkey generally enjoyed cordial diplomatic relations with both Israel and its Arab neighbors. Even during the 1967 Six-Day War and the 1973 Yom Kippur War and Arab oil embargo that followed it, Turkey continued its policy of neutrality in the Middle East.

Turkey's involvement in the 1955 Baghdad Pact, which was scorned by Muslim states except for Iraq and Iran, alienated Turkey from much of the Middle East, especially Egypt. In the early 1960s Turkey adopted a new Middle East foreign policy that meant less cooperation with the United States and a greater rapprochement with the Arab states. Nevertheless, Turkey's approach to the Arab-Israeli dispute remained staunchly neutral. Clearly, the Turkish government worried that assisting U.S. operations in the region would harm relations with the Arab states.

Turkey was among the 34-member international coalition that expelled Iraqi forces from Kuwait in the 1991 Persian Gulf War. In the immediate aftermath of the September 11, 2001, terrorist attacks on the United States, Turkey voiced support of the United States and the so-called war on terror, including the U.S. strike against the Taliban regime in Afghanistan. The United States had counted on active Turkish cooperation in the 2003 Iraq War that ousted Iraqi dictator Saddam Hussein from power, but the Turks balked at the last minute, in part because public opinion was strongly opposed to the war and in part over concerns of a possible breakup of Iraq and the creation of a Kurdish state in the north. This decision by the Turkish government denied the United States a secure northern base of operations and forced it to recast its military plans.

In the 1990s a unique entente developed between Turkey and Israel. Although overwhelmingly Muslim in religion, Turkey shared much in common with the Jewish state. Both are Western-oriented democratic states with close ties to the United States, and both seek closer ties with Europe. Leaders in Israel and in Turkey seek regional stability and worry about the threats to this posed by terrorism, Islamic radicalism, and perceived hostile regimes in Syria and Iran. The result of these shared concerns has been a growing cooperation in recent years between the two states. This has taken the form of growing trade and tourism as well as military cooperation in Israeli upgrades of Turkish military equipment, cooperation in training, and the sharing of intelligence. The principal factor inhibiting further cooperation is the concern in Ankara that this will damage relations with Arab nations. Turkish public opinion is strongly sympathetic toward the Palestinians.

KEITH LEITICH AND SPENCER C. TUCKER

See also

Baghdad Pact; Persian Gulf War; Six-Day War; Yom Kippur War

References

Barkey, Henri J., ed. *Reluctant Neighbor: Turkey's Role in the Middle East.* Washington, DC: U.S. Institute of Peace, 1996.

Karpat, H. Kemal. *Turkey's Foreign Policy in Transition, 1950–1974.* Leiden: Brill, 1975.

Mavkovsky, Alan, ed. *Turkey's New World: Changing Dynamics in Turkish Foreign Policy.* Washington, DC: Washington Institute for Near East Policy, 2000.

Robins, Philip. *Turkey and the Middle East.* New York: Council on Foreign Relations Press, 1991.

Turkmani, Hassan al-
Born: 1935

Syrian Army officer. Hassan al-Turkmani, an ethnic Turkman, was born in Aleppo, Syria, in 1935. He joined the Syrian Army in 1954,

Syrian Army chief of staff General Hassan al-Turkmani addressing new cadets at the Syrian Naval Academy in the Mediterranean port city of Latakia, October 22, 2003. (AP Photo)

and after graduating from the Syrian Military Academy at Homs, he served in the artillery. In the 1973 Yom Kippur War with Israel, he was the commander of a mechanized division. He was promoted to major general in 1978 and to lieutenant general in 1988.

On January 26, 2002, al-Turkmani became chief of staff of the Syrian armed forces. He set as the top national security goal the thorough modernization of the armed forces. Furthermore, he believed that the Syrian military should be trained to remain at a high level of readiness to repel any Israeli attack.

In May 2004 al-Turkmani, a Baath Party member, was appointed minister of defense. That October he became vice president of the Council of Ministers. Many saw his advancement as a move by President Bashar al-Assad to replace supporters of his late father, Hafez al-Assad, with younger loyalists.

On June 15, 2006, General al-Turkmani signed a defense agreement with Iran. It called for the elimination of weapons of mass destruction (WMDs), a clear reference to WMDs held by the Israelis and American forces operating in the region. On June 17, 2006, al-Turkmani sealed an agreement with Iran to purchase Iranian missiles as a defense against both Israel and the United States.

ANDREW J. WASKEY

See also

Assad, Bashar al-; Assad, Hafez al-; Baathism; Syria; Syria, Armed Forces

References

Al-Turkmani, Imad Hasan. *Al-Sira' al-Ma'lumanti.* Damascus, Syria: Al-Ula Li Al-Nashr Wa Al-tuzi, 2004.

Leverett, Flynt. *Inheriting Syria: Bashar's Trial by Fire.* Washington, DC: Brookings Institution Press, 2005.

Tz'va Haganah L'Yisrael

See Israel Defense Forces

U

U Thant
Born: January 22, 1909
Died: November 25, 1974

Burmese diplomat and secretary-general of the United Nations (UN) during 1961–1971. Born in Pantanaw, Burma, on January 22, 1909, Maha Thray Sithu (U Thant) attended the National High School in Pantanaw and graduated from University College, Rangoon, in 1929. He was a senior master at the National High School and became headmaster in 1935.

In 1947 U Thant became press director of the government of Burma. In 1948 he became director of broadcasting, and the following year he became secretary to the government of Burma in the Ministry of Information. In 1953 he became secretary for projects in the office of the prime minister, and in 1955 he was assigned additional duties as executive secretary of Burma's Economic and Social Board. He was the official secretary to the 1955 Bandung Conference, which gave birth to the Non-Aligned Movement.

In 1957 U Thant became Burma's representative to the UN. At the UN he was regarded as a moderate and soon attracted favorable attention for his efforts to end the war between nationalist rebels and the French in Algeria.

On November 3, 1961, U Thant was unanimously appointed by the UN General Assembly on the recommendation of the Security Council to fill the unexpired term of the late secretary-general Dag Hammarskjöld, who had been killed in a plane crash the previous September.

In the early years of his tenure as secretary-general, U Thant was deeply involved in efforts to settle major international disputes including the transfer of Netherlands New Guinea (now Papua and West Irian Jaya) to Indonesia in 1962, the removal of Soviet missiles

Burmese school headmaster and politician U Thant served as secretary-general of the United Nations (UN) during the 1960s, one of the most turbulent decades of the 20th century. (Corel)

from Cuba in 1962, ending the secession crisis involving the Congolese province of Katanga in 1963, and also in 1963 sending a UN observer team to Yemen, where a civil war had broken out. His most notable successes were the establishment of a peacekeeping force on Cyprus in 1964 and bringing about a cease-fire in the 1965 war between India and Pakistan. His efforts to sponsor negotiations between North Vietnam and the United States to end the Vietnam War met rebuff, however.

Elected to a second term in 1966, U Thant soon faced a crisis in the Middle East. Egyptian president Gamal Abdel Nasser had positioned himself as the leader of the Arab world and had steadily escalated tensions with Israel. On May 18, 1967, he demanded that UN Emergency Force (UNEF) troops be removed from the Sinai along the border with Israel. Endeavoring to secure a compromise, U Thant asked Israel to allow the stationing of UNEF within Israel, but the Israelis refused. In his most controversial decision as secretary-general, he then complied with Nasser's demand, and the UNEF troops departed from the Sinai on May 19. Both Israel and the Arab states then mobilized, and on May 22 Nasser announced a blockade of the Strait of Tiran, effectively closing the Israeli port of Eilat. On June 5 Israel launched a preemptive air strike against Egypt, destroying most of the Egyptian Air Force on the ground and precipitating the Six-Day War.

U Thant retired at the end of his second term in December 1971. He died of cancer in New York City on November 25, 1974.

KEITH A. LEITICH

See also

Hammarskjöld, Agne Carl Dag Hjalmar; Nasser, Gamal Abdel; Sinai; Six-Day War; United Nations, Role of; United Nations Peacekeeping Missions

References

Firestone, Bernard J. *The United Nations under U Thant, 1961–1971.* Lanham, MD: Scarecrow, 2001.

Nassif, Ramses. *U Thant in New York, 1961–1971: A Portrait of the Third U.N. General-Secretary.* New York: St. Martin's, 1988.

Oren, Michael B. *Six Days of War: June 1967 and the Making of the Modern Middle East.* Novato, CA: Presidio, 2003.

U Thant. *View from the UN.* New York: Doubleday, 1977.

Uganda Scheme

See East Africa Scheme

United Arab Republic
Start Date: February 1, 1958
End Date: September 1961

Union between Egypt and Syria. By late 1957 there was considerable interest in Arab unity. In the case of Syria and Egypt, the motivation was chiefly ideological—with ruling elites in both countries dedicated to Arab unity, social revolution, and neutralism in foreign affairs—and secondarily political. Egyptian president Gamal Abdel Nasser had supported Arab unity ever since a well-known speech in which he declared that the "Arab nation is one nation." On November 18, 1957, in Damascus, the Syrian parliament, dominated by the Baath Party, met jointly with a visiting Egyptian delegation and called for a Syrian-Egyptian federation. The Baathists were apparently prompted by the growing influence of a different political faction within their own party in Syria. Baathist leaders believed that Syria would benefit from the union, which would also destabilize various elements within the military and in the bourgeoisie in Syria.

Nasser was at first reluctant for a variety of reasons, including the sharp contrast in the two countries and their political and social configurations. Egypt's authoritarian military government differed sharply with Syria's multiparty parliamentary system and free press. Nasser responded to the Syrian overture by insisting that any union would have to be a unitary rather than a federal state and that Syria would have to dissolve its political parties. The ruling Baathists accepted Nasser's conditions including the elimination of all political parties, which he regarded as symbols of internal division and a potential political threat.

The union was formally approved by resolutions in both national parliaments and became official on February 1, 1958. The new unitary state was known as the United Arab Republic (UAR). In the new state, the president held the bulk of the power. He had executive authority, assisted by executive councils in the Egyptian and Syrian regions. Between these and the president there would be four vice presidents, two from each region. Legislative authority would be in the hands of an assembly appointed by the president. At least half of the assembly members were to be selected from the existing Syrian and Egyptian parliaments. At an unspecified future date a new constitution would be adopted, confirmed by a plebiscite.

On February 21, 1958, both the Egyptian and Syrian regions voted nearly unanimously for the union and for Nasser as its president. On March 5, Nasser proclaimed the provisional constitution in effect. Society would be organized along the lines of social solidarity and a planned economy according to principles of social justice. Political parties were abolished. In their place was a National Union, the principles behind which the president would define. Nasser then appointed the first UAR cabinet and the two regional executive councils.

On March 8, Yemen entered into a formal arrangement with the UAR, with the new entity to be known as the United Arab States. Although there was a Supreme Council of the heads of the member states—in sharp contrast to the UAR—in the United Arab States, each state retained its own form of government and, in most cases, maintained separate diplomatic representation abroad. In effect, the United Arab States was a very loose-knit organization, with Yemen largely going its own way. No doubt prompted by these developments, only weeks after the establishment of the UAR Iraq and Jordan announced the formation of their own federation.

In foreign affairs and in his regional radio communications,

Cheering crowds surround the car in which Egyptian president Gamal Abdel Nasser (*right*) and Syrian president Shukri al-Quwatli ride on their way to sign the papers making final the merger of Egypt and Syria into the United Arab Republic (UAR), Cairo, Egypt, February 1, 1958. (Corbis)

Nasser claimed that the Arab peoples supported the doctrine of Arab solidarity and that it was their governments that were preventing Arab unity. Tensions immediately developed between the UAR and a number of Arab states with which there were already strains, such as Saudi Arabia, and where the governments feared Nasserists among their own population, as in Tunisia and Lebanon. Then, in the late spring of 1958, Camille Chamoun, who was anti-Nasserist, began a political struggle in Lebanon. His foes protested, and he complained to the United States that Nasserists were threatening to take over the country. This came on the heels of a coup attempt against Jordan's King Hussein, who had other enemies as well. This possibility was stymied by the arrival in Jordan of British paratroopers, which widened the chasm between Pan-Arabists and pro-Westerners.

In internal developments, the UAR never worked out as Nasser had hoped. By the time of the union, Nasser had firmly consolidated his rule in Egypt, so the pressure was on Syria to conform to the Egyptian model. There were, however, strong elements, especially among the established political figures and the bourgeoisie in Syria,

that resented the union with Egypt and also among the growing numbers of Communist Party members in Syria, as Nasser had outlawed their party both in Egypt and in Syria.

To his credit, Nasser recognized the areas of Syrian reluctance regarding the UAR and at first pursued a deliberate, slow approach. For example, Syria was allowed complete economic autonomy in the first two years of the union. After about a year, however, Nasser did begin to eliminate certain Baath Party members from positions of leadership. In place of the multiparty system, he established the same National Union that existed in Egypt.

Two years after the UAR was established, Nasser did finally move, with fateful results, in the economic sphere to bring Syria in line with Egypt as far as its economic policies were concerned. In a number of speeches, he stated that the UAR meant a commitment to the goals of Arab socialism. In November 1958 he introduced agrarian reform in Syria. Opposition to such change from among the Syrian landholding classes, nostalgia for the former multiparty system, a stifling educational atmosphere in the schools and universities, and the desire to maintain a free enterprise economy all translated into opposition to the UAR itself. Syrians also resented certain heavy-handed Egyptian officials in the government. At the same time, as Nasser sought to play an increasing active role on the world stage, he involved the UAR in a host of matters that had no direct bearing on the people of either region.

In July 1961 Nasser met this growing Syrian discontent with a number of wide-sweeping decrees that virtually socialized the entire Syrian economy. Among the decrees were the nationalization of banks, insurance companies, and hundreds of large businesses and economic enterprises; controlling government stock interest in large corporations; new income taxes that ranged up to 90 percent for the highest incomes; and new real estate taxes. These decrees took Egyptians as well as Syrians by surprise. The crowning blows came, however, when Nasser abolished the three-cabinet system in favor of a single cabinet for the UAR, sweeping aside the last vestiges of local autonomy, and the introduction of a common currency for both regions.

Then on September 28, 1961, the Syrian military seized power in Damascus in a coup carried out without great bloodshed. The new leaders immediately announced the separation of Syria from Egypt. Although the new government's leaders expressed their support for Arab unity, they also insisted that this be based on equality rather than the dominance of one party over another. They also claimed that they sought socialism.

On learning of the coup Nasser at first ordered Egyptian paratroopers into action, but within hours he countermanded this and insisted that the Egyptian military in Syria surrender. According to journalist Muhammad Haykal, Nasser's longtime friend, Nasser intuitively knew that it was pointless to force an unwanted union, as it would undermine his desire to represent popular will. In public pronouncements, Nasser blamed the coup on "reactionaries" and "agents of imperialism."

The breakup of the UAR was greeted with great relief not only by Syria, but by the other Arab states of the region, especially Jordan. Jordan, Turkey, and Iran immediately recognized the new Syrian government.

SPENCER C. TUCKER

See also

Arab League; Arab Socialism; Baathism; Egypt; Nasser, Gamal Abdel; Pan-Arabism; Syria

References

Dawisha, A. I. *Egypt in the Arab World.* New York: Wiley, 1976.

Jankowski, James P. *Nasser's Egypt, Arab Nationalism, and the United Arab Republic.* Boulder, CO: Lynne Rienner, 2001.

Lenczowski, George. *The Middle East in World Affairs.* 4th ed. Ithaca, NY: Cornell University Press, 1980.

Podeh, Elie. *The Decline of Arab Unity: The Rise and Fall of the United Arab Republic.* New York: Sussex Academic, 1999.

Waterbury, John. *The Egypt of Nasser and Sadat: Political Economy of Two Regimes.* Princeton, NJ: Princeton University Press, 1983.

United Jewish Appeal

International Jewish fund-raising organization founded in New York City in 1939 through the merger of two American organizations dedicated to the charitable assistance of worldwide Jews. The United Palestine Appeal, formed in 1925, focused on assisting Jews to immigrate to Palestine and establish a Jewish national homeland. The American Joint Distribution Committee (JDC) placed more emphasis on assisting Jewish families within their home countries rather than urging them to transplant themselves to Palestine. The United Jewish Appeal (UJA) combined both goals under a single fund-raising umbrella, reducing the inherent competition for charitable gifts from American contributors. Much of the impetus for the creation of the UJA came from the Council of Jewish Federations and Welfare Funds (CJFWF), which considered the competing agencies to be a hindrance in local fund-raising efforts.

Despite initial problems reconciling the twin objectives of the new organization, the UJA's fund-raising ability steadily grew in its first decade of existence. In 1939 the UJA raised $16 million in 3,200 Jewish communities in the United States. However, divisions soon arose within the UJA, driving fund-raising down to only $3.5 million in 1940. In 1941 cochairs A. H. Silver and Jonah B. Wise announced that the UJA would dissolve by year's end. Such disunity was disheartening, particularly given that the UJA raised a total of $40 million in its first three years. Throughout U.S. involvement in World War II, the UJA limped along without formally dissolving. In 1946 donations to the UJA exploded, reaching $100 million. This number rose to $150 million in 1947 and topped $200 million in 1948.

After the proclamation of Israeli statehood in May 1948, donations fell largely due to a less urgent perceived need. However, during crisis periods in Israel donations spiked, particularly during Arab-Israeli wars. In the aftermath of the 1967 Six-Day War, calls for emergency funding more than doubled the contributions of the year before. Over the first four decades of its existence, the UJA received donations totaling more than $5 billion. Some 4 percent went to national operations, while the remainder went to subsidiaries for charitable operations. In the past three decades, the UJA has increasingly focused on its Major Gifts Program, which incorporates contributions of $10,000 or more. Approximately half of the UJA's annual funds come from the Major Gifts Program, and 80 percent of the organization's finances are derived from 20 percent of its donors.

The modern incarnation of the UJA contains two corporate arms: the American Jewish Joint Distribution Committee (AJJDC) and the United Israel Appeal (UIA). About 80 percent of the UJA's current revenues are channeled to Israel, with the rest used for operating costs and fund-raising. The vast majority of fund-raising is performed at the local level by affiliated federations, while the national organization devotes considerable effort to promoting issues related to Israel. Fund-raising follows a fairly well-established pattern of yearly campaigns. Once collected the funds are distributed, with approximately 50 percent given directly to the UIA. Although the UJA's explicit purpose is as a fund-raising organization, it also serves a subsidiary function building and strengthening Jewish Diaspora solidarity in the United States, and it continues to seek out new methods of charitable assistance for the worldwide Jewish community. The UJA has recently merged with the UIA and the Council of Jewish Federations to create the United Jewish Communities as an even larger umbrella organization for charitable fund-raising within the American Jewish community.

PAUL J. SPRINGER

See also
Galut Nationalism

References
Karp, Abraham J. *To Give Life: The UJA in the Shaping of the American Jewish Community.* New York: Schocken, 1981.
O'Brien, Lee. *American Jewish Organizations & Israel.* Washington, DC: Institute for Palestine Studies, 1986.
Raphael, Marc Lee. *A History of the United Jewish Appeal, 1939–1982.* Chico, CA: Scholars Press, 1982.

United Kingdom, Middle East Policy

Until 1914 the United Kingdom was, on the whole, content to exercise only informal influence in the Middle East. Only the small Crown Colonies of Aden and Cyprus (acquired in 1839 and 1878, respectively) were British in a strictly legal sense. The emirates along the southeastern coast of the Arabian Peninsula, from Qatar in the Persian Gulf to Muscat and Oman, were bound to Britain by defensive treaties. Aden, important to Britain with its port and fueling capacity, was actually under the rule of the British government of India, and Britain held protectorates over West Aden and East Aden. British leaders perceived the strongest area power, the moribund regime of the Ottomans, more as a dependent satellite than as an adversary and therefore enjoyed British protection from predatory neighbors such as czarist Russia.

The major exception to this hands-off approach was Egypt, occupied in 1882 in response to a nationalist coup and thereafter incorporated into the British imperial sphere under the veil of a puppet monarchy. With the opening of the Suez Canal in 1869, the old route from Europe to the Indies via the Cape of Good Hope had become obsolete, and with the majority of traffic passing through the canal of British registry, London deemed it a vital British interest to defend the maritime artery running through the Straits of Gibraltar to Port Alexandria and from there along the Red Sea corridor to Aden and the long transoceanic voyage to India. The security of this line of communication and transportation remained one of the core components of Britain's foreign policy, and control of Egypt's Canal Zone, which was eventually to become the world's largest military base, was thought crucial to imperial defense. The British, who had originally promised only a short-term intervention

to stabilize Egypt's faltering government and secure the extensive financial assets owned by European investors throughout the country, made periodic noises about leaving when conditions allowed. But with each passing year, the occupation grew more permanent.

An accident of geography made Egypt crucial to British interests, and an accident of geology would make the Middle East as a whole the geopolitical key to the 20th century. The otherwise economically worthless deserts of Arabia sat atop the world's largest reservoirs of crude petroleum, the energy resource that would eventually replace coal as the most critical strategic resource on the planet. The long-term significance of this was already becoming clear before the outbreak of World War I. In 1911 Winston Churchill, at the time first lord of the Admiralty, took the critical step of beginning the changeover of the Royal Navy from coal to more efficient oil-burning engines. Three years later, he seized the prescient opportunity of buying a government majority shareholding in the Anglo-Persian Oil Company, which was busy exploiting its newly drilled fields in what is today southwestern Iran. The economic and military implications of the Middle East's oil reserves would, by 1945, come to dominate the region's political fortunes.

Britain's traditional approach to Middle Eastern affairs ended in October 1914 when the Ottoman Empire's leaders took that country into World War I on the side of the Central Powers. Britain declared Egypt a formal protectorate and launched an extensive military effort across the eastern Mediterranean and the Fertile Crescent. The war there began badly for the British. An ambitious but poorly executed naval effort to force the Dardanelles, followed by the landing of an expeditionary force on the Gallipoli Peninsula, both in 1915, ended in ignominious evacuation, and there was another humiliating failure in Mesopotamia the following year when an Anglo-Indian expeditionary force moving up the Tigris and Euphrates was besieged and forced to surrender at Kut. But in early 1917, following reinforcement and a change of command, the Mesopotamian advance recovered its momentum, reaching and capturing Baghdad. British troops under Lieutenant General Sir Edmund Allenby launched a successful offensive from Egypt into Palestine, breaking the stubborn Ottoman line of resistance at the Third Battle of Gaza. Allenby entered Jerusalem on December 11, 1917, the first Christian general to seize the city since the Crusades. The following year, the Ottoman Empire imploded.

Britain's victory in World War I created new regional opportunities but also problems in the Middle East. In May 1916 Foreign Office envoy Mark Sykes had drawn up with his French counterpart François Georges Picot a plan to divide the former Ottoman territories in the Middle East. Britain would directly control Mesopotamia, France would control Lebanon and much of southern Anatolia, and the rest of the region would be carved up into informal spheres of European control. This, however, contradicted a promise already made by the high commissioner in Egypt to the sharif of Mecca, Hussein ibn Ali, that if the Arab chieftains revolted against Ottoman rule, the British would sponsor an independent Arab state in the

British forces under Lieutenant General Sir Edmund Allenby enter Jerusalem on December 12, 1917. (Israeli Government Press Office)

Middle East at the end of the war. To complicate things further, in 1917 Foreign Secretary Arthur Balfour had announced in his famous declaration that a postwar homeland would be established for the Jewish people in Palestine.

The final result was an untidy compromise. As a consequence of the Paris Peace Conference at the end of the war, Britain and France were awarded a number of mandate colonies under the auspices of the League of Nations. France received control over Syria and Lebanon. Britain received three mandate territories. Two of these, Iraq and Transjordan, were parceled out to the Hashemite princes Faisal and Abdullah, respectively, as consolation for the failure to create a Pan-Arab state. Palestine, the third, became the responsibility of the Colonial Office in London. Kuwait, at the mouth of the Mesopotamian delta, was detached from Iraq and declared a direct British protectorate.

The propping up of this shaky inheritance proved to be one of the British Empire's most intractable security problems of the 1920s onward. Nationalist feelings, both Arab and Zionist, had been permanently stirred up across the region by the rhetoric of Wilsonianism at the Paris peace talks, and tempers were flared with the widespread belief that the colonial powers had betrayed legitimate national aspirations for their own selfish benefit. A popular revolt

in Iraq during 1920–1922 was suppressed by the innovative (although later controversial) employment of military aircraft in so-called aerial policing by the Royal Air Force (RAF). In the spring of 1919, urban riots against British rule in Egypt led to a general uprising in which British troops killed hundreds of protestors. Although the protectorate was formally abandoned and a state of Egyptian independence declared in 1922—later modified by the Anglo-Egyptian Treaty of 1936—Britain retained control of key political and economic aspects of the country's life, and this transparently quasi-colonial situation continued to offend Egyptian national pride.

The situation in Palestine was if anything even worse. Britain was committed to the stewardship of a Jewish national homeland in the mandate, although the level of political autonomy that it would enjoy was not defined, and Britain insisted that "the civil and religious rights of existing non-Jewish communities" had to be left undisturbed, a demand that was easier to make than enforce. Jewish immigration quickly became the dominant issue. More than 100,000 Jews arrived in Palestine from Europe during the 1920s, and there were large transfers of land ownership as these migrants bought property from absentee landlords, displacing the Arab tenants who had traditionally worked the fields and orchards. As the resentment of the Arab fellahin (peasants and agricultural laborers) grew, the British authorities attempted to alleviate the tension by introducing immigration quotas. This angered Jewish residents and did little to heal the growing sectarian divide across the mandate.

Sporadic armed conflict between the two communities simmered until, in August 1929, 67 Jews were murdered by rioters in Hebron. This shocking event eroded what little confidence Jewish leaders had in a binational compromise future for the region and led to the rapid expansion of the paramilitary Jewish self-defense force known as the Haganah. For their part the British continued their increasingly unsuccessful policy of keeping the peace, trying to favor neither side and thereby alienating both. A British inquiry into the Arab riots, the Shaw Commission, acknowledged that previous government statements about the future of the mandate had been unhelpfully vague and contradictory, with politicians too eager to tell each community what it wanted to hear. But the subsequent 1930 Passfield White Paper could only suggest new and ultimately ineffectual restrictions on future Jewish land purchases.

The failure of Britain's efforts at de-escalation became clear in the spring of 1936 when a full-scale Arab revolt broke out across Palestine in protest against continuing Jewish immigration and land purchase. More than 20,000 British security troops spent three years suppressing the rebellion (often in unofficial cooperation with the Haganah) in a counterinsurgency that was marked by often bru-

tal policing tactics and the suspension of civil liberties. During the revolt the remaining economic ties between the Arab and Jewish communities were mostly severed, hampering the chance of any reconciliation between the two factions. Although in 1939 the revolt petered out, its containment did nothing to resolve the fundamental tensions that still plagued the mandate's political life.

Prime Minister Neville Chamberlain's government sought an opportunity to bring a final negotiated end to the conflict. Its first proposal was an Arab-Jewish summit, the 1939 St. James Conference, but this proved a failure because Arab representatives refused to even recognize the negotiating legitimacy of their Jewish counterparts. Forced to come up with a settlement of its own, Chamberlain's administration drafted a new White Paper later that year. It promised the creation within 10 years of an independent Palestinian state to be jointly governed by Arabs and Jews. More significant for the short term, however, it limited future Jewish immigration into the mandate to 75,000 people for the next five years.

The White Paper infuriated Jewish settlers while failing to satisfy Arabs, and it was only the outbreak of World War II that forestalled a more vigorous reaction to its proposals. Given the virulent anti-Semitism of Nazi Germany, mainstream Jewish organizations in Palestine were understandably willing to freeze the dispute for the duration of the war, although more extreme terrorist cells such as the Lohamei Herut Israel (also known as Lehi or the Stern Gang)

A Scots Dragoon plays the bagpipes during Operation TELIC in Kuwait on March 17, 2003. (Reuters/Corbis)

refused to abandon their struggle. In 1944 Lehi would assassinate Lord Moyne, the resident minister in Cairo and one of the most senior British officials in the region.

Britain faced multiple challenges to its military power in the Middle East during the war. An Italian army invaded Egypt in the fall of 1940 and, although this assault was expelled in a spectacular counteroffensive into Libya the following year, the fortunes of the desert war would soon be dramatically reversed in favor of the Axis by the arrival of the German Afrika Korps. Behind the front line, sedition openly flourished. In May 1941 British troops returned to Iraq (which had received independence nine years earlier) when a pro-German cabinet overthrew King Faisal II's government, headed by the regent Abd al-Ilah, and this performance repeated itself in Vichy-held French Syria a few weeks later and, in cooperation with the Soviet Union, in Iran in August. In July 1942, at a particularly desperate moment in the battle against German general Erwin Rommel, Egypt's King Farouk was ordered at gunpoint to dissolve his government and appoint a premier more accommodating toward British interests. Not until 1943 were North Africa and the Middle East secured by the Allies.

In 1945, the incoming Labour Party prime minister Clement Attlee and his foreign secretary, Ernest Bevin, faced the paradox that while the diplomatic importance of the Middle East had never been greater and Britain's nominal control over the region never stronger, the country was far less capable of exerting imperial authority than it had been before the war. According to the map, Britain's assets were impressive. Not only did it control a swath of occupied territory from Egypt to Iran, but the clearing out of Italian dictator Benito Mussolini's African colonies had left Britain in control of former Italian Somaliland, Eritrea, Tripolitania, and Cyrenaica. Only the vast and empty Arabian desert, ruled since 1927 by the Wahhabist House of Saud, remained—at least to some extent—outside the British orbit.

Britain's finances and manpower had, however, been exhausted by six years of war. The United States was now quite clearly the much stronger of the two powers, and it was evident to everyone—including Arab nationalists restless for greater autonomy and a fairer share of oil revenues—that the British Empire was on the decline. But Bevin refused to submit to despondency. In a September 1945 memorandum, he laid out his plan for a revitalized imperial role in the Middle East. While recognizing that gunboat diplomacy and informal rule through pliable puppet monarchs was no longer a feasible strategy, he proposed a new and more equitable set of partnerships that were to be based on British-funded economic development and Cold War defense cooperation. Bevin saw the Middle East as the keystone of his anti-Soviet strategy, with the Suez Canal base securing oil shipments to the West and long-range bomber airfields in Palestine threatening the Soviet Union's southern flank in the event of war.

Bevin's plans were bold but ultimately unrealistic. Insofar as Palestine in particular was concerned, they ignored the fact that the war had completely changed the character of Jewish politics in Europe. The Nazi so-called Final Solution had killed an estimated 6 million Jews and left at least 250,000 survivors of Hitler's death camps stranded in refugee facilities across the continent. Many of these displaced persons (DPs) sought to immigrate to Palestine in defiance of the White Paper quotas, and although British troops succeeded in intercepting and detaining many of them, the war-weary public back in the United Kingdom had little stomach for the distasteful spectacle of its soldiers imprisoning recent survivors of the Holocaust in new prisons. World sympathy for the DPs was strong particularly in the United States, where the new president, Harry Truman, was under pressure to use enhanced U.S. diplomatic leverage to change British policy in Palestine.

Britain's ability to maintain control of the region was also under pressure. Toward the end of the war Jewish militant groups such as the Irgun Tsvai Leumi (National Military Organization) had restarted their paramilitary campaigns against mandate rule, and a vicious insurgency campaign broke out that culminated in the July 1946 bombing of the King David Hotel, the British military headquarters in Jerusalem, in which 91 people died. In a period of rapid postwar demobilization and a dire manpower shortage at home, it was difficult to justify the presence of large numbers of British personnel in a province that looked increasingly headed toward civil war.

The Labour government's main political initiative was the 1946 Anglo-American Committee of Inquiry, which proposed the creation of a single binational state and the immediate entry of 100,000 Jewish DPs into Palestine. Although Attlee's administration was much more enthusiastic about the former recommendation than the latter, it cautiously welcomed the committee's findings, but President Truman torpedoed the delicate negotiation process when he made a blunt statement implying that the larger immigration quota was the only significant element to the report. Britain's determination to find a binational solution to Palestine came to an end the following February when, beleaguered by the mounting violence in the mandate, Attlee's government announced that it was referring the problem back to the United Nations (UN). In November 1947 the UN voted for partition, a vote on which the United Kingdom abstained. The following May, Britain abruptly withdrew its last remaining personnel from the mandate, precipitating the outbreak of the first Arab-Israeli war, the Israeli War of Independence (1948–1949). Britain expected the Arab League to win this conflict and would no doubt have welcomed the emergence of an independent Palestinian entity from the postmandate wreckage, but any chance of such a scenario was ruined by the poor military showing of the Arabs in the war.

The creation of the State of Israel in May 1948 greatly complicated Britain's subsequent Middle East policy. Recognition that the Jewish state was—however imperfectly—the region's only practicing democracy, a powerful anti-Soviet bastion, and a valued client of the United States had to be balanced against the British desire not to inflame Arab sensibilities elsewhere. Cold War Anglo-

Israeli relations were characterized by periods of cooperation interspersed with diplomatic prickliness, with Tel Aviv critical of what it saw as Britain's too-cozy attitude toward the Arabs and with London frustrated by the Israeli failure to settle the Palestinian question once and for all.

The 10 years that followed the end of World War II saw Britain's gradual withdrawal from many of its formal Middle East suzerainties. Nevertheless, it sought to retain key advisory links with the successor states, particularly with regard to oil exploration and defense issues. The success of this policy was mixed. In March 1946 the Transjordanian mandate was peacefully abolished, and two years later Emir Abdullah declared himself monarch of the new Anglophile Kingdom of Jordan. That same year, Britain negotiated the Treaty of Portsmouth, an attempt to define its ongoing security relationship with Iraq, particularly with regard to the retention of RAF bases there. The treaty failed, however, to appease Iraqi nationalists and was never ratified by Baghdad. Worse than this disappointment was the 1951 crisis in Iran, when populist prime minister Mohammad Mosaddeq nationalized the assets of the Anglo-Iranian Oil Company (AIOC), which forced a tense standoff with the British government. The crisis was relieved only when Mosaddeq was toppled from office through the covert actions of the U.S. Central Intelligence Agency (CIA) and Britain's Secret Intelligence Service (MI6). British Petroleum (BP), a reconstruction of the AIOC, retained a 40 percent share in Iranian oil production in the postcrisis settlement, but the net result was Iran's shift into an American rather than exclusively British sphere of influence, a pervasive theme of the postwar period.

That increasing U.S. involvement in Middle Eastern affairs might not always be in Britain's best interests was illustrated by the rise to power of Gamal Abdel Nasser in Egypt following the 1952 officers' coup that dethroned King Farouk. Violent protests had been brewing in Egypt even during the last days of the Hashemite monarchy because of Britain's procrastination over its withdrawal from the Canal Zone, originally scheduled to take place in 1949 but persistently delayed. London initially hoped to find in Nasser a more willing partner than Farouk, conceding an October 1954 treaty with Nasser that finalized the cession of the Suez base and offering to help fund the Aswan High Dam project.

However, in 1955 when Britain organized the anti-Soviet Baghdad Pact—also known as the Central Treaty Organization (CENTO)—with Turkey, Iran, Iraq, and Pakistan, an outraged Nasser denounced the agreement as neoimperialist and sought a rearmament deal with the Soviet Union. British prime minister Anthony Eden then followed the U.S. lead in withdrawing British assistance for the Aswan High Dam project. Egypt promptly nationalized the Anglo-French Suez Canal Company as compensation. Secret negotiations followed among Israel (already involved in an undeclared sniping war with Egypt) and the aggrieved British and French, and a plan was concocted to invade Egypt and unseat Nasser. Israel would invade the Sinai Peninsula, giving the European powers the excuse to intervene and seize the Canal Zone as neutral peacemakers. Because Nasser's refusal to accept this intervention was more or less guaranteed, the expeditionary force would then have a legal pretext to crush the Egyptian regime.

Israel duly attacked on October 29, 1956, and a few days later a mainly British amphibious force supported by strong airpower assaulted Port Said. Although militarily successful, the invasion was a diplomatic disaster for Britain, and when the Soviet Union threatened to intervene on Nasser's side, President Dwight D. Eisenhower's administration used its financial muscle to force the British into a cease-fire and a humiliating evacuation. The Suez Crisis was the last occasion in which Britain attempted a unilateral military solution to a Middle Eastern crisis and marked the collapse of Britain's already-tottering prestige in the region. During the crisis, CENTO proved ineffective in advancing British interests. As early as 1959, Iraq had dropped out of the organization following its republican revolution, and the pact was unable to influence the course of the Arab-Israeli conflict.

With the winding down of Britain's military presence in Jordan and the granting of independence to Kuwait in 1961, the only remaining remnants of empire were now along the Arabian shoreline. The old garrison town of Aden had, with the loss of Suez, become Britain's primary defense base in the Middle East, and although London recognized that its days as a Crown Colony were numbered, it was determined that any successor state should be friendly toward British interests. In January 1963, Prime Minister Harold Macmillan's government united Aden and the old Yemeni protectorate into the Federation of South Arabia (FOSA), which was promised independence within five years. However, terrorist resistance by the Egyptian-backed National Liberation Front prevented a peaceful transition of power, and after a fruitless campaign to pacify civil unrest, British troops abandoned the territory in November 1967. The failure to retain the Aden bridgehead coupled with parlous financial problems at home (set off in part by the rise in international oil prices after the 1967 Six-Day War) necessitated a comprehensive British defense review. This resulted in the decision to withdraw all remaining British forces east of Suez by the end of 1971. The political consequence of this decision for the Middle East was the reorganization of Britain's old Persian Gulf protectorates. Thus, they transformed themselves into the United Arab Emirates (UAE), and Qatar and Bahrain (which could not agree on a unified constitution with their UAE neighbors) became independent polities.

The end of empire did not of course end Britain's relationship with the Middle East. As one of the West's principal oil importers and a major supplier of advanced technology, Great Britain inevitably continued to display a strong interest in regional affairs. Although after the Suez debacle Britain no longer sought a leading role in the Arab-Israeli conflict, its position as a permanent member of the UN Security Council gave its opinions inherent significance. In general, Britain followed the lead of the United States throughout the remainder of the Cold War. But, bearing in mind its historical ties with the Arabian Peninsula, it was less publicly emphatic in its support of Israel.

   Until 1990 the story of Britain's military disengagement from the region followed a clear and consistent narrative. This was rudely reversed, however, with the Iraqi invasion of Kuwait in August 1990. Great Britain actively contributed to all of the U.S.-led multinational operations that followed it, including DESERT SHIELD and DESERT STORM. It also took part in the various airborne policing campaigns of Iraq in the 1990s, including Operation DESERT FOX, an air campaign launched in December 1998 designed to destroy suspected sites where weapons of mass destruction (WMDs) were allegedly being developed. After the September 11, 2001, terrorist attacks on the United States, Britain stood closely with its ally across the Atlantic and fully supported the operations to rid Afghanistan of the Taliban regime. And most recently, the unseating of Iraqi dictator Saddam Hussein's regime in Operation IRAQI FREEDOM (2003) —given the more prosaic title TELIC by British forces—involved direct involvement of British troops. In September 2007, British troops withdrew from their last base in Basra to an airport garrison on the outskirts of the city, and half of the 5,000 British troops remaining in Iraq were scheduled to return home by the spring 2008. Britain also maintained a substantial air and naval presence throughout the Persian Gulf area, an epilogue that would have seemed bizarre to those witnessing the lowering of the last Union Jacks in the region 35 years earlier.

ALAN ALLPORT

See also

Abdullah I, King of Jordan; Allenby, Sir Edmund Henry Hynman, 1st Viscount; Anglo-American Committee of Inquiry; Anglo-Egyptian Treaty; Anglo-Jordanian Defense Treaty; Arab Revolt of 1936–1939; Aswan High Dam Project; Attlee, Clement Richard; Baghdad Pact; Balfour Declaration; Bevin, Ernest; Churchill, Sir Winston; Decolonization; Eden, Robert Anthony; Eisenhower, Dwight David; Faisal II, King of Iraq; Farouk I, King of Egypt; Haganah; Hebron Massacre; Hussein, Saddam; Iraq War; Irgun Tsvai Leumi; Israeli War of Independence, Overview; Lohamei Herut Israel; London Round Table Conference; Macmillan, Maurice Harold; Nasser, Gamal Abdel; Palestine, British Mandate for; Palestine, Partition of; Shaw Commission; Six-Day War; Suez Canal; Suez Crisis; Sykes-Picot Agreement; Truman, Harry S.; United Nations Palestine Partition Plan; White Paper (1930); White Paper (1939); Woodhead Report; World War I, Impact of; World War II, Impact of

References

Abadi, Jacob. *Britain's Withdrawal from the Middle East, 1947–1971.* Middlesex, UK: Kingston, 1983.
Balfour-Paul, Glen. *The End of Empire in the Middle East.* New York: Cambridge University Press, 1991.
Brenchley, Frank. *Britain, the Six-Day War and Its Aftermath.* London: IB Tauris, 2005.
Cohen, Michael J., and Martin Kolinsky, eds. *The Demise of the British Empire in the Middle East.* London: Frank Cass, 1998.
Greenwood, Sean. *Britain and the Cold War, 1945–91.* New York: Macmillan, 2000.
Louis, William Roger. *The British Empire in the Middle East, 1945–1951: Arab Nationalism, the United States, and Postwar Imperialism.* New York: Oxford University Press, 1984.
Peterson, Tore. *The Middle East between the Great Powers: Anglo-American Conflict and Cooperation, 1952–57.* New York: Macmillan, 2000.
Ovendale, Ritchie. *Britain, the United States, and the Transfer of Power in the Middle East, 1945–1962.* Leicester, UK: Leicester University Press, 1996.

United Nations, Role of

The United Nations (UN) was created by 50 founding countries on October 24, 1945, as the successor to the post–World War I League of Nations (formed in 1919). The UN inherited the so-called Palestine question when London informed the UN on February 14, 1947, that Great Britain would no longer administer the British Mandate for Palestine that had been formally granted by the League of Nations on September 29, 1923.

   The UN Special Commission on Palestine (UNSCOP) was formed on May 13, 1947, and its 11 member states voted unanimously to terminate British administration of mandatory Palestine. On August 31, 1947, a majority of UNSCOP, 7 of 11 members, recommended that Palestine be partitioned into a Jewish state and an Arab state, with Jerusalem and Bethlehem remaining neutral. This recommendation was accepted by the UN General Assembly on November 29, 1947. Jews in Palestine agreed to the partition plan, but the Arab spokesmen rebuffed it.

   On March 12, 1948, UNSCOP informed the UN that it believed that dissolution would bring chaos and war to the region and on March 18 recommended that the UN attempt to maintain order and peace by assuming temporary trusteeship over Palestine from the British. The UN responded by creating the Truce Commission for Palestine (April 23, 1948) to assist the UN Security Council in bringing peace and order to Palestine as per UN Resolution 46 (April 17, 1948).

   The mandate was dissolved, partition was enacted, and the independent Jewish State of Israel was created at midnight Palestine time on May 14, 1948. Egypt, Syria, Jordan, Lebanon, and Iraq attacked Israel on May 15, and the UN dissolved UNSCOP on May 20 in the belief that an appointed mediator, Count Folke Bernadotte, UN mediator on Palestine (UNMP) and president of the Swedish Red Cross working with the Truce Commission, had a better chance at bringing peace to the region.

   On May 29, 1948, the UN Security Council called a four-week truce under the supervision of a UNMP and an international military observer team eventually known as United Nations Truce Supervision Organization (UNTSO). The truce lasted from June 11 until July 8. The Security Council initiated a second truce on July 15. The territories assigned to Palestine captured by the Israelis and the territory of the newly created Israel from 1948 to 1950 are well documented, but the number of Palestinian refugees who fled or were expelled from Jerusalem and other areas is disputed. The estimates range from the Israeli total of 400,000 to the Arab estimate of 950,000 to 1 million. The official UN estimate is 711,000.

The United Nations (UN) Security Council meets to discuss the Palestine question at UN headquarters in New York, April 1948. (UN photo)

Count Bernadotte was assassinated on September 17, 1948. The UNMP was then replaced by the UN Conciliation Commission for Palestine (UNCCP) headquartered in Jerusalem (January 1949), created by General Assembly Resolution 194 (III) on December 11, 1948. The UNCCP attempted to reach a settlement between the Arab states (Egypt, Saudi Arabia, the Hashemite Kingdom of Jordan, Iraq, Syria, and Lebanon), Israel, and the displaced Palestinians. Although armistice agreements were signed from February to July 1949 between Israel and Egypt, Jordan, Lebanon, and Syria, the UNCCP concluded after meeting with the concerned parties from March 21 through November 1951 that the entities involved were unwilling to comply with paragraph 11 of Resolution 194 (III) concerning Palestinian refugees and that reconciliation would be difficult to effectuate.

During 1952–1966 the UNCCP also determined the final valuations for approximately 453,000 abandoned or seized Arab-owned land parcels as well as Arab disposable property lost. The UNCCP completed its work in 1966 except for brief annual reports that it submits to the General Assembly and the maintenance of the property valuations and records on which the valuations were based. The General Assembly's 1996 Resolution 51/129 authorized that all

necessary means should be taken to "preserve and modernize the existing records" of the UNCCP. The UNCCP annual report to the General Assembly generates an annual resolution regretting that Resolution 194 (III), paragraph 11, concerning the repatriation or compensation of the refugees has not been accomplished and requesting that the UNCCP continue its efforts and annual reporting until such time that its original mandate is completely fulfilled.

Israel became a full member of the UN on May 11, 1949. The UN Relief and Works Agency for Palestine Refugees (UNRWA) began operation on May 1, 1951, after it was created on December 8, 1948, by UN General Assembly Resolution 302 (IV) to replace the UN Relief for Palestine Refugees (UNRPR) created on November 19, 1948, by Resolution 212 (III). The UNRWA was and still is the main provider of education, health, relief, social services, and other basic services to more than 4.3 million Palestinian refugees and their descendents who were displaced by Arab-Israeli wars during 1948–1949, 1956, 1967, 1973, 1982, and 2006 and Palestinian-Israeli conflicts such as the First Intifada (1987–1993) and the Second (al-Aqsa) Intifada (2000–2005). Although most refugees fall under the purview of the Office of the UN High Commissioner for Refugees (UNHCR) headquartered in Geneva, Switzerland, most Palestinian refugees are the responsibility of the UNRWA. The responsibility for all Palestinian refugees within Israel was the UNRWA's from 1948 until it was appropriated by Israel in 1952.

The UNRWA had an initial budget of $50 million but is the largest UN operation in the Middle East in the 21st century, employing 22,000 people in 900 facilities including the 59 camps with 1.3 million residents in the Gaza Strip, the West Bank, Jordan, Lebanon, and Syria. The UNRWA's mandate must be periodically renewed by the General Assembly.

The UNRPR was envisioned as a short-term agency coordinating the activities of international relief nongovernmental organizations (NGOs) that, along with other UN agencies such as the UN International Children's Emergency Fund (UNICEF), World Health Organization (WHO), Food and Agriculture Organization (FAO), and the International Refugee Organization were providing the direct relief services to the displaced Palestinians until what the UN anticipated would be a quick resolution of the Israeli-Palestinian crisis. The UN created the UNRWA when it became clear that there was to be no quick resolution of the displaced Palestinians. The UNRWA was headquartered in Beirut from 1950 to 1978 and in Vienna from 1978 to 1996 before it moved to Gaza in the Palestinian territories in 1996.

The UNRWA provides relief services to the Palestinian refugee camps in the Gaza Strip, the West Bank, Jordan, Lebanon, and Syria but does not participate in the administration of the camps. Half of the UNRWA's budget and two-thirds of its staff are committed to operating 647 elementary and secondary schools and 8 vocational training centers. The UNRWA also operates 122 health centers and provides environmental health services for the refugee camps. The agency develops infrastructure for the camps and provides loan assistance for enterprise development for all Palestinian refugees.

The UN helped end the 1956 Suez Crisis involving Egypt, Israel, France, and the United Kingdom by calling a cease-fire and deploying in November 1956 the UN's first peacekeeping force, the United Nations Emergency Force (UNEF). Egypt expelled UNEF from the buffer zone in the Sinai Peninsula in July 1967, however, and Israel responded to this and other provocations by launching the 1967 Six-Day War (June 5–10). Israel gained control of East Jerusalem, the West Bank, the Gaza Strip, the Sinai Peninsula, and the Golan Heights, and an additional 500,000 Palestinian refugees fled from these areas. On November 22, 1967, Security Council Resolution 242 urged both Israeli withdrawal from these territories and the correlative recognition of Israel as a state having the right to exist. Egypt and Jordan accepted the resolution contingent on the Israeli withdrawal, Syria and the Palestine Liberation Organization (PLO) rejected the resolution, and Israel accepted the resolution with the caveat that withdrawal was contingent on direct negotiations with the involved Arab states and the finalization of a comprehensive peace treaty.

Security Council Resolution 252 (1968) called on Israel to rescind its absorption and administration of East Jerusalem and return it to international administration. General Assembly Resolution 2443

(XXIII) of December 1968 created the three-member (Sri Lanka, Senegal, and Malaysia) Special Committee to Investigate Israeli Practices Affecting the Human Rights of the Palestinian People and Other Arabs of the Occupied Territories, also known as the Special Committee. The Special Committee was tasked with reporting on Israel's regard of the essential and inalienable human rights of the Palestinians and other Arabs under Israeli control, any Israeli looting of Palestinian and Arab real or disposable property, and any pillaging of Palestinian and Arab cultural and holy places. The Special Committee began submitting annual reports to the General Assembly in 1970 and then in 1989 began submitting two additional reports each year.

In 1972 UNTSO initiated a cease-fire and observation operation in southern Lebanon after Israel responded to PLO cross-border incursions by attacking PLO refugee camps in Lebanon.

The Security Council addressed the October 1973 Yom Kippur War by adopting Resolution 338 reaffirming Resolution 242 and the need for negotiations leading to "a just and durable peace in the Middle East." The Security Council cease-fire went into effect on October 23 and was followed on October 24 with the establishment of the second UN Emergency Force (UNEF II), which supervised the disengagement of Israeli and Egyptian forces. The mission of the UNEF ended with the 1979 Israel-Egypt Peace Treaty based on the 1978 Camp David Accords. In December 1973 the UN convened an International Peace Conference in Geneva that led in part to the disengagement agreements between Egypt and Israel (January 1974 and October 1975) and between Syria and Israel (May 1974). The UN created the UN Disengagement Force (UNDOF) to monitor the disengagement agreement between Israel and Syria.

In 1974 the UN granted the PLO observer status as the representative of the Palestinian people and on November 22 reaffirmed the inalienable rights of the Palestinian people to self-determination, national independence and sovereignty, and the right to return to their homes and property, a reaffirmation that continues to be made annually. In 1975 the General Assembly created the Committee on the Exercise of the Inalienable Rights of the Palestinian People (CEIRPP), also known as the Palestinian Rights Committee, and tasked it with developing a program that would enable the Palestinians to exercise these rights.

The PLO increased its incursions into northern Israel from the end of 1976 to early 1978. Israel responded by invading southern Lebanon in March 1978. The Lebanese government requested that the Security Council create the UN Interim Force in Lebanon (UNIFIL) to monitor the withdrawal of the Israel Defense Forces (IDF) from Lebanon and then to help restore peace, security, and Lebanese authority over southern Lebanon. The IDF withdrew in June 1978 and bypassed UNIFIL by creating a security zone roughly 62 miles long and 6–12 miles wide in southern Lebanon defended by the 2,000 member South Lebanon Army (SLA) backed by Israel.

On March 22, 1979, the Security Council and General Assembly determined in Resolution 446 that Israeli settlements in Palestinian areas captured since 1967 were against the 1949 Fourth Geneva

A view of the tabulation board as the United Nations (UN) General Assembly votes to grant observer status to the Palestine Liberation Organization (PLO), November 1974. (Corel)

Convention, had no legal basis, and created a great obstacle to a comprehensive peace in the area. The resolution also created a commission composed of Bolivia, Portugal, and Zambia tasked with investigating these settlements. The commission submitted reports in July 1979, December 1979, and November 1980 affirming that the settlement policy constituted a serious impediment to the establishment of a comprehensive peace agreement. It was after the first two reports that Israel began the process of making Jerusalem its capital. Security Council Resolution 476 (June 1980) called on Israel to follow all previous UN resolutions on the status of Jerusalem and was followed by Resolution 478 (August 1980) urging all UN member states not to establish diplomatic missions in Jerusalem. The assertion of Resolution 446 that Israeli settlements in these areas contravened the Geneva Convention was reaffirmed in December 1980 and in subsequent years.

During 1980–1982 the Lebanese Civil War intensified, and fighting increased throughout the country. Fearing the growing influence and power of the Syrians and the PLO in Lebanon and following the PLO attacks on Israeli diplomats in London and Paris, Israel invaded Lebanon on June 6, 1982. The Israeli invasion, known as Operation PEACE FOR GALILEE, was planned to move the PLO's Katyusha rockets out of the range of Israel's northern border and to destroy the terrorist infrastructure that had developed in Lebanon. The IDF bypassed or overran the UNIFIL positions, and the Security Council called for a cease-fire and the withdrawal of the IDF (Resolution 509). Israel continued its operation and eventually surrounded and blockaded Beirut. From June through August 1982, the Security Council demanded that Israel lift the blockade and withdraw. The Security Council also deployed UN military observers known as Observer Group Beirut to monitor the conflict.

At the request of the Lebanese government, a multinational force evacuated PLO forces from Beirut. This evacuation was achieved on September 1, 1982, and the multinational force withdrew over the next two weeks. Israel moved into West Beirut following the assassination of Lebanon's president-elect Bashir Gemayal on September 14, 1982. On September 17, 700–3,500 Palestinian civilians, including women and children, were massacred in the refugee camps of Sabra and Shatila by Lebanese Christian Phalangist forces along with some members of the SLA. A new multinational force reentered the area but failed to resolve the conflict, and all elements of this force withdrew by early 1984. In December 1983 PLO forces and PLO chairman Yasser Arafat were evacuated from Tripoli in northern Lebanon on ships flying the UN flag.

United Nations (UN) secretary-general Ban Ki-moon (*second from right*) prepares to lay a wreath at the tomb of former Palestinian president Yasser Arafat in Ramallah, Palestine, March 25, 2007. (Evan Schneider/UN photo)

The General Assembly convened the International Conference on the Question of Palestine, which met in Geneva from August 29 to September 7, 1983, despite opposition from Israel, the United States, and other countries. The conference, attended by 137 UN states and the PLO, adopted a Declaration on Palestine and approved a Program of Action for the Achievement of Palestinian Rights that included opposition to future Israeli settlements in the occupied territories, opposition to any change in status of Jerusalem, the right of all states to have internationally recognized secure borders, and respect for the inalienable rights of the Palestinian people.

Even though the PLO had been driven from Lebanon, the Israeli presence in force lasted until 2000 and resulted in such a high number of Palestinian civilian deaths that worldwide public opinion turned against Israel. A treaty ending the engagement was signed on May 17, 1983, only to be revoked by the Lebanese under Syrian pressure soon after Israeli prime minister Menachem Begin resigned. Israel continued to garrison soldiers and to operate in consort with the SLA in the southern security zone.

The First Intifada (1987–1993) erupted in December 1987. The Palestinian violence and the response of the Israelis were monitored by CEIRPP, the Special Committee, and the UNRWA. The UN was particularly disturbed by Palestinian deportations from the occupied territories and responded with Resolutions 607 and 608

in January 1988, Resolution 636 in July 1989, and Resolution 641 in August 1989 demanding that Israel cease and desist from deportations and allow the deportees to return.

The PLO's Palestinian National Council (PNC) meeting in Algiers formally created the State of Palestine in November 1988 in accordance with UN Resolution 181 (II). The General Assembly acknowledged the proclamation in December 1988 when the General Assembly changed the name of the UN delegation representing the Palestinian people from the "PLO" to "Palestine" and reaffirmed the borders of Palestine to be those preceding the 1967 war. From 1988 through 1990, the Security Council repeatedly condemned Israel for its disregard of the UN directions concerning Israel's handling of the First Intifada. In February 1993 the UN Commission on Human Rights appointed a Special Rapporteur on human rights violations in the occupied Palestinian and Arab territories.

The General Assembly supported the 1993 Oslo Accords, officially called the Declaration of Principles on Interim Self-Government Arrangements or simply the Declaration of Principles (DOP), and sought to actively participate in the ensuing peace process. The Oslo Accords and the creation of the Palestinian Authority (PA) effectively ended the violence of the First Intifada. The UN increased economic support to the Palestinians, established the High-Level Task Force on the Socioeconomic Development of the Gaza Strip and

Jericho; hosted a donor conference on October 1, 1993, in Washington, D.C., known as the Conference to Support Middle East Peace; and in June 1994 created the UN Special Coordinator (UNSCO) to enhance interagency cooperation. UNSCO was tasked with coordinating all UN and NGO operations in the West Bank and Gaza, representing the UN at donor coordination meetings and meetings concerning the Palestinian-Israeli Peace Accords, assisting the PA in its administration of international donations, and implementing the DOP as requested by the involved parties.

Three important events occurred in 1995 and 1996. First, the Israeli-Palestinian (PLO) Interim Agreement on the West Bank and the Gaza Strip (September 28, 1995), also known as Oslo II or Taba, directed the continuing redeployment of the IDF. Second, Israeli prime minister Yitzhak Rabin was assassinated on November 4, 1995. And third, Yasser Arafat was elected as the first president of the PA.

The UN secretary-general participated in the Summit of Peacemakers in Sharm al-Sheikh, Egypt, in March 1996 that condemned violence in the Middle East. The UN along with Norway also facilitated talks between Arafat and Israeli prime minister Benjamin Netanyahu on September 4, 1996. The secretary-general monitored the construction of new Israeli settlements in the occupied territories during this time and reported in June 1997 that the construction continued in spite of UN protestations. The General Assembly increased its scrutiny of Israeli actions in East Jerusalem and the Palestinian territories during 1997–1998 as Israel continued its redeployment per the 1997 Hebron Protocol. The General Assembly continued to express concern over what it determined to be persistent Israeli violations of the Geneva Convention.

The General Assembly enhanced Palestine's observer status on July 7, 1998, in Resolution 52/250 by expanding Palestine's rights and privileges of participation in the General Assembly. The UN played no role in the 1998 Wye River Memorandum signed by Netanyahu and Arafat.

On February 9, 1999, the General Assembly again declared that all legislative and administrative actions taken by Israel, called the "occupying power," in the areas it seized in 1967 were illegal, invalid, null, and void. The General Assembly convened a conference on July 15, 1999, concerning alleged continuing Israeli violations of the Geneva Convention. UNSCO was reconfigured in September 1999 into the Office of the Special Coordinator for the Middle East Peace Process and Personal Representative of the Secretary-General to the Palestine Liberation Organization and the Palestinian Authority. The Special Coordinator's Office was tasked with representing the UN secretary-general in all matters relating to the Middle East peace process.

The Special Rapporteur issued a report on the status of human rights in the Palestinian territories on March 15, 2000, asserting that Israeli settlement activity continued unabated through 1999 and that Israeli occupation forces conducted numerous punitive and violent demolitions of Palestinian homes and forcible evictions of entire Palestinian villages. The CEIRPP concurred and asserted (as it has annually) that Israel's settlement policy is a serious impediment to the establishment of a final comprehensive peace accord.

The July 2000 Camp David talks between Israel and the PA ended with no progress despite Israel's withdrawal of its forces from Lebanon on April 17, 2000, in full accord with Security Council Resolutions 425 (1978) and 426 (1978). The General Assembly asserted again on October 20, 2000, that all Israeli settlements in areas occupied since 1967 were illegal and an impediment to peace. On December 1, 2000, the General Assembly reaffirmed that all actions taken by Israel relative to what the UN deemed "occupied" East Jerusalem were illegal, invalid, null, and void.

The Second (al-Aqsa) Intifada began in September 2000 in Jerusalem after Israel's Likud Party opposition politician Ariel Sharon in the company of security forces visited the al-Aqsa Mosque. After demonstrations broke out, larger ones were met with violence by Israeli forces in the West Bank and Gaza. Security Council Resolution 1322 (2000) condemned all acts of violence and specifically condemned excessive force by Israel in dealing with the Palestinian uprising. The CEIRPP met in October 2000 and urged the UN to remain engaged in the peace process and to continue monitoring the conflict and safeguarding the inalienable rights of the Palestinian people. The intifada ended most discussions concerning the implementation of the DOP framework. As the violence increased and as suicide bombings became more prevalent, Israel responded by attacking PA infrastructure and facilities and reoccupied territory ceded to the PA. Israel also added to the tension by allowing the number of Jewish settlements in the West Bank to more than double the Israeli population within the autonomous region.

Although the Security Council considered deploying a UN observer group in the Palestinian territories in March 2001, the UN made no progress in resolving the conflict or the tangential issues. Mahmoud Abbas was elected president of the PA on January 9, 2005, after Arafat's death on November 11, 2004. The intifada essentially ended following a summit between Abbas and Israeli prime minister Ariel Sharon in early 2005. Despite Israeli withdrawals from Gaza and the Jericho area, Abbas's position was severely weakened when his Fatah party lost control of the Palestinian Legislative Council (PLC) to Hamas in the January 2006 elections. The United States, Canada, and the European Union (EU) withdrew financial support for the PA due to Hamas's unwillingness to recognize Israel's right to exist, and the UN was unable to make up the financial shortfall.

War raged again in Lebanon from July 12 to August 14, 2006, when Israel and Hezbollah fought in what is known in Lebanon as the July War and in Israel as the Second Lebanon War. Security Council Resolution 1701, passed on August 11, 2006, called for an end to militias in Lebanon, the withdrawal of Israeli forces from Lebanon, and the deployment of Lebanese soldiers and an enhanced UNIFIL in southern Lebanon. Unfortunately, the largest segment of the Lebanese population saw Resolution 1701 as a U.S.- and Israeli-supported mandate against Hezbollah that aimed to support only one side of the Lebanese government.

Richard Edwards

See also

Abbas, Mahmoud; Begin, Menachem; Camp David Accords; Expellees and Refugees, Palestinian; Hezbollah; Intifada, First; Intifada, Second; Israeli War of Independence, Overview; Israeli War of Independence, Truce Agreements; Lebanon; Lebanon, Civil War in; Lebanon, Israeli Invasion of; Jerusalem; Netanyahu, Benjamin; Oslo Accords; Palestine Liberation Organization; Palestinian Authority; Palestinian Refugee Camps; Rabin, Yitzhak; Right of Return, Palestinian; Settlements, Israeli; Sharon, Ariel; Sinai Campaign; Sinai I and Sinai II Agreements; Six-Day War; South Lebanon Army; Suez Crisis; Syria; United Kingdom, Middle East Policy; United Nations Conciliation Commission for Palestine; United Nations General Assembly Resolution 194; United Nations Relief and Works Agency for Palestine Refugees; United Nations Security Council Resolution 242; United Nations Security Council Resolution 338; United Nations Special Commission on Palestine; Wye River Agreement; Yom Kippur War

References

Berry, Mike, and Greg Philo. *Israel and Palestine: Competing Histories.* London: Pluto, 2006.

Gelvin, James L. *The Israel-Palestine Conflict: One Hundred Years of War.* New York: Cambridge University Press, 2005.

Grobman, Alex. *Nations United: How the United Nations Undermines Israel and the West.* Green Forest, AR: Balfour, 2006.

Harms, Gregory, and Todd Ferry. *The Palestine-Israel Conflict: A Basic Introduction.* London: Pluto, 2005.

Meisler, Stanley. *United Nations: The First Fifty Years.* New York: Atlantic Monthly Press, 1997.

Mingst, Karen A., and Margaret P. Karns, *United Nations in the Twenty-First Century.* 3rd ed. Boulder, CO: Westview, 2006.

Pappe, Ilan. *A History of Modern Palestine: One Land, Two Peoples.* Cambridge: Cambridge University Press, 2003.

United Nations, ed. *Basic Facts about the United Nations.* New York: United Nations, 2004.

———, ed. *The Origins and Evolution of the Palestine Problem, 1917–1988.* New York: United Nations, 1990.

———, ed. *Palestinians (the Work of the Committee on the Exercise of the Inalienable Rights of the Palestinian People).* New York: United Nations, 1997.

———, ed. *The Question of Palestine, 1979–1990.* New York: United Nations, 1990.

United Nations Charter, Articles 41 and 42

Provisions that enable the United Nations (UN) Security Council to undertake specific measures to contain aggression and maintain peace. Articles 41 and 42 of the UN Charter established the enforcement power of the Security Council within the mechanism of the charter. These articles are part of Chapter VII of the UN Charter, entitled "Action with Respect to Threats to the Peace, Breaches of the Peace, and Acts of Aggression."

Article 41 authorizes the Security Council to enact nonmilitary measures to deter acts of aggression such as "complete or partial interruption of economic relations and of rail, sea, air, postal, telegraphic, radio, and other means of communication and the severance of diplomatic relations."

Article 42 authorizes the Security Council to enact military measures, should Article 41 prove inadequate, such as "demonstrations, blockade, and other operations by air, sea, or land forces of Members of the United Nations."

Articles 41 and 42 were a direct result of the shortcomings of the League of Nations, the predecessor organization to the UN. World War II was preceded by the complete failure of the League of Nations to preserve peace. There were two significant factors that contributed to the demise of the League of Nations: the failure of the United States to ratify the League of Nations Covenant and the organization's lack of enforcement powers. President Franklin D. Roosevelt, who had been an early supporter of the League of Nations, hoped to create an organization to succeed it that would not contain any of its flaws.

The United States had chosen not to join the League of Nations because of the language contained in Article 10 of the League of Nations Covenant, which obligated members "to undertake to respect and preserve, as against external aggression, the territorial integrity and existing political independence of all Members of the League." Some American officials believed that this concept of collective security appeared to endanger the sovereignty of the United States. Furthermore, Article 16 of the covenant enjoined its members to participate in protecting other members suffering from aggression. These two articles were soon proven meaningless, however, during Italy's invasion of Ethiopia in 1935. The invasion proceeded with virtual impunity.

Unlike Articles 10 and 16 of the covenant, Articles 41 and 42 of the UN Charter gave the Security Council the sole prerogative of deciding what situations would involve the use of force. One reason the League of Nations failed was that it did not have any such mechanism to deliberate in situations that might have required the use of force. Second, the language of Article 16 proved to be the undoing of the League of Nations by placing an obligation on its members to intervene with nonmilitary measures. Article 41 differs in language by using the words "call upon" rather than "obligate." By placing the responsibility on the Security Council in determining what kinds of measures should be taken, the UN maintained its credibility rather than allowing each individual member to decide what kinds of actions to take.

Article 42 specifically placed military and other security measures in the hands of the Security Council. Under the League of Nations, it was impossible to find a consensus among the members to devote their armed forces toward enforcement. Thus, through Article 42 a system was devised whereby national military forces would be placed under international jurisdiction but only for specified objectives. As a result of these measures, the UN has maintained a credibility that the League of Nations could not uphold.

The UN, largely through Articles 41 and 42, has been heavily involved in the Middle East since 1945. Most of its work has come in the form of peacekeeping, monitoring, and enforcement. Some of its actions there include the UN Observation Group in Lebanon, dispatched in 1958 to ensure that no illegal infiltrations of personnel or materials made their way into Lebanon after the uprising there that same year. In November 1956 following the Suez Crisis and the Sinai Campaign, the UN established the first UN Security Force whose job was to oversee the withdrawal of French, Israeli, and British forces from Egypt and then to maintain a buffer zone between Egyptian and Israeli troops. This lasted until June 1967. In October 1973 following the Yom Kippur War, the second UN Emergency Force was dispatched to the Middle East to enforce the cease-fire between Israel and Egypt. UN forces also created and maintained a buffer zone between the two nations that lasted until July 1979. In August 1988 the UN established the UN Iran-Iraq Military Observer Group, which was charged with enforcing the terms of the cease-fire after the Iran-Iraq War (1980–1988). The UN Iraq-Kuwait Observation Commission, in operation from April 1991 to October 2003, was charged with deterring any aggression between the two nations and monitoring the demilitarized zone.

Ongoing UN activities in the Middle East include an observation force in the Golan Heights, first created in 1974, to supervise the cease-fire and withdrawal agreements made between Syria and Israel. The UN Interim Force in Lebanon, dispatched in 1978, continues the struggle to enable the Lebanese government to assert control over its territory and keep Israeli troops from occupying Lebanese lands. The UN Truce Supervision Organization, in existence since 1948, continues to monitor truces, observe military movements, enforce cease-fires, and perform other peacekeeping responsibilities in the region.

Articles 41 and 42 have also been invoked numerous times during Middle Eastern conflicts to effect embargoes, blockades, and economic sanctions against aggressor states. For example, after the Iraqi invasion of Kuwait in August 1990, the UN Security Council almost immediately passed Resolution 660, which condemned the Iraqi attack and demanded an immediate withdrawal. Just a few days later the Security Council passed Resolution 661, which slapped international economic sanctions on Iraq. After more diplomatic wrangling while Iraq still occupied Kuwait, the UN passed Resolution 678 in November 1990. This resolution gave the Iraqis a firm deadline of January 15, 1991, to withdraw entirely from Kuwait. It also authorized "all necessary means" to implement and enforce Resolution 660, which was a de facto authorization for the use of force. When Iraq refused to leave Kuwait, an international coalition led by the United States forcibly expelled it. Indeed, the 1991 Persian Gulf War was an almost textbook case of the effectiveness of the UN and specifically of Articles 41 and 42.

The same cannot be said, however, of the 2003 U.S.-led coalition that invaded Iraq and ousted Iraqi dictator Saddam Hussein from office. Although the UN had passed a number of resolutions entreating Hussein to cooperate with UN weapons inspectors, it had not passed a clear-cut measure that specifically authorized force as it had done in 1991. The United States continued to push the case for war, however, citing clear evidence that the Iraqis were concealing weapons of mass destruction (WMDs). Thus, the United States and its allies went to war with Iraq in March 2003 lacking any pretense of UN authorization. This engendered bitter condemnations from many nations, including old allies of the United States and Britain.

UN secretary-general Kofi Annan termed the invasion "illegal" in September 2004. The lack of international support has bedeviled the Anglo-American war in Iraq, as have reports that no WMDs were found in Iraq even after many months of careful hunting by military professionals.

DINO E. BUENVIAJE AND PAUL G. PIERPAOLI JR.

See also

Biological Weapons and Warfare; Golan Heights; Iran-Iraq War; Iraq War; Lebanon; Persian Gulf War; Sinai Campaign; Six-Day War; Suez Crisis; United Nations, Role of; Yom Kippur War

References
Goodrich, Leland, and Edvard Hambro. *Charter of the United Nations: Commentary and Documents.* 2nd rev. ed. Boston: World Peace Foundation, 1949.
Nothedge, F. S. *The League of Nations: Its Life and Times, 1920–1946.* Leicester, UK: Leicester University Press, 1986.
Roberts, Adam, and Benedict Kingsbury, eds. *United Nations, Divided World: The UN's Role in International Relations.* New York: Oxford University Press, 1994.
Schlesinger, Stephen C. *Act of Creation: The Founding of the United Nations.* Boulder CO: Westview, 2003.
Ziring, Lawrence, Robert E. Riggs, and Jack C. Plano. *The United Nations: International Organization and World Politics.* Chicago: Wadsworth, 1993.

United Nations Conciliation Commission for Palestine

The United Nations Conciliation Commission for Palestine (UNCCP), headquartered in Jerusalem, was created by United Nations (UN) General Assembly Resolution 194 (III) on December 11, 1948, in an attempt to resolve issues remaining from the 1948 Arab-Israeli war. That conflict had followed the May 1948 UN partition of the former British Mandate for Palestine and the creation of the State of Israel on May 14, 1948. The UN had originally attempted to avoid a war and any accruing issues by developing a plan through the UN Special Commission on Palestine (UNSCOP) for the equitable division of the mandate west of the Jordan River between the Jewish and Arab populations of the area.

The Arab states' rejection of the UNSCOP plan and UNSCOP attempts at reconciliation prior to partition led the UN to create the Truce Commission for Palestine on April 23, 1948, to assist the UN Security Council in bringing peace and order to Palestine per UN Resolution 46. The UN dissolved UNSCOP on May 20, 1948, believing that an appointed UN mediator on Palestine (UNMP), created by General Assembly Resolution 186 (S-2) on May 14, 1948, working with the Truce Commission, had a better chance at bringing peace to the region. The mediator was Count Folke Bernadotte. The UN terminated the mediator's position when it created the UNCCP and then mandated that the UNCCP assume the responsibilities of the UNMP.

The UNCCP was created when a General Assembly committee recommended that a continuing Conciliation Commission comprised of five states (China, France, the Soviet Union, the United Kingdom, and the United States) be mandated to act in three areas: conciliation, Jerusalem and the holy places, and Palestinian refugees. The UNCCP was authorized to appoint subsidiary bodies and employ technical experts as needed to effectuate its mandate.

The UNCCP began its tasks by asking the Arab nations and Israel to sign a protocol summarizing the UNCCP mandate and an accompanying map drawn per the November 1947 General Assembly Partition Resolution 181 (II) that formed the framework within which the UNCCP had to bring about conciliation. The UNCCP began to explore ways of reconciling the combatants and resolving the Palestinian refugee problem by visiting the Arab states (Egypt, Saudi Arabia, the Hashemite Kingdom of Jordan, Iraq, Syria, and Lebanon) and Israel in an effort to define the issues and exchange ideas on possible resolutions. The UNCCP then held in-depth meetings with the Arab nations in Beirut from March 21 to April 15, 1949, and a concurrent meeting with Israeli prime minister David Ben-Gurion on April 7, 1949.

These talks ended without any clear pathway to reconciliation or resolution of the refugee issue. A series of joint exchanges among all of the pertinent parties, known as the Lausanne Meetings, were held in Switzerland from April 27 to September 15, 1949, and again in Geneva from January to July 1950, with additional meetings following in Paris from September to November 1951. The UNCCP concluded at the close of the Paris meetings that both Israel and the Arab states were unwilling to comply with paragraph 11 of Resolution 194 (III) concerning the Palestine refugees and that reconciliation would be very difficult to achieve.

The UNCCP created the Committee on Jerusalem and Its Holy Places that initially gathered information on how best to establish Jerusalem as an international city, interviewed local and regional authorities and religious representatives who would be affected by the internationalization of Jerusalem, and then began to promote the internationalization of Jerusalem. The Arab representatives generally accepted internationalization contingent upon UN guarantees. Israel accepted only the international control of the holy places. The UNCCP submitted a draft proposal on the status of Jerusalem to the General Assembly in September 1949 that included a General Council composed of representatives of the Arab and Jewish populations of the city, an international tribunal to oversee the plan, a guarantee of unencumbered free access to the holy places by people of all faiths, and the governance of Jewish sections by Israel and the Arab sections by Jordan. The proposal was never implemented.

The General Assembly mandated that the UNCCP work closely with the director of the UN Relief for Palestine Refugees, other UN agencies, local governments, and other relief organizations to assist Palestinian refugees with the social, legal, and economic issues of repatriation (resettlement) and compensation for any losses of real or disposable property. The UNCCP created the Technical Committee in June 1949 to determine the number of refugees and to pursue any additional factual studies that might be needed. The Technical Committee determined the number of Palestinian refugees to be 711,000 but did not determine the number of Jewish refugees. The Technical Committee was soon dissolved, and the UN Economic Survey Mission (UNESM) was created in August 1949. The UNESM was tasked with determining the economic and social impact of the refugee problem on the countries affected by the outmigration, the appropriate compensation for the losses sustained by the refugees, and possible repatriation scenarios. The UNESM interim report to the General Assembly led to Resolution 302 (IV) and the creation of the UN Relief and Works Agency for Palestine Refugees (UNRWA) on December 8, 1949.

The UNCCP established a Refugee Office in Jerusalem in May 1951 per General Assembly Resolution 394 (V), adopted on December 14, 1950. The office's first task was to determine the total valuation of the real and disposable Arab refugee property abandoned, seized, or lost during 1948–1949. The office estimated that the Palestinians' lost land was worth 100 million Palestine pounds sterling and that disposable property was worth another 20 million Palestine pounds sterling. The Refugee Office prepared an initial assessment of refugee properties. The Arabs asserted that the valuation was too low, and a special office called the Commission's Office for the Identification and Valuation of Arab Refugee Properties, also known as the Technical Office, made the final valuations during 1952–1966 for the approximately 453,000 abandoned or seized Arab-owned land parcels by using microfilmed British Mandate for Palestine (BMP) land registries cross-referenced with BMP land taxation records held by the Israeli and Arab governments. The office also estimated the current market value of the real and disposable property lost by the Palestinian refugees. The office revalued the land at just under 200 million Palestine pounds sterling and the disposable property at 30 million Palestine pounds sterling. The final valuations also factored in hardship allowances and other compensation. The Arabs again rejected the valuation and were unhappy that the value of the Negev lands assigned to Israel in the partition was excluded. The Arabs also sought repatriation as well as compensation. Israel reserved comment.

A UNCCP special representative attempted to resolve the issues concerning the Palestinian refuges from 1961 to 1962. The UNCCP initiated at the behest of the United States a series of talks in 1963 among Israel, Jordan, Syria, Egypt, and Lebanon. All of these efforts proved fruitless, however. The UNCCP completed its work in 1966 except for brief annual reports that it submits to the General Assembly and the maintenance of the property valuations and the records on which those valuations were based. The General Assembly's 1996 Resolution 51/129 authorized that all necessary means be taken to preserve and modernize the existing records of the UNCCP. The UNCCP annual report to the General Assembly generates an annual resolution regretting that paragraph 11 of resolution 194 (III) concerning the repatriation or compensation of the refugees has not been accomplished and requesting that the UNCCP continue its efforts and its annual reporting until such time that its original mandate is completely fulfilled.

RICHARD M. EDWARDS

See also

Expellees and Refugees, Palestinian; Israeli War of Independence, Overview; Jerusalem; Right of Return, Palestinian; United Nations, Role of; United Nations Relief and Works Agency for Palestine Refugees

References

Gelvin, James L. *The Israel-Palestine Conflict: One Hundred Years of War.* New York: Cambridge University Press, 2005.

Grobman, Alex. *Nations United: How the United Nations Undermines Israel and the West.* Green Forest, AR: Balfour, 2006.

Harms, Gregory, and Todd Ferry. *The Palestine-Israel Conflict: A Basic Introduction.* London: Pluto, 2005.

Meisler, Stanley. *United Nations: The First Fifty Years.* New York: Atlantic Monthly Press, 1997.

Pappe, Ilan. *A History of Modern Palestine: One Land, Two Peoples.* Cambridge: Cambridge University Press, 2003.

United Nations, ed. *Basic Facts about the United Nations.* New York: United Nations, 2004.

———, ed. *The Origins and Evolution of the Palestine Problem, 1917–1988.* New York: United Nations, 1990.

———, ed. *Palestinians (the Work of the Committee on the Exercise of the Inalienable Rights of the Palestinian People).* New York: United Nations, 1997.

———, ed. *Teaching about Palestine.* New York: United Nations, 1990.

United Nations Educational, Scientific and Cultural Organization

A specialized agency of the United Nations (UN) formally established in 1946. Comprised of 166 member nations, the UN Educational, Scientific and Cultural Organization (UNESCO) promotes international collaboration through the dissemination of knowledge as well as multilateral cultural, educational, and scientific exchanges. The primary goal of UNESCO is the encouragement of peace by appealing to the common welfare of all nations.

The highest governing body of UNESCO is the General Conference, which is composed of representatives of all member nations and meets every two years. The Executive Board, composed of 58 representatives of member states, prepares the program for the General Conference and convenes two or three times a year. The

Palestinian leader Yasser Arafat and Israeli foreign minister Shimon Peres attend a UNESCO meeting in 1997. The two, along with Israeli prime minister Yitzhak Rabin, were joint winners of UNESCO's 1993 Félix Houphouët-Boigny Peace Prize. (Jean-Bernard Vernier/Corbis)

organization is administered by a Secretariat, which is headed by the director-general and the director of the Executive Office.

There are five regional UNESCO coordinators. They oversee Africa, Latin America and the Caribbean, Asia and the Pacific, the Arab states, and Europe and North America. Within these five regions are 14 subregional offices. There are also national commissions in most member states to help integrate UNESCO's work with the work of individual member states.

UNESCO sponsors programs to spread literacy, provide adult education, and encourage universal primary education. These services particularly emphasize support for disabled people and women as well as the role of literacy in rural development. UNESCO routinely sends experts to member nations on request to advise them on educational matters. It also provides educational fellowships and grants, with priority going to rural residents of developing nations who are UNESCO members.

UNESCO operates programs at the international, regional, subregional, and national levels that emphasize the use of science and technology in aiding developing countries. It also promotes collaboration between industrialized countries. International-level programs have encouraged intergovernmental collaboration in environmental sciences and natural resources research, established cooperation between developed and underdeveloped nations in the computer sciences, and worked with the world scientific community in all the basic sciences. UNESCO also develops cooperative agendas at the regional and subregional levels. At the national level, the organization sends experts on request to advise member nations on matters involving science and technology and organizes training and research programs. In addition, UNESCO has services encouraging study and research in the social sciences.

The organization's cultural heritage program has three parts. First, UNESCO promotes the application of international conventions on the protection of cultural properties and artifacts. Second, it helps member states preserve and restore cultural monuments and sites. Third, it operates training programs for museum managers, preservationists, archivists, and archaeologists.

UNESCO also promotes the international flow of information. To this end, the organization provides advisory services and assists member nations in developing training programs in communications, public information, media services, computer technology, and the like.

In the Middle East, UNESCO maintains offices in Jordan, Lebanon, Egypt, Iraq, Ramallah (a Palestinian city in the West Bank), Morocco, and Qatar. UNESCO's programs for Israel fall under its Europe and North America region. UNESCO has worked constantly and diligently to promote peace in the region by promoting mutual cooperation and dialogue between the Israelis and Arabs. Because many of the nations in the Middle East are considered developing nations, UNESCO has played a prominent role in education and poverty-mitigation efforts. It has also worked closely with nations such as Egypt to preserve its rich cultural past. Natural resource programs, meanwhile, have helped to increase crop

irrigation in the arid region, lessen the impact of seasonal flooding and erosion, and manage precious freshwater supplies. In 1993 the organization awarded its Félix Houphouët-Boigny Peace Prize to Israel's Yitzhak Rabin and Shimon Peres and to Yasser Arafat of the Palestine Liberation Organization (PLO) in recognition of the progress made at the Oslo Accords. In 2005 UNESCO helped to establish the Israeli-Palestinian Science Organization, a nongovernmental multilateral endeavor that brings Palestinian and Israeli researchers and scientists together.

PAUL G. PIERPAOLI JR.

See also

United Nations, Role of

References

Janello, Amy, and Brennon Jones, eds. *A Global Affair: An Inside Look at the United Nations.* New York: Jones and Janello, 1995.

Spaulding, Seth. *Historical Dictionary of the United Nations Educational, Scientific and Cultural Organization (UNESCO).* Lanham, MD: Rowman and Littlefield, 1997.

Ziring, Lawrence, Robert E. Riggs, and Jack C. Plano. *The United Nations: International Organization and World Politics.* Chicago: Wadsworth, 1993.

United Nations General Assembly Resolution 194
Event Date: December 11, 1948

Resolution passed by the United Nations (UN) General Assembly on December 11, 1948, that among other things called for the conditional return of hundreds of thousands of displaced Palestinian refugees. Contained in Article 11, the so-called right of return has been a sticking point in Arab-Israeli relations for decades.

The UN, in fulfillment of its mission to bring about world peace and security, has tried repeatedly to solve the Arab-Israeli conflict and bring lasting peace to the Middle East. The UN began to take direct action in the region upon the request of the British government, which by 1947 had decided that its position in Palestine was untenable. The UN General Assembly approved the partitioning of Palestine on November 29, 1947, by a two-thirds majority. The plan envisaged Palestine being divided into a Jewish state and an Arab state, with Jerusalem to come under the control of an international oversight agency. The Arabs promptly rejected the plan, and both sides prepared for war.

The British brought their mandate in Palestine to an official end at midnight on May 14, 1948. That same day, the National Assembly in Tel Aviv proclaimed an independent State of Israel in the areas allotted to the Jews under the partition plan. The Israeli War of Independence began the following day. The combined armies of Jordan, Egypt, Syria, Lebanon, and Iraq invaded Israel but ultimately were soundly defeated. Estimates vary as to how many Palestinians became refugees during the fighting, with numbers ranging from a low of 400,000 to a high of 1 million.

A Palestinian casts a paper ballot with "The Right of Return list, Resolution 194" written on it during symbolic voting in the Palestinian refugee camp of Ain el-Helweh in southern Lebanon, January 24, 2006. (AFP/Getty Images)

By the end of 1948 the UN hoped to end the conflict, in which several cease-fires had been promptly violated, by engaging both sides in multilateral diplomacy. Resolution 194, passed by the General Assembly on December 11, 1948, contained 15 articles. Collectively, these called for the following actions. A UN Conciliation Commission was to be formed to mediate the Arab-Israeli conflict and to deal with the repercussions of the war. Holy places—both Jewish and Muslim—were to be protected from intrusions or violence, and access to them was to remain unfettered. Jerusalem was to be demilitarized, and access to it would remain open to all residents of Palestine, Arab and Jewish alike. Finally, all refugees displaced by the war—almost all of whom were Palestinian—were to be allowed to return to their homes. In addition, compensatory payments were to be made to those refugees who chose not to return or to those whose property had been damaged or destroyed, with the costs to be borne by the responsible parties. It was this last item—Article 11—that would prove the most difficult to enact and would become the most controversial part of Resolution 194.

United Nations Resolutions Regarding the Arab-Israeli Conflict

Resolution Number	Date	Passed by	Effect
181	November 29, 1947	General Assembly	Called for the partition of the British Mandate for Palestine
194	December 11, 1948	General Assembly	Established the right of return
273	May 11, 1949	General Assembly	Admitted Israel to UN
242	November 22, 1967	Security Council	Called for peace and withdrawal from occupied territories
338	October 22, 1973	Security Council	Called for cease-fire, implementation of UNSC 242, and negotiations
350	May 31, 1974	Security Council	Created United Nations Disengagement Observer Force
3237	November 22, 1974	General Assembly	Granted the PLO observer status in UN
497	December 17, 1981	Security Council	Called on Israel to withdraw from the Golan Heights
1559	September 2, 2004	Security Council	Called for removal of foreign forces from Lebanon
1701	August 11, 2006	Security Council	Called for end to hostilities between Israel and Hezbollah

Not surprisingly, Resolution 194 generated much controversy. Article 11 begins: "The refugees wishing to return to their homes . . . should be permitted to do so at the earliest practicable date." There was no mention of "Arab" or "Palestinian" before the word "refugees." Both sides could claim "the right to return." However, the term obviously applied to the Palestinian refugees, as it was they who were driven from or had fled their homes, and it was they who remained refugees. There were few Jewish refugees as a consequence of the 1948 war. Although Article 11 spoke of compensation, the resolution did not specify whether Israeli or Arab governments would pay.

Recommendations of the UN General Assembly, unlike those of the UN Security Council, are not binding. Ultimately, the recommendations of the resolution were not fully implemented, and hostilities continued between the Arabs and Jews. When the resolution came up for a vote on December 11, 1948, the Arab states universally rejected it. The resolution had failed to satisfy either side and thus became something of a dead letter. It did, however, showcase the intractability of the Arab-Israeli conflict and proved that even the slightest ambiguity in language can hamstring the best of diplomatic intentions.

PATIT PABAN MISHRA

See also

Expellees and Refugees, Palestinian; Israeli War of Independence, Overview; Palestine, British Mandate for; United Nations, Role of; United Nations Conciliation Commission for Palestine; United Nations Special Commission on Palestine

References

Barker, A. J. *Arab-Israeli Wars.* New York: Hippocrene, 1980.
Dupuy, Trevor N. *Elusive Victory: The Arab-Israeli Wars, 1947–1974.* Garden City, NY: Military Book Club, 2002.
Eban, Abba. *Voice of Israel.* New York: Horizon, 1957.
Herzog, Chaim. *The Arab-Israeli Wars: War and Peace in the Middle East from the War of Independence to Lebanon.* Westminster, MD: Random House, 1984.
Meisler, Stanley. *United Nations: The First Fifty Years.* New York: Atlantic Monthly Press, 1997.

United Nations Palestine Partition Plan
Event Date: November 29, 1947

On February 18, 1947, British foreign secretary Ernest Bevin announced to the House of Commons that Britain no longer held out hope of reaching agreement with the Arabs and Jews of Palestine and would turn the future of the mandate over to the United Nations (UN) for resolution. On April 2 the British UN delegation requested a special session of the General Assembly to establish a committee to study the matter and then to report its findings to the regular General Assembly fall session.

The General Assembly special session met on April 27. The five Arab states immediately demanded consideration of a new agenda item, to wit an immediate end to the British mandate and its inde-

pendence. This was overwhelmingly defeated. On the other hand, the General Assembly heard from Arab spokesmen but refused to receive a Jewish representative, despite the fact that the American Section of the Jewish Agency had requested that it be heard as "a matter of simple fairness." The rejection was on the basis that the agency was a nongovernmental body. Subsequently, the General Assembly voted 44 to 7 with 3 abstentions to instruct the committee to grant a hearing to the Jewish Agency as the sole spokesman for the Jewish people.

Three prominent members of the Jewish Agency—David Ben-Gurion, Abba Hillel Silver, and Moshe Shertok—all addressed the First Committee (Political and Security Committee) and presented the Jewish case. This was a precedent, the first time that Jewish representatives had been able to address the community of nations.

The first debate was over the composition of the investigating committee itself. Ultimately, it consisted of representatives from 11 member nations. None of the big powers or Arab states was represented. Debate also occurred on the issue of whether the committee should visit the displaced persons (DP) camps in Europe, which the Jewish Agency sought. The Arab states claimed that this had nothing to do with the situation in Palestine, while the Jewish Agency claimed that it went to the very heart of the matter. The instructions to the committee gave it the "widest powers to ascertain all questions and issues relative to the problem of Palestine."

Over the next three months the UN Special Commission on Palestine (UNSCOP) gathered information in Europe and in Palestine, where it met with representatives of both the Jewish Agency and the Arabs, hearing 34 witnesses and holding 13 public meetings and 18 closed sessions. It also toured Palestine. The Arab High Committee decided to boycott the hearings, so most of the testimony came from the Jewish Agency and Palestinian government officials. At the same time, militant Arab groups staged anti-Zionist demonstrations in the cities. UNSCOP then went to Beirut, Lebanon, where it met with representatives of the Arab governments. Then a subcommittee visited certain DP camps in Austria and Germany.

UNSCOP spent most of August debating alternative solutions. Its final report was signed in Geneva on August 31, 1947. The committee could not reach unanimous opinion, and both majority and minority reports were presented. A majority of the representatives (Canada, Czechoslovakia, Guatemala, the Netherlands, Peru, Sweden, and Uruguay) voted for the partition of Palestine into two separate states, one Arab and the other Jewish, to be joined in an economic union. Following a transition period of two years, both states were to be completely independent, provided they had adopted a constitution, guaranteed minority and religious rights, and made provision for the protection of holy places. Jerusalem would be placed under a UN trusteeship.

Three of the representatives (India, Iran, and Yugoslavia) objected to the majority report and produced a minority report. It called for a brief transition period and then the creation of a federal state of Palestine. It would have both a Jewish and Arab state within it and two federal legislative bodies, one on the basis of proportionate

UN PARTITION PLAN, 1947

LEBANON

SYRIA

N

Hanita
Eilon
Matzuva
Gaaton
Nahariya
Acre
Yehiam
Safed
Haifa

Sea of Galilee

Mediterranean Sea

Kfar Hahoresh

Jenin

Hadera

Nablus

Jordan R.

Tel Aviv
Jaffa
Ben Shemen
Atarot
Neve Yaakov
Kfar Menachem
Hartuv
Nitzanim
Bet Haatava
Kedma
Galon
Kallia
Ein Tzurim
Gat
Gush Etzion
Yad Mordechai
Revadim
Hebron
Kfar Darom
Massout Yitzhak
Dead Sea
Nirim
Beersheba

El Arish

Negev

EGYPT

Sinai

Peninsula

TRANSJORDAN

- - - Boundary of the British
Palestine Mandate, 1922–1947

Proposed Jewish state

Proposed Arab state

⊙ Jewish settlements to be
included in the Arab state

Jerusalem and its suburbs
(to be an international zone)

0   10   20 mi
0 10 20 km

Eilat
Aqaba

34°E

36°E

33°N

32°N

31°N

30°N

representation and the other with equal representation from both Arabs and Jews. The Australian delegate refused to endorse either plan.

On September 23, 1947, at its regular fall session, the UN General Assembly referred the reports of the committee to the Special Committee on the Question of Palestine, which had representatives of all member states. It was before this committee that Silver, speaking on behalf of the Jewish Agency, stated that while the partition plan presented by the majority report would impose hardship on the Jewish people, the Jewish Agency was prepared to accept it. On October 11 the U.S. delegate stated his government's support for the partition plan. Two days later, the Soviet Union followed suit.

Nonetheless, the committee continued its deliberations. It divided into two subcommittees. Subcommittee No. 2 worked on the minority report, and Subcommittee No. 1 worked on the majority report. The major stumbling block in the latter was over the territorial arrangements for partition. The investigating committee had come up with a map of three Jewish and three Arab sections and additional enclaves. The Jewish Agency pressed for an additional 200,000 acres for the Jewish state for future settlement and defensible borders. On the other hand, the United States initially sought a reduction in the area allocated to the Jewish state, and it was because of this that the port and city of Jaffa became an Arab enclave and that most of western Galilee was assigned to the proposed Arab state. Jewish hopes were dealt another blow in the planned internationalization of Jerusalem. On the other hand, the Jewish state was awarded the Bet Ntofa Valley and Lydda (Lod) Airport as well as gains in Lower Galilee, the Beit She'an Valley, and the Gilboa area of the Jezreel Valley. Also, thanks to a last-minute visit by Chaim Weizmann with President Harry S. Truman, Israel was awarded the thinly populated but large Negev region, which the Jews hoped to use for future settlement. The plan also included the Arab-Jewish economic union. Thus, of the some 10,000 square miles of Mandate Palestine, the final report awarded the Jewish state 5,579 square miles. This area also contained an estimated Arab population of 397,000 people, or 46.5 percent of the total there.

On November 25, 1947, the committee voted on the two reports. The minority report from Subcommittee No. 2 was rejected by 29 to 12 votes with 16 abstentions. The majority report of Subcommittee No. 1 was accepted in a vote of 25 to 13 with 17 abstentions and 2 members absent. This was 1 vote short of the two-thirds vote that would be required in the final vote to be taken by the General Assembly.

The General Assembly voted on November 29, 1947. There were 33 votes for partition, 13 opposed, 10 abstentions, and 1 absent (Siam). Those voting no were Afghanistan, Cuba, Egypt, Greece, India, Iran, Iraq, Lebanon, Pakistan, Saudi Arabia, Syria, Turkey, and Yemen. States abstaining included the United Kingdom, China, and a number of Latin American countries.

While the Jewish Agency accepted the vote, the Arabs did not. Immediately on learning of the UN decision, Arabs in Palestine began attacking Jewish settlements in Palestine. This marked the beginning of the Arab-Jewish Communal War (November 3, 1947–May 14, 1948).

SPENCER C. TUCKER

See also
Arab-Jewish Communal War; Ben-Gurion, David; Palestine, British Mandate for; Palestine, Partition of; Truman, Harry S.; Weizmann, Chaim

References
Sachar, Howard M. *A History of Israel: From the Rise of Zionism to Our Time.* 3rd ed. New York: Knopf, 2007.
Shepherd, Naomi. *Ploughing Sand: British Rule in Palestine, 1917–1948.* New Brunswick, NJ: Rutgers University Press, 1999.

United Nations Peacekeeping Missions

The United Nations (UN) has played an important role in peacekeeping operations to prevent or limit hostilities between Israel and its Arab neighbors. The success of these peacekeeping missions has varied, but the effort began in 1948 and has been the largest such mission in UN history.

Blue-helmeted UN peacekeepers have become an iconic image for the world. Their missions have ranged from separating warring parties within the same state to observing cease-fires between rival states. Missions consist of either unarmed observers or lightly armed infantry forces. The peacekeepers do not have military superiority over the parties they are separating. The moral authority of the UN peacekeepers is their greatest weapon.

Surprisingly, the peacekeeping mission was not one anticipated for the UN when it was created. The idea of sending observers to limit the scope of wars and to keep combatants apart had its origin in the partition of Palestine. In April 1947 British diplomats brought the issue of Palestine to the UN to consider. The UN General Assembly appointed a special committee to study the problem and devise a proposed solution. The committee proposed a partition plan in November 1947, awarding the Jewish population just over half the disputed territory. Palestinians and the Arab countries rejected the plan out of hand.

Several months later, the UN reported that nearly 3,000 people had died in December 1947 and January 1948 in conflicts between Jews and Palestinians. Calls for cease-fires failed to halt the violence. When Great Britain announced its plan to end its mandate on May 14, 1948, the UN appointed a Truce Commission consisting of Belgium, France, and the United States to arrange a truce between the two sides. Later, a mediator was appointed, to be assisted by the Truce Commission, to bring about a settlement between Jews and Arabs. After the Jewish Agency proclaimed the State of Israel on May 14, 1948, open warfare broke out between surrounding Arab states and the new country. On May 22 the Security Council called for a cease-fire within 36 hours. To ensure that both sides complied with the cease-fire, the Security Council authorized military

Canadian major general E. L. M. Burns, head of the United Nations Emergency Forces (UNEF), and Israel Defense Forces (IDF) chief of staff Moshe Dayan on their way from the landing strip to a conference room at Lod Airport, Israel, December 6, 1956. (Israeli Government Press Office)

observers to be stationed between the two sides on May 29. The new organization was known as the UN Truce Supervision Organization (UNTSO).

UNTSO was the first peacekeeping mission undertaken by the UN. Within weeks, the number of observers grew to 572. The troops were drawn from different countries that did not have ties to either side. The goal was to have objective observers who could report violations of the truce to the Security Council. Rules of engagement for UNTSO personnel were strict, and the troops were virtually unarmed. Any sidearms could be used only to defend themselves. Indeed, UNTSO soldiers were not expected to enforce the truce but were present only to observe.

Fighting broke out again on July 9, 1948, after the truce expired with no peace settlement. Once again, the Security Council ordered a cease-fire and called on UNTSO to report violations. Incidents continued, including the assassination of Count Folke Bernadotte, the UN mediator, on September 17, 1948. On November 16 the Security Council ordered an armistice to which the various parties agreed. Between February and July 1949 Israel made bilateral agreements, known as the General Armistice Agreements of 1949, with the neighboring Arab states. The mediator's role was declared at an end in

August 1949, but UNTSO observers remained on the ground to make sure the borders separating Jews and Arabs were not violated. Mixed armistice commissions from the different states oversaw the peace with assistance from UNTSO. The failure to reach a permanent peace agreement led to UNTSO observers remaining on Israel's borders for the coming decades. They reported on commando raids by Palestinians on Israeli targets and on Israeli retaliations during that time.

In 1956 tensions between Israel and neighboring Egypt reached the boiling point. President Gamal Abdel Nasser had nationalized the Suez Canal and broken with the Western powers and had begun to receive arms shipments from the Soviet Union, threatening the balance of power in the Middle East. Israel, Great Britain, and France reached an agreement to defeat Egypt, using an Israeli attack as an excuse for the other powers to occupy the Suez Canal. On October 29, 1956, Israeli forces attacked the Egyptian Army in the Sinai. Great Britain and France demanded that both sides pull back to either side of the Suez Canal, an objective far in the Egyptian rear. When Egypt refused, as expected, allied forces landed in Egypt and occupied the canal. On November 5 the UN General Assembly authorized the UN Emergency Force (UNEF). When a cease-fire was worked

Indonesian troops board an aircraft in Jakarta, Indonesia, on November 10, 2006, en route to Lebanon to serve in the United Nations Interim Force in Lebanon (UNIFIL). (John M. Foster/U.S. Department of Defense)

out between the different sides, UNEF units began to land in the Sinai. Israeli forces pulled back to the prewar frontiers, with UNEF ensuring that they withdrew unmolested. Israel refused to allow UNEF units to be stationed on its side of the border, so they took up positions in Egyptian territory.

UNEF was initially comprised of 6,000 men commanded by Canadian general E. L. M. Burns. UNEF was headquartered in Ballah. The units were contributed by 10 countries that were not aligned with Arab countries or Israel. Over the next 10 years, UNEF remained along the border to prevent incursions by either side. Its strength gradually declined to 3,000 men.

By 1967, tensions between Israel and its Arab neighbors were once again at the boiling point. In November 1966 Israeli commandos raided Jordanian villages that were suspected of housing terrorists. In April 1967 Israeli artillery fired on Syrian positions in the demilitarized zone between the two states. Israeli authorities blamed other incidents in May on Syria. On May 13 the Soviet Union advised Nasser that the Israelis were planning to attack, a charge that was later admitted to be false. Nasser responded by strengthening his forces in the Sinai. He apparently hoped to bluff the Israelis out of any aggressive movements by presenting overwhelming force. On May 16 the Egyptian chief of staff requested that the UNEF

forces be removed. UN secretary-general U Thant recognized that Egypt had the right to request that the peacekeepers be moved and ordered UNEF to evacuate.

The removal of the peacekeepers was seen as a sign in Israel that Egypt was preparing to attack. UNEF had not completely cleared the area by June 5, when Israel launched a surprise attack on the neighboring Arab states. Within a week, Israeli forces had reached the Suez Canal. During the attack, 15 UNEF peacekeepers were accidentally killed by the Israelis. The remaining observers were out of Egypt by June 17.

Israel's overwhelming victory over the Arabs in the Six-Day War of 1967 did not bring peace. During the next six years, the Egyptians continued low-intensity attacks around the Suez Canal. UN attempts to negotiate a peace failed, but neither side would agree to a peacekeeping force to separate them. By 1973, the Egyptians were ready to attack Israeli forces in an attempt to force a settlement. On October 6, 1973, on the Jewish holy day of Yom Kippur, Egyptian and Syrian forces struck in the Sinai and on the Golan Heights. Although the Israelis were at first forced back, they rallied with heavy logistical support from the United States. By October 15 they had surrounded the Egyptian Army on the canal and were approaching Damascus. The Soviet Union threatened to intervene, making a confrontation with the United States possible. The two super-powers negotiated a resolution and took it to the UN.

On October 22 the Security Council adopted Resolution 338, which called for a cease-fire and an end to military activities. When the Israelis refused to comply, the situation threatened to get out of control. On October 25 the Security Council passed Resolution 340, which called for a return to the positions of October 22 and the creation of a peacekeeping force to separate the two sides. Israel agreed to the cease-fire.

On November 15 the new force took up positions between Israeli and Egyptian forces. Named UNEF II, the force was organized similarly to the earlier peacekeeping force. UNEF II supervised the cease-fire, reported violations, and controlled the buffer zone that was established between the Egyptians and Israelis in the Sinai. UNEF II continued from 1973 to 1979. At that time, the signing of a peace treaty between the two countries removed the need for UNEF II. The force was dissolved in July 1979 as relations normalized.

In 1974 another UN peacekeeping mission took up positions on the Golan Heights. Israel and Syria signed an armistice agreement on May 31, 1974, that created three buffer zones between their forces. To monitor the armistice, the UN created the UN Disengagement Observer Force (UNDOF). UNDOF interposed between Israeli and Syrian forces to prevent violations. UNDOF remains in existence, as no permanent peace treaty has been signed between Israel and Syria.

The most recent peacekeeping mission undertaken by the UN between Israel and its Arab neighbors was in Lebanon. Palestine Liberation Organization (PLO) forces relocated to Lebanon after being expelled from Jordan following the Black September fighting in 1970. PLO commandos raided from Lebanon into Israel during the 1970s. On March 11, 1978, PLO forces seized an Israeli bus. In the fighting that followed, 37 Israelis were killed. Three days later, Israeli prime minister Menachem Begin ordered an invasion of southern Lebanon. On March 19 the UN Security Council passed Resolution 425 calling for a cease-fire, an Israeli withdrawal, and the establishment of the UN Interim Force in Lebanon (UNIFIL). UNIFIL was originally authorized to have 4,000 men, lightly armed with infantry weapons. In May 1978 this was increased to 6,000 men. The mandate for the force was originally good for six months. As a result, UNIFIL has been reauthorized every six months since 1978.

UNIFIL was largely ignored by both the Israelis and Palestinians, and it failed to prevent PLO infiltration into northern Israel. It also could not help the Lebanese government reestablish its authority in southern Lebanon. In May 1982 the Israelis again invaded southern Lebanon in retaliation for PLO terrorist attacks and simply pushed UNIFIL forces out of the way. In 1985 the Israelis withdrew but remained in control of a buffer zone in southern Lebanon, with a local militia providing much of the manpower. Fighting continued between the PLO and Israel and its client forces. During operations in April 1996, Israeli artillery bombarded a UNIFIL post at Qana, killing more than 100 civilians who had gathered there under UN protection.

In June 2000 Israeli forces withdrew from the buffer zone. A month later the Security Council passed Resolution 1310, authorizing UNIFIL to assist the Lebanese government in reestablishing its authority over all of southern Lebanon. By January 2001 the Lebanese government had still taken no decisive action. The Security Council renewed UNIFIL's mandate but reduced the number of soldiers in the force from 5,800 to 4,500. The situation has changed little since that time, and UNIFIL's authorized strength continued to decline. By the middle of 2004, UNIFIL had only 1,995 soldiers from seven countries (China, France, Ghana, India, Ireland, Italy, and Poland) and 400 civilian workers. Another 50 observers from UNTSO assisted them.

During the summer of 2006 Hezbollah fighters in southern Lebanon launched a series of attacks on Israeli military outposts in northern Israel. Israeli soldiers were captured and taken to bases in Lebanon. In retaliation, Israeli forces launched an invasion of southern Lebanon in July. The UN was much criticized by Lebanese for the severe damage to the country and to civilians, which went far beyond areas where Hezbollah fighters were located. Hezbollah fighters resisted stubbornly, firing rockets into northern Israel. During the fighting, an observation post with members of UNTSO was bombed by Israeli warplanes. Four UN observers were killed. Although Israel claimed that it was an accident, letters from the observers in the days leading up to the bombing talked about previous near-misses and protests to the Israeli military. The letters also indicated that Hezbollah was using the post as a shield for firing rockets. Israeli forces later pulled out of Lebanon, leaving UNIFIL and the Lebanese Army to watch over the border.

Tim J. Watts

See also

Hezbollah; Lebanon, Civil War in; United Nations, Role of

References

Benton, Barbara, ed. *Soldiers for Peace: Fifty Years of United Nations Peacekeeping.* New York: Facts on File, 1996.

Coulon, Jocelyn. *Soldiers of Diplomacy: The United Nations, Peacekeeping, and the New World Order.* Toronto: University of Toronto Press, 1998.

Daniel, Donald C. F., and Bradd C. Hayes, eds. *Beyond Traditional Peacekeeping.* New York: St. Martin's, 1995.

Hill, Stephen M., and Shahin P. Malik. *Peacekeeping and the United Nations.* Aldershot, UK: Dartmouth, 1996.

Hillen, John. *Blue Helmets: The Strategy of UN Military Operations.* Washington, DC: Brassey's, 1998.

Macqueen, Norrie. *The United Nations since 1945: Peacekeeping and the Cold War.* New York: Addison Wesley Longman, 1999.

United Nations Relief and Works Agency for Palestine Refugees

The principal provider of education, health, relief, social services, and other basic services to more than 4.3 million Palestinian refugees and their descendents who have been displaced by Arab-Israeli wars from 1951 to the present. Also among these refugees are those displaced during Palestinian-Israeli conflicts such as the First

Intifada (1987–1993), the Second (al-Aqsa) Intifada (2000–2004), and the ongoing violence in the Palestinian territories. Although most refugees fall under the purview of the Office of the United Nations High Commissioner for Refugees (UNHCR) headquartered in Geneva, Switzerland, most Palestinian refugees are the responsibility of the United Nations Relief and Works Agency for Palestine Refugees (UNRWA). The responsibility for all Palestinian refugees within Israel fell to the UNRWA from 1951 until it was appropriated by Israel in 1952.

The UNRWA began operations on May 1, 1951, but was created on December 8, 1948, by UN General Assembly Resolution 302 (IV) to replace the United Nations Relief for Palestine Refugees (UNRPR) created on November 19, 1948, by Resolution 212 (III). The UNRWA mandate must be periodically renewed by the General Assembly. The UNRWA had an initial budget of $50 million. However, in the early 21st century it is the largest UN undertaking in the Middle East, employing 22,000 people in 900 facilities in the Gaza Strip, the West Bank, Jordan, Lebanon, and Syria.

The UN had envisioned the UNRPR as a short-term agency coordinating the activities of international nongovernmental organizations (NGOs), other UN agencies such as the United Nations International Children's Emergency Fund (UNICEF), the World Health Organization (WHO), the Food and Agriculture Organization (FAO), and the International Refugee Organization, which were providing direct relief services for displaced Palestinians until what the UN anticipated would be a quick resolution of the Israeli-Palestinian crisis. The UN created the UNRWA when it had become clear that there would not be a quick resolution of the displaced Palestinians.

The UNRWA was originally designed to replace the UNRPR's direct relief responsibilities that it had assumed with public works and economic development in cooperation with local governments, other UN agencies, NGOs, the World Bank, and any Palestinian governmental structure that developed. The UNRWA was headquartered in Beirut (1950–1978) and Vienna (1978–1996) before moving to Gaza in the Palestinian territories in 1996.

Although the fact that large numbers of Palestinians fled or were expelled from Jerusalem during the Israeli War of Independence (1948–1949) is well documented, the number of refugees is disputed. The numbers range from the Israeli estimate of 400,000 to the Arab and Palestinian estimate of 950,000–1 million, with an official UN estimate of 711,000. The UN originally defined a Palestinian refugee as a person and his or her descendants whose "normal place of residence was Palestine between June 1946 and May 1948 and who lost both their homes and means of livelihood as a result of the 1948 Arab-Israeli conflict," but the definition was expanded to include those displaced by the 1967 Six-Day War as well. The designation of Palestinian refugee applies only to those meeting this definition and residing in the Gaza Strip, the West Bank, Jordan, Lebanon, and Syria, whether or not they reside in a refugee camp.

The UNRWA provides relief services to the 1.3 million Palestinian residents in the refugee camps but does not participate in the administration or governance of these camps. Half of the UNRWA's budget and two-thirds of its staff are committed to operating 647 elementary and secondary schools and 8 vocational training centers. The UNRWA also operates 122 health centers and provides environmental health services for the refugee camps. The agency develops infrastructure for the camps and provides loan assistance for enterprise development for all Palestinian refugees.

The majority of UNRWA funding is derived from the voluntary contributions of donor states. The largest donors are the United States, the European Commission, the United Kingdom, Japan, Canada, the Gulf Arab states, and the Scandinavian countries. The UN funds 110 UNRWA staff positions, and UNESCO and WHO fund some of the staff positions in the UNRWA education and health programs. Other funding comes from NGOs, private individuals, and refugee copayments and participation fees. The UNRWA has operated in the red since 2000, despite reducing its annual expenditure per registered refugee to roughly $70 from its 1970s' average of $200.

RICHARD M. EDWARDS

See also

Expellees and Refugees, Palestinian; Palestinian Refugee Camps; Right of Return, Palestinian; United Nations, Role of

References

Dumper, Michael, ed. *Palestinian Refugee Repatriation: Global Perspectives.* New York: Routledge, 2006.

Grobman, Alex. *Nations United: How the United Nations Undermines Israel and the West.* Green Forest, AR: Balfour, 2006.

Harms, Gregory, and Todd Ferry. *The Palestine-Israel Conflict: A Basic Introduction.* London: Pluto, 2005.

Meisler, Stanley. *United Nations: The First Fifty Years.* New York: Atlantic Monthly Press, 1997.

Mingst, Karen A., and Margaret P. Karns. *United Nations in the Twenty-First Century.* 3rd ed. Boulder, CO: Westview, 2006.

Morris, Benny. *The Birth of the Palestinian Refugee Problem Revisited.* 2nd ed. Cambridge: Cambridge University Press, 2004.

Pappe, Ilan. *A History of Modern Palestine: One Land, Two Peoples.* Cambridge: Cambridge University Press, 2003.

Peteet, Julie Marie. *Landscape of Hope and Despair: Palestinian Refugee Camps.* Philadelphia: University of Pennsylvania Press, 2005.

United Nations, ed. *Basic Facts about the United Nations.* New York: United Nations, 2004.

———, ed. *The Origins and Evolution of the Palestine Problem, 1917–1988.* New York: United Nations, 1990.

———, ed. *Teaching about Palestine.* New York: United Nations, 1990.

Yiftachel, Oren. *Ethnocracy: Land and Identity Politics in Israel/Palestine.* Philadelphia: University of Pennsylvania Press, 2006.

United Nations Security Council Resolution 242

Event Date: November 22, 1967

United Nations (UN) Security Council resolution passed in the wake of the June 1967 Six-Day War and designed to lessen Arab-Israeli tensions and pave the way for a comprehensive Middle East peace settlement. Resolution 242 was unanimously adopted by the Security Council on November 22, 1967, following the Six Day-War that had pitted Israel against Egypt, Jordan, Syria, and Iraq. The conflict resulted in a decisive Israeli victory and the capture and occupation of the Sinai Peninsula and the Gaza Strip from Egypt, the West Bank and East Jerusalem from Jordan, and the Golan Heights from Syria.

Resolution 242 expressed concern over the "grave situation in the Middle East," emphasized the "inadmissibility of the acquisition of territory by war," and stressed the need for "a just and lasting peace in which all states in the region could live in peace and security." It also emphasized that all member states of the UN had accepted the UN Charter and undertaken to live in accordance with its Article 2. The resolution specifically called for the "withdrawal of Israeli armed forces from territories occupied in the recent conflict [and the] termination of all claims or states of belligerency and respect for and acknowledgment of the sovereignty, territorial integrity and independence of every State in the area and their right to live in peace within secure and recognized boundaries free from threats or acts of force."

The resolution went on to "affirm the necessity" for guaranteeing free navigation of all international waterways in the region, the achievement of a lasting solution to the refugee dilemma, and a guarantee of "the territorial inviolability and political independence of every State in the area, through measures including the establishment of demilitarized zones."

Finally, Resolution 242 requested that the Security Council designate a special representative to the Middle East to negotiate with the states of the region to achieve a settlement in accordance with the resolution. The Security Council also requested that the UN secretary-general report to it the efforts of the special representative.

The resolution was the Security Council's formula for a successful resolution of the Arab-Israeli conflict. Insistence on freedom of navigation through international waterways was clearly aimed at Egypt's closing of the Strait of Tiran to Israeli shipping in May 1967, one of the most important factors in Israel's decision for a massive preventive strike against Egypt. The resolution called for a solution to the refugee problem but did not specifically use the word "Palestinian" or stipulate how the Palestinian refugee situation would be resolved.

The resolution's most important feature was the so-called land for peace formula: an Israeli withdrawal from occupied Arab territories in exchange for peace with its neighbors, along with "the termination of all claims or states of belligerency" between the warring parties. It also stipulated that all parties respect and acknowledge "the sovereignty, territorial integrity, and political independence" of every state in the area.

The resolution imposed obligations on both the Arab states and Israel, yet the warring parties refused to comply with the resolution until the other side complied first. While both Israel and its Arab neighbors accepted the legitimacy of the resolution, they interpreted it quite differently. The Israelis chose to emphasize the end of "all states of belligerency." The refusal of the Arab states to end the state of war was, therefore, a major barrier to negotiations, even

with the more moderate states of Egypt and Jordan. The Arab states demanded an immediate and unconditional Israeli withdrawal from the occupied Arab territories of the Gaza Strip, the West Bank, and the Golan Heights without offering any security guarantees to Israel. On the other hand, as a precondition to any withdrawal on their part, the Israelis demanded that the Arab states first recognize the existence of the State of Israel by establishing diplomatic relations and renouncing their commitment to seeking its destruction. Israel also insisted on an end of terrorism as a precondition to negotiations regarding the return of territory to the Palestinians, while radical Palestinians have stated that the refusal of Israel to return land is the basis for their own military actions. The Palestinians have also seized on the wording in the resolution regarding settlement of "the refugee problem" to demand that any peace settlement recognize the right of all Palestinians to return to their places of origin within the former British Mandate for Palestine, regardless of whether these locations are now part of Israel. Israel says that a massive influx of Palestinians would undermine the Jewish character of the State of Israel and holds that Palestinian refugees must be settled where they presently live or in the territory of a new Palestinian state.

On November 23, 1967, UN secretary-general U Thant appointed Gunnar Jarring as the special envoy called for in the resolution to negotiate a settlement with the states in the region. His mission was not successful. Although Israel, Egypt, Jordan, and Lebanon all recognized the legitimacy of his appointment and agreed to participate in his shuttle diplomacy between their capitals, Syria did not. Damascus held that Israeli withdrawal from conquered land was a precondition to negotiations. Jarring continued his effort for the next six years but without success.

In 1973 following the Yom Kippur War, the UN Security Council reaffirmed Resolution 242 and strengthened it by passing Resolution 338. Until the 1978 Camp David Accords and the resultant 1979 Israel-Egypt Peace Treaty, Israel retained control of the Sinai. Israel continues to occupy the Golan Heights. Israel withdrew from the Gaza Strip in 2005, and the Palestinian Authority (PA) now governs that territory. Jordan renounced its claim over the West Bank in 1988, and the Palestinians now exercise limited authority over part of the West Bank, pending a final negotiated settlement with Israel.

STEFAN BROOKS AND SPENCER C. TUCKER

See also

Camp David Accords; Expellees and Refugees, Palestinian; Gaza Strip; Gaza Strip Disengagement; Golan Heights; Israel-Egypt Peace Treaty; Palestinian Authority; Sinai; Six-Day War; United Nations Security Council Resolution 338; West Bank; Yom Kippur War

References

Herzog, Chaim. *The Arab-Israeli Wars: War and Peace in the Middle East from the War of Independence to Lebanon.* Westminster, MD: Random House, 1984.

Mansfield, Peter, et al. *A History of the Middle East.* New York: Penguin, 2004.

Said, Edward W., and Christopher Hitchins, eds. *Blaming the Victims: Spurious Scholarship and the Palestinian Question.* London: Verso, 2001.

Smith, Charles D. *Palestine and the Arab-Israeli Conflict: A History with Documents.* 6th ed. New York: Bedford/St. Martin's, 2006.

United Nations Security Council Resolution 338

Event Date: October 22, 1973

United Nations (UN) Security Council resolution passed late in the Yom Kippur War. The war began on October 6, 1973, when Egypt and Syria launched a surprise attack on Israel. The war is called the Yom Kippur War or the Ramadan War because Egypt and Syria began their attacks on the Jewish holy day of Yom Kippur, which also coincided with the Muslim month-long fast of Ramadan. The primary motivations for the attack on Israel date to the 1967 Six-Day War in which Israel captured significant Arab territories, including the Sinai Peninsula from Egypt and the Golan Heights from Syria. Six years later, with these lands still in Israeli hands, Egypt and Syria decided to initiate a war to regain the territory or at least to oblige the United States and the Soviet Union to bring that about through diplomacy.

Israel was caught by surprise and suffered initial heavy losses in the first few days of the war. By the time of the resolution, however, Israel had regained the initiative, repulsed the Egyptian and Syrian attacks, and occupied additional Arab territory in Egypt across the Suez Canal and in Syria approaching Damascus.

International efforts to halt the fighting intensified, and U.S. secretary of state Henry Kissinger flew to Moscow on October 20 to meet with Soviet leaders. Two days later, on October 22, the UN Security Council adopted Resolution 338 by a vote of 14 votes to 0, with the People's Republic of China (PRC) abstaining.

UN Resolution 338 was quite short and contained only three provisions. First, it called for all parties to cease fighting and terminate all military activity no later than 12 hours from the moment of the adoption of the resolution and to remain in the positions that they presently occupied. Second, it called for immediate implementation of UN Resolution 242, which had been passed on November 22, 1967, following the Six-Day War between Israel and Egypt, Syria, Jordan, and Iraq. Third, the resolution stated that "immediately and concurrently with the cease-fire, negotiations [would] start between the parties concerned under appropriate auspices aimed at establishing a just and durable peace in the Middle East." The term "appropriate auspices" was assumed to refer to the United States, the patron and principal ally of Israel, and the Soviet Union, the patron and ally of the Arab states, rather than to the UN.

Egypt and Israel exchange dead under the auspices of the Red Cross and the United Nations (UN) on the Baluza-Kantara Road in the Sinai on November 25, 1973, three days after UN Security Council Resolution 338. (Shlomo Arad/Israeli Government Press Office)

By explicitly calling for the implementation of Resolution 242, Resolution 338 recognized Israel's refusal to withdraw from occupied Arab lands captured in 1967. It also acknowledged, per the September 1, 1967, Khartoum Resolution, the refusal of the Arab states to recognize, negotiate, or make peace with Israel, which prevented the establishment of "a just and durable peace in the Middle East peace."

U.S.-led diplomacy resulted in an armistice in March 1974 between Egypt and Israel. Two months later, an armistice was negotiated between Syria and Israel. The Soviet Union's diplomatic role in the peacemaking process was minimal, mainly because Egypt agreed to an American request not to ask for Soviet assistance, particularly military resupply.

Impatient at the slow pace and seeming lack of progress in the peace process with Israel, Egyptian president Anwar Sadat took the unprecedented step of visiting Israel in November 1977, becoming the first Arab head of state to do so and thus implicitly recognizing Israel. Sadat's visit jump-started the peace process with Israeli prime minister Menachem Begin, and following mediation by U.S. president Jimmy Carter, led to the Camp David Accords in 1978 whereby Israel withdrew from the Sinai in exchange for diplomatic relations and peace with Egypt. The accords were followed by a formal rapprochement in the Israel-Egypt Peace Treaty of 1979. Egypt became the first Arab state to make peace with Israel and recover its territory occupied by Israel in 1967. The Israeli-Egyptian settlement also allowed for the partial implementation of UN Resolutions 242 and 338.

Stefan Brooks

See also

Begin, Menachem; Camp David Accords; Israel-Egypt Peace Treaty; Kissinger, Henry Alfred; Sadat, Anwar; Six-Day War; United Nations Security Council Resolution 242; Yom Kippur War

References

Herzog, Chaim. *The Arab-Israeli Wars: War and Peace in the Middle East from the War of Independence to Lebanon.* Westminster, MD: Random House, 1984.

Mansfield, Peter, et al. *A History of the Middle East.* New York: Penguin, 2004.

Rabinovich, Abraham. *The Yom Kippur War: The Epic Encounter That Transformed the Middle East.* New York: Schocken, 2005.

Said, Edward W., and Christopher Hitchins, eds. *Blaming the Victims: Spurious Scholarship and the Palestinian Question.* London: Verso, 2001.

Smith, Charles D. *Palestine and the Arab-Israeli Conflict: A History with Documents.* 6th ed. New York: Bedford/St. Martin's, 2006.

United Nations Security Council Resolution 1559

Event Date: September 2, 2004

United Nations (UN) resolution passed by the UN Security Council on September 2, 2004, dealing with the political and military situation in Lebanon. Resolution 1559 received nine favorable votes (Angola, Benin, Chile, France, Germany, Romania, Spain, the United Kingdom, and the United States). There were six abstentions. The resolution essentially reiterated the UN's support of a free and fair presidential election in Lebanon and called for the removal of all foreign forces from the country. The resolution had been triggered by Syria's continuing meddling—both militarily and politically—in Lebanon's affairs. Since 1976 at the beginning of the Lebanese Civil War, Syria occupied parts of Lebanon and had exerted great influence on Lebanon's foreign and domestic politics. It also continued to sponsor various militia groups in Lebanon, most notably Hezbollah, a militant organization and Lebanese political party and sponsor of terrorism in the region against Israel. When the Syrians attempted to amend the Lebanese constitution in the early summer of 2004 so that their favored presidential candidate (Émile Lahoud) would emerge victorious, the members of the Security Council decided to act and passed Resolution 1559. In so doing, the Security Council reinforced its previous resolutions vis-à-vis Lebanon, including resolutions 425 (1978), 426 (1978), 520 (1982), and 1553 (2004).

At the crux of the UN's resolution was the disengagement of Syria from Lebanese affairs and the call for the disbandment of all armed militias within Lebanon's borders. For its part, the Lebanese government requested that Israel withdraw from Shaba Farms and Kfar-Shuba and return Lebanese prisoners being held in Israel. This, it argued, was a precondition for any full implementation of Resolution 1559.

The Syrians made little attempt to abide by the UN resolution, and the weak Lebanese Army had no mandate to disarm Hezbollah's militia in the south. Finally, in the spring of 2005 and following the February 2005 assassination of Rafik Hariri, Lebanon's former prime minister, Syria agreed to withdraw its troops (still numbering some 14,000 men) from Lebanon. On April 26 the last of the Syrian troops departed Lebanon, and Syria's 29-year-long occupation of Lebanon came to an end.

The Syrian withdrawal did not, however, bring any peace or stability to the region. First, the Syrians had many Lebanese allies, and these were of various religious sects. Perhaps most importantly, those in politics and government feared a purge. Also, in December 2005 Hezbollah rockets (operated from southern Lebanon) were fired at Israel, landing in Kiryat Shmona and injuring three people. In late January 2006 the UN, frustrated by additional assassinations of anti-Syrian figures in Lebanon, implored the Lebanese government to crack down on militants and militias operating in their country. It also asked Syria to take concrete steps to aid the Lebanese in this mission. The Syrians showed no will to cooperate with the UN or abide by Resolution 1559, and the Lebanese government remained adamant that the continued Israeli occupation of Shaba Farms represented a foreign force on its soil. However, the new majority, called the March 14 Coalition, feared the large popular support for Hezbollah.

Lebanon's major political factions argued over Hezbollah. Some called for Hezbollah's immediate disarmament, while others, including Prime Minister Fuad Siniura, claimed that Hezbollah was not a foreign force and was therefore exempt from the dictates of Resolution 1559. Yet others believe that Hezbollah should be disbanded and integrated into the regular Lebanese armed forces.

After the outbreak of the Israeli-Hezbollah War (Israeli-Lebanese War) in July 2006, Prime Minister Siniura insisted that Israel's continuing occupation of Lebanese territory in Shaba Farms was the primary cause of Hezbollah's activities. However, UN secretary-general Kofi Annan stated directly in January 2005 that Lebanon's position on Shaba Farms is invalid and that Israel's 2000 withdrawal from Lebanon was in accordance with the mandates set forth by various UN resolutions. In retrospect, UN Resolution 1559 may have been wishful thinking. To ask the still-weak Lebanese government and its army to disband all militias within Lebanon and to secure the nation from outside forces was not terribly realistic. Indeed, given the factionalism within Lebanese politics, the power of organizations such as Hezbollah, and the fact that Lebanon has been home to numerous militia groups for many years and retains other militias than Hezbollah, the likelihood of a peaceful and prosperous Lebanon was highly unlikely.

Paul G. Pierpaoli Jr.

See also

Hezbollah; Israel; Lebanon; Lebanon, Armed Forces; Lebanon, Civil War in; Lebanon, Israeli Operations against; Shaba Farms; Syria; United Nations, Role of

References

Gabriel, Richard. *Operation Peace for Galilee: The Israeli-PLO War in Lebanon.* New York: Farrar, Straus and Giroux, 1985.

Khalaf, Samir. *Civil and Uncivil Violence in Lebanon: A History of the Internationalization of Communal Conflict.* New York: Columbia University Press, 2004.

United Nations Special Commission on Palestine

Start Date: May 13, 1947
End Date: August 31, 1947

The United Nations Special Commission on Palestine (UNSCOP) was the United Nations (UN) committee that on August 31, 1947, recommended the partitioning of Palestine into a Jewish state and an Arab state with Jerusalem and Bethlehem remaining neutral areas. UNSCOP was formed on May 13, 1947, to study the so-called Palestine problem after the British government had informed the UN on February 14, 1947, that it would no longer administer the British Mandate for Palestine as directed by the League of Nations on September 29, 1923. UNSCOP's 11 member states (Australia, Canada, Czechoslovakia, Guatemala, India, Iran, the Netherlands, Peru, Sweden, Uruguay, and Yugoslavia) voted unanimously to terminate British administration. Seven of the 11 members issued the report eventually accepted by the UN General Assembly on November 29, 1947, that divided Palestine into independent Jewish and Arab states with well-defined borders. A minority report recommended a federal state uniting the two factions. No member recommended the Arab state proposal favored by the Arab Higher Committee.

World War II had left the United Kingdom unwilling and unable to bare the expense of its empire. The British were also facing a rising tide of violence in Palestine, where 80,000 British soldiers continued to be garrisoned. The Zionists, comprising just over a third of the population of Palestine, saw the British as pro-Arab and orchestrated legal and illegal immigration to Palestine in an attempt to bolster their numbers for what both they and the Arabs saw as an eventual war for Palestine. Other more radical Zionists, some of whom had fought with the British in World War II, attacked British facilities in Palestine. Both the Jews and the Arabs fought one another, and the British seemed incapable of quelling the violence. The British held a conference in London on February 7, 1947, seeking to resolve the issues between the Jews and the Arabs, but this proved impossible and led to the decision to cede the problem to the UN. The British government offered its recommendations on the future of Palestine when it detailed its administration of the mandate on April 2, 1947.

UNSCOP began its study in Palestine on June 15, 1947. The Jewish Agency cooperated with UNSCOP, but the Arab Higher Committee boycotted all the meetings and hearings and demanded the immediate creation of an independent Arab state. UNSCOP held two hearings, receiving reports and testimonies from the Jewish Agency and the government of Arab government Palestine before touring Jerusalem and Arab and Jewish settlements and cities throughout the mandate on July 4–17.

UNSCOP departed Palestine on July 20 and traveled to Lebanon, a visit that included an informal side trip to Damascus, Syria, on July 21. Hamid Franjiyya (Frangie) communicated the views of the Arab states to UNSCOP at a meeting in Beirut on July 22. UNSCOP's study included 13 public hearings and 4 private hearings involving testimony by representatives of 6 Arab states, 31 Jews, and 17 Jewish organizations.

The committee divided itself into four subcommittees and three working groups. One of these subcommittees visited King Abdullah I of Transjordan on July 25. During August 8–14 a subcommittee or its members met with Austrian, American, and British officials dealing with displaced persons (DP) in Europe and visited a hospital and camps in Germany and Austria servicing more than 26,000 adult and child DPs. More than 100 DPs were interviewed. The drama of the 1947 *Exodus* transport ship incident with 4,515 DP passengers (all Jewish, some orphaned children) occurred during the UNSCOP visit to Palestine. Two UNSCOP members were at the port of Haifa when the *Exodus* was towed there and the passengers deported on ships to Toulon, France. The *Exodus* deportees rejected disembarkation in France and began a 24-day hunger strike. UNSCOP members testified later that the plight of the DPs, the *Exodus* deportees in particular, helped shape their recommendations.

The whole committee held 39 private meetings. Additional meetings of its subcommittees and working groups were also held before UNSCOP began writing its report in Geneva on July 28. UNSCOP'S report began with a preface and was followed by four chapters of factual information and analysis. As part of this analysis, the report asserted that the League of Nations had committed itself to the creation of a Jewish state in Palestine and had not fulfilled that promise. UNSCOP also asserted that British policies had unfairly restricted Jewish immigration and land purchases to less than 6 percent of the land. Chapters 5–7 contained UNSCOP'S recommendations and proposals. The final chapter listed reservations voiced by some UNSCOP members and then detailed those reservations and some observations in the appendix.

UNSCOP'S August 31 partition plan allotted 56 percent of the land remaining in the mandate to the Jewish state. Although Palestine and Transjordan remained a single administrative unit until 1946, Transjordan was removed, over Zionist protests, on September 11, 1922, by the League of Nations from the geographical area to which the 1917 Balfour Declaration applied. Transjordan comprised 77 percent of the original mandate, leaving only 23 percent to be divided in UNSCOP'S partition. Jerusalem and its environs comprised 2 percent of the partition, leaving 42 percent of the non-Transjordan land for an Arab state. The land allotted to the Jewish state was 75 percent desert and was 61 percent Jewish in population. The population of the Arab partition was just over 2 percent Jewish, and the Jerusalem trusteeship was almost equal in Arab, Christian, Muslim, and Jewish inhabitants. UNSCOP's partition plan was rejected by the Arab Higher Committee on September 29, 1947, but was accepted by the Jewish Agency on October 2.

In early November UNSCOP determined May 14 as the recommended date for the dissolution of the British Mandate for Palestine and its partition. The UN General Assembly adopted Resolution 181, UNSCOP recommendations with minor revisions, with a two-thirds majority (33 to 13 and 9 others abstaining) on November 29, 1947. On March 12, 1948, UNSCOP informed the UN that it believed that dissolution would bring chaos and war to the region and on March 18 recommended that the UN attempt to maintain order and peace by assuming temporary trusteeship over Palestine. The UN responded by creating the Truce Commission for Palestine on April 23, 1948, to assist the UN Security Council in bringing peace and order to Palestine per UN Resolution 46.

The British Mandate for Palestine was dissolved, the partition was enacted, and the independent Jewish State of Israel was created at midnight Palestine time on May 14, 1948. Egypt, Syria, Jordan, Lebanon, and Iraq attacked Israel on May 15. The UN dissolved UNSCOP on May 20 believing that appointed mediator Count Folke Bernadotte, working with the Truce Commission, had a better chance at bringing peace to the region.

RICHARD M. EDWARDS

See also
Abdullah I, King of Jordan; *Exodus* Incident; Palestine, British Mandate for; Palestine, Partition of; Revisionist Zionism; United Kingdom, Middle East Policy; United Nations, Role of; United Nations Palestine Partition Plan

References
Berry, Mike, and Greg Philo. *Israel and Palestine: Competing Histories.* London: Pluto, 2006.
Gelvin, James L. *The Israel-Palestine Conflict: One Hundred Years of War.* New York: Cambridge University Press, 2005.
Grobman, Alex. *Nations United: How the United Nations Undermines Israel and the West.* Green Forest, AR: Balfour, 2006.
Harms, Gregory, and Todd Ferry. *The Palestine-Israel Conflict: A Basic Introduction.* London: Pluto, 2005.
Pappe, Ilan. *A History of Modern Palestine: One Land, Two Peoples.* Cambridge: Cambridge University Press, 2003.
United Nations, ed. *Basic Facts about the United Nations.* New York: United Nations, 2004.
———, ed. *The Origins and Evolution of the Palestine Problem, 1917–1988.* New York: United Nations, 1990.
———, ed. *Teaching about Palestine.* New York: United Nations, 1990.
Yiftachel, Oren. *Ethnocracy: Land and Identity Politics in Israel/Palestine.* Philadelphia: University of Pennsylvania Press, 2006.

United States, Middle East Policy

U.S. interest in the Middle East from a strategic perspective did not begin until the early 1940s, when the exigencies of World War II dictated that it pay increased attention to that region. Before that time, the U.S. government expressed little interest in the Middle East. It maintained only loose diplomatic and political relations with the region, deferring to the British and the French, who controlled the area after World War I. In the early 20th century, American petroleum companies had secured oil concessions in Iraq, Kuwait, Bahrain, and Saudi Arabia, but that was the extent of U.S. involvement until World War II. Worried about German and Italian efforts to seize oil fields and the strategic Suez Canal, the Americans assisted and fought with the British in defeating German and Italian forces in North Africa during 1941–1942. From this point on, securing the Middle Eastern oil fields became a major foreign policy objective of the United States.

In early 1943 as the tide of the war began to turn in favor of the Allies and the Axis threat to the Middle East receded, the United

U.S. Military and Economic Assistance to Israel (1950–2000)

Year	Assistance
1950	0
1955	32,700,000
1960	56,200,000
1965	65,100,000
1970	93,600,000
1975	778,000,000
1980	2,121,000,000
1985	3,376,700,000
1990	3,034,900,000
1995	3,102,400,000
2000	4,129,100,000

U.S. and Israeli flags fly over Tel Aviv on the day of U.S. ambassador James MacDonald's accreditation, March 29, 1949. (Hugo Mendelson/Israeli Government Press Office)

States began to challenge European colonialism in the region. President Franklin D. Roosevelt and his successor, Harry S. Truman, supported in principle the independence of Arab states in the Middle East. The government of Prime Minister Winston Churchill objected to the American position, but by the end of war, bankrupt and war-weary, the new Labour government of Clement Attlee was willing to release its hold on much of the region, although it retained a considerable interest in Egypt and the Suez Canal. With the onset of the Cold War, the British government increasingly deferred to the United States. For their part, the Americans sought to fill the power vacuum in the Middle East following the end of British and French rule and to challenge efforts by the Soviet Union to project its power and influence in the region.

The U.S. government sought to deny Soviet efforts to gain control of the Persian Gulf's oil fields, to acquire military bases and especially a port in the region, and to sponsor or promote procommunist or Soviet-inclined regimes. The creation of the Jewish State of Israel in May 1948 greatly complicated the politics of the Middle East and U.S. foreign policy, as it sparked the enduring Arab-Israeli conflict. It also put the United States in a delicate and arguably

untenable position. Washington supported Israel but at the same time sought to maintain friendly relations with Arab states, whose support for the Palestinians conflicted with close U.S. ties with Israel.

Owing to the strategic location of Greece and Turkey to the Middle East and the Mediterranean Sea, both countries became a part of U.S. Middle East policy in 1947. Bankrupt and facing severe domestic troubles from the war, Britain announced that it was abandoning its military and financial support for Greece against communist insurgents and its efforts to protect Turkey against Soviet encroachments. This prompted the United States in March 1947 to assume Britain's responsibilities in these nations. As such, the U.S. Congress appropriated $400 million in aid and secured the pro-Western governments of both countries. Thus, the Truman Doctrine, which pledged U.S. assistance to any nation fighting communism, began in the Middle East.

After including Greece and Turkey in the North Atlantic Treaty Organization (NATO), the United States sought to create a similar collective security arrangement for the Middle East proper. Initially known as the Baghdad Pact and signed in 1955, after an Iraqi nationalist government seized power in July 1958 it was renamed the Central Treaty Organization (CENTO) and then included Iran, Turkey, and Pakistan. Because of the weak military positions of its members, however, both the Baghdad Pact and CENTO offered a poor deterrence to Soviet aggression. In addition, once Iraq withdrew from the Baghdad Pact In 1958, none of the remaining members were Arab states. Even Arab countries friendly to the United States, such as Saudi Arabia, refused to align with either organization, preferring to maintain their independence and avoid being seen as American puppets and accused of serving American and, in the view of many Arabs, neocolonial and imperial interests.

Iran also figured prominently as an American ally until the 1979 revolution there. In August 1953, U.S. and British intelligence agencies engineered a coup that deposed the nationalist prime minister of Iran, Mohammad Mosaddeq, after he nationalized the Anglo-American Oil Company. The bloodless coup restored to full power the pro-Western shah Mohammad Reza Pahlavi II. In the ensuing decades, the United States equipped the shah's military with advanced weapons and trained his secret police, the Sazeman-e Ettelaat va Amniyat-e Keshvar (SAVAK, National Information and Security Organization), to consolidate and secure the shah's power and crush all political dissent. Indeed, by the early to mid-1970s, Iran was the bulwark of U.S. foreign policy in the Middle East. In 1979 an Islamic fundamentalist revolution deposed the shah and installed a theocratic government, which because of staunch U.S. support for the shah was rabidly anti-American. The United States and Iran remain bitter rivals to this day, and as recently as 2003 President George W. Bush labeled Iran a member of the so-called axis of evil along with North Korea and Saddam Hussein's Iraq.

Successive U.S. administrations regarded Israel as an important ally against Soviet efforts to influence the region. This was particularly the case after 1953, when the Soviet Union under Nikita Khrushchev actively sought to challenge and undermine American

The U.S. Navy Military Sealift Command supply ship *Spica* (T-AFS 9) and aircraft carrier *George Washington* separate following a scheduled underway replenishment in the Persian Gulf. The ships were involved in enforcing United Nations (UN) sanctions against Iraq, November 26, 1997. (Erik Kenney/U.S. Department of Defense)

influence in the region by fostering closer ties and providing economic and military aid to Arab states such as Egypt, Syria, and Iraq.

The United States has enjoyed a close and strong relationship with Israel since 1948. Various reasons explain this special relationship, as it is sometimes called. Humanitarian factors—guilt over the Holocaust and the sympathy it created for both its victims and survivors—was a major reason behind U.S. support for the establishment of Israel. In addition, the fact that Americans regarded Jews arriving in Palestine as settlers or pioneers, much like the early English colonists to North America, almost certainly elicited a sense of communion. Culturally, despite obvious differences in faith, because many Jews were Westernized and thus viewed as less foreign or alien than Arabs, this fostered a sense of cultural affinity among many Americans. Also, the establishment of a democratic government in Israel created an instant political bond between both nations. Many Evangelical Christians supported the establishment of Israel and remain among its staunchest defenders. Finally, along with his Christian faith, electoral considerations certainly played a role in President Truman's decision to recognize Israel in 1948. Indeed, the powerful Jewish bloc of voters clearly contributed to his reelection that November. Since then, the political and financial success of Jewish interest groups—such as the American Israeli

Public Affairs Committee (AIPAC)—continues to exert major influence on both Congress and the White House, far surpassing the influence of the Arab states. Given Israeli's strategic location and growing military might, Washington believed that the Jewish state would become the regional power and offer an effective way to check Soviet ambitions. Not surprisingly, over time many Arab states either allied themselves or at least fostered closer ties with the Soviet Union because of the strong U.S. support for Israel.

Although the United States has provided economic assistance to Israel since its inception, until the late 1960s France was Israel's main patron and supplier of military aid. The United States remained decidedly neutral or aloof from the Arab-Israeli conflict until the late 1960s. After the June 1967 Six-Day War, however, U.S. president Lyndon B. Johnson fostered much closer ties with Israel, and the United States became its main supplier of military weapons, thereby establishing the precedent for subsequent U.S. military sales to the Jewish state, a policy that has continued to this day. Acting on the belief that by the late 1960s many Arab states, particularly Egypt and Syria, had decisively drifted into the Soviet orbit, Washington established much closer ties with Tel Aviv. The Soviets, meanwhile, severed diplomatic relations with Israel in 1967. In this context, Israel became a far more important ally to the Americans and was a key player in its foreign policy. During the October 1973 Yom Kippur War, the United States mounted a major airlift to resupply Israel's besieged military after it suffered heavy casualties in the opening days of the war following the surprise Egyptian-Syrian attack.

With respect to the Arab-Israeli conflict, the United States has generally been very supportive of Israel despite sometimes pressuring Israel to negotiate with its Arab neighbors or relinquish its control of occupied Arab lands. Such was the case during the 1956 Suez Crisis, when President Dwight D. Eisenhower ordered the Israelis to pull back from the Suez Canal. It was also evident in the late 1970s, when President Jimmy Carter sought to secure a peace treaty—the 1978 Camp David Accords—between Israel and Egypt that brought Israel's withdrawal from the Sinai, which it had captured in 1967. By the 1980s, U.S. aid to Israel was approximately $3 billion annually, and Washington continued its policy of equipping Israel with some of the most advanced weapons to assure its military superiority. It also implemented a free trade agreement in 1985 eliminating all tariffs between both countries.

At the same time, however, over Israeli objections, the United States has repeatedly sold military weapons to friendly Arab states, particularly Egypt and Saudi Arabia. Saudi Arabia figured prominently in U.S. foreign policy owing to its large oil reserves and generally pro-American leaders. As early as 1943, in fact, the United States provided military aid to the kingdom and constructed an air base at Dhahran. American policymakers especially relished King Ibn Saud's anticommunism.

One area of noticeable friction between the United States and Israel, particularly during the late 1980s and 1990s, was the Israeli policy of constructing settlements in the occupied Arab territories of the Gaza Strip and the West Bank. In 1989, U.S. secretary of state James Baker went so far as to denounce Israel's expansionist policies, and President George H. W. Bush refused to grant loans to Israel if such funds were to be used to construct Israeli settlements in the occupied territories. This caused significant friction with Israeli prime minister Yitzhak Shamir.

Following the Persian Gulf War of 1991, the Middle East peace process accelerated with the hosting of the Madrid Peace Conference followed by the signing of the Oslo Peace Accords on September 13, 1993, between Israel and the Palestine Liberation Organization (PLO) and a peace treaty between Israel and Jordan in 1994. Subsequent negotiations between Israel and the Palestinians have failed to build on the Oslo Accords, however, despite active U.S. sponsorship and participation in such talks by U.S. presidents Bill Clinton and George W. Bush.

Peace talks between Israel and Syria remain deadlocked and show no sign of resolution in the near future. Under President George W. Bush, the United States supports an independent Palestinian state but insists that parties such as Hamas must formally recognize Israel and cease all talk of resistance and that all acts of terrorism against Israel must end. The United States has consistently favored the land for peace option to resolving the Arab-Israeli conflict and regards states that sponsor or support terrorism against Israel (such as Syria and Iran) as enemies of peace.

Iraq's invasion of Kuwait on August 2, 1990, led the United States to organize a multinational coalition to compel Iraq's withdrawal and, following the failure of diplomacy, launch Operation DESERT STORM, a sustained air and then ground offensive that routed and expelled the Iraqi military from Kuwait in late February 1991. The decision of the United States to repel Iraq's invasion of Kuwait was prompted by the fear that Iraq might invade Saudi Arabia and seize its northern oil fields located near the border with Kuwait. If Iraq were allowed to retain control of Kuwait's vast oil reserves, much less seize those of Saudi Arabia, Iraq would control a large share of the world's oil supply and thus potentially might engage in oil blackmail. Highly dependent upon Middle Eastern oil for its economy, the United States was unwilling to allow the free flow of oil to be threatened. Arab states were members of the coalition against Iraq, and for that reason the United States put heavy pressure on Israel not to attack Iraq in response to Iraqi Scud surface-to-surface missiles launched against Israel. Washington feared that if Israel entered the war, the Arab states would leave the coalition. The United States supplied Patriot missiles to Israel and was able, despite the missile attacks, to keep the Jewish state from intervening.

The September 11, 2001, terrorist attacks on the United States committed President Bush to waging the so-called war on terror against the terrorist organization Al Qaeda and other terrorist groups and any country that harbors or supports them. The Americans launched an attack and invasion of Afghanistan in early October 2001 (Operation ENDURING FREEDOM) to overthrow the Taliban government that had offered sanctuary to the Al Qaeda terrorist network. By December the Taliban had been routed, but the extent

of Al Qaeda's losses remains unknown. A provisional government for Afghanistan was established that same month followed by democratic elections for president in 2004 and for the legislature in 2005. A recent escalation in Taliban attacks in Afghanistan has raised fears of a resurgent threat posed by the Taliban. There are currently 20,000 U.S. troops in Afghanistan along with 40,000 troops from NATO member countries. These troops remain active in defending the country and government against Taliban and Al Qaeda forces.

In March 2003 the United States and Great Britain invaded Iraq—with a weak coalition of several other nations—and overthrew Hussein's government. President Bush justified the invasion by alleging Hussein's pursuit of weapons of mass destruction (WMDs) and ties to terrorism, including Al Qaeda. Following the end of the Persian Gulf War in 1991, per United Nations (UN) Resolution 687 (April 3, 1991) Hussein agreed to disable all of his WMDs. After 12 years of defiance and violating 10 subsequent UN resolutions demanding Iraqi disarmament, Bush justified the invasion as the only way to enforce the will of the UN and assure that Iraq would never pose a threat to the region.

The U.S. government claimed that Iraq had failed to disarm and remained in possession of stockpiles of WMDs, including biological, chemical, and nuclear materials. As of late 2007, however, no WMDs have been found. Nor have any direct links between Hussein and Al Qaeda ever been determined. This has led critics of the Bush administration to suggest that the president at the very least deliberately exaggerated the threat posed by Iraq to convince Congress and the American public to support the war. Defenders of the administration point out that before the war many of these same critics believed that Hussein had not disarmed and remained a threat. The Bush administration failed, however, to persuade the UN to authorize military action against Iraq and invaded Iraq on March 20, 2003. While most of the world denounced the invasion as illegal, the Bush administration defended its actions, claiming that UN Resolution 687 authorized any state "to use all necessary means . . . to restore international peace and security in the area." What has become abundantly clear, however, is that U.S. intelligence gathering and the interpretation of that intelligence leading up to the war were deeply flawed.

As to the claim that Iraq had ties with Al Qaeda, in his 2003 State of the Union address Bush declared that "Saddam Hussein aids and protects terrorists, including members of Al Qaeda," and warned that he might even supply WMDs to Al Qaeda. Bush therefore sought to link the overthrow of Hussein with the war on terror. No links between Al Qaeda and Hussein have yet to be uncovered. In the absence of finding stockpiles of WMDs, Bush has recast the reason for going to war from one of disarming Hussein to promoting democracy in Iraq. In a speech on September 11, 2006, he equated the war on terror with the U.S. struggle against fascism during World War II.

Less than one month after the invasion of Iraq, Hussein's government fell. Although the war resulted in a seemingly quick and decisive victory with limited resistance from Iraq's military, the aftermath of the invasion has proven far more problematic and bloody. American forces faced much difficulty and were criticized for not aggressively restoring order in the wake of the collapse of Hussein's government. They were also blamed for allowing mass looting, including that of military depots, providing a significant source of ammunition and weapons for the subsequent insurgency. The disbanding of the Iraqi Army immediately after the war is regarded as another critical mistake contributing to the disorder, if not anarchy, in the country.

By the summer of 2003 remnants of Hussein's military forces began attacking American forces, leading to an insurgency characterized by guerrilla warfare and acts of terrorism including hundreds of car bombings. In response, a series of American military operations was launched to suppress the insurgency. Also since 2003, the insurgency included radical Islamist militias in Iraq. Elections were held in January 2005 to select an assembly to draft a new constitution followed by elections in December of that year to seat a new parliament. Despite the establishment of a democratically elected government, the violence continues and has escalated into intersectarian conflict, mainly between Sunnis and Shias, as well as attacks on coalition troops and the newly reconstituted Iraqi military and police.

Critics of the war in Iraq contend that it has not only distracted the nation from the war on terror but has actually made the United States less safe because the war has served as a rallying call for Islamic terrorism. In the meantime, the United States also faces a challenge from Iran in a generally held belief that Iran is seeking to acquire nuclear weapons. Resolution to that crisis remains elusive.

STEFAN BROOKS

See also

France, Middle East Policy; Iraq War; Persian Gulf War; Sinai Campaign; Six-Day War; Soviet Union and Russia, Middle East Policy; Suez Crisis; Terrorism; United Kingdom, Middle East Policy; Yom Kippur War

References

Buckley, Mary, et al. *The Bush Doctrine and the War on Terrorism: Global Reactions, Global Consequences.* New York: Routledge, 2006.
Gaddis, John Lewis. *Surprise, Security and the American Experience.* Cambridge: Harvard University Press, 2005.
Hahn, Peter L. *Crisis and Crossfire: The United States and the Middle East since 1945.* Dulles, VA: Potomac Books, 2005.
Little, Douglas. *American Orientalism: The United States and the Middle East.* Chapel Hill: University of North Carolina Press, 2004.
Terry, Janice. *U.S. Foreign Policy in the Middle East: The Role of Lobbies and Special Interest Groups.* London: Pluto, 2005.

United States Coordinating and Monitoring Mission

Start Date: June 2003
End Date: January 2004

The United States Coordinating and Monitoring Mission (USCMM) was part of the peace initiative known as the Road Map to Peace in the Middle East. Established in June 2003 by the administration of President George W. Bush, the initial task of the USCMM was to test the hypothesis that both sides in the conflict were ready to take the hard steps necessary to achieve a two-state solution and a stable peace. The experience of the USCMM proved that this was an invalid assumption for both the Palestinian and Israeli sides in 2003 at the height of the Second (al-Aqsa) Intifada.

The chief of the USCMM was Ambassador John Wolf, the assistant secretary of state for nonproliferation. He assumed the USCMM mission while retaining his portfolio in the Nonproliferation Bureau. Wolf reported directly to both Secretary of State Colin Powell and National Security Adviser Condoleezza Rice. Wolf's chief of staff was Joseph Pritchard. Wolf was also assisted by a political adviser, an economics adviser, an intelligence adviser, and a police adviser. Initially there was no military representation on the USCMM. Recognizing the need for military expertise in dealing with the Israel Defense Forces (IDF) and the multitude of Palestinian security organizations, Wolf through the State Department requested the assignment of a general officer to serve as the senior security adviser.

The USCMM established its operating base at the U.S. Consulate in West Jerusalem. The U.S. embassy in Tel Aviv was the official U.S. policy mission to the Israelis. The U.S. consulate in Jerusalem, which unlike any other American consulate in the world reported directly to the State Department and not to an embassy, was the official policy mission to the Palestinians. In 2003 the USCMM was the only official U.S. element that talked to both sides.

In early August Wolf returned to Washington for the visits by Israeli prime minister Ariel Sharon and Palestinian prime minister Mahmoud Abbas. On August 10 Major General David T. Zabecki and his executive officer, Major Kevin Mills, joined the USCMM in Jerusalem. For the first several weeks Zabecki was also assisted by Colonel Philip J. Dermer, a former foreign policy adviser to Vice President Richard Cheney. Although Zabecki worked for Wolf, he also reported directly to the Joint Staff in Washington through the director for strategic plans and policy (J-5).

One of the major security challenges was the 11 or more Palestinian security organizations, each one its own little feudal fiefdom, reporting to different masters and competing for power with each other as well as the various militant groups. Another challenge was the initial truce, or *hudna,* that had been called unilaterally by Hamas and Palestinian Islamic Jihad—but not the al-Aqsa Martyrs Brigades and other militant groups—for a 45-day period. Israel continually accused the Palestinians of using the relative calm of the *hudna* to regroup and rearm in preparation for future attacks. The Palestinians accused Israel of using the *hudna* to expand settlements and outposts and to hunt down militant leaders. Finally, the Israelis claimed that outside actors, including Iran, Syria, and Hezbollah in Lebanon, were expending significant efforts and resources to defeat any possibility of peace and stability between the Israelis and Palestinians.

Wolf initially established a plan based on a matrix of nine spheres on which the USCMM would continually evaluate Israeli

Israeli prime minister Ariel Sharon, U.S. president George W. Bush, and Palestinian prime minister Mahmoud Abbas following their meeting about the Road Map to Peace at the Beit Behar Palace in Aqaba, June 4, 2003. (Menahem Kahana/epa/Corbis)

and Palestinian performance. He called these spheres "baskets." The Israeli baskets included Palestinian quality of life in the occupied territories, Israeli settlements and outposts, Palestinian prisoners, and Palestinian Authority (PA) revenues. The Palestinian baskets included PA institutional reform, incitement, and security performance, which meant bringing the militant groups under control. The shared basket between the two sides was security cooperation, which focused on the phased handover of West Bank cities to Palestinian security control. Progress in resolving the issues in the baskets was used as a gauge of political will, with the idea that additional monitoring assets would be committed as the performance on both sides produced concrete results.

To support the expanded monitoring, Zabecki and Dermer developed a plan to field five monitoring teams of two monitors and one translator each to engage both sides daily in the field. At any given time two teams would work in the West Bank, one team would work in the Gaza Strip, one team would be used for rapid response to any breaking incident, and one team would be off duty but available as a reserve. The plan called for the monitors to be recruited from retired military or State Department personnel with extensive experience in the region. Until the teams could be recruited, trained, equipped, and fielded, Zabecki, Dermer, and Mills plus Colonel

Roger Bass and Lieutenant Colonel Warren Gunderman of the U.S. Military Attaché's Office in Tel Aviv conducted numerous monitoring missions in the occupied territories to test out the monitoring procedures and to establish USCMM presence and freedom of movement.

Wolf returned to Washington briefly on August 16. At a meeting at Israeli Ministry of Defense headquarters in Tel Aviv on August 19, Major General Giora Eiland, the IDF chief of J-5, briefed Zabecki on the basic outline of a meeting he was to have with his Palestinian counterparts in the West Bank that night to negotiate the final details for the handover of several cities to Palestinian security control. That was one of the most hopeful signs of progress that the USCMM had seen so far. At about 9:30 p.m., however, as Eiland was en route to his meeting, a Palestinian suicide bomber blew up a bus in Jerusalem, killing 23 and wounding 136. Eiland turned around before reaching his destination. On August 21 an IDF helicopter strike killed Hamas leader Ismail Abu Shanab in Gaza. Shortly thereafter, Hamas and PIJ called off the *hudna*. (Hamas reinstated a *hudna* later in 2004.)

Wolf returned to Jerusalem on August 20 and tried to keep both sides talking to each other. On August 26 Wolf and Zabecki met with Palestinian minister for state security Muhammad Dahlan in Gaza to discuss what to do with three arms smuggling tunnels in Rafah and a number of Qassam rockets that had been seized by Dahlan's Preventive Security Organization (PSO). Just as Wolf and Zabecki were leaving Gaza, the IDF launched an air strike into Gaza City in an attempt to kill another Hamas leader. The presence of the two senior members of the USCMM inside Gaza at the time of the strike was a blow to the mission's credibility with the Palestinians.

Wolf continued to work relentlessly on the senior political leadership on both sides, especially on issues related to the exact route of Israel's West Bank security barrier. Zabecki continued to work with the IDF and the wide range of various Palestinian security figures. On August 28 Zabecki, Bass, and Mills were conducting a reconnaissance mission inside Gaza when they received reports of a Qassam rocket firing that almost hit the main power plant at Ashkalon. Leaving the strip, the monitors proceeded to the impact site to access the damage, which was negligible. On September 3 Zabecki met with military intelligence officers at the IDF's Southern Command headquarters in Beersheba to discuss various options to help Dahlan's PSO deal with the Rafah tunnels.

The point at which the USCMM's prospects for any real success began a major decline came on September 6 with the resignation of Abbas as Palestinian prime minister following his long-running dispute with Yasser Arafat. No other Palestinian leader had the trust and credibility with both the Israelis and the Americans, not Abbas's successor, Ahmed Qurei, and certainly not Arafat himself, with whom the Americans and Israelis had long since refused to deal. Nonetheless, the USCMM continued to push forward. On September 13 Mills and Pritchard returned to Washington to conduct initial interviews for members of the monitoring teams. On September 23 Zabecki flew to Germany to interview the lead candidate to be the operations officer of the monitoring teams.

On September 24 a USCMM convoy was fired on in Gaza in the vicinity of Beit Hanoun while police adviser John Collins was visiting Palestinian police stations. Three members of Palestinian Islamic Jihad were later arrested and charged. Wolf, meanwhile, was recalled to Washington on September 25 while the U.S. government continued to access the developing situation with the new Qurei government.

Zabecki returned to Jerusalem on October 1. Maintaining daily phone and email contact with Wolf, Zabecki continued to work the circle of security contacts on both sides and develop the plans to field the monitoring teams. On October 6 Qurei issued a statement that his government would not clamp down on the Palestinian militant groups, further decreasing the chances that Wolf would return to Jerusalem any time soon.

On October 15 Zabecki, Mills, and Pritchard were conducting a reconnaissance mission in the West Bank's Jordan Valley when at 10:15 a.m. they received a report that a U.S. diplomatic convoy in Gaza had been hit by a roadside improvised explosive device. The convoy had been carrying personnel from the embassy in Tel Aviv to interview Fulbright Scholarship candidates in Gaza. The attack occurred at nearly the exact same point where the USCMM convoy

had been attacked almost three weeks earlier. This time three American security guards, John Eric Branchizio, John Martin Linde, and Mark Thaddeus Parsons, were killed in the blast. A fourth guard, Oscar Inhosa, was seriously wounded. Upon receiving the report, the USCMM team broke off their mission and immediately returned to Jerusalem. Despite all sorts of pronouncements from various Palestinian leaders, no one was ever brought to justice for the attack. Many Palestinian newspapers immediately accused the Mossad of conducting the attack.

The USCMM mission was now all but dead. From that point on Zabecki had no more official contact with Palestinian security officials and only pro forma contacts with the IDF. On October 20 the United States informed the Israeli government that Wolf would not be returning to the region for the time being. After a final out-briefing at IDF headquarters in Tel Aviv on October 30 with Eiland and his deputy, Brigadier General Eival Gilady, Zabecki and Mills departed Israel on November 1 and returned to their home base in Heidelberg, Germany. The remaining members of the USCMM left within days. For the next two months all the members of the USCMM remained on standby, assigned to the mission and ready to return should the situation change. As late as January 5, 2004, Secretary of State Powell told the *Washington Post* that Wolf might be sent back to the region. On January 23 the Defense Department withdrew General Zabecki from the mission.

DAVID T. ZABECKI

See also

Abbas, Mahmoud; Al-Aqsa Martyrs Brigades; Arafat, Yasser; Dahlan, Muhammad Yusuf; Hamas; Improvised Explosive Devices; Intifada, Second; Islamic Jihad, Palestinian; Mossad; Palestinian Authority; Preventive Security Organization, Palestinian; Qassam Rocket; Qurei, Ahmed Ali Mohammed; Rafah Tunnels; Rice, Condoleezza; Sharon, Ariel; Wolf, John Stern

References

Leverett, Flynt, ed. *The Road Ahead: Middle East Policy in the Bush Administration's Second Term*. Washington, DC: Brookings Institution Press, 2005.
Moens, Alexander. *The Foreign Policy of George W. Bush: Values, Strategy and Loyalty*. Aldershot, Hampshire, UK: Ashgate, 2004.

Unmanned Aerial Vehicles

Unmanned aircraft flown by remote control and formerly known as remotely piloted vehicles (RPVs). Israel has led the world in pioneering development and use of unmanned aerial vehicles (UAVs) as both reconnaissance and strike platforms. Equipped to provide instantaneous and nearly continuous transmission of their collected information, Israeli UAVs have provided the Israel Defense Forces (IDF) a significant advantage in any confrontation against their foes.

After suffering surprisingly heavy losses to Egyptian SA-6 surface-to-air missiles (SAMs) during the early days of the Yom Kippur War of 1973, the Israeli Air Force decided to examine more expendable

Journalists viewing a display of Israel's latest unmanned reconnaissance aircraft at the Israel Aircraft Industries workshop, May 1989. (Tsvika Israeli/ Israeli Government Press Office)

unmanned platforms to meet its battlefield reconnaissance requirements. The inventors Reginald Denny and Yehuda Manor built Israel's first UAV, then known as an RPV, in Manor's garage. The prototype, however, crashed.

Alvin Ellis, an engineer who had been born and raised in the United States but immigrated to Israel in 1967 to work on the Kfir fighter, thought that the Denny-Manor design had promise and convinced officials at Tadiran, the Israeli electronics conglomerate, to fund a second prototype. Designated the Mastiff, it first flew in 1973. It featured a pusher-propeller and twin-boom tail configuration. The Mastiff drew little official interest, despite its impressive TV and data-link system that provided live video coverage of the targeted area.

Interest in the Mastiff changed with Operation PEACE FOR GALILEE, Israel's 1982 invasion of Lebanon. Operations there involved the air force's daily exposure to Syrian SAM systems in that country and necessitated nearly continuous surveillance of Hezbollah and other terrorist group movements in the Bekáa Valley and other difficult terrain areas. The Mastiff has a launch weight of 304 pounds and a payload of 81 pounds. It has a wingspan of 13.9 feet and a length of 10.8 feet. Its 7.5-hour flight endurance fulfilled Israel's area surveillance requirements, and it proved all but impervious to Syrian

and terrorist air defense systems. It has a speed of about 115 miles per hour (mph) and a ceiling of 14,700 feet. By 1984, the Israelis were employing the Mastiff and the virtually identical in configuration but slightly smaller Scout, also known as Zahavan (Oriole), almost continuously over southern Lebanon, enabling Israeli forces to monitor and strike Hezbollah and other terrorist group movements there.

The Mastiff and Scout remained in service with the IDF until the early 1990s, when they were replaced by the larger Searcher, also known as the Meyromit ("high flier"). With a wingspan of 25 feet and a length of 16.7 feet, the Searcher is about twice the size of the Scout. It has an endurance time of 12 hours, a launch weight of 990 pounds, and a payload of 150 pounds. An improved Searcher II has a wingspan of 28 feet and a length of 19.2 feet. With an endurance time of 18 hours, it has a launch weight of 1,100 pounds. The Searcher has a speed of 124 mph and a ceiling of about 17,000 feet.

Additionally, Israel employed another UAV, the former Harpy target drones, to find and attack Syrian SAM and radar sites during its many confrontations with Syrian forces in Lebanon. The Harpy is an antiradar loitering attack drone. It is a delta-winged aircraft with finlets on its wingtips and is driven by a pusher propeller. It has an endurance time of about 6 hours and a speed of about 115 mph. It has a wingspan of 6.8 feet and a length of 8.8 feet. Harpies patrol over the battlefield. When they sense a radar being turned on, they hone in on it, destroying the radar with their blast-fragmentation warheads. Israel has sold its UAVs to the United States, among other countries.

Recognizing the effectiveness of Israeli reconnaissance and targeting UAVs, Syria requested and received Soviet-built Tu-143 Rey UAVs. The Tu-143s were larger (more than 26 feet long) and were considerably faster than the Israeli UAVs. They also had a higher operating ceiling and did not linger over the target. Syria used them to take imagery of the Israeli-occupied Golan Heights and the Israeli-Lebanese border areas. However, the Reys were fairly easy to detect and engage, making their survival dependent upon the Israelis' fire–no fire decision.

More significantly, the Rey UAV lacked the real-time video data link found in all Israeli UAVs. Therefore, its reconnaissance pod had to be recovered and processed in order for Syrian authorities to benefit from its collection. Generally, the information was several hours old before any Syrian officials saw it, making it all but useless in a fluid battlefield situation, particularly against the generally mobile and tactically flexible Israeli military.

No Arab intelligence or reconnaissance system could match that of Israel for depth of coverage, speed of information delivery, or on-station surveillance time. Equally important, UAVs are far cheaper than manned aircraft and more expendable than the pilots who fly those planes. More than 32 nations now operate UAVs, all of which can be traced conceptually to the first Israeli models and to operations introduced over Lebanon in 1982.

CARL OTIS SCHUSTER

See also

Aircraft, Reconnaissance; Artillery, Antiaircraft; Hezbollah; Israel Defense Forces; Lebanon, Israeli Invasion of; Missiles, Surface-to-Air; Syria, Armed Forces; Yom Kippur War

References

Dunstan, Simon. *The Yom Kippur War, 1973.* 2 vols. Westport, CT: Praeger, 2005.
Munson, Kenneth. *Jane's Unmanned Aerial Vehicles and Targets, 1995–1996.* London: Jane's, 1996.
———. *World Unmanned Aircraft.* London: Jane's, 1988.
Taylor, John William Ransom. *Jane's Pocket Book of Remotely Piloted Vehicles.* New York: Collier, 1977.

Ussishkin, Menahem

Born: 1863
Died: 1941

Russian Zionist leader and president of the Jewish National Fund. Born in 1863 in Dubrovno, Mogilev District, Russia, Menahem Ussishkin received a traditional Jewish education and then attended the Moscow Technical Institute, from which he graduated as an engineer. A committed Zionist, as early as 1881 he had established a Jewish youth group and was working to promote the Hebrew language and Jewish culture as well as Jewish settlement in Palestine. He visited Palestine briefly in the mid-1890s and then returned to Russia to organize a Palestine settlement society there.

Ussishkin met Theodor Herzl in Vienna in 1896 and attended the First Zionist Conference at Basle, Switzerland, in 1897, where he acted as the Hebrew secretary. At the Second Zionist Congress Ussishkin was elected to the Actions Committee. He was heavily involved in fund-raising for settlements in Palestine. At the All-Russian Zionist Conference at Minsk in 1902, he suggested that Zionist youth cadres be established whereby young people would agree to work for the movement for a period of one or two years. Ussishkin visited Kishinev after the 1903 pogrom in that city and arranged for the settlement of pogrom orphans in Palestine.

Ussishkin strongly opposed the East Africa Scheme advanced at the Sixth Zionist Conference in Basle in 1903, considering it a "betrayal of historic Zionism," and was one of Herzl's principal opponents on this issue. Ussishkin's pamphlet *Our Program,* which he published in 1904, was a strong statement of his belief that Zionist activity in Palestine had to be centered on practical efforts such as land purchase and the establishment of settlements based on Labor Zionism. He also urged the establishment in Palestine of agricultural training farms and called for the formation of worker groups, the members of which would agree to work in Palestine for several years. Ussishkin's pamphlet proved a great inspiration to youths in the Second Aliya (1904–1914).

In 1906 Ussishkin became chairman of the Odessa Committee, which helped raise considerable settlement funds. Following the Young Turk Revolution of 1908, he visited Constantinople and set up a Zionist Office there. During World War I he opposed the establishment of a Jewish fighting force on the British side, believing that this would jeopardize the Jews of Palestine, which he also did his utmost to assist.

Ussishkin was one of the Jewish representatives at the 1919 Paris Peace Conference following World War I and settled in Palestine later that same year. In 1923 following differences with Chaim Weizmann, Ussishkin failed to win reelection to the Zionist Executive, but that same year he was chosen president of the Jewish National Fund, an organization he headed until his death. Ussishkin was actively involved in land acquisition in Emek Hefer and in the Jezreel and Beit She'an valleys and in the establishment of both agricultural settlements and the Hebrew University of Jerusalem. A strong opponent of the British plan to partition Palestine, he participated in the London Round Table Conference (St. James Palace Conference) of 1939. Ussishkin died in the British Mandate for Palestine in 1941.

SPENCER C. TUCKER

See also

Aliya, Second; East Africa Scheme; Herzl, Theodor; Jewish National Fund; Kishinev Pogrom; Labor Zionism; Minsk Conference; Weizmann, Chaim; World Zionist Organization Executive; Zionism; Zionist Conference

References

Bar-Gal, Yoram. *Propaganda and Zionist Education: The Jewish National Fund, 1924–1947*. London: Boydell and Brewer, 2003.

Hirschmann, Ira. *The Awakening: The Story of the Jewish National Fund.* New York: Shengold, 1980.

Lehn, Walter. *The Jewish National Fund.* London: Kegan Paul, 1988.

Sachar, Howard M. *A History of Israel: From the Rise of Zionism to Our Time.* 3rd ed. New York: Knopf, 2007.

Shilonv, Zvi. *Ideology and Settlement: The Jewish National Fund, 1897–1914.* Jerusalem: Magnes Press, Hebrew University, 1998.

V

Valley of Tears, Battle of the
Start Date: October 6, 1973
End Date: October 9, 1973

When Syria launched its surprise attack at 2:05 p.m. on October 6, 1973, to open the northern front of the Yom Kippur War, Israel had only 177 tanks and 11 batteries of artillery on the Golan Heights. The Syrian attack force had some 900 tanks and 140 batteries of artillery, with another 600 tanks in reserve. Most of the Israeli tanks were British Centurions and American M-48s, and both types had been upgraded by the Israelis. Each of the three attacking Syrian infantry divisions had an armored brigade with Soviet T54/55 tanks. The two follow-on armored divisions and the brigade-sized Assad Republican Guard operated Soviet T-62s. The Syrian tanks were equipped with the most current night sights. The Israeli tanks had no such equipment.

Only days prior to the attack, Israeli armored presence on the Golan Heights had been even less. The entire front had been held by the 188th Armored Brigade, also known as the Barak Brigade, under the command of Colonel Yitzhak Ben Shoham. On September 26 the 77th Armored Battalion, known as Oz 77, was detached from the 7th Armored Brigade and deployed to the Golan Heights as a counterattack force in support of the Barak Brigade. On October 4–5, the remainder of the 7th Armored Brigade, commanded by Colonel Avigdor Ben Gal, also deployed to the Golan Heights.

When the Syrian attack came, the 74th Armored Battalion, commanded by Lieutenant Colonel Yair Nafsi, was occupying pre-established firing positions on high ground that ran from Tel Hermonit about three miles south to a strong point that the Israelis called Booster and the Arabs referred to as Tall al-Mehafi. The valley floor below the Israeli positions was covered by minefields and antitank barriers. In the first wave of the Syrian attack, Nafsi's tanks destroyed some 60 tanks of the Syrian 7th Infantry Division, commanded by Brigadier General Omar Abrash.

Late on October 6 Israeli northern front commander, Major General Yitzhak Hofi, ordered the 7th Armored Brigade to assume responsibility for the Golan Heights line from Quneitra north, with the Barak Brigade covering the southern sector. The 36th Armored Division, under Brigadier General Rafael Eitan, was the higher headquarters for the two brigades. Since the sector assigned to the 7th Armored Brigade also included the Booster position, the 74th Armored Battalion was detached from the Barak Brigade and reassigned to the 7th Armored Brigade.

Israeli tactics centered on long-range precision engagement and first-round hits. During the day, with the sun to their backs, the Israelis held the advantage. But after dark, the Israelis could no longer engage at the longer ranges. The Syrians, with their advanced night sights, then held the advantage. The Israelis also counted on their airpower to counter any enemy numerical advantages in tanks, but from the very start it became clear that the Syrian air defenses rendered any Israeli air attacks near suicidal. The opening phases of the fight for the Golan Heights became an almost pure tank-on-tank battle.

As the Syrians attacked throughout the night, the engagement ranges closed to as little as 100 yards. By dawn on October 7, more than 100 knocked-out Syrian tanks littered the valley floor in front of the Israeli positions. Later that morning the Syrian 78th Armored Brigade renewed the attack, as Ben Gal constantly shifted his battalions to meet the threat. Later that afternoon the 77th Armored Battalion, under Lieutenant Colonel Avigdor Kahalani, moved to the Booster positions. At 10:00 p.m. the Syrians attacked again, this time augmented by the 81st Armored Brigade of the 3rd Armored

Israeli Centurian tanks breaking through the Syrian lines on the Golan Heights, October 9, 1973. (Rami Lahover/Israeli Government Press Office)

Division, commanded by Brigadier General Mustafa Sharba. The Israelis had 40 tanks against 500. Using the darkness, the Syrian tanks got to within 50 yards, while Syrian infantrymen armed with rocket-propelled grenades attempted to infiltrate the Israeli positions.

About 1:00 a.m. on October 8 the Syrians broke off the attack and attempted to recover knocked-out vehicles. The Israelis called in artillery fire and rearmed and refueled their surviving tanks. The Syrians attacked again at 4:00 a.m., with Abrash withdrawing his decimated first echelon and committing his second. The battle waxed and waned throughout the day. Abrash planned another all-out assault for that night, but he was killed just at dusk when his command tank took a direct hit. Resumption of the Syrian attack was postponed.

Early on October 9 the Syrians hit the Israeli positions with a massive barrage of accurate artillery and rocket fire. Ben Gal ordered Kahalani to pull his battalion back 500 yards and then rush back into position as soon as the fire lifted. The Syrians, however, moved too fast and seized the Booster crest before the 77th Armored Battalion could reach it. Charging headlong into the smoke and dust and firing at point-blank range, Kahalani's command tank knocked out four Syrian T-62s within a minute and a half. In short order Oz 77 decimated two battalions of the Assad Republican Guard.

Other elements of the Republican Guard had managed to break through in the north and were driving toward El Rom, west of Tel Hermonit. General Eitan ordered the 71st Armored Battalion under Lieutenant Colonel Menachem Ratess to block the thrust, but Ratess was killed almost immediately. Ben Gal then ordered Kahalani to absorb the remnants of the 71st Armored Battalion and stop the Republican Guard. With a total of only 15 tanks, Kahalani attacked.

As the fighting on October 9 ground on, the 7th Armored Brigade was down to only 7 of the 105 tanks with which it had started the battle. Each tank had only about four rounds remaining. The remnants of the 7th Armored Brigade were completely surrounded and fighting at 360 degrees. Just as Ben Gal was about to order his surviving units to break contact and escape and evade, a relief force under Lieutenant Colonel Yosi Ben Hannan arrived on the battlefield. By scrounging tanks from the rear-area repair depots and pulling together pick-up crews of replacements and the lightly wounded, Ben Hannan had managed to assemble a force of 13 tanks.

Crashing into the Syrian left flank, Ben Hannan's tiny force knocked out 30 Syrian tanks in short order. The unexpected attack stunned the Syrians, who assumed that Ben Hannan's force was the point element of a large Israeli reserve that had finally reached the battlefield after mobilization. Just on the verge of punching through into northern Galilee, the Syrians broke contact and started to withdraw along the line. Behind them they left 260 tanks and 500 antipersonnel carriers and other vehicles littering the low ground beneath the Booster-to-Tel Hermonit ridge, a place that would become known as the Valley of Tears. The surviving members of the 7th Armored Brigade had been in combat for more than 50 straight hours.

Kahalani was later awarded the Medal of Valor, Israeli's highest combat decoration. He became one of only 40 Israeli soldiers ever so honored. Only eight Medals of Valor were awarded for the entire Yom Kippur War. Kahalani retired from the IDF as a brigadier general and in 1992 was elected to the Knesset (Israeli parliament).

DAVID T. ZABECKI

See also

Golan Heights; Hofi, Yitzhak; Israel Defense Forces; Tank Warfare; Tanks

References

Dunstan, Simon. *The Yom Kippur War, 1973.* 2 vols. Westport, CT: Praeger, 2005.

Herzog, Chaim. *The War of Atonement: The Inside Story of the Yom Kippur War.* London: Greenhill, 2003.

Kahalani, Avigdor. *The Heights of Courage: A Tank Leader's War on the Golan.* Westport, CT: Praeger, 1992.

Vanunu, Mordechai
Born: October 13, 1954

Israeli nuclear technician who made public Israel's possession of nuclear weapons. Mordechai Vanunu was born in Marrakech, Morocco, on October 13, 1954. His father was a rabbi. In 1963 the family immigrated to Israel, and Vanunu subsequently served three years in a sapper unit in the Israel Defense Forces (IDF), leaving as a sergeant. Following his military service he entered Ben-Gurion University, where he studied philosophy but did not graduate. Reportedly he joined several peace groups while a student.

Between 1976 and 1985 Vanunu was employed as a low-level technician at the Negev Nuclear Research Center near Dimona, involved in the development of nuclear weapons. Although most Western intelligence agencies assumed that Israel had indeed developed an atomic bomb, the Israeli government steadfastly refused to confirm or deny it. Laid off from his job in 1985, Vanunu left Israel. Traveling to Nepal, he considered converting to Buddhism. The

Israeli nuclear engineer Mordechai Vanunu (*center*) following his release from Shikma prison in Israel, April 21, 2004. (Avi Ohayon/Israeli Government Press Office)

next year he was in Sydney, Australia, where he worked at odd jobs. There he began to attend a local Anglican church and converted to Christianity and was baptized as John Crossman. In Sydney he also met Peter Hounam, a reporter for the London *Sunday Times.*

In September 1986 Vanunu flew to London with Hounam and, in violation of the nondisclosure agreement he had signed with the Negev Nuclear Research Center, sold the story of the Israeli development of nuclear weapons to the *Sunday Times* and also supplied photographs that he had secretly taken while an employee. Anxious to confirm the story (the *Sunday Times* had earlier paid a substantial sum to serialize a diary by Adolf Hitler that turned out to be an elaborate hoax), the paper consulted with experts before it would publish the story. Frustrated by the delay, Vanunu then went to the London *Sunday Mirror,* which may or may not have informed the Israeli government. In any case, aware of Vanunu's activities and anxious not to embarrass the British government of Prime Minister Margaret Thatcher, the Israeli Mossad intelligence service arranged for an attractive female agent, masquerading as an American tourist, to convince Vanunu to fly with her on vacation to Rome. Once there, Vanunu was drugged and smuggled out to Israel on a freighter.

Meanwhile, the *Sunday Times* published the Vanunu story and claimed in its report that Israel possessed perhaps 100 nuclear warheads. Vanunu was interrogated and subsequently brought to trial on camera in Israel. On February 27, 1988, he was sentenced to 18 years imprisonment to date from the time of his arrest. He was then kept in near total isolation for more than 11 years and refused any contact with the media. The Israeli government alleged that this was because it feared he would reveal more sensitive information, although foreign experts have disputed this, claiming that he did not possess any truly important information. Human rights organizations have claimed that this treatment was mere vindictiveness.

Vanunu was released from prison on April 21, 2004. Although he has expressed the desire to emigrate, the Israeli government has repeatedly refused to allow him to do so and has restricted his travel within Israel and denied him access to foreigners. It has also briefly retained him on several occasions since his release from prison. Numerous individuals, especially abroad, have claimed that Vanunu was a mere whistle-blower. Many in Israel, however, consider him to be a traitor.

Spencer C. Tucker

See also

Dimona, Israel; Mossad; Nuclear Weapons; Osiraq Raid

References

Cohen, Avner. *Israel and the Bomb.* New York: Columbia University Press, 1998.

Cohen, Yoel. *The Nuclear Ambiguity: The Vanunu Affair.* London: Sinclair-Stevenson, 1992.

Feldman, Shai. *Nuclear Weapons and Arms Control in the Middle East.* Cambridge, MA: MIT Press, 1997.

Gaffney, Mark. *Dimona: The Third Temple? The Story behind the Vanunu Revelation.* Brattleboro, VT: Amana, 1989.

Vatican, Relations with Zionism and Israel

Since Israel's founding in May 1948, relations between the Jewish state and the Vatican—the Holy See and city-state of Roman Catholicism—have been troubled. Although Israel and the Vatican established formal diplomatic relations in 1993, the Vatican has continued to criticize Israeli policies in the occupied territories and, most recently, in Lebanon during the July–August 2006 war between Israel and Hezbollah.

Prior to Israel's foundation, the Vatican had maintained a negative attitude toward the Zionist movement. Theodor Herzl, a Viennese journalist considered to be the founder of political Zionism, met with Pope Pius X in Rome in 1904, just prior to Herzl's death, hoping to establish relations with the Catholic Church. This kind of diplomacy was part and parcel of Herzl's maneuvering, as he was well aware of his movement's need to attract foreign support. Unfortunately for the Zionists, Pope Pius X claimed that he could not recognize the rights to the Holy Land of the group that the Catholic Church held responsible for the death of Jesus Christ. Furthermore, from a theological standpoint Pius indicated that the Jews would be welcome to become Catholics, but until that day he could not support their rights to Palestine.

The Catholic Church continued to ignore the Zionist movement through World War II and the Holocaust, and the Church under Pope Pius XII was criticized for its inaction in the face of the German extermination of some 6 million Jews. Following these calamitous events, most of the Western world came to support the need for a Jewish state. Just prior to the United Nations (UN) vote on partition in late November 1947, the Zionists were unsure of their chances to receive the two-thirds majority necessary to divide Palestine into an Arab and Jewish state. The Zionist leader, David Ben-Gurion, who later became the first prime minister of Israel, and other prominent Zionist politicians worried that the Vatican might lobby majority Catholic nations to oppose partition. Yet the Vatican, while never openly supporting partition or the creation of a Jewish state, chose not to lobby against Zionist goals. This was apparently because of the impending internationalization of Jerusalem, a city where the Catholic Church believed that it would be able to exert direct influence for the first time since the early crusade period.

During the Israeli War of Independence (1948–1949), which followed the UN decision to partition Palestine, Israeli forces occupied the western portion of Jerusalem while the Jordanians captured the eastern part, which included the Old City with its many key Jewish and Christian religious sites. This created an intolerable situation for the Vatican, which now went on the diplomatic offensive and successfully lobbied UN members to pass a resolution in 1949 stating that the international community still supported the internationalization of Jerusalem.

The Vatican, however, tended to view communism as the most significant threat to the post–World War II world order. Because of alleged Zionist sympathy for communism, the Vatican leadership came to fear that Israel would drift into the Soviet orbit, which added to Vatican animosity against the new state. The Israeli leadership in this period, however, continued to pursue a pro-Western orientation yet consistently refused Western and Church demands to internationalize Jerusalem. In fact, Israel shifted its capital from Tel Aviv to Jerusalem in this period, thus demonstrating its intent to retain permanent control over West Jerusalem. Zionist leadership believed that if they consolidated their position in the holy city, then the rest of the world would eventually accept the status quo. Furthermore, Jordan also announced its intent to annex East Jerusalem, making internationalization even less likely.

During the 1950s, Israel continued to send diplomatic feelers to the Vatican leadership but was repeatedly rebuffed. Domenico Tardini, a Catholic cardinal and the Vatican secretary of state in the late 1950s, was a constant thorn in Israel's side, as he refused to budge on the issue of Jerusalem. Israel hoped that its now avowed pro-Western orientation and the spread of Arab nationalism, believed to be linked to Soviet designs by many in the West, would convince the Vatican to open dialogue with the Jewish state. The Vatican, however, seems to have understood that while Arab leaders promoted pro-Soviet sentiments in international circles, in their own countries they cracked down on communist parties that were deemed hostile to their respective regimes. Israel was therefore unable to use anticommunism as a means by which to enter into negotiations with the Vatican.

By the 1960s, Israeli leaders had concluded that no progress could be made on the Vatican front and abandoned their diplomatic initiatives. In fact, even the Vatican's attempts at reconciliation with worldwide Jewry in the 1960s did not help Israel's quest to establish relations with the Church, although at least officially the Church no longer held the Jews responsible for the death of Jesus. In June 1967, believing itself about to be attacked by the Arab states, Israel preemptively attacked Egypt and Syria, sparking the Six-Day War. It also found itself at war with Jordan. During this conflict, Israel captured the Sinai Peninsula and the Gaza Strip from Egypt, the Golan Heights from Syria, and the West Bank and East Jerusalem from Jordan. Therefore, for the first time since the British Mandate period that had ended with partition, Jerusalem was again a united city, this time under Israeli jurisdiction. Israel's conquest of East Jerusalem, the West Bank, and Gaza also reintensified the Israeli-Palestinian conflict.

The Vatican was somewhat slow to abandon the idea of internationalization, but by the 1970s and 1980s the Vatican had begun to search for ways to resolve the Israeli-Palestinian conflict and to create a Palestinian national state. Although the Vatican was long preoccupied with the Jerusalem issue, it was also consistently concerned with the status of Christians, specifically Catholics, in the Holy Land. A significant number of Catholics also live in Lebanon.

Although the 1970s and 1980s witnessed the first high-level meetings between popes and Israeli prime ministers, it was not until the 1990s that Israeli-Vatican relations markedly improved. In November 1991 in the aftermath of the Persian Gulf War and in the midst of the First Intifada, U.S. president George H. W. Bush pressured Arab and Israeli leaders to come together for the first time to discuss the possibility of peace agreements. This meeting was held in Madrid and also led to back-channel negotiations between Israelis and Palestinians, which culminated in the signing of the Oslo Accords in 1993.

The Madrid Conference convinced the Vatican that the time was finally right to establish formal diplomatic relations with the Jewish state. Following a year of negotiations, Israel and the Vatican officially established diplomatic relations with one another on December 20, 1993. Since then, however, Israeli-Vatican relations have experienced problems. The breakdown of the Oslo-inspired peace process, the beginning of the Second (al-Aqsa) Intifada in 2000, and most recently Israel's 2006 war in Lebanon have led to public criticisms from the Vatican. From the Israeli perspective, however, the opening of relations with the Vatican in 1993 marked the official acceptance by world Catholicism that the Jews indeed deserved a state of their own and also implied that the Church accepted the Holy Land as the Jews' homeland.

Despite these setbacks, however, Vatican-Israeli relations were revolutionized in the 1980s and 1990s, due in no small measure to the efforts of Pope John Paul II, a great believer in ecumenical dialogue with other denominations and faiths. Indeed, the pope went to great lengths to heal the long and deep scars that had marred Jewish-Catholic relations. In 1979 he became the first pope to visit a Nazi death camp in Poland, his home nation. The pope reportedly had lost Jewish friends in the Holocaust. In 1986 he became the first pope to officially visit a synagogue. And in March 2000, the old and frail pontiff made a moving visit to Israel, where he prayed at the Yad Vashem Holocaust Memorial and touched the holiest place in Judaism, the Western (Wailing) Wall in Jerusalem. Most notably, he placed a letter into the wall in which he offered Jews an apology for their treatment by the Church in decades and centuries past. When John Paul II died in 2005, the Anti-Defamation League issued a tribute to the pope by saying that Vatican-Jewish relations had changed more in the pope's 27-year reign than in the previous 2,000 years. It remains to be seen whether John Paul II's successor, Pope Benedict XVI, will be as ecumenical in his dealing with Israel and Judaism. He has, however, incited controversy with his remarks about Islam.

PAUL G. PIERPAOLI JR.

See also

Herzl, Theodor; Holocaust; Jerusalem; Jerusalem, Old City of; John Paul II, Pope; Madrid Conference; Oslo Accords; Pius XII, Pope; Six-Day War; Western Wall; Yad Vashem Holocaust Memorial; Zionism

References

Berger, Marshall J. *The Vatican-Israel Accords: Political, Legal, and Theological Contexts.* South Bend, IN: University of Notre Dame, 2004.

Bialer, Uri. *Cross on the Star of David: The Christian World in Israel's Foreign Policy, 1948–1967.* Bloomington: Indiana University Press, 2005.

Kreutz, Andrej. *Vatican Policy on the Palestinian-Israeli Conflict: The Struggle for the Holy Land.* Westport, CT: Greenwood, 1990.

W

Wadi Araba

See Arabah

Wafd Party

See New Wafd Party

Wahhabism

A Muslim religious reform movement that appeared in central Arabia in the 1740s. The term "Wahhabi" was coined by foes of the reform movement in reference to the movement's founder, Muhammad ibn Abd al-Wahhab (1702–1792). Wahhabism derives its influence from its association with the Saudi dynasty. The unique feature of Wahhabism as a religious doctrine is its view of other Muslims as unbelievers, which makes them legitimate targets of Muslim holy war, or jihad. This view provided justification for the Saudi dynasty's military expansion in much of Arabia. In the modern kingdom of Saudi Arabia, Wahhabism is the official religious doctrine propagated in mosques and schools. When it comes to Saudi policy on the Arab-Israeli conflict, however, Wahhabism is subordinate to government calculations of the national interest.

Muhammad ibn Abd al-Wahhab was a religious scholar from a small town near the present-day Saudi capital of Riyadh. In 1740 he composed a theological essay condemning common Muslim religious practices. For example, many Muslims went to holy men to seek their blessings. Other Muslims visited the tombs of holy men to ask that they intercede with God on their behalf. Sheikh Muhammad considered such actions to be idolatry because they violated Islam's central belief in worshiping God alone without any inter-mediaries. Because Muhammad branded other Muslims as unbelievers, he became a controversial figure. He was expelled from two Arabian towns before he formed an alliance with Muhammad ibn Saud in 1744. Sheikh Muhammad gave religious legitimacy to Saudi military expeditions in the guise of Muslim holy war against unbelievers in return for Saudi political support.

By 1800, Saudi-Wahhabi forces had conquered much of Arabia. The major Muslim power of the time, the Ottoman Empire, responded to the Saudi conquest of the holy city of Mecca with a military campaign to crush the first Saudi state. That war lasted from 1811 to 1818 and ended in an Ottoman victory. However, the Saudis staged a comeback in the early 1820s to rule over a smaller Arabian realm. The second Saudi state refrained from aggression against Ottoman territories. Because the Saudis would not wage holy war, Wahhabi leaders urged followers to avoid all contact with outsiders, such as Egyptian or Iraqi Muslims, on the grounds that strangers were unbelievers whose company would threaten the purity of true Muslims' belief. The second Saudi state fell to a rival Arabian power in 1891.

The present Kingdom of Saudi Arabia began to emerge when Saudi prince Abd al-Aziz ibn Saud, also known as Ibn Saud, seized Riyadh in 1902. Over the next 30 years, he conquered the territories that presently comprise the Kingdom of Saudi Arabia. A major element in those conquests was a new branch of the Wahhabi movement called Ikhwan (Brethren). The Brethren were tribesmen who gave up their nomadic way of life to settle in agricultural communities, where they learned Wahhabi doctrine. The Brethren became fierce warriors for Wahhabism and gained a fearsome reputation for their savage treatment of defeated enemies. They provided the shock troops for Ibn Saud's military campaigns, but in the mid-1920s he had to restrain them from pursuing holy war against tribes in Iraq and Transjordan. At the time, those two countries were governed by British-appointed monarchs. Consequently, Brethren raids threatened to embroil Ibn Saud in a confrontation with Great Britain. When he ordered the Brethren to cease their raids they rose up in rebellion, but he was able to crush them by 1930.

Three years later, Ibn Saud granted American oil companies the right to explore for petroleum. Wahhabi clerics were unhappy to see Americans permitted into the kingdom, but Ibn Saud and the oil companies minimized contact between Saudis and foreign workers by creating special residential compounds for non-Saudis. The first test of U.S.-Saudi relations came in 1947, when the United States supported the United Nations (UN) resolution for the partition of Palestine into Jewish and Arab states. Ibn Saud made clear his opposition to the creation of Israel but was careful not to jeopardize his ties with American oil companies. The only time that Saudi opposition to U.S. support for Israel disrupted relations came during the October 1973 Yom Kippur War. Saudi Arabia's King Faisal responded to the U.S. emergency airlift of military supplies to Israel by imposing an embargo on oil sales and joining with other major oil producers to dramatically raise the price of oil.

Throughout the Cold War, Saudi Arabia joined forces with the United States to combat the spread of communism in the Muslim world. Saudi efforts included support for exporting Wahhabi doctrine, which is firmly anticommunist. It is also firmly anti-Jewish because of its attachment to historical religious texts emphasizing early clashes between the Prophet Muhammad and Jewish clans in Arabia. When it comes to setting foreign policy, however, Saudi rulers take a practical approach and only consult Wahhabi leaders when seeking their approval for sensitive initiatives. Hence, Saudi Arabia supported the Madrid peace process of the 1990s and announced a peace initiative in March 2002 for a comprehensive settlement of the Arab-Israeli conflict.

DAVID COMMINS

See also

Faisal, King of Saudi Arabia; Ibn Saud, King of Saudi Arabia; Jihad; Saudi Arabia

References

Bronson, Rachel. *Thicker than Oil: America's Uneasy Partnership with Saudi Arabia.* New York: Oxford University Press, 2006.
Commins, David. *The Wahhabi Mission and Saudi Arabia.* London: Tauris, 2006.
Kostiner, Joseph. "Coping with Regional Challenges: A Case Study of Crown Prince Abdullah's Peace Initiative." Pp. 352–371 in *Saudi Arabia in the Balance,* edited by Paul Aarts and Gerd Nonneman. London: Hurst, 2005.
Piscatori, James. "Islamic Values and National Interest: The Foreign Policy of Saudi Arabia." Pp. 33–53 in *Islam in Foreign Policy,* edited by Adeed Dawisha. Cambridge: Cambridge University Press, 1983.

Wailing Wall

See Western Wall

Waqf

Muslim religious trust or endowment. A Muslim must leave certain set shares of his estate to his heirs, but he may also create a waqf prior to his death from that estate. A waqf (plural awaqf) refers to a property that produces income and that may have been deeded to benefit a community. It is property that is not supposed to be seized by any state or government, and its legal status is mortmain. Awaqf have been the source of political conflicts in the Middle East, because both religious and political authorities could benefit from their control. Modern nations that do not strictly follow Islamic law have taken over awaqf in contravention to their intent. The status of awaqf under Israeli rule has been a very sensitive issue, since all awaqf were claimed by the Israeli government and administered by councils that were entirely non-Muslim or included non-Muslims.

The waqf apparently originated in Arabia before the rise of Islam. According to at least one story, the Prophet Muhammad established an endowment for the poor from an orchard that was willed to him. Over the next three centuries, more formalized rules for creating a waqf were established. The most important aspect was that a waqf was intended to be permanent and in perpetuity. Once property was included in a waqf, it could no longer be sold to other owners. The waqf might consist of real property that had permanence. An administrator was appointed by a religious court to manage the waqf and to ensure that its income went to the designated purpose. Wealthy Muslims often used the waqf to circumvent the laws of inheritance by having themselves or a single heir appointed to the administrative position. Income from the waqf was used to support religious institutions such as mosques, educational institutions, libraries, or charitable endeavors, including water systems or fountains for neighborhoods or hospitals.

In Palestine, up to 15 percent of the land was part of awaqf. Before Israel's independence in 1948, Jewish settlers controlled about 10 percent. The Israeli government saw the awaqf as a source of additional land. Before and during the Israeli War of Independence (1948–1949), most of the Muslim officials charged with administering awaqf in Israel fled the country. To administer the awaqf, the Israeli government established the office of the Custodian of Abandoned Property. The income from waqf lands was supposed to be used to support the religious and secular needs of Muslims who remained in Israel's borders. Funds for religious purposes were distributed by the custodian, while funds for secular needs were released by the Ministry of Religious Affairs.

On February 2, 1965, the Knesset (Israeli parliament) revised the method under which the waqf property was administered. The Alien Property Law, Regulation No. 3, released property from the waqf system. All awaqf that were established for individual families were liquidated, and the funds from their sale were given to the rightful heirs if they were not refugees or could establish a claim. Any waqf established for religious or charitable purposes was placed under appointed boards with the power to manage, sell, or dispose of the real property in the waqf. Critics charged that the legislation was only a cover for confiscating Arab land, however.

Following the 1967 Six-Day War, the waqf system in the West Bank survived with little change in ownership. Its survival helped to establish a national identity among the Palestinians in the region. Yasser Arafat appointed new officials in the Ministry of Awaqf after the establishment of the Palestinian Authority (PA).

The administration of the waqf in East Jerusalem is especially controversial and important because it administers Haram al-Sharif, which also claims ownership of the Wailing Wall. The Haram al-Sharif itself as well as the area of the Wailing Wall were within a historic waqf, and its seizure by the Israeli government was the source of the earliest disputes over the wall.

TIM J. WATTS

See also

Haram al-Sharif; Religious Sites in the Middle East, Jewish; Religious Sites in the Middle East, Muslim

References

Dumper, Michael. *Islam and Israel: Muslim Religious Endowments and the Jewish State.* Washington, DC: Institute for Palestinian Studies, 1994.

Heyneman, Stephen P. *Islam and Social Policy.* Nashville: Vanderbilt University Press, 2004.

Owen, Roger, and Martin P. Bunton. *New Perspectives on Property and Land in the Middle East.* Cambridge: Harvard University Press, 2000.

Reiter, Yitzhak. *Islamic Institutions in Jerusalem: Palestinian Muslim Organization under Jordanian and Israeli Rule.* Boston: Kluwer Law International, 1997.

Warburg, Otto
Born: July 20, 1859
Died: January 10, 1938

German botanist, Zionist, and president of the World Zionist Organization (WZO). Otto Warburg was born in Hamburg on July 20, 1859. He studied philosophy, mathematics, and science at the universities in Bonn and Berlin and at Strasbourg, where he earned a doctorate in 1883. He then pursued additional study in chemistry at Munich and botany at Tübingen. During 1885–1889 he traveled in Australia and the Far East studying plants. His scholarly books and articles soon made him a recognized authority in the field of botany. Active in German colonization efforts in Africa, he also founded several companies for producing cocoa and coffee and published monographs dealing with their production.

Although an assimilated Jew, Warburg became active in the Zionist movement through the influence of his father-in-law. He first met Zionist leader Theodor Herzl in 1898. Warburg was always interested in what he termed practical Zionism as opposed to theoretical Zionism. In 1899–1900 he toured the Middle East and visited Cyprus, where he explored the possibility of establishing Jewish

Otto Warburg, German botanist, Zionist, and president of the World Zionist Organization (WZO), May 1, 1911. (Zoltan Kluger/Israeli Government Press Office)

---

settlements. He also visited Palestine and Anatolia. Upon his return to Germany, he contributed articles to Zionist publications.

In 1902 Herzl asked Warburg to investigate the possibility of establishing a settlement at El Arish, but he refused because he did not think the area was an appropriate one for settlement, primarily because of the lack of water for irrigation. At the 1903 Zionist Conference in Basle, Switzerland, Herzl asked Warburg to chair the committee that would explore the possibility of a Jewish settlement in British East Africa, and he was also made chairman of the new Palestine Commission. In 1904 he reported his findings from the Uganda mission without expressing his own negative views about the proposal. He also participated in fund-raising to finance Jewish cultural activities in Palestine.

In 1905 Warburg was elected to the WZO's Inner Actions Committee, and he also became a governor of the Jewish National Fund. In 1911 he was elected president of the WZO, a position he held until 1920. He used this post to promote what he regarded as practical Zionist activity in Palestine, including the establishment of private companies to further economic development. In 1921 he traveled to the United States to raise funds, and in 1922 he went to Palestine to head, with Isaac Wilkansky, an agricultural research station at Tel Aviv, which later moved to Rehovot. On the opening of Hebrew

University, Warburg headed its Botany Department. He continued to spend some months out of every year in Germany, and he died in Berlin on January 10, 1938. The Otto Warburg Minerva Center for Agricultural Biotechnology of the Hebrew University of Jerusalem is named for him.

SPENCER C. TUCKER

See also

Assimilation; East Africa Scheme; El Arish Scheme; Herzl, Theodor; Jewish National Fund; World Zionist Organization

References

Brenner, Michael. *Zionism: A Brief History.* Translated by Shelley Frisch. Princeton, NJ: Markus Wiener, 2003.

Laqueur, Walter. *A History of Zionism: From the French Revolution to the Establishment of the State of Israel.* Reprint ed. New York: Schocken, 2003.

War of Atonement

See Yom Kippur War

War of Attrition

See Attrition, War of

Ward, William E.
Born: June 3, 1949

U.S. Army general and security coordinator for the Israel-Palestinian Authority (February–December 2005). William "Kip" Ward was born in Baltimore on June 3, 1949. He graduated from Morgan State University with a bachelor's degree in political science in 1971 and received a commission as an infantry officer through the Reserve Officers Training Corps (ROTC). In October 1993 he was a brigade commander in the 10th Mountain Division in Mogadishu, Somalia, when two Blackhawk helicopters were shot down and 19 American soldiers died in the subsequent rescue operation.

Promoted to brigadier general in March 1996, from February 1998 to July 1999 Ward served as the chief of the Office of Military Cooperation, Egypt, working out of the U.S. embassy in Cairo. Promoted to major general in February 1999, he then commanded the 25th Infantry Division in Hawaii and served as vice director for operations of the Joint Staff in Washington. Promoted to lieutenant general in October 2002, he was appointed to command the North Atlantic Treaty Organization (NATO) Stabilization Force in Sarajevo, Bosnia-Herzegovina and held that post until October 2003.

Ward was serving as the deputy commanding general of the U.S. Army, Europe, when in February 2005 during a trip to the Middle East, Secretary of State Condoleezza Rice announced his appointment to the newly established position of U.S. security coordinator, Israeli-Palestinian Authority. The coordinator's job was twofold: to

U.S. Army brigadier general William E. Ward, 1995. (U.S. Department of Defense)

---

assist the U.S. administration in its efforts to encourage the Israeli government to stay on track with its promise to disengage from Gaza and the northern West Bank and simultaneously to support new Palestinian Authority (PA) president Mahmoud Abbas in his efforts to bring the various Palestinian militant organizations under control and to gain positive control over the disparate and fractured Palestinian security organizations.

It was that second task, where all of Ward's predecessors had failed, that came close to being mission impossible. Under the long reign of Palestine Liberation Organization (PLO) head Yasser Arafat, the Palestinian military, police, and intelligence functions had evolved into a Byzantine network of overlapping feudal empires, as much in competition with each other as with the Israelis and the various militant groups. Compounding the problem, all too many of the members of the security forces were also members of militant groups. In May 2005 Ward announced the establishment of the Security Sector Working Group, composed of donors interested in supporting Palestinian security reform. The group was cochaired by Ward and Nasir Yusuf, Palestinian minister of the interior and national security.

In December 2005 Major General Keith Dayton replaced Ward as the U.S. security coordinator. Ward returned to U.S. Army, Europe, headquarters in Heidelberg, Germany. Shortly after his return to Europe he was appointed deputy commanding general of the U.S. European Command. He was promoted to general in May 2006.

Ward is currently the senior ranking African American in the U.S. Army.

DAVID T. ZABECKI

See also

Abbas, Mahmoud; Arafat, Yasser; Palestinian Authority; Rice, Condoleezza; United States Coordinating and Monitoring Mission; Wolf, John Stern; Zinni, Anthony

References

Balaban, Oden, and Michael Graham Fry, eds. *Interpreting Conflict: Israeli-Palestinian Relations at Camp David II and Beyond.* New York: Peter Lang, 2005.

Leverett, Flynt, ed. *The Road Ahead: Middle East Policy in the Bush Administration's Second Term.* Washington, DC: Brookings Institution, 2005.

Warships, Surface

The Israelis and Arab nations in the Middle East have generally given financial priority to their armies and air forces. Nevertheless, the navies of Egypt, Israel, and Syria increased significantly over time, and their development sheds light on changing technology, the international arms market, and the influence of the superpowers on the region. Much earlier in history, the Fatimid and Ottoman navies had been an important adjunct to armies in the region. In the first half of the 19th century, Muhammad Ali Pasha of Egypt built a large fleet and established a naval academy. However, by the mid-20th century the navies of the region had relatively few warships, generally aging gifts from the former colonial powers or converted civilian ships.

In the 1950s the Middle Eastern states took advantage of the ready availability of retired World War II warships to expand their fleets. As funds became available, they ordered new warships from a variety of West European shipyards. After 1955, the Soviet Union supplied Egypt and Syria with a growing number of modern warships. Israel countered this first by increasing its European purchasing and later by building its own warships, including missile-armed fast attack craft to counter Soviet-supplied missile boats in the Egyptian and Syrian navies.

Egypt returned to European builders in the 1980s, and both Egypt and Syria purchased warships from the People's Republic of China (PRC), which produces many designs similar to Soviet warships. Without Soviet financial support, however, Syria could purchase few new warships, and its navy declined markedly in the 1990s. Egypt continued to buy warships from the Chinese, but it also returned to purchasing from European builders and recently from the United States. Israel continued to develop its shipbuilding

An Egyptian Ramadan-class fast-attack missile craft, August 1983. (U.S. Department of Defense)

The Israeli Navy's prototype Barak missile-launching platform, INS *Hetz*, first of the Hetz-class guided missile boats, August 1991. (U.S. Department of Defense)

capacity and even exported warships to several countries, but it too ordered its newest warship from the United States.

The primary naval powers in the Arab-Israeli wars were Egypt, Israel, and Syria. Jordan and Lebanon never built significant navies, contenting themselves with a few patrol craft to police their ports. Israel's more distant antagonists, such as Iraq, never deployed their naval forces in these wars. The Egyptian Navy formed after World War II around a nucleus of former British warships, including minesweepers, fast patrol craft, and eventually frigates and destroyers. The Israeli Navy emerged from the preindependence force that smuggled Jewish refugees past the British blockade and into Palestine. Along with a handful of civilian ships and small craft suited to running the British blockade, it acquired one warship, the former U.S. Coast Guard icebreaker *Northland,* renamed *Matzpen.*

Both navies added a variety of armaments to their existing warships during the Israeli War of Independence (1948–1949) and managed to evade the international arms embargo to purchase a few small warships. The only significant naval engagement of that war demonstrates the improvised nature of these naval forces. On October 22, 1948, Israeli commandos steered explosive-laden boats into the flagship of the Egyptian Navy, the armed royal yacht *Amir Faruq,* and promptly sank the vessel.

Following the first Arab-Israeli war, Syria purchased some small craft from France. Israel and Egypt purchased a variety of warships from European governments or builders for their fleets. The largest of these warships were destroyers, destroyer escorts, and frigates, terms often used interchangeably in these small navies. These ships had seen service in World War II, and many of them were available for purchase in the late 1940s and early 1950s. The largest mounted a main armament of several 4.5-inch guns, while the smaller frigates carried 3-inch guns. All carried torpedoes and antisubmarine weapons. Fairly typical of these ships were the Z-class destroyers purchased by both Egypt and Israel from Britain in 1955. Built during World War II, they displaced 1,710 tons, had a main armament of four 4.5-inch guns in single turrets, and also mounted 40-mm and 20-mm antiaircraft guns, depth charges, and torpedoes. Egypt also purchased two smaller 1,000-ton Hunt-class destroyer escorts from Britain. Designed to escort convoys during World War II, they mounted four 4-inch guns and a variety of antisubmarine weapons.

Cash-strapped Middle Eastern navies could afford few of these warships and, given the nature of the Arab-Israeli wars, required few of them. Israel, Egypt, and Syria purchased increasing numbers of fast-attack craft from European builders in the 1950s. Armed with a variety of machine guns and torpedoes, they required only a small crew and became the workhorses of their respective navies. In time of war they patrolled friendly waters, raided the enemy coast, and often delivered commandos for attacks on enemy installations. Typical were the Vosper torpedo boats of the Egyptian and Israeli navies. Armed with several machine guns and four torpedoes, they required a crew of only 13 men and could reach speeds in excess of 40 knots.

Egypt and Israel also purchased a variety of landing craft to stage larger raids and support operations along the Sinai coast. As with the destroyers and frigates, these were easily and cheaply purchased in the 1950s. The largest of them, World War II–vintage LSTs (Landing Ship, Tank), could carry two dozen tanks or other vehicles. In the 1960s, Israel began building its own landing craft— a modernized LST (designated LCT for Landing Craft, Tank) and a smaller LCP (Landing Craft, Personnel) to carry 200 troops.

By the 1956 Suez Crisis, Egypt and Israel had built respectable navies. The Egyptian navy included 2 Z-class destroyers, 7 frigates, several landing craft, 8 minesweepers, and more than two dozen British- or Italian-built torpedo boats plus a few recently arrived from Czechoslovakia. The Israeli Navy included 2 Z-class destroyers, 3 frigates, 3 landing craft, and 14 European-built torpedo boats. Egypt kept most of its fleet in home waters to defend the Suez Canal from Britain and France. However, it did dispatch the Hunt-class destroyer escort *Ibrahim al-Awal* to bombard Haifa. Two Israeli and 1 French destroyer engaged and captured the *Ibrahim al-Awal* on October 31, 1956. The Israelis renamed the ship *Haifa,* and it joined the Israeli Navy after the war.

Egypt's conclusion of an arms deal with the Soviet Union helped trigger the Suez Crisis, and after the war Soviet and East European arms significantly bolstered both the Egyptian and Syrian navies. These included 3,000-ton Skoryi-class destroyers, torpedo boats, patrol craft armed with machine guns, and eventually Komar- and Osa-class missile-armed fast-attack craft. Armed with SS-N-2 Styx missiles (two on the 80-ton Komar class, four on the 200-ton Osa class), they dramatically changed naval warfare in the Middle East. The Styx missile, with a 1,000-pound warhead and 27-mile range, could sink any ship in the Israeli Navy, which lacked both missiles and missile defense systems.

To counter this threat, Israel began work on its own antiship missile, the Gabriel, and commissioned a West German firm to design the modified torpedo boat that would carry it, the Saar. Built in France, none of the 12 Saar-class missile boats that Israel ordered were completed in time for the 1967 Six-Day War, which again featured little naval combat. The Israeli Navy was not ready for war, and the Egyptians proved unwilling to risk their warships against overwhelming Israeli airpower. After the war, however, aggressive Israeli patrolling along the newly conquered Sinai coast triggered several naval battles. The Israelis sank several Egyptian torpedo boats, and Egyptian missile boats sank the Israeli destroyer *Eilat* with Styx missiles. This conclusively demonstrated the obsolescence of the World War II–era ships in these navies and accelerated the transition to missile-armed fast-attack craft.

Following the Six-Day War, Egypt and Syria continued replacing their aging warships with Soviet designs. Israel, benefiting from its experience with the Saar, increasingly built its own warships, the most notable of which was the Reshef-class or Saar 4. The original Saar (designated as Saar 1, 2, or 3 depending on its armament) was a versatile 250-ton fast-attack craft armed with a variety of machine guns, 20-mm and 35-mm cannon (or a 76-mm Oto Melara gun that replaced several of these), and some combination of Gabriel missiles, torpedoes, and antisubmarine weapons that varied according to mission. The first two Reshef-class missile boats joined the fleet shortly before the 1973 war and boasted substantial firepower for their 450-ton size, including eight Gabriel missiles, a 76-mm gun, various 20-mm cannon and machine guns, and a variety of systems to protect the ship from enemy missiles. Israel also built a variety of small high-speed patrol craft, including the Dabur class and the slightly larger Dvora class, and generally has maintained at least 20 of them in its fleet. The Dabur is an enlarged version of the U.S. Swift boat that saw extensive service in the Vietnam War and carries two twin .50-caliber machine guns and two 20-mm cannon.

During the 1969–1970 War of Attrition, the Israeli Navy landed commandos and participated in numerous raids into Egypt. Meanwhile, the Israeli Air Force sank several Egyptian warships including a destroyer and a Komar-class missile boat. Egyptian commandoes twice raided the Israeli port of Eilat, damaging several Israeli landing craft.

The 1973 Yom Kippur War featured the most sustained naval combat of the Arab-Israel wars, and Israel's Saar and Reshef missile boats proved themselves in battle. In two engagements off Ladhakiyya, Syria, Israeli missile boats sank a minesweeper, two Osas, and three Komars without losing any of their number as Israeli countermeasures jammed incoming Styx missiles. This allowed Israel's Saars and Reshefs to close range and fire their shorter-range but more accurate Gabriel missiles with devastating effect. The Israeli Navy repeated this performance in several battles off the Egyptian coast, sinking four Osas and two Komars without any loss of their own. Both Arab navies withdrew their warships to port and refused to engage the Israelis for the remainder of the war, despite Israeli raids on coastal installations.

Despite these losses, new Soviet arms shipments enlarged the Syrian Navy in the 1970s. After the signing of the 1978 Camp David Accords, Egypt found new arms suppliers in China (which produced copies of many Soviet warships) and Western Europe. Israel continued to construct its own ships, building more than a dozen Reshef-class missile boats after the war (some for export) and two versions of a slightly larger version, the Saar 4.5. One version, the *Aliya,* has a platform for a helicopter, making it the smallest warship to carry a chopper. The other version, the *Hetz,* carries additional missiles.

In the 1980s, the Israelis acquired U.S.-made 70-mile-range Harpoon missiles and Phalanx Close-In Weapons Systems (CIWS) capable of shooting down incoming missiles and added them to their larger warships. Israel has continued to upgrade the electronics and weapons of its warships since then, adding Israeli-made

Barak point defense missiles to the Saar 4.5 in the 1990s. When it needed a still larger warship, however, Israel turned to the Ingalls Shipyard in the United States, which built three Saar 5 1,000-ton multimission corvettes for Israel. The largest ships in the Israeli Navy, these vessels are each armed with eight Harpoon and eight Gabriel II missiles, Barak and Phalanx systems for missile defense, and a variety of antisubmarine weapons and carry a helicopter to help locate targets.

While the Syrian Navy continued to expand after the 1973 War, it avoided clashes with Israeli warships even during Israel's 1982 invasion of Lebanon, which featured substantial Israeli naval operations. By 1985, the Syrian Navy included 22 missile boats, 10 of them the advanced Osa II class, and 20 smaller warships. The collapse of the Soviet Union, though, has virtually crippled the Syrian Navy. Syria has purchased parts and a few warships from China, but its warships rarely leave port. Many have rusted at anchor since the mid-1990s.

In marked contrast, Egypt invested heavily in its navy in the 1980s and 1990s, purchasing warships from China, West European builders, and eventually the United States. Egypt built a modified version of the Osa, the October class, armed with Otomat antiship missiles. But it ordered its larger warships from foreign builders: six 300-ton Ramadan-class missile boats armed with Otomat missiles from Britain, two 1,500-ton Descubierta-class frigates armed with Harpoon missiles from Spain, and two 1,900-ton Jianghu-class frigates equipped with Silkworm missiles from China. In the 1990s, Egypt arranged to purchase four 3,700-ton Oliver Hazard Perry–class frigates from the United States and to lease two 4,250-ton Knox-class frigates. These highly capable warships carry a variety of weapons systems including Harpoon missiles, Phalanx CIWS, and antisubmarine torpedoes. Their acquisition made Egypt's navy the largest and most powerful in the region.

STEPHEN K. STEIN

See also

Arms Sales, International; Attrition, War of; Baltim, Battle of; Egypt, Armed Forces; *Eilat* Sinking; Iraq, Armed Forces; Israel, Defense Industry; Israel Defense Forces; Israeli War of Independence, Overview; Jordan, Armed Forces; Latakia, Battle of; Lebanon, Armed Forces; Reshef-Class Guided-Missile Boat; Six-Day War; Submarines; Syria, Armed Forces; Yom Kippur War

References

Horgen, James. "Ali's Navy." *Saudi Aramco World* (November/December 1970): 18–21.

Jane's Information Group. *Jane's Fighting Ships, 1947–1948 to 2003–2004.* London and New York: Sampson, Low, Marsh, 1947–2004.

Rabinovich, Abraham. *The Boats of Cherbourg: The Secret Israeli Operation That Revolutionized Naval Warfare.* New York: Seaver, 1988.

Tzalel, Moshe. *From Ice-Breaker to Missile Boat: The Evolution of Israel's Naval Strategy.* Westport, CT: Greenwood, 2000.

Water Rights and Resources

Water rights and resources lie at the heart of the Arab-Israeli conflict. In a land of limited resources and inequitable distribution, water is a polarizing force. Israel has controlled the lion's share of water since 1948, and since that time both Jews and Arabs have argued over who owns which resources and who is using them irresponsibly. The main problem facing the human population in the region is one of uneven water distribution. Although experts insist that there is enough water for all current inhabitants, Israel has controlled most of the water resources available to the Palestinians since 1967, and Palestinians claim that Israel has routinely denied them access to their fair share of the precious resource.

Israel, Palestine, and Jordan all have very limited water resources. Water is naturally scarce in the region because of the arid climate, and available resources cannot accommodate all proposed uses. The main water source for Israel is the Jordan River drainage basin, which includes the Sea of Galilee, also called Lake Tiberias or Lake Kinneret.

The headwaters of the Jordan lie in northern Israel, in the Golan Heights, and in southern Lebanon. These waters feed Lake Tiberias. Runoff from the West Bank, Syria, and Jordan adds water to the lower Jordan. Israel uses all of the water from the Jordan River. The Palestinians on the West Bank do not receive any of it, although geographically the Palestinians are riparian. In fact, only 30 percent of the water in Palestine comes from surface sources. The remainder comes from underground aquifers.

The Mountain Aquifer, or West Bank Aquifer, supplies most of the water to the West Bank, while the water in Gaza comes from the Gaza Strip Aquifer, part of the Coastal Aquifer. Because the Gaza Strip Aquifer has been overused for many years to supply the needs of the large population of Gaza and Israel, the water table can no longer recharge. The water has now been contaminated with enough seawater that it is no longer drinkable, representing a major water crisis for the area.

In 1953 Israeli foreign minister Moshe Sharett insisted on Israel's right to use the waters from the Jordan as it wished for hydroelectric power, agriculture, and other needs. He claimed that Israel was willing to engage in negotiations with Jordan, Syria, and Lebanon to come up with a just apportionment of regional resources but that the neighboring countries refused to meet with Israel on the subject. The Israeli government felt justified, therefore, in treating the waters of the Jordan as its own and in using them for development in the north and elsewhere.

Between 1953 and 1965 U.S. ambassador Eric Johnston traveled between Israel and the neighboring Arab states endeavoring to reach some agreement on an equitable division of water rights. Experts from the affected nations agreed on a plan to divide and exploit existing resources, but the Arab League rejected it because it did not want to imply recognition of Israel. If the agreement had taken effect, Jordan would have been required to supply the West Bank with a large amount of water. It has never done so, and Israel claims that it has been forced to supply the West Bank from its own resources.

Palestinians and others accuse Israel of mismanaging the region's water, in part because many Israelis live a consumer-oriented lifestyle that depends on an ample water supply. Green lawns and swimming pools are common, and Israelis have continuously developed the land for the past 100 years, building homes, kibbutzim, and farms. The government subsidizes water for Israelis, which discourages conservation. In 1995 the Ministry of Agriculture recommended ending subsidies to agriculture, but the Water Commissioner's office rejected this idea. Almost half of the land in Israel is irrigated for agricultural purposes, and agriculture uses 75 percent of the nation's water resources.

In the 1960s Israel was a leader in drip irrigation research, which greatly reduces the amount of water needed to grow crops, but most of this experimentation ended after Israel took control of more water resources in 1967. Nevertheless, drip irrigation together with other dry farming techniques are being used in some neighboring countries such as Syria and Egypt. Most Arab countries, however, use much less water for agriculture than does Israel. Fewer than 10 percent of cultivated fields in Palestine are irrigated, and only about 8 percent of Jordan's farmland receives irrigation. Critics note that agriculture supplies only 6 percent of Israel's gross domestic product (GDP) and suggest that the scarce water resources might be better used to nourish nonirrigated traditional crops.

Since 1967, Palestinians living in the West Bank have been prevented from digging new wells, while Israelis have been exploiting the water resources underlying land inhabited by Arabs. Palestinians pay between 3 and 8 times more for water than do Israelis, while the average consumption per Israeli is 3.5 times that for individual Palestinians. Palestinians living in the occupied territories receive on average less than 26 gallons of water per day, which is well below the 40 gallons daily water allotment recommended by the World Health Organization (WZO). Palestinians have learned to conserve water, saving rainwater in rooftop cisterns and recycling water used for cooking and cleaning.

Under international law, the water resources should be shared equitably, but inequity has been the rule since the State of Israel was established. Palestinians argue in particular that Israel's taking control of the West Bank in 1967 has also given Israel those water resources. Israel has countered with the claim that international law gives priority to past and existing uses of water at the expense of potential uses and that because it has been using that water for years, it has the right to continue to use it.

The Sea of Galilee and the Coastal Aquifer are both entirely within Israel's pre-1967 borders, and Israel claims these completely. Israel also notes that most of the water from the Western Aquifer emerges from springs in Israel and that it has used the Western Aquifer's water since the early 1950s. Israelis argue that Palestinians are in fact benefiting from Israeli water because Palestinian settlements in the West Bank use water sources developed by Israel. Israeli water also goes to settlements in Gaza, Jordan, and southern Lebanon. Under the 1994 peace agreement between Israel and Jordan, Israel and Jordan agreed to share the Jordan River, and Israel agreed to supply a large amount of water to Jordan. Israel has been investigating the use of desalinization plants to purify saltwater.

Experts, however, fear that if the population of the region continues to grow at current rates, there will soon be a severe water shortage even if distribution problems are resolved.

AMY HACKNEY BLACKWELL

See also
Climate of the Middle East; Jordan River; Lake Kinneret

References
Amery, Hussein A., and Aaron T. Wolf, eds. *Water in the Middle East: A Geography of Peace.* Austin: University of Texas Press, 2000.

Gleick, P. H. "Water, War and Peace in the Middle East." *Environment* 36(3) (1994): 6–11.

Shapland, Greg. *Rivers of Discord: International Water Disputes in the Middle East.* London: Palgrave Macmillan, 1997.

Smith, Charles D. *Palestine and the Arab-Israeli Conflict: A History with Documents.* 6th ed. New York: Bedford/St. Martin's, 2006.

Wauchope, Sir Arthur Grenfell
Born: 1874
Died: 1947

British general and high commissioner of the British Mandate for Palestine (1931–1938). Born in Edinburgh in 1874, Arthur Grenfell Wauchope fought in the South African (Boer) War of 1899–1902 and was severely wounded. He was stationed in India during 1903–1912. He served on the western front in France during World War I until 1916, when he was transferred to the Mesopotamia Front and was again wounded. In 1923 he was a member of the overseas settlement delegation to Australia and New Zealand. During 1924–1927 he was chief of the British section of the Inter-Allied Commission of Control (IMCC) in Berlin. During 1927–1929 he served in Northern Ireland.

In 1931 Wauchope was appointed British high commissioner for Palestine, a post he held until 1938. He chose to interpret British immigration regulations liberally, and during his administration the Jewish population in Palestine expanded rapidly, including many German, Austrian, and Czech Jews. Wauchope endeavored to meet growing Arab opposition to the increased Jewish immigration by establishing a Legislative Council.

Wauchope received considerable criticism as a consequence of the Arab Revolt that began in April 1936. At first his administration took firm steps to end the rioting. Wauchope, however, continued his liberal immigration policy but at the same time did not move to arrest Arab leaders inciting the riots. A temporary halt in the violence occurred during the visit of the fact-finding Peel Commission to Palestine in 1938, but the violence resumed after the commission's departure. This time Wauchope moved against the Arab leaders. Following the assassination of acting district commissioner Louis Y. Andrews in the Galilee District, Wauchope declared the Arab Higher Committee and other Arab nationalist groups to be illegal associations. British authorities deported a half dozen Arab leaders, and Haj Amin al-Husseini, mufti of Jerusalem, was removed

Sir Arthur Wauchope (*center*) reviewing an honor guard on his arrival in Palestine as British high commissioner, November 20, 1931. (Library of Congress)

from office. In November 1937 Wauchope authorized the emergency establishment of military courts.

Wauchope's relief from his post and departure from Palestine in March 1938 signaled the beginning of a much harsher British policy toward Jewish immigration and land sales as well as a more pro-Arab policy in the mandate, carried out under his successor Sir Harold MacMichael. Wauchope retained his interest in Palestine following his retirement. He died in London in 1947.

SPENCER C. TUCKER

See also

Arab Higher Committee; Arab Revolt of 1936–1939; Husseini, Haj Amin al-; MacMichael, Sir Harold; Palestine, British Mandate for; Palestinian Legislative Council; Peel Commission

References

Sachar, Howard M. *A History of Israel: From the Rise of Zionism to Our Time.* 3rd ed. New York: Knopf, 2007.
Shepherd, Naomi. *Ploughing Sand: British Rule in Palestine, 1917–1948.* New Brunswick, NJ: Rutgers University Press, 1999.

Wazir, Khalil al-
Born: October 10, 1935
Died: April 16, 1988

Palestinian military strategist and cofounder of Fatah. Khalil al-Wazir, also known as Abu Jihad, was born in the town of Ramla in the British Mandate for Palestine on October 10, 1935. After the

Israeli War of Independence (1948–1949), he was forced to move to the al-Burauj refugee camp, as were many other Palestinians. He came to the attention of Egyptian officials in 1954 for his affiliation with the Muslim Brotherhood and in 1955 was briefly detained by Egyptian authorities for his connection to that group. He attended the University of Alexandria but did not graduate. He then moved to Kuwait, where he worked as a teacher until 1963.

During his time in Egypt, al-Wazir had received military training. While in Kuwait he met Salah Kalaf (Abu Iyad), Mahmoud Abbas (Abu Mazen), Khalid and Hani al-Hassan, Yasser Arafat, and others who would form the nucleus of Fatah. Al-Wazir was in charge of *Filastinuna*, the official publication of Fatah. He also headed up the recruitment of members for the military wing of the group and created one of the first armed units, known as Al-Asifa (the storm). It was al-Wazir who strengthened Fatah's ties to the communist bloc, although he himself was a devout Muslim and did not support leftist ideologies.

Al-Wazir traveled extensively in the socialist world on behalf of the Palestine Liberation Organization (PLO) and Arafat, its chairman. Some disputed reports claim that al-Wazir received specialized military training while in the communist bloc. Nevertheless, he became expert in the Maoist principles of people's war developed by Mao Zedong in China. In 1965 al-Wazir moved to Damascus, Syria, to help coordinate a guerrilla fight inside Israel.

In the wake of the June 1967 Six-Day War, al-Wazir, then considered the preeminent military thinker within the PLO, became the

See also
Arafat, Yasser; Black September; Black September Organization; Fatah; Mossad; Muslim Brotherhood; Palestine Liberation Organization; Sayeret Matkal

References
Cobban, Helena. *The Palestinian Liberation Organization: People, Power and Politics.* New York: Cambridge University Press, 1984.
Rubin, Barry, and Judith Colp Rubin. *Yasir Arafat: A Political Biography.* New York: Oxford University Press, 2003.
Yusuf, Samir. *Abu Jihad.* Cairo: al-Markaz al-Misri al-Arabi, 1989.

Weinberger, Caspar
Born August 18, 1917
Died: March 26, 2006

U.S. politician and secretary of defense (1981–1987). Born in San Francisco, California, on August 18, 1917, Caspar Willard Weinberger attended Harvard University, where he earned a bachelor of arts degree in 1938 and a law degree in 1941. He served in the U.S. Army during World War II, rising to captain.

Leaving the military in 1945, Weinberger clerked for a federal judge and then entered politics. Elected to the California State Assembly in 1952, he was chairman of the state Republican Party, then worked in Gov. Ronald Reagan's cabinet in the late 1960s and early 1970s. Moving to Washington, Weinberger served as director of the Federal Trade Commission (1970), deputy director (1970–1972) and then director (1972–1973) of the Office of Management and Budget, and secretary of the Department of Health, Education and Welfare (1973–1975).

Weinberger served as an adviser to Reagan's 1980 presidential campaign, and Reagan appointed him secretary of defense in 1981. Many conservatives feared that Weinberger, known as "Cap the Knife" for his budget-cutting ways, might oppose Reagan's plans to increase defense spending. Such worries proved groundless, as Weinberger presided over the largest peacetime defense buildup in U.S. history. He was also an enthusiastic supporter of Reagan's Strategic Defense Initiative (SDI) to establish a laser-guided defense system in outer space that would be able to destroy ballistic missiles aimed at the United States.

In Middle Eastern affairs, Weinberger opposed the stationing of U.S. marines in Lebanon in 1982, believing that the objective was not clearly defined. His fears over the vulnerability of this force were realized when 241 marines died in their Beirut barracks in a terrorist bombing in October 1983. Weinberger actively sought the prosecution of U.S. Navy intelligence analyst Jonathan Pollard, subsequently convicted of spying for Israel and sentenced to life imprisonment.

Weinberger opposed the secret transfer beginning in late 1985 of 500 U.S. TOW antitank missiles to Iran in exchange for the freeing of American hostages being held in the Middle East. The Reagan administration then illegally diverted some of the funds to the anticommunist Contra forces fighting the Sandinista government

Khalil al-Wazir, also known as Abu Jihad, a key figure in the Palestine Liberation Organization (PLO), shown at a preparatory meeting for the Palestinian National Council, February 13, 1983. (Alain Nogues/Corbis Sygma)

head of its Supreme Military Council. He also had charge of all guerrilla operations within Israel. It was widely believed by his colleagues in the PLO that the Maoist style of insurrection was the only way to win the struggle against Israel and Zionism.

During the September 1970 crisis in Jordan known as Black September, al-Wazir was instrumental in supplying embattled Palestinian forces fighting Jordanian troops. Following the Jordanian fiasco al-Wazir, along with most of the PLO leadership, shifted his base of operations to Beirut, Lebanon. He actively supported militants of the Black September organization, formed in November 1971, and also planned attacks such as the Coastal Road Massacre in Israel (March 1978). He fled Lebanon during the 1982 invasion of that country by Israeli forces. He reestablished himself in Tunis, as did most of the PLO hierarchy.

The Israeli intelligence agency Mossad placed al-Wazir under close surveillance and sought to eliminate him if possible. On April 16, 1988, boats carrying commandos from Israel's elite Sayeret Matkal landed in Tunis. In the span of just 13 seconds, Israeli forces dispatched al-Wazir's guard and burst into his bedroom, firing 75 shots into his body. His wife lying next to him was unharmed.

ROD VOSBURGH

Caspar Weinberger, U.S. secretary of defense (1981–1987). (U.S. Department of Defense)

in Nicaragua. This activity became public in late 1986 and was known as the Iran-Contra Affair. Weinberger resigned his post in November 1987, citing his wife's poor health.

In the fall of 1992 Special Counsel Lawrence Walsh indicted Weinberger on four felony counts of lying to a congressional committee and to the independent counsel's office and one count of obstruction of justice. The case never came to trial, as defeated incumbent president George H. W. Bush pardoned Weinberger on December 24, 1992. Weinberger died in Bangor, Maine, on March 26, 2006.

FRANK J. SMITH

See also

Bush, George Herbert Walker; Reagan, Ronald Wilson

References

Cannon, Lou. *President Reagan: The Role of a Lifetime.* New York: Simon and Schuster, 1991.

Weinberger, Caspar W. *Fighting for Peace: Seven Critical Years in the Pentagon.* New York: Warner, 1990.

Weinberger, Caspar W., with Gretchen Roberts. *In the Arena: A Memoir of the 20th Century.* Washington DC: Regnery, 1998.

Weis, Isaac Mayer

See Wise, Isaac Mayer

Weizman, Ezer
Born: June 15, 1924
Died: April 24, 2005

Israeli general and commander of the Israeli Air Forces (IAF) and then president of Israel (1993–2000). Born in Tel Aviv on June 15, 1924, Ezer Weizman was the nephew of Israel's first president, Chaim Weizmann, and was immersed in politics from his youth. Weizman's Zionist convictions and family background soon brought him into Haganah, the Jewish self-defense organization.

Weizman joined the Royal Air Force (RAF) in September 1942, first as a truck driver in the British campaigns in North Africa. In 1943 he was allowed to attend pilot training school at Bulawayo, Rhodesia. As one of 20–25 Palestinians who flew with the RAF in the war, he won his wings at the beginning of 1945 as a sergeant. He was then stationed in Egypt, where he learned to fly the Republic P-47 Thunderbolt. He ended the war and his RAF service in India.

During 1946–1947 Weizman studied aeronautics in Britain. There he joined the underground group Irgun Tsvai Leumi (National Military Organization), but his activities with it caused the British police to request that he return to Palestine. There he joined Haganah's clandestine air service of a half dozen light aircraft at Tel Aviv Airport, in effect Israel's first air squadron.

Weizman fought as a pilot in the Israeli War of Independence (1948–1949). He remained with the IAF after the war and is generally considered the father of that organization. During 1951–1952 he attended the RAF Staff College in Britain, and upon his return to Israel he set up the IAF Staff Command School. In 1953 he took command of a squadron, and in 1956 he supervised the clandestine ferrying of 60 French Dassault Mystère jet aircraft from France to Israel as part of the secret preparations for the joint French-Israeli-British campaign against Egypt. He then participated in the subsequent 1956 Sinai Campaign. During 1958–1966 he commanded the IAF as a major general. He then became deputy chief of staff of the Israel Defense Forces (IDF), where he played a major role in planning and directing the highly successful air campaign that ensured Israeli success in the 1967 Six-Day War. He retired as a major general in 1969.

Upon leaving the IDF, Weizman joined the Gahal parliamentary bloc (Gush Herut Liberalim) that later merged to become the conservative Likud Party. During 1969–1970 he served as minister of transport. He then led the Gahal bloc until 1972, when he left it. He returned to Herut in 1976. During 1977–1980 he was minister of defense in Prime Minister Menachem Begin's government. During Weizman's tenure, in March 1978 Israel launched Operation LITANI against the Palestine Liberation Organization (PLO) in southern Lebanon. He then quit the government and considered establishing a new political party with Moshe Dayan, which brought his expulsion from Herut. During 1980–1984 Weizman pursued business interests.

Weizman had now turned dovish and actively sought to secure

Ezer Weizman, Israeli general and commander of the Israeli Air Force and then president of Israel (1993–2000). (Ya'acov Sa'ar/Israeli Government Press Office)

peace with Israel's Arab neighbors. He strongly supported the negotiations with Egypt that led to the Camp David Accords in 1978. Being too progressive for the Herut government in the late 1970s, he founded his own party, Yachad, that won three seats in the Knesset (Israeli parliament). During 1984–1988 he was minister of Arab affairs. In 1986 the Yachad Party joined the Labor Party. During 1988–1990 Weizman was minister of science and technology.

Weizman seemed an ideal candidate for the largely ceremonial position of president in 1993. Taking office as head of state in May 1993, he became well known for his outspoken views and informal manner. He regularly visited the families of victims of terror attacks, slain soldiers, and wounded soldiers in hospitals. He supported the efforts toward peace of the Oslo Peace Process. He was the first Israeli president to visit Britain and West Germany. In 1996 he invited PLO leader Yasser Arafat to a private meeting in his residence. Weizman also supported an Israeli withdrawal from the Golan Heights in exchange for peace with Syria. Reelected president in 1998, he resigned from office in July 2000 over press charges that he had accepted bribes from businessmen. These charges were never pursued, however. Weizman died in Caesarea on April 24, 2005.

ULRIKE WUNDERLE AND SPENCER C. TUCKER

See also

Aircraft, Fighters; Arafat, Yasser; Begin, Menachem; Camp David Accords; Haganah; Irgun Tsvai Leumi; Israeli Air Strikes Beginning the Six-Day War; Oslo Accords; Palestine Liberation Organization; Six-Day War; Weizmann, Chaim

References

Shaul, Moshe Ben, ed. *Generals of Israel.* Tel Aviv: Hadar, 1968.
Weizman, Ezer. *The Battle for Peace.* New York: Bantam, 1981.
———. *On Eagles' Wings: The Personal Story of the Leading Command of the Israeli Air Force.* New York: Macmillan 1977.

Weizmann, Chaim
Born: November 27, 1874
Died: November 9, 1952

British scientist and Zionist leader, president of the World Zionist Organization (WZO), and first president of the State of Israel (1948–1952). Chaim Weizmann was born on November 27, 1874, in the village of Motol near Pinsk in imperial Russia (now Belarus). He studied chemistry and biochemistry at the polytechnic institutes of Darmstadt and Berlin and at the University of Freiburg, where he earned a doctorate with honors in 1899. At the forefront of his field, in 1901 he was appointed a lecturer at the University of Geneva, but in 1904 he accepted the position as reader in biochemistry at the University of Manchester in Britain.

Weizmann had become involved in Hoveve Zion (Love of Zion) activities at an early age. As a student in Berlin he also had occasion to meet a number of future Zionist leaders. Although he was selected as a delegate to the First Zionist Congress in Basle in 1897, he lacked the financial resources to make the trip and did not attend. He did attend the Second Zionist Congress the next year, where he met Theodor Herzl. Weizmann believed that a Jewish state would be established not through high-level diplomacy but by securing the support of the Jewish people as a whole. Toward that end he worked for the establishment of educational and cultural programs as well as practical settlements in Palestine. At the Sixth Zionist Congress in Berne he voted against the East Africa Scheme to establish a Jewish settlement in Uganda. He was an early advocate of the establishment of a Jewish institution of higher learning in Palestine, the future Hebrew University. He also believed that the interests of Britain and Zionists coincided, and this was one of the reasons he

Presidents of Israel (1948–Present)

Name	Term	Political Party
Chaim Weizmann	1948–1952	Mapai
Yitzhak Ben-Zvi	1952–1963	Mapai
Zalman Shazar	1963–1973	Labor
Ephraim Katzir	1973–1978	Labor
Yitzhak Navon	1978–1983	Labor
Chaim Herzog	1983–1993	Labor
Ezer Weizman	1993–2000	Labor
Moshe Katsav	2000–Present	Likud

Chaim Weizmann, British scientist and Zionist leader, president of the World Zionist Organization (WZO), and first president of the State of Israel (1948–1952). (Library of Congress)

decided to accept the academic position there in 1904. He first traveled to Palestine in 1907, the occasion being to investigate the possibilities of establishing a chemical industry there.

Weizmann's most important contributions to the Zionist cause came during World War I. He was firmly convinced that Britain and the Entente powers would win the war and that Palestine would pass from Turkish to British control. He worked hard to promote the Zionist program, meeting with both British politicians and the press.

Weizmann had offered his services to the British government at the beginning of the war, and his ability to promote the Zionist agenda was greatly enhanced by his important contribution to the Allied victory. During his studies in Germany, Weizmann had developed a fermentation process that produced acetone, a vital material in producing cordite for explosives from maize. Britain had previously depended on wood-distilled acetone from Germany. First Lord of the Admiralty Winston Churchill now asked Weizmann to produce vast quantities of acetone. Such work proved critical for the British war effort. In 1916 Weizmann moved to London to become director of the Admiralty laboratory, a post he held until 1919. He declined payment for his acetone process.

Weizmann's presence in London greatly increased the range of his political contacts, and in February 1917 in London he met Sir Mark Sykes, assistant secretary to the War Cabinet. This was the

beginning of talks that led to the 1917 Balfour Declaration. Weizmann also became close friends with Minister of Munitions David Lloyd George. At this time Weizmann held no official position in the WZO other than being a member of its Zionist Actions Committee. Aware of his important political work and to facilitate his important lobbying efforts with the British government, English Zionists in 1917 elected him the president of the English Zionist Federation. Weizmann played a key role in the negotiations with the British government that led Foreign Secretary Arthur James Balfour to issue the Balfour Declaration of November 2, 1917, in which Britain committed itself to the establishment of a Jewish home in Palestine. Weizmann also met with American diplomat Henry Morgenthau in an effort to promote the idea of a British mandate over Palestine at the end of the war.

At the end of the war Weizmann traveled to Palestine as the head of the Zionist Commission to study the situation and advise the British government on the future development of Palestine. While there he laid the cornerstone for the Hebrew University. During this trip he also met at Aqaba with Emir Faisal, a leading Arab statesman and the son of Sharif Hussein ibn Ali of Mecca, and secured his tentative support in a signed document for Jewish development work in Palestine. Weizmann then led a Zionist delegation to the Paris Peace Conference in 1919.

In 1920 the WZO elected Weizmann its president, and he served in that capacity during 1920–1930 and again in 1935–1946. He also headed the Jewish Agency established in 1929. Beginning in 1921 Weizmann made the first of a number of trips to the United States. Accompanied by the American physicist Albert Einstein, Weizmann helped raise money for the Hebrew University and the Palestine Foundation Fund. Convinced that Britain would not betray the Balfour Declaration, he reluctantly accepted the severance of Transjordan and supported the British government's 1922 White Paper that limited future Jewish immigration to Palestine on the grounds of the inability of the country to sustain it, and he secured the support of the Zionist Executive for the declaration. Weizmann presented the Zionist case before the 1936 Peel Commission that proposed partitioning Palestine. He also bitterly attacked the British White Paper of 1939 that set restrictions on Jewish immigration into Palestine and halted land transfers there.

In the 1930s Weizmann helped establish the Daniel Sieff Research Institute in Rehovot, where he moved in 1937. It subsequently became the Weizmann Institute, an important force in Israeli scientific research.

During World War II Weizmann again loyally supported Britain and urged the British government to establish a Jewish fighting force. He was honorary adviser to the British Ministry of Supply and worked on a variety of wartime scientific projects, including research on synthetic rubber and high-octane gasoline. During his long scientific career, he registered 110 different patents, some with collaborators.

During and after the war, Weizmann also actively lobbied for the creation of a Jewish state. He played a major role in securing passage in the United Nations (UN) of the partition plan for Palestine on November 29, 1947. He also helped convince U.S. president Harry Truman to recognize Israel in 1948.

In recognition of his great accomplishments on behalf of the Jewish state, in 1948 Weizmann became Israel's first president, largely a ceremonial position. He was also honorary president of the Hebrew University in the same period. Following a long illness, Weizmann died in office on November 9, 1952, at his home in Rehovot, Israel.

STEPHEN K. STEIN AND SPENCER C. TUCKER

See also

Balfour Declaration; Churchill, Sir Winston; East Africa Scheme; Einstein, Albert; Herzl, Theodor; Hoveve Zion; Jewish Agency for Israel; Lloyd George, David; Palestine, British Mandate for; Peel Commission; Truman, Harry S.; White Paper (1922); White Paper (1939); World Zionist Organization; Zionism

References

Reinharz, Jehuda. *Chaim Weizmann: The Making of a Statesman.* New York: Oxford University Press, 1993.
———. *Chaim Weizmann: The Making of a Zionist Leader.* New York: Oxford University Press, 1987.
Stein, Leonard, et al., eds. *The Letters and Papers of Chaim Weizmann.* London: Oxford University Press, 1968–.
Weizmann, Chaim. *Trial and Error: The Autobiography of Chaim Weizmann.* New York: Harper, 1949.

West Bank

The West Bank is the common name for the territory that lies west of the Jordan River and south of the Sea of Galilee. It was also known as Cisjordan (for "this side of the Jordan River") and by its biblical names of Judea in the south and Samaria in the north. Today about 40 percent of the area and 98 percent of the population is under the jurisdiction of the Palestinian Authority (PA), although Israel, which has occupied the territory since the 1967 Six-Day War, controls, has settlements in, and maintains forces in much of the remainder. East Jerusalem, although located in the West Bank, was annexed by Israel in the same war (a step not recognized by the international community) and is usually treated as a separate issue in peace negotiations. However, East Jerusalem is contiguous to the West Bank.

Until the end of World War I the West Bank was part of the territory of the Ottoman Empire, after which it was part of the League of Nations British Mandate for Palestine. The West Bank was captured by Jordanian forces in the Israeli War of Independence (1948–1949) despite the fact that it had been designated as part of a proposed Palestinian state by the United Nations (UN) in 1947. Following that war the boundary separating Israel and Jordan and Jordanian occupied territory became known as the Green Line. Palestinian Arab refugees from Israel flooded into the area. Jordan annexed the West Bank in 1950, although the move was not recognized by any country except the United Kingdom.

Despite Israel's effort to persuade Jordan to remain neutral in the 1967 Six-Day War, Israeli forces moved into and occupied the West Bank after Jordan entered the conflict. UN Security Council Resolution 242 of 1967 called for the withdrawal of Israeli forces from all the territories occupied in the Six-Day War, which included East Jerusalem, the West Bank, the Gaza Strip, the Golan Heights, and the Sinai Peninsula. Israel refused to comply with the resolution and throughout the 1970s established Jewish settlements in all the occupied territories, with the most being in the West Bank.

After almost 20 years of Israeli occupation and the expanding encroachment of Palestinian land by the settlements, the First Intifada started in 1987. The following year Jordan's King Hussein relinquished all claims to the West Bank, partly to support Palestinian claims and partly to reinforce Jordanian national identity.

The Palestine Liberation Organization (PLO) proclaimed the West Bank independent in 1988, although Israel did not recognize either the area's independence or the PLO as a legitimate governing body. The promise of a breakthrough came with the 1993 Oslo Accords, when Israel and the Palestinians agreed to a conditional withdrawal of Israeli troops from some West Bank areas. The Oslo Accords, however, stipulated that the status of the territory would not be determined finally until both sides entered into a permanent agreement.

Frustrated by the torturously slow peace process and the ever-encroaching Israeli settlements, Palestinian patience finally ran out. And when Ariel Sharon enraged the Palestinian public by visiting the al-Aqsa Mosque area of the Haram al-Sharif with Israeli security forces, the Second (al-Aqsa) Intifada erupted in 2000. Far more violent than the First Intifada, the Palestinian attacks and suicide bombings of the Second Intifada initially led Israel to send large military and security forces back into the West Bank.

Convinced that they had no reliable negotiating partner on the Palestinian side who could make agreements and deliver on them, the Israelis finally initiated steps that were intended to lead to a unilateral disengagement between the two peoples. In 2001 the Israelis obtained Israeli Jewish signatures on petitions supporting the construction of a security wall, and in 2002, despite strong Palestinian protests against the project, the Israelis began constructing the controversial security barrier around the West Bank. But rather than conforming to the boundary of the pre-1967 Green Line, the planned line of the Israeli Security Fence cut deep into the West Bank in various sectors to encompass Israeli settlements established since 1967. The Palestinians, along with much of the rest of the world, have condemned the Israeli move as nothing short of a blatant land grab.

In 2004 Sharon began the process of unilaterally withdrawing all Israeli settlements from the Gaza Strip as well as four smaller settlements in the West Bank. Meanwhile, the Israelis have continued to expand some of their larger settlements in the West Bank, resettling some of those Israelis evicted from the Gaza settlements.

In 2006 the West Bank was home to as many as 2.4 million Palestinians and more than 400,000 Israeli settlers (260,000 inhabitants of East Jerusalem are excluded). About 30 percent of the Palestinian population are refugees or their descendants from the

GROWTH OF JEWISH SETTLEMENTS ON THE WEST BANK & GAZA STRIP, 1967-1978

Legend:
- Principal Arab towns
- Arab villages
- Jewish settlements established between Jun 1967 and Aug 1978
- The cease-fire line between Israel and Jordan, 1949 – 1967
- The Jordan River boundary following the Six-Day War of Jun 1967

1948 war. Among the more populous Palestinian cities of the West Bank are East Jerusalem, Nablus, Ramallah, Bethlehem (home to a large number of Palestinian Christians), Hebron, Tulkarem, and Qlaquilla.

DAVID T. ZABECKI

See also

Expellees and Refugees, Palestinian; Hussein, King of Jordan; Intifada, Second; Israeli Security Fence; Oslo Accords; Palestine Liberation Organization; Palestinian Authority; Sharon, Ariel; Six-Day War

References

Oren, Michael B. *Six Days of War: June 1967 and the Making of the Modern Middle East.* Novato, CA: Presidio, 2003.

Said, Edward W. *The End of the Peace Process: Oslo and After.* New York: Vintage Books, 2001.

Smith, Charles D. *Palestine and the Arab-Israeli Conflict: A History with Documents.* 6th ed. New York: Bedford/St. Martin's, 2006.

Western Wall

Judaism's most sacred religious site, dating to King Herod the Great's reconstruction of the Second Temple in 19 BC. The First Temple was built in the 10th century BC on Mount Moriah (Temple Mount) in Jerusalem by King Solomon. It was destroyed by the Babylonians in 586 BC. The Second Temple was built on the same spot starting in 515 BC. Starting in 19 BC, the Second Temple was completely rebuilt by King Herod the Great. The Western Wall (also known as the Wailing Wall) is actually a section of the retaining wall at the base of the Temple Mount, built during Herod's reconstruction.

The surviving massive stone blocks of the Western Wall are some 1,600 feet long and nearly 200 feet high. Herod's spectacular renovations made the Second Temple one of the architectural wonders of the age. Its destruction by the Romans marked the end of the Great Revolt (AD 66–70) and the beginning of Jewish exile.

The Temple Mount today is sacred to Muslims as the Haram al-Sharif (Noble Sanctuary), the site of Muhammad's ascent to heaven following his Night Journey to Jerusalem. The Dome of the Rock stands over the rock from which Muhammad is believed to have ascended. Some Jews also believe that the rock marks the spot where the Sanctum Sanctorum (Holy of Holies) of King Solomon's Temple stood. The al-Aqsa Mosque, built during the seventh and eighth centuries AD, stands close to the Dome of the Rock.

Denied entrance to the Temple Mount, Jews in the Middle Ages made the Western Wall the preeminent place of prayer and pilgrimage. In the late 16th century, Ottoman sultan Suleiman the Magnificent gave Jews control of a portion of the wall and a narrow enclosed pavement, which became the now-familiar prayer area. The lamentations over the destruction of the Temple led to the Arabic name El-Mabka, or Place of Weeping, although the term "Wailing Wall" arose only during 20th-century British rule. The Western

The Western Wall, also known as the Wailing Wall, in Jerusalem. (PhotoDisc, Inc.)

Wall is the literal translation of the traditional Hebrew ha-Kotel ha-Ma'aravi, preferred in Israel because the term "Wailing Wall" smacks of exile and Christian triumphalism.

By the mid-19th century, although they were the majority population in Jerusalem, the Jews lost authority over the Western Wall and found their worship hampered by official restrictions and popular harassment. Under the British Mandate for Palestine (1922–1948), the wall was contested territory and a flash point between Muslims and Jews, as both groups invested holy places with new meaning and asserted their rights in ways that the other found provocative and exclusionary. As the wall became a more regular place of Jewish prayer and symbol of national revival, Muslims began to identify the western rather than eastern or southern portions of the wall as the al-Buraq Wall, to which Muhammad tethered the magical beast that carried him on his miraculous Night Journey.

British maintenance of the late Ottoman Empire status quo regarding holy places strengthened the hand of Arab authorities. The Supreme Muslim Council and in particular the mufti of Jerusalem Haj Amin al-Husseini exploited concern for the Temple Mount, its mosque, and the Dome of the Rock to mobilize anti-Zionist sentiment among the Palestinian masses and the international Muslim community. They denounced any presumed innovation in Jewish

activity at the wall as an attempt to create a synagogue and thus a dire threat.

Conflict over the Western Wall broke out in 1928 and erupted into full-scale violence in 1929 when armed Arab attacks on Jews spread from Jerusalem throughout Palestine. As a result, 133 Jews died and 399 others were wounded, while 87 Arabs lost their lives and 98 more were wounded. The fighting foreshadowed the Arab-Jewish Communal War, accelerating the British tilt toward the Arabs and, in turn, the growth of Haganah, the Jewish underground military organization.

After the Arab states rejected the 1947 United Nations (UN) partition plan for Palestine and the internationalization of Jerusalem, Transjordan seized Jerusalem's Old City in 1948 during the Israeli War of Independence (1948–1949). In direct violation of the 1949 armistice agreements, Jordan denied Jews access to the Western Wall.

Responding to a Jordanian attack on June 5, 1967, Israeli Central Command under Major General Uzi Narkiss launched a hasty counterattack that encircled the Old City of Jerusalem after heavy fighting. On June 7, paratroops under Colonel Mordechai (Motta) Gur took the Temple Mount and linked up with other forces at the Western Wall. This emotional climax of the Six-Day War was broadcast live on Israeli radio as troops spontaneously prayed and sang the national anthem and the popular song "Jerusalem of Gold," coincidentally written just weeks earlier.

Defense Minister Moshe Dayan arrived on the scene to proclaim that Israel had returned to its holy places, never to leave, while also promising freedom of religion to non-Jews. Jerusalem mayor Teddy Kollek soon ordered the demolition of the adjoining Maghribi neighborhood, replacing the old enclosed worship area with a much larger open plaza capable of accommodating large numbers of worshipers. On June 14, 1967, some 250,000 worshipers converged on the Western Wall on the holiday of Shavuot. Legislation passed on June 27, 1967, united Jerusalem under Israeli administration and law.

The unanticipated return to the Western Wall struck Israelis across the political spectrum as miraculous. An ultraobservant Jewish minority took the turn of events literally. They saw it as a sign to advance claims on the Temple Mount through provocative statements and sometimes direct action. For the majority of secular Israelis, the Western Wall, as the only surviving physical remnant of the Temple and symbol of historic national sovereignty, served the needs of both Judaism and civil identity. It has since been used as a site for activities as diverse as prayer and the swearing in of military units. The plaza area today still awaits an aesthetically satisfying architectural plan capable of expressing the complex interrelation of functions and meanings.

The fraught interrelation between the Western Wall/Temple Mount and Haram al-Sharif has led in recent years to much strife and violence. In 1996 clashes led to the greatest outbreak of bloodletting since the beginning of the 1993 Oslo Peace Process. The Western Wall lay at the heart of the failed Camp David peace talks and the subsequent resumption of armed conflict by Palestinians following Ariel Sharon's provocative visit to the Temple Mount in 2000, resulting in the Second (al-Aqsa) Intifada.

Palestinians define the Temple Mount as inalienable Muslim property and are prepared to discuss only worship rights on sufferance at the traditional Wailing Wall, which was actually part of an inalienable waqf to which valid documentation exists. The Israelis demand control over the entire length of the Western Wall, and some groups insist on formal sovereignty over the Temple Mount as well.

Up until Sharon's venture onto the Haram al-Sharif, there had been a tacit understanding that Palestinians should control the Haram al-Sharif but should also contain any disturbances that threatened Jewish access to the Wailing Wall. The increasing tendency in Islamic and Arab discourse is to elevate the religious importance of all Jerusalem and portray it as under threat by Jews, thus resurrecting the al-Aqsa in danger theme from the period of the British Mandate.

Among the many proposals for dividing or sharing sovereignty over the Temple Mount and the Western Wall, the suggestion to sidestep the political problem by assigning sovereignty to God, is perhaps no less realistic than any other. Nevertheless, it presupposes the willingness of each side not to question the faith of the other.

JAMES WALD

See also

Al-Aqsa Mosque; Arab-Jewish Communal War; Arafat, Yasser; Church of the Holy Sepulcher; Dome of the Rock; Gur, Mordechai; Haganah; Haram al-Sharif; Husseini, Haj Amin al-; Intifada, First; Intifada, Second; Israeli War of Independence, Overview; Israeli War of Independence, Truce Agreements; Jerusalem; Jerusalem, Old City of; Oslo Accords; Religious Sites in the Middle East, Christian; Religious Sites in the Middle East, Jewish; Religious Sites in the Middle East, Muslim; Sharon, Ariel; Six-Day War

References

Ben-Dov, Meir, Mordechai Naor, and Zeev Aner. *The Western Wall.* Translated by Raphael Posner. Jerusalem: Ministry of Defence Publishing House, 1983.

Dumper, Michael. *The Politics of Sacred Space: The Old City of Jerusalem in the Middle East Conflict.* Boulder, CO: Lynne Rienner, 2002.

Oren, Michael B. *Six Days of War: June 1967 and the Making of the Modern Middle East.* Novato, CA: Presidio, 2003.

Ross, Dennis. *The Missing Peace: The Inside Story of the Fight for Middle East Peace.* New York: Farrar, Straus and Giroux, 2004.

White Paper (1922)
Event Date: June 3, 1922

British government position paper on Palestine issued on June 3, 1922. The White Paper of 1922 was prompted by increasing Arab resistance to Jewish immigration and land purchases in the British Mandate for Palestine. It also closely followed establishment of Transjordan, constituting the land of Palestine east of the Jordan River that was part of Britain's League of Nations Palestine mandate. In 1921 the British government recognized Abdullah ibn Hussein as de facto king of Transjordan, which was nonetheless still considered part of the British Mandate. Abdullah would reign rather than rule. The British government merely promised to confer independence at some future date.

Zionists were slow to realize the implications of the creation of Transjordan, which in effect excluded land east of the Jordan River as falling under the provisions of the Balfour Declaration. The Arabs' position was quite clear. They wanted a complete repudiation of the Balfour Declaration and an end to Jewish immigration. They also claimed that the land being settled by Jews had been specifically promised to the Arabs in letters exchanged during World War I between British high commissioner for Egypt Sir A. Henry McMahon and Hussein ibn Ali, emir of the Arabian Hejaz and sharif of Mecca.

The White Paper of 1922 was commonly known as the Churchill White Paper because it was issued under the authority of Colonial Secretary Winston Churchill. It was based on correspondence among Churchill, the Arab Palestine delegation, and the World Zionist Organization (WZO). The paper was prompted by the return to London in May 1922 of British high commissioner for Palestine Sir Herbert Samuel, who impressed on Churchill the need to issue some statement to allay growing Arab concerns over the future of Palestine. The high commissioner is generally assumed to have had a major hand in the preparation of the declaration, which was intended to be a definitive statement on the Balfour Declaration and British intentions regarding Palestine.

In his official response on June 3, Churchill denied that the McMahon-Hussein correspondence had promised Palestine to the Arabs. While Churchill reaffirmed British support for a Jewish national home in Palestine, he also denied that the British government had at any time contemplated "that Palestine as a whole should be converted into a Jewish National Home." He noted that there were then some 80,000 Jews in Palestine, a great many of them working in agricultural pursuits, and 25,000 of them having arrived under the mandate. He identified the national home as "not the imposition of a Jewish nationality" upon all Palestine but the further development of the existing Jewish community so that it might become a center "in which the Jewish people as a whole may take, on grounds of religion and race, an interest and a pride." Toward that end, the British government supported additional immigration into Palestine but only enough so as to not exceed the economic capacity of Palestine to receive them. He also specified that the immigration should not deprive from employment "any section of the present population." Churchill called for the establishment of a special committee in Palestine, drawn entirely from the new elected Legislative Council, to confer on immigration matters and then report any concerns to the British government for decision.

Zionist leaders denounced the White Paper as a dilution of the Balfour Declaration and as a British government attempt to restrict Jewish immigration. Nonetheless, the WZO, fearful of losing British support altogether, reluctantly accepted the declaration. The Arab delegation rejected it altogether, however. In testimony before the Peel Commission in 1936, Churchill maintained that the White Paper of 1922 did not preclude the establishment of a Jewish state in Palestine.

SPENCER C. TUCKER

See also

Abdullah I, King of Jordan; Balfour Declaration; Churchill, Sir Winston; Immigration to Palestine/Israel; Jordan; McMahon-Hussein Correspondence; Samuel, Sir Herbert Louis

References

Sachar, Howard M. *A History of Israel: From the Rise of Zionism to Our Time.* 3rd ed. New York: Knopf, 2007.

Shepherd, Naomi. *Ploughing Sand: British Rule in Palestine, 1917–1948.* New Brunswick, NJ: Rutgers University Press, 1999.

White Paper (1930)
Event Date: October 31, 1930

British policy statement on Palestine, issued by the London government on October 31, 1930, under the authority of Colonial Secretary Sidney Webb, Lord Passfield. Prompted by the Arab Uprising in Palestine of 1929–1930, it incorporated the recommendations of both the Shaw Commission and the Hope-Simpson Report. The latter had recommended that the London government issue a dec-

Sidney James Webb (1859–1947), Lord Passfield, British Labour politician, socialist reformer, historian, economist, and, as secretary of state for the colonies, chief proponent of the 1930 Passfield White Paper. (Getty Images)

laration that would clarify its position regarding the future of the British Mandate for Palestine.

The Passfield White Paper was clearly pro-Arab and anti-Zionist in its approach and was an effort to reinterpret the 1917 Balfour Declaration so as to placate the Arab population of Palestine by arresting the movement toward a Jewish state. While it committed Britain to the development of a Jewish national homeland in Palestine, it also said that this was not considered central to the mandate. It stressed that Britain had an equal obligation to both Jews and Arabs in Palestine and that the British authorities had the task of reconciling any differences that arose between them.

Based on the Hope-Simpson findings and alleged shortages of arable land, the Passfield White Paper held that there was no land available in Palestine for agricultural use by new immigrants. It stated that the Palestine government did not hold any land that it might be able to assign to immigrants, and even if it did have such land available, it would have to be assigned to landless Arab farmers. It noted that the Arab population had sharply increased in numbers, while at the same time the amount of land available for Arab farmers had decreased because of land sales to Jews.

The White Paper was also critical of a number of Jewish organizations, including the Jewish Agency and the Histadrut (General Federation of Labor). It accused these groups of stipulating the employment of Jewish labor only on holdings owned by them or under their auspices. Although Jews who had purchased land would be able to continue to develop it, in the future Jews would be required to secure approval from the British authorities for any land purchases. In considering such requests, the authorities would take into consideration the ability of the land to absorb the population as well as the unemployment rates of both Arabs and Jews. It implied future restraints on Jewish immigration, for it held that if economic conditions would not allow, it was the duty of the mandatory power to suspend immigration.

The Passfield White Paper caused an outcry among Zionists and Zionist organizations worldwide, which in turn prompted a debate in Parliament on it during November 17, 1930, in which there was considerable criticism of the government position. Chaim Weizmann and other leading members of the Jewish Agency resigned in protest. As a consequence, British prime minister Ramsay MacDonald wrote a conciliatory letter to Weizmann on February 12, 1931. Made public the next day, this letter somewhat eased the offensive language in the report. MacDonald also said that he would encourage further Jewish settlement in Palestine while at the same time working to safeguard the interests of all groups in the country.

SPENCER C. TUCKER

See also

Balfour Declaration; Hope-Simpson Report; Palestine, British Mandate for; Shaw Commission; United Kingdom, Middle East Policy

References

Sachar, Howard M. *A History of Israel: From the Rise of Zionism to Our Time.* 3rd ed. New York: Knopf, 2007.

Shepherd, Naomi. *Ploughing Sand: British Rule in Palestine, 1917–1948.* New Brunswick, NJ: Rutgers University Press, 1999.

White Paper (1939)
Event Date: May 17, 1939

A British government policy statement that sought to mollify mounting Arab anger over increasing Jewish immigration into Palestine.

Members of the Yemeni community enter a stadium in Tel Aviv for a mass rally against the British White Paper policy, May 27, 1939. (Zoltan Kluger/Israeli Government Press Office)

British efforts to formulate a partition plan for Palestine met staunch opposition both from Arab leaders, who were adamantly opposed to partition, and from Zionist leaders, who objected to the small area assigned to the proposed Jewish state. During February 7–March 17, 1939, the British government hosted a conference in London in the hopes of reaching some solution to the Palestinian problem. This London Round Table Conference (also known as the St. James Palace Conference) was a failure, and two months later, on May 17, 1939, the British government issued a White Paper spelling out its Palestine policy. Colonial Secretary Malcolm MacDonald had already revealed its basic provisions to the Jewish delegation at the end of the London talks.

In the White Paper, the British government stated that 450,000 Jews had settled in Palestine and that the British government had, in consequence, fulfilled its pledges under the Balfour Declaration of 1917 to establish a Jewish national home in Palestine. It called for the establishment of an independent Palestine state within 10 years to be governed jointly by Arabs and Jews. The British government held that it was not the intention of the Balfour Declaration that Palestine be converted into a Jewish state against the will of its Arab population and that London had an obligation to the Arabs to prevent that from happening.

The White Paper sharply restricted Jewish immigration to 75,000 people over the next five years, with immigration thereafter to be entirely contingent on Arab agreement. The White Paper also noted that land sales by Arabs to Jews risked sharply reducing the Arab standard of living, and the document therefore invested the British high commissioner in Palestine with full authority to prohibit and regulate transfers of land.

The House of Commons approved the White Paper in a vote of 208 to 179. The White Paper represented a clear tilt to the Arab position. Jews in Palestine bitterly resented the White Paper, regarding it as a severe check to their hopes of a Jewish state. The immigration restrictions were particularly onerous, given the persecution of Jews in Germany and in Poland. Arabs also opposed the White Paper, however. The Arab Higher Committee, representing the Palestinian Arabs, opposed any new immigration of Jews to Palestine and the establishment of a state there in which the Jews would have a joint governing role. The Arab side sought a complete repudiation of the principle of a Jewish national home in Palestine.

Implementation of the White Paper proceeded slowly, and when the government fell in May 1940 and Winston Churchill became prime minister, it was dropped. Nonetheless, the British government was anxious to maintain Arab support during World War II and worked to prevent wide-scale Jewish immigration to Palestine, turning away Jews there even after full knowledge of the Holocaust. On May 15, 1948, however, the new government of Israel officially abolished the provisions of the White Paper.

SPENCER C. TUCKER

See also

Balfour Declaration; Holocaust; London Round Table Conference

References

Bethell, Nicholas. *The Palestine Triangle: The Struggle for the Holy Land, 1935–48.* New York: Putnam, 1979.

Hurewitz, J. C. *The Struggle for Palestine.* New York: Schocken, 1976.

Sachar, Howard M. *A History of Israel: From the Rise of Zionism to Our Time.* 3rd ed. New York: Knopf, 2007.

Wilson, Thomas Woodrow
Born: December 28, 1856
Died: February 3, 1924

U.S. academic, politician, and president of the United States (1913–1921). Born in Staunton, Virginia, on December 28, 1856, Woodrow Wilson grew up in Augusta, Georgia. The son of a Presbyterian minister and seminary professor, he was raised in a strict religious and academic environment. Wilson studied history and politics at Princeton University, graduating in 1879. He then studied law at the University of Virginia for a year and passed the Georgia bar examination in 1882. Wilson practiced law for a time in Atlanta, but he abandoned it to earn a doctorate in constitutional and political history at Johns Hopkins University in Baltimore in 1886. By then he had joined the faculty at Bryn Mawr College. Wilson returned to Princeton in 1890, first as professor of jurisprudence and political economy and then as president of the university in 1902. He won national acclaim for his academic reforms there.

Woodrow Wilson, president of the United States (1913–1921). (Library of Congress)

Turning to politics, Wilson won election as governor of New Jersey in 1910 as a Democratic Party progressive. His progressive agenda led to his selection as the Democratic Party nominee in the 1912 presidential election, which he won. As president, Wilson was preoccupied with domestic policy and his New Freedom policy, the belief that government should encourage free and competitive markets. He pushed through a tariff that sharply reduced import duties and increased the number of duty-free items. He also introduced the federal income tax, partly a consequence of World War I. On his initiative Congress also passed the Federal Reserve Act of 1913, and he secured passage of the Federal Trade Commission Act and the Clayton Anti-Trust Act.

Wilson was less successful in his foreign policy, where he sought to implement diplomacy based on morality and international law. He pledged that the United States would forgo territorial conquests, and he and his first secretary of state, William Jennings Bryan, worked to establish a new relationship between the United States and Latin America whereby Western Hemisphere states would guarantee each others' territorial integrity and political independence.

Despite Wilson's best intentions to avoid conflict with U.S. neighbors, he sent forces to occupy Veracruz, Mexico, in April 1914. Incidents along the border caused him two years later to mobilize the National Guard and dispatch a regular army force into northern Mexico under Brigadier General John J. Pershing in a vain attempt to capture the Mexican revolutionary Pancho Villa. Although the operation was unsuccessful in its stated intent, it did provide useful training for the army.

Wilson proclaimed U.S. neutrality when World War I began in August 1914, calling on Americans to be neutral in thought as well as action. The German Navy's sinking of the passenger liner *Lusitania* on May 7, 1915, and the deaths of 128 Americans led Wilson to threaten war, compelling Germany to halt unrestricted submarine warfare. Wilson won reelection in 1916 primarily on the platform of having kept the United States out of the war. Nonetheless, the National Defense Act of 1916 greatly enlarged the peacetime army and National Guard and provided for the establishment of reserve formations and the Reserve Officers' Training Corps (ROTC).

German acts of sabotage against the United States and publication of the Zimmermann Telegram, in which the German government proposed an alliance with Mexico, alienated American opinion. But the great blow to Wilson's efforts to keep the United States neutral came when Germany resumed unrestricted submarine warfare in February 1917. The sinking of U.S. merchant ships and the loss of American lives led Wilson to seek a declaration of war, which Congress approved on April 6, 1917.

Wilson made it clear that the country was merely an associated power, fighting the same enemy, and he refused to bind the United States to an annexationist peace settlement. With no military experience of his own, he deferred to his military advisers. He instructed American Expeditionary Forces (AEF) commander General Pershing to cooperate with the forces of other countries fighting Germany but to preserve the separate identity of the AEF. Wilson supported Pershing in his refusal to have the Allies employ AEF units piecemeal, but in the spring 1918 crisis, Wilson made it clear that Pershing was subordinate to new Allied generalissimo Ferdinand Foch of France.

Wilson's peace platform was to "make the world safe for democracy." He also unwisely referred to the conflict as "the war to end all wars." In January 1918 he announced his Fourteen Points as a basis of peace. Two key points were the support of self-determination for all peoples and the forming of a League of Nations, a supranational group that would work collaboratively to prevent war and international discord. U.S. forces had decisively tipped the balance in favor of the Allies, and Wilson played this to full advantage.

Wilson decided to head the U.S. delegation to the Paris Peace Conference in 1919. He traveled widely before the conference began and was lionized by the peoples of Europe, convincing him that they wanted him to be the arbiter of the peace and that they favored a settlement based on rightness rather than on narrow national self-interests. The president erred in not including key Republicans in the U.S. delegation and not leaving diplomatic wrangling to seasoned diplomats.

Wilson developed a close working relationship with British prime minister David Lloyd George. The two men stood together on most key issues against French premier Georges Clemenceau. The League of Nations was based on an Anglo-American draft, and Wilson strongly opposed French efforts to detach the Rhineland from Germany. The resulting Treaty of Versailles with Germany and the general peace settlement were essentially Wilson's work.

Wilson early favored Zionist aspirations in Palestine, not only because of his strong Christian background but also because of his friendship with such prominent American Zionists as Louis D. Brandeis, Felix Frankfurter, and Stephen S. Wise. Despite Secretary of State Robert Lansing's opposition, Wilson officially supported the British government's 1917 Balfour Declaration that called for the establishment of a Jewish national homeland in Palestine after the war. In 1920 after the Paris Peace Conference, Wilson opposed French efforts to secure a strip of territory from the British Mandate for Palestine to add to the French Mandate for Syria.

When Wilson returned to the United States from Paris in July 1919, popular sentiment had moved toward isolationism. The Republicans, led by Senator Henry Cabot Lodge, insisted upon restricting the League of Nation's power. Even some Democrats wanted amendments. Wilson embarked upon a cross-country speaking tour in an effort to sway public opinion, but he suffered a serious stroke on October 2, 1919, that left him virtually incapacitated for the remainder of his administration. When he insisted that Democrats in the Senate reject any compromises in the agreements, the Senate refused twice to ratify the Treaty of Versailles or enter the League of Nations. In the end, Wilson's call for self-determination that had heartened peoples in the Middle East and elsewhere did not come to fruition. Instead, Britain and France secured mandates over large swaths of the region that would last for another generation. Wilson died in Washington, D.C., on February 3, 1924.

Spencer C. Tucker

See also
Balfour Declaration; Brandeis, Louis Dembitz; World War I, Impact of; Zionism

References
Knock, Thomas J. *To End All Wars: Woodrow Wilson and the Quest for a New World Order.* Princeton, NJ: Princeton University Press, 1995.
MacMillan, Margaret. *Paris 1919: Six Months That Changed the World.* New York: Random House, 2002.
Nordholt, John Willem Schulte. *Woodrow Wilson: A Life for World Peace.* Berkeley: University of California Press, 1991.
Thompson, John A. *Woodrow Wilson.* London: Longman, 2002.

Wingate, Orde Charles
Born: February 23, 1903
Died: March 24, 1944

British Army general. Orde Wingate was born to a military family in Naini Tal, India, on February 23, 1903. He attended Charterhouse Public School and then the Royal Military Academy at Woolwich, from which he graduated in 1923 with a commission in the Royal Artillery. From 1928 to 1933 he served with the Sudan Defense Force, where he learned Arabic and honed his skills in small unit leadership by conducting patrols and ambushes along the Ethiopian border.

Wingate was assigned to the British Mandate for Palestine as an intelligence officer in 1936, just after the start of the Arab Revolt. Although most British officers and official British government policy were openly pro-Arab, Wingate became fervently pro-Jewish. His mother had come from a missionary family affiliated with the Plymouth Brethren, and Wingate grew up imbued with Christian Zionist ideals. He soon set about learning Hebrew, which he never really mastered.

Wingate first convinced resistant British commanders to permit him to arm and train Jewish volunteers to counter the increasing Arab raids and guerrilla attacks, and then he overcame the skepticism of the leaders of the Jewish Agency and Haganah. In 1938 Wingate formed, trained, and commanded the Special Night Squads (SNS) comprised of Haganah volunteers and a cadre of British regulars. The SNS mission was to defend Jewish settlements that were completely surrounded by Arab territory.

Up until that point, Haganah had relied almost exclusively on passive defensive tactics, waiting until a settlement was attacked and then defending from inside the perimeter. Wingate taught the Jews to take the battle to the Arabs, mounting active defenses of the settlements in the form of night patrols and ambushes near the exits to Arab villages to stop the attackers even before they could get started. Stressing leadership from the front, Wingate taught the importance of speed, surprise, imagination, and psychological leverage. A soldier's most important weapon was his mind.

Wingate's extreme views helped bring about his transfer back to Britain in May 1939. He subsequently gained fame as one of the most aggressive and innovative special operations commanders of

British Army officer Orde Wingate, who helped form, train, and command the Special Night Squads that defended Jewish settlements in Palestine from Arab attack. (Corbis)

World War II. Sent to the Sudan to drive the Italians from Ethiopia (Abyssinia), he commanded Gideon Force during the East African Campaign of 1941 and was awarded the Distinguished Service Order. Exhausted and ill, he attempted suicide in Cairo in June 1941. In early 1942 he went to the China-Burma-India theater and formed the Chindits, a long-range penetration group designed for operations against the Japanese in Burma. Although his large-scale raids had only mixed military results, they raised Allied morale in a theater in which the Japanese had heretofore enjoyed only success. On March 24, 1944, Major General Wingate was returning to India from a Chindit base in Burma when the American B-25 bomber in which he was a passenger crashed into a jungle-covered mountain, killing all on board.

Wingate was a dynamic small unit leader and a brilliant tactician. He was also a man with huge personal eccentricities and some would also say psychological problems. Nonetheless, he completely changed Haganah's thinking about military operations, and his influence can be clearly seen in the Israel Defense Forces (IDF) approach to war fighting to this day. Two of his protégés in the SNS, Yigal Yadin and Moshe Dayan, would become two of the most important leaders in the IDF. Israel's National Center for Physical Education and Sport is known as the Wingate Institute.

DAVID T. ZABECKI

See also
Arab Revolt of 1936–1939; Dayan, Moshe; Haganah; Israel Defense
   Forces; Yadin, Yigal

References
Bierman, John, and Colin Smith. *Fire in the Night: Wingate of Burma,
   Ethiopia, and Zion.* New York: Random House, 1999.
Royle, Trevor. *Orde Wingate: Irregular Soldier.* London: Weidenfeld and
   Nicolson, 1995.
Sykes, Christopher. *Orde Wingate.* London: Collins, 1959.

Wise, Isaac Mayer
Born: March 29, 1819
Died: March 26, 1900

Chief architect of Reform Judaism in the United States. Born Isaac
Weis on March 29, 1819, in Steingrub, Bohemia (now part of the
Czech Republic), he received a traditional Jewish upbringing, devot-
ing himself to mastering Hebrew and the tenets of the Jewish faith.
At age 12 he moved to Prague to study the Talmud and Jewish law
at various yeshivas. Educated at universities in Prague and Vienna,
Austria, he became a rabbi in 1842, moving to a congregation in
Radnitz, Bohemia, the following year.

Learning of the movement in Germany to reform traditional
Judaism, Weis attended the conference of Reform rabbis in Frankfurt, Germany, in 1845. A year later he decided to immigrate to the
United States in order to escape from the government restrictions
on Jews and also to advance the new religious ideas in the freer
atmosphere of America. He and his family arrived in New York City
in July 1846. There he changed his name to Wise.

Becoming rabbi of a synagogue in Albany, New York, that same
year, Wise immediately set to work to reform his congregation. At
the time, most of the nearly 60,000 Jews living in the United States
still followed traditional practices. Among the reforms suggested at
the Frankfurt conference and now proposed by Wise were limiting
the use of Hebrew in favor of the native language at services, employing choirs and organs, seating men and women together, and eliminating the prayer for the return of the Jewish people to Palestine.

These reforms so divided Wise's congregation that it split into
two factions. In 1851 the faction favoring reform broke away to
establish a separate congregation with Wise as its rabbi. Over the
next years he worked to spread the ideas of Reform Judaism by contributing columns to national Jewish periodicals, writing books and
scholarly articles, and preparing *Minhag America,* a prayer book
of American Reform rites.

In 1854 Wise was elected rabbi for life of the Bene Yeshurun synagogue, a large, wealthy reform congregation in Cincinnati, Ohio.
Soon after his arrival in the city, he began publication of a weekly
newspaper, the *Israelite* (later the *American Israelite*). Under his
leadership, Cincinnati became the center of Reform Judaism in
America.

Wise defended the rights of Jews in the United States and encouraged immigrant Jews to become Americanized. He was sharply

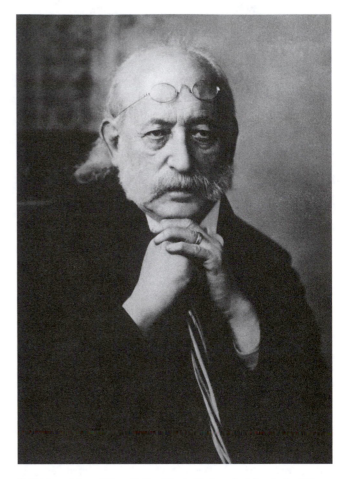

Rabbi Isaac Mayer Wise, chief architect of Reform Judaism in the 19th
century in the United States. (Bettmann/Corbis)

---

critical of Ohio governor Salmon P. Chase for calling the United
States a "Christian nation." Before the American Civil War, Wise had
frequently locked horns with abolitionists because of his willingness to accept slavery as the price of maintaining the Union. Wise
was also outspoken in his opposition to the Zionist movement that
sought to establish a Jewish homeland in Palestine.

Eager to bring about unity among the various Jewish groups in
the United States, Wise founded the Union of American Hebrew
Congregations (UAHC) in July 1873. He hoped that this organization would include Orthodox Jews (who were arriving from Eastern
Europe in large numbers) and Sephardic Jews (who had been in
America since pre-Revolutionary days) as well as the Reform Jews
of mostly German background. But the UAHC attracted only Reform
congregations.

Wise's second major project was to start a seminary to train
rabbis for the American Reform movement. On October 3, 1875, the
Hebrew Union College was established in Cincinnati with Wise as
its president, a position he held for the rest of his life. He influenced
a generation of graduates who carried his ideas to congregations
throughout the country.

The third part of Wise's agenda involved establishing a rabbinical organization, which he accomplished in July 1889 with the

founding of the Central Conference of American Rabbis. Wise served as president of the conference for the remainder of his life. Regarded as the most prominent American Jew of his lifetime in the United States, Wise died in Cincinnati on March 26, 1900.

SPENCER C. TUCKER

See also
Reform Judaism and Zionism; Zionism

References
May, Max B. *Isaac Mayer Wise, the Founder of American Judaism: A Biography*. New York: Putnam, 1916.
Wise, Isaac M. *Reminiscences*. New York: Central Synagogue of New York, 1945.

Wolf, John Stern
Born: September 12, 1948

U.S. State Department official, chief of the U.S. Coordinating and Monitoring Mission (USCMM), and assistant secretary of state for nonproliferation. John Stern Wolf was born in Philadelphia on September 12, 1948. He graduated from Dartmouth College in 1970 with a BA in English. He then entered the U.S. Foreign Service. His first posting was to Vietnam. He subsequently served in Australia, Greece, and Pakistan. From 1989 to 1982 he was principal deputy assistant secretary of state for International Organization and Affairs. From 1992 to 1995 he served as ambassador to Malaysia. In January 1996 he was appointed coordinator for the Asia-Pacific Economic Cooperation (APEC), and in February 1997 the U.S. Senate confirmed him as ambassador to APEC.

On September 11, 2001, President George W. Bush nominated Wolf to be assistant secretary of state for nonproliferation. In June 2003 he was asked to serve as chief of the USCMM while simultaneously retaining his duties as assistant secretary for nonproliferation. The mission of the USCMM was to monitor and facilitate the so-called Road Map to Peace in the U.S. Middle East peace initiative. Reporting directly to then–National Security Adviser Condoleezza Rice, Wolf established a plan based on a matrix of nine spheres on which the USCMM would continually evaluate Israeli and Palestinian performance. In early August 2003 he returned to Washington for the visits of Israeli prime minister Ariel Sharon and Palestinian Authority (PA) prime minister Mahmoud Abbas.

Despite some hopeful signs of progress in late August and early September 2003, several suicide bombings stalled much of the momentum of the peace process. Meanwhile, infighting and endless turf wars on the Palestinian side all but produced complete gridlock on any of the much-needed internal reforms. In late September, Wolf was recalled to Washington for consultations. On October 15, 2003, just prior to his scheduled return, a Palestinian terrorist group attacked a U.S. diplomatic convoy in Gaza, killing three security guards.

Wolf never returned to Jerusalem. The U.S. government waited for two weeks for the PA to take some action regarding the attack.

When nothing was done, the remaining USCMM members were withdrawn in early November.

Wolf retired from the State Department in June 2004. In August 2004 he assumed the presidency of the Eisenhower Fellowships.

DAVID T. ZABECKI

See also
Abbas, Mahmoud; Palestinian Authority; Rice, Condoleezza; Sharon, Ariel; United States Coordinating and Monitoring Mission

References
Balaban, Oden, and Michael Graham Fry, eds. *Interpreting Conflict: Israeli-Palestinian Relations at Camp David II and Beyond*. New York: Peter Lang, 2005.
Leverett, Flynt, ed. *The Road Ahead: Middle East Policy in the Bush Administration's Second Term*. Washington, DC: Brookings Institution, 2005.

Wolffsohn, David
Born: October 9, 1856
Died: September 15, 1914

Zionist leader, businessman, and second president of the World Zionist Organization (WZO) from 1905 to 1911. David Wolffsohn was born in Darbenai, Lithuania, on October 9, 1856. He was educated in a traditional Jewish fashion and moved to East Prussia in 1872, where he met several proto-Zionist rabbis.

Possessing a keen sense for business, Wolffsohn became involved in a major lumber operation in Köln (Cologne), Germany, where he would live for much of his life. There he also became involved with a Jewish literary society, a group to which he lectured on a variety of topics including Zionism. Becoming more and more interested in Zionism, Wolffsohn was mesmerized by Theodor Herzl's 1896 publication *Der Judenstaat* (*The Jewish State*). That same year Wolffsohn was determined to meet Herzl in person. Thus, Wolffsohn traveled to Vienna to meet with Herzl, an encounter that was the beginning of a lifelong partnership and friendship between the two men.

Herzl and Wolffsohn made a rather curious pair. Herzl was highly theoretical and not well versed in business. Wolffsohn, on the other hand, was a masterful business strategist and had a deep knowledge of Jewish life in Eastern Europe. In 1898 Herzl dispatched his associate to London to expound on political Zionism and raise money from Jewish businessmen and financiers. Shortly thereafter, Wolffsohn created the Jewish Colonial Trust, which would become the chief source of money for the WZO. In spite of their friendship, Herzl and Wolffsohn locked horns many times during the former's tenure as president of the WZO. Much of the discord involved money. Herzl was inclined to treat the Colonial Trust as a political tool, whereas Wolffsohn sought to run the trust as a business. Be that as it may, Wolffsohn remained Herzl's closest associate and confidant.

When Herzl died in 1904, Wolffsohn appeared to be the heir apparent in regard to the WZO. Yet he was not anxious to take on

David Wolffsohn (1856–1914), German businessman and Zionist leader, circa 1890. (Imagno/Getty Images)

in 1918 and went on to become Israel's premier university. Wolff-sohn died on September 15, 1914, in Hamburg, Germany.

PAUL G. PIERPAOLI JR.

See also

Der Judenstaat; Herzl, Theodor; Weizmann, Chaim; World Zionist Organization; Zionism

References

Cohn, Emil Bernhard. *David Wolffsohn: Herzl's Successor.* New York: Zionist Organization of America, 1944.

Laqueur, Walter. *A History of Zionism: From the French Revolution to the Establishment of the State of Israel.* Reprint ed. New York: Schocken, 2003.

Robertson, Ritchie, and Edward Timms, eds. *Theodor Herzl and the Origins of Zionism.* Edinburgh, UK: Edinburgh University Press, 1997.

Woodhead Report
Event Date: November 9, 1938

British government report of November 9, 1938, designed to address the partition of the British Mandate for Palestine in light of the Peel Commission findings of July 1937. Faced with mounting Arab violence in Palestine, the British government appointed yet another commission to study the Palestine situation. The government hoped that the commission might reassure the Arabs and reduce Arab violence.

The commission was charged with making recommendations to Parliament regarding the partition of the mandate into separate Arab and Jewish states as called for by the Peel Commission and providing specific delineation of the borders of the two proposed states. Sir John Woodhead, a former official in the British administration in India, headed the four-man commission. The members of the commission traveled to Palestine in April 1938. Arab leaders there, who were resolutely opposed to partition, refused to meet with the commission, and as a result it met almost exclusively with British officials and representatives of the Jewish community.

The Woodhead Commission remained in Palestine until August. The members then discussed their findings and duly delivered a report to Parliament on November 9, 1958. This 310-page document held that no plan would win the support of both Arabs and Jews. It also stated that while a Jewish state might be viable economically, this was unlikely to be the case for an Arab state without the Jewish hinterland. Indeed, the commission itself was in sharp disagreement on any specific recommendations. The report rejected the Peel Commission plan and proposed two alternatives. Plan B would reduce the size of the proposed Jewish state by the addition of Galilee to the permanently mandated area and the addition of the southern part of the region south of Jaffa to the Arab state. Plan C would limit the Jewish state to the coastal plain between Zikhron Yaagov and Rehovoth, while northern Palestine and all of southern Palestine would be under a separate mandate. Two commission members favored Plan C, one favored Plan B, and one declared that no partition plan was possible.

such a visible leadership role, and a faction within the WZO (known as the practical Zionists) would not support his candidacy. Nevertheless, he was elected president in 1905. He threw himself headlong into his work, traveling extensively and trying to pull the WZO together by championing political Zionism. From 1906 to 1908 he was constantly traveling. He visited Russia, Palestine, Hungary, Turkey, and even South Africa while advancing the Zionist vision. In Hungary and Russia he conferred with top-level government officials in an attempt to ease conditions for Jews there and to gain support for the Zionist cause. When he traveled to Constantinople (Istanbul) to meet with officials there, he negotiated with Sultan Abdulhamid II via a Turkish diplomat, although Wolffsohn's efforts were diluted by the rise to power of the Young Turks in 1908.

When Wolffsohn's term was completed in 1911, growing opposition within the WZO to his leadership blocked his reelection, for which the reluctant leader may have been grateful. He stayed actively engaged in the Zionist movement, however, and in Vienna in 1913 he presided over the Eleventh Zionist Congress. After Zionist pioneer Chaim Weizmann introduced his plans for the Hebrew University to the congress, Wolffsohn was the first individual to make a major contribution to this project. The university opened

Upon publication of the Woodhouse Report, the British government issued a statement to the effect that the report proved that partition was impracticable. At the same time, however, the government suggested that some sort of accommodation might yet be possible between Arabs and Jews. This hope led to the futile London Round Table talks (St. James Palace Conference) of February–March 1939.

SPENCER C. TUCKER

See also

Balfour Declaration; Peel Commission; White Paper (1939)

References

Bethell, Nicholas. *The Palestine Triangle: The Struggle for the Holy Land, 1935–48.* New York: Putnam, 1979.

Hurewitz, J. C. *The Struggle for Palestine.* New York: Schocken, 1976.

Sachar, Howard M. *A History of Israel: From the Rise of Zionism to Our Time.* 3rd ed. New York: Knopf, 2007.

World Jewish Congress

The World Jewish Congress (WJC) was officially founded in Geneva in 1936 as a representative assembly dedicated to solving the problems of the worldwide Jewish Diaspora. The WJC traces its roots primarily to two institutions, the American Jewish Congress (AJC) and the Committee of Jewish Delegations (CJD). Both were founded in the immediate aftermath of World War I. The AJC concentrated on the United States and North America, with headquarters in New York City, while the CJD focused on the European Jewish population and maintained its offices in Paris. Both sought to provide a voice to the Jewish population of Europe in the treaty negotiations at Versailles in 1919. The CJD also explicitly sought the creation of a worldwide organization to promote Jewish causes, eventually realized in the WJC.

The initial meeting dedicated to creating the WJC was held in August 1932 in Geneva. It was titled the First Preparatory World Jewish Conference and was followed by two more conferences, each dedicated to creating the WJC. In August 1936 Rabbi Stephen S. Wise called to order the First Plenary Assembly of the WJC. He was promptly elected president of the WJC, a position he held until his death. Cofounder Nahum Goldmann assumed the post after Wise's death, holding the position until 1977. Only three more presidents have led the organization: Philip M. Klutznick from 1977 to 1979, Edgar M. Bronfman from 1979 to June 2007, and Ronald S. Lauder from June 2007 to the present.

From its inception, the WJC was dedicated to the creation and preservation of a Jewish national state in Palestine, although it has rarely weighed in on the internal politics of Israel. The WJC argued

Israeli prime minister Ehud Barak (*third from right*) attends a meeting of the World Jewish Congress in Stockholm, Sweden, on January 26, 2000. The meeting coincided with a forum on the Holocaust. (Amos Ben Gershom/Israeli Government Press Office)

that the creation of a Jewish state was vital to the survival of the Jewish people, the foremost goal of the organization. The events of World War II, particularly the Nazi-inspired Holocaust, served to demonstrate the urgency of the Zionist position.

As Nazism became more prevalent in Germany and began to strongly influence the rest of Europe, the need for a coordinating body such as the WJC became self-evident. Throughout the 1930s as German persecutions of Jews increased, the leaders of the eventual WJC began to coordinate resistance efforts aimed at protecting the rights of Jewish individuals. In August 1932 the First Preparatory World Jewish Conference convened in Geneva and was chaired by Goldmann. Even before the Preparatory Committee coalesced into the WJC, he began requesting audiences with European governments and the League of Nations. In addition to pursuing political and diplomatic contacts, the Preparatory Committee organized and led an economic boycott of worldwide Jews against Germany. The committee coordinated efforts to increase Jewish emigration from Germany while documenting injustices against the Jews of Europe. However, the world was unwilling to devote significant energy to alleviating the plight of Jews in Europe. Thus, relief efforts proved woefully inadequate to counter the depredations of the Nazi regime.

The first headquarters of the WJC was in Paris with a subsidiary office in Geneva. As such, the early efforts of the WJC were clearly dedicated to the Jews of Europe, with the worldwide Jewish population a secondary concern. The WJC continued and expanded the efforts of the Preparatory Committee with a broader effort to combat anti-Semitism and protect the political and economic rights of Jews. Much of the WJC's focus was on short-term problems, including providing immediate economic relief to victims of the German government's anti-Jewish laws.

When World War II commenced in Europe, the WJC shifted its headquarters operations to the Geneva office in neutral Switzerland. This move alleviated communications difficulties across embattled Europe but also reduced the influence of the WJC on Allied war aims. The move proved short-lived. In 1940 the WJC headquarters moved to New York City, occupying offices belonging to the AJC. The move was prompted by the virtual conquest of Europe by Germany, which greatly hindered WJC operations even in Geneva. A special European office was established in London, but the vast majority of WJC leadership transferred to the United States for the duration of the conflict. As the war continued, WJC operatives began planning for postwar activities, including the creation of war crimes tribunals and the preparation of reparations claims against the Axis powers. WJC efforts to publicize the Holocaust during the war fell upon deaf ears in Europe and America, increasing the belief of WJC leadership that an independent Jewish state was a vital means to safeguarding the worldwide Jewish population.

At the end of World War II, the WJC became quite active in the reconstruction of Jewish communities in Europe. Its myriad activities included short-term charitable assistance as well as long-term efforts to influence Allied leadership to demand reparations from Germany. The WJC helped Holocaust survivors immigrate to Palestine and also pushed the British government to uphold promises of the creation of a Jewish state. The WJC contributed to modern definitions of war crimes as a means to avoid future genocides such as the Holocaust.

One of the foremost goals of the WJC was realized on May 14, 1948, with the proclamation of the State of Israel. The WJC immediately offered support and assistance to the new nation, particularly by influencing Western powers to recognize and supply Israel. After 1948 the WJC broadened its focus, devoting more attention to Jewish communities outside of Europe and Israel. In particular, the Jewish populations of North Africa and the Soviet Union received considerable attention. However, efforts to punish the perpetrators of the Holocaust remained paramount within the WJC. For 30 years after the war, the WJC assisted Holocaust survivors in pursuing reparations claims.

In the 1990s the WJC became involved in lawsuits demanding the return of property confiscated by the German government from its Jewish citizens. Much of the confiscated property is believed to have been deposited in Swiss banks. The WJC has increased its partnerships with other humanitarian organizations, including the Red Cross and the Red Crescent. It has also increased interfaith initiatives to reduce religious tensions threatening worldwide Jewish communities, especially in Israel.

The headquarters of the WJC remains in New York, with secondary offices throughout the world. The primary research offices of the WJC are currently located in Jerusalem. The organization holds a diplomatic seat in the United Nations (UN), where it serves as a worldwide leader pushing for the recognition and protection of the rights of Jewish citizens throughout the world. The WJC is open to all Jewish communities in the world and scrupulously avoids advocating a political creed to avoid antagonizing national governments. The WJC remains dedicated to promoting worldwide Jewish solidarity and the peaceful existence of Israel.

PAUL J. SPRINGER

See also

Goldmann, Nahum; Holocaust; Zionism

References

Laqueur, Walter. *A History of Zionism: From the French Revolution to the Establishment of the State of Israel.* Reprint ed. New York: Schocken, 2003.

Linzer, Norman, David J. Schnall, and Jerome A. Chanes, eds. *A Portrait of the American Jewish Community.* Westport, CT: Praeger, 1998.

O'Brien, Lee. *American Jewish Organizations & Israel.* Washington, DC: Institute for Palestine Studies, 1986.

World War I, Impact of
Start Date: June 28, 1914
End Date: November 11, 1918

World War I (1914–1918) was perhaps the most important political event in the evolution of the modern Middle East. The issues that

British troops march through the Jebel Hamrin Mountains during the Mesopotamian Campaign, 1917. (National Archives and Records Administration)

fuel the current Arab-Israeli dispute and serve as roadblocks to peace originated during World War I in the Middle East and its immediate aftermath. The war had three notable effects on the development of what would become an ongoing war between Arabs and Zionists in Palestine. The first was the destruction of the Ottoman Empire and its division into a number of smaller political units that ultimately became independent states in the modern Middle East. The second was the assumption of direct administrative responsibility for the territories in and around Palestine by Britain and France, two of the victors in that war. The third was the British declaration of support for the central goal of the Zionist movement, a Jewish homeland in Palestine. This was accomplished with the 1917 Balfour Declaration.

The war accelerated political and social trends that had been eroding the strength of the Ottoman Empire for the preceding century and a half. Meanwhile, the great powers of Europe had been steadily expanding their influence in Turkish-controlled areas. Britain's worldwide influence and its strategic presence in the Middle East had grown considerably since the construction of the Suez Canal in 1869. Indeed, safeguarding the route to India was a cornerstone of British policy in the Middle East. As such, the British sought to dominate the territories near Suez and the Persian Gulf—Egypt, Palestine, and Iraq—in order to keep their passage to India

and the Far East secure. France, for its part, sought to control Syria and Lebanon to safeguard the Maronite Christian population and give France a presence in the Eastern Mediterranean. Czarist Russia sought an opening through the Dardanelles and the protection of Orthodox Christian sites in Jerusalem. Germany wanted to influence the region and tap its resources through the construction of the Berlin to Baghdad Railway.

In addition to the growing encroachment of the European powers, the Ottoman Empire faced growing ethnic unrest among its minority populations. This was particularly the case among the Armenians, the growing Jewish population in Palestine (most of whom were fleeing persecution in Russia), and the Bedouin Arab tribes in the Arabian Peninsula.

The outbreak of war in August 1914 and the Turkish entry into the conflict on the German side in September along with wartime developments greatly accelerated the process of Ottoman disintegration. Wartime privations and Turkish repression (manifested in the Armenian massacres of 1915 and in intensified persecution of Jews in Palestine) triggered nationalist feelings and hatred of the Turks among these minorities. The British, hoping to take advantage of this, encouraged unrest among Arabs throughout the Ottoman Empire by promising them support for independence. At the same time, however, the British were negotiating postwar spheres of influence in the Middle East with the French. This was effected through the 1916 Sykes-Picot Agreement. Later, Italy and Russia would also become parties to these clandestine machinations.

Anglo-French imperial ambitions soon ran head-on into growing Arab and Jewish nationalism. The fall of the Ottoman Empire destroyed the state that had united Turks, Arabs, Armenians, and Jews within a single political and social framework for more than four centuries. Its disappearance brought the emergence of a variety of competing nationalist movements that offered their citizens alternate approaches of constructing their political identities and their cultural communities. Many times, one movement's goals were diametrically opposed to those of another. British pledges to the Arabs and their support for uprisings on the Arabian Peninsula fueled Arab nationalism that was to translate into resentment of Allied duplicity and a sense of betrayal when Britain and France established League of Nations mandates in Iraq, Syria, Lebanon, and Palestine after the war.

Britain's postwar difficulties with Palestinian Arabs were greatly compounded by the Balfour Declaration. Of all the wartime promises made by the British, the Balfour Declaration would have the most far-reaching consequences. In July 1917 British foreign secretary Arthur Balfour placed a notice in the *Times of London* promising British support for a Jewish homeland in Palestine. Based on a draft written by Baron Edmond de Rothschild (although Balfour modified it considerably before publication), it stated that the government favorably viewed the establishment of a Jewish national home in Palestine. The declaration avoided any mention of a Jewish state and stated clearly that there was to be no impingement on the civil and religious rights of indigenous non-Jewish populations.

Why the British chose to support Zionist ambitions in 1917 has been the subject of considerable controversy among scholars and analysts of British wartime Middle Eastern policies. Clearly, a number of factors were involved. Some observers have emphasized the strategic benefits that the British government believed Britain would derive from Jewish settlement in Palestine. Many British policymakers believed that a Jewish national homeland in Palestine, surrounded by a large Arab population and dependent on Britain for support and security, would provide an ideal safeguard for the Suez Canal and the route to India. Others argue that the British had one eye on influential Jews in the United States, particularly prominent Zionists such as Louis D. Brandeis and Felix Frankfurter who were close to the Woodrow Wilson administration. In this view, the British government was influenced by a patrician form of anti-Semitism that overestimated Jewish influence in the United States. Other viewpoints emphasize intense lobbying efforts by Zionist leaders, particularly Chaim Weizmann; fears that Germany might take over the Zionist movement; or efforts by Allied policymakers to reach out to the leaders of the Russian Revolution, many of whom were Jewish.

Whatever the reasons behind Balfour's action and however careful the Balfour Declaration's wording, the declaration ultimately poisoned Arab-Jewish relations in Palestine and undermined Britain's

credibility in both communities. The leadership of the Zionist movement and the Jewish community in Palestine took the declaration as a British commitment to a Jewish state in the long run and, in the short term, as support for unlimited Jewish immigration to Palestine.

Arabs, both in Palestine and in the wider Middle East, saw the Balfour Declaration as a great betrayal and evidence of Britain's lack of good faith. Arab nationalism now took on an intensely anti-British and anti-Western bent that could not be contained by the fragmented postwar order of protectorates dominated by the British and the French. The administrators of the British Mandate for Palestine were plagued by intensifying communal violence between the growing number of Jewish settlers and the indigenous Arab population. Nationalistic feelings in both Arab and Jewish camps—intensified by the persecution and suffering during World War I and, in the case of the Jews, fueled by persecution in Europe and the growing threat posed by the rise of Nazism in Germany—simply could not be reconciled. British and French wartime measures taken to aid the Allied war effort against the Ottoman Empire opened a Pandora's box that has not been closed.

WALTER F. BELL

See also

Arab Nationalism; Balfour Declaration; Geography of the Middle East; Iraq; Land Rights and Disputes; Lebanon; Palestine, British Mandate for; Sykes-Picot Agreement; Syria; Weizmann, Chaim; World War II, Impact of; Zionism; Zionist Conference

References

Fromkin, David. *A Peace to End All Peace: The Fall of the Ottoman Empire and the Creation of the Modern Middle East.* New York: Avon, 1989.
Gelvin, James L. *The Israel-Palestine Conflict: One Hundred Years of War.* New York: Cambridge University Press, 2005.
Morris, Benny. *Righteous Victims: A History of the Zionist-Arab Conflict, 1881–2001.* New York: Vintage Books, 2001.

World War II, Impact of
Start Date: September 1939
End Date: August 1945

When World War II began in September 1939, the political situation in the Middle East and particularly in Palestine was quite unsettled. Although British authorities had put down the Palestinian Arab Revolt of 1936–1939, there was still considerable unrest in the region. Meanwhile, the British government's White Paper of May 1939 caused great resentment in the Jewish community without satisfying the Arabs. World War II, however, put the three-sided struggle for control of Palestine on hold. Whatever their differences with Britain, the Palestinian Jewish community and Zionists worldwide were obliged to support Britain and the Allies against Nazi Germany. In terms of the Arab population, at least temporary quiescence with the British had been assured by wartime prosperity in the area, British restrictions on Jewish immigration, and the fact

Jewish sailors at the British Naval Base, Haifa, March 21, 1943. (Zoltan Kluger/Israeli Government Press Office)

that the Arab instigators of the Great Palestinian Rebellion had either fled or been imprisoned.

Although Palestine remained relatively calm during the World War II years, events outside the region changed the political balance of power dramatically and altered the parameters of the Palestine debate and the Arab-Zionist dispute. The war changed the politics of the area in three ways. First, the war left the British people exhausted and Britain deep in debt, making it imperative for the British government to reduce imperial commitments, including those in the Middle East. Second, the international Zionist community intensified its demands for the establishment of a Jewish state in Palestine. Third, the Holocaust and the ensuing need to find homes for tens of thousands of displaced Jewish survivors put great pressure on the victorious Allies to place them in Palestine, which then led to intensified violent resistance among Palestinian Arabs.

The most immediate of these three changes was the war's economic, social, and political impact on Britain. By 1943 it had become clear that Britain's financial and manpower resources were nearing exhaustion. British forces were spread thin around the globe, and Britain had been forced into increased reliance on the Dominions for manpower and production and on the United States for material and financial support through Lend-Lease assistance. Indeed, Britain ended the war $13 billion in debt, having borrowed heavily

from the United States and the Dominions and against its own sterling reserves in India and Egypt. At the same time, the British people were demanding concentration on long-neglected social programs that would ensure cradle-to-grave security. Most British policymakers, and especially the new Labour government that took power in July 1945, realized that London could no longer maintain the empire in its prewar form. In addition, the British believed that they would have to convince their more powerful ally, the United States, to become more involved in resolving the Palestinian question. The decline of British power in the Middle East and the corresponding rise of the United States and the Soviet Union radically changed the dynamics both between the Arab and Jewish disputants and among the outside powers with interests in the area.

The second significant change generated by the war concerned the demands of the international Zionist community. Zionists, both in the Jewish community in Israel (the Yishuv) and overseas in Britain and the United States, felt a sense of entitlement to a Jewish state in Palestine. They believed that this was due them because of their unstinting support for the Allied war effort and because of reports emanating from German-occupied Europe concerning the Holocaust. The Zionists hoped that Britain and the Allies would repay loyalty and wartime service with the abrogation of the White Paper and support for a Jewish state.

As the war went on, however, Zionists became increasingly suspicious of British policy and motives and agitated for a more assertive stance to pursue their goals. In May 1942 the Zionist leadership convened an Extraordinary Zionist Conference at the Biltmore Hotel in New York City. The resolution that grew out of this meeting became known as the Biltmore Program. The resolution cited the catastrophe faced by the European Jews and called for the establishment of a Jewish commonwealth in all of Palestine, although it did not reject the possibility of partition.

Many historians view the Biltmore Program as evidence of the ascendancy of the hard-line faction of the Zionist movement. This faction, led by David Ben-Gurion of the Yishuv-based Jewish Agency, was eclipsing the more moderate elements led by Chaim Weizmann of the World Zionist Organization (WZO). Weizmann had supported gradualism, the partition of Palestine between Jews and Arabs, and negotiations with the British. Ben-Gurion and his followers, on the other hand, advocated immediate statehood and threatened armed resistance against the British if necessary to achieve this end.

Ben-Gurion's position and the Biltmore Program gained wide popular support both in the Yishuv and among Zionists worldwide because of the treatment of European Jews by the Nazis and an increasingly conspiratorial perception of British policy and motives. Many Zionists believed that the British were willing to renege on their promises of a Jewish homeland to appease the Arabs. In this view, British steps to restrict Jewish immigration to Palestine, beginning with the White Paper of 1939, seemed aimed at decreasing the Jewish community in Palestine. These suspicions fed the drive for a Jewish state that would be able to control immigration and its own destiny. However, the Biltmore Program was still not strong enough for right-wing revisionists led by the Irgun Tsvai Leumi (National Military Organization) and the Lohamei Herut Israel (Lehi), both of which resumed attacks on the British in Palestine in 1944.

The final change brought on by the war was the Holocaust and the ensuing refugee problem. The mass murder of European Jews by the Nazis gave a powerful moral force to Zionist arguments for a Jewish state and generated widespread sympathy in the United States and Western Europe for the Zionist cause. The more immediate problem growing out of the collapse of Nazi Germany in 1945 and the overrunning of the concentration camps in Germany and Poland was the disposition of the survivors and hundreds of thousands of homeless Jewish refugees. Most were reluctant to return to their home countries, particularly those from Germany and Eastern Europe where anti-Semitism remained rife. The admission of 100,000 Jewish Holocaust survivors into Palestine became an increasingly thorny issue. Indeed, growing pressure from Zionists in Palestine and the United States to allow them into Palestine conflicted with British intransigence and violent Arab resistance.

The relative wartime calm did not survive the defeat of Germany. Britain's efforts to maintain stability by holding the line on Jewish immigration proved unworkable. This was the result of pressure in the United States from President Harry S. Truman's administration, which was still divided and ambivalent, and grow-

ing resistance from both stepped-up illegal immigration and terrorist violence among Palestinian Jews. The crisis in Palestine was further compounded by factional violence among the Palestinian Arabs themselves and acts of terrorism against both Jews and the British. The wartime truce had not resolved any of the differences among the contending factions in the British Mandate for Palestine but instead had only intensified them.

WALTER F. BELL

See also

Anti-Semitism; Arab Revolt of 1936–1939; Ben-Gurion, David; Biltmore Program; Holocaust; Irgun Tsvai Leumi; Jewish Agency for Israel; Lohamei Herut Israel; Palestine, British Mandate for; United Kingdom, Middle East Policy; United States, Middle East Policy; Weizmann, Chaim; White Paper (1939); World Zionist Organization; Zionism; Zionist Conference

References
Bauer, Yehuda. *From Diplomacy to Resistance: A History of Jewish Palestine, 1930–1945.* Translated by Alton M. Winters. Philadelphia: Jewish Publication Society of America, 1970.
Gelvin, James L. *The Israel-Palestine Conflict: One Hundred Years of War.* New York: Cambridge University Press, 2005.
Morris, Benny. *Righteous Victims: A History of the Zionist-Arab Conflict, 1881–2001.* New York: Vintage Books, 2001.
Segev, Tom. *The Seventh Million: The Israelis and the Holocaust.* Translated by Haim Watzman. New York: Hill and Wang, 1993.

World Zionist Organization

The Zionist Conference held in Basel (Basle), Switzerland, on August 29–31, 1897, created the World Zionist Organization (WZO), elected Theodor Herzl the first WZO president, and determined the goals of both Zionism and the WZO to be the creation of a legal (guaranteed) Jewish homeland in Palestine (Israel). Membership in the WZO was extended to anyone who accepted the Basle Program and purchased the Zionist shekel (dues).

The first WZO constitution was passed by the Third Zionist Congress in 1899 and amended over the years. The Zionist Congress is the supreme governing institution and legislative authority of the WZO. The congress met biennially from 1897 to 1939 but did not meet again until 1946, after World War II, and has met since on a semiregular basis every four to five years, with the Thirty-Fifth Congress held during June 19–22, 2006, in Jerusalem.

The WZO is managed by two elected institutions: the Zionist General Council and the Zionist Executive. The congress also elects the Zionist Supreme Court, the attorney of the WZO, and the comptroller of National Institutions. The Zionist Executive administers the policies of the WZO and is headed by a chairman who also serves as the president of the WZO.

The WZO created companies and institutions designed to accomplish its policies. Prominent among many of these are the Jewish Colonial Trust (1899); the Jewish National Fund (1901); the Jewish Colonial Trust's subsidary, the Anglo-Palestine Bank (1902); and Keren Hayesod (1920). The Jewish Colonial Trust manages the

Executive Head of the World Zionist Organization (1897–Present)

Name	Term
Theodor Herzl	1897–1904
David Wolffsohn	1905–1911
Heinrich Warburg	1911–1921
Chaim Weizmann	1921–1931
Nahum Sokolow	1931–1935
Chaim Weizmann	1935–1946
David Ben-Gurion	1946–1956
Nahum Goldmann	1956–1968
Ehud Avriel	1968–1972
Louis Arie Pincus	1972–1973
Arie Leon Dulzin	1973–1975
Pinhas Sapir	1975
Arie Leon Dulzin	1975–1976
Joseph Almogi	1976–1978
Arie Leon Dulzin	1978–1987
Simcha Dinitz	1987–1994
Yehiel Leket	1994–1995
Avraham Burg	1995–1999
Sallai Meridor	1999–2005
Zeev Bielski	2005–Present

finances of the WZO, and the Jewish National Fund acquires land. Prior to the formation of the State of Israel, Keren Hayesod funded Zionist and Yishuv (the Jewish community in Palestine) activities and created companies such as the Palestine Electric Company, the Palestine Potash Company, and the Anglo-Palestine Bank. Keren Hayesod continues to raise support for the Zionist movement and the Zionist enterprise in 60 countries apart from the United States, where the fund-raising arm of the WZO is known as the United Jewish Appeal.

In 1922 the League of Nations established a Jewish Agency in its Palestine mandate that would serve as the representative of the Jewish people to the British mandatory government and cooperate with it establishing the Jewish national homeland. The WZO initially served in the capacity of the Jewish Agency. A more comprehensive and somewhat autonomous Jewish Agency was established on August 11, 1929, by the WZO at its Sixteenth Zionist Congress in Zurich to serve as a partnership between the WZO and non-Zionist Jewish organizations and leaders such as Louis Marshall, Leon Blum, and Felix Warburg. Dr. Chaim Weizmann, then president of the WZO, was elected president of the new Jewish Agency, and its leadership was initially divided equally between representatives of the WZO and the non-Zionist Jewish organizations. This equal representation eroded over the years, and the Executive of the Jewish Agency and the Zionist Executive eventually merged into a single position.

The Jewish Agency became a quasi-Jewish government in Palestine under David Ben-Gurion's leadership when he chaired the Jewish Agency Executive (1935–1948) prior to the creation of Israel (1948), during which time the agency was responsible for both legal and illegal Jewish immigration into Palestine. The agency administered the assimilation of these immigrants into Jewish Palestine,

founded Youth Aliya in 1933 to rescue Jewish youth from Nazi Germany, and created and oversaw the labor, settlement, and industry departments as well as the defense of the Jewish communities in Palestine.

The primary goal of the WZO, the creation of a legal Jewish homeland in Palestine (Israel), changed after the formation of the State of Israel. The WZO's status was redefined by the Knesset (Israeli parliament) on November 24, 1952, with the passage of the Zionist Organization–Jewish Agency for Israel Status Law. This law and later covenants delineated the structure of the relationship between the government of Israel and the Zionist Executive, making the WZO responsible for immigration (aliya) and immigrant assimilation and settlement.

The relationship between the WZO and the Jewish Agency changed again in August 1970 when the membership structure of the assembly of the expanded Jewish Agency was changed as follows: representatives of the WZO, 50 percent; representatives of the United Jewish Communities (United States), 30 percent; and representatives of organizations affiliated with Keren Hayesod, 20 percent. The responsibilities for immigration were also changed, with the Jewish Agency overseeing immigration from countries of persecution and the WZO overseeing immigration from all other countries.

The WZO, the Jewish Agency, and the government of Israel again redefined their relationship in June 1979, making the Jewish Agency responsible for all issues related to immigration in Israel as well as support services for educational and youth activities and welfare services. The WZO assumed all responsibilities relating to Diasporic Jewry.

The WZO now comprises the territorial Zionist Federations, the territorial and interterritorial Zionist organizations, the territorial and interterritorial Jewish bodies, and the World Zionist Unions.

RICHARD M. EDWARDS

See also

Ben-Gurion, David; Herzl, Theodor; Jewish Agency for Israel; Weizmann, Chaim; Zionism; Zionist Conference

References

Brenner, Michael. *Zionism: A Brief History*. Translated by Shelley Frisch. Princeton, NJ: Markus Wiener, 2003.

Laqueur, Walter. *A History of Zionism: From the French Revolution to the Establishment of the State of Israel*. Reprint ed. New York: Schocken, 2003.

World Zionist Organization Executive

The executive organ of the World Zionist Organization (WZO). Also known until 1921 as the Inner Actions Committee, the WZO carries out decisions of the Zionist Congress and the Zionist General Council (Greater Actions Committee). The Executive is the leadership body of the WZO but is responsible to the Congress and to the General Council. Founded by Theodor Herzl, the WZO held its first meeting in Basel, Switzerland, in 1897. The main organ of the WZO was the

Zionist Congress, the elected assembly of the movement. In between congresses, however, the Zionist Executive carried out the organization's policies.

Under Herzl there was no clear-cut distinction between the Zionist Executive and the representative bodies. The General Council, comprised of representatives of Zionist organizations worldwide, was the leading body, but actual control of the movement fell to the five-man Greater Actions Committee. All men were located in the same area.

In the course of the Eighth Zionist Congress, held at The Hague in 1907, the Greater Council was officially proclaimed the WZO Executive. It was restricted to a membership of between 21 and 60 people, of whom 3 to 7 constituted the Inner Actions Committee. Because both the chairman of the WZO and the Inner Actions Committee were elected by separate votes of the Congress, this conferred on them an independent status. At the Tenth Zionist Congress at Basel in 1911, membership of the Greater Council was reduced to 25 people.

The Twelfth Zionist Congress of 1912 formally replaced the Inner Actions Committee with the Zionist Executive and specified a membership of 9–15 people. Members of the Executive living in Palestine constituted a Palestine branch, and all others constituted the remainder of the Executive, which until 1948 was located in London. Gradually, most functions of the Executive were transferred to its Palestine branch, while the portion of the Executive in London dealt primarily with political issues involving the British government, the mandatory power in Palestine.

When the Jewish Agency was founded in 1929, half the members of the Agency's Executive were also to be members of the Zionist Executive with the remainder drawn from non-Zionist Jewish groups. This arrangement proved unworkable because of a lack of interest on the part of non-Zionist groups. The Jewish Agency became the de facto government of the Jewish community in prestate Palestine involved in immigration, labor, and settlement. From 1931 the Executive has been based on a coalition of the leading Zionist parties. In 1960 a new WZO constitution provided that the General Council (the Greater Actions Committee) consist of 96 members, representing the Zionist parties on a proportional basis. The Twenty-Sixth WZO Congress of 1964–1965 increased membership in the General Council to 129.

SPENCER C. TUCKER

See also

Herzl, Theodor; Palestine, British Mandate for; World Zionist Organization; Zionism

References

Hertzberg, Arthur, ed. *The Zionist Idea: A Historical Analysis and Reader.* Philadelphia: Jewish Publication Society, 1997.

Herzl, Theodor. *The Jewish State.* Mineola, NY: Dover, 1989.

Kolatt, I. "Executive, Zionist." Pp. 309–310 in *Encyclopedia of Zionism and Israel*, Vol. 1, edited by Raphael Patai. New York: Herzl/McGraw Hill, 1971.

Laqueur, Walter. *A History of Zionism: From the French Revolution to the Establishment of the State of Israel.* Reprint ed. New York: Schocken, 2003.

Unity in Dispersion: A History of the World Jewish Congress. New York: World Jewish Congress, 1948.

Wye River Agreement
Event Date: October 23, 1998

The Wye River Agreement was the second agreement between Israel and the Palestinians during Prime Minister Benjamin Netanyahu's time in office. For the first time, the United States took a direct role in guaranteeing the implementation of the terms of the agreement. Under the terms of the Wye River Agreement, Israel was to pull out of additional territories in the West Bank, while the Palestinians made concessions toward Israel's security. The strict timetable for implementing the agreements was not met, however.

On September 28, 1995, Israel and the Palestine Liberation Organization (PLO) signed an interim agreement in regard to the West Bank and the Gaza Strip following secret negotiations in Oslo, Norway. Moderates on both sides hoped that this treaty was the first step in a peace process for the Middle East. Instead, Prime Minister Yitzhak Rabin was assassinated by a right-wing Israeli fanatic. Continued terrorist attacks by Muslims on Israeli targets helped bring about the election of Netanyahu, a hard-liner. He suspended the withdrawal of Israeli troops from occupied sections of the West Bank to permit new Israeli settlements in the area. A focal point for both sides was the creation of a Jewish settlement named Har Homa near Jerusalem.

In an effort to get the peace process started again, U.S. president Bill Clinton arranged for Israeli and Palestinian representatives to meet in the United States. Beginning on October 14, 1998, the two sides got together under U.S. sponsorship at the Wye River Conference Center in Maryland. For nine days, tough negotiations continued before an agreement was hammered out. On October 23, the agreement was signed by Netanyahu and PLO leader Yasser Arafat. King Hussein of Jordan attended the ceremony as well. The treaty was criticized by many on both sides, but it marked the first time that the United States offered to take an active role in guaranteeing the security and implementation of an agreement between Israel and its neighbors.

Most of the provisions of the Wye River Agreement had to do with security and the turnover of certain areas to the control of the Palestinian Authority (PA). The first step was a withdrawal of Israeli forces from an additional 13 percent of the West Bank. The Israelis originally refused to accept that figure, requested by the United States. A compromise was reached in which the PA under Arafat would occupy 10 percent of the land, while the remaining 3 percent would be turned into nature preserves.

The second part had to do with improving Israel's security. Arafat agreed to take measures to halt terrorist attacks launched from the West Bank and Gaza against Israeli targets. Specific individuals accused of terrorist activities were to be apprehended by Palestinian police and prosecuted. A joint U.S.-Palestinian commit-

Israeli prime minister Benjamin Netanyahu, U.S. president Bill Clinton, and Palestinian Authority (PA) chairman Yasser Arafat sign the Wye River Agreement at the White House, October 23, 1998. (Avi Ohayon/Israeli Government Press Office)

tee was to be formed to review Palestinian plans to reduce terrorism. Representatives of the U.S. Central Intelligence Agency (CIA) were to be appointed to provide expertise and evaluation of Palestinian efforts. Another joint committee would review the prosecution of individuals accused of terrorism. The PA undertook to collect illegal weapons from individuals in areas under its control and to prevent the importation or manufacture of additional weapons. The United States agreed to assist in collecting the illegal weapons and in preventing the smuggling of additional weapons. To reduce incidents of terrorism, the Palestinian authorities were required to prohibit all forms of incitement to violence.

Other provisions of the Wye River Agreement included a reduction in the number of Palestinian policemen from 36,000 to 30,000. Arafat also confirmed that he would have the Palestinian Central Council amend the Palestinian Charter to remove references to the destruction of Israel as a goal. In return for their concessions, the Palestinians were to receive free passage from the Gaza Strip to the West Bank. Also approved was the Palestinian National Airport, which opened in Gaza on November 24, 1998. Palestinian prisoners held by the Israelis were to be released soon after the treaty was signed. A strict time line was included in the agreement for the two sides to meet their commitments and to get the peace process back on track.

The United States made several secret agreements with both sides to help the process along. In one, the United States agreed to overlook the Israeli settlement at Har Homa. The United States also arranged for Israel to agree to restrict building in West Bank settlements, with the exception of natural growth. Finally, the U.S. government promised both sides financial assistance to remove settlements and build infrastructure. The United States also promised Israel that it would meet any attack on that country by weapons of mass destruction (WMDs) with counterweapons.

The optimism after the Wye River Agreement was signed soon evaporated. Netanyahu refused to implement the treaty until it was approved by his cabinet and the Knesset. Several of the terms of the agreement were modified by the cabinet. Also, Israel refused to release any prisoner accused of causing Israeli bloodshed. On December 20, Netanyahu suspended implementation of the treaty. In the May 1999 elections, Ehud Barak was voted in as prime minister of Israel, and he opposed the Wye River Agreement.

In an effort to restart the process, the United States sponsored further negotiations. An agreement was signed at the Egyptian resort of Sharm al-Sheikh on September 5, 1999. Also known as Wye River Two, the Sharm al-Sheikh agreement committed Israel to withdrawal from another 11 percent of the West Bank and the release of 350 Palestinian political prisoners. Although a promising beginning was made to implement Wye River Two, the agreement ground to a halt by the end of 1999. Further negotiations at Camp David in July 2000 brought no results. The election of George W. Bush to the presidency at the end of 2000 further halted direct guarantees by the United States for implementing the Wye River Agreement.

TIM WATTS

See also

Arafat, Yasser; Barak, Ehud; Clinton, William Jefferson; Gaza Strip; Hussein, King of Jordan; Netanyahu, Benjamin; Oslo Accords; Palestinian Authority; Rabin, Yitzhak; Settlements, Israeli; Sharm al-Sheikh

References

Enderlin, Charles. *Shattered Dreams: The Failure of the Peace Process in the Middle East, 1995–2002.* New York: Other Press, 2003.

Kimmerling, Baruch, and Joel S. Migdal. *The Palestinian People: A History.* Cambridge: Harvard University Press, 2003.

Ojeda, Auriana. *The Middle East.* San Diego, CA: Greenhaven, 2003.

Ross, Dennis. *The Missing Peace: The Inside Story of the Fight for Middle East Peace.* New York: Farrar, Straus, and Giroux, 2004.

Rubenberg, Cheryl. *The Palestinians: In Search of a Just Peace.* Boulder, CO: Lynne Rienner, 2003.

Y

Yad Vashem Holocaust Memorial

Yad Vashem, the national Holocaust memorial, was created by act of the Knesset (Israeli parliament) in 1953 and opened in 1954. It is located on the Har Hazikaron (Mount of Remembrance) beyond Mount Herzl near Jerusalem. The Hebrew words "Yad Vashem" mean "a monument and a name" and come from Isaiah 56:5: "I will give them, in My House and within My walls, a monument and a name . . . which shall not perish." The memorial is best known for its iconic Hall of Remembrance, which has become an obligatory stop for visiting dignitaries, but the institution is in fact a complex of memorials stretching over many acres and reflecting its multiple and not always easily reconcilable functions of commemoration, research, and education.

A candlelit cavern commemorates the estimated 1.5 million children who died in the Holocaust. The vast open-air Avenue and Garden of the Righteous and Valley of Communities (2.5 acres) honor 20,000 non-Jewish rescuers and 5,000 devastated towns. A new museum opened its doors in 2005. At 13,800 square feet, it is three times as large as its predecessor of 1973 and meets modern standards of preservation, technology, museology, and scholarship. Other recent additions include an art museum (10,000 works), greatly enhanced research and educational facilities (including the world's largest Holocaust archive of some 62 million pages of documents and 267,500 photographs), the International School for Holocaust Studies (more than 100 educators versus only 5 a decade ago), and the International Institute for Historical Research. Output of the publication program has risen from 2 titles in 1960 to more than 200 today, from monographs to massive lexica as well as the respected journal *Yad Vashem Studies*.

Yad Vashem was a crucial element in commemorating the Holocaust. The resultant debates about the behavior of the victims, the response of world leaders and world Jewry, and the causal connection between the Diaspora and the Holocaust mirrored the larger divisions of Israeli society: Right and Left, orthodox and secular, survivors and others. Commemorative activities came to emphasize resistance as well as suffering. Yad Vashem Rashut ha-Zikaron la-Shoah ve ha-Gevurah, the Holocaust Martyrs' and Heroes' Remembrance Authority, is also the official site for marking Yom HaShoah ve ha-Gevurah, Holocaust Martyrs' and Heroes' Remembrance Day. Falling midway between the end of Passover and military Memorial Day, which precedes Independence Day, the new holiday, on the Hebrew date of the Warsaw Ghetto Uprising, establishes a modern narrative of suffering and redemption to parallel that of the Old Testament of the Bible. Topography reinforces chronology, for Yad Vashem shares Mount Herzl with the grave of the founder of Zionism and the national military cemetery, together constituting Har ha-Zikaron, the Mount of Remembrance.

The task of the new museum on the threshold of the so-called fourth post-Holocaust generation is at once more simple and more complex than that of its predecessor. On the one hand, awareness of the Holocaust and its importance is widespread. On the other hand, intellectual standards are higher, old pieties no longer suffice, and simple models of power versus powerlessness no longer resonate well as history or policy. As Israeli society has become more diverse in background and attitude, the interpretation of the Holocaust has become less stable and monolithic. Above all, as the last survivors die, the events pass definitively from lived experience into history. Indeed, for the first time the chairman of Yad Vashem is not a Holocaust survivor.

In order to overcome the danger of abstraction and distance, the new museum more consistently uses individual stories, represented by testimony and artifacts, to convey the collective fate. Moshe

The Hall of Remembrance, part of the Yad Vashem Holocaust Memorial. (Courtesy of Yad Vashem, the Holocaust Martyrs' and Heroes' Remembrance Authority)

Safdie's spare and striking architecture provides a figurative linear narrative framework in concrete, stone, and glass. A 590-foot-long subterranean prismatic structure illuminated by a skylight and intersected by galleries leads to the Hall of Names with a circular platform suspended between two cones, representing the known and unknown victims. The light upper one displays photographs of the dead. The dark lower one of living rock holds a pool of water. The repository for the records of the decades-old attempt to give every victim a name by soliciting pages of testimony from relatives and friends (online since November 2004) holds 3.2 million records. Visitors exit into the light via a cantilevered balcony offering a striking panorama of Jerusalem.

Two snapshots from 2005 offer a sort of balance sheet. The dedication of the new museum in March marking the Yad Vashem jubilee and the 60th anniversary of the Liberation was attended by United Nations (UN) secretary-general Kofi Annan and dignitaries from 40 nations. Toward the end of the year, the UN General Assembly for the first time passed a resolution by Israel that was backed by 104 cosponsors and designated the anniversary of the Auschwitz Liberation as an annual Holocaust Remembrance Day. The Holocaust is commemorated in some 250 museums around the world from Houston, Texas, to Japan. One of the most important comprehensive museums is in Washington, D.C.

JIM WALD

See also

Anti-Semitism; Eichmann, Karl Adolf; Herzl, Theodor; Holocaust; Zionism

References

Gutterman, Bella, and Avner Shalev. *To Bear Witness: Holocaust Remembrance at Yad Vashem.* 2nd ed. Jerusalem: Yad Vashem, 2005.

Segev, Tom. *The Seventh Million: The Israelis and the Holocaust.*
    Translated by Haim Watzman. New York: Hill and Wang, 1993.
Zertal, Idith. *From Catastrophe to Power: Holocaust Survivors and the
    Emergence of Israel.* Berkeley: University of California Press, 1998.

Yadin, Yigal
Born: March 20, 1917
Died: June 28, 1984

Israeli general and chief of staff of the Israel Defense Forces (IDF), archeologist, and political leader. Yigal Yadin was born in Jerusalem on March 20, 1917. His father was the noted archeologist Eliezer Sukenik. In 1933 Yadin joined Haganah, the Jewish self-defense force, and along with Moshe Dayan quickly became one of its rising stars. In 1938 Yadin and Dayan worked closely with and were profoundly influenced by British Army captain Orde C. Wingate. Yadin resigned from Haganah in 1946 after he and Yitzhak Sadeh disagreed over whether infantry squads should include the machine gun as standard equipment.

Yadin began university studies in archeology but was recalled to military service by Prime Minister David Ben-Gurion just before Israel declared its independence in May 1948. During the ensuing Israeli War of Independence (1948–1949), Yadin served as Haganah's operations officer, contributing to many of the key operational and strategic decisions.

Yadin became the second chief of staff of the IDF on November 9, 1949. He completely reorganized the standing military, the reserves, and the system of compulsory military service that continues to define the IDF to this day. He resigned from his post on December 7, 1952, after clashing over cuts to the military budget with his old mentor Ben-Gurion, who was then both prime minister and defense minister.

Returning to Hebrew University, Yadin earned his PhD in archeology in 1955. The following year he received the Israel Prize for his dissertation, which was based on the translation and interpretation of one of the Dead Sea Scrolls. He went on to become one of the towering figures in Israeli archeology. He played a key role in acquiring the Dead Sea Scrolls for Israel, and his fieldwork included the important excavations at the Qumran Caves, Tel Megiddo, Masada, and Hazor. In 1970 he became the head of the Institute of Archeology at Hebrew University.

Just prior to the Six-Day War in 1967, Yadin became the military adviser to Prime Minister Levi Eshkol. Following the Yom Kippur War in 1973, Yadin served on the Agranat Commission that investigated the failures that contributed to the Israelis being taken by surprise by the Egyptian-Syrian attack. In 1976 Yadin was one of the founders of the Democratic Movement for Change. Although the political party dissolved into fragmented factions a few years later, it did win 15 Knesset seats in the 1977 elections. Forming a coalition with Menachem Begin's Likud Party, the new government was the first in Israeli history to exclude the Labor Party. Yadin

Israeli general Yigal Yadin, chief of staff of the Israel Defense Forces (IDF), January 3, 1949. On his retirement from the military, Yadin became a distinguished archeologist. (Israeli Government Press Office)

served as deputy prime minister from 1977 to 1981, when he retired from public life and returned to the university. He died in Jerusalem on June 28, 1984. He was both a warrior and a scholar, viewed by many as the prototype of the new Israeli ideal. In addition to his impressive list of very important archeological discoveries, he contributed greatly to making archeology a less arcane field and far more accessible to the average person.

DAVID T. ZABECKI

See also
Begin, Menachem; Ben-Gurion, David; Dayan, Moshe; Haganah; Israel Defense Forces; Sadeh, Yitzhak; Wingate, Orde Charles

References
Collins, Larry, and Dominique Lapierre. *O Jerusalem!* New York: Simon and Schuster, 1972.
Herzog, Chaim. *The Arab-Israeli Wars: War and Peace in the Middle East from the War of Independence to Lebanon.* Westminster, MD: Random House, 1984.
Yadin, Yigael. *Masada: Herod's Fortress and the Zealots' Last Stand.* New York: Welcome Rain, 1998.

Yair
See Stern, Avraham

Yassin, Ahmed Ismail
Born: 1929 or 1938
Died: March 22, 2004

Cofounder and spiritual adjunct of Hamas until his death in 2004 at the hands of the Israeli military who was often quoted as saying, "We chose this road and will end with martyrdom or victory." Ahmed Ismail Yassin was born in the British Mandate for Palestine in either the late 1920s or late 1930s. He claimed to be born in 1938, but his passport listed his year of birth as 1929. During the 1948–1949 Israeli War of Independence, his family relocated to the Gaza Strip. Because of an accident he was a quadriplegic from a young age, but he attended secondary school and then went to the College of Religious Studies at al-Azhar University in Cairo. It was there that he first became involved with the Muslim Brotherhood, a group that advocated Islamic principles in society and government. While participating in the Muslim Brotherhood, he advocated fierce opposition to Israel. He firmly opposed any peaceful agreements between the Palestinians and the Jewish state.

In 1987 Yassin, who had already been involved with an important charitable mosque-based undertaking, cofounded with Abd al-Aziz Rantisi and other figures Hamas, a militant Palestinian group aimed at the destruction of Israel. Two years later, Yassin was arrested by Israel and sentenced to life imprisonment for allegedly ordering the deaths of captured Israeli soldiers. However, as part of a 1997 deal with Jordan, he was released in a prisoner exchange on condition that he refrain from calling for suicide bombings against Israel. Upon his release he resumed leadership of Hamas and immediately resumed calls for suicide bombings and other violence against Israeli military forces and citizens alike. The Palestinian Authority (PA) frequently placed Yassin under house arrest, but the Israeli government criticized the PA for releasing him each time under pressure from his supporters.

Yassin became one of Israel's prime targets in its fight against terrorist group leaders. In September 2003 he was injured when Israeli aircraft bombed the building where he was staying. He vowed revenge and refused to go into hiding. Six months later, on March 22, 2004, he was once again directly targeted by Israel. As he was leaving a prayer service, an Israeli helicopter gunship, acting on the

Sheikh Ahmed Ismail Yassin, cofounder of Hamas and leader of the organization until his death in 2004. (Reuters/Corbis)

direct orders of Israeli prime minister Ariel Sharon, fired air-to-surface Hellfire missiles at Yassin as he was being wheeled out of an early morning prayer service, killing not only the Hamas leader but also his two bodyguards and six bystanders. Another dozen people were injured.

The assassination of Yassin brought immediate and widespread condemnation from the international community, including both the U.S. and British governments. Many feared that the killing of a revered Palestinian leader who was both blind and wheelchair-bound would harm the peace process. Even some Israeli leaders, including former prime minister Shimon Peres, were troubled by the assassination. However, most Israeli government officials and citizens believed the move to be legitimate, as Yassin was held responsible for many violent attacks on Israelis.

Thousands of Palestinians and other Arabs took to the streets to protest Yassin's assassination, and an estimated 200,000 people attended his funeral. Leadership of Hamas passed to Rantisi, also one of Israel's targets who was assassinated in a similar helicopter rocket attack less than a month later on April 17, 2004.

SPENCER C. TUCKER

See also

Gaza Strip; Hamas; Muslim Brotherhood; Palestinian Authority; Peres, Shimon; Sharon, Ariel

References

Derfner, Larry. "The Assassination of Sheikh Yassin: Sharon Opens the 'Gates of Hell'; Fear and Loathing in Israel." *Washington Report on Middle East Affairs* 23(4) (2004): 12–15.

Hroub, Khaled. *Hamas: Political Thought and Practice.* Washington, DC: Institute for Palestine Studies, 2000.

Mishal, Shaul, and Avraham Sela. *The Palestinian Hamas: Vision, Violence, and Coexistence.* New York: Columbia University Press, 2000.

Yemen

Middle Eastern nation located in the southern part of the Arabian Peninsula with an estimated 2006 population of 21.45 million people. Yemen borders Saudi Arabia to the north, Oman to the east, the Arabian Sea and the Gulf of Aden to the south, and the Red Sea to the west. Not far off the western and southern coasts of the country are the East African nations of Eritrea, Djibouti, and Somalia. Yemen's total area encompasses 203,846 square miles.

Yemen had been divided into North Yemen and South Yemen since 1918. In 1970 when South Yemen declared itself a Marxist state, many hundreds of thousands of Yemenis fled north. This precipitated a virtual civil war between north and south that would endure for 20 years. Not until 1990 did the two states reconcile, forming a single state known as the Republic of Yemen. Since then, there have been several unsuccessful attempts by groups in the south to secede from the republic. The most serious secessionist move came in 1994.

As with most areas in this part of the world, Yemen's climate is characterized by torridly hot weather, especially in the eastern desert regions where rainfall is scant. The west coast has a hot and somewhat humid climate, while the mountainous regions in the west are more temperate with more rainfall. Much of the country can be characterized as a desert. Topographically, Yemen features a narrow strip of coastal plains and low hills immediately behind them that give way to high mountains. High-desert plains farther east descend to hot desert in the interior. The nation's chief resources include oil, marble, fish, minor coal deposits, gold, lead, nickel, and copper. The bulk of Yemen's arable land is located in the west and comprises less than 3 percent of the entire land mass.

Yemen's population is overwhelmingly Muslim and of Arabic descent, and Arabic is the official language. Of the nation's Muslims, about 52 percent are Sunni Muslims and 48 percent are Shia Muslims. The Sunnis live principally in the south and southeastern part of the country. Yemen has one of the world's highest birthrates, and as a result its population as a whole is quite young. Indeed, some 46 percent of the population is 14 years old and under, while less than 3 percent is older than 65. The median age is 16.

Yemen is a representative republic that has a popularly elected president and a prime minister appointed by the president. The executive branch shares power with the bicameral legislature. The legal system in Yemen is a mix of Islamic law, Turkish law (a vestige of the Ottoman Empire), English common law, and local tribal dictates. Nevertheless, Islamic laws almost always take precedence in accordance with the Koran. Ali Abdullah Salih has served as president of the Republic of Yemen since the 1990 unification. Before that, he had served as the president of North Yemen since 1978.

Recorded human habitation in the region of Yemen can be traced as far back as the ninth century BC. Its strategic location on the Red Sea and the Gulf of Aden has made it an important crossroads for East-West trade as well as trade from Asia to Africa. Around the seventh century AD, Muslim caliphs began to exert their influence over the region. They gradually ceded authority to dynastic imams, who retained the caliph's theocratic government until the modern era. Over the centuries, Egyptian caliphs also held sway in Yemen. The Ottoman Empire controlled some or most of Yemen sporadically between the 1500s and 1918, when the empire crumbled as a result of World War I. Ottoman influence was most keen in northern Yemen. In the south, imams tended to control the local scene but were usually overseen to some extent by the central authorities in Constantinople (Istanbul).

In 1918 North Yemen won its independence from the Ottoman Empire and finally became a republic in 1962, which precipitated an eight-year-long civil war. The conflict pitted royalists of the Mutawakkilite Kingdom of Yemen against republicans. In the south until 1967 the British dominated, having established a protectorate in Aden in 1839. Soon the British created a formal colony that incorporated Aden and southern Yemen. As such, the British had great command of the strategic waterways of the region. After World War II, however, Yemenis in the south came to greatly resent the British presence, and before long they had organized an anti-British insurgency with aid from the Egyptians.

Several attacks against British interests sponsored by Egypt's government under Gamal Abdel Nasser in addition to insurgents from the north essentially forced the British out in 1967. The former British colony of Aden now became South Yemen. In 1970 the South Yemen government declared a Marxist state and aligned itself squarely with the Soviet Union. As a result, several hundred thousand Yemenis from the south fled to North Yemen, overwhelming that nation's resources. The south did nothing to stop the mass exodus.

Before 1962 the ruling imams in North Yemen pursued an isolationist foreign policy. North Yemen did have commercial and cultural ties with Saudi Arabia, however. In the late 1950s the Chinese and Soviets attempted to lure North Yemen into their orbit with technological missions. By the early 1960s North Yemen had become dependent upon Egypt for financial and technical support. Later still, the Saudis supplanted the Egyptians as the main conduit of support. During the civil war the Saudis backed the royalists, while Egypt and the Soviet Union aided the republicans. In the 1970s and 1980s many Yemenis from the north found jobs in neighboring Saudi Arabia, boosting North Yemen's flagging economy.

After 1967 when South Yemen declared itself a Marxist state (with ties to the Soviet Union), it maintained tense—and sometimes hostile—relations with its conservative Arab neighbors. In addition to the ongoing conflict with the north, southern Yemeni insurgents engaged the Saudis in military actions first in 1969 and again in 1973. They also openly aided the Dhofar rebellion in Oman.

After the 1990 unification, the Republic of Yemen has generally pursued a pragmatic foreign policy. It is a member of the Non-Aligned Movement, is a signatory to the Nuclear Non-Proliferation Treaty, and attempted to stay impartial during the 1991 Persian Gulf War and subsequent wars in the Middle East. Its noncommittal stance in these areas, however, has not endeared it to the Gulf states or Western nations.

Yemen is among the poorest nations in the Arab world. The long civil war of 1962 to 1970 wrought great havoc on an already struggling economy, and the agricultural sector has been hit by periodic droughts. Coffee production, once a mainstay among northern Yemeni crops, has fallen off dramatically. The Port of Aden in the south suffered dramatic curtailments in its cargo handling after the 1967 Six-Day War and the British exit that same year. Since 1990, the return of hundreds of thousands of Yemenis from other Gulf states because of Yemen's nonalignment in the Persian Gulf War brought with it staggering unemployment. Reduced aid from other nations at this time and a brief secessionist movement in 1994 conspired to keep Yemen's economy depressed. Yemen does have significant oil deposits, but they are not of the same quality as Persian Gulf oil and so have not brought in a windfall profit. Yemen does have major natural gas reserves, but that industry remains underdeveloped. As of 2007, the Yemeni government continues to struggle with high inflation, excessive spending, widespread corruption, and Islamist militants.

PAUL G. PIERPAOLI JR.

See also
Egypt; Nasser, Gamal Abdel; Persian Gulf War; Saudi Arabia; Soviet Union and Russia, Middle East Policy; Yemen Civil War

References
Dresch, Paul. *A History of Modern Yemen.* New York: Cambridge University Press, 2001.
Jones, Clive. *Britain and the Yemen Civil War.* London: Sussex Academic, 2004.
Mackintosh-Smith, Martin. *Yemen: The Unknown Arabia.* Woodstock, NY: Overlook, 2001.

Yemen Civil War
Start Date: September 1962
End Date: 1970

Civil conflict in North Yemen (Yemen Arab Republic) lasting from 1962 until 1970 that pitted royalist forces of the Imamate of Yemen against those seeking to establish a republic. In addition to the ongoing civil divisions in North Yemen (the south was controlled by Great Britain until 1967), the immediate catalyst of the civil war was the death of Ahmad bin Yahya in September 1962. Bin Yahya was the ruling imam in the region and represented the hereditary monarchy, which had controlled northern Yemen for many years. His repressive reign, which had begun in 1948, had gained few new adherents over its 24-year history. He harbored visions of uniting all of Yemen but was unable to garner sufficient support to end British rule in the south. In 1955 he had to fend off a serious coup effort instigated by two of his brothers and disgruntled army officers.

To bolster his position, bin Yahya entered into a formal pact of union with Egypt in 1956 that placed Yemeni military forces under a unified command structure. That same year he also named his son Muhammad al-Badr crown prince and heir apparent and established formal ties with the Soviet Union. In 1960 bin Yahya left North Yemen to seek medical treatment. In his absence, Crown Prince al-Badr began to implement several reform measures that his father had promised to implement but had as yet gone unfulfilled. Outraged that his son made such moves without his knowledge or assent, bin Yahya promptly reversed the measures when he returned home. This did not, of course, endear him to his subjects, and several weeks of civil unrest ensued, which the government quashed with a heavy hand. The 1955 coup attempt and growing resentment toward bin Yahya rendered the last years of his rule both paranoid and reactionary.

Bin Yahya died at age 67 on September 18, 1962, and al-Badr became imam. One of his first official acts was to grant a blanket amnesty to all political prisoners who had been imprisoned during his father's reign. Al-Badr did so in hopes of maintaining power and keeping the kingdom's detractors at bay. But his tactics did not stave off discord for long. Indeed, on September 26, 1962, Abdullah as-Sallal, commander of the royal guard who had just been appointed to that post by al-Badr, launched a coup and declared himself president of the Yemen Arab Republic.

Al-Badr, meanwhile, managed to escape an assassination attempt and went to the northern reaches of the kingdom, where he was able to stir up support among the royalist tribes there. Within days, clashes began between royalist fighters and the republicans that soon grew into a full-scale civil war. Soliciting support from another hereditary kingdom, al-Badr gained the support of Saudi Arabia, the proximity of which to northern Yemen made it a natural ally. As-Sallal, meanwhile, rallied republican forces and had soon gained the support of Egypt. Both the Saudis and Egyptians dispatched military troops to Yemen, adding to the destructiveness of the civil conflict.

By the mid-1960s the royalists had also enlisted the help of Iran and Jordan, while the Soviets and several other communist nations backed the republicans. From a larger perspective, the Yemen Civil War saw the more conservative Middle East regimes (e.g., Saudi Arabia, Iran, and Jordan) pitted against the more radical and Pan-Arab forces in the region, as represented by Egypt's Gamal Abdel Nasser and the Soviet Union. The conflict also became politicized along Cold War lines, as the United States, Great Britain, and other Western powers tended to side with the royalists.

On several occasions, the United Nations (UN) attempted to mediate an end to the bloodshed, but the regional and international dynamics of the struggle made this task nearly impossible. At the height of its involvement in the Yemen Civil War, Egypt, which had sent the most forces into Yemen, was fielding some 75,000 troops there. This was not only acting as a huge drain on the Egyptian treasury and military but was also stoking inter-Arab enmity. Saudi-Egyptian relations were particularly tense. It was in fact the 1967 Six-Day War and Egypt's ignominious defeat in that conflict that began to turn the tide in the civil war. After June 1967, a weakened and chastened Nasser was compelled to begin withdrawing his troops from Yemen. That same year saw the British withdrawal from southern Yemen. This presented a diplomatic opening that would ultimately lead to an end to the fighting in 1970.

By 1969 both sides in the struggle agreed that the first step to ending the war would be the withdrawal of all foreign troops from Yemeni territory. Both Egypt and Saudi Arabia agreed. The removal of foreign forces ultimately led to the 1970 compromise that allowed for the continuation of the republican government in which several key positions would be occupied by royalists. There was, however, no role for Imam al-Badr, and part of the compromise stipulated that he and his family leave the country. He sought exile in Britain, where he lived until his death in 1996. Sadly, the Yemen Civil War left deep scars on that country's society and politics that have not yet healed. Worse yet, it is estimated that between 100,000 and 150,000 Yemenis lost their lives in the eight years of fighting.

PAUL G. PIERPAOLI JR.

See also
Egypt; Egypt, Armed Forces; Nasser, Gamal Abdel; Saudi Arabia; Saudi Arabia, Armed Forces; Six-Day War; Soviet Union and Russia, Middle East Policy; United Kingdom, Middle East Policy; Yemen

References
Dresch, Paul. *A History of Modern Yemen*. New York: Cambridge University Press, 2001.
Jones, Clive. *Britain and the Yemen Civil War*. London: Sussex Academic, 2004.
Pridham, Brian. *Contemporary Yemen: Politics and Historical Background*. London: Palgrave Macmillan, 1984.

Yesh Gvul

Israeli organization formed in 1982 to resist service in the Israel Defense Forces (IDF). Yesh Gvul is Hebrew for "there is a limit." Resistance to military service in Israel was not new, with such people being known as refuseniks. According to Israeli policy, Haredi Jews are exempt from service as long as they study in yeshivas (religious schools). Although service in the military is mandatory for young Jewish men and women, orthodox Jewish women can also avoid it by performing alternate national service work instead.

Yesh Gvul was formed during the 1982 Israeli invasion of Lebanon by reservists refusing to serve there. Some 3,000 reservists signed a petition to that effect that was presented to Prime Minister Menachem Begin and Defense Minister Ariel Sharon. Some of the individuals who refused to serve in Lebanon were indeed court-martialed and sentenced to terms in military prison. Yesh Gvul has as its credo assisting those military personnel who refuse duties of either a repressive or aggressive nature. It has also been involved in leftist political activities.

In January 2002, 51 reserve officers and soldiers signed "The Combatants' Letter" in which they refused to fight beyond Israel's 1967 borders "in order to dominate, expel, starve and humiliate an entire people." More than 600 individuals have signed this letter and joined Courage to Refuse. In September 2003, 27 reserve pilots and former pilots, including Yiftah Spector, a retired air force brigadier general and Israel's second-leading ace, signed a document known as "The Pilots' Letter" in which they opposed carrying out "illegal and immoral" attack orders of the type that Israel had been conducting in the occupied territories. In 2002 the Israeli High Court of Justice ruled that pacifism toward war in general constituted legal grounds for refusal to serve but that selective refusal was not legal.

The political right-wing in Israel has condemned such movements as giving comfort to the militant Arab enemy, and many Israelis of all political persuasions worry that a refusal to serve constitutes treason in what is a time of war. Indeed, in January 2004 a military court sentenced five young activists to one-year prison terms for their refusal to enlist in the IDF. Left-wing Israeli politicians have expressed the concern that what is perceived to be a leftist refusal to serve in the territories might actually encourage the political right-wing in its objection to the removal of Jewish settlements there.

SPENCER C. TUCKER

See also
Israel Defense Forces; Lebanon, Israeli Invasion of; Spector, Yiftah

References

Lerner, Michael. *Healing Israel/Palestine: A Path to Peace and Reconciliation.* Berkeley, CA: North Atlantic Books, 2003.

Tamir, Avraham. *A Soldier in Search of Peace: An Inside Look at Israel's Strategy.* New York: Harper and Row, 1988.

Yesha Council

Governing body of Jewish settlements in Israeli-occupied territory. The Yesha Council (Moetzet Yesha, or Settler's Council) was established in the late 1970s as an outgrowth of the settler movement. The council is responsible for ensuring that there is sufficient security for the settlements, that adequate funds are available for construction and development, and that the Israeli government addresses the general interests of the settler population. The council represents some 250,000 people.

In the wake of the June 1967 Six-Day War and the spectacular success achieved by the Israeli armed forces, an intensely Zionist movement gradually emerged that sought to consolidate control over the lands seized during the conflict. The conquest of East Jerusalem and the West Bank in particular brought under Israeli control lands of biblical, historical, and cultural significance for all Jews. Within months of the war's end, religious settlers moved to reestablish the Jewish communities that existed in those areas only decades earlier. Intent on making their presence permanent, they felt a sense of urgency about achieving that objective in the aftermath of the October 1973 Yom Kippur War when events on the battlefield suggested that future Israeli governments would favor a policy of exchanging land for peace. In response to such perceived dangers, the Gush Emunim (Bloc of the Faithful) settler movement emerged in 1974 with the express purpose of undermining any attempts to surrender Jewish control over the Promised Land. Through accelerated and widespread settlement and economic development of Yesha, the collective Hebrew acronym for the areas of the West Bank (Yehuda and Shomron) and Gaza (Anah), Gush activists hoped to translate physical possession into an irreversible and nonnegotiable fact on the ground.

The Yesha Council is the body tasked with ensuring that the settler dream becomes a reality. Formed in the late 1970s, the council remains a powerful and influential body of regional mayors and community leaders lobbying for settler interests. However, the drive to populate the areas with Jews, which during 1967–1977 saw the creation of 85 settlements, required an influx of many thousands of Israelis who were not particularly committed to the land by religious or nationalist ties. Through an ambitious government program of housing subsidies and low-interest loans initiated by the

A Jewish settler is forcibly taken away as Israel Defense Forces (IDF) soldiers and police evacuate the Ma'on Outpost, November 10, 1999. Ma'on, in the southern West Bank, was the only settlement outpost of 12 remaining to be evacuated under an agreement between Ehud Barak's administration and the Yesha Council of Settlements. (Getty Images)

Likud following its victory in the 1977 parliamentary elections, average citizens were lured to purchase homes in the lands beyond Israel's sovereign borders. Funding for settlements increased from just under $4 million in 1976 to more than $34 million in 1983, and under the direction of the new minister of agriculture Ariel Sharon, existing restraints on building activities were suspended in favor of a concerted effort to assert Jewish control of the land. Over the next four years, between 1977 and 1981, 64 additional settlements sprang up on the West Bank alone, and the Israeli population increased steadily throughout the occupied territories. Even in the face of growing international criticism over the settlements and the contention that such construction violates the principles of the Fourth Geneva Convention of 1949, successive Israeli governments have sustained their support for the Yesha Council and ongoing expanded claims to the land.

Israel's decision in 2005 to withdraw unilaterally from the Gaza Strip and dismantle its approximately 20 settlements there has hardly changed the dynamics of the controversy over the occupied territories. Officials on the Yesha Council certainly denounced the expulsion of Jews from Gaza, but unlike the early 1990s when public statements from the body incited an atmosphere that facilitated the assassination of Prime Minister Yitzhak Rabin, they stopped short of calling for violence to block government policy. This restraint can mainly be explained by the moderate views of most West Bank settlers and Israel's commitment to retain possession of the key settlement blocks. The largest of these is Maale Adumim, an urban area near Jerusalem with a population of 30,000 people. Designated as Israel's linchpin settlement, housing construction within its ample municipal borders is continuing apace and increasing the flow of Jews to the area. The Yesha Council was therefore ever expanding its constituency even as the Israeli presence in Gaza was brought to an end, and the body is determined to retain for the state large sections of the West Bank in any future peace settlement with the Palestinian Authority (PA).

JONAS KAUFFELDT

See also

Gaza Strip; Jerusalem; Promised Land; Rabin, Yitzhak; Settlements, Israeli; Sharon, Ariel; Six-Day War; West Bank; Yom Kippur War

References

Gazit, Shlomo. *Trapped Fools: Thirty Years of Israeli Policy in the Territories.* London: Frank Cass, 2003.

Gelvin, James L. *The Israel-Palestine Conflict: One Hundred Years of War.* New York: Cambridge University Press, 2005.

Karpin, Michael, and Ina Friedman. *Murder in the Name of God.* New York: Metropolitan Books, 1998.

Yoffe, Avraham
Born: October 25, 1913
Died: April 12, 1983

Israeli military officer and politician. Avraham Yoffe was born on October 25, 1913, in what was then Ottoman territory and is now

Israeli Army brigadier general Avraham Yoffe, October 1976. (Israeli Government Press Office)

Yavniel, Israel. He joined the paramilitary Jewish self-defense organization Haganah at age 16. During World War II he served as a captain in the British Royal Artillery.

Upon the formation of the State of Israel in May 1948, Yoffe joined the Israel Defense Forces (IDF). During the Israeli War of Independence (1948–1949) he served as a battalion commander and helped in the capture of Nazareth. In the 1956 Suez Crisis and resultant Sinai Campaign he led an armored brigade that captured the Egyptian port of Sharm al-Sheikh in the Sinai Peninsula. In 1957 he became commander of the officers' school as a brigadier general before heading the Southern Command from 1958 to 1962 and the Northern Command from 1962 to 1964. As head of the Southern Command he developed contingency plans for tank movement in the desert. He left the IDF in 1964 and went on inactive reserve status.

Shortly before the June 1967 Six-Day War, Yoffe was recalled to command a division with the rank of major general. He was one of a number of generals who were highly critical of Prime Minister Levi Eshkol for hesitating to initiate the conflict with a preemptive strike, given the presence of Egyptian forces in the Sinai. Eshkol continued to stall, but Israel did ultimately initiate hostilities.

Once the fighting began on June 5, the head of the Southern Command, Major General Yishayahu Gavish, ordered Yoffe's force, consisting of two reserve brigades with some 200 tanks and 100 half-tracks, to screen the flanks of two other advancing divisions led by Major General Ariel Sharon and Major General Israel Tal. Yoffe's force crossed the Wadi Haroudin, a desert that the Egyptians believed was impassable for tanks and therefore left undefended. For nine hours Yoffe's force crossed the sand dunes clearing minefields. The force finally made contact at Bir Lahfan. Yoffe's tanks then effectively blocked the path to El Arish and obstructed Egyptian reinforcements. The Israelis then fought a series of running tank battles while they advanced toward the Suez Canal. By the fourth day of the war, the Egyptians were effectively defeated.

With the conclusion of hostilities, Yoffe left active duty. He subsequently became head of the Israel Nature Preservation Authority, which established numerous nature preserves throughout the country. He also served in the Knesset (Israeli parliament) as a member of the Likud Party from 1973 to 1977. Yoffe died in Tel Aviv on April 12, 1983, following a long illness.

MICHAEL K. BEAUCHAMP

See also

Eshkol, Levi; Likud Party; Sharm al-Sheikh; Sinai Campaign; Six-Day War

References

Bowen, Jeremy. *Six Days: How the 1967 War Shaped the Middle East.* New York: Thomas Dunne, 2005.

Oren, Michael B. *Six Days of War: June 1967 and the Making of the Modern Middle East.* Novato, CA: Presidio, 2003.

Yom HaShoah ve ha-Gevurah

A solemn day of remembrance for the victims of the Holocaust, considered a national holiday in Israel and a religious holiday among Jewry worldwide. Yom HaShoah ve ha-Gevurah, or Holocaust Martyrs' and Heroes' Remembrance Day, was created by the Israeli government in 1959 to honor the victims of the Nazi-inspired Holocaust (the Shoah) and those who survived it. The precise day of its observation varies on the Gregorian calendar, but according to the Hebrew calendar it is observed on the 27th day of Nisan, or the seventh month of the Hebrew civil calendar. Each year the commemoration falls in either March or April on the Gregorian calendar.

The day is honored in a variety of ways and incorporates both civil and religious observations. After sundown on the day prior to Yom HaShoah ve ha-Gevurah, the state holds a solemn ceremony at Yad Vashem, the official Israeli memorial to the Holocaust located in Jerusalem. On the actual day of the observation, at 10:00 a.m. local time, air-raid sirens are sounded continuously for two minutes as the entire nation pauses in honor of the Holocaust victims. Most public offices are by law closed on HaShoah ve ha-Gevurah, as are many restaurants, cafés, and markets. Flags on all buildings are lowered to half-staff, and television and radio stations broadcast—without commercials—somber mourning music and programs that deal with the Holocaust.

Jews residing elsewhere mark the observance in numerous ways, many of which are held in synagogues or temples. Observances included guest speakers, educational programs for youths, special prayer services, fasting, and the reading of individual names of Holocaust victims in grim recognition that it would take many years of remembrances to read off 6 million names. A special ceremony is also held at Auschwitz, Poland, the largest and perhaps the most notorious of all of the Nazi death camps. This commemoration includes the March of the Living in which several thousand Jews from Israel and around the world parade around and through Auschwitz.

PAUL G. PIERPAOLI JR.

See also

Holocaust; Yad Vashem Holocaust Memorial

References

Hoffman, Eva. *After Such Knowledge: Where Memory of the Holocaust Ends and History Begins.* New York: PublicAffairs, 2005.

Young, James Edward. *The Texture of Memory: Holocaust Memorials and Meaning.* New Haven, CT: Yale University Press, 1993.

Yom Kippur War

Start Date: October 6, 1973
End Date: October 26, 1973

Arab Israeli conflict that occurred from October 6 to October 26, 1973, so-named because it began with a coordinated Egyptian-Syrian surprise attack against Israel on the Jewish holy day of Yom Kippur (Day of Atonement.) The war is therefore also known as the War of Atonement or, for Muslims, the Ramadan War because it began during the holy month of Ramadan.

In addition to the long-standing issues of the Arab-Israeli conflict dating to 1948, the more pressing causes of the Yom Kippur War were inherent in the results of the June 1967 Six-Day War. During that campaign, the Israel Defense Forces (IDF) not only humiliated the Arab armies but also seized large portions of Syrian, Jordanian, and Egyptian territory. Although possession of the Golan Heights and the Sinai Peninsula gave Israel much-needed strategic depth, this was absolutely intolerable to the highly nationalistic regimes in Damascus and Cairo. Israel's continued occupation of these lands transformed the abstract grievances of Palestinian rights into a deeply resented insult to the Arab governments and armies involved.

Paradoxically, therefore, Israel's very success in 1967 had made it more difficult, both politically and emotionally, for Arab leaders to reach a negotiated settlement with the Israelis. Israel naturally

Estimated Casualties of the 1973 Yom Kippur War

	Israel	Arab Nations
KIA	2,687	15,400
WIA	7,251	42,000
POW	314	8,400
Aircraft Lost	182	432

Egyptian soldier in front of the Suez Canal flashing the "V" for victory sign during the Yom Kippur War, October 13, 1973. (Mena/Corbis Sygma)

wished to use these territories as a bargaining chip for a possible diplomatic compromise, whereas its opponents demanded complete evacuation as a prerequisite to any negotiations. In addition, these Israeli-held territories brought with them a constant drain on the reservist Israeli military, which had to provide forces to defend large sectors that it had never previously possessed. In particular, the 35 positions of the so-called Bar-Lev Line along the Suez Canal required garrisons to provide early warning and deter Egyptian infiltrations. Moreover, the distance between Israel proper and the canal meant that in the event of war Israeli reserve units would take several days to mobilize and reach the southern front. For Egypt's part, a constant state of semimobilization in combination with the loss of revenues from the Suez Canal placed enormous strains on the economy, increasing pressure to resolve the situation at all costs.

Renewed warfare was therefore inevitable, waiting only until the frontline Arab states had rearmed and reorganized their forces. The question in 1973 was how the Arabs could overcome the enormous advantages possessed by the IDF. The 1956 Suez Crisis and Sinai Campaign and especially the 1967 Six-Day War had shown the IDF to be a master of flexible, offensive warfare reminiscent of World War II blitzkrieg tactics. Although individual Arab soldiers had exhibited bravery and skill in defending fixed positions in those wars, they could not easily match the Israelis' mechanized maneuvers, and few Arab pilots had the experience of their Israeli counterparts.

The problem for the Egyptians was further complicated by the fact that they had to begin their offensive by crossing the Suez Canal, whose concrete-lined banks and adjacent sand walls made the canal difficult to breach with heavy vehicles. Long before the Egyptians could build bridges to bring their armor across the canal, their first waves of dismounted infantry would face counterattacks from the lethal combination of Israeli tanks and fighter-bombers.

A number of people were involved in planning solutions to these tactical problems, but the most significant was undoubtedly Lieutenant General Saad el-Shazly, Egyptian armed forces chief of staff from May 1971 to December 1973. Recognizing the strength of his soldiers on the defensive, el-Shazly developed a bold program to provide his assault infantry with as many man-portable antitank and antiaircraft missiles as possible. Particularly important in this regard was the AT-3 Sagger antitank guided missile (ATGM), Soviet designation 9M14, a wire-guided weapon that could be "flown" by the operator to kill tanks at a range of up to two miles. El-Shazly stripped the rest of the Egyptian Army of such weapons in order to give his attacking brigades all the missiles they could carry forward. He also planned five different crossings on a wide front, with the troops rushing forward to assume shallow but coherent bridgeheads that could defeat the first Israeli armored counterattacks, giving Egyptian forces time to bring their armored vehicles across the canal. Thus, while conducting an offensive at the operational level, at the tactical level the Egyptians planned to stand on the defensive,

YOM KIPPUR WAR, 1973

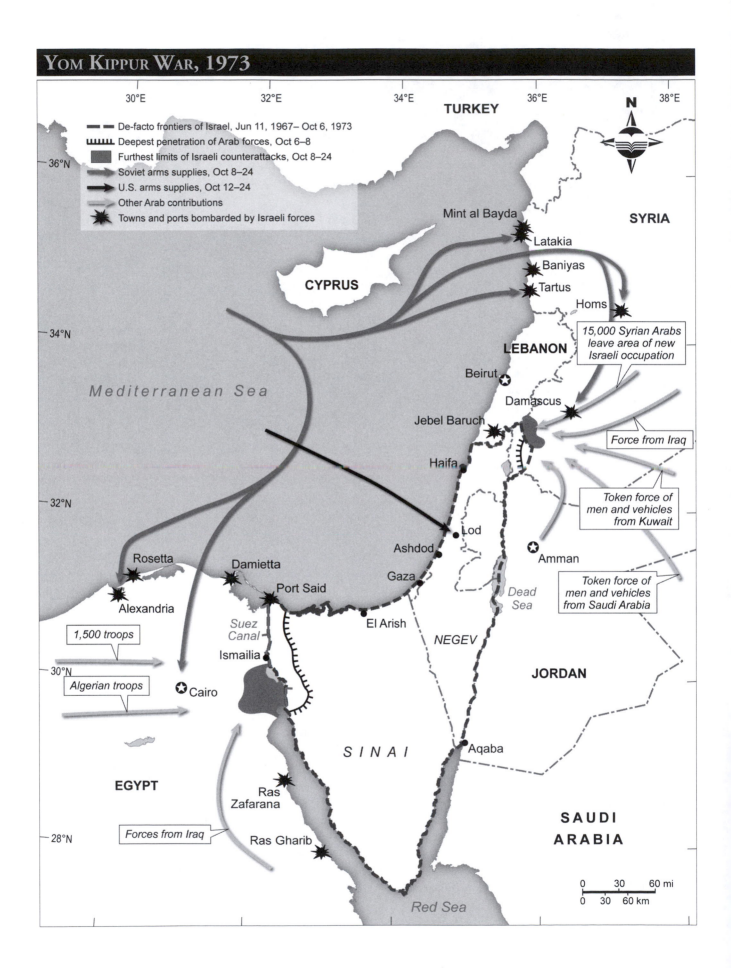

Legend:
- De-facto frontiers of Israel, Jun 11, 1967– Oct 6, 1973
- Deepest penetration of Arab forces, Oct 6–8
- Furthest limits of Israeli counterattacks, Oct 8–24
- Soviet arms supplies, Oct 8–24
- U.S. arms supplies, Oct 12–24
- Other Arab contributions
- Towns and ports bombarded by Israeli forces

TURKEY

SYRIA

CYPRUS

Mint al Bayda

Latakia

Baniyas

Tartus

Homs

Mediterranean Sea

LEBANON

Beirut

Damascus

15,000 Syrian Arabs leave area of new Israeli occupation

Jebel Baruch

Haifa

Force from Iraq

Token force of men and vehicles from Kuwait

Rosetta

Damietta

Lod

Amman

Ashdod

Alexandria

Port Said

Gaza

Dead Sea

Token force of men and vehicles from Saudi Arabia

1,500 troops

Suez Canal

El Arish

NEGEV

JORDAN

Ismailia

Algerian troops

Cairo

Aqaba

S I N A I

EGYPT

Ras Zafarana

SAUDI ARABIA

Forces from Iraq

Ras Gharib

Red Sea

0   30   60 mi
0   30   60 km

Israeli Army long-range 175-mm artillery in action on the Syrian front, October 11, 1973. (Menash Azouiri/Israeli Government Press Office)

forcing the IDF to attack them with little opportunity for outflanking maneuvers.

To span the Suez Canal, the Egyptians formed 40 battalions of assault and bridging engineers. A junior engineer officer suggested that to achieve an immediate breach of the huge sand walls that Israel had built on the eastern side of the canal, the attackers should use high-pressure water cannon rather than explosives or earthmoving equipment. During the event, 450 British- and German-made pumps enabled the attackers to create 60 gaps in the sand wall during the first six hours of the campaign.

At a time when most of his contemporaries still sought a single war of annihilation against Israel, el-Shazly decided to conduct a limited offensive, one that would capitalize on the abilities of his troops and shake the IDF's confidence in its own invincibility. Thus, Operation THE HIGH MINARETS intended to penetrate no more than six miles east of the Suez Canal. This meant that in order to attack the Egyptians, the Israeli Air Force would have to fly inside the overlapping range fans of the SA-2 and SA-3 air defense missiles located on the western bank of the canal. As they crossed the canal, Egyptian units took with them not only ATGMs but also a variety of more mobile air defense weapons, including the man-portable SA-7 missile and the vehicle-mounted ZSU-23–4 guns and SAM-6 missiles.

Working together, these Soviet-supplied weapons posed an integrated air defense capability that would degrade or neutralize the Israeli advantage in fighter-bombers.

Although there was general agreement on this first phase of the operation, most Egyptian officials expected far more from the war. In particular, the Egyptians had promised their Syrian allies that they would quickly move forward to the Sinai passes, denying Israel any defensible terrain in the desert. El-Shazly consistently opposed such plans because a deep advance would leave behind the air defense umbrella and tightly coordinated defensive positions that gave the Egyptians their initial advantages. Instead, el-Shazly envisaged forcing Israel to choose between a long stalemated war that it could not afford, unacceptably high casualties to retake the canal, or peace negotiations.

For its part, the Syrian plan was more conventional, relying on multiple attack echelons, each consisting of two to three mechanized or armored divisions, to overwhelm the IDF in the occupied Golan Heights before Israeli reserves could arrive. The leading brigades of infantry would cross the Israeli antitank ditch on foot, to be followed by vehicle-launched bridges to permit the tanks to cross. This concept was a highly stylized and overly centralized version of the offensive tactics that the Soviet Army had taught to its

Arab allies. From the beginning, therefore, Damascus was pushing for a total victory, a serious divergence from the Egyptian plans. Again, an integrated Soviet-manufactured air defense system, including 15 batteries of the mobile SA-6, would shelter the Syrian ground advance. Given the shallow (approximately 12.5-mile) depth of the IDF enclave on the Golan Heights, this plan appeared more feasible than an equivalent Egyptian effort to retake the entire Sinai.

Yet these plans would have been pointless had Israeli intelligence agencies detected Arab preparations in time to mobilize and counterattack. Indeed, the Egyptian intelligence services predicted that Israel would have unambiguous warning of the attack 15 days before it began. Therefore, planning and preparations for the attack included unprecedented secrecy and deception efforts. In this regard, it is worth noting that the 1973 attack was the first major conflict in which the Arab armed forces had actually planned their attacks and conducted those attacks at a time and place of their own choosing. It was also the first war in which the different Arab states coordinated their operations. This coordination was responsible for the unusual H-hour of 2:00 p.m., which was a compromise between the Syrian desire to attack at dawn and the Egyptian desire to conduct most of the canal crossing in darkness.

From August 21 to 24, 1973, the Syrian and Egyptian military planners met in civilian clothes for final staff talks regarding the approaching offensive, code-named Operation BADR after the AD 624 victory of the Prophet Muhammad. As a result of this meeting, the military commanders proposed a series of appropriate dates for the attack from which Presidents Anwar Sadat of Egypt and Hafez al-Assad of Syria chose October 6 as the starting date.

During the remaining weeks of intensive preparations, all concerned continued routine activities in public. Egypt in particular desensitized the Israelis by a series of field exercises and no fewer than 22 practice mobilizations and demobilizations of reservists during 1973. A major Egyptian troop concentration had passed without incident in the spring of 1973, further desensitizing observers. Meanwhile, the Egyptian General Staff maintained secrecy to the point that it did not inform its division commanders until three days before the attack.

Despite such tight security by the Egyptians, Israel's lack of strategic warning has been the subject of much debate. As early as January 1971, IDF chief of staff General David Elazar had recognized that the diplomatic stalemate virtually impelled the Arabs to attack. The only error was in estimating when that attack would occur. Fundamentally, the problem was a classic example of the intelligence conundrum of enemy capabilities versus intentions. In late September and early October 1973, Israeli and American intelligence reports clearly identified the fact that the Arab armies were fully mobilized and concentrated in attack positions. Indeed, the head of the IDF's Northern Command, Major General Yitzhak Hofi, reportedly concluded by mid-September that Syria was capable of attacking at any time without additional warning indications.

However, with certain exceptions, the Israeli intelligence and leadership structure was convinced that the Arab states did not intend to launch a war, because in Israeli eyes Syria knew that it could not win alone and Egypt supposedly felt too vulnerable to Israeli air attacks on its economy and population. Israeli leaders assumed that their opponents shared IDF views about the likely outcome of an immediate war. Indeed, the Israeli director of military intelligence, Major General Eliezer Zeira, was so convinced of this interpretation that he repeatedly delayed reporting key information to his superiors and downplayed the significance of the reports he did present. Thus, as recently as the day before the attack, Zeira estimated that a general attack was still improbable, although as a precaution the regular Israeli army moved to its highest state of alert on October 5.

During those final 24 hours before the war began, sufficient intelligence indications appeared to make the threat of attack seem real. In particular, after Sadat and al-Assad informed their Soviet military advisers that an attack was imminent, during October 4–6 Soviet aircraft urgently evacuated the families of their personnel from both countries. King Hussein of Jordan provided several specific warnings, as did one of Israel's highest human intelligence sources in Egypt. By the morning of October 6, therefore, the IDF belatedly began mobilization. The Israeli Air Force also prepared a preemptive strike against Arab targets, but low clouds made it impossible to strike the Golan Heights, and eventually Prime Minister Golda Meir cancelled the attack. She reportedly told U.S. ambassador to Israel Kenneth Keating that Israel wanted to avoid any accusation that it was responsible for the war.

As a result, the IDF began the conflict with only its active duty forces on the frontiers. Although IDF security makes exact order of battle analysis difficult, the overall weakness of these forces was obvious. The normal garrison on the Golan Heights was built around the 188th Brigade, which was deployed by platoons of three tanks each to support the infantry strong points, occupied in many cases by paratroopers, along the cease-fire line. As the threat of war loomed on October 5, this force received reinforcements including the famous 7th Armored Brigade and at least portions of the 1st (Golani) Infantry Brigade. These units were at full strength, but in the crisis the troops, airlifted from other parts of Israel, had to draw new vehicles while their commanders studied the unfamiliar terrain. Moreover, at least two companies of the 7th Brigade were composed of conscripts still undergoing initial training as tank crewmen. Overall, there were 177 IDF Centurion tanks and 44 artillery pieces on the Golan Heights, as compared to 700 T-55s and extensive artillery found in just the first echelon of Syrian attackers.

The Sinai was almost equally weak. The positions of the Bar-Lev Line required 800–3,000 infantrymen to occupy effectively, but at the time of the attack the positions contained only about 460 reservists, many of them middle-aged. These positions were poorly maintained, with wire obstacles buried by drifting sand and with shortages of ammunition. Behind them stood Major General Avraham Mandler's 252nd Armored Division. Major General Shmuel Gonen was the overall southern commander. Gonen had assumed command recently and was unaware of accurate intelligence con-

Israeli and Egyptian military representatives negotiate a cease-fire agreement in a United Nations (UN) tent at the kilometer 101 marker on the Cairo-Suez Road, November 11, 1973. (Corel)

cerning the wide frontage of the Egyptian attack plan. Although Mandler had 291 tanks and 48 artillery pieces, these troops expected the Egyptians to attack at dusk and were thus far from the canal when the attack began in midafternoon. In addition, the IDF had placed a low priority on mechanized infantry after the success of the tank–fighter-bomber team in 1967.

Consequently, many infantry troops were still in the mobilizing reserves, while tank units were in the habit of maneuvering without infantry support. Most mechanized infantry still rode in World War II–era M3 half-tracks, and the field artillery branch was almost equally neglected. The IDF plan for emergency defense in the south, Operation DOVECOTE, called for one battalion (36–40 tanks) from each of the three armored brigades to immediately advance to firing positions near the canal in order to break up any attack and support the Bar-Lev Line.

The initial attack began on both fronts with air strikes at 2:00 p.m. on October 6 followed immediately by brief artillery barrages to suppress the defenders in fortified positions. Preceded by reconnaissance engineers and commandos, the first wave of infantry crossed the canal in assault boats at 2:15. Subsequent waves followed every 15 minutes, so that 23,500 men—the assault elements of five infantry divisions—had crossed the canal by 4:15 p.m. The commandos and initial infantry troops shattered the quick-reaction

IDF tank units, which had not trained to deal with ATGMs. Additional losses followed as the Israelis repeatedly attempted to relieve and evacuate the Bar-Lev positions. The first floating bridge was completed by 8:30 that night, beginning the flow of tanks and heavy weapons. Only in the south did the Egyptians have difficulties. There, the different soil opposite the 19th Infantry Division meant that the water cannon turned the protective walls into impenetrable mud, restricting the number of crossing points. Meanwhile, an amphibious brigade successfully crossed the Great Bitter Lake, but its lightly armored vehicles suffered heavily when they tried to reach the Gidi Pass in mid-Sinai.

IDF tank crews quickly learned to disturb ATGM gunners' aim by weaving rapidly while firing at the gunners' positions. Still, in the first day the Egyptian Army achieved its objectives at a cost of only 280 killed. That evening, more commandos were airlifted forward to ambush arriving IDF reserve and supply columns. Although the Israelis shot down 20 of the 48 helicopters involved, these commandos seriously disrupted Israeli movements. On the coastal road alone, at least 21 Israelis died before they neutralized the tenacious commandos.

Matters for Israel were even worse on the Golan Heights. General Hofi and his chief of staff were both absent for meetings when the attack began, so the two tank brigades operated almost

Israeli troops withdraw from the Suez Canal area of Egypt in 1974 in accordance with an agreement reached by the United Nations Disengagement Observer Force. (Corel)

independently. Moreover, only two battalions defended the flatter, open southern portion of the Golan Heights, and in most instances these battalions were dispersed in small groups, trying to defend every inch of the Golan Heights territory rather than blocking major penetrations. While IDF commanders reported stopping the attackers in their sectors, they were unaware of large forces infiltrating between those sectors and advancing to the rear. Indeed, by the early evening of the first day, the 5th Syrian Infantry Division had in effect broken through in the south but turned its forces northward toward Nafakh, seeking to outflank the defenders rather than pushing forward into Israel. During this period both sides created epics of individual gallantry, such as that of Lieutenant Zvika Greengold whose single tank delayed the Syrian flanking movement for hours along the Tapline Road. Although equipped with infrared vision devices, many of the Syrian units were untrained for night fighting, causing them to pause in the darkness. Moreover, despite the bravery of individual Syrian soldiers, many of their commanders were slow to respond to changing situations.

At the start of the war, Syrian commandos had captured the key IDF observation point on Mount Hermon but failed to execute their plan to interdict the flow of reserves across the Jordan River bridges. That night, Israeli brigadier general Rafael Eitan's 36th Armored

Division headquarters assumed tactical responsibility for the Golan Heights. During the next two days, the 7th Armored Brigade and reinforcements fought the attackers to a standstill on the northern Golan Heights, destroying more than 260 tanks of the 7th Syrian Infantry Division and following echelons. On October 9 the remnants of the 7th Brigade performed another miracle, halting two Syrian tank brigades including the T-62s of the Presidential Guard Brigade, which outnumbered the Israelis four to one. Only seven original tanks of the 7th Brigade remained after that battle.

The Israeli Air Force suffered heavily, losing 49 aircraft in the first four days in large measure because it was unable to eliminate enemy air defense batteries. Instead, Defense Minister Moshe Dayan repeatedly changed priorities, insisting that the air force attack Syrian spearheads and Egyptian bridges to gain time until the reserves were mobilized. Although the latter attacks were effective, the Egyptians rapidly replaced damaged sections of their floating bridges. Only at sea did Israel enjoy its usual dominance, using electronic countermeasures to negate Arab Styx missiles.

On October 8 a poorly coordinated IDF counterattack by two armored divisions failed painfully in the Sinai, due as much to excessive optimism by General Gonen as to Egyptian defensive capabilities. Yet on that and the following day two reserve armored divisions,

Major General Dan Laner's 240th Division and Major General Moshe Peled's 146th Division, successfully retook the southern and central Golan Heights despite the dogged defense of Colonel Tawfiq Juhni's 1st Syrian Armored Division around Hushniyah. By darkness on October 10, Israel had destroyed some 870 Syrian tanks and retaken its prewar positions except for Mount Hermon. Still, the Syrian Army had withdrawn in good order. Fearing that an early cease-fire would leave Israel with a net loss in territory, Prime Minister Meir ordered an offensive into Syria to begin on October 11.

This offensive, in combination with Israeli air attacks against Syrian command and infrastructure targets, changed the course of the war. Damascus appealed to Cairo to divert Israeli attention by a renewed attack, and President Sadat overruled his field commanders, ordering the Egyptian Army to leave its air defense umbrella and advance to the Sinai passes on the morning of October 14. This attack by three understrength divisions, the 4th Armored and 6th Mechanized in the south and the 21st Armored in the north, was a predictable disaster, costing Egypt 250 tanks in a few hours. More significantly, it disrupted the integrity of Egypt's bridgehead defenses while committing most of the operational reserve.

Once these armored units (less one brigade of the 4th Division) crossed the Suez Canal going eastward, it was politically impossible for them to reverse course and defend the western bank. As a result, beginning on the evening of October 15, the IDF, led by Major General Ariel Sharon's 143rd Armored Division, was able to launch Operation GAZELLE, breaking through to the canal and pushing Colonel Danny Matt's 247th Paratroop Brigade across just north of Great Bitter Lake. Although the Egyptians attempted to pinch off this penetration by attacks on the eastern side of the canal, those attacks failed. Instead, over the next several days elements of the 143rd and 146th Armored Divisions crossed the canal and fanned out, disrupting the Egyptian air defense network by attacking individual batteries on the ground. Egyptian artillery took a considerable toll on Israeli engineers, who nonetheless maintained bridges across the canal. For days, Sadat refused to recall units from the east, and in fact senior Egyptian commanders were not informed of the threat until several days after the initial crossing.

The Egyptian failure was compounded by continued defeats in Syria, where the IDF continued to push toward Damascus while engaging other Arab forces as they arrived to fight. In the early morning of October 13, Laner's 240th Armored Division decimated the Iraqi 3rd Armored Division and repulsed the Jordanian 40th Armored Brigade. The Arab armies continued to fight bravely, but coordination among those armies was not always effective.

From the beginning of the conflict, the Soviet Union had attempted to impose a cease-fire, at first because it expected the Arabs to be defeated and later to preserve their gains. Sadat had refused such initiatives until the Israeli crossing endangered his forces. Meanwhile, U.S. secretary of state Henry Kissinger tried to delay cease-fire negotiations in order to afford Israel time to regain its initial positions. By mid-October such a cease-fire appeared imminent, accelerating the two IDF offensives.

At the same time, Kissinger had to persuade his own government and especially Secretary of Defense James R. Schlesinger that Israel urgently needed replacement tanks, aircraft, and ammunition. Many officials suspected a trick, but Kissinger argued that an IDF defeat would appear to be an American defeat as well. President Richard Nixon decisively supported Kissinger. Beginning on October 13, the United States defied Arab reactions, sending a total of 567 transport aircraft sorties moving 22,000 tons of supplies. Seventy-two fighter aircraft were also flown to Israel, while two Israeli ships moved 65 M-60 tanks, 23 M-109 howitzers, and 400 M-54 trucks from West Germany. Many of these vehicles arrived too late for immediate use, but the knowledge that they were on the way permitted the IDF to use all its available stocks in battle. The Soviet Union responded with 15,000 tons airlifted to replace the losses of its client states.

On October 22 the United Nations (UN) Security Council approved a cease-fire, but the agreement failed as each side blamed the other for violations. Regardless of who was at fault, the IDF used this excuse to push southward on the western bank of the canal, cutting off the Third Egyptian Army from its supplies. With the air defense umbrella ruptured, the Israeli Air Force could again excel in both air-to-surface and air-to-air operations, downing almost 100 Egyptian aircraft at a loss of only 3 Israeli planes. In defeat, the Egyptians continued to fight in a disciplined manner, and a combination of soldiers and local militia thwarted Israeli efforts to seize Suez City, at the southern end of the canal, on October 23 and 25.

The continued fighting, with the Third Army stranded and the IDF approaching Damascus, provoked a superpower confrontation at the end of the war. The Soviet Union had alerted some of its forces at the start of hostilities and reportedly increased the readiness of certain airborne units after an Israeli victory became apparent. On October 24 Soviet leader Leonid Brezhnev sent President Nixon a note threatening unilateral action if the United States did not join with him in curbing the Israelis. Kissinger had already told the Israelis that their further incursions violated the spirit of his agreements with Moscow, but this new message prompted the United States to alert its nuclear forces to Defense Condition (DefCon) 3 at 11:41 p.m. on October 24. Although Brezhnev's true intentions have never been established, the situation was defused peacefully when, after repeated UN Security Council resolutions, the fighting finally halted on October 26. Even then, Israel refused to permit resupply of the stricken Third Army until Egypt returned all prisoners.

Overall, Israel suffered at least 2,687 killed and 7,251 wounded. Some 314 more were taken prisoner. This compares to combined Arab losses that exceeded 15,400 dead, 42,000 wounded, and 8,400 prisoners.

Although like the previous conflicts the Yom Kippur War ended with Israeli victories, General el-Shazly's larger objectives were clearly accomplished. Because the Arabs rather than the Israelis had the advantages of preparation and surprise, the fighting value of the opposing sides was much closer than in previous conflicts. Egypt in particular had demonstrated that Israel could not occupy the Sinai indefinitely, thereby establishing the psychological pre-conditions for successful peace negotiations in 1978.

The conflict also contributed to Middle Eastern disenchantment with the superpowers. The Soviet Union had shown itself unwilling or unable to give the Arabs weapons equal in quality to those that the United States had provided to Israel. However, the open U.S. support for Israel offended many Arab governments and led directly to the crippling oil embargo by Arab nations during late 1973 and early 1974. That imbroglio wrought havoc on already-weak U.S. and West European economies and saw the near quadrupling of petroleum prices in the span of only a few months.

JONATHAN M. HOUSE

See also

Assad, Hafez al-; Bar-Lev Line; Dayan, Moshe; Egypt, Armed Forces; Eitan, Rafael; Elazar, David; Golan Heights; Gonen, Shmuel; Hofi, Yitzhak; Hussein, King of Jordan; Israel Defense Forces; Kissinger, Henry Alfred; Mandler, Avraham Albert; Meir, Golda; Sadat, Anwar; Sharon, Ariel; Shazly, Saad el-; Sinai; Sinai Campaign; Six-Day War; Suez Crisis; Syria, Armed Forces

References

Adan, Avraham. *On the Banks of the Suez: An Israeli General's Personal Account of the Yom Kippur War.* Novato, CA: Presidio, 1980.

Dunstan, Simon. *The Yom Kippur War, 1973.* 2 vols. Westport, CT: Praeger, 2005.

El Shazly, Saad. *The Crossing of the Suez.* San Francisco: American Mideast Research, 1980.

Gamasy, Mohamed Abdul Ghani el-. *The October War: Memoirs of Field Marshal El-Gamasy of Egypt.* Translated by Gillian Potter, Nadra Morcos, and Rosette Frances. Cairo: American University in Cairo Press, 1993.

Gawrych, George W. *The 1973 Arab-Israeli War: The Albatross of Decisive Victory.* Leavenworth Papers No. 21. Fort Leavenworth, KS: Combat Studies Institute, 1996.

Heikal, Mohammed Hasanyn. *The Road to Ramadan.* New York: Quadrangle/New York Times Book, 1975.

House, Jonathan M. *Toward Combined Arms Warfare: A Survey of 20th Century Tactics, Doctrine, and Organization.* Fort Leavenworth, KS: U.S. Army Command and General Staff College, 1984.

Kahalani, Avigdor. *The Heights of Courage: A Tank Leader's War on the Golan.* Westport, CT: Praeger, 1992.

———. "Israeli Defense of the Golan." *Military Review* 59(10) (October 1979): 2–13.

Kahana, Ephraim. "Early Warning versus Concept: The Case of the Yom Kippur War, 1973." *Intelligence and National Security* 17 (Summer 2002): 81–104.

Pollack, Kenneth M. *Arabs at War: Military Effectiveness, 1948–1991.* Lincoln: University of Nebraska Press, 2002.

Rabinovich, Abraham. *The Yom Kippur War: The Epic Encounter That Transformed the Middle East.* New York: Schocken, 2005.

Young Israel

A branch of Modern Orthodox Judaism founded in 1912 to combat the assimilation by young Jews into secular American society. Young Israel, also known as the National Council of Young Israel (NCYI), is a not-for-profit service organization headquartered in New York City with regional offices in Florida, California, New Jersey, and Jerusalem.

The Young Israel movement sought at its inception to provide a positive Orthodox Jewish synagogue experience as an alternative to the then exclusively Yiddish-speaking and East European-dominated Orthodox synagogues. Young Israel initially targeted newly arrived immigrants, the religiously disenfranchised youths of American Jewry, and poor Jewish communities with Friday night lectures in English. Young Israel introduced its first Model Synagogue in 1915. These synagogues provided traditional Jewish services and observances formatted to attract English-speaking American youths and introduced educational, religious, social, spiritual, and communal programming designed to attract its original target groups. At the time of its founding, there were a host of similar organizations tailored to specific immigrants and immigrant communities. Some ministered to specific ethnic groups and their newly arrived immigrants, while others focused on religious principles. Indeed, between 1880 and 1920, the United States witnessed a massive influx of immigrants, many of whom were from Eastern and Southern Europe.

There are nearly 150 North American NCYI Orthodox congregations, all of which meet the minimum standards of orthodoxy established by Jewish rabbinic law, custom, and tradition (or Halakha). These standards included a mechitza (divider) separating male and female worshipers, nonaccessible parking on the Sabbath and holy days, and synagogue (shul) officers who keep the Sabbath (Shomer Shabbos) according to halakic standards (the standards set by the Halakha). Many of Young Israel's affiliated rabbis are graduates of Haredi Lithuanian yeshivas (rabbinic academies), and this has led to closer ties with the Haredi (Hasidic Judaism).

NCYI's religious and sociocultural ethos arises from the Religious Zionist Movement (Mizrahic Judaism) that roots Zionism in the practice of Orthodox Judaism rather than in secular humanism and sociopolitical theories and agendas. This ethos manifests itself in NCYI's support of Israel as the homeland for the Jewish people and NCYI's 50 branches in Israel established through its sister movement, the Young Israel Movement in Israel (Yisrael Hatzair). Young Israel also encourages its membership to be politically active at all levels of the U.S. government.

RICHARD M. EDWARDS

See also

Hasidic Judaism; Mizrahic Judaism

References

Baer, Max F. *Dealing in Futures: The Story of the Jewish Youth Movement.* Washington, DC: B'nai B'rith International, 1983.

Brenner, Michael. *Zionism: A Brief History.* Translated by Shelley Frisch. Princeton, NJ: Markus Wiener, 2003.

Youth Aliya

Movement founded on May 10, 1933, by Recha Freier, a German teacher and pianist worried by the National Socialist assumption of power in Germany. The Youth Aliya was dedicated to assisting Jewish youths to emigrate from oppressive regimes in Europe to Palestine, where they could join a well-established Jewish community living under the British Mandate government. Immigration to Palestine was strictly controlled by the British, and thus Freier believed that the few immigration permits should be reserved for the young. As such, Youth Aliya pushed for the emigration of teenagers at the expense of all other hopeful candidates.

The Youth Aliya movement was soon adopted by Henrietta Szold, the founder of the Jewish women's organization Hadassah. With Szold's ample assistance, Youth Aliya became a department within the Jewish Agency, increasing the political leverage of the organization. Szold worked primarily as a facilitator in Jerusalem, while Freier remained in Germany.

All told, Youth Aliya facilitated the transfer of almost 25,000 youths to Palestine prior to World War II, with the first arrivals from Germany in 1934. Because the new immigrants arrived without parents or adult supervision, they were assimilated into new families. Most of the Youth Aliya children were sent to kibbutzim and moshavim. These collective settlements, dedicated to labor and agriculture, were ill-equipped to absorb the new arrivals, however, most of whom came from urban middle-class families and were thus poorly prepared for farm life. In the kibbutzim, the children joined the community at-large, participating as full members in the kibbutzim system. In the moshavim, where individual families maintained separate farms, the Youth Aliya children were adopted individually by single families, separating siblings where necessary. In both cases, Youth Aliya immigrants formed extremely strong bonds with their adoptive families.

During World War II Youth Aliya became virtually defunct, as all immigration virtually ceased from the Axis powers and the territories they conquered. However, immediately after the war the organization resumed its drive to help Jewish youths leave war-torn Europe and move to British-controlled Palestine. In the decade after the end of hostilities, Youth Aliya helped 15,000 more children emigrate, most of them Holocaust survivors. Once more, they assimilated into new households and communes without regard to kinship networks or nationalities. When the British Mandate period ended in Palestine in May 1948, the organization simply shifted its operations to assisting children to immigrate to the new State of Israel. Youth Aliya has continued its mission of aiding the transfer of disadvantaged children worldwide to Israel, although many of the new arrivals are not directly placed with new families. Instead, Youth Aliya has created a system of boarding school villages that accept custody and responsibility for the recent immigrants.

Youth Aliya adopted a broad new role in the decades after World War II. In addition to assisting in the immigration of at-risk youths, the organization has also instituted a service mission aimed at disadvantaged students within the Israeli educational system. Youth Aliya has established a series of boarding school villages that offer a second chance to Israeli children with educational or behavioral difficulties. The students at these schools receive a combination of intensive educational assistance and behavioral therapy and are housed in a stable residential community. Class sizes are kept small and are enhanced by extensive extracurricular activities. Some of the schools are coeducational, while others are designated solely for young boys. Many of the students at these schools were considered lost causes at their home institutions, and the Youth Aliya schools represent a final effort to create productive members of Israeli society.

The first measure of success for the graduates of the Youth Aliya schools is acceptance for service in the Israel Defense Forces (IDF). Because all young adults are responsible for service in the IDF, any individual who is rejected from service due to behavioral or psychological reasons faces a difficult transition to adulthood and a certain social stigma because of this rejection. The vast majority of Youth Aliya graduates are accepted into military service, however, and a large number go on to extremely successful careers in all segments of Israeli society. Israeli president Moshe Katsav, for example, studied at a Youth Aliya school in Ben Shemen village prior to undertaking his career in public service.

The modern incarnation of Youth Aliya operates more than 60 schools, serving more than 10,000 students. The Israeli Ministry of Education provides the majority of funding for the schools, a testament that they have become a vital support network for at-risk youths. Further budgetary assistance is supplied through the Jewish Agency and a series of Youth Aliya Committees throughout the world that raise funds exclusively for Israel's education system.

The number of Israeli youths living below the poverty line has quadrupled since 1980. The most recent census data indicated that almost 30 percent of Israeli children, more than 600,000 individuals, live in poverty. Some of the increase has been linked to economic hardships in Israel, but most of the increase is attributed to the increased immigration of poor families from the former Soviet republics and other poor nations. These immigrants present not only an educational and behavioral challenge but also a communication obstacle, as most of the new arrivals do not speak Hebrew. The Youth Aliya villages offer children an excellent chance for assimilation and reidentification as Israeli citizens, welcoming the diversity inherent in catering to a multinational population of children in need.

PAUL J. SPRINGER

See also

Hadassah; Holocaust; Jewish Agency for Israel; Kibbutz Movement; Moshavim; Zionism

References

Beilin, Yossi. *Israel: A Concise Political History.* New York: St. Martin's, 1992.

Brenner, Lenni. *Zionism in the Age of the Dictators.* Westport, CT: Lawrence Hill, 1983.

Laqueur, Walter. *A History of Zionism: From the French Revolution to the Establishment of the State of Israel.* Reprint ed. New York: Schocken, 2003.

Weintraub, D., M. Lissak, and Y. Azmon. *Moshava, Kibbutz, and Moshav: Patterns of Jewish Rural Settlement and Development in Palestine.* Ithaca, NY: Cornell University Press, 1969.

Yusuf, Hasan
Born: ca. 1955

Palestinian politician and senior Hamas leader who heads the political division of the organization's West Bank branch. The West Bank branch of Hamas is often considered to be somewhat more moderate than the Gaza Strip branch, and Sheikh Hasan Yusuf is likewise characterized as a moderate. Yusuf was born around 1955 and joined the Muslim Brotherhood, which was well established in Jordan during his university studies in that country. He obtained a bachelor's degree in Sharia (Islamic law) in the early 1970s. When Hamas formed from elements of the Muslim Brotherhood in 1987, Yusuf became part of the organization.

Yusuf used to travel from village to village throughout the West Bank to preach in the mosques, which added to his popularity throughout the region. Israeli authorities arrested and imprisoned him multiple times for his activities in Hamas. He was then exiled with a group of Palestinians who were left on a hillside near the town of Marj al-Zuhur in southern Lebanon in 1992 along with Sheikh Ahmed Yassin, Abd al-Aziz Rantisi, and 415 militants. They were permitted to return to the West Bank from Lebanon in 1993. Yusuf also served 28 months of solitary confinement at Ofar Prison (near Ramallah) until November 2004. He was pursued and arrested because of his high visibility as a political leader. Unable to locate and arrest members of the military wing of Hamas, Israeli authorities chose to hold the political leadership accountable.

Yusuf has said that he accepted the two-state solution to the Palestinian-Israeli conflict and has admitted directly negotiating with Israeli authorities, although in an informal way, about the daily needs of Palestinians in his area. He endeavored to promote brotherhood with Christians of the West Bank, who were included on the party's electoral list, and he supported the participation in women in the Hamas organization. He has also been eager to promote a better relationship and dialogue between the party and those in the West, where in particular the U.S. government takes a dim a view of Hamas. Yusuf nonetheless argued vigorously for greater freedom and rights for Palestinians, the release of Palestinian political prisoners, and an end to the erosion of Arab (East) Jerusalem. He has also advocated for Hamas to be permitted to operate its charitable institutions in return for complete transparency about its finances and dealings.

Hamas had initially refused to participate in the elections for a Palestinian president after Yasser Arafat's November 2004 death. However, Yusuf actively campaigned for Hamas in its January 2006 parliamentary elections in which the party defeated Fatah. Yusuf asserted that the organization could not afford passivity in the elections if it was to support the national cause and forward Islam. Yusuf was rearrested in September 2006 along with some 415 other West Bank Palestinians, including 250 Hamas members.

Sherifa Zuhur

See also
Arafat, Yasser; Fatah; Hamas; Muslim Brotherhood; West Bank

References
Karmi, Omar. "The Transformation of Hamas." *Wilberforce Quarterly* 1(1) (2006): 19–23.
Mishal, Shaul, and Avraham Sela. *The Palestinian Hamas: Vision, Violence, and Coexistence.* New York: Columbia University Press, 2000.
Zuhur, Sherifa. "From Gaza to the West Bank: An Interview with Shaykh Hasan Yousef of HAMAS on June 28, 2005." Strategic Studies Newsletter. Strategic Studies Institute, U.S. Army War College, August 2005.
———. *A Hundred Osamas: Islamist Threats and the Future of Counterinsurgency.* Carlisle Barracks, PA: Strategic Studies Institute, U.S. Army War College, 2006.

Z

Zaidan, Muhammad
See Abbas, Abu

Zaim, Husni al-
Born: 1894
Died: August 14, 1949

Syrian Army officer and briefly president of Syria in 1949. Of Kurdish origin, Husni al-Zaim was born in Aleppo, Syria, in 1894. During his long military career he served in the Ottoman Army, with the French armed forces during the mandate period, and in the army of independent Syria.

In March 30, 1949, Colonel al-Zaim seized power in Syria in a bloodless coup, which was initially quite popular with the wider Syrian public. Not only had he emerged as a stabilizing figure during the domestic unrest of late 1948, but as the army chief of staff he had also personally led the successful June 1948 offensive to capture and hold small bits of Israeli territory south of Lake Hula and around the Sea of Galilee during the Israeli War of Independence (1948–1949). His campaign served to partly rehabilitate the image of the army in the eyes of the Syrian public and to underscore his abilities as a leader.

Al-Zaim was unable to capitalize on the goodwill that surrounded his seizure of power. Over the few months of his rule, he attempted to institute a New Order that seems to have been largely influenced by the reforms of Kemal Ataturk of Turkey. Al-Zaim's proposed reforms included the virtual separation of religion and state, curbs on the clergy, extension of the suffrage to literate women, a new civil code based on Western models, and inauguration of a public works program.

Al-Zaim adopted a pragmatic approach in foreign affairs. In April he traveled to Cairo to confer with Egyptian leaders and received their recognition of his regime. Saudi Arabia and Lebanon followed suit, and the Saudis agreed to provide financial support. The price of Saudi aid, however, was al-Zaim's renunciation of the greater Syria scheme of his predecessors that would have brought close relations with Iraq and Jordan.

While he was not pro-Israel, al-Zaim also adopted a pragmatic approach toward the Jewish state. Here the aim was to secure recognition for his regime from abroad as well as aid from the United States. Toward the latter end, he also made several statements denouncing communism. In a bid to bypass the 1949 armistice talks, he posed that in exchange for the establishment of full diplomatic relations the Jewish state should make land and water rights concessions that reflected Syrian gains during the war. He also offered to resettle more than 250,000 Palestinian refugees inside his country. However, Israeli prime minister David Ben-Gurion distrusted al-Zaim's motives and his abilities to guarantee any agreement that might be signed. Israel opted instead to insist on a full Syrian withdrawal and settled for only an armistice, which was signed in July 1949.

Al-Zaim's Israeli policies deeply angered much of his army core constituency as well as Arab nationalists. His domestic reforms also upset many traditionalists, while his delay in instituting the promised public works program disillusioned many of his supporters. Many Syrians were also angered by what was seen as al-Zaim's personal ambition, which included promoting himself from colonel to field marshal in public ceremonies, moving into luxurious quarters, assuming the title of head of state after a questionable referendum, and banning political parties while failing to organize one of his own.

On August 14, 1949, just a few weeks after the armistice was reached with Israel, al-Zaim and his prime minister, Muhsin el-Barazi, were shot to death in Damascus, the victims of a coup from within the military led by Colonel Sami Hinnawi.

JONAS KAUFFELDT

See also

Ben-Gurion, David; Expellees and Refugees, Palestinian; Israeli War of Independence, Overview; Israeli War of Independence, Truce Agreements; Syria; Syria, Armed Forces; Water Rights and Resources

References

Rathmell, Andrew. *Secret War in the Middle East: The Covert Struggle for Syria, 1949–1961.* London: Tauris, 1995.

Seale, Patrick. *The Struggle for Syria: A Study of Post-War Arab Politics, 1945–1958.* New Haven, CT: Yale University Press, 1987.

Torry, Gordon H. *Syrian Politics and the Military, 1945–1958.* Columbus: Ohio State University Press, 1964.

Zayyad, Tawfiq
Born: May 7, 1929
Died: July 5, 1994

Palestinian poet, author, and Israeli politician. Tawfiq Zayyad was born in Nazareth in the British Mandate for Palestine on May 7, 1929. He studied in Moscow for a time but never earned a university degree. His community of Nazareth was taken by the Israelis in the Israeli War of Independence (1948–1949), which had erupted over the creation of the State of Israel. The Arab population of Nazareth was not evacuated during the conflict, although Arab refugees from surrounding areas poured into the city. This mass migration changed the majority population of the area from Christian to Muslim.

In the meantime, Zayyad began to make a name for himself, not only because of the haunting rhetorical lyricism found in his poetry but also because of his political stances and his championing of the Palestinian cause. A leftist who had been drawn to communism at a young age, Zayyad decided to enter Israeli politics. As such, he would be among a tiny minority of Arabs to hold elected office.

Zayyad served in the Knesset (Israeli parliament) from 1973 until his death in 1994. He was a member of Rakah, the Israeli Communist Party, which was adamantly opposed to policies that were prejudicial toward Palestinians. He usually voted with coalition groups such as the New Communist List and eventually headed Hadash, the Democratic Front for Peace and Equality. Hadash, a coalition of Rakah and other like-minded groups, opposed Israel's occupation of lands captured in the 1967 Six-Day War. Zayyad was also an outspoken opponent of the Israeli settlement program that sought to build Jewish communities on Arab land. Indeed, his outrage at Israel's land seizures in upper Nazareth led to his election as mayor of Nazareth in 1975.

The Israeli government opposed Zayyad's mayoral election, largely because of his ties to Palestine Liberation Organization (PLO) chairman Yasser Arafat. In its bid to keep Zayyad from the office,

Prominent Palestinian poet Tawfiq Zayyad. (Ya'acov Sa'ar/Israeli Government Press Office)

---

the Israeli government offered Arabs in Nazareth land should they vote against him. Nevertheless, Zayyad won the 1975 election and served in that post uninterrupted until his death in 1994. Despite his ties to Arafat, however, Zayyad was not a proponent of violence, and he recognized Israel's right to exist.

In 1976 Zayyad was a leader on the Committee for the Defense of the Land, which held a general strike called Land Day on May 30, 1976, during which Palestinians protested against Israeli land seizures. There was some violence during Land Day, much of it on the part of strikers against Arabs refusing to participate. Land Day was important in that it was an act of resistance, but by and large it was a peaceful resistance.

Zayyad's poetry expressed a national Palestinian sense of strength and perseverance in the face of Israeli aggression and usurpations. He was considered one of the best modern Arab poets and was revered by many Palestinians, particularly those in Nazareth. Zayyad died in a car crash on July 5, 1994, near Mishor Adumim while traveling on the road from Jericho to Jerusalem.

MICHAEL K. BEAUCHAMP

See also

Land Day; Literature of the Arab-Israeli Wars

References

Aruri, Naseer Hasan. *Enemy of the Sun: Poetry of Palestinian Resistance.* Washington, DC: Drum and Spear, 1970.

Sachar, Howard M. *A History of Israel: From the Rise of Zionism to Our Time.* 3rd ed. New York: Knopf, 2007.

Said, Edward W. *The Question of Palestine.* New York: Vintage Books, 1992.

Zinni, Anthony
Born: September 17, 1943

U.S. Marine Corps general, commander of U.S. Central Command, and special envoy for the United States to Israel and the Palestinian Authority (PA). Anthony Charles Zinni was born to Italian immigrant parents in Philadelphia on September 17, 1943. In 1965 he graduated from Villanova University with a degree in economics and was commissioned in the U.S. Marine Corps. In 1967 he served in Vietnam as an infantry battalion adviser to a South Vietnamese marine unit. In 1970 he returned to Vietnam as an infantry company commander. He was seriously wounded that November and was medically evacuated.

In 1991 as a brigadier general Zinni was the chief of staff and deputy commanding general of the Combined Joint Task Force

(CJTF) for Operation PROVIDE COMFORT, the Kurdish relief effort in Turkey and Iraq. During 1992–1993 he was the director of operations (J-3) for Operation RESTORE HOPE in Somalia. As a lieutenant general he commanded the I Marine Expeditionary Force (I MEF) from 1994 to 1996. In September 1996, as a full general, he became deputy commanding general of the U.S. Central Command (CENTCOM), the U.S. military combatant command responsible for most of the Middle East. He served as commanding general of CENTCOM from August 1997 until his retirement from the military in September 2000.

Upon leaving the military, Zinni participated in a number of different diplomatic initiatives. In late 2001 at the request of his old friend, Secretary of State Colin Powell, Zinni became the special envoy for the United States to Israel and the Palestinian Authority (PA).

Zinni arrived in Israel on November 25, 2001. He conducted several negotiating sessions with Prime Minister Ariel Sharon and PA president Yasser Arafat individually but never with the two together. On December 12 a Palestinian suicide bombing of a bus near the settlement of Emmanuel effectively cut off all dialogue between the two sides. Zinni returned to the United States on December 17.

Zinni made his second short trip to the region during January 3–7, 2002. While Zinni was conducting a meeting with Arafat, the

Israeli prime minister Ariel Sharon greets U.S. Middle East envoy General Anthony Zinni (*right*) in Jerusalem, November 27, 2001. (Moshe Milner/Israeli Government Press Office)

Israelis intercepted and captured an illegal Palestinian arms ship in the Red Sea. The *Karine A* was carrying some 50 tons of weapons ordered by the PA from Iran, a direct violation of the Oslo Agreement.

Zinni returned to the region for the last time on March 12, 2002. While he believed that he was starting to make some headway, a Palestinian suicide bomber on March 27 struck a Passover Seder being held at an Israeli hotel. The Israelis launched a massive military retaliation against the Palestinians and severed all ties with Arafat. Zinni departed the region on April 15.

Although Zinni resigned his position as a special envoy, he continued to serve as an unofficial consultant. On August 5, 2003, in Washington he spent several hours briefing Major General David T. Zabecki, incoming senior security adviser of the newly established U.S. Coordinating and Monitoring Mission. In an address Zinni gave at Harvard's Kennedy School of Government on December 8, 2004, he stressed that resuming the peace process between Israel and the Palestinians was the single most important step the United States could take to restore its stature in the world. But interestingly enough, he noted that it would be a mistake to assign more high-profile special envoys to the mission. He favored the presence of professional negotiators.

Following his retirement from the military, Zinni held visiting appointments at several U.S. universities and in May 2005 became the president of international operations for M.C.I. Industries, Inc. He also became a leading public critic of President George W. Bush's handling of the war in Iraq.

DAVID T. ZABECKI

See also

Arafat, Yasser; Sharon, Ariel; United States Coordinating and Monitoring Mission

References

Clancy, Tom, Tony Zinni, and Tony Koltz. *Battle Ready.* New York: Putnam, 2004.
Leverett, Flynt, ed. *The Road Ahead: Middle East Policy in the Bush Administration's Second Term.* Washington, DC: Brookings Institution, 2005.
Zinni, Tony, and Tony Koltz. *The Battle for Peace: A Frontline Vision of America's Power and Purpose.* London: Palgrave Macmillan, 2006.

Zion Mule Corps

World War I British Army auxiliary unit composed of Jewish volunteers. With the beginning of the war in 1914, the Ottoman authorities expelled from Palestine those foreigners unwilling to accept Turkish citizenship. Many went to Egypt, and the vast majority of these, perhaps 11,000 in all, were settled by the British in Alexandria. There Zionists Vladimir Jabotinsky and Joseph Trumpeldor promoted the idea of forming a Jewish military unit that would fight with the British Army during the war. Both men believed that the Allies would win the war and that a Jewish fighting unit campaigning against the Turks would greatly advance the formation of a Jewish state in Palestine.

Jabotinsky and Trumpeldor organized the Legion Committee, which in March 1915 began recruiting Jews for the military unit. Many Palestinian Jews were eager to join, but when the idea was presented to Lieutenant General Sir John Maxwell, British commander in Egypt, he said that regulations prohibited him from enlisting foreigners as British fighting troops. He also could not promise that the men would be sent to Palestine, which is where the Jews sought to fight, because the British were not then planning such an offensive.

Maxwell suggested that an auxiliary unit be formed, one that would transport ammunition and supplies to the front lines in support of the British Army. The leaders of the Legion Committee were disappointed, not only that the proposed unit would serve only in an auxiliary capacity but also that it would be deployed on a front other than Palestine. They voted to reject the proposal and dissolved their committee.

Trumpeldor, who had been a highly decorated soldier in the Russian Army and lost an arm in the Siege of Port Arthur during the Russo-Japanese War of 1904–1905, pointed out that there was nothing demeaning in an auxiliary unit that would serve an essential role, and he said that transporting ammunition to the front took great courage. He also noted that in order for a Jewish state to be created in Palestine, the Turks would first have to be defeated, and it did not matter how or where that was accomplished.

Trumpeldor then worked with British lieutenant colonel John Henry Patterson in recruiting Jews to serve in the unit, which became known as the Zion Mule Corps. Most of the volunteers were Palestinian, but there were also some Egyptian Jews. The men trained in Egypt and adopted the Magen David (Star of David) as their unit insignia. Colonel Patterson commanded the unit, while Trumpeldor was second-in-command as a captain.

The Zion Mule Corps deployed from Egypt on April 17, 1915, and landed on the Gallipoli Peninsula, where it provided invaluable support to British Empire forces in the Gallipoli Campaign. It transported supplies to the front and, on occasion, directly fought the Turks. In the summer of 1915 both Patterson and Trumpeldor returned to Egypt and recruited additional members for the Zion Mule Corps. In November 1915 when Patterson became seriously ill, Trumpeldor commanded the unit.

In mid-December 1915 the British cabinet decided to end the Gallipoli Campaign, and imperial forces were evacuated from the peninsula later that month and in early January 1916. The Zion Mule Corps returned to Egypt and was disbanded in the spring of 1916, despite Trumpeldor's appeals that it be retained in service for a subsequent British invasion of Palestine.

A total of 650 men served in the Zion Mule Corps, 562 of them at Gallipoli. In the course of their service, 9 died and 55 were wounded. Some 150 of the former corps members were accepted for British Army service and were sent on to Britain, where half of them formed a platoon in the 20th London Regiment. Later they served as trainers for the Jewish Legion raised in 1917.

SPENCER C. TUCKER

See also

Jabotinsky, Vladimir Yevgenyevich; Jewish Legion; Patterson, John Henry; Star of David; Trumpeldor, Joseph; Zionism

References

Jabotinsky, Vladimir. *The Story of the Jewish Legion.* New York: Bernard Akerman, 1945.

Katz, Shmel. *Lone Wolf: A Biography of Vladimir Ze'ev Jabotinsky.* 2 vols. Fort Lee, NJ: Barricade Books, 1996.

Sachar, Howard M. *A History of Israel: From the Rise of Zionism to Our Time.* 3rd ed. New York: Knopf, 2007.

Zionism

Zionism holds that Jews constitute a people and a nation. As a political movement, it supports the creation of a homeland for the Jewish people. Zionism began in the late 19th century, arising out of the general movement of nationalism and increased anti-Semitism. It soon became a well-organized and well-funded settlement movement focused on Palestine, which many Jews believe was the ancient homeland granted them by God. Zionism eventually contributed directly to the formation of the State of Israel and continued to influence the politics of Israeli Jews for the rest of the 20th century.

The word "Zionism" derives from Mount Zion, the high ground in Jerusalem just south of the Temple Mount and the traditional burial place of King David. The term was first used in 1890 by Austrian Jew Nathan Birmbaum. Zionists found justification for their movement in the Hebrew Bible (and Christian Old Testament) account of God giving the land of Israel to the Israelites in perpetuity and from the long-standing belief of Diaspora Jews that they would one day return to the Holy Land. Zionism also grew out of the rise of nationalism in the 19th century, as various European nations developed national identities and political systems. Many Jews at that time had a secular view of their Judaism. They abandoned their religious practices but embraced the concept of Jews as a people and a nation that deserved a national homeland. Other ideas, such as socialism and rationalism, also influenced early Zionists. Zionism was fueled by the persecution of Jews in many places in Europe, most notably the Russian Empire. Jews came to believe, with some justification, that only a Jewish state could protect them.

Although other locations were suggested, Palestine seemed to be the obvious choice for the establishment of a Jewish nation. It had biblical connotations, and many Jews believed that it was their historical homeland. In 1862 Moses Hess wrote *Rome and Jerusalem,* which urged Jews to settle in Palestine in an agrarian socialist state. Hess and other writers, such as Ber Borochov and Nahum Syrkin, believed that Jews had become weak and downtrodden as a result of their centuries of working as merchants and pawnbrokers and that they needed to redeem themselves with healthful outdoor labor and socialism. Zionism and socialism often went hand in hand in the late 1800s and early 1900s. Many Jews looked on the creation

Theodor Herzl at the First Zionist Congress in Basel, Switzerland, August 25, 1897. (Israeli Government Press Office)

of a Jewish state as an opportunity for them to build an ideal society, a religious community founded on the principles of socialism. This belief coalesced in a movement known as Labor Zionism, which held that the creation of a Jewish state must necessarily be part of a class struggle in which Jews would become agriculturists, living on collective socialist farms known as kibbutzim.

From the late 1870s through 1882 some Russian Jews went to Palestine, then a part of the Ottoman Empire, there to establish small farms in a movement that became known as the First Aliya. Beginning in 1882, thousands of Russian Jews immigrated to Palestine, fleeing from pogroms and Czar Alexander III's 1882 anti-Semitic May Laws. These settlers called themselves Biluim, after a verse from the book of Isaiah. Their goal was to establish a Jewish national homeland in the land they called Israel. These first settlers nearly starved during their attempt to support themselves on land without adequate freshwater, and many of them left. Baron Edmond de Rothschild provided the remaining settlers with money to establish a winery, which soon became successful. The settlers also used his money to found the town of Zichron Yaakov.

In 1894 the Dreyfus Affair in France, which triggered an explosion of anti-Semitism in that country, persuaded many European Jews that anti-Semitism was a growing problem, even in the supposedly enlightened Western Europe. Theodor Herzl, a Jewish-Austrian journalist who covered the trial, became a staunch supporter of Zionism in the course of the Dreyfus Affair. In 1896 Herzl wrote *Der Judenstaat* (*The Jewish State*), in which he called for the Jews to create their own homeland either in Palestine or in Argentina.

In 1897 Herzl organized the First Zionist Congress in Switzerland. It created the Zionist Organization (ZO), the goal of which was to raise money and buy land in Palestine so that Jews could settle there. Herzl was the group's first president. The group spent the next 52 years purchasing land and creating governmental procedures for the new Israeli state. It was later renamed the World Zionist Organization (WZO).

All Jews were allowed to join the ZO. People from countries all over the world came to the group's congresses, which were held every two years between 1897 and 1946. Members assembled in delegations according to ideology instead of geographic origin. Some Zionists were ardent socialists or communists. Many were vehemently secular or even atheists. Others had more religious leanings.

The ZO organized the Jewish Colonial Trust to handle financial matters. The Jewish National Fund, created in 1901, took responsibility for purchasing land. The Anglo-Palestine Bank, established in 1903, provided financial services for settlers. Gradually the group created an infrastructure for the Jewish homeland that made the process of settling in Palestine easier than it had been in the 1800s.

First Israeli prime minister David Ben-Gurion (standing under a portrait of Theodor Herzl, the founder of political Zionism), surrounded by members of the National Jewish Council, officially proclaims the State of Israel, at 6:00 p.m., May 14, 1948, in Tel Aviv. (AFP/Getty Images)

In the early years of the 20th century, Zionists debated whether Palestine was the ideal location for the Jewish homeland. In 1903 the British government proposed a Jewish homeland in modern Kenya. This plan was known as the British Uganda Program. Herzl suggested this to the Sixth Zionist Congress as a temporary safe haven for Russian Jews, but the Russian Jews themselves disliked the idea, and the Seventh Zionist Congress abandoned the idea in 1905. The Jewish Territorialist Organization wanted to create a Jewish homeland wherever it could, but it disbanded in 1917. In the 1930s the Soviet Union created a Jewish Autonomous Republic in the Far Eastern Federal District, but few Jews wanted to move there. For the most part, Palestine remained the sole focus of the Zionist movement.

During the early 1900s, many small groups of settlers went to Palestine. A number arrived there following the 1905 Revolution in Russia. Leaders such as Joseph Baratz and other settlers pooled their money, added to it contributions from Jews all over the world, and founded kibbutzim on plots of land that they lived on and farmed collectively. By 1914 there were kibbutzim throughout Palestine. Residents shared all work and all profits and governed themselves democratically.

Cultural Zionists looked on the settlement movement as an opportunity to create a unique Jewish culture. Many Jews were quite critical of Jewish culture in the late 19th century, which they saw as downtrodden and weak after centuries of diaspora. Some Zionist thinkers such as Asher Ginsberg and Eliezer Ben Yehudah thought that Palestine would be the ideal place to revive Hebrew language and culture, allowing Jews to replace their Germanic Yiddish language and speak to one another in a uniquely Jewish language that would unite diverse groups of Jews. Herzl wanted German to be the official language of Palestine, but most settlers and Zionists supported the use of Hebrew. Tel Aviv, founded in 1909, was the first city to make Hebrew its official language.

The United Kingdom was an important ally in the creation of the Jewish state. Jews were generally made welcome in Britain in the early 20th century, and many British people appreciated Jewish culture. During World War I the British government sought to mobilize the support of Jews for the war effort, and in 1917 British foreign secretary Arthur Balfour issued a statement (known as the Balfour Declaration) in which the British government expressed its support for the establishment of a Jewish homeland (not a state) in Palestine.

In Balfour's declaration, he said that a Jewish homeland should not harm the civil rights of non-Jewish people already living in Palestine. Zionists realized that the Muslim Arabs already living in Palestine would become a source of conflict, but many of them chose to ignore the issue or to suggest that Jewish immigration could only benefit the current residents. Zionist leaders such as Israel Zangwill concocted slogans such as "A land without a people, for a people without a land," which deliberately glossed over the presence of people in the land in question.

In the early days of settlement (the 1880s and earlier) Arabs did not object to the incursion of Jews. The first Jewish settlers had been unable to farm successfully, so they ended up hiring Arab laborers to work their farms. In the 1890s, however, as Arabs began to realize what the Zionists intended, they grew concerned about losing their farmland and water. The socialist agrarian settlers of the early 1900s did not employ Arabs because their whole raison d'être was to encourage Jews to work the land themselves. This, the Balfour Declaration, the partitioning of Palestine in 1918, and their increasing landless status and poverty all prompted Palestinian Arabs to agitate for a state of their own. Also around this time, some Zionists suggested that Palestinian Arabs should be expelled from the country or should be made to accept the Jewish presence through armed force.

In the early 1920s the ZO, having reached the conclusion that socialism was the only way to distribute available economic resources among a rapidly growing group of Jewish immigrants, decided that Jewish settlement in Palestine should be socialist. During the 1920s David Ben-Gurion, a leader of Histadrut, the Jewish Labor Zionist trade union that dominated Jewish Palestine, officially opposed the use of force against Arabs, claiming that it would be unnecessary because Arabs would soon decide that Zionism was good for them. In private, however, he said that conflict was inevitable because Arabs would never accept Zionist settlement. In the late 1930s Ben-Gurion and the Labor Zionists supported the idea of a Jewish state with no Arabs in it, the existing Arabs having been removed forcibly.

Zionism became somewhat more popular after the creation of the British Mandate for Palestine in 1922. Increasing numbers of Jews moved to Palestine, as the ZO and other Zionist organizations raised money and lobbied the British government not to allow the Palestinian Arabs to create their own state. Palestinian nationalism also increased during this time, as the Muslims saw their land and livelihood increasingly threatened by Jewish newcomers.

Zionism was made up of many different streams. "General Zionism" is the term used to describe the general or transcending beliefs held in common by all Zionists exemplified by the goals of the ZO. General Zionism sought unity by placing the importance of the Jewish homeland above class, party, political, social, religious, or personal interests. Political Zionism centered on the creation of a legal and political entity in Palestine, the existence and sovereignty of which would be sanctioned by the great world powers.

Socialist Zionism asserted that the fusion of Zionist and socialist ideals in Palestine would create a labor-based communal society (socialism) that would transform Palestine and become an attractive haven for the downtrodden of world Jewry. Socialist Zionism eventually evolved into the Labor Zionism of Ben-Gurion. Although the Socialist Zionists and the Labor Zionists were more ethnic Jews than religious Jews, both respected Jewish religious traditions as part of their national heritage.

Labor Zionism believed that the best foundation for a Jewish state was a strong economy and shared economic opportunity that benefited all of the society's members, such as collective settlements (kibbutzim). Labor Zionism generally believed that Arabs in Palestine should and could be encouraged to transfer out of Palestine.

Practical Zionism asserted that the best way to achieve the Zionist goal was through a massive immigration movement (aliya). The aliya would be oriented toward settling both rural and urban areas and the creation of industries, educational institutions, and social services.

Messianic Zionism effectively ignored the practical and simply asserted that the Jewish state would come to be and would last because it was part of the original divine decree given to Abraham, a promise on which those settling in Palestine could depend. Religious Zionism asserted that the formation of an ethnic Jewish state with no religious heart would be temporary. Religious Zionism argued that the only Jewish state that would survive and attract other Jews would be one that wove a conservative Torah-based Jewish religion into its political and social fabric. In other words, the state should be based on the commandments and laws of the Torah. Spiritual Zionism agreed with Religious Zionism but asserted further that the then-prevalent form of Judaism in the Zionist movement, the more liberal and intellectual Ashkenazic Judaism, had lost its guiding spirit. Spiritual Zionism believed that Palestine could not practically hold all of world Jewry, and even if it could, a Jewish state would not elevate the social and economic status of Jews, nor would it end persecution. Spiritual Zionism advocated a modest settlement plan and the formation of a national spiritual center in Palestine instead of a Jewish political state. Chaim Weizmann's Synthetic Zionism combined political, social, practical, and ethno-religious Judaism into a single entity that tried to incorporate all of the different ideals into a Jewish state reflecting all of the concerns of the Zionist spectrum.

Revisionist Zionism argued that the British Mandate for Palestine should be revised to create a sovereign Jewish state encompassing both sides of the Jordan River. Revisionist Zionists also held that Zionism should shift its emphasis from social and economic development in Palestine to the immediate creation of a Jewish state aligned with Great Britain.

Not all Jews supported the Zionist movement, of course. Some socialist Jews disliked the idea of a state because it smacked of un-socialistic nationalism. Communist Jews in Russia also rejected the idea of a Jewish state in Palestine. Many Jews believed that there was no need for a Jewish homeland because Jews could live perfectly well in other nations, such as the United States. American Jews argued that the United States was the Jewish homeland.

All these arguments changed after Adolf Hitler came to power in Germany in 1933. The United States, formerly so welcoming to Jews, closed its doors to Jewish immigration. Jews became refugees in the Europe that they had formerly considered a perfectly adequate home. Increasing numbers of Jews moved to Palestine in the 1930s, but this angered Palestinian Arabs. After riots broke out, in 1939 the British government restricted Jewish immigration to Palestine. Jews living in Palestine armed themselves and began fighting the Arabs and launching attacks on British targets.

After World War II, Zionism experienced a huge upsurge of popularity and support thanks to the horrific events of the Holocaust, Hitler's attempt to exterminate the Jews in Europe. The United States was one of the strongest backers of the formation of a Jewish state in Palestine. Jews themselves were almost unanimous in their support for the creation of Israel. Following the failure of British partition efforts, in 1947 the United Nations (UN) voted to create two states within Palestine, one Arab and one Jewish, with Jerusalem as a shared possession. The Jews accepted the plan, but the Palestinian Arabs rejected it. With the British withdrawal, Jewish leaders in Palestine declared the independent State of Israel on May 14, 1948.

Once the Jewish homeland was established, Israeli leaders turned their attention to expelling Arab agitators, welcoming a new influx of Jewish settlers, and organizing the Israel Defense Forces (IDF). International Zionist organizations continued their support for Israel, raising money and sponsoring immigration and development. In 1960 the Zionist Organization became the World Zionist Organization, dedicated to making Israel the center of Jewish life, preserving Jewish identity, and protecting the rights of Jews around the world.

AMY BLACKWELL

See also

Balfour, Arthur James; Balfour Declaration; Ben-Gurion, David; Israel; Kibbutz Movement; Labor Zionism; Revisionist Zionism; Weizmann, Chaim; Zionist/Israeli Socialism

References

Hertzberg, Arthur, ed. *The Zionist Idea: A Historical Analysis and Reader.* Philadelphia: Jewish Publication Society, 1997.

Herzl, Theodor. *The Jewish State.* Mineola, NY: Dover, 1989.

Laqueur, Walter. *A History of Zionism: From the French Revolution to the Establishment of the State of Israel.* Reprint ed. New York: Schocken, 2003.

Pappe, Ilan. *A History of Modern Palestine: One Land, Two Peoples.* Cambridge: Cambridge University Press, 2003.

Rose, John. *The Myths of Zionism.* London: Pluto, 2004.

Zionism, Revisionist

See Revisionist Zionism

Zionist Conference

Start Date: August 29, 1897
End Date: August 31, 1897

Conference held during August 29–31, 1897, in Basel, Switzerland, that gave birth to the World Zionist Organization (WZO). Also known as the First Zionist Congress and the Basel Congress, the Zionist Conference was organized by Austrian-Jewish journalist Theodor Herzl. The congress came in response to increased European anti-Semitism as revealed in the 1894 Dreyfus Affair in France and to Herzl's call for a Jewish state in his pamphlet *Der Judenstaat* (*The*

Jewish State), published in 1896. The First Zionist Congress created the WZO, elected Herzl its first president, and authorized the organization to establish branches in all countries with consequential Jewish populations. Perhaps most notably, it determined Zionism's goal to be the creation of a legal (guaranteed) Jewish homeland in Palestine (Israel).

The 204 voting delegates to the First Zionist Congress and several hundred spectators met in the Basel Municipal Casino Concert Hall. Voting delegates represented 17 countries. However, the majority of the delegates came from Ashkenazic Jewish communities in Russia and Central and Eastern Europe. There were also delegates from Western Europe and the United States. Seventeen women participated as nonvoting delegates. The delegates represented the social, political, economic, and religious spectrum of world Jewry. The spectators included Christians as well as international journalists. Biographies of the participants were compiled and published in the 1964–1965 *Herzl Year Book*.

Max Nordau (1849–1923), a Parisian physician and controversial author who was elected as one of three WZO vice presidents, opened the congress with an address detailing the plight of the Jewish people. Even though he was the son of a Hungarian Orthodox Sephardic rabbi, he had distanced himself from the Jewish community until the rising tide of French anti-Semitism led him to rediscover his Jewish heritage and to discover Zionism.

The planned focus of the conference was the creation of the WZO and the adoption of the Basel Program, an outline statement of the goals of Zionism. Delegates disagreed on whether an established Jewish homeland should be guaranteed by international law. Herzl proposed a compromise that sought to guarantee the Jewish homeland in Palestine by law. This was the exact phrase used when a committee headed by Nordau made the proposal that was unanimously adopted during the morning session on August 30.

The WZO was formed to unite the Jewish people politically so that Judaism might exert more power in addressing the plight of world Jewry and in creating a homeland in Israel. It was at the First Zionist Congress that the political Zionism of the Jews of Western Europe merged with the settlement activities in Turkish Palestine. Those activities had been promoted by and successfully engaged in by the East European Hovevei Zion. Zion, which had asserted that Jewish settlers could farm and develop the land of Ottoman Palestine, agreed that the goal of a secure Jewish homeland required international political and financial support. The hope was to include large-scale Jewish migration into and settlement of Palestine.

The First Zionist Congress's official language, both spoken and written, was German, but many delegates also spoke Yiddish (Hebrew-German vernacular), the language of Ashkenazic Judaism, and a Yiddish-like German known as Kongressdeutsch. Subsequent Zionist congresses followed the outline of the First Zionist Congress. They included reports on the condition of the Jewish people, lectures on Eretz Israel, reports on settlement activities, and discussions on the cultural differences within world Jewry. Subsequent congresses originally met annually (1897–1901), then biannually

(1903–1913, 1921–1939), and following World War II until the present every four years. An Inner Actions Committee and a Greater Actions Committee oversaw any issues or business that occurred between congresses.

RICHARD EDWARDS

See also

Ashkenazic Judaism; Sephardic Judaism; Zionism

References

Bein, Alex. *Theodor Herzl: A Biography*. London: Jewish Publication Society of America, 1943.

Brenner, Michael. *Zionism: A Brief History*. Translated by Shelley Frisch. Princeton, NJ: Markus Wiener, 2003.

Zionist/Israeli Socialism

A political and economic philosophy that calls for a society in which the community or state, rather than individuals, controls the economic aspects of society. This was the prevailing philosophy of most Jewish settlers in Palestine before it became Israel. It was also the guiding principle of the founders of the State of Israel. Jews began settling Palestine in the late 19th century with the intention of farming the land and living in egalitarian communities. They created a type of communal farm, called a kibbutz, in which all individuals ideally work together for the good of the community. In a kibbutz, no individual receives more goods than any other. Socialism was the dominant political sentiment in Israel from its formation in 1948 until the late 1970s. Since that time, the socialist Labor Party has faced stiff competition from the rightist Likud Party.

Socialist political movements tend to mobilize the working class in an effort to create a classless society, usually through revolution. In Marxist theory, socialism is a halfway point between capitalism and communism. Modern socialist governments provide numerous services to their citizens, usually creating a very extensive welfare state.

Zionism and socialism often went hand in hand in the late 1800s and early 1900s. Many Jews looked toward the creation of a Jewish state as an opportunity for them to build an ideal society, a religious community founded on the principles of egalitarian socialism. A large number of the founding settlers of Israel came from Russia, where they had suffered years of severe religious persecution and economic deprivation. They had also been exposed to Marxist ideas there.

Kibbutzim were created in the spirit of Zionist socialism, often called Labor Zionism. Labor Zionism held that the creation of a Jewish state must necessarily be part of a class struggle in which Jews would become agriculturists. The Jews who settled in Palestine during the 1880s and 1890s during the First Aliya (mass immigration to Israel) had to abandon their traditional trades and instead devote themselves to farming. Jews who had been accustomed to intellectual work disliked physical labor, but the initial settlers decided that the lack of hard labor had caused them to suffer both physically and spiritually. They could achieve redemption by working the land in Palestine, which would transform them into strong farmers. The first settlers to attempt the switch to farming were not successful, and the Jews ended up hiring Arabs to work the fields for them.

More Jews arrived in Palestine after the 1905 Russian Revolution. These new arrivals thought they were coming to an ideal socialist agricultural Jewish state. Instead, they found that the Jewish settlers had become employers of Arab workers. Leaders such as Joseph Baratz wanted to set themselves up as independent farmers, but individual farming proved almost impossible because of the harshness of the land and the capital needed to start a successful farm. Baratz and other settlers pooled their money, added to it contributions from Jews all over the world, and bought plots of land that they lived on and farmed collectively. This type of farm came to be called a kibbutz. By 1914 there were kibbutzim throughout Palestine in which residents shared all work and all profits and governed themselves democratically.

The founders of the State of Israel saw the new state as a perfect democratic socialist nation, with political freedom for all. David Ben-Gurion, the first prime minister of Israel, believed that Palestine and Russia were the only two nations on the correct political track. He considered himself a Bolshevist, idolized Russian revolutionary Vladimir Lenin, and dressed in the style of Soviet leaders. He was supported by an East European group called Poale Zion (Workers of Zion) that in 1919 merged with other Zionist organizations to create Ahdut Ha'avodah, a socialist organization. This group dominated the labor federation that served as a central government of the economic structure of Jewish Palestine. Ben-Gurion guided Ahdut Ha'avodah along Russian lines.

In the early 1920s the World Zionist Organization (WZO) accepted that Jewish settlement in Palestine would be socialist. The group came to believe that socialism was the only way to distribute available economic resources among a rapidly growing group of Jewish immigrants. During the 1920s Ben-Gurion was one of the leaders of Histadrut, the Jewish Labor Zionist trade union that dominated Jewish Palestine before the creation of the Israeli state.

Some socialists criticized Histadrut as not being a purely socialist vehicle. They noted that it was actually a centrist organization designed to prevent workers from organizing and overthrowing their employers. Socialist Zionists such as Menahem Elkind believed that Israel would be better organized as a commune of workers in which the workers themselves held all political power instead of vesting it in an executive such as Histadrut. Elkind eventually organized a group called the General Commune of Jewish Workers in Palestine in an effort to achieve this goal, but the organization folded in 1927 after several years of Ben-Gurion's campaigns against it.

Settlers who came to Palestine in the 1920s and 1930s were more likely to come from Germany and other East European countries rather than from Russia, but they were still influenced by Russian socialism. Labor Zionism was the prevailing political sentiment of the time. Many of these settlers were firm believers in voluntary socialism, convinced that all people, given a chance, would choose a socialist lifestyle because of its obvious benefits. They thought their settlement of Palestine would inspire other nations to adopt socialist principles.

Settlers tended to be young people who wanted to form a society in which all citizens would be equal and in which no one would be exploited. Everyone would hold property in common, and all would work for the good of the community. The community would satisfy individual needs, supplying residents with food, clothing, and housing. They put these principles into practice on their communal farms. In most kibbutzim, families did not live together, and children were raised in common. For the most part, settlers on kibbutzim were not overtly religious, considering hard physical work in the desert to be more spiritually redeeming than religious observance.

By the 1930s, Labor Zionism had become the most powerful political movement in Palestine. It controlled the Yishuv (the collective term for the Jewish settlers in the area), Histadrut, and the paramilitary force that later became known as the Palmach. Labor Zionists dominated the Israeli military before and after 1948. After the formation of the State of Israel, Labor Zionists formed several political parties, the most powerful of which was the Mapai Party, later the Israeli Labor Party. Histadrut, which became more important when Israel became a state, owned and operated a number of businesses on behalf of the state, including several industries and banks. It also provided a comprehensive health care system for all Israelis.

Radical socialism continued to be popular among Israelis through the 1960s and early 1970s. It also appeared among Palestinians during this time. The Marxist-Leninist group the Popular Front for the Liberation of Palestine (PFLP) used terrorism and airplane hijackings as a means of drawing attention to its plans to establish a socialist state for Palestinians.

The Labor Party dominated Israeli politics until the late 1970s, when the conservative Likud Party became more powerful. Indeed, socialism became less popular toward the end of the 20th century, and Histadrut declined in importance. Likud has claimed to prefer capitalist free market policies and insists that Histadrut is entirely too powerful and contributes to general laziness on the part of the population. After Menachem Begin became prime minister in 1977, Labor has not been able to regain control of the machinery of government for more than a few years at a time.

AMY HACKNEY BLACKWELL

See also

Arab Socialism; Begin, Menachem; Ben-Gurion, David; Kibbutz Movement; Labor Party; Likud Party; Palmach; Popular Front for the Liberation of Palestine; World Zionist Organization; Zionism; Zionist Conference

References

Sachar, Howard M. *A History of Israel: From the Rise of Zionism to Our Time.* 3rd ed. New York: Knopf, 2007.
Shafir, Gershon. *Land, Labor and the Origins of the Israeli-Palestinian Conflict, 1882–1914.* Berkeley: University of California Press, 1996.
Smith, Charles D. *Palestine and the Arab-Israeli Conflict: A History with Documents.* 6th ed. New York: Bedford/St. Martin's, 2006.

Sternhell, Zeev. *The Founding Myths of Israel.* Translated by David Maisel. Princeton, NJ: Princeton University Press, 1999.

Zionist Organization of America

Pro-Zionist association founded in 1897. Headquartered in New York City, the Zionist Organization of America (ZOA) currently has a paid membership of about 30,000 people and maintains chapter offices in numerous cities around the country including Chicago, Los Angeles, Cleveland, Dallas, Philadelphia, and Washington, D.C. from which it conducts its lobbying efforts. Billed as the oldest Zionist organization in the United States, the ZOA has been affiliated with a sister organization, Hadassah (Women's Zionist Organization of America).

In its early years, the ZOA was at the vanguard of the Zionist movement in the United States. Among its many prominent leaders was U.S. Supreme Court justice Louis D. Brandeis. The ZOA also served as the principal American liaison to the World Zionist Organization (WZO). As such, the ZOA adhered to political Zionism rather than the more radical Labor Zionism of other groups around the world.

Prior to the establishment of Israel in May 1948, the ZOA helped rally public support for Israel and maintained close contacts with Congress and the executive branch to keep the pressure on for the creation of a Jewish homeland. Today, the ZOA's mission is more diverse. It sponsors educational endeavors that strengthen the bonds between the United States and Israel, promotes public affairs activities in the public interest, and funds scholarships and educational opportunities for newly arrived Jewish immigrants and others. The ZOA works to promote pro-Israeli legislation in Congress and combats anti-Jewish bias and anti-Semitism in the media, on college campuses, and even in instructional textbooks. Masada, the youth arm of the ZOA, funds the largest program in the country that sends Jewish youths to Israel for educational purposes.

Yet the ZOA's efforts do not stop at the nation's shores. The group also funds and promotes cultural and educational programs throughout Israel. In Tel Aviv, the ZOA House is among the top cultural centers in the city. Near Ashkelon, Israel, the ZOA has established a large campus for the education and vocational training of new immigrants to Israel.

In addition, the ZOA claims that it is the only group that documents and makes public Arab violations of the Arab-Israeli peace process and of the so-called Road Map to Peace. It also exposes the victims of Palestinian terrorism. In recent years the ZOA has built its Campus Activism Network and Center for Law and Justice, which promotes activism and Jewish causes via the U.S. court system.

Morton Klein, national president of the Zionist Organization of America (ZOA), speaks at a demonstration held near the White House in Washington, D.C., on July 25, 2003. The demonstrators were protesting U.S. president George W. Bush's meeting with Palestinian prime minister Mahmoud Abbas. (Reuters/Corbis)

Finally, the ZOA publishes a wide array of newsletters, reports, periodicals, etc., and makes wide use of the Internet to disseminate information to its membership.

PAUL G. PIERPAOLI JR.

See also

Brandeis, Louis Dembitz; Hadassah; Lobbies, Jewish; World Zionist Organization; Zionism

References

Cohen, Naomi W. *The Americanization of Zionism, 1897–1948.* Waltham, MA: Brandeis University Press, 2003.

Klieman, Aaron S. *From Many, One: The Zionist Organization of America.* London: Routledge, 1991.

Meyer, Isidore S. *Early History of Zionism in America.* New York: American Jewish Historical Society, 1958.

Appendices

Air Force Ranks

	United States	Egypt	Iran	Iraq	Israel
Officers	General of the Air Force	Mushir			
	General	Fariq Awwal	Arteshbod	Fariq Awwal	
	Lieutenant General	Fariq	Sepahbod	Fariq	
	Major General	Liwa	Sarlanshkar	Liwa	Alúf
	Brigadier General	Amid	Satrip	Amid	Tat Alúf
	Colonel	Aqid	Sarhang	Aqid	Alúf Mishné
	Lieutenant Colonel	Muqaddam	Sarhang Dovom	Muqaddam	Sgan Alúf
	Major	Raid	Sargord	Raid	Rav Séren
	Captain	Naqid	Saravan	Naqib	Séren
	First Lieutenant	Mulazim Awwal	Setvan Yekom	Mulazim Awwal	Ségen
	Second Lieutenant	Mulazim	Setvan Dovom	Mulazim	Ségen Mishné
Enlisted	Chief Master Sergeant		Ostavar Yekom		Rav Nagád
	Senior Master Sergeant	Rais Awwal	Ostavar Dovom		Rav Samál Bakhír
					Rav Samál Mitkadém
	Master Sergeant	Rais Awwal	Ostavar Dovom		Rav Samál Rishón
	Technical Sergeant	Raqib	Goruhban Yekom		Rav Samál
	Staff Sergeant	Raqib	Goruhban Dovom	Rais Urafa	Samál Rishón
	Sergeant Senior Airman	Arif	Gorhban Sevom	Arif	Samál
	Airman First Class	Jundi Awwal	Sarboz Yekom	Naib Arif	Rav Turái
	Airman	Jundi Awwal		Jundi Awwal	Turái Rishón
	Airman Basic				Turái

	Jordan	Lebanon	Saudi Arabia	Syria
Officers	Mushir			
	Fariq Awwal	Fariq	Fariq Awwal	Fariq Awwal
	Fariq Awwal		Fariq Awwal	Fariq
	Liwa	Liwa	Liwa	Liwa
	Amid	Liwa	Amid	Liwa
	Aqid	Aqid	Aqid	Aqid
	Muqaddam	Muqaddam	Muqaddam	Muqaddam
	Raid	Raid	Raid	Raid
	Naqid	Rais	Naqid	Naqib
	Mulazim Awwal	Mulazim Awwal	Mulazim Awwal	Mulazim Awwal
	Mulazim	Mulazim	Mulazim	Mulazim
Enlisted	Wakil		Rais Ruquba	
	Wakil	Musaid Awwal	Rais Awwal	Raqib Thani
	Raqid Awwal	Musaid	Raqid	
	Raqid Awwal	Raqib Awwal	Wakil Raqib	Raqib Awwal
	Raqid	Raqib	Wakil Raqib	Raqib Awwal
	Arif	Arif Awwal	Arif	Raqib
	Wakil Arif	Arif	Jundi Awwal	Jundi Awwal
	Wakil Arif	Jundi Awwal	Jundi	
	Jundi			

		Soviet Union	United Kingdom	France	Turkey
Officers			Marshal of the RAF	Maréchal de France	Maresal
		General Armii	Air Chief Marshal	Général d'Armée Aérienne	Orgeneral
		General Polkovink	Air Marshal	Général de Corps Aérienne	Korgeneral
		General Leitenant	Air Vice Marshal	Général de Division Aérienne	Tümgeneral
		General Maior	Air Commodore	Général de Brigade Aérienne	Tuggeneral
		Polkovnik	Group Captain	Colonel	Albay
		Podpolkovink	Wing Commander	Lieutenant Colonel	Yarbay
		Maior	Squadron Leader	Commandant	Binbasi
		Kapitan	Flight Lieutenant	Capitaine	Yüzbasi
		Starshii Leitenant	Flying Officer	Lieutenant	Üstegman
		Mladshii Leitenant	Pilot Officer	Sous Lieutenant	Tegmen
Enlisted		Starshina	Warrant Officer Class 1	Major	Astsubay Kidemli Bascavus
		Starshii Serzhant		Adjudant Chef	Astsubay Bascavus
					Astsubay Kidemli Ustcavus
			Flight Sergeant Chief Technician	Adjudant	Astsubay Ustcavus
		Serzhant	Sergeant	Sergent Chef	Astsubay Kidemli Cavus
		Mladshii Serzhant	Corporal	Sergent	Astsubay Cavus
			Junior Technician	Caporal Chef	Cavus
		Efreitor	Senior Aircraftsman	Caporal	Onbasi
			Leading Aircraftsman	Soldat de 1ère Classe	
		Private (Ryadovi)	Aircraftsman	Soldat de 2ème Classe	Er

Army Ranks

	United States	Egypt	Iran	Iraq	Israel
Officers	General of the Army	Mushir		Mushir	
	General	Fariq Awwal	Arteshbod	Fariq Awwal	
	Lieutenant General	Fariq	Sepahbod	Fariq	Rav Alúf
	Major General	Liwa	Sarlanshkar	Liwa	Alúf
	Brigadier General	Amid	Satrip	Amid	Tat Alúf
	Colonel	Aqid	Sarhang	Aqid	Alúf Mishné
	Lieutenant Colonel	Muqaddam	Sarhang Dovom	Muqaddam	Sgan Alúf
	Major	Raid	Sargord	Raid	Rav Séren
	Captain	Naqid	Saravan	Naqib	Séren
	First Lieutenant	Mulazim Awwal	Setvan Yekom	Mulazim Awwal	Ségen
	Second Lieutenant	Mulazim	Setvan Dovom	Mulazim	Ségen Mishné
Enlisted	Command Sergeant		Ostavar Yekom		Rav Nagád
	Major Sergeant				
	Major				
	First Sergeant	Rais Awwal	Ostavar Dovom		Rav Samál Bakhír
	Master Sergeant				
					Rav Samá Mitkadém
	Platoon Sergeant	Raqid	Goruhban Yekom		Rav Samál Rishón
	Sergeant First Class				
	Specialist 7				
	Staff Sergeant	Wakil Raqib	Goruhban Dovom	Ra Is Urafa	Rav Samál
	Specialist 6				
	Sergeant	Wakil Raqib	Gorhban Sevom	Arif	Samál Rishón
	Specialist 5				
	Corporal Specialist 4	Arif	Sardjuhke	Na Ib Arif	Samál
	Private First Class	Jundi Awwal	Sarboz Yekom	Jundi Awwal	Rav Turái
	Private (E-2)	Jundi			Turái Rishón
	Private (E-1)	Jundi			Turái

	Jordan	Lebanon	Palestine	Saudi Arabia	Syria
Officers	Mushir			Mushir	
	Fariq Awwal	Fariq		Fariq Awwal	Fariq Awwal
	Fariq Awwal			Fariq Awwal	Fariq
	Liwa	Liwa		Liwa	Liwa
	Amid	Amid	Amid	Amid	Amid
	Aqid	Aqid	Aqid	Aqid	Aqid
	Muqaddam	Muqaddam	Muqaddam	Muqaddam	Muqaddam
	Raid	Raid	Raid	Raid	Raid
	Naqid	Rais	Naqib	Naqid	Naqib
	Mulazim Awwal	Mulazim	Mulazim Awwal	Mulazim Awwal	Mulazim Awwal
	Mulazim	Mulazim	Mulazim	Mulazim	Mulazim
Enlisted	Wakil			Rais Ruquba	
	Wakil			Rais Awwal	Raqib Thani
	Raqid Awwal	Raqib Awwal		Raqid	Raqib Awwal
	Raqid Awwal			Wakil Raqib	
	Raqid	Raqib		Wakil Raqib	Raqib
	Arif	Arif		Arif	Arif
	Wakil Arif	Jundi Awwal		Jundi Awwal	Jundi Awwal
	Wakil Arif			Jundi	
	Jundi	Jundi			

	Soviet Union	United Kingdom	France	Turkey
Officers	Marshal Sovetskogo Soyuza	Field Marshal	Maréchal de France	Maresal
	General Armii	General	Général d'Armée	Orgeneral
	General Polkovink	Lieutanant General	Général de Corps d'Armée	Korgeneral
	General Leitenant	Major General	Général de Division	Tümgeneral
	General Maior	Brigadier	Général de Brigade	Tuggeneral
	Polkovnik	Colonel	Colonel	Albay
	Podpolkovink	Lieutenant Colonel	Lieutenant Colonel	Yarbay
	Maior	Major	Commandant	Binbasi
	Kapitan	Captain	Capitaine	Yüzbasi
	Starshii Leitenant	Lieutenant	Lieutenant	Üstegman
	Mladshii Leitenant	Second Lieutenant	Sous Lieutenant	Tegmen
Enlisted	Starshina	Warrant Officer Class 1	Major	Astsubay Kidemli Bascavus
	Starshii Serzhant	Warrant Officer Class 2	Adjudant Chef	Astsubay Bascavus
				Astsubay Kidemli Ustcavus
		Staff Sergeant	Adjudant	Astsubay Ustcavus
	Serzhant	Sergeant	Sergent Chef Maréchal des Logis Chef	Astsubay Kidemli Cavus
	Mladshii Serzhant	Corporal Bombardier	Sergent Maréchal des Logis	Astsubay Cavus
		Lance Corporal	Caporal Chef	Cavus
		Lance Bombardier	Brigadier Chef	
	Efreitor		Caporal Brigadier	Onbasi
			Soldat de 1ère Classe	
	Ryadovi	Private Trooper	Soldat de 2ème Classe	Er
		Gunner Sapper		

Navy Ranks

	United States	Egypt	Iran	Iraq	Israel
Officers	Fleet Admiral	Mushir		Mushir	
	Admiral	Fariq Awwal	Darybod	Fariq Awwal	
	Vice Admiral	Fariq	Darsaklar	Fariq	
	Rear Admiral (Upper Half)	Liwa	Daryban	Liwa	Alúf
	Rear Admiral (Lower Half)	Liwa	Daryban	Liwa	Tat Alúf
		Amid		Amid	
	Captain	Aqid	Nakhoda Yekom	Aqid	Alúf Mishné
	Commander	Muqaddam	Nakhoda Dovom	Muqaddam	Sgan Alúf
	Lieutenant Commander	Raid	Nakhoda Sevom	Raid	Rav Séren
	Lieutenant	Naqid	Navsarvan	Naqib	Séren
	Lieutenant (Junior Grade)	Mulazim Awwal	Navban Yekom	Mulazim Awwal	Ségen
	Ensign	Mulazim	Bnavban Dovom	Mulazin	Ségen Mishné
Enlisted	Master Chief Petty Officer				Rav Nagád
	Senior Chief Petty Officer	Rais Awwal	Navostavar Yekom		Rav Samál Bakhír
					Rav Samá Mitkadém
	Chief Petty Officer	Raqid	Navostavar Dovom		Rav Samál Rishón
	Petty Officer First Class	Raqib	Navi Yekom		Rav Samál
	Petty Officer Second Class	Raqib			Samál Rishón
	Petty Officer Third Class	Arif	Navi Dovom		Samál
	Seaman	Jundi Awwal	Navi Sevom		Rav Turái
	Airman				
	Fireman				
	Seaman Apprentice	Navi Sevom			Turái Rishón
	Airman Apprentice				
	Fireman Apprentice				
	Seaman Recruit		Sardjuhke		Turái

	Lebanon	Saudi Arabia	Syria	Turkey
Officers				Büyük Amiral
	Fariq	Fariq Awwal		Oramiral
		Fariq Awwal	Fariq	Koramiral
	Liwa	Liwa	Liwa	Tümamiral
	Liwa	Amid	Liwa	Tugamiral
	Amid			
	Aqid	Aqid	Aqid	Albay
	Muqaddam	Muqaddam	Muqaddam	Yarbay
	Raid	Raid	Raid	Binbasi
	Rais	Naqid	Naqib	Yüzbasi
	Mulazim Awwal	Mulazim Awwal	Mulazim Awwal	Üstegman
	Mulazim	Mulazim	Mulazim	Tegmen
Enlisted		Rais Ruquba		Astsubay Kidemli Bascavus
	Musaid Awwal	Rais Awwal	Raqib Thani	Astsubay Bascavus
				Astsubay Kidemli Ustcavus
	Musaid	Raqid	Raqib Thani	Astsubay Ustcavus
	Raqib Awwal	Wakil Raqib	Raqib Awwal	Astsubay Kidemli Cavus
	Raqib	Wakil Raqib	Raqib	Astsubay Cavus
	Arif Awwal	Arif	Arif	Cavus
	Arif	Jundi Awwal	Jundi Awwal	Onbasi
	Jundi Awwal	Jundi		
				Er

	Soviet Union	United Kingdom	France
Officers	Admiral Flota Sovetskogo Soyuza	Admiral of the Fleet	
	Admiral Flota	Admiral	Amiral
	Admiral	Vice Admiral	Vice Amiral d'Escadre
	Vitse Admiral	Rear Admiral	Vice Amiral
	Kontr Admiral	Commodore	Contre Amiral
	Kapitan Prevogo Ramga	Captain	Capitaine de Vaisseau
	Kapitan Vtrogo Ramga	Commander	Capitaine de Frégate
	Kapitan Tretyego Ramga	Lieutenant Commander	Capitaine de Corvette
	Kapitan Leitenant	Lieutenant	Lieutenant de Vaisseau
	Leienant	Sub Lieutenant	Enseigne de Vaisseau de 1ère Classe
	Mladshii Leitenant		Enseigne de Vaisseau de 2ème Classe
Enlisted	Starshina	Warrant Officer Class 1	Major
	Glavnyy Starshina		Maître Principal
		Chief Petty Officer	Premier Maître
	Starshina Pervoy Stat'I	Petty Officer	Maître
	Starshina Vtoroy Stat'I	Leading Rate	Second Maître
			Quartier Maître de 1ère Classe
	Starshiny Matros	Able Seaman	Quartier Maître de 2ème Classe
			Maître Brevet
	Matros	Ordinary Seaman	Matelot

Country Profiles

ALGERIA

Location: Northern Africa
Capital: Algiers
Area (square miles): 919,591
Area (relative): slightly less than 3.5 times the size of Texas

	1950	1961	1970	1989	1999
Population Estimate	8,893,000	11,122,000	13,932,000	24,501,000	29,963,000
Population Density (per square mile)	9.67	12.09	15.15	26.64	32.58
Armed Forces Personnel		45,000	57,000	126,000	120,000
Armed Forces as % of Population		0.40%	0.41%	0.51%	0.40%
Military Expenditures as % of Gross National Product (GNP)		Unknown	2.4	3.0	4.0

EGYPT

Location: Northern Africa
Capital: Cairo
Area (square miles): 386,660
Area (relative): slightly more than three times the size of New Mexico

	1950	1961	1970	1989	1999
Population Estimate	21,198,000	27,523,000	33,574,000	56,694,000	69,067,000
Population Density (per square mile)	54.82	71.18	86.83	146.62	178.62
Armed Forces Personnel		215,000	300,000	450,000	430,000
Armed Forces as % of Population		0.78%	0.89%	0.79%	0.62%
Military Expenditures as % of Gross National Product (GNP)		5.7	12.8	4.7	2.7

FRANCE

Location: Western Europe
Capital. Paris
Area (square miles): 212,934
Area (relative): slightly less than twice the size of Colorado

	1950	1961	1970	1989	1999
Population Estimate	41,829,000	46,189,000	50,787,000	56,417,000	59,116,000
Population Density (per square mile)	196.44	216.92	238.51	264.95	277.63
Armed Forces Personnel		720,000	570,000	554,000	421,000
Armed Forces as % of Population		1.56%	1.12%	0.98%	0.71%
Military Expenditures as % of Gross National Product (GNP)		6.2	4.2	3.7	2.7

IRAN

Location: Middle East
Capital: Tehran
Area (square miles): 630,575
Area (relative): slightly larger than Alaska

	1950	1961	1970	1989	1999
Population Estimate	16,357,000	22,181,000	28,854,000	56,669,000	62,834,000
Population Density (per square mile)	25.94	35.18	45.76	89.87	99.65
Armed Forces Personnel		185,000	238,000	604,000	460,000
Armed Forces as % of Population		0.83%	0.82%	1.07%	0.73%
Military Expenditures as % of Gross National Product (GNP)		4.4	8.2	6.4	2.9

IRAQ

Location: Middle East
Capital: Baghdad
Area (square miles): 169,236
Area (relative): slightly more than twice the size of Idaho

	1950	1961	1970	1989	1999
Population Estimate	5,163,000	7,026,000	9,414,000	18,135,000	22,031,000
Population Density (per square mile)	30.51	41.52	55.63	107.16	130.18
Armed Forces Personnel		90,000	98,000	1,000,000	420,000
Armed Forces as % of Population		1.28%	1.04%	5.51%	1.91%
Military Expenditures as % of Gross National Product (GNP)		7.9	11.0	41.1	5.5

ISRAEL

Location: Middle East
Capital: Jerusalem (Tel Aviv)
Area (square miles): 8,019
Area (relative): slightly smaller than New Jersey

	1950	1961	1970	1989	1999
Population Estimate	1,286,000	2,217,000	2,903,000	4,344,000	5,743,000
Population Density (per square mile)	160.37	276.47	362.02	541.71	716.17
Armed Forces Personnel		63,000	105,000	191,000	173,000
Armed Forces as % of Population		2.84%	3.62%	4.40%	3.01%
Military Expenditures as % of Gross National Product (GNP)		7.0	25.2	12.5	8.8

JORDAN

Location: Middle East
Capital: Amman
Area (square miles): 34,444
Area (relative): slightly smaller than Indiana

	1950	1961	1970	1989	1999
Population Estimate	561,000	887,000	1,503,000	3,262,000	4,843,000
Population Density (per square mile)	16.29	25.75	43.64	94.70	140.61
Armed Forces Personnel		35,000	60,000	190,000	102,000
Armed Forces as % of Population		3.95%	3.99%	5.82%	2.11%
Military Expenditures as % of Gross National Product (GNP)		15.6	20.5	12.1	9.2

LEBANON

Location: Middle East
Capital: Beirut
Area (square miles): 4,015
Area (relative): about 0.7 times the size of Connecticut

	1950	1961	1970	1989	1999
Population Estimate	1,364,000	1,836,000	2,383,000	3,147,000	3,529,000
Population Density (per square mile)	339.73	457.29	593.52	783.81	878.95
Armed Forces Personnel		8,000	14,000	18,000	58,000
Armed Forces as % of Population		0.44%	0.59%	0.57%	1.64%
Military Expenditures as % of Gross National Product (GNP)		2.7	3.4	Unknown	4.0

LIBYA

Location: Northern Africa
Capital: Tripoli
Area (square miles): 679,359
Area (relative): slightly larger than Alaska

	1950	1961	1970	1989	1999
Population Estimate	961,000	1,389,000	1,999,000	4,140,000	4,993,000
Population Density (per square mile)	1.41	2.04	2.94	6.09	7.35
Armed Forces Personnel		8,000	15,000	86,000	85,000
Armed Forces as % of Population		0.58%	0.75%	2.08%	1.70%
Military Expenditures as % of Gross National Product (GNP)		4.1	1.4	12.8	Unknown

MOROCCO
Location: Northern Africa
Capital: Rabat
Area (square miles): 172,413
Area (relative): slightly larger than California

	1950	1961	1970	1989	1999
Population Estimate	9,343,000	12,736,000	15,909,000	24,686,000	29,597,000
Population Density (per square mile)	54.19	73.87	92.27	143.18	171.66
Armed Forces Personnel		40,000	60,000	195,000	195,000
Armed Forces as % of Population		0.31%	0.38%	0.79%	0.66%
Military Expenditures as % of Gross National Product (GNP)		2.8	2.8	5.1	4.3

PEOPLE'S REPUBLIC OF CHINA
Location: Eastern Asia
Capital: Beijing
Area (square miles): 3,696,100
Area (relative): slightly smaller than the United States

	1950	1961	1970	1989	1999
Population Estimate	562,580,000	644,670,000	820,403,000	1,130,729,000	1,260,107,000
Population Density (per square mile)	152.21	174.42	221.96	305.92	340.93
Armed Forces Personnel		2,200,000	2,850,000	3,903,000	2,400,000
Armed Forces as % of Population		0.34%	0.35%	0.35%	0.19%
Military Expenditures as % of Gross National Product (GNP)		7.1	13.5	3.4	2.3

SAUDI ARABIA

Location: Middle East
Capital: Riyadh
Area (square miles): 829,996
Area (relative): slightly more than one-fifth the size of the United States

	1950	1961	1970	1989	1999
Population Estimate	3,860,000	4,828,000	6,109,000	16,061,000	22,484,000
Population Density (per square mile)	4.65	5.82	7.36	19.35	27.09
Armed Forces Personnel		35,000	60,000	82,000	190,000
Armed Forces as % of Population		0.72%	0.98%	0.51%	0.85%
Military Expenditures as % of Gross National Product (GNP)		11.6	13.3	15.9	14.9

SOVIET UNION/RUSSIA

Location: Asia and Eastern Europe
Capital: Moscow
Area (square miles): 8,649,538
Area (relative): slightly less than 2.5 times the size of the United States

	1950	1961	1970	1989	1999
Population Estimate	201,300,000	218,100,000	241,700,000	288,700,000	147,352,000
Population Density (per square mile)	23.27	25.22	27.94	33.38	17.04
Armed Forces Personnel		3,000,000	4,300,000	3,700,000	900,000
Armed Forces as % of Population		1.38%	1.78%	1.28%	0.61%
Military Expenditures as % of Gross National Product (GNP)		15.8	14.0	11.5	5.6

SYRIA

Location: Middle East
Capital: Damascus
Area (square miles): 71,498
Area (relative): slightly larger than North Dakota

	1950	1961	1970	1989	1999
Population Estimate	3,495,000	4,681,000	6,258,000	12,437,000	15,889,000
Population Density (per square mile)	48.88	65.47	87.53	173.95	222.23
Armed Forces Personnel		52,000	70,000	400,000	310,000
Armed Forces as % of Population		1.11%	1.12%	3.22%	1.95%
Military Expenditures as % of Gross National Product (GNP)		13.5	13.8	14.3	7.0

TUNISIA

Location: Northern Africa
Capital: Tunis
Area (square miles): 63,170
Area (relative): slightly larger than Georgia

	1950	1961	1970	1989	1999
Population Estimate	3,517,000	4,216,000	5,098,000	8,053,000	9,459,000
Population Density (per square mile)	55.68	66.74	80.70	127.48	149.74
Armed Forces Personnel		18,000	26,000	40,000	35,000
Armed Forces as % of Population		0.43%	0.51%	0.50%	0.37%
Military Expenditures as % of Gross National Product (GNP)		3.5	1.9	3.0	1.8

TURKEY

Location: Southeastern Europe/Southwestern Asia
Capital: Ankara
Area (square miles): 299,158
Area (relative): slightly larger than Texas

	1950	1961	1970	1989	1999
Population Estimate	21,122,000	29,030,000	35,758,000	55,031,000	64,820,000
Population Density (per square mile)	70.60	97.04	119.53	183.95	216.67
Armed Forces Personnel		400,000	540,000	780,000	789,000
Armed Forces as % of Population		1.38%	1.51%	1.42%	1.22%
Military Expenditures as % of Gross National Product (GNP)		5.5	4.2	3.1	5.3

UNITED KINGDOM

Location: Western Europe
Capital: London
Area (square miles): 94,548
Area (relative): slightly smaller than Oregon

	1950	1961	1970	1989	1999
Population Estimate	50,127,000	52,807,000	55,632,000	57,324,000	59,293,000
Population Density (per square mile)	530.18	558.52	588.40	606.30	627.12
Armed Forces Personnel		475,000	375,000	318,000	218,000
Armed Forces as % of Population		0.90%	0.67%	0.55%	0.37%
Military Expenditures as % of Gross National Product (GNP)		4.2	4.8	4.1	2.5

UNITED STATES

Location: North America
Capital: Washington, D.C.
Area (square miles): 3,717,796
Area (relative): about half the size of Russia

	1950	1961	1970	1989	1999
Population Estimate	152,271,000	183,691,000	205,052,000	247,342,000	279,295,000
Population Density (per square mile)	40.96	49.41	55.15	66.53	75.12
Armed Forces Personnel		2,483,000	3,070,000	2,241,000	1,490,000
Armed Forces as % of Population		1.35%	1.50%	0.91%	0.53%
Military Expenditures as % of Gross National Product (GNP)		9.2	7.9	5.6	3.0

Chronology

3300–1550 BC   Early and Middle Canaanite Periods. Semitic-speaking Canaanites come from the area of present-day Lebanon, although other groups also settle in the area of Palestine, including those possibly from the Arabian Peninsula.

ca. 2100 BC   According to the traditions of the modern world's three major monotheistic religions—Judaism, Christianity, and Islam—they all trace their origins to the Prophet Abraham, who emigrates from Ur in present-day Iraq to Canaan, which is present-day Palestine. Abraham's two sons, Ishmael and Isaac, are the first Arab and Jew, respectively. On a hilltop in what later became Jerusalem, Abraham prepares to sacrifice one of his sons on God's order, but the boy is spared at the last moment. According to Jewish tradition, that son was Isaac. According to Muslim tradition, he was Ishmael.

1240–1200 BC   The Twelve Tribes of Israel under the leadership of Joshua conquer Canaan after wandering for 40 years following their escape from Egyptian bondage, as described in the book of Exodus.

1180–1150 BC   About the time of the Twelve Tribes' conquest of Canaan, the ancient Philistines also conquer the southern coast and adopt Canaanite culture. One theory is that the Philistines were one of the groups known as the Sea People.

1025–1000 BC   After Joshua's conquests, 11 of the Twelve Tribes are allotted their own land. A line of Judges rule the land of Israel, who periodically save Israel from hostile neighbors. Around 1025 BC, Saul becomes the first king of Israel, inaugurating a new chapter in Jewish history.

1000–970 BC   Following a power struggle, David succeeds Saul as king of Israel, inaugurating the House of David as the new ruling dynasty.

970–930 BC   Solomon becomes king after David's death. During Solomon's reign, Israel develops a more centralized government. The Bible describes the reign of Solomon as a period of unprecedented peace and prosperity. He was known for his wisdom and for the construction of the First Temple.

930–920 BC   After Solomon's death, the kingdom of Israel splits into two kingdoms. The Northern Kingdom is known as Israel and later Samaria. The Southern Kingdom is known as Judah, with Jerusalem as its capital. The Northern Kingdom holds 10 of the Twelve Tribes, while Judah consists of the tribes of Judah and Benjamin.

722 BC   The Assyrians under Sennacherib destroy the Northern Kingdom and displace the 10 tribes, which become the lost tribes of Israel. Other peoples brought in by the Assyrians repopulate Samaria. The Assyrians hold Samaria until 701 BC, when they are overthrown by the Babylonians.

597 BC   The Babylonian Captivity begins as the inhabitants of Judea are transferred to Babylon and dispersed throughout the Mediterranean and the Middle East. During this time, the Jewish people maintain their national and religious identity by codifying their rituals from the Torah.

586–312 BC   The Edomite people, who also lived in ancient Palestine, move into Judea. Then the Nabataeans, most probably an Arab people with an Aramaized culture, move into former Edomite territory, controlling the Gulf of Aqaba region. Later they are Roman clients and converts to Christianity.

539 BC   King Cyrus the Great of Persia conquers the Babylonians and allows a small group of Jews to return to Judah and rebuild Jerusalem.

521 BC   King Darius I of Persia allows the construction of the Second Temple under the prophets Haggai and Zechariah. Ezra restores the temple rituals, while Nehemiah, the cup-bearer to Artaxerxes I, returns to Jerusalem and rebuilds the walls of Jerusalem.

428 BC   The Samaritans build their temple on Mount Gerizim, which is not in accord with Jewish traditions and becomes the basis for enmity between the two groups.

333 BC   Alexander the Great of Macedonia conquers Persia, bringing Palestine under Greek rule.

323 BC   The death of Alexander the Great sparks a civil war among his generals over who will control his empire. Palestine falls under the control of the Seleucids.

168 BC   Antiochus IV begins his policy of Hellenizing Palestine by profaning the temple and outlawing Jewish practices.

167–164 BC   A Jewish revolt led by the Hasmoneans under Mattathias and Judah Maccabus gains control of the temple. The Jewish holiday of Hanukkah originates from this period.

142–63 BC   A Jewish state is established under the Hasmonean dynasty and expands into Samaria, Galilee, Idumea, and the lands beyond the Jordan River.

63 BC   The Romans under Pompey the Great conquer Judah, overthrow the Hasmonean dynasty, and rename the area Judea.

57–55 BC   The Romans divide Syria, Galilee, and Judea, which were formerly under the Hasmoneans, into separate provinces of the Roman Empire.

37–4 BC   The Romans appoint Herod the Great king of the Jews. Herod restores the Second Temple in 20 BC. His son, Herod Antipas, is made tetrarch of Galilee. Herod Archelaus becomes ruler of Judea. Jesus Christ is born toward the end of Herod's rule.

32 BC   Herod begins a war with the Nabataeans.

AD 26–36   The Romans consolidate their rule over the eastern Mediterranean. Caesarea is made the capital of Syria under the control of the governor Quirinius. Pontius Pilate serves as procurator of Judea and presides over the crucifixion of Jesus Christ.

41–44   The Roman emperor Claudius appoints Herod Agrippa I as king of the Jews. On his death in 44, Herod Agrippa II becomes king of the Jews.

50   The Council of Jerusalem convenes and approves the Apostle Paul's proposal to include the Gentiles. Christianity now becomes a growing religion, which the Romans deem a threat.

59–60   Paul goes before Herod Agrippa II and demands his right as a Roman citizen to be heard before Caesar.

64–69   Apostles Peter and Paul are executed as part of Emperor Nero's persecution of the Christians.

66–73   The First Jewish Revolt takes place. The Romans under Vespasian destroy Jerusalem and the Second Temple in AD 70 after a 134-day siege. The last pocket of Jewish resistance ends in the stronghold of Masada in AD 73. The crushing of the revolt results in the Second Diaspora of the Jews. There would not be another Jewish state until the mid-20th century.

132–135   The Romans crush the Simon Bar Kokhba Revolt. The Jewish population is evicted from Jerusalem, which is reconstructed as a pagan city and renamed Aelia Capitolina. Judea is renamed Palaestina. More of the Jewish population is dispersed throughout the Roman Empire.

312   Emperor Constantine converts to Christianity. He allows the Jews to visit Jerusalem and mark the anniversary of the destruction of the Temple.

326   Constantine's mother, Helena, makes a pilgrimage to Palestine and orders the construction of the Church of the Holy Sepulcher in Jerusalem and the Church of the Nativity in Bethlehem.

361–363   Emperor Flavius Claudius Julianus, known as Julian the Apostate, allows the Jews to resettle in Jerusalem.

622   The Prophet Muhammad flees from Mecca to Medina in the Hegira, or emigration, that marks the official beginning of Islam.

635   Khalid ibn Walid, Muslim general of the Umayyad caliph Umar ibn Khattab, conquers Damascus. Heraclius counterattacks, and then the Romans are defeated at the Battle of Yarmouk in 636.

637   Khalid ibn Walid conquers Jerusalem.

640–647   Palestine, a district of Syria, is controlled by the Umayyad caliphate until the Abbasid Revolution (747–750).

685–691   Under Caliph Abd al-Malik, the Dome of the Rock is constructed around the rock from which Muslims believe the Prophet Muhammad ascended to Heaven in the Miraj (Night Journey). This site lies above the Temple.

750–878   Palestine is under the Abbasid caliphate.

878–969   The Tulunid and Ilkhshid dynasties rule Palestine.

970–972 until 1073   The Fatimid dynasty, whose rulers were Shia Muslims, rule Palestine from Egypt.

1071   The Seljuk Turks conquer Jerusalem.

1098   Fatimid rulers reconquer Jerusalem.

1099   Christian Crusaders from Europe invade Palestine and conquer Jaffa and Jerusalem. The Latin Kingdom of Jerusalem is established.

1187   Salah al-Din, who later establishes the Ayyubid dynasty, defeats the Crusaders at the Battle of Hattin in Galilee and reclaims Jerusalem for the Muslims.

1191   King of England, Richard I the Lionheart, captures the city of Acre during the Third Crusade but cannot recapture Jerusalem.

1192 Richard the Lionheart reaches a settlement with Salah al-Din that includes a truce for years and Christian access to Jerusalem, and Richard then leaves for Europe.

1229 Frederick II of Germany, Holy Roman emperor, as part of the Sixth Crusade obtains rights to Nazareth, Bethlehem, and Jerusalem except for the Muslim holy sites there in a deal with the Ayyubids.

1244 The Khwarezmian forces, which fought for Baibars, the Mamluk ruler of Egypt, invade Jerusalem and swiftly defeat forces of the Seventh Crusade at Gaza.

1259 The Mongols battle the Mamluks and sack Jerusalem.

1260 The Mamluk forces of Baibars defeat the Mongols at the Battle of Ayn Jalut and retake Antioch in 1268.

1291–1517 The Mamluks conquer Acre, ending the Crusader states, and govern Syria and Egypt.

1348–1349 The Black Death, or plague pandemic, reaches Gaza and the cities of Palestine.

1516 Forces of the Ottoman Empire overthrow the Mamluk Sultanate and capture Syria, including Jerusalem, and Gaza. Egypt formally becomes a part of the Ottoman Empire in 1517, although the Mamluks remain powerful in Egypt, Baghdad, and other locations.

1535–1538 Sultan Suleiman the Magnificent orders the reconstruction of Jerusalem. In doing so, he seals the Golden Gate, where the Jewish Messiah was to enter.

1705 The Ottoman Empire restricts Jewish immigration after Judah the Pious and 1,000 immigrants settle in Jerusalem.

1831 Ibrahim Pasha, son of Muhammad Ali Pasha, the khedive or ruler of Egypt, conquers Syria and then Palestine. He overcomes a revolt against him there in 1834. Muhammad Ali Pasha authorizes this challenge to the Ottomans because the sultan failed to grant his father hereditary rights to various territories in exchange for quelling a Greek revolt. The Egyptian period aids centralized policies, and Jerusalem is opened. Ibrahim leaves the country in 1841. By 1844 there are 7,120 Jews in Jerusalem along with 5,760 Muslims and 3,390 Christians.

1839–1876 The Ottoman Empire initiates the Tanzimat, a series of reforms intended to restore Ottoman vitality and grant more rights to non-Muslims and non-Turks; create new financial, economic, military, and legal policies; and institute universal conscription.

1853–1856 The Crimean War erupts because of the dispute between the czar of Russia and the sultan of the Ottoman Empire over control of Christian sites in the Holy Land and the status of Orthodox Christians in the Balkans.

1882–1904 First wave of Jewish immigration to Palestine. The Jewish population of Palestine reaches 24,000 out of a total 400,000 as a result of immigration by East European Jews. By 1895 the population almost doubles to 47,000 out of 500,000.

1886 Palestinian villagers attack Petah Tikva colony, a Zionist settlement established in 1878.

1891 Palestinian notables protest Jewish immigration.

1894 Trial of Alfred Dreyfus.

1897 The First Zionist Congress, organized by Theodor Herzl, convenes in Basel (Basle), Switzerland, in response to the anti-Semitism of the Dreyfus Affair. The World Zionist Organization (WZO) emerges from the First Zionist Congress with the stated intention of establishing a Jewish homeland in Palestine.

1900 An Ottoman commission studies the effects of Zionist land purchases and settlement in Palestine.

1903 The British offer Zionists settlement in East Africa.

1904 Conflict breaks out between Palestinians and Jewish settlers in Tiberias.

1904 Najib Azoury's *The Awakening of the Arab Nation in Turkish Asia* expresses fears of Zionist goals in Palestine. This prompts the WZO to consider alternative locations for a Jewish homeland, such as Argentina or Uganda. Other Arabic publications raise alarms over Jewish settlement in Palestine, as the Jewish population totals 85,000 out of 700,000, or 12 percent of the total population, in 1913.

1910 The Sarsuq family, based in Beirut, sells a large area of land to the Jewish National Fund.

1911 Najib al-Nassar publishes the first book on Zionism in Arabic.

June 28, 1914 Archduke Franz Ferdinand and his wife are assassinated in Sarajevo, Bosnia-Herzegovina. In less than two months Austria-Hungary, Britain, France, Germany, and Russia rush into war, which would become the most devastating in history to date.

November 4, 1914 The Ottoman Empire formally enters World War I on the side of the Central Powers.

1915–1916 Correspondence between Sharif Hussein of Mecca and Sir Henry McMahon, British high commissioner of Egypt, promises Arabs an independent kingdom in certain areas in return for their support against the Ottoman armies in World War I.

1915 Herbert Samuel, an English politician of Jewish descent, proposes that Britain annex Palestine and settle it with 3–4 million Jews.

1916 Sharif Hussein leads an Arab revolt against the Ottoman Empire and declares himself the king of the Arabs.

May 16, 1916 Britain and France agree to the secret Sykes-Picot Agreement, which divides the Near East and areas of the Middle East between them.

November 2, 1917 The Balfour Declaration is issued by the British government and supports the establishment of a Jewish homeland in Palestine.

December 1917 The British Army under General Sir Edmund Allenby enters Jerusalem. All of Palestine falls under Allied control by September 1918.

November 11, 1918   World War I comes to an end with the Germans agreeing to an armistice.

January 18–21, 1919–January 1920   A peace conference is held in Paris and prepares treaties including the Treaty of Sèvres that deals with the former Ottoman Empire.

January 1919   The First Palestinian National Conference meets in Jerusalem and sends a demand for independence to the Paris Peace Conference and rejects the Balfour Declaration.

June 28, 1919   Germany signs the Treaty of Versailles, sowing the seeds of another war.

August 10, 1920   The Treaty of Sèvres is signed and formally dissolves the Ottoman Empire. The treaty is revised in the Treaty of Lausanne on July 24, 1923. The former Ottoman territories in the Middle East are partitioned into League of Nations mandates under Britain and France. Britain occupies Palestine, Transjordan, and Iraq, while France gains control of Lebanon and Syria.

1920   The British begin to implement the Balfour Declaration. Herbert Samuel is appointed the high commissioner over Palestine and seeks to elicit Jewish, Muslim, and Christian participation. Arab riots break out against the British Mandate for Palestine, and the Histadrut, or Jewish labor federation, is founded.

December 1920   The Third Palestine National Conference meets in Haifa and elects an executive committee.

1921   The British appoint Faisal, son of Sharif Hussein, as king of Iraq and his other son, Abdullah, as the ruler of Transjordan.

March 1921   The Haganah is founded. At first, it is an untrained militia that guards Jewish lands and repels attacks by Palestinian Arabs, but after 1929 it becomes a trained underground militia.

May 1921   Samuel appoints Haj Amin al-Husseini as the mufti of Jerusalem.

1922   The first census conducted by the British in Palestine counts the population as 757,182, of which 78 percent are Muslim Arabs, 9.6 percent are Christian Arabs, and 11 percent are Jewish, primarily new immigrants.

July 24, 1922   The League of Nations officially ratifies the mandate over Palestine. The Churchill White Paper further reinforces British support for a Jewish homeland in Palestine. The British Parliament issues the Palestinian Order in Council, calling for a legislative council made up of Jews and Arabs, but the order is rejected.

August 1922   The Fifth Palestine National Conference meets and approves an economic boycott of the Zionists.

August 1923   The British Mandate for Palestine formally begins.

1924–1928   A wave of Jewish immigrants arrives in Palestine.

1925   Vladimir Jabotinsky founds the Revisionist Party and calls for a Jewish state in Palestine and east of the River Jordan and a militarized Zionism.

1929   The Seventh Arab National Congress meets in Jerusalem. Riots erupt in Jerusalem over the presence of Jews at the Western Wall. In Jerusalem, Safed, and Hebron, 133 Jews and 116 Palestinians are killed. The Mapai, the Workers' Party of Israel, is founded.

1930   The Hope-Simpson Report on Jewish immigration and land shortages and the Passfield White Paper, which makes recommendations based on the question of immigration and unequal development of the two communities, are issued.

1931   The British MacDonald statement retracts the Passfield White Paper. By 1936, Jews account for 30 percent of the population, or 400,000.

1931   The Pan-Islamic Congress meets in Jerusalem.

1932   The Palestinian Istiqlal party is formed and calls for independence for Palestine.

1933   Adolf Hitler gains power in Germany. The rise of the Nazis prompts a mass emigration of Jews from Europe and into Palestine.

March 1933   The Nazis open Dachau concentration camp and then the Buchenwald, Sachsenhausen, and Ravensbrück camps.

April 11, 1933   Nazi decree defines non-Aryans.

1935   Nuremberg Race Laws against Jews are proclaimed and strip Jews of their citizenship and rights.

1936   The Arab Revolt of 1936–1939 breaks out against the British and Zionists. About 20,000 troops are sent to Palestine. Some 5,000 Arabs are killed, and thousands more are injured and arrested. The revolt is crushed only with assistance from Jewish groups.

1937   The Peel Royal Commission concludes that there is no hope for Jewish and Arab coexistence and recommends the partition of Palestine.

1938–1939   With increasing Nazi mistreatment and restrictions on Jews, the 1938 Anschluss (annexation of Austria) and the Kristallnacht pogrom create a refugee crisis as some 36,000 Jews leave Germany and Austria in 1938 and 77,000 leave in 1939.

April–August 1938   The Woodhead Commission meets and considers and rejects two partition plans.

July 26, 1938   Revisionist Zionists detonate a bomb in an Arab market in Haifa, killing 54.

September 1938   The Italian government passes racial legislation against Jews.

October 2, 1938   Palestinian militants kill 20 Jews at a settlement in Tiberias.

1939   The White Paper of 1939, also known as the MacDonald White Paper, calls for the establishment of an independent Palestinian state jointly governed by Jews and Arabs within 10 years. It limits Jewish immigration to 75,000 persons over five years. For the first time land transfers from Arabs to Jews are to be limited due to the growing number of landless and impoverished Arabs. The paper contrasts a Jewish "state," which the British feel should not be imposed against the will of the Arab population, with the Jewish "national home" as promised in the Balfour Declaration. The Zionists and Arab leadership reject the White Paper. World War II (1939–1945) erupts. The Nazis carry out the Holocaust in their attempt to systematically obliterate European Jews. Italian forces invade Egypt from Libya.

June 19, 1940 Twenty Palestinian Arabs are killed by explosives in a Haifa market, and then 13 more are killed in multiple shootings.

1941 British and Free French forces move through Palestine to invade Syria and Lebanon and replace the Vichy authorities. Britain also reoccupies Iraq, overthrowing the government.

1942 The Biltmore eight-point program is issued at the Extraordinary Zionist Conference. The program rejects the 1939 White Paper and calls for an independent Jewish state in all of Palestine and also stipulates that the Jewish Agency control immigration into the country.

1945 The Arab League is formed amid Jewish illegal immigration in Palestine. Jewish groups pressure the British government to allow Holocaust victims to settle into Palestine by sending refugee ships, forcing a confrontation with the Royal Navy.

1946 The Morrison-Grady Plan calls for the division of Palestine into a federalized state with Jewish and Arab areas and a neutral zone administered by the British. The Morrison-Grady Plan is rejected by Zionists. Although President Harry S. Truman first supports the plan, he is pressured against endorsing it.

1946 The Irgun Tsvai Leumi (National Military Organization) bombs the British headquarters at the King David Hotel in Jerusalem, killing 91 Britons, Jews, and Arabs.

1947 The majority of the United Nations Special Commission on Palestine (UNSCOP) recommends the partition of Palestine into Jewish and Arab states with Jerusalem as a neutral site, while a minority recommends a nonpartitioned nation. Thirteen member states including six Arab nations vote against United Nations (UN) Resolution 181 (a slightly different partition plan), arguing that 36 percent of the Arab population would be under Jewish control. The Arab states try to seek remedy at the International Court of Justice and are outvoted. Fighting then begins between Jewish and Palestinian groups.

January 10, 1948 The Palestinians have no regular army and only two small paramilitary groups, the Najjada of about 2,000 men in Jaffa and the Futuwwa of a few hundred men. An Arab volunteer force, the Arab Liberation Army (ALA) of less than 6,000 men, assembles in Syria and is supposed to fight in northern Palestine under the leadership of Fawzi al-Qawuqji from Syria. Other Arab countries commit forces ranging from a larger Egyptian contingent of 10,000 men (later in the war up to 20,000 men) to small groups from Lebanon, Saudi Arabia, and Yemen. They face Jewish forces of about 35,000 men in addition to the smaller groups of Irgun and Lehi, estimated at between 2,500 and 4,800 men.

January–April 1948 Violence continues to increase in Palestine as a war erupts between Jews and Arabs and also with the British, who are engaged in an evacuation of the area. Jews and Arabs wait for opportunities to seize areas that the British abandon. British major general Hugh Stockwell attempts in vain to maintain order in Haifa as Jewish forces surround the city. Jewish forces capture Tiberias on April 18 and Safad on May 12. In central Palestine, Jewish and Arab forces clash on the road between Tel Aviv and Jerusalem after the Jewish Agency, the organization representing Jewish interests in Palestine, attempts to supply 100,000 Jews in the New City of Jerusalem through Arab-controlled territory. In a battle at Kastel, Abd al-Qadir al-Husseini, the founder of the Organization of Holy Struggle, is killed on April 9 when citizens of Deir Yassin are massacred by Jewish forces. Between April 25 and May 13 the city of Jaffa is under siege, ending with the forced evacuation of its Arab population. At Kfar Etzion, south of Jerusalem, Arab Legion forces and irregulars, eager to avenge the killing of the villagers of Deir Yassin, massacre many Jewish defenders on May 14. Defenders of Gush Etzion surrender in the presence of the International Red Cross.

March 6, 1948 The Haganah calls for general mobilization.

April 9, 1948 While fighting for control of the road between Jerusalem and Tel Aviv, units from the Jewish organizations Irgun and the Lohamei Herut Israel (Lehi, or Stern Gang) attack the Arab community of Deir Yassin and massacre 254 noncombatant Arab men, women, and children. This massacre shocks Jews as well as Arabs and adds to the Arab bitterness toward the cause of Zionism.

April 25, 1948 Lebanon, Syria, Iraq, Transjordan, and Egypt agree to invade Palestine. These countries mobilize for an attack on the Jewish regions in Palestine. King Abdullah of Transjordan becomes the nominal leader of the Arab forces, which fight only in a limited area.

April 30, 1948 Haganah captures western Jerusalem and expels all Palestinians.

May 14, 1948 The independence of Israel is proclaimed. David Ben-Gurion becomes the first prime minister of the State of Israel.

Israeli War of Independence, May 14, 1948–January 7, 1949

Phase I: May 14–June 11, 1948

NORTHERN OPERATIONS

May 14–19, 1948   Syria and the small 1,000-member Lebanese force launch an invasion. Syria captures Zemach and then abandons it and next captures Mishmar Hayarden near the border but then fights on the defensive. The Lebanese are stopped at Malkya.

May 15–June 4, 1948   Iraq invades Israel from Mafraq in Jordan and crosses the Jordan River south of the Sea of Galilee. Between May 16 and 22, the Iraqis are unable to take Geshir. The Iraqis occupy Jenin and Samaria in the West Bank and proceed toward Natania on May 30. The Israelis attempt to take Jenin between June 1 and 4 but are held back by the Iraqis. The Iraqis, however, are forced to withdraw and participate no further in the war.

May 20, 1948   Count Folke Bernadotte of Sweden is appointed by the UN Security Council as a mediator between the Jews and Arabs.

June 6–10, 1948   Syria and Lebanon renew their offensive. The Syrians are unsuccessful in taking Ein Gev but capture Mishmar Hayarden. With the support from the ALA and the Syrians, the Lebanese capture Matka on June 6 and Ramat Naftali and Kadesh on June 7. As a result, the ALA occupies much of the area around Galilee.

OPERATIONS IN THE CENTRAL SECTOR

May 15–25, 1948   The Arab Legion under British general John Glubb gains control of the eastern and southern portions of New Jerusalem and occupies much of the Old City unopposed.

May 15–28, 1948   The Arab Legion lays siege to the Jewish Quarter in Old Jerusalem. With Palestinian Arab irregulars, the Arab Legion fights its way through the Jewish Quarter. Eventually the Jews are forced to surrender.

May 18–June 10, 1948   The Israelis under the command of American volunteer Colonel David "Micky" Marcus attempt to gain control of the Tel Aviv–Jerusalem Road but fail, and Marcus is mistakenly killed by a Jewish sentry.

May 25–30, 1948   The First Battle of Latrun begins. Lieutenant Colonel Habas al-Majali from the Arab Legion occupies Latrun on the way to Tel Aviv. The Israelis are unable to drive his forces out.

June 9–10, 1948   The Israelis make a second attempt to take Latrun in the Second Battle of Latrun. The Arab Legion again holds its ground against the Israelis.

SOUTHERN OPERATIONS

May 15, 1948   Two Egyptian brigade groups under Major General Ahmed Ali al-Mwawi move into Palestine. The larger of the two groups advances along the coast from El Arish to secure the Gaza Strip and to be within striking distance of Tel Aviv. The ALA advances toward Jerusalem from Abu Ageila through Beersheba.

May 16–June 7, 1948   The Egyptian Army marches through the Gaza Strip. Between May 19 and 24 the Egyptians seize Yad Mordechai and Ashdod, which are only 25 miles from Tel Aviv. The Egyptians rebuff an Israeli attempt to recapture Ashdod between June 2 and 3. The Egyptians take Nitzanin on June 7, which secures their lines of communication from El Arish.

May 16–June 10, 1948   The Egyptians capture Beersheba on May 20 and Hebron on May 21 and connect with the Arab Legion at Bethlehem on May 22.

June 11–July 9, 1948   After three weeks, Bernadotte negotiates a truce between both sides that is welcomed by the Israelis and opposed by the Arabs. The truce allows the Israelis to regroup their forces, which grew to 49,000 troops. On June 20 a UN police force of 49 guards arrives from New York.

Phase II: July 9–18, 1948

NORTHERN OPERATIONS

July 9–14, 1948   The Israelis are unsuccessful in driving out the Syrians from the upper Jordan River at the Third Battle of Mishmar Hayaden.

July 12–16, 1948   The Israelis begin their Nazareth Offensive by taking control of the coast north of Haifa and then take Nazareth.

OPERATIONS IN THE CENTRAL SECTOR

July 9–12, 1948   The Israelis launch their Lod Ramla Offensive with the goals of securing the Tel Aviv–Jerusalem Road and driving out the Arab Legion from the Coastal Plain. The Israelis take control of Lod and Ramla and a nearby airport.

July 9–18, 1948   The Second Battle for Jerusalem ends in failure, as the Israelis are rebuffed by the Arab Legion.

July 14–18, 1948   The Israelis fail for the third time to take Latrun.

SOUTHERN OPERATIONS

July 18–October 15, 1948   A second truce is declared between Israel and the Arabs. During the truce, the Israeli Army grows to 90,000 troops, giving Israel a numerical advantage over the Arabs.

September 17, 1948   Israel's success in the war causes many Israelis to oppose Bernadotte's efforts at a negotiated peace with the Arabs, which would have meant returning territories conquered during the conflict. Bernadotte is assassinated by three men from the Stern Gang. Dr. Ralph Bunche succeeds him as UN negotiator.

September 29–October 15, 1948   On the southern border with Egypt, neither side adheres closely to the cease-fire. The Israelis launch an offensive to cut Egyptian communications and to open a line of communications into the Negev region.

October 1, 1948   The Palestinian National Council meets and confirms Ahmad Hilmi Abd al-Baqi as president of the All Palestine Government, announced just a week earlier, and proclaims Palestine a free democratic state. King Abdullah opposes the All Palestine Government, although it continues on until 1963.

Phase III: October 6–November 5, 1948

SOUTHERN OPERATIONS

October 15–19, 1948   Israel launches a coastal offensive against the Egyptians to drive them out of the Ashdod-Gaza area. Despite some short-term successes, the Israelis do not gain control of any major positions.

October 19–21, 1948   Israel launches its Beersheba offensive. The Israelis are successful in opening lines of communication with the Negev. On October 19 the Israelis seize Huleiqat, which disrupts Egyptian communications, and capture Beersheba on October 21. Israeli success in these areas leaves the Egyptians at Hebron and Faluja isolated.

October 27–November 5, 1948   With its coastal communications severed, Egypt withdraws its forces from Ashdod and Majdal. Instead, the Egyptians concentrate their forces in the area along Asluj, Gaza, and El Arish.

CENTRAL SECTOR OPERATIONS

October–November 1948   The Israelis launch limited offensives along the Jerusalem–Tel Aviv Road to gain control of areas north and south of Jerusalem. The Arab League turns back an Israeli attack near Beit Jabrin.

November 30, 1948   Israel and Transjordan declare a cease-fire.

December 1, 1948   King Abdullah declares himself king of Arab Palestine and the Union of Transjordan and Arab Palestine at Amman.

NORTHERN OPERATIONS

October 22–31, 1948   Israel launches another offensive in northern Galilee in response to a probe by the ALA along the Lebanese border. At Tarshiham, the Israelis suffer a setback on October 28 but drive the ALA back into Lebanon after successes at Gish on October 29 and Sasa on October 30. Israelis then break Arab resistance in the Hula Valley, retake Manara, and seize a three-to-nine-mile area of southern Lebanon, expelling the villagers and also the Palestinian Arab residents of the Galilee.

November 30, 1948   The Israelis, Syrians, and Lebanese declare a cease-fire.

Phase IV: November 21, 1948–January 7, 1949

November 19–December 7, 1948   The Egyptians expand their control in the area east of Gaza and in Asluj but are unable to relieve their besieged forces in Faluja.

December 20, 1948–January 7, 1949   Israel launches its Sinai Offensive (Operation HOREF) with the goal of knocking Egypt out of the war. Israel surrounds Rafah on December 22, Asluj on December 25, and Auja on December 27. The Israelis have a column going toward Rafah, and another column take Abu Ageila on December 28. The Israelis head toward El Arish and seize an airfield and surrounding villages. The Egyptians, however, halt their advance on December 29.

January 7, 1949   The Egyptians ask for an armistice, which is granted by the Israelis.

February–June 1949   Israel signs separate armistice agreements with Egypt, Lebanon, Jordan, and Syria. Israel acquires 50 percent more territory than originally provided in the UN partition plan. According to United Nations figures, an estimated 710,000 Palestinians flee or are evicted from Jewish-held areas. Egypt gains control of Gaza, and Jordan holds the West Bank. As part of a secret agreement with Israel, Jordan later annexes the West Bank.

March 7–10, 1949   The Israel Defense Forces (IDF) capture the southern Negev, including Eilat, without difficulty in Operation UVDA.

April 27–September 1949   Representatives from Israel and Arab states meet at the Lausanne Conference. Although the conference is largely a failure, Israel gains a working recognition by Arab states. Both sides accept UN resolutions.

April 1950   Britain gives de jure recognition to Israel and Jordan (including the West Bank).

1950   The Israeli Knesset passes the Law of Return, specifying that any Jew who wishes to settle in the State of Israel will be granted immediate citizenship.

July 1951   King Abdullah of Jordan is assassinated. He is succeeded by King Talal, who is subsequently succeeded by King Hussein.

1951–1958   Israel begins a land reclamation project to drain the Hulah Valley as well as eradicate malaria.

July 23, 1952   Free Officers seize control of Egypt, and the July Revolution ends the monarchy.

January 18, 1953   The Soviet Union accuses so-called Zionist agents of murdering top Soviet leaders as part of its anti-Zionist position against Israel.

October 1953   Ariel Sharon leads the IDF Paratrooper Unit 101 in a raid against the Jordanian village of Qibya. The raid kills 69 civilians and destroys much property as retaliation for a raid on Tirat Yehuda.

July 1954   Defense Minister Pinhas Lavon orders Israeli spies to sabotage British and U.S. property in Egypt as part of a plan to strain relations against Britain and Egypt and postpone British withdrawal from the Suez Canal. The plan, called the Lavon Affair, fails, implicates Lavon, and precipitates his resignation. Egypt retaliates against Egyptian Jews because some of them were involved in the plot.

September 7, 1954   Ben-Gurion resigns as prime minister and is replaced by Moshe Sharett.

October 19, 1954   Britain and Egypt sign an agreement whereby British troops withdraw from the Suez Canal.

January 27, 1955   An Egyptian military court sentences two Israeli spies to death and executes them.

February 1955   Israel launches Operation HETZ SHAHOR (BLACK ARROW) against Egypt for incursions into Israel. The operation kills 38 Egyptians and causes Nasser to reconsider his plans toward Israel.

September 27, 1955   Egypt signs an arms deal with Czechoslovakia. The Israeli government is alarmed, and discussion of preemptive military action begins.

November 2, 1955   Ben-Gurion once again becomes prime minister, replacing Sharett.

December 11, 1955   Israel launches the Kinneret raid against Syria, a signatory to a defense pact with Egypt. Sharett, now foreign minister, requests U.S. arms and is turned down the next day.

1956 Suez Crisis (Suez or Sinai War), October 29–November 6, 1956

Background

June 1956   Sharett is ousted as foreign minister and is replaced by Golda Meir, who supports the subsequent Sinai Campaign.

June 13, 1956   British troops leave the Suez Canal Zone.

July 4–26, 1956   Tensions flare along Israel's borders with Jordan and along the Gaza Strip. UN secretary-general Dag Hammarskjöld visits the Middle East to restore the cease-fire between Egypt and Israel, first brokered at the end of the Israeli War for Independence (1948–1949).

July 18, 1956   Secretary of State John Foster Dulles announces that the United States will withdraw its financial support to Egypt for the construction of the Aswan High Dam.

July 26, 1956   President Nasser nationalizes the Suez Canal Company.

August 16–30, 1956   Violence erupts along Israel's borders with Egypt and Jordan. This raises fears that another Middle Eastern war will erupt.

October 5, 1956   Britain and France propose to the UN Security Council that the Suez Canal be placed under international control. The Soviet Union vetoes the proposal.

October 15, 1956   As a result of shooting incidents along the Israel-Jordan border, the Jordanians accuse Israel of aggression before the UN Security Council.

October 24, 1956   Israel, Britain, and France agree to take military action against Egypt at a secret meeting in Sevrès and coordinate their strategies. Britain and France will demand that Israel withdraw from the Suez Canal. Israeli forces will then move on the canal, and upon Nasser's sure refusal to withdraw, Britain and France will intervene militarily to save the canal from Israeli occupation.

Operations

October 29, 1956   Israel invades the Sinai.

October 30, 1956   The Israelis turn back an attack by Egyptian ground and air forces. Sharon's troops capture Thamad and rejoin with the paratrooper battalion. The Israeli Central Task Group under Colonel Yehuda Wallach captures Sabha and Kusseima and then proceedes to Abu Ageila. The Egyptian 4th Armored Division moves toward Bir Gifgafa and Bir Rud Salim.

October 30, 1956   The governments of Britain and France send an ultimatum that calls for Israel and Egypt to cease hostilities and withdraw from the Suez Canal and propose an Anglo-French occupation of Port Said, Ismailiyya, and Suez to ensure international access. As expected, Egypt rejects the ultimatum, and an Anglo-French force leaves Malta for Egypt.

October 31, 1956   Britain and France bomb airfields on the Suez Canal. Sharon's paratroopers are ambushed at Mitla Pass. The fighting is hard and includes hand-to-hand combat. Many Egyptians are taken prisoner, but the Egyptian forces hold their line. The Israelis overrun part of the Egyptian defenses at Abu Ageila but are repulsed. The Central Task Force captures Bir Hassnah, Jebel Libni, and Bir Hama.

October 31, 1956   The Egyptian destroyer *Ibrahim al-Awal* bombards naval and oil installations at Haifa. After a sea battle, the Israeli Navy captures the destroyer and tows it into Haifa Harbor.

October 31, 1956   The British bombard Egyptian air bases. Nasser orders Egyptian forces to withdraw from the Sinai.

November 1, 1956   Israeli forces are rebuffed again at Abu Ageila. The Israeli General Headquarters suspends further attacks at Abu Ageila. The Northern Task Group under Colonel Haim Laskov captures Rafah and proceeds toward El Arish. By midnight, all Egyptian troops in the Sinai begin withdrawing except for units in Gaza and Sharm al-Sheikh, which are surrounded by Israeli forces.

November 2, 1956   The Israeli 9th Infantry Brigade moves toward Sharm al-Sheikh along the Gulf of Aqaba. The Egyptians evacuate Abu Ageila and are pursued by the Israelis through Bir Gifgafa toward the Suez Canal. The 27th Armored Brigade under Chaim Bar-Lev captures El

Arish and heads toward Romani. The 11th Infantry Brigade under Colonel Aharon Doron captures the northern Gaza Strip, including the city of Gaza. The Egyptian forces not surrounded by the Israelis complete their withdrawal from Sinai.

November 2, 1956   The UN calls for a cease-fire between Egypt and Israel. Egypt accepts the UN call for a cease-fire, but Britain and France continue to bomb Egyptian airfields and military installations.

November 3, 1956   The Israeli 9th Brigade continues to advance down the Sinai coast. Paratroopers advancing down the Gulf of Suez capture Egyptian oil fields at Ras Sudar, Abu Znayma, and al-Tur. The 11th Brigade captures Khan Yunis, which brings the Gaza Strip under Israeli control. Colonel Ra'if Mahfuz Zaki, the commander of the garrison at Sharm al-Sheikh, withdraws his forces from Ras Nasrani to bolster his defenses.

November 3–4, 1956   Israel initially accepts the UN's call for a cease-fire, assuming that Sharm al-Sheikh would have been captured by the time the cease-fire takes effect. The British and French, however, pressure Ben-Gurion to continue hostilities since a cease-fire would negate intervention at the Suez Canal.

November 4, 1956   The 9th Brigade passes through Ras Nasrani and falls under heavy fire from the Egyptians.

November 5, 1956   The Israelis mount their first assault on Sharm al-Sheikh after midnight but are stopped by a minefield and Egyptian resistance. At 5:30 a.m. the Israelis resume their attack with air and mortar support, leading to the capture of Sharm al-Sheikh.

November 5, 1956   Britain and France send 500 paratroopers over El Gamil Airfield near Port Said at 8:30 a.m. Another 600 land near Port Fuad. The Anglo-French force captures the waterworks and isolates the cities. Despite a brief truce between local Egyptian and British commanders, fighting resumes late that evening.

November 6, 1956   Britain and France mount an amphibious assault on Port Said. At 7:30 p.m. Stockwell is ordered to cease fire at midnight.

March 23, 1957   The Suez Canal reopens to traffic.

1957   Israel signs a secret agreement with France to construct a nuclear breeder reactor, later discovered by American U-2 planes between 1960 and 1961.

February 1958   The United Arab Republic (UAR), the union of Egypt and Syria, is established.

1958   Palestinians form legislative and executive councils for Gaza shortly after establishment of the UAR. This is the first open political activity permitted in almost 10 years in the Diaspora.

1958   The Palestinian Arab Nationalist Union (al-Ittihad al-Qawmi al-'Arabi al-Filastini, PANU) is set up. The mufti objects and leaves Egypt. The PANU lacks an active role, deals with host governments, and provides water and electricity to camps until 1961.

July 14, 1958   The Iraqi government is overthrown in a coup led by Brigadier Abdul Karim Qassem and Colonel Abd al-Salam Arif, who establish a republic and execute the king and the regent.

July 15, 1958   The United States sends 14,000 troops to Lebanon in Operation BLUE BAT to shore up the government of President Camille Chamoun against his internal opposition.

October 23, 1958   The Soviet Union approves a loan to Egypt to finance the Aswan High Dam.

November 18, 1958   Israel begins the National Water Carrier Project to divert water from the Sea of Galilee, which will deplete the Jordan River.

1959   Yasser Arafat and other Palestinian leaders found Fatah, the reverse acronym of Harakat al-Tahrir al-Watani according to Salah Khalaf. However, another source dates the origins of the movement to late 1957.

1959   The General Union of Palestinian Students (GUPS) is formed at a meeting in Cairo. The GUPS demands mandatory conscription for Palestinians and comes to be a base of the Palestine Liberation Organization (PLO).

1960   Mossad agents capture Nazi war criminal Adolf Eichmann in Argentina and send him to Israel, where he is tried for ordering the deaths of millions of Jews and other minorities.

1961   Eichmann's trial is televised and seen throughout the world.

1961   Syria withdraws from the UAR.

June 1962   Eichmann is executed.

June 24, 1963   Ben-Gurion resigns as prime minister over the 1954 Lavon Affair.

1963   The General Union of Palestine Workers (GUPW) is founded and is centered in Cairo until the 1970s, when it moves to Damascus. Large numbers of fedayeen are recruited from the GUPW.

January 13–17, 1964   The First Arab Summit convenes at Cairo. The Arab states condemn Israel's diversion of the Jordan River and try to formulate a response to it, hinting at diversion of its headwaters. The summit also welcomes the African Unity Charter and supports the Arab struggle and the struggle against imperialism.

May 1964   The PLO is officially founded, as announced by the new Palestinian National Council. The PLO is headed by Ahmad Shukeiri.

September 13, 1964   The Second Arab Summit is held at Alexandria and focuses on the strengthening of Arab military forces with the goal of liberating Palestine from Israel. Israel submits its concerns to the UN Security Council.

September 18, 1965   The Third Arab Summit convenes in Casablanca. The most important aspects of this summit are the Casablanca Protocol, which addresses the treatment of Palestinians in Arab countries, and the acknowledgment of intra-Arab propaganda and conflict, which is to be minimized.

1965 The General Union of Palestinian Women is established and is then reorganized after a Beirut conference in 1974.

March–April 1965 President Habib Burjiba (Bourguiba) of Tunisia proposes that Arab states recognize Israel on the basis of the UN Partition Resolution of 1947.

1965 Egypt has sent 55,000 troops to Yemen, having started a military commitment with 5,000 troops in 1962.

November 13, 1966 Israeli troops launch an attack on the Jordanian village of Samu, killing 15 Jordanian soldiers and 3 civilians. Israeli troops destroy 125 houses in response to the deaths of 3 Israeli soldiers by a road mine. The UN Security Council censures Israel by issuing Security Council Resolution 228.

Six-Day War, June 5–10, 1967

Preliminary Moves

May 16, 1967 Egypt declares a state of emergency.

May 17, 1967 Egypt and Syria declare their readiness for combat, and Jordan begins mobilization.

May 18, 1967 Troops in Syria and Egypt are placed on maximum alert, and Kuwait announces its mobilization.

May 19, 1967 The UNEF troops withdraw from Sinai.

May 20, 1967 Israel completes a partial mobilization of forces.

May 23, 1967 Saudi Arabia begins mobilization of its troops.

May 24, 1967 Jordan completes its mobilization.

May 28, 1967 Sudan mobilizes its troops.

May 29, 1967 Egypt receives units from Algeria.

May 30, 1967 Egypt and Jordan sign the Mutual Security Treaty.

May 31, 1967 Iraqi troops move into Jordan.

The Sinai Front

June 5, 1967 Israel launches a preemptive air strike against Egypt's air bases, destroying its air force. Later in the day, the Israelis destroy the Jordanian and Syrian air forces while destroying Iraqi air units in Mosul.

June 5, 1967 Israeli ground forces consist of a mechanized brigade under Colonel Yehuda Resheff, a mechanized division commanded by Major General Israel Tal, an armored division under Major General Avraham Yoffe, and a mechanized division under Major General Ariel Sharon. Tal's division drives into the Rafah–El Arish area. Resheff advances into the Gaza Strip, while Sharon advances toward fortifications in the area of Abu Ageila and Kusseima. Yoffe heads southward toward central Sinai to cut off the Egyptian retreat.

June 6, 1967 Egyptian troops in Gaza surrender to Resheff. Tal joins Yoffe. Sharon sends part of his force to Rafah and El Arish, and the remainder advance toward Nakhl and Mitla Pass. Yoffe attacks the main Egyptian force at Jabal Libni

in central Sinai. The Egyptian field marshal Abdel Hakim Amer orders all units in the Sinai to withdraw.

June 7, 1967 Tal's main forces arrive at Bir Gifgafa, while his northern task force moves past Romani. Yoffe's leading brigade arrives at the eastern end of the Mitla Pass without fuel and short of ammunition. Egyptian forces quickly surround the unit. Yoffe's other brigade relieves its comrades soon after. Sharon advances closer to Nakhl, while other units capture northeastern Sinai and air and amphibious forces capture Sharm al-Sheikh.

June 8, 1967 Egyptian armored units attempt to provide cover for ground forces withdrawing from the Sinai. However, Tal's forces drive them back as he advances toward the Suez Canal between Qantara and Ismailiyya. Yoffe's division traverses Mitla Pass and reaches the canal opposite Port Suez. Sharon captures Nakhl and passes through Mitla Pass. The Sinai is firmly under the control of the Israeli Army.

The Jordanian Front

THE BATTLE FOR JERUSALEM

June 5, 1967 The Jordanians begin firing on Israel from Jerusalem. Israeli general Uzi Narkiss begins the offensive against Jerusalem with three brigades under Colonel Mordechai Gur. The Israelis surround the Old City, which is defended by Jordanian brigadier Ata Ali.

June 6, 1967 The Israelis continue their siege of the Old City but are hampered by Jordanian opposition. They frustrate Jordanian efforts to relieve the Old City. A tank brigade seizes Ramallah, and another captures Latrun. The road between Tel Aviv and Jerusalem is open to Jewish traffic for the first time since 1947.

June 7, 1967 Gur's forces storm the Old City, while the Jordanians withdraw. The Israelis subsequently capture Bethlehem, Hebron, and Etzion.

THE BATTLE OF JENIN-NABLUS

June 5, 1967 Major General David Elazar sends one division and an armored brigade toward Jenin, capturing it after fierce combat the next day.

June 7, 1967 The Israelis advance toward Nablus despite Jordanian counterattacks and seize it. The Jordanians withdraw across the Jordan River, and both Israel and Jordan call for a cease-fire by the UN.

The Syrian Front

June 5–8, 1967 The Syrians control the Golan Heights with six brigades and six more in reserve. Elazar engages in artillery duels against the Syrians for four days.

June 8, 1967 The UN calls for a cease-fire.

June 9, 1967 President Gamal Abdel Nasser offers his resignation, which is rejected by the Egyptian people in large public demonstrations. Elazar advances toward the Dan-Banyas area along the foothills of Mount Hermon, fighting through the first line of Syrian defenses in the northern Golan Heights, with three brigades to follow. Other units force their way north of the Sea of Galilee. Elazar orders units to attack the Golan Heights south of the Sea of Galilee.

June 10, 1967   The Syrian defenses are rapidly deteriorating, which is an advantage to the Israelis as they press through the northern Golan Heights. The Israelis push forward toward Quneitra from the north, west, and southwest. The troops from the Jordanian front drive northeastward toward the Yarmuk Valley to occupy the southern Golan Heights. The Israelis surround Quneitra, with a unit occupying the city. Israel and Syria soon enter into a cease-fire.

The Naval War

June 3–4, 1967   The Israelis wage a campaign of deception by transferring landing craft back and forth from the Mediterranean to Eilat. This leads the Egyptians to believe that the Israelis are massing toward Eilat, forcing the Egyptians to concentrate their forces toward the Red Sea. As a result, the Israelis redress the imbalance of forces in the Mediterranean.

June 5, 1967   An Israeli destroyer and several torpedo boats reach Port Said, where they are met by two Egyptian Osa-class missile boats. After an inconclusive battle, the Egyptian vessels withdraw into the harbor. Israeli frogmen enter the harbors of Port Said and Alexandria, where they inflict some damage on Egyptian vessels but are captured.

June 6, 1967   The Egyptians withdraw from Port Said after heavy Israeli air attacks and the threat of Tal's advance. The Egyptian Navy withdraws all of its vessels from Port Said to Alexandria.

June 6–7, 1967   The Israeli coast is bombarded by three Egyptian submarines near Ashdod and north and south of Haifa. Israeli air and naval forces return fire and drive off the submarines.

June 7, 1967   An Israeli task force captures Egyptian fortifications at Sharm al-Sheikh. This allows naval vessels to travel unobstructed through the Strait of Tiran to the Red Sea.

June 8, 1967   USS *Liberty,* an American electronics vessel, is attacked 14 nautical miles north of El Arish by Israeli fighter-bombers and naval forces. The Israeli government apologizes to the United States.

August–September 1967   The Arab Summit convenes in Khartoum and votes against peace or negotiations with Israel.

October 21, 1967   An Egyptian missile ship sinks the Israeli destroyer *Eilat.* Israel in turn bombards a refinery complex at Suez.

November 22, 1967   Security Council Resolution 242 calls for Israeli withdrawal and for peace.

1967   Seizure of Palestinian land in the West Bank and Gaza by Israel for military and security requirements.

March 21, 1968   Jordanian and Palestinian forces defeat an Israeli raid at the Battle of Karameh. Karameh serves as a base for PLO Fatah guerrillas, and it is from here that they will launch their attacks.

1968   The Popular Front for the Liberation of Palestine (PFLP) is formed.

June 1968   The War of Attrition between Egypt and Israel begins. Egypt launches attacks because of Israel's failure to withdraw from the Sinai Peninsula in accordance with UN Resolution 242. Egypt first violates the 1967 cease-fire along the Suez Canal.

July 23, 1968   Three PFLP members hijack an El Al 707 en route from Rome to Lod and divert it to Algiers. Negotiations take 40 days. Hostages are freed and not killed, and the hijackers are not apprehended.

Fall 1968   After a successful strike, UNRWA teachers together with PLO leadership establish the General Union of Palestinian Teachers.

October 26, 1968   Very heavy Egyptian artillery barrage on Egypt.

November 1, 1968   Israeli helicopter-borne commandos destroy Egypt's electrical transformers at Nag Hamadi, some 120 miles inside Egyptian territory. Israel fortifies its position on the east of the Suez Canal in the Bar-Lev Line. This action leads the Egyptians to more aggressive action in the War of Attrition the next spring.

1968–1970   Israel begins to build settlements in the West Bank, East Jerusalem, the Gaza Strip, and the Golan Heights.

December 26, 1968   The PFLP attacks an El Al airplane in Athens, killing an Israeli mechanic.

December 28, 1968   Israel launches a helicopter raid on Beirut International Airport, destroying 13 Arab planes and inflicting heavy damage on the airport. Security Council Resolution 262, passed on December 31, censures Israel.

1969   The Palestine Red Crescent Society, formerly the Fatah Medical Services formed to deal with the inadequacy of medical care in 1967, is declared the official health organization of the PLO.

January 6, 1969   Israel discloses a French ban on arms supplies.

1969   The Democratic Front for the Liberation of Palestine is formed.

January 27, 1969   The Iraqi government condemns and executes 14 people as Israeli spies, of whom 9 are Jews.

February 1–4, 1969   The Fifth Palestinian National Council (PNC) convenes in Cairo. Arafat becomes the chair of the Executive Committee. The PNC calls for a "secular democratic state" for Muslims, Christians, and Jews in Palestine.

February 18, 1969   The PFLP attacks an El Al airplane in Zurich.

February 20, 1969   The PFLP launches a bomb attack on a supermarket in Jerusalem.

February 24, 1969   Israel launches an air strike against two Fatah camps near Damascus, inflicting heavy casualties. The PFLP declares its intention to overthrow King Hussein of Jordan, whom it saw as a Western puppet.

March 1969   Israel and Egypt exchange missile attacks. Egypt shells the Bar-Lev Line heavily on March 8 and 9, firing some 40,000 shells. On March 9 when Israel shells the canal city of Ismailiyya, Lieutenant General Abd al-Munim Riyadh is killed.

March 11, 1969   Golda Meir becomes prime minister after the death of Levi Eshkol.

April 19, 1969   Egyptian commandos begin crossing the canal to attack Israeli units.

April 23, 1969   Egypt and Israel engage in heavy artillery bombardments and air strikes around the Suez Canal. The United States condemns Nasser's actions. Israel shells the town of Suez and its oil refineries as well as Ismailiyya, Port Said, and Port Tawfiq.

July 20, 1969   Israel employs air, land, and sea forces, briefly taking Jazirat al-Khadra in the Suez Canal, and shoots down five Egyptian aircraft, losing two of its own. Israel attacks numerous ground targets at Suez and inside Egypt.

July 24, 1969   Israel strikes Egypt's surface-to-air missile (SAM) sites at the Suez Canal.

August 21, 1969   An Australian tourist starts a fire at the al-Aqsa Mosque, sparking protests and demonstrations.

September–October 1969   Israeli forces destroy all of the Egyptian SAM sites and radar stations at the Suez Canal. In October the Israelis begin attacking the Gulf of Suez, then shift back again to the Suez Canal.

November 3, 1969   The Cairo Protocol is signed by General Emile al-Bustani of Lebanon and Arafat. The Egyptian government sponsors this agreement to prevent attacks on Palestinian armed groups in Lebanon who are within certain restrictions permitted to continue their revolution against Israel, with the unwritten understanding that they are to avoid Lebanese internal disputes and will not be naturalized.

December 9, 1969   U.S. secretary of state William Rogers proposes an Israeli-Egyptian settlement, which is rejected by both countries.

January 1970   Israel begins deeper air raids into Egypt on January 8, striking 30 miles from Cairo, and on January 18 at installations north of Helwan and a base at the Cairo International Airport. Bombing continues at Qantara and Suez. Seventy civilians are killed in the Delta area on February 12, and 30 children are killed at a school in Bahr al-Baqr on April 8. These activities continue until April, when Soviet advisers, pilots, and missiles arrive in Egypt.

August 7, 1970   The War of Attrition between Israel and Egypt ends with a cease-fire after pressure from the superpowers.

September 1970   Fighting between King Hussein of Jordan's forces and Palestinian guerrillas begins. The period is known as Black September for its violence and the expulsion of Palestinian fighters from Jordan. President Nasser of Egypt helps to negotiate the end of this conflict. A terrorist organization subsequently adopts the name Black September.

September 6, 1970   The PFLP hijacks Swissair, BOAC (later British Airways), PanAm, and TWA flights and diverts them to Jordan, where 310 passengers are held hostage. The hijackers agree to release the hostages in exchange for the release of Palestinian prisoners. Lufthansa and Air France pay protection money in the aftermath of the hijackings.

September 28, 1970   Nasser dies of cardiac arrest after 15 years in power and is succeeded by Sadat.

November 16, 1970   The Corrective Revolution takes place in Syria by Hafez al-Assad, divesting Salah al-Jadid and his supporters of power.

February 22, 1971   Al-Assad is elected president of Syria.

May 30, 1972   The PFLP and the Japanese Red Army launch an attack at Lod Airport, killing 27.

September 5, 1972   Black September massacres the Israeli Olympic team in Munich. Israel launches a major manhunt for the assassins.

Yom Kippur War, October 6–24, 1973

Preliminary Moves

September 26, 1973   Egypt and Syria conduct military maneuvers. Israel is placed on alert, and an armored brigade is dispatched to the Golan Heights.

October 4–5, 1973   Sadat expels 15,000 Soviet advisers and all dependents. This is part of his reshaping of Egyptian foreign and domestic policies and is also aimed at Nasserists.

October 6, 1973   General Eliezer Zeira, Israeli director of intelligence, warns Lieutenant General David Elazar of an imminent attack, but Prime Minister Meir decides not to launch a preemptive strike.

Sinai Front

October 6, 1973   Egypt sends a massive air strike against Israeli artillery and command positions. At the same time, the Egyptians bombard the Bar-Lev Line along the Suez Canal, and the Syrians attack from the Golan Heights. Israel gives priority to fighting the Syrians in the Golan Heights.

October 6–7, 1973   The Egyptians begin their offensive toward the Suez Canal by sending commandos followed by infantry, engineers, and tanks. Engineers construct bridges, allowing the Egyptians to cross the canal. By October 8, 500 tanks cross the canal. Two Israeli armored divisions under General Ariel Sharon and Avraham Adan are mobilized.

October 8, 1973   Adan and Sharon conduct counterattacks against the Egyptian Second Army but are repulsed. Israeli air support suffers heavy losses against Egyptian antiaircraft defense.

October 11, 1973   The Egyptians launch a second offensive in the Sinai.

October 13, 1973   Operation NICKLE GLASS, a U.S. effort to airlift supplies to Israel, begins.

October 14, 1973   The Egyptian offensive in the Sinai is unsuccessful. The Egyptians suffer heavy losses, particularly in tanks.

October 15–16, 1973   The Israelis mount an offensive across the Suez Canal. Sharon strikes between the Second Army and the Third Army and establishes a bridgehead with a brigade of paratroopers.

October 17, 1973   Arab members of the Organization of Petroleum Exporting Countries (OPEC) embargo oil shipments to any nation supporting Israel. The embargo results in a full-blown energy crisis in much of the West and wreaks havoc on Western economies.

October 16–18, 1973   The Egyptian Second Army isolates Sharon's division east and west of the Suez Canal. Adan's division breaks through, however. Egypt is unable to isolate the Israelis and suffers heavy losses in tanks.

October 18–19, 1973   Adan's division continues to push westward, capturing Egyptian targets. Israeli planes attack ground targets. Sharon, however, is unsuccessful in seizing Ismailiyya.

October 20–22, 1973   Sharon continues his attacks on Ismailiyya but is met with resistance by the paratroopers and armored reserves of the Second Army and the Third Army. Adan is more successful in cutting the Suez-Cairo Road northeast of Suez.

October 22, 1973   Egypt and Israel agree to a cease-fire, which is soon broken. Israel deploys reinforcements to the Suez Canal.

October 23–24, 1973   Adan is ordered to continue his drive toward the Gulf of Suez and isolate the Third Army. General Kalman Magen follows Adan and reaches Adabiya. The Israelis make an attempt to take Suez but are unsuccessful.

October 24, 1973   Egypt and Israel agree to a second cease-fire.

Golan Heights Front

October 6, 1973   Syria conducts a massive air strike against Israeli positions on the Golan Heights.

October 6–7, 1973   The Syrian 7th Infantry Division is unsuccessful in taking Amadiye, north of Quneitra, and suffers heavy tank losses. The 3rd Syrian Tank Division similarly suffers heavy losses west of Amadiye. The Syrian 5th Mechanized Division breaks through the Israeli 188th

Armored Brigade. In two days, the 188th Armored Brigade is practically destroyed. The Syrians surround the Israeli Golan Heights command post. The 5th Mechanized Division halts its progress to resupply.

October 8–9, 1973   The Israeli 7th Armored Division conducts a counterattack and drives back the Syrian 1st and 5th Divisions toward the original line. The Syrians suffer heavy tank losses. The 7th Brigade repulses another Syrian attack north of Quneitra.

October 10–12, 1973   The Israelis conduct a counteroffensive north of the Quneitra-Damascus Road. Three Israeli divisions break through the first and second Syrian lines of defense near Sasa, close to Damascus. The Israelis halt their advance and redeploy their forces to the Sinai front. The Iraqi 3rd Armored Division attacks an Israeli position on October 11 but is unsuccessful.

October 15–19, 1973   The Jordanians and Iraqis counterattack. The Iraqi 3rd Armored Division and the Jordanian 40th Armored Division are repulsed by the Israelis on October 16. Another Arab attack led by the Jordanians is similarly repulsed on October 19.

October 22, 1973   Fighting ceases between the Israelis and the Syrians.

The Air War

October 6–8, 1973   Israeli aircraft first appear over the Sinai and Golan Heights fronts 40 minutes after the Arab attack and encounter Soviet-made missiles. The Israelis lose more than 30 aircraft. Egyptian SAMs inflict heavy losses on Israeli aircraft. For the first few days, Israeli air support is ineffective.

October 8–16, 1973   Israeli aircraft make greater contributions to the ground campaign using electronic countermeasures. As a result, the Israelis destroy bridges over the Suez and Arab airfields.

October 9–21, 1973   Israel conducts an aerial campaign against Syria, striking targets within Syria including the Ministry of Defense in Damascus. The Israelis strike Syrian seaports, factories, and fuel storage, profoundly affecting the Syrian economy.

October 17–24, 1973   The Israelis regain their air superiority over the Suez Canal. Adan captures Egyptian missile and antiaircraft defenses, disrupting Egypt's effectiveness.

The Naval War

October 6–25, 1973   Egypt announces a blockade over the Israeli coastline, disrupting Israeli commerce in the Mediterranean. Egyptian destroyers and submarines at the Strait of Bab al-Mandab disrupt traffic to Eilat.

October 6, 1973   Israeli Saar missile boats strike the Syrian port of Latakia (Ladhaqiyya). A Syrian squadron engages them, and the Israelis sink four Syrian vessels. The remaining Syrians withdraw to the port. The Soviet Union flies its technical advisers home from Syria and Egypt.

October 7–8, 1973   The Israelis make a second strike at Latakia. The battle ends with no decisive victory on either side. Israeli and Egyptian forces engage each other on the Mediterranean Sea and the Red Sea. Neither side gains a decisive advantage.

October 8, 1973   Israel sends El Al aircraft as part of an airlift program to procure supplies from the United States.

October 8–9, 1973   Israeli missile boats make a strike off Damietta. Egyptian vessels suffer severe losses and withdraw.

October 9, 1973   The Soviet Union begins to send supplies to Syria and Egypt through Hungary and Yugoslavia.

October 9–10, 1973   Israeli missile boats bombard Latakia, Tartus, and Banias without opposition from Syrian vessels. Israeli and Egyptian missile boats engage each other off Port Said. The Israelis sink three Egyptian vessels. The Egyptians withdraw to Damietta and Alexandria.

October 12–13, 1973   Israeli vessels attack Tartus and Latakia with little success.

October 15–16, 1973   Israeli missile boats sink Egyptian landing craft on the Nile Delta.

October 21–22, 1973   Israel attacks Abu Kir Bay and Alexandria, sinking two Egyptian patrol boats.

October 13, 1973   The United States augments the Israeli airlifts by sending American C5A transport planes to Israel through the Azores. Between October 14 and 21, the United States airlifts 20,000 tons of supplies against 15,000 tons from the Soviet Union.

October 24, 1973   The Soviet Union places seven airborne divisions on alert to be ready to be sent to Egypt.

October 25, 1973   U.S. secretary of state Henry Kissinger announces that the United States has placed its forces—including its nuclear assets—on precautionary alert based on the possibility that the Soviet Union might intervene in the Middle East, implying that the United States will respond in such an eventuality.

October 27, 1973   The UN Security Council votes to establish a peacekeeping force to enforce the cease-fire in the Sinai Peninsula and the Golan Heights. The decision by the Security Council to establish the UNEF defuses superpower tensions in the Middle East.

November 11, 1973   Egypt and Israel agree to exchange prisoners of war on the cease-fire line. In all, 241 Israelis and 8,031 Egyptians are returned to their respective countries. However, talks between both countries break down because neither would agree on disengagement.

January 18, 1974   Israel and Egypt agree on a disengagement plan after a week of shuttle diplomacy by Kissinger. Israeli troops agree to withdraw within 40 days from their position to a line 15–20 km from the Suez Canal, while the Egyptians will remain on the east bank of the canal. A buffer zone is to be established and will be patrolled by the UNEF. The Israeli withdrawal begins on January 24 and is completed by March 4.

February 28, 1974   The United States and Egypt resume diplomatic relations.

February–May 1974   Israel and Syria engage in a war of attrition along the Golan Heights that consists of artillery fire along the cease-fire line between Quneitra and Damascus.

March 18, 1974   The OPEC oil embargo against the United States comes to an end.

April–May 1974   Palestinian guerrillas engage in attacks from Lebanon into Israel. The most significant attacks are on Qiryat Shemona on April 11 and Maalot on May 15. In retaliation, Israeli aircraft bomb Palestinian bases in Lebanon. Civilian death counts are high on both sides.

May 31, 1974   Israel and Syria agree to disengage their forces after 32 days of shuttle diplomacy by Kissinger between Jerusalem and Damascus. Israel relinquishes all territory taken from Syria in the Yom Kippur War, two small strips taken in 1967, and the town of Quneitra but retains all of the Golan Heights. A cease-fire line, to be patrolled by the UNEF, is established between both countries.

July 1974   The Twelfth Palestinian National Council votes to establish sovereignty "on every part of Palestinian land to be liberated."

September 1974   The UN General Assembly debates the question of Palestine, voting 82 in favor, 4 against, and 20 abstentions for inviting PLO chairman Arafat to New York to address the body.

October 28, 1974   The Arab Summit at Rabat, Morocco, recognizes the PLO as the legitimate representative of the Palestinian people.

November 10, 1975   The UN General Assembly adopts Resolution 3379, which determines that Zionism is a "form of racism and racial discrimination" that countermands the UN's Declaration on the Elimination of All Forms of Racial Discrimination. Resolution 3379 is revoked by Resolution 46/86 on December 16, 1991.

1975   The Lebanese Civil War begins. Multiple grievances exist due to a feudal elite in each community with political challengers, economic disparities, and a long-standing conflict over Lebanon's identity, whether it is Arab, and closely affiliated with Syria and the Arab world, or "Phoenician" and Mediterranean, and Christian, and closer to France. An additional stressor is the presence of Palestinian refugees and militants. Some of the progressive or younger parties in Lebanon support the Palestinian cause, while the Christian Phalangists and others regard the Palestinians as a threat to their dominance and defense of a Christian Lebanon. External parties such as

Syria, Israel, Libya, and other Arab states also fuel the civil war for their own reasons.

1976   The PLO makes gains in municipal elections in the West Bank.

July 4, 1976   Hijacking of an Air France flight from Israel by Palestinian and German terrorists to Entebbe Airport in Uganda. Israel carries out a rescue mission and frees 100 hostage passengers, but 1 Israeli soldier, 45 Ugandans, 3 hostages, and the hijackers are killed.

May 1977   The Likud Party under Menachem Begin wins the Knesset election. Begin promotes and expands the building of Jewish settlements in the West Bank, which he considers to be the liberated territories of Judea and Samaria.

November 19, 1977   Sadat shocks the Arab world and pleases the West when he travels to Jerusalem and addresses the Israeli Knesset. There he emphasizes that true peace in the Middle East will not be possible without a solution for the Palestinians.

1978   Palestinians for the first time bring cases against seizure of their lands to the Israeli Supreme Court, arguing that the "military and security requirements" of the seizure do not rationalize the establishment of Jewish settlements on these lands.

March 11, 1978   A group of Palestinians lands on the Israeli coast and massacres 35 people. Three days later in retaliation, the Israeli Army launches Operation LITANI, a massive offensive of 25,000 troops into southern Lebanon. Some 285,000 Lebanese are displaced and become refugees, and 1,100–2,000 Lebanese are killed. Israel's partial withdrawal and creation of a surrogate Maronite force add to intersectarian tensions in the Lebanese Civil War.

September 5–17, 1978   The Camp David Accords, mediated by President Jimmy Carter, take place between Begin and Sadat. Sadat and Begin draft the Framework for the Conclusion of a Peace between Egypt and Israel, which establishes normal relations between both countries. Sadat and Begin are awarded the Nobel Peace Prize in December. The Camp David Accords are condemned throughout the Arab world as a betrayal of the Palestinian people.

October 8, 1978   Four of the six surviving members of Egypt's Revolutionary Command Council publish a memorandum to President Sadat in the *al-Safir* newspaper decrying the Camp David Accords because they fail to resolve numerous outstanding issues necessary for peace.

March 26, 1979   Sadat and Begin sign the Treaty of Peace between the Arab Republic of Egypt and the State of Israel.

March 31, 1979   Egypt is expelled from the Arab League, and its headquarters move from Cairo to Tunis.

April 30, 1979   The first Israeli ship passes through the Suez Canal.

May 9, 1979   Egypt is expelled from the Islamic Conference.

May 25, 1979   Israel begins its withdrawal from Sinai.

1980   Order No. 59 of the Military Government of Judea and Samaria facilitates more land seizures from Palestinians when a "specific area is declared to be government property." Israel and Egypt normalize relations by exchanging ambassadors. The Egyptian National Assembly repeals the boycott of Israel, and passenger flights begin between Israel and Egypt. Israel gains access to Sinai oil. Israel officially annexes all of Jerusalem.

June 7, 1981   Israel launches an aerial attack on the Iraqi nuclear power plant at Osiraq, which violates the terms by which the United States supplies aircraft to Israel.

July 17, 1981   Israel bombs Beirut, killing more than 450 Lebanese and Palestinians after a week of fighting that includes a naval attack as well. The PLO headquarters in West Beirut is targeted, although not exclusively.

September 1981   Egyptian authorities arrest more than 1,600 activists, intellectuals, and political figures.

October 6, 1981   Sadat is assassinated by army officers who are members of the Jihad organization while he views the October 6 victory celebration that commemorates the Ramadan War. Hosni Mubarak succeeds him as president of Egypt.

December 14, 1981   Israel announces the annexation of the Golan Heights in defiance of the U.S. position that returning the Golan Heights is a prerequisite for peace with Syria.

April 1982   Israel withdraws the last of its troops from the Sinai.

Israeli Invasion of Lebanon, 1982

June 4–5, 1982   Israel bombs Palestinian refugee camps and other targets in Beirut and southern Lebanon, killing 45 people. The Palestinians launch mortar and artillery attacks on northern Israel.

June 6, 1982   Israel launches an invasion of Lebanon called Operation PEACE FOR GALILEE. The goal is to create a 40-km security zone in southern Lebanon. However, since the Israelis push far beyond that limit, it appears that the goal is to evict all Palestinians and bolster a Lebanese government more favorable to Israeli interests. Some 17,825 Lebanese, Palestinians, and Syrians are killed.

June 9, 1982   Israeli forces move through the southern cities. All males aged 16–60 thought to be Palestinians are arrested through July. Nine thousand to 10,000 Lebanese and Palestinians are imprisoned, and 7,000 to 9,000 are held at Ansar near Nabatiya.

June 10, 1982   Israeli forces land at the beaches of Beirut and take control of its southern and western routes.

July 1982   Israel begins an intensive bombardment over West Beirut.

August 1, 1982   Israelis begin a massive air raid over West Beirut consisting of 127 sorties that day alone. The bombardment lasts for 10 weeks. Calls for a cease-fire by the United States go unheeded.

August 12, 1982   Israel announces a cease-fire.

August 13, 1982   The PLO announces its evacuation from Beirut, transporting its guerrilla fighters by land and sea to other sympathetic Arab states.

August 21, 1982   A multinational force arrives in Lebanon to oversee the PLO's evacuation. France deploys its Foreign Legion to supervise the PLO evacuation to Yemen and Tunisia. The United States and Italy send troops to oversee the PLO evacuation to Syria. In all, about 15,000 PLO fighters evacuated Lebanon. Israel begins withdrawing troops from Lebanon. However, Israel occupies a broad swath of the south with a proxy Lebanese force.

September 1, 1982   President Ronald Reagan proposes a peace plan calling for self-government in the West Bank and Gaza. The plan is rejected by the Israelis.

September 9, 1982   The multinational force leaves Beirut, believing that a full-scale attack has been averted.

September 14, 1982   Lebanese president Bashir Jumayyil is assassinated. Israel halts its withdrawal from Lebanon and reoccupies West Beirut.

September 16–18, 1982   The refugee camps of Sabra and Shatila are attacked by the Phalangists, a right-wing Lebanese militia group in association with the Israelis. The Phalangists massacre between 800 and 2,000 civilians with assistance from the Israeli Army. News of the massacre sparks protests and a demonstration by 400,000 people in Tel Aviv, and international outcries prompt an inquiry by Begin. The occupation of southern Lebanon sparks a resistance movement and results in the formation of Islamic Amal and eventually Hezbollah.

September 28–29, 1982   Israel withdraws from West Beirut. A multinational force of American, French, Italian, and British troops arrives.

February 1983   The inquiry on Sabra and Shatila results in the dismissal of Sharon as defense minister and the resignation of Begin as prime minister. Yitzhak Shamir succeeds Begin as prime minister.

April 18, 1983   Robert Ames, a leading Central Intelligence Agency (CIA) Middle East analyst, is killed along with 62 others in a suicide van bombing at the U.S. embassy in Beirut.

May 17, 1983   U.S. secretary of state George Shultz attempts to bring stability to Lebanon but is unsuccessful. The multinational force in Lebanon falls victim to the escalating violence in that country.

October 23, 1983   French and U.S. bases are attacked by Shiite suicide car bombers, causing the deaths of 78 French and 241 American marines.

February 8, 1984   Reagan announces the redeployment of American marines to ships offshore followed by British, French, and Italians troops. This ends the multinational force in Lebanon.

October 7, 1985   Palestinian militants hijack the *Achille Lauro*, killing Jewish American Leon Klinghoffer.

First Intifada, 1987–1993

December 8, 1987   An Israeli civilian truck crashes into a car at the Jabalya refugee camp in the Gaza Strip. Four Palestinian passengers in the car are killed instantly, and the others are injured. Palestinians accuse the Israelis of deliberately attacking them in retaliation for the stabbing of an Israeli in Gaza two days earlier. As the victims are buried, thousands of protesters storm an Israeli military outpost in Jabalya.

December 9, 1987   Palestinian civilians stay home from work, and demonstrations take place throughout Gaza and the West Bank. This is the beginning of a period of protracted all-out confrontation between the IDF and Palestinians.

December 22, 1987   The UN Security Council condemns Israel for violating the Geneva Convention due to the high number of Palestinian deaths in the initial few weeks of the intifada.

December 1987   Formation of the first unit of Hamas (Harakat al-Muqawama al-Islamiyaa) by Abd al-Aziz Rantisi, Salah Shihadah, and Yayha al-Sinuwwar. The movement gains the approval of Sheikh Ahmed Yassin.

January–March 1988   The Unified National Leadership of the intifada issues communiqués and establishes popular and neighborhood committees. This formalizes the uprising.

February–June 1988   Palestinians boycott Israeli products. A commercial strike begins. Merchants close their shops, and Israeli forces break them open. Merchants are also active in a tax boycott. Israeli taxes on the occupied territories are disputed under international law. Police and tax collectors are asked to resign. Israelis jail Palestinians in response, imposing heavy fines while seizing and disposing of the equipment, furnishings, and goods from local stores, factories, and even homes.

February 15, 1988   Abd al-Jawad Salah, a former mayor of Ramallah-al-Bireh (north of Jerusalem) who was expelled to Jordan, attempts to embarrass the Israeli government by organizing a boatload of Palestinian refugees called *The Ship of No Return,* equating the plight of Palestinian refugees with those of Jewish refugees of the *Exodus* in 1947. However, the PLO officers who purchased the ferry in Limassol, Cyprus, are found killed by an explosive planted in their car, and the ferry that was to have carried the refugees is sabotaged. The evidence appears to be linked to Israel.

April 16, 1988   Khalil al-Wazir (also known as Abu Jihad), PLO chairman Arafat's second-in-command and likely successor, is assassinated by an elite team of Israeli Mossad and commando units.

July 1988   King Hussein renounces all claims to the West Bank and acknowledges the PLO's authority over Palestine. A civilian bus en route from Tel Aviv to Jerusalem is commandeered by a gunman from Islamic Jihad, signaling the broadening of the intifada inside Israel.

September 1988   An international arbitration panel returns Taba to Egypt, Israel's last remaining outpost on the Sinai Peninsula.

October 30, 1988   A fire bomb destroys a bus near Jericho, killing five Israeli civilians. The bus bomb influences Israeli general elections, which result in a rise of seats going to right-wingers.

November 1988   The Palestinian National Council issues the Palestinian Declaration of Independence for a Palestinian state in the West Bank and Gaza.

December 13, 1988   Arafat addresses the UN General Assembly in Geneva, Switzerland. He announces his acceptance of Security Council Resolution 242, which affirms the right of every nation in the Middle East to peace and security and thus recognizes Israel's right to exist.

September 1989   Sixty-two Lebanese parliamentarians meet in Taif, Saudi Arabia. The Taif Accord, which is meant to settle the Lebanese Civil War, is ratified on November 4. However, the conflict continues.

September 17, 1989   Improved Israeli security on busses thwarts an attack on a bus en route from Tel Aviv to Jerusalem.

November 22, 1989   Newly elected Lebanese president Rene Muawwad is assassinated.

1990   A large influx of Jews to Israel from the former Soviet Union begins.

February 16, 1990   Members of Hamas carry a campaign of murder against Israeli soldiers by abducting them and killing them.

October 8, 1990   Jews and Muslims clash as Jewish fundamentalists announce their intentions to march on the Temple Mount, also a site holy to Muslims, on the Jewish holiday of Sukkot. More than 3,000 Muslims gather at the al-Aqsa Mosque after hearing rumors of a Jewish takeover. Muslims throw stones at Jewish worshipers praying beneath them at the Western Wall, the sole remnant of the ancient Jewish Temple. Policemen storm the Haram al-Sharif based on misinformation. In all, 19 Palestinians are killed, and 200 Palestinians and 11 Israelis are injured.

October 13, 1990   The Syrian Air Force attacks the Lebanese Presidential Palace, and as President Michel Aoun takes refuge in the French embassy, the Lebanese Civil War ends.

The Persian Gulf War, August 2, 1990–March 6, 1991

August 2, 1990   After months of rancor between Hussein and the Kuwaiti government over oil prices, alleged transverse

drilling by the Kuwaitis, and Iraqi debts to Kuwait, Iraq invades and occupies Kuwait with 100,000 troops. Some fear that Hussein will then invade Saudi Arabia.

August 8, 1990   Hussein announces the annexation of Kuwait by Iraq. Because of Arafat's support of Hussein, the Gulf states interrupt funds to the PLO.

January 6, 1991   French president François Mitterand proposes linking Iraq's pullout from Kuwait with the Palestinian question, but this is opposed by the United States. This proposal had been made earlier by the Soviet Union's Yevgeni Primakov.

January 9, 1991   U.S. secretary of state James Baker meets with Iraqi deputy prime minister and foreign minister Tariq Aziz in Geneva and gives him President George H. W. Bush's message ordering Hussein to withdraw immediately and unconditionally from Kuwait. A similar plea by UN secretary-general Javier Perez de Cuellar goes unheeded.

January 16, 1991   The air campaign against Iraq begins. Between January 18 and February 25, Iraq launches missile attacks over Israeli targets such as Tel Aviv. In all, 39 Scud missiles are launched. The United States assures its Arab allies that Israel would have no role in the Persian Gulf War and impresses upon the Israelis the importance of restraint.

February 24, 1991   The ground campaign begins.

February 27, 1991   The ground campaign ends after Hussein agrees to a cease-fire on U.S. terms.

March 3, 1991   The Persian Gulf War comes to a close upon Iraqi acceptance of a UN-brokered cease-fire agreement. Kuwait severs ties with the PLO and expels or pressures most of the 450,000 Palestinians there to leave.

October 31, 1991   Bush and Baker organize an international summit in Madrid, Spain, that involves the heads of governments of the Middle East and is sponsored by the United States and the Soviet Union. The summit provides bilateral negotiations among Israel, Syria, and Lebanon and a joint Jordanian-Palestinian delegation. At the Madrid Summit, it is agreed that Moscow will host five multilateral meetings to address regional issues.

January 29, 1992   An international summit is held in Moscow, as provided in the Madrid Summit, and results in the creation of a five-nation multilateral working group dealing with issues pertaining to the Middle East such as economic development, arms control, water, refugees, and the environment. A variety of factors inhibit the success of this process.

1993   Israel drastically restricts Palestinian travel from the West Bank and Gaza (except for East Jerusalem) to Israel, constituting the start of constant closures and restrictions on Palestinian movements.

Oslo Accords, September 13, 1993–July 25, 2000

January 1993   Secret talks in Oslo begin between Israel and the PLO. The Israeli delegation is led by two academics who report to Deputy Foreign Minister Yossi Beilin and are later joined by Foreign Minister Shimon Peres and Prime Minister Yitzhak Rabin. The Palestinian delegation is headed by Dr. Haidar Abdel Shafi and is instructed by the PLO from Tunis despite Israeli objections.

August 3, 1993   Rabin secretly asks U.S. diplomat Warren Christopher to convey orally to Hafez al-Assad that Israel is ready to withdraw from the Golan Heights, provided its requirements for security and normalization are met. Apparently, this is simply a ruse to gain time for the Oslo Palestinian track.

August 1993   The Palestinian and Israeli delegations draft the Oslo Declaration of Principles.

September 11, 1993   Israel and Jordan agree to move toward a peace agenda, culminating in a peace treaty.

September 13, 1993   Rabin, Peres, and Arafat sign the Oslo Declaration of Principles at a White House ceremony over which President Clinton presides. A huge anti-Oslo demonstration is held in Damascus.

February 25, 1994   Dressed in his IDF uniform, Baruch Goldstein, a member of the extremist Kach movement, massacres 29–60 (sources differ) Palestinians and injures another 125 who are praying the dawn prayer at the mosque area of the Cave of the Patriarchs. Only 1 of the 9 Israeli armed guards who should have been there is present. Survivors kill Goldstein.

May 4, 1994   Israel and the PLO sign the Cairo Accord. According to the agreement, the IDF will withdraw from Gaza and Jericho in the West Bank.

July 1, 1994   Arafat returns to Gaza for the first time in 25 years. He then establishes the Palestinian Interim Self-Governing Authority in Gaza and Jericho as part of the Oslo Declaration of Principles.

August 29, 1994   The Early Empowerment Agreement transfers responsibilities for education, health, culture, social welfare, tourism, and taxation to the Palestinian Authority (PA).

October 26, 1994   Israeli prime minister Rabin and Jordan's King Hussein sign a peace treaty on the border between both countries.

January 1995   Jordan relinquishes authority over Muslim sites in Jerusalem to the PLO, provided the PLO gains control over East Jerusalem. The Jordanian dinar is accepted as the currency of the PA.

January 22, 1995   Two suicide bombers from Islamic Jihad strike a bus stop filled with Israeli soldiers in Bayt Lid near Netanya. The bombing kills 22 Israelis and wounds 63. Israeli public opinion blames the PA for the attack. Israeli president Ezer Weizman suggests that Rabin suspend further negotiations, which Rabin claims would favor the terrorists.

February 1995   Arafat, Rabin, Mubarak, and King Hussein attend a summit meeting in Cairo to discuss the peace process. Foreign ministers Peres and Omani meet at Aqaba, Jordan, to discuss mutual interests.

March 1995   Israel participates in the Cairo International Trade Fair for the first time since 1987.

April 1995   Israel and Jordan formally exchange ambassadors. Israel and the PA agree to accept $60 million from international donors as part of a plan to meet the PA's budget shortfall.

April 9, 1995   Two suicide bombers attack Israeli targets in the Gaza Strip, killing 7 soldiers and 1 civilian and wounding 34.

May 1995   The PA gains control of banking, energy, industry, labor, and securities in the West Bank.

June 1995   Israel agrees to hand over civilian powers to elected officials in the Palestinian-controlled areas of the West Bank and Gaza after elections to be held in 1996.

July 24, 1995   A suicide bombing in Ramat Gan, near Tel Aviv, kills 6 people and wounds 32.

August 21, 1995   A suicide bombing strikes a bus near Jerusalem, killing 4 and wounding 106.

September 24, 1995   Israeli and Palestinian officials meet in Taba and agree on elections for a Palestinian council, withdrawal of Israeli troops, and extending self-rule for the Palestinians.

September 27, 1995   The Israeli Knesset approves the Taba Agreement.

September 28, 1995   President Clinton, Hosni Mubarak, and King Hussein meet in Washington, D.C., to encourage further negotiations between Israel and the Palestinians regarding the West Bank. This results in the signing of the Palestinian-Israeli Interim Agreement on the West Bank and the Gaza Strip, also known as Oslo II. According to the terms, Israel will withdraw troops from much of the West Bank by March 30, 1996, and hand them over to Palestinian political institutions. The area is divided into Areas A, B, and C. In turn, the Palestinians will eliminate all language pertaining to Israel's destruction in their National Charter. This is accomplished on May 4, 1996.

October 6, 1995   The Knesset agrees to the terms of the Oslo II accords by a vote of 61 to 59.

November 4, 1995   A right-wing Israeli student, Yigal Amir, assassinates Rabin in Tel Aviv after a culmination of tensions from the suicide bombings throughout the year weaken the Rabin government. Arafat does not attend the funeral services because of the security risk, but he pays his respects to Rabin's widow. Peres succeeds Rabin as prime minister.

January 5, 1996   Yahya Ayyash, the mastermind known as "the engineer" behind the bombings by Hamas, is assassinated by Israeli operatives. Israel imposes closures on the West Bank and Gaza to prevent retaliations.

January 20, 1996   The West Bank and Gaza hold elections for the Palestinian Council. Arafat's leadership in the PLO is confirmed by the elections. Fatah emerges as the victorious party, having won the most seats.

February 1, 1996   Peres announces early elections for May 29, 1996.

February 25, 1996   A six-month lull in suicide bombings comes to an end when a Jerusalem bus is targeted, killing 24 people and injuring 70. This attack is followed by another suicide bombing in Ashkelon in the Gaza Strip. A week later another Jerusalem bus is attacked, killing 19 and wounding 10. The next day, a suicide bomber strikes in Tel Aviv outside a mall, where 14 people die and 100 are injured. These attacks show either the inability or unwillingness of Arafat to contain radical elements such as Hamas and Islamic Jihad. Only after the Tel Aviv attack does Arafat take action by rounding up suspected members of Hamas and Islamic Jihad.

April 11, 1996   Israel launches Operation GRAPES OF WRATH, bombing Hezbollah bases in southern Lebanon as well as southern neighborhoods of Beirut and locations in the Bekáa Valley.

April 18, 1996   More than 100 Lebanese refugees die when the Israelis bomb a UN base at Qana, Lebanon.

April 26, 1996   The United States negotiates a truce and promotes an agreement in which Hezbollah will not attack civilians in northern Israel but has a right to resist the Israeli occupation of southern Lebanon. Lebanon and Syria do not sign the agreement. The Israel-Lebanon Monitoring Group, with a five-country membership, is established.

May 29, 1996   The string of attacks throughout the year in the aftermath of Rabin's assassination erodes confidence in Peres's government. Rightist politician Benjamin Netanyahu becomes the next prime minister.

August 1996   Netanyahu and Arafat meet for the first time, reaffirming their commitment to the Oslo Accords.

September 23–24, 1996   Israeli workers complete excavation of an archaeological tunnel underneath the wall of the Temple Mount and the Haram al-Sharif and also complete the construction of the gate to the Via Dolorosa, ostensibly to facilitate tourist traffic. To Palestinians, however, it is an example of Israel's tightening control over Muslim sites and property in East Jerusalem. Riots break out in East Jerusalem, Ramallah, and Bethlehem. Israelis and Palestinian police exchange fire.

September 25, 1996   The PA calls for a general strike in the West Bank. Clashes and riots break out in Gaza. Demonstrators attack a religious school in Nablus near the Tomb of Joseph, killing six Israeli soldiers.

September 27, 1996   Rioting subsides throughout the West Bank and Gaza. In all, 84 Palestinians and 15 Israeli soldiers are killed.

January 2, 1997   Arafat and Netanyahu draft the Hebron Protocol from a meeting on December 24, 1996. The agreement is signed on January 15. Israel agrees to withdraw from 80 percent of Hebron after months of delay. Both Israelis and Palestinians oppose the Hebron Protocol between Arafat and the Likud Party because it means dividing the West Bank, and this is attractive to neither side.

October 1998   Netanyahu and Arafat draft the Wye River Agreement. Israel will make further pullouts from the West Bank, giving Palestinians control over 40 percent of the territory. The agreement makes Arafat responsible for security in the region with assistance from the CIA. The Wye River Agreement comes under heavy criticism by both Palestinians and Israelis. Hamas protests Arafat's agreement to the security measures. Netanyahu faces resignations from his cabinet, and this erodes confidence in his government.

December 13, 1998   President Clinton makes a three-day visit to the Middle East to endorse his support of the Wye River Agreement. During a visit to Gaza, he addresses the Palestinian National Council and watches it confirm the official removal of clauses for Israel's destruction in its National Charter.

February 7, 1999   King Hussein of Jordan, a pivotal figure in the Arab-Israeli conflicts and the peace process, dies of cancer. Clinton, Mubarak, Weizman, and other major world leaders attend the funeral. Hussein's son, Prince Abdullah, succeeds him.

May 17, 1999   Because of declining confidence in his government, Netanyahu calls for elections. A coalition led by the Labor Party gains control of the Knesset. Ehud Barak is sworn in as the next prime minister on July 7, 1999. Barak meets with Arafat shortly thereafter to show his commitment to a peace settlement. Barak's agenda is to reconcile the Israeli public to a settlement in the Israeli-Palestinian conflict. Barak hopes that Clinton will use his influence to persuade Arafat to control elements such as Hamas and Islamic Jihad and prevent them from derailing the peace process.

September 1999   Negotiations presided over by U.S. secretary of state Madeleine Albright result in an agreement to reach final borders and a final settlement over Jerusalem within one year.

October 25, 1999   A 40-km land route, known as the Southern Safe Passage, between the West Bank and Gaza is established to prevent Palestinians from traveling in any other way through the country. The Northern Safe Passage, scheduled to open in November, is delayed.

January 5, 2000   Israel and Syria enter into peace talks mediated by the United States. However, the talks stall, which is a setback for Barak. At the same time, Hezbollah has been attacking Israeli positions in southern Lebanon.

March 22, 2000   Pope John Paul II makes a pilgrimage to Israel, visiting biblical sites. The pope is in favor of a Palestinian homeland. He also supports forgiveness and understanding between Jews and Christians.

May 15, 2000   The anniversary of Israel's founding is marked by an exchange of fire between Israeli and Palestinian security forces. Confidence in Barak's government is steadily declining.

May 22–24, 2000   Israel withdraws troops from southern Lebanon after 18 years. The withdrawal takes place not as planned but due to the collapse of the South Lebanon Army and Israelis under Hezbollah's fire. Lebanon declares May 25 an annual national holiday, Resistance and Liberation Day.

July 5, 2000   Clinton announces that Barak and Arafat have accepted his invitation to come to Camp David to make a final settlement. This is Clinton's opportunity to establish his presidential legacy as a peacemaker, having brokered the Good Friday Agreement between Great Britain and Northern Ireland in 1998.

July 11–25, 2000   The Camp David Summit takes place. Barak's proposals include partial Palestinian control of the West Bank, a Palestinian capital in part of Jerusalem, and shared control of the Temple Mount but do not grapple with other issues deemed crucial by the Palestinians. President Clinton strongly endorses Barak's proposals and offers economic assistance to Arafat should he accept. Arafat objects to the terms of the proposals in accordance with the majority Palestinian stance, particularly over the status of Palestinian refugees and Jerusalem. The Camp David Summit ends in failure.

Second (al-Aqsa) Intifada, 2000–2004

September 28, 2000   Sharon visits the Haram al-Sharif (Temple Mount), inciting violence by Palestinians from rock throwing to demonstrations in the Second (al-Aqsa) Intifada, which lasts until 2004. Israeli settlers retaliate against Palestinians. In the violence that ensues through October, 15 Israeli Arabs, 3,000 Palestinians, and 1,000 Israelis are killed.

October 17, 2000   President Mubarak hosts the Sharm al-Sheikh Conference addressing the violence between Israelis and Palestinians, which prompts the formation of the Mitchell Commission.

October 21–22, 2000   Mubarak hosts the Arab League Summit, convened at the request of Arafat in Cairo. The summit issues a statement in support of the intifada along with other declarations.

December 2000   Israelis and Palestinians attempt to renew talks in Washington, D.C., and at different locations throughout 2001 but reach nothing conclusive.

January 21–27, 2001   Israelis and Palestinians meet without mediators in Taba to discuss final status agreements.

February 6, 2001   Sharon is elected prime minister and promises peace and security.

February 12, 2001   The Israeli Army shells the refugee camp at Khan Yunis, injuring 115 people and destroying 20 homes. There are numerous reports of 180 civilians sick from a toxic gas sprayed on them.

March 2, 26, and 30, 2001   Reports that the IDF used a new toxic gas against civilians east of Gaza City, in Nablus, and in Bethlehem.

March 26–27, 2001   The Thirteenth Arab League Summit calls for the renewal of the Arab League boycott against Israel.

April 2001   The Mitchell Commission makes recommendations for restoring peace and a renewal for negotiations.

April 17, 2001   The Israeli Army reoccupies territory ceded to the PA in Gaza under the Oslo Accords.

June 1, 2001   A suicide bomber strikes at a discotheque in Tel Aviv and kills 20 Israelis, mostly teenagers. Islamic Jihad and Hezbollah claim responsibility.

June 13, 2001   CIA chief George Tenet hosts Israeli and Palestinian security officials in order to forge a truce.

July 9, 2001   Israelis demolish Palestinian homes, prompting demonstrations.

August 9, 2001   A suicide bombing by Islamic Jihad strikes a pizzeria in Jerusalem, killing 15 and wounding 130.

August 27, 2001   Israeli agents assassinate Abu Ali Mustafa, the secretary-general of the PFLP.

September 11, 2001   The Islamic terrorist group Al Qaeda, headed by Osama bin Laden, hijacks four U.S. airliners. Two of the hijacked planes strike the World Trade Center in New York City. A third hits the Pentagon in Washington, D.C. A fourth, allegedly bound for the White House, crashes in Somerset, Pennsylvania. Nearly 3,000 people die in the attacks. President George W. Bush begins the so-called war on terror soon afterward.

September 16, 2001   Israelis raid Jenin, two nearby villages, and Jericho, prompting gun battles.

October 17, 2001   In retaliation for the assassination of Mustafa, the PFLP assassinates Rehavam Ze'evi, Israel's tourism minister, because of his extreme right-wing views. Israeli troops enter Palestinian areas in the West Bank and begin a siege of six cities.

October 24, 2001   The siege continues, and Israelis kill 15 Palestinians overnight.

December 11, 2001   For the first time in Israel, parliamentary immunity is lifted to try an Arab member of the Knesset, Azmi Bishara, for undermining the state due to his sympathy for his community expressed in speeches in Umm al-Fahm and in Syria. He is also charged because he arranged for elderly Palestinian citizens of Israel to visit their relatives in Syria whom they had not seen since 1948.

December 13, 2001   The Israeli Army attacks Arafat's compound.

January 3, 2002   Israelis capture a boatload of illegal weapons en route to the PA as General Anthony Zinni from the United States arrives to mediate a settlement.

January 21, 2002   Israelis take over the entire town of Tulkarem, impose a curfew, and make house-to-house searches.

January 27, 2002   The first female Palestinian suicide bomber blows herself up, killing 1 person and injuring 100.

February 19, 2002   Palestinians raid an army checkpoint in the West Bank, killing six Israeli soldiers.

February 26, 2002   Prince Abdullah of Saudi Arabia announces a peace plan offering Arab recognition of Israel if Israel relinquishes the West Bank and other occupied territories.

February 28, 2002   The Israeli Army storms the Balata and Jenin refugee camps.

March–April 2002   Israel initiates Operation DEFENSIVE WALL in retaliation for the suicide bombings of the previous year. Palestinian leaders, including Marwan Barghuti, are arrested, and Arafat is surrounded in his compound in Ramallah by Israeli troops while they attack it and the city. Israeli forces surround the Church of the Nativity in Bethlehem where militants are hiding. Suspicions of atrocities arise from the Israeli assault on the refugee camp in Jenin where 50 people, including civilians, are killed. Israel refuses to cooperate with a UN investigation.

March 8, 2002   Israeli forces kill 40 Palestinians in the West Bank and Gaza.

March 12, 2002   Twenty thousand Israeli troops invade refugee camps and Ramallah.

Spring 2002   Many Arab employees such as gardeners, guards, and drivers in Israeli townships are replaced with other workers. Guards are hired for nurseries and supermarkets.

April 12, 2002   Battle of Jenin.

May 2002   Israel lifts its sieges of Arafat's compound in Ramallah and the Church of the Nativity. The head of the PFLP orchestrates a suicide attack from his cell in Jericho.

May 30, 2002   Arafat signs the Basic Law, which implements reforms in the government of the PA.

May–June 2002   An Israeli group, Fence for Life, collects signatures in Israeli towns for a security fence, arguing that it will keep the terrorists out.

June 24, 2002   Bush gives a speech calling for Israeli withdrawal from the occupied territories, the establishment of a Palestinian state, and reforms within the PA as well as for Palestinians to replace Arafat with another leader. Israel sends troops to the West Bank with the exception of Jericho.

July 23, 2002   Saleh Shihadah, the head of Hamas Izz al-din al-Qassam Brigades, is assassinated by Israelis.

August 16, 2002   Abu Nidal, the head of the Fatah Revolutionary Council, is assassinated by Iraqi secret police.

November 3, 2002   Labor Party ministers resign from Sharon's government.

January 5, 2003   Two suicide bombings by Hamas strike Tel Aviv, killing 23 people.

January 14, 2003   The London Conference on Palestinian Reform convenes and expresses a commitment to the Road Map to Peace and to statements on economic, political, judicial, and security reforms. Islamist movements claim that the PLO no longer represents the Palestinian people.

January 28, 2003   Israeli elections result in a victory for Likud and continue the premiership of Sharon.

February 2003   Israel mounts offensives in the Gaza Strip and Nablus.

March 5, 2003   A Hamas suicide bombing in a Haifa bus kills 17 people. A day later, a Qassam rocket from Gaza precipitates the Israeli reoccupation of parts of Gaza around the Jabalya refugee camp.

March 10, 2003   The Central Council of the PLO in Ramallah approves Arafat's proposal to choose a prime minister, Abu Mazen (Mahmoud Abbas), as part of Israeli and U.S. pressure to reform the PA.

March 19, 2003   The United States launches its invasion of Iraq after Saddam Hussein's repeated lack of cooperation with UN nuclear weapons inspectors.

April 9, 2003   Baghdad falls to the United States, and Hussein's regime falls after a quarter of a century in power.

April 24, 2003   Abbas becomes prime minister of the PA. The Quartet, consisting of the United States, Britain, Russia, and Spain, encourages further PA reforms and the Road Map to Peace. Israel also backs Abbas.

April 30, 2003   The United States releases details of the Road Map to Peace in the Middle East.

June 4, 2003   Abbas and Sharon vow to end violence and adhere to the Road Map to Peace. However, Hamas and Islamic Jihad continue their campaign of violence by killing four Israeli soldiers in Gaza.

June 11, 2003   A Hamas suicide bomber kills 14 in Jerusalem.

August 20, 2003   A Hamas suicide bombing kills 21 people in a Jerusalem bus.

August 21, 2003   Israeli agents assassinate Hamas leader Ismail Abu Shanat and other Hamas members in the West Bank. Arafat undermines Abbas's government by replacing Abbas's appointee Muhammad Dahlan as security chief in Gaza.

September 6, 2003   Abbas resigns as prime minister. Israeli agents are unsuccessful in assassinating Ahmed Yassin, the spiritual leader of Hamas.

September 8, 2003   Arafat names Ahmed Qurei as prime minister to replace Abbas.

September 10, 2003   Suicide bombers kill 15 in Israel. Israeli forces surround Arafat's compound the next day.

October 4, 2003   An Islamic Jihad suicide bomber kills 20 in an Arab Jewish–owned restaurant in Haifa.

November 19, 2003   The UN Security Council passes Resolution 1515 supporting the Road Map to Peace.

November 24, 2003   Sharon announces the Disengagement Plan calling for a unilateral withdrawal of Israeli forces if the Road Map to Peace fails to end terrorism.

December 2003   Beilin and Yasser Abed Rabbo launch the Geneva Accord peace plan. The UN General Assembly meets in an emergency session to adopt Resolution ES-10/14 asking the International Court of Justice to rule on the legality of the Israeli Security Fence (which Palestinians call the Racial Segregation Wall or Apartheid Wall) being erected.

February 24, 2004   The International Court of Justice begins its hearings on the legality of the Israeli Security Fence.

March 22, 2004   The IDF assassinates Hamas leader Yassin.

April 14, 2004   Sharon meets with President Bush, who supports the Israeli disengagement plan.

April 17, 2004   Hamas leader Abd al-Aziz Rantisi is assassinated by the IDF.

May 2004   The Likud Party votes down Sharon's disengagement plan. Israeli forces launch Operation RAINBOW to prevent arms from crossing Egypt's border into Gaza. The IDF demolishes homes and kills more than 40 Palestinians. Marwan Barghuti is found guilty on five counts of murder, but he also manipulates the show trial, challenging Israel's rights to subsume PA sovereignty. Sharon proposes a new disengagement plan.

July 9, 2004   The International Court of Justice rules that the Israeli Security Fence violates international law and must be torn down. Israel ignores the ruling.

July 12–19, 2004   UN envoy Roede Larsen is sternly criticized by Palestinian leaders for his claims of instability in Palestinian-controlled areas. In Gaza, factions within Fatah erupt into violence.

August 31, 2004   A suicide attack on a Beersheba bus kills 16 Israelis. This is the first successful attack in several months.

September 22, 2004   A suicide bomber attack on the French Hill section of Jerusalem kills one Israeli as Israeli troops launch operations in Gaza and the West Bank to capture would-be terrorists.

September 26, 2004   Mossad agents assassinate Hamas leader Izz al-Din al-Shaykh Khali, prompting Hamas to consider targeting Israelis outside Israel. The United States pressures Syria to close organizational offices that the United States identifies as terrorist.

September 29, 2004   Two children in the Israeli town of Sderot are killed by Qassam rockets launched from Gaza. Operation DAYS OF REPENTANCE goes into effect as Israeli troops occupy northern Gaza, demolishing houses. More than 80 Palestinians die as a result.

October 7, 2004   Israeli tourists and Egyptians are targets of suicide attacks in the Sinai desert at the Taba Hilton Hotel and Ras al-Shaitan. About 27 people are killed. The Tawhid wa al-Jihad, a group similar to Al Qaeda, is responsible for the attacks.

October 25–26, 2004   The Knesset approves the disengagement plan calling for withdrawal from Gaza, supported by the Labor Party and the Yahad Party. The Likud Party and National Union demand a referendum.

November 11, 2004   Arafat dies. Prime Minister Qurei assumes control of the PA, former prime minister Abbas heads the PLO, and Foreign Minister Farouk Qaddumi takes over the leadership of Fatah.

December 5, 2004   Egypt releases Azzam Azzam, an Israeli Druze jailed for eight years on highly publicized charges of espionage.

December 12, 2004   Hamas and Fatah Eagles destroy an Israeli Joint Verification Team terminal near the Egyptian-Gaza border, killing five Israeli soldiers by using explosives that were tunneled into the Gaza side of the border.

December 14, 2004   Egypt, Israel, and the United States sign a three-way trade agreement to allow Egypt and Israel to send exports to the United States without tariffs.

January 9, 2005   Abbas is elected president of the PA.

February 8, 2005   Sharon, Abbas, Mubarak, and King Abdullah II of Jordan meet at the Sharm al-Sheikh Conference to call for an end to violence. Israel agrees to release 900 Palestinian prisoners, and Egypt and Jordan agree to return ambassadors to Israel. The Second (al-Aqsa) Intifada, which has killed more than 4,000 Palestinians and more than 1,000 Israelis, is declared over.

February 20, 2005   The Israeli cabinet approves a plan for disengagement.

February 25, 2005   Islamic Jihad launches a suicide bombing that kills five Israelis in Tel Aviv, prompting Israel to freeze plans of handing over Palestinian towns.

February 2005   U.S. Army lieutenant general William E. Ward, appointed to the new post of U.S. security coordinator for the Israel-Palestinian Authority, arrives in Israel and remains there until August 2005.

March 16, 2005   Palestinian militant groups agree to a cease-fire in order to participate in May elections for the Palestinian Legislative Council. Israel pulls out of Jericho.

May 26, 2005   Abbas is received in the White House by President Bush and is promised economic assistance. Israel releases 400 prisoners and agrees to withdraw from Palestinian cities in the West Bank.

June 20, 2005   Wafa Bis is arrested at Gaza on her way to carry out a suicide bombing in an Israeli hospital.

Summer 2005   Palestinian infighting, particularly between Fatah and the al-Aqsa Martyrs Brigades, occurs in the West Bank.

June 30, 2005   Violence escalates in Gaza as Israeli settlers take over buildings, stone Palestinian homes, and attempt to lynch a Palestinian youth in the Al-Mawasi area. The IDF raids the Maoz Yam Hotel and other buildings in Gaza to evict 100 right-wing disengagement activists.

July 13, 2005   Islamic Jihad launches a suicide bombing at a Netanya mall, killing five civilians. The IDF reoccupies Tulkarem, and Hamas fires rockets on Israeli settlements and inside Israel. Israeli forces launch a campaign to capture Hamas members in Hebron and Gaza and renew the policy of assassinating terrorist leaders.

August 15, 2005   Israel begins its evacuation of settlements in Gaza and the West Bank.

September 1, 2005   The last Israeli soldiers leave Gaza, handing over control of the settlements to Palestinians by September 12.

September 15, 2005   Sharon addresses the UN and calls for peace and recognition of Palestinian rights while reaffirming Israel's claim on a united Jerusalem and its determination to fight terror. The Israeli Supreme Court rules that the security fence is not a violation of international law.

September 26, 2005   Sharon wins a victory over opponents of disengagement in Likud's Central Committee.

September–October 2005   Israeli forces begin arresting Hamas officials, including some moderates slated to run in the upcoming elections. This is to be the first election in which Hamas will participate.

October 2005   Palestinian elections are held. Fatah wins 55 seats, and Hamas wins 24 seats.

November 2005   Sharon leaves the Likud Party and forms the Kadima Party due to disagreements with Likud over disengagement. The border between Gaza is opened for Palestinians. However, Palestinian militants fire Qassam rockets near Sderot, prompting Israel to go back on opening a passage between Gaza and the West Bank.

January 4, 2006   Sharon suffers a massive stroke. Ehud Olmert succeeds him as acting prime minister.

January 26, 2006   Hamas wins a major victory in the Palestinian Legislative Council elections. Israel and the United States refuse to deal with the new Hamas government.

March 2006   The southern town of Sderot is attacked by 40 Qassam rockets. The IDF responds by destroying launching sites and mounting raids to kill leaders of militant groups and also attacking civilians in Gaza.

Spring 2006   Ninety-six thousand Palestinians remain political prisoners in Israeli jails according to the Mandela Institute. This figure includes 130 women.

The Second Lebanon War, Summer 2006

June 25, 2006   An Israeli soldier is captured in Gaza. The Israeli government demands his release and begins a military campaign against Lebanon as well as Gaza, which they had evacuated only the previous summer. Palestinian militants begin launching rockets into Israel.

July 2006   Israeli forces destroy the Palestinian foreign ministry in Gaza. Israeli security forces arrest Hamas leaders connected with Syrians as leverage to release the Israeli soldier.

August 2006   Olmert's cabinet authorizes a ground campaign 30 km into Lebanon after a bombing campaign that consisted of 8,700 sorties and destroyed 74 roads, 146 bridges, and 100,000 homes in Lebanon. At the same time, Hezbollah launches rockets into Israel. About 1 million Lebanese take flight. The UN Security Council issues Resolutions 1559 and 1680 to call for an end to the hostilities and the disarming of Hezbollah.

August 14, 2006   A UN-brokered cease-fire takes effect.

July 27–30, 2006   The IDF sweeps through Gaza carrying out attacks.

August 4, 2006   The IDF occupies Rafah and carries out house-to-house searches.

August 5, 2006   Israeli forces arrest Abd al-Aziz Duaik, the Speaker of the Palestinian Parliament, at his home. Although Duaik is a PA official, as a Hamas member they claim they can arrest him.

September 8, 2006   The Second Lebanon War comes to a formal conclusion.

November 8, 2006   Israeli artillery fire kills 19 Palestinian civilians, mainly women and children, at Bayt Hanun in northern Gaza.

November 22, 2006   Israeli forces attack Bayt Hanun and the Jabalya refugee camp in Gaza.

December 2006–February 2007   Fighting between Hamas and Fatah results in more than 80 Palestinian deaths.

February 2007   The Mecca summit meeting produces an agreement between Fatah and Hamas, which form a Palestinian unity government.

February 19, 2007   A peace summit attended by officials from Israel, the PA, and the United States ends with no visible results.

June 14, 2007   After several days of struggle with Fatah, Hamas gains complete control of the Gaza Strip.

June 16, 2007   Members of the Fatah-linked al-Aqsa Martyrs Brigades attack Hamas-controlled government buildings in Ramallah, West Bank.

June 17, 2007   Abbas swears in a new emergency cabinet as a result of the Hamas takeover. All 11 members are independents. Salam Fayyad is named as the new interim prime minister.

June 20, 2007   Hamas leaders warn that if Fatah continues to meddle with Hamas in the West Bank, Fatah will be defeated there as it was in Gaza.

June 25, 2007   Al Qaeda announces that all Muslims should support Hamas with weapons and money.

July 4, 2007   Alan Johnston, a BBC reporter held captive by the Army of Islam for almost four months, is released thanks to efforts by Hamas and Abbas.

July 5, 2007   Israeli soldiers backed by tanks and air support launch a raid into the Gaza Strip, killing at least seven militants, six of whom are identified as members of Hamas.

July 9, 2007   Abbas announces that the PA will not have contact with Hamas and calls for international peacekeepers to be stationed in and around Gaza.

July 10, 2007   Israeli prime minister Olmert urges Syrian president Bashar al-Assad to open direct talks between the two countries rather than wait for U.S. intervention.

July 25, 2007   The foreign ministers of Jordan and Egypt meet with Israeli top officials. Olmert declares that he wants to reach an "agreement on principles" that would promise the establishment of a Palestinian state on all of the Gaza Strip and 90 percent of the West Bank. The visiting foreign ministers are promoting a peace initiative first developed by the Arab League in 2002. The initiative offers Arab recognition of the Jewish state in return for a full withdrawal from the occupied territories and a just solution to the Palestinian refugee problem.

August 6, 2007   Talks between Olmert and Abbas in Jericho regarding peace are considered constructive, but no significant progress is announced.

September 2, 2007   The three-month siege of the Nahr al-Bared Palestinian refugee camp in Lebanon by the Lebanese Army, perpetrated in order to rout out members of the militant group Fatah al-Islam, ends.

September 6, 2007   Israeli aircraft destroy an unidentified facility in Syria, believed by the Israeli government to be a partially constructed nuclear reactor.

September 19, 2007   The Knesset votes unanimously to declare the Gaza Strip, home to some 1.4 million Palestinians, an "enemy entity."

October 15, 2007   U.S. secretary of state Condoleezza Rice states that the administration of President George W. Bush supports the creation of a Palestinian state.

October 25, 2007   Israeli defense minister Ehud Barak approves a plan that will allow Israel to reduce electricity supplies to the Gaza Strip in retaliation for rocket attacks into Israel.

November 13, 2007   During an event in Gaza to commemorate the death of Yasser Arafat, Hamas forces fire on Fatah demonstrators, killing 7 and wounding more than 50.

November 26–28, 2007   U.S. officials convene a peace summit in Annapolis, Maryland, between Israel and the Palestinians at which both sides agree to work continuously toward a final status agreement by the end of 2008.

DINO E. BUENVIAJE, DAVID ZABECKI, AND SHERIFA ZUHUR

References

Bell, J. Bowyer, *The Long War: Israel and Arabs since 1946.* Englewood Cliffs, NJ: Prentice Hall, 1969.

Bickerton, Ian J., and Carla L. Klausner. *A Concise History of the Arab-Israeli Conflict.* 4th ed. Upper Saddle River, NJ: Prentice Hall, 2004.

Bregman, Ahron. *Israel's Wars, 1947–93.* London: Routledge, 2000.

Herzog, Chaim. *The Arab-Israeli Wars: War and Peace in the Middle East from the War of Independence to Lebanon.* Westminster, MD: Random House, 1984.

Ovendale, Ritchie. *The Origins of the Arab-Israeli Wars.* London: Longman Group, 1992.

Peretz, Don. *The Arab-Israeli Dispute.* New York: Facts on File, 1996.

Seale, Patrick. "The Syria-Israel Negotiations: Who Is Telling the Truth?" *Journal of Palestine Studies* 29(2) (Winter 2000): 65–77.

Glossary

AAA	Antiaircraft artillery.
AAMs	Air-to-air missiles.
Abd	Arabic term meaning "slave" or "servant," often used in compound names.
ABM	Antiballistic missile.
ADC	Aide de camp (personal assistant to a flag officer).
AFV	Armored fighting vehicle.
ahl al-sunna wal-jamaa	Arabic for "people of the way" (or the Prophet), used to describe the community of Muslims. Often shortened to Sunni.
AK47	Russian-designed assault rifle, Automat Kalashnikov, manufactured throughout the communist bloc and considered to be one of the most successful infantry weapons of the 20th century.
al-futuhaat	Arabic name for the seventh-century battles that brought Islam to the region.
alim	A trained Muslim religious scholar. The plural form is "ulama."
aliya	Hebrew term meaning "to ascend," used to refer to the immigration of Jews to Palestine.
Allah	Arabic for "God."
al-Quds	Arabic for "sacred" or "holy," only used in reference to the City of Jerusalem.
amphibious warfare	Military activity that involves landing from ships, either directly or by means of landing craft or helicopters.

annex	The action of one nation in which it takes control of another territory and makes it a part of itself.
anti-Semitism	Hostility against those of the Jewish faith.
armistice	An agreement between opposing sides in a conflict to suspend military actions for a period of time.
ASM	Air-to-surface missile.
autonomy	Self-government.
AWACS	The Airborne Warning and Control System is a mobile, long-range radar surveillance and control center for air defense.
awlama	Arabic word for "globalization."
ayatollah	Arabic for "sign of God" and a title used for high-ranking Shiite clerics in Iran.
ballistics	The science of projectiles, divided into interior and exterior ballistics. Its aim is to improve the design of shells and projectiles so that increased accuracy and predictability are the result. Ballistics also deals with rockets and missiles.
bombing raid	A military tactic in which airplanes and seaplanes drop a successive number of bombs on specified targets within a short period of time.
breastworks	A barricade usually about breast high that shields defenders from enemy fire.
buffer zone	A piece of territory between two opposing groups.

caliph From the Arabic word *khalifa,* or "successor," a title given to Muslim leaders who followed the Prophet Muhammad as leader of the community after his death.

cease-fire A cease-fire, which occurs during times of war, may involve a partial or temporary cessation of hostilities. A cease-fire can also involve a general armistice or a total cessation of all hostilities.

coastal defense The defense of a nation's coast from an enemy sea invasion or blockade, accomplished with heavy artillery, mines, small warships, and nets.

Cold War The period of economic and military competition between the communist nations, led by the Soviet Union, and the capitalist nations, led by the United States, from the late 1940s to the early 1990s.

concentration camp An installation where prisoners of war, political prisoners, or other perceived enemies are held.

Crusades A number of military pilgrimages blessed by the pope in Rome and determined to retake the holy sites of the Middle East for Christian Europe. The first Crusades initially set European dominance in the region, but subsequent actions returned many sites to the hands of the Muslim leaders.

death squads Clandestine and usually irregular organizations, often paramilitary in nature, that carry out extrajudicial executions and other violent acts against clearly defined individuals or groups of people.

defense perimeter A defense without an exposed flank, consisting of forces deployed along the perimeter of a defended area.

deforestation The removal of the forest cover from an area.

demilitarized zone A piece of territory between two opposing groups in which military forces cannot be stationed.

desertification The process of desiccation or drying of climate in areas that historically experience a deficiency of precipitation. Desertification may be caused by climatic change, but the process may be exacerbated by removal of vegetation on desert margins.

dislocation The displacement of populations of people from one geographic location to another, most often caused by sudden and extreme situations of a political, military, or economic nature.

domestication The process of bringing animals and plants under human control and altering their genetic makeup by artificial selection into forms amenable to human use.

draft Conscription, or compulsory military service.

Druze A religious group based mainly in Lebanon and Syria.

echelon attack A refused advance on an enemy position, meaning that the advance occurred in sequence from right to left or vice versa in parallel but nonaligned formations. Ideally, an echelon attack would compel the reinforcement of those parts of the enemy line first assailed thereby to weaken the latter parts and increase the chances of breaching them, but more frequently such an attack becomes disorganized and falters in confusion.

economic warfare Compelling an enemy to submit either directly by action against its economic basis or indirectly through blockade or boycott.

electronic warfare The use of the electromagnetic spectrum to gain knowledge of the presence and movement of an opposing force and also to deny any opposing force the use of that spectrum.

emir Arabic title meaning "commander" or "prince."

enfilade To fire upon the length rather than the face of an enemy position. Enfilading an enemy allows a varying range of fire to find targets while minimizing the amount of fire the enemy can return.

envelopment To pour fire along the enemy's line. A double envelopment means to attack both flanks of an enemy and is a risky venture. A strategic envelopment is not directed against the flanks but rather is a turning movement designed at a point in the rear whereupon the enemy had to vacate his position to defend it.

espionage The practice of spying to learn the secrets of other nations or organizations. Espionage has always been an important component of any military operation.

ethics of war Rules, principles, or virtues applied to warfare.

ethnic cleansing A policy by which government, military, or guerrilla forces remove from their homes members of different ethnic communities considered to be enemies of the country.

Euphrates One of the two great rivers of Mesopotamia. The Euphrates is located to the west of the Tigris.

exodus The departure from a location by a large group of people. Also, the second book of the Torah describing the movement of the Hebrew slaves from Egypt to the land promised to them by God.

fatwa A judicial opinion made by a qualified Islamic scholar or mufti based on the Sharia. Traditionally, fatwas were used to settle legal disputes and to establish precedence. In modern times, fatwas have been used to proclaim judgments against non-Muslims and to support political agendas.

firefight A brief and violent exchange of small-arms fire between two opposing units rather than combat action between two larger forces during an assault.

fossil fuels Materials rich in carbon and hydrogen, these compounds (primarily coal, petroleum oil, and natural gas) are produced by decayed living matter. They have served as the major fuels for the last 200 years.

friendly fire Friendly fire describes the incidence of casualties incurred by military forces in active combat operations as a result of being fired upon by their own or allied forces.

global positioning system (GPS) A series of satellites that broadcast navigational signals by ultraprecise atomic clocks, providing accurate positioning.

guerrilla A type of warfare involving small groups, not part of the official government forces. A type of military action involving hit and run tactics against more powerful forces.

hafiz Arabic for "guardian." A person who has memorized the entire text of the Koran in Arabic.

hajj The annual pilgrimage to Mecca (in present-day Saudi Arabia) during the month of Dhul-Hijja in the Islamic lunar calendar. The hajj brings Muslims from all around the world to worship together. It is the fifth of the Five Pillars of Islam.

hegemony The dominance of one nation over other nations, based on the dominant nation's transfer of core values and basic societal institutions rather than through military conquest.

hijab Arabic for "cover." In many modern Muslim societies, *hijab* is used to refer to the head coverings or veils of women in public view.

Ikhwan al-Muslimin Translated often in English as the Muslim Brotherhood (or Society of Muslim Brothers). Founded by Hasan al-Banna.

imam Arabic for "leader." Sunni Muslims use the term for the leader of the Islamic prayers. Shiite Muslims believe that the imam is the divinely chosen leader of the people.

indemnity An amount of money paid by a nation defeated in war to the victor as compensation for damages it inflicted.

intelligence community The intelligence community comprises the government agencies charged with gathering information (intelligence) about other countries' military abilities and general intentions in order to secure a country's foreign policy goals.

international waters All waters apart from nations' territorial waters.

intifada Arabic for "shaking off." Often used for the uprising of Palestinians against the Israeli occupation of the West Bank and the Gaza Strip.

Islamic lunar calendar The traditional dating system of most Muslim societies, also referred to as the *hijri* calendar. It takes as its starting point the *hijra* and is a purely lunar system; that is, each month is determined by the actual cycle of the moon. Because this calendar does not use any system of intercalating days, it is shorter than the solar calendar by an average of 11 days a year.

Islamist Term used to refer to the movement of political Islam.

Ithnaashari Shiites The largest subsect of Shiism, also referred to as the Twelvers or Imami Shiites. They follow the teachings of 12 Imams descended from Ali and Fatima and believe that the Twelfth Imam has been in a state of mystical occultation since the 10th century.

jet engine An internal combustion engine in which hot exhaust gases generated by burning fuel combine with air, causing a rearward thrust of jet fluid to propel an aircraft.

Jordan River A river that flows 198.4 miles (320 km) from northern Israel, with tributaries in Syria, to the Sea of Galilee and thence through the nation of Jordan and the West Bank to the Dead Sea. The Jordan River's waters are a matter of importance and controversy to the nations of the area.

Kaaba	Structure at the center of the mosque in Mecca housing a mystical black stone. Muslims all over the world pray in the direction of the Kaaba, where Islamic tradition says that God's presence is most felt on Earth.
kibbutz	A commune that is often used for farming.
Knesset	The legislative body within the government of Israel.
Kurds	A numerous people inhabiting Kurdistan, a region that is the combined areas of south-eastern Turkey, northern Iraq, and western Iran. The Kurds speak an Indo-European language distantly related to Farsi, the language of Iran.
Lake Nasser	The reservoir impounded on the Nile River by the Aswan High Dam. The lake extends upstream into Sudan, where it is called Lake Nubia.
Levant	The geographical area comprising Israel, the Palestinian territories, Jordan, Syria, and Lebanon.
MAD	Mutual Assured Destruction.
madrassa	Arabic for "school." In common usage the word is used for religious schools. Originally, madrassas were institutions developed for the instruction of Islamic law. Madrassa courses have been expanded for the instruction of Muslim children in the ways of their community.
mandate	Official command from authority organization.
martial law	Martial law is the temporary military governance of a civilian population when the civil government has become unable to sustain order.
melee	Hand-to-hand combat resulting from an advance that has brought a body of troops into close quarters with an enemy.
mercenaries	Hired professional soldiers who fight for a state or entity without regard to political interests or issues.
Mesopotamia	Greek for "land between the rivers," the Arabic word is "Ma Bayn Nahrain." Both refer to the region known in the west as the Cradle of Civilization. Watered by the Tigris and Euphrates rivers, this area saw the rise of the Sumerian, Akkadian-Babylonian, and Assyrian civilizations. It is now a part of the nations of Iraq and Kuwait and includes parts of Iran, Turkey, and Syria.
militant	A supporter of a particular cause who utilizes aggressive, often violent action to make his or her point.
militarism	The view that military power and efficiency are the supreme ideals of the state.
mufti	A Muslim religious scholar charged with issuing religious opinions, or fatwas.
mujahideen	A term, literally meaning "those who engage in jihad," used to refer collectively to disparate groups of Islamic militants who fought against the Soviet occupation of Afghanistan in the 1980s.
Nasserism	A term coined from the name of Egyptian president Gamal Adbel Nasser. A particular form of Islamic nationalism grown from the policies and actions of Nasser.
nationalism	The understanding that a people organized into a nation are superior to another nation.
Nile River	The longest river in the world at more than 4,000 miles long, it is the primary water source for Egypt. The origins of the river are found in East Africa.
Nobel Prize	The Nobel Foundation was established in 1900, and it awarded its first annual prize in 1901.
Non-Aligned Movement	The Non-Aligned Movement was initiated by many Third World nations during the 1950s and 1960s in an attempt to steer a course of neutrality between the United States and the Soviet Union in the atmosphere of the Cold War. These countries felt that they had nothing to gain from entering direct alliances with either of the two superpowers, although they frequently courted both sides in attempts to gain greater amounts of economic and military assistance. The Non-Aligned Movement first met at the Bandung Conference in Indonesia in 1955. International meetings were held periodically over the next two decades, but the neutral nations were never able to formulate any cohesive policies because of the wide variety of member countries. With the end of the Cold War, the Non-Aligned Movement lost any importance that it once held in international affairs.
nonproliferation	A collective term used to describe efforts to prevent the spread of weapons of mass destruction short of military means.
paramilitary	Something paramilitary is organized after a military fashion.

paramilitary organizations	Unofficial groups organized along military lines yet lacking the traditional role or legitimization of conventional or genuine military organizations.
pastoralism	A way of life in which people care for, subsist upon, and control the movements of herds of large herbivorous animals, using their products such as meat, milk, skins, and wool. In the Mediterranean area the animals involved in pastoralism are most notably sheep, goats, cattle, horses, and camels.
peaceful coexistence	An expression that describes the act of living together without hostility, peaceful coexistence is often a foreign policy goal of nations that wish to avoid war.
political machine	A party organization staffed by city workers who were hired by the party into patronage jobs as a reward for their loyalty or service.
propellants	Compounds used to move a projectile from the firing device to the target.
Prophet	Refers to Muhammad. Islam theorizes that God's final revelation, completing the message of the prophets of Christians and Jews, came through his final prophet, Muhammad.
Ramadan	A month of the Islamic lunar calendar when Muslims fast from dawn to dusk.
rationing	Often implemented during a war, famine, or national emergency or in times of scarcity, rationing is a government policy consisting of the planned and restrictive allocation of scarce resources and consumer goods.
rearmament	The process that a nation undertakes to rebuild its arsenal of weapons that were exhausted during a time of war or other military action.
refugee	An individual who moves or is moved to another location.
renewable resource	A resource that is constantly replenished so that it can be used sustainably. Examples are forests, fish, and other animal and plant populations.
retrograde	An orderly retreat usually designed to move away from an enemy.
salat	The five daily prayers conducted at dawn, midday, midafternoon, sunset, and evening. It is the second of the Five Pillars of Islam.
salient	A military position that extends into the position of the enemy.
salvo	The simultaneous firing of a number of guns.
SAM	Surface-to-air missile.
sanctions	Activities taken against a nation by other nations to pressure them into a change of policy. There are political, economic, and military sanctions.
sawm	Arabic term for "fasting," the fourth pillar of Islam.
satellite state	A country that is under the domination or influence of another. The term was used to describe the status of the East European states during the Cold War.
Scud missile	Name given to a type of tactical ballistic missile developed by the Soviet Union during the years of the Cold War.
Semitic	A family of languages including modern Arabic and Hebrew, based on ancient languages of the region of the Middle East.
shahada	The first of the Five Pillars of Islam, it is the profession of faith for all Muslims. The profession translates into English as "There is no god but God, and Muhammad is his messenger."
Sharia	General term connoting the whole of Islamic law.
Shatt al Arab	A tidewater estuary found at the mouths of the combined Tigris and Euphrates rivers and stretching to the Persian Gulf. A portion of it forms part of the boundary between Iraq and Iran.
sheikh	Term of respect for older men (fem., sheikha) referring to people of wisdom or religious knowledge.
Shiites	Arabic expression for "partisans," referring to the partisans of Ali ibn Abi Talib, the cousin and son-in-law of the Prophet Muhammad. The Shiites, who now constitute about 10 percent of Muslims worldwide, support the claim that Ali and his family are the legitimate religious and political successors to the Prophet.
sortie	One flight by one aircraft.
standing army	Used since the Middle Ages, a standing army is a permanent military unit of paid soldiers.
Sunnis	Arabic expression for "people of the way [of the Prophet] and the community" that refers to the majority Muslim community. After the death of the Prophet, the earliest Sunnis were those who supported determining Muhammad's successor through community consensus rather than through blood lineage.

takfir — Arabic term used to declare that a Muslim group has strayed from the precepts of Islam. Often used by radical militant groups to justify violent actions against other Muslims. Al Qaeda is an extension of these radical Islamic fundamentalist groups, although Al Qaeda does not declare ordinary Arabs to be infidels.

Tigris — One of the two great rivers of Mesopotamia. The Tigris is located to the east of the Euphrates. The major sources of the Tigris are in the eastern part of modern Turkey and in the Zagros Mountains of Iran, and with the Euphrates it flows into the head of the Persian Gulf.

traverse — Sandbags or other obstacles placed along a trench to prevent enfilading fire.

UHF — Ultrahigh frequency.

ulama — Arabic term for "scholars" that refers to the body of knowledgeable scholars in Muslim society. Ulama often refers to the experts who study Sharia.

umma — Arabic term for "people" that refers to the community of Muslims around the world.

urbanization — The origin and growth of cities as areas of human habitation that include transportation, markets, government and religious buildings, and other infrastructure.

VHF — Very high frequency.

VLF — Very low frequency.

VSTOL — Very short takeoff and landing.

VTOL — Vertical takeoff and landing.

Wahhabism — A movement of scripturalist reformism initiated in the Arabian Peninsula by Muhammad ibn Abd al-Wahhab (d. 1792).

waqf — Endowments of land revenue established for the financial support of religious institutions such as mosques, schools, and charitable facilities.

war crimes — Violations of the laws and customs of war entailing individual criminal responsibility directly under international law.

war reparations — Restitution usually imposed by the victorious party as part of the peace negotiations at the end of a war.

Zagros — A mountain range in Iran that separates the Mesopotamian lowlands from the Iranian plateau. The Zagros marks the eastern margin of Mesopotamia.

zakat — Arabic term for "almsgiving," the third pillar of Islam.

Selected Bibliography

Abbas, Mahmoud. *Through Secret Channels: The Road to Oslo; Senior PLO Leader Abu Mazen's Revealing Story of the Negotiations with Israel*. Reading, UK: Garnet, 1997.

Abed Rabbo, Samir, and Doris Safie. *The Palestinian Uprising*. Belmont, MA: Association of Arab-American University Graduates, 1990.

Aboul-Enein, Youssef, and Sherifa Zuhur. *Islamic Rulings on Warfare*. Carlisle, PA: Strategic Studies Institute, U.S. Army War College, 2004.

Abu Amr, Ziad. *The Intifada: Causes and Factors of Continuity*. 2nd ed. Jerusalem: PASSIA, 1994.

———. *Islamic Fundamentalisms in the West Bank and Gaza: Muslim Brotherhood and Islamic Jihad*. Bloomington: Indiana University Press, 1994.

Abu Baker, Khawla. *Women, Armed Conflict and Loss: The Mental Health of Palestinian Women in the Occupied Territories*. Jerusalem: Women's Studies Centre, 2004.

Abu Nowar, Maan. *The Jordanian-Israeli War, 1948–1951: A History of the Hashemite Kingdom of Jordan*. Reading, UK: Ithaca Press, 2002.

Aburish, Said K. *Arafat: From Defender to Dictator*. New York: Bloomsbury, 1998.

———. *Cry Palestine: Inside the West Bank*. Boulder, CO: Westview, 1993.

———. *Nasser: The Last Arab*. New York: St. Martin's, 2004.

Adams, Michael. *Suez and After: Year of Crisis*. Boston: Beacon, 1958.

Adan, Avraham. *On the Banks of the Suez: An Israeli General's Personal Account of the Yom Kippur War*. Novato, CA: Presidio, 1980.

Aharoni, Dov. *General Sharon's War against Time Magazine: His Trial and Vindication*. New York: Steimatzky/Shapolsky, 1985.

Ahlstrom, Gosta W. *The History of Ancient Palestine*. Minneapolis, MN: Augsburg, 1993.

Ahmad, Eqbal, and Sheila Ryan. *Indirect Guilt*. New York: Nation, 1983.

Ahmad, Hisham H. *From Religious Salvation to Political Transformation: The Rise of Hamas in Palestinian Society*. Jerusalem: Palestinian Academic Society for the Study of International Affairs (PASSIA), 1994.

Akram, Tanweer. *Peace for Palestine: A Collection of Essays on Politics, Philosophy, and Economics*. Dhaka, Bangladesh: House of Consultants, 1997.

Al-Asi, Mohammad H. *The Duality of the Palestinian Issue: Islam, Al-Intifadah, the Future*. Bethesda, MD: Islamic Trend of North America, 1988.

Alexander, Edward. *The Jewish Idea and Its Enemies: Personalities, Issues, Events*. New Brunswick, NJ: Transaction Books, 1988.

Ali, Jaffer. *Palestine and the Middle East: A Chronicle of Passion and Politics*. Tempe, AZ: Dandelion Books, 2003.

Alimi, Eitan. *The First Palestinian Intifada and Israeli Society: Political Opportunities, Framing Processes, and Contentious Politics*. London: Routledge, 2006.

Allen, Peter. *The Yom Kippur War*. New York: Scribner, 1982.

Allon, Yigal. *Battles of the Palmach*. Tel Aviv: Hakibbutz Hameuchad, 1965.

———. *The Making of Israel's Army*. New York: Universe Books, 1971.

Al-Nashif, Mohammad Qadri. *The Palestinian Uprising: Beyond the Human Suffering; The Environmental Agony*. Irbid, Jordan: Dar al-Ketab, 2003.

Alofs, Ben. *More than Tear-Gas: Harassing Agents and Their Use in Israeli Occupied Territories*. Amsterdam: Dutch Palestine Committee, 1988.

Appel, Elliot. *Violations of Human Rights in the Occupied Territories: Annual Report 1990*. Jerusalem: B'tselem, 1989.

Arian, Alan. *Israeli Public Opinion and the War in Lebanon*. JCSS Memorandum No. 15. Tel Aviv: Tel Aviv University, Jaffee Center for Strategic Studies, 1985.

Arnon, E. *The Undercover Units: An Informational Pamphlet*. Berkeley, CA: Yesh Gevul, 1992.

Aronson, Shlomo, and Oded Brosh. *The Politics and Strategy of Nuclear Weapons in the Middle East: Opacity, Theory, and Reality, 1960–1991; An Israeli Perspective*. Albany, NY: SUNY Press, 1992.

Ashiurakis, Ahmed M. *The Palestinian Stone Revolution against Zionist Colonialism*. Misrata, Libya: Al-Dar Al-Jamahiriya Li-Nashr, 1988.

Asmar, Marwan. *Intifada II: Media & Politics*. Amman: Ad Dustour Commercial Presses, 2001.

Assaraf, Robert. *Le Drame d'Israël: De la Paix à la Guerre* [The Drama of Israel: From Peace to War]. Paris: Ramsay, 2001.

Atallah, Susan, and Toine Van Teeffelen. *The Wall Cannot Stop Our Stories: Diaries from Palestine, 2000–2004*. Bethlehem: Terra Sancta School for Girls, Sisters of St. Joseph, 2004.

Ateek, Naim Stifan, Marc H. Ellis, and Rosemary Radford Ruether. *Faith and the Intifada: Palestinian Christian Voices*. Maryknoll, NY: Orbis Books, 1992.

Avneri, Aryeh. *Sabra Commandos*. Tel Aviv: Olive Books of Israel, 1972.

———. *The War of Attrition*. Tel Aviv: Olive Books of Israel, 1972.

'Ayid, Khalid. *Al-Intifadha al-Thawriyya fi Falastin: Al-Ab'ad al-Dakhiliyya*. Amman: Dar al-Shuruq, 1988.

Azad, Abul Kalam. *Intifada: The New Dimension to Palestinian Struggle*. Dhaka: Bangladesh Institute of International and Strategic Studies, 1990.

Azar, George Baramki. *Palestine: A Photographic Journey*. Berkeley: University of California Press, 1993.

Bailey, Sydney D. *Four Arab-Israeli Wars and the Peace Process*. New York: St. Martin's, 1982.

Ball, George W. *Error and Betrayal in Lebanon: An Analysis of Israel's Invasion of Lebanon and the Implications for U.S. Israeli Relations*. Washington, DC: Foundation for Middle East Peace, 1984.

Barakat, Halim, ed. *Toward a Viable Lebanon*. London: Croom Helm, 1988.

Barari, Hassan A. *Israel and the Decline of the Peace Process, 1996–2003*. Abu Dhabi: Emirates Center for Strategic Studies and Research, 2003.

Barkai, Haim. *Reflections on the Economic Costs of the Lebanon War*. Jerusalem: Maurice Falk Institute for Economic Research in Israel, 1986.

Barnea, Amalia, and A. Barnea. *Mine Enemy*. London: Halban, 1989.

Bar-On, Mordechai, ed. *A Never-ending Conflict: A Guide to Israeli Military History*. Westport, CT: Praeger, 2004.

Baroud, Ramzy, et al. *The Second Palestinian Intifada: A Chronicle of a People's Struggle*. London: Pluto, 2006.

Baroud, Ramzy, and Mahfouz Abu Turk. *Searching Jenin: Eyewitness Accounts of the Israeli Invasion, 2002*. Seattle: Cune, 2003.

Bar-Siman-Tov, Yaacov. *The Israel-Egyptian War of Attrition, 1969–1970: A Case-Study of Limited Local War*. New York: Columbia University Press, 1980.

———. *Israel and the Intifada: Adaptation and Learning*. Jerusalem: Leonard Davis Institute for International Relations, Hebrew University of Jerusalem, 2000.

Bar-Yaacov, Nissim. *The Israel-Syrian Armistice: Problems of Implementation, 1949–1966*. Jerusalem: Magnes Press, Hebrew University, 1981.

Bawley, Dan, and Eliahu Salpeter. *Fire in Beirut: Israel's War in Lebanon with the PLO*. Briarcliff Manor, NY: Stein and Day, 1984.

Bayne, E. A. *Economics of a Victor: Comments on the Impact of War on Israel's Economy*. New York: American Universities Field Staff, 1967.

———. *Palaestina Infelix*. Hanover, NH: American Universities Field Staff, 1968.

Beaufre, André. *The Suez Expedition, 1956*. Translated by Richard Barry. New York: Praeger, 1969.

Begin, Menachem. *The Revolt*. Los Angeles: Nash Publishing, 1972.

Beilin, Yossi. *Israel: A Concise Political History*. New York: St. Martin's, 1992.

———. *The Path to Geneva: The Quest for a Permanent Agreement, 1996–2004*. New York: RDV Books, 2004.

Beinin, Joel. *Was the Red Flag Flying There? Marxist Politics and the Arab-Israeli Conflict in Egypt and Israel, 1948–1965*. Berkeley: University of California Press, 1990.

Beinin, Joel, and Rebecca L. Stein. *The Struggle for Sovereignty: Palestine and Israel, 1993–2005*. Stanford, CA: Stanford University Press, 2006.

Beit-Hallahmi, Benjamin. *Original Sins: Reflections on the History of Zionism and Israel*. New York: Olive Branch, 1993.

Beitler, Ruth Margolies. *The Path to Mass Rebellion: An Analysis of Two Intifadas*. New York: Lexington Books, 2004.

Belenky, Gregory Lucas, C. Frederick Tyner, and Frank J. Sodetz. *Israeli Battle Shock Casualties, 1973 and 1982*. Washington, DC: Walter Reed Army Institute of Research, 1983.

Ben-Gurion, David. *Israel: Years of Challenge*. New York: Holt, 1963.

Ben-Porat, Yeshayahu, Eitan Haber, and Zeev Schiff. *Entebbe Rescue*. New York: Delacorte, 1977.

Bennis, Phyllis. *Understanding the Palestinian-Israeli Conflict: A Primer*. 2nd ed. Lowell, MA: TARI, 2003.

Bennis, Phyllis, and Neal Cassidy. *From Stones to Statehood: The Palestinian Uprising*. Brooklyn, NY: Olive Branch, 1990.

Benvenisti, Meron. *Intimate Enemies: Jews and Arabs in a Shared Land*. Berkeley: University of California Press, 1995.

Berberoglu, Berch. *Power and Stability in the Middle East.* London: Zed, 1989.

———. *Turmoil in the Middle East.* Albany, NY: SUNY Press, 1999.

Bergen, Kathy, David Neuhaus, and Ghassan Rubeiz. *Justice and the Intifada: Palestinians and Israelis Speak Out.* New York: Friendship Press, 1991.

Berkman, Ted. *Cast a Giant Shadow.* Garden City, NY: Doubleday, 1962.

Bernadotte, Folke. *To Jerusalem.* London: Hodder, 1951.

Bernier, Michelle. *Summer of Silence: Congressional Response to the Invasion of Lebanon.* Washington, DC: American-Arab Anti-Discrimination Committee, 1982.

Berry, Mike, and Greg Philo. *Israel and Palestine: Competing Histories.* London: Pluto, 2006.

Betz, Don. *Notes from the West Bank and Gaza.* Tunis: Palestine Liberation Organization, Unified Information, 1988.

Biale, David. *Cultures of the Jews: A New History.* New York: Schocken, 2002.

Bishara, Marwan. *Palestine/Israel: Peace or Apartheid: Occupation, Terrorism and the Future.* New York: Zed, 2002.

Bix, Herbert P. *The Occupied Territories under Israeli Rule: On the Origins of the Intifada.* Sheffield, UK: University of Sheffield, 1991.

Bleaney, C. H. Lawless. *The First Day of the Six Day War: A Day That Made History.* London: Dryad, 1990.

Blincoe, Nicholas. *Peace under Fire: Israel/Palestine and the International Solidarity Movement.* London: Verso, 2004.

Blum, Howard. *The Eve of Destruction: The Untold Story of the Yom Kippur War.* New York: Perennial Books, 2004.

Blum, Yehuda Zvi. *Judea, Samaria and Gaza: The Israeli Record.* Jerusalem: Ministry of Foreign Affairs, 1979.

Bowen, Jeremy. *Six Days: How the 1967 War Shaped the Middle East.* New York: Thomas Dunne, 2005.

Boykin, John. *Cursed Is the Peacemaker: The American Diplomat versus the Israeli General, Beirut 1982.* Belmont, CA: Applegate, 2002.

Boyle, Francis. *Palestine, Palestinians and International Law.* Atlanta: Clarity, 2003.

Boyne, Walter J. *The Yom Kippur War and the Airlift Strike That Saved Israel.* New York: St. Martin's Griffin, 2003.

Brand, Laurie A. *Palestinians in the Arab World: Institution Building and the Search for State.* New York: Columbia University Press, 1988.

Bregman, Ahron. *A History of Israel.* New York: Palgrave Macmillan, 2003.

———. *Israel's Wars, 1947–93.* London: Routledge, 2000.

Brenchley, Frank. *Britain, the Six-Day War and Its Aftermath.* London: Tauris, 2005.

Bright, John. *A History of Israel.* 4th ed. Louisville, KY: Westminster John Knox Press, 2000.

Brooman, Josh. *The Arab-Israeli Conflict.* New York: Longman, 1989.

Brown, Nathan J. *Palestinian Politics after the Oslo Accords: Resuming Arab Palestine.* Berkeley: University of California Press, 2003.

Brynen, Rex. *Echoes of the Intifada: Regional Repercussions of the Palestinian-Israeli Conflict.* Boulder, CO: Westview, 1991.

B'tselem. *A Wall in Jerusalem: Obstacle to Human Rights in the Holy City.* Jerusalem: B'tselem, 2006.

Bucaille, Laetitia. *Growing Up Palestinian: Israeli Occupation and the Intifada Generation.* Princeton, NJ: Princeton University Press, 2004.

Bunche, Ralph. *Truce: In Connection with the Agreement Reached between the Arab and Jewish Military Commanders in the Jerusalem Area for the Demilitarization of Mount Scopus Area, Commencing Wednesday, July 7, 1948.* New York: Ralph Bunche Collection, United Nations, 1948.

Carey, Roane. *The New Intifada: Resisting Israel's Apartheid.* London: Verso, 2001.

Carlton, David. *Britain and the Suez Crisis.* Oxford, UK: Blackwell, 1989.

Casey, Ethan, and Paul Hilder. *Peace Fire: Fragments from the Israel-Palestine Story.* London: Free Association Books in Association with BlueEar.com, 2002.

Chaitani, Youssef. *Dissension among Allies: Ernest Bevin and Palestine Policy between Whitehall and the White House, 1945–47.* London: Saqi, 2002.

Chomsky, Noam. *Middle East Illusions.* Lanham, MD: Rowman and Littlefield, 2003.

Claire, Rodger W. *Raid on the Sun: Inside Israel's Secret Campaign That Denied Saddam the Bomb.* New York: Broadway, 2004.

Clancy, Tom, Tony Zinni, and Tony Koltz. *Battle Ready.* New York: Putnam, 2004.

Clarke, Gordon M. *The 1982 Israeli War in Lebanon: Implications for Modern Conventional Warfare: A Research Report Submitted to the Faculty in Fulfillment of the Research Requirement.* Washington, DC: National War College, 1983.

Clawson, Patrick, Michael Eisenstadt, and Nicole Brackman. *The Last Arab-Israeli Battlefield? Implications of an Israeli Withdrawal from Lebanon.* Washington, DC: Washington Institute for Near East Policy, 2000.

Clovis, Samuel H. *The Decision to Fight.* Carlisle Barracks, PA: U.S. Army War College, 1992.

Cobban, Helena. *The Palestinian Liberation Organization: People, Power and Politics.* New York: Cambridge University Press, 1984.

Cohen, Michael J. *Palestine and the Great Powers, 1945–1948.* Princeton, NJ: Princeton University Press, 1982.

———. *Truman and Israel.* Berkeley: University of California Press, 1990.

Cohen, Mitchell. *Zion and State: Nation, Class, and the Shaping of Modern Israel.* New York: Columbia University Press, 1992.

Cohen, Saul Bernard. *The Geopolitics of Israel's Border Question.* Jerusalem: Jerusalem Post, 1986.

Collins, John. *Occupied by Memory: The Intifada Generation and the Palestinian State of Emergency*. New York: New York University Press, 2004.

Collins, Larry, and Dominique Lapierre. *O Jerusalem!* New York: Simon and Schuster, 1972.

Comay, Michael. *U.N. Peace-Keeping in the Israel-Arab Conflict, 1948–1975: An Israel Critique*. Jerusalem: Leonard Davis Institute for International Relations, Hebrew University, 1976.

Coopersmith, Nechemia, and Shraga Simmons. *Israel: Life in the Shadow of Terror; Personal Accounts and Perspectives from the Heart of the Jewish People*. Southfield, MI: Targum, 2003.

Cordesman, Anthony H. *The Arab-Israeli Military Balance and the Art of Operations: An Analysis of Military Lessons and Trends and Implications for Future Conflicts*. Washington, DC: American Enterprise Institute for Public Policy Research, 1987.

Cristol, A. Jay. *The Liberty Incident: The 1967 Israeli Attack on the US Navy Spy Ship*. Washington, DC: Brassey's, 2002.

Crosbie, Sylvia K. *A Tacit Alliance: France and Israel from Suez to the Six-Day War*. Princeton, NJ: Princeton University Press, 1974.

Damas, Michael J. *The Day Israel Died . . . And Lived*. Philadelphia: Dorrance, 1974.

Darraj, Susan Muaddi. *Bashar Al-Assad*. New York: Chelsea House, 2005.

———. *Hosni Mubarak*. New York: Chelsea House, 2007.

Davies, Rhona, and Peter R. Johnson. *The Uzi and the Stone: Images of Gaza*. Calgary: Detselig Enterprises, 1991.

Davis, M. Thomas. *40km into Lebanon: Israel's 1982 Invasion*. Washington, DC: National Defense University Press, 1987.

Davis, Uri. *Crossing the Border: An Autobiography of an Anti-Zionist Palestinian Jew*. 1st English ed. Ealing, London: Books and Books, 1995.

Dayan, Moshe. *Breakthrough*. New York: Knopf, 1981.

———. *Diary of the Sinai Campaign*. Cambridge, MA: Da Capo, 1991.

Dershowitz, Alan M. *The Case for Israel*. New York: Wiley, 2004.

Diehl, Paul F. *A Road Map to War: Territorial Dimensions of International Conflict*. Nashville: Vanderbilt University Press, 1999.

Drucker, Raviv. *Harakiri: Ehud Barak Be-Mivhan Ha-Totsaah*. Tel Aviv: Yedi'ot aharonot, Sifre hemed, 2002.

Drury, Richard Toshiyuki, Robert C. Winn, and Michael O'Connor. *Plowshares and Swords: The Economics of Occupation in the West Bank*. Boston: Beacon, 1992.

Dumper, Michael. *The Politics of Sacred Space: The Old City of Jerusalem in the Middle East Conflict*. Boulder, CO: Lynne Rienner, 2002.

Dunnigan, James F., and Austin Bay. *A Quick and Dirty Guide to War: Briefings on Present and Potential Wars*. 3rd ed. New York: William Morrow, 1996.

Dunstan, Simon. *The Yom Kippur War, 1973*. 2 vols. Westport, CT: Praeger, 2005.

Dupuy, Trevor Nevitt, and Paul Martell. *Flawed Victory: The Arab-Israeli Conflict and the 1982 War in Lebanon*. Fairfax, VA: Hero Books, 1986.

Eban, Abba. *Abba Eban: An Autobiography*. New York: Random House, 1977.

Eden, Anthony. *The Suez Crisis of 1956*. Boston: Beacon, 1968.

Eisenstadt, S. N. *The Internal Repercussions of the Lebanon War*. Jerusalem: Hebrew University of Jerusalem, Leonard Davis Institute for International Relations, 1986.

El-Awaisi, Abd al-Fattah. *The Muslim Brothers and the Palestine Question, 1928–1947*. New York: Tauris, 1998.

El Edross, Syed Ali. *The Hashemite Arab Army, 1908–1979*. Amman, Jordan: Central Publishing House, 1986.

El-Hajj, Jamal. *Unifil in Lebanon: The Past and the Future*. Carlisle Barracks, PA: United States Army War College 1998.

Ellerin, Milton, and Micki Alperin. *Israel's Military Campaign in Lebanon*. New York: American Jewish Committee, Institute of Human Relations, 1982.

Elon, Amos. *A Blood-Dimmed Tide: Dispatches from the Middle East*. Rev. ed. London: Penguin, 2001.

Elon, Ari. *From Jerusalem to the Edge of Heaven: Meditations on the Soul of Israel*. Philadelphia: Jewish Publication Society, 1995.

El Shazly, Saad. *The Crossing of the Suez*. San Francisco: American Mideast Research, 1980.

Emerson, Gloria. *Gaza: A Year in the Intifada; A Personal Account from an Occupied Land*. New York: Atlantic Monthly Press, 1991.

Ennis, James M., Jr. *Assault on the Liberty: The True Story of the Israeli Attack on an American Intelligence Ship*. New York: Random House, 1979.

Epstein, Leon D. *British Politics in the Suez Crisis*. Urbana: University of Illinois Press, 1964.

Eshel, David. *The Lebanon War, 1982*. Hod Hasharon, Israel: Eshel-Dramit, 1982.

Espinosa, William. *Defense or Aggression? U.S. Arms Export Control Laws and the Israeli Invasion of Lebanon*. Washington, DC: American Educational Trust, 1982.

Espy, Richard. *The Politics of the Olympic Games*. Berkeley: University of California Press, 1979.

Evron, Yair. *War and Intervention in Lebanon: The Israeli-Syrian Deterrence Dialogue*. Baltimore: Johns Hopkins University Press, 1987.

Farhat, Albir, and Hanna Salih. *The Sun Rises from the South: The Israeli Aggression against South Lebanon; Facts and Testimony*. Beirut: Dar Al-Farabi, 1978.

Farsoum, Samih K., and Naseer H. Aruri. *Palestine and the Palestinians: A Social and Political History*. 2nd ed. Jackson, TN: Westview, 2006.

Feldman, Shai. *The Raid on Osiraq: A Preliminary Assessment*. Tel Aviv: Center for Strategic Studies, Tel Aviv University, 1981.

Feldman, Shai, and Heda Rechnitz-Kijner. *Deception, Consensus, and War: Israel in Lebanon*. Tel Aviv: Tel Aviv University, 1984.

Finkelstein, Norman G. *The Rise and Fall of Palestine: A Personal Account of the Intifada Years.* Minneapolis: University of Minnesota Press, 1996.

Fischbach, Michael R. *Records of Dispossession: Palestinian Refugee Property and the Arab-Israeli Conflict.* New York: Columbia University Press, 2003.

Fisk, Robert. *Pity the Nation: Lebanon at War.* Oxford: Oxford University Press, 2001.

Ford, Peter S. *Israel's Attack on Osiraq: A Model for Future Preventive Strikes?* Colorado Springs, CO: USAF Institute for National Security Studies, United States Air Force Academy, 2005.

Freedman, Robert Owen. *The Intifada: Its Impact on Israel, the Arab World, and the Superpowers.* Miami: FL: International University Press, 1991.

———, ed. *The Middle East and the Peace Process: The Impact of the Oslo Accords.* Gainesville: University Press of Florida, 1998.

Friedman, Thomas. *From Beirut to Jerusalem.* New York: Anchor Books, 1995.

Fuller, Graham E. *The West Bank of Israel: Point of No Return?* Santa Monica, CA: RAND, 1989.

Gabriel, Richard. *Operation Peace for Galilee: The Israeli-PLO War in Lebanon.* New York: Farrar, Straus and Giroux, 1985.

Gamasy, Mohamed Abdul Ghani el. *The October War: Memoirs of Field Marshal El-Gamasy of Egypt.* Translated by Gillian Potter, Nadra Morcos, and Rosette Frances. Cairo: American University in Cairo Press, 1993.

Gat, Moshe. *Britain and the Conflict in the Middle East, 1964–1967: The Coming of the Six-Day War.* Westport, CT: Praeger, 2003.

Gaughen, Shasta. *The Arab-Israeli Conflict.* San Diego, CA: Greenhaven, 2004.

Gavron, Daniel. *Israel after Begin: Israel's Options in the Aftermath of the Lebanon War.* Boston: Houghton Mifflin, 1984.

Geddes, C. L. *The Arab-Israeli Dispute: An Annotated Bibliography of Bibliographies.* Denver, CO: American Institute of Islamic Studies, 1973.

Gelber, Yoav. *Israeli-Jordanian Dialogue, 1948–1953: Cooperation, Conspiracy, or Collusion?* Brighton, UK: Sussex Academic, 2004.

Gelvin, James L. *The Israel-Palestine Conflict: One Hundred Years of War.* New York: Cambridge University Press, 2005.

Gerson, Allan. *Management and Disposition: Israel, the West Bank and the Rule of International Law.* New Haven, CT: Yale Law School, 1976.

Ghabra, Shafiq. *Palestinians in Kuwait: The Family and Politics of Survival.* Boulder, CO: Westview, 1987.

Giacaman, George, and Dag Jorund Lonning, eds. *After Oslo: New Realities, Old Problems.* Chicago: Pluto, 1998.

Gilbert, Tony. *Israel—Where To? Constant War or Peace.* London: Liberation, 1982.

Glubb, John Bagot. *A Soldier with the Arabs.* New York: Harper and Brothers, 1959.

Golan, Matti. *The Road to Peace: A Biography of Shimon Peres.* New York: Warner Books, 1989.

Gold, Steven J. *The Israeli Diaspora.* Seattle: University of Washington Press, 2002.

Goldshtain, Yosi. *Eshkol: Biyografyah.* Yerushalayim: Keter, 2003.

Gordon, Hayim, Rivca Gordon, and Taher Shriteh. *Beyond Intifada: Narratives of Freedom Fighters in the Gaza Strip.* New York: Praeger, 2003.

Gordon, Matthew. *Hafez Al-Assad.* New York: Chelsea House, 1989.

Goremberg, Gershom. *The Accidental Empire: Israel and the Birth of Settlements, 1967–1977.* New York: Times Books, 2006.

Goren, Amos. *Mordekhai Maklef: Perakim Be-Hayav Shel Ha-Ramatkal Ha-Shelishi.* Tel Aviv: 'Am 'oved, 2002.

Gorst, Anthony, and Lewis Johnman. *The Suez Crisis.* London: Routledge, 1997.

Gowers, Andrew, and Tony Walker. *Behind the Myth: Yasser Arafat and the Palestinian Revolution.* 1st American ed. New York: Olive Branch, 1992.

Grant, Michael. *The Jews in the Roman World.* New York: Scribner, 1973.

Greffenius, Steven. *The Logic of Conflict: Making War and Peace in the Middle East.* Armonk, NY: M. E. Sharpe, 1993.

Haber, Eitan. *Menahem Begin: The Legend and the Man.* New York: Delacorte, 1978.

Hadawi, Sami. *Bitter Harvest: Palestine between 1914–1967.* New York: New World Press, 1967.

———. *The Middle East Reality: Between War and Peace.* Dallas, TX: American-Arab Society, 1974.

———. *The Realities of Terrorism & Retaliation.* 2nd ed. Toronto: Arab Palestine Association, 1987.

Hahn, Peter. *Caught in the Middle East: U.S. Policy toward the Arab-Israeli Conflict, 1945–1961.* Chapel Hill: University of North Carolina, 2004.

———. *The United States, Great Britain, and Egypt, 1945–1956: Strategy and Diplomacy in the Early Cold War.* Chapel Hill: University of North Carolina Press, 1991.

Hajjar, Sami G. *Hezbollah: Terrorism, National Liberation, or Menace?* Carlisle Barracks, PA: Strategic Studies Institute, U.S. Army War College, 2002.

Hall, John G. *Palestinian Authority: Creation of the Modern Middle East.* Langhorne, PA: Chelsea House, 2002.

Hammel, Eric. *Six Days in June: How Israel Won the 1967 Arab-Israeli War.* New York: Scribner, 1992.

Hammer, Joshua. *A Season in Bethlehem: Unholy War in a Sacred Place.* New York: Free Press, 2004.

Hammer, Julianne. *Palestinians Born in Exile: Diaspora and the Search for a Homeland.* Cairo: American University in Cairo Press, 2005.

Hamzeh, Muna. *The Language of Occupation: Refugees in Our Own Land; Chronicles from a Palestinian Refugee Camp in Bethlehem.* London, UK, and Sterling, VA: Pluto, 2001.

Hamzeh, Muna, and Todd May. *Operation Defensive Shield: Witnesses to Israeli War Crimes.* London: Pluto, 2003.

Hanf, Theodor. *Coexistence in Wartime Lebanon: Decline of a State and Rise of a Nation.* London: Centre for Lebanese Studies and Tauris, 1993.

Harik, Judith Palmer. *Hezbollah: The Changing Face of Terrorism.* London: Tauris, 2005.

Harms, Gregory, and Todd Ferry. *The Palestine-Israel Conflict: A Basic Introduction.* London: Pluto, 2005.

Hart, Alan. *Arafat: A Political Biography.* Rev. ed. London: Sidgwick and Jackson, 1994.

Hass, Amira. *Drinking the Sea at Gaza: Days and Nights in a Land under Siege.* New York: Henry Holt, 1996.

Hasso, Frances S. "Modernity and Gender in Arab Accounts of the 1948 and 1967 Defeats." *International Journal of Middle East Studies* 32(4) (November 2000): 491–510.

Hastings, Max. *Yoni, Hero of Entebbe.* New York: Dial Press/J. Wade, 1979.

Hatina, Meir. *Islam and Salvation in Palestine: The Islamic Jihad Movement.* Syracuse, NY: Syracuse University Press, 2001.

Heiburg, M., and G. Hovensen, eds. *Palestinian Society, 1993.* Oslo: Falch Hurtygtrykk, 1993.

Heikal, Mohammed Hasanayn. *The Road to Ramadan.* New York: Quadrangle/New York Times Book Company, 1975.

Hentoff, Nat. *The Silence of American Jews.* New York: News Group Publications, 1982.

Hertling, Mark Phillip. *Insights Garnered and Gained: Military Theory and Operation Peace for Galilee.* Fort Leavenworth, KS: School of Advanced Military Studies, U.S. Army Command and General Staff College, 1988.

Herzog, Chaim. *The Arab-Israeli Wars: War and Peace in the Middle East from the War of Independence to Lebanon.* Westminster, MD: Random House, 1984.

———. *The War of Atonement: The Inside Story of the Yom Kippur War.* London: Greenhill, 2003.

Heydemann, Steven, ed. *War, Institutions and Social Change in the Middle East.* Berkeley: University of California Press, 2000.

Hill, Christopher. *Olympic Politics.* 2nd ed. Manchester, UK: Manchester University Press, 1996.

Hiltermann, Joost R. *Behind the Intifada: Labor and Women's Movements in the Occupied Territories.* Princeton, NJ: Princeton University Press, 1991.

Hirst, David, and Irene Beeson. *Sadat.* London: Faber and Faber, 1981.

Hirszowicz, Lukasz. *The Third Reich and the Arab East.* London: Routledge, 1966.

Hof, Frederic C. *Beyond the Boundary: Lebanon, Israel, and the Challenge of Change.* Washington, DC: Middle East Insight, 2000.

Holliday, Laurel. *Children of Israel, Children of Palestine: Our Own True Stories.* New York: Washington Square Press, 1999.

Holt, Maria. *Half the People: Women, History and the Palestinian Intifada.* East Jerusalem: PASSIA, 1992.

Horovitz, David Phillip. *Shalom, Friend: The Life and Legacy of Yitzhak Rabin.* New York: Newmarket Press, 1996.

———. *Still Life with Bombers: Israel in the Age of Terrorism.* New York: Knopf, 2004.

Hroub, Khaled. *Hamas: A Beginner's Guide.* Ann Arbor, MI: 2006.

———. *Hamas: Political Thought and Practice.* Washington, DC: Institute for Palestine Studies, 2000.

Hudson, Michael C. *The Palestinians: New Directions.* Washington, DC: Center for Contemporary Arab Studies, Georgetown University, 1990.

Hunter, F. Robert. *The Palestinian Uprising: A War by Other Means.* Berkeley: University of California Press, 1991.

Hunter, Robert E., and Seth G. Jones. *Building a Successful Palestinian State: Security.* Santa Monica, CA: RAND, 2006.

Hussain, Mehmood. *The Revolutionary Arabs: The Unfinished Agenda.* Delhi: Independent Publishing, 2003.

Ichilov, Orit. *Political Learning and Citizenship Education under Conflict: The Political Socialization of Israeli and Palestinian Youngsters.* London: Routledge, 2004.

International Crisis Group. *The Jerusalem Powder Keg.* Middle East Report 44, August 2, 2005.

Irmiya, Dov. *My War Diary: Israel in Lebanon.* London: Pluto, 1984.

Israelyan, Victor. *Inside the Kremlin during the Yom Kippur War.* University Park: Pennsylvania State University Press, 1995.

Jaber, Hala. *Hezbollah: Born with a Vengeance.* New York: Columbia University Press, 1997.

Jansen, Michael E. *The Battle of Beirut: Why Israel Invaded Lebanon.* Boston: South End Press, 1983.

Jiryis, Sabri. *The Arabs in Israel.* Translated by Inea Bushnaq. New York: Monthly Review Press, 1976.

Jones, Clive. *Between Terrorism and Civil War: The Al-Aqsa Intifada.* London: Routledge, 2005.

Josephus Flavius. Translated by G. A. Williamson. *The Jewish War.* Baltimore: Penguin, 1959.

Kahalani, Avigdor. *Derekh Lohem.* Tel Aviv: Stimatski, 1989.

———. *The Heights of Courage: A Tank Leader's War on the Golan.* Westport, CT: Praeger, 1992.

———. *A Warrior's Way.* New York: S.P.I. Books, 1993.

Kahalani, Avigdor, and Gil-Tani Mikhal. *Be-Khoah Ha-Emet.* Tel Aviv: Stimatski, 2002.

Kaleh, Hala, and Simonetta Calderini. *The Intifada: The Palestinian Uprising in the West Bank and Gaza Strip: A Bibliography of Books and Articles, 1987–1992.* Oxford, UK: Middle East Libraries Committee, 1993.

Karetzky, Stephen, and Norman Frankel. *The Media's Coverage of the Arab-Israeli Conflict.* New York: Shapolsky, 1989.

Karsh, Efraim. *The Cautious Bear: Soviet Military Engagement in Middle East Wars in the Post-1967 Era.* Jerusalem: Jaffee Center for Strategic Studies and the Jerusalem Post, Boulder, CO, 1985.

Kaspit, Ben Kafir Ilan. *Netanyahu: The Road to Power.* London: Vision, 1999.

Kassem, Maye. *Egyptian Politics: The Dynamics of Authoritarian Rule.* Boulder, CO: Lynne Rienner, 2004.

Katz, Samuel M. *Israeli Tank Battles: Yom Kippur to Lebanon.* London: New York, 1988.

Kaufman, Asher. *The Shebaa Farms: A Case Study of Border Dynamics in the Middle East.* Jerusalem: Hebrew University of Jerusalem and Gitelson Peace Publications, 2002.

Kayyali, Abd al-Wahhab al-. *Tarikh filastin al-hadith.* Beirut: al-Mu'asasa al-arabiyya lil-dirasat wa al-nashr, 1970.

Kazak, Ali. *The Jerusalem Question.* London: Radical History, 2006.

Kedourie, Elie, and Sylvia Kedourie. *Zionism and Arabism in Palestine and Israel.* London: Frank J. Cass, 1982.

Keller, Werner. *The Bible as History.* London: Hodder and Stoughton, 1956.

Kellerman, Barbara, and Jeffrey Z. Rubin. *Leadership and Negotiation in the Middle East.* New York: Praeger, 1988.

Kelly, Saul, and Anthony Gorst, eds. *Whitehall and the Suez Crisis.* London: Routledge, 2000.

Kennedy, David, and Richard Haass. *The Reagan Administration and Lebanon.* Pittsburgh, PA, and Washington, DC: Pew Charitable Trusts, 1994.

Khalid al-Faisal, Prince. *Jihad in Palestine & Afghanistan: The Second Exhibition of Paintings by H.R.H. Prince Khalid Al Faisal.* Riyadh: Al-Khozama Center, 1989.

Khalidi, Rashid. *Palestinian Identity: The Construction of Modern National Consciousness.* New York: Columbia University Press, 1997.

———. *Under Siege: P.L.O. Decisionmaking during the 1982 War.* New York: Columbia University Press, 1986.

Khalidi, Walid, ed. *All That Remains: Palestinian Villages Occupied and Depopulated by Israel in 1948.* Washington, DC: Institute for Palestine Studies, 1992.

———, ed. *From Haven to Conquest: Readings in Zionism and the Palestine Problem until 1948.* Washington, DC: Institute for Palestine Studies, 1987.

Khomeini, Imam. *Islam and Revolution.* Translated by Hamid Algar. Berkeley: Mizan, 1981.

Khouri, Fred J. *The Arab-Israeli Dilemma.* 3rd ed. Syracuse, NY: Syracuse University Press, 1985.

Kidron, Peretz. *Refusenik! Israel's Soldiers of Conscience.* London: Zed, 2004.

Kimmerling, Baruch. *Politicide: Ariel Sharon's Wars against the Palestinians.* London: Verso, 2003.

Kimmerling, Baruch, and Joel S. Migdal. *Palestinians: The Making of a People.* New York: Free Press, 1993.

Klein, Menachem. *Jerusalem: The Contested City.* Translated by Haim Watzman. New York: New York University Press, 2001.

Knohl, Dov, et al. *Siege in the Hills of Hebron: The Battle of the Etzion Bloc.* Abridged ed. New York: Thomas Yoseloff, 1994.

Koch, Howard Everard. *Permanent War: A Reappraisal of the Arab Israeli War.* Stanford, CA: Koch, 1973.

Kook, Rebecca B. *The Logic of Democratic Exclusion: African-American Citizens in the United States and Palestinian Citizens in Israel.* Lanham, MD: Lexington Books, 2002.

Korany, Bahgat, Paul Noble, and Rex Brynen, eds. *The Many Faces of National Security in the Arab World.* London: Macmillan, 1993.

Kramer, Michael. *Israel's Dream for Lebanon: Updating Ben-Gurion.* New York: News Group Publications, 1982.

Krishna Rao, K., ed. *The Arab-Israeli Conflict: Documents and Comments.* New Delhi: Indian Society of International Law, 1967.

Kurzman, Dan. *Ben-Gurion, Prophet of Fire.* New York: Simon and Schuster, 1983.

Lacouture, Jean. *Nasser, a Biography.* New York: Knopf, 1973.

Lamb, Franklin P., and John E. Dockham. *Israel's War in Lebanon: Eyewitness Chronicles of the Invasion and Occupation.* 2nd ed. Boston: South End Press, 1984.

Laqueur, Walter, and Yonah Alexander, eds. *The Terrorism Reader: The Essential Source Book on Political Violence Both Past and Present.* New York: Signet, 1987.

Lawrence, E. V. *Egypt and the West: Salient Facts behind the Suez Crisis.* New York: American Institute of International Information, 1956.

Lawrence, T. E. *Seven Pillars of Wisdom.* 1936. Reprint, New York: Anchor, 1991.

Legrain, François. "A Defining Moment: Palestinian Islamic Fundamentalism." In James Piscatori, ed., *Islamic Fundamentalism and the Gulf Crisis.* Chicago: American Academy of Arts and Sciences, 1991.

———. *Les Palestines du quotidien: Les élections de l'autonomie.* January 1996. Beirut: CERMOC, 1999.

Lenczowski, George. *American Presidents and the Middle East.* Durham, NC: Duke University Press, 1990.

———. *The Middle East in World Affairs.* 4th ed. Ithaca, NY: Cornell University Press, 1980.

Leone, Bruno. *The Middle East: Opposing Viewpoints.* St. Paul, MN: Greenhaven, 1982.

Lesch, David W. *The Middle East and the United States: A Historical and Political Reassessment.* New York: Perseus, 2006.

Levite, Ariel, Bruce W. Jentleson, and Larry Berman. *Foreign Military Intervention: The Dynamics of Protracted Conflict.* New York: Columbia University Press, 1992.

Lewis, Bernard. *The Crisis of Islam: Holy War and Unholy Terror.* London: Orion, 2004.

———. *What Went Wrong? The Clash between Islam and Modernity in the Middle East.* New York: Oxford University Press, 2002.

Lieblich, Amia. *Seasons of Captivity: The Inner World of POWs.* New York: New York University Press, 1994.

Livingstone, Neil C., and David Haley. *Inside the PLO.* New York: William Morrow, 1990.

Lockman, Zachary. *Comrades and Enemies: Arab and Jewish Workers in Palestine, 1906–1948.* Berkeley: University of California Press, 1996.

Lockman, Zachary, and Joel Beinin. *Intifada: The Palestinian Uprising against Israeli Occupation.* Toronto: Between the Lines, 1989.

Lorch, Netanel. *The Edge of the Sword: Israel's War of Independence, 1947–1949.* Norwalk, CT: Easton, 1991.

Louis, William Roger. *The British Empire in the Middle East, 1945–1951: Arab Nationalism, the United States, and Postwar Imperialism.* New York: Oxford University Press, 1984.

Louis, William R., and Roger Owen, eds. *Suez, 1956: The Crisis and Its Consequences.* New York: Oxford University Press, 1989.

Lukacs, Yehuda Battah Abdalla M. *The Arab-Israeli Conflict: Two Decades of Change.* Boulder, CO: Westview, 1988.

Lunt, James D. *Hussein of Jordan: Searching for a Just and Lasting Peace.* 1st U.S. ed. New York: W. Morrow, 1989.

Lustick, Ian. *Arabs in the Jewish State: Israel's Control of a National Minority.* Austin: University of Texas Press, 1980.

———. *From War to War: Israel vs. the Arabs, 1948–1967.* New York: Garland, 1994.

Maddy-Weitzman, Bruce, and Shimon Shamir. *The Camp David Summit: What Went Wrong? Americans, Israelis, and Palestinians Analyze the Failure of the Boldest Attempt Ever to Resolve the Palestinian-Israeli Conflict.* Sussex, UK: Sussex Academic, 2005.

Makovsky, David. *A Defensible Fence: Fighting Terror and Enabling a Two-State Solution.* Washington, DC: Washington Institute for Near East Policy, 2004.

———. *Making Peace with the PLO: The Rabin Government's Road to the Oslo Accord.* Boulder, CO: Westview, 1996.

Mandelbaum, Michael. *Israel and the Occupied Territories: A Personal Report on the Uprising.* New York: Council on Foreign Relations, 1988.

Mandell, Brian S. *The Sinai Experience: Lessons in Multi-Method Arms Control Verification and Risk Management.* Ottawa: The Division, 1987.

Mann, Peggy. *Golda: The Life of Israel's Prime Minister.* New York: Coward, McCann and Geoghegan, 1971.

Manna, Adil. *The Notables of Palestine at the End of the Ottoman Period (1800–1918).* (Arabic). Washington, DC: Institute for Palestine Studies, 1997.

Manor-Tamam, Keren. *Images in Times of Conflict: Al-Aqsa Intifada, As Reflected in Palestinian and Israeli Caricatures.* Jerusalem: Harry S. Truman Research Institute for the Advancement of Peace, Hebrew University of Jerusalem, 2003.

Mark, Clyde R. *The Arab-Israeli Conflict over Palestine: A Catalog of Issues and Problems As Defined by Opposing Arguments.* Washington, DC: Library of Congress, Congressional Research Service, 1971.

Marshall, S. L. A. *Sinai Victory.* New York: William Morrow, 1967.

Martin, Ralph G. *Golda: Golda Meir, the Romantic Years.* New York: Scribner, 1988.

Mattar, Philip. *The Mufti of Jerusalem.* New York: Columbia University Press, 1988.

Matusky, Gregory, and John Phillip Hayes. *King Hussein.* New York: Chelsea House, 1987.

McCormack, Timothy L. H. *Self-Defense in International Law: The Israeli Raid on the Iraqi Nuclear Reactor.* New York: St. Martin's, 1996.

McDowall, David. *Palestine and Israel: The Uprising and Beyond.* London: Tauris, 1989.

McNamara, Robert. *Britain, Nasser and the Balance of Power in the Middle East, 1952–1967: From the Egyptian Revolution to the Six-Day War.* New York: Frank Cass, 2003.

Meir, Golda. *My Life.* New York: Putnam, 1975.

Meisler, Stanley. *United Nations: The First Fifty Years.* New York: Atlantic Monthly Press, 1997.

Meital, Yoram. *Peace in Tatters: Israel, Palestine, and the Middle East.* Boulder, CO: Lynne Rienner, 2006.

Meo, Leila M. T. *The Arab Boycott of Israel.* Detroit: Association of Arab-American University Graduates, 1976.

Middleton, Drew. *Crossroads of Modern Warfare.* Garden City, NY: Doubleday, 1983.

Milgram, Norman A. *Stress and Coping in Time of War: Generalizations from the Israeli Experience.* New York: Brunner/Mazel, 1986.

Miller, Anita, Jordan Miller, and Sigalit Zetouni. *Sharon: Israel's Warrior-Politician.* Chicago: Academy Chicago Publishers, 2002.

Mingst, Karen A., and Margaret P. Karns. *United Nations in the Twenty-First Century.* 3rd ed. Boulder, CO: Westview, 2006.

Mishal, Shaul, and Avraham Sela. *The Palestinian Hamas: Vision, Violence, and Coexistence.* New York: Columbia University Press, 2000.

Mohammad Reza Pahlavi, Shah of Iran. *Answer to History.* New York: Stein and Day, 1980.

Mohammad Reza Pahlavi, Shah of Iran, and Teresa Waugh. *The Shah's Story.* London: M. Joseph, 1980.

Morris, Benny. *Israel's Border Wars, 1949–1956: Arab Infiltration, Israeli Retaliation, and the Countdown to the Suez War.* Oxford, UK: Clarendon, 1993.

———. *Righteous Victims: A History of the Zionist-Arab Conflict, 1881–2001.* New York: Vintage Books, 2001.

———. *The Road to Jerusalem: Glubb Pasha, Palestine and the Jews.* New York: Tauris, 2002.

Motro, Helen Schary. *Maneuvering between the Headlines: An American Lives through the Intifada.* New York: Other Press, 2005.

Nacer, Zabout. *A Child of the Intifada.* London: Minerva, 2001.

Nakdimon, Shelomoh. *First Strike: The Exclusive Story of How Israel Foiled Iraq's Attempt to Get the Bomb.* New York: Summit Books, 1987.

Nakhla, Muhammad. *Tatawwur al-mujtama' fi filastin.* Kuwait: Mu'assasat Dhat al-Salasil, 1983.

Nakhleh, Khalil, and Clifford A. Wright. *After the Palestine-Israel War: Limits to U.S. and Israeli Policy.* Belmont, MA: Institute of Arab Studies, 1983.

Nashashibi, Nasser Eddin. *Jerusalem's Other Voice: Ragheb Nashashibi and Moderation in Palestinian Politics, 1920–1948.* Exeter, UK: Ithaca Press, 1990.

Nassar, Alison Jones, and Frederick M. Strickert. *Imm Mathilda: A Bethlehem Mother's Journal.* Minneapolis, MN: Kirk House, 2003.

Netanyahu, Iddo. *Entebbe: A Defining Moment in the War on Terrorism; The Jonathan Netanyahu Story.* Toronto: Balfour, 2003.

Nir, Amiram. *After the Awali Line Redeployment: A Proposed Model for IDF Withdrawal from Lebanon.* Tel Aviv: Tel Aviv University, 1983.

Norton, Augustus R. *External Intervention and the Politics of Lebanon.* Washington, DC: Washington Institute for Values in Public Policy, 1984.

———. *Hezbollah: Extremist Ideals vs. Mundane Politics.* New York: Council on Foreign Relations, 2000.

———, ed. *Civil Society in the Middle East.* 2 vols. Leiden: Brill, 1996.

Nusaybah, Sari. *Palestine: A State Is Born.* The Hague: Palestine Information Office, 1990.

Nusse, Andrea. *Muslim Palestine: The Ideology of Hamas.* London: Routledge, 1999.

O'Ballance, Edgar. *The Arab-Israeli War, 1948.* London: Faber, 1956.

———. *The Palestinian Intifada.* New York: St. Martin's, 1998.

Olson, Steven P. *The Attack on U.S. Marines in Lebanon on October 23, 1983.* New York: Rosen, 2003.

Oren, Michael B. *Power, Faith, and Fantasy: America in the Middle East, 1776 to the Present.* New York: Norton, 2007.

———. *Six Days of War: June 1967 and the Making of the Modern Middle East.* Novato, CA: Presidio, 2003.

Oz, Amos. *The Slopes of Lebanon.* New York: Vintage International, 1992.

Pappe, Ilan. *Britain and the Arab-Israeli Conflict, 1948–51.* Basingstoke, UK: Palgrave, 1988.

———. *A History of Modern Palestine: One Land, Two Peoples.* Cambridge: Cambridge University Press, 2003.

———. *The Israel/Palestine Question: Rewriting Histories.* Minneapolis: Augsburg, 1999.

Parker, Richard Bordeaux. *The Ethnic Cleansing of Palestine.* New York: Oneworld, 2006.

———. *The Politics of Miscalculation in the Middle East.* Bloomington: Indiana University Press, 1993.

———, ed. *The Six-Day War: A Retrospective.* Gainesville: University Press of Florida, 1996.

Parsons, Nigel Craig. *The Politics of the Palestinian Authority: From Oslo to Al-Aqsa.* London: Routledge, 2003.

Patai, Raphael. *The Arab Mind.* New York: Scribner, 1976.

Pearlman, Wendy. *Occupied Voices: Stories of Everyday Life from the Second Intifada.* New York: Thunder's Mouth Press/Nation Books, 2003.

Pell, Claiborne. *Lebanon and the Prospects for Peace in the Middle East: A Report to the Committee on Foreign Relations, United States Senate.* Washington, DC: U.S. Government Printing Office, 1982.

Peres, Shimon. *Battling for Peace: A Memoir.* Edited by David Landau. New York: Random House, 1995.

Perlmutter, Amos. *The Life and Times of Menachem Begin.* Garden City, NY: Doubleday, 1987.

Perlmutter, Amos, Michael Handel, and Uri Bar-Joseph. *Two Minutes over Baghdad.* 2nd ed. London: Frank Cass, 2003.

Petran, Tabitha. *The Struggle over Lebanon.* New York: Monthly Review Press, 1987.

Pollack, Kenneth M. *Arabs at War: Military Effectiveness, 1948–1991.* Lincoln: University of Nebraska Press, 2002.

Pollock, David. *The Politics of Pressure: American Arms and Israeli Policy since the Six Day War.* Westport, CT: Greenwood, 1982.

Posner, Michael H., and Virginia Sherry. *An Examination of the Detention of Human Rights Workers and Lawyers from the West Bank and Gaza and Conditions of Detention at Ketziot.* New York: The Committee, 1988.

Prittie, Terence. *Eshkol: The Man and the Nation.* New York: Pitman, 1969.

Qattush, Atallah. *Shams al-Layl.* Jerusalem: Union of Palestinian Writers, 1988.

Qouta, Samir, and Eyad El Sarraj. *Palestinian Children under Curfew.* Gaza Strip: Gaza Community Mental Health Programme, 1993.

Qouta, Samir, Eyad El Sarraj, and Raija-Leena Punamäki-Gitai. *Impact of Peace Treaty on Psychological Well-Being: A Follow-up Study of Palestinian Children.* Gaza Strip: Gaza Community Mental Health Programme, 1994.

Raas, Whitney, and Austin Long. *Osirak Redux? Assessing Israeli Capabilities to Destroy Iranian Nuclear Facilities.* Cambridge: Security Studies Program, Massachusetts Institute of Technology, 2006.

Rabil, Robert G. *Embattled Neighbors: Syria, Israel and Lebanon.* Boulder, CO: Lynne Rienner, 2003.

Rabin, Lea. *Rabin: Our Life, His Legacy.* New York: Putnam, 1997.

Rabin, Yitzhak. *The Rabin Memoirs.* 1st English-language ed. Boston: Little, Brown, 1979.

Rabinovich, Abraham. *The Yom Kippur War: The Epic Encounter That Transformed the Middle East.* New York: Schocken, 2005.

Rabinovich, Itamar. *The War for Lebanon, 1970–1985.* Rev. ed. Ithaca, NY: Cornell University Press, 1986.

RAND Palestinian State Study Team. *Building a Successful Palestinian State.* Santa Monica, CA: RAND, 2005.

Raz, Eyal, and Yael Stein. *Operation Defensive Shield: Soldier's Testimonies, Palestinian Testimonies.* Jerusalem: B'Tselem, the Israeli Information Center for Human Rights in the Occupied Territories, 2002.

Reddaway, John. *Israel and Nuremberg: Are Israel's Leaders Guilty of War Crimes? A Preliminary Study.* London: International Organization for the Elimination of All Forms of Racial Discrimination, 1983.

Reese, Scott. *Colonial Pursuits: Settler Violence during the Uprising in the Occupied Territories.* Chicago: Database Project on Palestinian Human Rights, 1989.

Reinhart, Tanya. *The Road Map to Nowhere: Israel/Palestine since 2003.* London: Verso, 2006.

Rejwan, Nissim. *Israel's Years of Bogus Grandeur: From the Six-Day War to the First Intifada.* Austin: University of Texas Press, 2006.

Rigby, Andrew. *Economic Aspects of the Intifada.* East Jerusalem: Palestinian Academic Society for the Study of International Affairs, 1988.

Rikhye, Indar Jit. *The Sinai Blunder: Withdrawal of the United Nations Emergency Force Leading to the Six-Day War of June 1967.* London: Frank Cass, 1980.

Robertson, Terence. *Crisis: The Inside Story of the Suez Conspiracy.* New York: Atheneum, 1965.

Robinson, Glenn E. *Building a Palestinian State: The Incomplete Revolution.* Bloomington: Indiana University Press, 1997.

Rogers, Mary Eliza. *Domestic Life in Palestine.* 1862. Reprint, London: Kegan Paul International, 1989.

Rohr, Janelle. *The Middle East: Opposing Viewpoints.* St. Paul, MN: Greenhaven, 1988.

Roosevelt, Kermit. *Arabs, Oil, and History.* New York: Harper and Brothers, 1949.

Roth, Stephen J. *The Impact of the Six-Day War: A Twenty-Year Assessment.* London: Palgrave Macmillan, 1988.

Roy, Sara. *Failing Peace: Gaza and the Palestinian-Israeli Conflict.* Ann Arbor, MI: Pluto, 2006.

———. *Gaza Strip.* Washington, DC: Institute for Palestine Studies, 1995.

Rozenman, A. *Ha-Shamashim, Rupin Ve-Eshkol.* Jerusalem: Ha Histadrut ha-Tsiyonit ha-'olamit, 1992.

Rubenberg, Cheryl. *The Palestinians: In Search of a Just Peace.* Boulder, CO: Lynne Rienner, 2003.

Rubin, Barry. *The PLO: A Declaration of Independence?* Washington, DC: Washington Institute for Near East Policy, 1988.

———. *Revolution until Victory? The Politics and History of the PLO.* Reprint ed. Cambridge: Harvard University Press, 2003.

Rubin, Barry, and Thomas A. Keaney, eds. *Armed Forces in the Middle East: Politics and Strategy.* Portland, OR: Frank Cass, 2002.

Ruebner, Joshua. *The Current Palestinian Uprising: Al-Aqsa Intifadah.* Washington, DC: Library of Congress, Congressional Research Service, 2001.

Saad-Ghorayeb. *Hizbu'llah: Politics & Religion.* London: Pluto, 2002.

Sachar, Howard Morley. *Egypt and Israel.* New York: R. Marek, 1981.

———. *A History of Israel: From the Rise of Zionism to Our Time.* 3rd ed. New York: Knopf, 2007.

Sadat, Anwar. *In Search of Identity: An Autobiography.* New York: Harper and Row, 1978.

———. *Revolt on the Nile.* London: Wingate, 1957.

Sahliyeh, Emile. *In Search of Leadership: West Bank Politics since 1967.* Washington, DC: Brookings Institution, 1988.

Said, Edward W. *Intifada: The Palestinian Uprising against Israeli Occupation.* Boston: South End Press, 1989.

———. *Out of Place: A Memoir.* New York: Knopf, 1999.

———. *The Question of Palestine.* New York: Vintage Books, 1992.

Said, Edward W., and Christopher Hitchins, eds. *Blaming the Victims: Spurious Scholarship and the Palestinian Question.* London: Verso, 2001.

Salman, Rida, Randa Charara, and Yola Batal with revisions by Samir Jabour and Khalid Ayid. *Israel and the War in Lebanon: Assessments by Israeli Experts.* (Arabic). Washington, DC: Institute for Palestine Studies, 1986.

Saraste, Leena. *For Palestine.* London: Zed, 1985.

Sarraj, Eyad El. *Peace and the Children of Stone.* Gaza Strip: Gaza Community Mental Health Programme, 1993.

Sarraj, Eyad El, and Fadel Abu Hein. *Trauma, Violence and Children: The Palestinian Experience.* Gaza Strip: Gaza Community Mental Health Programme, 1993.

Satloff, Robert B. *Islam in the Palestinian Uprising.* Washington, DC: Washington Institute for Near East Policy, 1988.

Satloff, Robert B., ed. *War on Terror: The Middle East Dimension.* Washington, DC: Washington Institute for Near East Policy, 2002.

Sayigh, Rosemary. *Palestinians from Peasants to Revolutionaries.* London: Zed, 1979.

Sayigh, Yezid. *Armed Struggle and the Search for State: The Palestine National Movement, 1949–1993.* New York: Oxford University Press, 2000.

Schechla, Joseph. *The Iron Fist: Israel's Occupation of South Lebanon, 1982–1985.* Washington, DC: American-Arab Anti-Discrimination Committee, 1985.

Schechtman, Joseph B. *The Mufti and the Fuehrer.* New York: Yoseloff, 1965.

Schiff, Zeev. *The Green Light.* Washington, DC: Carnegie Endowment for International Peace, 1983.

———. *Israel's Lebanon War.* London: Unwin Paperbacks, 1986.

Schleifer, Ron. *Psychological Warfare in the Intifada: Israeli and Palestinian Media Politics and Military Strategies.* Sussex, UK: Sussex Academic, 2006.

Schoenman, Ralph. *Homage to Palestine.* Santa Barbara, CA: Veritas, 1991.

Schou, Arild. *The Emergence of a Public Political Elite in the West Bank during the Palestinian Uprising (1987–1991).* Oslo: NIBR, 1996.

Schow, Kenneth C. *Falcons against the Jihad: Israeli Airpower and Coercive Diplomacy in Southern Lebanon.* Maxwell Air Force Base, AL: Air University Press, 1995.

Schulze, Kirsten E. *Israel's Covert Diplomacy in Lebanon.* New York: St. Martin's, 1998.

Seikaly, May. *Haifa: Transformation of Arab Society, 1918–1939.* London: Tauris, 1995.

Sela, Avraham, and Moshe Ma'oz. *The PLO and Israel: From Armed Conflict to Political Solution, 1964–1994.* Basingstoke: Macmillan, 1997.

Selfa, Lance. *The Struggle for Palestine.* Chicago: Haymarket Books, 2002.

Senker, Cath. *Defiance: Palestinian Women in the Uprising.* London: Israeli Mirror, 1989.

Segev, Tom. *One Palestine, Complete: Jews and Arabs under the British Mandate.* New York: Owl Books, 2001.

Shamir, Yitzhak. *Summing Up: An Autobiography.* London: Orion, 1994.

Shapira, Anita. *Yigal Alon, Aviv Heldo: Biografyah.* Tel Aviv: Ha-Kibuts ha-meuhad, 2004.

Sharon, Ariel, and David Chanoff. *Warrior: An Autobiography.* 2nd ed. New York: Simon and Schuster, 2001.

Sheffer, Gabriel. *Moshe Sharett: Biography of a Political Moderate.* New York: Oxford University Press, 1996.

Shepherd, Naomi. *Ploughing Sand: British Rule in Palestine, 1917–1948.* New Brunswick, NJ: Rutgers University Press, 1999.

Shindler, Colin. *Ploughshares into Swords? Israelis and Jews in the Shadow of the Intifada.* New York: St. Martin's, 1991.

Silver, Eric. *Begin: The Haunted Prophet.* 1st American ed. New York: Random House, 1984.

Smith, Charles D. *Palestine and the Arab-Israeli Conflict: A History with Documents.* 6th ed. New York: Bedford/St. Martin's, 2006.

Snow, Peter John. *Hussein: A Biography.* Washington, DC: R. B. Luce, 1972.

Sofer, Amon. *Rivers of Fire: The Conflict over Water in the Middle East.* Lanham, MD: Rowman and Littlefield, 1999.

Solecki, John. *Hosni Mubarak.* New York: Chelsea House, 1991.

Sorkin, Michael. *Against the Wall: Israel's Barrier to Peace.* New York: New Press: 2005.

Souryal, Sam. *Islam, Islamic Law, and the Turn to Violence.* Huntsville, TX: Office of International Criminal Justice, Sam Houston State University, 2004.

Spedding, David. *The Leadership of the Intifada.* Oxford: St. Antony's College, 1991.

Spier, Howard. *From the Sidelines: The USSR and the Lebanese Crisis.* London: Institute of Jewish Affairs, in association with the World Jewish Congress, 1982.

St. John, Robert. *Ben-Gurion: The Biography of an Extraordinary Man.* Garden City, NY: Doubleday, 1959.

Stein, Kenneth W. *The Intifadah and the 1936–1939 Uprising: A Comparison of the Palestinian Arab Communities.* Atlanta: Carter Center of Emory University, 1990.

Stephens, Robert Henry. *Nasser: A Political Biography.* New York: Simon and Schuster, 1972.

Steven, Stewart. *The Spymasters of Israel.* New York: Macmillan, 1980.

Stevens, Janet D. *The Israeli Use of U.S. Weapons in Lebanon: A Report in Two Parts.* Belmont, MA: AAUG Press, 1983.

Stevenson, William. *90 Minutes at Entebbe.* New York: Bantam, 1976.

Sullivan, George. *Sadat: The Man Who Changed Mid-East History.* New York: Walker, 1981.

Swisher, Clayton E. *The Truth about Camp David: The Untold Story about the Collapse of the Middle East Peace Process.* New York: Thunder's Mouth, Nation Books, 2004.

Sykes, Christopher. *Orde Wingate.* London: Collins, 1959.

Tamari, Salmi. *Jerusalem 1948: The Arab Neighbourhoods and Their Fate in the War.* Beirut, Lebanon: Institute of Palestine Studies, 1999.

Tamir, Avraham. *A Soldier in Search of Peace: An Inside Look at Israel's Strategy.* New York: Harper and Row, 1988.

Telhami, Shibley. *Power and Leadership in International Bargaining: The Path to the Camp David Accords.* New York: Columbia University, 1990.

Templeton, Malcolm. *Ties of Blood and Empire: New Zealand's Involvement in Middle East Defence and the Suez Crisis.* Auckland: Auckland University Press in association with the New Zealand Institute of International Affairs, 1994.

Teveth, Shabtai. *Ben-Gurion: The Burning Ground, 1886–1948.* Boston: Houghton Mifflin, 1987.

Thompson, Thomas L. *Early History of the Israelite People: From the Written & Archaeological Sources.* Leiden: Brill Academic, 2000.

Timerman, Jacobo. *The Longest War: Israel in Lebanon.* New York: Knopf, 1982.

Towell, Larry. *Gaza.* Kingston, Ontario: Quarry Press, 1994.

———. *No Man's Land.* London: Chris Boot in association with the Archive of Modern Conflict, 2005.

Towell, Larry, Mahmud Darwish, and René Backmann. *Then Palestine.* New York: Aperture, 1998.

Toye, Patricia D., and Angela Seay. *Israel: Boundary Disputes with Arab Neighbours, 1946–1964.* 10 vols. Slough: Archive Editions, 1995.

Trever, John C. *The Bible and the Palestinian-Israeli Conflict.* Claremont, CA: School of Theology at Claremont, 1983.

Twersky, David. *With the Israeli Army in Lebanon: How Much Has Changed and How Much Hasn't.* New York: Partisan Review, 1982.

United Nations, ed. *Basic Facts about the United Nations.* New York: United Nations, 2004.

———, ed. *The Origins and Evolution of the Palestine Problem, 1917–1988.* New York: United Nations, 1990.

———, ed. *Palestinians (the Work of the Committee on the Exercise of the Inalienable Rights of the Palestinian People).* New York: United Nations, 1997.

———, ed. *The Question of Palestine, 1979–1990.* New York: United Nations, 1990.

Usher, Graham. *Palestine in Crisis: The Struggle for Peace and Political Independence after Oslo.* London: Pluto, 1995.

Van Creveld, Martin. *Military Lessons of the Yom Kippur War.* London: Sage, 1976.

———. *The Sword and the Olive: A Critical History of the Israeli Defense Force.* New York: PublicAffairs, 2002.

Vardi, Ronit. *Bibi: Mi Atah, Adoni Rosh Ha-Memshalah?* Jerusalem: Keter, 1997.

Villiers, Gérard de Bernard Touchais, and Annick de Villiers. *The Imperial Shah: An Informal Biography.* 1st American ed. Boston: Little, Brown, 1976.

Wagner, Heather Lehr. *King Abdullah II.* New York: Chelsea House, 2005.

Wald, Êmanuel. *The Wald Report: The Decline of Israeli National Security since 1967.* Boulder, CO: Westview, 1992.

Waldman, Adir. *Arbitrating Armed Conflict: Decisions of the Israel-Lebanon Monitoring Group.* Huntington, NY: Juris, 2003.

Wallach, Janet, and John Wallach. *Arafat: In the Eyes of the Beholder.* Rocklin, CA: Prima, 1991.

Warschawski, Michel. *On the Border.* Cambridge, MA: South End Press, 2005.

Watt, Donald Cameron, ed. *Documents on the Suez Crisis, 26 July to 6 November 1956.* London: Royal Institute of International Affairs, 1957.

Weinberger, Peter. *Co-opting the PLO: A Critical Reconstruction of the Oslo Accords, 1993–1995.* New York: Rowman and Littlefield, 2006.

Weizman, Ezer. *The Battle for Peace.* New York: Bantam, 1981.

Weizmann, Chaim. *Trial and Error: The Autobiography of Chaim Weizmann.* New York: Harper, 1949.

Westwood, J. N. *The History of the Middle East Wars.* London: Bison, 1991.

Winternitz, Helen. *A Season of Stones: Living in a Palestinian Village.* New York: Atlantic Monthly Press, 1991.

Yamani, Mai. *Cradle of Islam: The Hijaz and the Quest for Arabian Identity.* London: Tauris, 2004.

Yapp, M. E. *The Near East since the First World War: A History to 1995.* 2nd ed. London: Longman, 1996.

Yariv, Aharon, et al. *The War in Lebanon.* Tel Aviv: Center for Strategic Studies, Tel Aviv University, 1983.

Younes, Fayez, and Jamileh Saad. *The Uprising: December 8, 1987–March 8, 1988.* Nicosia, Cyprus: Bisan Press, 1988.

Young, Elise G. *Keepers of the History: Women and the Israeli-Palestinian Conflict.* New York: Teacher's College Press, 1992.

Zereik, Elia. *The Palestinians in Israel: A Study in Internal Colonialism.* London: Routledge and Kegan Paul, 1979.

Zinni, Tony, and Tony Koltz. *The Battle for Peace: A Frontline Vision of America's Power and Purpose.* London: Palgrave Macmillan, 2006.

Zuhur, Sherifa. "Arabs and Arab Culture." In Wim Melis, ed., *Nazar, Photography and Visual Culture of the Arab World.* Leeuwarden, Netherlands: Stichting Fotografie Noorderlicht, 2004.

———. *Asmahan's Secrets: Woman, War, and Song.* Austin, TX: Center for Middle Eastern Studies, 2000; London: Al Saqi Books, 2001.

———. *Asrar Asmahan.* Damascus, Baghdad, and Beirut: Dar al-Mada, 2007.

———, ed. *Colors of Enchantment: Theater, Music, Dance, and Visual Arts of the Middle East.* Cairo: American University in Cairo Press, 2001.

———. *Egypt: Security, Political, and Islamist Challenges.* Carlisle Barracks, PA: Strategic Studies Institute, U.S. Army War College, 2007.

———. *A Hundred Osamas: Islamist Threats and the Future of Counterinsurgency.* Carlisle Barracks, PA: Strategic Studies Institute, U.S. Army War College, 2006.

———. *The Middle East: Politics, History and Neonationalism.* Carlisle, PA: Institute of Middle Eastern, Islamic, and Diasporic Studies, 2005

———. *Saudi Arabia: Islamic Threat, Political Reform and the Global War on Terror.* Carlisle Barracks, PA: Strategic Studies Institute, 2005.

———. "State Power and the Progress of Militant and Moderate Islamism in Egypt." In James Forest, ed., *Combating Terrorism in the 21st Century,* Vol. 3. Westport, CT: Praeger Security Series, 2007.

List of Editors and Contributors

Volume Editor
Dr. Spencer C. Tucker
Senior Fellow
Military History, ABC-CLIO, Inc.

Editor, Documents Volume
Dr. Priscilla Roberts
Associate Professor of History, School of
    Humanities
Honorary Director, Centre of American
    Studies
University of Hong Kong

Associate Editor
Dr. Paul G. Pierpaoli Jr.
Fellow
Military History, ABC-CLIO, Inc.

Assistant Editors
Dr. David Zabecki (Retired)
Major General
U.S. Army

Dr. Sherifa Zuhur
Research Professor of Islamic and
    Regional Studies
U.S. Army War College, Strategic Studies
    Institute

Contributors
Dr. Aref Abu-Rabia
Ben Gurion University of the Negev

Dr. Alan Allport
University of Pennsylvania

Ralph Martin Baker
Independent Scholar

Lacie A. Ballinger, MA
The Sixth Floor Museum at Dealey
    Plaza

Dr. John H. Barnhill
Independent Scholar

Dr. Michael B. Barrett
Department of History
The Citadel

Michael K. Beauchamp
Texas A&M University

Walter F. Bell
Reference Librarian
Aurora University

Dr. Berch Berberoglu
Professor and Director of Graduate
    Studies in Sociology
University of Nevada, Reno

Amy Hackney Blackwell
Independent Scholar

Scott Blanchette
Information Security Officer
Stanford University Medical Center

Dr. Stefan Marc Brooks
Department of Political Science
Morehead State University

Robert M. Brown
U.S. Army Command and General Staff
    College

Dino E. Buenviaje, MA, RPH
University of California, Riverside

Dr. J. David Cameron
Associate Professor
Southeast Missouri State University

Dr. Stanley D. M. Carpenter
Professor of Strategy and Policy
United States Naval War College

Dr. James F. Carroll
Iona College

Sergio Catignani
Department of War Studies
King's College London

Dr. Justin P. Coffey
Bradley University

Dr. David Commins
Dickinson College

Dr. Seif Da'Na
University of Wisconsin–Parkside

Dr. Everett Dague
Department of History
Benedictine College

Lieutenant Colonel Louis Dimarco
   (Retired)
Associate Professor
U.S. Army Command and Staff College

Yuanyuan Ding
Georgia State University

Dr. Paul W. Doerr
Associate Professor
Acadia University

Michael Doidge
University of Southern Mississippi

Dr. Richard M. Edwards
Senior Lecturer
University of Wisconsin Colleges and
   Milwaukee School of Engineering

Mary J. Elias
ITT Technical Institute

Dr. Chuck Fahrer
Georgia College and State University

Dr. Elun Gabriel
Assistant Professor of History
St. Lawrence University

Brent Geary
Ohio University

Trista Grant
Doctoral Fellow
University of Western Ontario

Dr. Steven W. Guerrier
James Madison University

Dr. Michael R. Hall
Associate Professor of History
Armstrong Atlantic State University

Dr. Maia Carter Hallward
Kennesaw State University

Neil Hamilton
Independent Scholar

Dr. Neil Heyman
San Diego State University

Dr. Jonathan M. House
Professor
Gordon College

Dr. Charles Francis Howlett
Molloy College

Dr. Timothy D. Hoyt
Associate Professor of Strategy and
   Policy
U.S. Naval War College

Dr. Harry Hueston
Associate Professor of Criminal Justice
West Texas A&M University

Jonas Kauffeldt
Florida State University

Carool Kersten
School of Oriental and African Studies
King's College London

Laura Khoury
University of Wisconsin-Platteville

Dr. Robert Kiely
Illinois Mathematics and Science Academy

Rana Kobeissi
Katholieke Universiteit Leuven

Daniel W. Kuthy
Georgia State University

Dr. Jeremy Kuzmarow
Assistant Professor
Brandeis University

Dr. Tom Lansford
Assistant Dean
University of Southern Mississippi

Dr. Debbie Yuk-fun Law
Open University of Hong Kong and Shue
   Yan College

Keith A. Leitich
North Seattle Community College

Dr. LaVonne Jackson Leslie
Howard University

Jonathan H. L'Hommedieu
University of Turku

Shawn Livingston
Librarian
University of Kentucky, William T.
   Young Library

Clare M. Lopez
Middle East Strategic Policy and
   Intelligence Analyst
Private Consultant

Dr. Adam Lowther
Assistant Professor
Arkansas Tech University

Paul J. Magnarella
Professor and Director of Peace and
   Justice Studies
Warren Wilson College

Dr. Antoinette Mannion
Department of Geography
University of Reading, United Kingdom

Dr. James Matray
Professor and Chair of History
Department of History
California State University, Chico

Dr. Terry Mays
Associate Professor, Department of
    Political Science
The Citadel

James R. McIntyre
Instructor
Moraine Valley Community College

Dr. Jay A. Menzoff
Armstrong Atlantic State University

Dr. Patit Paban Mishra
Professor
Sambalpur University, India

Josip Mocnik
Bowling Green State University

Dr. Gregory Moore
Associate Professor of History
Notre Dame College

Gregory Morgan
University of Southern Mississippi

Dr. Irina Mukhina
Department of History
Assumption College

Dr. Keith Murphy
Professor
Fort Valley State University

Dr. Jaime Ramón Olivares
Professor
Houston Community College–Central

Dr. Peter Overlack
Independent Scholar

Brian Parkinson
Independent Scholar

Dr. James D. Perry
Independent Historian

Dr. Allene S. Phy-Olsen
Professor of English
Austin Peay State University

Dr. Paul G. Pierpaoli Jr.
Associate Editor
Military History, ABC-CLIO, Inc.

Dr. Michael Polley
Associate Professor
Columbia College

Carolyn Ramzy
Florida State University

Dr. Dave Rausch
Associate Professor
West Texas A&M University

Dr. Priscilla Roberts
Associate Professor of History,
    School of Humanities
Honorary Director, Centre of American
    Studies
University of Hong Kong

Mark M. Sanders
Reference Librarian
East Carolina University

Captain Carl Otis Schuster (Retired)
U.S. Navy
Hawaii Pacific University

Jessica Sedgewick
Independent Scholar

Vadim Konstantine Simakhov
Virginia Military Institute

Dr. Cathy Skidmore-Hess
Associate Professor
Georgia Southern University

Dr. Dan Skidmore-Hess
Professor
Armstrong Atlantic State University

Dr. Frank J. Smith (PhD, DD)
Presbyterian International News
    Service

Dr. Yushau Sodiq
Associate Professor
Texas Christian University

Dr. Daniel E. Spector
U.S. Army Chemical Corps

Dr. Paul Joseph Springer
Visiting Assistant Professor
United States Military Academy

Robert Stacy
Independent Scholar

Dirk Steffen
Independent Scholar

Dr. Stephen K. Stein
Department of History
University of Memphis

Luc Stenger
Director, Culture & Society in the NIS,
    Central & Oriental Europe
University Paris VIII

Dr. Nancy L. Stockdale
Assistant Professor
University of North Texas

Dr. David Tal
Professor
Tel Aviv University

Dr. Ghada Talhami
Lake Forest College

Dr. Moshe Terdiman
Director, Islam in Africa Project
Senior Research Fellow, PRISM
Gloria Center, IDC

Dr. Wallace Andrew Terrill
U.S. Army War College, Strategic
    Studies Institute

Andrew Theobald
Queen's University

Dr. Spencer C. Tucker
Senior Fellow
Military History, ABC-CLIO

Dallace W. Unger Jr.
Independent Scholar

Dr. Peter Vale
Nelson Mandela Professor of Politics
Rhodes University

Dr. Thomas D. Veve
Associate Professor of History
Dalton State College

Dr. Bryan Vizzini
West Texas A&M University

Roderick Vosburgh
Independent Scholar

Lisa Roy Vox
PhD Candidate
Emory University

James Wald
Associate Professor
Hampshire College

Dr. Andrew Jackson Waskey
Division of Social Sciences
Dalton State College

Tim J. Watts
Humanities Librarian
Kansas State University

Thomas J. Weiler
Associate Professor
Universities of Bonn, Erfurt, and
    Trier

Kurt Werthmuller
Assistant Professor
Geneva College

Dr. James H. Willbanks
Director
Department of Military History
U.S. Army Command and General Staff
    College, Fort Leavenworth

Dr. Paul Wingrove
University of Greenwich

Dr. Anna M. Wittmann
Department of English
University of Alberta

Ulrike Wunderle
University of Tübingen

Dr. David T. Zabecki
Major General
Army of the United States, Retired

David Zierler
Thomas Davis Fellow in Force and
    Diplomacy
Temple University

General Anthony C. Zinni (Retired)
U.S. Marine Corps

Dr. Sherifa Zuhur
Research Professor of Islamic and
    Regional Studies
U.S. Army War College, Strategic Studies
    Institute

Dr. Stephen Zunes
Professor
University of San Francisco

Categorical Index

Index